ISBN 978-0-260-71000-0
PIBN 10965623

FB &c Ltd, Dalton House, 60 Windsor Avenue, London, SW19 2RR.
Company number 08720141. Registered in England and Wales.

For support please visit www.forgottenbooks.com

PRIVATE LAWS

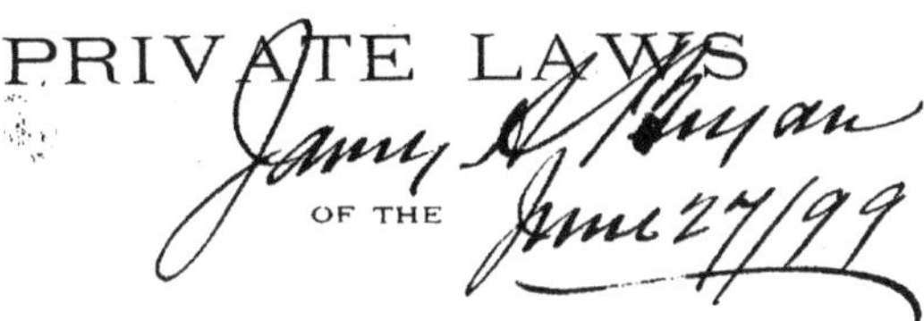

OF THE

State of North Carolina

PASSED BY THE

GENERAL ASSEMBLY

AT ITS

SESSION OF 1899,

BEGUN AND HELD IN THE CITY OF RALEIGH

ON

Wednesday, the Fourth Day of January, A. D. 1899.

PUBLISHED BY AUTHORITY.

RALEIGH:
EDWARDS & BROUGHTON, AND E. M. UZZELL, STATE PRINTERS AND BINDERS.
1899.

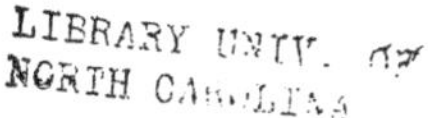

CAPTIONS

OF THE

PRIVATE LAWS,

SESSION 1899.

PRIVATE LAWS

OF THE

STATE OF NORTH CAROLINA.

SESSION 1899.

PRIVATE LAWS

OF THE

State of North Carolina.

SESSION 1899.

CHAPTER 1.

An act to repeal chapter three hundred and sixteen of the private laws of eighteen hundred and ninety-five.

The General Assembly of North Carolina do enact:

Repeals chapter 316, private acts 1895, concerning construction of turnpike from Paris Gap to Hickory Nut Gap.

Section 1. That chapter three hundred and sixteen (316) of the private acts of the general assembly of North Carolina of the session of eighteen hundred and ninety-five, entitled "An act to construct a turnpike from the Rutherford county line at Paris Gap to the Buncombe county line in Hickory Nut Gap," and all laws amendatory of said act be and the same are hereby repealed.

Sec. 2. This act shall be in force from and after its ratification.

Ratified the 14th day of January, A. D. 1899.

CHAPTER 2.

An act to authorize the town of Louisburg to issue bonds for public improvements, and to levy a special tax, and for other purposes.

The General Assembly of North Carolina do enact:

To provide for water-works, sewerage, lights, etc., the board of commissioners may issue bonds.

Section 1. That for the purpose of providing a system of water-works, sewerage, and electric lights for the town of Louisburg, or of making other public improvements in the said town, and for refunding the outstanding bonded indebtedness of said town, or for either or all of said purposes, as and when the board of commissioners may determine, the board of commissioners of the town of Louisburg, in the county of Franklin, are hereby authorized and empowered to issue bonds from time to time, to an amount not exceeding, in the aggregate, thirty thousand dollars, of such denominations and in such proportions as said board may deem advisable, bearing interest from the date thereof, at a rate not exceeding six per centum per annum, with interest coupons attached, payable annually at such times and at such place or places as may be deemed advisable by said board, said bonds to be of such form and tenor, and transferable in such way, and the principal thereof payable or redeemable at such time or times, not exceeding fifty years from the date thereof, and at such place or places as the board of commissioners may determine.

Aggregate amount not to exceed $30,000.

Interest not to exceed 6 per cent.

Bonds to run not exceeding 50 years.

Bonds not to be disposed of for less than par.

Sec. 2. That none of the bonds provided for in the above section shall be disposed of, either by sale, exchange, hypothecation or otherwise, for a less price than their par value, nor shall said bonds or their proceeds be used for any other purpose than those those declared in said section.

Proceeds applied to special purposes.

Bonds not taxable by town till after maturity and tender of payment.

Sec. 3. That the bonds authorized to be issued by section one hereof and their coupons shall not be subject to taxation by the said town until after they become due, and tender of payment shall have been made by the board of commissioners, and the coupons shall be receivable in payment of town taxes or other town dues, for any fiscal year in which said coupons become due, or thereafter, and if the holder of any of said bonds or coupons shall fail to present the same for payment at the time or times, and at the place or places therein named, he shall not be entitled to any interest thereon for the time they have been outstanding after maturity.

Coupons receivable for town taxes.

Interest ceases upon maturity, if bonds or coupons not presented for payment when due.

To provide for payment of principal and interest, commissioners to levy special tax.

Sec. 4. That for the purpose of providing for the payment of the interest accruing on, and the principal at maturity of the bonds herein authorized, the board of commissioners of said town shall annually and at the time of levying other town taxes, levy and lay a particular tax on all persons and subjects of taxation on which the said board of commissioners now are or may hereafter be authorized to lay and levy taxes for any purpose whatever; said tax shall be so levied and laid as to raise a sum sufficient to pay off the interest upon said bonds and to provide for the payment of the principal of said bonds at maturity, and shall be collected in the manner and at the times other town taxes are collected, and shall be accounted for and kept separate from other town taxes, and shall be applied exclusively to the purposes for which they are levied and collected.

Upon all subjects of taxation.

Manner and time of collection.

How accounted for and applied.

Sec. 5. All profits resulting to the said town from the operation of said system of water-works and electric lights, over and above the cost and expense of operation, and all moneys which may be derived from the rental or sale of said systems, in the event that the same shall at any time hereafter be rented or sold, shall be held for the exclusive purpose of paying the interest and principal of the bonds above provided for. So much of the moneys derived from the operation, rental, or sale of the said system of water-works and electric lights, and from the taxes which shall be levied in accordance with the provisions of the next preceding section hereof, as may not be necessary to pay the interest on the bonds issued as it falls due, and cannot be applied to the purchase or discharge of the said bonds, shall be invested by the town treasurer under such rules and regulations as the board of commissioners shall from time to time prescribe, so as to secure the payment of the principal of said bonds at the maturity thereof. And the town treasurer shall also do and perform all such other services in connection with said bonds as said board of commissioners may prescribe, and shall give bond and receive such compensation for his services as said board of commissioners may determine.

Profits of system of water-works and electric lights, and proceeds of rental or sale, to be applied to payment of bonds.

If in excess, how invested to secure payment at maturity.

Duties, bond, and compensation of town treasurer.

Sec. 6. That before any of the bonds herein provided for shall be issued, the question of issuing the same shall first be submitted to the qualified voters of said town. The said election shall be advertised for thirty days prior to the day of election in a newspaper published in said town, also at the court-house door and two other public places in said town. The board of commissioners shall appoint a registrar and three judges of election who shall hold and conduct said election according to the same rules and regulations as are now prescribed by law for election of municipal officers in said town, except as herein otherwise provided. No new registration shall be required, but all persons whose names have heretofore been registered on the registration books of said town, and have not died, removed, or in any way been disqualified according to law, shall be entitled to vote in said election, and the board of commissioners shall appoint at least three days for the registration of voters not already registered. The qualification of the voters shall be the same as are provided now by law, or may be provided at the time of holding said election. Those qualified voters approving the issue of such bonds and the levying of the taxes to pay the same shall deposit in the ballot box a written or printed ticket, with the words "For Bonds" thereon, and those disapproving the same shall deposit a like ticket with the words "Against Bonds" thereon. The result of said election shall be ascer-

The question of bond issue to be submitted to qualified voters.

Election, how advertised.

Election officers, how appointed.

Election, how conducted.

Who entitled to vote.

Commissioners to fix three days for registration.

Ballots to be "For Bonds" and "Against Bonds."

Result of election, how ascertained and recorded.

tained by the aforesaid registrar and judges, and returned by them over their signatures to the mayor and commissioners of said town, who shall cause the same to be recorded in the minutes of the town. If a majority of the qualified voters of said town shall vote "For Bonds" then the said board of commissioners shall issue the bonds provided for in this act, to such an amount as they shall deem necessary for the purposes aforesaid, and shall levy and order the collection of the taxes authorized by this act; but if a majority of the qualified voters of said town shall fail to vote "For Bonds" at such election, then this act shall be of no force or effect.

If "For Bonds," commissioners to issue bonds and levy tax.

If "Against Bonds" then this act invalid.

Mayor and commissioners may lease and sell water-works and electric lights.

Sec. 7. If said water-works, sewerage and electric lights are procured as provided for in this act, then the mayor and commissioners of said town shall have full power over and control of the same, and may lease and sell to any person or persons in said town, or owning property therein, or desiring to so purchase or lease, the right to use the said water, lights or sewerage upon such terms and under such arrangements as may be agreed upon between such person and the commissioners of said town; and all proceeds arising from the sale or lease of such rights, shall be applied as hereinbefore directed.

Proceeds, how applied.

Sec. 8. All laws and clauses of law in conflict with this act are hereby repealed.

Sec. 9. This act shall be in force from and after its ratification.

Ratified on the 14th day of January, A. D. 1899.

CHAPTER 3.

An act to amend the charter of Saint Mary's School.

The General Assembly of North Carolina do enact:

Amends section 3, chapter 86, private laws 1897, so as to include South Carolina.

Section 1. That section three of chapter eighty-six of the private laws of eighteen hundred and ninety-seven be amended by repealing the proviso therein and inserting the following in lieu thereof: Provided, that said corporation shall be under the jurisdiction, control and direction of the Protestant Episcopal Church in the states of North Carolina and South Carolina as represented by the bishops and legislative bodies of said church within the limits of said states, as is hereinafter more particularly specified.

Sec. 2. That section five of said act be amended by striking out the word "three" at the end of the seventh line of the section and inserting the word "six" in lieu thereof; by striking out the word "sixteen" in the eleventh line of the said section five and inserting the word "thirty" in lieu thereof; and by striking out the words "State of North Carolina" wherever they occur in said section five and inserting in lieu thereof the words "States of North Carolina and South Carolina." Amends section 5 of the act.

Sec. 3. That this act shall be in force from and after its ratification.

Ratified the 16th day of January, A. D. 1899.

CHAPTER 4.

An act authorizing the mayor and commissioners of the town of Reidsville in the county of Rockingham to issue bonds for the establishment of a system of water-works for said town.

The General Assembly of North Carolina do enact:

Section 1. That for the purpose of raising money to build, erect, construct and establish a system of water-works for the town of Reidsville, in the county of Rockingham, the mayor of said town in conjunction with its board of commissioners are hereby authorized and empowered to issue bonds to an amount not exceeding twenty-five thousand dollars ($25,000), payable at such place as they may designate. Mayor and commissioners authorized to issue bonds not exceeding $25,000 in amount for water-works. Said bonds shall bear not exceeding six per cent. interest per annum, which interest shall be payable annually, and each bond shall have coupons attached thereto for the amount of interest due thereon for each year they have to run, Rate of interest not to exceed six per cent. payable annually. and said coupons after their maturity shall be receivable in payment of town taxes, Coupons receivable for town taxes. and if the holder of said bonds or coupons shall fail to present the same for payment at the time and place therein named, he shall not be entitled to more than fifteen days' interest thereon for the time they have been outstanding after maturity. Interest on bonds and coupons to cease unless presented within fifteen days after maturity. Said bonds shall be in denominations and forms as shall be determined upon by said mayor, and board of commissioners, Form and denomination determined by mayor and board of commissioners. and shall mature and be made payable in not less than thirty years nor more than fifty years from the date of their issue, Bonds to run thirty to fifty years. and shall be signed by the said mayor and countersigned by the clerk of said board, and said clerk shall keep a record of the number and amount of each class of bonds issued, the date of issue when the same matures, and to whom payable. Signed by mayor and countersigned by clerk, who keeps a record.

Bonds not to be disposed of for less than par.

Sec. 2. That said bonds shall not be sold, hypothecated or otherwise be disposed of for less than their par value, nor shall said bonds or their proceeds be used for any purpose other than the purpose mentioned in section one of this act.

To provide for payment of interest and principal, special tax authorized to be levied and collected as other taxes.

Sec. 3. That for the purpose of providing for the payment of the annual interest on said bonds as well as the redemption of the same at their maturity, said mayor and board of commissioners shall annually at the time of levying other town taxes, levy and lay a special and particular tax on all persons, property and subjects of taxation, which are now subject to taxation under the charter of said town, and the various amendments thereto, or which hereafter by future amendments may become subject to taxation sufficient to meet the annual accruing interest on said bonds; the taxes provided for in this section shall be collected in the same manner and at the same time the other town taxes are collected and shall be accounted for and kept separate and apart from the other town taxes, and shall be applied exclusively to the purpose for which they are collected; and it is further provided that after the expiration of five years from the issuance of said bonds, or any part of them, an additional special tax (if that be deemed expedient and desirable) may in like manner be levied, laid and collected each and every year sufficient in amount to redeem, retain and take up each and every year thereafter five per cent. of said bonds issued and outstanding, otherwise all of them at their maturity.

Special taxes kept separate for exclusive purpose.

After five years additional special tax may be levied.

No bonds to issue until this act is ratified by a majority of qualified voters.

Sec. 4. That none of said bonds shall be issued until this act shall be submitted to and approved by a majority of the qualified voters of said town of Reidsville at an election to be held in said town on a day to be designated and fixed by said mayor and board of commissioners at any time after ten days from and after the ratification of this act, and after the expiration of a public notice for thirty days preceding said election, giving time when and place where the said election shall be held; which said notice shall contain a synopsis of the object and purpose of this act, and shall be published once a week for four consecutive weeks immediately preceding said election in the newspapers published in said town; said election shall be held and returns thereof made under the same provisions, rules and regulations as exist in cases of elections for mayor and board of commissioners of said town. Those qualified voters approving the provisions of this act shall vote "Issue," and those not approving its provisions shall vote "No issue." If it shall appear from the returns of said election that a majority of the qualified voters of said town have voted in favor of the issuance of said bonds then the same may be issued in accordance with the provisions of this act, otherwise not.

Mayor and board to give thirty days' notice of election.

Notice, what to contain and how published.

How election held and returns made.

Ballots to be "Issue" and "No Issue."

If majority of qualified voters favor "Issue," bonds to be issued.

Sec. 5. That all laws and clauses of laws in conflict with the provisions of this act are hereby repealed.

Sec. 6. This act shall be in force from and after its ratification.

Ratified the 18th day of January, A. D. 1899.

CHAPTER 5.

An act to incorporate the ".St. Luke's Circle of the King's Daughters" for charitable purposes.

The General Assembly of North Carolina do enact:

Section 1. That the "St. Luke's Circle of the King's Daughters," composed of the following members, to-wit: Mrs. Lucy Blake, Mrs. S. B. Foy, Mrs. M. E. Scarlett, Mrs. C. S. Lambeth, Mrs. M. A. Johnson, Mrs. A. M. Harward, Mrs. E. E. Moffitt, Miss M. E. Moore, Miss Anna Maynard, Miss Julia Royster, Miss Florence Telfair, Miss Anna L. Lagergren, Mrs. Ella Williamson, Mrs. Mary Sherwood, Mrs. M. A. Leard, Miss Lucy Brown, Mrs. M. L. Pace, Miss ...... Montgomery, Mrs. Nora Atkinson, Mrs. Mattie Hall and Mrs. Annie Rogers, and their successors, are hereby constituted a body corporate under the name and style of "St. Luke's Circle of the King's Daughters."

Names of the corporators.

Sec. 2. That the corporators above named, or any seven of them, whenever one hundred and fifty dollas shall have been subscribed and paid in for the purposes hereinafter designated, may meet, after giving ten days' notice thereof to a majority of the members of said circle as now constituted, and named above, and if seven thereof be present in person or by proxy, they may organize, and by a majority vote of those present, elect a president and such other officers as they may deem necessary, and make a constitution and by-laws, to carry out the provisions of this charter, and for the further government of the corporation.

When $150 paid in, the corporators, or seven of them, may organize and elect officers and make constitution.

Sec. 3. That the business to be conducted hereunder shall be the caring for and the support and maintenance of old or infirm, or other women, such as the management of said corporation shall select or determine upon, and for such period of time and upon such conditions as said management may elect: and said corporation through its said mangement may make charge or charges for such support or maintenance, or not, as in the judgment of said management may be just and proper, according to the means of the person or persons seeking aid

The purpose of the corporation.

May make charges if management deems proper.

No member shall derive remuneration, but paid assistance may be had.

therefrom. In no event shall any member of this corporation derive any remuneration therefrom; but if, in the opinion of said management it should become necessary to employ paid assistants, or help, to further the provisions of this charter, it may do so at an expenditure therefor, and in such manner as said management may, in its discretion, deem wise and proper.

Corporation may acquire, hold or sell property, and may appoint trustees for that purpose.

Sec. 4. That the said corporation may hold and possess real, personal or mixed property by gift, deed, grant or otherwise, for the purposes herein mentioned, or may sell or transfer the same; and shall appoint one or more trustees by a majority vote at any meeting of the members thereof, seven being present for such length of time as they may specify, to hold such property in trust according to the intent of this charter, and may remove such trustee, or trustees, through the said management: and the trustee, or trustees so appointed, may select any bank or banks in the city of Raleigh, North Carolina, as a place of deposit; and if such bank or banks should become insolvent or in any manner jeopardize any property of said corporation, such trustee, or trustees, thus to be appointed, shall not, in any manner be held liable therefor; nor shall such trustee, or trustees, be liable for any property paid out, or transferred upon the order of the management of said corporation lawfully given. No property of said corporation shall be subject to taxation.

Trustees may deposit in Raleigh banks without personal liability, and so transfer upon order of management.

Property not taxable.

Raleigh the place of business.

Sec. 5. That the place of business of said corporation shall be in Raleigh, North Carolina; but it may establish branches thereof anywhere within the limits of the said state.

No personal liability for debts of corporation.

Sec. 6. That no member of this corporation shall be held personally liable for any debt or other obligation that the said corporation may incur.

Incorporated for thirty years.

Sec. 7. That the powers, privileges and franchise herein conferred shall extend for a period of thirty years from the date of organization hereunder.

Sec. 8. That this act shall be in force from and after its ratification.

Ratified the 18th day of January, A. D. 1899.

CHAPTER 6.

An act to amend the charter of the Bingham School.

The General Assembly of North Carolina do enact:

Section 1. That chapter eighty-one of the private laws of the session of eighteen hundred and ninety-five be and the same is hereby amended by striking out the word "captain" in section two of said act and inserting in lieu thereof the word "major." "Major" substituted for "Captain" in section 2, chapter 81, private laws 1895.

Sec. 2. That this act shall be in force from and after its ratification.

Ratified the 18th day of January, A. D. 1899.

CHAPTER 7.

An act to authorize the city of Charlotte to issue negotiable bonds for water-works and sewerage purposes, and to ratify the action of the board of aldermen and of the qualified voters of said city in authorizing the issue of bonds for said purposes.

The General Assembly of North Carolina do enact:

Whereas, the board of aldermen of the city of Charlotte on or about January sixth, eighteen hundred and ninety-six, duly passed an ordinance providing for the submission to the voters of the city of the question whether bonds of the city to an amount not to exceed three hundred thousand dollars should be issued, and the money derived from their sale be applied to obtaining a more abundant and cheaper supply of water for both public and private uses, and a corresponding increase and improvement of the city sewers, as appears by the said ordinance; and also duly provided by ordinance for the holding of an election of the qualified voters in said city to vote upon the said question, and caused due notice to be given of said election, and afterwards, on or about February eighteen, eighteen hundred and ninety-six, an election was held in said city, at which the said question was submitted, and the issue of the said bonds to an amount not to exceed three hundred thousand dollars for the said purpose was duly approved by a vote of a majority of the qualified voters in said city; and Preamble.

Whereas, the said city, acting through its board of aldermen and other proper officers, has made an agreement with the Charlotte City Water-works Company, a corporation organized under the laws of this state, owning and operating a water-works system in the said city of Charlotte, in and by which agreement it has been provided that the said water-works company shall sell and said city shall buy the water-works and other property of the said water-works company; now, therefore,

ote of the people 1896 made effecve and the board aldermen are au-ıorized to issue onds.

Section 1. That, in consideration of the premises and to give effect to the aforesaid election and vote of the people, the board of aldermen of the city of Charlotte be and they are hereby authorized to issue negotiab.e bonds for the purpose of procuring money to enable the said city to obtain a more abundant and cheaper supply of water for both public and private uses, and to make payment for such increase and improvement of the city sewers as have been or shall be made pursuant to the said vote of the people, and to pay the purchase price of the water-works property of the Charlotte City Water-works Company on such terms as have been or may be agreed, acting upon and between the company and the said city of Charlotte through the board of aldermen, and to pay for any extension and improvement of such water-works as may be determined by the said board of aldermen:

he total issue of onds shall not ex-.ed three hundred ıousand dollars.

Provided, the total issue of bonds authorized by this act shall not exceed the sum of three hundred thousand dollars.

he form, denomi-ation, time and ace of payment, also the rate of iterest, deter-ined by the board aldermen.

Said bonds shall be in such form, and of such denomination, and shall be payable at such time or times and place, and shall bear such rate of interest, payable semi-annually, as the board of aldermen of said city have determined or may hereafter determine.

ow the bonds and oupons shall be gned and attest-d.

Said bonds shall be signed by the mayor, countersigned by the treasurer, and sealed with the corporate seal of the city, attested by the city clerk. The coupons on said bonds shall bear the engraved or lithographed signature of the clerk. The purchaser of said bonds shall not be bound to see to the application of the purchase money.

he action of the oard of aldermen d the qualified ectors in 1896 au-horizing the issue f bonds is ratified d approved.

Sec. 2. That the action of the board of aldermen and the qualified electors in said city in authorizing the issue of bonds for the purpose mentioned in section one of this act, the aforesaid ordinance of January six, eighteen hundred and ninety-six, and the said election hereinbefore recited, be and the same are hereby ratified and approved:

roviso.

Provided, however, that the total issue of bonds authorized by the said ordinance and by the said election and by this act shall not exceed the sum of three hundred thousand dollars. And the bonds so issued are hereby declared to be the valid and legally binding obligations of the said city.

oard directed to vy additional tax roperty.

Sec. 3. That the board of aldermen of the city of Charlotte are hereby required and directed to levy and collect, in addition to all other taxes in said city, an ad valorem tax upon all the taxable property in said city sufficient to pay the interest on said bonds as the same becomes due; and, also, at or before the time when the principal of said bonds becomes due, a further ad valorem tax upon all the taxable property in said city sufficient to pay the same or to provide for the payment thereof. Such taxes shall be levied and collected at the same time and in the same manner as other taxes upon the property in said city.

Sec. 4. That the board of aldermen of the said city of Charlotte are hereby authorized to operate, manage and control the said water-works, and for this purpose to appoint such agent, servants and employees as they may deem proper, and pay the same out of the revenues from the said water-works, or from any other revenues of the said city not otherwise appropriated. The board authorized to operate, manage and control water-works.

Sec. 5. This act shall take effect from and after its passage.

Ratified the 23d day of January, A. D. 1899.

CHAPTER 8.

An act to incorporate the "Southern Conservatory of Music" in the town and county of Durham.

The General Assembly of North Carolina do enact:

Section 1. That Gilmore Ward Bryant, J. H. Southgate and T. C. Williams, Jr., their associates and their successors, be and they are hereby constituted a body politic and corporate by the name of the "Southern Conservatory of Music," for the musical training and instruction of students in all departments of the science, with all the powers, rights and privileges conferred on corporations by chapter sixteen, volume one of The Code. Southern Conservatory of Music made a body politic.

Sec. 2. That they are authorized and empowered in their corporate name to purchase and hold such real estate as they may deem necessary for the purposes above-named, and may convey the same at pleasure. May purchase and hold real estate.

Sec. 3. That under this act of incorporation power shall be conferred upon said Southern Conservatory of Music to grant diplomas and issue such other certificates of merit as they may deem advisable. Corporation may grant diplomas and issue certificates.

Sec. 4. That this act shall be in force from and after its ratification.

Ratified the 24th day of January, A. D. 1899.

CHAPTER 9.

An act to enable the tax collector of Salem to collect taxes.

The General Assembly of North Carolina do enact:

Chapter 40, private laws of 1891, amended so as to give tax collector of Salem same power as sheriff to collect tax by garnishee or otherwise in any portion of county.

Section 1. That chapter forty of the private laws of eighteen hundred and ninety-one be amended by adding after the last word in section thirty-two of said act the following, to-wit: The tax collector of Salem shall have the same power and authority to collect taxes due the said town by garnishee or otherwise, in any portion of Forsyth county that is conferred by law upon the sheriff of Forsyth county in the collection of state and county taxes.

Sec. 2. That this act shall be enforced from and after its ratification.

Ratified the 23rd day of January, A. D. 1899.

CHAPTER 10.

An act to repeal chapter five (5) private laws of eighteen hundred and ninety-five.

The General Assembly of North Carolina do enact:

Repeals act to incorporate the Swain Lumber and Boom Company.

Section 1. That chapter five, private laws of eighteen hundred and ninety-five, be and the same is hereby repealed.

Sec. 2. That this act shall be in force from and after its ratification.

Ratified the 24th day of January, A. D. 1899.

CHAPTER 11.

An act to amend chapter one hundred and sixty-three of the private laws of eighteen hundred and ninety-five.

The General Assembly of North Carolina do enact:

Chapter 163, private laws of 1895, relates to charter of Bank of Fayetteville. Minimum capital stock may be $100,000.

Sec. 1. That section one hundred and sixty-three of the private laws of eighteen hundred and ninety-five be amended by striking out the word "two" in line ten and inserting the word "one."

Sec. 2. That this act shall be in force from and after its ratification.

Ratified the 23d day of January, A. D. 1899.

CHAPTER 12.

An act to change the corporate limits of the town of Kelford in Bertie county.

The General Assembly of North Carolina do enact:

Section 1. That the corporate limits of the town of Kelford, in Bertie county, shall be as follows:

A square, each of whose sides is seven hundred yards in length, and commencing on the Norfolk and Carolina Railroad at a point five hundred yards from its crossing with the Roanoke and Tar River Road and in the direction from said crossing towards the Roanoke river, and thence at right angles from said Norfolk and Carolina Railroad, turning towards the west a distance of three hundred and fifty yards; and thence turning to the right and at right angles and parallel to said Norfolk and Carolina Railroad track a distance of seven hundred yards; and thence at right angles turning to the right and parallel with the Roanoke and Tar River Railroad a distance of seven hundred yards; and thence turning to the right at right angles and parallel with the Norfolk and Carolina railroad track a distance of seven hundred yards; and thence turning to the right at right angles a distance of three hundred and fifty yards to the point of beginning on the Norfolk and Carolina Railroad track. Kelford, corporate limits, metes and bounds.

Sec. 2. That all laws in conflict with this act are repealed. Repeal.

Sec. 3. That this act shall be in force from and after its ratification.

Ratified the 24th day of January, A. D. 1899.

CHAPTER 13.

An act for the relief of Miss Fannie B. Alston and Florence Williams.

The General Assembly of North Carolina do enact:

Section 1. That the treasurer of Vance county is hereby authorized and instructed to pay to Miss Fannie B. Alston, a white school teacher of Vance county, and Florence Williams, a colored school teacher of Vance county, the sums of fifteen dol- Treasurer Vance county authorized to pay Fannie B. Alston and Florence Williams for schools taught in 1897.

lars and fourteen dollars and sixty cents, respectively, out of any school funds now in his hands (not otherwise appropriated) or that may hereafter come into his hands. Said sums of fifteen dollars and fourteen dollars and sixty cents are respectively due to Miss Fannie B. Alston and Florence Williams each for teaching a public school in Vance county in the year eighteen hundred and ninety-seven.

Sec. 2. That this act shall be in force from and after its ratification.

Ratified the 24th day of January, A. D. 1899.

CHAPTER 14.

An act to repeal chapter two hundred and ninety-seven of the private laws of eighteen hundred and ninety-five.

The General Assembly of North Carolina do enact:

Repeals the act incorporating the North Carolina Treasure Association.

Section 1. That chapter two hundred and ninety-seven, private laws of the session of eighteen hundred and ninety-five, ratified the thirteenth day of March, eighteen hundred and ninety-five, be and the same is hereby repealed.

Sec. 2. That this act shall be in force from and after its ratification.

Ratified the 24th day of January, A. D. 1899.

CHAPTER 15.

An act to repeal the charter of the town of Dudley in Wayne county.

The General Assembly of North Carolina do enact:

Chapter 72, private laws of 1897, repealed.

Section 1. That chapter seventy-two of the private laws of eighteen hundred and ninety-seven incorporating the town of Dudley be and the same is hereby repealed.

Sec. 2. That this act shall be in force from and after its ratification.

Ratified the 24th day of January, A. D. 1899.

CHAPTER 16.

An act to amend the charter of the Cabarrus Savings Bank.

The General Assembly of North Carolina do enact:

Section 1. That section four of chapter one of the private laws of North Carolina, passed at session of eighteen hundred and ninety-seven, be and the same is hereby amended by striking out the word "nine" in the second line of said section and inserting in lieu thereof the word "twelve." Section 4 amended

Sec. 2. That said Cabarrus Savings Bank is hereby fully authorized and empowered to subscribe for, hold and possess stock in any other banking corporation to such an amount as its board of directors may authorize. May subscribe for, hold and possess stock in other banking corporations to any amount determined upon by its board of directors.

Sec. 3. That said Cabarrus Savings Bank may under such rules and regulations as its board of directors may prescribe, establish, operate and control a branch of its said bank at Albemarle, Stanley county, North Carolina, and that said branch when so established shall have all the rights, privileges and powers granted to the said Cabarrus Savings Bank. Bank may establish, operate and control a branch bank at Albemarle, Stanley county. Branch bank, rights, privileges and powers.

Sec. 4. That when the directors of said Cabarrus Savings Bank shall establish a branch in said town it shall be known and designated as the Cabarrus Savings Bank of Albemarle, North Carolina. Branch bank, name and designation.

Sec. 5. That all checks, drafts or other orders for money drawn upon said branch shall be due and payable at the banking house in the town of Albemarle where said branch is so established, and at no other place: Provided, that this act shall not release said Cabarrus Savings Bank of Concord, North Carolina, from the debts and obligations of its branch. Branch bank, cheques and orders of, payable, where. Proviso.

Sec. 6. That this act shall take effect from and after its ratification.

Ratified the 26th day of January, A. D. 1899.

CHAPTER 17.

An act to amend the charter of the town of Jamesville, Martin county, North Carolina.

The General Assembly of North Carolina do enact:

Section 1. That section two (2), chapter one hundred and fifty-eight (158), private laws of eighteen hundred and ninety-one (1891) be stricken out, and the following inserted in lieu thereof: Chapter 158, private laws of 1891, entitled a act to incorporate the town of Jamesville, amended.

2

Corporate limits of town of Jamesville.

That the corporate limits of said town shall be as follows: Beginning on Roanoke river at the northern end of Smithwick street; thence southerly along Smithwick street to the northeast corner of W. T. Stallings' dwelling-house tract of land, on said Smithwick street; thence westerly along said Stallings' back fence to New street; thence southerly to Washington street; thence a southerly course continued one hundred and twenty yards (120) to a corner post; thence easterly to the southwest corner of Mrs. Fannie Lilly's dwelling-house lot; thence southerly to the southwest corner of the A. J. Davis dwelling-house lot; thence easterly to the center of Maple branch; thence northerly along the center of said branch to Hardison street; thence easterly along Hardison street to the eastern end of said street; thence southerly one hundred and twenty yards (120) to a post; thence easterly to the Jamesville and Washington Railroad track; thence northerly along said railroad track to Roanoke river; thence up said Roanoke river along the water's edge to Smithwick street on said river, the beginning.

Conflicting laws repealed.

Sec. 2. That all laws and clauses of law coming in conflict with this act are hereby repealed.

Sec. 3. That this act shall be in force from and after its ratification.

Ratified the 26th day of January, A. D. 1899.

CHAPTER 18.

An act to amend chapter one hundred and fifty-three, private laws of eighteen hundred and ninety-three, entitled an act to incorporate the city of Fayetteville.

The General Assembly of North Carolina do enact:

An act entitled an act to incorporate the city of Fayetteville. Section 23 of said act amended.

That chapter one hundred and fifty-three of the private laws of eighteen hundred and ninety-three be amended as follows:

Section 1. Amend section twenty-three so as to read as follows:

Mayor shall have no fees in any trial before him.

Salary of mayor to be fixed by boards of aldermen and audit and finance. Salary of mayor payable at such periods as aldermen may prescribe.

"Section 23. The mayor of the said city shall not receive any fee in any case tried before him, whether he has final jurisdiction or only to act as a committing magistrate, but all fees shall be collected and paid into the treasury of the said city. The mayor shall receive as compensation for his services such salary as the board of aldermen and board of audit and finance may fix, payable out of the city treasury in such sums and at such periods as the board of aldermen may prescribe."

Sec. 2. Amend section thirty-two so as to read as follows: "Section 32. The board of aldermen when convened shall have the power to make and provide for the execution thereof such ordinances, by-laws, rules and regulations for the better government of the city as they may deem necessary, provided the same be allowed by the provisions of this act, and are consistent with the constitution and by-laws of the state. This chapter in its amended form, together with all ordinances, by-laws, rules and regulations heretofore adopted, and now in force and which may hereafter be adopted, shall be properly recorded in a separate book to be known as the 'Book of Laws and Ordinances.' All ordinances shall be properly indexed and, excepting in cases of emergency, ordinances hereafter adopted shall not become operative until they have been published at least once in a newspaper of the said city, or by printed posters for ten days."

Board of aldermen shall have power to make and enforce ordinances, by-laws etc.

Proviso.

Ordinances, rules and by-laws to be recorded in separate book.

Ordinances, etc., not operative till published.

Sec. 3. Amend section thirty-three so as to read as follows: "Section 33. The board of aldermen at the first meeting after their election shall appoint a clerk and treasurer who shall respectively hold their offices during the official term of the aldermen who appointed them; subject, however, to be removed at any time and others appointed in their stead, for misbehavior or negligence in office. Before acting the clerk and treasurer shall execute a bond payable to the city of Fayetteville in such sums as the board of aldermen may determine."

Boardof aldermen shall appoint a clerk and treasurer

Clerk and treasurer to be sworn. Bond.

Sec. 4. Amend section thirty-four to read as follows: "Sec. 34. The clerk shall have a reasonable salary, to be fixed by the board of aldermen, and it shall be his duty to keep regularly correct minutes of the proceedings of the board of aldermen and to preserve all books, papers and articles committed to his care during his continuance in office, and to deliver them to his successor, and generally to perform such other duties as may be prescribed by the board of aldermen and this charter."

Clerk's salary.

Clerk's duties.

Sec. 5. Amend section thirty-five so as to read as follows: "Sec. 35. The treasurer shall make out annually a full and correct transcript of receipts and disbursements on account of the city for the general inspection of the citizens, and cause the same to be posted before the door of the mayor's office at the end of the fiscal year, and printed in some newspaper published in the city of Fayetteville. The treasurer's salary shall be such as may be fixed by the board of aldermen."

Treasurer to make annual transcripts.

Treasurer's salary.

Sec. 6. Amend section thirty-seven so as to read as follows: "Sec. 37. All orders drawn upon the treasurer shall be issued by the clerk from the regular city scrip book, specifying the name of the payee, on what account paid, the amount, date and number signed by him and countersigned by the mayor, and an accurate stub of the same shall be kept, and the treasurer shall

Orders drawn upon treasurer shall be issued by the clerk from regular scrip book, and shall specify name of payee and what account charged to, orders signed by him and countersigned by mayor

Treasurer to keep stub-book, and specify purpose for which money is paid, and sources from which it is derived.

specify in his accounts the purposes to which all moneys are applied and also the sources whence are derived the moneys received by him."

Sec. 7. Amend section thirty-nine so as to read as follows:

Duties of board of audit and finance.

"Sec. 39. It shall be the duty of the board of audit and finance to consider and act upon the charges fixed for privileges of various kinds and to make recommendations to the mayor and board of aldermen as to all such matters as shall affect the finances of the city of Fayetteville, and no appropriation of moneys or expenditures or contracts affecting the finances of the city shall be made by the mayor and board of aldermen until the same shall be approved by at least two members of the board of audit and finance, but said board of audit and finance shall have no power or authority to do anything binding upon the city of Fayetteville otherwise than to concur in or veto the action of the board of aldermen in matters of finance and contracts affecting the finances of the said city: Provided, that upon a veto by the board of audit and finance of the action of the board of aldermen, it shall be the duty of said board of audit and finance to report to the board of aldermen in writing, at the next regular or called meeting of said board of aldermen, such veto, together with the cause of the same, and such communication from the board of audit and finance to the board of aldermen shall be spread upon the minutes of the board of aldermen, and at the next regular or called meeting of the board of aldermen the mayor, after having caused such communication to be read, shall submit the question on the 'aye and nay' vote, 'Shall the vote be sustained?' and thereupon, if eleven of the board of aldermen shall vote 'nay,' such veto shall be of no effect, and the original action of the board of aldermen shall prevail."

No appropriation of money or expenditures or contracts shall be made or entered into till approved by board of audit and finance

Board of audit and finance may concur in or veto the action of aldermen in all matters of finance and in contracts affecting the finances of said city

Proviso.
Board of audit and finance.

Report of veto to be spread upon minutes of the aldermen.

Mayor shall cause an aye and nay vote to be taken on measure vetoed, the question being "Shall the veto be sustained?"

Number necessary to sustain veto.

Sec. 8. Amend section forty-nine so as to read as follows:

Sinking fund to be created.

"Sec. 49. The board of aldermen and board of audit and finance of the city of Fayetteville shall create a sinking fund for the payment of all its bonded indebtedness, and to that end they may appropriate the taxes to be derived from railroads, licenses, or any other sources, which in their judgment would be adequate and proper; and the board of aldermen, subject to the approval and ratification of the board of audit and finance as heretofore provided, shall have power to establish ordinances fixing a schedule of rates to be charged as a license or privilege tax upon any business, trade, occupation or profession conducted in the corporate limits of the said city, including railroads, express companies, steamboat companies, telegraph companies, telephone companies, gas companies, electric light companies, water companies, and fire and life insurance companies, or any agent or agencies of the same or any of the same on business done wholly

What taxes applied to sinking fund.

The board of aldermen, with the approval of the board audit and finance, may prescribe privilege tax upon trades, etc.

What business shall pay privilege taxes.

within the State. In the event that the sale of liquor shall hereafter be authorized by law within the limits of Cumberland county, the board of aldermen shall have no authority or power to grant any retail license to sell spirituous, vinous or malt liquors in Fayetteville at a less sum than five hundred dollars per annum, payable quarterly in advance, and said board of aldermen shall be the sole judges of the character and fitness of all applicants for liquor license in Fayetteville; it shall exercise strict supervision over same, and for violation of law or other just cause may rescind any license granted."

Board shall grant licenses to sell liquor, under what circumstances, and what sums shall be charged for such licenses. Who to be sole judges of fitness of persons to sell liquor.

Sec. 9. Amend section fifty-two so as to read as follows:

"Sec. 52. There shall be and is hereby levied a tax of one per centum on property, thirty per centum of which shall be applied to the liquidation of the debt, and three dollars poll tax, and the said mayor and board of aldermen shall have no power or authority to create any new bonded indebtedness, unless with the assent of the majority of the qualified voters of the city of Fayetteville at an election or elections to be held for that purpose under the express authority to be granted by the general assembly of the state; nor shall they have power to issue orders on the treasurer for payment of any obligation due by the city when the issue of such orders will increase the amount of unpaid scrip to more than one thousand dollars."

What taxes shall be levied, and how applied.

Mayor and board of aldermen shall create no new bonded debt only with assent of majority of voters, under express authority of General Assembly.

No orders to issue on treasurer when such orders would increase amount of unpaid scrip.

Sec. 10. Amend section fifty-three so as to read as follows:

"Sec. 53. The board of aldermen shall set aside thirty per centum of the poll and property tax collected each year, which shall be applied to the debt, and twenty per centum of the tax, if necessary, shall be set aside for water-works, and the board of aldermen shall have the power to regulate water charges for private consumption by any water company doing business, or the plant or pipes of which are wholly or partially located in the city of Fayetteville.

Portion of taxes to be set apart for debt, portion to be set apart for water-works.

Water charges, how and by whom regulated.

Sec. 11. Amend section fifty-five so as to read as follows:

"Sec. 55. The assessment of property for the purpose of taxation under the provisions of this charter shall be the same as that fixed by the assessors appointed by the board of county commissioners of Cumberland county, to assess the property of Cross Creek township for state and county purposes, and the board of aldermen of the said city shall place on the tax lists of the said city the property owned by the people of said city in the limits thereof or subject to taxation therein at the sum assessed by said county assessors for Cross Creek township, returned by them to the county authorities, and place said lists with the tax collector of the said city and direct that he shall proceed to collect the same."

Property, how assessed for taxation.

Property, upon what tax lists to be placed.

Tax lists to be placed in hands of collectors.

Sec. 12. Between section fifty-five and section fifty-six insert section 55b to read as follows:

City board of health, who shall constitute.

"Sec. 55b. The mayor, chairman of the board of audit and finance, city engineer, and the white physicians residing and practicing in the corporate limits of said city of Fayetteville, shall constitute the city board of health, which board shall meet at such times as the said board may determine, or upon the call of the mayor or any two physicians belonging to said board for the purpose of making recommendations to the board of aldermen concerning health and sanitation within the corporate limits of said city. The said board of health may elect its chairman and secretary."

Board of health meetings. Board of health, meetings of, by whom called.

Board of health, officers of, by whom elected.

Sec. 13. This act shall be in force from and after its ratification, and all laws and parts of laws in conflict herewith are hereby repealed.

Conflicting laws repealed.

Ratified the 26th day of January, A. D. 1899.

CHAPTER 19.

An act to amend the charter of the town of Salem, North Carolina.

The General Assembly of North Carolina do enact:

Charter of Salem amended.

Section 1. That the preamble to chapter three hundred and sixty-six of the laws of eighteen hundred and ninety-one, being "An act to extend the police jurisdiction of the town of Salem," be and the same is hereby amended by striking out the word "two" in line six and inserting in lieu thereof the word "four," so as to extend the police jurisdiction of said town to a distance of four thousand feet in place of two thousand feet.

Police jurisdiction extended, to what boundaries.

Sec. 2. That the police jurisdiction of the mayor and commissioners of Salem be further extended as follows, to-wit: From the point where the present line crosses Lexington road, southwardly along said road to Glencoe street, thence westwardly along Glencoe street to Glendale street, thence southwardly along Glendale street to Edgewood street, thence westwardly along Edgewood street to the boundary line of the property now known as Sherwood heights, and with the boundaries of said property in its various courses until it meets Wachovia brook, and thence eastwardly along said brook until it reaches the boundary line of Salem; all the provisions of said act of eighteeen hundred and ninety-one and all the powers contained therein shall apply to the territory embraced in the foregoing extent of jurisdiction.

Provision and powers of act 1891 extended.

Sec. 3. That this act shall be enforced from and after its ratification.

Ratified the 26th day of January, A. D. 1899.

CHAPTER 20.

An act to authortze the town of Morganton to purchase and operate an electric light and power plant.

Whereas, the board of commissioners of the town of Morganton have entered into a contract with F. H. Busbee and W. C. Erwin, commissioners, to purchase the plant of the Morganton Electric Light and Power Company, and to pay therefor five thousand dollars in coupon bonds of the town of Morganton, provided an issue of bonds to that amount is duly authorized by a vote of the qualified voters of said town; now therefore, Preamble.

The General Assembly of North Carolina do enact:

Section 1. That the board of commissioners of the town of Morganton be and they are hereby authorized and empowered to purchase, hold and, as hereinafter provided, to operate and maintain all that certain electric plant in said town, known as the Morganton Electric Light and Power Company's plant, with all and singular the real and personal property constituting the same, and to use, exercise and enjoy as hereinafter provided, all the privileges and franchises conferred upon the Morganton Electric Light and Power Company by its charter, and to issue and pay therefor five thousand dollars ($5,000) in coupon bonds of said town, said bonds to be of such denomination as said board of commissioners may determine, to run for twenty (20) years from the issue of the same, and to bear interest at the rate of six (6) per cent., payable semi-annually. That said coupon bonds shall be signed by the mayor and secretary of the town of Morganton and shall have the corporate seal thereto affixed. The coupons of said bonds shall be receivable by the tax collector and treasurer of the town of Morganton in payment of taxes and all dues to said town, but said bonds shall not be sold for less than par, and shall not be issued unless and until duly authorized by a majority of the qualified voters of said town at an election held as hereinafter provided.

Commissioners authorized to purchase electric light plant, and to hold, use and enjoy the same.

Coupon bonds to the amount of $5,000 authorized.

Bonds to run twenty years; what rate of interest.

Bond, by whom signed.

Coupons receivable for taxes and all dues to town of Morganton.

Bonds must be sold at par.

Bonds to be authorized by majority of voters.

Sec. 2. That it shall be lawful for the board of public works of the town of Morganton (as hereinafter provided for) to operate and maintain said electric light and power plant, and from time

Board may opearte plant and extend it from time to time.

May furnish light and power for public and private use, and may charge for such service.
Proviso.

to time to extend and enlarge the same, and to furnish electric lights for lighting the streets of said town, and to provide lights and motive power for private use, and to charge such reasonable rentals as may be agreed upon: Provided, that all charges and rentals shall be uniform and without discrimination against any citizen of said town.

Board of public works, how and upon what conditions created.

Term of office of board.

Board shall manage plant, and appoint employees, fixing their compensations, etc.

Sec. 3. That if at the election held as hereinafter provided, a majority of the qualified votes shall be cast in favor of issuing said bonds, the said board of commissioners are authorized and directed at their first meeting after said election to elect five resident voters of said town, who shall constitute, and are hereby denominated "The Board of Public Works" of the town of Morganton, whose term of office shall begin at their election, and shall continue for six years, and until their successors are duly elected for a like term by the voters of the town of Morganton at the next regular town election, after said term of office shall expire. That said "Board of Public Works" shall have full management and control of said electric light plant; shall appoint all employees, fix their compensation, adopt uniform schedule of rates, and do and perform all and singular the acts and duties necessary or convenient to the maintenance, operation and control of said electric light plant.

Income, how paid over, how held, and how paid out.

Surplus, how applied.

Special tax, when and upon what property to be levied.
Sum set aside to meet bonds at maturity.
Extent of special tax.

Sec. 4. That all income derived from the operation of said electric light plant shall be paid over to the treasurer of the town of Morganton, and shall be kept separate and apart from the other funds of said town as "the electric light fund," and shall be paid out on the order of the "board of public works" for meeting the costs of operating and maintaining said plant and making such improvements and extensions thereof as may be determined upon by said board, and any surplus remaining after the payment of such costs and charges shall be applied to the payment of the coupons on the bonds issued for the purchase of said plant, and for the creation of a sinking fund to meet said bonds at maturity: Provided, that the board of commissioners are authorized, and it shall be their duty, if the surplus aforesaid is not sufficient therefor, each and every year to levy a special tax upon all taxable property and polls in said town sufficient to pay the coupons on said bonds as the same become due, and to set aside the sum of two hundred and fifty dollars ($250) for each year to meet said bonds at maturity, but said special tax levied for such purpose shall not exceed eight and one-third (8 1-3) cents on the hundred dollars worth of property and twenty-five cents on the poll.

Election, when to be ordered.

Sec. 5. That within fifteen days after the ratification of this act the board of commissioners of Morganton shall order an election to be held in said town upon the question of issuing said five thousand dollars ($5,000) in coupon bonds as aforesaid for the purchase of said plant, at such time and place as the said board of commissioners of Morganton shall appoint, at which election those in favor of issuing said bonds and levying the special tax hereinbefore provided for shall vote a ballot on which is written or printed "For electric lights," and those opposed to said issue of bonds shall vote a ballot on which is written or printed "Against electric lights," and it shall be the duty of said board of commissioners to give notice of said election by publication in some newspaper published in the town of Morganton for four successive weeks prior thereto.

Ballot, what to contain.

Notice of election.

Sec. 6. That at the time of ordering said election said board shall select a registrar and two judges of election, and shall give notice of a registration for all unregistered voters in said town by publication, for four successive weeks, in some newspaper published therein, and by posting said notice for ten days at the court-house door in said town. Notice of their appointment shall be served on said registrar and judges of election by the sheriff. It shall be the duty of said registrar to open his books at such times and place in said town as may be designated by said board of commissioners, and to erase from said registration books the names of all persons who by death, removal or otherwise are not legally entitled to vote in said town.

Registrar and judges of election.

Notice of registration.

Notice of their election, how served on registrar and judges.

Sec. 7. That all persons entitled to vote in the county of Burke for members of the general assembly, and who shall have been bona fide residents of the town of Morganton ninety days immediately preceding the election shall be entitled to register and vote hereunder.

Who may vote in election.

Sec. 8. Any person applying to be registered under the provisions of this act shall take the following oath, to be administered by the registrar: "I . . . . do solemnly swear that I have been a citizen and resident of the state of North Carolina for the last twelve months, and a bona fide resident of the town of Morganton for the last ninety days. So help me God."

Oath administered to applicants for registration.

Sec. 9. The judges appointed by said board of commissioners, together with the registrar, shall hold and conduct the election, and shall, before opening the polls, take an oath before some justice of the peace, or other person authorized to administer oaths, to hold said election fairly and impartially according to the constitution and laws of this state.

Who shall hold election—oath.

Sec. 10. The polls shall be opened on the day of election from seven o'clock in the morning until sunset of the same day. No person whose name has not been duly registered shall be allowed to vote, and any one offering to vote may be challenged at the polls, and if the judges of election shall sustain the challenge, such person's ballot shall not be received.

Polls, when opened and when closed.

Challenge.

Abstract of vote vote cast.

Sec. 11. The judges of election shall make an abstract of the vote cast at said election "For electric lights," and "Against electric lights," and return same to the board of commissioners of Morganton, and shall certify to said board the number of qualified voters in said town as shown by the registration books, and said board of commissioners shall thereupon canvass said vote, and judicially determine and declare the result, and enter the same upon the minutes of said board. If upon the canvass of said vote as aforesaid it shall appear that a majority of the qualified voters of the town of Morganton have voted "For electric lights," said commissioners shall issue said bonds, and complete the purchase of said electric light plant, and elect "the board of public works," as hereinbefore provided.

Votes, canvassed by whom.

Who may invest in bonds.

Sec. 12. All administrators, executors and guardians and persons acting in a fiduciary capacity, having funds to invest, are hereby authorized and empowered to invest the funds intrusted to them in said bonds, if issued as hereinbefore set forth.

Vacancies, how filled.

Sec. 13. That all vacancies occurring in "the board of public works," as hereinbefore provided for, by death, resignation or otherwise, shall be filled by the members of said "board of public works," and the successors to said "board of public works," elected as provided for in section three of this act, shall be elected at the regular town election in the year nineteen hundred and five, and at the regular town election held during each recurring sixth year thereafter and shall serve for six years, and until their successors are elected.

Conflicting laws repealed.

Sec. 14. All laws and parts of laws in conflict with this act are hereby repealed.

Sec. 15. This act shall be in force from and after its ratification.

Ratified the 26th day of January, A. D. 1899.

CHAPTER 21.

An act for the relief of Maggie F. Hughie of Wilkes County.

The General Assembly of North Carolina do enact:

County treasurer to pay out of school fund.

Section 1. That the county treasurer of Wilkes county be directed to pay out of the school funds of Wilkesboro township the sum of thirteen dollars and thirty-five cents ($13.35) to Maggie F. Hughie, this being the balance due her for teaching school at Eschol in said township.

Sec. 2. That this act shall be in force from and after its ratification.

Ratified the 31st day of January, A. D. 1899.

CHAPTER 22.

An act to repeal the charter of the town of Redmon.

The General Assembly of North Carolina do enact:

Section 1. That chapter sixty-nine of the private laws of the session of eighteen hundred and ninety-seven be and the same is hereby repealed. Repealed.

Sec. 2. That this act shall be in force from and after its ratification.

Ratified the 31st day of January, A. D. 1899.

CHAPTER 23.

An act to authorize the treasurer of Haywood county to pay school fund.

The General Assembly of North Carolina do enact:

Section 1. That the treasurer of Haywood county is hereby authorized and directed to pay J. W. Scot the sum of twenty-eight dollars and fifty cents out of the first unapportioned school funds that may come into hands of the county treasurer. Treasurer of Haywood county to pay J. W. Scot $28.50.

Sec. 2. That this act shall be in force from and after its ratification.

Ratified the 31st day of January, A. D. 1899.

CHAPTER 24.

An act to pay Sarah M. Leary for service as teacher in public school, district No. 24, for colored race in Cape Fear district, Chatham county, North Carolina.

Whereas, Sarah M. Leary performed the duties of teacher in public school No. 24 district, under contract with the school committee, and there is a balance due her of twenty dollars and sixty-seven cents, as per certificate held by her, dated June eighth, eighteen hundred and ninety-seven, which has never been paid by the county for alleged want of funds, Preamble.

The General Assembly of North Carolina do enact:

Sec. 1. That the treasurer of Chatham county be and is hereby authorized and directed to pay Sarah M. Leary the sum of twenty dollars and sixty-two cents for said services upon her receipting to him for the same.

Sec. 2. That this act shall be in force from and after its ratification.

Ratified the 31st day of January, A. D. 1899.

CHAPTER 25.

An act to amend chapter thirty-seven, private laws of eighteen hundred and ninety-seven.

The General Assembly of North Carolina do enact:

Chapter 37, private laws 1897, relating to Tar River Bank, Rocky Mount. Amended.

Section 1. That the title of chapter thirty-seven, private laws of eighteen hundred and ninety-seven, be amended by striking out the words "Tar river" and inserting in lieu thereof "Planters."

Amended.

Sec. 2. That section one of said act be amended by striking out in line five of said section the words "Tar river" and inserting in lieu thereof the word "Planters."

Amended.

May own and lease warehouses, carry on business of warehousemen, forwarders, etc.

May collect interest, etc.

Preferred lien on property held or deposited.

Property may be sold for charges.

Sale—notice.

Sec. 3. That section six of said act be amended by adding thereto the following, viz.: and the said corporation shall have power to own, maintain or lease warehouses and storage-houses, and carry on the business of warehousemen and forwarders; to receive on storage or deposit any and all kinds of produce, merchandise or other personal property; to make advances in money or merchandise or produce; and to carry on and transact all kinds of business usually transacted by warehousemen; and to collect and receive interest, commission compensation for storage, and all labor and expenses incident thereto; and all advances made by said corporation on property received for storage or deposit, and compensation for all charges and expenses thereon shall be a preferred lien on said property, which shall be satisfied and paid before said corporation can be required to deliver said property to any one: and if the charges aforesaid are not paid when due, according to the terms of the agreement upon which the advances thereon were made, the said property of whatever nature may be immediately sold for cash, at public auction, after due advertisement by posters posted at the court-house door in the county where said property is situated, and at three other public places near said property for ten days. From the proceeds of said sale shall be taken the charges aforesaid, and also the costs of said sale, and the surplus paid to the owner thereof.

Sec. 4. This act shall be in force and effect from the date of its ratification.

Ratified the 1st day of February, A. D. 1899.

CHAPTER 26.

An act to repeal chapter thirteen of the public laws of eighteen hundred and ninety-five.

The General Assembly of North Carolina do enact:

Section 1. That chapter thirteen of the acts of the general assembly at its session of eighteen hundred and ninety-five be and the same is hereby repealed. Chapter 13, laws 1895, relating to name of town of Lamoth.

Sec. 2. That chapter sixty-three of the laws of eighteen hundred and eighty-nine be and the same is hereby re-enacted.

Sec. 3 That this act shall be in force from and after its ratification.

Ratified the 31st day of January, A. D. 1899.

CHAPTER 27.

An act to amend chapter two hundred, private laws of eighteen hundred and ninety-three.

The General Assembly of North Carolina do enact:

Section 1. That chapter two hundred (200), private laws of North Carolina, passed March third, eighteen hundred and ninety-three, be amended by striking out in lines five and six of section one the words "North Carolina Savings Bank," and inserting in lieu thereof the words "Central Savings," and by striking out in section eleven all that follows the word "purpose" in line sixteen, to-wit, the second proviso of said section. Chapter 200, private laws 1893, relating to N. C. Savings Bank and Trust Company. Change of name.

Sec. 2. That this act shall be in force from and after its ratification.

Ratified the 1st day of February, A. D. 1899.

CHAPTER 28.

An act to repeal chapter four hundred and ninety-one of the public laws of eighteen hundred and ninety-three, and to amend chapter one hundred and six of the public laws of eighteen hundred and eighty-fiue.

The General Assembly of North Carolina do enact:

Section 1. That chapter four hundred and ninety-one of the public laws of eighteen hundred and ninety-three be and the same is hereby repealed. Repealed. Relating to impounding stock in Edgecombe county

Amended.

Sec. 2. That section three of chapter one hundred and six of the public laws of eighteen hundred and eighty-five be amended by striking out the words "fifty cents" in line five and inserting in lieu thereof the words "twenty-five cents."

Sec. 3. That this act shall be in force from and after its ratification.

Ratified the 1st day of February, A. D. 1899.

CHAPTER 29.

An act to change the name of Harriston, Pitt county, North Carolina.

The General Assembly of North Carolina do enact:

Repealed—name restored.

Section 1. That chapter four hundred and fifty-two of the public laws of eighteen hundred and ninety-five be and the same is hereby repealed and the name Ayden is hereby restored to said town.

Sec. 2. That this act shall be in force from and after its ratification.

Ratified the 1st day of February, A. D. 1899.

CHAPTER 30.

An act to amend the charter of the city of New Bern.

The General Assembly of North Carolina do enact:

Charter, amendments and laws repealed.

Section 1. That the charter of the city of New Bern and all amendments thereto, and all laws constituting the said charter and amendments, be and the same are hereby repealed, and all offices created by and under said charter, laws and amendments be and the same are hereby abolished.

Property of city delivered to certain persons, trustees.

Trustees shall take, hold and protect property; powers to own property, for what purposes.

Sec. 2. That all the property, real, personal and mixed which belonged to or was vested in the said city of New Bern shall be delivered to Wm. Dunn, S. H. Cutler, T. A. Green, K. R. Jones and G. H. Roberts, trustees, who shall take and hold possession thereof and diligently keep, protect and preserve the same with full power and authority to use the same for the protection and benefit of the inhabitants of the territory formerly constituting the said city of New Bern and for the protection of the property of said inhabitants of said territory.

Sec. 3. That any and all persons who may have control of or possession of any of said property shall deliver the same to said trustees or such other persons as may be entitled thereto upon demand made by them, and any person refusing to so deliver any part of said property shall be guilty of a misdemeanor and fined not more than five hundred dollars and imprisoned not more than six months or either: Provided, that said trustees or other person entitled to receive the same may extend the time for any such person or persons to comply with their demands.

Persons in possession of property must deliver it to Trustees upon demand.

Persons refusing to deliver property guilty of misdemeanor—fine and imprisonment.

Proviso.

Sec. 4. That said trustees shall keep, hold, preserve and use said property as aforesaid until further directed by law, and shall deliver up the said property to such person or persons as may be designated by law.

Trustees shall keep property, how long; shall deliver it to whom.

Sec. 5. That this act shall take effect seven days after its ratification.

Ratified the 3d day of February, A. D. 1899.

CHAPTER 31.

An act to incorporate the Citizens Bank of Elizabeth City.

The General Assembly of North Carolina do enact:

Section 1. That O. McMullan, F. M. Grice, C. E. Kramer, W. C. Glover, John Sharber, T. G. Skinner, M. N. Sawyer, George W. Ward, C. H. Robinson, J. B. Flora, D. B. Bradford, Mrs. Nellie Baxter, R. B. Martin, A. L. Pendleton, J. B. Blades, Charles Blades, Toms and McMullan, Blanchard and Brother, McCabe and Grice, C. W. Grice, Charles Overman, George H. Wood, R. J. Mitchell, James Parker, George M. Scott, W. T. Old, W. J. Woodley, Thomas P. Nash, their associates, successors and assigns are hereby created a corporation under the name of "The Citizens Bank of Elizabeth City," for the period of sixty years, with full power to sue and be sued in any court of the state or the United States, to acquire, own and convey real and personal property, and to adopt and use a common seal which may be altered when deemed expedient.

Incorporators.

Corporation and body politic; name. Limit of corporate life.

May sue and be sued.

May own and convey real property.

Sec. 2. The capital stock of the corporation shall be twenty-five thousand ($25,000) dollars, divided into shares of one hundred ($100) dollars each, which may be increased from time to time by the vote of two-thirds (2-3) of said stock to one hundred thousand ($100,000) dollars. The bank may commence business as soon as twenty-five thousand ($25,000) dollars is subscribed and two-fifths (2-5) thereof paid in.

Amount of capital stock—shares.

Capital stock may be increased—limit of increase.

May commence business, when.

Location of office.

Sec. 3 The principal office and banking house of the corporation shall be located in Elizabeth City, North Carolina.

Board directors, how many.

Directors, how elected, and whom.

Term of office.

Directors' meetings.

Quorum.

Directors to meet, how often.

Sec. 4. The affairs of the bank shall be managed by a board of directors consisting of seven, but may be a greater or less number, not less than five (5) nor more than nine (9), as the stockholders may decide, which board shall be elected at the annual meeting of the stockholders to be held on the second Tuesday of each January, beginning with January nineteen hundred (1900), and hold their offices for one year and until their successors are elected and qualified. The directors shall hold meetings as often as the by-laws of the company shall require, and a majority of them shall constitute a quorum for the transaction of all business: Provided, however, that such meetings of said directors shall be held at least once in every week.

First meeting of directors—election of officers.

Officers' terms.

Directors elect cashier and other employees—term of employment.

Bonds—amounts.

Sec. 5. The board of directors shall meet as soon after their election as practicable, and elect from among themselves a president and vice-president of the bank, who shall hold their office for one year and until their successors are duly elected. The said board shall also elect, not from among themselves, a cashier and such other officers and employees as the board may deem best, to hold office during the pleasure of the board. The president, cashier, teller and all clerks shall be required by the directors to give bond as follows: The president and cashier in a sum of not less than ten thousand dollars each, the bonds of all other officers to be fixed by the directors.

Powers, rights, etc.

Sec. 6. The said corporation shall have all powers, rights, privileges and immunities granted to any banking institution under the laws of North Carolina, especially by chapter four, volume two of The Code entitled "Banks," shall also have power to receive and pay out money, to deal in mercantile paper, to receive deposits of money and other valuables, may discount, buy and sell notes, drafts and all other securities and evidences of debt; may loan money upon mortgages of real or personal estate or other mortgages of real or personal estate or other security, and charge for money loaned by it such rate of interest as may be agreed upon, not exceeding the rate allowed by law, which interest it may take and receive at the time of making such loan.

Provision for protection of married women, minors, etc.

Sec. 7. That when married women, minors or apprentices shall deposit money or other thing of value in said bank, generally or specially, to their own credit, the same may be withdrawn on their check, draft or other order, and they and all other persons shall be bound by such check, draft or order, and the same shall be an absolute release and discharge of said bank from liability for the same.

Sec. 8. That any real estate held by the said corporation at any time may be duly conveyed by a deed signed by the president and cashier with its seal affixed to the same. The said corporation may buy any real or personal property sold by any one for it under deeds of trust or other assurance for debts due it, when necessary for its protection in its judgment.

May convey real estate.

May buy real estate under certain circumstances.

Sec. 9. This corporation is authorized to organize in connection with its general banking business a department for savings, and do a savings bank business for the convenience of small depositors, and to make regulations in regard thereto, and in that event said bank may receive deposits in the savings department and give certificates therefor, and pay such interest as the directors authorize, not exceeding the legal rate.

Savings bank business may be annexed to other business.

Sec. 10. In the event any subscriber to the stock of this corporation shall fail to pay for his stock, or any part of it, hereafter or heretofore subscribed, the amount so due on said stock may be recovered by the directors by civil action or the directors may sell such stock at public biddings at the banking house of the corporation, after giving thirty days' (30) public notice of such sale and like notice to the holders of such defaulting stock, and the amount realized at such sale shall be applied to the payment of the cost of such sale, the amount remaining due and unpaid for such stock and entered on same, and any balance to the owner of said stock; if the amount realized be sufficient to pay the balance due, then such balance may be recovered by civil action of the subscriber for the same.

Unpaid stock, how recovered.

Unpaid stock may be sold; notice; proceeds of sales, how applied.

Sec. 11. Subscriptions already made or which may be made to the stock of the Citizens Bank of Elizabeth City, the election of directors, officers and employees heretofore had and other acts done or which may be done, before the granting of this charter, for and in the name of said bank, not inconsistent with said charter, are hereby expressly ratified, confirmed and made valid and binding in all respects as if they had been done after the charter is granted.

Subscriptions made and acts done before the ratification of this act, ratified.

Sec. 12. That said corporation is hereby authorized to receive on deposit all valuables, gold, silver, precious metals, jewels, plate, certificates of stock, bonds, evidences of debt, instruments of title, and all other things of value which may be left on deposit with said company for safe keeping and shall be entitled to charge such commissions or compensation as may be agreed upon, and that said bank is authorized and empower to accept and exercise any trust of any and every other description which may, by its consent, be committed or transferred to it by any person or persons whomsoever, by any bodies politic or corporate, public or private, and to accept the office of executor, administrator, collectors, guardian or assignee wherever such appoint-

May receive special deposits of valuables, etc., and may charge commissions for custody thereof.

May accept and exercise trusts, etc.

ment is made or conferred by any person or persons or court in the state or of the United States, and shall be clothed with the same powers and shall be under the same restrictions as private individuals are in the same capacity.

Liability of stockholders to bank; liability to depositors.

Sec. 13. That the stockholders shall be liable to said bank for the amount subscribed by each stockholder, and in addition thereto each stockholder shall be individually liable to depositors or other creditors of said bank for an amount equal to the stock which he owns therein and no more.

Annual meetings; omissions, etc.

Sec. 14. If for any cause, any annual meeting or other meeting of the directors shall not be held as provided herein, or being held, any duty required to be done at such meeting be not then done, such omitted meeting may be subsequently held and such duties subsequently performed.

Stock transferred only on books of corporation in person or by power of attorney. No one indebted shall transfer stock until indebtedness paid.

Sec. 15. No stock held in this corporation shall be transferred except on the books of the corporation in person or by the written power of attorney, and no stock shall be transferred at all by any one indebted in any way to said corporation until said indebtedness has been fully paid, without the consent of a majority of the directors in meeting expressed, and all stock shall be liable for all debts due by such stockholders and shall be affected with a lien for such indebtedness.

Officers.

Sec. 16. The following shall constitute the officers who for the first year are to manage the affairs of this bank, viz.: O. McMullan, president; W. C. Glover, vice-president; directors, M. N. Sawyer, T. G. Skinner, W. C. Glover, O. McMullan, F. M. Grice, J. W. Sharber, C. E. Kramer.

Forfeiture of powers, etc.

Sec. 17. The immunities, powers and privileges herein granted shall be forfeited if not used in two years.

Sec. 18. This act shall be enforced from and after its ratification.

Ratified the 3d day of February, A. D. 1899.

CHAPTER 32.

An act to change the name of the South Atlantic Life and Endowment Company of North Carolina.

The General Assembly of North Carolina do enact:

Name changed.

Section 1. That section one of chapter two hundred and nine (209) of the private laws of eighteen hundred and ninety-five be and the same is hereby amended by striking out the word "south" in line nine of said section; and also striking out the word "endowment," in said line of said section, and by inserting in place of the said word "endowment" the word "annuity."

Sec. 2. That section seven of said chapter be and the same is hereby amended by striking out the word "south," in line one thereof; and also by striking out the word "endowment," in line two thereof, and inserting in place of the word "endowment" the word "annuity." Name changed.

Sec. 3. That the time for completing the organization of said company, pursuant to the provisions of said chapter, as amended by this act, be extended for two years from and after the ratification of this act. Time for organization extended.

Sec. 4. That this act shall be in force from and after its ratification.

Ratified the 8th day of February, A. D. 1899.

CHAPTER 33.

An act to incorporate the Carolina Bonding and Surety Company.

The General Assembly of North Carolina do enact:

Section 1. That F. H. Fries, R. B. Glenn, W. H. Ragan, C. D. Ogburn, and such other persons as may be associated with them, their successors or assigns, are hereby created and declared a body politic and corporate, with perpetual succession, under the name and style of the "Carolina Bonding and Surety Company." In that name may sue and be sued, plead and be impleaded in any court of this state or United States. Said corporation shall have power to adopt a common seal, and shall be capable of taking by purchase, gift, or any other way, real and personal property, and holding, leasing or conveying the same; it shall have power to buy and sell stocks, bonds or other evidences of debt; it shall have power to borrow money and to pledge or convey its property or any part thereof in any form to secure the same; it shall have and enjoy all the rights, powers and immunities which corporate bodies may lawfully exercise, and make all necessary regulations, by the adoption of by-laws, for the government of the corporation not inconsistent with the laws of the United States and the state of North Carolina. Stockholders shall not be individually liable for the obligations or debts of the corporation. Incorporators, successors, etc. Body politic and corporate. Name. May sue and be sued. Common seal. May hold real and personal property; holding, leasing, conveying; buy and sell stocks, bonds, etc. May borrow money; may pledge, etc., property. Rights, powers, etc. By-laws, regulations, etc.

Sec. 2. This company shall be located and its principal place of business shall be in the cities of Winston-Salem, N. C., but it may establish such branches and agencies throughout the United Location—principal place of business, where. Branches.

States and elsewhere as may be necessary and deemed advisable for the transaction of business.

Capital stock, amount. Shares. Books opened, by whom; places.

Sec. 3. The capital stock of the company shall be one hundred thousand dollars, divided into one thousand shares of one hundred dollars each. The incorporators shall have the power to open books of subscription in person, or by agents duly appointed by a majority of them, at such place or places as they may determine, and keep the same open for such time, and under such rules and regulations as may be deemed necessary or expedient. Ten thousand dollars shall be the minimum subscription on which the company may be organized. When said sum has been duly subscribed, the incorporators shall give ten days' notice to the subscribers of a meeting for the purposes of organization, and said subscribers shall then complete the organization of said company by electing a board of directors. The capital stock of the company may be increased from time to time by a vote of two-thirds of the stockholders to an amount not exceeding one million dollars.

Minimum subscription for organization. Notice to subscribers. Board of directors. Increase of capital stock.

Business of the corporation.

Sec. 4. Said corporation shall have the power to guarantee the fidelity of persons holding places of public or private trust, to execute as surety all bonds or undertakings of any official; to guarantee the performance of contracts other than insurance policies and to execute or guarantee bonds and undertakings required or permitted in all actions or proceedings in law or equity.

Corporate powers, by whom exercised. Delegation of powers. Officers, by whom elected; duties; salaries. Executive committee; powers.

Sec. 5. All the corporate powers of the company shall be exercised by a board of directors, annually elected by the stockholders; and said board of directors shall have authority and power to delegate any of the powers or rights of the corporation to any officer, agent or committee. The board of directors shall elect all officers, and prescribe their duties and salaries, and employ all agents or servants, and prescribe their duties and salaries. The board of directors may also appoint an executive committee, and such committee shall have such power as may be conferred upon it by the by-laws or by the resolution of the board.

Annual meeting of stockholders, when held. Directors, by whom elected; term of service. Election; ballot; number of votes; how cast; how many votes. Directors, how divided.

Sec. 6. The annual meeting of the stockholders of the company shall be held the last Tuesday in each and every year. The directors of the company shall be elected by the stockholders, and shall serve until their successors are elected. All elections shall be by ballot, and every stockholder shall have the right either in person or by proxy to cast one vote for every share of stock held by him. The directors shall be divided into three equal classes, and at the first election of the directors one-third shall be elected for one year, and one-third for two years, and one-third for three years, and annually thereafter there shall be elected to succeed the retiring members a number equal to those retiring to serve for a period of three years. All vacancies in the board of directors shall be filled by the board for the unexpired term. Vacancies.

Sec. 7. The president of the board of directors may from time to time appoint such agents, resident vice-presidents and resident secretaries in various places as may be necessary or deemed advisable for the transaction of the business of the company, and such agents or officials may be removed at any time either by the president or board of directors. Who may appoint agents, etc. Removal of agents, etc.

Sec. 8. This act shall be in force from and after its ratification.

Ratified the 8th day of February, A. D. 1899.

CHAPTER 34.

An act to amend the charter of the city of Southport.

The General Assembly of North Carolina do enact:

Section 1. That an act entitled "an act to incorporate the town of Southport," ratified the fifth day of March, eighteen hundred and eighty-nine, chapter seventy-eight, private laws of North Carolina, be amended as follows: that sections four and five be stricken out, and the following substituted therefor: Act amended.

Sec. 2. That the city of Southport is hereby divided into three wards, to be known and designated as wards one, two and three, and the following are declared to be the boundary lines of said wards: The first ward shall constitute and embrace that part of the city of Southport west of the centre line of Howe street, including West street to the western line of the corporate limits of said city. Wards; boundaries. First ward.

Sec. 3. The second ward shall constitute and embrace that part of said city east of the centre line of Howe street, including West street to the eastern line of the corporate limits of said city. All that part of the city not embraced within the foregoing boundaries shall be known as the third ward. Boundaries second ward.

Sec. 4. It is hereby declared and understood by this act that all qualified electors residing within the limits of the first ward, as above defined, shall be qualified voters of the first ward, and all qualified electors residing within the limits of the second ward, as above defined, shall be qualified voters of the second ward, and all qualified electors residing within the limits of the third ward, as above defined, shall be qualified voters of the third ward. Qualified voters of several wards.

Sec. 5. There shall on the first Monday in May, eighteen hundred and ninety-nine, and on the first Monday in May biennially thereafter, be elected six aldermen for said city, who shall hold Aldermen, election. Term of office.

their office until their successors are qualified, of whom two shall be elected from the first ward, two from the second ward, and two from the third ward. Such aldermen shall be residents of the wards for which they are chosen, and shall be elected by the qualified voters of such wards, respectively.

Distribution amongst wards.

Registrar, when and by whom elected.

Judges of election.

Notice; publication.

Registration.

Notice of election, how given.

Sec. 6. The board of aldermen of the city of Southport shall select at their regular meeting in March, eighteen hundred and ninety-nine, and biennially thereafter, a registrar of voters and two judges of election for each of the three wards of the city of Southport, and shall cause publication thereof to be made at the court-house door, and notice to be served on persons selected by the chief of police of said city, and shall give ten days' public notice of a registration of voters in and for said wards, specifying time and place and names of registrars and judges, and at the same meeting shall cause to be published by posters or by publication in a newspaper published at Southport, N. C., a notice, calling an election for the first Monday in May, eighteen hundred and ninety-nine, and biennially thereafter, for an election by the qualified voters of said city of Southport, of six aldermen, viz.: two from the first ward, two from the second ward, and two from the third ward.

Registrar's books; duties.

Registration books open, how long.

Persons registered.

Separate lists of white and colored voters.

Residences designated.

Electors, qualifications.

Residence in ward where elector offers to vote.

Alderman, qualification.

Sec. 7. The registrars shall be furnished by said aldermen with registration books, and it shall be the duty of said registrars to open and keep open their books at such places in the city of Southport as may be designated by said aldermen, thirty days before the first Saturday preceding the election, and to register therein the names of all persons applying for registration and entitled to register and vote in the ward for which such registrar has been appointed, keeping the names of the white voters separate and apart from those of the colored voters, and designating on the registration books opposite the name of each person registering the place of his residence in his ward. At the municipal election herein provided for the qualifications of the elector shall be the same as prescribed in the general election law of the state for members of the general assembly, with the additional qualification that he shall have resided ninety days immediately preceding the election in the ward in which he offers to vote; the qualification of an alderman shall be the same as an elector as herein stated.

Registration, oath; what oath shall specify.

False swearing; felony; punishment.

Proviso.

Sec. 8. Any person offering to register shall take an oath that he is an elector as above defined. In such oath he shall specify the place of his residence in such ward; if any person shall wilfully swear falsely in such affidavit he shall be deemed guilty of a felony, and on conviction thereof shall be punished as for felony: Provided, that after the first registration shall have been made as provided for herein, a new registration shall not be biennially held unless the board of aldermen shall at their regular meeting in March determine that the same is necessary, and by due advertisement give notice of the same and the place where the books of registration shall be opened; but a revision of the registration shall be made, beginning on Saturday next preceding each election to be held for said city of Southport. Revision of registration.

Sec. 9. On the first Saturday preceding the election the registrars and judges of election shall meet at the polling place in their respective wards, there to hear and decide challenges and approve the registration books, from the hour of nine o'clock A. M. until the hour of four o'clock P. M. Challenges to be heard, when and by whom.

Sec. 10. The registrars and judges of election shall, on the first Monday in May, eighteen hundred and ninety-nine, and biennially thereafter, open the polls of their respective wards for said election at the hour of seven o'clock A. M. and keep open for qualified electors to cast their votes until sunset of the same day. Polls, when and by whom opened. Ballots shall be on white paper and without device. The aldermen of each ward shall be voted for on one ballot. Ballots; who voted for on ballots. After the ballots are counted they shall be carefully preserved, and shall be, together with the poll-list, which shall be signed by the judges of election, and the registration books, delivered to the mayor of Southport for preservation. Ballots; count; preserved; poll list. Signed, by whom.

Sec. 11. If, among the persons voted for in any ward, two or more should have an equal number of votes, and either would be elected but for the equal vote, the judges of election and registrars in such ward shall decide the election between such persons. Tie, who shall decide. As soon as the result of the election in any ward is determined a certificate thereof shall be made under the hands of the registrars and judges, setting forth in writing and in words the number of votes each candidate received, which certificate they shall deliver to the mayor, who shall at twelve o'clock M. on the day after election make proclamation thereof at the door of the mayor's office, and have same recorded in minute book of the city of Southport. Result, determination; certificate, what to set forth. Certificate, to whom delivered; proclamation; recordation.

Sec 12. That on the Tuesday next succeeding the day of election the aldermen elected thereat shall qualify by taking the oath now provided by law, and shall succeed to and have all the rights, powers and duties now provided by law for such board, as well as those conferred upon them by the provisions of this act. Aldermen, when to qualify and how. Succession; rights; powers, etc.

Sec. 13. The board of aldermen upon their organization shall elect some person of their own number to be mayor of said city of Southport, to hold his office for two years, and until his successor shall qualify. Mayor, by whom elected. Term of office.

Sec. 14. That all laws and clauses of laws in conflict with the provisions of this act be and the same are hereby repealed. Conflicting laws repealed.

Sec. 15. That this act shall be in force from and after its ratification.

Ratified the 8th day of February, A. D. 1899.

CHAPTER 35.

An act to amend chapter two hundred and twelve of the private laws of eighteen hundred and fifty-one entitled "An act to incorporate the Wilmington Gas Light Company."

The General Assembly of North Carolina do enact:

Section 1. That chapter two hundred and twelve of the private laws of eighteen hundred and fifty and fifty-one, entitled "An act to incorporate the Wilmington Gas Light Company," ratified the twenty-seventh day of January, eighteen hundred and fifty-one, be amended by adding thereto the following section:

Increase of capital stock, limit; shares, how divided.

That the said corporation shall have power to increase its present capital stock from time to time to a sum not exceeding five hundred thousand dollars, in shares of like amount (fifty dollars) as its capital stock is now divided; but no such increase shall be made unless authorized by a majority in interest of the stockholders at a regular meeting or special meeting called for that purpose.

Increase of stock to be authorized by stockholders.

May borrow money; may make notes, drafts or bonds to secure loans.

Sec. 2. It shall be lawful for the said corporation to borrow money, and to make, negotiate and dispose of its promissory notes, drafts or bonds given for money borrowed or given in liquidation of any debt due or owing by the said corporation, or made for the purpose of raising money, and to secure the payment of any such obligation or obligations by a mortgage, deed of trust or pledge of any or all of its property, plant and franchises.

May secure obligations by mortgage, deed of trust, etc.

May amalgamate with other corporations.

Sec. 3. That it shall be lawful for and authority is hereby given to said corporation to unite, amalgamate or consolidate with the "Wilmington Street Railway Company" or with the "Wilmington Sea Coast Railroad Company," or with both of said corporations, either by the sale and transfer by one or more of said corporations to the other of its or their capital stock or corporate franchises, property and effects, or in any other manner: Provided, that the terms and conditions of such consolidation be mutually agreed upon by the vote of two-thirds of all the shares of stock of each of said corporations at any regular meeting of the stockholders thereof or at a special meeting called for that purpose; and the corporation to which such sale and transfer of either the capital stock or franchises, property and effects are made as aforesaid, or with which consolidation is effected in any other manner, shall have the power to purchase, take, hold, use and enjoy the said stock, franchises, property and effects.

Proviso.

Power to purchase, take, hold, etc., property.

Franchises, rights, powers, privileges and property shall inure to purchasing corporation.

Sec. 4. That upon the said amalgamation or consolidation of said corporations, as hereinbefore provided, all the franchises, rights, privileges and immunities held, owned and enjoyed by the said corporation or corporations selling and transferring its or their capital stock or franchises and property, or consolidating with the other in any manner, shall inure to the benefit, and become a part of the capital stock, franchises, rights, privileges and immunities of the corporation purchasing the same or with which consolidation is made, as fully and to all intents and purposes as if the same were set forth and expressly granted by the original charter of said corporation and all amendments thereto.

Sec. 5. That the said consolidated corporations may adopt the name of the corporation with which said consolidation or merger is made, or they may select some other for the consolidated corporation. Name.

Sec. 6. That as soon as the consolidation aforesaid is completed the presidents of each of the corporations so consolidating shall send to the secretary of state a joint certificate signed by each of them and under the seal of each of said corporations, stating the name of each corporation so consolidating, the fact of said consolidation the name adopted for and the amount of capital stock of said consolidated corporation, which said certificate the secretary of state shall file in his office and furnish to each of said presidents, under his official seal, a certificate of such filing, and the presidents of said corporations shall also jointly give notice of said consolidation, and the name of said consolidated corporation by the publication of said notice in some newspaper published in the city where said corporations are located once a week for four successive weeks. Presidents' certificates sent to secretary of state. What certificate shall state. Secretary of state shall file certificate. Joint notice of consolidation by publication.

Sec. 7. That all laws and parts of laws in conflict with this act are hereby repealed. Conflicting laws repealed.

Sec. 8. That this act shall be in force from and after its ratification.

Ratified the 8th day of February, A. D. 1899.

CHAPTER 36.

An act to incorporate the Greensboro Loan and Trust Company.

The General Assembly of North Carolina do enact:

Section 1. Tnat J. A. Odell, C. H. Ireland, C. D. McIver, John Gill and J. W. Fry and their associates, successors and assigns are hereby constituted a body corporate by the name of the "Greensboro Loan and Trust Company," by which name said corporation shall have all franchises, rights, powers and privileges incident to a corporation. Incorporation; body corporate. Name. Rights, powers, etc.

Books of subscription; notice; organization.

Sec. 2. The corporators above-named or any three of them may open books of subscription, and after five hundred shares of one hundred dollars each have been subscribed, upon ten days' notice issued by said corporators or any three of them, the subscribers may meet and organize by the election of a board of five or more directors, who shall manage the affairs of the company for one year or until their successors are elected, and who shall elect all necessary officers and agents. The company shall have authority to transact business whenever one thousand shares of one hundred dollars each have been subscribed to the capital stock and ten per centum paid thereon. Further assessments shall be paid in as called for by the directors. The capital stock may be increased from time to time to an amount not to exceed two hundred and fifty thousand dollars, either by additional subscriptions of stock or by application of the surplus earnings of the corporation, and not more than one hundred thousand dollars of the same to be invested in real estate; and if such increase shall be from the earnings of the corporation the directors shall have the power to declare stock dividends to the shareholders pro rata. At all stockholders' meetings each share shall be entitled to one vote, either in person or by proxy.

Directors, their powers; term of office.
Officers, elected by directors.
Company may transact business, when.
Payment of assessments.
Capital stock, increase of; limit.
Investments in real estate, limit.
Stock dividends, how declared.
Votes at stockholders' meetings.

Power to contract; seal; may sue and be sued, complain and defend.
Purchase and conveyance of real estate.
By-laws; regulations.
Powers and privileges.

Sec. 3. The corporation hereby created shall have power to make contracts; to have and use a common seal; to sue and be sued, complain and defend in any court as fully as natural persons; to buy, hold, possess and convey real and personal property; to make by-laws for the regulation and management of the business of the company; to do all lawful acts and things and exercise all lawful powers and privileges which a corporate body may do.

May borrow money; may issue notes, certificates or bonds.
May receive money on deposit, etc.
May receive special deposits of valuables.
May charge commissions.

Sec. 4. That said company shall have power to borrow money in such amounts and at such rate of interest and payable at such times and places as the board of directors may determine, and issue its notes, certificates or registered or coupon bonds under its corporate seal. It may receive money on deposit, on open account or on certificate of deposit and pay interest thereon or not. It may receive on deposit for safe-keeping gold, silver, paper money, bullion, precious metals, jewels, plate, certificates of stock, evidences of indebtedness, deeds or muniments of title or other valuables of any kind, and charge commission or compensation therefor.

May loan money, on what security.
May buy and sell real estate, stock, etc.
May discount bills, etc.

Sec. 5. The said company may loan money on mortgage or deed of trust conveying real or personal property or on other security; may buy and sell real estate, stocks, bonds and other security; may discount bills of exchange, foreign and domestic, promissory notes and other negotiable papers. In case any borrower from said company fails to meet his obligations it may exact and collect such amount or percentage as may have been agreed upon, not exceeding the legal rate of interest, and reasonable costs, charges and expenses, and in case of sale of either real or personal security make title to the purchaser.

May collect interest, etc.
May make title, etc.

Sec. 6. The said company may act as the fiscal or transfer agent of or trustee for any state, county, municipality, body politic or corporation, or for any person or persons, and in such capacity may receive and disburse money, and negotiate, sell, transfer, register and countersign certificates of stock, bonds or other evidences of indebtedness.

May act as agent.

Sec. 7. The said company shall have power to act as executor, administrator, guardian, trustee, receiver or depository, and to take, accept and execute any and all such trusts and powers of whatever nature or description as may be conferred upon or entrusted or committed to it by any person or persons or by any corporation, by agreement, grant, assignment, transfer, devise, bequest or otherwise or by order of any court [of] record, and to receive, take, hold, manage and convey any property or estate, real or personal, which may be the subject of any such trust, and for compensation shall have such commission as may be fixed by law or as may be agreed on. In lieu of the bond required by law to be given by an administrator, guardian, trustee, receiver or other fiduciary, it shall be lawful, and before assuming any such trust under order of any court the said company shall file in the office of the clerk of the superior court of Guilford county an undertaking with sufficient security, with either personal sureties or bonds of the state of North Carolina or of the United States or of any county or city of the state of North Carolina or any other security satisfactory to the court, and to be approved by the said clerk, and the said undertaking so secured may be accepted by the said clerk and held as such security in the sum of ten thousand dollars, conditioned for the faithful performance of any trust which may be committed to the said company by order of any court of North Carolina as aforesaid. In case of willful default in the performance of any trust so committed to said company, as aforesaid, the said undertaking may be sued upon by the party injured or his personal representative in the superior court of any county of North Carolina where such default may have been made (and the superior court of Guilford county, whenever it shall be made satisfactorily to appear by sworn testimony that it is necessary in order to secure the faithful performance of all said trusts may require the said undertaking to be enlarged sufficiently to secure the faithful performance of the same). A copy of such undertaking, duly certified by the seal of the superior court of Guilford

May act as executor, etc.
May take, accept and execute trusts.

Compensation.

Undertaking to be filed when; security.

Clerk may take undertaking so secured; amount.

Wilful default; undertaking to be sued on, when.

Copy of undertaking, duly certified, to be evidence.

county, and if secured by the bonds of the state or of the United States or of any county or city or other security, as aforesaid, a statement thereof so certified shall be evidence in all the courts of North Carolina. And the superior court wherein the said company shall have been appointed guardian, executor, administrator, receiver, trustee or depository shall have the power to make orders respecting such trusts, and to require the said company to render all accounts which said court might lawfully make or require if such trustees were a natural person. And in accepting any of the trusts or powers hereunder the said corporation may qualify by any of its executive officers.

Court to make orders.

May qualify, by whom.

Investments, discretion.

Sec. 8. The said company shall have discretionary power to invest the funds received by it in trust in the bonds of the United States, or of any state, or in the bonds duly authorized to be issued by any county or incorporated city or other good securities, or in safe and personal securities; but all such investments shall be at the sole risk of the company, and for any losses by reason of such investments the capital stock, property and effects of said corporation shall be absolutely liable. The company shall use due diligence to enhance the income, rents and profits of any trust estate within its hands; but shall not be liable for any greater income, rents and profits than can be reasonably earned by safe and prudent investments.

Investments at risk of company.

Enhancement of income, rents, etc., of trust estates.

Offices, where established.

Sec. 9. The said company may establish offices and agencies or transact business at such places as it may deem proper, but the principal office shall be in Greensboro, in Guilford county, North Carolina.

Sec. 10. This act shall be in force from and after its ratification.

Ratified the 8th day of February, A. D. 1899.

CHAPTER 37.

An act to authorize the city of Fayetteville to receive one-fourth of the taxes listed in eighteen hundred and ninety-eight, in full settlement, and fixing the tax year for said city.

Preamble.

Whereas, the city of Fayettevile is now one year behind in the collection of its taxes, and much will be saved to said city by the collection of the taxes in the year for which they are listed,

The General Assembly of North Carolina do enact:

Tax list to be placed in the hands of collector, when.

Sec. 1. That the tax books of the city of Fayettevlle, containing the taxes listed in June, eighteen hundred and ninety-eight, shall be placed in the hands of the tax collector as soon as possible, and not later than March first, eighteen hundred and ninety-nine, and said collector is hereby authorized and empowered to accept twenty-five per centum of the poll and property taxes listed in June, eighteen hundred and ninety-eight, in full satisfaction and settlement: Provided, said twenty-five per centum of said taxes shall be paid before September first, eighteen hundred and ninety-nine, on and after which date said collector shall collect said taxes of eighteen hundred and ninety-eight in full.

Collector empowered to accept 25 per centum of poll and property tax in satisfaction, etc.

Proviso.

Sec. 2. The authorities of the city of Fayetteville are authorized and empowered to settle with the city tax collector on the basis of section first of this act.

Basis for settlement with city tax collector.

Sec. 3. The tax books containing the taxes listed in the year eighteen hundred and ninety-nine, shall be placed in the hands of the collector on the first Monday in September, eighteen hundred and ninety-nine, or as soon thereafter as possible, and thereafter the tax year shall be from September the first to September the first.

Tax books to be placed in hands of collector, when.

Sec. 4. The city tax collector shall have all the rights and powers concerning the collection of taxes which are or may hereafter be given to any sheriff or collector of Cumberland county.

Rights and powers of city tax collector.

Sec. 5. All laws and parts of laws in conflict with this act are hereby repealed.

Conflicting laws repealed.

Sec. 6. This act shall be in full force and effect from and after its ratification.

Ratified the 8th day of February, A. D. 1899.

CHAPTER 38.

An act to amend chapter one hundred and thirty-four, private laws of eighteen hundred and ninety-seven.

The General Assembly of North Carolina do enact:

That chapter one hundred and thirty-four of the private laws of the general assembly of eighteen hundred and ninety-seven be amended as follows:

Chapter 134, private laws 1897, relating to underwriters, Goldsboro.

Section 1. By striking out the words "of Goldsboro" wherever it occurs in the caption or body of said act and substituting therefor the words "of Greensboro."

Amended.

Sec. 2. By adding the following section, to be known as number four: That the principal office and place of business of said cor-

Office and place of business.

Liability of stockholders.

poration shall be Greensboro, N. C., and no stockholder shall be individually liable for the debts, contracts or torts of the corporation; and no policy-holder shall in any event be liable to any assessment or to pay more than the premium which he contracts to pay.

Sec. 3. By adding the following section, to be known as number five:

Fund created to belong to stockholders.

Deficit, how to be made up.

After paying all losses and expenses for each year an amount up to ten per cent. of the gross premiums for such year shall be set aside to create a fund which shall belong to the stockholders. That if the sum left after paying losses and expenses for any year is less than ten per cent. of the gross premiums this deficit shall be made up from the profits of any succeeding year or years. That after paying losses and expenses and setting aside the ten per cent. to stockholders as provided for above such part of the remaining premium receipts as the executive committee may ascertain to be necessary to reinsure the outstanding policies of the company shall be carried to a fund to be known as the emergency fund or insurance fund. That any residue of premium receipts that may be left at the end of any year shall be distributed among the policy-holders in such manner as the by-laws may determine.

Emergency fund.

Surplus, how distributed.

Sec. 4. By changing the numbers of sections four and five to six and seven, respectively.

Sec. 5. That this act shall be in force from and after its ratification.

Ratified the 8th day of February, A. D. 1899.

CHAPTER 39.

An act to allow the town of Edenton to sell certain lands for school purposes.

The General Assembly of North Carolina do enact:

Sale of land; consideration; purpose

Section 1. That power and authority are hereby given the town of Edenton, in the county of Chowan, and state of North Carolina, to sell and convey to the county of Chowan, the consideration to be agreed upon between said town and county, a site for a school-house for the colored race. That said land to be sold and conveyed is bounded and described as follows:

Boundaries.

One lot of land situated in the town of Edenton. Beginning at the corner of Oakum and Free Mason streets and runs along Free Mason street to Sawyer's lot; thence with Sawyer's lot to the town common and continuing in a straight line to Peterson street; thence along Peterson street to Oakum street; thence along Oakum street to Free Mason street.

Sec. 2. That the mayor of said town of Edenton shall have the power, and the power and authority is hereby given him, for and in behalf of said town to make title to said land in fee to the county of Chowan, and do all such acts and things as is necessary to carry out the purposes of this act. The said deed to be attested by the secretary of said town. Mayor; power; title, etc.

Sec. 3. That this act shall be in force from and after its ratification.

Ratified the 10th day of February, A. D. 1899.

CHAPTER 40.

An act to amend the act incorporating the town of Graham, Alamance county, and to consolidate and amend the acts amendatory thereof.

The General Assembly of North Carolina do enact:

Section 1. That the town of Graham, in the county of Alamance, be and the same is hereby incorporated under the name and style of "The Town of Graham," and that McBride Holt, W. S. Vestal, J. B. Thompson, T. C. Montgomery and A. L. Bain, the present commissioners of said town, and their successors in office, shall be and they are hereby declared a body corporate and politic, with succession during the corporate existence of said town, and shall be styled the commissioners of the town of Graham. Corporation; name. Body politic.

That E. S. Parker, Jr., the present mayor of said town, and the commissioners aforesaid shall continue in office as such, and perform all the duties pertaining to their offices of mayor and commissioners of said town until their successors shall be elected and qualified as hereinafter provided. Continuance in office. Election, etc.

Sec. 2. That the corporate limits of said town are hereby declared to be as follows: The southern boundary shall be one-half mile south of the centre of the court-house in and for said county of Alamance, and said boundary shall be a true east and west line; the eastern boundary shall be one-half mile east of the centre of the said court-house, and said boundary shall be a true north and south line, extending from the point of its intersection with the southern boundary to and across the North Carolina Railroad to a point ten feet beyond the centre of the track of the said North Carolina Railroad; thence westward with Corporate limits, metes and bounds.

said railroad track at a distance of ten feet north of the centre of said track to a point ten feet west of the cotton platform near to and west of the depot at Graham Station; thence southward a straight line to a point where the said straight line shall intersect the southern boundary at a point one mile due west of the intersection of the southern and eastern boundaries.

Officers: election, when held.

Sec. 3. The officers of said town shall consist of a mayor and five commissioners, to be elected by the qualified voters of said town annually on the first Monday in May.

Election, when to be held; voters, etc

Sec. 4. Said election of said mayor and commissioners shall be held in one of the jury rooms in the court-house in said town, and no person shall be entitled to vote in said election or at any election in said town for municipal purposes unless he shall be an elector of the state of North Carolina, and shall have resided ninety days next preceding the day of election within the said corporation.

Registrar and judges of election, appointment of.

Sec. 5. It shall be the duty of the commissioners of the said town at the first meeting in March in each year to appoint a registrar and two judges of election, one of whom shall be of a different political party from the other two, who shall be qualified voters of said town, and who shall, within ten days thereafter be notified of their appointment by the constable of said town.

Publication, when made.

The registrar so appointed shall immediately make publication at the postoffice in said town and at three other public places in said town of his appointment as such. He shall be furnished with a registration book by the commissioners of said town, and it shall be his duty to revise the existing registration book of said town in such a manner that said book shall show an accurate list of electors previously registered and still residing in said town without requiring such electors to register anew. He shall also, between the hours of seven o'clock A. M. and sunset (Sundays excepted), on each day for thirty days preceding each election keep open said books for the registration of any electors residing in said town entitled to register, whose names have not before been registered, and any of the electors shall [be] allowed to object to the name of any person appearing on said book. In case of any such objection the registrar shall enter upon his book opposite to the name of the person so objected to the word "Challenged," and shall appoint a time on the election day when he, together with the said judges of election, shall hear and decide the said objection, giving due notice to the voter so objected to. If any person challenged or objected to shall be found not duly qualified as provided for in this charter, his name shall be erased from the registration book and he shall not be allowed to vote at that election. The commissioners may, if they think proper, upon giving thirty days' notice at four public places in

Registration books. Revision of registration.

Registration books, how long kept open.

Objection to registration, when entered.

Challenges, when and by whom heard; notice.

Not qualified, name erased.

said town and in a newspaper published in said town, require an entire new registration of the voters before any election held therein. New registration, notice, etc.

Sec. 6. The registrar and judges of election, before entering upon the discharge of their duties, shall take the oath prescribed by article six, section four, of the constitution of North Carolina, before some justice of the peace of Alamance county. Oath, etc.

Sec. 7. That the registration book of said town shall be at all times open to the inspection of the electors of said town. Registration book, inspection.

Sec. 8. The said judges of election, together with the registrar, who shall take with him the registration book, shall assemble at the polling place on the day of election held in said town and shall open the polls at seven o'clock A. M. They shall superintend said election and keep the polls open till sunset, when the polls shall be closed, and the votes for mayor and commissioners shall be counted out by them, and they shall certify to the town clerk the result of said election. They shall keep poll books and write in them the name of every person voting at said election, and at the close thereof shall certify said poll-list and return them, together with the registration books, into the hands of the clerk of said town. If for any cause any of the judges of election shall fail to attend, the registrar shall appoint some discreet person or persons from the same political party as the absent judge or judges to fill the vacancy, who shall be sworn by him before acting. That the registrar shall receive as compensation for the performance of his duties three cents for each name registered and one dollar for the day of election. That the judges shall receive one dollar each for their services in holding said election. Election; registrar and judges of election, duties. Polls opened when, and how long kept open. Vote counted; certification of result. Names written in poll books; certificate, etc. Return. Vacancies in judges of election, how filled. Registrar, compensation. Judges, compensation.

Sec. 9. The voters shall vote by ballot, having the name of the mayor and commissioners on one ballot, either in writing or printed on white paper and without any device. And the person having the highest number of votes shall be declared elected by the judges of election, who shall certify said fact to the town clerk. Ballot; paper; what to contain. Person declared elected; certification.

Sec. 10. That no person shall be eligible to any office in said town unless he shall be a qualified voter therein. Eligibility to office.

Sec. 11. That immediately after the election it shall be the duty of the town clerk to notify in writing the mayor and commissioners elect of their election. Town clerk, duty

Sec. 12. That the mayor and commissioners-elect shall, within three days after having been notified by the town clerk of their election, before some justice of the peace in said county, take the oath prescribed for public officers, and an oath that they will faithfully and impartially discharge the duties imposed on them by law. Oaths of office.

Quorum.

Sec. 13. That [a] majority of said commissioners shall constitute a quorum for the transaction of business.

Mayor, duties; called meetings.

Tie vote.

Sec. 14. That the mayor when present shall preside at all meetings of the commissioners; he shall also have power to call meetings when he may deem it necessary and may only vote in case of a tie. In the absence or sickness of the mayor the commissioners of said town shall elect one of their own number to act as mayor pro tempore, who shall while acting as such have all the powers and authority conferred by this charter on the mayor of said town.

Mayor pro tem.

Clerk and treasurer

Term of office.

Sec. 15. That said commissioners shall at the first meeting after their election select some one, who may or may not be one of their number, as town clerk and treasurer, who shall hold office for one year or until his successor is duly elected and qualified. He shall act as secretary to said board of commissioners and as treasurer of said town, and before entering upon the discharge of his duties as such shall be required to give a bond with good and sufficient sureties, in such sum as the commissioners may see fit, conditioned upon the faithful discharge of his duties as clerk to the said board, and the faithful accounting for and paying over to the proper authorities of all moneys that may come into his hands as treasurer of said town.

Bond, how conditioned.

Constable, by whom elected.

Term of office.

Bond, how conditioned.

Sec. 16. The said commissioners shall at the first meeting after their election select some one to act as constable and tax collector for said town. The said constable and tax collector shall hold office for one year, or until his successor is duly elected and qualified, and before entering upon the discharge of his duties he shall enter into bond in such sum as the said commissioners may see fit, with good and sufficient sureties, to be approved by the board, conditioned upon the faithful discharge of his duties as said constable and tax collector, and the faithfully accounting for and paying over to the proper authorities of all moneys that shall come to his hands as constable or tax collector.

Officers, compensation.

Sec. 17. That the said board of commissioners shall have the right, and it shall be their duty, to fix the compensation of all officers herein mentioned and of all officers in connection with the government of said town of Graham.

Streets, powers of commissioners.

Sec. 18. That said commissioners shall have the right to open new streets in said town when and where they shall deem necessary. They shall have the right to widen or straighten, make narrower or discontinue any of the streets now in said town. When in the exercise of this power it shall become necessary to take the lands of any individual, firm or corporation, they shall pay full compensation to such individual, firm or corporation, and if the said commissioners and the individuals, firm or corporation who own the land cannot agree, then the said commis-

Land taken for streets, compensation.

Disagreement; damages, how determined.

sioners shall proceed in the manner for county commissioners in opening public roads, to have the damage done the individual, firm or corporation assessed, and this amount they shall pay said individual, firm or corporation, and by this proceeding and payment shall acquire the right to open and maintain a street on said land.

By-laws; ordinances.

Sec. 19. The commissioners of said town shall have the power to make such by-laws and adopt such ordinances for the government of said town as a majority of them may deem necessary to promote the interests and insure the good order of said town; for the improvement of the streets and the preservation of the health in the same, and to make all such other police regulations as the interests, comfort and convenience of the citizens of the said town may require.

Improvement of streets; health.

Ordinances, violation of misdemeanor; punishment.

Sec. 20. Any person or persons violating any ordinance of said town shall be deemed guilty of a misdemeanor, and in all cases where an offender has been convicted before the mayor of said town for the violation of any of the ordinances thereof, and a fine has been imposed on such offender for such violation, the mayor of said town, at the time of entering the judgment against such offender may order that on the failure to pay such fine to the constable of said town for the space of one day, such offender shall be by the constable put to work on the streets of said town for a time to be fixed by the mayor, not exceeding thirty days, when he shall be discharged.

Failure to pay fines; work on streets.

Taxes, how levied and collected.

Sec. 21. The board of commissioners of said town shall have the power annually to levy and cause to be collected taxes for necessary town purposes on all real property, all moneys, credits, investments in bonds, stocks, joint stock companies, and all other personal property, and on the taxable polls within the limits of said town: Provided, however, that the taxes levied by them shall not exceed forty cents on the hundred dollars valuation on all real and personal property, and one dollar and twenty cents on each taxable poll, and the valuation of all property within said town as taxed by said town commissioners shall be the same at which it is assessed for taxation for state and county purposes.

Proviso.

Tax lists, tax books, etc.

Duty of clerk and treasurer.

Sec. 22. That it shall be the duty of the town clerk and treasurer before the first Monday in September of each year to make out from the county tax lists a tax list for the town of Graham, and from this list shall be made out the tax books for the town of Graham, and that it shall be the duty of the town clerk and treasurer to place said tax books in the hands of the constable and tax collector by the said first Monday in September of each year. That the compensation of the said town clerk and treas-

Compensation of town clerk and treasurer.

urer for the making out of said tax lists and tax books shall be fixed by the said commissioners.

Taxes, when due.

Sec. 23. That all taxes levied by said town commissioners shall be due and payable on or before the first day of December of each year, and if there shall be parties who have failed to pay their taxes by the said first day of December, then the said constable and tax collector may collect the same in the manner prescribed by law for sheriffs in collecting delinquent taxes.

Failure to pay taxes, how collected.

Privilege taxes, power to levy and collect.

Sec. 24. The commissioners of said town shall have the power to annually levy and cause to be collected for the necessary expenses of said town such privilege taxes as shall seem to them fair and equitable on the professions, callings, trades, occupations and all other business carried on in said town.

Sale of spirituous liquors; control, in whom vested.

Sec. 25. The board of commissioners of said town shall have full and complete control of the sale or vending of spirituous, vinous or malt liquors or wines, save those manufactured and sold by the manufacturer on the premises, within the limits of said corporation and one-half mile from the limits of said corporation in every direction. They may permit the same to be sold by persons of good character, after a license first had and obtained; they shall prescribe the rules and regulations under which the same shall be sold and the amount of the license tax therefor, which shall not be less than one hundred nor more than five hundred dollars per annum. That said commissioners shall have the power to grant license for less than one year, but that it shall be at a rate of not less than one hundred nor more than five hundred dollars per annum. That they shall prescribe the time when the said license tax shall be due and payable, and shall have full power and authority at any time to annul and revoke any license by them granted, and in that event they shall return to the party the amount of said license tax paid by him, which shall justly be due him at the rate above set out.

Character of vendors of liquors, etc.

Rules and regulations.

License tax, limit.

Revocation of liquor licenses, etc.

Conflicting laws repealed.

Sec. 26. That all laws heretofore passed for the better government of the town of Graham, in conflict with this act, be and the same are hereby repealed.

Sec. 27. That this act shall be in force from and after its ratification.

Ratified the 10th day of February, A. D. 1899.

CHAPTER 41.

An act to authorize the town of Lexington to issue bonds.

The General Assembly of North Carolina do enact:

Bonds; issuance; denominations; forms; limit.

Section 1. That the board of commissioners of Lexington is hereby authorized and empowered to issue bonds in the name of the town of Lexington in such denomination and forms as it may determine to an amount not exceeding thirty thousand dollars, bearing no greater interest than six per centum per annum, which shall be paid semi-annually, and said bonds shall be made payable at such time and place as shall be determined by said board of commissioners: Provided, that the time of payment shall not be fixed at less than twenty nor more than thirty years.

Interest, limit.

Payable, when and where.

Sec. 2. That said bonds shall in no case be sold, hypothecated or otherwise disposed of for less than their par value, and all moneys arising from the sale thereof shall be used for the purpose of internal improvements, construction of water-works, erection or purchase of electric light plant, or otherwise providing for the lighting of the town, the purchase or erection of school buildings, and for no other purpose whatsoever.

Bonds, sold for par.

Proceeds, to be used for what purpose.

Sec. 3. That said bonds shall not be issued until authorized by the majority of the qualified voters of said town at a public election, to be held at such time and place as said board shall appoint, of which notice shall be given for twenty days in some newspaper published in said town, and at said election those favoring the issue of said bonds shall vote "Issue," and those opposing it shall vote "No issue": Provided, that said board may, in its discretion, order a new registration of the voters of said town, and if a majority of the qualified voters of said town shall vote to issue said bonds then the said board of commissioners shall issue the same, which shall be signed by the mayor and attested by the town treasurer, and have interest coupon bonds attached thereto, and said bonds and their coupons shall be exempt from town taxation until after they become due, and the coupons shall be receivable in payment of town taxes.

Authorized by a majority of voters.

Election; notice.

Question on ballots.

Proviso.

Bonds, signed by whom.

Coupons.

Coupons receivable for town taxes.

Sec. 4. That for the purpose of paying said coupons as they become due, it shall be the duty of the board of commissioners, and they are hereby empowered to do so, to levy and collect a sufficient special tax each year upon all subjects of taxation which are now or may hereafter be embraced in the subjects of taxation under the charter of said town, said levy not at any time to exceed one dollar and twenty cents on the poll and forty cents on the one hundred dollars valuation of property, which taxes when collected shall be used for no other purpose; and it shall be the duty of the town treasurer as said coupons are paid off and taken up to cancel the same, and he shall report not less than twice a year to the board of commissioners the number and amounts of the coupons so cancelled.

Coupons, due; special taxes.

Limit on taxation.

Purpose of special taxes.

Coupons, cancellation.

Treasurer report, how often.

Sec. 5. That all acts and parts of acts in conflict with the provisions of this act are hereby repealed.

Conflicting acts repealed.

Sec. 6. This act shall be in force from and after its ratification

Ratified the 10th day of February, A. D. 1899.

CHAPTER 42.

An act to incorporate Winston-Salem Trust and Deposit Company.

The General Assembly of North Carolina do enact:

Corporators.

Section 1. That W. A. Lemly, Jas. A. Gray, R. J. Reynolds, Frank Miller, P. H. Hanes, J. W. Hanes, Eugene E. Gray, J. W. Hunter, W. T. Vogler, Joseph Jacobs, E. S. Gray, Frank L. Matthews, T. W. Huske, W. B. Lemly, N. D. Sullivan, Bowman Gray, T. B. Fitzgerald, W. L. Floyd, B. F. Watkins, and their associates, successors and assigns, and all other persons who may hereafter become stockholders in the company hereby incorporated, shall be a body corporate by the name and style of "Winston-Salem Trust and Deposit Company," and by that name shall have all franchises, rights and privileges belonging to a corporation, and shall by that name sue and be sued, plead or be impleaded, complain, answer and defend as any natural person in any court whatsoever.

Body corporate.

Capital stock; shares.

Increase of capital stock, limit.

Books of subscription to be opened.

Directors, election of; conditions; term of office.

Powers of directors.

Increased capital stock, how distributed.

Sec. 2. That the capital stock of said corporation shall consist of two hundred shares of the par value of one hundred dollars each, being two hundred thousand dollars, with the privilege to increase the same at any time or from time to time by a majority vote of all the stock, at any regular annual meeting, or at any special meeting to be called for that purpose, to any amount not to exceed one million dollars; and the above-named incorporators, or any number of them not less than three, shall have power to open books for subscription at such times and places as they may deem expedient; and when not less than one thousand shares have been subscribed and fully paid for, the stockholders may elect seven or more directors to serve until the ensuing annual election or until their successors have been duly elected and qualified, and the directors of said company so elected may and they are hereby authorized and empowered to, have and exercise in the name and on behalf of the company all rights and privileges which are intended to be hereby given; and should the capital stock be at any time increased, the stockholders at the time of such increase shall be entitled to a pro rata share of such increase upon the payment of the par value of the same, and of such price in excess of the par value as the board of directors may prescribe.

Election of directors.

President, vice-president, secretary, treasurer, cashier, other officers, agents, etc.

Sec. 3. That the directors shall be elected annually by the stockholders on the second Tuesday of January of each year, and they shall elect from their number, at the first meeting of the board after their election as prescribed by section second of this act, and after all subsequent elections, a president and a vice-president or vice-presidents; and the said directors shall also have the power to elect a secretary and treasurer or cashier, and to appoint and employ such other officers, clerks and agents as the business of said company from time to time may require. All elections shall be by ballot, and at such elections and meetings of stockholders every stockholder shall be entitled to one vote for every share of stock held by him; that no person shall be eligible as director who is not a stockholder to the amount of at least ten shares of stock.

Elections by ballot.

Eligibility of directors.

Sec. 4. That ten days' notice shall be given by publication in a daily newspaper published in the city of Winston, North Carolina, of the time and place of said annual election and annual meeting, and when a meeting shall be held in pursuance of such notice it shall be organized and its proceedings shall be conducted as may be prescribed by the by-laws of the company.

Notice of annual meetings, etc.

Sec. 5. That the directors shall have the power to declare such dividends of profits of the said company as they may deem proper: Provided, that no dividend shall be declared when the capital stock would be impaired thereby.

Dividends.

Proviso.

Sec. 6. That the president, vice-president and directors of the corporation hereby created shall have power to enact and adopt such rules, regulations and by-laws for the government and management of the affairs of said corporation as they may deem advantageous to the interests thereof.

Rules and regulations.

Sec. 7. That said corporation be and it is hereby authorized and empowered to accept and execute as fully as a natural person, trusts of any and every description which may be committed or transferred to it with its consent by any person or persons whomsoever, or by bodies corporate, public or private, upon such terms as may be agreed upon by and between the said corporation and said person, natural or corporate, or by any court in the state of North Carolina, or by the courts of the United States, or of any of the states or territories thereof; and in all cases where application shall be made to any court of this state for the appointment of any receiver, trustee or assignee, it shall and may be lawful for such court to appoint the said corporation such receiver, trustee or assignee, and the accounts of said corporation as such receiver, trustee or assignee shall be regularly settled before the court making such appointment, and all proper legal and customary charges, costs and expenses shall be allowed said corporation for its care and management of the trusts and estate aforesaid, in accordance with the practice of the court so appointing in the case of natural persons when so appointed, and the said corporation as such receiver, trustee and assignee shall be subject to all lawful orders or decrees made by the said court.

Acceptance and execution of trusts.

Terms.

May be appointed receiver, trustee or assignee.

Accounts, settlement.

Charges.

Subjection to orders of court.

Collector, committee, guardian, trustees, etc., power

Sec. 8. That the said corporation shall have power to act as collector, committee, executor, administrator, guardian, trustee, receiver or custodian, and to accept, perform, and execute any and all such trusts and powers of whatever nature or description as may be conferred upon or intrusted or committed to it, with its consent, by agreement, grant, assignment, transfer, devise, bequest, or otherwise by any person or persons natural or corporate, or by any order of court of record, and to receive, take, hold, manage and convey any property or estate, real, personal or mixed, which may be the subject of any such trust, and for compensation shall have such compensation as may be fixed by law, or as may be agreed upon.

May hold, manage and convey. Compensation.

Receive, keep on deposit, money, bullion, papers, or other property.

Sec. 9. That the said corporation be and is hereby authorized and empowered to receive and keep on deposit, storage or otherwise, all such valuables as gold, silver or paper money, bullion, precious metals, jewels, plate, certificates of stock, evidences of indebtedness, promissory notes, contracts or muniments of title, or other valuable papers of any kind, or any other article or thing whatsoever, and take charge and custody of real and personal estate and securities, and advance money thereupon on such terms as may be established or approved by said corporation; and it may be lawful for any court of this state or any United States court into which moneys, stocks, bonds or other property may be paid or deposited by agreement of parties, order, judgment or decree of said court, to order and direct the same to be deposited with said corporation; and that any executor, administrator, or other trustee or receiver, agent or other public officer having control of any bonds, stocks, security, moneys or other valuables belonging to others is allowed the discretion, if it be safe to do so, to deposit the same for safe keeping with said corporation; and for the complete preservation of all articles or things so deposited for safe keeping, the said corporation may construct, erect, purchase or lease such suitable buildings, and all other means which may be or become necessary, and to maintain and let for hire vaults, safes, boxes and all like receptacles.

Advance of money.

Provisions for safe keeping of property.

Sec. 10. That whenever any court shall appoint the said corporation a receiver, trustee or assignee, or shall order the deposit of money or other valuables of any kind with the said corporation, or whenever the said corporation becomes executor, administrator, guardian, collector or committee, the capital stock of said corporation shall be taken and considered as security required by law for the faithful performance of any duty imposed upon it by the order or decree of such court, unless the said court shall deem proper or require further security, and said corporation shall be absolutely liable in case of any default whatever; such court may from time to time and whenever

Capital stock may be taken as security for deposits.

Liability of corporation.

deemed advisable by such court, appoint suitable persons to investigate the affairs and management of said corporation, who shall report to such court the manner in which such funds so held as receiver, trustee or assignee, executor, administrator, guardian, collector, or committee are invested or held, and the expenses of such investigation shall be borne by the said corporation, and such court may, if it deem necessary, examine the officers of said corporation under oath or affirmation as to such investments.

Investigation of affairs by courts; expenses of investigation.

Examination under oath, etc.

Sec. 11. That the said corporation shall have power to receive and hold on deposit and in trust, and as security, estate, real, personal and mixed, including notes, bonds, obligations of states, companies, corporations and individuals, and the same to purchase, collect, adjust, settle, sell, convey and dispose of, upon such terms as may be agreed upon between it and the parties contracting with it.

May receive and hold on deposit and in trust real and personal property, etc.

Sec. 12. That the said corporation shall have power to receive deposits of money, securities and other personal property from any person or persons or public or private corporation upon such terms as may be agreed upon, and to loan money on mortgage or deed of trust, conveying real or personal property, and may loan money on personal security or other security; may buy and sell real estate, stocks, bonds and other securities; may discount and deal in bills of exchange, foreign or domestic, promissory notes or other negotiable papers; it may receive money on deposit, on open account or on certificate of deposit, and pay interest thereon or not. In case any borrower or borrowers fails or fail to meet his, her, its or their obligations, the said corporation may exact and collect such amount and percentage as may have been agreed upon, not exceeding the legal rate of interest and reasonable costs, charges and expenses, and in case of sale of real or personal property make title to the purchaser or purchasers.

Deposits of money, etc.

Loans, mortgages, etc.

May buy and sell real estate, etc.

Failure of borrower; collection of amounts, etc.; limit.

That said corporation may receive on deposit all sums of money which may be offered for the purpose of being invested, in such sums and at such times and on such terms as the by-laws of the corporation shall prescribe, and which shall be repaid to such depositors at such times and with such interest, not exceeding the lawful rate, and under such regulations as the board of directors shall from time to time prescribe; and if money is deposited by any minor such money may be withdrawn by the minor without the consent of the parent or guardian of such minor. That said corporation shall have power to make loans and discounts, to loan its own or depositors' funds, to act as agent for borrowers in obtaining loans from any third person, company or partnership or corporation, and to charge such a commission for its services in procuring such loans as may be

May receive money for investment.

Interest to depositors, limit.

Deposit by minor, withdrawal, etc.

Loans and discounts, etc.

Commissions, etc.

agreed upon between it and the borrower; to loan and invest its own money or the money of others in or upon the security of mortgage, pledge, deed or otherwise; and in all loans made by said corporation, either for itself or others, it may charge interest for the full time and include the same in the note or notes or other evidences of debt given therefor and collect the same by monthly or other installments, if the debtor so agree, without any rebate or interest thereon, and in such cases the laws relating to loans made by building and loan associations are hereby made applicable. That said corporation shall have power to borrow money in such amounts and at such rate of interest and payable at such times and places as the board of directors may determine, or in such manner as may be set forth or prescribed in the by-laws of the corporation, and for such money borrowed the said corporation may issue its notes, certificates or registered or coupon bonds under its corporate seal. The said corporation may act as the fiscal or transfer agent of or trustee for any state, county, municipality, body politic, corporation, public or private, or for any person or persons, and in such capacity may receive and disburse money and negotiate, sell, transfer, register and countersign certificates of stock, bonds and other evidences of indebtedness. The said corporation may act as agent, general agent, or special agent, or manager for any purpose or business for any corporation, either public or private, or for any person or persons that may appoint or select said corporation, with its consent, as such agent, general agent, special agent or manager for any purpose or business not inconsistent with the laws of this state or of the United States. Said corporation may guarantee, endorse and secure the payment and collection of notes, debts, bills of exchange, contracts, bonds, mortgages, evidences of debt, certificates of property or value checks, and the titles to property, real or personal, indebtedness of companies, partnerships, loans of cities, states, counties, municipalities on such terms or commissions as may be agreed upon or established by said corporation and the person or corporation dealing therewith. The said corporation may subscribe to the capital stock of other corporations, and may vote said stock, and may hold, transfer or sell the same. It may conduct warehouses and depots for the storage of personal property, and the certificates or receipts issued therefor shall be negotiable by delivery, entitling the holder to the property mentioned in said certificates or receipts without regard to the disposition of the property, and the said corporation shall exercise care in the custody or protection of property stored with it. The said corporation is hereby authorized and empowered to insure the fidelity of persons holding places of trust or responsibility into

Laws building and loan associations made applicable.

Notes, certificates, bonds.

Fiscal agent, etc.

May act as agent, general or special.

May guarantee, etc.

Subscription to capital stock of other corporations.

May insure fidelity of persons in places of trust, etc.

or under any state, county, city, corporation, company, person or persons whatsoever or whomsoever: to become surety on the bonds of executors, administrators, guardians and agents, and to become security for the faithful performance of any trust, office, duty, contract or agreement, and to supersede any judgment, or to go upon any appeal or other bond; and it is further authorized to become sole surety in all cases where by law two or more sureties are required for the faithful performance of any trust or office, and it shall and may be lawful for any court, register, clerk or other officer to approve said corporation as sole surety in all such cases, if in the opinion of such court or officer the same shall be sufficient; but in such cases the officers and affairs of said corporation may be subject to examination by such court, register, clerk or other officer, and it shall be lawful for said corporation to stipulate and to provide for indemnity from the parties aforesaid, for whom it shall be or become responsible, and to enforce any bond, contract, agreement, pledge or other security made or given for that purpose. And the said corporation may charge for all such bonds of suretyship, as well as for all other acts and all other business it undertakes to perform authorized by this act such compensation as may be agreed upon, not inconsistent with the laws of this state or of the United States.

Sole surety, etc.

Examination of officers, etc.

Charges, etc.

Sec. 13. That the said corporation shall have the power to invest its capital and increment thereof, or such funds as may be deposited with said corporation for that purpose from time to time, in the public funds or bonds of the United States or in the bonds of any state, county or municipality in the United States, or in any stock or property whatsoever, and to dispose of said bonds, stocks, money and property in any such manner (not contrary to law) as may appear most advantageous to the said corporation, and to take, have, hold, enjoy all such estates, real, personal and mixed, as may be obtained by the investment of the capital of said corporation and all other moneys or funds that may come into its possession in the course of its dealings and business, and the same to sell, grant, mortgage, lease and dispose of at pleasure, and to execute, acknowledge and deliver all deeds and other instruments of writing concerning the same.

Investment of capital, etc.

Sec. 14. The stockholders of said corporation shall be held individually responsible, equally and ratably, and not one for another, for all contracts, debts and agreements of this corporation to the extent of the amounts of their stock therein at the par value thereof in addition to the amount invested in such share or shares; but beyond this the stockholders shall not be individually liable.

Responsibility of stockholders.

Total liability of corporation, limit.

Sec. 15. The total liabilities to this corporation of any person, or of any company, corporation or firm for money borrowed (including in the liabilities of a firm the liabilities of the several members thereof), shall at no time exceed one-tenth part of the amount of the capital stock of this corporation then actually paid in: Provided, however, that the said amount of money so borrowed may be any amount not in excess of twenty per cent. (20 per cent.) of said capital stock actually paid in, in such cases as may be authorized by order of the board of directors. But the discount of bills of exchange drawn in good faith against actually existing values, and the discount of commercial or business paper actually loaned by the person negotiating the same, shall not be considered money borrowed. The liabilities referred to in this section shall refer only to liabilities for money borrowed.

Corporate life, limit.

Principal place of business.

Sec. 16. That the said corporation shall have a duration of forty years; that it may adopt, have and use a common seal, and change or alter the same at its pleasure; that its principal place of business shall be in the city of Winston, North Carolina, with power and privilege to establish branches and agencies at any place in or out of this state for the transaction of its business.

Change of corporate name.

Seal.

Sec. 17. That the stockholders of said corporation shall have the power at their first meeting, by majority vote of the stock, to change the corporate name from "Winston-Salem Trust and Deposit Company" to "Wachovia Bank, Trust and Deposit Company," and to adopt a seal to correspond with its change of name; and this corporation, if and when so named "Wachovia Bank, Trust and Deposit Company," shall be the same corporation, with all the powers, franchises, rights and privileges as if its name had not been so changed from "Winston-Salem Trust and Deposit Company" to "Wachovia Bank, Trust and Deposit Company."

Conflicting laws repealed.

Sec. 18. That all laws or parts of laws inconsistent with this act be and the same are hereby repealed.

Sec. 19. That this act shall be in force from and after its ratification.

Ratified the 10th day of February, A. D. 1899.

CHAPTER 43.

An act to establish a stock law for a certain part of Carver's Creek township, Cumberland county, North Carolina.

The General Assembly of North Carolina do enact:

Stock law extended to certain territory.

Section 1. That the provisions of the stock law as contained in chapter twenty, volume two of The Code, are hereby made applicable to the following territory in Cumberland county, North Carolina, viz.: Beginning at or near McNeill's bridge on lower Little river, and thence by such route as may be adopted as most expedient to the Cape Fear river at or near the mouth of Troutham's creek, and thence up the Cape Fear river and lower Little river to the beginning; and the provisions of said chapter are hereby adopted and made applicable to said territory in the same manner as if said territory had adopted the stock law in the manner prescribed therein. Boundaries.

Sec. 2. That said Cape Fear river and lower Little river are hereby declared to be lawful fences for the purposes of this act, and W. B. Ray, J. O. Adams, J. E. Lucas, S. R. Surles and A. B. Walker are hereby appointed commissioners for building and keeping in repair the fence and necessary gates across public highways, and under the supervision and direction of the commissioners of Cumberland county shall do any and all things expedient and necessary for the prompt establishment of the fences and gates as contemplated by this act and carrying its provisions into effect. Any three of them shall constitute a quorum to act, and any vacancy in their members shall be filled by the county commissioners from the land-owners within said territory. Lawful fences. Commissioners. Quorum.

Sec. 3 They shall make report annually to the county commissioners on or before the first Monday in June, giving as near as may be the amount that may be necessary to build and keep in repair the fences and gates; and it shall be the duty of the county commissioners to levy a tax on all real estate within said boundaries, which tax shall in no case exceed fifty cents on one hundred dollars worth of real estate. Annual reports of commissioners to show amounts necessary to make and repair.

Sec. 4. The provisions of chapter two hundred and thirteen, acts of eighteen hundred and ninety-three, in regard to the territory therein mentioned, are hereby made applicable and as part of this act, so far as same is not inconsistent with this act and chapter twenty, volume two of The Code. Former laws applicable.

Sec. 5. The fence commissioners shall as soon as the fence and gates as contemplated by this act have been erected, give notice by posters at five (5) public places in said territory, and from and after five days from such publication this act shall be in full force and effect. Notice, etc.

Ratified the 10th day of February, A. D. 1899.

CHAPTER 44.

An act to repeal an act incorporating the town of Yanceyville.

The General Assembly of North Carolina do enact:

Repealed.

Section 1. That chapter one hundred and twenty-nine, laws of eighteen hundred and eighty-five, be and the same is hereby repealed.

Sec. 2. That this act shall be in force from and after its ratification.

Ratified the 10th day of February, A. D. 1899.

CHAPTER 45.

An act to amend the charter of the town of Franklinton.

The General Assembly of North Carolina do enact:

Former laws; exception.

Section 1. That all the rights, powers and privileges heretofore granted to the town of Franklinton by any laws now in force, together with the powers conferred on incorporated towns by chapter sixty-two of The Code, shall remain in full force except as changed by or inconsistent with this act.

Poll tax.

Sec. 2. That the board of commissioners of said town may collect annually on all property taxed by the state and county a tax not to exceed thirty-three and one-third cents on the hundred dollars, and a poll tax not to exceed one dollar.

License tax on bar-rooms, etc., limit.

Billiard, pool and other tables, limit.

Sec. 3. That the said commissioners may furthermore collect semi-annually as a license tax on drinking saloons, bar-rooms, or places where spirituous liquors are sold, not exceeding seventy-five dollars; on billiard, pool or bagatelle tables, not exceeding fifty dollars; on dogs, not exceeding one dollar.

Default in payment of fines and costs, imprisonment.

Sec. 4. That in default of the payment of any fine or costs in any action under an ordinance of the town, the person against whom such judgment for fine or costs, or both, shall have been rendered, may be imprisoned in the county jail till such costs and fine be paid or he be discharged by law.

Buy real estate.

Sec. 5. That the commissioners of said town shall have the power to buy, sell and hold for and in the name of the town any real estate.

Commissioners may borrow money, limit.

Sec. 6. That the said commissioners are hereby empowered to borrow for the town not to exceed five hundred dollars with which to erect for the town a suitable jail or guard-house, together with a market-house, if they see fit: Provided, that the

Proviso.

money shall be borrowed and the work commenced not later than May 1st, 1900.

Sec. 7. This act shall be in force from and after its ratification.

Ratified the 10th day of February, A. D. 1899.

CHAPTER 46.

An act for the relief of Trinity Land Company.

The General Assembly of North Carolina do enact:

Section 1. That Trinity Land Company of Durham county, North Carolina, is hereby authorized to remove the bodies of all the parties who are buried on the lands near the North Carolina Railroad west of Durham, lying between Trinity College and the Erwin Cotton Mills, under the conditions hereinafter named. Removal of bodies buried at certain point.

Sec. 2. That such land company shall purchase a lot in the town cemetery of Durham, North Carolina, and shall re-inter said bodies in such lot in said cemetery in an appropriate manner. Reinterment of bodies.

Sec. 3. That each separate body shall be carefully disinterred by a competent person, and shall be placed in a coffin and removed in a becoming manner to the place of reinterment and there reburied as above provided. Manner of disinterment.

Sec. 4. That all laws and parts of laws in conflict with this act are hereby repealed. Conflicting laws repealed.

Sec. 5. That this act shall be in force from and after its ratification.

Ratified the 10th day of February, A. D. 1899.

CHAPTER 47.

An act to amend chapter two hundred and thirteen, private laws of eighteen hundred and ninety-seven.

The General Assembly of North Carolina do enact:

Section 1. That section two (2) of chapter two hundred and thirteen, private laws of eighteen hundred and ninety-seven, be amended as follows: By striking out all after the word "that" Chapter 213, private laws 1897, relating to Cullowhee High School. Amended.

in line three (3) thereof down to and including the word "Bryson" in line five (5) thereof, and inserting in lieu thereof the following: L. J. Smith, Felix E. Alley, J. Robert Long, D. D. Davies, John R. Long and J. D. Coward; and that said section be further amended by striking out all of said section two (2) after the word "department" in line nine (9) thereof.

Repealed. Sec. 2. That section three (3) of said chapter two hundred and thirteen, private laws of eighteen hundred and ninety-seven, be and the same is hereby repealed.

Vacancies, how filled. Sec. 3. That in case of a vacancy by death, resignation or otherwise in said board as constituted in section one (1) of this act, such vacancy shall be filled by the remaining members of said board electing his or their successors, which successor shall have the same powers, authority and privilege as his or their predecessor.

Repealed. Sec. 4 That section four (4) of said chapter two hundred and thirteen, private laws of eighteen hundred and ninety seven, be and the same is hereby repealed.

Conflicting laws repealed. Sec. 5. That all laws and clauses of laws in conflict with this act are hereby repealed.

Sec. 6. That this act shall be in force from and after its ratification.

Ratified the 13th day of February, A. D. 1899.

CHAPTER 48.

An act to amend the charter of Edenton.

The General Assembly of North Carolina do enact:

Amendment. Section 1. That section one of chapter thirty-nine of private laws of eighteen hundred and ninety-five, entitled "An

Change in wards. act to amend the charter of the town of Edenton," be stricken out, and in lieu thereof the following be inserted: That the town of Edenton, in Chowan county, North Carolina, shall be divided into four wards as follows: That portion of said town embraced

Limits of wards. within the following boundaries, to-wit: Beginning on west side of Broad street at a point midway between Water street and King street, then running westerly parallel to Water street to Granville street, then north along Granville street to north side of Blount street, then westerly along north side of Blount street to Mosely street, then north along Mosely street to a point midway between Church and Gale streets, then easterly parallel to Church street to a point one hundred feet west of Broad street, then south parallel with Broad street to Queen street, then east along Queen street to Broad street, then south along west side of Broad street to place of beginning, shall constitute and be known as the first ward.

That portion of said town embraced within the following boundaries: Beginning at the southeast corner of Water and Broad streets, then running along the water's edge easterly to Oakum street, then northerly along west side of Oakum street to King street, then easterly along King street to a point one hundred feet east of Oakum street, then north parallel to Oakum street to Queen street, then west along south side of Queen street to Court street, then north along Court street to Church street, then west along Church street to a point one hundred feet east of Broad street, then south parallel with Broad street to Queen street, then west along Queen street to Broad street, then south along Broad street to place of beginning, shall constitute and be known as the second ward. Second ward.

That portion of said town embraced within the following boundaries: Beginning on north side of Queen street at a point one hundred feet west of Broad street, then running north parallel to Broad street to Freemason street, then along south side of Freemason street to a point one hundred feet east of Broad street, then south parallel with Broad street to Queen street, then west along Queen street to place of beginning, shall constitute and be known as the third ward. Third ward.

That portion of said town not embraced within the boundaries of the first, second and third wards as set out above shall constitute and be known as the fourth ward. Fourth ward.

Sec. 2. That section two of said chapter be amended by inserting the words "and other officers" in line seven of said section between the word 'mayor" and the word "from." Officers.

Sec. 3. That the words "and other officers" in section six of said chapter be and the same are hereby stricken out; and the words and figures eighteen hundred and ninety-five in said section be changed to eighteen hundred and ninety-nine; and words "old Love and Charity Hall" be changed to "C. Tarkinton's store." Amendment.

Sec. 4. That the officers of said town shall receive such pay as the councilmen shall vote them, not exceeding twenty-four dollars per year for each councilman, one hundred dollars per year for the mayor, and fifty dollars per month for the constable; Provided, the board of councilmen may discontinue any salary or pay voted any officer [who] has not faithfully discharged his duties. No officer shall receive any pay unless same is fixed by a vote of said councilmen. Pay of officers, limit.

Conflicting laws repealed.

Sec. 5. That all laws and clauses of laws in conflict with this act be and the same are hereby repealed.

Sec. 6. That this act shall be in force from and after its ratification.

Ratified the 13th day of February, A. D. 1899.

CHAPTER 49.

An act to amend chapter one hundred and nine, private laws of eighteen hundred and ninety-seven.

The General Assembly of North Carolina do enact:

Chapter 109, private laws 1897, relating to police justice in Asheville.

Vacancies, how filled.

Section 1. That section seventeen of chapter one hundred and nine, private laws of session of eighteen hundred and ninety-seven, be and the same is hereby amended by adding at the end of said section the following words: "And all vacancies in the said office of police justice shall be filled by the board of aldermen of the city of Asheville."

Sec. 2. That this act shall be in force from and after its ratification.

Ratified the 13th day of February, A. D. 1899.

CHAPTER 50.

An act to incorporate the Inter-state Telephone and Telegraph Company.

The General Assembly of North Carolina do enact:

Corporators.

Created body corporate and politic; name.

May sue and be sued, etc.; may contract and be contracted with; privileges.

Section 1. That L. A. Carr, Julian S. Carr and George W. Watts of Durham, North Carolina, together with all other persons and corporations who shall be associated with them and become stockholders in the corporation hereby incorporated, their successors and assigns, be and they are hereby created and constituted a body politic and corporate, by and under the name and style of the "Interstate Telephone and Telegraph Company," by which name the said corporation may sue and be sued, plead and be impleaded, appear, prosecute and defend in any court whatsoever all actions; may contract and be contracted with, and shall have the privileges hereby specially granted, and such others as may be necessary to the full exercise and enjoyment of the same.

Sec. 2. That the said corporation shall enjoy all the rights, privileges, liberties, immunities, franchises and powers conferred upon and pertaining to other corporate bodies and not forbidden by the laws of the United States and of the state of North Carolina.

Rights, powers, privileges, etc.

Sec. 3. That the said corporation shall have the right to make, adopt and use a common seal, which it may break and alter at its pleasure.

Seal.

Sec. 4. That said corporation is hereby authorized and empowered to conduct, transact and carry on in all their branches the business usually done by telephone and telegraph companies in the transmission of messages, charging for such services just and reasonable charges, rates and compensation as may be agreed upon between said corporation and its patrons and customers, or such rates or charges as may be established by said corporation, not exceeding the amount fixed therefor under such rules and regulations as may be prescribed by law or fixed by duly constituted legal authority regulating the same from time to time. And said corporation is also authorized and empowered to manufacture for its own use and for use to others in course of business, all such articles, appliances and supplies as may be necessary and useful in carrying on the business usually done by telegraph and telephone companies.

Business of the corporation.

Charges for services limited to rates prescribed by law.

May manufacture for its own use and for sale certain articles.

Sec. 5. That the said corporation, its successors and assigns, is hereby authorized and empowered to buy, own, lease, deal in or otherwise acquire and hold, sell and convey lands, tenements and hereditaments, easements and privileges, and all manner of real, personal and mixed property whatsoever, to such extent as it may deem proper and necessary in conducting its business, and as fully as other citizens of the state may do, and may sell and convey or lease the same to other persons or corporations; and said corporation is authorized to pay for such real estate and personal property, tenements and hereditaments, easements and privileges as it may purchase or otherwise acquire with and by its capital stock or any portion thereof. It may borrow money and contract debts and issue bonds therefor, and to secure the payment thereof it may execute mortgages or deeds of trust upon any or all of its property and rights of property, privileges and franchises. It may also subscribe to the capital stock of any other telephone or telegraph company, and any other telephone or telegraph company may subscribe for stock in said corporation. It may, upon such terms as may be agreed upon between it and the Interstate Telephone and Telegraph Company of Frederick, Maryland, purchase from said Interstate Telephone and Telegraph Company of Frederick, Maryland, all the property and property rights, franchises and privileges belonging to said

May acquire, sell and convey real estate, personal and mixed property, etc.

May sell or lease to other corporations.

May borrow money, contract debts, execute mortgages, deeds in trust, etc.

May subscribe to capital stock of other corporations.

May purchase the property of Interstate Telephone Co. of Maryland, or consolidate with same.

company, and consolidate or merge its property and business with that of said Interstate Telephone and Telegraph Company of Frederick, Maryland, or with any other telephone or telegraph company, upon such terms as may be agreed upon between the contracting parties interested: Provided, such consolidated corporation or corporations shall be a domestic corporation under the laws of North Carolina.

Proviso.

Powers and privileges secured by Code of N. C.

Sec. 6. That said corporation shall have all the powers and privileges and be subject to the provisions relating to telegraph companies contained in chapter forty-nine, volume one, Code of North Carolina, to-wit: Sections number two thousand and seven, number two thousand and eight, number two thousand and nine, number two thousand and ten, number two thousand and eleven, number two thousand and twelve and number two thousand and thirteen.

Capital stock, limit.

When corporation may organize.

Capital stock may be increased, limit.

May issue stocks, both common and preferred.

Certificates of stock, par value; shall be issued only when fully paid for.

Stock non-assessable.

Shares deemed personal property; transfer, etc.

Sec. 7. That the capital stock of said corporation shall be twenty-five thousand ($25,000) dollars, and the said corporation shall have authority to organize and transact business whenever ten (10) per cent. thereof shall have been subscribed, payable either in money or in property which said corporation is authorized to hold; the capital stock of said corporation may be increased from time to time or at any time to an amount not exceeding two millions ($2,000,000) of dollars by the consent of a majority of the stockholders. The said corporation may issue stock both common and preferred under such regulations as to the issue thereof as may be prescribed by a majority of the stockholders. The certificates for shares of stock shall be of par value one hundred ($100) dollars each, and shall be issued only when the same are fully paid for, either in money or property, at an agreed valuation, and the shares of stock when issued shall not thereafter be liable to assessment for any corporate purpose whatever. The shares of stock shall be deemed personal property, and be transferable upon the books of said company, in the manner provided for in the by-laws, but no share or right to a share of stock shall be transferable on the books of said corporation until all previous calls thereon for unpaid subscriptions therefor shall have been fully paid or satisfied, or until declared forfeited for non-payment of call thereon. And the directors may refuse the entries or transfers of any shares into the books of the corporation whereon any call for an unpaid subscription has been, which has not [been] paid in or satisfied according to the terms of the subscription.

Directors may refuse entries of transfers.

Not individually liable for debts, etc.

Sec. 8. That the corporators, subscribers for stock and stockholders in said corporation, their successors and assigns, shall not be individually or personally liable or responsible for the acts, liabilities, contracts, engagements, defaults, omissions or commissions or torts of said corporation, or for any claim, payment, loss, damages, injuries, transaction, matter or thing whatsoever related to or connected with the business affairs of said company, and no stockholder or subscriber for stock shall be liable to pay for more stock than he subscribed.

Principal office.

Sec. 9. That the principal office of or place of business of said corporation shall be in Durham county, North Carolina, but said corporation may establish branch offices and branches of its business at any other places, either within or outside of the state of North Carolina, as its business interest may require.

Branch offices.

By-laws, etc.

Sec. 10. That the said corporation may adopt such by-laws for its government as a majority of the corporators, subscribers for stock or stockholders may deem proper, not inconsistent with the laws of the United States and of the state of North Carolina, and therein provide for the election or appointment of all necessary officers or agents of said corporation.

Property, etc., liable to ad valorem tax.

Sec. 11. That all the property and franchises of said corporation shall be liable to an ad valorem tax, including shares of stock belonging to its stockholders, and said property and franchises, including such shares of stock, shall be listed and given in for taxation, and the taxes thereon paid by the proper officers of the corporation, and assessed for taxation only in the county where its principal office is located, unless otherwise expressly provided by general law, and shall be liable for taxation there and not elsewhere, and upon its assessed valuation, unless otherwise expressly provided by general law, except that in case said corporation establishes branches of its business in other counties, towns and cities in North Carolina. The amount of its stock and franchises shall be listed therein by the proper officers of the corporation pro rata, the same being estimated according to the value of such plant or plants in the respective counties, cities and towns bears to the whole valuation of the property, stock and franchises of said corporation, the aggregate of said valuations to be deducted from the total assessment in the county wherein the principal office of said corporation is situated, so as to avoid double taxation thereon.

Shares of stock, etc., shall be listed for taxation.

Assessed valuation for taxation.

Branches, etc.

Listed for taxation, how.

By-laws and regulations prima facie evidence.

Sec. 12. That a copy of any by-laws or regulation of the corporation under its corporate seal, and purporting to be signed by the president or vice-president thereof, shall be received as prima facie evidence for and against the corporation in any action or judicial proceeding.

That this act shall be in force from and after its ratification.

Ratified the 13th day of February, A. D. 1899.

CHAPTER 51.

An act to amend chapter seventy-one (71) of the public laws of North Carolina, passed at the session of eighteen hundred and eighty-nine.

The General Assembly of North Carolina do enact:

Chapter 71, laws 1889, relating to Aberdeen and West End Railroad Co. Amended as to line of road.

Section 1. That chapter seventy-one (71) of the public laws of eighteen hundred and eighty-nine be and the same is hereby amended as follows: In section two (2) of said chapter in line eight (8) after the word "counties" strike out the words "thence through Montgomery county to Albemarle in Stanley county," and insert the words "thence by way of Troy in Montgomery county to the town of Mt. Gilead in said county, thence to Mangum in Richmond county."

Conflicting laws repealed.

Sec. 2. That all laws in conflict with this act be and the same are hereby repealed.

Sec. 3. That this act shall be in force and effect from and after its ratification.

Ratified the 13th day of February, A. D. 1899.

CHAPTER 52.

An act to incorporate the town of Lattimore in Cleveland county.

The General Assembly of North Carolina do enact:

Incorporation of town; name; benefits, etc.

Section 1. That the town of Lattimore, in the county of Cleveland, be and the same is hereby incorporated by the name and style of the town of "Lattimore," and it shall have the benefit of and be subject to all the provisions of law now existing in reference to incorporated towns, not inconsistent with this act.

Corporate limits.

Sec. 2. The corporate limits of said town shall be as follows: One-half of a mile north and south and one-half of a mile east and west from the centre of the railroad crossing.

Officers, etc.

Sec. 3. That the officers of said town shall consist of a mayor and three aldermen and a marshal, to be elected in accordance with the general laws regulating elections in cities and towns.

Persons appointed, term.

Sec. 4. That until their successors shall be elected and qualified, the following persons shall be the officers of said town, to-wit: Mayor, A. M. Lattimore; aldermen, C. A. McCord, S. G. Price and W. T. Colton; marshal, J. P. Lattimore.

Sec. 5. That this act shall be in force from and after its ratification.

Ratified the 13th day of February, A. D. 1899.

CHAPTER 53.

An act to incorporate the Brevard Banking Company at Brevard, North Carolina.

The General Assembly of North Carolina do enact:

Section 1. That W. A. Gosh, J. W. McMinn, T. D. England, N. E. McMinn, Z. W. Nichols, W. H. Allison, N. McMinn, and their associates, successors and assigns, are hereby constituted and declared a body politic and corporate by the name and style of the "Brevard Banking Company," with its principal office and place of business at Brevard, North Carolina, and by that name may sue and be sued, plead and be impleaded in any court in the state, and have a continual succession for the term of fifty years. Corporators. Body politic, etc. Name. May sue and be sued, etc. Limit on corporate life.

Sec. 2. That the capital stock shall not be less than fifteen thousand dollars in shares of one hundred dollars each, and such capital stock may be increased from time to time as said corporation may elect to a sum not to exceed one hundred thousand dollars. Minimum capital stock; increase of capital stock; limit of increase.

Sec. 3. That the corporators named herein or any three of them are hereby empowered to open books of subscription to the capital stock of said corporation, at such time or times, at such places and for such periods as they may determine; and the stockholders representing a majority of the stock may at any time, at any general meeting called after the organization of said corporation, at their discretion re-open books of subscription to said capital stock, until the same as herein limited is wholly taken. Books of subscription, who may open. Majority of stockholders may reopen books of subscription.

Sec. 4. Whenever fifteen thousand dollars shall be subscribed and paid into the capital stock of said bank, the beforementioned corporators, or any three of them, may call a meeting of the subscribers to said stock at such time and place, and upon such notice as they may deem sufficient, and such stockholders may elect such directors and so many as they deem proper and sufficient, who shall hold their office one year, or until their successors are elected, with power in said board of directors to fill all vacancies occurring in their body until any general election thereafter; and said directors may elect a president, vice-president, cashier and all other such officers as may by them be deemed necessary, to serve during their continuance in office, or until their successors shall be elected or appointed by said board of directors. Stockholders' meetings called by corporators; may elect directors; notice. Terms of directors. Vacancies in directors, how filled. Election of president, vice-president, cashier, etc.

Sec. 5. The president and directors of said corporation may adopt and use a common seal, and alter the same at pleasure; may make and appoint all necessary officers and agents and fix their compensation; shall exercise and have all such powers and Common seal. May appoint officers, agents, etc.

authority as may be necessary for governing the affairs of the corporation, consistent with such by-laws as may be adopted by such stockholders; they may regulate the terms and rates on which loans may be made and discounts received, not to exceed the rate allowed by law, and deposits taken; and when dividends of the profits and the amount thereof shall be made and declared, they shall fill all vacancies occurring among the officers or agents of said corporation; they may call meetings of the stockholders at such time and upon such notice as they may deem proper, and [at] all such meetings of the stockholders said stockholders may be represented by written proxy, and each share shall be entitled to one vote.

May regulate terms of loans, etc.; limit. Dividends, discounts, etc.

Vacancies, how filled, etc. Meetings stockholders; representation in person or by proxy.

Bank may receive and pay out currency of its own issue, etc.

Sec. 6. That said bank may receive and pay out all lawful currency of its own issue, under all rights, powers and authority and under such instructions as may be imposed by the laws of this state and of the United States as to circulation by state banks; may deal in exchange, gold and silver coin, current and uncurrent paper, public, municipal and other securities, and for the purpose of aiding planters, manufacturers and others, said bank shall and may have power to loan any sum or sums of money, and to secure the repayment of same by taking in writing a lien or liens upon the crops to be raised or upon any article or articles then in existence, and shall have power to make loans upon mortgages of real estate and personal property, with power of sale inserted upon default of payment; said bank may discount notes and other evidences of debt, buy or sell or otherwise deal in all commercial paper of every kind; may loan money to and receive deposits of the same from any and all persons, including corporations, minors, married women, upon such terms and the manner and time of collections and payment as may be agreed upon, and may charge such rate of interest as allowed by the laws of this state, and may take and receive such interest at the time of making such loans, or at such time as may be agreed upon; said bank may invest in stocks, bonds or other securities of this state, the United States, or any corporation, public or private, of this or any other state in the Union, and may borrow money in such amounts and at such rate of interest, and payable at such times and places as the board of directors may determine, and issue its notes, certificates or registered or coupon bonds under its corporate seal.

May deal in exchanges, etc.

Loan of money; liens, etc.; loans upon mortgages.

Discounts.

Loans, deposits for persons and corporations.

Rate of interest.

Investments in securities, etc.

May issue notes, etc.

May guarantee or become security upon official bonds, etc.

Sec. 7. That the said bank may guarantee or become surety upon any official or other bonds or undertaking required or authorized by law; and it may likewise guarantee or become surety upon all kinds of fiduciary bonds or undertakings made by those having possession, custody or control, or who may come in the possession, custody or control of trust money or funds, either as guardians, executors, administrators, collectors, receivers or trustees of any sort, or as employees of any person, company or corporation however or by whomsoever chosen or appointed, under such regulations as may be provided in the by-laws, and may receive therefor compensation: Provided, the above and other things of similar nature done by the bank shall be consistent with the laws of the State.

Compensation. Proviso.

Sec. 8. The said bank may purchase and hold property, real, personal or mixed, and such may be conveyed to it to secure or satisfy any debt due it, or for any other purpose, or any sold under any mortgage, execution, or order of court to satisfy any debt due it, and may sell and convey the same at pleasure, and use or reinvest the proceeds thereof, as it may deem best.

May purchase and hold property.

Sec. 9. That when married women, minors or apprentices deposit money or other things of value in said bank, either generally or specially to their own credit, they, or any of them, may draw the same on their check or order and be bound thereby; and such married women, minors or apprentices shall be bound by such individual check or order, and the said check or order shall be valid and sufficient release to said corporation against such married women, minors or apprentices.

Deposits by minors, married women, apprentices, etc.

Sec. 10. That if any subscriber shall fail to pay for his stock or any part thereof, as the same is required of him, the entire residue of his stock shall be deemed to be due and may be recovered in the name of the corporation by an ordinary civil action, or the entire stock of such delinquent may be sold by order of the directors for cash at the banking house of said corporation in the town of Brevard, after advertisement of such sale for ten days, in some newspaper published in said town or in three public places in said town, and the proceeds of such sale may be applied to the payment of the balance of unpaid subscription, with all the cost of such sale.

Failure to pay for stock; residue to become due. Unpaid stock, how recovered.

Sec. 11. That if any subscriber shall assign his stock before its full payment, he and his assigns, and all subsequent assigns thereof, shall be liable for its payment and may be sued jointly or severally as aforesaid or by civil action; in every case of delinquency in a subscriber or others, the subscription shall be deemed a promissory note payable to said corporation, as well in respect to the remedy for recovering the same, as in the distribution of the assets of any deceased subscriber.

Assignor and assignee, liability of.

Sec. 12. That the said bank shall have the right to act as agent, factor or trustee for any state, county, township, town or other municipality or corporation, company or individual, on such terms as to compensation as commission as may be agreed upon.

May act as agent, factor or trustee. Terms, etc.

In registering, selling, countersigning, collecting, acquiring, holding, deeding and disposing of on account of any state, county, township, town, municipality, corporation, company or individual, any bonds, certificates of stock, notes, or any description of property, real or personal, or for endorsing or guaranteeing the payment of said bonds, certificates of stock, notes, etc., and generally for managing such business; and for doing any and all other matters and things authorized by this charter, said corporation may charge such premium, commissions or rate of compensation as may be agreed upon, and which is not prohibited by law.

Charges for services, etc.

May receive valuables on deposit.

Sec. 13. That said corporation is hereby authorized to receive on deposit all valuables, gold, silver, precious metals, jewels, plate, certificates of stock, bonds, evidences of debt, instrument of title and all other things of value which may be left on deposit with said corporation for safekeeping, and shall be entitled to charge such commission or compensation as may be agreed upon; and that said bank is authorized and empowered to accept and exercise any trust of any and every other description which may by its consent be committed or transferred to it by any person or persons whomsoever, by any bodies politic or corporate, public or private, and to accept the office of executor, administrator, collector, guardian or assignee, whenever such appointment is made or conferred by any person or persons or court of this state or of the United States, and shall be clothed with the same powers, and shall be under the same restrictions as private individuals in the same capacity. In lieu of the bond required by law to be given by an administrator, guardian, trustee, receiver or other fiduciary, it shall be lawful, and before assuming any such trust under order of any court the said bank shall file in the office of the clerk of the superior court of Transylvania county an undertaking, with sufficient security with either personal securities or bonds of the state of North Carolina or of the United States or of any county or city of the state of North Carolina, or any other security satisfactory to the court, and to be approved by the said clerk, and the said undertaking so secured may be accepted by the said clerk and held as security in the sum of ——— dollars, conditioned for the faithful performance of any trust which may be committed to the said bank by order of any court of North Carolina as aforesaid. In case of wilful default in the performance of any trust so committed to said bank as aforesaid, the said undertaking may be sued upon by the party injured or his personal representative in the superior court of any county of North Carolina where such default may have been made (and the superior court of Transylvania county, whenever it shall be

Commissions to be charged, etc.

May accept and exercise trusts, etc.

May secure administrators, etc., by undertaking to be secured by bonds of North Carolina, or of any city or town, or of the United States, to be approved by clerk of court.

Default in performance of trusts, undertakings may be served upon.

made satisfactorily to appear by sworn testimony that it is necessary in order to secure the faithful performance of all of said trust, may require the said undertaking to be enlarged sufficiently to secure the faithful performance of the same), a copy of such undertaking duly certified by the seal of the superior court of Transylvania county, and if secured by bonds of the state or of the United States or of any county or city or other security as aforesaid, a statement thereof so certified shall be evidence in all courts in North Carolina; and the superior court wherein the said company shall have been appointed guardian, executor, administrator, receiver, trustee or depository shall have the power to make orders respecting such trusts, and to require the said company to render all accounts which said court might lawfully make or require if such trustees were a natural person. And in accepting any of the trusts or power hereunder, the said corporation may qualify by one of its executive officers.

Undertaking to be enlarged.

Certified statement to be evidence.

Power of court to make orders, etc.

Acceptance of trusts; qualification, etc.

Sec. 14. The said bank shall have discretionary power to invest the funds received by it in trust in bonds of the United States, or any state, or in the bonds duly authorized to be issued by any county or incorporated city or other good securities, or in safe real or personal securities; but all such investments shall be made at the sole risk of the bank, and for any losses by reason of such investment the capital stock, property and effects of said corporation shall be absolutely liable. The bank shall use due diligence to enhance the income, rents and profits of any trust estate within its hands, but shall not be held liable for any greater income, rents and profits than can be reasonably earned by safe and prudent investments.

Discretionary power over investment of trust funds.

Investments, at whose risk.

Use of diligence to enhance value of trust estates, etc.

Sec. 15. No stockholder shall be in anywise individually liable or responsible for any debts, obligation, contracts or engagements of said bank beyond the amount of stock subscribed by such stockholder, and no stockholder shall be individually liable to depositors or other creditors of said bank beyond the amount of stock subscribed by each stockholder.

Stockholders not individually liable beyond amount of their stock.

Sec. 16. That the said bank is hereby authorized to organize in connection with its general business a savings bank department, and do a savings bank business for the convenience of small depositors, receive deposits in any sum, and pay the same with interest as may be agreed upon; to regulate the time of payment and notices of demand; may receive deposits from minors without guardians or married women, and pay the same upon their checks or receipts, which shall be valid.

May organize a savings bank.

Deposits from minors and married women.

Sec. 17. The president and directors may establish agencies of this bank at such time and places as they may designate, and such agencies may be removed or terminated at any time; and such agencies shall have the same powers as are prescribed for

May establish agencies, etc.

Powers, etc.

the corporation hereby chartered, and shall be subject to such rules and regulations as may be prescribed by the president and board of directors of the said bank: Provided, the license tax be paid to the treasurer of the state of North Carolina and a receipt for said tax from the treasurer shall be sufficient power and authority to establish the said agency under this act.

Proviso.

Organized, when.

Sec. 18. The said corporation may be organized under this act at any time within five years from the date of its passage.

Sec. 19. This act shall be in force from and after its ratification.

Ratified the 13th day of February, A. D. 1899.

CHAPTER 54.

An act to ratify the consolidation of the Wilmington, Columbia and Augusta Railroad Company and the Cheraw and Darlington Railroad Company with the Atlantic Coast Line Railroad Company of South Carolina, and to incorporate the said Atlantic Coast Line Railroad Company of South Carolina in North Carolina.

Preamble.

Whereas, The Atlantic Coast Line Railroad Company of South Carolina, a corporation created by the laws of the state of South Carolina, has by virtue of the power and authority given by its charter, acquired the ownership of the railroad and property of the Wilmington, Columbia and Augusta Railroad Company and of the Cheraw and Darlington Railroad, including that portion of each which is located in this state; and the said Wilmington, Columbia and Augusta Railroad Company, and the said Cheraw and Darlington Railroad Company have, by virtue of the powers in them vested, become consolidated with other railroads under the name of the said Atlantic Coast Line Railroad Company of South Carolina; now therefore:

The General Assembly of North Carolina do enact:

Constitution ratified.

Section 1. That the consolidation of the said Wilmington, Columbia and Augusta Railroad Company and the Cheraw and Darlington Railroad Company with the Florence Railroad Company, the Manchester and Augusta Railroad Company and the North Eastern Railroad Company, under the charter of and by the name of the Atlantic Coast Line Railroad Company of South Carolina, and the conveyance and delivery of that portion of the railroads and other property and branches of the said Wilmington, Columbia and Augusta Railroad Company and [the] Cheraw and Darlington Railroad Company which is situate in this state to the said Atlantic Coast Line Railroad Company of South Carolina, are hereby ratified and approved.

Sec. 2. That the Atlantic Coast Line Railroad Company of South Carolina, a corporation created by an act of the general assembly of the state of South Carolina, approved the fifth day of March, A. D. eighteen hundred and ninety-seven, is hereby created a body politic and corporate in the state of North Carolina, under and by the aforesaid name of The Atlantic Coast Line Railroad Company of South Carolina, and by such name may sue and be sued, adopt a common seal and change the same at will, and have all the general powers and be subject to all general restrictions granted and imposed by the laws of this state to and upon railroad companies.

Atlantic Coast Line, etc., Railroad, made a body politic and corporate.

Name; may sue and be sued.

May adopt common seal.

General powers.

Sec. 3. The said Atlantic Coast Line Railroad Company of South Carolina is hereby authorized and empowered to maintain and operate the railroads and branches which formerly belonged to the said Wilmington, Columbia and Augusta Railroad Company and the said Cheraw and Darlington Railroad Company in this state, and is hereby given all the rights, powers and privileges, and made subject to all the restrictions granted and imposed by the respective charters of each of said companies, or any amendments to the same in the state of North Carolina.

Authorized to operate certain railroads and branches

Rights, powers, etc.

Restrictions.

Sec. 4. The powers given by this act to the Atlantic Coast Line Railroad Company of South Carolina are granted upon the express condition that the property of the Atlantic Coast Line Railroad Company of South Carolina in this state shall always be liable to taxation under the constitution and laws of this state, and that the said company shall be subject to the tariffs, rules and regulations prescribed by the board of railroad commissioners.

Condition upon which powers and privileges are granted.

Sec. 5. That this act shall be in force from and after its ratification.

Ratified the 13th day of February, A. D. 1899.

CHAPTER 55.

An act to declare the Southeastern Railroad Company a duly incorporated company, and to amend and enlarge its charter.

The General Assembly of North Carolina do enact:

Section 1. That the Southeastern Railroad Company, a corporation organized under the general laws of this state by articles

Declared a duly incorporated company.

of association duly filed in the office of the secretary of state on the fourth day of August, eighteen hundred and ninety-seven, and the persons named therein as incorporators, and such other persons as are now or that may be hereafter associated with them, or any of them, as stockholders, their successors and assigns, are hereby declared to be a duly incorporated company and are hereby created a body politic and corporate under the laws of this state, under and by the aforesaid name of the Southeastern Railroad Company, and by such name may sue and be sued, adopt a common seal and change the same at will, and shall have all the general powers granted to and be subject to all the general restrictions imposed upon railroad companies by the laws of this state.

Body politic and corporate; name.

Seal. Powers.

Sec. 2. The said Southeastern Railroad Company shall have the right to maintain and operate its railroad as already constructed from Elrod in the county of Robeson to Ashpole in the same county, and shall have the power at any time hereafter to construct an extension of its said road and maintain and operate the same from a point in the town of Ashpole to a point in or near the town of Hub in the county of Columbus in this state, and to that end shall have the right to acquire by purchase, gift or condemnation such lands as may be necessary for its purposes, as provided in the general laws of this State.

May operate railroads, when.

Extensions, when.

May acquire, purchase and condemn property.

Sec. 3. That the capital stock of the said company may be fixed by the stockholders thereof in any annual or special meeting so that the same shall not be less than fifty thousand dollars nor more than five hundred thousand dollars, anything in the original charter of the company to the contrary notwithstanding.

Capital stock to be fixed by company; limit.

Sec. 4. That the said company shall have the right to make, issue and negotiate its bonds, either coupon or registered, to such an amount as may be deemed proper by the stockholders thereof, and to cause the same to be secured by one or more mortgages or deeds in trust to such trustee or trustees and on such terms and conditions as to the board of directors of said company may seem proper.

Bonds, coupon or registered.

Security, etc.

Sec. 5. That the principal office of the said company shall be in the city of Wilmington, North Carolina, and that the stockholders thereof may in any annual or special meeting adopt all such by-laws, rules and regulations for the government of the affairs of the company as may be deemed necessary: Provided, the same shall not be inconsistent with the laws of this state or of the United States.

Principal offices; by-laws, etc.

Sec. 6. The said company shall have the right to consolidate with any other railroad company organized under the laws of this state with which it may connect on such terms as may be agreed upon by the stockholders of this company, such consoli-

Right of consolidation; terms.

Consolidation, how effected.

dation to be effected by the conveyance of this company's property to the company with which it may become consolidated, or to lease its road and property to any other person, persons or corporation upon such terms and on such conditions as to the stockholders may seem proper: Provided, the same is approved by the affirmative vote of the holders of at least two-thirds of the capital stock of the said company. Lease, etc.; terms and conditions.

Sec. 7. This act shall be in force from and after its ratification.

Ratified the 15th day of February, A. D. 1899.

CHAPTER 56.

An act to incorporate the Bank of Chapel Hill.

The General Assembly of North Carolina do enact:

Section 1. That J. S. Carr, C. L.Lindsay, David McCauley, T. B. Lloyd, J. C. Biggs and R. W. Winston, and their associates, successors and assigns, be and they are hereby created and constituted a body corporate under the name, style and title of "The Bank of Chapel Hill," whose place of business shall be Chapel Hill, North Carolina, and by that name may have perpetual succession, and shall be able and capable in law to have and use a seal, the same break, alter and renew at pleasure, to sue and be sued, to plead and be impleaded, and are hereby made able and capable in law to have, purchase, receive, take, hold, possess, enjoy and retain to them and their successors, lands, rents, tenements, hereditaments, stock, goods, chattels and effects of whatever kind, nature or quality, whether real, personal or mixed, by gift, grant, demise, bargain and sale, devise, bequest, testament, legacy, loan, deposit or advance, or by any other mode of conveyance or transfer whatever, and the same to give, grant, sell, devise, convey, assure, transfer, alien, pay, release and dispose of for the whole or any less estate or property than they have in the same, and also to improve and augment the same in such manner and form as the said company by its by-laws and regulations shall direct; and shall and may apply the rents, issues, income, interest and profits of such estate, and the moneys arising from the sale, alienation, disposal or employment thereof, to the uses, ends and purposes of their creation and institution, according to the rules, regulations and orders of the company, as fully and effectually as any natural person or body politic or corporate within this state can or may do or perform. The said company Corporators, etc. Body corporate and politic; name. May sue and be sued, etc. May take, use and enjoy property, etc. May grant, devise, sell and convey property. Application of income, etc.

By-laws, etc.

shall have power to make, ordain or establish and put into execution such by-laws, ordinances and regulations as shall to it hereafter seem meet or convenient for the government of such corporation, not being contrary to the constitution and laws of this state or the United States, and generally to do and execute all and singular such acts, matters and things which to the said corporation shall or may appertain and be necessary for the purposes thereof.

General powers.

May receive and pay out currency and deal in exchanges.

SEC. 2. That said corporation shall have the right to receive and pay out the lawful currency of the country, deal in exchange, gold and silver coin, stocks, bonds, notes and other securities, to loan money to or receive deposits from any and all persons, firms, associations and corporations, including apprentices, minors and femes covert, or other persons, on such terms and time and manner of collection and payment as may be prescribed by this charter, or by the by-laws or as may be agreed on by the parties; and for the use and loan of money may charge not exceeding six per centum per annum, and may take and receive said interest at the time of making said loan or otherwise, free from all other control, contract or liability whatever; to invest in the stocks, bonds or other securities of this or any other state or territory, or of the United States, or of any corporation organized under the laws of this or any other state or territory or of the United States; and to take such real, personal or mixed property upon such terms, trusts and conditions for the security and payment of money loaned, advanced or expended as may be considered safe, expedient and beneficial; to elect such officers as they see fit, and prescribe their duties, compensation and term of service.

Loan of moneys; deposits, etc.

Charges for loans, etc., limit.

Investments, etc.

Security, etc.

May elect officers.

May receive deposits of valuables.

SEC. 3. That said corporation shall be and is hereby authorized and empowered to receive and keep and deposit all such valuables, gold, silver and paper money, bullion, precious metals, jewels, plate, certificates of stock, bonds, notes, evidences of debt, dues, muniments of title or any other valuable papers of any kind, or any other article or thing whatsoever, which may be left or deposited for safe keeping with said company, and shall be entitled to charge, demand and receive such commission or compensation therefor as may be agreed upon; and for the complete preservation and safe keeping thereof may construct, erect and purchase such fire and burglar-proof building, vaults, iron and composition safes or other means which may be or become necessary, and generally to transact and perform all business relating to such deposit and safe keeping and preservation of all such articles or valuables as may be deposited with said company; and also to invest the capital or funds as may be deposited with said company for that purpose from time to time in such stocks, bonds and securities as may be regarded as advantageous

Charges, etc.

Safes, vaults, etc.

May invest capital or funds deposited, etc.

and desirable; they shall have power to receive and hold on deposit and in trust, and as security, estate real, personal and mixed, including notes, bonds, obligations of states, muncipalities, corporations, companies and individuals, and the same to purchase, collect, adjust, settle, sell and dispose of, and upon such terms as may be agreed upon between them and the parties contracting with them.

Funds on deposit, in trust as security, etc. notes, bonds, etc.

Sec. 4. That said corporation shall also have power and authority to accept and execute trusts of any and every description which may be committed or transferred to them with their consent by any person whomsoever, corporations, or by any court in this or any other state or territory or of the United States; and for its services as such said corporation shall receive such usual and customary fees, emoluments and charges as are allowed individuals in like capacities and like cases.

May accept and execute trusts, etc.

Fees, etc.

Sec. 5. That any executor, administrator, guardian, receiver, or other trustee or public officer having the care, custody or control of any bonds, stocks, securities, moneys or other valuable things whatsoever, shall be and is hereby authorized and empowered to deposit the same generally or specially with said company.

Executors, administrators, receivers, etc., may deposit funds, etc., in bank.

Sec. 6. That the capital stock of said corporation shall be ten thousand dollars, divided into two hundred shares of fifty dollars each, which said capital stock may be increased at any time or from time to time by the vote of the majority of the stockholders to any sum not exceeding fifty thousand dollars. The corporators and stockholders of said corporation and their successors and assigns shall not be individually or personally liable or responsible for any of the debts, liabilities, obligations, engagements, contracts or torts of the company, except to an amount equal to the stock held by each stockholder. When twenty-five hundred dollars of the capital stock is subscribed and paid in, the corporators named herein, or a majority of them or their assigns, shall be deemed and held ready and capable to organize, which they shall do by electing a board of directors to consist of not less than five nor more than fifteen, who shall serve for one year or until their successors are elected and qualified, unless it is otherwise provided in and by the by-laws adopted at said meeting, and these directors so chosen shall proceed to elect a president, whose term shall expire at the expiration of the term of said directors, unless the by-laws otherwise provide, and said board of directors shall elect at such time as they see fit, a first vice-president and such other officers as they think necessary and increase or diminish the number of said officers at pleasure, and no person shall be elected director, president or vice-president unless he is a stockholder in said corporation; and the

Capital stock, shares.

Increase of capital stock, limit.

Corporators, stockholders, etc., not individually liable.

Organization, when entered into.

Directors, number of.

President, by whom elected.

Vice-president and other officers.

Eligibility to office in company.

Bonds of officers.

directors shall require of the subordinate officers such bonds and security for the honest and faithful discharge of their duties as they may order, and may require such bonds of the president if they may see fit to do so.

May guarantee payments, etc.

Sec. 7. That said corporation shall have and is hereby granted power and authority to guarantee the payment of principal and interest of notes, bonds, bills of exchange, acceptances, checks and other securities or evidences of debt, including the obligations of such corporations and individuals as may have secured their payment by deed of trust made to this corporation, and to charge and receive for any guaranty such compensation as may be agreed on by the parties, and may take and receive interest at the time of making said transaction, or at any other time.

Charges, etc.

Deposits; minors, married women, etc.

Sec. 8. Whenever any deposit shall be made by or in the name of any person being a minor, or a female being or thereafter becoming a married woman, the same shall be held for the exclusive benefit of such depositor, and free from all control or lien of any persons except creditors, and shall be paid to the persons in whose name the deposit shall have been made, and the receipt or acquittance of such minor or female shall be valid and sufficient release and discharge for such deposit, or any part thereof, to the corporation; and whenever any deposit shall be made by any person in trust for another, and no other or further notice of the existence and terms of a legal and valid trust shall have been given in writing duly attested to the company, in the event of the death of the trustee, the said deposit or any part thereof may be paid to the person for whom the deposit was made.

Deposits in trust, by whom withdrawn.

Property sold under liens may be bought by president.

Sec. 9. Whenever any real estate or person property upon which the company may have a lien of any kind shall be exposed to sale under authority of law, the president of this company may purchase the same for and on behalf of the company, and such purchase, though made at a sale by the company as trustee, shall be valid and binding upon all parties having or claiming an interest therein.

Sec. 10. That this act shall be in force from and after its ratification.

Ratified the 15th day of February, A. D. 1899.

CHAPTER 57.

An act to amend section nine, chapter fifteen, private laws of eighteen hundred and ninety-five.

The General Assembly of North Carolina do enact:

Chapter 15, private laws 1895, relative to fire insurance.

Section 1. That section nine of chapter fifteen, private laws of eighteen hundred and ninety-five, be and the same is hereby amended by striking out the word "two" in line two of said section and inserting the word 'four" in lieu thereof.

Sec. 2. That this act shall be in force from and after its ratification.

Ratified the 15th day of February, A. D. 1899.

CHAPTER 58.

An act to amend chapter one hundred and eleven of the private laws of eighteen hundred and seventy-one and eighteen hundred and seventy-two.

The General Assembly of North Carolina do enact:

Section 1. That chapter one hundred and eleven of the private laws of eighteen hundred and seventy-one and eighteen hundred and seventy-two be amended by striking out of section two of said chapter all after the word "follows" in the second line of said section, and inserting in lieu thereof the following, to-wit: "Beginning at the southwest corner of the court-house in said town, a line to be surveyed running due west forty (40) chains, thence due south forty (40) chains, then due east eighty (80) chains, then due north to Cape Fear river, then up the river with its meanderings eighty (80) chains, then direct to the second corner. Relative to incorporation of town of Lillington, Amended.

Sec. 2. That this act shall take effect from and after its ratification.

Ratified the 15th day of February, A. D. 1899.

CHAPTER 59.

An act to amend the charter of the Saint Peter's Home and Hospital, chapter ten of the private laws of eighteen hundred and seventy-nine, and chapter two hundred and seventy-one of the private laws of eighteen hundred and ninety-three, and to authorize the said corporation to establish a training school for nurses.

The General Assembly of North Carolina do enact:

Section 1. That chapter ten of the private acts of eighteen hundred and seventy-nine and chapter two hundred and seventy-one of the private acts of eighteen hundred and ninety-three be and Amended.

the same are hereby amended by striking from the name of Saint Peter's Home and Hospital the words "Home and," so that the name of the corporation created by the said acts shall hereafter be "Saint Peter's Hospital."

May establish a training school for nurses.

Sec. 2. That said corporation shall have power and authority to establish and maintain in connection with its hospital a school or department for the education and training of nurses, and to award certificates of proficiency or diplomas to the pupils as graduates of the said school or department, under such rules and regulation as may be prescribed by the board of directors or managers of the said institution; and the said board shall have the power to make, establish and enforce such rules and regulations for the management of said school or department, and for the general conduct and administration of the affairs of the said hospital as to them may seem fit and proper.

Diplomas, etc.

Rules and regulations.

Addition to charter.

Sec. 3. That section two (2) of this act shall be an additional section to the charter of said institution as contained in chapter ten of the private laws of eighteen hundred and seventy-nine, and amended by chapter two hundred and seventy-one of the private laws of eighteen hundred and ninety-three, and shall be known as section six of the said act of eighteen hundred and seventy-nine, section six of the said act of eighteen hundred and seventy-nine being changed to section 7.

Sec. 4. That this act shall take effect and be in force from and after its ratification.

Ratified the 15th day of February, A. D. 1899.

CHAPTER 60.

An act to incorporate the Golden Rule Benevolent Association.

The General Assembly of North Carolina do enact:

Corporators.

Section 1. That H. H. Falkner, Smith Donnell, Rev. C. H. King, Rev. P. J. Jordan and J. W. Patterson, and their associates, successors and assigns, be and they are hereby created a body politic and corporate under the name and style of the "Golden Rule Benevolent Association," whose motto shall be "Do unto others as you would have them do unto you," and as such shall be capable of suing and being sued, shall have and use a corporate seal, shall exist for sixty years, and shall have all the powers and privileges belonging to corporations under the laws of North Carolina.

Body corporate and politic.

May sue and be sued.

Limit of corporate life.

General powers.

Sec. 2. That the object of the corporation shall be the relief of the widow and orphan, of the sick and of those injured by accident, and the burial of the dead; and to this end the corporation may issue certificates to its members agreeing to pay at their death or in the event of their injury by accident sums of money to the beneficiaries named therein; may provide for the payment of sick benefits and for the further care of the sick and for the burial of the dead, and adopt such by-laws, rules and regulations fixing the assessments, dues and premiums to be paid to it by its members, the manner of electing the directors, the numbers necessary to make a quorum of the members of the corporation and of the directors, the time and place of meeting, and generally for the government of the corporation as are not contrary to law.

Objects of the corporation. By-laws, rules, etc. Assessments; election of directors; times and places of meeting.

Sec. 3. That the principal lodge or office of said corporation shall be in Greensboro, North Carolina, but the board of directors may establish lodges or branch offices anywhere in this or other states, and the said corporation, its lodges and property shall be exempt from all taxation, and from the rules governing insurance companies.

Principal lodge, location. Branch lodges.

Sec. 4. That the said association or corporation shall have the right to take by gift, purchase or otherwise, property, both real and personal, and to hold and dispose of same at its pleasure.

May take real and personal property, and dispose of the same.

Sec. 5. That none of the members of the corporation shall be individually liable for its debts, contracts or torts, except to the extent of the assessments, dues and premiums agreed to be paid by them.

Liability of members.

Sec. 6. That a certain per cent. of the proceeds, to be fixed by the board of directors, shall be turned over to the Pigford Sanitarium at Southern Pines.

Per cent. to sanatarium.

Sec. 7. That this act shall be in force from and after its ratification.

Ratified the 15th day of February, A. D. 1899.

CHAPTER 61.

An act to incorporate the Burial Society No. 2 of Edenton.

The General Assembly of North Carolina do enact:

Section 1. That Stephen Abrams, Major Perkins, William Ellis, Noah Best, Butler Davis, Archer Baker, William Jenkins, Isaac Welch, Simon Skinner, Jerry Beasley, Alfred Foxwell, Henry Stanley, and such other persons as may associate themselves

Corporators.

together with them and become members of said society, and their successors, are hereby incorporated under the name and style of the Benevolent Burial Society Number Two of Edenton, and by such name and style shall have perpetual succession and the right to establish and charter subordinate branches under the terms of this charter.

Incorporated; name. Shall have perpetual succession. Subordinate branches, etc.

Object of the Society, etc.

Sec. 2. The object and business of the society shall be the promotion and cultivation of its members socially, morally and intellectually, and to extend material aid and benefit to those who may become dependent members of the society, and to aid the sick and the poor, and to bury the destitute and indigent dead.

May sue and be sued. Corporate seal. By-laws.

Sec. 3. That the society and the subordinate branches thereof may sue and be sued, plead and be impleaded, and each may have a corporate seal of its own for making and delivering of all legal acts and proceedings, and all necessary by-laws for its government not inconsistent with the laws of the state of North Carolina or the United States government, which they may change or alter from time to time as they may deem desirable or best.

May acquire and hold land free from taxation; purposes.

Sec. 4. That the society may acquire title to and hold land and other property, free from taxation, for the purposes of establishing and maintaining home or homes for the infirm, indigent and invalid persons and for burying the dead.

Donations; gifts; deeds; devise, etc.

Sec. 5. That the society may receive donations from any source by gift, deed, grant or devise, for the promotion of the purposes and objects of the society.

Misnomer not to invalidate instruments or contracts, if corporation shall be described.

Sec. 6. That a misnomer of the corporation in any gift, deed, grant or devise, or in any other instrument or contract, or in any suit against them, shall not invalidate the same, if the corporation shall be sufficiently described therein to ascertain the meaning and the intention of the parties.

Means and devices; lottery forbidden.

Sec. 7. That the society may employ any lawful means or proper device to add to its revenue, it being understood that it will not and shall not resort to any lottery to effect such purpose.

Officers, etc. Election of officers, when to take place. Terms of office.

Sec. 8. That the principal officers shall be a president, vice-president, marshal, deputy marshal, secretary, treasurer, chaplain, outside and inside sentry and five trustees, who shall be elected by the members, or a majority of them, who at the time of the said election shall be in good standing in said society, on the first Saturday of November, A. D. eighteen hundred and ninety-nine, and annually thereafter on the day named, unless the date shall be changed to some other day by a majority of the members of the said society, at any annual meeting thereof, and said officers and trustees shall hold their office from the time of the annual election until their successors shall be chosen and qualified.

Sec. 9. That until the said election shall be held for said officers and trustees under this charter, Stephen Abrams shall be president; Major Perkins, vice-president and treasurer; William Ellis, secretary; Isaac Welch, marshal; Archer Baker, deputy marshal; Simon Skinner, chaplain; Butler Davis, outside sentry, and Henry Stanley inside sentry. Temporary officers.

Sec. 10. That its chief office shall be located at Edenton in Chowan [county] and state of North Carolina, with power to create and establish subordinate branches anywhere in the state of North Carolina or United States. Principal office, location.

Sec. 11. That the president of said society shall have the power to call a meeting of the trustees whenever he may deem proper. Called meetings.

Sec. 12. That the trustees, officers and members of the society shall not be individually liable for any liability of said corporation, or any of its branches. Not individually liable for debts.

Sec. 13. That said Stephen Abrams, a member of and president of the society, under this charter is hereby duly authorized to call the first meeting of the trustees. First meeting, who may call.

Sec. 14. That the said society, and such subordinate branches thereof as it may establish and charter, shall provide for the election of such officers in connection therewith as it may deem best for the transaction of the business of the corporation and such subordinate branches in promoting its objects, and these officers shall hold their office until their successors are chosen and qualified. Provision for election of officers. Term of office.

Sec. 15. That the said society shall have power to collect, hold and disburse the funds named in its objects for promoting charity, relieving the sick and poor, and burying the destitute and indigent dead, under such regulations as it may deem necessary to adopt, and said fund and its property, both real and personal, shall be exempt from execution and liable under no circumstances for the debts of any of its living or dead members. Collection of funds, power. Property exempt from execution.

Sec. 16. The trustees of the society shall have full power to fill any vacancy which may occur among themselves or other officers of the corporation. Vacancies, by whom filled.

Sec. 17. This act shall be in full force and effect from and after the date of its ratification.

Ratified the 15th day of February, A. D. 1899.

CHAPTER 62.

An act to amend the charter of Elizabeth City, North Carolina.

The General Assembly of North Carolina do enact:

Section 1. That chapter eighty-five of the private laws of eighteen hundred and ninety-five entitled "An act to repeal the present charter of Elizabeth City and re-charter the city," be amended as follows:

Amended.

Corporate limits of city.

Sec. 2. By striking out sections one and two and inserting instead thereof the following: The corporate limits of Elizabeth City shall be bounded as follows: Beginning at a point on Pasquotank river at the southern mouth of Knobb's creek near Blade's mills, thence up the centre of said creek to a bend in the same to a point immediately opposite an angle of Road street near Knobb's creek bridge, thence a westerly course a straight line from the angle in Knobb's creek to the angle of Road street near the Norfolk and Southern Railroad, thence along the eastern side of said Road street southerly to a point opposite the division line between the Gregory and Skinner property and the line of M. M. Sawyer (the present city lines), thence westerly to and along the line of the Gregory and Skinner property straight to the Norfolk and Southern Railroad, thence southerly and westerly along the Norfolk and Southern Railroad to a point one thousand five hundred feet westerly from Parsonage street, thence due south (magnetic) through the Improvement Company's property to and across Main street to the westerly projection of Church street on the Baxter property, thence along the north side of said projection of Church street easterly to Doughty's lane (the present city limits), then along the east side of Doughty's lane southerly and in a direct straight line with its projection to the "Body road," thence a northeasterly course in a direct straight line to a point on the "Pear Tree road" at the northeast corner of Alexander Wadsworth's property on said road, thence along the west side of the "Pear Tree road" northerly to opposite Road street, thence along the north side of the main road leading to the almshouse southerly and easterly to the southern end of Factory avenue, thence along the east side of Factor avenue to Park street, thence easterly along Park street to Butler's lane through Pryortown, thence along the centre of said Butler's lane (the present city limits) northerly and easterly to a point on said Butler's lane two hundred and fifty (250) feet southerly from Riverside avenue, then through the properties of J. B. Fearing and R. O. Pryor and others in an easterly direction parallel with said Riverside avenue to Pasquotank river, thence a due north course to the northeast side of Pasquotank river at the Camden county line, then binding the shore line of Pasquotank river on the Camden side by its various meanders to a point which will suit a position due south from the beginning at the mouth of Knobb's creek near Blade's mills, thence north to the said beginning.

Sec. 3. By striking out section three and inserting instead thereof the following: The said Elizabeth City shall be divided into seven (7) wards, to be known respectively as the first, second, third, fourth, fifth, sixth and seventh wards. The first ward shall be bounded as follows: Beginning on Pasquotank river at the mouth of Knobb's creek at the city limits, thence up said Knobb's creek to Road street binding the city limits, thence along Road street binding the city limits to the Gregory and Skinner and M. N. Sawyer line, thence westerly binding the city limits to swamp on the northern branch of Poindexter creek, thence down the centre of said swamp southerly to a point on the western projection of Burgess on Pleasant street, through the Vaugn property to Road street, thence easterly along Burgess or Pleasant street to Pasquotank river, thence northerly along the westerly projection of Burgess or Pleasant street through the Vaugn property, thence easterly from said point along the said river to the place of beginning at the mouth of Knobb's creek.

Number of wards.

First ward; boundaries.

The second ward shall be bounded as follows: Beginning at the corner of Parsonage and Poplar streets, thence northerly along Poplar street to the centre of Poindexter creek swamp to the line of the first ward, thence binding the line of the first ward through the centre of the north branch of Poindexter creek swamp to Gregory and Skinner line, thence westerly binding their line and the city limits to the Norfolk and Southern Railroad, thence along the Norfolk and Southern Railroad westerly to Parsonage street, thence along Parsonage street easterly to Poplar street, place of beginning.

Second ward; boundaries.

The third ward shall be bounded as follows: Beginning on Pasquotank river at the eastern end of Burgess or Pleasant street thence westerly along said Burgess or Pleasant street to Road street, thence westerly along said street through the Vaugn property to the centre of Poindexter creek swamp, thence southerly through the centre of said Poindexter creek swamp and in a line with Poplar street to Parsonage street, thence westerly along Parsonage street to the city limits at the Norfolk and Southern Railroad, thence binding the city limits along the Norfolk and Southern Railroad to the western boundary of the city, thence binding the city limits south to Cherry street on the Improvement Company's property, thence easterly along Cherry street to Harney street, thence a direct straight line to the centre of Matthews street at Dyer street, thence easterly along Matthews street to Pasquotank river, then northerly along Pasquotank river to the place of beginning.

Third ward; boundaries.

The fourth ward shall be bounded as follows: Beginning at the corner of Road and Matthews streets, thence westerly along Matthews street to Dyer street, thence binding the line of the third ward a straight line to the centre of Cedar street at Har-

Fourth ward; boundaries.

ney street, thence westerly along Cherry street to the city limits, thence due south along the city limits to the westerly projection of Church street, thence along Church street and the city limits easterly to Doughty's lane, thence along Doughty's lane southerly to the first lane south of and parallel with Church street, thence easterly along said lane to African street (north of colored Methodist church), thence a direct straight line easterly to "Canal bridge" on Road street, thence along Road street northerly to Matthews street, place of beginning.

Fifth ward; boundaries.

The fifth ward shall be bounded as follows: Beginning on Pasquotank river at Matthews street, thence westerly along Matthews to Road street, thence southerly along Road street to "Canal bridge," thence along new Tiber creek canal easterly to Pasquotank river, thence northerly along Pasquotank river to the place of beginning at Matthews street.

Sixth ward; boundaries.

The sixth ward shall be bounded as follows: Beginning at "Canal bridge" on Road street, thence westerly a direct straight line to centre of a lane on African street, the line of the fourth ward (said lane being the first lane south of Church street on African street), thence westerly along said lane to Doughty's lane, thence along Doughty's lane westerly and binding the city limits to the "Body road," thence binding the city limits northeasterly to the "Pear Tree road," thence binding the city limits northerly and easterly along the "Pear Tree road," thence binding the city limits northerly and easterly along the "Pear Tree road" and the road leading over Harrington's bridge to the almshouse to the southern end of Factory avenue, thence binding the city limits along Factory avenue, Park street and Butler's lane to an angle in said lane at a black-gum tree near a branch of Charles creek swamp, thence through the same swamp southerly and westerly to "Bud Johnson's" stables on Factory Avenue, thence across Factory avenue westerly a straight line with Kirby's fence to the southwest corner of his lot, thence northerly a straight line parallel with Factory avenue to Charles creek, thence easterly along Charles creek to the bridge, thence along Factory avenue northerly to southern line of L. W. Madrin's lot, thence along said Madrin's line westerly to his southwest corner, thence northerly along his western line fence to Barnett street, thence westerly along Barnett street to Green street, thence along Green street northerly to Lawrence street, thence westerly along Lawrence street about one hundred and fifty (150) feet to the west line of the Fenwick lot line fence, thence northerly with said line fence straight to Tiber creek canal, thence down said canal westerly to "Canal bridge," place of beginning on Road street.

The seventh ward shall be bounded as follows: Beginning on Pasquotank river at mouth of Tiber creek canal, thence westerly up Tiber creek canal to a point opposite the west line of the northern projection of Fenwick lot line fence, thence southerly along said projection of Fenwick's line fence to a point on Lawrence street about one hundred and fifty (150) feet from Green street the line of the sixth ward, thence along Lawrence street easterly to Green street, thence southerly along Green street to Barnett street, thence easterly along Barnett street to L. W. Madrin's western line fence, thence southerly along said Madrin's line fence to the southwest corner of his lot the line of the sixth ward, thence easterly along said Madrin's southern line to Factory avenue, thence southerly along Factory avenue to the bridge over Charles creek, thence westerly along Charles creek to a point to suit a position by the northerly projection of Lee Kirby's line fence, thence southerly said projected line to said Kirby's southwest corner of his lot, thence easterly binding his southern line easterly to and across Factory avenue to "Bud Johnson's" stables on Factory avenue, thence a direct straight line along the line of the sixth ward to a black-gum tree at a bend in Butler's lane near branch of Charles creek swamp, thence northerly along Butler's lane binding the city limits to a point on said lane two hundred and fifty (250) feet southerly from Riverside avenue the city limits, thence binding the city limits easterly through the property of J. B. Fearing, R. O. Pryor and others to Pasquotank river at the city limits, thence along Pasquotank river westerly to the place of beginning at Tiber creek canal. Seventh ward; boundaries.

Sec. 4. By striking out section four and inserting instead thereof the following: The first election for aldermen (in place of the name commissioners) shall be held on the second Monday in May, eighteen hundred and ninety-nine, and shall be called and notice thereof given by the sheriff of Pasquotank county not later than the first Monday in April, eighteen hundred and ninety-nine. He shall order an entire new registration of voters, shall appoint one registrar and two poll-holders in each ward who shall be qualified voters in the ward in which they are appointed. He shall also designate the polling places in each ward and provide boxes for the ballots. First election, when held. Sheriff shall call; notice. New registration. Designation of polling places.

Sec. 5. By striking out section five and inserting instead thereof the following: The next election shall be held on the second Monday in April, nineteen hundred and one, and succeeding elections biennially thereafter. These elections shall be ordered by the board of aldermen and notice thereof given at least four weeks preceding the same, and they shall appoint the Next election, when to be held. Elections ordered by board of aldermen. Appointment of registrars, etc.

registrars and poll-holders and designate the polling places and provide ballot boxes as named in section four hereof.

Qualification of voters, etc.

Sec. 6. By striking out section six and inserting instead thereof the following: Every male person of the age of twenty-one years who is or may hereafter be qualified to vote for any representative in the legislature of North Carolina, and who has resided in the corporation ninety days, and in the ward in which he offers to vote for thirty days immediately preceding the election, shall be a qualified voter in said ward.

Registration books, when opened.

Sec. 7. By striking out section seven and inserting instead thereof the following: The registrars in their respective wards shall open their books for the purpose of registering such persons as apply for registration one week prior to the coming election, and keep the same open until sunset of the Saturday preceding the election.

Oath to be administered by registrar.

Sec. 8. By striking out section eight and inserting instead thereof the following: The said registrars shall register all such qualified voters as make application, and take oath to be administered by said registrar as follows: "I do solemnly swear (or affirm) that I will support the constitution of North Carolina and of the United States; that I am twenty-one years of age, and have lived in North Carolina for one year, in the corporation of Elizabeth City ninety days, and in the ward thirty days. So help me God."

Oath of registrar.

Sec. 9. By striking out section nine and inserting instead thereof the following: Before entering upon the discharge of his duties each registrar shall make oath before some one authorized by the laws of North Carolina to administer oaths that he will faithfully and impartially perform the duties of his office. A certificate of the administering of said oath shall be made in the registration book by the party administering the same, with the date of administration.

Certificate of registrar's oath to be registered in registration book.

Challenges, when and by whom heard

Sec. 10. By striking out section ten and inserting instead thereof the following: The registrars and poll-holders shall meet at the polling places in their respective wards on the Saturday before the election, to hear and determine challenges made to any person registered in said ward. But before they proceed to determine the right of any person to vote they may require proof of notice to the party challenged which may be signed by any voter in the city, but must be served by the chief of police or any police officer, or by any officer of the county authorized to execute civil process.

Proof of notice may be required. Notice, how served.

Names of persons not entitled to vote erased.

Sec. 11. By striking out section eleven and inserting instead thereof the following: Whenever it is decided that a party registered is not entitled to vote the registrar shall erase his name from the book, writing opposite the date of the erasure and the cause thereof. In case the poll-holders cannot decide, the registrars shall.

Sec. 12. By striking out section twelve and inserting instead thereof the following: On the morning of the election the registrars and poll-holders of each ward shall meet at the polling place of their respective wards, and after being duly sworn shall proceed to open the polls at sunrise and receive the votes, depositing the same in the box prepared for that purpose. The polls shall be closed at sunset.

Registrars and poll-holders to meet, take oath and open polls.

Polls opened and closed, when.

Sec. 13. By striking out section thirteen and inserting instead thereof the following: The registrars shall check off the name of each man as he votes, and the poll-holders shall keep a list of those who vote.

Names checked off; list of those who vote.

Sec. 14. By striking out section fourteen and inserting instead thereof the following: Immediately after the closing of the polls the poll-holders and registrars shall proceed to count the votes cast in the presence of such voters as may desire to attend, and make three certificates thereof, one to the clerk of the board of aldermen, one to the sheriff of Pasquotank county and one to the aldermen elect; said certificates shall state the number of votes cast for each candidate, the ward in which they were cast, the date of the election, and be signed by at least two of the poll-holders, or by the registrar and one of the poll-holders.

Votes, counted by whom; who may be present.

Certificates, how many and to whom sent; what certificates shall state.

Sec. 15. By striking out section fifteen and inserting instead therof the following: Should there be more votes in the box than the recorder's list shows have been cast, and the poll-holders shall be of the opinion that the excess was placed there fraudulently, and the result of the election is thereby affected, they shall certify such to the aldermen-elect at their first meeting, who shall declare the election in said ward void and proceed to fill the vacancy. But shold the excess appear to the poll-holders to be accidental they shall elect some child who cannot read to draw said excess from the box one vote at a time. Should two or more votes be folded together the poll-holders shall reject them. The ballots shall contain the name of only one person, printed or written, on white or colored paper, with or without device.

Fraudulent votes affecting result of election to be reported; election to be declared void; vacancy filled.

Excess, accidental, to be drawn from box, how.

Votes folded together rejected.

Ballots.

Sec. 16. By striking out section sixteen and inserting instead thereof the following: The certificates to the clerk, the books of registration and the lists kept by the poll-holders and registrar shall be filed with the clerk of the board within three days after the election, and the clerk shall notify the aldermen-elect of their election within five days thereafter.

Certificates, books, etc., filed, when and where.

Sec. 17. By striking out section seventeen and inserting instead thereof the following: Should the present board of commission-

Failure of commissioners or clerk to perform duties, sheriff shall perform them.

ers or the clerk fail to perform the duties imposed upon them in any of the preceding sections within five days from the time the same ought to have been done, the sheriff of Pasquotank county is hereby directed and empowered to make the appointments and perform the acts imposed upon said commissioners and clerk.

Aldermen, oath; continuance in office, etc.

Sec. 18. By striking out section eighteen and inserting instead thereof the following: On the first Monday in June, eighteen hundred and ninety-nine, the aldermen-elect, after having taken and subscribed an oath or affirmation before some justice of the peace for said county to support the constitution of the United States, the constitution of North Carolina, and to perform faithfully the duties of their offices (which oath or affirmation shall be entered upon the minutes of the corporation, subscribed as aforesaid and attested by some justice), shall take their seats and continue in office until their successors have been elected and qualified. They shall organize by appointing one of their number chairman, and shall first proceed to fill vacancies caused by death or failure to elect in any ward, whether by virtue of a tie or on a certificate of fraud: Provided, that upon the election to be held on the second Monday in April, nineteen hundred and one, the aldermen-elect shall take their seats of office on the first Monday in May, and so each succeeding election thereafter.

Term of office.
Organization of aldermen; filling vacancies, etc.
Proviso.

Election of city officers by aldermen.

Sec. 19. By striking out section nineteen and inserting instead thereof the following: After the said board may have been organized they may proceed to the election of a mayor, clerk, treasurer, chief of police, city attorney, street commissioner, two fire commissioners, health officer, and harbor master, and as many policemen as they may deem necessary, who shall hold office during the term of the board of aldermen appointing the same, subject to be removed at any time for misconduct or other causes. But no person shall be eligible for any office under this charter who is not a citizen of North Carolina and a bona fide resident of said city: Provided, that the board can at any time, even after their appointment, reduce the number or discontinue the whole of the police force.

Term of office.
Removal for cause.
Eligibility to office.
Proviso.

Ordinances, who has power to make.

Sec. 20. By striking out section twenty and all amendments to the same and inserting instead thereof the following: The board of aldermen of Elizabeth City shall have power to make and provide such ordinances for the government of said city as they may deem necessary, not inconsistent with the laws of the land, and they shall have power by all needful ordinances to secure order, health, quiet and safety within the city limits and for one mile beyond; to establish one or more markets, and to require the sale of such articles therein as they may deem proper; to take all necessary means to prevent and extinguish fires; to

Police and health, limits.
Markets and sales therein.
Prevention and extinguishment of fires.

make regulations for the observance of the Sabbath; suppress and remove nuisances; control and regulate keeping of powder in the city; to regulate the speed of riding and driving on the public streets; to keep or require to be kept the sidewalks clear of all obstructions; to cut and remove all limbs, branches and parts of trees or shrubbery extending upon or overhanging the sidewalks or streets at the expense of the owners of the adjacent lots who may refuse to do the same on five days' notice from the mayor of the town, and regulate building and building material within specified limits. They shall also have the right to regulate the charge for the carriage of persons, baggage and freight by omnibus or other vehicle, and issue license for the same.

Nuisances; speed of riding and driving; obstructions on sidewalks; removal of limbs, expense of whom.

Building and building material.

Charges for carriage of persons, baggage, etc.

Sec. 21. By striking out section twenty-one and inserting instead thereof the following: The board of aldermen shall have power to fill any vacancies in the board that may occur during their term of office, and also to appoint all officers that they may deem necessary for the efficient administration of the regulations, ordinances and by-laws of the town, and shall prescribe their terms of office.

Filling vacancies; appointment of necessary officers.

Terms of office.

Sec. 22. By striking out section twenty-two and inserting instead thereof the following: The board of aldermen may take such means as they deem effectual to prevent the entrance into the town of any contagious or infectious disease; may stop, detain and examine for the purpose every train, conveyance or vehicle coming from places believed to be infected with such diseases; may establish and regulate hospitals within the town or within three miles thereof; may cause any person in the town suspected to be infected with such diseases and whose stay may endanger health to be removed to the hospitals; may remove from the town or destroy any furniture or other articles which may be suspected of being tainted or infected with contagious or infectious disease, or which there shall be reasonable cause to apprehend that they may pass into such a state as to generate disease. With the view of preserving the health of the city a health officer may be appointed when deemed necessary.

Quarantine against diseases.

Establishment of hospitals, etc.

Removal of infected persons; removal or destruction of furniture.

Health officer.

Sec. 23. By striking out section twenty-three and inserting instead thereof the following: That in case any person be removed to the hospital, the board of aldermen may obtain before the mayor or any justice of the peace a judgment against such person for the expense of his or her removal, support, nursing and medical attendance, and in case of death against his or her legal representative, and in that event burial expenses also if the city incur that expense.

Judgment against infected person for expense of removal, etc., how obtained.

Sec. 24. By striking out section twenty-four and inserting instead thereof the following: That the board of aldermen shall

Laying out and opening streets.

have power to lay out and open any new street or streets within the corporate limits of the city whenever by them deemed necessary, and shall have power at any time to widen, change or extend or discontinue any street or streets, or any part thereof, within the corporate limits of the city, and shall have full power and authority to condemn, appropriate and use any land or lands necessary for any of the purposes named in this section, upon making a reasonable compensation to the owner or owners thereof. In case the owners of the land and the board of aldermen cannot agree upon the price, the said board of aldermen shall appoint five disinterested freeholders, residents of Elizabeth City, who shall assess the land to be condemned and make report to the board of aldermen. If the board of aldermen accept the report they shall pay or tender to the said land-owner the amount assessed in legal tender of this country, and thereupon the title shall become vested in said board of aldermen and their successors. If the land-owner shall think the amount assessed is below the actual value of the land taken, nothing herein shall be construed to deprive him of his right to appeal or suit de novo for damages against the corporation for the value of the land taken.

May widen, change or extend streets.

Condemnation of land, etc., compensation.

Non-agreement of aldermen and land-owners, what proceedings to be had.

Right of appeal, etc.

Sec. 25. By striking out section twenty-five and all amendments to the same and inserting instead thereof the following: The board of aldermen of the city shall have power annually to impose, levy and collect a tax for general corporation purposes, not exceeding seventy-five cents on the one hundred dollars assessed valuation, as made and accepted by the county commissioners of Pasquotank county, upon all real and personal estate within the corporate limits of said city, and a poll tax not greater than two dollars and twenty-five cents from each resident of said city who is not exempt from poll taxation under the general laws of the state, and may levy a tax equal to the state tax upon all other subjects of taxation taxed by the general assembly for public purposes.

Levy and collection of taxes for general purposes, limit.

Poll tax, limit.

Sec. 26. By striking out section twenty-six and inserting instead thereof the following: That in addition to subjects liable to taxation for state purpose the aldermen shall have power to levy and collect a specific or license tax on the following subjects, to-wit: All itinerant auctioneers, merchants or peddlers vending or offering to vend in the town; each electric light company; each telephone company; each street railroad company; each express company; each telegraph company; each broker or banker; dealer in patent right; commission merchants and commercial brokers; each junk dealer; each distiller of fruit or grain; each livery-stable keeper; every non-resident huckster or

Specific or license tax, subjects, etc.

trader or agent of such, who buys produce for sale in other markets; each rectifier and compounder of spirituous liquors; each gift enterprise or lottery; each dray; each omnibus; each circus; each traveling theatrical company; each person or company making any exhibit or show for compensation; each billiard table; each ten-pin alley used by the public.

Sale of spirituous liquors, license.

Sec. 27. By striking out section twenty-seven and inserting instead thereof the following: That no person shall retail or sell any spirituous liquors, wine, cordial ale, porter, lager beer, or any other spirituous, vinous or malt liquors by a less measure or in less quantities than three gallons within the corporate limits without first having obtained a license therefor from the board of aldermen.

Abatement of nuisances, at whose expense.

Sec. 28. By striking out section twenty-nine and inserting instead thereof the following: That the board of aldermen may require and compel the abatement and removal of all nuisances within the town at the expense of the person causing the same, or the owner or tenant of the ground, wherever the same may be. They may also prevent the establishment of, and regulate, if allowed to be established, any slaughter-house or place, or the exercise within the town of any offensive or unhealthy business, trade or employment.

Slaughter-houses, etc.

Taxes for fire-engines, etc., limit.

Sec. 29. By striking out section thirty and inserting instead thereof the following: In addition to the tax hereinbefore permitted to be levied on real and personal property within the corporate limits of the city, the aldermen are hereby empowered to levy a tax not to exceed seven cents on the one hundred dollars assessed valuation of said real and personal property and a poll tax not greater than twenty-one cents upon every resident of said town who is not exempt from poll taxation under the general laws of the state for the purpose of defraying the necessary expense of keeping the fire engine and extinguishing apparatus in good condition and repair, and of defraying the expense of the fire department. The fire commissioners shall have control of the fire department, but shall have no authority to disburse the funds without the approval of the board of aldermen; they shall take receipted bills for money expended and file the same with the clerk of the board of aldermen at the end of each year, with the report of their expenses, of the fires extinguished, estimated amount saved, labors and general services of the fire department, the loss of property estimated, and such other statements as may be deemed proper.

Control of fire department.

Receipted bills, taken and filed with whom.

Annual reports, what to show.

Presence of one fire commissioner. Pulling down of houses, etc.

Sec. 30. By striking out section thirty-one and inserting instead thereof the following: One of said fire commissioners shall be present at each fire and have control of the engine, and if he deem it necessary to check the progress of any fire he may cause any house or houses to be pulled down or blown up, ar shall not be liable to any person for the damage caused thereb But should neither fire commissioner be present, the mayor, (if he be absent, a member of the board of aldermen present : the fire shall be vested with the powers herein conferred on tl fire commissioners.

Absence of commissioner, who vested with power.

Sec. 31. By striking out section thirty-two and insertir instead thereof the following: The fire commissioners shall u: their best endeavors to have the engine at each fire, and for th: purpose they may use such means and aid as they deem bes and the board of aldermen are hereby authorized and permitt(to make appropriations from the amount collected from the sp cial tax mentioned in section thirty, to be disbursed and used ; they direct: Provided, the appropriations shall never exceed ti amount in the hands of the fire commissioners.

Fires, means.

Appropriations.

Proviso.

Sec. 32. By striking out section thirty-three and insertir instead thereof the following: The board of aldermen sha allow fire commissioners a sum for their services, not exceedin twenty-five dollars per annum, together with their actual nece sary expenses, to be paid out of the special tax mentioned in se tion thirty.

Compensation of fire commissioners, limit.

Sec. 33. By striking out section thirty-four and insertin instead thereof the following: The board of aldermen shall ha the authority to put to and keep at work on the streets of th town any person or persons who may fail to pay any tax or fin penalty or forfeiture, which may be imposed on such person o persons for violation of any ordinance, by-law or regulation (said town, and the said aldermen shall have authority by thei ordinances and by-laws to confine, control and manage such pe sons until the said fines and penalties or forfeitures, togethe with cost thereof, shall be fully paid and satisfied, under suc rates for labor and board as the aldermen may adopt.

Persons compelled to work out taxes, fines, penalties, forfeitures, etc.; powers to enforce labor.

Confinement and management of delinquents, etc.

Rates of labor, etc.

Sec. 34. By striking out section thirty-five and insertin instead thereof the following: The mayor shall preside at th meetings of the board of aldermen but shall have no vote excep in case of a tie.

Mayor to preside at meetings of board; may vote, when.

Sec. 35. By striking out section thirty-six and inserting instea thereof the following: It shall be the duty of the mayor to com municate in writing, whenever it shall be deemed expedient, general statement of the situation and condition of the city i relation to its government and improvement; second, to recom mend to the adoption of the board of aldermen all such measure connected with the police, security, health and cleanliness of th city, as he may deem expedient; third, to be vigilant and activ in causing the laws and ordinances for the government of th

Mayor, duties; to communicate in writing certain things.

Recommendation of police measures.

Execution of laws and ordinances.

city to be duly executed and enforced; fourth, to keep a faithful minute of all precepts issued by him and of his judicial proceedings, and to report in writing at every regular monthly meeting of the board of aldermen the total amount of costs and fines that may have been imposed by him in all his judicial proceedings for the violation of city ordinances during the previous month.

Precepts, minutes of, and of his judicial proceedings; reports in writing, etc.

Sec. 36. By striking out section thirty-seven and inserting instead thereof the following: Whenever there shall be a vacancy in the office of mayor, and when the mayor shall be absent from the city or be prevented by sickness or any other cause, from attending to the duties of his office, the board of aldermen may appoint one of their number to act as mayor, who shall possess all the rights and powers of mayor during the continuance of such vacancy, absence or disability.

Temporary vacancies in office of mayor, how filled.

Rights, powers, etc.

Sec. 37. By striking out section thirty-eight and inserting instead thereof the following: That the mayor of said city is hereby constituted an inferior court, and as such shall, within the corporate limits of the city, have all the powers, jurisdiction and authority of a justice of the peace to preserve and keep the peace, to issue process, to hear and determine all causes of action which may arise upon ordinances and regulations of the city, to enforce penalties by issuing executions upon adjudged violations thereof, and to execute the by-laws, rules and regulations made by the aldermen. The mayor shall further be a special court within the corporate limits of the city, to arrest and try all persons who are charged with a misdemeanor for violating any ordinance of the city, and if the accused be found guilty he shall be fined at the discretion of the mayor or court not exceeding the amount specified in the ordinance or ordinances so violated; or at the discretion of the mayor or court trying the same, such offender may be imprisoned not more than thirty days in the common county jail. If the accused is dissatisfied with the judgment of the mayor or court, he may appeal in a like manner as prescribed for appeal from judgments of a justice of the peace.

Mayor constituted an inferior court; powers, jurisdiction and authority.

Mayor made a special court with corporate limits, jurisdiction, etc.; power to fine and imprison, limits.

Accused may appeal.

Sec. 38. By striking out section thirty-nine and inserting instead thereof the following: That the mayor may issue his precepts to the chief of police or any policeman who may execute the same anywhere in Pasquotank county, or such other officers to whom a justice of the peace may direct his precepts. An endorsement by the mayor of the name and witnesses upon a summons or warrant shall be authority for the officer to execute the same. The mayor shall keep a faithful minute of the precepts issued by him and of all his judicial proceedings.

Mayor; issuance of precepts, by whom executed.

Endorsement of names of witnesses upon summons or warrant, officer's authority.

Minutes of precepts, etc.

Sec. 39. By striking out section forty and all amendments

Mayor, salary of, limit.

thereto, and inserting instead thereof the following: The mayor shall be paid a salary from the general funds of the city, not exceeding two hundred dollars per annum, to be fixed by the board of aldermen at their first meeting. In the trial of criminal matters the mayor shall be allowed the same fees as are allowed to justices of the peace.

Mayor, fees in criminal matters.

Sec. 40. By striking out section forty-one and inserting instead thereof the following: The treasurer shall give bond payable to the corporation of Elizabeth City in a sum to be fixed by the board of aldermen, with sureties to be approved by said board. For his services he shall be paid a sum not exceeding two hundred dollars per annum to be fixed by the board of aldermen at their first meeting. He shall disburse no funds except on orders signed by the clerk of the board of aldermen and countersigned by the mayor. He shall make report of the funds coming into his hands at the end of his term, and for failure to do so he shall be fined two hundred and twenty-five dollars to be recovered by suit in the superior court, for which his bond shall be responsible.

Treasurer, bond, sureties, amount, by whom fixed.

Compensation of treasurer, limit.

Disbursement of funds, order, signed, countersigned.

Report of treasurer, failure, fine, recovered, how.

Sec. 41. By striking out section forty-two and inserting instead thereof the following: The clerk shall keep a faithful record of all proceedings of the board of aldermen; he shall keep and file all papers presented to the board, all reports made to same, and all bonds; he shall also keep an order book with stub; the orders shall be consecutively numbered, and shall state on the face for what the order is issued; he shall not deliver the order to the payee until countersigned by the mayor; he shall sign all licenses granted by the board and collect the money thereof; he shall collect all taxes levied upon real and personal property, except the huckster tax; he shall collect all rents from the market or other properties of the city; he shall settle with the treasurer at the end of each month. On failure to settle at the said times he shall be fined for each failure the sum of ten dollars; he shall give bond payable to the corporation of Elizabeth City, and with security, to be approved by the board, in a sum to be fixed by them. His compensation shall be fixed by the board, not to exceed five hundred dollars ($500) per annum, and no other fees, which is to be in full for all services rendered. He shall carefully preserve all books, papers and articles committed to his care, and deliver the same to his successor.

Clerk to aldermen, duties.

Papers, etc., filed.

Order book, stub. Orders, how numbered.

Licenses signed by clerk; collection of money; collection of taxes; collection of rents.

Settlement with treasurer.

Failure to settle, fine.

Bond of clerk, security, sum of bond.

Compensation of clerk, limit.

Preservation of books; delivery of books to successor.

Sec. 42. By striking out section forty-three and inserting instead thereof the following: The board of aldermen shall appoint a fit and proper person, who shall be a qualified voter of the city, to the office of chief of police, who shall give bond, with approved sureties, in a penal sum to be fixed by the board and

Chief of police; appointments, qualifications, bond and sureties; penal sum of bond, payable to whom, conditioned.

payable to the corporation of Elizabeth City, with conditions that he will diligently perform all the duties imposed upon him by virtue of his office and faithfully pay to the treasurer or sums of money collected or recovered by him to and for the use of the city and shall hold the office during the term of the board appointing him, subject to be removed at any time for misconduct. The chief of police and other police officers shall wear a regular uniform to be adopted by the aldermen. His compensation shall be fixed by the board, not to exceed five hundred dollars per annum.

Term of office, removal for cause.

Officers, uniforms. Compensation of chief of police.

Sec. 43. By striking out section forty-four and inserting instead thereof the following: It shall be the duty of the chief of police to pay over to the city treasurer all the money that may be collected by him, to and for the use of the city, at least once every month, and shall communicate to the board of aldermen at their monthly meetings, in writing, a full statement of all costs, fines, taxes, fees collected, and the disposition made of same.

Chief of police to pay over money for use of city, how often.

Statement to aldermen, etc.

Sec. 44. By striking out section forty-five and inserting instead thereof the following: It shall be the duty of said chief of police and the policemen to preserve the peace by suppression of disturbance and the apprehension of all offenders, and the chief of police or any policeman shall have the power to summon as many persons as he may deem necessary to assist in the performance of the above duties.

Chief of police and policemen, duties of.

May summon persons.

Sec. 45. By striking out section forty-six and inserting instead thereof the following: The street commissioner shall be vested with the power of a policeman, and it shall be his duty to keep in repair all the streets, bridges, wells, pumps, drains, ditches, canals, sidewalks, crossings, et cetera, within the city boundary, and the board of aldermen shall direct all labor due the city from all sources to be at his disposal, and the chief of police shall notify as many persons as said commissioner may need from time to time from a list to be furnished him by said commissioner—the board of aldermen to furnish such material and tools, horses and carts, et cetera, as they may deem necessary, on requisition made by the commissioner. But said commissioner shall be liable to be removed from office at any time during his term on charges preferred by a majority vote of the board of aldermen, and shall have such compensation as the board may direct, but shall be paid only for the time actually employed.

Street commissioner a policeman, duties, etc.

Labor, at whose disposal; notification to laborers.

Material, tools, etc., furnished by whom

Removal of commissioner.

Compensation.

Sec. 46. By striking out section forty-seven and inserting instead thereof the following: That all suits on bonds given by any officer under this charter shall be in the name of the corpo-

Suits on officers' bonds, in whose name.

Moneys collected upon suits, to whom paid.

ration of Elizabeth City, and moneys collected from said bonds shall be paid to the treasurer of the city. That all suits and actions by or against said corporation of Elizabeth City, and by the name of the corporation of Elizabeth City; the said corporation is hereby incorporated a body politic with power to sue and defend, hold property and do all other works which a corporation can do.

Corporated; power to sue and be sued, etc.

Sec. 47. By striking out section forty-eight and inserting instead thereof the following: All able bodied male persons residing within the corporate limits, between the ages of twenty-one and forty-five years, shall be liable to contribute or work upon the streets or public improvements of the corporation for two days in each year, or to pay the sum of one dollar per day, and any person after being duly notified by the mayor, and refusing to work, shall be fined not exceeding five dollars.

Who liable to contribute or work on streets.

Number of days work each year; money to be paid in lieu of work; notification. Refusing to work, etc., fine.

Sec. 48. By striking out section forty-nine and inserting instead thereof the following: The board of aldermen shall have the power to require every owner of real estate in Elizabeth City to furnish material for paving the sidewalks in front of his or her land in the improved portion of said town with such material, either brick, stone or other durable material, and enforce such requirements by proper fines and penalties: Provided, however, the said board of aldermen may in their discretion assess against the owner or owners of said lots only a portion of the costs of the same, as in their judgment and discretion may seem just, and upon the failure of such owner or owners to furnish said material the said corporation of Elizabeth City may have the same done, and the cost thereof may be assessed against the property of such delinquent and added to the taxes against him or her and collected in the same manner that other taxes or assessments are collected, or judgment may be taken by the corporation of Elizabeth City before any justice of the peace or the mayor of Elizabeth City if under fifty dollars, or in the superior court of Pasquotank county if over fifty dollars, for the actual cost of such material delivered at the place of paving.

Land-owners to furnish material for paving, etc. Enforcement of requirements; fines and penalties.

Proviso.

Failure of land-owners to furnish material, city may have it done; assessment and addition to taxes.

Judgment, how taken.

Sec. 49. The board of aldermen shall have the right to regulate and establish rates of wharfage and prescribe the limits of the part of said town, also the power to appoint wood inspectors whose duty shall be to inspect all firewood brought to the city for sale.

Regulation of rates of wharfage, etc. Wood inspectors.

Sec. 50. It shall be the duty of the harbor master to enforce all rules and regulations which the board of aldermen may prescribe for the government of the port of Elizabeth City within its limits, for the proper anchorage of vessels in the harbor, and designate the same, and he shall have the right to settle all mat-

Harbor master, enforcement of rules, etc.

Anchorage, settlement of disputes, etc.

ters of dispute between masters of boats, vessels or steamboats as to the priority of right to land or fasten to a wharf in said city and to cause the same to be removed upon the demand of the owner of any wharf.

Sec. 51. The board of aldermen shall appoint annually a finance committee, to be composed of three freeholders and citizens of the city, who shall examine the books, accounts, vouchers and papers of the clerk, chief of police, street commissioners and treasurer, and make a report in writing to the said board at a regular monthly meeting in July, eighteen hundred and ninety-nine (1899), June, nineteen hundred, and May, nineteen hundred and one, and thereafter on each monthly meeting in May of each year. The said committee shall receive such compensation as the board may designate, not exceeding one hundred dollars.

Finance committee, how often and by whom appointed; examination of books, etc.

Reports, when to be made.

Compensation of finance committee.

Sec. 52. That chapter fifteen of the laws of eighteen hundred and eighty-five, entitled "An act to amend the charter of the town of Elizabeth City," ratified February the sixth, eighteen hundred and eighty-five, and all sections thereof from one to and including section fifty-four, be and the same are hereby repealed. Repealed.

Sec. 53. That chapter fifty-eight, laws of eighteen hundred and eighty-nine, entitled "An act to permit the town of Elizabeth City to issue bonds and levy a special tax," ratified February the twenty-fifth, eighteen hundred and eighty-nine, and all sections from one to and including section seven, be and the same are hereby repealed. Repealed.

Sec. 54. That chapter one hundred and twenty-six, laws of eighteen hundred and eighty-nine, entitled "An act to amend the charter of the town of Elizabeth City, North Carolina," and ratified March the ninth, eighteen hundred and eighty-nine, and all sections thereof from one to and including fifteen, be and the same are hereby repealed. Repealed.

Sec. 55. That chapter one hundred and nine, laws of eighteen hundred and ninety-one, page nine hundred and twelve, entitled "An act to amend the charter of the town of Elizabeth City," and ratified February the twenty-fifth, eighteen hundred and ninety-one, and all sections thereof from one to and including section seven, be and the same are hereby repealed. Repealed.

Sec. 56. That chapter two hundred and fifty, private laws of eighteen hundred and ninety-three, entitled "An act to amend the charter of Elizabeth City," and ratified March the fourth, eighteen hundred and ninety-three, be and the same is hereby repealed. Repealed.

Sec. 57. That chapter ninety-seven of the private laws of eighteen hundred and ninety-seven, entitled "An act to amend chapter eighty-five, laws of eighteen hundred and ninety-five, to Repealed.

amend charter of the town of Elizabeth City," and ratified March the third, eighteen hundred and ninety-seven, be and the same is hereby repealed.

Conflicting laws repealed.

Sec. 58. All acts in conflict with these laws heretofore enacted are hereby repealed.

Sec. 59. This act shall take effect from and after its ratification.

Ratified the 15th day of February, A. D. 1899.

CHAPTER 63.

An act to authorize William Howard to practice pharmacy without license.

The General Assembly of North Carolina do enact:

Wm. Howard authorized to practice pharmacy.

Section 1. That William Howard of Edgecombe county be and [he is] hereby authorized to register and practice pharmacy without the examination and license prescribed by the general law.

Sec. 2. That this act shall be in force from its ratification.

Ratified the 8th day of March, A. D. 1899.

CHAPTER 64.

An act to incorporate the Raleigh Storage Warehouse Company.

The General Assembly of North Carolina do enact:

Body politic. Corporate name. Corporate powers.

Section 1. That Claud B. Barbee, John Gatling and W. W. Robards, all of Raleigh, North Carolina, and such other persons as may be hereafter associated with them, their successors and assigns, be and they are hereby created and declared a body politic and corporate under the name and style of "Raleigh Storage Warehouse Company," and may exercise and enjoy all the privileges, franchises and immunities incident to a corporation; may sue and be sued, plead and be impleaded, complain and defend in all courts of law and equity, of record and otherwise.

Capital stock.

Sec. 2. The capital stock of the said company shall be ten thousand dollars ($10,000), which may be increased at the option of the company to any amount not exceeding two hundred and fifty thousand dollars ($250,000). So soon as five thousand dollars ($5,000) of said capital stock shall have been subscribed and ten per cent. thereof paid in cash, it shall be lawful for the company to organize and commence business. The said capital stock shall be divided into shares of one hundred dollars ($100) each; shall be deemed personal property; shall be transferable as may be prescribed by the by-laws of the company, and each share shall entitle its holder to one vote in all meetings of the stockholders. The capital stock of the said company shall be forever unassessable, and there shall be no personal liability of the stockholders of said company beyond the full payment for such stock as they shall subscribe for.

Division of stock.

Stock unassessable.

Sec. 3. The said company shall have all the general powers and be subject to all the general restrictions conferred and imposed upon corporations and chartered companies generally by the laws of North Carolina, save so far as the same may conflict with the provisions of this act.

Powers and privileges of corporation.

Sec. 4. The said company shall have power and authority to carry on a general warehouse, storage and commission business; may lease, purchase, hold, convey and assign all such real and personal property as it or its officers may deem necessary or convenient for its business not exceeding in value the amount of two hundred and fifty thousand dollars ($250,000); may rent, lease, buy or construct warehouses and other buildings for its business; may receive on storage or deposit raw cotton, cotton and woolen goods, tobacco and other agricultural products and all other kinds of general merchandise and personal property, to include bonds, notes, accounts or other securities and evidences of debt for safe keeping, sale or shipment; may transact and carry on all kinds of business usually transacted and carried on by warehouse companies or commission merchants; may collect and receive compensation for storage, selling or shipment and all labor incident thereto, including expenses of receiving and delivering, handling, sampling, cooperage, bagging, baling, compressing, insurance and custody, or any other service rendered or expense incurred, on all property received on storage or deposit, at such rates and on such terms as may be agreed on by and between said company and the owners of such property or their respective agents; may make advances in money, negotiable notes, acceptances, endorsements or other evidences of indebtedness on raw cotton, cotton and woolen goods, tobacco or other agricultural products, merchandise or other property stored or deposited with it, and may guarantee payment of notes, acceptances, bonds or other like obligations of persons or corporations storing or depositing such property with it, and all such advances or guarantees so made by said company on property received on storage or deposit, and compensation for all charges and expenses thereon, shall be a preferred lien on said

Corporate powers.

property, which shall be satisfied and paid before the said company shall be called on for the delivery of said property; and for such advances in money or otherwise, acceptances, notes or guarantees, the said company shall be entitled to charge and collect such commissions as may be agreed upon between said company and the owners of such property or their agents; said corporation shall have authority to construct and operate a branch railway track or tracks, each track not exceeding three-quarters of a mile in length from its warehouse or warehouses, to connect with any railroad or railroad tracks running within one-half of a mile of its warehouse or warehouses; said connection to be at such place and upon such terms as may be agreed upon, and for the purposes of survey and rights of way said corporation shall have the same powers and be subject to the same restrictions as are contained in chapter forty-nine of The Code and acts amendatory thereof in the location and construction of its lines: Provided, that nothing herein contained shall authorize the said corporation to charge for the use of money advanced a greater rate of interest than the rate prescribed by law.

Liability of corporation for execution of contracts.

SEC. 5. For all raw cotton, cotton and woolen goods, tobacco or other property received by the company on storage or deposit and which it is authorized to receive under this act, the receipt or certificate of the company shall be given, binding the company to deliver the said raw cotton, cotton or woolen goods, tobacco or other thing to the party in whose favor the receipt or certificate is given, or to his or her assignee, on payment of all dues to the company for which the same is liable, which receipt or certificate shall be negotiable, and by endorsements or assignment and delivery thereof shall transfer the title to the property therein mentioned and described to the holder of the said receipt or certificate. The holder of the said receipt or certificate shall be entitled to receive the property therein mentioned and described from the company on delivery of the said receipt or certificate properly endorsed, and paying to the company whatever may be due on the said property for advances, endorsements, guarantees, charges, storage, labor and expenses, with interest thereon, if any have accrued: Provided, however, that said company shall not be held responsible for losses arising from the act of God or of the common enemies. And said company [may] make such stipulations in its warehouse receipts or contracts as to loss or damage arising by fire or other cause as it may deem necessary and proper. All advances, endorsements and guarantees made by the company on any property stored or deposited with it, shall be endorsed or stated on the receipt or certificate given for such property. In the event of the loss or destruction of a receipt given by the company for property on storage or deposit, the bona fide holder of such receipt or certificate at the time of its loss or destruction, his representatives or assigns, shall have the same right to receive the said property from the said company that he would have had on the delivery of the said receipt on proof of its said loss or destruction, and on the delivery to the said company of a proper bond of indemnity with satisfactory security to said company.

Sec. 6. Whenever from any cause any raw cotton, cotton or woolen goods, tobacco or other property on storage or deposit with the said company shall so decrease in value as in the opinion of the said company to render the preferred lien of the same a doubtful security for advances, endorsements, guarantees, charges, storage, labor and expenses due the said company thereon, or whenever on any raw cotton, cotton or woolen goods, tobacco or other property left on storage or deposit with the said company the advances, endorsements, guarantees, charges, labor, storage and expenses due the said company thereon shall not have been satisfied and paid at such time or times as may be required by the regulations established by said company for the conduct of its business, it shall be lawful for the said company to give notice to the party entitled to said raw cotton, cotton or woolen goods, tobacco or other property personally (or by mailing such notice to him or her by registered mail), or his or her agent, at his or her agent's last known place of business or residence, requiring the said party within fifteen days after the receipt of such notice to pay to the said company all such advancements, endorsements, guarantees, charges, storage, labor and expenses, with any interest that may have accrued thereon; and if within twenty-five days after the personal service (or receipt of registered notices) the same be not paid, it shall be lawful for the said company to sell such property at public sale, after ten days' public notice, as to the said company may seem best for all concerned; and after reserving the amount due the said company and paying the costs of the sale, the said company shall pay over the balance of the proceeds of the property to the party entitled thereto on his or her surrender of the receipt or certificate given for said property. If the holder of the receipt or certificate be unknown to the said company, the said notice may be given to the party to whom the said receipt or certificate was originally issued, or if he or she be deceased, to his or her personal representative. But nothing in this section contained shall be construed to prevent the said company from making any such sale at such earlier or later time and in such other manner as may be provided for in any contract or agreement made by any person or persons with said company.

Remedy in case of doubtful security.

Notice shall be to owner.

Corporate powers.

Sec. 7. It shall be lawful for the said company to borrow such sums of money from time to time as may be necessary to carry out the provisions of this act; and to issue and dispose of its promissory notes or bonds for the amounts so borrowed; and the said company may mortgage, pledge or hypothecate any part of its corporate property and franchises to secure the payment of such notes or bonds.

Duties and powers of stockholders.

Sec. 8. The stockholders in general meeting shall make and establish such by-laws, rules and regulations not inconsistent with the laws of the state of North Carolina or of the United States, and not inconsistent with this act, as they may deem proper for the management and control of its affairs and business of the said company and the government of its officers, agents, clerks and other employees, which shall be binding upon themselves and all other persons in the employment of the said company.

Board of directors.

Sec. 9. The persons named in the first section of this act shall constitute the board of directors, who shall serve until the first annual meeting of the stockholders and until their successors are elected. So soon as the said company is authorized to organize and commence business by having complied with the requirements of the second section of this act, the board of directors shall call a meeting of the stockholders at such time and place as they may appoint, which shall be their first annual meeting. At their first and every subsequent annual meeting the stockholders shall elect such of their number as the by-laws may prescribe to constitute a board of directors, to remain in office until their next annual meeting or until their successors are elected: but in no event shall the existence of the company be in any way affected or be dissolved by reason of a failure to elect officers.

Election of directors. Term of office. Failure to elect directors shall not affect existence of company.

Powers of board of directors.

Sec. 10. Subject to the by-laws, rules and regulations of the company, the board of directors shall have the management and control of its affairs and business. They shall appoint or elect such officers, agents and clerks as they may find necessary for the management of the company's business; and they shall provide for receiving subscriptions to the capital stock of the company, which they shall make payable at such time and in such installments as they or the stockholders may determine.

Place of business.

Sec. 11. The principal office and place of business of the said company shall be located in the city of Raleigh, and such other offices, buildings or places of business may be established in such place or places as the board of directors or the stockholders of the company in general or special meeting may determine; and the said corporation shall exist for sixty years from the date of its organization.

Sec. 12. This act shall be in force from and after its ratification.

Ratified the 15th day of February, A. D. 1899.

CHAPTER 65.

An act to incorporate the Olivia Raney Library.

The General Assembly of North Carolina do enact:

Section 1. That Richard H. Battle, Joseph G. Brown, Joseph B. Cheshire, Jr., Bryan G. Cowper, Frank B. Dancy, John C. Drewry, William B. Grimes, Frank P. Haywood, Jr., Herbert W. Jackson, Wesley N. Jones, Matthias M. Marshall, Samuel F. Mordecai, Charles W. Raney, Richard B. Raney and Gustave Rosenthal and their successors, be and they are hereby created a body corporate by the name of the "Olivia Raney Library," and by that name may sue and be sued; may have a common seal, may acquire, receive and hold real estate to the value of thirty thousand dollars in the city of Raleigh, North Carolina, by purchase, gift, devise or otherwise, and may acquire, receive and hold personal property, money and choses in action to the value and amount of thirty thousand dollars by purchase, gift and bequest by will or otherwise; may sell, dispose of, lease and convey its real and personal property and estate under such circumstances as are provided for in this act; may contract and be contracted with for the purposes provided in this act, and as limited and restricted by this act, and may make such by-laws for its government and the exercise of its powers and may alter the same from time to time as shall not be in conflict with the laws of this state and of the United States and not repugnant to this act.

Corporators. Body corporate. Corporate name. Seal. Corporate powers.

Sec. 2. The powers, purpose and duties of said corporation shall be as follows: To establish and maintain a free library for the use, without any charge whatever, of the white citizens of the city of Raleigh, and to that end said corporation may acquire real estate as is hereinafter provided, and construct and maintain thereon a suitable building or buildings for a library, and may let such portion or portions of such building or buildings as may be unnecessary for the library to other persons, and appropriate the rents and profits derived from such letting to the maintainance and current expenses of the library. And said corporation may apply the personal estate it may acquire as is hereinbefore provided to the proper furnishing, equipment and maintainance of the library, including current expenses of the corpo-

Corporate powers.

ration, and may invest its money in interest-bearing securities to such an extent as to provide a suitable income to defray the necessary expenses of maintaining said library; may extend the privileges of said library to white persons who may visit the city of Raleigh under such circumstances and with such reasonable regulations as the said corporation may prescribe in its by-laws; but no charge shall be made for the use of the said library by such visitors; may make from time to time reasonable regulations as to the use of the library and for the preservation of the books and other property of the corporation, and the maintainance of decency and order on the premises of the corporation.

Compensation of officers.

Sec. 3. The members of the corporation, other than the treasurer, shall receive no compensation for their services.

Employees and their salaries.

Sec. 4. The corporation may employ a librarian, janitor, and such other employees and servants as it may deem essential, and pay their salaries and wages out of any funds of the corporation.

Corporate powers.

Sec. 5. The corporation shall not have the power to mortgage or incumber its property, nor shall it have the power to contract any debt exceeding five hundred dollars without the written assent of three-fourths of its members; nor shall its members and officers contract for the corporation in such manner that the aggregate of its outstanding indebtedness shall at any one time exceed one thousand dollars. It shall not have the power to sell and convey its real estate without the assent of the general assembly of this state.

Membership, vacancy.

Sec. 6. Whenever a vacancy shall occur in the membership of the corporation, such vacancy shall be filled by the election of another member by the remaining members. Any member may resign by tendering his written resignation to the president or vice-president. Any member may be removed for physical or mental incapacity by a vote of three-fourths of other members.

Officers of corporation.

Sec. 7. The officers of the corporation shall be a president, a vice-president, a secretary and a treasurer (but the offices of secretary and treasurer may be filled and held by the same person), and an executive committee of five of the members. All of the said officers shall be elected at the first meeting of the members of the corporation, and those so elected shall hold their offices until their successors are duly elected. There shall, after the first meeting, be another regular meeting held on the third Thursday in December, eighteen hundred and ninety-nine, at which meeting the successors to the officers elected at the first meeting shall be elected, and thereafter the regular annual meeting of said corporation shall be held on the third Thursday of December in each and every year, at which meetings all of the officers of the corporation shall be elected; but if for any cause no election of officers or any one or more officers shall be had at

Term of officers.

Regular annual meeting.

any regular meeting, such election or elections may be held at any subsequent special meeting. All officers of the corporation shall hold their offices until their successors shall be duly elected. No one shall be eligible as an officer of the corporation except a member thereof. Eligibility to office.

Sec. 8. The first and all other meetings of the members of the corporation shall be held in the city of Raleigh, North Carolina. The first meeting shall be held at such time and place in said city as any three members may designate in written notices signed by them and delivered to each of the other members. The time and place in said city at which all subsequent annual meetings shall be held, and the times and places in the said city and upon what notice special meetings may be held, shall be fixed and regulated by the by-laws of the corporation. Meetings of said corporation. Special meetings.

Sec. 9. The president shall preside at the meetings of the corporation; shall sign all contracts on behalf of the corporation; shall be the custodian of the corporate seal and set the same to such instruments as the corporation may properly and legally direct to be executed by the corporation, and perform such other acts as he may be authorized and empowered to perform by the by-laws, or by resolution of the corporation. Duties of president.

Sec. 10. The vice-president shall perform all the duties of the president when the president shall be absent from a meeting or from the city of Raleigh. Duties of vice-president.

Sec. 11. The secretary shall keep the records of the corporation and do such other acts as may be prescribed by the by-laws. The treasurer shall receive and disburse all the funds of the corporation under the direction of the executive committee, or as may be directed by the by-laws of the corporation, and do such other acts as the by-laws may prescribe. He shall be required to give bond in such amount as may be fixed by the corporation, and may be paid a reasonable salary or commission. Duties of secretary. Duties of treasurer.

Sec. 12. The executive committee shall have general supervision and control of the affairs of the corporation and shall perform such duties as may be prescribed by the by-laws of the corporation, but shall not have the power to do any act inconsistent with the other provisions of this act, and the corporation at any regular or special meeting may take charge and control of any matter or matters which the executive committee would otherwise have under their control. Duties of executive committee.

Sec. 13. No member of this corporation shall be liable personally or individually for any contract, obligation or other liability of any kind of the corporation. Liability of corporators.

Sec. 14. At all meetings of the corporation a majority of its members shall constitute a quorum. Majority of members shall constitute a quorum.

Sec. 15. The general assembly being authorized by the consti-

Corporation exempt from taxation. tution, article six, section five, to exempt from taxation property held for education, literary and charitable purposes, the property and estate which this corporation may acquire, hold and use according to the provisions of this act, shall be exempted from all state, county and municipal taxation.

Corporate existence. Sec. 16. The corporate existence of this corporation shall be one hundred years.

Injury to property a misdemeanor. Sec. 17. Any person who shall wilfully deface, injure, mutilate or destroy the books, or works of art, or furniture of the corporation, shall be guilty of a misdemeanor, and upon conviction shall be fined or imprisoned in the discretion of the court.

Violation of rules of conduct a misdemeanor. Sec. 18. Any person who shall use indecent or profane language in the library room or rooms of the corporation, or who shall conduct himself in an indcent or boisterous manner in such library room or rooms, or who shall wilfully and wantonly violate any reasonable rule of the corporation regulating the use of the library, shall be guilty of a misdemeanor, and upon conviction shall be punished by a fine not exceeding fifty dollars or imprisoned for thirty days.

Sec. 19. This act shall be in force from and after its ratification.

Ratified the 15th day of February, A. D. 1899.

CHAPTER 66.

An act to incorporate the town of Manteo.

The General Assembly of North Carolina do enact:

Incorporation; name of town. Subject to all provisions of law. Section 1. That the town of Manteo, in the county of Dare, be and the same is hereby incorporated by the name of the town of Manteo, and shall be subject to all provisions of law now in force or hereafter enacted relating to incorporated towns and cities, except as herein provided.

Corporate limits. Sec. 2. That the boundaries and corporate limits of said town shall be as follows: Beginning on the Manteo creek, at the south line of the John T. Wescott place, running thence with said line across the main road, thence southerly along the main road to abreast of the cemetery gate, thence westerly to the westward line of the Fannie Hassell land, thence southerly to the westward line of R. C. Evans and Mack Simmons, thence southerly to the north line of Levinia Brinkley, thence along the said Brinkley line to Shallowback bay, thence along said bay and Manteo creek to the first station.

Town officers. Sec. 3. That the officers of said town shall consist of a mayor, seven commissioners, marshal and treasurer. The treasurer shall be ex officio the clerk to the board of commissioners, and the following named persons shall fill said offices until the first Monday in May, eighteen hundred and ninety-nine, viz.: Wm. G. Forbes, mayor; James A. Evans, Richard C. Evans, Augustus G. Sample, Jabez B. Jennett, Hilliard G. Peel, Lewis S. Hooper and Daniel W. Etheridge, commissioners; Leonard D. Hassell, marshal, and Samuel E. Mann treasurer.

Term of office.
Temporary officers.

Sec. 4. That there shall be an election held for the various officers mentioned in this act on the first Monday in May, eighteen hundred and ninety-nine, and each succeeding year thereafter under the same regulations and restrictions that county and state elections are held, and all citizens who shall have resided in the State one year and within said corporate limits ninety days previous to the day of election shall be entitled to vote therein.

First election.
Succeeding elections.
Qualified voters.

Sec. 5 That the said commissioners shall have power to pass all by-laws and regulations for the good government of said town not inconsistent with the laws of this state and the United States, and may levy a tax on all objects of state taxation, not to exceed sixteen and two-third cents (16 2-3) on each one hundred dollars worth of taxable property therein and fifty (50) cents on each poll, and to impose fines for the violation of the town ordinances and collect the same for the use of the town.

Power of commissioners.
Tax levy.
Fines for violation of town ordinances.

Sec. 6. That the treasurer and marshal shall each enter with a bond of not less than two hundred (\$200) dollars, to be approved by the town commissioners and payable to the state of North Carolina, to the use of the town of Manteo, conditioned for the faithful performance of their respective duties.

Bond of treasurer and marshal.

Sec. 7. That the officers of said town shall receive such compensation for their services as the town commissioners in their discretion may authorize: Provided, the cost in all cases of violation of town ordinances shall not exceed the amounts allowed justices of the peace and constables for similar services by the general state laws.

Compensation of officers.
Proviso.

Sec. 8. That this charter shall be subject to all the conditions and restrictions and regulations as to sale of spirituous and other intoxicating drinks, heretofore enacted and now in force as to Dare county.

Charter subject to conditions.

Sec. 9. That it shall be the duty of the officers appointed by this act, within thirty days after its ratification, to go before some justice of the peace of Dare county or other officer therein authorized to administer oaths and take the oath of office prescribed by law for such officers.

When officers shall qualify.

Sec. 10. That this act shall be in force from and after its ratification.

Ratified the 16th day of February, A. D. 1899.

CHAPTER 67.

An act to incorporate the town of North Brevard.

The General Assembly of North Carolina do enact:

Incorporated.

Section 1. That the town of North Brevard, in the county of Transylvania, be and the same is hereby incorporated by the name and style of North Brevard, and shall be entitled to all the rights and privileges and be subject to the restrictions and liabilities as now provided by law for incorporated towns in this state.

Name of town. Privileges and restrictions.

Corporate limits.

Sec. 2. That the corporate limits of said town shall be as follows: Beginning at a stake in corporate line of Brevard, where said line crosses the public road leading from Brevard to Henderson county near Cooper's creek, and runs with said corporation line east and southeast to Cooper's creek, then with said creek to the public road near T. S. Woods to a stake on the east bank of said road and south bank of said creek, then a direct line to the east end of M. J. Neely's dwelling, then a direct line to the east side of Manning Gallamore's house, then north and along the line between W. K. Osborn and E. Allison and along the line between Osborn and J. A. Miller to L. C. Neil's land, then north to the H. and B. Railroad, then along said railroad in a westerly direction to corporation line or town of Brevard, thence with said line to the beginning.

Town officers.

Term of office.

Temporary officers.

Sec. 3. That the officers of said corporation shall consist of a mayor and three commissioners and a marshal, and the commissioners shall have the right to appoint a secretary and treasurer and the following named persons shall fill said offices until the first Monday in May, eighteen hundred and ninety-nine, or until their successors are duly elected and qualified, viz.: M. J. Orr, mayor; T. S. Boswell, G. C. Witmer and Manning Callamore, commissioners; and J. A. Miller, marshal, who shall take the oath of office within thirty days after the ratification of this act before some justice of the peace of Transylvania county or other officer qualified to administer oaths.

When officers shall qualify.

Time of holding town elections.

Sec. 4. That the election for mayor, three commissioners and marshal shall be held on the first Monday in May, eighteen hundred and ninety-nine, and annually thereafter under the same rules and regulations as prescribed by law for holding municipal elections in this state.

Fines, how applied.

Sec. 5. That all fines collected for violation of any of the town ordinances shall be paid into the treasury for the benefit of the town.

Sec. 6. That this act shall be in force from and after its ratification.

Ratified the 16th day of February, A. D. 1899.

CHAPTER 68.

An act to amend the charter of the Raleigh and Gaston Railroad Company, and to authorize said Raleigh and Gaston Railroad Company to consolidate with other railroad, transportation or other companies, or to lease or otherwise acquire the property and franchises of the same.

The General Assembly of North Carolina do enact:

Section 1. That authority is hereby given the Raleigh and Gaston Railroad Company to consolidate with the Seaboard and Roanoke Railroad Company, the Raleigh and Augusta Air Line Railroad Company, the Carolina Central Railroad Company, the Georgia, Carolina and Northern Railway Company, the Durham and Northern Railway Company, the Roanoke and Tar River Railroad Company, the Louisburg Railroad Company, and any other railroad, transportation or other company now incorporated or hereafter to be incorporated under the laws of the United States, or any of the states thereof, or of this state, not parallel competing, or to lease or otherwise acquire the property and franchises of said companies; and authority is hereby given all and each of said railroad companies and other railroad, transportation or other company now incorporated or hereafter to be incorporated, as aforesaid, not parallel competing, to make, enter into and carry out an agreement whereby the said Raleigh and Gaston Railroad Company shall become consolidated with or shall lease or otherwise acquire the property and franchises of said other company or companies, as one railroad company.

Raleigh and Gaston R. R. Company empowered to consolidate with certain other non-competing and non-parallel roads.

Sec. 2. That such consolidation, lease or acquisition shall be made on such terms and conditions as may be agreed to by the stockholders in each of said companies by resolution to be adopted in a general meeting of the stockholders of each of said companies, duly called for the purpose of considering the same: Provided, that such resolution shall be adopted in each of such meetings by the affirmative vote of those owning or representing at least a majority of the entire capital stock of said companies.

Stockholders of companies affected shall agree to terms of consolidation, lease or acquisition.

Sec. 3. That when such consolidation, lease or acquisition shall have been agreed to in the manner and form hereinbefore prescribed, then the same shall be effected by the execution of and delivery of a deed or other proper conveyance from the railroad, transportation or other company agreeing to such consolidation, lease or acquisition to the Raleigh and Gaston Railroad Company, conveying by proper description all of the property, real, personal and mixed, including the road-bed, right of way and superstructures, as well as all equipment and other personal property, and all the rights, powers, privileges and franchises of the said railroad, transportation or other company agreeing and consenting thereto, as aforesaid, to the said Raleigh and

How consolidation, lease or acquisition shall be effected.

Subject to existing liens.

Gaston Railroad Company, subject to any and all existing liens on each of said railroad, transportation or other companies, respectively, and the said Raleigh and Gaston Railroad Company shall have the right to covenant to assume and to assume as a part of the consideration of such conveyance the payment of the principal and interest of any or all such liens, and upon the execution and delivery of such conveyance, the said Raleigh and Gaston Railroad Company shall immediately be and become vested with the complete and full title to all the property, rights, powers, privileges and franchises conveyed thereby, upon the conditions therein contained, with the right to own, maintain and operate the railroads and all branches heretofore owned and operated, and other works of the transportation or other companies agreeing thereto, as one railroad company.

Corporate powers and privileges.

May sell and purchase stocks.

Sec. 4. That the Raleigh and Gaston Railroad Company is hereby authorized to make and carry out any agreement that may be made for the transfer and delivery of shares of its capital stock to the holders of the shares of stock in any of said railroad, transportation or other companies consenting thereto, in exchange for such stock on such terms and at such rates as may be mutually agreed upon; and said company is hereby authorized to purchase from the holders thereof any of the shares of stock in any of said railroad, transportation or other companies agreeing thereto, which may not be exchanged as aforesaid.

Authorized to increase capital stock on approval of stockholders.

Maximum price to be paid.

Sec. 5. That the said Raleigh and Gaston Railroad Company is hereby authorized to increase its capital stock from time to time to such an amount as may be authorized or approved by the stockholders thereof in any annual or general meeting assembled, not to exceed in the aggregate the sum of twenty-five thousand dollars per mile of main line and branch roads, now constructed or hereafter to be constructed and now owned or hereafter to be acquired under the provisions of this act, or otherwise; said stock to be divided in one or more series or grades with such preferences, conditions and voting power as shall be provided by the stockholders in general meeting as herein provided.

Division of stock.

Corporate power.

Authorized to borrow money and to issue bonds.

Sec. 6. That the said Raleigh and Gaston Railroad Company, in addition to the rights which it now has as to the issue of bonds, shall have the right at any time hereafter to borrow money and issue bonds or other evidences of indebtedness therefor and may secure the same from time to time by a mortgage or deed of trust upon any or all of its property and franchises now owned or hereafter to be acquired, and may issue and sell its bonds and its capital stock at such prices and on such terms as a majority in amount of the stockholders shall approve at any annual or general meeting, and may receive in payment therefor property, security or shares in any corporation mentioned in this act, and any stock so issued shall be deemed fully paid and free from any liability.

May acquire stock in other railroads.

Sec. 7. That the said Raleigh and Gaston Railroad Company is hereby authorized from time to time to purchase, own or hold bonds or other evidences of debt and shares of the capital stock of any railroad, transportation or other company formed under the laws of this state or of any other state, and from time to time may guarantee or assume the bonds, evidences of indebtedness or capital stock of any such railroad, transportation or other company: Provided, it shall not be lawful for the said Raleigh and Gaston Railroad Company to sell or lease a majority of its capital stock to any competing parallel railroad company, or to acquire or hold a majority of the capital stock of any competing parallel railroad company.

Proviso.

May not acquire or sell majority of stock from or to competing parallel lines.

Corporate power.

Sec. 8. That the said Raleigh and Gaston Railroad Company may from time to time acquire or guarantee the bonds and stocks, or either, of any inland, coast or ocean transportation company or companies, and it may develop or aid in the development of its business by acquiring or guaranteeing the stocks and bonds, or either, of hotel, lighterage, wharf, elevating and such other enterprises convenient in connection therewith, or as a part thereof.

Property of corporation.

Sec. 9. That notwithstanding the conveyance of the property of the railroad, transportation or other companies herein referred to, to the said Raleigh and Gaston Railroad Company, as hereinbefore provided, the existence of the said railroad, transportation and other companies as a corporation shall respectively continue so long as any of its shares of capital stock shall not be sold to or exchanged with the said Raleigh and Gaston Railroad Company for the purpose only of protecting the interest of the said stockholders in said railroad, transportation or other companies as such, and in all meetings of the said railroad, transportation or other companies, respectively, thereafter held, the said Raleigh and Gaston Railroad Company shall have the right to represent all the stock which it may have acquired or purchased or exchanged, as aforesaid, in the railroad, transportation or other companies, respectively, casting such vote as it may be entitled to on the number of shares so acquired by it and standing in its name on the books of the said railroad, transportation or other company, respectively, and to that end the said Raleigh and Gaston Railroad Company may keep alive and hold for that purpose only all the shares of stock in any of said railroad, transportation or other companies which it may acquire by purchase or in exchange as aforesaid, until it shall have acquired the whole of said stock in the said railroad, transpor-

Right of representation.

tation or other companies, respectively, when the same shall be cancelled and the existence of the railroad, transportation or other company whose entire stock shall be so acquired shall cease and be at an end.

Stockholders refusing to convert acquired stock.

Sec. 10. That any stockholder in any of the railroads, transportation or other companies herein referred to or included who shall refuse to convert his stock into the stock of the Raleigh and Gaston Railroad Company under the terms of the agreement of consolidation may on reasonable notice to said company demand that it shall purchase the said stock at its actual value in cash, and if the price can be agreed upon it shall be the duty of the said company to purchase and take the same, and if the price cannot be agreed upon or the said company shall fail to take and pay for the same at the agreed price, then such stockholders may apply by petition as in other special proceedings to the superior court of Wake county, to appoint three disinterested persons to fix the value of said stock, whose award shall be final and conclusive when confirmed by the said court, and it shall be the duty of the said company to take and pay for the said shares of stock at the valuation thereof as fixed by such appraisers upon its being transferred and delivered to it, and upon its failure to take and pay for the same within thirty days after the confirmation of said award, then the amount of said award shall be a judgment against said company and collected as other judgments of said court are by law collected: Provided, however, that said company shall not be required to pay the said judgment except upon the surrender and delivery to it of the certificate for said shares, legally transferred.

When price cannot be agreed upon.

Proviso.

Election of president and directors.

Sec. 11. That the stockholders of the Raleigh and Gaston Railroad Company may, at any annual or general meeting thereof, elect a president and a board of directors not to exceed twenty-five in number.

Empowered to change name.

Sec. 12. That said company shall have the right at any time to change its name to the Seaboard Air Line Railway Company by a majority vote in annual or general meeting of its stockholders, such change of name to be evidenced by a certificate signed by the president of said company with the corporate seal affixed and attested by its secretary and treasurer, and recorded in the office of the register of deeds of Wake county; such change of name shall be without prejudice to the rights of any creditor or to the exercise of any of the powers and privileges granted by this act.

Right of actions not impaired.

Sec. 13. That nothing herein contained shall be construed as in anywise impairing or changing any right of action which the state of North Carolina, or any of its agents, or any county of the state, or any person or party whomsoever, may now or hereafter have against any of the corporations or railroad companies hereinbefore referred to; but such right of action shall remain unchanged, and may be enforced against any such corporation and against the rights, property and franchises thereof, the same as it might have been before the passage of this act or any transfers in pursuance thereof.

Sec. 14. That all corporations formed or consolidated under the provisions of this [act], or affected thereby, shall be domestic corporations of North Carolina, and shall be subject to the jurisdiction and laws of North Carolina. Shall be domestic corporations.

Sec. 15. This act shall be in force from and after its ratification.

Ratified the 16th day of February, A. D. 1899.

CHAPTER 69.

An act to incorporate the town of Mayodan in Rockingham county.

The General Assembly of North Carolina do enact:

Section 1. That the town of Mayodan, in the county of Rockingham, be and the same is hereby incorporated by the name and style of the town of Mayodan, and shall be subject to all the provisions and have all the rights and privileges contained in chapter sixty-two, volume two of The Code of North Carolina, not inconsistent with this act. Incorporated. Corporate name. Rights and privileges.

Sec. 2. That the corporate limits of said town shall be as follows, to-wit: Beginning at a point on the west bank of Mayo river in the county of Rockingham, North Carolina, the said point being at the intersection of the land of the estate of W. N. Mebane, deceased, and the land of the Piedmont Land and Manufacturing Company; thence following the branch in said line to a stake; thence north fifty-one degrees fourteen seconds west three hundred and three feet to a stake; thence with the division line of the land of the estate of W. N. Mebane, deceased, and the land of the Piedmont Land and Manufacturing Company to the Ayersville road; thence following the Ayersville road in the direction of Ayersville to the intersection in the line of division between the property purchased by the Piedmont Land and Manufacturing Company from Highfield and the land purchased by said company from Robert Lewis; thence following the division line between the Joyce, Highfield and Lewis tracts eastwardly to the east bank of the Mayo river; thence following the east bank of the Mayo river to a point opposite the first named Corporate limits.

point; thence across the Mayo river to the point of beginning. The said corporate limits being shown on its map of the land of the Piedmont Land and Manufacturing Company.

Town officers.

Sec. 3. That the officers of said town shall consist of a mayor and three commissioners and a marshal, and the commissioners when qualified, as required by law, may elect an officer to be called either a town clerk or a secretary and treasurer, and the said secretary and treasurer and the said town clerk or secretary and treasurer may be elected by said commissioners from among the citizens of the town of Mayodan, or from the members of said commissioners, as the said commissioners may determine.

Temporary officers.

Sec. 4. That until the election hereinafter provided for, the mayor and three commissioners provided for in the preceding section of this act shall be as follows: Mayor, W. C. Ruffin; commissioners, L. W. Blackwell, C. G. Carter and F. B. Kemp, who shall hold their respective offices until their successors are elected and qualified. The commissioners after taking the oath prescribed by law shall elect a town marshal, and may, if they think best, elect a town clerk or secretary and treasurer, as above provided for, and require of them such bond payable to the state for the faithful performance of their several duties, as to the said commissioners may seem just and reasonable.

Duties of commissioners.

First election.

Sec. 5. That there shall be held on the first Monday in May, eighteen hundred and ninety-nine, and every year thereafter, in some convenient place in the town to be designated by said commissioners by notice of the time and place thereof, posted in three public places in said town, an election for mayor and three commissioners, who shall hold their offices until their successors are qualified.

Term of office.

Commissioners may dispense with notice of election after certain time.

Sec. 6. That after the first election held in pursuance to the provisions of the preceding section, the commissioners may dispense with the notice of the time and place for holding the election provided for in this act: Provided, they shall establish by ordinance a permanent polling place in said town.

Proviso.

Qualified electors.

Sec. 7. That any qualified elector in this state shall be eligible as mayor or commissioner: Provided, he shall have resided within the corporate limits of said town for twelve months next preceding the day of election.

Sec. 8. That all persons entitled to vote in the county of Rockingham for members of the general assembly, and who shall have been bona fide residents of the town of Mayodan ninety days next preceding the day of election, and shall be otherwise qualified to vote, as required by law, shall be entitled to vote at any and all municipal elections for said town.

Corporate powers.

Sec. 9. That in addition to the powers conferred on the commissioners of incorporated towns, enumerated in chapter sixty-two (62) of The Code of North Carolina, the said mayor and commissioners shall have power to lay out and open any new streets within the corporate limits of said town whenever by them deemed necessary within the said corporation, and of the necessity thereof the said mayor and commissioners are to be sole judge, and they shall have power at any time to widen, enlarge, change, extend or discontinue any street or streets or any part thereof within the corporate limits of said town, and shall have power and authority to condemn, appropriate or use any land or lands necessary for any of the purposes named in this section upon making reasonable compensation to the owner or owners thereof; but in case the owner or owners of the land sought to be condemned or appropriated for public use by the mayor and commissioners, and if the mayor and commissioners and owner or owners cannot agree as to the compensation, the matter shall be referred to arbitration, the commissioners and the owners of the land each choosing one freeholder and a qualified elector of said town, and in case the owner of the land sought to be condemned shall refuse to choose such an arbitrator, then the mayor shall in his stead choose such an arbitrator for him, and in case the two chosen as aforesaid cannot agree, then the arbitrators so chosen shall elect an umpire like qualified as themselves, the duty of which board of arbitrators it shall be to examine the land sought to be condemned, and ascertain the damages that will be sustained by and the benefit accruing to the owner in consequence of the taking and appropriating of said land, and award to the said owner, the amount, if any, that shall be paid by the town for the use of the land so taken, and shall assess against the property adjoining any new street or streets such benefits as they shall have decided shall be taxed against said property, and the award of the arbitrators shall be conclusive of the rights of the parties, and shall vest in the mayor and commissioners the right to use the land for the purposes for which it is condemned, and the damages agreed upon between the owner of the land and the mayor and commissioners, or awarded by the arbitrators, shall be paid as other liabilities, and the benefits assessed against any property shall be a lien upon real property, and may be collected in the manner provided by law for the collection of such unpaid state and county taxes: Provided, that either party may appeal to the superior court of Rockingham county.

Streets.

May condemn land.

When there is disagreement, arbitrators shall decide.

Condemned land.

Lien upon property.

Sec. 10. That the said mayor and commissioners shall have the right to prohibit the running at large of horses, cattle, hogs, sheep, jacks, jennets, goats and other live stock in the corporate limits of said town, and are hereby empowered to make such

Running at large of stock.

rules and regulations as they may deem best for the impounding and sale of all the animals mentioned, found roaming at large in the corporate limits of said town, contrary to the ordinances of said town.

Sale of liquors, etc.

Sec. 11. That no spirituous, vinous or malt liquors shall be sold within the corporate limits of the said town of Mayodan, and the mayor and commissioners shall have no right to issue or grant license to any one for such purpose: Provided, however, the said mayor and commissioners may have the right to grant such license only after three-fifths of the qualified voters of the said town of Mayodan shall have voted for license, in an election ordered by said board of commissioners, submitting the question of "License" and "No license" to the qualified voters of said town. Such election shall be ordered on May first, eighteen hundred and ninety-nine, in case three-fifths of the qualified voters of said town shall petition said mayor and commissioners to order said election.

Proviso.

On petition of three fifths of voters.

When election is ordered.

Sec. 12. The mayor and commissioners, in ordering the election provided for in section eleven, shall order the same to be held in the same manner as the election for municipal officers.

Unlawful to sell liquor without license.

Sec. 13. Any person convicted of selling vinous, spirituous or malt liquors in said town of Mayodan shall be fined not less than fifty dollars or may be imprisoned thirty days.

License tax.

Sec. 14. The said mayor and commissioners, in the event that three-fifths of the qualified voters vote for "License," as hereinbefore provided, shall have the right to levy and collect from all persons to whom license shall be granted for the sale of spirituous, vinous or malt liquors, such tax for the benefit of said town, as they, the said mayor and commissioners, shall prescribe.

Conflicting laws repealed.

Sec. 15. That all laws and parts of laws in conflict with the provisions of sections eleven, twelve, thirteen and fourteen of this act, be and the same are hereby repealed.

Sec. 16. That this act shall be in force from and after its ratification.

Ratified the 16th day of February, A. D. 1899.

CHAPTER 70.

An act to incorporate the North Carolina Society of the Cincinnati.

The General Assembly of North Carolina do enact:

Corporated.

Section 1. That John Gray Blount, John Myers Blount, John Collins Daves, Richard Bradley Hill, Wilson Gray Lamb, James

Iredell McRae, William Law Mufree, William Johnson Saunders, Lee H. Yarborough, and all such persons as may from time to time be associated with them, and their successors, be and they are hereby constituted a body politic and corporate by the name of the "North Carolina Society of the Cincinnati," to be located at Raleigh, for the purpose of carrying out the principles of said society and to succeed to all the rights, property and privileges of said society as originally organized at Hillsborough in October, seventeen hundred and eighty-three, with the power to hold real and personal estate by subscription, grant, purchase or devise, and to sell or invest the same for the benefit of said society and the beneficiaries thereof; to have a common seal; to make contracts in relation to the objects of the charitable fund of the said society, to sue and be sued, to establish by-laws and rules for the regulation of said society and the preservation and application of the funds thereof, not inconsistent with the laws of the state of North Carolina or of the United States. Body politic. Corporate name. Location. Corporate rights and powers.

Sec. 2. This act shall be in force from and after its ratification.

Ratified the 16th day of February, A. D. 1899.

CHAPTER 71.

An act to amend chapter one hundred and sixty-eight, private laws of eighteen hundred and eighty-seven, entitled an act to reincorporate the town of Roxboro, and to extend the corporate limits thereof.

The General Assembly of North Carolina do enact:

Section 1. The board of commissioners of Roxboro are hereby authorized and empowered to issue from time to time, to an amount not exceeding twelve thousand dollars, bonds in the name of the town of Roxboro, in such denominations and form, and payable at such place and time, but running not less than ten years nor more than thirty years, and bearing interest at no greater rate than six per centum per annum, and payable annually or semi-annually, as said board of commissioners may determine. Commissioners of Roxboro authorized to issue bonds. Denomination. Interest. When payable.

Sec. 2. That none of said bonds shall be issued until approved by a majority of the qualified voters of said town, at a public election to be held at such time or times and under such regulations as the board of commissioners may prescribe, first giving thirty days' notice of same in some newspaper published in said town, at which election those favoring the issue of bonds shall vote "Issue," and those opposing it shall vote "No Issue." When bonds shall be issued.

Bonds shall not be disposed of for less than par.

Sec. 3. That said bonds shall in no case be sold, hypothecated or otherwise disposed of for a less sum than their par value.

Proceeds, how applied.

Sec. 4. That the money arising from the sale of said bonds shall be used by said commissioners for the purpose of liquidating the present indebtedness of said town, for the purpose of supplying the town with water, making, grading and improving streets, erecting electric lights and putting in sewerage system.

Sec. 5. That this act shall take effect from and after its ratification.

Ratified the 16th day of February, A. D. 1899.

CHAPTER 72.

An act to incorporate the town of Sylva, North Carolina.

The General Assembly of North Carolina do enact:

Body politic.

Section 1. That the inhabitants of the town of Sylva shall be a body politic and corporate, and in the name of the commissioners of the town of Sylva shall have the right to sue and be sued, contract and be contracted with, to purchase, hold and convey real and personal property for the purpose of the government of said town, its welfare and improvement, and under the name and style aforesaid, is hereby invested with and shall be subject to any and all the provisions of law now existing or may subsequently be enacted in reference to incorporated cities and towns.

Corporate rights and powers.

Corporate limits.

Sec. 2. That the corporation boundary lines of the town of Sylva shall be as follows, to-wit: Beginning at the southeast corner of the depot, as now located, shall run three-fourths of a mile each north, south, east and west with the cardinal points of the compass, and intermediate points of same a like distance of three-fourths of a mile so as to form an exact octagon.

Town officers.

Sec. 3. That the officers of said town shall be a mayor, five commissioners and a marshal, who shall be chief of police, and such additional police officers as the commissioners of said town may provide for by an ordinance for that purpose; and the commissioners of said town shall have the power to elect a secretary and treasurer, and a tax collector, who shall be required to give bond for the faithful discharge of any duties devolving upon said secretary and treasurer and tax collector in such amounts as the said commissioners may exact.

Election of secretary and tax collector.

Temporary officers

Sec. 4. That for the purpose of carrying this act into immediate operation, and until their successors are elected on first Monday of May, A. D. nineteen hundred, and qualified in accordance with this act, the following-named persons shall fill said offices of mayor, commissioners and marshal, to-wit: Mayor, Dr. J. H. Wolff; commissioners, R. A. Painter, M. D. Cowan, M. Buchanan, A. B. Dills and B. C. Grindstaff; marshal, James H. Robinson; and such officers shall have the same power and authority as are conferred upon like officers by law, and such additional authority as may be conferred upon the commissioners of the town of Sylva by this act.

Sec. 5. That an election shall be held in the town of Sylva for the officers mentioned in this act on the first Monday in May, A. D. nineteen hundred, and annually thereafter, under the same regulations and restrictions that govern state and county elections; that all male citizens over twenty-one years of age, who have resided in the state for a term of twelve months and in the corporate limits of said town for ninety days, in addition to the same qualifications as are required by the laws of the state of North Carolina governing state and county elections, shall be deemed as duly qualified electors in such election.

Date of regular election.

How conducted.

Sec. 6. That after any election, upon the qualification of the newly-elected officers so elected, the preceding officers of the town of Sylva, without delay, shall turn over to their successors all corporate moneys, bonds, titles, contracts, papers, books, minutes, dockets and any and all properties whatsoever, both real and personal, and thereupon their duties shall cease and determine; and all officers, agents, servants and employees whatsoever of said commissioners shall, immediately upon the qualification of the mayor and aldermen and marshal, provided for in this act, report to and be subject to the authority of said mayor and aldermen.

Preceding officers shall turn certain moneys, etc., over to successors.

Sec. 7. That the commissioners of the town of Sylva shall have and exercise all corporate powers and duties as are conferred and demanded of like commissioners of incorporated cities and towns under the law, and in addition thereto they shall have power to pass ordinances, by-laws, rules and regulations for the government of said town of Sylva, not inconsistent with the laws of the state and the United States, and to impose and collect fines and penalties for the violation of town ordinances or common law offenses, not inconsistent with the constitution and laws of the state.

Powers of commissioners.

Fines.

Sec. 8. That the mayor shall issue his precepts to the marshal or chief of police of the town of Sylva, and said marshal or chief of police may execute the same anywhere in the county of Jackson; and the mayor may in the absence of the marshal or chief of police, or in case of a vacancy of said office, issue his precepts to any voter or male citizen of the town of Sylva by deputing said person as marshal pro tem., or to any such officers to whom

Power of mayor to issue precepts.

a justice of the peace may issue his precepts, who shall execute same as is provided by law in reference to justices of the peace.

Jurisdiction of mayor's court.

Sec. 9. That all proceedings in the mayor's court for the town of Sylva, shall be the same as are now, or may hereafter be prescribed for courts of justices of the peace, and in all such cases there shall be a right of appeal to the superior court of Jackson county. That whenever a defendant, witness, or other person, shall be adjudged as in contempt, the same procedures may be had as are prescribed by law governing trials in justices of the peace courts; and in case such person or persons shall be adjudged to be imprisoned by said mayor's court, to sentence such persons to imprisonment in the county jail or town prison for a term not exceeding thirty days, and to adjudge also that such person or persons work during the period of their confinement on the public streets or works of the town of Sylva, and that a commitment directed to the sheriff or jailor of Jackson county and signed by the mayor of said town directing said sheriff or jailor to receive such prisoner or prisoners he shall incarcerate according to law, as in cases provided in justice of the peace courts.

Persons guilty of contempt.

Penalty.

May be sent to public roads.

Mayor shall keep record of precepts issued.

Sec. 10. That the mayor shall keep a truthful minute of the precepts issued by him, and the disposition of same, in a book furnished by the commissioners of said town and known as the Mayor's Docket, said book to be paid for out of the town funds not otherwise appropriated; that the judgments issued by the mayor of said town shall have all the force, virtue and validity of judgments rendered by a justice of the peace, and may be executed and enforced against any defendant or defendants within the county of Jackson or elsewhere, in the same manner and by the same means as if the same had been rendered by a justice of the peace for the county of Jackson.

Effect of judgment.

Compensation of mayor.

Sec. 11. That the mayor of said town shall be entitled to receive such fees as by law are allowed justices of the peace for similar or like service; and that the marshal, policeman, or other officer deputed by the mayor, shall be entitled to receive such fees as by law are allowed sheriffs for similar or like services.

Presiding officer at meeting of commissioners.

Sec. 12. That the mayor shall preside at all the meetings of the commissioners of said town when present, but shall not be entitled to vote on any proposition which may be considered by said commissioners except in case of a tie, when he may be allowed the casting vote. In case of the absence of the mayor at any meeting of the said commissioners they shall choose from their number a temporary presiding officer, and in case of the absence or other inability of the mayor to execute the duties of his office, the commissioners of said town shall appoint one of their number to act as mayor whenever said mayor is absent;

such appointments shall be recorded by the secretary of said town in the minutes of the meetings of the commissioners, and such mayor pro tem. and such acting mayor during the absence of the mayor of said town, before assuming the duties of such office shall take the oath prescribed for the mayor of said town, and such official acts of said acting mayor shall be valid and shall be entitled to full credence as prescribed by law relating to mayor pro tem. governing cities and towns.

Oath administered to mayor.

Sec. 13. That the mayor, on Thursday after his election, and before entering upon the duties of his office, shall take and subscribe to, before some justice of the peace, or other person authorized by law to administer oaths, the following oath, to-wit:

Form of oath.

"I . . . . do solemnly swear that I will diligently endeavor to perform faithfully, truthfully and impartially, according to my best skill and ability, all the duties of the office of mayor of the town of Sylva while I continue therein; that I will cause to be executed as far as in my power lies, all the laws, ordinances and regulations enacted for the government of the town of Sylva; and in the discharge of my duties I will strive to do equal justice in all cases whatsoever. So help me God." And a copy of this said oath shall be placed on the minutes of the commissioners of said town by the secretary, which shall be signed by said mayor on said minute book and attested by the officer administering the same.

Fines, how applied.

Sec. 14. That all fines collected for violation of any town ordinance, or in anywise collected as benefits, privileges and forfeitures, shall be paid into the town treasury for the benefit of said town, and may be expended as the commissioners of the town of Sylva shall direct.

Persons failing to pay fines may be put at labor.

Sec. 15. That the board of commissioners have authority to put to and keep at work upon the street or public grounds or public property whatsoever of the town of Sylva any person or persons who may fail to pay any fine, cost, penalty or forfeiture which may have been imposed on such person or persons by the mayor of the town of Sylva; and the said commissioners of said town shall have authority by the ordinances and by-laws of said town to provide a town hall, known as the mayor's and commissioners' office, for the use of the mayor in his official capacity and for assembling of the commissioners of said town, at their regular meeting, or for the transaction of any business pertaining to their official duties, also a safe place for the confinement of any person or persons for failure to pay fines, costs, penalties or forfeitures, and during such time may manage, work, hire out any such ones until fully paid and satisfied, under such rates for labor, board and guarding as the said town commissioners may establish.

Town hall may be built.

Commissioners and marshal when to qualify.

Sec. 16. That on Thursday succeeding the day of election, the commissioners and marshal elected thereat shall qualify as such by taking the oath of office before a justice of the peace, or some other officer authorized by law to administer oaths as prescribed for commissioners and marshals of incorporated towns according to section three thousand seven hundred and ninety-nine, chapter sixty-two, volume two of The Code of North Carolina, and when so organized shall constitute a body corporate, under the name and style of the "Board of Commissioners of the town of Sylva," and shall succeed to all moneys, books, papers, titles, all manner of property whatsoever heretofore belonging to the town of Sylva, and have all the rights and powers of a corporate body as prescribed by law; may have a corporate seal, sue and be sued in its corporate capacity.

Taxes levied.

Sec. 17. That in order to raise funds for the expenses incident to the proper government of said town, the board of commissioners of said town shall by this act be empowered to levy and collect taxes on the following persons and subjects of taxation situate, being and lying within the corporate limits of said town, payable in the existing national currency, and shall be assessed and collected under the rules and regulations prescribed by law, viz.:

Poll tax.

Exempted from poll tax.

First—That on each poll or male person residing within the corporate limits of said town between the ages of twenty-one and fifty years, except those poor and infirm persons whom the board of commissioners of said town may exempt, there shall be levied and collected annually a tax not exceeding one dollar and fifty cents, the collection of which may be enforced in the same manner by the tax collector of said town as is provided for the collection of poll tax for state and county purposes by existing law.

Ad valorem tax.

Second—On all real estate and personal property, money on hand, solvent credits, investments in bonds, stocks, joint stock company, copartnerships or otherwise situated and being within the corporate limits of said town, there may be levied and collected annually an ad valorem tax not to exceed fifty cents on every one hundred dollars valuation thereof, this to be levied and collected as prescribed by law in relation to county and state taxes.

License taxes.

Liquor license.

Third—A special license or privilege tax on all professions and trades, on all persons exhibiting or offering to exhibit any show, magic lantern, sleight-of-hand, or slot machine or lottery of any kind not mentioned; on all persons who shall buy and sell spirituous, vinous or malt liquors, on merchants, jewelers, grocers, druggists, livery-men, hotels, boarding-houses, or other dealers who shall buy and sell goods, meats as peddlers, wares or merchandise of whatsoever name or description not specially taxed elsewhere in this act, may be levied and collected by the board of commissioners of said town in such manner as they may prescribe by ordinances and regulations for that purpose not in conflict with the laws of the state in relation to the same.

Sec. 18. That the assessment of poll and property for the purposes of taxation under the provisions of this charter shall be the same as that fixed by the assessors appointed by the board of commissioners of Jackson county to assess the poll and property of Sylva township for state and county purposes, and the commissioners of the town of Sylva shall place on the tax lists of said town the polls and property owned by the people of said town, in the limits thereof, or subject to taxation therein, at the sums assessed by the said county assessors for Sylva township as returned by them to the county authorities, and place said list with the treasurer or tax collector of said town between the first Monday of June or July, eighteen hundred and ninety-nine, and each year thereafter, and direct that said tax collector collect and pay over the same in manner and form as regulated by law the collection of state and county taxes. Assessors of Jackson county to fix tax rate

Sec. 19. That the mayor and commissioners of the town of Sylva shall be empowered to appoint registrars and judges for town elections in said town in accordance with the law governing state and county elections. Appointment of registrars and judges.

Sec. 20. The marshal of the town of Sylva shall be present at each regular meeting of said commissioners when possible, and shall notify each commissioner of said town of any called meeting by the mayor. It shall be the duty of said marshal at the town elections to perform all the duties, and be subject to the same penalties as are by law imposed upon sheriffs in relation to holding general elections under the law. The town marshal or any one deputed as special policeman of said town, shall have all the powers and authority vested in sheriffs and constables for the preservation of the peace of the town, by suppressing disturbances and apprehending offenders of the law; they shall execute all processes directed them by the mayor, or others, and in pursuance of such shall have the same powers which sheriffs and constables are by law given. Town marshal shall attend meetings. Power of marshal.

Sec. 21. That for any breach of his official bond by the secretary and treasurer, and marshal, tax collector, or any other officer who may, by town commissioners, be required by ordimance to give an official bond, such officer and his sureties shall be liable in an action on the same in the name of the town, at the suit of the town, or any person aggrieved by such breach; and the same may be put in suit without assignment from time to time until the whole amount of penalty be recovered. Breach of official duty.

Sec. 22. The commissioners of the town of Sylva shall have

Commissioners may grant certain privileges.

power to grant unto any corporation, copartnership, person or persons whatsoever the right to build or construct any railway, electric, horse or tramway line, or erect poles for electric, telephone or telegraph lines whatsoever upon the streets of the town of Sylva for the successful operation of the same, but nothing in this act shall be construed to grant special privileges to any such corporation, company, person or persons to the exclusive rights of others, under such time as to payment for such rights as they, the town commissioners, may contract.

Commissioners may condemn land

Sec. 23. That the commissioners of said town of Sylva shall have the power when any land or right of way either within the corporate limits of said town of Sylva, shall in the opinion of the commissioners of said town be required for the purpose or purposes of laying sewer-pipes and making manholes, extending present streets, or laying out of new streets in and for the benefit of said town, shall condemn such land with rights of way; and when the owners of such lands and rights of ways cannot agree with the commissioners of said town as to the damage or benefit to such land or rights of way by reason of such condemnation, the owners thereof shall select three disinterested male persons, and the town commissioners shall select three disinterested male persons from among citizens of said incorporated town of Sylva, whom together shall select an additional male person, who as a court of inquiry shall sit, hear evidence sworn to and decide as to the damages or benefits arising to said owners of such condemned land, who shall report their findings to the town commissioners who shall proceed to carry into effect such findings; that from the findings of such a court there shall be no appeal.

Assessors of damage

Commissioners may order an election to vote on bonds.

Sec. 24. That the commissioners may, when in their opinion it is for the good and material interest of the town of Sylva, order an election to be held for the purpose of submitting to the qualified voters of said town the question of an issue of Sylva municipal bonds, not exceeding in amount the sum of ten thousand dollars in any one year, bearing interest at the rate of six per cent. per annum, payable semi-annually, bonds to run for fifteen years; notice of said election to be caused to be posted at three public places in said corporate limits of said town, of which the question to be voted upon shall be "For Bonds," and this either printed or written upon a single ballot, and "Against Bonds" either printed or written upon a single ballot, notice to [be] given shall be thirty days prior to election. If in the election so ordered and held, the result of such an election shall be declared in favor of an issue of bonds as above specified, then the commissioners of said town of Sylva shall cause them to be printed and engraved, or gotten up in artistic appearance at the cost of the said town, and sold at not less than ninety per cent. of their face

Form of ballot.

value. The placing of said bonds upon the market when so ordered by an election as above set forth shall be determined by ordinance of town commissioners at some subsequent meeting of commissioners after election. The denominations shall be in fifty dollars, one, two and five hundred denominations. Disposition of bonds. Denomination of bonds.

Sec. 25. That the mayor of the town of Sylva may issue process without complaint when he is satisfied there has been a violation of law, or any town ordinance, and his endorsement of the names of witnesses upon a summons or warrant shall be authority for the marshal or any other like officer to execute the same. Mayor may issue process without complaint.

Sec. 26. That at the regular meeting in June, eighteen hundred and ninety-nine, and annually thereafter the commissioners of the town of Sylva shall elect a tax collector for said town, who shall be required to give a justified collectible bond in double the amount of the taxes assessed and discoveries to be collected for such year, who shall hold his office for one year, and until his successor is elected and qualified; but the commissioners of said town shall have the power to remove him from office for inefficiency or misconduct in office and elect his successor to fill his unexpired term. Such tax collector shall have the exercise of the powers as by law are given to tax collectors for state and county purposes. Election of tax collector. Duties of tax collector.

Sec. 27. That this act shall be in force from and after its ratification, and all other acts in conflict or otherwise are hereby repealed.

Ratified the 16th day of February, A. D. 1899.

CHAPTER 73.

An act for the relief of I. W. West of Mt. Airy, North Carolina.

Whereas, I. W. West of Mount Airy, North Carolina, has been in the pharmaceutical business for more than ten years, and during that period has had constant practical experience in the preparation of physicians' prescriptions, in compounding and vending medicines and poisons; Preamble.

And whereas, by reason of his ignorance of the passage of the act, chapter one hundred and eighty-two, laws of eighteen hundred and ninety-seven, he omitted to apply to the state board of pharmacy for license, on account of said practical experience, within the ninety days mentioned in section three thousand one hundred and thirty-nine of The Code. Preamble.

The General Assembly of North Carolina do enact:

I W. West authorized to apply to secretary of state board of pharmacy for license.

Section 1. That the said I. W. West be and he is hereby authorized to apply to the secretary of the state board of pharmacy, on payment of the fee therefor, for license to conduct a pharmacy to prepare physicians' prescriptions and to compound and vend medicines and poisons as permitted by law on account of his aforesaid practical experience in said business: Provided, that such application be made within ninety days after the ratification of this act.

Sec. 2. This act shall be in force from and after its ratification.

Ratified the 17th day of February, A. D. 1899.

CHAPTER 74.

An act to incorporate the town of Hoffman.

The General Assembly of North Carolina do enact:

Incorporated. Corporate name.

SECTION 1. That the town of Hoffman, in Richmond county, be and the same is hereby incorporated under the name and style of Hoffman, and as such shall be subject to all the provisions contained in chapter sixty-two, volume two, of The Code in relation to incorporated towns.

Corporate boundaries.

SEC. 2. The corporate boundaries of said town shall be as follows, viz: Beginning at a point on the Raleigh and Augusta Air Line Railroad, two hundred (200) yards north fifty-six east of the eighty-three mile post and running north thirty-four west four hundred and forty yards to a stake; thence north fifty-six east one thousand nine hundred yards to a stake; thence south thirty-four east one thousand one hundred and forty yards to a stake; thence south fifty-six west one thousand nine hundred yards to a stake; thence north thirty-four west seven hundred yards to the beginning.

Officers, how elected.

SEC. 3. That the officers of said town shall consist of a mayor and five commissioners, a constable and such other officers as said board of commissioners may elect, and that until the next election John W. Butler shall be mayor and William Godfrey, A. H. McDonald, D. T. Blue, E. C. Whitaker and A. H. Page shall be commissioners of said town.

Temporary officers.

Corporate powers.

SEC. 4. That said board of commissioners shall have all the powers as enumerated in the said chapter of The Code, and may issue license for the sale of liquor and charge and collect reasonable license taxes therefor.

SEC. 5. That this act shall be in force from and after its ratification.

Ratified the 23d day of February, A. D. 1899.

CHAPTER 75.

An act to incorporate The North State Electrical Power Company, and for other purposes.

The General Assembly of North Carolina do enact:

SECTION 1. That D. A. Lowe, M. Foster, W. B. Ellis and W. C. Atwell and their associates be and they are hereby created a body corporate under the name of "The North State Electrical Power Company," for the purposes hereinafter described, and by that name and style shall for a term of sixty years have succession and power to sue and be sued, to plead and be impleaded, defend and be defended in all courts, whether in law or in equity, and may make and have a common seal and alter and renew the same at pleasure; and shall have, possess and enjoy all rights and privileges of a corporation or body politic in the law and necessary for the purpose of this act. Corporators. Body corporate. Corporate name. Corporate powers.

SEC. 2. That the said company is authorized and empowered to supply to the public, including both individuals and corporations within the state of North Carolina and elsewhere, power in the forms of electric current and hydraulic, pneumatic and steam pressure, or any of the said forms, and in any or all other forms for use in driving machinery, and for light, heat and all other uses to which the power so applied can be made applicable, and to fix charges, collect and receive payment therefor; and for the purpose of enabling the company to supply power as aforesaid, the company is authorized and empowered to buy or otherwise acquire, generate, develop, store, use, transmit and distribute power of all kinds, and to locate, acquire, construct, equip, maintain and operate from any place in the state where the said company may establish plants to any distributing points in the state where they may elect, and from the same to any other points by the most practicable routes, to be determined by the board of directors of the company, lines for the transmission of power by wire on poles or under ground, and by cables, pipes, tubes, conduits and all other convenient appliances for power transmission, with such connecting lines between the lines above mentioned, and also with such branch lines as a majority of the stockholders of the company may locate or authorize to be located, for receiving, transmitting and distributing power; and as appurtenances to the said lines of power transmission and their branches the company may acquire, own, hold, sell or otherwise dispose of water-powers and water privileges in the state of North Carolina and elsewhere, and may locate, acquire, construct, equip, maintain and operate all necessary plants for generating and developing by water, steam or any other means, and for storing, using, Corporate powers. Corporate powers. Corporate powers.

transmitting, distributing, selling and delivering power, including dams, gates, bridges, tunnels, stations and other buildings, boilers, engines, machinery, switches, lamps, motors and all other works, structures and appliances in the state of North Carolina; also may build, own, control and operate electric railway lines, and may own, rent, lease or sell power for any other uses to which electricity, steam or water-power can be applied: *Provided*, that the amount of land which the company may at any time hold within the state of North Carolina for any one water-power and other works, except the land flowed or submerged with water accumulating at any one dam, shall not exceed ten thousand acres exclusive of right of-way: *And provided further*, that lines and appurtenances hereinbefore authorized for distributing power and light are to be constructed when on public streets or highways of any county, city or town under such reasonable regulations as the authorities respectively thereof shall upon application from the company prescribe.

Corporate powers.

Capital stock.

SEC. 3. The capital stock of the said company shall be not less than fifty thousand dollars, and may, with the consent of a majority of its stockholders, be increased from time to time to one million dollars or any additional amount by the issue and sale of shares of preferred or common stock or both upon such terms and conditions and under regulation as the board of directors, with the approval of the majority in interest of the stockholders of said company, shall prescribe, but the par value of every share of stock shall be one hundred dollars; and the directors, with like approval of the stockholders, may receive cash, labor, material, bonds, stock, contracts, real or personal property in payment of subscriptions to the capital stock, and under the directions of a majority of the corporators hereinbefore named, or such of them as shall be subscribers, may organize the said company by electing a board of directors and providing for the election or appointment of such other officers as may be necessary for the control and management of the business and affairs of said company, and thereupon they shall have and exercise all the powers and functions of a corporation under their charter and the laws of this state. Every subscriber to or holder of the stock of the said company shall be liable for the debts of the company to an amount equal to the amount unpaid on the stock subscribed for and held by him, and no more.

May be increased.

Division of stock.

Individual liability.

May borrow money.

SEC. 4. It shall be lawful for the said company to borrow money and issue and sell its bonds from time to time for such sums and on such terms as its board of directors may deem expedient and proper, for any of the purposes of the company, and may secure the payment of said bonds by mortgages or deeds of trust upon all or any portion of its property, real, personal or mixed; its contracts and privileges, and its charter rights and franchises, including its franchise to be a corporation, and it may, as the business of the company shall require, sell, lease, convey and encumber the same; and it shall be lawful for the said company to subscribe to and hold the stock and bonds of manufacturing or other corporations, and any manufacturing or other corporations may subscribe to and guarantee and hold the stock and bonds of said company.

May subscribe to and hold stock in other companies.

SEC. 5. The said company may connect or unite its lines for the transmission of power with those of any other company or companies, or consolidate and merge its stock, property and franchises with and into those of any other company or companies incorporated under the laws of this state or any other states of the United States, operating or authorized to operate lines for the transmission of electric or other power, upon such terms and under such name as may be agreed upon between the companies so uniting or collecting, merging or consolidating; and the said company may lease or sell any or all its property, real or personal or mixed, its contracts and privileges and its charter rights and franchises to any such other company upon such terms as may be agreed upon between them, and may in like manner acquire by lease or purchase any or all the property, real or personal or mixed, the contracts and privileges and the chartered rights and franchises of any such other company or companies, and full power and authority is hereby given to the said company or companies to make and carry out all such contracts as will facilitate and consummate such consolidation or merges and changes of name of such leases and sales.

May unite and consolidate with other companies.

Corporate powers.

Corporate powers.

SEC. 6. The board of directors shall, as soon as they deem it practicable, proceed to locate the works of said company, and may have one or more locations from time to time as they may deem expedient, and the construction of some of the said works shall be begun within five years after the ratification of this act.

Works of company, when located.

SEC. 7. That the principal office of said company shall be located at Charlotte, North Carolina, and such branch offices as may be desirable for the purposes of the corporation shall be established at such places as the by-laws of the corporation shall designate and prescribe. But by consent of the board of directors and a majority of the stockholders the principal office may be removed to any place within the state most expedient to the management of its works.

Principal office.

Principal office may be removed.

SEC. 8. It shall be lawful for the president and directors, their agents, superintendents, engineers or others in their employ to enter at all times upon lands or water for the purpose of exploring and surveying the works of said company and locating the same, doing no unnecessary damage to private property; and

Representatives of company may enter upon lands of others for necessary purposes.

when the location of said works in whole or in part shall have been determined upon and a survey of the same deposited in the office of the secretary of state, then it shall be lawful for the said company by the officers, agents, engineers, superintendents, contractors and others in its employ to enter upon, take possession of, hold, use and excavate any such lands and to erect all structures necessary and suitable for the completion or repairing as is hereinafter provided: *Provided always*, that payment or tender of payment of the value of all lands upon which the said works may be laid out are made before the said company shall enter upon or break ground upon the premises, except for surveying or locating said works, unless the consent of the owners thereof be first obtained.

Five commissioners may fix valuation of property.

SEC. 9. When any land or right-of way and trees within danger a ...... inuity to lines may be required by said company for the purpose of constructing its works or building its roads, and for want of agreement as to the value thereof or for any other cause the same can not be purchased from the owner, the same may be taken at a valuation to be fixed by five commissioners, or a majority of them, to be appointed by any superior court judge. In making the said valuation the said commissioners shall take into consideration the loss or damage which may occur to the owner or owners in consequence of the land being surrendered:

Proviso.

Provided, nevertheless, that if any person or persons on whose lands the said works may be located, or if said company shall be dissatisfied with the valuation of said commissioners, then and in that case the party so dissatisfied may have an appeal to the

Either party may appeal.

superior court in the county wherein the valuation has been made, or in either county in which the land may be when it shall be in more than one county, subject to the same rules, regulations and restrictions as in other cases on appeal. The proceedings of said commissioners, with a full description of the land, shall be returned under their hands and seals or a majority of them to the court from which the commission was issued, there to remain a matter of record, and the lands so valued shall vest in the said company as soon as the valuation shall have been

Proviso.

paid or tendered: *Provided*, that upon application for the appointment of a commissioner under this section it shall be made to appear to the satisfaction of the court that at least ten days' notice had been previously given of the application to the owner or owners of the land so purposed to be condemned, or if the owners be under disability or the guardians of such owners as are under disability can not be found within the county, or the owner or owners are not known, then that such notice of such application has been published once a week for at least four weeks in some newspaper printed in the vicinity of the court-house of the county in which the application is to be made: *And provided further*, that the valuation provided for in this section shall be made on oath by the commissioners aforesaid, which oath may be administered by any clerk of the court, justice of the peace or other person authorized by law to administer oaths: *And provided further*, that the rights of condemnation herein granted shall not authorize said company to remove or invade the yard or garden around the private dwelling, the burial grounds of any individual without his or her consent; and the lands aforesaid, for the purpose of this act, are hereby condemned for public purposes. Proviso.

SEC. 10. All land not heretofore granted to any person lying within the locations made by the company for its works shall vest in the said company as soon as the works are definitely laid out, through or upon it, and any grant of said land thereafter shall be void. Lands vested in the company.

SEC. 11. A part of the works of said company at any of its plants may be constructed without completing its entire works, and the said works may be operated and electric current may be transmitted and delivered and charges may be collected therefor, notwithstanding the entire work of the company have not been completed. Part of works may be completed and works operated.

SEC. 12. Every stockholder in the company shall at all meetings or elections be entitled to one vote for every share of stock registered in his name. The stockholders of the said company may enact such by-laws, rules and regulations for the management of the affairs of the company as they may deem proper and expedient. Meetings of the stockholders and directors may be held at such times and places as the stockholders may in the by-laws or otherwise prescribe. Representation of stockholders in meeting. Time of meeting.

SEC. 13. The board of directors shall be composed of stockholders of said company and shall consist of such members as the stockholders may prescribe from time to time by the by-laws, and shall be elected at the stockholders' annual meeting, to be held on such days as the by-laws of the company may direct, and shall continue in office for the term of one year from and after the date of their election and until their successors are elected and accept the duties of the office; and they shall choose from among their number a president, vice-president, secretary and treasurer, but one or more of said offices may be held by the same person. In case of death, resignation or incapacity of any member of the board of directors during his term of office the said board shall choose his successor for the unexpired term. Board of directors. When elected. Term of office. Officers elected by directors.

SEC. 14. This act shall be deemed and taken to be a public act, and a copy of any by-laws or regulations of the said company under its corporate seal, purporting to be signed by the presi- By-laws of company signed by president prima facie evidence.

dent shall be received as prima facie evidence for and against the said company in any judicial proceedings.

Persons injuring property of company guilty of a misdemeanor.

SEC. 15. That any person who shall willfully and maliciously deface, injure, destroy, remove or obstruct said works, or any fixtures, property or machinery thereof or its structures or appliances of any kind shall be guilty of a misdemeanor, and fined or imprisoned within the discretion of the court.

Persons shooting into or otherwise damaging property guilty of a misdemeanor.

SEC. 16. That any person or persons who shall willfully and maliciously cast throw, shoot, propel or project, or in anywise put in motion any stone, rock, shot, torpedo or other missile of any kind or nature at, against or into any of the property of said company shall be guilty of a misdemeanor, and shall be fined or imprisoned within the discretion of the court.

Employees vested with certain powers.

SEC. 17. That the conductors, drivers and other agents and servants of said company, while in the active service of said company or the discharge of any duty connected therewith are hereby vested with the same power, authority and privileges which belong to similar officers and agents of railroad companies in this state, and in addition to the general powers conferred upon such agents and officers they may eject and remove all drunken, profane and disorderly persons from any of the conveyances, cars or property of said company at any time, whether the fare of said drunken, disorderly or profane persons has been paid or not. and the said company shall not be liable or responsible in damages therefor, and such agent or officer shall not be liable, civilly or criminally therefor unless he uses greater force than is necessary to eject such person.

SEC. 18 This act shall take effect from and after its ratification, and all acts or parts of acts inconsistent herewith are hereby repealed.

SEC. 19. This act shall be in full force and effect from and after its ratification.

Ratified the 21st day of February, A. D. 1899.

CHAPTER 76.

An act to incorporate The Black Diamond Company.

Be it enacted by the General Assembly of the State of North Carolina, and the General Assembly of North Carolina do enact:

Corporators.

SECTION 1. That Albert E. Boone. William Kirkby, Kope Elias, John Bane. Samuel B. Dow, John B. Harrison, James L. Tribble, Judge S. Fowler and William F. Cox, and all other persons who shall become stockholders with them, and their successors and assigns, be and they are hereby created a body corporate, to be known and styled "The Black Diamond Company," and by that

Body corporate.

Corporate name.

name and style shall have perpetual succession, and all the privileges, franchises and immunities incident to a corporation; may sue and be sued, implead and be impleaded, complain and defend in all courts of law and equity of record or otherwise; may purchase, receive, hold and enjoy to them, their successors and assigns all such lands, tenements, leasehold estates and hereditaments, goods and chattels, securities and estates, real, personal and mixed, of what kind and quality soever, as may be deemed necessary to erect depots, engine houses, tracks, shops and other purposes of the said corporation as hereinafter defined in this act, and the same from time to time sell, convey, mortgage, encumber, charge, pledge, grant, lease, sub-lease, alien and dispose of, and also make and have a common seal and the same to alter and renew at pleasure, and ordain, establish and put in execution such by-laws or ordinances, rules and regulations as may be necessary or convenient for the government of the said corporation, not being contrary to the constitution and laws of this commonwealth, and generally may do all and singular the matters and things which to them shall appear necessary to do for the well-being of the said corporation and the management and ordering of the affairs and business of the same: *Provided*, that nothing herein contained shall be so construed as to give to the said corporation any banking privileges or franchises or the privilege of issuing their obligations as money.

Corporate powers.

Proviso.

SEC. 2. That the said corporation hereby created shall have power to contract with any person or persons, firm, corporations, or any other party however created, formed or organized or existing or that may hereafter exist in any way that said parties or any of them may have authority to do, to build, construct, maintain or manage any work or works, public or private, which may tend or be designed to improve, increase, facilitate or develop trade or the transportation and conveyance of freight, live stock, passengers and any other traffic, by land or water, from or to any part of the United States or the territories thereof; and the said corporation shall have power and authority to supply or furnish all needful material, labor, instruments, implements and fixtures of any and every kind whatsoever on such terms and conditions as may be agreed upon between the parties respectively; and also to purchase, erect, construct, maintain or conduct in its own name for its own benefit or otherwise any such work, public or private, as they may by law be authorized to do (including also herein lines for telegraphic communication), and to aid, cooperate and unite with any other company, person or firm in so doing

SEC. 3. The company hereby created shall also have the power to make purchases and sales of or investments in the bonds and securities of other companies, and to make advances of money of

May invest in stock of other companies.

credit to other companies, and to aid in like manner contractors and manufacturers, and to receive and hold on deposit or as collateral or otherwise any estate or property, real or personal, including the notes, obligations and accounts of individuals and companies, and the same to purchase, collect, adjust and settle and also to pledge, sell and dispose thereof on such terms as may be agreed upon between them and the parties contracting with them, and also to indorse and guarantee the payment of the bonds and the performance of the obligations of corporations, firms and individuals, and to assume, become responsible for, execute and carry out any contracts, leases or sub-leases made by any company to or with any other company or companies, individuals or firms whatsoever.

May condemn land.

Sec. 4. The company hereby created shall also have power and authority to enter upon and occupy the lands of individuals or of companies on making payment therefor or giving security according to law for the purpose of erecting, constructing, maintaining or managing any public work, such as is provided for,

Corporate powers.

mentioned and contemplated by this act, and to construct and erect such works thereon and also such buildings, improvements, structures, roads, tracks or fixtures as may be deemed necessary by said company or convenient for the uses and purposes of the said company under the powers herein granted; and may lay off and survey lands for its road and tracks not exceeding two hundred (200) feet in width, and for the purpose of cutting material for any embankments and for obtaining gravel or other material may take as much land as may be necessary for the purpose of constructing and operating said road, or to cut down any tree or trees that may be liable to fall on the tracks, or of obstructing the right-of-way or telegraph lines. To construct its road across, along or upon any stream of water, water-course, street, highway, canal, wherever the route of the road may intersect or touch; to cross, intersect or join or unite its road with any other railroad heretofore constructed or that may hereafter be constructed at any point on its route or line or upon the grounds of

Corporate powers.

any other railroad company with all necessary turn-outs, side-tracks and switches and other contrivances necessary in the construction and operation of its road, and may run over any part of any other railroad's rights-of-way necessary or proper to reach its freight or passenger depots in any city, town or village, or to reach any other point or points of its right-of-way otherwise inaccessible through or near which its road may run; and to purchase, make, use and maintain any works or improvements connected or intended to be connected with the works of the said company, and to merge or consolidate or unite with the said company, the improvements, property and franchise of any ther company or companies on such terms and conditions as the aid company may agree upon, and to fix and regulate the tolls r charges to be charged or demanded for any freights, property r passengers travelling or passing or to be transported over any nprovements erected, managed or owned by the said company r on any merchandise or property transported over any road hatever by the said company. and to make from time to time ividends from the profits made by said company. The several ailroads managed by said company shall continue taxable as ther like taxable property in this state in proportion to their ength within this state respectively, and the said "The Black Diamond Company" shall be taxable only on the proportion of ividends on its capital stock and upon net earnings or income, nly in proportion to the amount actually carried by it within his state, and all its earnings or income derived from its business eyond the limits of this state shall not be liable for taxation in his state.

Liability for taxation.

SEC. 5. The capital stock of said company shall consist of two housand shares of the value of fifty dollars each, being one undred thousand dollars ($100,000), and with the privilege of in- reasing the same by a vote of the holders of a majority of the tock present at any annual or special meeting to such an amount s they may from time to time deem needful, and the corporators, r a majority of them named in the first section of this act shall ave power to open books for subscription at such times and laces as they may deem expedient; and when not less than one undred shares shall have been subscribed and twenty per cen- um thereon shall have been paid in, the shareholders may elect ot less than three nor more than nine directors to serve until he next annual election or until their successors shall have been uly elected and qualified; and the directors so elected are au- horized and empowered to elect from their number a president, ice-president, secretary and treasurer, and the said officers and irectors so elected may and they are hereby authorized and mpowered to have and to exercise in the name and behalf of he said company all the rights, powers and privileges which are ntended to be given under this act, subject only to such liabili- ies as other shareholders are subject to, which liabilities are no nore than for the payment to the company the sums due on the hares held by said shareholders respectively; and should the apital stock at any time be increased the stockholders at the ime of such increase shall be entitled to a pro rata share of such ncrease upon the payment of the same as determined by the oard of directors, and said shareholder desiring his pro rata hare of such increase shall notify the board of directors within hirty days from the time said increase of the capital stock has

Capital stock.

Election of directors.

Election of officers.

Powers of officers and directors.

Individual liability.

Increase of capital stock.

credit to other companies, and to aid in like manner contract and manufacturers, and to receive and hold on deposit or as co lateral or otherwise any estate or property, real or personal, i cluding the notes, obligations and accounts of individuals a companies, and the same to purchase, collect, adjust and sett and also to pledge, sell and dispose thereof on such terms as m be agreed upon between them and the parties contracting wi them, and also to indorse and guarantee the payment of t bonds and the performance of the obligations of corporatio firms and individuals, and to assume, become responsible for, e ecute and carry out any contracts, leases or sub-leases made any company to or with any other company or companies, ind viduals or firms whatsoever.

May condemn land.

SEC 4. The company hereby created shall also have power a authority to enter upon and occupy the lands of individuals of companies on making payment therefor or giving security a cording to law for the purpose of erecting, constructing, mai taining or managing any public work, such as is provided fo

Corporate powers.

mentioned and contemplated by this act, and to construct a erect such works thereon and also such buildings, improvement structures, roads, tracks or fixtures as may be deemed necessa by said company or convenient for the uses and purposes of t said company under the powers herein granted; and may lay and survey lands for its road and tracks not exceeding two hu dred (200) feet in width, and for the purpose of cutting materi for any embankments and for obtaining gravel or other materi may take as much land as may be necessary for the purpose of co structing and operating said road, or to cut down any tree trees that may be liable to fall on the tracks, or of obstructi the right-of-way or telegraph lines. To construct its road acro along or upon any stream of water, water-course, street, hig way, canal, wherever the route of the road may intersect touch; to cross, intersect or join or unite its road with any oth railroad heretofore constructed or that may hereafter be co structed at any point on its route or line or upon the grounds

Corporate powers.

any other railroad company with all necessary turn-outs, sid tracks and switches and other contrivances necessary in the co struction and operation of its road, and may run over any part any other railroad's rights-of-way necessary or proper to reach i freight or passenger depots in any city, town or village, or reach any other point or points of its right-of-way otherwise i accessible through or near which its road may run; and to pu chase, make, use and maintain any works or improvements co nected or intended to be connected with the works of the sa company, and to merge or consolidate or unite with the sai company, the improvements, property and franchise of an other company or companies on such terms and conditions as the said company may agree upon, and to fix and regulate the tolls or charges to be charged or demanded for any freights, property or passengers travelling or passing or to be transported over any improvements erected, managed or owned by the said company or on any merchandise or property transported over any road whatever by the said company, and to make from time to time dividends from the profits made by said company. The several railroads managed by said company shall continue taxable as other like taxable property in this state in proportion to their length within this state respectively, and the said "The Black Diamond Company" shall be taxable only on the proportion of dividends on its capital stock and upon net earnings or income, only in proportion to the amount actually carried by it within this state, and all its earnings or income derived from its business beyond the limits of this state shall not be liable for taxation in this state.

Liability for taxation.

Capital stock.

SEC. 5. The capital stock of said company shall consist of two thousand shares of the value of fifty dollars each, being one hundred thousand dollars ($100,000), and with the privilege of increasing the same by a vote of the holders of a majority of the stock present at any annual or special meeting to such an amount as they may from time to time deem needful, and the corporators, or a majority of them named in the first section of this act shall have power to open books for subscription at such times and places as they may deem expedient; and when not less than one hundred shares shall have been subscribed and twenty per centum thereon shall have been paid in, the shareholders may elect not less than three nor more than nine directors to serve until the next annual election or until their successors shall have been duly elected and qualified; and the directors so elected are authorized and empowered to elect from their number a president, vice-president, secretary and treasurer, and the said officers and directors so elected may and they are hereby authorized and empowered to have and to exercise in the name and behalf of the said company all the rights, powers and privileges which are intended to be given under this act, subject only to such liabilities as other shareholders are subject to, which liabilities are no more than for the payment to the company the sums due on the shares held by said shareholders respectively; and should the capital stock at any time be increased the stockholders at the time of such increase shall be entitled to a pro rata share of such increase upon the payment of the same as determined by the board of directors, and said shareholder desiring his pro rata share of such increase shall notify the board of directors within thirty days from the time said increase of the capital stock has

Election of directors.

Election of officers.

Powers of officers and directors.

Individual liability.

Increase of capital stock.

been decided; and after that time the board is authorized to place said increased stock as may be deemed advisable for the best interest of said company. Whenever an increase of the capital stock is made a certificate thereof duly executed under the corporate seal of the company, signed by the president and attested by the secretary shall be filed with the secretary of state before the same shall be deemed valid.

Secretary of state shall be notified of increase of stock.

Preferred and common stock.

SEC. 6. That the capital stock of The Black Diamond Company when increased in the mode and manner prescribed herein may be in the whole common or in part preferred stock, as the said company may from time to time determine, and the said company are hereby authorized and empowered to issue said stock or any portion thereof in payment of any debt or liability incurred in the purchase of any property, or they may sell or dispose of any portion of said common or preferred stock on such terms and conditions as the company may agree upon with any party or parties, company or companies or in the doing of any other act authorized herein.

Company authorized to issue bonds.

SEC. 7. That The Black Diamond Company be and it is hereby authorized to create and issue bonds, bearing not to exceed five per centum gold interest to an amount not exceeding the full paid capital stock of said company as it may exist from time to time, and to secure the same by one or more mortgages upon the corporate rights and franchises and all or any part of the real and personal or other property of said company as may be described in said mortgage or mortgages: *Provided, however*, that no bond or mortgage shall be created without being first submitted to a meeting of the stockholders and approved by a majority of the capital stock.

Proviso.

Question of bonds must be first submitted to stockholders.

Principal office.

SEC. 8. The principal office of said company may be located wherever the board of directors may by resolution fix, and they may establish branch offices and agencies or agents in such parts of this state or elsewhere as they may deem advisable for the interest of said company, and all of the directors of said company shall be citizens of the United States and reside therein.

Annual election of directors.

SEC. 9. The directors shall be elected annually by the stockholders on the first Tuesday of April of each year, after the organization of said company hereunder, and from their number elect the officers hereinbefore designated and such other officers, agents and clerks as the business of the company may require; all elections for directors shall be by ballot and every stockholder shall be entitled to one vote for each share of stock held by him, but no person shall be eligible as director who is not a stockholder to the amount of ten shares; at the annual or special meetings a quorum shall consist of stockholders owning at least one-half of the capital stock.

SEC. 10. Ten days' notice shall be given by the secretary of the company by publication in such newspaper as the secretary may deem most likely to give the stockholders notice of the time and place of any meeting of the stockholders, or in lieu thereof he may mail to each stockholder a postal card giving notice of the time and place of said meeting, and all elections of directors and officers shall be conducted under such rules as the stockholders may adopt. Notice shall be given of meeting.

SEC. 11. The board of directors shall be charged with the duty of managing the affairs of the company and make all by-laws and rules necessary for conducting the business of the company, which by-laws and rules shall at all times be accessible to persons transacting business with said company; the said directors shall have power to remove any officer, clerk or agent elected or appointed by them and fill the vacancy caused by such removal or resignation should any officer or director resign as often as they shall deem it advisable for the best interest of said company, and shall have power to prescribe the duties of the several officers or agents elected or appointed by them, and should it be deemed advisable at any time to change the name of said corporation, the board of directors shall have power to do so by a vote of a majority of said directors, in which event the secretary shall notify the secretary of state, and all persons holding shares in said company upon surrendering same shall be entitled to a like number of shares and amount in the company under the new name, and upon the filing of the certificate with the secretary of state the company under the changed name shall succeed to all the rights, powers and privileges of the company named in the act. Directors shall make by-laws. Directors may remove officers Vacancies.

SEC. 12. That this act shall take effect from its ratification.

Ratified the 21st day of February, A. D. 1899.

CHAPTER 77.

An act to incorporate "The Ohio River, Franklin and Tide Water Railway Company," to confer certain powers and privileges, and for other purposes.

Be it enacted by the General Assembly of the State of North Carolina, and the General Assembly of North Carolina do enact:

SECTION 1. That Kope Elias, E. Everett, D. Dehart, John T. Cunningham, N. L. Barnard, R. L. Porter, J. F. Ray, F. S. Johnston, W. N. Allman, John T. Berry, John A. Hall, S. J. May, J. J. Smith, A. C. Brabson, A. P. Munday, D. W. Penland and John Gray, of Macon and Swain counties, North Carolina, and J L. Tribble, P. K. McCully, J. S. Fowler, W. F. Cox, J. E Corporators.

Breazeale, R. S. Ligon, R. C. Strother, J. D. Maxwell and R. T. Jaynes, of Anderson, South Carolina, and all other persons who shall be stockholders and their successors and assigns be and they hereby are created a body politic and corporate under the name of "The Ohio River, Franklin and Tide Water Railway Company," with power under said name to sue and be sued, plead and be impleaded in the courts of law and equity in this state; to have and use a corporate seal, and the same to alter and renew as often as said corporation may desire; to make such by-laws, rules and regulations for the government thereof as shall be deemed necessary, not inconsistent with the constitution and laws of this state, to buy, hold, use, sell and enjoy and convey all such real and personal property as may be necessary to and will advance the interests of said company, together with such other powers as are herein conferred, as well as those which by the laws of this state are conferred generally on railroad corporations.

Body corporate.

Corporate name.

Corporate powers.

Corporate power.

SEC. 2. That said company be and it is hereby authorized and empowered to survey, locate, build, construct, equip, maintain and operate a railroad in this state, connected with and being a continuation of a railroad leading from Knoxville, Tennessee, so as to run near or through Chilhowe Gap or near the line between North Carolina and the state of Tennessee and through Swain county and Macon county via Franklin, and from thence though Rabun Gap, Rabun county, Georgia, to connect with The Ohio River, Anderson and Tide Water Railway Company, with the privilege of building branch roads to such other points in this state as said company may deem advisable for its interest, the object and purpose of which is to carry freight and passengers.

Territory penetrated and roads with which connected.

SEC. 3. That for the purpose of constructing, maintaining and operating said lines of railroads said company is hereby empowered:

Necessary surveys, etc.

1st. To cause such examinations and surveys to be made as shall be necessary to the selection of the most advantageous route, and for such purpose is hereby empowered by its officers and agents, servants and employees to enter upon the lands and waters of any person for that purpose.

May hold voluntary grants of real estate.

2d. To take and hold such voluntary grants of real estate or other property as may be made to it to aid in the construction, maintenance and accommodation of its road, which shall be used for that purpose only.

May hold such real estate as is necessary.

3d. To purchase, hold and use all such real estate and other property as may be necessary for the construction and maintenance of its roads or stations, wharves, docks and terminal facilities and all other accommodations necessary to accomplish the objects of its incorporation, and to sell, lease or buy any land necessary for its use.

4th. To lay out its roads not exceeding two hundred feet in width and to construct the same: and for the purpose of cutting material for any embankment and for obtaining gravel or other material, may take as much land as may be necessary for the purpose of construction, operation and security of such road, or to cut down any trees that may be in danger of falling on the track or of obstructing the right of-way. Maximum width of road.

5th. To construct its road across, along or upon any stream of water, water-course, street, highway or canal which the route of the road shall intersect or touch. May construct road across streams.

6th. To cross, intersect or join or unite or consolidate its road with any other railroad heretofore or hereafter to be constructed on its route, or upon the ground of any other railroad company, with the necessary turn-outs, side tracks and switches and other contrivances necessary in the construction of its road, and may run over any part of any other railways' rights-of-way necessary or proper to reach its freight depot in any city, town or village, or to reach any other point of its right-of-way otherwise inaccessible, through or near which its road may run. May unite or consolidate with other roads.

7th. To take and convey persons and property over their road by use of steam or other mechanical power, and to secure compensation therefor, and to do all things incident to railroad business. May convey passengers.

8th. To erect and maintain convenient buildings, wharves, docks, stations, fixtures and machinery, whether within or without a city, town or village, for the accommodations and use of their passengers and freight business. May erect certain buildings.

9th. To regulate the terms and manner in which passengers and freight shall be transported, and the compensation to be paid therefor, subject to any laws of this state upon the subject. Transportation, manner and charges.

10th. To borrow such sum or sums of money at rates of interest not contrary to law, and upon such terms as said company or its board of directors shall authorize or agree upon and may be necessary or expedient, and may execute one or more trust deeds or mortgages or both if occasion may require on its road or branches or both in process of construction by said company for the amount or amounts borrowed or owing by said company as its board of directors shall deem expedient; said company may make deed or mortgage for transferring their railroad track or tracks, depots, grounds, rights, privileges, franchises, immunities, machine houses, rolling stock, furniture, tools, implements, appendages and appurtenances used in construction with its road in any manner then belonging to said company or which shall hereafter belong to it as security for any bonds, debts or May borrow money. Corporate powers.

sums of money as may be secured by said trust deeds or mortgages as they shall think proper.

When road may condemn land.

SEC. 4. In the event said company does not procure from the owner or owners thereof a contract, lease or purchase the title to the land or right-of-way or other property necessary or proper for the construction or constructions of said road and its branches and extensions, or its depots, wharves docks, and its other necessary terminal facilities necessary or proper for it to reach its freight or passenger depot in any city, town or village in this state, or for the purpose of reaching some other inaccessible point of its right-of-way as hereinbefore provided it shall be lawful for such corporation to construct its railroad or branches over any lands belonging to other persons, or own such rights-of-way or tracts of railroads as aforesaid, upon paying or tendering the owner or owners of, or to his or her or its legally authorized representative, just and reasonable compensation, [which,] when not agreed upon otherwise, shall be assessed and determined in the following manner, to-wit: And said company shall have all the rights and privileges for the condemnation of lands for the rights-of-way and other purposes as are conferred by the general laws of this state relating to railroad corporations: *Provided*, that not more than one hundred feet of land on each side of the center of the road shall be condemned for right-of-way, and only necessary lands for station houses, depots, etc., shall be condemned.

When disagreement as to price.

Capital stock.

SEC. 5. That the capital stock of said company shall be one million dollars, divided into two hundred thousand shares of the face value of five dollars each, with the right to increase the same from time to time to any amount required for the purpose aforesaid by a two-third vote of the stockholders at an annual meeting or at a meeting called by the directors for that purpose, not exceeding three million five hundred thousand dollars, divided into seven hundred thousand shares of five dollars each; notice must be served on them in person or by mail post-paid, directed to them at the post-office nearest their place of business, twenty days prior to said meeting; that said company may organize when ten thousand dollars of said stock shall be subscribed and which may be paid in money or material or labor and services as hereinafter provided for.

May increase.

Notice must be served on directors previous to each meeting.

Number of directors.

SEC. 6. That the board of directors, which shall not consist of less than five or more than thirteen members, at the option of the corporation, are hereby authorized to open books of subscription at such time and place in or out of the state as they may deem proper, and subscription to the capital stock of said company may be made in the shape of a general contract or promissory note of such form as the directors may decide, and certificates of stock shall be issued on the basis of one share for every

Subscription to stock.

twenty-five dollars so paid. All such stock so subscribed shall be payable in such settlements as may be agreed upon or determined by the board of directors, and if any stockholder shall neglect or refuse to pay any installment when it becomes due, if required by the directors, such board may declare his stock forfeited as well as all previous payments thereon to the benefit and use of the company; but before declaring it forfeited said stockholder shall have served upon him a notice in writing, in person or by depositing said notice in the post-office post-paid, directed to him at the post-office nearest his place of abode, stating that he is required to make such payment within sixty days from date of said notice at such time and place as is therein named; said notice shall be served or mailed sixty days prior to the day on which such payment is required to be made: that all subscriptions may be paid in real estate or property or money or both, or labor or services as agreed upon by the subscriber, and the directors either before or after subscribing, and in case any kind of property is received as payment of subscription the directors shall have the right to sell, hold, lease or otherwise dispose of it to the best interest of the company; that said board of directors shall elect one of their number president, and may appoint such other officers, agents and employees as they may deem necessary and proper to carry on the business of said company. Said board of directors shall manage the affairs of the company for the first year and until others are elected and fill all vacancies that may occur between the annual elections, and that all future boards of this company shall be elected by the stockholders at their annual meeting, which time and place shall be determined by the by-laws of the company. And in all meetings of the stockholders each stockholder shall be entitled to as many votes as the shares owned by him or her. All elections shall be by ballot cast in person or by proxy duly given in writing. The directors shall have power to adopt a corporate seal make by-laws and regulations and declare dividends, but the stockholders shall have power to regulate and limit the powers of the board and modify and change the by-laws.

When stock is forfeited.

When notice shall be served.

Election of officers.

Duties of directors.

Representation of stockholders.

SEC. 7. That the stock in said company shall only be transferred on the books of the company under regulations to be prescribed by the by-laws.

Stock transferable.

SEC. 8. That the stockholders in said railroad company shall in their private capacity be bound to any creditor of the company for the amount of stock subscribed for by him or her, until such subscription is fully paid up or to an amount equal to his unpaid subscription and not otherwise.

Individual liability.

SEC. 9. That the principal office of said road shall be in Franklin, Macon county, North Carolina.

Principal office.

Sec. 10. That this act of incorporation shall be in force from and after its ratification.

Ratified the 21st day of February, A. D 1899.

CHAPTER 78.

An act to re-enact and amend chapter one hundred and seventy-two of the laws of eighteen hundred and ninety-three, and to extend the time for the organization of the said corporation authorized thereby.

The General Assembly of North Carolina do enact:

Chapter 172, private laws of 1893, re-enacted. Authorized incorporation of High Point Loan and Trust Company.

Section 1. That chapter one hundred and seventy-two of the private laws of eighteen hundred and ninety-three, which authorized the incorporation of the High Point Loan and Trust Company, be and is hereby re-enacted.

Time granted for incorporation.

Sec. 2. That three years from the date hereof shall be allowed to the incorporation for the purposes of organization.

Sections 2 and 18 amended.

Sec. 3. That section two and section eighteen of the said chapter be amended [so] as to read as follows: "Ten thousand" instead of "fifty thousand."

Sec. 4. That this act shall be in force from and after its ratification.

Ratified the 22d day of February, A. D. 1899.

CHAPTER 79.

An act to amend and re-enact section one of an act entitled "An act to amend an act to provide for the enlargement, increase of depth and completion of the Albemarle and Chesapeake canal, ratified the second day of February, eighteen hundred and fifty-seven, and to repeal certain statutes," ratified the thirty-first day of March, eighteen hundred and seventy-one.

The General Assembly of North Carolina do enact:

Section 1 of an act ratified February 2, 1857, and an act to repeal certain statutes ratified March 31st, 1871, amended.

Section 1. That section one of an act entitled "An act to provide for the enlargement, increase of depth and completion of the Albemarle and Chesapeake canal, ratified the second day of February, eighteen hundred and fifty-seven, and to repeal certain statutes," ratified the thirty-first day of March, Anno Domini eighteen hundred and seventy-one, be amended by striking out after the words "the general assembly of North Carolina do enact" the following words, to-wit: "That provided a majority of the directors shall be resident citizens of North Carolina," and by striking out in the last line thereof the words, "several sec-

Proviso.

tions" and inserting in lieu thereof the words "said sections," so that the said section as thus amended shall read:

"Sec. 1. The General Assembly of North Carolina do enact:

"That the second section of chapter forty-six of the private laws of North Carolina, ratified on the second day of February, Anno Domini eighteen hundred and fifty-seven, entitled an act to provide for the enlargement, increase of depth and completion of the Albemarle and Chesapeake canal be and the said section is hereby repealed." Section 2, chapter 46, private laws of 1857, amended.

SEC. 2. That all other sections of the charter of the Albemarle and Chesapeake Canal Company or any amendments thereto not repealed by this act or otherwise than under said second section of chapter forty-six above mentioned are hereby continued in force. Sections not repealed by this act in force.

SEC 3. That this act shall be in force from and after its ratification.

Ratified the 22d day of February, A. D. 1899.

CHAPTER 80.

An act supplemental to an act to unite the Richmond, Petersburg and Carolina Railroad Company, ratified January thirty-first, eighteen hundred and ninety-nine.

The General Assembly of North Carolina do enact:

SECTION 1. That the preamble of said act be amended by inserting in the blanks twenty-seventh day of April, eighteen hundred and ninety-two. Preamble of act uniting the Richmond, Petersburg and Carolina Railroad Company ratified January 31st, 1899, amended.

SEC. 2. That section two be amended by inserting after the word "company" where it first occurs in said section the words, "a corporation incorporated under the laws of the state of Virginia be and they are hereby constituted stockholders of the Richmond, Petersburg and Carolina Railroad Company." Section 2 amended.

SEC. 3. That this act shall be in force from and after its ratification.

Ratified the 22d day of February, A. D. 1899.

CHAPTER 81.

An act to incorporate the Pee Dee News Transit Company.

The General Assembly of North Carolina do enact:

SECTION 1. That William A. Smith, Joseph I. Dunlap, J. T. Bundy and W. H. Wilhoit, together with such persons as may be associated with them, their successors and assigns, be and they are hereby created a body politic and corporate for sixty years Corporators. Body politic.

Corporate name. Corporate powers. under the corporate name of the Pee Dee News Transit Company, and by that name may sue and be sued, plead and be impleaded, appear, prosecute and defend in any court of law or equity whatsoever in all suits and actions, may contract and be contracted with, may have and use a common seal and alter the same at pleasure, and in addition to the powers given by this act shall have and enjoy all the rights, privileges and immunities, liberties and franchises pertaining to corporations created under the general laws of the state.

Corporate powers. SEC. 2. That said corporation may erect, construct, own and operate telephones and telephone lines in any county in this state, receive and transmit news and messages and charge and receive pay for the same, take, receive and acquire the real and Corporate powers. personal property, rights-of-way and franchises necessary to effectively carry on the business herein authorized; may condemn in the manner provided by law for telegraph companies, right-of-way, privileges and easements over lands of persons, corporations, municipalities and over and through streets of towns and cities and over public highways, and may acquire such by gift or purchase, and the proceedings and powers for such condemnation shall be such as are granted telegraph lines and companies by chapter forty-nine of The Code, section two thousand and seven to two thousand and thirteen, both inclusive, and such other sections as may be provided for like cases; said corporation Corporate powers. may erect its poles and lines along public highways so as not to obstruct and interfere with public travel, may establish its offices and news depots and agencies at such places and such intervals as will best promote an efficient news and message service, and may acquire all such property, real and personal, as may be necessary for the purposes of said corporation.

Capital stock. SEC. 3. The capital stock of said corporation shall be two thousand five hundred dollars, with the privilege of increasing the same to twenty-five thousand dollars. Books of subscription shall be opened for subscripton to the stock of said corporation, the shares of stock shall be twenty-five dollars each, when two thousand five hundred dollars of stock shall have been subscribed or ten per cent of the subscription therefor paid, said corporation When authorized to begin operations. shall be authorized to begin its operations and to exercise the powers and privileges herein granted.

Place of business. SEC. 4. The principal office or place of business shall be at Wadesboro, North Carolina, but the directors of said corporation may change the location of said principal office. Said corporation shall be governed by a board of directors not less than Directors, how elected. three in number and not exceeding eleven; said directors shall be elected by the stockholders and said directors may elect a Directors may elect president, secretary and treasurer. president and secretary and treasurer, and may elect one person to fill any one or more of said offices. Said corporation may make such by-laws rules and regulations for its government not inconsistent with the laws of the state, as may be deemed expedient. It may buy and lease telephone lines and acquire the rights, privileges and franchises of such, and may lease, sell or mortgage its own lines and property, together with all such as it may by any means acquire. Corporate powers.

SEC. 5. Said corporation shall be subject to such general laws as may be made governing like corporations in this state. Shall be subject to general laws governing corporations.

SEC. 6. Any person violating and willfully damaging or impairing the poles, wires, offices, instruments or other property of said corporation shall be guilty of a misdemeanor, and any person or corporation interfering with its wires poles, offices, news depots in any unlawful and willful manner shall be guilty of a misdemeanor, and any person or corporation unlawfully and willfully hindering or obstructing the work of construction and operation herein provided for shall be guilty of a misdemeanor. Interference with or damage to property a misdemeanor.

SEC. 7. That the stockholders of said corporation shall not be individually liable for the debts and obligations thereof. Liability of stockholders.

SEC. 8. That this act shall be in force from and after its ratification.

Ratified the 22d day of February, A. D. 1899.

CHAPTER 82.

An act to incorporate The City of New Bern.

The General Assembly of North Carolina do enact:

SECTION 1. That the inhabitants residing within the boundaries set out in second section hereof be and the same are hereby incorporated, and that the corporate name shall be "The City of New Bern." Incorporated. Corporate name.

SEC. 2. That the corporate limits of the said city shall be as follows: Beginning at the southwest corner of the church lot, number sixty-six in the plan of the former city of New Bern, where stands a cannon fixed in the ground, and running thence eastwardly with the north side of Pollock street and said street extended to the channel of Neuse river; thence northwardly with the channel of Neuse river to a point in said channel one hundred and fifty feet north of where the G. S. Atmore line intersects said channel; thence westwardly and parallel with the said Atmore line to the eastern line of the right-of-way of the Atlantic and North Carolina Railroad; thence westwardly with said line of said right-of-way to a point where the south side of Wil- Corporate limits.

liam street in Mechanicsville extended will intersect said line; thence southwardly with said William street extended and said William street to the extension of the western line of End street; thence southwardly with the western line of End street extended and End street to the channel of Lawson creek; thence eastwardly with the channel of Lawson creek to the channel of Trent river; thence eastwardly with the channel of Trent river to the channel of Neuse river; thence northwardly with the channel of Neuse river to the northern side of Pollock street extended.

Corporate limits.

Corporate power vested in a mayor and twelve aldermen.

SEC. 3. That the corporate power and authority hereby granted to The City of New Bern shall be vested in and exercised by a mayor and twelve aldermen; that no person shall be eligible as alderman unless he shall be eligible to be a member of the general assembly of this state and shall have resided in the city and ward from which he shall be chosen ninety days next preceding the day of election.

Eligible for aldermen.

Eligible for mayor.

SEC. 4. That no person shall be eligible as mayor unless he shall be a qualified voter for a member of the general assembly of this state, and shall have been a resident of The City of New Bern for twelve months immediately preceding his election, and no person who has been elected mayor for two full terms shall be eligible as his own immediate successor.

Division of wards.

SEC. 5. That The City of New Bern shall be divided into six wards, bounded and described as follows:

Boundaries of first ward.

First ward—Beginning at a point in Neuse river where Broad street extended will intersect the channel and running thence west with Broad street to Middle street; thence south with Middle street to the channel of Trent river; thence with the channel of Trent river to the intersection of said Trent river with Neuse river; thence with the channel of Neuse river to the beginning.

Boundaries of second ward.

Second ward—Beginning at a point in the channel of Neuse river where Broad street extended will intersect said channel, and running thence west with Broad street to Hancock street; thence north with Hancock street to Johnson street; thence west with Johnson street to Metcalf street; thence with Metcalf street to Queen street; thence eastwardly with Queen street to the track of the Atlantic and North Carolina Railroad Company; thence westwardly with said track to the switch which leads to the said company's freight depot on Neuse river to the channel of Neuse river; thence southwardly with the channel of said river to the beginning.

Boundaries of third ward.

Third ward—Beginning at a point in the channel of Trent river where Middle street extended will intersect said channel and running thence northwardly with said street extended and said street to Broad street; thence west with Broad to Hancock street; thence north with Hancock street to Johnson street; thence west with Johnson street to Metcalf street; thence south with Metcalf street to New street; thence west with New street to George street; thence south with George [street] to the channel of Trent river; thence east with the channel of Trent river to the beginning.

Fourth ward—Beginning at a point in the channel of Trent river where George street extended will intersect said channel and running thence northwardly with George street extended and George street to New street; thence west with New street to Bern street; thence southwardly with Bern street to Broad street; thence west with Broad street to Fleet street; thence southwardly with Fleet street to Pollock street; thence west with Pollock street to German street; thence southwardly with German street to the channel of Lawson's creek; thence eastwardly with the channel of Lawson's creek and the channel of Trent river to the beginning. **Boundaries of fourth ward.**

Fifth ward—Beginning at a point in the channel of Lawson's creek where German street extended will intersect said channel and running thence northwardly with German street to Pollock street; thence eastwardly with Pollock street to Fleet street; thence northwardly with Fleet street to Broad street; thence eastwardly with Broad street to Bern street; thence northwardly with Bern street to Queen street; thence westwardly with Queen street to West street; thence northwardly with West street and West street extended to the boundary of the city; thence westwardly with the boundary of the city to another of the boundary lines of said city; thence southwardly with said boundary line to a point where End street extended will intersect said boundary; thence southwardly with End street extended and End street to the channel of Lawson's creek; thence eastwardly with the channel of Lawson's creek to the beginning. **Boundaries of fifth ward.**

Sixth ward—Beginning at the intersection of West and Queen streets and running thence eastwardly with Queen street to Bern street; thence southwardly with Bern street to New street; thence eastwardly with New street to Metcalf street; thence northwardly with Metcalf street to Queen street, thence eastwardly with Queen street to Hancock street; thence eastwardly with the track of the Atlantic and North Carolina Railroad Company and the switch leading to said company's freight depot on Neuse river to the channel of Neuse river; thence northwardly with the city boundary to another of the boundaries of said city; thence westwardly with said boundary to right-of-way of the Atlantic and North Carolina Railroad, another of the said boundaries; thence westwardly with said right-of-way to a point where West street extended will intersect said right-of-way; **Boundaries of sixth ward.**

thence southwardly with West street extended and West street to the beginning.

Ward representation.

When aldermen shall qualify.

SEC. 6. That two aldermen shall be elected biennially on the first Tuesday in May for each of the six wards of the city by the qualified voters of said wards respectively, and within five days after their election they shall convene and qualify before a justice of the peace. The board of aldermen shall after convening and qualifying elect one of their number chairman, who shall preside until a mayor is elected and qualified, and in case of a tie shall give the casting vote. The board of aldermen or a majority of them shall elect at their meeting in May from outside their number a mayor, who shall within five days after his election and before entering on the duties of his office qualify before a justice of the peace.

Election of chairman of board of aldermen.

Election of mayor.

Vacancies occurring.

SEC 7. If any vacancy shall occur in the board of aldermen by reason of the failure of any alderman to qualify within the time prescribed or his failure to serve after qualifying, or for any cause, the board of aldermen who have qualified shall fill the vacancy by the election of some person qualified to serve as alderman. If the election of mayor shall have been prevented by a vacancy in the board of aldermen such election shall be had after the vacancy is filled.

Persons elected mayor and aldermen failing to qualify.

Penalty.

Proviso.

Proviso.

SEC. 8 Any person who has been elected an alderman or mayor who shall fail to qualify or who after qualifying shall fail to serve during the term for which he has been elected for any cause, inability from sickness and absence from the city excepted, shall forfeit and pay one hundred dollars, to be recovered in the name and for the benefit of The City of New Bern: *Provided*, that this section shall not apply to any person who has served in any such office within six years last preceding such election: *Provided further*, that any officer whose resignation after his qualification shall be accepted by the board of aldermen shall be exempt from the penalty herein imposed.

Persons entitled to vote.

SEC. 9. Every person shall be entitled to vote at all elections held under the provisions of this act who is qualified to vote for members of the general assembly of this state and who shall have resided in the ward in which he offers to vote for ninety days immediately preceding the day of election. The residence of a married man shall be in the ward in which his family resides, unless he be separated from them, in which case it shall be the ward of his residence, and that of a single man shall be in the ward in which he sleeps. Any person knowingly registering or voting in any other ward than that of his bona fide residence shall be guilty of a misdemeanor, and on conviction shall be fined five hundred dollars and imprisoned six months.

SEC. 10. The first election for aldermen under this act shall be held on the first Tuesday in May, eighteen hundred and ninety-nine (1899) and shall be called and notice thereof given by the board of aldermen appointed by the general assembly under the provisions of this act. The said board of aldermen shall order an entire new registration of voters, shall appoint one registrar and two poll holders in each ward, who shall be qualified voters in the ward in which they are appointed, and shall designate the polling places in each ward and provide boxes for the ballots.

First election under this act, when held.

New registration.

SEC. 11. The next or second election shall be held on the first Tuesday in May, nineteen hundred and one, and succeeding elections biennially thereafter on the first Tueday in May. These elections shall be ordered by the board of aldermen, and they shall appoint the registrars and poll holders and designate the polling places and provide ballot boxes as provided in section ten hereof.

Second election, when held.

SEC. 12. If any person appointed as registrar shall fail or refuse to discharge the duties of registrar, the other registrars shall fill the vacancy. If any person appointed as a poll holder shall fail or refuse to discharge the duties of poll holder, the registrar for the ward in which the vacancy shall occur shall appoint to fill the vacancy.

Vacancies among registrars.

SEC. 13. The registrars in their respective wards shall open their books for the purpose of registration at some convenient place in the ward and shall give ten days' notice of the time and place in some newspaper in said city prior to the commencement of such registration. The registration books shall be kept open from and including the second Monday preceding the first Tuesday in May, eighteen hundred and ninety-nine, to and including the following Saturday, and for each election thereafter on Thursday, Friday and Saturday preceding the election between the hours of eight a. m. and six o'clock p. m. of each day. After the first election held under this act, the registrars may transfer from the old registration books the names of such persons as they know are entitled to be transferred. The registrars and poll holders shall receive two dollars per day each for the time they are engaged in registering voters and holding the elections and hearing challenges.

Notice shall be given of registration.

When books shall be kept open for registration.

Compensation for registrars and poll holders.

SEC. 14. The registrars shall before registering any voter administer the following oath: "I do solemnly swear (or affirm) that I will support the constitution of the United States and of North Carolina; that I am twenty-one years of age and have lived in North Carolina for one year and in this ward ninety days prior to this election. So help me, God."

Oath administered to elector.

SEC. 15. The registrars before entering upon the discharge of their duties shall make oath before some person authorized by law to administer oaths that they will faithfully and impartially

Registrars shall make oath.

perform the duties of their office, and a certificate of the administering of said oath shall be made in the registration books by the party administering it, with the date of administration.

Challenges of electors.

SEC. 16. The registrars and poll holders shall meet at the polling places in their respective wards on the Monday preceding any election to hear and determine challenges. The party challenged must have been notified in writing of such challenge but such notice may be served by any person; no challenge shall be considered on the day of election.

When person is not allowed to vote.

SEC 17. Whenever it is decided that a person registered is not entitled to vote the registrars shall erase his name from the book, writing opposite his name the date and cause thereof. The registrar shall only be entitled to vote upon a challenge if the poll holders can not agree.

When polls shall be opened and closed.

SEC. 18. The registrars and poll holders shall meet at the polling places on the day of election, and after being duly sworn shall open the polls at seven o'clock a. m., receive the votes and deposit them in the ballot box. The polls shall be closed at seven o'clock p. m.

Poll holders and registrars shall count ballots.

SEC. 19. Immediately after the closing of the polls the poll holders and registrars shall proceed to count the votes cast in the presence of such voters as may choose to attend, and make three certificates thereof, one of which shall be delivered to the mayor of the city for the board of aldermen and one to each of the aldermen elect; said certificates shall state the number of votes cast for each candidate, the ward in which they were cast, the date of the election, and shall be signed by at least two of the poll holders or by one poll holder and the registrar. If no two candidates shall receive the highest number of votes by reason of a tie the registrar shall cast the deciding vote.

Certificate of votes.

Announcement of result, how made.

SEC. 20. The mayor and retiring board of aldermen shall meet at the city hall on Friday night after the election at eight o'clock, when they shall inspect the certificates and shall declare the two candidates receiving the highest number of votes in each ward duly elected.

Temporary aldermen.

SEC. 21. That S. B. Parker and Fernie Gaskill are hereby appointed aldermen for the first ward and C. E. Foy and Edward S. Gerock aldermen for the second ward; C. T. Watson and John W. Bowden aldermen for the third ward; W. S. Phillips and B. B Davenport aldermen for the fourth ward; Thomas F. McCarthy and J. A. McKay aldermen for the fifth ward, and W. H. Bishop and R. J. Disosway aldermen for the sixth ward. That said aldermen shall qualify within ten days after the ratification of this act and shall hold their offices until their successors are elected and qualified under the first election to be held hereunder in May, eighteen hundred and ninety-nine. That said alder-

When temporary aldermen shall qualify.

men shall at their first meeting proceed to fill all the offices of said city provided for in this act in the manner herein provided, which officers shall hold their respective offices until their successors are elected and qualified under the election to be held in May, eighteen hundred and ninety-nine.

SEC. 22. That no person who shall have been elected and who shall qualify as aldermen shall be eligible to any office to be filled by the board of which he has been elected a member. No aldermen shall be elected to office to be filled by board of which he is a member

SEC. 23. It shall be the duty of the mayor to have a general supervision over the streets, public water supply, city lights, security, health and cleanliness of the city, the enforcement of all the ordinances thereof, and to keep a faithful minute of all precepts issued by him and of his judicial proceedings, and report in writing at each regular meeting of the board of aldermen the total amount of costs and fines which have been imposed by him in all judicial proceedings during the previous month, stating the general situation and condition of the city, particularly the condition of its streets, public water system and lights, and shall recommend to the board the adoption of such measures as will promote the interest of said city and its inhabitants. The mayor shall preside at all meetings of the board of aldermen, but shall have no vote except in case of tie. Duties of mayor. Mayor shall report amount of costs and fines at each meeting.

SEC. 24. That the board of aldermen may from time to time elect a mayor pro tem, who shall act as mayor whenever the mayor shall be absent from the city or be prevented by sickness or any other cause from attending to the duties of his office, and who shall possess all the rights and powers of mayor during the continuance of such vacancy, absence or disability. Election of mayor pro tem.

SEC. 25. That the mayor shall have power to commit any person convicted of a violation of any city ordinance to the county or city prison until the fines and costs are paid, or require such person so imprisoned to work on the streets until the fines and costs and prison fee are paid, and such person can only be released as is provided in like cases in other courts. Powers of mayor to work persons on streets.

SEC. 26. That all costs, fees and fines imposed by the mayor in any process in connection with any breach of any city ordinance shall be collected by the chief of police and paid over to the treasurer for the use of the city. Costs, fines, etc., how collected.

SEC. 27. That the board of aldermen shall have power to make and provide for the execution thereof of such ordinances for the government of the city as it may deem necessary, not inconsistent with the laws of the land. It shall have power by all needful ordinances to secure order, health, quiet and safety within the same and for one mile beyond the city limits. It may require the abatement of all nuisances within the city at the expense of the person causing the same, or of the owner or tenant of the Aldermen shall have power to make necessary ordinances. Abatement of nuisances.

ground whereon the same shall be; and it is hereby especially vested with the power and authority to pass ordinances to prohibit the sale of spirituous, vinous or malt liquors on Sunday and enforce the same by fines or imprisonment or both, and otherwise enforce the due observance of the Lord's day; also to prohibit and close up houses of ill fame and punish the inmates thereof by fine or imprisonment or both; also to punish by fine or imprisonment or both any person or persons owning and renting or renting for others any houses to be used as bawdy houses by women of ill fame.

Sale of liquors, etc., on Sunday.

Houses of ill fame.

Measures against contagious or infectious diseases.

SEC. 28. That the board of aldermen may take such measures as it may deem effectual to prevent the entrance into the city of any contagious or infectious disease; may stop, detain and examine for that purpose every person coming from places believed to be infected with such disease; may establish and regulate hospitals within the city or within three miles thereof; may cause any person in the city suspected to be infected with such disease and whose stay may endanger health to be removed to the hospital; may remove from the city or destroy any furniture or other articles which shall be suspected of being tainted or infected with such diseases or which there shall be reasonable cause to apprehend may be the cause of any such disease.

Costs of removal to hospital, etc., may be recovered.

SEC. 29. That in case any person be removed to the hospital the corporation may recover before the mayor or any justice of the peace from such person the expense of his removal, support and medical attendance, and in case of his death of his legal representative the burial expense also, if the corporation incurs such expense.

May stop and examine trains, etc.

SEC. 30. That the board of aldermen may adopt such measures as it may deem effectual to stop, detain and examine within three miles of the city limits all railroad trains and other public conveyances bringing passengers or goods to said city, and that the compensation of the port physican for visiting said trains or other conveyances shall be paid by the owner or owners thereof: *Provided, however*, that the compensation shall not exceed two dollars for each visit and that this section shall not apply to vessels or steamers or subjects now governed by the general quarantine law.

Compensation for port physician.

Animals roaming at large.

SEC. 31. That the board of aldermen is empowered to make such rules and regulations as it may deem best for the sale of all animals found roaming at large in the street contrary to the ordinance of the said city but no estrays shall be sold without being first advertised for five days in some daily paper in said city or three public places in said city, all such sales to be made at the court-house door, and the mayor is hereby empowered to make title to the purchaser of all such estrays sold as aforesaid.

SEC. 32. That the board of aldermen is authorized to make such rules and regulations as it may deem proper for the erection, continuance or discontinuance of all sheds, awnings and signs over sidewalks, and all platforms and bridges on or over sidewalks or ditches of the city. Regulation of sheds, awnings, etc.

SEC. 33. All ordinances passed by the board of aldermen shall be entered in the minutes of the meeting at which they are passed and recorded in a book to be kept for that purpose, which record shall state the number of the ordinance and the date of its passage. All ordinances shall be recorded.

SEC. 34. No ordinance shall take effect until it shall have been published in a daily paper in the city or posted at the city hall for five days. Ordinance shall be published before effective.

SEC. 35. That the board of aldermen shall appoint a chief of police, who shall be a qualified voter of the city, and who shall give a bond with approved sureties in a penal sum to be fixed by the board and payable to The City of New Bern, conditioned that he will diligently perform all duties imposed upon him by virtue of his office and faithfully pay the treasurer all sums of money collected or recovered by him for the use of the city. He shall hold his office for two years, subject to removal by the board of aldermen at any time for cause. Chief of police. Bond. Term of office.

SEC. 36. It shall be the duty of the chief of police to pay over to the city treasurer all money that may be collected by him for the use of the city at least once every week, and he shall communicate in writing to the board of aldermen at their regular monthly meeting a full statement of all costs, fines and fees collected by him and the disposition thereof. Duties of chief of police.

SEC. 37. It shall be the duty of the said chief of police and the policemen to preserve peace by the suppression of disturbances and the apprehension of offenders, and the chief of police or policemen shall have power to summon as many persons to assist in the performance of said duties as may be necessary. Duties of chief and policemen.

SEC. 38. That the board of aldermen may appoint a port physician, a city attorney, a sexton for each cemetery and six policemen. That the port physician, city attorney and the sexton shall hold their offices during the term of the board of aldermen appointing them. That the policemen shall hold their offices for three years, but may be removed by the board of aldermen at any time for cause. The board shall have authority on special occasions to appoint as many special policemen as it may deem necessary to preserve order in the city. Power of aldermen to appoint certain officers. Term of office.

SEC. 39. The mayor shall have power to suspend the chief of police or any policeman temporarily for misconduct by an order in writing, a copy of which shall be served on the suspended officer by any one whom the mayor shall direct. In all cases of Officers may be suspended.

suspension the mayor shall report his action in writing to the board of aldermen at their meeting next after such suspension, and in his report shall give the name of the suspended officer and the reason for his suspension. No officer who has been suspended by the mayor shall receive any compensation for the time of his suspension unless otherwise ordered by the board of aldermen. The board of aldermen may upon the hearing of such charges suspend such officer for a definite time without pay, discharge him altogether or reinstate him. The mayor or any member of the board of aldermen may prefer charges against any police officer for misconduct, incompetence or dereliction of duty. The charges shall be in writing, and a copy shall be served on such officer as the mayor or aldermen shall direct twelve hours before the time set for the trial, and the officer shall be notified in writing at the same time to appear before the board of aldermen at a time and place named to answer the charges, at which time and place the board of aldermen shall proceed to hear and determine such charges. If such officer shall be adjudged guilty by a majority of the board of aldermen he may be suspended for a definite time without pay or removed from his position, as a majority of the board of aldermen may decide. All votes upon charges against any police officer shall be by ballot.

Suspended officers shall not receive compensation.

Charges shall be preferred in writing.

Board of aldermen shall hear charges.

Voting by ballot.

Tax collector, how and for what time appointed.

Sec. 40. The board of aldermen shall appoint a tax collector for two years, who shall be a resident of the city and a freeholder, and who shall before entering upon the discharge of his duties give bond in the sum of five thousand dollars with sufficient sureties, to be approved by the board, and which shall be justified according to law, said bond to be payable to The City of New Bern, and conditioned for the due collection, payment and settlement of the taxes imposed by the board of aldermen. The board of aldermen may at any time, upon a notice in writing of twenty days, require said collector to give additional sureties upon his said bond, and if he fail after such notice to give additional security satisfactory to the board, the board of aldermen may declare his office vacant and elect his successor. The said tax collector shall take the tax list of said city and collect all taxes imposed by the board of aldermen of said city, and for said purpose said collector is hereby vested with the same power and authority to collect said taxes, as well those contained in the list of taxables as those due from delinquents, by distress or otherwise, as the sheriffs of the state have or may have, and it shall be sufficient notice of any sale of property for taxes to advertise the same in a newspaper published in The City of New Bern for four weeks. The said tax collector shall receive five per centum on the gross amount of collections made by him until his commissions, fees and emoluments shall amount to the sum of one

Collector may be required to give additional securities.

Duties and powers of tax collector.

Compensation for collector.

thousand dollars, and after his said commissions, fees and emoluments shall have amounted to said sum he shall account to the board of aldermen for all sums received by him by virtue of his said office from any source whatever. If said tax collector shall fail to collect and pay over all taxes within the year for which said taxes are levied, except insolvent as herein provided, he shall forfeit all compensation for collection, and it shall be lawful for the superior court of Craven county, on motion of the mayor and the board of aldermen, after ten days' notice in writing, to give judgment against said tax collector and his sureties, their executors and administrators, for all moneys with which said collector may be chargeable, except such as may be allowed by the mayor and board of aldermen as insolvent, and such as may be shown to be insolvent upon the hearing of said motion. That any tax collector who shall misapply any funds received by him shall be guilty of a misdemeanor. That the tax collector shall act as clerk of the board of aldermen without compensation.

Failure to turn over all collectible taxes.

Funds misapplied a misdemeanor.

SEC. 41. That the board of aldermen shall appoint from outside their number a treasurer, who shall be a resident of said city and who shall give bond in the sum of five thousand dollars, with two or more sureties, to be approved by the board of aldermen, payable to The City of New Bern, conditioned for the faithful discharge of his duties as treasurer. He shall publish monthly by posting in every ward of the city and at the court-house door an itemized statement of money received and disbursed by him, which statement shall be sworn to. He shall hold his office for two years.

Treasurer.

Treasurer's bond.

SEC. 42. The board of aldermen shall appoint from outside their number an auditing committee consisting of three, who shall be familiar with accounts, to whom the treasurer of the city, tax collector and all other officers into whose hands any money may go belonging to the city shall exhibit their books, accounts and moneys once every three months, and oftener if the board of aldermen shall deem it necessary. And it shall be the duty of the auditing committee to examine the books and accounts of such officers to see that the accounts are correctly and properly kept, and to count the money in the hands of any such officers and see that it corresponds with the amount shown by the books and accounts to be in such officer's hands; and if at any time there shall be a deficit in the amount of money in the hands of any such officer, the auditing committee shall so report to the board of aldermen, whose duty it shall be to institute proceedings in the superior court against such officer and his bond for violating his official duty. The auditing committee, upon the completion of each examination, shall prepare and post at the door of the city hall a statement showing the amount of

Auditing committee.

Duties of auditing committee.

Auditing committee shall report.

money collected and received by such officer, the amount turned over or disbursed by him and the amount, if any, in his hands, and the amount credited by the treasurer to the account of each of the different departments of the city, and the amounts paid out by him on account of each of said departments, and the amounts of any other money which may be paid out by said treasurer and the purpose for which the same may have been disbursed. The board of aldermen shall allow to each of the auditing committee who examines the books, accounts and moneys and prepares and posts reports as herein specified the sum of two dollars as full compensation for each examination.

Compensation for auditing committee.

Authority of chief of fire department.

SEC. 43. That the chief of the fire department of said city shall have authority to direct the pulling down, demolishing or blowing up of any house or building which he shall deem necessary to pull down, demolish or blow up for the purpose of preventing the spread of any fire which may occur in said city, and during the continuance of any fire he shall have free control of the territory contiguous to any fire, and any person failing to obey any command given by him for the purpose of extinguishing such fire, preventing its spread or protecting adjacent property, shall be guilty of a misdemeanor and fined five dollars.

Failure to obey order of chief of fire department in case of fires a misdemeanor.

Tax levy.

SEC. 44. The board of aldermen are authorized and empowered to levy an annual tax on the first Tuesday in July in each year upon all property subject to taxation in said city, and upon the polls, which said tax shall not exceed the sum of sixty cents on the one hundred dollars valuation of property and one dollar and eighty cents upon the poll, and at the time the taxes are so levied the board of aldermen shall divide the same money among various departments of the city government, apportioning to each such proportion thereof as in their judgment each department may need, or as the amount levied will permit; and it shall be the duty of the treasurer to open and keep a separate account with each department of the city government, to enter and credit therein all moneys appropriated to its use and to charge it with all moneys expended on its account. And there shall be a fund to be known as the general fund, a separate account for which shall be opened and kept by the treasurer, to which account may be credited all moneys received from license tax and from all other sources except the tax levied on property and polls and the money received from the sale of cemetery lots. And the board of aldermen may at any time appropriate any part of the general fund to the use of any of the various departments of the city. All moneys received from the sale of cemetery lots shall be credited to a fund to be known as the cemetery fund.

Treasurer shall keep separate accounts.

Cemetery fund.

License taxes.

SEC. 45. That the board of aldermen shall have power to levy and collect the following license tax for the privilege of carrying on the trade, profession, business or doing the acts named, and nothing in this schedule shall be construed to exempt or relieve any person from the payment of the ad valorem tax on property:

On all dealers in spirituous, vinous and malt liquors a tax not exceeding three hundred dollars per annum, and on all persons following any trade, profession, occupation or calling, and on all banks, bankers, express, telegraph and insurance companies a tax not exceeding fifty dollars per annum: *Provided*, that the total amount collected from any person or firm shall not exceed fifty dollars per annum.

Dealers in spirituous liquors.

Banks, express, telegraph and insurance companies.

SEC. 46. That any person who shall [follow] any trade, profession or use any franchise taxed according to law by the board of aldermen without first obtaining a license for the same, shall be guilty of a misdemeanor, and on conviction fined not more than fifty dollars or imprisoned thirty days.

Persons using franchise without license guilty of a misdemeanor.

Penalty.

SEC. 47. That the board of aldermen shall have power to divide the license taxes into monthly installments to be paid in advance, and may allow a reduction of five per centum on said license tax to such persons as shall pay for twelve months in advance.

License taxes may be divided into installments.

SEC. 48. The board of aldermen shall have power to impose an annual tax on each dog running at large or kept within said city limits, and may require all such dogs to wear such tax badge as it may designate. Any person having or owning any such dog who shall fail to return it for taxation or to pay the tax, after fifteen days' public notice that such tax has been imposed, shall be guilty of a misdemeanor, and on conviction fined not exceeding five dollars or imprisoned not exceeding two days, and such dog may be treated as a nuisance and destroyed.

Dogs.

Persons owning dogs shall return them for taxation

Misdemeanor.

Penalty.

SEC. 49. That the tax collector is hereby authorized and empowered to sell the real estate in the city for taxes, whether such real estate belongs to residents or non-residents or persons unknown, and to sell any lot or subdivision of a lot or so much thereof as may be necessary to pay the tax due. The board of aldermen may purchase any real estate sold for any tax, and in such event the deed conveying same shall be made to The City of New Bern, and all such real estate so purchased may be redeemed as other real estate, and when so redeemed the mayor shall reconvey the same to the owner at the expense of the owner. The land of an infant, lunatic or person non compos mentis shall not be sold for any tax, and when the same shall be owned in common with others free from disability the sale shall be made according to section two, chapter ninety-nine of the Revised Code. The owner of any mortgage or person having any lien may redeem any property sold for tax at any time within two years on paying the purchaser, or city treasurer for him, the amount of tax,

Real estate may be sold for taxes.

Aldermen may purchase real estate

Deed shall be made to New Bern in certain events.

Land of certain persons which shall not be sold.

Property may be redeemed within two years.

cost and expenses, with twenty-five per centum added, and two dollars for the expenses of re-conveyance.

Sale shall not be invalid on account of certain irregularities.

Sec. 50. That no sale of real estate for a tax shall be invalid on account of the same having been assessed as belonging to any other than the owner, or as the property of an unknown owner, or on account of any informality or irregularity whatever in any proceedings for its assessment or sale, unless the person impeaching said sale shall show that the tax due on said property and all the penalties and cost accruing on such assessment and proceedings for sale were paid at the time of the sale of said property.

After two years property thus purchased shall be conveyed in fee simple.

Sec. 51. That if any real estate sold for tax shall not be redeemed within the time specified the tax collector shall convey the same in fee to the purchaser or his assigns, and the recitals in such conveyance or in any other conveyance of land designated, sold for taxes due the city, shall be prima facie evidence of the truth of the facts recited.

City documents shall be kept open to inspection of public.

Sec. 52. All tax lists, minutes of all meetings of the board of aldermen, and all documents or books containing any record relative to the city government shall be kept open to the inspection of the public.

Power to improve streets.

Sec. 53. The board of aldermen shall have full power and authority to straighten or widen streets or lay off and establish new streets when in their opinion the same shall be required to the best interest of the city. Whenever it shall be necessary to straighten, widen or establish new streets, and the owner of the land which may be required for such purposes shall claim damages, the owner of the land shall file his claim with the clerk of the city, and it shall be the duty of the board of aldermen forthwith to appoint three freeholders resident in said city connected with the said claimant neither by consanguinity or affinity, who shall forthwith go upon the premises and view the same and assess the damages which will accrue to such property for the improvement, and report the same to the board of aldermen who shall pay the said damages assessed, if any, and proceed to establish said street. If the owner or the city is dissatisfied with such assessment either party may appeal from the finding of the commissioners to the next term of the superior court, when the same shall be tried before a jury, but such appeal shall not have the effect to stay the improvements on the streets. All the provisions of this section shall apply when the board of aldermen of The City of New Bern shall deem it necessary to condemn for the purpose of enlarging, improving or protecting the cemetery or cemeteries of said city.

Owner of land condemned may claim damages.

Committee to assess damages.

Either party may appeal.

Aldermen empowered to construct and maintain electric light plant.

Sec. 54. That the board of aldermen are authorized and empowered to construct or buy, maintain and operate an electric light plant for the purpose of furnishing lights to the inhabitants of said city, waterworks system and sewerage system, and the said board of aldermen is authorized and empowered to charge reasonable prices for the use of said light, water and sewerage when furnished to private consumers.

Commissioners may issue bonds.

SEC. 55 That if the board of aldermen shall conclude to buy or erect and construct an electric light plant, waterworks system or system of sewerage it is hereby authorized and empowered to issue for said purpose city bonds of the denomination of not less than ten dollars each, payable in not less than twenty and not more than thirty years, bearing interest at not more than five per centum, payable semi-annually, which said bonds may be issued directly in payment for such or sold at not less than par and the proceeds so applied: *Provided*, that before any bonds are issued as herein provided, the question shall be submitted to a vote of the qualified voters of the city and a majority of the votes cast at such election shall be in favor of the issuing of said bonds.

Denomination of bonds.

Proviso.

Shall be voted upon.

No officers of city shall contract for any work, etc., done for city.

SEC. 56. That no officer of the city shall directly or indirectly become a contractor for work to be done for or property sold to the city, and no contract shall be awarded any contractor without good and sufficient sureties, and no officer of the city shall receive directly or indirectly any compensation from any contractor with the city.

Magistrates' or other fees shall not be assessed upon city.

SEC. 57. That no fees or costs of magistrates or other officers for the arrest or trial of persons charged with misdemeanor shall be assessed upon or collected from the city.

All work for city above $200 shall be let out by contract

SEC. 58. All work to be done for the city wherein the total amount for material and labor exceeds the sum of two hundred dollars shall be let out on contract to the lowest bidder, after advertisement for not less than ten days in a newspaper published in the city. That no work or contract shall be subdivided so as to defeat the operation of this section.

No work or contract shall be subdivided.

Votes taken on making contracts shall be entered on minutes.

SEC. 59. That all votes taken in making appropriations or contracts shall be entered upon the minutes of the meetings and shall designate the names of the aldermen voting in the affirmative and in the negative.

Salaries of officers.

SEC. 60. That the salaries of the officers of the city shall not exceed the following sum: The mayor, six hundred dollars per annum, without cost or fees; the treasurer, two hundred dollars per annum; the chief of police, fifty dollars per month; the city attorney, two hundred dollars per annum; sexton, twenty dollars each per month; policemen, thirty-five dollars per month.

All moneys shall be paid to treasurer.

SEC. 61. All moneys arising from taxation, donation or other sources shall be paid to the treasurer of the city, and no appropriation thereof shall be made except for necessary expenses.

SEC. 62. That all the property of every description, real, per-

Property, etc., vested in the city of New Bern incorporated hereby.

sonal and mixed, and all choses in action which were owned by the city of New Bern whose charter has been heretofore repealed are hereby granted to, vested in and assigned to The City of New Bern, incorporated by the provisions hereof. That all valid subsisting debts, obligations and contracts of the city of New Bern are hereby declared to be valid, binding upon and forceable against The City of New Bern incorporated hereby.

Duties of tax collector elected by board appointed by this act.

Sec. 63. That the tax collector who shall be elected by the board of aldermen appointed by the general assembly as provided in section twenty-one in this act shall receive the tax list levied in eighteen hundred and ninety-eight and prior thereto and proceed to collect the balance of taxes that may remain unpaid as per said lists, which said lists and the levies and assessments made thereby are hereby declared to be in all respects legal and valid, and the said collector shall have full power and authority to collect the taxes that are unpaid on said list in the same manner as provided for the tax collector to be elected, and shall account for the same to the city authorities as provided in this act; and the said tax collector shall proceed to collect all license taxes which may have been levied by the mayor and councilmen of the city of New Bern, whose charter has been heretofore repealed, and all such licensed taxes are hereby declared to be legal and valid, and said tax collector shall have all remedies that are provided for collection of license taxes in this act.

Numbering of lots shall remain the same.

Sec. 64. That the numbering of all lots situated in the territory heretofore constituting the city of New Bern shall remain the same under the present corporation, and all plots of said territory which have heretofore been lawfully adopted laying the same off in lots and streets are hereby re-adopted.

Persons having in charge books or other property belonging to city of New Bern shall surrender same.

Sec. 65. That any person or persons having in charge or possession any property, books or papers formerly belonging to the city of New Bern shall deliver the same to the board of aldermen appointed by the general assembly under the provisions hereof. Any person other than those appointed hereunder or elected by the board of aldermen appointed hereby, who shall exercise or attempt to exercise or hold any office in said city shall be guilty of a misdemeanor and upon conviction shall be fined one thousand dollars and imprisoned one year.

Persons other than those appointed by this act attempting to hold office guilty of a misdemeanor.

Sec. 66. That this act shall be in force from and after its ratification.

Ratified the 20th day of February, A. D. 1899.

CHAPTER 83.

An act to amend chapter three hundred and forty of the private laws of eighteen hundred and ninety-five.

The General Assembly of North Carolina do enact:

SECTION 1. That chapter three hundred and forty of the private laws of eighteen hundred and ninety-five be amended by striking out all of section second and inserting in lieu thereof the following: Chapter 340, private laws of 1895, amended.

SEC. 2. That the corporate limits of the town of Jonesboro shall be as follows: Beginning at the point where the south side of Carthage street intersects the present boundary line of said town at a point near A. E. Kelly's, running thence with said south side of Carthage street to McIver's alley; thence with McIver's alley and continuation thereof in the same course to the right-of-way of the Cape Fear and Yadkin Valley Railway; thence with said right-of-way in a southeasterly direction with the present boundary line of said town; thence in a northern direction with the present boundary line of said town; thence in a northern direction with the present boundary line of said town and following the present boundary lines in their several courses to the beginning. Corporate limits of the town of Jonesboro described.

SEC. 3. That this act shall be in force from its ratification.

Ratified the 22d day of February, A. D. 1899.

CHAPTER 84.

An act to amend the charter of the Levi Bank and change the name thereof.

The General Assembly of North Carolina do enact:

SECTION 1. That chapter twenty-seven and chapter fifty-one of the private laws of eighteen hundred and ninety-seven be amended by striking out the words "the Levi Bank" whenever they occur in said chapters and the title to said chapters and insert instead thereof "The Merchants' and Planters' Bank." Chapters 27 and 51, private laws of 1897, amended. Name of Levi Bank changed to Merchants' and Planters' Bank.

SEC. 2. That the corporators shall be allowed two years from the date of the ratification of this act to organize said bank and commence business. Corporators allowed two years to organize and commence business.

SEC. 3. That all laws and clauses of laws in conflict with this act be and the same are hereby repealed. Conflicting laws repealed.

SEC. 4. That this act shall be in force from and after its ratification.

Ratified the 22d day of February, A. D. 1899.

CHAPTER 85.

An act to incorporate Chapel Hill School.

The General Assembly of North Carolina do enact:

Corporators. Section 1. That J. W. Canada, C. S. Canada and S. M. Wilson and those who hereafter may be associated with them be incorporated for educational purposes under the name and style of Corporate name. "Chapel Hill School," in the town of Chapel Hill, Orange county, and as such may have all the power of trustees of like institu- Corporate powers. tions; may sue and be sued, may plead and be impleaded at law.

Seal. Corporate powers. Sec. 2. That the said corporation may have a common seal, and may have power to pass all needful rules and regulations for its own government, not inconsistent with the constitution and laws of this state and the United States.

Power of trustees. Sec. 3. That the said trustees shall have power to hold and acquire such real and personal property as may be necessary and suitable for maintaining a school for boys and girls at Chapel Hill.

Power conferred to award certificates of proficiency. Sec. 4. That under this act of incorporation power shall be conferred upon said "Chapel Hill School" to award certificates of proficiency to such pupils as have completed in a satisfactory manner the courses of study prescribed in the school.

Sec. 5. That this act shall be in force from and after its ratification.

Ratified the 22d day of February, A. D. 1899.

CHAPTER 86.

An act to amend the charter of the Goldsboro Lumber Company.

The General Assembly of North Carolina do enact:

Section 2, chapter 169, private laws of 1889, amended. Section 1. That section two (2) of chapter one hundred and sixty-nine (169) of the private laws of eighteen hundred and eighty-nine (1889), entitled "An act to incorporate the Goldsboro 5,000 stricken out in line 2 and 20,000 substituted therefor, etc. Lumber Company" be amended by striking out the figures "five thousand" in line two (2) and by inserting in lieu thereof the word "twenty thousand" and by inserting between the words "purchase" and "standing" in line three (3) of said section the words "and. hold," and between the words "timber" and "or" in said line three (3) the words "not exceeding one hundred thousand acres."

Section 3, chapter 169, private laws of 1889, amended. Sec. 2. That section three (3) of said chapter one hundred and sixty-nine (169) be amended by striking out the words "one hundred" in line three (3) and by inserting in lieu thereof the words "three hundred and fifty."

SEC. 3. That all laws in conflict with this act are hereby repealed. Conflicting laws repealed.

SEC. 4. That this act shall be in force from and after its ratification.

Ratified the 22d day of February, A. D. 1899.

CHAPTER 87.

An act to change the manner of electing officers for the town of Hertford, in Perquimans county.

The General Assembly of North Carolina do enact:

SECTION 1. That the town of Hertford shall be divided into three wards as follows: Ward divisions of the town of Hertford, North Carolina

The first ward shall be all that portion of the said town lying and being east of Church street and north of Grub street. Boundaries of first ward

The second ward shall be all that portion of said town west and south of the following boundaries: Beginning at the southern terminus of Church street at the corporate limits and running north along said street to Dobb street, and west along Dobb street to Hyde Park street, and north along Hyde Park street to Main street, and west along Main street and Main street extended to the corporation limits. Boundaries of second ward.

The third ward shall be all of said town not included in the first and second wards. Each of said wards shall be entitled to one member of the board of commissioners for said town, to be elected by the voters of each ward respectively. Boundaries of third ward. Representation on board of commissioners.

SEC. 2. The present board of commissioners of said town is hereby directed and empowered to appoint a registrar and two judges of election for each of said wards, and the registrars shall make a new registration of the voters of each of the said wards, and shall keep the books open for registration for thirty days preceding the day of election. The necessary registration books shall be provided by the board of town commissioners and the registrar of election and the judges shall hold the town election on the first Monday in May of the year eighteen hundred and ninety-nine and each succeeding year. Present board of commissioners authorized to provide for a new election. Time for holding election.

SEC. 3. That the commissioners who shall be chosen at the next and all succeeding elections in said town shall meet on the Wednesday following their election at the hour of noon in the court-house, and after taking the oath of office before any person authorized to administer oaths, proceed by ballot to elect the Time of meeting for new commissioners.

Officers to be elected by commissioners. Powers of officers.

following offices for said town, to-wit: A mayor, a town constable, a town clerk, a town treasurer, which officers shall take the oaths and have and execute the powers conferred upon such officers in the charter of said town where such officers were named therein, and when not so named they shall have such powers as the board of commissioners may confer upon them.

Powers of mayor and commissioners.

SEC. 4. That the mayor and commissioners hereafter elected under this act shall have all the powers conferred upon said officers in the charter of said town and in chapter sixty-two of The Code.

Conflicting acts repealed.

SEC. 5. That all acts of incorporation for said town in so far as they conflict with this act are hereby repealed and this act shall be in force from and after its ratification.

SEC. 6. That the secretary of state shall send a certified copy of this act within ten days after its ratification to the mayor of the town of Hertford.

Ratified the 22d day of February, A. D. 1899.

CHAPTER 88.

An act to incorporate the Carolina Northern Railroad Company.

The General Assembly of North Carolina do enact;

Corporators.

SECTION 1. That Alfred A. Sparks, George Wertener, C. E. Lent, A. B. Pearson, Lewis C. Leidy, John W. Leidy, W. H. P. Barnes, John C. Davis, Jr., Harry A. Powell, Peter E. Bird, Ellis Pugh, Robert S. Huston, William R. Lee, E. N. McCollin, M. M. Freeman, A. Topham, E. A. Ryan, J. Dixon Andrews, Myers W. Davies, George A. McFetridge, Henry Neater, A. D. Phillips, John R. Phillippi, John F. Farrell, O. B. Jones, George H. Mecke, W. J. Moore and all of Philadelphia, Pennsylvania, their associates, successors and assigns, be and they are hereby constituted a body politic and corporate under the name of the "Carolina Northern Railroad Company," and under that name and style they and their successors and assigns shall have succession for sixty years and shall have power in their corporate name to sue and be sued, appear, prosecute and defend to final judgment and execution in any court of competent jurisdiction in this state or elsewhere; shall have a common seal, which they may use and alter at pleasure, and they and their successors and assigns, under the said corporate name and style, shall have power to purchase, hold and convey any lands, tenements, goods and chattel whatsoever necessary or expedient to the purpose and object of the said corporation; they shall have power to make such by-

Body politic. Corporate name. Corporate powers. Seal. Corporate power.

laws and regulations for their own government and for the due and orderly conducting of their affairs and the management of their property as may be deemed necessary.

SEC. 2. That the said company is hereby authorized and empowered to lay out, construct, equip, maintain and operate railroads in this state with one or more tracks, with the necessary cars and fixtures, from the town of Lumberton, in Robeson county, through said county to some point in North and South Carolina state line near Page's Mill, South Carolina, and from said town of Lumberton, North Carolina, through Robeson and Bladen counties to some point on the Cape Fear river, between Fayetteville and Elizabethtown, North Carolina, and from thence through the counties of Bladen, Sampson and Wayne to the city of Goldsboro, North Carolina, and the said company may in its discretion construct and operate any part of its road before the whole thereof shall be completed, and may establish such gauge as they may think proper and may construct and operate branch lines, and may consolidate with the Carolina Northern Railroad Company recently chartered under the general laws of this state in the office of the secretary of state. Corporate power. Corporate power. Corporate power.

SEC. 3. That the capital stock of said company shall be five hundred thousand dollars, with the privilege and power of increasing the same to one million five hundred thousand dollars, divided into shares of ten dollars each. The capital stock of said company may be paid in money, labor, land, material, bonds or other securities and in any manner that may be agreed upon by the company and the subscribers. Capital stock. Privileged to increase. Division of shares.

SEC. 4 That at the time of said organization and annually thereafter such stockholders or subscribers or a majority thereof shall elect from their number not less than three or more than seven directors of said company, who shall hold their offices one year and until their successors shall be elected and qualified, and the directors chosen at such meeting and annually thereafter shall elect one of their number as president of said company, and shall elect a treasurer and secretary and such other officers as may be provided for in the by-laws of said company, who shall hold their office one year and until their successors are elected and qualified, and shall fill any vacancy that may occur in any of said offices by death, resignation or otherwise; that in all elections provided for in this act each share of stock represented in person or by proxy shall be entitled to one vote, each proxy to be verified in the manner prescribed in the by-laws of said company. The meetings of the stockholders and directors of said company shall take place at such times and places as may be provided for by said by-laws. Election of directors. Election of president, treasurer, etc. Term of office. Manner of elections. Place and time of meetings.

SEC. 5. The said company shall issue certificates of stock to its

Certificates of stock may be transferred.

members, and stock may be transferred upon the books of said company in such manner and form as the by-laws may prescribe.

Shall have right to condemn land for right-of-way, etc.

SEC. 6. That said company shall have the right to have land condemned for right-of-way and for necessary warehouses and other buildings according to existing laws, the width of the right-of-way not to exceed two hundred feet; and shall have full power and authority to sell or lease its road bed, property and franchise to any other corporation or person, and to consolidate with any other railroad company now created or which may hereafter be created by the laws of this state, and may change its name whenever a majority of the stockholders so desire, and shall have power to contract with individuals, firms and corporations for the construction or operation of said road and also for the equipment thereof.

Corporate powers.

Corporate powers.

Empowered to construct bridges.

SEC. 7. That said company is hereby authorized and empowered to construct, maintain and use bridges for the transportation of its cars across the Cape Fear river, Lumber river and other rivers in the line of its said railroads: *Provided*, that said bridges shall be so constructed as not to interfere with rafts on said rivers which may be crossed by said railroads, and that said company shall provide drawbridges at such points on said rivers where it shall be necessary for the convenience of boats navigating said rivers

Proviso.

Corporate power.

SEC. 8. That said company is hereby empowered to build and operate telegraph and telephone lines on its right-of-way or any part thereof.

Corporate power.

SEC. 9. That said company shall have the right to borrow money and to make, issue, negotiate and use its bonds in such sums and to such amounts as to the directors may seem expedient, and the said bonds shall bear no greater rate of interest than six per centum per annum, and shall be payable at such times and places as the board of directors may determine, and the said company shall have power to cause the payment of the same, principal and interest, to be secured by one or more mortgages or deeds of trust on its property, rights and franchises, including its road bed, superstructures and real estate and personal estate of whatever kind on such terms and to such trustee as the board of directors may order.

Corporate power.

Corporate power.

SEC. 10. That said company is hereby empowered to purchase and hold such lands, timber and personal property as it may deem necessary and proper for the efficient conduct of its business, all of which property may be acquired, held, used and disposed of at the discretion of the company in any manner not inconsistent with law: *Provided*, that said company shall have power to hold at the same time for terminals, stations, depots,

Proviso.

warehouses, etc., any number of acres of land even exceeding hree hundred acres.

SEC. 11. That no assessment shall be made on any of the stock of said corporation after the same has been fully paid, nor shall the owners thereof be liable for the obligation, indebtedness or any liability whatever of said corporation. No assessment shall be made on certain conditions.

SEC. 12. That said corporation, besides the powers herein granted, shall be invested with all the powers and privileges granted to corporations by chapters sixteen and forty-nine of The Code and amendments thereto not inconsistent with the provisions of this act. Invested with powers and privileges granted by chapters 16 and 49 of The Code and all amendments thereto.

SEC. 13. That the principal offices of said corporation shall be located at the town of Lumberton, North Carolina, unless hereafter changed by order of the stockholders of said company. Principal office at Lumberton.

SEC. 14. That this act shall be in force from and after its ratification.

Ratified the 22d day of February, A. D. 1899.

CHAPTER 89.

An act to incorporate the Peoples Storage and Mercantile Company.

The General Assembly of North Carolina do enact:

SECTION 1. That J. J. Thomas, B. P. Williams[on], H. W. Jackson, S. W. Brewer, C. J. Hunter, B. S. Jerman and H. C. Thomas, their associates, successors and assigns, are hereby constituted and created a body politic and corporate under the name and style of the Peoples Storage and Mercantile Company. Corporators. Body politic. Corporate name.

SEC. 2. The capital stock of the said company shall be twenty-five thousand dollars ($25,000), which may be increased at the option of said company to an amount not exceeding one hundred and twenty-five thousand dollars ($125,000), and when ten thousand dollars ($10,000) of said capital shall have been subscribed and five thousand dollars ($5,000) thereof paid in cash it shall be legal for the said company to organize and commence business. The said capital stock shall be divided into shares of fifty dollars ($50) each and shall be deemed personal property, and shall be transferable as may be prescribed by the by-laws of said company, and each share entitle the party to whom issued or bona fide holder to one vote in any or all meetings of the stockholders. Capital stock. May be increased at the option of company. When permitted to organize and commence business. Division of shares.

SEC. 3. The said Peoples Storage and Mercantile Company shall have power to sue and be sued, plead and be impleaded, prosecute and defend actions and special proceedings in any Corporate powers.

Seal. court, and have a common seal; shall have authority to transact and carry on a general warehouse, storage, commission and mercantile business; may lease, purchase, hold, convey and assign all such real and personal property as it may deem necessary for its business, not exceeding in amount the capital stock of the company; may build, erect and maintain buildings and warehouses for its business; may receive on storage or deposit cotton and other agricultural products, and all other kinds of general merchandise and personal property for storage, shipment or sale; may carry on and transact all kinds of business usually carried on and transacted by warehousemen, commission merchants and general dealers in any and all kinds of supplies; may collect and receive compensation for storage, selling or shipment and expenses for receiving, delivering and all labor incident thereto; may act only as agents for its patrons in making contracts with insurance companies on cotton or other goods stored or in transit; may make advances in money or acceptances on cotton, supplies, goods, property of any kind whatsoever received on storage or deposit, and compensation for all expenses and charges thereon, to include any advances in money or acceptances or otherwise, shall be and constitute a preferred lien on said property which shall be satisfied and paid before the said company shall be called upon for the delivery of said property; before any advances in money or acceptances upon cotton or other property such cotton or property must actually be in the possession of said company or satisfactory bills of lading or order for the same.

Corporate powers. Corporate powers. Corporate powers. Corporate powers.

Corporate powers. SEC. 4. That said company shall have power to carry on and conduct said business for a period of fifty years from the date of incorporation, and shall have all the general powers conferred and imposed upon corporations and chartered companies generally by the laws of North Carolina.

Receipts may be given for property deposited. SEC. 5. For all cotton or property of whatsoever kind received by said company for storage, deposit or sale, a receipt may be given for the same, said receipt or certificate issued shall be and are hereby declared to be negotiable instruments; such receipt or certificate having been properly transferred the holder shall be entitled to receive such property as called for in such receipt or certificate, after paying all advances, charges or expenses, with interest and cost, if any have accrued.

Holder shall be entitled to receive property called for in receipt.

When preferred liens are of doubtful security. SEC. 6. Whenever from any cause cotton or property of any kind whatsoever shall so decline in value as to render the preferred lien on same of doubtful security for advances or acceptances, it shall be lawful for the company to give notice to the party entitled to said cotton or other property personally or by mailing such notice to him or his agents at last known place of business or residence by registered mail, requiring said party within five days after issuing such notice to pay the said company all such advances and charges with any interest that may have accrued, or provide further adequate security for same; and upon failure to do so the said company may sell such cotton or property at public sale after giving not less than thirty days' notice in a newspaper published in the city of Raleigh and at the court-house door in Wake county, the cost of said notice to be paid by said debtor upon such terms as may seem best to the company for all parties concerned, and after reserving the amount due the said company and paying all cost of said sale, pay over any balance of the net proceeds to the party entitled thereto on his surrender of the receipt or certificate given for such property.

When said company may sell property.

Notice of sale required.

How proceeds of sales applied.

SEC. 7. It shall be lawful for the said company to borrow such sums of money from time to time as the needs of the company may require and to issue and dispose of its promissory notes or bonds, and said company may mortgage, pledge or hypothecate any part of its corporate property or franchises to secure the payment of such bonds or promissory notes.

May borrow money, mortgage property, etc.

SEC. 8. The stockholders in general meeting shall make and establish such by-laws and rules and regulations not inconsistent with the laws of North Carolina and the United States as they may deem best for the management and control of the affairs and business of said company.

Stockholders shall make by-laws.

SEC. 9. At their first and every subsequent annual meeting the stockholders shall elect not less than three (3) and may elect five (5) of their number to constitute a board of directors, to remain in office until their next annual meeting or until their successors are elected.

Election of board of directors.

SEC. 10. Subject to the by-laws, rules and regulations of the company the board of directors shall have the management and control of its affairs and business. From its own body shall elect a president, who shall preside at all meetings of the board; they may choose a vice-president from the board or stockholders; they shall also appoint all such officers, clerks or agents as may be needed in the management of the business of the company.

Powers of directors.

Election of president and other officers.

SEC. 11. The corporators, stockholders and their assigns shall not be liable or in any way responsible, individually or personally, for the contracts, obligations, debts or torts of the corporation beyond the amount of stock subscribed individually. The powers and privileges granted herein shall not be deemed forfeited by non-use: *Provided*, the corporation is organized within four (4) years from the date of ratification of this act.

Liability of stockholders.

Powers not forfeited by non-use. Proviso.

SEC. 12. That this act shall be in force from and after its ratification.

Ratified the 22d day of February, A. D. 1899.

CHAPTER 90.

An act to incorporate the town of Mount Gilead, in the county of Montgomery.

The General Assembly of North Carolina do enact:

Incorporated. SECTION 1. That the town of Mount Gilead, in Montgomery county, be and the same is hereby incorporated by the name and Name of town. style of the town of Mount Gilead, subject to all the provisions of law now existing in regard to incorporated laws as contained Provisions of general law. in chapter sixty-two, volume two, Code of eighteen hundred and eighty-three, and all laws amendatory thereto.

Corporate limits SEC. 2. That the corporate limits of said town shall extend one mile in all directions from the point where the Allenton Ferry road crosses the Turnpike road.

Officers. SEC. 3. That the officers of said town shall consist of a mayor, three commissioners and a constable The following-named persons shall fill said offices until their successors are elected and Temporary officers. qualified, viz: Mayor, W. S. Ingram; commissioners, R. H. Sheen, W. F. McAuley and L. P. Byrd. The constable shall be elected by the present board of commissioners, and his successor may be either elected by the people at the election for the other officers or appointed by the commissioners.

Elections, when held. SEC. 4. That the election for officers shall be held on the first Tuesday in May, eighteen hundred and ninety-nine, and every two years thereafter.

No intoxicating liquors shall be sold within corporate limits. SEC. 5. That no intoxicating liquors of any kind shall be sold within the corporate limits of said town.

Mayor shall have power to work persons failing to pay fines on the streets SEC. 6. That the mayor shall have power to cause all persons failing to pay their fines to work out the same on the streets at such price as the commissoners shall fix.

SEC. 7. That this act shall be in full force and effect from and after the first day of March, eighteen hundred and ninety-nine.

Ratified the 22d day of February, A. D. 1899.

CHAPTER 91.

An act to incorporate the Oriental Insurance Company.

The General Assembly of North Carolina do enact:

Corporators. SECTION 1. That Henry R. Bryan, Jr., Samuel H. Boyd, Alexander Webb and all other persons who may hereafter succeed or be associated with them, be and they are hereby constituted a Body politic. body politic and corporate under the name and style of the Name of corporation. "Oriental Insurance Company," to have succession for sixty years, and by and under that name may sue and be sued, appear, plead and be impleaded, protect and defend to final judgment and execution in any court of record or other court or places whatsoever, and may have and use a common seal, which it may alter at pleasure, and may purchase, acquire and hold such real or personal estate as may be deemed necessary, convenient or desirable, and may sell, dispose of and convey the same at pleasure; and may make such by-laws and regulations consistent with the laws of the state for its government and for the due and orderly conducting of its affairs and the management of its property, and generally do and perform any and all such acts and things as may be necessary, convenient or desirable to carry on their business and to carry into effect the provisions of this act. Corporate powers. Corporate powers.

SEC. 2. That the said company shall have power and authority to insure all kinds and classes of property, real, personal or mixed, against loss or damage by fire, lightning, water, winds or tornadoes, marine or inland navigation, inland transportation or any other risk whatsoever, and issue policies of insurance therefor, and for any such insurance may charge such premium or premiums as may be agreed upon between said company and the persons, firms or corporations whose property is so insured, and the said company shall be liable for and make good and pay to the several persons, firms and corporations whose property it may insure the losses which they may sustain in accordance with the terms of the contract or policy issued to them respectively by said company, but no policy or other contract of insurance shall bind said company unless it be signed by the president and secretary thereof; and the said company shall have power and authority to reinsure any and all of its risks, and further said company is hereby vested with all the powers, rights and privileges that any and all other insurance companies doing business in this state have or that may hereafter be granted them. Corporate power. Corporate power. Liability of company. When policy or contract is not binding

SEC. 3. That the home office or principal place of business of said company shall be at such place in said state as the stockholders may select at the time of their organization or thereafter; and said company may have and maintain branch offices, establish agencies and appoint agents at such other place or places in this or any other state as its board of directors may determine. Home office to be selected by stockholders. May establish agencies.

SEC. 4. That the capital stock of this corporation shall be one hundred thousand dollars, which may be increased from time to time in the discretion of the stockholders to a sum not exceeding five hundred thousand dollars; such stock shall be divided into shares of twenty-five dollars each and shall be subscribed and paid for in such manner and form and on such terms and subject to such restrictions as shall be prescribed by the by-laws of said company. Capital stock. May be increased.

Stock transferable.

SEC. 5. That the stock of the said company shall be transferable and assignable according to such rules and subject to such restrictions and regulations as shall be prescribed by the by-laws; and it shall be lawful for the company to reserve a first lien upon its stock for any indebtedness or liability of the owner thereof to the said company.

Company may reserve a first lien.

Privileges granted when capital stock becomes impaired, etc

SEC. 6. That should the paid up capital stock of the company at any time hereafter become impaired by reason of losses or depreciation in the value of assets the directors may at any time and from time to time, after being duly authorized and empowered so to do by a resolution approved by the votes of the stockholders in person or by proxy, representing at least three-fifths of all the paid up stock of the company at a regular or special meeting of the stockholders called for the purpose, reduce, scale or write off the paid up capital stock of the company by the amount or to the extent such capital has been impaired.

Directors may increase the paid up stock.

SEC. 7. That the directors may from time to time, out of the profits of the company, by declaring a stock dividend or bonus or otherwise, increase the paid up stock of the company by an amount or amounts not exceeding the amount or amounts by which the same may have been reduced under the provisions of section six preceding.

When stockholders shall not be individually liable.

SEC. 8. That the stockholders of said company shall not be individually liable for its debts, contracts or obligations, nor shall any stockholder be liable to the company or any creditors thereof for more than the unpaid portion of his or her individual stock subscription.

Business of company shall be governed by directors.

SEC. 9. That the business and affairs of said company shall be regulated, governed and managed by a board of directors, to consist of not less than three nor more than twenty members, as may from time to time be determined upon by the stockholders; and it shall be the duty of such board of directors and they are hereby vested with power and authority to choose officers, to whom or any of whom they may delegate any or all of the powers possessed by such board itself, fix salaries, fill vacancies caused by death, resignation or otherwise, and generally to do and perform all such acts and duties as the by-laws of the company shall prescribe, when said by-laws shall have been ratified by a majority in number and value of the stockholders voting thereon, and the company in their by-laws designate the number of such board of directors necessary to constitute a quorum at any meeting of the same. Such directors to the number then determined upon shall be elected at the organization meeting of said company and shall hold office for one year or until the first regular annual meeting of the stockholders (to be held at such time as shall be prescribed by the by-laws) and until their successors

Duties of directors.

When directors elected.

shall have been selected and qualified. No person shall be such director unless he shall also be a stockholder in said company. Only stockholders shall be directors.

SEC. 10. That in all meetings of the stockholders of said company, whether regular or special, each share of stock represented either in person or by proxy shall be entitled to one vote on any question that may be presented for determination. Stock representation.

SEC. 11. That the said company shall have full power and authority, subject to the provisions of the by-laws, to invest the capital stock paid in and other funds coming into its possession in real estate or personal property, stocks, bonds, mortgages, notes, choses in action or securities of any kind, character or description, and to lend upon personal or real security, and shall have the power to sell, dispose of, and convey any such property or securities, and to change the character of the investments of the company from time to time as may be deemed expedient or desirable, and it may borrow money for the prompt payment of losses or otherwise, and may secure its payment in such manner as may be deemed advisable. Company shall have power to invest capital stock paid in.

SEC. 12. That the persons named in section one hereof or any of them are hereby authorized, so soon as the capital stock of the said company shall have been subscribed to the amount of fifty thousand dollars, to call a meeting of such subscribers by giving ten days notice in writing to each and every one of them for the purpose of organizing said company and electing a board of directors, and so soon thereafter as twenty-five thousand dollars of said stock shall have been paid in shall have the power to commence the business operations of the company. Meeting, when to be called.

SEC. 13. That nothing herein contained shall be so construed as to prevent this company from receiving any of the benefits of or complying with any general insurance law that may hereafter be enacted. Company shall receive all benefits and comply with general insurance law.

SEC. 14. That all laws and parts of laws in conflict with this act be and they are hereby repealed. Conflicting laws repealed.

SEC. 15. That this act shall be in force from and after its ratification.

Ratified the 22d day of February, A. D. 1899.

CHAPTER 92.

An act to incorporate the Elizabeth City and Western Railroad Company.

The General Assembly of North Carolina do enact:

SECTION 1. That for the purpose of constructing and operating a railroad with one or more tracks from or near Elizabeth City, in the county of Pasquotank, in the state of North Carolina, to some point on the Norfolk and Carolina Railroad, through the Points of operation.

Corporators. counties of Pasquotank, Perquimans and Gates, C. H. Robinson, G. M. Scott, J. B. Blades, J. B. Flora, W. W. Griggs, O. McMullen and E. F. Aydlett, and such other persons and corporations as may be associated with them and their successors and assigns, be and they are hereby created a body politic and corporate by the name and style of the "Elizabeth City and Western Railroad Company," and by that name may sue and be sued, plead and be impleaded, may make by laws, appoint all necessary officers and prescribe their duties, and may accept and hold and convey any property either real or personal necessary for the purposes herebefore [hereinbefore] and hereinafter named, to make contracts, to have and to use a common seal, and to do all other lawful acts incident to and connected with said corporation and necessary for the control and transaction of business, and shall have all the rights and privileges possessed and enjoyed by other railroad companies under the laws of North Carolina as are conferred by chapter forty-nine of The Code of North Carolina and all amendments thereto.

Body politic. Corporate name. Corporate powers. Seal. Privileges.

Authority to construct, maintain and operate a railroad. SEC. 2. That this said company be and is authorized to construct, maintain and operate a railroad, extending from and between the places mentioned in the first section of this act, with the privilege of connecting with such other companies and at such other places as may be deemed advisable by such company.

Capital stock. SEC. 3. That the capital stock of said company shall be one hundred thousand dollars in shares of one hundred dollars each, with the privilege of increasing the capital stock to such an amount as may be found necessary to carry out the intention and purpose of this act, and not to exceed three million dollars, and the shares shall be transferable in such a manner as the by-laws may direct: *Provided*, that when the sum of ten thousand dollars shall have been subscribed to the capital stock of said company as hereinafter directed, the said corporators or a majority of them shall within a reasonable time thereafter appoint a time and place for the meeting of said stockholders of which thirty days' notice shall be given in such newspapers of this state as they may deem necessary, at which time and place said stockholders may proceed to the organization of said company by the election of a president and nine directors, and which board may in their by-laws prescribe the time and manner of holding their subsequent annual election for president and directors, subject to the approval of the stockholders at their ensuing annual meeting.

Privilege of increasing capital stock. Stock transferable. Proviso. Notice shall be given of first meeting. Organization. Election of president and directors.

Cities, towns and townships subscribing stock may be represented in stockholders meeting. SEC. 4. That in conventions of the stockholders of said company such city, town or township as may subscribe to the capital stock thereof may be represented by not less than three and not more than five delegates, who shall be chosen as such city, town r township may direct, and private stockholders shall represent heir own stock in person or by proxy duly executed.

SEC. 5. That for the purpose of raising the capital stock of aid company it shall be lawful to open books for private sub-criptions at such times and places and under the direction of uch persons as the said company may appoint, and that said ubscription to capital stock may be made in money, bonds, and, material and work, at such rates as may be agreed upon by he said company, and the said railroad company shall have ower to mortgage the property and franchise and issue bonds n such terms and conditions and for such purposes and uses of aid corporations as the said company may deem necessary.

Books may be opened for private subscription.

Corporate powers.

SEC. 6. At any time after its organization said company may ›urchase or receive title to any land or lands, houses, tenements, ights-of-way or other property necessary for the construction of he line or lines or any of the offices, stations or works. But in ase said company is not able to agree with the owner or owners f any land or property necessary for the construction of said ine or lines or any of the works or operations, that the value of he same shall be fixed by arbitration, each side choosing one rbitrator or appraiser who, in not being able to come to an agreement, shall choose a third, whose decision shall be final. In all cases of appraision or arbitration it shall be lawful for the appraisers or arbitrators to take in consideration the enhanced value of the property of the owner in consequence of the construction of the said railway as an effect, in whole or in part, for the right-of-way of lands or other property necessary for the construction of the line or the purpose before named; or said company may of its option acquire any property required for its lines, operations, objects or purposes in manner provided by section five, chapter one hundred and seventy-six of the laws of eighteen hundred and seventy-one and eighteen hundred and seventy-two, ratified ninth February, eighteen hundred and seventy-two.

May purchase or receive title to property.

Where difference arises over value of property, dispute shall be settled by arbitration.

Decision final.

SEC. 7. The said railroad shall have the privilege to consolidate and unite with any other railroad company or companies within or without the limits of this state, under any general railroad laws, terms or rules as may be agreed upon not inconsistent with the laws of this state, and such consolidated company shall be a corporation of this state and amenable to the laws of this state.

May consolidate and unite with any other railroad company.

SEC. 8. That nothing in this act contained shall be construed to exempt the property of said railroad company from taxation for state, county and town purposes.

Property shall not be exempt from taxation.

SEC. 9. This charter shall continue for sixty years.

Charter continues sixty years.

SEC. 10. This act shall be in force from and after its ratification.

Ratified the 22d day of February, A. D. 1899.

CHAPTER 93.

An act to incorporate The North and South Carolina Railroad Company.

The General Assembly of North Carolina do enact:

Corporators. SECTION 1. That Henry S. Haines, Alfred P. Thom, John S. Cunningham, James A. Lockhart, John N. Vaughan, W. B. Hatcher, Richard B. Tunstall, F. W. Tatem, W. S. Stirling, James A. Leak, W. C. Hardison, John D. Leak, J. A. Long and John C. Drewry and such other persons as are now or may hereafter be associated with them are hereby created and declared to be a body politic and corporate, to exist for the term of sixty years, under the name and style of "The North and South Carolina Railroad Company," and in that name may sue and be sued, plead and be impleaded, contract and be contracted with; shall have power to adopt a common seal and to change the same at will, and shall be capable of taking by purchase, gift or in any other way real and personal property and of holding, leasing, conveying or in any other manner dealing with the same, and the said corporation shall also have and enjoy all the rights, privileges and immunities which corporate bodies may lawfully exercise or enjoy, and may make ordinances, by-laws and regulations consistent with the laws of this state and of the laws of the United States for the government of all under its authority, for the management of its estates and for the due and orderly conduct of its affairs. It may build branch roads not exceeding fifty miles in length from any points on its main line, and for this purpose shall have all the powers, privileges and rights contained in this act, which are hereby made to apply to such branch roads as well as to the main line.

Body politic. Term of years chartered. Corporate name. Corporate powers. Seal. Rights and privileges.

Corporate power. SEC. 2. Said company upon its organization as hereinafter provided for shall have power to survey, lay out, construct and equip, maintain and operate, by steam or other motive power, a railroad with one or more tracks, and telegraph and telephone line or lines from some point to be selected by it on the line between the state of Virginia and the state of North Carolina in the county of Granville or in the county of Person, and from such point through the counties of Granville, Person, Caswell, Orange, Alamance, Durham, Chatham, Guilford, Randolph, Moore, Montgomery, Richmond, Stanly, Union and Anson to the boundary line between the state of North Carolina and the state of South Carolina, or through or into such of said counties as the said corporation may from time to time elect.

Counties through which road shall run.

Corporate powers. The said company shall also have power to connect its tracks with any other railroad company now or hereafter chartered, and to lay down and use tracks through or into any town or city along its proposed lines by and with the consent of the corporate authorities of such town or city upon such terms as they may prescribe.

SEC. 3. The capital stock of said company shall be not less than ten thousand dollars ($10,000) nor more than five million dollars ($5,000,000), to be divided into shares of one hundred dollars ($100) each, and may be from time to time increased between the minimum and maximum limits hereby provided, as the stockholders thereof may determine. The holder of stock in this company shall in all meetings of the stockholders be entitled either in person or by proxy to one vote for each share of stock held by him, and a majority of the stock shall constitute a quorum at all meetings of the stockholders. As soon as the minimum amount above provided for shall be subscribed the said company may be organized. Subscriptions to the stock may be made in money, land or other property, bonds, stocks, credits, contracts, leases, options, mines, minerals or mineral rights, rights-of-way, and other rights or easements, labor or services upon such terms as may be agreed upon or approved by the subscriber and the board of directors of the company, and there shall be no individual liability upon the takers or holders of said stock beyond the unpaid subscriptions thereto.

Capital stock.

Division of shares. May be increased.

Representation of stockholders.

When company may be organized

Subscriptions, how made.

Individual liability.

If any subscriber to the stock of this company shall neglect or refuse to pay any installment of his subscription amount when it becomes due, as required by the board of directors, said board may declare his stock forfeited as well as all previous payments thereon to the use and benefit of said company; but before so declaring it forfeited said stockholder shall have served upon him a notice in writing, in person, or by depositing said notice in the post-office, postage paid, directed to him at the post-office nearest his usual place of abode, or to his post-office address as given opposite to his signature to the subscription paper, stating that he is required to make such payment within sixty days from the date of such notice at such time and place as is named therein, and at the expiration of such period of sixty days, if the subscriber is still in default, the board of directors may exercise the power of forfeiture above conferred.

Failure or refusal to pay stock subscribed when due.

Notice to be served on subscriber failing to pay stock.

SEC. 4. The incorporators mentioned in this act or a majority of them shall have power to open books of subscription in person or by agent or agents at such place or places, either within or without this state, as they or such majority may fix, and with or without notice and if with notice then upon such notice as they or such majority may determine, and to keep the same open for such time and under such conditions, rules and regulations as they or such majority may deem necessary or expedient. And said incorporators or a majority of them may, when they or such

Incorporators shall have power to open books of subscription.

Incorporators may call meeting of stockholders and complete organization.

majority deem proper, after ten days' notice served upon or mailed to the subscribers at such address as may be given opposite their names to such subscription paper, call together the subscribers to said shares of stock at any place in or out of this state; and said subscribers or such of them as shall attend may then complete the organization of said company by electing a board of directors, to consist of such number as they may determine and of such officers as they may see fit, and the said directors shall thereupon proceed to elect one of their number as president and to elect such other officers as the by-laws of said company may prescribe, and to appoint such agents as they may deem necessary or expedient, and may do and perform all other acts necessary and convenient to the complete organization of said company and to carry into effect the objects of this act.

Election of president. Empowered to appoint agents and complete organization.

Annual meeting, when held.

Sec. 5. The annual meeting of the stockholders shall be held on such day as is or may be prescribed by the by-laws, or if none be so prescribed, on such day as the stockholders may in general meeting from time to time appoint, or in the absence of such appointment by the stockholders on such day as the board of directors may designate and at such place within or without this state as shall be fixed from time to time by the board of directors. Notice of the annual meeting of the stockholders shall be published in a newspaper for two successive weeks.

Notice of meeting shall be published.

A general meeting of stockholders may be held at any time on call of directors

Sec. 6. A general meeting of the stockholders may be held at any time upon the call of the board of directors, or of stockholders holding together one-tenth of the capital stock, upon their giving notice of the time and place of such meeting for ten days in a newspaper published in or near the place at which the last annual meeting was held. At such general meeting all the powers of the company may be exercised and any business transacted that might be transacted at an annual meeting.

Powers that may be exercised at such meeting.

Election of directors by ballot, when held. Term of office.

Sec. 7. The election of directors shall be by ballot and shall be held at the annual meeting unless otherwise determined from time to time by the stockholders. The directors shall hold office until the succeeding annual meeting or until their successors are duly elected and assume their duties. The board may fill any vacancy that may occur in it during the term for which its members have been elected. The president of the company and such other elective officers as may be provided for by the by-laws shall be annually elected by the directors from among their number in such manner as the regulations of the company shall prescribe, and shall hold their offices until their successors shall be elected and assume their duties. The secretary and treasurer shall also be elected by the board of directors and may be one and the same person.

May fill vacancies. Election of president and other officers.

Term of office.

Election of secretary and treasurer.

In the absence at any meeting of the board of directors of the president and vice-president, if there be a vice-president, or of the secretary, the board may appoint a president or secretary pro tempore. Appointment of temporary officers.

The board of directors shall have power to adopt by-laws, subject, however, to amendment or repeal by the stockholders. Directors may adopt by-laws subject to approval of stockholders

SEC. 8. The company shall issue certificates of stock to its members and the stock may be transferred in such manner and form as may be prescribed by the by-laws of the company. Stock may be transferred.

SEC. 9. The said company shall have power to take by purchase, lease or otherwise the railroad franchises and property of any other railroad now constructed or that may hereafter be constructed in this state or elsewhere. It shall have power to consolidate its franchises and property with any other company upon such terms and under such name as may be agreed upon. It may assign or lease its property and franchises or any part thereof to any other railroad company incorporated by the laws of this state or of any other state, and the railroad company leasing or purchasing this road shall hold, own and enjoy all the property and franchises so leased or purchased as though the same had been originally held or constructed by the railroad company so leasing or purchasing, and the railroad company so purchasing or leasing shall be entitled to all property, franchises, privileges and immunities belonging or pertaining to the company incorporated by this act. Any of the powers and privileges conferred and authorized by this section may be exercised and carried into effect by the directors of the companies concerned in such manner and on such terms as the stockholders of each company may determine. The company incorporated by this act may subscribe to or purchase the capital stock, bonds or other securities of any other corporation now in existence or hereafter projected in this state or elsewhere, and any other such company may subscribe to or purchase the capital stock, bonds or other securities of this company. This company shall have power to use any section or portion of its road or other lines before the whole of the same shall have been completed, and may charge tolls for the transportation of passengers and freight on its road and for the transmission of messages on or use of its telegraph or telephone lines, and on any such section or portion of said road or lines. Corporate powers. Corporate powers. Directors of companies concerned may carry into effect powers and privileges granted by this charter. Corporate powers. Corporate powers.

SEC. 10. This company shall have the right and power, when necessary or convenient, to construct their said road across any public road or street at such point as it may determine, or along or alongside of any public road: *Provided*, said company shall not obstruct any public road without first constructing one equally as good and convenient as the one taken by the company; it shall likewise have power to construct dams, culverts, May construct road across any public road or street. Proviso.

May construct dams, culverts, trestles, bridges, etc

trestles and bridges over or across streams, valleys and depressions, and to cross any navigable stream or canal or its route; it shall likewise have the right and power to cross at grade or over or under any other railroad constructed or that may hereafter be constructed in this state at any point on its route; to intersect, join or unite its line of railway with any other such railroad upon the ground of such other companies at any point on its route, and to build turnouts, sidings, switches and any other conveniences in furtherance of the object of its construction, and may, in making any intersection or connection with any other railroad, have all the rights, powers and privileges conferred upon railroads by the laws of this state.

When company is unable to agree with owners of land desired over price, clerk of court shall appoint five disinterested freeholders who shall assess value of property desired.

SEC. 11. Whenever from any cause this company is unable to agree with the owners of the land over or near which it is proposed to extend its road for the purchase of such land for its depots, road beds, station grounds, yards, shops, gravel pits, quarries or other purposes of the company, the said company may file a petition before the clerk of the superior court of the county wherein the land lies, specifying the object for which the land is desired, with a description and plat thereof. A copy of such petition with a notice of the time and place, when and where the same shall be heard by the clerk, must be served on all persons whose interests are to be affected by the proceedings at least ten days prior to the hearing of the same by the said clerk in the manner provided by law, and in the event that any of the persons interested in said company are unknown or non-residents of this state, such notice may be served by advertisement, stating briefly the object of the application and giving a description of the land to be taken, published in a paper, if there be one published in the county in which the land to be taken is situate, once in each week for four successive weeks next previous to the presentation of the petition, and if there be no paper published in said county, then in some paper published in the city of Raleigh, or such notice may be given in any other way provided for the giving of notices relative to the condemnation of land by chapter forty-nine of the first volume of The Code of North Carolina. The clerk of the superior court shall thereupon appoint five disinterested freeholders, who shall be summoned by the sheriff to meet on the premises at a time to be fixed in the order of appointment, not more than ten days after the appointment unless a later day be fixed by consent, to assess the damages to the land proposed to be taken. In assessing the damages the appraisers shall take into consideration the actual value of the land, together with the damage to the residue of the tract beyond the peculiar benefit to be derived in respect to such residue from the work to be constructed. The assessment shall be of the fee sim-

Assessment of value by freeholders.

Manner of appraising value of land desired by company.

ple value of the property proposed to be taken by the company. The appraisers shall make their report to the clerk of the superior court within ten days from the time of their meeting on the premises. Said report shall be recorded in the office of the register of deeds after approval by the clerk and payment of the damages assessed to the clerk or to the parties interested, and shall have the force and effect of a deed conveying such property to the company in fee simple. Either party may appeal to the superior court in term from the approval or disapproval of the action of the clerk, provided such appeal be prayed within ten days from the approval or disapproval of the clerk, and on such appeal may present such evidence as they may desire and have a hearing de novo before the court, but the burden of proof shall be upon the party objecting to the ruling of the appraisers.

Appraisers shall make report within ten days.

Shall have the force and effect of a deed in fee simple.

Either party may appeal.

Burden of proof shall rest upon parties objecting to ruling of appraisers.

In the event that the true owner of any property taken as above mentioned is not notified as above provided, then such owner may within two years but not afterwards petition the superior court of the county in which the land lies for assessment of the value thereof, as aforesaid, but no action of ejectment shall be brought by him nor the possession or occupation of this company in any way disturbed unless it shall within the time to be fixed by the said court fail to pay such damages as may be assessed for the value thereof: *Provided, however*, that in case the true owner be at the time of such condemnation and occupation under any legal disability he may file a petition for the assessment of such damages within two years from the removal of such disability.

Effect of failure to notify owner of property of proceedings.

No action of ejectment arises.

Proviso.

SEC. 12. The right of said company to condemn and take land under this act shall be limited to the space of fifty feet on each side of its road bed, measuring from the middle line of the same, except in cases of deep cuts or high embankments, when said company shall have the right to condemn as much in addition thereto as may be necessary for the construction of its road; and except also that if for depot, warehouse, station grounds, shops, yard, gravel pits, quarries or other purposes necessary for the construction and operation of said road it may condemn not exceeding ten acres in any one place.

Right of said company to condemn land.

SEC. 13. It shall be lawful for the said company, through its agents, superintendents, engineers or other persons in its employ, to enter at any and all times upon all lands or waters for the purpose of exploring, surveying and locating its line upon the same and of making a plat thereof.

Privileged to [illegible] enter upon lands, etc.

SEC. 14. Any county, township, city or town along or near the line of the constructed or proposed road of this company may subscribe to the capital stock of the company in the following manner: Upon presentation of a petition in writing signed by

Counties, townships, cities or towns may subscribe to capital stock.

When election or subscription may be ordered.

not less than twenty-five per centum of the voters of the county, township, city or town to the board of commissioners of such county or to the proper authorities of said city or town, requesting them to submit to the qualified voters of the county, city, township or town where such petitioners may reside a proposition to subscribe a definite sum, to be named in said petition, to the capital stock of this company, the board of commissioners of said county or proper authorities of said city or town shall within thirty days order an election to be held in such county, township, city or town and submit to the qualified voters therein the question of subscribing to the capital stock of the said company the amount specified in said petition, at which election all those qualified to vote who are in favor of such subscription and shall vote shall vote a ballot on which shall be written or printed the words "For subscription," and those opposed to such a subscription shall vote a ballot on which shall be written or printed the words "Against subscription"; and the election for this purpose shall be conducted in the same manner and subject to the same rules and regulations as are provided for the election of county, township, city or town officers by the general election laws of this state. Such election shall be held after thirty days' notice thereof, specifying the amount of the proposed subscription, shall have been posted at the court-house of said county and at every polling place of said county, township, town or city where the said election shall take place, and the returns thereof shall be made to the board of commissioners of said county or proper authorities of said city or town. If a majority of the qualified voters vote for subscription, then the board of commissioners of said county or proper authorities of said city or town shall immediately make such subscription and shall issue coupon bonds to the amount of said subscription in order to pay the same, and the bonds shall upon their face indicate on account of what county, township, city or town they are issued.

Form of ballots.

Manner of holding elections.

Returns of election to be made to commissioners.

Coupon bonds shall be issued.

Denomination of bonds.

They shall be in denominations of not less than one hundred dollars ($100) and not more than one thousand dollars ($1,000) each, and shall run for such number of years and bear such rate of interest as the petition and order of election shall indicate. They shall be signed, if issued by a county or township, by the chairman of the board of county commissioners and by the clerk of said county, and if issued by a city or town, by the mayor and one of the commissioners of such city or town.

Rate of interest, etc.

Bonds, how signed.

Commissioners empowered to levy additional taxes for bond purposes.

SEC. 15. The county authorities in any county voting for subscription or in which there is a township voting for subscription, or the proper authorities in the city or town voting for subscription who are legally empowered to levy taxes, shall, in order to provide for payment of the bonds and interest thereon, to be issued under the preceding section, compute and levy each year at the time of levying their taxes a sufficient tax upon the property and polls in said county, township, city or town to pay the interest on the bonds issued on account of such county, township, city or town, and shall also levy a sufficient tax to create a sinking fund to provide for the payment of said bonds at maturity.

Shall levy sufficient tax to create a sinking fund for payment of bonds.

The taxes levied as above provided shall be annually collected as other taxes and shall be paid by the collecting officer of such county, township, city or town to the treasurer thereof, and the taxes levied and collected for these purposes shall be kept distinct from all other taxes and shall be used for the purpose for which levied and collected and for no other. The sinking fund shall be invested as may be directed by the board of commissioners of the county issuing said bonds or in which there is a township issuing such bonds, or by the proper authorities of the city or town issuing said bonds: *Provided*, that whenever possible the sinking fund shall be invested in the purchase of the identical bonds issued under this act at a price not exceeding the par value thereof. In the event that the properties, rights and franchises or any part thereof of this company are hereafter acquired under the provisions of this act by any other company the board of commissioners of any county making such subscription or in which there is a township making such subscription or the proper authorities of any city or town making such subscription shall be and are hereby authorized to transfer such subscription to such other company as the payee and beneficiary thereof.

Taxes levied, when collected.

Sinking fund shall be invested.

Subscriptions may be transferred to purchasing company.

SEC. 16. For the purposes of this act all the townships and counties along or near the line of the constructed or proposed road of this company which may vote to subscribe to the capital stock of the company as provided by this act shall be and are declared to be respectively bodies politic and corporate and vested with full power to subscribe as provided in this act and to assume the contract of indebtedness for the payment of said subscription, and shall have generally all the powers necessary and convenient to carry out the provisions of this act, and shall have all the rights and be entitled to all the liabilities in respect to any rights or causes of action growing out of the provisions of this act. The county commissioners of the respective counties in which any such township is located are declared to be corporate agents of said townships so incorporated and situated within the limits of the said counties respectively for the purpose of issuing the bonds of said township or townships and to provide for the levy and collection of taxes on property and polls to pay the principal and interest of such bonds, and to provide for the sinking fund hereinabove mentioned.

Townships and counties subscribing stock constituted bodies politic.

Counties corporate agents of townships subscribing.

Company may issue coupon or registered bonds.

SEC. 17. It shall be lawful for this company to issue coupon or registered bonds in such denominations, running for such time, bearing such rate of interest and payable at such time and place as the board of directors may direct, and to secure the payment of the same the company is authorized to execute one or more mortgages or deeds of trust to such person or corporation as it may select on all or any part of its real and personal property, franchises and privileges, or in case the road be divided and built in sections such mortgages or deeds of trust may be placed upon such separate sections or on all or any part of its franchises and in such manner as the company may direct, and it is hereby further provided that the registration of any mortgage or deed of trust provided to be executed in this section may be made in each county where the property lies, and upon the registration thereof it shall be a lien upon the property and franchises conveyed in said mortgage or deed of trust.

Registered mortgage or deed of trust shall constitute lien on property and franchise.

Company may dispose of bonds through directors.

This company may, by the action of the stockholders or through its board of directors, sell, hypothecate or otherwise dispose of the bonds authorized by this section to be issued, or any other of its stock, bonds or securities.

Empowered to employ state convicts on approval of governor.

SEC. 18. The board of directors of the penitentiary may, on the application of the president of this company, approved by the governor, turn over to said company convicts not otherwise appropriated or needed, in the discretion of said board, not less than two hundred and fifty in number, to be worked on the construction of said road, upon such terms as may be agreed upon, the said convicts to be guarded and superintended by the authorities of the penitentiary, and to be hired to said company as provided by law.

Personal liability of stockholders.

SEC. 19. The stockholders of this company, whether private individuals or corporations, public, private or municipal, shall not be personally liable for the debts of the company.

SEC. 20. This act shall be in force from and after its ratification.

Ratified the 22d day of February, A. D. 1899.

CHAPTER 94.

An act to repeal certain acts whereby the town of Shelby, and townships Numbers One and Three of Cleveland county were exempt from the local option law.

The General Assembly of North Carolina do enact:

Chapter 67, private laws of 1893, relative to sale of intoxicating liquors in Shelby, repealed.

SECTION 1. That chapter sixty-seven of the private laws of North Carolina of eighteen hundred and ninety-three, entitled "An act relative to the sale of intoxicating liquors in the town of

Shelby, Cleveland county," and all laws amendatory thereof, be and the same are hereby repealed.

SEC. 2. That chapter two hundred and thirty-three of the public laws of North Carolina of eighteen hundred and ninety-five, entitled "An act to allow Number One and Number Three townships, in Cleveland county, to vote on the question of prohibition or license," be and the same is hereby repealed. Chapter 233, public laws of 1895, allowing townships Nos. 1 and 3 to vote on question of prohibition or license, repealed

SEC. 3. That chapter one hundred and thirty-nine of the laws of eighteen hundred and seventy three—eighteen hundred and seventy-four, also chapter one hundred and fifteen of the laws of eighteen hundred and seventy-six—eighteen hundred and seventy-seven, and also all of that part of section forty-two, chapter one hundred and one, private laws of eighteen hundred and eighty-one, relative to the sale of liquors, wines, cordials or other spirituous liquors in the town of Shelby are hereby re-enacted. Certain chapters relative to the sale of whiskey in Cleveland county re-enacted.

SEC. 4. The effect of this act shall be to restore prohibition in the town of Shelby and in Number One and Three townships, in Cleveland county, as it existed in said territory prior to the enactment of chapter sixty-seven, private laws of eighteen hundred and ninety-three, and chapter two hundred and thirty-three of the public laws of eighteen hundred and ninety-five. Effect of this act to restore prohibition to Shelby and Nos. 1 and 3 townships, Cleveland county.

SEC. 5. That all laws and clauses of laws in conflict with this act are hereby repealed. Conflicting laws repealed.

SEC. 6. That this act shall be in force from and after the thirtieth day of June eighteen hundred and ninety-nine.

Ratified the 23d day of February, A. D. 1899.

CHAPTER 95.

An act to incorporate the Thompson Institute.

The General Assembly of North Carolina do enact:

SECTION 1. That S. S. Stephens, W. C. Copeland, Derry Lewis, Rev. B. W. Williams, Rev. J. D. Harrell, Harrison Singletary, Rev. S. Atkinson, P. B. Peacock and J. C. Inman, and their successors, as trustees, duly elected in the manner hereinafter prescribed be and they are hereby made and created a corporation and body politic, to have perpetual succession under the name and style of the Thompson Institute. Corporators. Body politic. Corporate name.

SEC. 2. That said corporation shall have a seal, may purchase or receive by gift or devise or otherwise real and personal property, to hold in fee simple or otherwise, amounting in the aggregate to ten thousand dollars; may sue and be sued and enjoy any and all rights incident to and appropriate for conducting an institution for education of males and females. Corporate powers.

Term of office of trustees.

SEC. 3. That said trustees shall hold their offices as follows: S. S. Stephens, W. C. Copeland and Derry Lewis, one year from January first. eighteen hundred and ninety nine; Rev. B. W. Williams, Rev. J. D. Harrell and Harrison Singletary, two years from January first, eighteen hundred and ninety-nine; and Rev. S. Atkinson, P. B. Peacock and J. C. Inman, three years from January first, eighteen hundred and ninety-nine; and that hereafter at each annual session of the Lumber River Baptist Association three trustees shall be elected to succeed the three whose terms expires with that year, each trustee, however, to be subject to removal at any time by a majority of the others for inefficiency or neglect of duty.

Election of trustees by Lumber River Baptist Association.

Five trustees shall constitute quorum.

SEC. 4. That five members of said board of trustees shall constitute a quorum for the transaction of business; and when a vacancy shall occur in said board by death, resignation, refusal to act, removing from state or otherwise, such vacancy or vacancies may be filled at any regular meeting of the board by a majority vote of the trustees present, but such trustees shall hold their office only until the next meeting of the Lumber River Baptist Association, when their successors shall be regularly elected.

Vacancies occurring.

Election of officers.

SEC. 5. That such trustees shall have the right to elect a president, secretary and treasurer of said board under such rules and regulations as they may prescribe, who shall hold their offices not longer than one year, and the treasurer elect, before entering upon the discharge of his duties, may be required to enter into bond to said trustees as trustees and their successors in a sum not exceeding five hundred dollars, conditioned for the faithful performance of his duties as treasurer.

Treasurer may be required to give bond.

Presiding officers.

SEC. 6. That the president shall preside at all meeting of the board of trustees when present, and when absent the president pro tempore designated by those present shall preside. The secretary shall keep a record of all the proceedings of the board, and all the by laws made by said trustees for the government of said corporation and record the same in a book to be kept for that purpose.

Record of proceedings.

Compensation.

SEC. 7. That the said trustees shall receive no compensation for their services, but the treasurer and secretary of said board may receive such compensation as the trustees may allow.

No individual liability.

SEC. 8. That the individual property of the said trustees shall not be liable for the debts or obligations of said corporation.

May open books for receiving donations.

Proviso.

SEC. 9. That said trustees shall have the right to open books for the purpose of receiving donations to said school, to be used for any purpose in connection therewith: *Provided, however*, where the donor provides in the instrument making the donation to said school as to what uses and purposes the donation shall be used for, that the said trustees and their successors

Trustees shall comply with provisions of donor.

forever shall comply with the directions of the donor as near as practicable in the use of the donation.

SEC. 10. That it shall be the duty of the treasurer to issue to all persons making donations to said corporation for the benefit of said school a certificate stating the amount or nature thereof under his hand and seal of said corporation, and to make a permanent record of same in the records of said corporation.

Treasurer shall issue certificate of donations.

SEC. 11. That should a majority of the aforesaid trustees or their successors at any time conclude that the purposes and objects for which the donations were received have failed, then it shall be the duty of said trustees to make advertisement thereof for four weeks in a newspaper published in the town of Lumberton, North Carolina, and to convert all the funds received by donation to said corporation into money on such terms as they may think right and just and for the best interest of all parties concerned, and paying all debts and obligations against them as trustees of said school, and retaining all costs and expenses incurred in making sale of the property of said corporation; to divide the surplus, if any, among all the donors or their legal representatives equally in proportion to the amount donated to said school. And when such conclusion as aforesaid shall have been published and declared and the distribution of the assets of said corporation shall have been made as herein provided, then the said corporation shall cease to exist to all intents and purposes in law.

How corporation may be dissolved.

SEC. 12. That the board of trustees and their successors aforesaid shall have full power to employ such teachers and other employees in and for said school as they may deem qualified to discharge the duties of their several offices and as are necessary for the management of said school, and may remove the same at any time for good cause. They shall also have the power to make all necessary by-laws, rules and regulations for the government of said school and for the government of the corporation not inconsistent with the laws and constitution of North Carolina and the United States. They shall have power to erect and fully equip suitable buildings near the town of Lumberton, North Carolina, for school purposes, and such other building as they may think proper to use in connection therewith, and to exercise a general supervision and control over the school at all times.

Powers of trustees.

SEC. 13. That all laws and clauses of laws in conflict with this act are hereby repealed so far as this the said corporation is concerned, and no further.

Conflicting acts repealed.

SEC. 14. That this act shall be in force from and after its ratification.

Ratified the 23d day of February, A. D. 1899.

CHAPTER 96.

An act for the government of the town of Beaufort, Carteret county.

The General Assembly of North Carolina do enact:

Corporate powers of the town of Beaufort, in whom vested.

SECTION 1. That the corporate powers and authority granted to the town of Beaufort shall be vested in and exercised by a mayor and eight (8) commissioners. No person shall be eligible as mayor or commissioner unless he shall be eligible as a member of the legislature of this state and shall have resided within the town ninety days next preceding the election, and every commissioner elected by the people shall be a resident of the ward for which he shall be chosen ninety days next preceding the day of election.

Eligibility for mayor.

Commissioners, how elected.

SEC. 2. That the commissioners shall be elected by the qualified voters of each ward respectively as hereinafter set forth in the several sections of this act.

Qualifications for voting.

SEC. 3. That no person shall be entitled to register and vote in said town of Beaufort in any other ward than the one in which he is an actual and bona fide resident on the day of election; that every elector shall have resided in the ward in which he offers to vote thirty days prior to the day of registration and in the state twelve months and county ninety days; that the registration books shall be open for the registration of electors for three days (Thursday, Friday and Saturday) next preceding the day of election; and that all challenges shall be on the day of election.

Registration.

Registrar and poll holders, how and when appointed.

SEC. 4. That the registrar and poll holders shall be appointed by the mayor and commissioners at least thirty days preceding the day of election and shall consist of one registrar and two poll holders of different political persuasion and who shall be able to read and write and be otherwise competent to fill said position.

Representation of wards.

SEC. 5. That the first and second wards shall each elect two commissioners, the third, fourth and fifth wards shall each elect one commissioner; that the first and second wards shall elect one commissioner at large. The commissioners thus elected shall within five days after their election qualify by taking the oath of office before some officer qualified to administer oaths and immediately and at the first meeting of said board of commissioners they shall elect some man and permanent resident of said town, who is legally and otherwise well qualified, as mayor of said town; said mayor shall duly qualify by taking the oath of office before some officer qualified to administer oaths within three days after his election. The mayor thus elected and qualified shall preside at all meetings, and in case of a tie shall give the casting vote. The board thus elected shall hold their office for the term of one year or until their successors are elected and qualified.

When commissioners shall qualify.

Mayor, how elected.

Term of office.

SEC. 6. That the town of Beaufort shall be divided into five wards, bounded as follows, to-wit: The first ward shall consist of that part of the town included within these boundaries: Beginning at the west end of Broad street and running with Broad street to Orange street, and thence with Orange street to Ann street, and thence with Ann street to Turner street, and thence with Turner street southerly to the water, and with the water to the beginning. The second ward shall consist of that part of the town included within these boundaries: Beginning at the water, the southern extremity of Turner street and running with Turner street to Ann; thence with Ann street to Orange street; thence with Orange street to Broad street; thence with Broad street to Queen street; thence with Queen street to Ann street, and with Ann street to Live Oak street southerly to the water, and with the water to the beginning. The third ward shall consist of that part of the town east of Live Oak and south of Broad streets. The fourth ward shall consist of that part of the town west of Turner street and north of Broad street. The fifth ward shall consist of that part of the town not included in the former wards. Ward boundaries.

SEC. 7. That the election shall be held at the town hall, except in case of fire or other good cause, when the registrar and poll holders may move to some other convenient place; that the votes shall be cast in separate boxes for each ward properly and legibly labeled; that the hours for registration shall be from eight o'clock in the morning to five o'clock in the evening of each day; that the polls shall be opened at seven o'clock in the morning and closed at sundown of the same day. Election, when held. Hours for registration. Polls, when opened and closed.

SEC. 8. That chapter seventy-two (72), laws eighteen hundred and ninety-five, and all laws and clauses of laws in conflict with this act shall be and the same are hereby repealed. Chapter 72, laws of 1895, providing form of government for Beaufort, and other conflicting laws repealed.

SEC. 9. That this act shall go into effect immediately, and all of its provisions be carried out at the next general election of the town of Beaufort, to be held on the first Monday in May, eighteen hundred and ninety-nine. Effective at once.

Ratified the 23d day of February, A. D. 1899.

CHAPTER 97.

An act to extend the corporate limits of the city of Hickory.

WHEREAS, the corporate line of the city of Hickory takes in about one-half of the dwelling of N. C. Deal and runs near the dwelling and takes in a part of the lands of L. S. Whitener; and Preamble.

WHEREAS, the said N. C. Deal and the said L. S. Whitener desire to become citizens and be attached to said city.

The General Assembly of North Carolina do enact:

Extension of corporate limits of Hickory.

SECTION 1. That the dwellings of the said N. C. Deal and of the said L. S. Whitener be attached to and made a part of the said city of Hickory: and that the inmates of said dwellings shall be entitled to all the rights and privileges appertaining to the citizens of said city of Hickory, and that they shall be liable for and bound to the discharge of all the duties and obligations appertaining to the citizens of the said city of Hickory.

Conflicting laws repealed.

SEC. 2. That all laws and clauses of laws in conflict with this act are hereby repealed.

SEC. 3. That this act shall be in force from and after its ratification.

Ratified the 23d day of February, A. D. 1899.

CHAPTER 98.

An act to incorporate the Atlantic and Yadkin Railway Company.

Preamble.

WHEREAS, the purchasers of the Cape Fear and Yadkin Valley Railway Company have, in the deed conveying the property to them and otherwise under the statutes of this state, declared themselves a corporation under and by the name of Atlantic and Yadkin Railway Company; have elected officers and performed

Preamble.

other acts as such corporation, and it is now desired that the same shall be ratified and that the said company shall be incorporated by this general assembly; therefore,

The General Assembly of North Carolina do enact:

Purchasers.

SECTION 1. That H. Walters, B. F. Newcomer, Michael Jenkins and Warren G. Elliott, purchasers of the property of the Cape Fear and Yadkin Valley Railway Company, and such other persons as are now or that may hereafter be associated with them, their successors and assigns, are hereby created and de-

Body politic.

clared to be a body politic and corporate under and by the name

Corporate name.

of Atlantic and Yadkin Railway Company, and as such shall have all the powers, rights and franchises which were enjoyed by

Corporate powers.

the Cape Fear and Yadkin Valley Railway Company, and shall have all the general powers and be subject to all the general restrictions given to or imposed upon railroad companies or other corporations by the laws of this state.

Action already taken ratified.

SEC. 2. That such action as may have been already taken by the said purchasers and their associates in the organization of the said company as a corporation under the laws of this state, and the acts and things so far done by such corporation under such organization are hereby ratified.

SEC. 3. That the said company shall have the right from time to time to issue its capital stock to any amount not exceeding the amount of the outstanding capital stock of the Cape Fear and Yadkin Valley Railway Company at the time of the sale of the property thereof, to-wit: the sum of one million nine hundred and seventy-two thousand nine hundred dollars ($1,972,900), divided into shares of one hundred dollars each, and may issue the same either as preferred or common stock. Capital stock. Division of stock.

SEC. 4. That the said company shall have the right to borrow money and to make, issue and negotiate on such terms as to its directors may seem proper, its bonds, either coupon or registered, to such an amount as it may deem proper and necessary for the general uses and purposes of the company, and to cause the same to be secured by one or more mortgages or deeds in trust conveying the property, rights and franchises of such company to such trustee or trustees and upon such terms and conditions as to the directors may seem proper. Corporate power. May borrow money, issue bonds, etc.

SEC. 5. The said company shall have the right to issue and deliver so much of its capital stock and as many of its mortgage bonds as it may deem proper in settlement of the purchase of the property, rights and franchises of the Cape Fear and Yadkin Valley Railway Company conveyed to it as aforesaid. May issue and deliver capital stock in settlement of purchase of property.

SEC. 6. The said company shall have the right to consolidate with any other railroad company organized under the laws of this state with which it may connect directly or indirectly on such terms and conditions as may be agreed upon by and between the stockholders of this and any other such company: *Provided*, that any corporation or company consolidated under the provisions of this act shall be a domestic corporation and subject to the laws and jurisdiction of North Carolina. Empowered to consolidate with other roads. Proviso. Subject to laws and jurisdiction of North Carolina.

SEC. 7. That this act shall be in force from and after its ratification.

Ratified the 23d day of February, A. D. 1899.

CHAPTER 99.

An act to extend the time for organizing The American Trust and Savings Bank.

The General Assembly of North Carolina do enact:

SECTION 1. That the time for organizing The American Trust and Savings Bank, which was incorporated by an act entitled "An act to incorporate The American Trust and Savings Bank," being chapter seventy eight of the private laws of eighteen hun- Time for organizing The American Trust and Savings Bank extended.

dred and ninety seven, be and the same is hereby extended to the first day of January, nineteen hundred and one.

Sec. 2. That this act shall be in force from and after its ratification.

Ratified the 23d day of February, A. D. 1899.

CHAPTER 100.

An act to incorporate the Bank of Mooresville, North Carolina

The General Assembly of North Carolina do enact:

Corporators.

Section 1. That J. E. Sherrill, W. C. Johnston, J. P. Mills, C. K. McNeely, J. R. McLelland, G. C. Goodman, T. O. Brawley, S. C. Rankin, R. W. Freeze, J. L. Harris, A. Leazar and S. A. Lawrence, their present and future associates and successors are hereby constituted and declared to be a body politic and corporate by the name and style of the Bank of Mooresville, and shall so continue for the term of sixty years, with capacity to take, hold and convey real and personal estate, and with all the powers, rights and privileges granted to any bank by this or any preceding legislature of this state, together with the rights, powers and privileges incident to corporations as set forth or referred to in the first, second and third sections of chapter sixteen of The Code, entitled "Corporations."

Body politic. Corporate name. Corporate powers.

Capital stock.

Sec. 2. The capital stock of said corporation shall not be less than fifteen thousand dollars, in shares of one hundred dollars each, and such capital stock may be increased from time to time as said corporation may elect to a sum not exceeding one hundred thousand dollars.

May be increased.

Empowered to open books to take subscriptions for stock.

Sec. 3. The corporators in the first section named, or a majority of them, are hereby authorized and empowered to open books of subscription to the capital stock of said bank at such times and places as they shall determine, and the stockholders at any general meeting called after the organization of said bank may at their discretion from time to time reopen books of subscription to said capital stock until the same be wholly taken.

When stockholders shall organize.

Sec. 4. Whenever fifteen thousand dollars shall be subscribed and ten thousand dollars paid into the capital stock of said bank the before-named corporators or a majority of them shall call a meeting of the subscribers to said stock at such time and place and on such notice as they may deem sufficient; and such stockholders shall elect such directors as they may think proper, who shall hold office for one year and until their successors are elected, and said directors shall choose a president to serve during their continuance in office.

SEC. 5. The president and directors of the bank may adopt and use a common seal and alter the same at pleasure, may make and appoint all necessary officers and agents, fix their compensation and take security for the faithful discharge of their duties, prescribe the manner of paying for stock and the transfer thereof; may do a general banking business on such terms and rates of interest and discount as may be agreed on, not inconsistent with the laws of the state, and in general have the privileges conferred on corporations by the general laws of the state. The bank shall have a lien on the stock for debts due it by the stockholders before and in preference to other creditors of the same dignity.

Seal.

Corporate powers.

SEC. 6. That said bank may receive and pay out the lawful currency of the country, deal in exchange, gold and silver coin, bullion, uncurrent paper and public or other securities; may purchase and hold such real and personal estate and property as may be conveyed to secure debts to the bank or may be sold under execution to satisfy any debt due to said bank, and may sell and convey the same; may purchase and hold real estate for the transaction of business and at pleasure sell or exchange the same; may discount notes or other evidences of debt, may lend money on such terms as may be agreed on not inconsistent with the laws of the state. It may receive on deposit moneys on terms agreed on between the officers and depositors.

Corporate powers.

Corporate powers.

SEC. 7. If any subscriber shall fail to pay his stock or any part thereof as the same is required of him the entire residue of his stock shall be deemed to be due and may be recovered in the name of the bank either by motion to the court of the county wherein the delinquent may reside upon giving ten days' notice of the motion, or by civil action; or the entire stock may be sold by order of the directors for cash at the banking house in Mooresville, after advertisement of sale for twenty days in a newspaper published in the town or county; and if at such sale the price should not be sufficient to discharge the amount unpaid, with all costs attending the sale, the subscriber shall be liable for the deficiency in a civil action.

Remedy against subscriber failing to pay stock.

SEC. 8. If any subscriber shall assign his stock before its full payment, he and his assignee and all subsequent assignees thereof shall be liable for its payment, and may be sued jointly or severally by motion as aforesaid or by civil action, and in every case of delinquency by a subscriber or others the subscription shall be deemed a promissory note payable to the bank as well in respect to the remedy for recovering the same as in the distribution of the assets of any deceased subscriber.

Assignment of unpaid for stock. Remedy.

SEC. 9. The president and directors shall exercise all such powers and authority as may be necessary for the governing of the affairs of the corporation; shall have power to prescribe the

Powers of president and directors.

rules for the conduct of the bank, the same being consistent with the rules, regulations and by laws established by the stockholders, and may regulate the terms and rates on which discounts and loans may be made and deposits received by the bank; and they shall direct when dividends of profits may be made. They may call a meeting of the stockholders whenever they may think proper; and any number of stockholders holding together one-fifth of the stock may call a special meeting on giving thirty days' notice in a newspaper published in the town or county. At all meetings stockholders may be represented by proxy, each share being entitled to one vote.

May call meeting.

Corporate power.

SEC. 10. Said bank shall have power to make loans upon mortgages of real estate and personal property, with power of sale upon default of payment inserted, and also to receive in storage or warehouse any cotton or other agricultural or manufactured product whatsoever as a pledge for the repayment of money loaned upon the faith of the same; the said liens, pledges or mortgage being duly recorded and registered as in the case of mortgage and deeds of trust, and any sales thereunder according to the terms therein recited shall be good and valid in law.

SEC. 11. This act shall be in force from and after its ratification.

Ratified the 23d day of February, A. D. 1899.

CHAPTER 101.

An act supplementary to an act entitled "An act authorizing and empowering the town of Reidsville, in Rockingham county, to issue bonds for the establishment of waterworks in said town."

The General Assembly of North Carolina do enact:

Word "retain" stricken out and "retire" substituted.

SECTION 1. That the word "retain," it being the twenty-fourth word from the end of section three, be stricken out and the word "retire" be inserted in lieu thereof.

SEC. 2. That this act shall be in force from and after its ratification.

Ratified the 23d day of February, A. D. 1899.

CHAPTER 102.

An act to amend the charter of the Southern Guarantee and Investment Company.

The General Assembly of North Carolina do enact:

Charter of Southern Guarantee Investment Company, formerly the Worth-

That the charter of the Southern Guarantee and Investment Company, formerly the Worth-Wharton Real Estate and Investment Company, a corporation duly incorporated under the laws of this state on the fourth day of August, eighteen hundred and ninety, with its principal office at Greensboro in this state, be amended so that the same shall read as follows: Wharton Real Estate and Investment Company, amended.

SECTION 1. E. P. Wharton, A. W. McAlister and I. M. Wharton, together with such other persons as they may associate with them, their successors and assigns, be and they are hereby created a body politic and corporate under the name and style of the Southern Loan and Trust Company, by which name they may sue and be sued, plead and be impleaded, adopt and use a common seal, which they may alter at their pleasure; may make bylaws, rules and regulations for the government of said corporation, not inconsistent with law; shall exist for the term of sixty (60) years and enjoy all the rights, privileges, powers and immunities usually pertaining to corporations. Corporators, as amended. Body politic. Corporate name. Corporate powers. Term of existence.

SEC. 2. That the capital stock of said corporation shall be twenty-five thousand dollars, to be divided into shares of the par value of one hundred dollars each, with the privilege to said corporation of increasing the same to an amount not exceeding one hundred and fifty thousand dollars. Capital stock. Division of shares. Stock may be increased.

SEC. 3. That the principal office of said corporation shall be in Greensboro, North Carolina, but the board of directors may establish branch offices and agencies in this and other states as it may deem convenient and useful for the business of the corporation. Principal office.

SEC. 4. That the officers of the corporation shall be a president, vice-president, secretary and treasurer, and a board of directors, which shall consist of such number as the by-laws may determine; and two or more of such offices may be held by one person if the board of directors so elect. Officers.

SEC. 5. That said corporation shall have full power to buy, lease, own, hold and improve real estate and personal property of all kinds and to sell, lease, convey and dispose of the same in such lots and upon such terms as the board of directors may determine; and may engage in manufacturing enterprises of any kind, and may build, equip and operate for itself or others mills, factories, furnaces, stores and warehouses and other buildings; it may deal in stock, bonds, mortgages and other securities; it may borrow and lend money, and make, accept, endorse, issue and purchase promissory notes, bonds with or without coupons, bills and mortgages, and mortgage and pledge its property, both real and personal; may act as factors, brokers or agents in borrowing and lending money, buying and selling stocks, bonds and securities and in doing other acts not inconsistent with law, and investing such money as may be entrusted to its care or management for investment in bonds, stocks or other securities and property; may subscribe to stock in other corporations and accept subscrip- Corporate powers. Corporate powers.

Corporate powers.

tions for stock in this company, either in real estate or personal property or in the bonds or stocks of other incorporated companies; it may insure or guarantee the payment of any dividends, bonds, notes, undertakings, mortgages or other securities or evidences of indebtedness to any person, partnership or corporation; and may guarantee the title to any and all real estate situate within or without this state; it may guarantee or become surety upon all kinds of fiduciary and other bonds or undertakings not prohibited by law, including those of guardians, executors, administrators, collectors, receivers, trustees of any sort, suitors in any court, public officers of the United States or of any state, county or municipality, and of employees and agents of any person, company or corporation, under such regulations as may be determined upon by the board of directors.

Corporate powers.

Corporate powers.

SEC. 6. That the said company shall have power to act as executor, administrator, guardian, trustee, receiver, assignee or depositary, and to take, accept and execute any and all such trusts and powers of whatsoever nature or description as may be conferred upon or entrusted or committed to it by any person or persons, or by any corporation by agreement, grant, assignment, transfer, devise, bequest or otherwise, or by order of any court of record, and to receive, take, hold, manage and convey any property or estate, real or personal, which may be subject to any such trust. In lieu of the bond required by law to be given by any administrator, guardian, trustee, receiver or other fiduciary, the said company shall, before assuming any such trust under order of of any court, filed [file] in the office of the clerk of the superior court of Guilford county an undertaking with sufficient surety with either personal sureties or bonds of the state of North Carolina or the United States, or any county or city of the State of North Carolina, or any security satisfactory to the court and to be approved by the said clerk, and the said undertaking so secured may be accepted by the said clerk and held as such security in the sum of ten thousand dollars, conditioned upon the faithful performance of any trust which may be committed to the said company by order of the court of North Carolina as aforesaid. In case of default in the performance of any trust so committed to said company as aforesaid, the said undertaking may be sued upon by the party injured or his personal representatives in the superior court of any county of North Carolina where such default may have been made or in the superior court of Guilford county whenever it shall have been made satisfactorily to appear by sworn testimony that it is necessary to secure the faithful performance of all the said trusts. The court may require the said undertaking to be enlarged sufficiently to secure the faithful performance of the same. A copy of such undertaking duly certified

Corporate powers.

In event of company's default in the performance of any trust. Remedy.

by the seal of the superior court of Guilford county shall be evidence in all the courts of North Carolina, and the superior court wherein the said company has been appointed guardian, executor, administrator, receiver, trustee or depositary shall have the power to make orders respecting such trusts, and to require the said company to render all accounts which said court might lawfully make or require if such trustee were a natural person, and in accepting any of the trusts or powers hereunder, the said corporation may qualify by its president, vice-president, secretary or treasurer.

Copy of undertaking duly certified shall be evidence.

SEC. 7. That the said company may act as the fiscal or transfer agent of or trustee for any state, county, municipality, body politic or corporation, or for any person or persons, and in such capacity may receive and disburse money and negotiate, sell, transfer, register and countersign certificates of stocks, bonds or other evidences of indebtedness.

Corporate power.

SEC. 8. That the said company shall have discretionary power to invest the funds received by it in trust in bonds of the United States or of any state, or in the bonds duly authorized to be issued by any county or incorporated city or other good securities, or in safe real or personal securities, but all such investments shall be at the sole risk of the company, and for any losses by reason of such investments, the capital stock, property and effects of said corporation shall be absolutely liable. The company shall use due diligence to enhance the income, rents and profits of any trust estate within its hands, but shall not be held liable for any greater income, rents and profits than can be reasonably earned by safe and prudent investments.

Company given discretionary power to invest funds, etc.

Investment at risk of company.

Company shall use due diligence.

SEC. 9. That in addition to the powers above conferred said corporation may build, erect, maintain, conduct and operate one or more warehouses or depots for the storage of goods, wares, merchandise, cotton and other produce, and to charge and receive commissions, rents and compensation for the storage and keeping thereof, which charge shall constitute a first lien upon the property so stored, make rules, regulations, contracts and by-laws fixing terms and prices for storage, manner of inspection, form of receipts, insurance of property stored, and all other matters affecting the safe and prudent conduct of such business, make advances of money or credit upon cotton or other products and merchandise stored as aforesaid, and the receipts issued by said company shall be and are hereby declared to be negotiable instruments and pass by endorsement and delivery and to entitle the holder thereof to the property marked and designated therein in like manner as the original holder would be had not such an assignment been made.

Corporate powers.

SEC. 10. That said corporation may receive and pay out the

Corporate powers.

lawful currency and deal in exchange, gold and silver coin and bullion: may discount notes, drafts and other securities: may issue bills or notes to circulate as currency in such denominations as the board of directors may authorize and under such regulations as may be hereafter authorized and provided by the laws of this state and the United States, and shall have all the rights, powers, privileges and franchises incident to banking institutions in this state, and if money be deposited with said coporation by a minor or feme covert either as an investment or otherwise, such money may be withdrawn by such minor or feme covert without the consent of the parent or guardian of such minor or the husband of the feme covert, and his or her check or receipt therefor shall be as binding upon such minor or feme covert as though he or she were of full age or unmarried.

Money deposited by minor or feme covert may be withdrawn by them.

May establish branch houses.

SEC. 11. That the said corporation shall have the right to establish branch banks at such other places in the state of North Carolina as the stockholders and board of directors may from time to time agree upon: *Provided, however*, that all branch banks established under this section shall pay such license tax as may be provided by law, shall be under the supervision and control of the directors and officers of the said corporation, and the said corporation shall be liable for all the debts and other liabilities of any such banks so established: *Provided further*, that nothing herein shall be so construed as to prevent the election of local boards of directors and other officers to take immediate supervision and control of any branch bank to be established under the provisions of this section, but such local boards and officers shall at all times be amenable to the direction and control of the principal directors and officers of the said corporation hereinbefore referred to.

Proviso.

Branch houses shall pay such license tax as is provided by law.

Proviso.

Local boards may be elected.

Corporate powers.

SEC. 12. That said company may receive on deposits for safe keeping, gold, silver, paper money, bullion, precious metals, jewels, plate, certificates of stock, evidences of indebtedness, deeds or muniments of title or other valuables of any kind, and charge commission or compensation therefor, which said charge shall be a lien upon said deposit until paid.

Courts may order money deposited with the company.

SEC. 13. Any and every court in which moneys may be paid, lodged or deposited by agreement of parties or by order, judgment or decree of such court, may order or direct the same to be deposited with the said company, and when such deposits shall have been made the same, like all moneys deposited with said company by individuals or corporations, shall be at all times subject to withdrawal by the check or order of the person entitled and duly authorized to withdraw the same; and any executor or administrator, guardian or other trustee or public officer having the control of any bonds, stocks, securities, moneys or other valuables belonging to others shall be and is hereby authorized to deposit the same for safe keeping with said company.

Sec. 14. This corporation is especially invested with the power and authority to carry on. conduct and operate a savings banking business in all its branches, and may receive deposits in small sums, the limits to be fixed by its board of directors, and pay interest thereon by way of dividends out of the net earnings or at fixed rates, according as it may be agreed between the company and its depositors; and the board of directors are hereby fully authorized to make all needful by-laws and regulations for conducting and carrying into effect the different features of this branch of this corporation.

Authorized to conduct a savings bank business.

Sec. 15. That said corporation shall have the power to insure buildings, furniture, stocks of goods and other property against loss or damage by fire, lightning and water, and may issue policies therefor, and shall have power to issue policies of accident and life insurance payable upon the injury by accident or death of the person insured to the beneficiary named in the policy, under such rules and regulations as may be fixed by the by-laws and not inconsistent with law.

Corporate powers.

Sec. 16. That said corporation shall have the power to charge and receive for all services or risks undertaken by it as herein provided, such a compensation as may be provided by law, and in the event no compensation is provided by law then it may charge and receive therefor such compensation as may be agreed upon between said corporation and the party to be charged therewith.

Corporate powers.

Sec. 17. That no stockholder shall be individually liable for any debt, contract or tort of the corporation.

Individual liability.

Sec. 18. That the stock of this corporation held by any one shall be transferred only on the books of the company, either in person or by attorney, and no stockholder shall transfer his stock except by the consent of the directors of the corporation, if he be indebted to the corporation as principal, surety or otherwise, until such indebtedness is paid off and discharged, and for all such indebtedness said corporation shall have a lien superior to all other liens upon the stock of said stockholders.

Stocks transferable only on books of company.

Shall have lien for indebtedness.

Sec. 19. That all acts performed by the Southern Guaranty and Investment Company prior to the ratification of this act and done in pursuance of supposed powers given by amendments to its charter granted by the clerk of the superior court of Guilford county be and the same are hereby in all respects ratified and confirmed.

Former acts of Southern Guaranty and Investment Company ratified.

Sec. 20. That this act shall be in force from and after its ratification.

Ratified the 23d day of February, A. D. 1899.

CHAPTER 103.

An act to amend the charter of the city of Winston.

The General Assembly of North Carolina do enact:

Chapter 161, private laws of 1895, and chapter 83, laws of 1897, relative to charter of city of Winston, repealed.

SECTION 1. That chapter one hundred and sixty-one, private laws of the general assembly of North Carolina of eighteen hundred and ninety-five (1895) and chapter eighty-three of the private laws of the general assembly of North Carolina, eighteen hundred and ninety-seven (1897), and all the provisions thereof, together with each and every section of said chapter be and the same are hereby repealed.

Act ratified March 7th, 1891, to consolidate and revise the charter of Winston, re-enacted and amended.

SEC. 2. That an act entitled "An act to consolidate and revise the charter of the city of Winston," ratified the seventh day of March, eighteen hundred and ninety-one (1891), chapter three hundred and seven, private laws of eighteen hundred and ninety-one (1891), be and the same is hereby re-enacted and amended as follows:

Corporate boundaries.

SEC. 3. Strike out all after the word "Winston" in second line and insert the following: "Shall be as follows, to-wit: Beginning at the northeast corner of the town of Salem and running thence with the old corporation line the three following courses: North eighty-one east eighty poles; thence north one east three hundred and forty-five poles to the northeast corner of the present limits of the Winston corporation; thence north eighty-nine west along the old corporation line to the east side of the old town road; thence in a southerly direction along the east side of the railroad to Peters creek; thence in a southwestwardly direction down Peters creek to the north side of Shallow Ford road; thence in an easterly direction along the north side of Shallow Ford road to the point at which the road forks (the north fork running to Winston and the south fork to Salem); thence in a southeasterly direction to the northwest corner of the Salem corporation; thence north eighty east along the boundary line between Winston and Salem to the place of beginning.

Corporate boundaries.

Corporate boundaries.

SEC. 4. That section five of said chapter three hundred and seven, acts of eighteen hundred and ninety-one (1891), be amended by striking out all after the word "the" in line seven and insert the following: "Boulevard, thence along the center line of the Boulevard running on the north side of the Zinzendorf site to Glade street; thence along the center line of Glade street to Sunset drive; thence west to Peters creek; thence in a southerly direction down Peters creek to the north side of Shallow Ford road; thence east along the north side of Shallow Ford road to the point at which the road forks (the north fork leading to Winston and the south fork to Salem); thence in a southeasterly direction to the northwest corner of the Salem corporation; thence east along the boundary line between Winston and Salem to the beginning. The second ward shall begin at the corner of First and Chestnut streets; thence east along First street with the boundary line between Winston and Salem to the northeast corner of the Salem corporation; thence with the Winston corporation line the five following courses, to-wit: North eighty-one east eighty poles to southeast corner of the Winston corporation; thence north one degree east three hundred and forty-five poles to the northeast corner of the Winston corporation; thence north eighty-nine west to the east side of the old town road; thence south along the east side of the old town road to Peters creek; thence down Peters creek to the N. C. Midland Railroad trestle, the northwest corner of the third ward; thence in a southeasterly direction to the western terminus of Seventh street; thence east along the center line of the street to the center line of Chestnut street; thence south along the center line of Chestnut street to the beginning. The third ward shall begin at corner of Chestnut and Fourth streets; thence north along the center line of Chestnut street to the center of Seventh street; thence west along the center line of Seventh street to its western terminus; thence in a northwest direction to the N. C. Midland Railroad trestle over Peters creek; thence down Peters creek to the north corner of the first ward; thence east to the corner of Sunset drive and Glade street; thence along the center line of Glade street to the Boulevard; thence along the center line of the Boulevard running north of the Zinzendorf site to Fourth street; thence east along the center line of Fourth street to the beginning."

Corporate boundaries.

Corporate boundaries.

Corporate boundaries.

Corporate boundaries.

Sec. 5. That section six of said chapter three hundred and seven be amended as follows: Strike out all of said section down to the word "be" in third line and insert in lieu thereof the following: "There shall on the first Monday in May, nineteen hundred (1900), and on the first Monday in May biennially thereafter," and after the word "respectively" in ---- line of said section insert the following: "Provided, that no aldermen [alderman] thus elected shall be eligible to hold an office of profit or trust to which he may be elected by the board of aldermen, and if at any time the board of aldermen should deem best to relieve the mayor of a part of his duties, they may appoint or elect some person not from their body to be known as the city recorder, whose duties shall be to preside over the municipal court of the city of Winston and in no other respect to interfere with the duties now imposed on the mayor. The person so elected city recorder shall be vested with all power to try and determine all matters coming before him as now given to the mayor, and shall be ex officio a justice of the peace of Winston township. The aldermen shall

Municipal elections, when held.

No alderman shall be eligible to hold an office of trust or profit to which he may be elected by board of aldermen.

Mayor may be relieved of part of his duties by election of a recorder.

Duties of recorder.

Powers vested in recorder.

Compensation fixed by aldermen.

have the power to fix the compensation of the mayor and the recorder in such amounts as to them may seem best, not to exceed the sum of one thousand dollars in the aggregate.

Section 7, private laws of 1891, amended. Time of selecting registrars changed.

SEC. 6. That section seven be amended by striking out in line two the words "December, eighteen hundred and ninety-one" and insert in lieu thereof the following: "March, nineteen hundred."

When books shall be opened for registration.

SEC. 7. That section eight of said act be amended as follows: Strike out the word "January" in line four and insert in lieu thereof the word "April."

Section 11, in reference to oath as to previous residence, amended.

SEC. 8. That section eleven of said act be amended by striking out the words "third Tuesday in February" and insert in lieu thereof the words "first Monday of May."

Section 12, in reference to time of appointment of judges of election, amended

Section 12, referring to time of holding election, amended.

SEC. 9. That section twelve of said act be amended as follows: Strike out the words "December, eighteen hundred and ninety-one" in line two and insert in lieu thereof the words "March, nineteen hundred," and strike out in line five and six thereof the words "third Tuesday of February" and insert in lieu thereof the words "first Monday of May."

Section 17, referring to day when aldermen shall qualify, amended.

SEC. 10. Strike out the word "Tuesday" in line one of section seventeen and insert in lieu thereof the word "Monday."

Oath of mayor and recorder.

SEC. 11. That section twenty be amended by inserting in line one after the word "mayor" the words "or recorder, if such officer shall have been elected."

Biennial election of aldermen.

SEC. 12. That section twenty-two of said act be amended by striking out in line two the word "Tuesday in February, one thousand nine [eight] hundred and ninety-two" and insert in lieu thereof the words "first Monday in May, nineteen hundred,"

Election of mayor.

and strike out the word "Tuesday" in line five of said section and insert in lieu thereof the word "Monday."

Election of tax collector.

SEC. 13. That section twenty-three of said act be amended by striking out the word "May" in line one and insert in lieu thereof the word "September," and striking out in lines two and three the words "eighteen hundred and ninety-one."

Contagious diseases, prevention of.

SEC. 13½. That after the word "disease" in line five, section seventy-six, insert the following: "Shall have power to establish and maintain quarantine against communities or territories where the board may declare prevails any infectious disease."

SEC. 14. That section fifty of said act be amended by striking out all after the word "for" in line eight down to the word "principal" in line nine.

Aldermen empowered to adopt ordinances as to dogs.

SEC. 14½. That after the word "larceny" at the end of line sixteen, section fifty, insert the following: 'And said board of aldermen shall have power to adopt ordinances regulating the keeping of dogs and sluts within the city limits during the months of June, July, August and September, and may kill and destroy any dog or slut kept within the city limits or impose a fine and imprisonment on any person for a violation of any of said ordinances.

SEC. 14¾. That the board of aldermen of the city of Winston shall have power and are hereby authorized to pass ordinances for the protection of the waterworks and the water supply of the city of Winston, and may in said ordinances by fine and imprisonment, within the jurisdiction of the mayor, punish all persons violating said ordinances so passed. Protection of waterworks and water supply.

SEC. 15. That section fifty-one of said act is hereby repealed. Section 51, providing for application of certain taxes to school fund, repealed.

SEC. 16. That section fifty-five of said act be amended by striking out the words "of" and "one" in line four and insert in lieu thereof the words "not less than two," and strike out all of said section after the word "city" in line nine. Corporation tax for liquor dealers.

SEC. 17. That section fifty-nine of said act be amended by striking out the word "January" in line ten and insert in lieu thereof the word "April." Additional levy on unpaid taxes, amended.

SEC. 18. That section sixty-one of said act be amended by striking out the word "January" in line three of said section and insert in lieu thereof the word "April," and strike out all of said section after the word "sold" in line seven and insert in lieu thereof "subject to the rules and regulations and the law providing for the sale of lands for taxes by the sheriff." When tax unpaid, real property to be advertised and sold. Lien of taxes. Manner of sale.

SEC. 19. That said act be amended by striking out all after the word "city" in line one, section sixty-six, subsection three, down to the word "stage" in line two. Amend subsection five under section sixty six by striking out all after the word "reward" in line two down to the word "in" after subsection thirteen under section sixty-six, and subsection fourteen to read as follows: "And power is hereby granted the board of aldermen to impose and collect such reasonable license tax on merchants and others buying, selling or in any way dealing in second-hand clothing, bedding, wearing apparel and furniture of all kinds, as in their discretion they may deem necessary for the protection of the public against infectious diseases, and the said aldermen are further authorized and empowered to make from time to time such ordinances as they may deem necessary for the protection of the public against any disease by regulating the importation into the city and the sale therein of second-hand clothing, beds and furniture of all kinds. Tax on theatrical exhibitions. License tax on merchants. Aldermen empowered to make ordinances in interest of public health.

SEC. 20. That said acts be amended by striking out all after the word "repair" in line three down to the word "they" in line five, and adding after the word "mortality" in the last line the following: "The city of Winston is hereby authorized to purchase suitable grounds for cemeteries, one for the white people and one for the colored people, to be under the supervision and City authorized to purchase suitable grounds for cemeteries.

control of the city, with power to make such regulations as may be proper for regulating the burying of the dead therein, and to have police jurisdiction thereon; that the cemeteries of the city of Winston as now laid off shall not be enlarged nor shall the dead be buried within the corporate limits of said city other than within the boundaries as now laid off. Any person violating the provisions of this section shall be guilty of a misdemeanor, and upon conviction shall be fined not more than fifty dollars or imprisoned for not more than thirty days.

Present cemeteries shall not be enlarged.

Violation of ordinance a misdemeanor. Penalty.

SEC. 21. That said act be amended by inserting after the word "proper" in line three, section seventy-four, the following: "That they may elect at any regular meeting after the passage of this act a committee of three citizens and taxpayers, to be known as the 'fire commissioners'—one for one year, one for two years and one for three years; that immediately upon their election their term of office shall begin and continue until the election of their successors; that annually after the first election aforesaid one commissioner shall be elected for a term of three years: *Provided*, that one alderman and no more shall be one of the three members; that said commissioners shall have full and complete control of the fire department, and may do such acts and make such expenditures as they may deem best for the equipment and organization of such department, including the purchase of apparatus, erection of buildings, employment of firemen, and all other things essential to its establishment and maintenance; said commissioners shall have a chairman and a secretary, and the city treasurer shall pay all warrants drawn on him by said chairman and countersigned by said secretary: *Provided*, said warrant specifies the object thereof: *And provided further*, that it shall be the duty of said fire commissioners to make application to the board [of] aldermen at their regular meeting on the first day of each and every year for such sum or sums of money as they desire to expend in the fire department during the coming year: *And provided further*, that such expenditure shall not exceed such sum as the board of aldermen upon such application may grant; that the board of aldermen may pass ordinances clothing firemen with police powers."

Aldermen empowered to elect a fire commission.

Term of office.

When term of office begins.

Proviso.

No aldermen shall be a member of the fire commission.

Power of fire commissioners.

Proviso.

Proviso.

Duty of fire commisioners.

Fire commissioners shall make application for moneys to be expended during following year.

Firemen may be clothed with police powers.

SEC. 22. That said act be amended by striking out all after the word "fifth" in line thirteen and section eighty-six and inserting in lieu thereof the following: "That the aldermen of the city at their first regular meeting in September, eighteen hundred and ninety-nine, and annually thereafter, shall appropriate a sufficient sum of money out of the general fund for the support of the graded schools, to be known as the 'graded school fund,' the sum to be appropriated for this purpose to be determined by the

Appropriation to graded schools.

graded school commissioners and approved by the board of aldermen."

SEC. 23. That said act be amended by inserting after the word "require" in last line of said section eighty-nine the following: And in case when required the citizens living along the lines of sewer or owning property along said lines or in the vicinity thereof shall neglect or refuse to connect their premises, drains or other pipes with said sewerage, then in that event it shall be lawful for the aldermen after notice to said owners or their qualified agents (which notice, in case of non-residence, having no resident agent, may be made by publication) may cause said premises to be properly arranged for health purposes and properly connected with the city sewerage pipes; and the expenses of making said repairs and alterations and connections with the main sewerage pipes shall be paid by the person when property shall be thus corporated, and said expenses shall be a lien upon said premises or lot, and if not paid on demand such lot or so much as may be necessary shall be sold by the tax collector to pay said expenses and costs under the same rules and regulations and restrictions as are required by law for the sale of lands for unpaid taxes.

Citizens along sewerage lines refusing to connect.

Aldermen may cause premises to be connected after notice.

Expenses incurred in connecting, a lien on property.

That said act be amended by adding after the word "punishment" in last line of section one hundred and three the following: "That the board of aldermen of the city of Winston, acting for the city of Winston alone or jointly with the city of Salem, shall have the authority to purchase such land as may be necessary and to establish thereon a workhouse for men and for women and for minors, and that in said workhouse or on said land, men, women or minors convicted of misdemeanors by the city authorities may be sentenced and confined at hard labor at such work as the board of aldermen may prescribe. That the superior court of Forsyth county with criminal jurisdiction or such criminal court as may be established for such county is given full power, with the consent of the city of Winston and Salem, to confine all women and minors convicted in said superior or criminal court in the workhouse so established.

Empowered to purchase land and establish a workhouse.

Courts may with consent of city confine women and minors in workhouse.

SEC. 24½. That section two, chapter one hundred and fifty-one, private laws of eighteen hundred and ninety-three, is hereby re-enacted.

Section 2, chapter 151, private laws of 1893, giving city officers jurisdiction over offenses committed one mile from corporate limits, re-enacted.

SEC. 25. That the city of Winston shall have power to annually appropriate and pay over to The Twin City Hospital Association, out of funds not otherwise appropriated, a sum not exceeding six hundred dollars.

Empowered to pay over to Twin City hospital certain money.

SEC. 26. That all acts or parts of acts in conflict with this act are hereby repealed.

Conflicting laws repealed.

SEC. 27. This act shall be in force from and after its ratification.

Ratified the 23d day of February, A. D. 1899.

CHAPTER 104.

An act to extend the time for the organization of "The Southern Trust and Guarantee Company."

The General Assembly of North Carolina do enact:

Time for organization of Southern Trust and Guarantee Company extended two years.

SECTION 1. That the time within which the organization, "The Southern Trust and Guarantee Company," chartered by chapter sixt y-five of the private laws of eighteen hundred and ninety-seven, may be perfected be and is hereby extended two years from the ratification of this act.

Corporate name changed.

SEC. 2. The name of said company is hereby changed to the "Carolina Banking, Guarantee and Trust Company," and this latter title shall be and is hereby inserted in lieu of and wherever the title "Southern Trust and Guarantee Company" occurs in said act, chapter sixty-five, private laws of eighteen hundred and ninety-seven.

SEC. 3. This act shall be in force and effect from its ratification.

Ratified the 23d day of February, A. D. 1899.

CHAPTER 105.

An act to amend and re-enact chapter two hundred and eighty-four of the laws of eighteen hundred and ninety-three, concerning the Wilmington and Weldon Railroad Company, and to authorize that company to change its name to the Atlantic Coast Line Railroad Company of North Carolina.

The General Assembly of North Carolina do enact:

Chapter 284, private laws of 1893, concerning Wilmington and Weldon Railroad, amended.

SECTION 1. That chapter two hundred and eighty-four of the private laws of eighteen hundred and ninety-three, ratified March six, eighteen hundred and ninety-three, concerning the Wilmington and Weldon Railroad Company be and the same is hereby amended and re-enacted so as to read as follows, to-wit:

Empowered to consolidate or merge with other railroads, etc.

That authority hereby is given to the Wilmington and Weldon Railroad Company to consolidate or to merge its railroads with or to buy or lease the railroad or railroads of any other railroad company with which it may connect, either directly or indirectly, organized under the laws of this state or of any adjoining state which, under the laws of this or such other state, may have power to consolidate, merge, sell or lease its road; and any such other

Additional corporate powers.

company shall have the right to consolidate, merge, sell or lease its railroad in whole or in part with or to the Wilmington and Weldon Railroad Company; and such consolidation, merge, sale or lease may be made between the Wilmington and Weldon Railroad Company and any other such company upon such terms and conditions as may be agreed upon by a majority of the stockholders of each corporation entitled to vote at all stockhlders' meetings; and on like terms and conditions the said Wilmington and Weldon Railroad Company may sell or lease in whole or in part any of its railroads to any other such railroad company, and power hereby is given to any other such railroad company organized under the laws of this or of any adjoining state, to take such lease or to make such purchase: *Provided*, that nothing herein contained shall be construed to exempt said railroad company or any other road with which it may be consolidated or otherwise acquire under this act from any taxes imposed by any general law of the state upon railroad property or franchises, and if said railroad company shall consolidate with or acquire under this act any other road whose property or franchises are now exempt from taxation, such exemption shall cease and such property and franchises of any and all such companies as may be consolidated or acquired under the provisions of this act shall be subject to taxation in like manner as the property and franchises of companies which are subject to taxation under the laws of this state: *Provided*, that this act shall not have the effect of ousting the jurisdiction of the courts of this state over causes of action arising within the state: *Provided further*, that any and all corporations consolidated, leased or organized under the provisions of this act shall be domestic corporations of North Carolina and shall be subject to the laws and jurisdiction thereof.

Proviso.

Subject to general laws of the state.

Shall be subject to taxation.

Proviso.

Jurisdiction of courts of this state retained.

Proviso.

Corporations consolidated, leased or organized under this act shall be domestic corporations.

SEC. 2. That authority is hereby given to the said Wilmington and Weldon Railroad Company at any meeting of its stockholders' by a majority vote thereof, to change its name to the Atlantic Coast Line Railroad Company of North Carolina.

May change name.

SEC. 3. This act shall be in force from and after its ratification.

Ratified the 24th day of February, A. D. 1899.

CHAPTER 106.

An act to incorporate "The Home Protection Insurance Company."

The General Assembly of North Carolina do enact:

SECTION 1. That John B. Kenney, Thomas C. Guthrie and D. R. Julian, and all other persons who may hereafter be associated with them, in the name and style of "The Home Protection Insurance Company," are hereby constituted a body politic and corporate, to have succession for ninety-nine years, and by

Corporators.

Corporate name.

Body politic.

Corporate powers. that name may sue and be sued, appear, prosecute and defend in any court of record or any other court or places whatsoever, and may have and use a common seal, and may purchase and hold such real estate and personal property as may be deemed necessary to effect the object of this association, and may sell and convey the same at pleasure, and may make, establish and put in execution such by-laws, ordinances and resolutions, not being contrary to the laws of this state and of the United States, as may be necessary and convenient for their regulation and government and for the management of their affairs, and to execute all such acts and things as may be necessary to carry into effect the provisions of this act.

Number of directors. SEC. 2. That the affairs of this company shall be governed and managed by a board of directors to consist of not less than three nor more than fifteen members or stockholders as may be regulated by the by-laws of the company, and the president and two directors may constitute a quorum for the transaction of business unless the by-laws prescribe a greater number.

Temporary directors. SEC. 3. The persons named in the first section of this act are hereby constituted a board of directors to serve as such until others are chosen, which may be done by them.

Election of officers. SEC. 4. That the board of directors shall elect a president and secretary and such other officers as they may see fit, who shall hold their offices for one year and until other officers are chosen and qualified in their places.

Home office. SEC. 5. That the home office of this company shall be in the city of Charlotte, in the state of North Carolina, and may be removed to any other place in the state whenever the directors may deem it necessary or convenient to promote the business of the company.

Corporate powers. SEC. 6. That this company may insure or reinsure against loss or damage by fire, lightning, wind or tornado or any other insurance whatever that the directors may deem proper, including life, accident and surety business; and this company is hereby vested with all powers that any insurance company has or may have to transact business in this state; and they may charge and receive such premiums as may be agreed upon by their company and the parties insured; and the payment of such premiums may be made in cash or by note, as may be decided upon by the board of directors.

Character of company. SEC. 7. That this company shall have authority to transact business as a mutual or a joint stock insurance company, or may combine the two as the stockholders or members may decide.

When authorized to commence business. SEC. 8. If the company should transact business as a mutual company only, they shall be authorized to commence business as soon as twenty-five or more persons shall have agreed in writing to become policy holders and have made application for at least fifty thousand dollars insurance.

Sec. 9. If the company should transact business as a stock company it shall be authorized to commence business as soon as twenty-five thousand dollars shall have been subscribed to the capital stock and ten thousand dollars paid in or properly secured. When authorized to commence business.

Sec. 10. If the company should decide to transact business as a stock and mutual company, it shall be authorized to commence business when the provisions of both the preceding sections shall have been complied with. When authorized to commence business.

Sec. 11. That the stockholders of said corporation shall not be liable for any loss or damage or responsibility in their person or property other than the property they have in the capital stock or funds of said corporation to the amount of shares respectively held by them and any profit therefrom not divided. Individual liability.

Sec. 12. That the policy holders of said corporation who may hold policies which participate in the profits of the company, may be held liable in the event the funds of the company may not be sufficient to meet any losses for an amount equal to twice the sum of one annual premium on their respective policies. Liability of policy holders.

Sec. 13. That nothing herein contained shall be so construed as to prevent the company receiving any of the benefits or from complying with any general insurance law that may hereafter be enacted. Shall be governed by general insurance laws.

Sec. 14. That the board of directors may invest and employ the funds of the company in such way and manner as they may judge that the interest and the welfare of the company may require. Funds of company may be invested.

Sec. 15. That in the event this company should transact business as a mutual company each policy holder shall have one vote in all meetings of policy holders and may authorize any other policy holder to act as his proxy. In the event the company transact business solely as a joint stock company, or should it transact business as a mutual and stock company, the affairs shall be managed by the subscribers to the capital stock only under the usual rules applicable to joint stock companies, subject to such by-laws as may be adopted. Policy holders may vote in meetings under certain conditions.

Sec. 16. That said company shall have power to represent as agent or attorney any life, fire, marine, accident, surety or trust company or any corporation or individual authorized to do business under the laws of the state of North Carolina. Corporate powers.

Sec. 17. This act shall be in force from and after its ratification.

Ratified the 24th day of February, A. D. 1899.

CHAPTER 107.

An act to amend section twelve of the act to amend the charter of the Raleigh and Gaston Railroad Company, ratified the sixteenth day of February, eighteen hundred and ninety-nine, and to authorize said Raleigh and Gaston Railroad Company to change its name.

The General Assembly of North Carolina do enact:

Section 12 of amended charter of Raleigh and Gaston Railroad Company ratified February 16th, 1899, amended.

SECTION 1. That in line three, section twelve, after the word "company" add the words "or any other name that may be selected and agreed upon."

SEC. 2. This act shall be in force from and after its ratification.

Ratified the 24th day of February, A. D. 1899.

CHAPTER 108.

An act to incorporate The Fire Insurance Company of Robeson county.

The General Assembly of North Carolina do enact:

Corporators. Body politic. Corporate name. Duration of charter.

SECTION 1. That B. Godwin, L. R. Hamer, E. F. McRae, K. M. Barnes, J. A. McAllister, B. Stansel, A. H. McLeod, A. C. Oliver, Sr., John H. McEachern, L. Shaw and R. R. Barnes, and all others who may become members thereof be and they are hereby constituted a body politic and corporate under the name of "The Fire Insurance Company of Robeson County" for a period of fifty years, and under that name shall have all the powers, privileges and franchises incident to such corporation under the laws of North Carolina.

Corporate powers. Seal.

SEC. 2. That said corporation shall have the right to mutually insure the respective dwelling houses, barns and other property, real and personal, of its members in the said county of Robeson in said state against loss by fire, wind and lightning, upon such terms as and under such conditions as may be fixed by the by-laws of said corporation. The said corporation may sue and be sued in any court in this state, and may have and use a common seal, and may acquire and own such real estate and erect such buildings thereon as may be necessary for its use in carrying on its business not exceeding ten thousand dollars in value.

Corporate power.

SEC. 3. That the said corporation may make by-laws fixing the number of its board of directors and other officers and defining the duties and powers of the directors and officers.

The said corporation may also make rules and regulations for governing the conduct of its business: *Provided*, the same be not inconsistent with the laws of this state or the United States.

SEC. 4. That every member of said corporation shall be bound to pay his pro rata share (in proportion to the amount of insurance held by him), and no more, of all losses and expenses that may accrue against the same while he shall be a member thereof: *Provided*, that any member may at any time surrender his insurance therein by paying up his pro rata share of the losses and expenses accrued up to the time of surrendering his policy. Members liable for losses and expenses. Proviso.

SEC. 5. That the principal office of said company shall be at Lumberton, North Carolina, and it may have branch offices at other places in Robeson county. Principal office.

SEC. 6. That this act shall be in force and effect from and after its ratification.

Ratified the 27th day of February, A. D. 1899.

CHAPTER 109.

An act to incorporate the R. J. Reynolds Tobacco Company.

The General Assembly of North Carolina do enact:

SECTION 1. Richard J. Reynolds, William N. Reynolds, Walter R. Reynolds and Robert C. Critz, of Winston, North Carolina, and John F. Parlett, of Baltimore, Maryland, their successors and assigns, are hereby created a body politic and corporate under the name of "R. J. Reynolds Tobacco Company," with the capital stock of one million two hundred thousand dollars, with the liberty and authority to increase the same from time to time or at any one time not to exceed twelve million dollars, to be divided into shares of one hundred dollars each; said stock shall be common and preferred stock, issued in the proportion of two shares of common stock to one share of preferred stock. Said preferred stock shall entitle the holder to receive in each year a dividend to be fixed at the time of the issue of the stock, of not more than eight per centum, payable half-yearly, before any dividend shall be set apart or paid on said general or common stock, and if the net proceeds in any year shall not be sufficient to pay the dividend aforesaid on said preferred stock, that such dividend shall be paid thereon as the net profits of the year will suffice to pay. The holders of the preferred stock shall have a preference on the assets of the company, but the dividends thereon are not to be cumulative, but shall be payable each year out of the profits of that year or out of any unused surplus of subsequent years; and on payment of the preferred stock at its par value with all dividends due thereon, said preferred stock shall not further participate in the assets of the corporation and may be called in and paid as prescribed by the by-laws. Said preferred Corporators. Body corporate. Corporate name. Capital stock. Division of stock. Holders of preferred stock shall have preference on assets.

stock and the certificates therefor may be issued by the board of directors by resolution. Said corporation shall have the privilege and rights hereby specifically granted, and also those conferred upon corporations by the laws of North Carolina.

Corporate powers.

Books may be opened for subscription.

SEC. 2. That any three of the persons herein incorporated to effect the purpose of this act may open books of subscription and receive subscription to the capital stock of the company at such time and place as they may appoint, and when twenty-five per centum of the capital stock herein first authorized, to-wit: One million two hundred thousand dollars shall have been subscribed and paid in, then the stockholders may organize the company. That property of every kind may be received in payment of the capital stock at such valuation as may be agreed upon between the subscriber or subscribers and said stockholders. The stockholders shall not be individually liable for debt or liabilities of the corporation.

Individual liability.

Corporate powers.

SEC. 3. That said corporation is hereby authorized and empowered to conduct, transact and carry on in all its branches and in every manner or form the business of curing, manufacturing, buying and selling tobaccos; and said corporation may manufacture, buy, sell and deal in wares and merchandise of every kind and description; shall have the power to own, hold, lease, purchase, sell and convey real estate and all other kinds of property wherever situate, and own and conduct any business at its will and pleasure; banking, insurance and operating a railroad excepted. The company proposes to carry on its operation in all the other states and territories in the United States, and in all foreign countries and territories.

Corporate powers.

SEC. 4. That the stcokholders of the said corporation shall have the power to make all rules and regulations for the government of said corporation and transaction of its business. They shall have power to elect, in such manner as the majority of the stock may prescribe, such officers as they deem necessary, prescribe their duties, compensation and term of service; and, in general, said stockholders may make such by-laws and regulations for the government and conduct of the said corporation and its business, not inconsistent with the laws of this state and the laws of the United States, as they may consider best calculated to serve their interest.

Seal.

SEC. 5. As such corporation they may have a common seal, which they may break, change and alter at their pleasure.

Certain powers granted the R. J. Reynolds Tobacco Company.

SEC. 6. That the present corporation, known as the R. J. Reynolds Tobacco Company, chartered under the general law of North Carolina by articles of agreement duly filed in the office of the clerk of the superior court of Forsyth county and doing business in Winston, North Carolina, shall have power and authority to sell, convey and transfer to a corporation formed under this act all its assets, franchise and property of every kind, and to merge itself therein. And the corporation organized under this act shall have power and authority to purchase, receive, take into possession and hold all the assets, franchise and property of every kind belonging to said existing corporation. Corporate power.

SEC. 7. That this act shall be in force from and after its ratification.

Ratified the 27th day of February, A. D. 1899.

CHAPTER 110.

An act to amend chapter two, private laws of eighteen hundred and eighty-three, entitled "An act to perfect the organization of the Odell Manufacturing Company."

The General Assembly of North Carolina do enact:

SECTION 1. That section seven (7), chapter two (2), private laws of eighteen hundred and eighty-three (1883), be and the same is here [hereby] repealed, and the following be substituted in lieu thereof: "The general meeting of the stockholders shall be held at such times as may be prescribed by the by-laws of said corporation." Section 7, chapter 2, private laws of 1883, amended. Time of meeting.

SEC. 2. That this act shall be in force from and after its ratification.

Ratified the 27th day of February, A. D. 1899.

CHAPTER 111.

An act to amend section two, chapter one hundred, private laws of eighteen hundred and seventy-four and eighteen hundred and seventy-five, in regard to the Bank of Reidsville, in the county of Rockingham.

The General Assembly of North Carolina do enact:

SECTION 1. That section two of chapter one hundred, private laws of eighteen hundred and seventy-four and eighteen hundred and seventy-five, entitled "An act to incorporate the Bank of Reidsville, in the county of Rockingham," be and the same is hereby amended as follows: Strike out the word "five" in line seven of said section and insert "seven." Section 2, chapter 100, private laws of 1874 and 1875, amended.

SEC. 2. That this act shall be in force from and after its ratfiication.

Ratified the 27th day of February, A. D. 1899.

CHAPTER 112.

An act to incorporate the town of Union City, in Robeson county.

The General Assembly of North Carolina do enact:

Incorporated. SECTION 1. That the village now known as Ashpole, in Robeson county, be and the same is hereby incorporated under the name and style of "Union City," and shall be subject to all the provisions of chapter sixty-two (62) of second volume of The Code of North Carolina.

Corporate name. Corporate powers.

Corporate limits. SEC. 2. That the corporate limits of said town shall be as follows, viz: Beginning at the point where the Inman and Ionia roads intersect and runs north one-half mile; thence east one-half mile; thence south one mile; thence west one mile; thence north one mile; thence east one-half mile, making one mile square.

Officers. SEC. 3. That the officers of said town shall consist of mayor, five aldermen, a marshal and a clerk and treasurer.

Temporary officers. SEC. 4. That until their successors have been duly elected and qualified the following-named persons shall fill said offices, to-wit: Mayor, Robert E. Lee; aldermen, Dr. John P. Brown, Charles B. Thompson, Prof. G. E. Lineberry, A. L. Jones and A. A. Floyd; clerk and treasurer, F. S. Floyd; marshal, Henry G. Braswell.

Election, when held. SEC. 5. That there shall be an election held on the first Monday in May, eighteen hundred and ninety-nine, and annually thereafter for said officers under the rules and regulations governing other elections in North Carolina.

Vacancies occurring. SEC. 6. That whenever a vacancy occurs in said offices the aldermen shall appoint one of their number mayor *pro tem.*

Powers of aldermen. SEC. 7. That the aldermen of said town shall have power to pass ordinances, rules and by-laws for the government of the town not inconsistent with the laws of the state of North Carolina and of the United States.

Mayor empowered to impose fines. SEC. 8. The mayor is hereby empowered with the right to impose fines and penalties for the violation of the ordinances established by the aldermen of said town.

Fines, how applied. SEC. 9. That all fines collected for the violation of the ordinances established by the aldermen for the government of said town shall be paid into the treasury of said town for the use and benefits of said town.

Treasurer and marshal shall give bond. SEC. 10. That the treasurer and marshal shall each be required to enter into a bond in the sum of two hundred dollars ($200) for the faithful performance of their duty, payable to the state of North Carolina, subject to the approval of the board of aldermen of said town.

Sec. 11. That the manufacture and sale of all spirituous, vinous nd malt liquors, wine and cider are hereby prohibited. Manufacture and sale of liquor, etc., prohibited.

Sec. 12. That all laws and clauses of laws in conflict with this ct are hereby repealed. Conflicting laws repealed.

Sec. 13. That this act shall be in full force and effect on and fter its ratification.

Ratified the 27th day of February, A. D. 1899.

CHAPTER 113.

An act to amend the charter of Red Springs Séminary, chapter two hundred and ten, private laws eighteen hundred and ninety-seven.

The General Assembly of North Carolina do enact:

Section 1. That section one of chapter two hundred and ten, private laws eighteen hundred and ninety-seven, be amended by inserting in line two after the name of J. L. McMillan, "A. L. Bullock, A. B. Pearsall, A. T. McCallum." Section 1, chapter 210, private laws of 1897, amended.

Sec. 2. That section three thereof be amended by striking out the word "six" in line two and insert "nine," and by striking out the word "four" in line three and insert the word "five," and by striking out the word "two" in line ten and inserting the word "three." Section 3, chapter 210, private laws of 1897, amended.

Sec. 3. That A. T. McCallum, the trustee above named, is hereby assigned to class one as mentioned in section three; A. B. Pearsall to class two, and A. L. Bullock to class three, and their terms of office shall be deemed to have commenced at the spring session eighteen hundred and ninety-seven, of Fayetteville Presbytery. Assignment to classes.

Sec. 4. That this act shall be in force from and after its ratification.

Ratified the 27th day of February, A. D. 1899.

CHAPTER 114.

An act to amend chapter thirty-three, laws of eighteen hundred and eighty-three, authorizing the Yadkin Mineral Spring Academy to grant certificates of proficiency.

The General Assembly of North Carolina do enact:

Section 1. That section five, chapter thirty-three, private laws of eighteen hundred and eighty-three, be amended by adding thereto the following words, viz: That the faculty and trus- Additional power granted Yadkin Mineral Spring Academy.

tees of said academy be empowered and authorized to grant certificates of proficiency to pupils who shall complete the course prescribed in said institution.

SEC. 2. That this act shall be in force from and after its ratification.

Ratified the 27th day of February, A. D. 1899.

CHAPTER 115.

An act to amend and consolidate the charter of the town of Greenville.

The General Assembly of North Carolina do enact:

Town of Greenville, Pitt county, continues municipal corporation.

SECTION 1. That the inhabitants of the town of Greenville, in the county of Pitt, shall be and continue as they heretofore have been a municipal corporation and shall be known as the town of Greenville, and by that name may sue and be sued, plead and be pleaded, contract and be contracted with, purchase, hold and convey all needful property.

Corporate powers.

Corporate limits.

SEC. 2. That the corporate limits of said town shall be as follows: beginning on the Tar river where the branch on the east side of the town as located prior to this act empties into said river, and thence running up said branch to the point where it crosses the old road leading from Greenville to Greene's old mill pond; thence southwardly along the west side of said road to a point where Twelfth street extended eastwardly would intersect said road; thence westwardly along north side of Twelfth street to the western limit of the right-of-way of the Scotland Neck and Kinston branch of the Wilmington and Weldon Railroad; thence northwardly along the western limit of the said right-of-way to the northwestern side of Broad street; thence along the northwestern side of said street to the line of E. A. Moye's land; thence with said Moye's line to the old plank road; thence a northeasterly course to the southwestern corner of the college property; thence along the western line of the college property to its northwestern corner; thence a straight line to the southeastern corner of the lands of R. J. Cobb and R. L. Davis, on the Greenville and Farmville road; thence north with their eastern line to Tar river, and thence down the river to the beginning.

Affairs of town, by whom managed.

SEC. 3. That the affairs of said town shall be managed by a mayor, eight aldermen and such other officers as may be provided for by this charter or as the board of aldermen may from time to time deem necessary and create.

Mayor, how chosen.

SEC. 4. The aldermen shall be chosen annually on the first Monday in June of each and every year by the qualified voters residing in the several wards of said town in the following numbers or proportion; that is to say, the first and fifth wards shall elect one alderman each, and the second, third and fourth wards two aldermen each.

Division of wards and aldermanic representation of each.

SEC. 5. That the said town is hereby divided into five wards, whose boundaries and limits shall be as follows, towit: The first ward shall begin at the railroad bridge across Tar river and from that point run southwardly along the railroad to Third street; thence eastwardly with Third street to the line of lot No. 6; thence a northwardly course with the line of lots Nos. 6 and 5 to Second street; thence an easterly course with Second street to Reade street; thence a southerly course to the branch; thence down said branch to Tar river; thence up said river to the beginning. The qualified voters residing within the above boundaries shall elect one alderman. The second ward shall begin at the same point with the first and run with the first to Greene street; thence with Greene street to Fifth [street]; thence with Fifth street and the road or street leading between the Latham and Flanagan residences to the southeast corner of the lands of R. J. Cobb and R. L. Davis; thence with their line to Tar river, and thence down the river to the beginning. The qualified voters residing within the above boundaries of the second ward shall elect two aldermen. The third ward shall begin at the intersection of Second and Greene streets, and running with Greene street to Fifth street; thence with Fifth street to Reade street; thence with Reade street to Second street; thence with Second street to the beginning. The qualified voters residing within the said limits of the third ward shall elect two aldermen. The fourth ward shall begin at the intersection of Reade and Fifth streets and run a southerly course with Reade street to the branch, the town limits; thence up the branch and town limits to Greene's mill road; thence along said road and town limits to Twelfth street; thence along Twelfth street and the town limits to the west side of the right-of-way of the Scotland Neck and Kinston Branch of the Wilmington and Weldon railroad; thence with the right-of-way and the town limits to the northwestern side of Broad street; thence along the northwestern side of said street to E. A. Moye's land; thence with said Moye's line to the old Plank road; thence with the said old plank road, now known as Dickinson avenue; thence with said Dickinson avenue to its intersection with Greene street; thence with Greene street to Fifth street, and thence with Fifth street to the beginning. The qualified voters residing within the said limits of the fourth ward shall elect two aldermen. The Fifth ward shall begin at the intersection of Greene and Fifth streets and run with Greene street to Dickinson avenue, and thence westwardly with said avenue to the town limits, as fixed by this act, and thence with the said town limits to the Greenville and Farmville road, and thence an easterly direction with said road and Fifth street to the beginning. The qualified voters residing within the said boundaries of this ward shall elect one alderman.

First election to be held first Monday in June, 1899.

SEC. 6. That the first election to be held under this act for aldermen shall take place on the first Monday in June, eighteen hundred and ninety-nine, and that the persons now composing the present board of councilmen shall continue in office until the persons chosen at said election be qualified, and the said board of councilmen shall be clothed with all the powers and authority herein given to the board of aldermen. The present mayor, treasurer and tax collector shall likewise continue in office until their successors are chosen and qualified.

Term of office of aldermen and officers.

Powers of aldermen.

SEC. 7. That the board of aldermen are hereby fully authorized and empowered to do and to perform the following acts: (1) To make and publish all needful ordinances, rules and regulations for the peace, good order and government of said town. (2) To levy and to cause to be collected sufficient taxes for the efficient administration of the public affairs of said town upon the following subjects, to-wit: A tax not to exceed sixty-six and two-thirds cents on each one hundred dollars worth of real and personal property in said town, including money on hand, solvent credits and all other classes of property required to be listed as property by the laws of this state; a poll tax not to exceed two dollars on each poll within said town liable under the laws of this state to pay a poll tax; a license tax on druggists, merchants, hotels, boarding house or restaurant keepers; on all opera houses or other halls used for hire or rent for exhibitions of any kind; on all travelling or theatrical companies giving exhibitions within the town; on all travelling concert or musical companies or persons giving exhibitions in said town; on all exhibitions of museums of waxworks or curiosities for profit; on every exhibition of a circus or menagerie; on each billiard or pool table kept for hire or public use; on each skating rink, bagatelle table, merry-go-round, hobby-horse or stand or place for any other game or play used for profit; on every person every billiard or pool table kept for hire or public use; on each skating rink, bagatelle table, merry-go-round, hobby-horse or stand or place for any other game or play used for profit; on every person or firm that keeps horses or mules for sale or hire; on every dray or other vehicle used on the streets for hire; on every lawyer, doctor or dentist practicing his profession in said town; on every bank, banker, broker, or other persons or firm doing a banking or brokerage business of any kind in said town; on every mercantile agency, association, person or firm which has for its business selling goods, wares or merchandise by samples; on all dogs running at large in said town, with power to enforce the payment of the tax by the owner or the killing of the dog; on all retail dealers in liquors,

Levy taxes.

License taxes.

License taxes.

License taxes.

spirituous, vinous or malt; on all persons vending or advertising from a stand or vehicle any drugs, nostrums or medicines or goods, wares or merchandise of any kind; and on any and all other subjects taxed by the laws of this state, whether expressly herein enumerated or not. (3) To lay out and open new streets and sidewalks in any part of said town. (4) To extend, widen, straighten, grade or otherwise improve any street or sidewalk now existing in said town, and to this end the board shall have full power and authority to remove or cause to be removed any and all obstructions to any of the streets or sidewalks, no matter whether such obstructions be of a temporary or of a permanent kind, or caused by porches, sheds or buildings, or parts of buildings erected on, upon, or over any of said streets or sidewalks. (5) That the board of aldermen may require property owners to construct and keep in repair such sidewalks adjacent to their property in such manner as said board may direct; and should any owner of such property refuse or fail to so construct or repair such sidewalks after twenty days' notice, the board may have the same constructed or repaired and the cost thereof shall be added to the taxes paid on said property on the tax list of the next succeeding year, and collected as taxes are collected upon property listed for taxation. (6) To adopt such plans or methods and to make such contracts as the board may deem best for lighting the streets and sidewalks of said town (7) To adopt such plans or methods, to make such contracts and to take such action as the board may deem best to procure a water supply for said town. (8) To contract for, purchase, keep in repair and provide for the use of all such engines, hose or other apparatus or appliances for the prevention or extinguishing of fires as the board may deem needful and proper. (9) To suppress and remove nuisances, and to make all needful rules and regulations to preserve the health of the inhabitants of the town from contagious, infectious or other diseases. (10) To make and enforce regulations for the due observance of the Sabbath and to prescribe the hours at which bar-rooms, billiard or pool rooms or other places where liquors are sold or billiards or pool are played, shall be closed at night: *Provided*, that such regulations shall not be in conflict with other provisions of this act or any law of the state. (11) To prescribe the places and regulate the manner in which the business of marketing shall be carried on in said town. (12) To regulate the speed of riding or driving on the streets or other public places in said town. (13) To regulate the sale and keeping of powder or other explosives within the corporate limits of said town. (14) To prohibit, regulate or contract the sale or use of fire-crackers, Roman candles, bombs, torpedoes or other explosives: *Provided*, that such prohibition, regulation or contract shall not conflict with other provisions of this act, or any law of this state. (15) To elect all such policemen, guards or night watchmen, fix their compensation and prescribe

May lay out and open streets.
Street improvements.
Aldermen may make certain requirements for property owner.
Refusal of property owner.
Costs added to taxes.
For lighting streets.
Water supply.
Fire apparatus.
Nuisances.
Regulations for observance of Sabbath.
To prescribe place in which marketing may be carried on.
Speed of riding and driving.
Sale of explosives.
Sale of fire crackers, etc.
Election of policemen.

their duties as may be necessary to enforce the ordinances, preserve the peace and secure good government to the inhabitants of the town. And the policemen, guards or watchmen shall hold office and be subject to removal at the pleasure of the board. (16) To employ such labor and to purchase such machinery and material and to make such contracts and to do all such things as may be necessary to put and keep the streets and sidewalks, public wells, tanks and reservoirs and other town property in proper condition. (17) To execute and employ all other powers and functions conferred by the general laws of this state upon boards of commissioners, councilmen or aldermen of cities and towns and which may not be herein specifically mentioned.

Street machinery.

Other powers.

Fiscal year, when commences.

Sec. 8. That the fiscal year for said town shall commence on the the first day of July and end on the 30th day of June each and every year, and the term of office of the aldermen chosen at any election shall begin on the first day of July next after their election and each alderman before he enters upon the duties of his office shall take, subscribe and file with the records of the board an oath for the faithful discharge of the duties of aldermen.

When persons elected aldermen shall meet.

Sec. 9. That the persons chosen as aldermen on the first Monday of June, eighteen hundred and ninety-nine, and at the election held on the first Monday of June each and every year thereafter, shall meet in the mayor's office on the first day of July next after their election (unless such a day fall on Sunday, and in that event the day after), and organize by the election of one of their number as president *pro tem.*, and a clerk of their board, who shall not be one of their number.

Mayor, tax collector and treasurer, how elected.

Term of office.

Sec. 10. That the board shall also proceed to elect from outside their number a mayor and tax collector, and shall select a treasurer from their number, each of whom shall be a qualified elector in said town and shall serve one [year] from the first day of July of the year in which the election occurs and until his successor is qualified, unless he is sooner removed by the board for cause, of which the board shall be the judge.

Duties of mayor.

Sec. 11. That the mayor, in addition to his other duties, shall preside at the meetings of the board of aldermen, but shall have no vote on any question, unless the board be equally divided, and in that case he shall cause a record to be made of that fact, and he shall then record his vote and declare the result. In case of the absence of the mayor at any meeting, the president *pro tem.* shall preside, but he shall have no casting vote in case of a tie, if he has already voted, and in that case he shall declare the question lost. In the absence of both the mayor and the president *pro tem.*, any member of the board may preside.

In absence of mayor.

Tax collector and treasurer shall give bond.

Sec. 12. That the persons chosen as treasurer and tax collector shall enter into bonds with sureties to be approved by the board in such sums as the board may prescribe for the faithful discharge of their duty.

SEC. 13. That the board may fix the compensation of the mayor, treasurer, tax collector and clerk. Compensation.

SEC. 14. That the mayor-elect shall immediately after his election, and before he enters upon the duties of his office, take and subscribe before some one authorized to administer oaths and file with the clerk of the board the following oath: I, A. B., do solemnly swear that I will support and maintain the constitution and laws of the United States, and the constitution and laws of North Carolina not inconsistent therewith, and that I will diligently and faithfully and truly perform, according to the best of my skill and ability, all the duties of the office of mayor of the town of Greenville while I continue therein, and I will cause to be executed as far as in my power, all laws, ordinances and regulations made for the government of said town, and in the discharge of my duties I will do equal justice in all cases whatsoever. So help me, God. Oath of mayor.

SEC. 15. That the mayor of said town is hereby constituted an inferior court, and as such, shall, within the corporate limits of said town, have all the power, jurisdiction and authority of a justice of the peace to preserve and keep the peace, to issue process, to hear and determine all causes of action which may arise upon the ordinances and regulations of the town; to enforce penalties by issuing executions upon any adjudged violations thereof, and to enforce and execute the ordinances, by-laws, rules and regulations made by the board of aldermen. And the mayor shall further be a special court, within the corporate limits of said town, to arrest and try all who are charged with misdemeanors for violating any ordinance, rule or regulation of the town, and if the accused be found guilty, he shall be fined not exceeding fifty dollars or imprisoned not exceeding thirty days, at the discretion of the mayor or court trying the case. If the accused is dissatisfied with the judgment of the mayor, or court, he may appeal to the superior court in like manner as appeals may be taken from judgments of a justice of the peace. He shall also have all the authority of a justice of the peace to cause the arrest of any person charged with any criminal offense, and to detain, try and deal with them, within the corporate limits of said town, in like manner as a justice of the peace might do. Mayor constituted inferior court. Powers and jurisdiction. Mayor a special court. Violation of ordinances. Penalty. Accused may appeal. Power of mayor.

SEC. 16. That if for any cause a vacancy shall occur in the office of either the mayor, treasurer, clerk or tax collector, the board shall fill such vacancy, and the appointee shall hold for the unexpired term; and an absence of five days from the town without special permission from the board shall be deemed a vacancy. Vacancies occurring. Absence without permission.

SEC. 17. That in the absence of the mayor from the town, or in case of his inability to act, the president *pro tem.* of the board of aldermen shall be acting mayor during such absence or inability, and Absence of mayor.

while so acting he shall have all the authority and power herein given to the mayor.

whom warts may be ued.

SEC. 18. That the mayor may issue his warrant or other process to any policeman of the town or to such other officer to whom a justice of the peace might direct his warrant or other process, and such policeman or other officer may execute such warrant or other process anywhere in the county of Pitt.

yor shall keep cord.

SEC. 19. That the mayor shall keep a faithful record or minute of all warrants or other process issued by him and of all the judicial proceedings, and all judgments rendered by him shall have the same force and validity as if rendered by a justice of the peace, and may be enforced anywhere in the county of Pitt, in the same manner and by the same means as if rendered by a justice of the peace.

es and costs.

SEC. 20. That the fees and cost in the mayor's court shall be the same as the fees and cost in a justice's court for like services, and the fees and costs shall be collected and accounted for as the board of aldermen may direct.

rsons failing to y fine may be nt to public ads.

SEC. 21. That the board of aldermen shall have authority to put and keep at work on the streets any person or persons who may fail to pay any tax, fine, cost, penalty or forfeiture which may have been imposed on such person or persons by the mayor. And the said board shall have the authority to make such rules and regulations for the control and management of such persons until said fines, penalties and costs are paid under such rates for labor as they may fix.

le of spirituous uors, etc.

SEC. 22. That after the 30th day of June, 1899, no person shall retail or sell within the corporate limits of said town, or within half a mile of said limits in any direction around it, any spirituous, vinous, malt or other intoxicating liquors, in quantities less than one gallon, without first having obtained a license from the board of aldermen, and paid to the town tax collector therefor the tax assessed by the board of aldermen for such license for the privilege of carrying on his business in said town or within a half a mile of the limits thereof, which tax shall not be less than one hundred dollars nor more than five hundred dollars for one year, or half these amounts for six months: *Provided*, that no license shall be given or tax paid for a less time than six months: *And provided further*, that all license shall begin on the first day of January and July, and shall end in one year or six months, as the case may be, from those dates. The above amounts not to apply to malt dealers, their tax being fixed by the board of town commissioners.

x for selling uors.

oviso.

me of license.

oviso.

hen license gins.

SEC. 23. That all applicants for license as a retailer of liquors under the preceding section shall make their application to the board in writing, in which they shall state the place and character of their business for the succeeding twelve months, the length of time for which license is desired, and the building and location in which it is proposed to carry on said business. The board may make

plicants for ense shall ake application writing and te certain ts.

such investigation as it may deem proper as to the person or place and may in its discretion refuse to grant the license applied for.

Board may refuse license

SEC. 24. That it shall be unlawful for any person or firm to keep any billiard table, pool table, bagatelle table or other like thing for hire or public use in said town without first obtaining a license from the board of aldermen, and paying to the town tax collector the tax levied by the board for such license.

Billiard and pool tables, etc., shall secure license.

SEC. 25. That all licensed bar-rooms or other places where liquor are sold, and all billiard rooms, pool rooms or other places where billiard tables, pool tables, bagatelle tables or other like things are kept for hire or public use shall be closed not later than eleven o'clock at night, and opened not earlier than four o'clock in the morning. And it shall be unlawful for any liquor to be sold or games played within these places within these hours. And the said board may prescribe the hours for closing all other places of business within said town. Any person violating any of the provisions of this section, or any of the ordinances or regulations passed by the board in reference thereto, shall be guilty of a misdemeanor, and on conviction shall be fined not more than fifty dollars or imprisoned not more than thirty days, provided such violation did not occur between the hours of closing Saturday night and the opening Monday morning. But if any person shall be guilty of violating any of the provisions of this section between the hours of closing on Saturday night and opening on Monday morning, he shall be guilty of a misdemeanor, and upon conviction he shall be fined or imprisoned in the discretion of the court, and shall, in addition thereto, forfeit his license: *Provided*, the retail dealer may, within these prohibited hours, fill a regular practicing licensed physician's prescription in which the name of the patient and the necessity for the stimulants shall be certified to without being guilty of violating this section.

Hour at which bar rooms, etc., shall be opened and closed.

May prescribe hours for closing of other business houses.

Proviso.

Violators guilty of a misdemeanor.

Penalty.

Proviso.

May fill physicians' prescriptions.

SEC. 26. That the exploding of fire crackers, roman candles, bombs, torpedoes or other explosives within the corporate limits of said town, being dangerous to property and a nuisance to its citizens, is hereby prohibited, and it shall be unlawful for any person to sell any such explosives in said town, no matter by what name called, without first having obtained a license from the board of aldermen, and paid a tax to the town tax collector, to be fixed by the said board, which shall not be less than ten dollars nor more than two hundred and fifty dollars for carrying on said business twelve months.

Explosion of firecrackers.

Sale of firecrackers.

Penalty.

SEC. 27. That when it shall become necessary to condemn property for public uses, the board of aldermen shall designate and describe the property to be condemned, and if the board and the owner or owners of said property can not agree upon the damages, then the board shall appoint one arbitrator, the owner or owners of the property one, and a third shall be named by the clerk of the superior court of

Property condemned

Arbitrator.

Minors without guardian.

Pitt county. But if any of the owners of the property are minors and without a general guardian, then the board shall file petition before the clerk of the superior court, setting out the facts, and the said clerk shall appoint some suitable person to represent such infant or infants, and such guardian *ad litem* shall appoint the arbitrator to represent such minors, and report the name of the person so selected to said clerk, who shall make a record of these proceedings, which shall, when approved by said clerk, be as conclusive as to said minors so made of record as if they were of full age. The three arbitrators chosen as provided for in this section shall take an oath before entering upon their duties to do even and exact justice between the town and the owners of the property to be condemned, to the best of their ability. The board shall deliver to the three arbitrators a description of the property to be condemned, and thereupon the arbitrators shall view the property, hear the testimony, if any may be offered, and make and sign their award, which shall be filed with the board, and a copy delivered by them to the owners. The award, when signed by a majority of the arbitrators, shall be final and conclusive as to all parties, in case there is no appeal. If the town or the owners of the property is dissatisfied with the award, either may appeal to the superior court of Pitt county in term time, by giving ten days' notice of such appeal to the opposite party, and giving a bond to be approved by the clerk of the superior court to secure the cost of such appeal. The notice shall state the grounds of the appeal, and to be effective, must be served within ten days after the award is filed with the board and a copy delivered to the owner. If the appeal be on a question of law, the judge shall render his decision thereon; if it be on the amount of damages, then that question shall be tried by a jury. Upon the payment to the owner of the amount found by the arbitrators, if there be no appeal, or of the amount adjudged by the court, if there be an appeal, the board of aldermen may proceed with the contemplated improvements for the public convenience in the use of the property so condemned.

Duty of arbitrators.

Award of arbitrators final.

May appeal.

Aldermen may proceed.

No wooden building shall be constructed on certain streets.

Sec. 28. That no wooden building shall be built on that part of Evans street lying between Second street on the north, and the town sewer at the academy grove on the south: *Provided, however,* that any dwelling between these points now standing, that may be removed, burned or otherwise destroyed, may be replaced.

Claims against town.

Sec. 29. That all claims against said town shall be presented to the board of aldermen to be examined, passed upon and audited, and the board shall cause a record to be made of all claims allowed by them, and shall cause an order to be issued upon the treasurer therefor, which order shall state what it is for, and be signed by the presiding officer and countersigned by the clerk.

Treasurer shall keep a record.

Sec. 30. That the treasurer shall keep a book in which he shall charge himself with all moneys that come into his hands, which shall show the source or sources from which they were derived, and in which he shall record the amount and date of all orders paid by him, the date of payment and to whom paid, and he shall pay out no moneys except upon the order of the board. He shall make a full report to the board at the end of each fiscal year, which shall show the financial condition of the town, and he shall make such other reports from time to time as the board may direct.

Annual report.

Duties of tax collector.

SEC. 31. That the tax collector shall collect and account for all the taxes due the town under the direction and supervision of the board of aldermen, and shall pay the same over to the treasurer, from time to time, as the board may direct, and he shall make his report to the board at the end of each fiscal year, which shall show the amounts received by him, the sources from which they were received, and the times and the amounts when paid to the treasurer. In addition to this report he shall make such other reports as the board may direct.

Tax lister shall be appointed by aldermen.

SEC. 32. That the board of aldermen, at some meeting in May of each and every year, shall appoint some suitable person to take and make a list of all taxable property and all subjects of taxation within the town, which he shall return to the board at its first regular meeting in July following, unless directed by the board to make his return at another time. Upon the return of the list the board shall give ten days' notice of a meeting, when complaints shall be heard, if any are to be made. And at a regular meeting to be held during the first week in August the board shall levy the tax for the current fiscal year. The board shall then cause a tax list to be made out and delivered to the tax collector, which shall have all the force and effect of an execution. The tax collector shall collect said taxes, and pay them over to the treasurer as fast as collected, and he shall have all the rights and remedies, authority and power to enforce the payment of said taxes that are given to sheriffs or tax collectors for the collection of state and county taxes by the laws of this state.

Complaints heard.

Tax levy made in August.

Appointment of registrars and poll holders.

SEC. 33. That thirty days prior to any election to be held in said town for aldermen, the board of aldermen shall appoint a registrar and two poll-holders for each ward in said town to conduct the registration and hold the election in said town, which shall be conducted and held in accordance with the general election laws of this state, so far as the same are applicable to town elections. No person shall vote in said election unless he be a qualified voter under the laws of this state and a *bona fide* resident of the ward in which he offers to vote. The board of aldermen shall at the time of the appointment of the registrar and poll-holders, designate the place in each ward where the election shall be held, and the registrar shall attend the place three days immediately preceding the Saturday next preceding the election. He shall remain at said place from nine o'clock a. m. to five o'clock p. m., during said three days, with his book of regis-

Elections, how conducted.

Duties of registrar.

tration; prepared to register such persons as may be entitled to register. He shall give at least ten days' notice of the time and place of registration, in one or more newspapers published in the town, and at some public place in his ward. The returns of said election shall be made to the board of aldermen, who shall declare and publish the result.

Returns of election.

Conflicting laws repealed.

SEC. 34. That all laws and clauses of laws heretofore passed either chartering or amending the charter of the town of Greenville, inconsistent with this act, are hereby repealed.

SEC. 35. That this act shall be in force from and after its ratification.

Ratified the 27th day of February, A. D. 1899.

CHAPTER 116.

An act to incorporate The Eureka Mining, Land and Manufacturing Company.

The General Assembly of North Carolina do enact:

Corporators.

SECTION 1. That I. Bluford, J. N. Gorman, D. Morgan, J. H. Wissler and George E. Harelson, together with such other persons as now or may hereafter be associated with them and their successors and assigns, be and they are hereby made and created a body politic and corporate under the name, "The Eureka Mining, Land and Manufacturing Company," and under that name may sue and be sued, prosecute and defend actions and special proceedings in all the courts of the land, contract and be contracted with, and adopt and use a common seal, which may be altered at pleasure, make, alter and amend such by-laws and regulations as may be deemed by them proper, not repugnant to the constitution and law of the land, and shall have a corporate existence for twenty-five years.

Body politic.
Corporate name.
Corporate powers.

Capital stock.
May be increased.

SEC. 2. That the capital stock of the said company shall be twenty-five thousand dollars, and the same may be increased from time to time as a majority of the stockholders may determine up to fifty thousand dollars. That the stock of said company shall be in shares of ten dollars each, for which certificates shall be issued, and each share shall be entitled to one vote. Said stock shall be deemed personal property and be transferable upon the books of said corporation. Books of subscription may be opened by any two of the incorporators at such time and place as they may prescribe. That the said corporators, or a majority of them, acting in person or by proxy, after the sum of five thousand dollars ($5,000) has been subscribed, shall call a meeting of

Division of stock.

the subscribers to the said capital stock for the purpose of completing the organization of the company, giving three days' notice to each subscriber of said stock or two weeks' notice in some paper published in Chatham county, if there be any; if not, then in some paper published in Raleigh. North Carolina. That at such meeting the stockholders may elect a board of directors consisting of five members, who shall immediately elect one of their number president of the company.

When meeting may be called.

Subscribers shall be notified

Election of directors.

SEC. 3. That the corporators and stockholders of said company and their associates and assigns shall not be individually or personally liable or responsible for the debts, contracts, engagements or torts of said corporation, and no stockholder shall be liable to pay for more stock than he subscribes for.

Individual liability.

SEC. 4. That subscriptions to the capital stock of said company may be made in money, land, labor or material necessary for carrying on the work intended, in bonds, stocks or other valuable credits in such manner and on such terms as may be agreed upon by the president and a majority of the directors of the said company.

Subscriptions, how taken.

SEC. 5. That said company is authorized to borrow such sums of money from time to time as may be necessary for its purposes, and for such loans to issue its bonds bearing interest not exceeding six per centum per annum, to sell, exchange, hypothecate said bonds on such terms as it may deem advisable, and to secure said bonds and interest thereon by deed of trust or mortgage conveying its works, lands, minerals property and franchises in whole or in part; or to issue shares of preferred stock which, in case of a dividend, shall be paid six per centum out of the proceeds of the company in preference to any other stock of the company, but shall not be entitled to a per share vote in the stockholders' meeting.

Empowered to borrow money, etc.

Dividend.

SEC. 6. That meetings of stockholders shall be held annually at such time and place in this state as may be determined by them, and at all annual meetings the president and directors shall render to the stockholders an account of the affairs of the company; special meetings may be called by the president or a majority of the directors by notice mailed to each stockholder ten days before said meeting, and notice of such meeting shall likewise be published in some newspaper in Chatham county or in one of the Raleigh papers.

Meeting of stockholders.

Officers shall render account.

Special meetings.

SEC. 7. That the president and directors shall have power to elect a vice-president, secretary and treasurer, and also to appoint such other officers as may be necessary for conducting the work as authorized by this act, and to prescribe their duties, compensation and terms of service. The directors shall be elected annually by the stockholders and shall remain in office one year

Powers of officers.

Compensation.

Directors, when elected.

or until their successors are elected and qualified, and in case of a vacancy occurring by death, removal or resignation in the office of director the same may be filled by the president until the next meeting of the stockholders.

President and directors may contract debts.

SEC. 8. That the president and directors being authorized by the stockholders shall have power to make such expenditures and contract such debts as may be necessary.

Character of business.

SEC. 9. That said company shall have power to carry on the business of mining from the ground any ores, minerals or metals; to manufacture the same into any shape or shapes and prepare for home or foreign market, or to manufacture as they may determine such other goods, and for said purposes they may erect such mills, sawmills, buildings, machine shops, stores, dwellings and other houses and other works as may be requisite or necessary to carry on such branches of industry as this act may provide for.

May subscribe to stock of other companies.

SEC. 10. That this company shall have power to subscribe to the capital stock of any other corporate company, and any other corporate company may have the right to subscribe to the stock of this company.

Chief office.

SEC. 11. That the chief office of the said company shall be in the town of Moncure, in the state of North Carolina, but it shall have the power and authority to establish branch offices and agencies in this state or elsewhere when in the opinion of the board of directors it may be necessary to do so for the proper conduct of its business and the due development of the aims and purposes of its organization.

SEC. 12. That this act be enforced from and after its ratification.

Ratified the 27th day of February, A. D. 1899.

CHAPTER 117.

An act to re-enact chapter three hundred and twenty-seven of the laws of eighteen hundred and ninety-three, and to extend the time for organization of the said corporation authorized thereby.

The General Assembly of North Carolina do enact:

Chapter 327, laws of 1893, re-enacted. Relating to Thomasville Banking Company.

SECTION 1. That chapter three hundred [and] twenty-seven of the laws of eighteen hundred [and] ninety-three, which authorized the incorporation of the Thomasville Banking and Trust Company be and the same is hereby re-enacted.

Extension for time of organization.

SEC. 2 That three years from the date hereof shall be allowed to said incorporation for the purpose of organization.

SEC. 3. That said chapter three hundred and twenty-seven, laws of eighteen hundred and ninety-three, be amended by striking out the words "The Thomasville Banking and Trust Company" in line [lines] four and five of section one, chapter three hundred and twenty-seven, private laws eighteen hundred and ninety-three, and insert instead thereof the words "The Bank of Thomasville," and by striking out "ten" in line six of section three of said chapter and inserting "five" in lieu thereof. Corporate name changed.

SEC. 4. That this act shall be in force from and after its ratification.

Ratified the 27th day of February, A. D. 1899.

CHAPTER 118.

An act to authorize the city of Fayetteville to establish and operate a system of electric lights and motive power.

WHEREAS, a proper system for lighting public streets is a necessity to the inhabitants of the city of Fayetteville and is conducive to the advancement and prosperity of said city; and Preamble

WHEREAS, by reason of its revenues from other sources and because under the provisions of chapter one hundred and fifty-three (153) of the private laws of eighteen hundred and ninety-three (1893) and the act amendatory thereof, passed by the general assembly of eighteen hundred and ninety-nine (1899), entitled "An act to amend chapter one hundred and fifty-three (153) of the private laws of eighteen hundred and ninety-three (1893)," etc., and ratified on January twenty-sixth, eighteen hundred and ninety-nine, sufficient taxes are now levied and not otherwise appropriated to amply provide for the payment of interest on the coupon bonds hereinafter provided for as it falls due and the creation of a sinking fund sufficient to fully pay off said bonds, as well as to meet all the other obligations and liabilities of the said city: Preamble continued.

The General Assembly of North Carolina do enact:

SECTION 1. That the city of Fayetteville be and is hereby authorized and empowered to purchase, hold, erect and establish all necessary lands, works and machinery wherewith to furnish electric lights and motive power for the use of the city and its citizens and of the persons living in its suburbs. City of Fayetteville authorized to purchase water and electric lights.

SEC. 2. For the foregoing purpose it shall be lawful for the said city of Fayetteville to issue and sell at a price not less than par the coupon bonds of said city to the amount of fifteen thousand ($15,000) dollars, said bonds to be in denominations of one hun- May issue and sell bonds to amount of $15,000.

dred ($100) dollars and five hundred ($500) dollars, and to run for a period of thirty years from the issue of the same, and to bear interest at a rate not exceeding six (6) per centum per annum, payable semi-annually on the first (1st) day of June and December of each year after their issue.

Bonds, how signed and numbered.

SEC. 3. Said coupon bonds shall be consecutively numbered and signed by the mayor and the clerk of the city of Fayetteville, and it shall be the duty of the said clerk to keep an accurate account of the same.

Coupons receivable for taxes.

SEC. 4. The coupons of said bonds shall be receivable by the tax collector and treasurer of the city of Fayetteville in payment of all taxes and dues to the city.

May provide lights for private use.

SEC. 5. It shall be lawful for the said city of Fayetteville, in addition to lighting the streets and public buildings of the city, to provide lights and motive power for private use at such rentals as may be agreed upon or at rates to be fixed by the proper authorities of the said city, and the receipts arising from said rentals shall be kept by the treasurer of said city and shall be applied to the payment of interest on said bonds as the coupons may fall due, and to the further purpose of creating a sinking fund of five hundred ($500) dollars per annum, which sinking fund it shall be the duty of the authorities of said city to lay aside annually from any funds in the treasury not otherwise appropriated, and from any surplus from said rentals in excess of an amount sufficient to pay the interest on said bonds; and the sinking fund above provided for may temporarily be applied to the payment of the operating expenses of the plant, and any deficiency in the amount necessary for the payment of either interest, sinking fund or operating expenses of said system of electric lights and motive power shall be paid from the current tax receipts of said city and shall be charged as necessary "light expense." Should there be any excess from private rentals over the amount necesary to pay said interest, sinking fund and operating expenses, such excess shall be used for the payment of the ordinary expenses and liabilities of said city.

Application of receipts.

Sinking fund.

How sinking fund may be temporarially applied.

Excess from rentals.

Power of aldermen to create uniformity of bond numbers.

SEC. 6. The board of aldermen of said city may at any time it deems proper cause the numbers of all bonds herein provided for and then outstanding to be placed on uniform slips of paper in a hat, from which the mayor shall draw by lot one or more numbers until the amount represented by the number of the bonds so drawn equals that part of the sinking fund which said board shall have decided to apply toward the liquidation of said bonds, and thereupon the treasurer of said city shall issue a call for the presentation to him for payment of the bond or bonds so drawn by lot, giving the number, date of issue and amount of the same, which call shall be published at least once a week for four con-

Treasurer shall issue call.

sective weeks in some newspaper published in Fayetteville, and may be published in any other newspaper designated by said board and as said board may direct, and after such advertisement for four consecutive weeks the interest on such called bonds shall cease, but when the holders of such bond or bonds are certainly known a written notice to such holder or holders in accordance with the requirements of the publication above provided for and mailed to his or their address shall have the same effect as would such publication; in either event the holders of the bond or bonds so called shall be entitled to interest on such bond or bonds until the expiration of the call, and shall further be paid two (2 per centum) per centum upon the principal as a premium for such call.

Interest shall cease.

Rate of interest.

SEC. 7. All administrators, executors and guardians and other persons acting in a fiduciary capacity are hereby authorized and empowered to invest the funds intrusted to them in said bonds.

Funds may be invested in bonds by administrators, etc.

SEC. 8. An election shall be held at the market house in the city of Fayetteville on the first (1st) Tuesday in April, eighteen hundred and ninety-nine (1899), for the purpose of ratifying or disapproving by a majority of the qualified voters of the said city the issuance of the bonds herein provided for. It shall be the duty of the mayor to cause daily publication of this act in full to be made in some newspaper published in said city for not less than ten (10) days immediately preceding said election, not including Sundays.

Election, when held.

SEC. 9. The board of aldermen of the city of Fayetteville shall appoint a registrar of voters for said city of Fayetteville, who shall register such citizens of said city as are not at present registered and who would be entitled to vote at the election, or the board of aldermen may by a majority vote, twenty or more days prior to such election order a new registration, and shall cause publication and notice to be given as provided by section seven (7) of chapter one hundred and fifty-three (153) of the private laws of eighteen hundred and ninety-three (1893).

Appointment of registrar.

New registration may be ordered.

SEC. 10. The duties of registrar so to be appointed, the registration and the oath of election shall be as provided by sections eight (8), nine (9) and ten (10) of chapter one hundred and fifty-three (153) of the private laws of eighteen hundred and ninety-three (1893).

Duty of registrar.

SEC. 11. The board of aldermen of said city shall appoint two judges of election to hold said election, and the duties and powers and qualifications of said judges of election shall be the same as are provided by said chapter one hundred and fifty-three of the private laws of eighteen hundred and ninety-three (1893), and all matters and questions as to the election herein provided for shall be determined according to the provisions of chapter

Appointment of judges of election.

Duties and powers of judges.

one hundred and fifty-three (153) of the private laws of eighteen hundred and ninety-three (1893), sections seven (7) to fourteen (14), inclusive of both.

Form of ballots.

Sec. 12. The ballots to be used at the election herein provided for shall be on white paper and without device and shall contain the word "Lights" or the words "No lights," and the bonds herein provided for shall be issued only in case a majority of the qualified voters of the said city shall vote "Lights."

Conflicting laws repealed.

Sec. 13. All laws and parts of laws in conflict with this act are hereby repealed.

Sec. 14. This act shall be in force from and after its ratification.

Ratified the 27th day of February, A. D. 1899.

CHAPTER 119.

An act to change the corporate limits of the town of Waynesville.

The General Assembly of North Carolina do enact:

Section 1, chapter 156, private laws of 1893 relative to boundaries of town of Waynesville, amended.

Section 1. That section first of chapter one hundred and fifty-six of the private laws of eighteen hundred and ninety-three be amended by inserting at the end of said section the following: *Provided*, that that portion of said territory embraced in the following description shall be excluded from the corporate limits of the said town:

Beginning at a stake on Powell's branch, in Howell and Fitzgerald's line and runs down the meanderings of branch north thirty-eight west sixty-eight poles to a stake on branch; thence north twenty eight east forty-two poles; thence north ten west sixty-two poles to a maple on the north side of Powell's branch and Pigeon street; thence along the side of hill west of colored Baptist church north seventy-five east seventy-two poles to a Spanish oak at a point on the ridge and north side of Thomas road; thence with said road south sixty-five east thirty poles; thence north sixty east thirty poles to the gap of ridge; thence up the ridge south fifty east about fifty poles to the outer line of the corporate limits of the said town as constituted by the said act of eighteen hundred and ninety-three; thence with the said line south twenty-five west sixty poles; thence south thirty-five west sixty poles; thence south fifty-five west sixty-eight poles to the beginning.

Sec. 2. That this act shall be in force from and after its ratification.

Ratified the 27th day of February, A. D. 1899.

CHAPTER 120.

An act to incorporate The Bank of Cumberland, Fayetteville, North Carolina.

The General Assembly of North Carolina do enact:

Section 1. That F. R. Rose, Joseph W. Hollingsworth, Charles Haigh, S. H. Strange, Herbert Lutterloh, A. J. Cook, A. G. Brady, H. C. Bash, A. E. Rankin, John R. Tolar, George Overbaugh, S. H. McRae, John A. Pemberton, James C. McRae, W. L. Holt, W. M. Morgan, L. A. Williamson, H. McD. Robinson and Dr. J. W. McNeill and their present and future associates, successors and assigns be and they are hereby constituted, created and declared to be a body politic and corporate under the name and style of "The Bank of Cumberland." And shall so continue for the period of sixty years, with capacity to sue and be sued, maintain and defend actions and special proceedings in its corporate name, to take, hold, buy, sell, lease and exchange and convey real and personal estate, and to conduct, transact and carry on in its full scope and import a general banking business, with all the powers, rights, privileges and immunities hereby specially granted, and in addition those contained in chapter four, volume two of The Code, entitled "Banks." Corporators. Body corporate. Corporate name. Duration of charter. Corporate powers.

Sec. 2. That the capital stock of said bank shall be fifty thousand dollars ($50,000) in shares of one hundred dollars ($100) each, with liberty to the stockholders or a majority of them to increase said capital stock at any time or from time to time to any sum not exceeding finally two hundred and fifty thousand dollars ($250,000), and said corporators may at the beginning of business or at any time thereafter purchase the business, good-will and assets of any private bank or bankers or banking institution and issue the whole or any part of its capital stock in payment thereof. Capital stock. May be increased.

Sec 3. That the corporators named in section one of this act or any three of them may open books of subscription to the capital stock of said corporation at such times and places as they may choose; and when twenty-five thousand dollars ($25.000) is subscribed and paid in the said corporators who have opened said books may call a meeting of the subscribers in the city of Fayetteville at such time and place and on such notice as they may choose, and a majority of such stockholders shall constitute a quorum qualified to do any act which the corporation is allowed to do, and they may adopt such by-laws and regulations for the government of the corporation and conduct of its business as they please: *Provided*, the same be consistent with the constitution of and laws of the United States and of this state. And Books of subscription may be opened. When organized. Proviso.

Election of officers.

they may then or at any adjourned meeting elect such officers as they see fit to elect and prescribe their duties, compensation and terms of service, and require bonds of such officers as they choose; but if said stockholders prefer, they may elect a board of directors only, to consist of as many members as they may desire, and clothe said board of directors with the power of electing their officers and prescribing their duties and fixing their terms of office and salaries.

Directors.

Election of president.

SEC. 4. The directors shall at their first meeting and annually thereafter elect one of their own members president of the corporation, and he shall be ex officio chairman of the board of directors. Any vacancy in the board of directors or any of their officers shall be filled by the remaining members of said board at any election held at any general or special meeting.

Vacancies occurring.

Powers of directors.

SEC. 5. The said board of directors may adopt, use, break and alter a seal, prescribe the manner and times of paying for stock and transferring the same, regulate the method of conducting the business of the corporation, lend money and charge and retain and receive the interest in advance or at any other time or times, discount, buy, sell and exchange notes, drafts, bills and any and all other evidences of debt or securities for debt; deal in stocks, bonds or securities of any kind, loan money at not above the legal rate of interest on mortgages of real or personal estate or both (or upon liens upon crops planted or unplanted), may build, buy or lease a banking house or houses, and when any stockholder or subscriber shall be indebted to the corporation for unpaid subscriptions no transfer of his stock shall be valid or effectual against said corporation while said indebtedness exists, and the corporation shall have and is hereby given a lien on all stocks and interest in stock to the full amount of such indebtedness of each such stockholder or subscriber to the bank, and after three days notice to the owner of said stock, as shown by the stock book of said corporation, or to the holder thereof, the same may be sold by any officer of the corporation under its directions at public auction for cash at the market house or court-house door in Fayetteville, after having advertised said sale for twenty days at three public places in the city of Fayetteville, North Carolina, and the proceeds applied to the payment of such indebtedness and interest, and the surplus, if any, paid to the owner of stock as shown by the bank book, or his assignee.

Powers of directors.

Principal office.

SEC. 6. The principal office and place of business of the corporation shall be at Fayetteville, North Carolina.

Deposits by married women and minors.

SEC. 7. When married women, minors or apprentices deposit money or other things of value in said bank, either generally or specially to their own credit, they or any of them may draw the same on their check or order and be bound thereby, and such individual check of such minor, married women or apprentice shall be a valid and sufficient release and receipt to said corporation against said minors, married women and apprentices and all other persons.

When property of debtor is sold.

SEC. 8. When said bank shall sell the property of its debtors on which it has a lien to secure a debt, or when such property shall be sold for its benefit, it may bid for and buy and hold any and all such property free from lien or incumbrance, and its title thereto shall be absolute and unconditional and shall be in all respects valid and binding against all persons.

SEC. 8. This act shall be in force from and after its ratification.

Ratified the 27th day of February, A. D. 1899.

CHAPTER 121.

An act to amend the charter of the town of Mount Olive, in Wayne county.

The General Assembly of North Carolina do enact:

Charter of town of Mount Olive amended.

Commissioners have power to open streets, etc.

SECTION 1. That the charter of the town of Mount Olive be amended as follows: That the board of commissioners of said town of Mount Olive shall have power to lay out and open new streets within the corporate limits of the said town whenever by them deemed necessary, and shall have power at any time to widen, enlarge, change, extend or discontinue any street or streets or any part thereof within the corporate limits of the said town, and shall have full power and authority to condemn, appropriate or use any land or lands necessary for any of the purposes named in this section, upon making a reasonable compensation to the owner or owners thereof. But in case the owner of the land and the said board of commissioners can not agree as to the damages then the matter shall be referred to arbitrators, each party choosing one, who shall be a freeholder and a citizen of the said town; and in case the owner of the land shall refuse to choose such arbitrator, then the sheriff of the county shall in his stead select one for him; and in case the two chosen can not agree, they shall select an umpire, whose duty it shall be to examine the land condemned and ascertain the damages sustained and the benefits accruing to the owner in consequence of the change, and the award of the majority of those so chosen shall be conclusive of the rights of the parties, and shall vest in the board of commissioners the right to use the land for the purposes specified, and all damages agreed upon by the board of commissioners or awarded by a majority of the arbitrators and umpire shall be paid as other town liabilities, by taxation: *Provided,*

Shall have power to condemn land.

When disagreement as to damages.

Arbitrators to be chosen.

Proviso.

that either party may appeal to the superior court as now provided by law.

Corporate limits extended.

That the corporate limits of said town be extended on the north so as to include the following land, to-wit:

Corporate limit extension.

Beginning at the present northwestern corner of the corporate limits and runs thence north thirty-eight degrees forty minutes east two hundred and forty feet; then parallel with the present northern boundary line of said town south fifty-one degrees twenty-one minutes east two thousand six hundred and forty feet to a stake; then south thirty-eight degrees forty minutes west two hundred and forty feet to the present corporate limits; then with said corporate limits to the beginning.

SEC. 2. That this act shall be in force from and after its ratification.

Ratified the 27th day of February, A. D. 1899.

CHAPTER 122.

An act to incorporate Cooleemee Water Power and Manufacturing Company.

The General Assembly of North Carolina do enact:

Corporators. Body corporate. Corporate name. Capital stock.

SECTION 1. That F. L. Fuller, Frank C. Hairston and Robert W. Winston and their associates, successors and assigns be and they hereby are created a body politic and corporate under the name and style of "Cooleemee Water Power and Manufacturing Company," with capital stock of ten thousand dollars ($10,000), divided into one hundred shares of the par value of one hundred dollars each, with liberty and authority to the majority of the stockholders to increase said capital stock at any time or from time to time to any amount not exceeding in the aggregate five hundred thousand dollars ($500,000), divided into shares of the par value of one hundred dollars each, and with privilege to said company to commence business when one thousand dollars ($1,000) of its capital stock has been subscribed for and paid in; and by unanimous vote of all the stockholders the capital stock of said company, after it has been increased, may at any time or from time to time be reduced: *Provided*, it shall never be less than its original capital stock of ten thousand dollars ($10,000).

May increase stock. When authorized to commence business.

Term of succession. Corporate powers.

SEC. 2. That said corporation shall have perpetual succession for the term of sixty years. It may adopt a common seal, which it may break or alter at pleasure. In its corporate name it may sue and be sued, prosecute and defend actions and special proceedings in all courts of the land; it may divide its capital stock into such classes and issue it upon such terms and conditions as its stockholders may desire, and after the original or any increase thereof has been issued its stockholders may by unanimous consent convert one class of stock into another or modify and change the terms and conditions upon which any or all of it has been issued; it may issue the whole or any part of its capital stock in payment for property acquired for the company upon such terms and conditions as its board of directors may deem advisable; it may buy, lease, exchange, hold, sell and convey real and personal property at its will and pleasure: *Provided*, that it shall not at any time [own] more than twenty thousand (20,000) acres of land in fee; it may construct, build and erect such buildings, works and improvements upon property of its own or of others by their permission as may be deemed proper, and may equip, operate, use and maintain the same; it may purchase, lease, use and maintain any works or improvements connected or intended to be connected with the works and improvements of said company; it may consolidate or unite with any other company now created or to be hereafter under the laws of this or any other state, retaining its own name or that of the company united or consolidated with, or by a vote of those holding a majority of its outstanding share capital, adopt a new name; it may borrow money and as security therefor it may issue its notes, bonds or other obligations, and if deemed advisable secure the payment of the same by a mortgage or deed of trust upon its franchises and property or any part of it; it may acquire, hold, own and enjoy stock in the capital of any company now in existence or hereafter to be created under the laws of this state or any other state or country, and stock in its capital may be owned, held and enjoyed by any company now created or to be hereafter created; for the purposes of its business it may build, equip and maintain a railroad or railroads operated by such motive power as it may see fit to adopt; it may acquire, construct, equip and operate telephone and telegraph lines and electric light and power plants; and it may construct or in any other way acquire, maintain and operate boats or vessels of such character as it may deem best or in any other way provide means for transportation of persons and goods.

Corporate powers.

Corporate powers.

Sec. 3. That the principal office of said company shall be in Davie county, North Carolina, but it may establish and maintain branch offices, agencies, factories, depots, warehouses, stores, and works anywhere in the United States or elsewhere that its directors may deem advisable.

Principal office.

Sec. 4. That it may make such by-laws, rules and regulations as the stockholders may desire not inconsistent with the constitution and laws of this state.

By-laws and rules.

Individual liability.

Sec. 5. That the corporators and stockholders of said company and their associates, successors and assigns shall not be individually or personally liable or responsible for the debts, contracts, obligations, engagements or torts of said corporation.

Notice of first meeting not required.

Sec. 6. That no notice or publication whatever of the first meeting of said corporation shall be given or required: *Provided*, all of the corporators named herein waive in writing such notice and fix a time and place for such meeting.

Sec. 7. That this act shall be in force from and after its ratification.

Ratified the 27th day of February, A. D. 1899.

CHAPTER 123.

An act to incorporate Cooleemee Cotton Mills.

The General Assembly of North Carolina do enact:

Corporators. Body corporate. Corporate name. Capital stock. May increase capital stock. Proviso.

Section 1. That F. L. Fuller, Frank C. Hairston and Robert W. Winston and their associates, successors and assigns be, and they hereby are created a body politic and corporate under the name and style of Cooleemee Cotton Mills, with capital stock of ten thousand dollars ($10,000), divided into one hundred shares of the par value of one hundred dollars each, with liberty and authority to the majority of the stockholders to increase said capital stock at any time and from time to time to any amount not exceeding in the aggregate five hundred thousand dollars ($500,000), divided into shares of the par value of one hundred dollars each, and with privilege to said company to commence business when one thousand dollars ($1,000) of its capital stock has been subscribed for and paid in; and by unanimous vote of all the stockholders the capital stock of said company, after it has been increased, may at any time or from time to time be reduced, provided it shall never be less than its original capital stock of ten thousand dollars ($10,000).

Term of succession. Corporate power.

Sec. 2. That said corporation shall have succession for the term of sixty (60) years; it may adopt a common seal which it may break or alter at pleasure; in its corporate name it may sue and be sued, prosecute and defend actions of special proceedings in all courts of the land; it may divide its capital stock into such classes and issue it upon such terms and conditions as its stockholders may desire, and after the original or any increase thereof has been issued its stockholders may, by unanimous consent, convert one class of stock into another or modify and change the terms and conditions upon which any or all of it has been issued; it may issue the whole or any part of its capital stock in payment for property acquired for the company upon such terms and conditions as its board of directors may deem advisable; it may buy, lease, exchange, hold, sell and convey real and personal property at its will and pleasure; it may construct, build and erect such buildings, works and improvements upon property of its own or of others, by their permission, as may be deemed proper, and may equip, operate, use and maintain the same; it may in any way it may desire manufacture, handle and deal in cotton, wool, jute, hemp, silk or any other textiles, either singly or in combinations of two or more of them; it may buy, sell and exchange goods, wares and merchandise of all kinds; it may purchase, lease, use and maintain any works or improvements connected, or intended to be connected with the works and improvements of said company; it may consolidate or unite with any other company now created or to be hereafter created under the laws of this or any other state, retaining its own name or that of the company united or consolidated with, or by a vote of those holding a majority of its outstanding share capital, adopt a new name; it may borrow money and as security therefor it may issue its notes, bonds or other obligations, and if deemed advisable, secure the payment of the same by a mortgage or deed of trust upon its franchises and property or any part of it; it may acquire, hold, own and enjoy stock in the capital of any company now in existence or hereafter to be created under the laws of this state or any other state or country, and stock in the capital may be owned, held and enjoyed by any company now created or to be hereafter created; it may acquire, construct, equip and operate telephone and telegraph lines and electric light and power plants.

Corporate power.

May consolidate.

May borrow money.

Sec. 3. That the principal office of said company shall be in Davie county, North Carolina, but it may be establish and maintain branch offices, agencies, factories, depots, warehouses, stores and works anywhere in the United States or elsewhere that its directors may deem advisable.

Principal office.

Sec. 4. That it may make such by-laws, rules and regulations as the stockholders may desire not inconsistent with the constitution and laws of this state.

By-laws and rules.

Sec. 5. That the corporators and stockholders of said company and their associates, successors and assigns shall not be individually or personally liable or responsible for the debts, contracts, obligations, engagements or torts of said corporation.

Individual liability.

Sec. 6. That no notice or publication whatever of the first meeting of said corporation shall be given or required: *Provided*, all of the corporators named herein waive in writing such notice and fix a time and place for such meeting.

Notice of first meeting not required.

Proviso.

Sec. 7. That this act shall be in force from and after its ratification.

Ratified the 27th day of February, A. D. 1899.

CHAPTER 124.

An act to incorporate the Butler Institute in the county of Martin.

The General Assembly of North Carolina do enact:

Corporators. Section 1. That Thomas P. Moore, Isaiah Davis, Charles A. Willis, Thomas G. Gray, Kemp Price, Rev. George Jarvis, Joseph J. Walker, George Alexander, William G. Holomon, and their Body politic. successors be, and they are hereby constituted a body politic and Corporate name. corporate by the name and style of Butler Institute, and by that Corporate powers. name may sue and be sued, plead and be impleaded, may acquire by purchase, gift or otherwise, to them and their successors, estates real and personal for the use of said Butler Institute, in the town of Jamesville, in the county of Martin, and have all the other rights, privileges and immunities conferred by law upon bodies corporate of a like nature.

Quorum. Sec. 2. That any five of the corporators shall constitute a quorum for the transaction of business, and in case of vacancy Vacancies occurring. by refusal to act, or by death, removal, resignation or otherwise, such vacancy shall be filled at a general meeting of the colored citizens of Jonesville [Jamesville] and vicinity, called by the trustees for that purpose.

Sec. 3. That this act shall be in force from and after its ratification.

Ratified this 27th day of February, A. D. 1899.

CHAPTER 125.

An act to incorporate the "Southern Real Estate, Loan and Trust Company."

The General Assembly of North Carolina do enact:

Corporators. Section 1. That W. S. Alexander, P. M. Brown, J. C. McNeely, and J. H. Weddington, their present and future associates, successors and assigns, are hereby constituted and declared to be Body corporate. a body corporate by and under the name and style of the "Southern Real Estate, Loan and Trust Company," and shall so con- Corporate name. tinue for a period of sixty (60) years, with principal place of Principal office. business in the city of Charlotte; and as such may, and shall be Corporate rights. capable to, in their corporate name, sue and be sued, appear, prosecute and defend to final judgment and execution in all actions in any courts or elsewhere; to have a common seal, which they may alter at pleasure; to elect in such manner as they shall determine to be proper all necessary officers and agents and define their duties and obligations; to fix the compensation of such officers and agents, and if they deem proper, to take bonds with security, payable to the corporation, for the faithful performance of their duties; to make by-laws and regulations not inconsistent herewith, the laws of this state and of the United States, for the due and orderly conduct and government of themselves and the management of the affairs, business and property of the said company, and alter the same as they may provide in said by-laws; to determine the manner of calling and conducting all meetings, the number of membres that shall constitutea quorum, the number of shares that shall entitle the members to one or more votes, the mode of voting by proxy, the mode of selling and transferring stock, the term of office of the several officers, the manner in which vacancies in any of the offices shall be filled until a regular election, and such other things as may be for the best interest of said company; and to do any and all things exercised by or incident to other corporations of similar character and purpose by force of the common or general statutory laws of the state. Make by-laws.

SEC. 2. The capital stock of said corporation shall not be less than ten thousand dollars ($10,000), divided into shares of the par value of one hundred dollars ($100), with power in said corporation to increase the same from time to time as said corporation may elect, to an amount not exceeding five hundred thousand dollars ($500,000), divided into shares of the par value as above. Capital stock.

SEC. 3. That said Southern Real Estate, Loan and Trust Company shall have power to buy, take, acquire, hold and own all kinds of real, mixed and personal estates and property as owner thereof or in trust for itself or others, to convey the same or any part thereof absolutely or by way of mortgage or lease or otherwise as natural persons can or are authorized to do under the laws of this state, and to and with the same effect, according to law, and to buy, sell, rent and deal in real estate and mixed and personal property of every kind, class and description, and to take and accept conveyances to itself of any such property by way of trust or mortgage, as security for debts due to itself or others, and to sell any such property or foreclose any such deed of conveyance in trust or mortgage, as shall be provided by the terms of any such instrument, as if it were a natural person, and with the same effect. Corporate power. Corporate power.

SEC. 4. That said company shall have power to receive money in trust and accumulate the same at such legal rate of interest as may be obtained or agreed on, or to allow interest not to exceed the legal rate; to accept and execute trusts of every description as fully as natural persons could, which may be committed to said company by any person or persons whatso- Corporate power.

ever, or by any corporation, or by order, decree or authority of any court of record, upon such terms as may be agreed upon, provided or declared thereto; to act as agent for the purpose of selling, issuing, registering or countersigning certificates of stock, or other evidences of debt of any state, corporation, association, municipality, or public authority, on such terms as may be agreed upon; to lease and rent real estate, and collect rents from the same on commission; to accept from and execute trusts for married women, in respect to their separate property or estate, whether real, personal or mixed, and to act as agent for them in the management, sale and disposition of their properties, charging such compensation for its services as shall be allowed by law or shall be agreed upon by the parties; that said company shall have the right and power to act as agent and broker for fire, tornado, accident and other insurance, for the sale of real estate, and for the management of all estates, real, personal or mixed, of partnerships or persons living or deceased; and nothing in this act shall be construed to relieve any guardian or other trustee from personal liability according to law in case of loss.

Corporate power.

Courts shall have power to appoint this company guardian, etc.

SEC. 5. That in all cases where an application may be made to any court having jurisdiction to appoint a curator, guardian of an infant, committee of an idiot, or insane person, administrator of any person dying testate or intestate, trustee or receiver, such court shall have power to appoint said company as such curator, guardian, committee, trustee or receiver, upon the like application that any natural person might be appointed; and it shall be lawful for any person, natural or artificial, by deed, will, or other writing, to appoint said company a trustee, executor, guardian of an infant, committee of an idiot, or insane person, administrator, trustee, executor, assignee or receiver. Said company may lawfully act, and as such shall be subject to all the obligations and liabilities of natural persons acting in like capacities, and in accepting any of the trusts or powers hereunder, the said corporation may qualify by any of its executive officers authorized by the rules and regulations of the company to do so.

Liability.

May receive deposits from executors, administrators, etc.

SEC. 6. That it shall be lawful for any individual, executor, administrator, guardian, committee, receiver, assignee, trustee, public officer or other person having the custody of any bonds, stocks, securities, moneys or other valuables, to deposit the same for safe keeping with said company.

Courts may make company render accounts.

SEC. 7. That every court wherein said company shall be appointed, or shall be allowed to qualify as guardian, committee, executor, administrator, trustee or receiver, or in which it is made the depository of moneys or other valuables, shall have power to make all orders and compel obedience thereto, and require said company to render all accounts, which said courts might lawfuly make or require, if such company were a natural person.

Corporate powers.

SEC. 8. That said company is authorized to invest moneys received on deposit, and to take, have and hold estates, real, personal and mixed, obtained with the moneys aforesaid, or with funds belonging to said company, and to sell, grant, mortgage or otherwise incumber, lease or dispose of the same, and to that end may execute all deeds or other instruments, concerning the same, as hereinbefore provided; to subscribe for and take stock in any other incorporated companies; to borrow and lend money, and give or take notes therefor, as the case may be; discount, buy and sell notes, bonds, drafts, and other securities, or evidences of debt; to lend money upon such rates of interest as may be agreed upon, subject to the general laws of the state as to the rate, and secure the payment thereof by mortgages, or deeds in trust, made directly to said company, or to others in trust for it, on all kinds of property; to act as agent for others in borrowing and lending money, charging such compensation therefor, by way of commissions, as may be agreed upon by said company and the party for whom it is acting; to deal in exchange, foreign or domestic, securities, mortgages, lands, certificates of indebtedness, stock of incorporated companies, notes, loans, bonds of the United States or of any city, county, or any incorporated company or individual; and is granted all other powers and privileges usually possessed by or appertaining to loan and trust companies.

Corporate power.

SEC. 9. That said company shall have power to guarantee, endorse and secure the payment and punctual performance and collection of notes, debts, bills of exchange, contracts, bonds, accounts, claims, rents, annuities, mortgages, choses in action, evidences of debt, certificates of property of value, checks, and the title to property, indebtedness of companies, partnerships, cities, counties, municipalities, et cetera, in this state and others, on such terms or commissions as may be agreed upon or established, by said company and the parties dealing therewith.

Corporate powers.

SEC. 10. And be it further enacted, that the said corporation shall be, and is hereby, authorized and empowered to receive and keep on deposit all such valuables as gold, silver or paper money, bullion, precious metals, jewels, plates, certificates of stock or evidences of indebtedness, deeds or muniments of title or other valuable papers of any kind, or any other article or thing whatsoever which may be left or deposited for safe keeping with said corporation; and it may be and shall be lawful for any of the courts of this state, into which moneys, stocks, bonds or other property may be paid or deposited by agreement of parties, order, judgment or decree of said court, to order and direct the same to be deposited with said corporation; and it shall be entitled to charge such commission or compensation therefor as may be agreed upon; and for the complete preservation and safe keeping thereof, may construct, erect, purchase or lease such fire and burglar-proof buildings, vaults, iron and composition safes or other buildings or means, which may be or become necessary, and generally to trans[act] and perform all the business relating to such deposit and safe keeping or preservation of all such articles or valuables as may be deposited with it.

Deposits, etc , by married women and minors.

Sec. 11. That when married women, minors or apprentices, lend money to, or deposit same, or other things of value, with said company, in the course of the business herein provided for, or in the course of doing a savings banking business, hereinafter provided for, either generally or specifically, in their own, or to their own name or credit, they, or any of them, may collect or draw the same, in their own name, or on their own check or order, and they and all other persons be bound thereby; and such collection, draft, checks or order, shall be a valid and sufficient release and discharge of said company.

Corporate powers.

Sec. 12. That said corporation is authorized to organize, in connection with its general business, a department for savings bank business, and do a savings bank business for the convenience of small depositors, and to make such regulations in regard thereto, not inconsistent with the laws of this state or of the United States, as the stockholders may deem proper; in which the said company may receive deposits in the savings department and give books, certificates or other evidences of deposit, and to pay such interest as the company may authorize, and as may be agreed upon, not exceeding the legal rate of interest, and also to regulate the time of payment and notice of demand.

Corporate powers.

Sec. 13. That said corporation shall be capable of subscribing for, holding, buying, selling and dealing in the stock of any building and loan asociation, now in existence or hereafter incorporated and organized, and is authorized and empowered to act either as general agent, manager or secretary and treasurer, as the case may be, for any such association; to act as trustee in any and all deeds of trust executed by any member of any such association conveying real estate as security for any loan and to execute, carry out and perform any and all powers and trusts in regard thereto which may be granted to or conferred upon it by any person or corporation, with full power and authority to the said corporation to do all acts and things, execute and perform all the trusts and to hold and exercise the offices and agencies in this section mentioned and set out as fully and effectually as if it were a natural person under no disabilities and possessing like rights, powers, authority and privileges.

SEC. 14. That said corporation shall have its chief office at Charlotte, Mecklenburg county, North Carolina, with branch offices at such other places as the stockholders may fix upon at any time. Chief office.

SEC. 15. That whenever ten thousand dollars ($10,000) of the capital stock of the said company is *bona fide* subscribed for, then by agreement signed by said corporators and subscribers, a meeting for the purpose of organization of the company may be held, at such time and place as the said corporators and subscribers may agree upon, or after stock has been subscribed as above, then a majority of said corporators and subscribers may give notice in some newspaper published in the city of Charlotte, North Carolina, for the space of ten days, that there will be a meeting of said corporators and subscribers for the purpose of organization at a time and place therein named, in said city; and if at a meeting called as herein provided for there shall be present such persons as have subscribed for a majority of said stock (if not, then another meeting shall be called in one of the foregoing ways), they, the said corporators and subscribers, may proceed to an exercise of all the powers and privileges, etc., herein granted. When company may be organized.

SEC. 16. The corporators and stockholders of said corporation and their successors and assigns shall not be individually or personally liable or responsible for any of the debts, liabilities, obligations, engagements, contracts or torts of the said corporation. Individual liability.

SEC. 17. That said corporation shall exist, and be in force and effect, with all the rights, powers, privileges and capacities hereinbefore conferred, for the term of sixty (60) years from and after the ratification of this act, and this act shall be in force from and after its ratification. Duration of existence.

Ratified the 27th day of February, A. D. 1899.

CHAPTER 126.

An act to amend chapter two hundred and twelve, private laws of eighteen hundred and ninety-seven.

The General Assembly of North Carolina do enact:

SECTION 1. That chapter two hundred and twelve (212) of the private laws of 1897, be, and the same is hereby amended by striking out section three (3) of said chapter. Chapter 212, private laws of 1897, amended by striking out section 3, which forbids anyone to build poultry pens within 300 feet of a dwelling in Sparta.

SEC. 2. This act shall be in force from and after its ratification.

Ratified the 27th day of February, A. D. 1899.

CHAPTER 127.

An act to amend chapter one hundred and fifteen of the private laws of eighteen hundred and ninety-three, entitled "An act to incorporate the Piedmont Toll Bridge Company."

The General Assembly of North Carolina do enact:

Amendment to chapter 115, private laws of 1893, relating to incorporation Piedmont Toll Bridge Company. Extension of time for commencement of operations.

SECTION 1. That section one of the private laws of 1893 be amended as follows: By striking out the names of W. V. Clifton and B. Arendell and inserting in lieu thereof L. S. Overman and N. P. McCanless.

SEC. 2. That section three thereof be amended by extending the time for the commencement of the operations under this charter for two years from the ratification of this act.

SEC. 3. That this act shall be in force from and after its ratification.

Ratified the 27th day of February, A. D. 1899.

CHAPTER 128.

An act to amend chapter twenty-six of the private laws of eighteen hundred and ninety-one, the same being "An act to amend and consolidate the acts incorporating the town of Wadesborough."

The General Assembly of North Carolina do enact:

Chapter 26, private laws of 1891, relating to charter of Wadesborough, amended.

SECTION 1. That "An act to amend and consolidate the acts incorporating the town of Wadesborough," the same being chapter 26 of the private laws of 1891, be and the same is hereby added to and amended as follows:

Commissioners authorized to order election.

SEC. 2. That the commissioners of the town of Wadesborough are hereby authorized, empowered and directed to submit to the qualified voters of said town, on a day to be fixed by said commissioners, not later than the first Monday in June A. D. 1900, the question whether the said town of Wadesborough shall issue coupon bonds of said town in an amount not exceeding thirty thousand dollars, for the purpose of providing, erecting and maintaining a system of waterworks, electric lights, and sewerage, or any or either of the same for said town. The said election shall be held in the same manner and under the same rules and regulations as are provided by said chapter 26, of private laws of 1891, for the election of mayor and commissioners for said town, or as may be provided by law in force at the time said election shall be held, for holding and conducting elections for said officers; and at said election each elector or voter shall vote a ballot with the words "For Coupon Bonds" or "Against

Purpose of election.

Manner of election.

Form of ballot.

Coupon Bonds" written or printed thereon. At the close of the polls said ballots shall be counted by the election officers provided by law, and they shall make out and subscribe a paper writing showing the result of said election and seal up the same and direct to the mayor and commissioners of the town of Wadesborough, and shall designate one of their number to carry and deliver said return, on or by the day next after said election, to the mayor of said town, or in his absence, to the town clerk and treasurer, and on said day at the hour of 12 o'clock m. the said commissioners of said town shall meet at their accustomed place of meeting, and a majority being present, shall open said returns and declare the result and have the same recorded in the minutes of their meetings. Delivery of returns.

SEC. 3. That if at said election a majority of said qualified electors shall vote for coupon bonds, then said board of commissioners are authorized, empowered and directed to prepare, or cause to be prepared, said coupon bonds in denominations to be fixed by them, not less than one hundred dollars nor more than one thousand dollars, and to run for such period or periods of years not exceeding thirty years, as said commissioners may determine, at a rate of interest not exceeding six per centum per annum, which interest shall be represented by coupons attached to said bonds, and shall be payable semi-annually on the first days of January and July in each and every year, and said bonds and coupons shall be payable at the First National Bank of Wadesborough, in the town of Wadesborough; said coupons shall bear date and number corresponding with the date and number of the bond to which the same is attached. Said bonds shall be called bonds of the town of Wadesborough and shall be signed by the mayor of said town and countersigned by the clerk and treasurer of said town, and shall have the impress of the seal of said town thereon; said coupons shall be signed by the mayor of said town, and shall state the day when and where the same are payable. Said coupons shall be receivable for all municipal taxes levied by said town. Bonds shall be issued by commissioners if proposition prevails. Denomination of bonds. When interest on bonds payable. When payable. Bonds, how signed.

SEC. 4. That when said bonds are prepared and issued the same shall be disposed of by and under authority of said commissioners, at a price not less than their par value, and shall only be issued and sold as the necessity for the prosecution of the work shall require. The proceeds of said bonds and sales thereof shall not be used for any other purpose than for the providing, erecting and constructing of waterworks, electric lights and sewerage, or such of said improvements as said commissioners may determine upon. Said commissioners shall cause to be made in their minutes an exact record of the numbers of said bonds, Sale of bonds. Proceeds of bonds, how to be applied. Record shall be kept.

when issued and to whom sold or disposed of, and the price received for the same.

Commissioners empowered to make special tax levy for interest and sinking fund.

SEC. 5. That said commissioners, for the purpose of paying the interest of said bonds as the same may become due, and to provide a sinking fund for the redemption of said bonds, shall annually, at the time of the general levy of taxes for said town, levy and cause to be collected a tax on all of the real and personal property in said town subject to taxation by the charter of said town, not exceeding forty cents on the one hundred dollars worth of property and one dollar and twenty cents on each taxable poll, which said tax shall be levied and collected as other taxes for said town; and said commissioners may provide for the collection of rents, water and light charges and other revenues for the use of water, lights and sewerage privileges, and fix and agree upon charges for the same, and said rent charges and revenues shall be held and kept solely for the purpose of maintaining said system of improvement herein provided for and determined upon, and the surplus after paying the expenses of maintaining said improvements shall be applied to the sinking fund for the redemption of said bonds until the same shall be fully paid. In all levies of taxes for the purpose of this act the constitutional equation between property and polls shall be observed.

Maximum special tax.

Commissioners may fix rates.

Commissioners empowered to purchase bonds.

SEC. 6. That in case said sinking fund herein provided shall be sufficient for the purchase of one or more of said bonds at any time before the maturity of the same, said commissioners are hereby authorized and empowered to purchase the same at a sum not exceeding their par value, and in case no one shall offer to sell any such bond or bonds, then said commissioners are authorized to designate such bonds as they may desire to purchase, and after the designation of such bond or bonds and notice thereof given through a newspaper published in Anson county, if the holder or holders of such bond or bonds shall refuse to surrender the same and receive the par value of the same with accrued interest to the date of the maturity of the coupon next due after said notice, then the holder shall not receive any interest subsequently accruing: *Provided*, the said [bond] shall be affected with the conditions of this section only when said conditions are expressed on the face of the bond.

When bonds or coupons are paid.

SEC. 7. That when any bond or coupon shall be paid said commissioners shall cause a record of the same to be made and shall cause them to be canceled and destroyed by fire in the presence of said commisioners and record thereof shall be made.

Notice of election shall be given.

SEC. 8. That said commissioners shall for thirty days before holding any election herein provided for give public notice thereof at the court-house door in Wadesborough and by publication for five successive weeks in one or more newspapers published in the town of Wadesborough, and said notices shall state clearly and succinctly the objects of said election and the amount of bonds to be authorized to be issued. Said commissioners may, under such regulations as are prescribed by law as aforesaid, order a new registration for said election, giving such length of notice and time for registration as said laws may prescribe.

SEC. 9. That said commissioners shall have power and authority to provide water and waterworks for said town, electric lights and sewerage or such of the same as they may determine ; shall have power and authority to acquire by purchase or condemnation sites and right-of-way, either within or outside of said town, for the construction of all the necessary plants, mains, piping and other works necessary to effectively carry out the objects of improvement here provided for. That when for the purposes of this act it shall be necessary to condemn any site or right-of-way in said town, said condemnation shall be had in the manner provided for condemnation of right-of-way for streets by the charter of said town; and when it shall be necessary to condemn any right-of-way for the construction of any aqueduct or water main to carry water to or from said town, outside the limits of said town, said condemnation proceedings shall be instituted by and in the name of the commissioners of said town in the same manner and the proceeding shall be the same as provided for condemnation of right-of-way for telegraph lines by chapter 49 of The Code. Said commissioners may use the streets of said town for all such purposes as may be necessary to carry on and construct and operate the works and improvements contemplated by this act.

Certain property commissioners may acquire.

When condemnation of land is necessary.

SEC. 10. That section 34 of chapter 26 of the private laws of 1891 be amended as follows: Strike out all of said section down to and including the word "notice," in the sixth line thereof, and substitute the following therefor: "The town clerk and treasurer, or such persons as shall be appointed by the commissioners of said town to list the taxes, shall for twenty days next preceding the first day of June in each year, by advertisement at the court-house door and four other public places in said town, notify all persons subject to poll or property tax in said town to come forward and list with him their polls and property for taxation at the same time and place they render the same for taxation to the tax-lister who lists the taxes for general county purposes. And said commissioners may appoint as such tax-lister the same tax-lister who may be appointed by the county commissioners to list the same property for county purposes.

Section 34, chapter 26, private laws of 1891, amended.

SEC. 11. That this act shall be in force from and after its ratification.

Ratified the 27th day of February, A. D. 1899.

CHAPTER 129.

An act to incorporate The Bank of Wadesboro, Anson county, North Carolina.

The General Assembly of North Carolina do enact:

Corporators. SECTION 1. That Charles M. Burns, F. C. Allen, T. J. Covington, T. R. Tomlinson, W. K. Boggan, J. L. Adams, K. W. Ashcraft, H. D. Pinkston, L. D. Robinson, H. Williams and J F. Medley, their present and future associates, successors and assigns, are hereby declared to be a body politic and corporate by the name and style of "The Bank of Wadesboro," situate in Wadesboro, North Carolina, and shall so continue for the period of twenty-five years, with capacity to take, hold and convey real and personal estate; to sue and be sued, and with all the powers, rights and privileges granted to any bank or banking institution by this or any preceding legislature of this state, together with the rights, powers and privileges incident or belonging to corporations of a like character, set forth or referred to in the first, second and third sections or any other section contained in chapter sixteen, volume one, of The Code, entitled "Corporations," and chapter four, volume two of The Code, entitled "Banks."

Body corporate. Corporate name. Place of business. Corporate powers.

Capital stock. SEC. 2. The capital stock of said bank shall be twenty-five thousand dollars, divided into shares of twenty-five dollars each, and such capital stock may be increased from time to time by the stockholders or a majority of them as said stockholders may elect to a sum not exceeding fifty thousand dollars. The office and place of business of said bank corporation shall be Wadesboro, North Carolina; and its officers shall consist of a president, vice-president cashier and a board of not less than five nor more than nine directors, exclusive of the president and vice-president, who shall be ex officio members of said board. The said directors may if they see proper elect a teller who, together with the cashier and president, shall be required to give bonds with approved security for the faithful performance of their respective duties. The stockholders shall meet annually and at such other times as their directors may designate, and shall elect a board of directors at their said annual meeting, who shall serve for a period of twelve months and until their successors are elected and qualified; the directors so elected shall immediately elect the officers aforesaid and fix the term of their offices and their compensation.

Stock may be increased. Officers. Officers shall give bonds. Stockholders' meeting.

When books for subscription open. SEC. 3. The corporators named in the first section, or a majority of them, are hereby empowered to open books of subscription to the capital stock of said bank at such time and place and for such a period of time as they shall determine whenever twenty-five thousand dollars are paid in. The said corporators or a majority of them may call a meeting of the stockholders in the town of Wadesboro and the stockholders shall proceed to adopt bylaws and regulations for the government of said bank not inconsistent with the laws of the state, and may elect such number of directors as may be necessary, to serve for one year and until their successors shall be chosen, or for such term as they may prescribe.

SEC. 4 The said board of directors may adopt and use a seal, and break and alter the same at pleasure; may prescribe the manner of paying for stock and transferring the same; may regulate the method of conducting the business of the said bank; may do a general banking business and exercise all the powers, rights and privileges conferred by the public laws of the state on banks and corporations of a like character; may lend money upon such rates of interest as may be agreed upon, not to exceed the legal rate; may discount, buy and sell notes, drafts and all other securities or evidence of debt; may loan money on mortgages of real and personal property; may buy, build or lease a banking house and sell or exchange the same at pleasure, may negotiate loans on mortgages, real or personal estate, or both, and they shall direct when dividends or profits shall be made and declared: *Provided,* said bank shall not charge a greater rate of interest than is allowed by law, to wit: six per centum.

Seal.

Corporate powers.

Corporate powers.

Proviso.

SEC. 5. That to aid planters, manufacturers and others the said banking company shall and may have power to advance or loan to any planter, farmer, manufacturer or other person any sum or sums of money, and to secure the payment of the same, take a lien in writing on the crop or crops to be raised, whether planted or unplanted, or upon any article then existing or thereafter to be made, purchased, manufactured or otherwise acquired, and any lien so taken shall be good and effective in law.

Advances to planters.

SEC. 6. That if any subscriber shall fail to pay for his or her stock hereafter or heretofore subscribed or any part thereof as the same may be required of him or her, the same or any part thereof remaining unpaid may be recovered in the name of the corporation by ordinary civil action or the entire stock of such delinquent may be sold by order of the directors for cash at the banking house of the said corporation, after three months' notice of such sale in writing to the said delinquent, and after ten weeks' advertisement published in some newspaper in said town, and the proceeds of such sale may be applied to the payment of the balance of the unpaid subscription; and if the proceeds shall not be sufficient to discharge the amount of the unpaid subscription, with all costs of sale, the balance may be secured by civil action as hereinbefore provided.

Unpaid subscriptions.

Corporate powers.

Sec. 7. The said corporation shall have the power to own, maintain or lease warehouses and carry on the business of warehousemen and forwarders, in case the said corporation by stock vote shall so determine; to receive on storage or deposit all kinds of produce, merchandise or other personal property; to make advances in money or merchandise or produce, and to carry on and transact all kinds of business usually transacted by warehousemen; also to advance money and take legal liens for all such advances, and collect and receive interest and commissions, compensation for storage and all labors and expenses incident thereto. All advances made by said corporation or property received for storage or deposit and compensation for all charges and expenses thereon shall be a preferred lien on said property, which shall be satisfied and paid before said corporation can be required to deliver said property.

Corporate powers.

Advances, etc., on property a preferred lien.

Deposits by married women or minors.

Sec. 8. That when married women, minors or apprentices deposit money or anything of value in said bank, either generally or specifically to their own credit, they or any of them may draw the same on their check or order and be bound thereby, and such married woman, minor or apprentice shall be bound by such individual check or order, and the same shall be valid relative to said corporation against such married woman, minor or apprentice and all other persons whatsoever.

Corporate powers.

Sec. 9. That said corporation shall have the right to act as agent, factor or trustee for any state, county, township, town or other municipality or corporation, company or individual, on such terms or compensation and commission as may be agreed on, in registering, selling, countersigning, collecting, acquiring, holding, dealing and disposing of, on account of any county, township, town, municipality, corporation, company or individual, any bond, certificate of stock, note or any description of property, real or personal, or for endorsing or guaranteeing the payment of said bonds, certificate of stock, notes, etc., and generally for managing such business, and for doing any of the matters and things authorized by this charter. The said corporation may charge such premium, commissions or rate of compensation as may be agreed upon.

Individual responsibility.

Sec. 10. All stockholders shall be held individually responsible, equally and ratably, and not one for another, for all contracts, debts and engagements of said bank to the extent of the amount of their stock therein at the par value thereof in addition to the amount invested in such shares, and no more.

Stockholders' representation in meeting.

Sec. 11. That each stockholder shall be entitled in all meetings of the stockholders to cast one vote for each share of stock of the par value of twenty-five dollars owned by him or her.

Transfer of stock.

Sec. 12. That the stock held by any one shall be transferred only on the books of said corporation either in person or by power of an attorney.

Sec. 13. That said corporation shall have power to receive money in trust and to accept and execute any trust that may be committed to it by any court, corporation, company, person or persons; and it shall have power to accept any grant, assignment, transfer, devise or bequest, and to hold any real or personal estate or trust created in accordance with the laws of this state, and then to execute the same on such terms as may be established or agreed upon by the board of directors. And said corporation is hereby fully authorized and empowered to act as trustee or assignee and to receive any deposit of funds in litigation in the various courts of this state and pay therefor such interest as may be agreed upon not exceeding the lawful rate. In case its stockholders shall so elect it shall have power and authority to receive for safe keeping on deposit all money, bonds, stocks, diamonds and silver plate and other valuables and collect reasonable compensation for same, which charge shall be a lien on such deposit until paid, and generally do and carry on the business of a safe deposit and trust company.

Corporate power.

Sec. 14. That said bank is authorized to organize in connection with its general banking business a department for savings and do a savings bank business for the convenience of small depositors, and to make such regulations in regard thereto not inconsistent with the laws of the state as will enable said bank to receive small deposits in the earnings department, and to give certificate or other evidence of deposit and to pay such interest and to regulate the time of payment and notice of demand.

Authorized to organize department for savings.

Sec. 15. That when this bank shall sell the property of its debtors on which it has a lien to secure a debt, or when such property shall be sold for its benefit, it may bid for, buy and hold any and all such property free from lien or incumbrance, and its title thereto shall be absolute and unconditional and shall be in all respects valid and binding against all persons.

Sale of company's property.

Sec. 16. The directors of said bank are empowered to appoint such other clerks as they may see fit and proper, to serve at the discretion of the directors. The directors shall prescribe their duties and shall take them [their] bonds with security for the faithful discharge of their duties and shall fix their compensation.

Directors empowered to appoint clerks.

Sec. 17. Any vacancy in the board of directors shall be filled by appointment by the remaining directors, and any director so appointed shall hold his place until the next election.

Vacancies in board of directors.

Sec. 18. Said corporation may be organized under this act at any time within five years from the date of its ratification.

Time for organization.

Sec. 19. This act shall be in force from and after its ratification.

Ratified the 27th day of February, A. D. 1899.

CHAPTER 130.

An act to incorporate Buies Creek Academy and Commercial College in Harnett county.

The General Assembly of North Carolina do enact:

Corporators. SECTION 1. That J. A. Campbell, J. V. DeVeany, P. D. Woodall, J. S. Pearson and their associates and successors be and are hereby created a body politic and corporate under the name and style of "Buies Creek Academy and Commercial College," and by that name to remain for sixty years for the purpose of maintaining a school of high grade in Harnett county, and in that name may acquire, hold and convey property, real and personal, may sue and be sued, contract and be contracted with, plead and be impleaded, in their corporate capacity; may exercise such rights and acts as may be deemed needful for the promotion of education as aforesaid; may have and use such a common seal, may make and alter from time to time such by-laws as they may deem necessary for the government of said institution: *Provided*, such by-laws shall not be inconsistent with the constitution and laws of the United States and of this state.

Body politic. Corporate name. Purpose of organization. Corporate powers. Proviso.

Certificates of proficiency. SEC. 2. That the corporation shall have power to issue to students who complete the prescribed course of study certificates of proficiency.

Capital stock. SEC. 3. This corporation and its stockholders may, as they see proper from time to time, in order to best promote the interest of the institution, issue, offer for sale and sell shares of the capital stock of the corporation, which may if so desired be divided into dividend bearing and non-dividend bearing shares: *Provided*, that each share shall be of the par value of twenty dollars.

Control of corporation. SEC. 4. That the members of this corporation, together with such stockholders as may be admitted from time to time by sale of shares of stock, shall control the affairs of the corporation, elect such officers as they see fit, fix times of meetings and transact such business as may be incident to the success of the corporation: *Provided*, that in all meetings of the corporation and stockholders all questions shall be decided by a majority vote of the stock represented, each share having one vote: *Provided*, that a majority of the whole stock shall be represented in order to constitute a legal meeting of the corporation or stockholders.

Proviso.

Empowered to create debts. SEC. 5. That in order to make improvements or advance the purposes of the corporation this corporation shall have power to create a debt or debts, and if so desired to secure the same by a mortgage or mortgages or deed or deeds of trust.

Individual liability. SEC. 6. That the stockholders shall not be individually liable for the contracts or torts of this corporation.

SEC. 7. That it shall not be lawful for any person or persons to set up any gaming table or any device whatever, or play at any game of hazard by whatever name called, or to gamble in any manner, or to keep a house of ill fame, or to manufacture intoxicating liquors, or otherwise sell or convey for a certain consideration, or to carry by pretense of gift to any person or persons, any intoxicating liquors, wines, cigarettes or cordials within three miles of said Buies Creek Academy, and any person who shall violate any of the provisions of this section shall be guilty of a misdemeanor. Games of chance prohibited. Manufacture and sale of intoxicants. Misdemeanor.

SEC. 8. That the first meeting of the stockholders or incorporators shall be held within the next six months from or after the ratification of this act at such time and place in Harnett county as said J. A. Campbell shall designate. Notice of said meeting to be given to each stockholder or incorporator. First meeting.

SEC. 9. That this act shall be in force from and after its ratification.

Ratified the 27th day of February, A. D. 1899.

CHAPTER 131.

An act to incorporate the City and Suburban Electric Company of Charlotte.

The General Assembly of North Carolina do enact:

SECTION 1. That George W. Watts, M. P. Pegram, Rev. C. B. King, James T. Anthony, P. M. Brown, D. P. Hutchinson, J. A. Durham, John B. Ross, Charles F. Wadsworth, J. H. Weddington, C. Gresham, James W. Wadsworth, Osmond L. Barringer, Giles M. McAden, John Van Landingham, E. M. Andrews, Walter S. Alexander. Dr. C. A. Misenheimer, Dr. John R. Irvin, Jonas Schiff, John P. Long, J. M. Morrow, H. C. Dotger, S. E. Linton, D. E. Allen, James C. Long, Edward S. Reid, W. W. Phifer, A. C. Summerville, Dr. C. L. Alexander, J. K. Wolfe, C. Valaer, T. M. Barnhardt, A. H. Washburn, C. H. Wolfe, William R. Wearn, James M. Davis, R. E Cochrane, S. J. Torrence, T. M. Shaw, H. G. Link, McD. Watkins, W. S. Pharr, John W. White, S. H. Hilton, and their associates, successors and assigns be and they are hereby created a body politic and corporate by and under the name of "City and Suburban Electric Company of Charlotte," North Carolina, and by that name shall exist for sixty years, the right to have and use a common seal, to sue and be sued, to contract and be contracted with, to purchase or acquire by gift or demise, property, real, personal or mixed; to hold, lease Corporators. Body corporate. Corporate name. Corporate rights.

or sell the same as the interest of said company may require, and shall have all the rights and enjoy all the privileges and immunities possessed and enjoyed by any other street railway or railroad company under the laws of North Carolina.

Capital stock.

Sec. 2. That the capital stock of said company shall be one hundred thousand dollars, divided into shares of one hundred dollars each, to be created by subscription, contribution or donation by individuals, townships, municipal or other corporations, and such subscriptions may be paid in money, labor, land, material, stocks, bonds or other securities, as may be stipulated between the company and the subscribers; and said company may, by a concurrence of two-thirds in value of all its stock, increase its capital stock from time to time to an amount not exceeding five hundred thousand dollars.

May increase stock.

Subscription books may be opened.

Sec. 3. That for the purpose of creating capital stock for said company any three of the corporators above named may open books of subscription to such capital stock at such times and places as they may appoint and keep the same open for such time as they may determine, under such rules and regulations as a majority of all the corporators may prescribe.

When company may be organized.

Sec. 4. That when the sum of ten thousand dollars shall have been subscribed to the capital stock of said company it shall be the duty of at least three of the corporators above named to call a general meeting of the corporators and subscribers for stock of said company, of which meeting ten days' notice of the time and place thereof shall be given to each corporator and to each subscriber for stock, and if a majority of the stock then subscribed for shall be represented in person or by proxy at said meeting, such stockholders shall proceed to elect a board of directors, to consist of five stockholders, which may at any time be increased to nine; and the said directors shall thereupon at said meeting or thereafter proceed to elect one of their number president and shall also elect such other officers as the by-laws may prescribe, and may do and perform all other acts necessary to the complete organization of said company. In all its meetings of stockholders each share of stock shall be entitled to one vote.

Directors.

Election of officers.

Corporate powers.

Sec. 5. That said company is hereby given power and authority to make, construct, equip, operate and maintain a line or lines of railway, with one or more tracks and with such cars, trolley wires, cable-posts, side-tracks, switches, appliances, crossings, bridges, turnouts and branches as it may deem necessary, through, along and over the streets and avenues of the city of Charlotte and of the towns and villages of Elizabeth College, Belmont, Highland Park, Atherton, Seversville, Biddle University and all other towns and villages within a radius of twenty-five miles from the centre of said city, and over and along the public highways and avenues connecting said city with said towns and villages and any of said towns and villages with each other, and to such points in the vicinity thereof and within the radius aforesaid, as the said company by its board of directors may determine; to cross any track of any street railway or railroad company now incorporated or hereafter to be incorporated: *Provided*, that it conform to the grade of the track to be crossed, subject to such rules and regulations as may be prescribed by the board of aldermen; to erect and equip such stations, warehouses, offices, power plants, shops and other buildings as its said board of directors may deem necessary; to buy or otherwise acquire, generate, develop, store, use, transmit and distribute power in the forms of electric current, hydraulic, pneumatic and steam pressure, and in any and all forms now or hereafter in use for driving machinery and for propelling cars or carriages; to charge and collect such sums of money for the carriage of passengers and transportation of property as the board of directors may reasonably fix as the fare or rate of transportation between given points: *Provided, however*, that its cars or carriages shall be operated over and along the streets and avenues of the city of Charlotte with electric power or with such power as shall be approved by the board of aldermen of said city: *Provided further*, that its line or lines of railway shall be constructed over and along streets within the corporate limits of said city by and with the consent of the board of aldermen of said city, and over and along the public highways and avenues without said corporate limits by and with the consent of the authorities having lawful supervision and control of said public highways and avenues: *And provided further*, that said company shall begin the construction of its line or lines of railway within two years, and shall finish and put in operation such line or lines as may be built within the corporate limits of said city within five years from the passage of this act.

Corporate powers.

Proviso.

Proviso.
When construction of line to begin.

SEC. 6. That said company is hereby given power and authority also to make, transmit and furnish to individuals and corporations within said city and within a radius of twenty-five miles from the center of said city, power, light and heat in the form of electricity, gas or other forces, currents or fluids used for such purposes; to construct, maintain and operate a plant or plants in or near the city of Charlotte or at some initial point within a radius of twenty-five miles from the center of said city for the purpose of generating, manufacturing and transmitting the same, and either above or under ground, by wires, cables, tubes, pipes, conduits and all other ways and means now used or which may be devised for transmission of power, light and heat, to transmit and distribute the same directly to consumers or users within the

Authorized to furnish power to certain persons.

radius aforesaid, or to a distributing point therein and from such distributing point to consumers and users as aforesaid; to make, buy, deal in, furnish, supply and sell electricity, gas and any and all other kinds of powers, forces, fluids, currents, matters and materials now used or which may be discovered, for the purposes of illumination, heat and power; to carry on any and all business in anywise connected with the manufacturing and generating, distributing and furnishing of electricity, gas and any other fluids, forces, currents, matters and materials now used or which may be discovered for light, heat and power purposes, including the transaction of any and all business in which such are now or hereafter may be utilized, and all matters incidental or necessary to the use and distribution of light, heat and power; to manufacture and repair, buy, sell and deal in any and all necessary machinery, apparatus and appliances used in or which may be required or deemed advisable for or in connection with the utilization of any and all such forces, fluids and powers or in anywise appertaining thereto or connected therewith; to own and operate within the radius aforesaid cars and carriages, with all such forces, fluids or powers and without tracks when found practicable; to purchase, acquire, hold, improve, lease, operate and maintain water powers, water rights and privileges; to supply water to persons, corporations, towns and cities for domestic or public purposes for use as power and for manufacturing purposes, and to charge and collect such rents and rates therefor as may be deemed advisable or expedient; to purchase, acquire, rent, lease, own, hold, improve and develop real property in such quantities as may be deemed expedient, to build dwelling houses and to build, own and operate stores, mills, schools, factories, warehouses and any and all other structures desirable or convenient; to sell and dispose of the same on such terms and conditions and payments, including installments and installment plans as may be desirable or convenient; to lay out and plat any real property belonging to or acquired by the corporation into lots blocks, squares, factory sites and other convenient forms; and to lay out, plat and dedicate to public use or othewise streets, avenues, alleys and parks: *Provided*, that none of the powers or privileges enumerated in this section and the next preceding section shall be exercised within a radius of four miles from the center of Concord in Cabarrus county.

Corporate power.

Corporate powers.

Proviso.

Privileges, where exercised.

May borrow money.

SEC. 7. That said company is also given power and authority to borrow such sums of money as may be necessary for its purposes from time to time, and for such loans to issue its bonds, bearing interest not exceeding six per centum per annum; to sell, exchange and hypothecate said bonds on such terms as it may deem advisable, and to secure the said bonds and interest thereon by deed of trust or mortgage, conveying its road bed, property and franchises in whole or in part.

SEC. 8. That in order to carry into effect the purposes of this act said company may survey such routes for its line or lines of railway and for its ways and means for transmission and distribution of power, light and heat as may be deemed practicable, and if any lands of individuals or corporations or any easement, privilege or right-of-way therein shall be found necessary for the construction and operation of its said line or lines of railway, its branches and sidings of the standard width, and of its wires, cables, tubes, pipes and conduits for the purposes of transmission and distribution of power, light and heat, and if unable to agree with the owners thereof upon the compensation therefor, said company shall have the right to acquire title to the same or to an easement, privilege or right-of-way therein in the manner and by the special proceedings prescribed by chapter forty-nine of The Code of North Carolina, entitled "Railroad and Telegraph Companies": *Provided, however*, that said company shall not have the power under this act to condemn for its use any of the tracks of the "Charlotte Electric Railway, Light and Power Company," or any of its easements or other property or any of the property now owned by the "Charlotte Consolidated Construction Company."

Rights to survey, etc.

When unable to agree on price of land condemned

SEC. 9. That any person who shall deface, injure, destroy, remove or obstruct said railway or any part thereof, or any of the cars, trains, coaches or carriages thereof, or any of the fixtures, property or machinery thereof or its structures or appliances of any kind shall be guilty of a misdemeanor, and fined or imprisoned within the discretion of the superior court.

Persons injuring property guilty of a misdemeanor.

Penalty.

SEC. 10. That any person or persons who shall cast, throw, shoot, propel or project or in anywise put in motion any stone, rock, shot, torpedo or other missile of any kind or nature at, against or into any car, carriage, coach or train of said railway, whether the same be in motion or at rest, with intent to injure any such car, carriage or coach, or any person or persons therein or thereon, or the property of said company, shall be guilty of a misdemeanor and fined or imprisoned within the discretion of the superior court.

Persons shooting at or in certain other ways damaging property of company guilty of a misdemeanor.

Penalty.

SEC. 11. That the conductors and drivers and other agents and servants of said company while in the active service of said company or the discharge of any duty connected therewith are hereby vested with the same power, authority and privileges which belong to similar officers and agents of railroad companies in this state; and in addition to the general powers conferred upon such agents and officers they may eject and remove all drunken, profane and disorderly persons from any of the conveyances or cars

Certain powers vested in employees of company for protection of property, etc.

of said company at any time, whether the fare of said drunken, disorderly or profane persons has been paid or not, and the said company shall not be liable or responsible in damages therefor, and such agent or officer shall not be liable, civilly or criminally therefor unless he use greater force than is necessary to eject such perons.

Individual liability.

Sec 12. That the stockholders shall not be individually or personally liable for any of the contracts, obligations, indebtedness, defaults or torts of the corporation, and no stockholder shall be liable to pay for more stock than he has subscribed for.

Principal office.

Sec. 13. That the principal office of said corporation shall be at Charlotte, North Carolina, and such branch offices as may be desirable for the purposes of the corporation shall be established at such places as the by-laws of the corporation shall designate and prescribe.

Sec. 14. That exclusive rights granted to other corporations shall not prevent the exercise of the powers granted in this act: *Provided, however*, that nothing herein contained shall authorize the company hereby created to run its line or lines of railway along those parts of Trade and Tryon streets in said city which are now occupied and used by the "Charlotte Electric Railway, Light and Power Company," except for purposes of crossing on West Trade street in such manner as may be prescribed by the board of aldermen of said city, and in making such crossing the line of railway of the "Charlotte Electric Railway, Light and Power Company" may be paralleled for a distance of not more than one square on West Trade street, if the board of aldermen of said city in their discretion may so allow: *And provided further*, that the company created by this act may lay its track on East Morehead street between Tryon and Brevard streets if said part of Morehead street shall be so widened by the said city as to provide sufficient space for that purpose, and the board of aldermen of said city shall authorize said track to be laid in said part of Morehead street.

Sec. 15. That this act shall be in force from and after its ratification.

Ratified the 27th day of February, A. D. 1899.

CHAPTER 132.

An act for the relief of the sureties on the official bond of J. H. Able, former tax collector for the town of Waynesville.

The General Assembly of North Carolina do enact:

Certain relief for sureties of J. H. Able, former tax collector of Waynesville.

Section 1. That D. F. Rhinehart, one of the sureties on the official bond of J. H. Able, former tax collector for the town of Waynesville, be and is hereby authorized and empowered to collect for the benefit of himself and his co-sureties on said bond all arrears of taxes due the said town of Waynesville for the year eighteen hundred and ninety-six under such rules and regulations as are or may be prescribed for the collection of taxes in said town.

SEC. 2. That the authority herein given shall cease and determine on the first day of January, in the year nineteen hundred. When this authority shall cease.

SEC. 3. That this act shall be in force from and after its ratification.

Ratified the 28th day of February, A. D. 1899.

CHAPTER 133.

An act to change the name of Berryville, in Catawba county, to West Hickory.

The General Assembly of North Carolina do enact:

SECTION 1. That the name of the town of Berryville, in Catawba county, be changed to West Hickory; and that in the act incorporating said town the name of Berryville is stricken out and the name of West Hickory is substituted therefor. Name of Berryville, Catawba county, changed to West Hickory.

SEC. 2. This act shall be in force from and after its ratification.

Ratified the 28th day of February, A. D. 1899.

CHAPTER 134.

An act to amend chapter one hundred and fifty-six, private laws eighteen hundred and ninety-five.

The General Assembly of North Carolina do enact:

SECTION 1. That section two of chapter one hundred and fifty-six of the private laws of eighteen hundred and ninety-five be amended as follows, viz: Strike out all after the word 'town" in the fourth line of said section and substitute the following in lieu thereof, viz: "Thence with Swanzy street to Ben street; thence with the Bladenboro road forty yards; thence a direct line parallel with Swanzy street to a point opposite the lower edge of Cypress street; thence with said street to Main street; thence with Main street to Lower street; thence with Lower street to the Cape Fear river; thence up the river to the beginning." Chapter 156, private laws of 1895, relating to incorporation of town of Elizabethtown, amended.

SEC. 2. That section three of said chapter is hereby repealed and the following substituted in lieu thereof, viz: "That the offi- Officers of town.

cers of said town shall consist of a mayor and two commissioners and such other officers as they may elect, and the following-named persons shall fill the offices of mayor and commissioners till the first Monday in May, nineteen hundred and one, and until their successors are elected and qualified, viz: For mayor, Frances M. Willis; for commissioners, John W. Hall and G. F. Melvin."

Commissioners may license sale of liquor.

Sec. 3. That section four of said chapter is hereby repealed and the following substituted as section four, viz: "That said commissioners shall have power and authority to tax all liquor dealers and manufacturers of liquor doing business in said town, a license tax of not exceeding one hundred dollars per annum."

Said chapter as amended, re-enacted.

Sec. 4. That said chapter as amended by this act is hereby re-enacted.

Sec. 5. This act shall be in force from and after its ratification.

Ratified the 28th day of February, A. D. 1899.

CHAPTER 135.

An act to extend the time for the organization of the "Bank of Maxton," chapter one hundred and thirty-six, private laws of eighteen hundred and ninety-seven.

The General Assembly of North Carolina do enact:

Time for organization of bank of Maxton extended.

Section 1. That the time for the organization and commencing business under the charter granted in chapter three hundred and fifty, private laws of eighteen hundred and ninety-three, and amendments thereto be and the same is hereby extended for two years from the ratification of this act.

Sec. 2. That this act shall be in force from and after its ratification.

Ratified the 28th day of February, A. D. 1899.

CHAPTER 136.

An act to authorize J. L. Welch to pay over surplus road tax to treasurer of Cherokee county.

The General Assembly of North Carolina do enact:

Certain road taxes ordered to be paid to treasurer of Cherokee county.

Section 1. That J. L. Welch is directed to pay over the surplus of road tax of Valley Town township now in his hands to the treasurer of Cherokee county, to be paid out by order of the county commissioners on any indebtedness for the public now existing or that may hereafter accrue on the public roads in Valley Town township.

Sec. 2. That this act shall be in force from and after its ratification.

Ratified the 28th day of February, A. D. 1899.

CHAPTER 137.

An act to amend chapter three hundred and two, private laws of eighteen hundred and ninety-one, entitled "An act to charter The Murphy Banking Company."

The General Assembly of North Carolina do enact:

SECTION 1. That section one of the said act be and the same is hereby amended by adding the names of W. T. Corder, R. L. Cooper and W. C. Kenyon as corporators.

Section 1, chapter 302, private acts of 1891, relating to organization of Murphy Banking Company, amended.

SEC. 2. That said act be amended by striking out of said section one of said act the words, "The Murphy Banking Company," and by inserting in the said [stead] thereof the words "The Bank of Murphy."

Corporate name changed.

SEC. 3. That sections two and three of the said act be amended by striking out the words "twenty-five" in said sections and by inserting in the stead thereof the word "twenty"; so that the same will be read "twenty thousand" in the stead of "twenty-five thousand"; that the said act, chapter three hundred and two, is hereby re-enacted as amended by this act.

Capital stock.

SEC. 4. That this act shall be in force from and after its ratification.

Ratified the 28th day of February, A. D. 1899.

CHAPTER 138.

An act to amend chapter fifty, laws of eighteen hundred and eighty-three.

The General Assembly of North Carolina do enact:

SECTION 1. That section four of chapter fifty, laws of eighteen hundred and eighty-three, be and the same is hereby repealed and the following substituted therefor, viz: That the trustees, five (5), in number, provided for in said chapter fifty, laws of eighteen hundred and eighty-three, shall be elected by the qualified voters of the town of Kings Mountain, and they shall be elected by said qualified voters at the general town election in May, eighteen hundred and ninety-nine, and every three years thereafter at the general town election. The qualification of voters or electors under this act shall be the same as the qualification for electors in the annual town elections of Kings Mountain.

Chapter 50, laws of 1883, relative to incorporation of Kings Mountain High School, amended.

Trustees elected by voters of Kings Mountain.

SEC. 2. That all laws and clauses of laws in conflict with this act are hereby repealed.

Conflicting laws repealed.

SEC. 3. That this act shall be in force from and after its ratification.

Ratified the 28th day of February, A. D. 1899.

CHAPTER 139.

An act to extend the time for collecting the taxes of the town of Rutherfordton.

The General Assembly of North Carolina do enact:

Time for collection of taxes by collector of Rutherfordton extended.

SECTION 1. That it shall be lawful for the tax collector of Rutherfordton for the year eighteen hundred and ninety-seven to collect the taxes for the year aforesaid until January, nineteen hundred, under the same rules and regulations and with the same powers and rights as he had in eighteen hundred and ninety-seven.

May levy on any property in Rutherford county to make such collection.

SEC. 2. That said tax collector shall have the right to levy on property anywhere in Rutherford county for the collection of said taxes.

Persons making affidavit that tax has been paid.

SEC. 3. That any person who will make affidavit that said tax has been paid shall not be required to pay under the provisions of this act.

SEC. 4. This act shall be in force from and after its ratification.

Ratified the 28th day of February, A. D. 1899.

CHAPTER 140.

An act to amend chapter one hundred and six of the private laws of eighteen hundred and seventy-three and eighteen hundred and seventy-four of North Carolina, the same being an act to incorporate the "Pee Dee Manufacturing Company," in the county of Richmond.

The General Assembly of North Carolina do enact:

Chapter 106, private laws of 1873 and 1874, relative to incorporation of Pee Dee Manufacturing Company, amended.

SECTION 1. That chapter one hundred and six of the private laws of eighteen hundred and seventy-three and eighteen hundred and seventy-four of North Caolina be amended by striking out all between the word "Fabricks" in line seven of section one and the word "near" in line eight of said section; and by inserting between the words "organization" and the words "and" in line twenty of said section one, "may do a general mercantile business in their corporate capacity."

Amended.

SEC. 2. That section nine of said act be amended by striking out the word "fifty" in line three of said section nine and inserting in lieu thereof the words "one hundred."

Boundaries of municipal corporation.

SEC. 3. That section ten of said act be amended by adding thereto: "That the boundaries of the municipal corporation created by this act shall extend to all the land on which Pee Dee Mill Number Two is erected, and shall include the fifty acres of land owned by said corporation around said Pee Dee Mill Number Two."

SEC. 4. That section eleven of said act be amended by striking out the two last lines thereof and inserting in lieu of the same the words "twenty-eighth day of February, Anno Domini nineteen hundred and thirty-four." Amended.

SEC. 5. That this act shall be in force from and after its ratification.

Ratified the 28th day of February, A. D. 1899.

CHAPTER 141.

An act to incorporate "The Aurora High School."

The General Assembly of North Carolina do enact:

SECTION 1. That Alex. Hudnall, B. H. Thompson, Robert T. Bonner, John B. Whitehurst, Lee T. Thompson. F. F. Cherry, W. H. Roberts, J. H. Jarvis, R. T. Pickering, R. T. Hodges, B. B. Nicholson, W. B. Rodman, J. L. Fowle, J. M. Litchfield, W. T. Hudnall, J. Havens, John M. Griffin, their associates and successors, be and are hereby created a body politic and corporate under the name and style of "The Aurora High School," and by that name may sue and be sued, plead and be impleaded, and have the power to adopt a common seal, which they may change at will. Corporators. Body politic. Corporate name. Corporate powers

SEC. 2. That the said corporation shall exist for sixty years, unless sooner dissolved according to law. Time of existence of corporation.

That the capital stock of the said company shall be one thousand dollars, divided into two hundred shares of the par value of five dollars each. That the stockholders may at any time increase the capital stock to an amount not exceeding five thousand dollars. That the incorporators above named or a majority of them may open the books of subscription at such time and place as they or a majority of them may direct. That as soon as sixty shares shall have been subscribed a general meeting of the stockholders shall be called, of which meeting five days' notice shall be given to the subscribers. Capital stock. May increase stock. When subscribers may meet and organize.

That the corporation can organize whenever sixty shares of stock shall be bona fide subscribed for and ten per centum thereof paid in. That the whole of the capital stock need not be issued. That at such general meeting the stockholders shall elect not more than seven and not less than three directors, and a president, who shall ex officio be a director, and shall do all other things necessary to organize said company and carry out the Election of directors and officers.

objects of the charter. That the stockholders shall hold annual meetings at such time and place as the stockholders may designate. That all said officers of the said company shall hold their offices for one year and until their successors are elected and qualify. That the said corporation may adopt such by-laws and rules and regulations as it may desire, not inconsistent with the laws of the state of North Carolina.

Annual meetings.

Term of office.

Empowered to acquire property.

Sec. 3 That the said corporation shall have power to acquire by purchase, gift or in any other way property, personal, real or mixed, and may hold same for the use of said company, and may sell, exchange, mortgage or otherwise dispose of their property and holdings.

Location of school.

Sec. 4. That the said company shall have full power to provide and establish a school or schools in the town of Aurora, Beaufort county, for the white children of said town and of Richland township, and the said company shall have power to make the tuition such sum as the said company may designate, or may make the tuition free to white children of said village, township or county.

Tuition.

School authority of Aurora may contract for free tuition for white children of said territory.

Sec. 5. That the school committee or authority having charge of the public school for white children in the district or territory in which Aurora is located shall have power to contract with the said company to provide public schools, free of tuition to the parties privileged to attend the public school of said district or territory, and may use the public school fund to pay said company for such service.

Stock non-assessable.

Sec. 6. That the stock shall be non-assessable, and the stockholders shall not be liable for any of the debts, liabilities or obligations of said corporation.

Conflicting laws repealed.

Sec. 7. That all laws or parts of laws in conflict with this act are hereby repealed.

Sec. 8 That this act shall be in force from and after its ratification.

Ratified the 28th day of February, A. D. 1899.

CHAPTER 142.

An act to allow the city of Greensboro to issue bonds.

The General Assembly of North Carolina do enact:

Aldermen of Greensboro empowered to issue bonds.

Section 1. That the board of aldermen of the city of Greensboro is hereby authorized and empowered to issue bonds in the name of the city of Greensboro, in such denominations and forms as it may determine to an amount not exceeding three hundred thousand dollars, payable at such times and such places as the board of aldermen may prescribe: *Provided*, that the time of payment of such bonds shall be not less than thirty and not more than fifty years from their date.

Proviso.

Bonds, when payable.

SEC. 2. That the said bonds shall bear interest at no greater rate than five per centum per annum, and the interest shall be made payable annually or semi-annually as the board of aldermen may prescribe, and said bonds shall in no case be sold, hypothecated or otherwise disposed of for less than their par value.

Rate of interest.

When payable.

SEC. 3. The said bonds shall be signed by the mayor, attested by the city treasurer and sealed with the corporate seal of the city, and shall have interest coupons attached thereto, which said bonds and their coupons shall be exempt from city taxation until after they become due, and the coupons shall be receivable in payment of city taxes. That for the purpose of paying said bonds at maturity and the said coupons as they become due, it shall be the duty of the board of aldermen and they are hereby empowered so to do, to levy and collect each year a sufficient special tax upon all subjects of taxation which are now or may hereafter be embraced in the subjects of taxation under the charter of said city, and in the manner and at the same time as other taxes are collected under said charter: *Provided*, that the total rate of taxation for both general and special purposes shall never exceed one dollar and thirty cents on each one hundred dollars valuation of property and three dollars and ninety cents on each poll: *Provided further*, that the taxes collected under this act for the payment of said bonds and interest coupons as aforesaid shall be used for no other purpose, and it shall be the duty of the city treasurer, as said coupons are paid off and taken up, to cancel the same and report not less than twice a year to the board of aldermen the numbers and amounts of the coupons so cancelled.

Coupons exempt from taxation.

May levy and collect special tax for reserve fund.

Proviso.

Maximum of tax rate.

Proviso.

Shall be used for no other purpose.

SEC. 4. That the board of aldermen shall not issue said bonds nor any of them, nor levy nor collect said tax until they shall have been authorized and empowered so to do by a majority of the qualified voters at [of] said city at an election or elections to be held at such times and places as the said board shall appoint, of which notice shall be given for twenty days in some newspaper published in said city; and at said election or elections those favoring the issue of said bonds or of any of them as specified in the call of such election or elections and the levy and collection of the tax for the payment of said bonds and coupons shall vote "Issue," and those opposing it shall vote "No issue": *Provided*, that the said board may in its discretion order a new registration of voters.

Election ordered by commissioners.

Form of ballot.

SEC. 5. That said board may call an election under this act at

When election may be called.

Succeeding elections may be ordered.

any time it may see fit, after giving the proper notice; and the rejection by the voters of any proposition submitted to them under this act shall not prevent a submission of the same or other propositions to the said voters at any other time that the board of aldermen may appoint, and that the said board may continue to call elections under this act until the whole amount of three hundred thousand dollars shall have been issued.

Purpose of issuance of bonds.

SEC. 6. That the said bonds may be issued for the purpose of building or buying, conducting and operating an electric light and power plant or gas plant, or both, to furnish lights for the streets of said city. and lights and power to its citizens if the board of aldermen sees fit; for the purpose of building or buying a waterworks plant and maintaining and operating the same, to furnish water for the use of the city and its citizens; to build, construct, enlarge and maintain the sewerage system; to build a city hall and market and other necessary buildings; and to grade, curb, macadamize, pave and improve the streets of the city:

Proviso.

Provided, however, that the said board shall, in the resolution calling the election and in the notice to the people of said election, state the maximum amount of bonds to be issued under said election and the purpose or purposes for which the said bonds are to be issued, specifying the maximum amount to be used for each purpose. and the bonds shall be used for no other purpose than that specified as aforesaid: *Provided*, that the purchasers of said bonds shall not be required to see to the application of the purchase-money.

In ordering election commissioners shall state maximum amount of bonds to be issued.

Board of aldermen shall have entire supervision of works created under this act

SEC. 7. That the said board of aldermen shall have entire supervision and control of any and all of the plants or works established under this act, and is hereby authorized to elect all such agents, servants and employees as it may deem proper, and pay the same from any of the revenues of the city not otherwise appropriated, and do all other proper things to carry into effect the true intent of this act.

SEC. 8. This act shall be in force from and after its ratification.

Ratified the 28th day of February, A. D. 1899

CHAPTER 143.

An act to incorporate the "Dismal Swamp Railroad Company."

Preamble.

WHEREAS, by an act ratified the ninth day of March. eighteen hundred and ninety-five, the general assembly of North Carolina did create O. Emerson Smith, R. N. Musgrave, Arthur Emmerson, J. C. Emmerson, T. J. Pope, and such other persons as they might associate with them, and their successors and assigns, a body politic and corporate for the term of fifty years, under the name, style and title of the "Norfolk and Camden Railroad Company," and by that name might have succession and a common seal, might sue and be sued, plead and be impleaded, and have all the rights and privileges conferred upon corporations by chapter sixteen of The Code, entitled "Corporations"; and

Whereas, by said act certain other rights and privileges were conferred upon said body politic and corporate as in said act contained; and

Whereas, certain proceedings have been had in the superior court of Camden county, state of North Carolina, by C. W. Steele, receiver of the Portsmouth Lumber Manufacturing Company; B. F. Scott, Nathaniel Hathaway, Annie C. Smith, R. E. Wren, John C. Emmerson, and Cole and Shultice as plaintiffs against said Norfolk and Camden Railroad as defendant; and Preamble.

Whereas, in said proceedings the court did by an order entered October the twelfth, eighteen hundred and ninety-eight, direct that the Norfolk and Camden Railroad, running through the counties of Camden and Currituck to the Virginia line, and all the timber lands belonging to said railroad, its franchises, road bed, iron, cars, engines, lands, timber and all rights and interests belonging to said corporation be sold at public auction before the court-house door in Camden county on November the eighteenth, eighteen hundred and ninety-eight; and Preamble. Preamble.

Whereas, at said sale Gustavus Milhiser and T. K. Parrish became the purchasers of said railroad, its franchises, rights, privileges and property, which sale to them was confirmed by said superior court of Camden county and title directed to be made them by an order entered in said proceedings; and Preamble.

Whereas, the said Gustavus Milhiser and T. K. Parrish do not desire to own, control and operate said railroad individually, but desire the same to be owned, controlled and operated by a corporation to be composed of themselves, C. R. Johnson and such other persons as they may associate with them, their successors and assigns; now therefore,

The General Assembly of North Carolina do enact:

Section 1. That Gustavus Milhiser, T. K. Parrish and C. R. Johnson, and such other persons as they may associate with them, and their successors and assigns, be and they are hereby created a body politic and corporate under the name of "Dismal Swamp Railroad Company" for a term of forty-six years, and by that name may have succession and a common seal, may sue and [be] sued, plead and be impleaded, and shall have all the rights Corporators. Body corporate. Corporate name. Corporate powers.

and privileges conferred upon corporations by chapter sixteen of The Code, entitled "Corporations," and all acts amendatory thereof.

Corporate powers.

Sec. 2. That said corporation may buy and hold such lands as may be necessary for the purpose of its business, not exceeding ten thousand acres; may purchase standing timber, may sell and convey the same; may sell, mortgage or otherwise dispose of its lands; may construct, own and operate sawmills, planing mills and all kinds [of] wood-working machinery and appliances; may purchase or otherwise legally acquire from Gustavus Milhiser and T. K. Parrish all such rights, privileges, franchises and property, real, personal and mixed, as was sold to them under the order of the superior court of Camden county, state of North Carolina, and may control and operate the railroad lately owned by the Norfolk and Camden Railroad Company as at present located, which was sold to Gustavus Milhiser and T. K. Parrish under the order of court aforesaid, and may pay for the same in shares of its capital stock.

Capital stock. May be increased.

Sec. 3. That the capital stock of said company shall not be less than fifteen thousand dollars, and may be increased from time to time by a vote of the stockholders to a sum not to exceed one hundred thousand dollars. The shares shall be of the par value of one hundred dollars each, and the stockholders shall not be individually liable for the debts or liabilities of the corporation.

Rights and privileges.

Sec. 4. That said property shall have all the rights and privileges conferred on railroads and be subject to all the liabilities imposed on them by the general laws of the state of North Carolina, and nothing in this act contained shall be construed as depriving said company of said rights and privileges.

May open books for subscriptions to capital stock.

Sec. 5. That the persons named in section one of this act shall have power to open books of subscription to the capital stock, and when the same shall have been subscribed and paid for in money or property, may call a meeting of the stockholders and organize the company. Until the election of directors the persons named in section one shall constitute the directors of the company and all vacancies shall be filled by the board of directors. The principal office of the company and the place of holding the meetings shall be determined by the stockholders and may be in the city of Richmond, in the state of Virginia.

Sec. 6. This act shall be in force from and after its ratification.

Ratified the 28th day of February, A. D. 1899.

CHAPTER 144.

An act to amend chapter two of the private laws of one thousand eight hundred and ninety-one, incorporating "The Great Falls Water Power Manufacturing and Improvement Company."

The General Assembly of North Carolina do enact:

Section 1. That section three (3) of chapter two (2) of the private laws of eighteen hundred and ninety-one, entitled "An act to declare The Great Falls Water Power Manufacturing and Improvement Company" a duly incorporated company, and to amend and enlarge its charter, be amended by adding thereto the following sentence, to-wit: "If the number of shares issued or authorized to be issued shall at any time legally exceed in amount the value of the property and assets of the company, the same may from time to time be scaled and reduced to such a number as the stockholders at any special meeting called for that purpose and at which four-fifths of the capital stock is represented, may authorize and prescribe: *Provided*, that the capital stock shall never be less than two hundred thousand dollars: *Provided further*, that at the time the reduction is made the amount to which the capital stock is reduced shall not be below their assessed value for taxation of the property of the company.

Section 3, chapter 2, private laws of 1891, incorporating Great Falls Water Power Manufacturing and Improvement Company, amended.

When shares of stock exceed assets, they may be scaled.

Proviso.

Maximum capital stock.

Proviso.

Sec. 2. That this act shall be in force from and after its ratification.

Ratified the 28th day of February, A. D. 1899.

CHAPTER 145.

An act to amend an act entitled "An act to incorporate The Biddle University," etc., ratified the eighth day of February, eighteen hundred and eighty-seven.

The General Assembly of North Carolina do enact:

Section 1. That chapter seventeen (17) of the private laws of eighteen hundred and eighty-seven, being an act to amend an act, entitled "An act to incorporate The Biddle University," etc., ratified the eighth day of February, eighteen hundred and eighty-seven, be amended by adding thereto the following: That the board of trustees of the said university are authorized and empowered to establish schools in the said university for the purpose of educating and qualifying students for any of the learned professions, including that of the law and medicine: *Provided*, that the requirements for graduation of said school of medicine

Chapter 17, private laws of 1887, incorporating Biddle University, amended.

Schools of medicine, law, etc., may be established.

Proviso.

be approved by "the board [of] medical examiners of the state of North Carolina." Also to establish training schools in mechanics and agriculture, and to establish, carry on and conduct such other schools as are usual in the universities in the United States, although express power so to do may not be specifically granted in this act.

SEC. 2. That this act shall be in force from and after its ratification.

Ratified the 28th day of February, A. D. 1899.

CHAPTER 146.

An act to incorporate the Sylva High Training School in Jackson county,

The General Assembly of North Carolina do enact:

orporators.

SECTION 1. That M. D. Cowan, A. B. Dills, E. P. Lewis, L. W. Allen, John Bumgarner, C. W. Allen, A. L. Ensley, H. D. Welch, and the two public school committeemen of Sylva township R. A. Painter and J. W. Divelbiss and their successors in office, and the successors of the first named eight, who may be elected as hereinafter provided, be and the same are hereby created a body politic and corporate under the name and style of the "Sylva High Training School" for the purpose of establishing and maintaining a high training school at Sylva, in Jackson county, North Carolina, with the privilege of a common seal, to be altered at their pleasure, and with power in their corporate name to sue and be sued, plead and be impleaded, contract and be contracted with, hold real estate and personal property by purchase, donation or otherwise as they may consider necessary or convenient for the establishment and maintenance of said Sylva High Training School, not to exceed twenty-five thousand dollars, and make all rules, regulations, by-laws and agreements needful or necessary for the government of their body and the said Sylva High Training School, and for carrying into effect the aforesaid purposes of their institution and do all other acts pertaining to similar corporations and not inconsistent with the laws of this state or of the United States.

Body politic.
Corporate name.
Purpose of corporation.
Corporate powers.
Rules and regulations.

Term of office of trustees.

SEC. 2. That the terms of office of the eight trustees named in section one of this act shall be one year from the date of its incorporation by this general assembly and until their successors are elected.

Election of trustees by mass meeting of citizens.

SEC. 3. That the election of the eight trustees provided for in section one of this act shall be by a mass meeting of the citizens on the first Monday in May, nineteen hundred, and every two years thereafter, and that said trustees shall have power to elect a president and secretary of the board from among their number.

SEC. 4. That said board shall have power to prescribe a course of study for "Sylva High Training School" and to change the same at any time deemed proper; and upon the completion of said course of study so provided it shall be the duty of the principal of said "Sylva High Training School" to give to the student so completing said course a certificate of proficiency. Board of trustees empowered to prescribe course of study.

SEC. 5. That said board of trustees shall have power to receive by donation, gift or otherwise any money or property of any kind or nature and disburse the same for the benefit of the said "Sylva High Training School." Trustees may receive donations, etc.

SEC. 6. That the said board of trustees shall have power to elect a principal teacher in said "Sylva High Training School," and as many assistants, either male or female, as may be necessary to carry on the said school. Election of principal.

SEC. 7. That the individual property of the aforesaid trustees shall not be liable for the debts of said corporation. Individual liability.

SEC. 8. That it shall be unlawful for any person or persons to sell any spirituous, vinous or malt liquors within two miles of said Sylva High Training School. Sale of spirituous liquors within two miles of said school a misdemeanor.

SEC. 9. That any five members of the said board shall constitute a quorum for the transaction of any business coming before said board. Quorum.

SEC. 10. That any person violating the provisions of section eight of this act shall be deemed guilty of a misdemeanor and fined or imprisoned in the discretion of the court. Violations of provisions of this act a misdemeanor.

SEC. 11. That this act shall be in force from and after its ratification.

Ratified the 28th day of February, A. D. 1899.

CHAPTER 147.

An act to amend the charter of The Town of Columbia.

The General Assembly of North Carolina do enact:

SECTION 1. That The Town of Columbia shall be and continue, as heretofore, a body politic and corporate, and by the corporate name of "The Town of Columbia," may purchase and hold for the purpose of its government, welfare and improvement all such estate, real and personal, as may be deemed necessary therefor, or as may conveyed, devised or bequeathed to it, and the same may, from time to time, sell, dispose of and reinvest as shall be deemed advisable by the proper authorities of the corporation. Corporate powers of The Town of Columbia.

SEC. 2. The corporate limits of The Town of Columbia shall Corporate limits.

hereafter be defined and located as follows: Beginning on the east side of the Scuppernong river, at the mouth of a ditch or canal, known as the William McCleese ditch, thence southwestwardly up and along the margin of the Scuppernong river one hundred and ten poles to a large cypress bearing two chops on the south side and two chops on the north side; thence south fifty-six degrees east fifteen poles to a cluster of three small marked cypresses; thence north eighty-two degrees east, forty-nine and one-half poles to the southeast corner of the lot whereon Thomas J. Davenport now lives; then north thirteen and one-half poles to the north corner of said lot; thence north seventy-seven degrees east along a new street ten poles to the east side of Back street; thence north twenty-five degrees east along Back street fifteen poles to a post on the east side of Back street; thence east sixty poles to the Martha Fouso road; thence north eighty-five poles to William McCleese ditch or canal; thence along said ditch or canal westwardly to its mouth at the Scuppernong river, the place of beginning.

Annual elections. Sec. 3. There shall, on the first Monday in May in each and every year, be elected by the qualified voters of the town of Columbia, a mayor and five commisioners, who shall be residents within corporate limits of said town of Columbia and qualified voters therein. Mayor and commissioners.

Election, how held. Sec. 4. That the election above provided for shall be held under the same rules and regulations as elections are now or may be hereafter held for members of the general assembly, except as herein provided, and every citizen residing within the corporate limits of The Town of Columbia, who may be qualified to vote for member of the general assembly if an election year for members of the general assembly (or would [be] qualified if it was an election year for members of the general assembly), shall be entitled to vote for one mayor and for five commissioners; each elector shall vote one ballot on which shall be placed the names of the persons voted for, either written or printed, and of the persons voted for as mayor, the one who shall receive the greatest number of votes cast at said election shall be declared elected mayor of The Town of Columbia, and of the persons voted for as commissioners, the five who shall have received the greatest number of votes cast shall be declared elected commissioners of The Town of Columbia. Immediately upon the result of the election being ascertained by the judges thereof, it shall be their duty or the duty of any one of them thereto authorized by the others, to make proclamation at the door of the house in which the election was held, and then and there declare the result of the same. It shall also be the duty of the judges within the next twenty-four hours thereafter to

Persons entitled to vote.

Result of election, how declared.

certify under their hands and seals to the mayor of The Town of Columbia, the result of the said election, which certificate shall be placed in the mayor's office, and he shall have the same recorded on the records of the minutes of the commissioners of The Town of Columbia. Upon the receipt of said certificate the mayor shall immediately notify the persons of their election, requesting them to immediately appear before him to be qualified and enter upon the duties of their respective offices. If among the persons voted for there shall be any two or more who shall receive an equal number of votes for the same office and either of them would be elected but for the equal vote, the question as to which of such parties is elected shall be decided by the judges of election, and in case they fail to decide, the registrar or registrars shall decide betwen the persons thus having an equal number of votes: *Provided*, the judges of election and other election officers shall not receive any compensation except as is provided or permitted by the state election law governing the elections of members of the general assembly: *Provided, further*, that the mayor shall receive nothing for notifying the officers elected.

Duty of judges to certify result of election.

Result shall be recorded.

Persons elected, how notified.

In case of tie vote.

Proviso.

Compensation of registrars and judges.

Proviso.

SEC. 5. That the mayor immediately after his election and before entering on the discharge of the duties of his office shall take and subscribe before his predecessor in office or other person authorized and empowered by law to administer oaths, the following oath:

Mayor shall take oath.

"I, ..., do solemnly swear that I will diligently endeavor to perform faithfully and truly, according to my best skill, judgment and ability, all the duties of the office as mayor of The Town of Columbia, while I continue therein, and will cause to be executed as far as in my power lies, all laws ordinances and regulations made for the government of the town, and in the discharge of my duties I will do equal justice in all cases whatsoever. So help me, God." The oath shall be recorded by the clerk of the board of town commissioners, and filed with the records of the board.

Form of oath for mayor.

SEC. 6. That each commissioner, before entering upon the duties of his office, shall likewise take an oath that he will truly and impartially perform the duties of commissioners for The Town of Columbia, according to the best of his ability, skill and judgment.

Commissioners shall take oath.

SEC. 7. That the mayor and commissioners shall hold their office respectively until the succeeding election, and until their successors are elected and qualified.

Term of office.

SEC. 8. That if the person elected mayor of The Town of Columbia shall refuse to qualify, or shall die before qualifying, or if, having qualified, there is any vacancy in the office of mayor by reason of death, resignation or disability to discharge the duties

When mayor refuses to qualify.

Vacancy occurring.

of the office, or if the mayor, during his term of office, shall become a non-resident of the town, the commissioners shall choose some discreet and well-qualified person to serve as mayor for the term, or for the unexpired portion of the term, as the case may be, and either from their own number or from some of the qualified residents of the town; and if in like manner and for like cause vacancies shall occur in the board of commissioners, the remaining commissioners shall elect some suitable person from the qualified residents and voters of the town to fill such vacancies.

Jurisdiction of mayor.

Sec. 9. That the mayor of said town of Columbia, while acting as such, is hereby constituted an official court with all the jurisdiction and powers over criminal offenses occurring within the limits of The Town of Columbia which are now or may hereafter be given to justices of the peace, and shall also have jurisdiction to hear and determine all misdemeanors consisting of a violation of the ordinances and by-laws of the said town. The proceedings of said court shall be the same as are now prescribed by the charter of the said town and the amendments thereto, and are now, or may be hereafter prescribed for the courts of justices of the peace, not inconsistent with the charter of the said town or the amendments thereto. In all cases there shall be a right of appeal to the superior court of Tyrrell county, having jurisdiction of the case, and in all cases of appeal from the mayor's judgment, the mayor shall require bond with sufficient security to insure the defendant's appearance at the next succeeding term of the appellate court, and on failure to furnish said bond the mayor shall commit the defendant to the common jail of Tyrrell county.

In cases of appeal from mayor's court.

Persons failing to pay fines may be worked on public roads.

Sec. 10. That in all cases where judgment may be entered up against any male person or persons for fine or penalties according to laws and ordinances of The Town of Columbia, and the male person or persons against whom the same is adjudged refuses or is unable to pay the said judgment, it may and shall be lawful for the mayor of said town to order and require said male person or persons convicted to work on the streets or other public works of said town under the supervision of the person whose duty it is to oversee the working of the streets or other public works of said town, until at a fair rate of wages such male person or persons shall have worked out the full amount of the judgment and costs of the prosecution.

Warrants may be issued by mayor to certain officers.

Sec. 11. That warrants and other processes issued by the mayor of Columbia may be issued by him to any officer that a warrant or other process of a justice of the peace may by law be.

Mayor shall keep record of judicial acts.

Sec. 12. That the mayor shall keep a faithful minute of his judicial proceedings, and all warrants and processes by him issued for violation of the ordinances and by-laws of The Town of Columbia, and other offenses committed in said town, shall have all of the force, virtue and validity of warrants or other process issued by a justice of the peace, and shall be executed and enforced anywhere in Tyrrell county and elsewhere in all cases where the warrant or other process of a justice of the peace would be.

Mayor shall preside over meetings of commissioners.

Sec. 13. That the mayor shall attend at and preside over the the meetings of the board of commissioners, and where there is an equal division upon any question, or in the election of officers by the board, he shall determine the matter by his vote. He shall vote in no other cases, and if he shall be absent, the board shall appoint one of their members *pro tempore* chairman; in the event of his extended absence or sickness, the board of commissioners may appoint one of their own members mayor *pro tempore* to exercise each and every duty of the mayor.

Mayor pro tempore.

Quorum.

Sec. 14. That a majority of the commissioners shall constitute a quorum and be competent to perform all the duties prescribed for the commissioners. Within five days after their election they shall convene for the transaction of business and shall then fix stated days of meeting for their term of office, which shall be as often as once in each calendar month. Special meetings may be called by the mayor or a majority of the commissioners.

Commissioners shall hold first meeting within five days after election.

Fees of mayor.

Sec. 15. That the mayor shall receive the fees of his office, which shall be the same as that of a justice of the peace. He shall receive no salary, and the commissioners shall receive no salary.

Power of commissioners to make ordinances.

Sec. 16. That the commissioners, when convened, shall have power to make and provide for the enforcement of such ordinances, by-laws, rules and regulations for the better government of the town as they may deem necessary.

Powers of commissioners.

Streets.

Sec. 17. That among the powers hereby conferred upon the board of commissioners are the following: To provide for the constructing, laying out, cleaning and repairing streets and sidewalks and to condemn land for any of the purposes, establish and regulate a market, take all proper and effectual means to prevent and extinguish fire, make regulations to cause the due observance of Sunday, suppress and remove nuisances, take all necessary measures to preserve the town from contagious or infectious diseases, appoint special policemen or other officers where necessity arises, take measures to preserve the peace of the town, and to execute the laws and ordinances thereof and maintain good order, establish one or more cemeteries outside of the town of such dimensions as they may deem necessary, and lease or sell burial plots therein to individuals and families on such terms as may be thought best, and also to provide a common place of burial

Contagious diseases.
Policemen.

Cemeteries.

therein, and the right to take up and remove from any part of the cemetery, now belonging to the town, the remains of any person or persons, and remove and re-inter them in some other part of the cemetery, for the improvement and better arrangement of the said cemetery, or for the advancing the interests of the town; to enact and pass such laws and ordinances as they deem necessary to preserve the health of the town; determine, when necessary, the boundaries of streets and alleys, and establish new streets, lanes and alleys; to provide for licensing and regulating auctions, to restrain and prohibit gambling and to provide for licensing and restraining shows, theatrical and public amusements in the town; to impose and appropriate fines, penalties or forfeitures for the breach of its by-laws and ordinances, to levy and collect taxes on the real and personal property in the town and on all trades, callings and franchises for carrying all necessary measures into operation in the town for the benefit of the town; to regulate the business of carrying persons, baggage and freight or merchandise on the streets, and to issue license to persons wishing to engage in such business and lay tax on the same; to appoint, pay and prescribe the duties of all such officers and employees as may be deemed necessary, except as otherwise provided.

Health.

Auctions. Gambling. Shows.

Trades, callings, etc.

Buggies for hire.

Officers appointed, salary and duty.

Clerk and treasurer.

SEC. 18. The commissioners at their first meeting after their election shall appoint a clerk and also a treasurer, who may be from their own number, and also a collector of taxes, who may be also the constable of the town, and a constable, all of which officers shall respectively hold their offices during the official term of the commissioners, or until their successors are duly appointed and qualified; subject, however, to be removed at any time for misbehavior or neglect of duty, and others appointed in their stead by the commissioners, who alone shall be the judges of such misconduct or neglect of duties. Before entering upon the duties of their offices, each of said officers shall be sworn by the mayor or other person competent to administer oaths, at the expense of the officer sworn, to the faithful discharge of their duties, and to execute a bond, payable to the state of North Carolina in such sum as the commissioners shall determine, with security approved by the commissioners, which bond shall be duly probated and recorded in the office of the register of deeds of Tyrrell county, in the book prepared for the official bonds of the officers of said county. The original bond shall be deposited with the mayor, and a copy of the same, duly certified by the register of deeds, shall at all times be received as evidence in any court of law for the enforcement of the penalty, or for any other purpose: *Provided*, the amount of the bond of the treasurer shall never be less than twice the

Term of office.

May be removed.

Officers shall take oath.

Security.

Original bond of officers shall be deposited with mayor.

Proviso.

amount of the taxes received and disbursed by the treasurer for the fiscal year previous, and the bond may be required to be enlarged or strengthened at any time, and the official bond of the constable, as constable, shall be in the amount of five hundred dollars, and the tax collector's bond shall be at least as much as the treasurer's bond, or more, if deemed necessary.

Amount of bond of treasurer.

Bonds of tax collector and constable.

SEC. 19. The officers provided for in the preceding section shall receive the following compensation: Treasurer, five per centum on the total amount received and disbursed, as commissions. The constable shall receive the fees of his office, as provided by law, and such additional compensation as the commissioners shall allow. The clerk's salary shall be fixed by the commissioners.

Compensation of officers.

SEC. 20. It shall be the duty of the treasurer to call on all persons who may have in their hands any moneys or securities belonging to the town, which ought to be paid or delivered into the treasury, and to safely keep the same for the use of the town; to disburse the funds according to such orders as may be drawn on him in the manner hereinafter specified. He shall keep in a book, provided for that purpose, a fair and correct account of all moneys received and disbursed by him, and shall submit said book and accounts to the mayor or commissioners whenever required to do so; on the expiration of his term of his office, he shall deliver to his successor all the books, moneys, securities and other property entrusted to him for safe keeping or otherwise, and during his continuance in office he shall faithfully perform all duties imposed upon him as town treasurer.

Duties of treasurer.

Shall submit books to commissioners.

SEC. 21. That all orders drawn on the treasurer shall be signed by the mayor and clerk, and shall state the purpose for which the money is applied, and the treasurer shall specify the said purpose in his accounts and also the sources from whence are derived the moneys received by him.

Orders drawn on treasurer, how signed.

SEC. 22. It shall be the duty of the constable to see that the laws, ordinances and orders of the commissioners are enforced, and to report all breaches thereof to the mayor; to preserve the peace of the town by suppressing disturbances and apprehending offenders, and for that purpose he shall have all the powers and authority vested by law in sheriffs or other constables, he shall execute all warrants, precepts or process lawfully directed to him by the mayor or others; and in the execution thereof shall have the same power anywhere in Tyrrell county as the sheriff or constables have; he shall have the same fees on all warrants, precepts or process executed and returned by him, which may be allowed to any constable under like circumstances, and also such other compensation as the commissioners may allow.

Duty of constable.

Power of constable.

Fees of constable.

SEC. 23. That the sheriff or jailer of Tyrrell county is hereby required, without a mittimus, to receive into the common jail

Sheriff of Tyrrell county required to receive in jail

certain persons arrested in Columbia.

of said county as his prisoner, any person taken up in the night by the constable or police of the town of Columbia, and to keep such person safely until the following morning at eight o'clock, except as herein otherwise provided, when the offender shall be brought before the mayor or some justice of the peace, resident in the town, and be lawfully dealt with, and for such service the sheriff or jailer shall be entitled to such fees as he is in other like cases. If the offender is charged with the violation of the law of the state, the fee shall be paid by him if guilty, and if not, by the county of Tyrrell; if the offender is charged with violation of the ordinances of the town, the fee shall be paid by him if guilty, and if not by the town.

Sheriff or jailer shall be entitled to fee.

By whom paid.

Commissioners may take measures to prevent entrance of contagious diseases.

SEC. 24. The board of commissioners may take such measures as they may deem effectual to prevent the entrance into the town of any contagious or infectious disease; may stop, detain and examine for that purpose, any steamboat or water craft, conveyance or vehicle or any passenger coming from places believed to be infected with such disease, and if necessary, turn them back. They may establish and regulate hospitals and pest houses within the town, or within three miles thereof, may cause any person in the town suspected to be infected with such disease, and whose stay may endanger health, to be removed to a hospital or pest house, in or out of said town; and may remove from the town or destroy any furniture or other articles which may be suspected of being tainted or infected with contagious or infectious diseases, or of which there shall be reasonable cause to apprehend that they may pass into such a state as to generate disease.

Hospitals and pest houses may be established.

Commissioners may recover certain costs in removing persons to pest houses, etc.

SEC. 25. That in case any person be removed to any hospital or pest house, as provided for in the preceding section, the board of commissioners may recover before the mayor or any justice of the peace the expense of his or her removal, support, nursing and medical attendance in an action to which such person shall be party defendant; in the event of the death of such person, in addition to the above, the burial expenses also, if the commissioners incur that expense, in an action against the personal representative of the deceased.

SEC. 26. The board of commissioners may take such measures as they may deem best to stop, detain, examine and turn back, within three miles of the town limits, any boats, conveyances, passengers, or travellers to more effectually prevent entrance to the town of any contagious or infectious disease.

Persons interfering with officers guilty of a misdemeanor.

SEC. 27. If any person shall threaten or resist the officers of the said town in the performance of any duty or privilege upon them conferred, the person so offending shall pay to the town one hundred dollars and moreover be deemed guilty of a misdemeanor.

Sec. 28. That in order to guard against the introduction or spread of smallpox in the town, the commissioners may require all persons not sufficiently vaccinated to be forthwith vaccinated.

Commissioners may require vaccination.

Sec. 29. That in making arrests the constable or policeman shall be governed by the regulations provided for and clothed with the powers conferred upon its officers by the state of North Carolina, and when arrests have been made, the prisoner or prisoners shall be immediately carried before the mayor, or some other competent officer for trial, except in the following cases: (1) When the arrest is made between sunset on Saturday and eight o'clock on Monday morning. (2) When the arrest is made in the night. (3) When the person arrested is found in an inebriated or intoxicated condition. (4) When for the safe keeping of the party arrested, imprisonment is necessary. In any of which cases the prisoner may be committed without mittimus to the county or town jail until his trial before the mayor or other officer, which can not be compelled, except between the hours of eight o'clock in the morning and sunset on all days of the week except Sunday, and not at all on Sunday. And in such case the keeper of the county or town jail shall receive prisoners under this act without mittimus.

Powers of officers in making arrests.

When persons shall be tried.

Except.

Sec. 30. That arrests shall be made by the constable or any policeman of the town in the following cases: (1) Whenever he shall have in his hands a warrant duly issued by the mayor of Columbia or a justice of the peace of Tyrrell county. (2) Whenever any misdemeanor or the violation of any town ordinance shall be committed in his presence. (3) Whenever a misdemeanor or violation of any ordinance has been committed and he has a reasonable cause to believe that the suspected party may make his escape before a warrant can be obtained. Whenever any arrest is made by any town offcer, it shall be lawful for him to summons any of the by-standers or witnesses as witnesses, and such summons shall be as binding as though made by a subpœna issued from any authority or officer whatever.

In what cases arrests shall be made.

Officers may summon by-standers.

Sec. 31. That for the purpose of protecting the town from fires, they may prevent the erection of wooden buildings where they may increase the danger by fire; they may order the removal or repairs of old structures or dangerous structures, where they increase the danger of fires, or in such manner as they may deem best, and in the event of a refusal to comply with the orders and demands of the commissioners, the owners, their agents, lessees or occupants, as the case may be, shall be subject to a fine of one hundred dollars, and be guilty of a misdemeanor. And in the event of a fire in the town the commissioners may direct, command, permit or suffer a house or

Protection from fires.

Refusal to comply with this ordinance a misdemeanor.

Houses may be destroyed by order of commissioners in event of fire.

houses to be blown up or otherwise removed for the purpose of arresting the progress of the fire, without subjecting themselves or the town, or any officer of the same to any action for damage for the same, upon objection being made to the board of commissioners. No building shall be built, rebuilt, repaired or altered in said town without a permit first had and obtained from the commissioners; *Provided*, no charge shall be made for a permit.

Permit for rebuilding must be had from commissioners.

Nuisances.

Sec. 32. The commissioners may require and compel the abatement and removal of all nuisances within the town at the expense of the person causing the same, or at the expense of the owner or tenant of the property whoever the same may be. They may also prevent the establishment of, and may regulate, if allowed to be established, any slaughter house or place, or the exercise in town of any offensive, dangerous or unhealthy business, trade or employment.

Slaughter house.

Shall levy annual tax.

Sec. 33. That the board of commissioners of the town shall have the power not oftener than annually, to impose, levy and collect a tax for general corporation purposes not exceeding thirty-three and one-third cents on the hundred dollars assessed valuation upon all real and personal property within the corporate limits of said town and on all taxable polls residing in said town on the first day of June each year, a tax not exceeding one dollar.

Tax rate.

Clerk shall procure certified list of assessments of value of property.

Sec. 34. That the clerk of the board of commissioners shall procure from the register of deeds of Tyrrell county a duly certified list of the assessments of the value of property, real and personal, which have been returned to him for taxation and upon which town taxes can be levied under this act, situated within the corporate limits of The Town of Columbia, and such other records pertaining to matters taxable by the town as may be kept in his office. The board of commissioners shall have all the powers given to the authorities of Tyrrell county pertaining to the revision of the tax list, except the power to alter the valuation of real estate: *Provided*, that when any piece or parcel of real estate is situated partly within and partly without the corporate limits of the town, the commissioners of said town shall have the said real estate so situated, valued on the town tax list, so that only the part thereof situated within the corporate limits shall be subject to town tax.

Power of commissioners to revise tax list.

When and to whom taxes shall be listed.

Sec. 35. That the citizens of Columbia, and others liable to pay taxes under this act, shall on the day prescribed by law for listing state and county taxes, render under oath to the clerk of the town, who is hereby constituted a commissioner of affidavits for that purpose, a list of such property taxable under this act, and which is not liable to state and county tax, under all the rules and penalties prescribed for listing state and county taxes; and if any person shall fail to render such list within the time prescribed for listing state and county taxes he shall pay double the tax assessed on any article for which he is liable to be taxed under this act:

Persons failing to list taxes shall be liable for double amount of taxes.

Annual tax levy.

SEC. 36. That the clerk shall make out said tax list, and after it is completed and not later than the regular meeting of the commissioners in September in each year, they shall proceed to levy the tax upon such subjects of taxation as they shall determine and shall place the tax list containing the order of the clerk to the tax collector to collect the same, which shall be substantially the same as that required and used by the clerk of the county commmissioners to the sheriff of the county, to collect the taxes due the county, which said order and tax list when delivered to the tax collector, shall have all the force and virtue of a judgment and execution against the property named therein without the right of homestead or personal property exemptions, as in the case of taxes due the state and county. The said constable or tax collector shall proceed with the collection of the said tax list and complete the same by the first of December following: *Provided*, that the commissioners may extend the time for the completion of such collection to a date not later than June first next ensuing, and the tax collector shall pay over all moneys as collected at least as often as once a week, to the treasurer, and take his receipt therefor; and the tax collector shall receive for his fees for the collection of taxes the same compensation allowed by law to county tax collectors. On the first day of December, or the time fixed by the commissioners, not later than June first, there shall be one per centum added to all taxes due, and on the first day of each month thereafter, one per centum additional, until the tax is paid. And the tax collector of The Town of Columbia shall be the constable thereof, unless the commissioners shall elect another person, which they are authorized to do.

Tax list shall have force of a judgment.

Time in which taxes shall be collected.

Proviso. Commissioners may extend time for completion of collection.

Persons liable and failing to return tax guilty of a misdemeanor.

Penalty.

SEC. 37. That all persons who are liable for a poll tax to said town and shall willfully fail to make return thereof, and all persons owning property subject to tax and who willfully fails to list the same as provided herein, shall be deemed guilty of a misdemeanor to the same extent as for a failure to list state and county taxes, and on conviction thereof before the mayor of the town, shall be fined not more than twenty dollars or imprisoned not more than ten days, and it shall be the duty of the tax collector to prosecute offenders against this section: *Provided*, any person prosecuted under this section may be discharged by the mayor upon the payment of double the amount of tax found to be due by him to the town, together with the cost of the prosecution.

Persons failing to pay tax.

SEC. 38. That if any person liable to pay any tax shall fail to pay the same, within the time prescribed for collection, the collector shall proceed to colect the same forthwith by distress and sale, after public advertisement for a space of ten days at the court-house door in said town, if the property be personal. That when the tax due on any lot or other real estate or interest in the same shall remain unpaid on the first day of December, or the time prescribed by the commissioners for completing the collection of taxes, the tax collector shall proceed to collect the same by distress and sale of personal property belonging to the owner of said lot, real estate or interest in real estate, if enough of such personal property can be found; or if enough of personal property can not be found, the tax collector shall report the facts to the commissioners, together with a particular description of said lot, real estate or interest therein, and thereupon they shall direct the same to be sold at the court-house door in The Town of Columbia, by the collector. The collector shall, before selling the same, make a full advertisement of said real estate at the court-house door and three other public places in said town for twenty days, and shall also serve upon the owners or agents of the owners, if the owner or his agent reside in town, a written or printed notice of the taxes due and of the day of sale, or if the owner or his agent be, one or both, non-residents of the town, he shall mail notices above to them or either of them, if their place of residence is known. In default of the payment of the taxes by the hour and day of sale designated in the notice, the tax collector shall sell at the court-house door, in The Town of Columbia, the lot, real estate, or interest in real estate, to the highest bidder for cash, and if no person will bid enough to pay the taxes, penalties and expenses for the said property offered, the tax collector shall bid on behalf of the town, the amount of said taxes, penalties and expenses, and no higher bid being offered, the same shall be struck off to the town, and if not redeemed as hereinafter provided, shall belong to the town absolutely. The collector shall return to the commissioners a statement of his proceedings, specifying the purchaser and the price, which shall be entered upon the book of the proceedings of the commissioners, and if there shall be a surplus after paying said taxes, penalties and expenses, the same shall be paid into the town treasury subject to the demand of the owner.

Failure to pay tax on real estate.

Sale of property for failure to pay taxes.

Real estate sold for taxes may be redeemed within a year.

Sec. 39. That the owner of any lot, real estate or interest in real estate, sold under the provisions of this act, his heirs, executors, administrators or any person acting for them, may redeem the same within one year from the date of sale by paying to the purchaser the amount by him paid, and twenty-five per centum in addition thereto.

Sec. 40. That if the lot, real estate, or interest in real estate, sold as aforesaid, shall not be redeemed within the time specified, the collector or his successor, under the direction of the mayor of the town, shall convey the same to the purchaser, or to his assigns in fee. In the event the town is the purchaser, the collector, or his successor, shall convey to the corporation of Columbia, and the recitals in such conveyance or in any other conveyance, made by any tax collector of said town, shall be *prima facie* evidence of the truth of the same and can not be attacked, except on the ground that the taxes were not due and unpaid at the date of sale.

When to be conveyed to purchaser.

When town is purchaser.

SEC. 41. That in addition to the tax on real and personal property hereinbefore provided for, the commissioners shall have power to levy and collect a specific or license tax on the following subjects, trades, callings, professions or occupations, to-wit, merchants, peddlers, oculists, vendors of any articles whatever, hotels, restaurants, circuses, shows, plays, theatricals or exhibitions of any kind in the town or within one mile of the corporate limits of the same, concerts, strolling musicians, auctioneers, conveyances, lawyers, doctors, photographers (resident or itinerant), brokers, soliciting agents, telegraph and telephone companies, sawmills, agents of all kinds, including sewing machine, lightning-rod and insurance agents, dentists, dealers in fresh meats, fish, etc., fertilizer agents, ice cream and other saloons, draymen, livery stables, and those keeping horses for hire, dealers in millinery goods, coach-makers and repair shops.

Commissioners shall have power to levy certain special taxes.

Special taxes.

SEC. 42. The commissioners may pass ordinances, rules and regulations regulating the amount of taxes to be paid upon any of the foregoing subjects of taxation and the manner of paying the same, and the time of paying the same. Any person exercising any of the professions, trades, callings or occupations named in the preceding section, without first having obtained a license therefor, shall be guilty of a misdemeanor, and upon conviction before the mayor, shall be fined five dollars for each day he shall exercise such trade, calling or occupation, and the cost of the prosecution.

Power of commissioners to pass ordinances, fix tax rate, etc.

Failure to pay license tax.

SEC. 43. The commissioners may place a tax on dogs and enforce the collection of same with sufficient penalty for nonpayment of same, and may, if the tax be not paid, have the dogs killed.

Tax on dogs.

SEC. 44. The clerk of the board of commissioners herewith provided for, shall attend at all meetings of the board, and be the clerk thereof; he shall keep a correct minute of the proceedings of the board and perform any and all other duties herein involved upon him.

Clerk shall keep record of meetings.

Laws heretofore constituting charter of Columbia repealed.

Sec. 45. That this act shall be in force from and after its ratification: *Provided*, that all laws heretofore constituting the charter of The Town of Columbia, and affecting the government thereof, are continued in full force, unless in direct conflict with the provisions of this act.

Ratified the 28th day of February, A. D. 1899.

CHAPTER 148.

An act to amend the charter of the town of Gastonia, North Carolina.

The General Assembly of North Carolina do enact:

Body corporate. Corporate name. Corporate powers.

Section 1. That the inhabitants of the town of Gastonia, in the county of Gaston, shall be and continue as they have been, a body corporate under the name and style of the town of Gastonia, and they shall have full power to make all by-laws, rules, regulations and ordinances for the benefit and good governmetn of said town, not inconsistent with the constitution of the state of North Carolina or the United States, to contract and be contracted with, to sue and be sued, to plead and be impleaded, to purchase and to hold and convey real and personal estate. And they are hereby invested with all the powers and rights necessary or belonging to or usually appertaining to municipal corporations.

Term of office of present mayor and aldermen continued.

Sec. 2. That J. Lee Robinson, mayor; George A. Gray, J. D. Moore, Edgar Love, Thomas W. Wilson and A. C. Williamson, heretofore styled commissioners, elected on the first Monday of May, eighteen hundred and ninety-eight, shall continue to hold their office until an election shall be held as hereinafter provided for, and shall constitute the mayor and board of aldermen respectively.

Corporate limits.

Sec. 3. That the corporate limits of the town of Gastonia shall be as follows, to-wit: Beginning at a stone one-half mile due north of the crossing of the Southern and Narrow Gauge Railroads in the present town of Gastonia, running thence due east one mile to a stone; thence due south one mile to a stone; thence due west two miles to a stone; thence due north one mile to a stone; thence due east one mile to the beginning.

Division of wards

Boundaries of ward No. 1.

Sec. 4. That the said town shall be divided into five (5) wards to be known as follows, to-wit: That portion of the town bounded on the north by the line of the corporate limits, on the east by the line of the corporate limits, on the south by the Southern Railroad, and on the west by Marrietta street and the extension of Marrietta street to the corporate limits, shall be known as ward number one. That portion bounded on the north by the line of the corporate limits, on the east by Marrietta street and the extension of Marietta street to the line of the corporate limits, on the south by the Southern Railroad, and on the west by the line of the corporate limits, shall be known as ward number two. That portion bounded on the north by the Southern Railroad, on the west by York street and the extension of York street to the corporate limits, on the south by the line of the corporate limits, and on the west by the line of the corporate limits shall be known as ward number three. That portion bounded on the north by the Southern Railroad, on the east by Oakland avenue and the extension of Oakland avenue to the corporate limits, on the south by the line of the corporate limits, and on the west by York street and the extension of York street to the line of the corporate limits shall be known as ward number four. That portion bounded on the north by the Southern Railroad, on the east by the line of the corporate limits, on the south by the line of the corporate limits, and on the west by Oakland avenue and the extension of Oakland avenue to the line of the corporate limits shall be known as ward number five.

Ward No. 2.

Ward No. 3.

Ward No. 4.

Ward No. 5.

SEC. 5. That on the first Monday in May, eighteen hundred and ninety-nine, and annually thereafter, there shall be an election held as hereinafter provided for a mayor and five (5) aldermen, one alderman so elected to reside in each ward.

Annual election for mayor and aldermen.

SEC. 6. That it shall be the duty of the board of aldermen to declare at what place or places elections shall be held in said town; and they shall give due notice of the establishment of said voting place or places by publication in some newspaper published in said town for four weeks before the election or by posting such notices at three or more public places in said town. The said board of aldermen shall at their first regular meeting in March, eighteen hundred and ninety-nine, and annually thereafter, appoint a registrar for said election and shall give notice of registration by causing publication to be made at three public places in said town of Gastonia, giving in said notice the name of said registrar and the place of registration. The aldermen shall furnish such registrar with registration books, and it shall be the duty of the registrar appointed by the year eighteen hundred and ninety-nine and thereafter for four consecutive Saturdays next preceding the election, between the hours of seven a. m. and seven p. m., to open the registration books at such place or places as has been advertised as aforesaid, and to register therein the names of all persons applying for registration and entitled to register and vote, keeping the names of the white voters separate and apart from those of the colored voters. Any person offering to register shall be required to take an oath that he is a citizen of North Carolina and has resided in the county

Aldermen shall give notice of election places.

Registration notice shall be given.

Duties of registrar.

Days for registration.

Persons offering to register shall take oath.

ninety days and in the town of Gastonia thirty days, and if any person shall willfully swear falsely he shall be deemed guilty of a misdemeanor, and on conviction be sentenced to pay a fine of fifty dollars or imprisoned for thirty days in the county jail: *Provided, however*, that after the first registration shall have been made a new registration shall not be made annually, but such registration books may be revised so as to show an active list of electors previously registered and still residing in said town without requiring said electors to be registered anew. And such registration books shall on the fourth Saturday before the first Monday in May, eighteen hundred and ninety-nine, and annually thereafter, be opened for the registration of any elector entitled to registration whose names have never before been registered in said books or do not appear in the revised list: *Provided, however*, that the board of aldermen may at any time order a new registration. The said registrar and the two judges appointed as above set forth shall compose the judges or inspectors of election to open the polls, receive and deposit the ballots in the boxes provided for that purpose, and to superintend and have control of the voting.

Persons falsely registering. Penalty.

Proviso.

Registration after first new registration.

Proviso. Board of aldermen may order new registration.

Registration books, when closed.

SEC. 7. That the registration books shall be closed on the Saturday before the first Monday in May in each year at the hour of seven o'clock p. m., and after the same are closed no person shall be allowed to register, but the registrar shall on application before said books are closed register all persons not then qualified to vote who will become so qualified on or before the day of election. Immediately after said books are closed, they shall be deposited in the office of the secretary of the board of aldermen, and citizens desiring to do so may inspect them. The secretary shall write in each of the said books the exact time they are deposited with him and the same shall not be taken from his office until the day of election. Any registrar failing to deposit his registration book with the said secretary at the time prescribed shall receive no compensation for making said registration.

Citizens may inspect registration books.

Registrars failing to deposit book with secretary.

When polls shall be opened.

SEC. 8. The polls shall be opened on the day of election from seven o'clock in the morning until sunset of the same day. No person whose name has not been duly registered shall be allowed to vote, and anyone offering to vote may be challenged at the polls, and if the judges of election shall sustain the challenge, such person's ballot shall not be received. Ballots shall be on white paper and without device. The aldermen and mayor shall be voted for on one ballot, and every qualified elector shall be allowed to vote for all five aldermen.

Ballots.

Aldermen and mayor on one ballot.

Result of election, how certified.

SEC. 9. After the ballots are counted they shall be carefully preserved, and shall be, together with the poll list, which shall be signed by the judges of election, and the registration books, delivered to the secretary of the board of aldermen for preservation.

SEC. 10. If among the persons voted for for mayor and aldermen there should be any two or more having an equal number of votes the judges of election shall decide the election between such persons. As soon as the result of the election shall be determined two certificates thereof shall be made under the hands of the judges of election, setting forth in writing the number of votes each candidate received, one of which shall be delivered to the chief of police, who shall at once make proclamation thereof at the door of the town hall, and the other shall be delivered to the secretary of the board of aldermen for preservation. The board of aldermen shall fill all vacancies occurring in their board or in the office of the mayor, by death, resignation or otherwise.

Elections resulting in a tie vote.

Certificates of result.

Vacancies occurring.

SEC. 11. That on the second day after the election the mayor and board of aldermen so elected shall meet at the town hall or some other place by them appointed, and shall there and then take an oath to support the constitution and laws of the United States and the constitution and laws of North Carolina, and to discharge the duties imposed upon them by virtue of their office as mayor and aldermen with fidelity and integrity and to the best of their ability, which oath shall be administered by a justice of the peace or by the former mayor.

When officers shall qualify.

Shall take oath.

SEC. 12. The mayor of the said town of Gastonia while acting as such is hereby constituted an official court with all the jurisdiction and power in criminal offenses occurring within the limits of said town which now or may hereafter be given by law to justices of the peace, and shall have exclusive jurisdiction to hear and determine all misdemeanors consisting of all the violations of the ordinances of the said town. The proceedings in said court shall be the same as now or hereafter shall be prescribed for courts of justice of the peace, and in all cases there shall be the right of appeal, and in all cases where a defendant may be adjudged to be imprisoned by the said mayor it shall be competent for him to adjudge also that such person work during the period of his confinement on the public streets or other public works of said town of Gastonia.

Jurisdiction of mayor.

Right of appeal.

Certain persons may be worked on public roads.

SEC. 13. That the mayor may issue his precepts to the policemen of the town and to such other officers to whom a justice of the peace may direct his precepts.

To whom mayor may issue precepts.

SEC. 14. That the mayor shall keep a faithful minute of all the precepts issued by him and all of his judicial proceedings. The judgments rendered by him shall have all the force, virtue and validity of judgments rendered by a justice of the peace, and may be executed and enforced against the parties in the same

Mayor shall keep record of official acts.

manner and by the same means as if the same had been rendered by a justice of the peace.

Presiding officer at meeting of aldermen.

SEC. 15. That the mayor when present shall preside at all meetings of the board of aldermen and when there is an equal division upon any question or in the election of officers by the board he shall determine the matter by his vote. He shall vote in no other cases, and if he shall be absent the board may appoint one of their number pro tempore to exercise his duties.

Power of majority of aldermen.

SEC. 16. That the aldermen shall form one board and a majority of them shall be competent to perform all the duties prescribed, unless otherwise provided. At their first meeting they shall fix stated days of meeting for the year, which shall be as often at least as once in each month. Special meetings of the aldermen may also be held on the call of the mayor or a majority of the aldermen, and of every such meeting when called by the mayor, all the aldermen shall be notified, and when called by a majority of the aldermen the mayor and such aldermen as shall not join in the call shall be notified.

Stated days of meeting for aldermen.

Power of aldermen to make ordinances.

SEC. 17. That the board of aldermen when convened shall have power to make and provide such ordinances, by-laws, rules and regulations for the better government of the town, as they may deem necesary, not inconsistent with this act, or with the laws of the land

Powers of aldermen.

SEC. 18. That among the powers hereby conferred on the board of aldermen, they may provide water, provide for macadamizing, repairing and cleaning the streets, regulate markets and take all proper means to prevent and extinguish fires; make regulations to cause the due observance of Sunday; appoint and regulate a police force to execute such precepts as the mayor or other persons may lawfully issue to them, to preserve the peace and order of the town, and to execute the ordinances thereof; to suppress and remove nuisances, preserve the health of the town from contagious or infectious diseases and appoint and provide for the pay and prescribe the duties of all such officers as may be deemed necessary.

Police force.

Nuisances.

Appointment of police.

SEC. 19. That the board of aldermen shall have power to appoint a police force, to consist of a chief of police and such number of policemen as the good government of the town may require, who shall hold office during the term of the board appointing them and until their successors are appointed. The chief of police shall give bond in such sum as the board of aldermen may prescribe for the faithful discharge of the duties imposed by law and the ordinances of the town, and to faithfully account for all moneys that may come into his hands from fines, penalties, etc. The chief of police shall have the supervision and control of the police force, and it shall be his duty to report to the mayor any

Term of office.

Chief of police shall give bond.

Duties of chief of police.

dereliction of duty on the part of any member of the police force. It shall be the duty of the chief of police to attend the mayor's court each day and report any violation of laws or ordinances of the town, to collect all fines and penaties imposed and pay the same to the town treasurer; to execute the orders and judgments of the said court; to see that the laws and ordinances of the town are enforced and to do such other things as may be required of him by the board. The chief of police and each member of the police force shall have all the power and authority vested in sheriffs and constables for the preservation of the peace of the town, by suppressing disturbances and apprehending offenders; they shall execute all processes directed to them by the mayor or others, and in the execution thereof shall have the same powers which sheriffs and constables have. The chief and members of the police force shall take an oath before the mayor for the faithful performance of the duties required by law and the ordinances.

Power of police.

Police shall take oath.

SEC. 20. That the salary and compensation of the policemen shall be fixed by the board of aldermen and they shall receive no other pay whatever for their services.

Salary of policemen.

SEC. 21. That in the time of exigency the mayor may appoint temporarily additional policemen for such time as may appear necessary.

Additional temporary policemen may be appointed.

SEC. 22. The mayor may at any time, upon charges being preferred, or upon finding said chief or any member of said police force guilty of misconduct, have the power to suspend such member from service until the board of aldermen shall convene and take action in the matter, and upon hearing proofs in the case the board may discharge or restore such member, and the pay of such member so suspended shall cease from the time of his suspension until the time of his restoration to service. Any violation of the regulations or orders of any superior shall be good cause for dismissal, and the mayor may suspend the chief or any member of the police force if found drunk while on duty.

Policemen, when guilty of misconduct.

Cause for dismissal.

SEC. 23. The board of aldermen shall require the entire police force to wear badges and to be so armed and uniformed as to be readily recognized by the public as peace officers. And the police shall generally have power to do whatever may be necessary to preserve the good order and peace of the town and secure the inhabitants from personal violence and their property from loss or injury.

Aldermen shall require officers to be uniformed.

SEC. 24. That in order to raise a fund for the expenses incident to the proper government of the town of Gastonia, the board of aldermen of said town may annually levy and collect the following taxes:

Aldermen empowered to levy tax.

Ad valorem tax. I. On real estate and personal property situated in the town a tax not exceeding one dollar on every hundred dollars value.

Poll tax. II. On all taxable polls a tax not exceeding three dollars on all residents in the town on the first day of June in each year or who may have been so resident within sixty days next preceding that day, preserving the constitutional eqation.

Public vehicles. III. On every four-horse omnibus a tax not exceeding fifty dollars. On every two-horse omnibus a tax not exceeding forty dollars.

IV. On every dray or express wagon drawn by one or two horses a tax not exceeding twenty-five dollars; if drawn by more than two horses a tax not exceeding fifty dollars.

Public vehicles. V. On all carriages, buggies, sulkies and other vehicles used in the city for the carriage of persons or for pleasure a tax not exceeding fifteen dollars.

Dogs. VI. On every dog a tax not exceeding ten dollars: *Provided*, a discrimination may be made within this limit on the different species and sexes of dogs.

Dealers in cider. VII. On all dealers in cider a tax not exceeding one hundred dollars.

Itinerant merchants, etc. VIII. On all itinerant merchants or peddlers selling or offering to sell in the city a tax not exceeding fifty dollars.

Bowling alley, billiard tables, etc. IX. On every bowling alley and every billiard table, and every bagatelle table and every pool table, and every gambling contrivance, the object of which is gain and for the use of which a charge is made, a tax not exceeding two hundred dollars, reserving the right to remove it or them at any time as a nuisance.

Restaurants, fish markets, etc. X. On all keepers of eating houses or restaurants, fish or meat or vegetables or bread stuff or fruiters a tax not exceeding one hundred dollars per year.

Circuses. XI. On every circus which shall exhibit within the town or within a mile thereof a tax not exceeding two hundred dollars for each day, the tax to be paid before the exhibition, and if not to be doubled.

Theatrical plays. XII. On every person or company exhibiting in the town or within a mile thereof stage or theatrical plays, sleight-of-hand performances, rope dances, tumbling wire dancing or menagerie, a tax not exceeding two hundred dollars for every day they exhibit.

Exhibitions for reward. XIII. Upon every exhibition for reward of artificial curiosities (models of useful inventions excepted) in the town, or in one mile thereof, a tax not exceeding fifty dollars, to be paid in advance.

Shows and exhibitions. XIV. On each show or exhibition of any other kind, and on each concert for reward, and on every strolling musician, a tax not exceeding twenty dollars, to be paid before exhibiting.

XV. On every goat or hog running at large in the town there

may be levied a tax not exceeding ten dollars and every such goat or hog may be seized or impounded, and if the owner, on being notified, will not pay the tax the animal shall be sold therefor, after three days' notice at the town hall. Goats and hogs running at large.

XVI. Upon every horse or mule or bull going at large a tax not exceeding ten dollars. Horses, mules and bulls running at large.

XVII. On every life, accident, fire or other insurance company a tax not exceeding twenty-five dollars. Insurance companies.

XVIII. On every barber shop a tax not exceeding twenty-five dollars. Barber shops.

XIX. On every shoe shine outside of barber shops a tax not exceeding ten dollars. Boot blacks.

XX. On every dray for hire a tax not exceeding twenty-five dollars. Drays.

XXI. On every photographer a tax not exceeding twenty-five dollars. Photographers.

XXII. On every livery stable a tax not exceeding fifty dollars. Livery stables.

XXIII. On every meat market a tax not exceeding fifty dollars. Meat markets.

XXIV. On every trade stable a tax not exceeding fifty dollars. Trade stables.

XXV. On every company, person or manufacturer who shall engage in the selling of pianos or organs by sample, list or otherwise a tax not exceeding twenty-five dollars. Piano and organ agents.

SEC. 25. That the board of aldermen shall at the first regular meeting in April, eighteen hundred and ninety-nine, and annually thereafter appoint some competent person, who shall on the third Monday of May in each and every year make advertisement in some newspaper notifying all persons residing in the town of Gastonia who own or have control of taxable property in the town on the first of June to return to him on or before the last day of June a list of their taxable property in said town; said list shall state the number of lots or parts of lots and all other property now taxable or that hereafter may be made taxable by the laws of the state or the ordinances of the town, and the list so returned shall be sworn to, and the person taking said list is hereby authorized to administer the following oath: "I, ------, do solemnly swear that the tax return made out and signed by me contains a full and accurate list of the number of lots owned by me in said town, a full and accurate list of all personal property of Gaston county bonds and a full and accurate list of all other stocks, bonds, income, solvent credits and other property subject to taxation with [under] the laws of the state and ordinances of said city, according to my best knowledge, information and belief. So help me, God." From the returns so made the person appointed as aforesaid to protect such tax return shall, within thirty days after the expiration of the time for taking said list, make out in a book kept for that purpose an Tax lister. Oath administered by tax lister.

alphabetical list of the persons and owners of property who have so made their returns, in the same manner as tax lists are made out by law for the collection of state taxes, and the tax lister appointed as aforesaid shall copy in said book the assessment made by the county of said assessors of all property within the town limits, which assessment may be revised, corrected or amended by the board of aldermen, but must at all times be the same in value as to property assessed as the state and county assessment.

Persons failing to list taxes.

Sec. 25½. That if any person liable to taxes on subjects to be listed shall fail to pay them in the time prescribed for collection the collector shall proceed forthwith to collect them by distress and sale, after public advertisement for the space of ten days in some newspaper published in the town, if the property to be sold be personalty, and of thirty days if the property be realty.

Taxes due and remaining unpaid after certain time.

Sec. 26. That when the tax due on any lot or other land (which is hereby declared to be a lien on the same) shall remain unpaid on the first day of January, and there is no other visible estate, but such lot or land of the person in whose name it is listed, liable to distress and sale, known to the collector, he shall report the fact to the aldermen, together with a particular description of the real estate, and thereupon the aldermen shall direct the same to be sold at the door of the town hall by the collector, after advertising for thirty days in some newspaper published in the city, which the collector shall do. And the collector shall divide the said land into as many parts as shall be convenient (for which purpose he is authorized to employ a surveyor), and shall sell as many parts as may be required to pay said taxes and all expenses attendant thereon. If the same can not be conveniently divided the collector shall sell the whole, and if no person will pay the whole taxes and expenses for the whole land, the same shall be struck off to the town, and if not redeemed as hereinafter provided, shall belong to the said town in fee.

When sale shall be ordered.

Tax collector shall return account of proceedings to aldermen when sale is made.

Sec. 27. The collector shall return an account of his proceedings to the aldermen, specifying the portions into which the land was divided and the purchaser or purchasers thereof and the prices of each, which shall be entered on the book of proceedings of the board, and if there shall be a surplus after paying said taxes and expenses of advertising and selling the same, it shall be paid into the town treasury, subject to the demand of the owner.

Owner of land sold may recover within a year.

Sec. 28. That the owner of any land sold under the provisions of this charter or any person acting for them may redeem the same at any time within one year after the sale by paying the purchaser the sum paid by him and twenty-five per centum on the amount of taxes and expenses, and the treasurer shall refund to him, without interest, the proceeds, less double the amount of taxes.

When real estate is not redeemed in time specified.

SEC. 29. That if the real estate sold as aforesaid shall not be redeemed in the time specified the tax collector shall convey the same in fee to the purchaser or his assigns; and the recitals in such conveyance or in any other conveyance of land sold for taxes due the town, that the taxes were due or any other matter required to be true or done before the sale might be made, shall be prima facie evidence that the same was true and done.

How taxes shall be levied.

SEC. 30. That taxes for town purposes shall be levied on all real and personal property, trades, licenses and other subjects of taxation as provided in section three, article five, of the state constitution. That all moneys arising from taxes, donations or other sources shall be paid to the treasurer and no appropriation of the same shall be made but by a board constituted of a majority of the board of aldermen.

Power to improve streets.

SEC. 31. That the board of aldermen shall have the power to grade, macadamize and pave the streets and side-walks and to lay out and open new streets or widen those already open and make such improvements thereon as the public convenience may require. That when any land or right of-way shall be required for the the purpose of opening new streets or for widening those already open, or for other objects allowed by this charter, and for the want of agreement as to the value thereof, the same can not be purchased from the owner or owners, the same may be taken at a valuation thereof to be made by three freeholders of the town, to be chosen by the aldermen; and in making said valuation the said freeholders, after being duly sworn by the mayor or a justice of the peace or clerk of a court of record, shall take into consideration the loss or damages that may accrue to the owner in consequence of the land or right-of-way being surrendered, also any benefit the owner may receive from the opening or widening of such streets or other improvement and ascertain the sum which shall be paid to the owner of said property, and report the same to the board of aldermen under their hands and seals, which report on being confirmed by the board and spread upon their minutes shall have the effect of a judgment against said board of aldermen, and shall pass the title to the board of aldermen in their corporate capacity of the land so taken: *Provided*, that if any person over whose land the said street may pass or improvement be erected, or the aldermen be dissatisfied with the valuation thus made, then in that case either party may have an appeal to the next superior court: *Provided, however*, that such appeal shall not hinder or delay the aldermen in opening or widening such street or erecting such improvement.

May condemn land necessary.

Assessment of damages.

Proviso.

Either party may appeal.

SEC. 32. That the board of aldermen shall have power to regu-

Cemeteries.

late the manner and terms on which bodies may be interred in the public cemetery and have said cemetery kept in proper repair; they shall also have power to purchase, when they deem it proper, land adjoining the cemetery for its enlargement; they shall also have the power to forbid any and all interments of dead bodies within the limits of said town whenever they shall deem it expedient.

Fire companies.

SEC. 33. That they may provide for the establishment, organization, equipment and pay of such number of fire companies as they shall deem necessary and proper. That in case of a fire occurring in said town the mayor, or in his absence, a majority of the aldermen who may be present, may order the blowing up or pulling down or destroying of any house or houses deemed necessary to stop the progress of the fire; and no person shall be held liable civilly or criminally for acting in such case in obedience to such orders. They shall also have the power to establish fire limits within said town, within which it shall not be lawful for any person to erect or build any wooden houses or cover any building with any material other than metal or slate. They may prohibit wooden buildings from being removed from without into said fire limits or from being removed from one place to another within the same, under such penalties as the board of aldermen may establish, and said penalty may be sued for and recovered from the owner in an action of debt in any court having jurisdiction.

Buildings may be destroyed when necessary in case of fire.

Aldermen may prohibit the erection of certain buildings.

Trades or occupations becoming nuisances prohibited.

SEC. 34. They shall have the power and it shall be their duty to prohibit all trades or occupations which are a nuisance from being carried on in said town, and the power and authority of said board of aldermen for the abatement and removal of nuisances shall extend one mile beyond the town limits. They shall have power and it shall be their duty to cause all ponds, sunken lots and other places in which water stands and stagnates, to be drained and filled up, and to recover from the owner or occupier the expenses as above, which expense shall be a lien on the lot: *Provided*, the owner or occupant of said lots, after a reasonable notice, to be fixed by the board of aldermen, shall neglect or refuse to remove or abate said nuisance. They shall have authority to cause all nuisances arising within and for one mile without the town limits to be removed or abated, and for removing or abating such nuisance the person creating the same shall pay the expenses as above required.

Ponds and stagnates.

Nuisances within a mile of town limits.

Regulation of streets and markets.

SEC. 35. That the said board shall have power to regulate the manner in which provisions and other articles shall be sold in the streets and markets of said town, and to regulate the manner in which the streets and markets in said town shall be used and kept.

SEC. 36. That all fines and penalties imposed by this act or which are or may be imposed by the ordinances of the said town or the laws of the state, when tried and recovered before the mayor of said town, shall be paid to the town treasurer for the use of the said town. **Fines, to whom paid.**

SEC. 37. That the board of aldermen may establish all public buildings necessary and proper for the town and prevent the erection or establishment of wooden buildings in any part of the town where they may increase the danger of fire. **Public buildings may be established.**

SEC. 38. That for the violation of any ordinance or by-laws made by said board of aldermen they may prescribe penalties not exceeding fifty dollars for each offense, to be recovered before the mayor, without stay of process, mesne or final; and when judgment shall be given for such penalty the party convicted may, unless the penalty and costs be paid, be immediately committed to the county jail or the town calaboose for a term not exceeding thirty days or until such penalty and costs be paid: *Provided*, nothing herein contained shall prevent the said defendant from being guilty of a misdemeanor for the violation of the said ordinance of the town or shall prevent the working of said defendant on the public streets or other public works of the town. **Fines for violation of ordinances.** **Proviso.**

SEC. 39. That all penalties imposed relating to the town by this act or by any ordinance of the town shall be recoverable in the name of the town of Gastonia before the mayor or other tribunal having jurisdiction thereof. **Fines recoverable in name of town.**

SEC. 40. That all penalties incurred by any minor for the breach of any of the provisions of this act or of any ordinances passed in pursuance thereof shall be recovered from his parent, guardian or master (if the minor be an apprentice) of such minor. **Offenses by minors.**

SEC. 41. That the mayor shall be entitled to the following fees in the cases herein enumerated whereof he may have jurisdiction as mayor: For every warrant issued by him for the recovery of any penalty or for other cause of action, fifty cents; for every judgment rendered thereon, not more than one dollar, to be fixed by the board of aldermen, to be taxed among the costs; for every warrant issued by him as mayor to apprehend an offender against the criminal laws of the state under which he may be arrested and recognized to appear before a court of record, not more than one dollar, to be fixed by the board of aldermen, to be taxed on submission or conviction, among other costs; for every warrant to arrest individuals who may have fled from other states or counties, two dollars, to be paid on removal of offender by such as may carry him away; for the use of the town seal for other than town purposes one dollar; for every certificate for other than town purposes, fifty cents. **Fees of mayor.**

Persons violating ordinances guilty of a misdemeanor.

SEC. 42. That any person or persons violating any ordinances of the town shall be deemed guilty of a misdemeanor, and shall be punished as provided in chapter sixty-two of The Code of North Carolina.

Salaries of officers.

SEC. 43. That the compensation or salaries of the mayor and board of aldermen and the secretary and the treasurer of the board shall be fixed by the board of aldermen at their first regular meeting after their qualification.

Chief of police ex officio tax collector.

Shall give bond.

SEC. 44. That the chief of police of the town of Gastonia shall be ex officio tax collector of said town, and before entering upon the discharge of his duties shall enter into a bond with sureties and of an amount to be approved by the board of aldermen, said bond to be made payable to the town of Gastonia and conditioned for the faithful performance of his official duties.

Defendants shall have right of appeal.

SEC. 45. That section nine hundred and seven of The Code of North Carolina shall not be construed to apply to trials by the mayor for the violation of town ordinances, but the defendant in all such cases shall have the right of appeal.

Health officer.

SEC. 46. That the board of aldermen of the town of Gastonia may appoint a health officer for said town, who shall be called the sanitary policeman, and may prescribe his duties and fix his compensation.

Election of cotton-weigher.

Vacancy occurring.

Compensation.

SEC. 47. That the mayor and board of aldermen of the town of Gastonia shall at their first regular meeting after their election in each year elect one cotton weigher for the town, and any vacancy occurring in said office of cotton weigher by death, resignation or otherwise shall be filled at a call or regular meeting of the board of aldermen; and they shall elect all assistant weighers and inspectors and shall prescribe their duties, fix their compensation. The mayor and board shall also fix the price to be paid for weighing each bale, and same shall be collected by the weigher and paid to the treasurer.

Duties of cotton weigher.

SEC. 48. That it shall be the duty of the said cotton weigher to weigh all baled cotton sold in the town of Gastonia at its true weight, making all proper deductions for water or damage.

Oath of cotton weigher.

SEC. 49. That the said cotton weigher before entering upon his duties shall take the following oath before some justice of the peace or other officer authorized by law to administer oaths, viz: "I do solemnly swear that I will faithfully perform the duties of the office of cotton weigher, and that I will take no interest near or remote in buying or selling cotton in the town of Gastonia."

Bond of cotton weigher.

SEC. 50. That the said cotton weigher shall give bond in an amount to be fixed by the board of aldermen, conditioned for the faithful performance of his duty, payable to the town of Gastonia.

SEC. 51. That no other person than said cotton weigher shall weigh any cotton sold in Gastonia, and any person violating the provisions of this section, on conviction before the mayor, shall pay a fine of not more than fifty dollars or be imprisoned not more than fifty days. Cotton weigher alone shall weigh cotton.

SEC. 52. That any cotton weigher elected under the provisions of this act who shall willfully or corruptly abuse the power or trust conferred on him by this act shall upon conviction thereof be dismissed from his office; and any damage sustained by any person by reason of any such willful or corrupt abuse of trust or power shall be recoverable out of the bond of such cotton weigher so offending. Cotton weigher abusing trust.

SEC. 53. That whenever the board of aldermen shall determine that the welfare of the town requires the establishment of a system of waterworks and sewerage, they shall so declare by ordinance, in which shall be set forth the amount to be expended for that purpose, which shall not exceed sixty-five thousand dollars, and shall also hold an election to ascertain the will of the people as to issuing bonds for that purpose. The election shall be held not less than thirty days after the adoption of said ordinance, and notice shall be given as provided in this act for other elections, and it shall be held under such rules and regulations as are prescribed by law for other elections for this town. A registrar shall be appointed by the board of aldermen, who shall keep open at a convenient place in said town the registration books as for other elections in said town for three consecutive Saturdays next preceding the said election, and shall enter on said books the names of all qualified voters in said town whose names do not appear thereon. The board of aldermen shall also appoint two judges or inspectors of election. And the said registrar and judges shall compose the board of election and have control of the same. In all other respects the election shall be conducted, except where otherwise herein provided, as is required for municipal elections for mayor and aldermen, and may order a new registration. Those in favor of issuing bonds for waterworks and sewerage, as set forth in the ordinance, shall vote a ticket on which shall be the words, "For waterworks"; and those in favor of not issuing bonds will vote a ticket on which shall be the words, "Against waterworks." The inspectors or judges composing the board of election shall meet as soon as the poll is closed, and shall declare the result and shall make and sign a certificate thereof, and shall deliver the same to the secretary of the board of aldermen, who shall record it in the minute book of said board. If a majority of the qualified voters of said town shall have voted in favor of waterworks the board of aldermen may issue coupon bonds of the said town for an amount not exceeding the amount designated in the ordinance declaring for

Waterworks and sewerage. Maximum amount. Shall order election. Election, when held. Registrar. Days for registration. Judges. Board of election. How election conducted. Form of ballot. Certificate of result. If a majority of voters favor bonds, when issued.

Date of maturity of bonds.

Sale of bonds.

Proceeds from bonds.

Management of works.

Necessary land may be condemned.

Special tax levy for interest, etc.

said election, maturing in not more than thirty years, bearing interest not exceeding six per centum in such denominations and payable at such places as the board may fix, and may sell the said bonds for not less than par. The proceeds of said sale shall be expended under the direction of the board in the erection or purchase of waterworks for said town and the laying of sewers therein as the board may deem necessary. The board of aldermen shall have the power to appoint such agents as may be necessary to manage such waterworks, to regulate the charges for water, and generally to do all that may be necessary for the maintenance and preservation of said waterworks. If land or right-of way is required in the construction of said works or in laying of said sewer, and the same can not be purchased at a price which the board considers fair and reasonable, the said land and right of-way may be condemned and taken for waterworks and sewerage purposes as is provided in this act for the condemning and taking of land for street purposes. It shall be the duty of the board of aldermen to levy and collect taxes for the payment of the interest on said bonds and to próvide for the payment of the principal at maturity.

Aldermen empowered to issue bonds for construction of electric light plant.

SEC. 54. That the board of aldermen of the town of Gastonia whenever they shall deem it to the best interest of said town, are hereby authorized and empowered to issue bonds to an amount not exceeding twenty-five thousand dollars in the name of the said town in such denominations and form as the said board of aldermen may determine with which to establish, construct or purchase or otherwise secure and maintain a system of electric lights for the use of the said town and its inhabitants, and to levy taxes to pay the principal and interest thereon.

Time of maturity of bonds.

SEC. 55. That said bonds shall be made payable at such place and time as may be determined upon by said board of aldermen, but the time of payment of the principal of said bonds shall be fixed at not more than thirty years.

Rate of interest on bonds.

SEC. 56. That said bonds shall bear interest at not more than six per centum per annum, and the interest shall be made payable at such time as the board of aldermen shall fix, and said bonds shall in no case be sold, hypothecated or otherwise disposed of by the board of aldermen for less than their par value, and the money arising from the sale thereof shall be used for the purchase of an electric light plant and appurtenances, including such real estate and other próperty and machinery as may be necessary in establishing the same, and for no other purpose.

Bonds shall not be issued until authorized by voters.

SEC. 57. That said bonds shall not be issued until authorized by a majority of the qualified voters of the said town at a public election to be held at such time and place as the board of aldermen shall appoint, at which election those favoring the issue of said bonds shall vote "For issue of electric light bonds," and those opposing it shall vote "Against issue of electric light bonds"; and it shall be the duty of the said board of aldermen to give notice of the time, place and purpose of such election for thirty days in some newspaper published in the town of Gastonia; that said election shall be held in like manner and under the same rules and regulations as far as the same are pertinent and applicable as other elections are held in said town.

When commissioners may issue bonds

Sec. 58. That if the powers hereby conferred and hereinbefore provided shall be exercised, and a majority of the qualified voters of the said town shall vote for the issue of the said bonds, then the said board of aldermen shall issue the said bonds, and they shall be signed by the mayor, attested by the treasurer of the town and sealed with the corporate seal of the town, and said bonds and their coupons shall be exempt from town taxation until after they shall become due, and the coupons thereon shall be receivable in payment of town taxes.

Bond coupons shall be exempted from taxation.

Empowered to establish and maintain electric light plant.

Sec. 59. That the said town of Gastonia shall have power to establish, construct or purchase, and at all times maintain in the said town an electric light and power plant, including all machinery and appliances necessary and appurtenant to the same, and all rights and privileges required to accomplish and maintain the same, and to secure the full benefit thereof to the said town, and its customers or the consumers of each such light and power within or near the said town; and the said town shall and may charge and contract for special rates for the use and privileges of electric lights and motive power furnished to such persons or corporations as may desire to use the same; and the said town shall have full power and right to purchase and hold such real estate and personal property as shall be necessary to enable it to build and maintain such electric light and power plant in the said town, and to use the streets of said town for planting its poles and other purposes, and may enter by its officers, agents and servants upon the lands of other persons and corporations for the above purposes, and contract for and purchase the same; and if unable to agree for the purchase of said lands with the owners of the same, then the said town shall have the right, by its board of aldermen, to condemn the same to its use in the manner now provided in the charter of said town for the condemnation of land for streets and other purposes; and the said town shall at all times have the right to enter upon the land for the repairing, improving or replacing of the poles and lamps, et cetera; also the right to enter at all proper hours the stores, hotels, business houses, dwellings or other premises where said electric lights and motive power, fixtures, wires, lamps, et cetera,

May condemn land.

are located, for the purpose of repairing, removing or replacing the same.

Empowered to order election for street railway.

SEC. 60. That whenever the board of aldermen may determine that the welfare of the town requires the establishment of a street railway in the town of Gastonia they shall so declare by ordinance, in which shall be set forth the amount to be expended for that purpose, which shall not exceed seventy five thousand dollars; and shall also hold an election to ascertain the will of the people as to issuing bonds for that purpose. Said election shall be held as to notice and other rules and regulations as provided in this act for providing the town with a system of waterworks and sewerage, and those in favor of street railways shall vote a ticket on which shall be the words "For a street railway," and those voting against street railways shall vote a ticket on which shall be the words "Against street railways"; and if a majority of the qualified voters in said town shall have voted in favor of street railways the board of aldermen shall issue bonds in denominations and to bear interest and on other terms as is provided in this act for providing the said town with a system of waterworks and sewerage, and shall levy taxes to pay said bonds and interest thereon.

Form of ballot.

Empowered to equip and operate electric light plant.

SEC. 61. The board of aldermen is hereby authorized to make, construct, equip, maintain and operate lines of street railway with one or more tracks, and all necessary branches, turnouts and switches, using such motor power as shall be determined by the board through and along the streets within the corporate limits of the town of Gastonia and to points within the vicinity thereof, and erect such depots, stables, offices, shops and other buildings as are necessary and proper for conducting the business of the said street railway, and to demand and receive such sums of money for the carriage of passengers as the board may think proper, not to exceed ten cents for each person on any line within the corporate limits of the town nor more than twenty-five cents to points beyond the town limits; and if the board shall determine to carry freight or parcels, such compensation for these services as may be reasonable: *Provided*, that the tracks of the said railway shall conform to the grades of the streets through which they pass, and shall be laid so as to present no unnecessary obstacles to wagons or other vehicles turning in or crossing the streets or roads through or over which said railways, branches, turnouts or switches may be laid, and shall repair and put in as good condition as they were previous to the laying of the tracks the streets through which the said railways may be constructed.

Maximum car fare.

Proviso.

Persons damaging said property.

SEC. 62. That any person who shall remove, obstruct, injure, deface or destroy any part of said railway, cars, fixtures, machinery or structures of any kind shall be deemed guilty of a misdemeanor and fined and imprisoned at the discretion of the court.

SEC. 63. That the conductors and other agents and servants of said street railway are hereby invested with the same authority, powers and privileges which belong to similar officers and agents of railway companies now operating in this state.

Authority and power of employees.

SEC. 64. That whenever the board of aldermen of the town of Gastonia may determine that the welfare of the said town requires the establishment of a public school in said town, they shall so declare by an ordinance duly adopted, in which shall be set out the maximum rate of taxation which in their opinion shall be levied for that purpose, and also the number of school commissioners who shall be elected. The ordinance shall fix the date, not earlier than thirty days after its adoption, when an election shall be held to ascertain the will of the people of the town upon the subject. At said election those in favor of levying the tax shall vote a ticket on which shall be the words, "For graded schools," and those opposed to levying the tax shall vote a ticket on which shall be the words, "Against graded schools." The inspectors shall meet as soon as the polls are closed and shall declare the result and certify the same to the secretary of the board, who shall record the same. If a majority of the qualified voters of the town shall vote in favor of said school it shall be the duty of the board of aldermen to levy and collect annually for the use of the said school a tax, the rate of which shall be fixed by the school commissioners, not, however, to exceed the rate mentioned on the aforesaid ordinance. This tax shall be collected as other town taxes and shall be paid to the treasurer of said town, who shall be ex officio secretary and treasurer of the board of school commissioners The mayor shall be president of such board. Within ten days after their election the board shall meet and organize; they shall hold office until the next regular election and until their successors are qualified. At the said regular election five school commissioners shall be elected under the same rules and regulations as may be provided for the election of the aldermen of the town. The board of school commissioners of the town of Gastonia, provided for, shall be a corporation, and shall have power to acquire and hold all such personal and real property as may be needed for the schools to be maintained and established under the provisions of this act; they shall employ teachers, fix their pay and make all rules and regulations for the government of said teachers: *Provided, however*, that the said board must establish and maintain separate schools for the children of [the] white race and for the children of the colored race. It shall be the duty of the school commissioners of the county of Gaston, as soon as the schools herein provided for

Election shall be ordered to vote on public school.

Form of ballot.

Aldermen may levy annual tax for school purposes.

How collected.

Election of school commissioners.

Powers of school commissioners.

Commissioners shall lay off school district.

are established, to lay off, as one of the school districts of said county, all that part of said county which is within the limits of the said town of Gastonia, to be known as Gastonia school district, and all moneys apportioned to said district under the provisions of the school laws of the state shall be paid by the county treasurer to the treasurer of the school commissioners of said town, to be by them expended in the maintenance of said schools: *Provided*, that the privilege of attending is granted to all children who would be entitled to attend the public schools of this state.

Proviso.

Under what rules election shall be held.

SEC. 65. The election provided for in the preceding section shall be held upon such notice and under such rules and regulations as are required in this act for elections for providing a system of waterworks and sewerage for the town of Gastonia, except as otherwise provided in the preceding section.

Aldermen shall set forth in ordinance amount required for schools.

SEC. 66. That if the board of aldermen shall declare in the ordinance, mentioned in section sixty-four of this act, that it is expedient that the town shall provide houses for said schools, they shall set forth in said ordinance the amount which in their opinion the town should expend in the purchase of lots and erection of buildings for that purpose, not to exceed, however, twenty-five thousand dollars. If after the adoption of an ordinance containing such declarations and due publication a majority of the qualified voters of the town shall vote "For graded schools" at the election held under the provisions of section sixty-four of this act, it shall be lawful for the board of aldermen to issue and sell for not less than par coupon bonds of the town, bearing interest at not more than six per centum per annum, to be known as "Gastonia school bond," to be payable not more than thirty years after date at such place as the aldermen may designate. The interest on such bonds shall be paid semi-annually at the places designated for the payment of the principal, and there shall be levied annually taxes to pay said interest and the principal at maturity.

Style of bond.

Date of maturity.

Proceeds of sale of bonds, how applied.

SEC. 67. That with the proceeds of the sale of the bonds issued under the provisions of the last section the aldermen of the town shall provide suitable buildings for the school established under the provisions of this act and proper furniture for the same. The title to said property shall be taken in the name of the town of Gastonia, but it shall be under the management and control of the school commissioners, who may make all such rules and regulations as may be proper for its safety and to prevent intruders from coming thereon.

Title to property.

Vagrancy a misdemeanor.

SEC. 68. That any person found in the town of Gastonia who may be able to labor and who has no apparent means of subsistence and neglects to apply himself to some honest occupation for the support of himself or family and goes about from place to place begging or subsisting on charity, shall be a tramp and upon conviction before the mayor shall be fined not exceeding fifty dollars or imprisoned not exceeding thirty days, and the mayor shall have authority to require any person convicted under this section, in lieu of imprisonment or on non-payment of the fine, to work on the streets or other public works of the town. Penalty.

SEC. 69. That it shall be unlawful to sell or manufacture intoxicating liquors in the town of Gastonia, except druggists or pharmacists, who shall not sell or dispose of intoxicating liquors to any person who has not first obtained a prescription from a practicing physician. Sale of liquor prohibited.

SEC. 70. That the board of aldermen shall have power by ordinance to prohibit all persons from any place or places wherein contagious or infectious diseases are believed to exist or to have existed, from entering the town of Gastonia and all goods and chattels from being brought from said place or places into said town, and to fix a penalty for the breach of any of the ordinances established by them on the subject; they shall also have power to take such other precautionary measurers to prevent the introduction or spreading of all infectious or contagious diseases in the said town as they may deem expedient. Places wherein contagious diseases exist.

SEC. 71. That the board of aldermen may purchase and hold such land as in their judgment may be needed for municipal purposes, and shall have authority to sell all lands belonging to the town which in their opinion is not required for their purposes. May purchase and own land

SEC. 72. That chapter fifty-two of the laws of eighteen hundred and seventy-six and eighteen hundred and seventy-seven, entitled "An act to incorporate the town of Gastonia, in Gaston county," and chapter two hundred and thirty-three of the laws of eighteen hundred and eighty-nine, entitled "An act to amend chapter fifty-two of the laws of eighteen hundred and seventy-six and eighteen hundred and seventy-seven, being an act to incorporate the town of Gastonia, in Gaston county," and chapter one hundred and sixty of the private laws of eighteen hundred and ninety-five, entitled "An act to amend the charter of the town of Gastonia," and all other laws or parts of laws in conflict with the provisions of this act are hereby repealed. Conflicting laws repealed.

SEC. 73. That this act shall be in force from and after its ratification.

Ratified the 28th day of February, A. D. 1899.

CHAPTER 149.

An act to amend the charter of the town of Albemarle, Stanly county.

The General Assembly of North Carolina do enact:

Body corporate. SECTION 1. That the inhabitants of the town of Albemarle shall be and continue as they have been, a body corporate and shall Corporate name. bear the name and style of the town of "Albemarle," and shall Corporate power. have power to purchase and hold real estate for the benefit of the town, and that said town shall have the power to sue and be sued, to plead and be impleaded, as any other corporation, and that said town shall be subject to the general laws of the state in relation to corporations of like kind not inconsistent with this act.

Corporate limits. SEC. 2. The corporate limits of said town shall extend from the center of the public square in said town one-fourth of a mile west; thence north five-eighths of a mile; thence east one mile; thence south one mile; thence west one mile; thence north three-eighths of a mile.

Town officers. How elected. SEC. 3. The officers of said town shall consist of a mayor, seven commissioners and a marshal all of which shall be elected at the regular elections to be held as provided by this act, except the Marshal marshal, who shall be appointed by the board of town commis- Proviso. sioners for a term of two years: *Provided*, that said board of com- Commissioners may revoke appointment of marshal. missioners shall have the right to revoke said appointment at any time on failure of any marshal to perform the duties of his office satisfactorily. Said marshal to be paid for his services in any lawful way that said board may see fit.

Persons entitled to vote SEC. 4. That all resident citizens who are qualified voters of this state within said corporation that have resided in the county for ninety days and in the town for thirty days next preceding any election held in said town shall be entitled to vote, and all Eligibility to office. citizens who have resided in the incorporation for six months shall be eligible to hold office in said corporation.

Mayor and commissioners shall take oath and organize within five days after election. SEC. 5. That it shall be the duty of the mayor of said town to take the oath of office prescribed by law within five days after his election, and that the commissioners elected at any election for said town shall meet and organize within five days next after their election, and they shall take the oath of office that they as a body will faithfully and impartially perform the duties of commissioners to the best of their knowledge and their ability for ensuing term.

Bond of marshal. SEC. 6. The marshal appointed by said board of commissioners shall enter into a bond payable to the town of Albemarle or the state of North Carolina, the amount of which shall be fixed by the board of town commissioners.

Sec. 7. The commissioners of said town shall have power to levy a tax for each year, not to exceed one dollar and fifty cents on the poll and fifty cents on the one hundred dollars valuation of property, said valuation to be the same that is placed thereon to raise revenue for state and county purposes, and that all taxes shall be levied according to article five, section three, of the constitution of the state.

Commissioners empowered to levy tax.

Taxes, how levied.

Sec. 8. That the board of commissioners of said town shall have power to grade, macadamize and pave the streets and sidewalks and to lay out, change and open new streets or widen those already opened, and to make such improvements thereon as the public convenience may require, and that the board shall be the sole judges of the improvements required. The board may condemn any land for public use under the same rules and regulations as are hereafter provided for the laying out of public streets in this act.

Empowered to improve streets.

Commissioners may condemn land.

Sec. 9. That when any land or right-of-way be required for the purpose of opening new streets or for other objects allowed by this charter and for want of agreement as to the compensation therefor, the same may be taken at a valuation to be made by three freeholders of the town, one to be chosen by the board of commissioners and one to be selected by the land owner, and these two to select a third, and in case the land owner refuses to select one, then the commissioners shall select all three, and in making said valuation said freeholders, after being duly sworn by the mayor, shall at once proceed to condemn said lands and take into consideration the loss or damage which may accrue to the owner in consequence of the lands or right-of-way being surrendered; also any benefit or advantage such owner may receive from the opening or widening of such streets or other improvements and ascertain the sum which shall be paid to the owner of said property and report the same to the board of commissioners under their hands and seals, which, on being confirmed by the board and spread upon their minutes, shall have the effect of a judgment against said board of commissioners, and shall pass the title to the board of commissioners in their corporate capacity of the lands so taken, and the lands may at once be condemned and used by said town for the purpose intended: *Provided*, that if any person over whose land the said street may pass or improvements be created, or the commissioners be dissatisfied with the valuation thus made, then in that case either party may have an appeal to the next term of the superior court: *Provided, however*, that such appeal shall not hinder or delay the commissioners from opening or widening such streets or creating such improvements.

Disagreement as to compensation.

Selection of arbitrators.

Title shall pass when purchase money paid.

Proviso.

May appeal.

Proviso.

Sec. 10. That all freeholders appointed to assess damages shall

Assessors refusing to serve guilty of a misdemeanor.

receive one dollar per day each for their services, and any freeholder who shall refuse to take the oath prescribed and to act according to law, after having been duly appointed by the board and after having been notified in writing by the marshal, shall be deemed guilty of a misdemeanor and fined twenty dollars for each offense by the mayor.

Penalty.

Taxes levied by commissioners, when due and collectible.

Sec. 11. That all taxes levied by the commissioners of said town shall be due and collectible at any time after the first day of October in each year, and that the commissioners may expend all moneys collected either by fines or taxes as they may deem best for the interest of the town.

Jurisdiction of mayor.

Sec. 12. That the mayor shall have the same jurisdiction as a justice of the peace in all criminal actions within the incorporate limits; that all fines collected by him in criminal actions under the law of this state shall be paid into the town treasury.

Term of office.

Sec. 13. That all officers elected at any election in the town of Albemarle shall hold office for the term of two years and until their successors are elected and qualified. That in the absence of any officer from the town, or during sickness of any of the officers, the commissioners may appoint a man to fill the office during his absence or during his inability and no longer. If the absence be caused by resignation the board may appoint an officer to fill the unexpired term.

Vacancies occurring.

Election of secretary and treasurer.

Sec. 14. That the commissioners shall at their first meeting after being qualified elect for the ensuing term a secretary and treasurer, and that the treasurer shall enter into a bond payable to the town of Albemarle or to the state, the amount of which shall be fixed by the board, and that said bond shall be recorded in the office of register of deeds for Stanly county as other bonds for county officers.

Marshal shall give bond.

Sec 15. That the marshal appointed shall enter into a bond payable to the state of North Carolina, the amount of which shall be fixed by the board of commissioners, and that the board shall appoint the marshal or some other competent person as tax collector for said town, and he shall collect all taxes for said town under the same laws and regulations as are prescribed for the sheriff of the county.

Appointment of tax collector.

Fire company.

Sec. 16. That the commissioners may provide for the establishment and equipment of a fire company for said town.

Sanitary committee.

Sec. 17. That the commissioners of said town shall constitute a sanitary committee, and that all orders made by them for the preservation of the health of the citizens of the town shall be put into effect by the marshal. Any person who shall fail to comply with any order made by the board, after having been notified in writing by the marshal, shall be deemed guilty of a misdemeanor, and fined by the mayor for each and every offense.

Persons failing to comply with orders of board.

SEC. 18. That all tax lists or books which have or may hereafter be placed in the hands of the town tax collector shall be subject at all times to the control of the authorities imposing said tax and subject to correction, and shall be open for inspection by the public.

Control of tax books.

SEC. 19. That if any person shall be found violating the laws of this state or any of the town ordinances by the marshal or other officer appointed to act as such within the incorporate limits he shall forthwith arrest the offender without a warrant and carry him before the mayor to answer the charge and be dealt with according to law.

Officers may arrest persons without warrant.

SEC. 20. That all proceedings in the mayor's court shall be the same as are now or hereafter shall be prescribed for courts of justice of the peace, and in all cases there shall be a right of appeal to the superior court of Stanly county. That whenever a defendant or witness or other person shall be adjudged to be imprisoned by said court, it shall be competent for the said court to sentence such person to imprisonment in the county jail or town prison for a term not to exceed thirty days, and to adjudge also that such person work during the period of his confinement on the streets or on the public works of the town as provided for in section twenty-two of this act.

Proceedings in mayor's court.

Persons may be required to work on streets.

SEC. 21. The board of commissioners of the said town are hereby authorized and empowered to establish a fire limit within a reasonable distance from the center of the town, and to pass an ordinance or ordinances to the effect that none other than brick or stone or metal buildings shall be built or erected within said limits; and that they may repeal said ordinances at any time they may deem it necessary for the interest of the town and property holders therein.

Protection from fire.

SEC. 22. The commissioners of said town of Albemarle are hereby authorized and empowered to organize a "chain gang" in said town and work the streets by convict labor. The chairman of said board of commissioners, together with the concurrence of the other members shall have full control of and make all orders concerning the working of said streets that they may deem necessary for the improvement of the same: *Provided*, that the said board of commissioners are hereby authorized and empowered to make any order or orders that may be necessary for the purpose of compelling convicts to perform reasonable duty, as may be directed by the overseer of said "chain gang," said overseer to be appointed by said board of town commissioners at a salary to be fixed by them.

Empowered to organize chain gang.

Proviso.

Overseer of chain gang.

SEC. 23. The judges of the different terms of the superior court of Stanly county are authorized and empowered to sentence convicts to work on the Albemarle "chain gang" from said court un-

Persons convicted at Stanly court may be worked on road.

less there be more than the town can use, then in that event he or they may sentence them to any other point allowed by law, except so many as the town may call for.

Care of convicts. SEC. 24. The board of town commissioners shall provide a place of safe keeping for convicts at all times while not on duty.

Appointment of marshal. SEC. 25. That the board of town commissioners of the town of Albemarle shall appoint a marshal for the town at their first meeting after the passage of this act, who shall serve until the next general election and until his successor is appointed as is provided for in section three of this act.

License taxes. SEC. 26. That the board of commissioners shall have power to tax circuses, shows, liquor dealers, theatres. artificial curiosities, venders of patent proprietary medicines, or any entertainments, musical or otherwise, and exhibits of any character for money or reward, as they may see fit and proper, not inconsistent with the laws of the state.

Commissioners failing to attend meetings shall be fined. SEC. 27. That if any commissioner who shall fail to attend a regular meeting of the board of commissioners, or call meeting of which he shall have had notice, unless permitted by such cause as shall be satisfactory to the board, he shall forfeit and pay for the use of the town one dollar for each and every offense, and it shall be the duty of the mayor to enforce such forfeiture as in all other criminal actions.

Salary of mayor. SEC. 28. That the commissioners may allow the mayor such reasonable salary as they may see fit and proper, the amount depending upon services needed and rendered.

Term of office of present commissioners. SEC. 29. That the commissioners now in office shall hold office until the next regular election on the first Monday in May, eighteen hundred and ninety-nine (1899), and until their successors are elected and qualified.

SEC. 30. That the board of commissioners shall have power to enact any ordinance or ordinances and to pass all laws and regulations not incorporated in this charter they may deem necessary for the better government of the town, not inconsistent with the general laws and constitution of the state.

Conflicting laws repealed. SEC. 31. That all laws and clauses of laws heretofore enacted inconsistent with the charter of Albemarle, and all other laws conflicting with this act, are this day repealed and this charter substituted.

SEC. 32. That this act shall be in force from and after its ratification.

Ratified the 28th day of February, A. D. 1899.

CHAPTER 150.

An act supplemental to an act ratified February twenty-first. eighteen hundred and ninety-nine, being "An act to incorporate the Ohio River, Franklin and Tidewater Railway Company."

The General Assembly of North Carolina do enact:

Section 1. That section two of an act ratified February the twenty-first, eighteen hundred and ninety-nine, it being an act to incorporate the "Ohio River, Franklin and Tidewater Railway Company," be amended by striking out the word "cap" where it occurs in said section, between the words "Rabun" "Rabun," and insert in lieu thereof the word "Gap," so that it will read Rabun Gap Rabun. **Act to incorporate Ohio River, Franklin and Tidewater Railway Company ratified February 21st, 1899, amended.**

Sec. 2. That this act shall be in force from and after its ratification.

Ratified the 28th day of February, A. D. 1899.

CHAPTER 151.

An act to incorporate The North Carolina Electrical Power Company, and for other purposes.

The General Assembly of North Carolina do enact:

Section 1. That H. E. Fries, Jno. W. Fries, C. A. Reynolds, J. Spach, W. B. Ellis, and their associates be and are hereby created a body corporate under the name of "The North Carolina Electrical Power Company," for the purposes hereinafter described, and by [that] name and style shall, for a term of sixty years, have succession and power to sue and be sued, to plead and be impleaded, defend and be defended in all courts, whether in law or in equity, and may make and have a common seal and alter and renew the same at pleasure; and shall have, possess and enjoy all rights and privileges of a corporation or body politic in the law and necessary for the purpose of this act. **Corporators. Body corporate. Corporate name. Corporate powers.**

Sec. 2. That the said company is authorized and empowered to supply to the public, including both individuals and corporations, within the state of North Carolina, and elsewhere, power in the forms of electric current, and hydraulic, pneumatic and steam pressure, or any of the said forms, and in any or all other forms for use in driving machinery, and for light, heat and all other uses to which the power so applied can be made applicable, and to fix, charge, collect and receive payment therefor; and for the purpose of enabling the company to supply power as aforesaid, **Empowered to supply electric power.**

Corporate powers. the company is authorized and empowered to buy or otherwise acquire, generate, develop, store, use, transmit and distribute power of all kinds, and to locate, acquire, construct, equip, maintain and operate from any place in the state where the said company may establish plants to any distributing points in the state where they may elect, and from the same to any other points, by the most practicable routes, to be determined by the board of directors of the company, lines for the transmission of power by wire on poles or under ground, and by cables, pipes, tubes, conduits and all other convenient appliances for power transmission, with such connecting lines between the lines above mentioned, and also with such branch lines as a majority of the stockholders of the company may locate or authorize to be located, for receiving, transmitting and distributing power; and as appurtenances to the said lines of power transmission and their branches, the company may acquire, own, hold, sell or otherwise dispose of water powers and water privileges in the state of North Carolina and elsewhere, and may locate, acquire, construct, equip, maintain and operate all necessary plants for generating and developing by water, steam or any other means, and for storing, using, transmitting, distributing, selling and delivering power, including dams, gates, bridges, tunnels, stations and other buildings, boilers, engines, machinery, switches, lamps, motors and all other works, structures and appliances, in the state of North Carolina; also may build, own, control and operate electric railway lines, and may own, rent, lease or sell power for any other uses to which electricity, steam or water power can be applied: *Provided*, that the amount of land which the company may at any time hold within the state of North Carolina for any one water power and other works, except the land flowed or submerged with water accumulating at any one dam, shall not exceed ten thousand acres, exclusive of right-of-way: *And provided further*, that lines and appurtenances hereinbefore authorized for distributing power and light are to be constructed, when on public streets or highways of any county, city or town, under such reasonable regulations as the authorities respectively thereof shall, upon application from the company, prescribe.

(Margin notes: Corporate powers. Proviso. Maximum amount of land to be held by company. Proviso.)

Capital stock. SEC. 3. The capital stock of the said company shall be not less than thirty thousand dollars, and may, with the consent of a majority of its stockholders, be increased from time to time, to one million dollars, or any additional amount by the issue and sale of shares of preferred or common stock or both, upon such terms and conditions and under regulation as the board of directors, with the approval of the majority in interest of the stockholders of said company, shall prescribe, but the par value of every share of stock shall be one hundred dollars,

(Margin note: May be increased.)

and the directors, with like approval of the stockholders, may receive cash, labor, material, bonds, stock, contracts, real or personal property in payment of subscriptions to the capital stock, and under the direction of a majority of the corporators hereinbefore named, or such of them as shall be subscribers, may organize the said company by electing a board of directors and providing for the election or appointment of such other officers as may be necessary for the control and management of the business and affairs of said company, and thereupon they shall have and exercise all the powers and functions of a corporation under their charter and the laws of this state. Every subscriber to or holder of the stock of the said company, shall be liable for the debts of the company to an amount equal to the amount unpaid on the stock subscribed for and held by him, and no more.

Par value of stock.

Election of officers.

Individual liability of stockholders.

Sec. 4. It shall be lawful for the said company to borrow money and issue and sell its bonds, from time to time, for such sums and on such terms, as its board of directors may deem expedient and proper, for any of the purposes of the company, and may secure the payment of said bonds or mortgages, or deeds of trust, upon all or any portion of its property, real, personal or mixed, its contracts and privileges, and its charter rights and franchises, including its franchise to be a corporation; and it may, as the business of the company shall require, sell, lease, convey and encumber the same; and it shall be lawful for the said company to subscribe to and hold the stock and bonds of manufacturing or other corporations, and any manufacturing or other corporations may subscribe to, and guarantee and hold the stock and bonds of the said company.

May borrow money.

May hold stock in other corporations.

Sec. 5. The said company may connect or unite its lines for the transmission of power with those of any other company or companies, or consolidate and merge its stock, property and franchises with and into those of any other company or companies incorporated under the laws of this state or any other states of the United States, operating or authorized to operate lines for the transmission of electric or other power upon such terms and under such name as may be agreed upon between the companies so uniting or connecting, merging or consolidating; and the said company may lease or sell any or all its property, real or personal, or mixed, its contracts and privileges, and its charter rights and franchises, to any such other company, upon such terms as may be agreed upon between them, and may, in like manner, acquire by lease or purchase, any or all the property, real or personal, or mixed, the contracts and privileges, and the chartered rights and franchises of any such other company or companies; and full power and authority is hereby given to the said company or companies to make and carry out all such con-

May unite with other companies.

tracts as will facilitate and consummate such consolidation, or merges and changes of name of such leases and sales.

When works of company shall be located.

Sec. 6. The board of directors shall, as soon as they deem it practicable, proceed to locate the works of said company, and may have one or more locations from time to time, as they may deem expedient, and the construction of some of the said works shall be begun within five years after the ratification of this act.

Principal office.

Sec. 7. That the principal office of said company shall be located at Winston, North Carolina, and such branch offices as may be desirable for the purposes of the corporation shall be established at such places as the by-laws of the corporation shall designate, and prescribe. But by consent of the board of directors, and a majority of the stockholders, the principal office may be removed to any place within the state expedient to the management of its works.

Agents of company may lawfully enter upon certain lands.

Sec. 8. It shall be lawful for the president and directors, their agents, superintendents, engineers, or others in their employ, to enter, at all times, upon lands or water, for the purpose of exploring and surveying the works of said company and locating the same, doing no unnecessary damage to private property, and when the location of said works, in whole or in part, shall have been determined upon, and a survey of the same deposited in the office of the secretary of state, then it shall be lawful for the said company, by the officers, agents, engineers, superintendents, contractors, and others in its employ, to enter upon, take possession of, hold, use, and excavate any such lands, and to erect all structures necessary and suitable for the completion or repairing as is hereinafter provided: *Provided always*, that payment or tender of payment of the value of all lands upon which the said works may be laid out are made before the said company shall enter upon, or break ground upon, the premises, except for surveying or locating said works, unless the consent of the owners thereof be first obtained.

Proviso.

Payment for lands condemned.

When necessary land can not be purchased assessing commissioners shall be appointed.

Sec. 9. When any land or right-of-way, and trees within danger and proximity to lines, may be required by said company for the purpose of constructing its works, or building its roads, and for want of agreement as to the value thereof, or for any other cause, the same can not be purchased from the owner, the same may be taken at a valuation to be fixed by five commissioners, or a majority of them, to be appointed by any superior court judge. In making the said valuation, the said commissioners shall take into consideration the loss or damage which may occur to the owner or owners in consequence of the land being surrendered: *Provided, nevertheless*, that if any person or persons on whose lands the said works may be located, or if said company shall be dissatisfied with the valuation of said commissioners,

Proviso.

then and in that case the party so dissatisfied may have an appeal to the superior court in the county wherein the valuation has been made, or in either county in which the land may be when it shall be in more than one county, subject to the same rules, regulations and restrictions as in other cases on appeal. The proceedings of said commissioners, with a full description of the land, shall be returned under their hands and seals, or a majority of them, to the court from which the commission was issued, there to remain a matter of record, and the lands so valued shall vest in the said company as soon as the valuation shall have been paid or tendered: *Provided*, that upon application for the appointment of commissioners under this section, it shall be made to appear to the satisfaction of the court, that at least ten days' notice had been previously given of the application to the owner or owners of the land so purposed to be condemned, or if the owners be under disability, or the guardians of such owners as are under disability can not be found within the county, or the owner or owners are not known, then that such notice of such application has been published once a week for at least four weeks, in some newspaper printed in the vicinity of the court-house of the county in which the application is to be made: *And provided further*, that the valuation provided for in this section shall be made on oath by the commissioners aforesaid, which oath may be administered by any clerk of the court, justice of the peace, or other person authorized by law to administer oaths: *And provided further*, that the right of condemnation herein granted shall not authorize said company to remove or invade the yard or garden around the private dwelling, the burial grounds of any individual, without his or her consent; and the lands aforesaid for the purpose of this act, are hereby condemned for public purposes.

Either party may appeal.

Proceedings of commissioners shall be returned.

Proviso.

Notice shall be given owners of property

Valuation by commissioners shall be made on oath.

SEC. 10. All land, not heretofore granted to any person, lying within the locations made by the company for its works, shall vest in the said company as soon as the works are definitely laid out, through or upon it, and any grant of said land thereafter shall be void.

Lands that shall vest in company.

SEC. 11. A part of the works of said company, at any of its plants, may be constructed without completing its entire works, and the said works may be operated, and electric current may be transmitted and delivered, and charges may be collected therefor, notwithstanding the entire works of the company have not been completed.

Operation may begin before works are completed.

SEC. 12. Every stockholder in the company shall, at all meetings or elections, be entitled to one vote for every share of stock registered in his name. The stockholders of the said company may enact such by-laws, rules and regulations for the

Representation of stockholders in meeting.

Rules and regulations. Meeting of stockholders and directors.

management of the affairs of the company as they may deem proper and expedient. Meetings of the stockholders and directors may be held at such times and places as the stockholders may in the by-laws or otherwise prescribe.

Directors, of whom composed. Term of office. Officers of company. Vacancies occurring.

Sec. 13. The board of directors shall be composed of stockholders of said company, and shall consist of such members as the stockholders may prescribe, from time to time by the by-laws, and shall be elected at the stockholders' annual meeting, to be held on such days as the by-laws of the company may direct, and shall continue in office for the term of one year from and after the date of their election, and until their successors are elected and accept the duties of the office, and they shall choose from among their number a president, vice-president, secretary and treasurer; but one or more of said offices may be held by the same person. In case of death, resignation or incapacity of any member of the board of directors during his term of office, the said board shall choose his successor for the unexpired term.

By-laws prima facie evidence.

Sec. 14. This act shall be deemed and taken to be a public act, and a copy of any by-laws or regulations of the said company under its corporate seal, purporting to be signed by the president, shall be received as *prima facie* evidence for and against the said company in any judicial proceedings.

Sec. 15. That any person who shall willfully and maliciously deface, injure, destroy, remove or obstruct said works, or any fixtures, property or machinery thereof, or its structures or appliances of any kind, shall be guilty of a misdemeanor, and fined or imprisoned within the discretion of the court.

Persons injuring property guilty of a misdemeanor.

Sec. 16. That any person or persons who shall willfully and maliciously cast, throw, shoot, propel or project, or in any wise put in motion any stone, rock, shot, torpedo or other missile of any kind or nature, at, against or into any of the property of said company, shall be guilty of a misdemeanor, and shall be fined or imprisoned within the discretion of the court.

Powers vested in employees.

Sec. 17. That the conductors, drivers and other agents and servants of said company, while in the active service of said company or the discharge of any duty connected therewith, are hereby vested with the same power, authority and privileges which belong to similar officers and agents of railroad companies in this state; and in addition to the general powers conferred upon such agents and officers they may eject and remove all drunken, profane and disorderly persons from any of the conveyances, cars or property of said company at any time, whether the fare of said drunken, disorderly or profane persons has been paid or not, and the said company shall not be liable or responsible in damages therefor, and such agent or officer shall not be liable, civilly or criminally therefor, unless he uses greater force than is necessary to eject such person.

SEC. 18. This act shall take effect from and after its ratification, and all acts or parts of acts inconsistent herewith are hereby repealed.

SEC. 19. This act shall be in full force and effect from and after its ratification.

Ratified the 28th day of February, A. D. 1899.

CHAPTER 152.

An act to incorporate The Troy Manufacturing Company at Troy, North Carolina.

The General Assembly of North Carolina do enact:

SECTION 1. That Milton L. Jones, Arthur Jones and J. Peece Blair, together with their associates and successors, be and they are hereby created and constituted [a] body corporate under the name of "The Troy Manufacturing Company," and by that name shall be entitled to sue and be sued, plead and be impleaded, in any court in or out of the state of North Carolina, shall have and use the common seal and order [alter] the same at pleasure, and have all the rights and privileges and be subject to all the regulations and restrictions now existing and applicable to such corporations under the laws of this state. Corporators. Body corporate. Corporate name. Corporate powers.

SEC. 2. That said corporation may acquire, buy, sell and hold lands and timber and personal property in this state; may conduct a general lumber business in all its branches; it may maintain sawmills, planting [planing] mills, dry-kiln; it may acquire, manufacture, hold and sell all kinds of machinery; it may manufacture, buy and sell sash, blinds, doors and everything of whatever nature or kind that is made from lumber; it may manufacture, buy, sell and dispose of furniture of every description, it may manufacture cotton goods of all kinds, and also woolen goods; it may conduct in all of its branches the business of mining, smelting, forging and casting and the working of iron, copper, silver and gold; it may conduct in all of its branches the business of carrying on and operating a flour and grist mills; to that end may buy, sell and dispose of corn, wheat, barley, oats, rye, flour, meal and the products of all the cereals, and grain of every description; it may conduct and carry on in all of its branches the general mercantile business. Corporate powers. Corporate powers.

SEC. 3. That said corporation is hereby authorized to make, construct, equip, maintain and operate lines of tramway with Corporate powers.

one or more tracks, and all necessary branches, turnouts, switches and sidings, using such motive power as may be determined upon by the board of directors from any point on the Aberdeen and Ashboro Railroad and the Yadkin Railroad, in the counties of Montgomery and Stanly, through, along, over and across any portion of said counties of Montgomery and Stanly to any point or points in said counties, and erect such depots, stables, offices, shops and other buildings, structures, fixtures and appliances as are necessary and proper for conducting the business of said tram-roads and company, and to demand and receive such sum or sums of money for the carriage of passengers and freight as the directors may think proper, not to exceed five cents per mile for passengers and not exceed one cent per mile for each one hundred pounds of freight by the tram carload, and for parcels such compensation as may be reasonable.

Rates for transportation.

Condemnation of land.

SEC. 4. That whenever any land may be required for the purpose of constructing, equipping, maintaining and operating the said line or lines of tramway, or for constructing, maintaining, equipping and operating all necessary branches, switches, turnouts and sidings and the erection and maintaining of the necessary depots, stables, offices, shops and other buildings, structures, fixtures and appliances proper for conducting the business of the said tramway by said company, it shall have the power to have the same assessed and condemned for its purposes in the manner prescribed in The Code of North Carolina, chapter forty-nine, of volume one, section one thousand nine hundred and forty-three, and the sections following.

May lease or sell property.

SEC. 5. That the said company shall have the right to lease or sell its road, property and franchise or any part thereof to any person or persons or corporation, and may acquire the property and franchises of or interest in any other corporation, by purchase, lease, subscription to or purchase of its capital stock or otherwise.

Capital stock.

Division of shares.

SEC. 6. That the capital stock of the company shall be ten thousand dollars ($10,000), divided into one hundred shares of one hundred dollars ($100) each, and may from time to time be increased to any amount, not exceeding one hundred thousand dollars, whenever a majority of the stockholders in value shall determine. Said capital stock may be divided into preferred and common shares in such proportions and with such privileges, qualities and characteristics as a majority of the stockholders in value may determine.

May issue bonds, etc.

SEC. 7. That the said company shall have power to contract debts and borrow money for the legitimate purposes of the corporation, and to make and issue notes, and shall have power to issue bonds and other evidences of debt and indebtedness for any obligation incurred in the conduct of its business, and shall have power to execute a mortgage or mortgages or deeds in trust upon or conveying its property, franchise and income to secure the payment of any indebtedness of said company as it may deem expedient.

SEC. 8. That the officers of said corporation shall consist of a president, secretary and treasurer, whose duty shall be prescribed by the by-laws of said company, and to be elected at their first meeting, and that the president, secretary and treasurer shall constitute the board of directors of said corporation, and that upon the election of said officers the said company shall be deemed to be fully organized, and may obtain subscriptions, issue stocks, bonds and other evidence of indebtedness, and begin the operations of such manufacturing establishments, mills, mining, smelting works, tramroads as they may have already erected, and may enter into contracts for the construction of buildings, tramroads and purchase any articles connected with the business herein mentioned, and do any and all other lawful things necessary to carry out the purposes of the company. Officers of corporation.

SEC. 9. That the principal office of said company shall be kept at Troy, Montgomery county, North Carolina, and it may establish such branch offices at such points in this state as it may deem necessary, and this corporation shall continue for a period of sixty years, subject to the general law regulating corporations. Principal office.

SEC. 10. That any person who shall unlawfully and willfully remove, obstruct, injure, deface or destroy any part of the property of said company shall be deemed guilty of a misdemeanor, and upon conviction be fined and imprisoned in the discretion of the court. Persons damaging property of company guilty of a misdemeanor.

SEC. 11. That the stockholders of said company shall not be individually liable for any of its debts or engagements. Individual liability.

SEC. 12. That this act shall be in force from and after its ratification.

Ratified the 28th day of February, A. D. 1899.

CHAPTER 153.

An act to amend, revise and consolidate the charter of the City of Raleigh, in the county of Wake, and state of North Carolina.

The General Assembly of North Carolina do enact:

SECTION 1. That the territory bounded by and included within the following lines, to-wit: On the north by a line centered upon the center of Union Square and lying two thousand eight hundred and ninety-three and five-tenths feet to the northward Territory comprising city of Raleigh, Wake county.

thereof parallel with the true center of Hillsboro street and Newbern avenue; south by a line centered as aforesaid and lying four thousand three hundred and fifty-one and five tenths feet to the southward of said center parallel with said first described line, and on the east and west by a line parallel with the true center of Fayetteville and Halifax streets, lying three thousand three hundred and seventy nine and five-tenths feet to the eastward and westward thereof respectively, thereby intersecting and closing the extremities of the first and second described lines, shall constitute the external boundaries: *Provided*, that these boundaries do not extend the corporate limits of the city, and the inhabitants residing therein shall be and remain a body politic and corporate under the name and style of "The City of Raleigh," and under such name and style may adopt a corporate seal, sue and be sued, plead and be impleaded, acquire by purchase, devise, bequest or other conveyance such real and personal property anywhere within Raleigh township as may be requisite and necessary for the proper government of the city; hold, invest, improve, use, govern, control and protect, and under the hand of the mayor and two aldermen, attested by the corporate seal, may sell or dispose of the same, and have all the powers, rights and privileges necessary, belonging or usually pertaining to municipal corporations; and within twelve months after the ratification of this act the board of aldermen may cause an accurate survey to be made of the exterior boundaries of the city as herein provided, and it shall be their duty to erect upon each corner and upon every natural elevation intercepting the line of sight from any one corner to the next corners, a firm and durable monument of stone, to be maintained by the city, and protected from obstruction, removal, defacement or other injury by a rigid enforcement of the penalties herein denounced against such crimes: *Provided*, that the tract of land conveyed to the city of Raleigh by R. S. Pullen, Esquire, by deed dated March the twenty-second, eighteen hundred and eighty seven, as recorded in book ninety-five, page four hundred and sixty-three, register of deeds office of Wake county, and known as "Pullen Park," and all other territory which may be required [acquired] by the city of Raleigh by purchase or donation or otherwise for park purposes, and the cemetery for the burial of deceased white persons, located northeast of the city of Raleigh, known as "Oakwood Cemetery," and the cemetery for the burial of colored deceased persons, located southeast of the city of Raleigh, known as "Mount Hope Cemetery," shall also be included in the corporate limits of the city of Raleigh, and all ordinances now in force or hereafter enacted by the board of aldermen of said city shall be applicable to the territory included in said Pullen Park or other park and

Body corporate.

Corporate name.

Corporate powers.

Board of aldermen may order survey.

Proviso.

Certain other lands included in corporate limits.

in said cemeteries as fully as if the said territory was embraced within the limits of the City of Raleigh defined (as fully as in any other part of the City of Raleigh).

SEC. 2. That said city shall be divided into four wards, with centers of Hargett and Fayetteville streets as intersections, to-wit: The northwest portion of said area included between the centers of Hargett street on the south and Fayetteville and Halifax streets on the east, and as they now are or hereafter may be to the exterior boundaries, shall be known as the first ward; the northeast portion of said area included between the centers of Halifax and Fayetteville streets on the west and Hargett street on the south, and as they now are or hereafter may be to the exterior boundaries, shall be known as the second ward; the southeast portion of said area included between the centers of Hargett street on the north and Fayetteville street on the west, and as they now are or hereafter may be to the exterior boundaries, shall be known as the third ward; and the remainder of said area between the centers of Hargett street on the north and Fayetteville street on the east, and as they now are or hereafter may be to the exterior boundaries, shall be the fourth ward.

Division of wards.

Boundaries of first ward.

Boundaries of second ward.

Boundaries of third ward.

Boundaries of fourth ward.

SEC. 3. That the wards so laid off shall be divided into eight election districts as follows: Beginning at a point in the center of Hargett and Fayetteville street and running west along the center of Hargett street to the city limits; thence north along the line of the city limits to the center of Jones street; thence east along the center of Jones street to the center of Halifax street; thence south along the center of Halifax and Fayetteville streets to the beginning, and shall be known as the first election district of the first ward. Beginning at a point in the center of Halifax and Jones street and running west along the center of Jones street to the city limits; thence north along the line of the city limits to the city limits on the northwest; thence east along the line of the city limits to the center of Halifax street; thence south along the center of Halifax street to the beginning, and shall be known as the second election district of the first ward. Beginning at a point in the center of Hargett and Fayetteville streets and running east along the center of Hargett street to the city limits; thence north along the line of the city limits to the center of Jones street; thence west along the center of Jones street to the center of Halifax street; thence south along the centers of Halifax and Fayetteville streets to the beginning, and shall be known as the first election district of the second ward. Beginning at a point in the center of Halifax and Jones streets and running east along the center of Jones street to the city limits; thence north along the line of the city limits to the city limits on the northeast; thence west along the line of the

Division of election districts.
Boundaries of first election district of first ward.

Boundaries of second election district of first ward.

Boundaries of first election district of second ward.

Boundaries of second election district of second ward.

city limits to the center of Halifax street; thence south along the center of Halifax street to the beginning and shall be known as the second election district of the second ward. Beginning at a point in the center of Hargett and Fayetteville streets and running east along the center of Hargett street to the city limits; thence south along the line of the city limits to the center of Cabarrus street; thence west along the center of Cabarrus street to the center of Fayetteville street; thence north along the center of Fayetteville street to the beginning, and shall be known as the first election district of the third ward. Beginning at a point in the center of Cabarrus and Fayetteville streets and running east along the center of Cabarrus street to the city limits; thence south along the line of the city limits to the city limits on the southeast; thence west along the line of the city limits to the center of Fayetteville street; thence north along the center of Fayetteville street to the beginning, and shall be known as the second election district of the third ward. Beginning at a point in the center of Hargett and Fayetteville streets and running west along the center of Hargett street to the city limits; thence south along the line of the city limits to the center of Lenoir street; thence east along the center of Lenoir street to the center of Fayetteville street; thence north along the center of Fayetteville street to the beginning, and shall be known as the first election district of the fourth ward. Beginning at a point in the center of Fayetteville and Lenoir streets and running west along the center of Lenoir street to the city limits; thence south along the line of the city limits to the city limits on the southwest; thence east along the line of the city limits to the center of Fayetteville street; thence north along the center of Fayetteville street to the beginning and shall be known as the second election district of the fourth ward: *Provided*, that the territory embraced in "Pullen Park" and "Mount Hope Cemetery" shall be and compose a part of the second election district of the fourth ward, and the territory embraced in "Oakwood Cemetery" shall be and compose a part of the second election district of the second ward.

Boundaries of first election district of third ward.

Boundaries of second election district of third ward.

Boundaries of the first election district of the fourth ward.

Boundaries of the second election district of the fourth ward.

Proviso.

SEC. 4. That on the first Monday in May, eighteen hundred and ninety-nine, and on the same Monday biennially thereafter, there shall be elected at large of and by the qualified voters of said city a mayor, city clerk and tax collector, and in each of said election districts there shall be elected separately of and by the qualified voters therein two aldermen for each district; and the aldermen so elected shall constitute "the board of aldermen" of said city, and all of said officers so elected shall hold office for two years or until their successors shall have been duly elected and qualified: *Provided*, that no officer of said city shall be qualified

Annual election of city officers.

Aldermen, how elected.

Term of office of aldermen.

or enter upon his duty until a good and sufficient bond conditioned for the faithful discharge of the duties of his office shall have been tendered, accepted, approved and filed with the clerk, in case a bond is required by the provision of this act: *Provided*, that the registrars appointed under the provisions of this act for the election to be held on the first Monday in May, eighteen hundred and ninety-nine, shall take a new registration of all qualified voters residing in the wards and election districts named in this act: *Provided further*, that no person shall have the right to vote at any election held in said city unless he shall have been a bona fide resident of the ward or election district in which he proposes to register and vote for thirty days prior to such election.

Bonds of officers.

Proviso.

Registrars shall take new registration.

Proviso.

Persons entitled to vote.

SEC. 5. That the biennial elections herein provided for officers of said city and any other election herein authorized for city purposes, shall be called, held, conducted and concluded under the direction of the mayor and board of aldermen by officers designated and appointed by them for that purpose, in manner and form in every respect and detail as near as may be and under the same provisions of law and practice as near as may be as elections for county and state officers are held and conducted by county officials under the general law relating to such elections in North Carolina in force at the time of such city election, including all the penalties prescribed for the violation of such law: *Provided*, that when any certain duties are prescribed under the general election law to be done and performed by state or county officials unknown to municipal corporations, which are likewise required to be done and performed in such city election, then and in that case such duties shall be done and performed by city officer or officers whose office and duties bear the greatest analogy to those of the officer named in the general election law for such duty; as chief of police to sheriff, city clerk to clerk of the superior court, etc.: *And provided further*, that the election herein provided to be held on the first Monday in May, eighteen hundred and ninety-nine, shall be called, held, conducted and concluded under the direction of the clerk of the city of Raleigh, who shall designate the polling places in the precincts and appoint the registrars and poll holders, judges of election for each in the city; provided [provide] the requisite ballot boxes, books and blanks at the expense of the city; receive, count, tabulate and aggregate the returns and announce the result as required by law for the conduct and conclusion of general elections in the county.

Biennial elections, how conducted.

Proviso.

Duties required by general election law.

Proviso.

Election herein provided for shall be held under direction of city clerk.

SEC. 6. That the board of aldermen so elected and constituted shall, during the month of May after election and qualification, elect the following officers, none of whom shall be of their num-

Election of officers by aldermen.

ber: A chief of police, two captains of police, sanitary inspector, street commissioner, auditor, treasurer, commissioner of sinking fund, and such other officers as they may deem necessary for the government of the city. All of said officers so elected shall hold their office during the official term of the board of aldermen or until their successors shall have been duly elected and qualified.

Term of office.

OF THE MAYOR.

Oath of city officers.

SEC. 7. That the mayor and every other officer of said city before entering upon the duties of his office shall take, subscribe and file with the city clerk the following oath of office:

I, ______, do solemnly swear (or affirm) that I will support and defend the constitution of the United States and the constitution and laws of North Carolina not inconsistent therewith, and I will faithfully perform the duties of the office of ______, on which I am about to enter according to may best skill and ability. So help me, God.

Subscribed and sworn before me, ____, this __ day of ____, 189__

Mayor's office.

SEC. 8. That the mayor shall have and keep his office in the city hall or in some other convenient building provided by the board of aldermen. He shall have the custody of the corporate seal; preside when present over all meetings of the board of aldermen; have a casting vote in all cases of equal division therein; a general custody, direction, supervision and control of all the public employees, work and works, improvements, grounds, buildings and property of the city not otherwise provided for by this act or by the board of aldermen; may, after a full and fair hearing, suspend for cause until the next meeting of the board of aldermen any officer or employee of the city charged with dereliction of official duty or the violation of any of the provisions of this act (except members of the police force, who shall be given a preliminary hearing by the police committee upon charges preferred by the chief of police, and their act even thereon shall be reported to the next meeting of the board of aldermen), and shall perform such other duties as are or may be prescribed by this act or the ordinances of said city.

Duties and privileges of mayor.

May suspend officers or employees of city for cause.

Mayor constituted special court.

Jurisdiction of mayor.

SEC. 9. That the mayor of the City of Raleigh is hereby constituted a special court, to be known as "the mayor's court," with exclusive original jurisdiction of all offenses arising from the violation of the provisions of this act or of the ordinances, by-laws, rules and regulations of the board of aldermen made in pursuance hereof, and with all the jurisdiction, power and authority which is now or hereafter may be given to justices of the peace for the trial and determination of such civil and criminal causes as may arise within the corporate limits of said city under the general laws of North Carolina, and to that end he may issue his summons, warrant or other process, and if criminal, have the party brought before him; hear, determine and give judgment thereon; issue execution, impose fines, penalties and forfeitures as the case may be, and direct the enforcement thereof, subject to the limitations of this act as to the amounts of such penalties, and subject also to the same right of appeal as is provided for courts of justices of the peace: *Provided*, that no cause arising upon the violation of any of the provisions of this charter or of any ordinance, rule or regulation made in pursuance hereof, shall be removed from the mayor's court to a justice of the peace for trial: *And provided further*, that in case a defendant, a witness or other person shall be adjudged to be imprisoned by the said mayor's court, it shall be competent for the said court to sentence such person to imprisonment in the county jail for a term not exceeding thirty days, and to adjudge also that such person work during the period of his or her confinement on the public streets or works of the city or on the public roads or works of the county of Wake; and in case such imprisonment be for the non-payment of a fine, a penalty or costs, he shall have credit thereon at the rate of one dollar per day for every day in which he shall so work upon the public streets, roads or other works of the city or county.

Power to issue summons, etc.

Proviso.

Certain causes not removable from mayor's court.

Proviso.

Empowered to execute sentences.

Persons who may be worked on public streets.

Sec. 10. That the mayor may issue process to the chief of police or to the city police or to any other officer in the county of Wake to whom a justice of the peace may issue similar process, and such process when attested by the corporate seal shall run anywhere in the state of North Carolina, and they shall execute the same: *Provided*, that neither the chief of police nor the city police shall execute any process beyond or outside of the boundaries of Raleigh township unless the offense was committed or cause of action arose within the corporate limits of the city and in violation of the provisions of this act.

Process issued to officers.

Proviso.

Execution of process beyond corporate limits.

Sec. 11. That the judgments rendered by the mayor under the provisions of this act shall have all the force, virtue and validity of judgments rendered by a justice of the peace; may be enforced and executed against the parties in the county of Wake and elsewhere in the same manner and by the same means. The fines and penalties imposed by him shall be collected by or paid over to the chief of police, who shall pay over and account for the same as hereinafter directed, to the use of the city of Raleigh.

Validity of judgment rendered by mayor.

Fines, how collected.

Sec. 12. That it shall be the duty of the mayor to keep an exact account and true record of all fines, penalties and forfeitures by him imposed under any of the provisions of this act or for the violation of any ordinance, by-law, rule or regulation made in pur-

Mayor shall keep record.

suance hereof, in a separate book to be furnished by the board of aldermen therefor, showing the name and residence of each offender, the nature of the offense, the date of hearing of trial, the amount of the fine or penalty imposed and, if known, when and by whom paid to the chief of police.

Failure of mayor to qualify.

SEC. 13. That if any person who has been elected mayor shall fail, neglect or refuse to qualify, or if a vacancy shall occur in the office after election and qualification other than by expiration of term, or if the mayor be absent from the city or unable to attend or discharge the duties of his office from any other cause, then and in such case the board of aldermen shall choose some qualified person to perform the duties of the absent mayor during the period of his absence or disability or to the end of the term, as the case may be, and the mayor so chosen shall have all the power and authority which is vested in the regularly elected mayor under this act; and the board of aldermen shall in like manner fill all vacancies for the unexpired term which may occur in the city government, choosing only such persons as are eligible to original election under the provisions of this act: *Provided*, that in case a vacancy shall occur in the office of mayor of the city during the first year of the term of such mayor, then the board of aldermen shall call and hold an election and the vacancy shall be filled by the vote of the people qualified to vote thereon in the city within forty days of the date on which such vacancy occurred or was first known.

Board of aldermen shall elect.

Other vacancies occurring filled by aldermen.

Proviso.

Vacancies occurring during first year of incumberancy of mayor, special election shall be held.

Mayor shall present annual report to aldermen.

SEC. 14. It shall be the duty of the mayor as soon after the close of each fiscal year (including the last year thereof) as is practicable, to present to the board of aldermen a report of the several departments of the city government for the previous year, reviewing the same, with such recommendations in relation thereto as may seem to him advantageous to the public service. It shall be the duty of the clerk of the city to cause the same to be printed and bound in the usual form with the other reports of the city officers.

Clerk shall have report printed and bound.

OF THE CITY CLERK.

Clerk shall keep record of meeting, have custody of city books, etc.

SEC. 15. That it shall be the duty of the city clerk to be present at all meetings of the board of aldermen; to keep and record in a book to be provided therefor regular and fair minutes of the proceedings of the board, and, when thereto required, of the mayor's court; to preserve all the books, records, documents, papers and other articles committed to his use, care or custody during his term of office and deliver them in good order and condition to his successor, and generally to perform such other duties as may be prescribed by this charter or by the board of aldermen.

OF THE CHIEF OF POLICE.

Sec. 16. That the chief of police shall be the chief executive officer of the police force. He shall be chargeable with and responsible for the execution of all laws and the rules and regulations of the department; he shall assign to duty the officers and members of the police force and shall have power to change such assignment from time to time whenever in his judgment the exigencies of the service may require such change. He shall have power to suspend without pay, pending the trial of charges, any member of the police force: *Provided, however*, that no such suspension shall be continued for a period of more than ten days without affirmative action to that effect by the police committee. If any member of the police force so suspended shall not be convicted by the police committee of the charges so preferred, he shall be entitled to full pay from date of suspension, notwithstanding such charges and suspension. Said chief of police may grant leave of absence to members of the force for a period not exceeding five days; he shall report to the police committee all changes or assignments of officers and all leave of absences granted. He shall have general care of the peace of the city and see that all subordinates do their duty in preserving the same. He shall have control over the entire police force and see to the execution of every ordinance · He shall have general supervision over the subject of nuisances and the abatement of the same, and shall exercise and discharge all such powers and functions as pertain to the office of chief of police and as the board of aldermen may from time to time prescribe. He shall make monthly report to "the board of aldermen" of the general condition of the department, together with such other matters as pertain to his office and perform such other duties as may be required of him by ordinance. In case of the absence or disability of the chief of police, then a member of the police force may be designated by the chief of police to serve during such absence or disability, and the member so designated shall be competent to discharge all the duties of the chief of police.

Chief of police chief executive officer of police force.

Assignment of policemen.

Suspension of policemen without pay. Proviso.

When suspension of policemen not sustained, entitled to full pay.

Leave of absence.

Supervision over subject of nuisances.

Monthly report to aldermen.

In absence of chief of police.

Sec. 17. That said chief of police may appoint with the consent of the mayor special police whenever the exigencies of the times in his judgment demand it; he may appoint or employ, with the consent of the mayor, detectives and assign them to specific duties.

When special police may be appointed.

Sec. 18. If any member of the police force, or if any two or more householders, shall report in writing under his or their signature to the chief of police that there are good grounds (stating the same) for believing any house, room or premises within the said city to be kept or used as a common gambling house, com-

Report of gambling houses to chief of police

mon gaming room or common gaming premises for therein playing for wagers of money at any game of chance, or to be kept or used for lewd and obscene purposes or amusements or the deposit or sale of lottery tickets or lottery policies, it shall be lawful for the chief of police to authorize in writing any member or members of the police force to enter the same, who may forthwith arrest all persons there found offending against law, but none others, and seize all implements of gaming or lottery tickets or lottery policies and convey any person so arrested before the mayor and bring the articles so seized to the station-house. It shall be the duty of the said chief of police to cause such arrested persons to be vigorously prosecuted and such articles seized to be destroyed, as the orders, rules and regulations of the police committee may direct.

Chief of police may admit persons charged with violation of ordinances to bail.

SEC. 19. That the chief of police shall have the authority to admit to bail any person arrested for violation of the city ordinance in the sum of not less than three dollars or more than fifty dollars for their appearance for trial before the mayor, and should any person so admitted to bail fail to appear for trial before the mayor, then such bail shall be forfeited to the city, and the chief of police shall report the money so forfeited in the same way that he does other moneys collected by him.

Observation of dinances, etc.

SEC. 20. That it shall be the duty of the chief of police and of the city police force under his immediate charge and direction to see that the laws of the city and the ordinance of the board of aldermen and the orders of the mayor are executed and enforced, and all breaches thereof reported to the mayor; to preserve the peace and order of the city, to suppress disturbances and arrest and carry before the mayor all offenders against any laws, city, state or national, who may be found within the corporate limits or within one mile thereof; to execute all warrants or other process lawfully directed to him by the mayor or other competent authority against any person or persons charged with the commission of any crime or misdemeanor within the corporate limits of the city or within one mile thereof, and if in violation of any of the provisions of this act, they may pursue and continually follow and arrest such offender anywhere within the county of Wake; and in the performance of such duties they shall have all the power and authority of and be governed by the same provisions of the law as sheriffs and constables in their respective jurisdictions.

Persons violating ordinances may be pursued beyond corporate limits.

Shall attend police courts.

SEC. 21. That it shall also be the duty of the chief of police to attend upon the police court, to collect such fines, penalties and forfeitures as may be imposed by the mayor upon offenders for the violation of any of the provisions of this character [charter] or of the ordinances, rules and regulations of the board of aldermen made in pursuance hereof, of which he shall keep an exact record in a book to be furnished by the board of aldermen, showing the name and residence of the offender, the nature of the offense, the date of the hearing thereon before the mayor, the amount of the fine, penalty or forfeiture imposed, the date of its collection and the date of payment thereof by the chief of police to the treasurer. And the signature of the treasurer on the last column and the same line of each entry shall be the only sufficient voucher of the chief of police for such payment in each case.

Record shall be kept by chief of police.

DUTIES OF POLICE.

SEC. 22. It is hereby made the duty of the police department and force at all times of day or night, and the members of such force are hereby thereunto empowered to especially preserve the public peace, prevent crime, detect and arrest offenders, suppress riots which obstruct the free passage of public streets, sidewalks, parks and places; protect the rights of persons and property, guard the public health, preserve order at elections and all public meetings and assemblages, regulate the movement of teams and vehicles in streets, bridges, squares, parks and public places, and remove all nuisances in public streets, parks and highways, arrest all street mendicants and beggars, provide proper police attendance at fires, assist, advise and protect strangers and travellers in public streets and at railroad stations, carefully observe and inspect all places of public amusement, all places of business having licenses to carry on any business, all gambling houses, cock pits, rat pits and public common dance houses, and to repress and restrain all unlawful and disorderly conduct or practices therein; enforce and prevent the violation of all laws and ordinances in force in said city, and for these purposes to arrest all persons guilty of violating any law or ordinance for the suppression or punishment of crimes or offenses; to prevent as far as possible all injury to the city property and buildings, streets and sidewalks, to report to the chief of police any repairs needed and to perform such other duties as may be required of them by the board of aldermen or the chief of police or the mayor.

Duties and powers of police department.

They shall have authority, if resisted in the execution of their official duties, to summon a sufficient number of men to aid them in enforcing the law; and if any person so summoned shall refuse to assist, the policemen are hereby directed to report the names of such persons to the mayor, who is required to proceed against them as the law directs. They shall have power to enter the enclosure and house of any person without warrant, when they have good reason to believe that a felony or infamous crime has been or is about to be committed, for the apprehension of any person

May summon others to assist in making arrest.

May enter residences without warrant.

so offending, and if necessary to summon a posse to aid them, and all persons so summoned shall have like authority of entry and arrest.

Jailer shall receive certain persons without committment.

SEC. 23. That upon demand by a city policeman the sheriff or jailer of the county of Wake is hereby required, without a mittimus, to receive into the jail of the county as prisoner any person taken up in the night by the police force and to keep such person safely until morning, when the offender shall be taken before the mayor and shall be lawfully dealt with; and for such services the jailer shall be entitled to such fees as in other like cases.

Compensation of jailer.

Exempt from military and jury duty.

SEC. 24. No person holding office under the police department shall be liable to military or jury duty, and no officer or patrolman, while actually on duty, shall be liable to arrest on civil process.

OF THE TREASURER.

Trsasurer, custodian of public moneys.

SEC. 25. That it shall be the duty of the treasurer to call on all persons who may have in their hands any moneys or securities belonging to the city, which ought to be paid or delivered into the treasury, to receive and faithfully keep the same for the use of the city, and to disburse the funds upon the appropriation of the board of aldermen according to such orders as may be duly drawn on him in the manner hereinafter specified; he shall keep in a book provided for that purpose a fair and correct account of all moneys received and disbursed by him, together with the sources from whence they came, and the purposes for which they were appropriated, except the proceeds of fines, penalties and forfeitures imposed by the mayor, and collected and paid over to him by the chief of police, of which he shall keep an exact account in a separate book to be furnished by the board of aldermen, showing the name and residence of the offender, the nature of the offense, the date of the hearing thereon before the mayor, and the date and amount of the payment thereof by the chief of police to the treasurer, the information for which shall be filed by the chief of police at the time of payment, and shall submit said accounts to the aldermen whenever required to do so. During his continuance therein he shall faithfully perform all duties lawfully imposed on him as city treasurer, and at the expiration of his term of office, he shall deliver to his successor all the moneys, securities, books of record, and other property entrusted to him for use, safe keeping, disbursement or otherwise.

Shall keep record.

Orders drawn on treasurer.

SEC. 26. That all orders drawn on the treasurer shall be signed by the mayor and countersigned by the clerk and shall state the purpose for which the money was appropriated by the board of aldermen.

Sec. 27. That no claim against the city shall be paid until it shall have been audited and approved by the auditor and attested by his signature thereon. He shall keep a record and make monthly reports of such claims as are audited by him to the board of aldermen, and shall perform such other duties as the board may order. Claims against city, how verified.

THE COMMISSIONER OF THE SINKING FUND.

Sec. 28. That the commissioner of the sinking fund shall receive from the tax collector the whole of the special taxes collected for the purpose of paying the principal and interest of the bonds issued under chapter eighty, private acts of eighteen hundred and seventy-four and eighteen hundred and seventy-five, chapter thirty-five, private acts of eighteen hundred and eighty-five, and chapter one hundred and seventeen, private acts of eighteen hundred and eighty-nine, chapter one hundred and twenty-nine, private acts of eighteen hundred and ninety-three, and such other acts as may hereafter be passed which provide for the levying of a special tax by said city, and the commissioners shall give receipts to the collector for said payments, and pay the interest on the bonds issued under said acts at the time the said interest becomes due. And it shall be the duty of the said commissioner to demand said special taxes from time to time from the collector, and if not paid, to report the fact to the board. Moneys received by commissioner of sinking fund.

Sec. 29. That the said commissioner shall, from time to time, under the provisions of the acts set forth in the above section, when he shall have sufficient money in his hands, advertise for ten days in the daily newspapers for sealed proposals for the sale of the bonds of the city issued under said acts. Bids shall be opened in the presence of the mayor and treasurer, and such bids as are most advantageous for the city shall be accepted. But said officers, in their discretion, may refuse to accept any bids made, and advertise for additional proposals. Bonds of the city so purchased shall be cancelled by them. Sale and redemption of city bonds.

Sec. 30. That if, after reasonable diligence, none of said bonds can be purchased at their value or less, then the commissioner shall in like manner purchase any other bonds of the city, which bonds shall be made payable to the commissioner of the sinking fund, in trust for the City of Raleigh, and shall be held by him in trust for the holders of the bonds authorized by the said acts, mentioned in section twenty of this chapter, or shall make such investment of the funds in his hands as the finance When bonds can not be purchased. Investment of funds of city.

committee of the board of aldermen shall approve, preference being given to loans upon real estate in this city.

Annual report of commissioner.

SEC. 31. That the said commissioner shall make a report to the board annually at their meeting in the month of May, of the condition of the fund, and of his action since the last report.

OF THE ALDERMEN.

Majority of board of aldermen shall be competent to perform certain duties.

SEC. 32. That a majority of the board of aldermen shall be competent to perform all the duties herein provided for them, and for the proper government of the city, except as herein otherwise provided. They shall convene within five days next following their election for the transaction of business and fix regular stated times for meeting—not less than once a month during their term of office. Special meetings may also be held on the call of the mayor, with written notice to all of the aldermen, and on a call of a majority of the board, with written notice to the mayor and to such aldermen as shall not have joined in the call.

Time of meeting.

Special meetings.

Power of majority of aldermen to make ordinances, etc.

SEC. 33. That it shall be the duty of the aldermen to attend all the meetings of the board, unless unavoidably prevented from doing so, and when convened a majority of the board shall have power to make and to provide for the execution of such ordinances, by-laws, rules and regulations, and such fines, penalties and forfeitures for their violation as may be authorized by this act, consistent with the laws of the land, and necessary for the proper government of the city: *Provided*, that no penalty prescribed by the board of aldermen for the violation of any of the provisions of this act, or of any ordinance, by-law, rule or regulation made in pursuance hereof, shall exceed fifty dollars fine or thirty days' imprisonment.

Penalties prescribed by aldermen.

Powers of alder- to elect certain officers.

SEC. 34. That among the powers conferred on the board of aldermen are these: They may elect a chief of police, a street commissioner, a commissioner of the sinking fund and an auditor, neither of whom may be of their number; ascertain the location, increase, reduce and establish the width and grade, regulate the repairs and keep clear the streets, sidewalks and alleys of the city, extend, lay out, open, establish the width and grade, keep clean and maintain others; establish and regulate the public grounds, including Moore Square, Nash Square and Pullen Park, have charge of, improve, adorn and maintain the same, and protect the shade trees of the city; appoint and regulate a police force, and fix their salary, prohibit vagrancy and street begging; regulate, control, tax, license or prevent the establishment of junk and pawn shops, their keepers or brokers, and the sale of spirituous, vinous and malt liquors; regulate the speed of railroad locomotives, trains, and electric cars; the

Improvement of streets.

Shade trees.

Power to levy certain taxes.

charge for the carriage of persons, baggage and freight for hire and the license or prevention of the same; provide for the proper observance of the Sabbath, and the preservation of the peace, order and tranquillity of the city. They may provide a board of health, with prescribed powers and duties, and ways and means for the collection and preservation of vital statistics, promote the establishment and maintenance of public schools and educational facilities by the acquisition of land and the erection of buildings thereon, and the equipment thereof within the corporate limits of the city. They may also construct or contract for the construction of a system of sewerage for the city, and protect and regulate the same by adequate ordinances, and if it shall be necessary in obtaining proper outlets for the said system, to extend the same beyond the corporate limits of the city, then in such case, the board of aldermen shall have the power so to extend it, and both within and without the corporate limits to condemn land for the purpose of right-of-way, or other requirements of the system, the proceedings for such condemnation to be the same as those prescribed in chapter forty-nine, section six, of the private laws of eighteen hundred and sixty-two and eighteen hundred and sixty-three, or in the manner prescribed in chapter forty-nine, volume one, of The Code: *Provided*, that they shall contract no debt of any kind or degree, without the money in the treasury available for its payment, except for the actual and necessary current expenses of the city.

Board of health.

Public schools.

Sewerage.

May condemn land for sewerage purposes.

Proviso.

Certain debts shall not be incurred unless money is in treasury.

SEC. 35. That they may, from time to time, for the purpose of groding, paving, and otherwise improving the streets of the City of Raleigh, create and establish "assessment districts," within said city, and they may require every owner of real estate abutting the streets in any of the said districts, to pave one-fourth of the street fronting such lot, in such manner, and with such material as the street commissioner of said city may at the same time pave one-half thereof, and to enforce such requirement by proper fines and penalties, and upon the failure of such owner to do such paving, after twenty days' notice given by the chief of police to said owner, or if he be a non-resident of Wake county, to his agent, or if such non-resident have no agent in said county, or if personal notice can not be served upon the owner or agent, then after publication of a notice by the chief of police for thirty days in some newspaper published in said city, notifying said owner to do such paving, the City of Raleigh may have the same done, and the cost thereof may be assessed upon said property, and entered on the tax list of said city against said property for the current year, and the said assessment so entered on said tax list shall constitute a

Assessment districts.

Owner of property abutting may be required to share certain expenses.

lien upon said property, and the same may be collected either in the same manner that other taxes are collected, or by an action instituted in the name of the City of Raleigh against said owner in the superior court of Wake county, in the nature of an action of foreclosure, in which action judgment may be taken for the sale of the said property, to satisfy the amount due the said city from the owner thereof, as aforesaid.

License tax upon surface privies.

Sec. 36. That they may levy a license tax not exceeding one dollar a year upon each and every surface privy within the corporate limits of said city, and enforce the payment thereof by the occupant of the lot or premises upon which such surface privy is maintained and used by proper fines and penalties: *Provided*, that such occupant shall be thereby relieved from any and all liability as to the cleansing and condition of such surface privy, and the same shall be cleansed in a regular, systematic and sanitary manner by the City of Raleigh, under such laws, ordinances, rules and regulations as may be prescribed by the board of aldermen.

Proviso.

May establish sanitary districts.

Sec. 37. That they may, from time to time, whenever the health of the city may demand the same, establish and create anywhere in Raleigh township such sanitary district or districts as they may deem expedient, and the provisions of the foregoing section, as well as all sanitary laws, ordinances, rules and regulations as may now or hereafter exist under the provisions of this charter, shall apply to the householders or occupants of lots within said sanitary districts established as aforesaid as if the same were within the corporate limits and said occupants or householders residents of said city.

May compel abatement of nuisances.

Sec. 38. That they may require and compel the abatement of all nuisances within the city, or within one mile of the city limits, at the expense of the person causing the same, or the owner or tenant of the ground whereon the same shall be; they may also prevent the establishment within the city, or within one-half mile of the city limits, and may regulate, if allowed to be established, any slaughter-house or place, or the exercise within the city, or within one-half mile of the city limits, of any dangerous, offensive or unhealthy trade, business or employment.

May regulate establishment of slaughter houses.

May prevent running at large of dogs, cattle, etc.

Rate of speed at which horses, etc., may be driven.

Firing of guns, pistols, etc.

Sec. 39. That they may prohibit and prevent by penalties the running at large of dogs, hogs, cattle and other brutes; the riding or driving of horses or other animals at a speed greater than six miles per hour, or in a reckless manner within the city limits, and also the firing of guns, pistols, crackers, gun powder, or other explosive, combustible or dangerous materials in the streets, public grounds or elsewhere within the city.

Sec. 40. That they may establish and regulate the market,

and prescribe at what time and place and in what manner, within the corporation, marketable articles shall be sold; in what manner, whether by weight or measure, may be sold, grain, meal, flour (if not packed in barrels), fodder and unbaled hay, or oats in straw; may erect scales to weigh the same, appoint a weighmaster and fix his fees, and direct by whom they shall be paid; appoint a keeper of the market, prescribe his duties and fees, and shall also have power to prevent forestalling and regrating.

May establish and regulate market.

Keeper of market may be appointed.

SEC. 41. That they may establish all public buildings necessary and proper for the city, and prevent the erection or establishment of wooden buildings in any part of the city where they may increase the danger by fire.

Public buildings.

SEC. 42. That they may require the owner or lessee of any lot or premises within the city who shall desire to erect a building thereon, or to add to, remodel or alter any building or buildings already built thereon, or make other improvements on the same, if said buildings, additions, alterations or other improvements shall cost the estimated sum of one hundred and fifty dollars, to take out a building permit, before the clerk of said city, for which a fee not exceding twenty-five cents may be charged, under such rules and regulations as may be prescribed by ordinance, and to enforce the same by proper fines and penalties against said owner or lessee.

Owners of certain buildings may be required to take out building permits.

Fee.

SEC. 43. That they may appoint a board of building inspectors to consist of not less than three, or more than five freeholders, of said city, to which the chief of fire department shall be added as chairman *ex offcio*, and prescribe the duties of said board of building inspectors, and provide by ordinance such rules and regulations concerning the construction and material of buildings within the corporate limits of said city, with a view of protecting life and health, in case of fire, accident or other causes, as they may deem necessary, and enforce the same by proper fines and penalties.

Board of building inspectors.

Duties.

SEC. 44. That they may provide graveyards in or near the city, and regulate the same; may appoint and pay a keeper, and compel the keeping and return of bills of mortality, and they may prohibit further interments in the city cemetery.

Provision for cemeteries.

SEC. 45. That they may provide for the establishment, organization, equipment and government of fire companies, and appoint fire commissioners from their number, and in all cases of a fire, a majority of the fire commissioners may, if they deem it necessary to stop the progress of the fire, cause any house to be blown up or pulled down, and the removal of any other property, for which they shall not be responsible to any one in damages; and in case the presence of a majority of the fire commis-

Fire companies.

Fire commissioners in certain cases may order buildings destroyed.

sioners can not be had, the mayor, together with two aldermen of the city, to be selected by him, shall perform the duties prescribed for the fire commissioners in this section.

Precaution against contagious diseases.

SEC. 46. That they may take such measures as they deem effectual to prevent the entrance into the city, or the spreading therein of any contagious or infectious disease; may stop, detain and examine for that purpose every person coming from places believed to be infected with such disease; may establish and regulate hospitals within the city, or within three miles thereof; may cause any person in the city suspected to be infected with such disease, and whose stay may endanger its health, to be removed to the hospital; may remove from the city or destroy any furniture or other articles which shall be suspected of being tainted or infected with contagious or infectious disease, or of which there shall be reasonable cause to apprehend that they may pass into such a state as to generate and propagate disease; and in case any person shall be removed to the hospital, the corporation may recover of such person before the mayor the expense of his removal, support, nursing and medical attendance, and burial expenses, in case of death.

Hospitals

REVENUE.

Moneys raised from certain sources

SEC. 47. That all moneys arising from taxes, fines, penalties, forfeitures, or any other sources whatsoever, shall be the property of the city, and be paid into the city treasury, where it shall remain until lawfully appropriated by a majority of the board of aldermen in specific items, for the exclusive use and benefit of the city, and the people resident therein, unless otherwise expressly provided in this act.

SEC. 48. That in order to raise a fund for the expenses incident to the proper government of the city, the aldermen may annually levy and collect the following taxes, namely:

Ad valorem tax.

(1) On all real and personal property within the corporate limits, including money on hand, solvent credits, investments in bonds, stocks, and all other subjects taxed by the general assembly *ad valorem*, except incomes, a tax not exceeding one dollar on every hundred dollars value.

Polls.

(2) On all taxable polls resident in the city on the first day of June of each year, or so resident within sixty days next preceding that day, a tax not exceeding three dollars a poll.

Laws regulating attachment and garnishment applicable.

(3) That in the collection of all city taxes, upon property or polls, the general law of the state regulating attachment and garnishment shall be applicable, and the mayor and chief of police shall have the same power as that allowed by the general law to justices of the peace and sheriffs in such cases.

(4) Upon every omnibus used for the carriage of persons for

hire, a license tax not exceeding fifteen dollars a year; upon every hack, carriage, or other vehicle, including express wagons used for the carriage of persons or baggage for hire, and upon every dray used for the transportation of freight or other articles for hire, a license tax not exceeding five dollars a year; and a discrimination shall be made between one- and two-horse vehicles. Omnibuses, hacks for hire, etc

(5) Upon all male dogs kept in the city and which may be so kept on the first day of June, a tax not exceeding three dollars; and upon every bitch, not exceeding five dollars. Dogs.

(6) Upon all swine and goats not prohibited by the aldermen to remain in the city, when confined, a tax not exceeding three dollars a head. Swine and goats.

(7) Upon all encroachments on the trees [streets], or sidewalks by porches, piazzas, stairways, passages or other projections or excavations suffered, or allowed by the aldermen, a tax not exceeding one dollar nor less than twenty-five cents per square foot. On porches, etc. Encroaching on sidewalks.

(8) Upon every express company, and upon every telegraph or telephone company doing business in the city, a tax not exceeding one per centum of its gross receipts in the city, to be given in upon oath by the managing agent of such company annually, at the time when other taxes are listed, and under the same penalty as that prescribed in the law of the state for the failure to give in. Express, telephone and telegraph companies.

(9) Upon all shares and certificates of stock issued by every bank, banking association or other incorporated institution located within the corporate limits, whether such institution [or] banking association has been organized under the laws of this state or of the United States, *ad valorem*, a tax not exceeding one dollar on every hundred dollars value: *Provided*, that the owners of such shares or certificates of shares of stock are residents of the city, and that the assessment shall be with regard to the value of the stock on the first day of June annually: *And provided further*, that the value of the property of such bank or association otherwise taxed by said city and its property exempt from taxation, be deducted from the aggregate amount of such bank or association's capital stock. Shares and certificates of stock. Proviso. Proviso. Certain deductions.

(10) Upon every stud-horse, jackass or bull used for the purpose of breeding within the corporate limits of said city, a license tax not exceeding twenty-five dollars a year. Stud-horse, jackasses and bulls.

Sec. 49. That the citizens of Raleigh, and others liable to be taxed under this charter, shall, on the day prescribed for listing state and county taxes, render on oath to the clerk of the city, who is hereby constituted a commissioner of affidavit for that purpose, on a blank to be prepared and furnished by the board Tax returns under oath.

of aldermen, a list of their property and subjects for which they may be liable to be taxed, under all the rules and penalties prescribed in this charter. The list shall state the age of the party with reference to his liability to a poll tax, and shall also contain a verified statement of all the real and personal property of every kind, and such interest and estates therein as are taxable, moneys, credits, investments in bonds, stocks, joint stock companies, annuities or otherwise not herein excepted, and all other subjects taxed by this charter and by the general assembly in possession or under control or in charge of the person required to render said list, either as owner or holder thereof, or as parent, husband, guardian, trustee, executor, administrator, receiver, accounting officer, partner, agent, factor or otherwise. The party listing shall also swear to the true value of all property, choses in action and other subjects listed, except land, which oath shall be in the following form, to-wit: "I ...., do solemnly swear (or affirm) that the list furnished by me contains a true and accurate list of all property which by law I am required to list for taxation, and that the value affixed thereon by me is a true valuation of the same, according to my best knowledge, information and belief. So help me, God." Any person making a false return shall be deemed guilty of perjury. Property held in trust, or as agent, guardian, executor or administrator, or in right of a *feme covert*, shall be returned on separate lists. Persons owning shares in incorporated companies within the city limits taxable by this charter are not required to deliver to the clerk a list thereof, but the president or other chief officer of such corporation shall deliver to the clerk a list of all shares of stock held therein, and the value thereof, and the tax assessed on shares of stock in such corporations shall be paid by the corporations respectively.

Tax list shall contain verified statement.

Form of oath.

Persons making false return guilty of perjury.

Presidents of incorporated companies required to deliver list of stock.

Companies having their principal office in Raleigh shall make certain sworn statement.

SEC. 50. That all bridge, express, gas, manufacturing, street railroad and transportation companies, and all other companies and associations incorporated under the laws of this state, situate, or having its principal place of business within the corporate limits of the city, shall, in addition to the other property required by this act to be listed, make out and deliver to the clerk a sworn statement of the amount of its capital stock, setting forth particularly: First, the name and location of the company or association; second, the amount of capital stock authorized and the number of shares into which such capital stock is divided; third, the amount of capital stock paid up; fourth, the market value, or if no market value, then the actual value of the shares of stock; fifth, the assessed valuation of all its real and personal property, which real and personal property shall be listed and valued as other real and personal property is listed and assessed under this charter. The aggregate amount of the fifth item shall be deducted from the aggregate value of its shares of stock as provided by the fourth item, and the remainder, if any, shall be listed by the clerk in the name of such company or corporation as capital stock thereof. In all cases of failure or refusal of any person, officer, company or association to make such return or statement, it shall be the duty of the clerk to make such returns or statement from the best information which he can obtain.

Refusal to make such returns.

SEC. 51. That every bank (not incorporated), banker, broker, or stock jobber, shall, at the time fixed by this charter for listing personal property, make out and furnish the clerk a sworn statement showing:

Sworn statements to be furnished by banks, brokers and jobbers.

(1) The amount of property on hand or in transit.

Property on hand or in transit.

(2) The amount of funds in the hands of other banks, bankers, brokers or others subject to draft.

Funds.

(3) The amount of checks or other cash items not included in either of the preceding items.

Checks and other cash items.

(4) The amount of bills receivable, discounted or purchased and other credits due or to become due, including accounts receivable and interest accrued but not due, and interest due and unpaid.

Bills receivable, etc.

(5) The amount of bonds and stocks of every kind, state and county warrants and other municipal securities, and shares of capital stock of joint stock or other companies or corporations held as an investment, or any way representing assets.

Bonds and stocks on hand.

(6) All other property pertaining to said business other than real estate, which real estate shall be listed and assessed as other real estate is listed and assessed under this act.

All other property.

(7) Amount of deposits made with them by other parties.

Deposits.

(8) The amount of all accounts payable other than current deposit accounts.

Accounts payable.

(9) The amount of bonds and other securities exempt by law from taxation, specifying the amount and kind of each, the same being included in the preceding fifth item.

Bonds and other securities exempt from law.

The aggregate amount of the first, second and third items in said statement shall be listed as moneys. The amount of the sixth item shall be listed the same as other similar personal property is listed under this charter. The aggregate amount of the seventh and eighth items shall be deducted from the aggregate amount of the fourth item of said statement, and the amount of the remainder, if any, shall be listed as credits. The aggregate amount of the ninth item shall be deducted from the aggregate amount of the fifth item of such statement, and the remainder shall be listed as bonds or stocks.

How listed.

SEC. EB. That all the real and personal property of any railroad, or so much thereof as may be located within the corporate limits

Real and personal property of railroads.

of said city, including road beds, rights-of-way, main and side-tracks, depot buildings and grounds, section and tool-houses, machine and repair shops, general office buildings and store-houses, rolling-stock and personal property necessary for the construction, maintenance and successful operation thereof, shall be listed for purposes of taxation by the principal officers or agents of such companies with the clerk in the manner provided by law for the listing and valuation of real and personal property, and shall be taxed as other real and personal property, under the rules, regulations and methods now or hereafter to be provided by the general assembly of North Carolina for ascertaining and listing the value thereof.

Companies and persons failing to render list shall pay double tax.

Sec. 53. That if any person or company shall fail to render to the clerk the list of property and other taxables required to be rendered by this charter within the time prescribed for listing state and county taxes, such person or company shall pay double the tax assessed on any subject for which said person is liable to be taxed.

Clerk shall examine persons on oath.

Sec. 54. That the clerk shall be particular to examine each person on oath as to whether he has other property than that stated in his return which he may claim is not liable to taxation. Such property, except bonds of the United States and of this state, shall be entered and noted on the tax list.

Clerk shall make out alphabetical list of persons making returns.

Sec. 55. That from the returns and lists made as provided by this charter, the clerk shall, within thirty days after the expiration of the time for taking said lists, make out in a book kept or provided for that purpose an alphabetical list of the persons, companies and owners of property who have so made their returns, in the same manner as tax lists are made out by law for the state and county taxes. And the said clerk shall copy in said book the assessments on file in the register of deeds office for Wake county, of all property within the city limits.

BOARD OF EQUALIZATION.

Three persons to be appointed by aldermen and to be known as board of equalization.

Sec. 56. That in the month of May, eighteen hundred and ninety-five, and biennially thereafter, the board of aldermen shall appoint three discreet and proper persons among the electors of the City of Raleigh, to be constituted and who shall constitute and be styled "the board of equalization of the City of Raleigh," and the persons so appointed shall continue in office for two years, and until their successors are duly appointed and qualified, unless removed from office or otherwise incapacitated to hold office as herein provided. No member of the board of aldermen, and no person holding an office or appointment under the board of aldermen, shall be eligible or qualified to act as a member of the board of equalization.

Term of office.

Who is qualified.

SEC. 57. That before entering on their duties the members of said board shall take and subscribe before the mayor or some justice of the peace the oath prescribed in section four of article six of the constitution of the state, and cause the same to be filed in the office of the clerk of said city.

Members of said board shall take oath.

SEC. 58. That said board shall elect from their number a chairman, who shall have power to administer oaths and issue subpœnas for witnesses to appear before the board, who shall be required to appear and testify, under like pains and penalties as if summoned to the superior court. In the absence of the chairman at any meeting of the board, a temporary chairman shall be chosen who, during such meeting, shall have and exercise the powers of the regular chairman.

Election of chairman of board.

SEC. 59. That as soon as the tax list can be completed by the city clerk, the same shall be by him delivered to the board of equalization, which board shall have the power, and it shall be their duty, to act conjointly with the board of county commissioners of Wake county in equalizing the valuation of all property within the corporate limits of said city, and said boards conjointly shall have all the powers given to the board of commissioners of a county to revise a tax list.

Tax list shall be delivered by clerk to board of equalization.

SEC. 60. That said boards shall conjointly and carefully examine the tax lists of the city and county and shall equalize the valuations of all property within the city limits, so that each tract or lot of land, or article of personal property, and all other subjects of taxation shall be entered on the respective tax lists of the city and county at its true value in money, and shall cause the respective tax lists to conform as nearly as possible, and for this purpose they shall have power to increase, modify, add to and change the tax lists as made out, so that the valuations of all property within the city limits, so that each near uniform as possible, and in doing so they shall observe the following rules and shall have the following powers:

Duty of board.

Empowered to increase or modify returns.

(1) They shall, after notifying the owner or agent, raise the valuation of such tracts or lots of real property, or articles of personal property, and all other subjects taxed by the charter, as in their opinion have been returned below their true value, to such price or sum as they may believe to be the true value thereof.

After notifying owner or agent may raise value of tracts.

(2) They shall reduce the valuation of such tracts and lots of real property or articles of personal property, and other subjects taxed by the charter, as in their opinion have been returned above their value as compared with the average valuation of real and personal property of said city. In regard to real property, they shall have due regard to the relative situation,

May reduce valuations.

quality of soil, improvements, natural and artificial advantages possessed by each tract or lot and the uses thereof.

Shall correct certain returns.

(3) Whenever said board of equalization shall have reasonable ground to believe that any person, company or corporation has failed to give in a true and accurate list of such personal property and other subjects taxable by the charter as he, it or they are required to furnish, with the true value thereof, it shall be their duty to ascertain the same and insert the same and the true value thereof in the tax list.

May subpœna witnesses, examine certain records, etc.

(4) In performing the duties required of them, the said board of equalization shall have power to subpœna, compel the presence of and examine witnesses and parties who list or fail to list, and send for and require to be brought before them and examine records, books, papers and such other things as they may deem proper to be used in evidence before them, upon the same rules and penalties as are provided for superior courts.

Certain powers to ascertain true value of property.

(5) The said board of equalization, on tendering the prescribed oath, may take a list of any person, company or corporation applying to list his or its taxables at any meeting held on or before the first day of October, upon the applicant paying the clerk twenty-five cents for recording the same; and in ascertaining the value of property and taxables thus listed, said board shall have the same powers to investigate and ascertain the true value thereof as is herein given them in other cases.

Aldermen shall levy tax when lists have been revised.

Sec. 61. That as soon as the tax list can be revised by the board of equalization, the board of aldermen shall proceed to levy the tax on such subjects of taxation as they shall determine, and shall place the tax list in the hands of the tax collector for collection, who shall proceed forthwith in the collection and shall complete the same on or before the first day of December next ensuing, and shall pay the moneys as they are collected to the treasurer. On the first day of December there shall be a penalty of one per centum added to the amount of all taxes due, and an additional one per centum on the first day of each month thereafter until the same are paid.

When tax collector shall collect taxes.

Penalty for failure to pay taxes before December 1st.

Tax on shares of bank stock to be paid by cashier.

Sec. 62. The taxes imposed upon the shares or certificates of shares of stock in any bank or banking association (state or national), shall be paid by the cashier or other principal officer of such bank or banking association, directly to the city tax collector, within thirty days after notice from said tax collector of the amount of tax due, and upon the failure of said cashier or principal officer to pay the tax collector as aforesaid, he shall forthwith institute an action against the bank or banking association for the recovery of the same in the proper court in said county of Wake.

Action against bank on failure to pay said tax.

the price of each, which shall be entered on the book of pro-

When taxes may be collected by distress.

Sec. 63. That if any person liable to taxes on subjects directed to be listed shall fail to pay them within the time prescribed for collection, the collector shall proceed forthwith to collect the same by distress and sale, all sales to be made after public advertisement for the space of ten days in some newspaper published in the city if the property to be sold be personalty, and of twenty days if the property be realty. And the said collector shall have the right to levy upon and sell any personal property situated outside of the limits of the city and within the county of Wake belonging to a delinquent taxpayer of the city in order to enforce the payment of taxes due the city by said delinquent.

Empowered to sell certain personal property.

Tax on lot a lien

Sec. 64. That the tax due on any lot or other subdivision of land is hereby declared to be a lien on the same, and if it shall remain unpaid on the first day of December next after the assessment, the tax collector shall either proceed to collect the same by a levy and sale of personal property belonging to the owner of said lot, or shall report the fact to the aldermen, together with a particular description of the real estate, and thereupon the aldermen shall direct the same to be sold at the court-house door in the city of Raleigh by the collector. The collector shall, before selling the same, make a full advertisement of the said real estate at the court-house door, an at three or more public places in said city for twenty days, and shall also serve upon the owners thereof a written or printed notice of the taxes due and the day of sale, but such notice need not be given to any person having or claiming any lien on said land by way of mortgage or otherwise. Whenever the owners are not in the city, or for any cause can not be served with notice, then the advertisement of real estate belonging to such owners shall be made for one week in some newspaper published in the city of Raleigh, and the collector shall divide the said land into as many parts as may be convenient (for which purpose he is authorized to employ a surveyor), and he shall sell as many thereof as may be required to pay said taxes and all expenses attendant thereon. If the same can not be conveniently divided, the collector shall sell the whole; and if no person shall pay the whole of the taxes and expenses for the whole land, the same shall be struck off to the city, and if not redeemed as hereinafter provided, shall belong to the said city in fee: *Provided*, that such sale shall in no case affect the lien of any lawful incumbrance which can be shown to have been listed and taxes paid thereon to the city.

Advertisement shall be made of property to be sold for taxes.

City may become purchaser

Collector shall return account of proceedings to aldermen.

Sec. 65. That the collector shall return an account of his proceedings to the aldermen, specifying the portions into which the land was divided, and the purchaser or purchasers thereof, and

ceedings of the aldermen; and if there shall be a surplus after paying said taxes, the same shall be paid into the city treasury, subject to the demands of the owner.

Owner or agent of land may redeem same within a year.

SEC. 66. That the owner of any land sold under the provisions of this charter, his heirs, executors and administrators, or any person acting for them, may redeem the same within one year after the sale by paying to the purchaser the sum by him paid, and twenty-five per centum on the amount of taxes and expenses, and the treasurer shall refund to him, without interest, the proceeds, less double the amount of taxes.

When real estate thus sold and not redeemed.

SEC. 67. That if the real estate sold as aforesaid shall not be redeemed within the time specified, the corporation shall convey the same in full to the purchaser or his assigns, by deed executed under the hand of the mayor and two aldermen, attested by the corporate seal; and the recitals in such conveyance, or in any other conveyance of land sold for taxes due the city, that the taxes were due, or of any other matter required to be true or done before the sale might be made, shall be *prima facie* evidence that the same was true and done.

Real estate of infants and persons non compos mentis shall not be sold.

SEC. 68. That the real estate of infants or persons *non compos mentis* shall not be sold for tax; and when the same shall be owned by such, in common with other persons free of such disability, the sale shall be made according to section ninety-two of chapter ninety-nine of the Revised Code.

Special taxes, aldermen may levy.

SEC. 69. That in addition to the subjects listed for taxation the aldermen may levy a tax on the following subjects, the amount of which tax, when fixed, shall be collected by the chief of police instantly, and if the same be not paid on demand, the same may be recovered by suit, or the articles upon which the tax is imposed, or any other property of the owner, may be forthwith distrained and sold to satisfy the same, namely:

Itinerant merchants.

(1) Upon all itinerant merchants or peddlers offering to vend in the city, a license tax not exceeding fifty dollars a year, except such only as sell books, charts, maps or wares of their own manufacture, but not excepting vendors of medicine by whomsoever manufactured, and not more than one person shall peddle under a single license: *Provided*, that such itinerant merchants or peddler, shall comply with such rules and regulations as the board of aldermen may make in respect to the times, places and manner of vending under such licenses.

Proviso.

Billiard tables, bowling-alleys, etc.

(2) Upon every billiard table, bowling-alley or alley of like kind, bowling saloon, bagatelle table, pool table, or table, stand, or place for any other game or play, wheels of fortune or any game of chance, with or without a name, kept for hire or kept in a house where liquor is sold, or a house used or connected with such a house, or used or connected with a hotel a restaurant, or continuous [contiguous] or adjacent thereto, a license tax not exceeding fifty dollars.

(3) Upon every permission by the board of aldermen to retail spirituous, vinous or malt liquors, a tax of three hundred dollars, and for every permission to sell spirituous, vinous or malt liquors in quantities of one quart and less than five gallons, a license tax of one hundred dollars, and in quantities of five gallons or more, a license tax of one hundred dollars: *Provided*, that they may issue a single license for the sale of beer only, and charge therefor not exceeding one hundred dollars a year. Retailers of spirituous, vinous or malt liquors.

(4) Upon every company of circus-riders or performers, by whatever name called, who shall exhibit within the city or within one mile thereof, a license tax not exceeding fifty dollars for each performance or separate exhibition, and upon every side-show connected therewith, a license tax not exceeding ten dollars, the tax to be paid before exhibition, and if not, to be doubled. Circus-riders. Side-shows.

(5) Upon every person or company exhibiting in the city, or within one mile thereof, any stage or theatrical plays, sleight-of-hand performances, rope dancing, tumbling, wire dancing or menageries, a tax not exceeding twenty dollars for every three hours allowed for exhibiting, the tax to be paid before exhibiting, or the same shall be doubled. Theatrical plays.

(6) Upon every exhibition for reward, of artificial curiosities (models of useful inventions excepted), in the city or within one mile thereof, a tax not to exceed twenty dollars, to be paid before exhibition, or the same shall be doubled. Exhibitions for reward.

(7) Upon each show or exhibition of any other kind, and on each concert for reward, in the city or within one mile thereof, and on every strolling musician, a tax not exceeding ten dollars, to be paid before exhibition, or the same shall be doubled. Shows or exhibitions of any other kind.

(8) Upon every cow, goat or hog running at large in the city may be levied a tax not exceeding three dollars, and upon every horse, mule or bull going at large, not exceeding ten dollars, and every such animal may be seized and impounded in an enclosure, which shall be established and kept by the city therefor, and if the owner, on being notified, will not pay the tax, the animal shall be sold therefor at the pound, after three days' notice at the court-house. Cows, goats and hogs running at large. Animals shall be sold on failure of owner to pay tax.

(9) Upon every dog which may be kept or brought into the city, after the first day of June, to be kept therein, a tax not exceeding two dollars for the permission to keep such dog in the city, which permission shall not extend further than the last day of May, next ensuing. Upon dogs brought into the city after June 1st.

(10) Upon every auctioneer or crier of goods at public auction, subject to the limitations provided in section 2281 of The Code, a license tax not exceeding fifty dollars a year. Auctioneers and criers of goods.

(11) Upon every stock and bond broker, junk dealer and pawn-

Stock brokers, sewing machine agents, etc.

broker, sewing machine or bicycle company or agent for such company, dealer in or manufacturer's agent of musical instruments, keeper of sales stables or stock yards, doing business in the city, a license not exceeding twenty-five dollars a year.

Lawyers, physicians, dentists, etc.

(12) Upon every lawyer, physician, dentist, cotton broker, bill poster, street huckster, photographer, merchandise or produce broker, ice dealer, dealer in wood and coal or either, insurance company or insurance agency for every company represented, and every skating rink or shooting gallery, a license tax not exceeding ten dollars a year.

Surface privies.

(13) Upon every surface privy as provided in this charter a license tax not exceeding one dollar a year for each of said licenses.

Other occupations and professions.

(14) Upon every other occupation, profession or business not herein specially named a license tax not exceeding ten dollars a year.

Auctioneers shall give bond.

SEC. 70. That every auctioneer licensed by the board of aldermen shall give bond in the sum of five thousand dollars with approved security, and shall be entitled to charge two and a half per centum commission on the amount of his sales unless otherwise agreed between him and the owner of the goods sold; and every person who cries or sells goods at auction shall be considered an auctioneer.

License shall not be granted by commissioners of Wake county to retail liquor within corporate limits of Raleigh without permission.

SEC. 71. That it shall not be lawful for the commissioners of Wake county to grant any license to sell spirituous, vinous or malt liquors within the limits of the city or within one mile thereof without permission in writing, attested by the clerk of the board of aldermen and exhibited to the county commissioners and filed with the clerk of the board of county commissioners; the same shall be utterly void, and the person obtaining such license shall be liable to indictment as in other cases of selling without license, and for every offense of selling shall moreover forfeit and pay to the city the sum of twenty dollars.

Necessary land may be condemned by city.

SEC. 72. That when any land or right-of-way shall be required by said City of Raleigh for the purpose of opening new streets or for other objects allowed by this charter, and for want of agreement as to the value thereof the same can not be purchased from the owner or owners, the same may be taken at a valuation to be made by five freeholders of the city, to be chosen by the aldermen, who shall receive a per diem of one dollar each; and in making said valuation said freeholders, after being duly sworn by the mayor or a justice of the peace of the county, or a clerk of a court of record, shall take into consideration the loss or damage which may accrue to the owner or owners in consequence of the land or right-of-way being surrendered, also any special benefit or advantage such owner may receive from the opening of such street or other improvement, and shall state the value and

Arbitrators.

Duty of arbitrators.

amount of each, and the excess of loss or damage over and above the advantages shall form the measure of valuation of said land or right-of-way: *Provided, nevertheless*, that if any person over whose land the said street may pass or improvement be erected, or the aldermen shall be dissatisfied with the valuation thus made, then and in that case either party may have an appeal to the next superior court of Wake county to be held thereafter; and the said freeholders shall return to the court to which the appeal is taken their valuation, with the proceeding thereon, and the land so valued by the freeholders shall vest in the city so long as it may be used for the purposes of the same as soon as the valuation may be paid or lodged in the hands of the clerk of the superior court (in case of its refusal by the owner of the land): *Provided further*, that in case of the discontinuance of the use of the land and its reversion to the owner, the city may remove any improvement erected under its authority and expense within sixty days of such reversion.

Proviso.

Either party may appeal.

Proviso.

SEC. 73. That every owner of a lot, or person having as great an interest therein as a lease for three years, which shall front any street on which a sidewalk has been established and graded shall improve in such manner as the aldermen may direct such sidewalk as far as it may extend along such lot, and on failure to do so within twenty days after notice by the chief of police to said owner, or if he be a non-resident of the county of Wake, to his agent, or if such non-resident have no agent in said county, or if personal notice can not be served upon the owner or agent, then after publication of a notice by the chief of police for thirty days in some newspaper in Raleigh, calling on the owner to make such repairs, the aldermen may cause the same to be repaired either with brick, stone or gravel, at their discretion, and the expenses shall be paid by the person in default.

Owners of property may be required to repair sidewalks fronting property.

Said expense shall be a lien upon said lot, and if it is not paid within sixty days after completion of the repairs such lot or the interest of said lessee may be sold, or enough of the same to pay such expenses and costs, under the same rules, regulations and restrictions, rights of redemption and savings as are prescribed in this charter for the sale of land for unpaid taxes, or an action of the collection of the costs of said repairs may be instituted in the superior court of Wake county in the name of the City of Raleigh against said owner or lessee in the nature of an action of foreclosure, in which action judgment may be taken for the sale of said lot or the interest of said lessee as the case may be, to satisfy the amount due the city by the owner or lessee as aforesaid.

Expenses for repairs a lien on property.

Rights of redemption.

SEC. 74. That no basement, cellar, area, passage, entrance or other opening shall be excavated, made, built or permitted to

Regulations regarding cellars, verandas, piazzas, etc.

remain under any sidewalks; nor shall any veranda, piazza, platform, entrance, stairway, passage, building or other projection or construction whatsoever be permitted to occupy any space on or over any sidewalk in the city whereby the free and safe passage of persons may be hindered, obstructed, delayed or in anywise endangered, unless annually licensed and taxed by the board of aldermen.

Books, records, etc., of city shall be open to inspection.

SEC. 75. That all the books, records, documents and papers of every name and nature belonging to the city government or to the officers thereof in the performance of their official duties shall be open to the inspection of any citizen and taxpayer of the city at all times during ordinary business hours.

Officers of city shall make out annual statement of receipts and disbursements.

SEC. 76. That on the first Monday of March in each year all of the officers of the city shall make out and file with the city clerk a fair transcript of all receipts and disbursements in the departments over which they preside; all the officers of the city having any of the property of the city in their charge shall report an inventory of the same, and each committee of the board of aldermen shall submit annual reports, all of which the board of aldermen shall cause to be printed in book form for the general information of the citizens.

Officers and employees not elected by vote of people, how removed.

SEC. 77. That any officer or employee not elected by a vote of the people may be removed from office or employment at any time by a two-thirds vote of the board for misbehavior or neglect of official duty; and if any officer shall fail to give the bond required by the board or by this act his office shall ipso facto be vacant.

Mayor or aldermen shall not become contractors for work to be done by the city.

SEC. 78. That no mayor or alderman or other officer of the city shall directly or indirectly become a contractor for work to be done by the city.

OF CRIMES AND PENALTIES.

Additional crimes and misdemeanors.

SEC. 79. That in addition to the crimes and penalties hereinbefore enumerated and in addition to the crimes and penalties denounced by the public laws of North Carolina applicable hereto are these:

Persons illegally registering and voting.

(1) Any person who having entered, sojourned and remained in the City of Raleigh in the capacity of a state or county officer, clerk or employee, or as a teacher, student or employee of any public or private school therein, or as an officer, employee or inmate of any hospital, asylum, soldiers home or other institution of temporary employment, residence or detention whatsoever, and while so sojourning or remaining in any such capacity shall offer or attempt to register as a voter or to vote therein, or who shall register or vote therein, and any person who shall advise, counsel, aid or assist any such person to register or to vote

therein; and any registrar, judge, poll holder or other officer of registration or election in the city whatsoever who shall willfully or knowingly register the name or poll the vote of any such person or permit it to be done in his precinct, shall for every such offense forfeit and pay a fine of fifty dollars, or be imprisoned at hard labor thirty days, and if at the expiration of thirty days from the filing of authentic information of such offense before the mayor he shall have failed to prosecute the offender or to enforce the penalty herein provided, then any elector who will first sue in the name of the city before the mayor or the superior court of Wake county, may recover such fine or fines to his own use, and enforce the payment thereof and of the costs as herein provided in case of non-payment to the city.

Penalty.

(2) Every mayor of the city of Raleigh who shall fail, neglect or refuse to attend at and keep open his office for the transaction of official business as required by this act, without good and sufficient reasons satisfactory to the board of aldermen, shall be removed from office by the board of aldermen, three-fourths of the members concurring therein.

On failure of mayor to attend to duties of his office.

(3) Any mayor or member of the board of aldermen who shall fail, neglect or refuse in due time to call and provide for the election by the people of city officers and for other purposes prescribed in this act; every officer of the city of Raleigh who shall fail, neglect or refuse to keep proper books of account showing all their transactions with the city, or to make proper returns and reports thereof, or to keep the books of his office open to public inspection, or to turn over and account for all the proceeds of all the fines, penalties and forfeitures imposed by the mayor as required by the provisions of this act; or who, having been elected to the office of mayor, alderman or other officer of the city, with his full knowledge and consent, shall fail, neglect or refuse to qualify; or who, having been elected to such office, shall enter upon duty, or attempt to do so, without having first taken, subscribed and filed with the clerk the oath of office, nor given bond (if any required by the provisions of this act), shall be guilty of a misdemeanor, and upon satisfactory proof thereof before the mayor or before the superior court of Wake county in case the mayor be accused, shall be adjudged to pay a fine not exceeding fifty dollars or to be imprisoned not exceeding thirty days.

Failure of mayor or other city officers to perform certain duties a misdemeanor.

Penalty.

(4) Any alderman of the city who shall fail, neglect or refuse to attend any regular meeting of the board or any special meeting called by a majority of the board in which he joined, or who, having had written notice by mail or otherwise of a special meeting of the board called by the mayor or a majority of the board in which he did not join, shall fail, neglect or refuse to attend such regular or special meeting or to give to the board on or before

Failure or neglect of aldermen to perform certain duties.

the next ensuing regular meeting thereof a satisfactory excuse therefor, shall forfeit and pay to the chief of police to the use of the city the sum of three dollars for each offense: *Provided*, that if any alderman be absent from three successive regular meetings of the board without a satisfactory excuse therefor, it shall be the duty of the board of aldermen to declare his office vacant and proceed to elect his successor.

Penalty.

Aldermen or other officers making contracts, debts, etc., for other than certain purposes guilty of infamous crime.

(5) Any alderman or other officer of the city who shall vote for, support or contract any debts against the city for purposes other than the necessary current expenses of the city, without money in the treasury available for its payments, or who shall make any appropriation, donation, gift, sale, transfer or payment directly or indirectly of any money, property or credit of the city for any use or purpose other than for the exclusive use and benefit of the City of Raleigh and of the people resident therein unless herein otherwise provided, shall be guilty of an infamous crime, and upon conviction thereof in the superior court shall be adjudged to pay a fine not less than one thousand dollars nor more than five thousand dollars, or to be imprisoned not less than one year nor more than five years, or both such fine and imprisonment in the discretion of the court, and shall be liable to an action at law for the recovery of the whole amount so unlawfully contracted or misappropriated, paid or transferred.

Penalty.

Agents and attorneys failing or refusing to list property or performing certain acts guilty of a misdemeanor.

(6) Any person whose duty it shall be as principal, agent, attorney, trustee, officer or otherwise, for an individual, company, association, corporation or otherwise to make, return, list or report of property or poll for taxation under the provisions of this act, who shall fail, neglect or refuse to list the same or shall list the same in the name of any other than the true owner, or who, being interrogated by the clerk or any member of the board of equalization respecting such property, shall refuse to answer, or shall answer falsely concerning the same, or who shall refuse to fill out, subscribe and make oath to his returns of such property or poll for taxation; and any person who shall interfere and by threats, force or violence prevent or attempt to prevent the lawful removal of any person into any hospital within or without the city by the authorities thereof; or who shall excavate, construct, build, use, keep or mantain any cellar, basement, area, passage, entrance or way under any sidewalk, or build, construct, keep, use or maintain any veranda, piazza, platform, building or stairway or other projection or construction upon or over any sidewalk in the city, whereby the free and safe passage of persons may be hindered, delayed, obstructed or in any way endangered, or who shall engage in the business of any auctioneer or the keeping of a bucket, junk or pawn shop, or the sale of spirituous, vinous or malt liquors, without having first taken out a

license therefor; or who, being a resident freeholder, shall refuse to serve as such for the condemnation of land when threunto required by the board of aldermen, shall be guilty of a misdemeanor, and upon satisfactory proof before the mayor shall be adjudged to pay for every such offense a fine not exceeding fifty dollars or be imprisoned not exceeding thirty days. **Penalty.**

(7) Any person who shall remove, deface, injure or destroy any monument placed at the central intersection or prolongation of the line of any public street or on the line of any ward or on the exterior lines and points of intersection of the corporate limits of the city, or who shall place or maintain upon any of said lines or any of the prolongations of the public streets of the city to the exterior boundaries any obstruction to the line of sight from any one corner, intersection, monument or natural elevation to any next corner, intersection, monument or natural elevation thereof, or who shall aid, advise or procure any such removal, defacement, injury, destruction or obstruction shall be guilty of a misdemeanor, and upon conviction thereof before the mayor he shall forfeit and pay for every such offense the sum of fifty dollars, and in addition thereto for every day in which such obstruction is maintained, after five days' notice to remove the same, he shall forfeit and pay the sum of five dollars, and he shall be imprisoned until such fine or fines and the costs are paid by work upon the public streets, roads or other works of the city or county at the rate of one dollar a day, and one-half of all such fine or fines shall go to any complainant or informer other than a city official, who shall also furnish evidence sufficient to convict the offender. **Defacement of monuments and obstruction of streets, etc., a misdemeanor.** **Penalty:** **Certain fees to informers.**

(8) That any person not lawfully authorized who shall give or knowingly cause to be given any false alarm of fire by means of the fire-alarm telegraph of said city, or who shall willfully and deliberately injure any part of the same, shall be guilty of a misdemeanor, and shall upon conviction be fined fifty dollars or imprisoned thirty days. **Giving false alarms of fire a misdemeanor.** **Penalty.**

Sec. 80. That all penalties imposed under the provisions of this act or of any ordinance, by-law or regulation of the city, unless herein otherwise provided shall be recoverable in the name of the City of Raleigh before the mayor, and all such penalties incurred by any minor shall be recovered from the parent, guardian or master, as the case may be, of such minor. **Penalties recoverable in the name of the City of Raleigh.**

BONDS IN SECURITY COMPANIES.

Sec. 81. That each of the following-named officers shall before entering upon duty give a good and sufficient bond conditioned for the faithful performance of the duties of his office, with two or more sureties, justified in a sum not less than the penalty of the bond over and above all their just debts and liabilities and **Bonds of security of city officers.**

the exemptions allowed by law, to be approved and certified as satisfactory by the board of aldermen and recorded by the clerk as follows, to-wit:

Bonds. Chief of police. (1) The chief of police shall give bond in the penalty of five thousand dollars.

City clerk. (2) The city clerk shall give a bond in the penalty of two thousand dollars.

Street commissioner. (3) The street commissioner shall give a bond in the penalty of two thousand dollars.

Tax collector. (4) The tax collector shall give a bond in a penal sum not less than thirty-five thousand dollars.

Treasurer. (5) The treasurer shall give a bond in a penal sum not less than thirty-five thousand dollars.

Commissioner of sinking fund. (6) The commissioner of the sinking fund shall give a bond in a penal sum not less than twenty thousand dollars.

Sanitary inspector. (7) The sanitary inspector shall give a bond in the penalty of two thousand dollars.

Proviso. Bond may be given with surety company. *Provided*, that the bonds herein provided for may be given with such surety company as surety thereto as are now or may hereafter be allowed to execute similar bonds under the general laws of the state. Such bonds shall be carefully examined and certified anew by the board of aldermen annually during the month of May. Examination of bonds. If the security of any of such bonds shall have become impaired, or if for any cause the security shall be adjudged insufficient to cover the amount of public money or other property in the custody of the officer, then the bond shall be renewed and the insufficient security shall be increased and the impaired shall be made good, but such renewal shall not make "cumulative," thereby doubling the penalty of the bond, any "judge made law" to the contrary notwithstanding. And for Breach of bond. any breach of any such bond by any officer required to give an official bond he shall be liable in an action on the same in the name of the city at the suit of the city or any person aggrieved by such breach, and the same may be put in suit without assignment from time to time until the whole penalty is recovered.

SALARIES AND FEES.

SEC. 82. That in addition to the salaries, fees and allowances hereinbefore prescribed, there shall be allowed the following:

Salary of mayor. (1) To the mayor, for his services to the city as such, per month, payable monthly by the city, one hundred dollars. For his services in the performance of magisterial duties in the mayor's Fees of mayor. court under the provision of this act he shall be entitled to such fees and allowances as justices of the peace and clerks of the superior court are entitled to receive for the performance of like duty, to be taxed on the papers as part of the cost in each case and paid by the state, county or person usually charged with costs in like cases in courts of justices of the peace or the superior court, as the case may be, and in no event by the city.

(2) To the chief of police for his services to the city as such, per month, payable monthly by the city, eighty-three dollars and thirty-three cents. For his services in the execution of process issued by the mayor and actually executed by him under the provisions of this act he shall be entitled to such fees and allowances as sheriffs and constables are entitled to receive for the performance of like duty, to be taxed on the papers as part of the costs in each case and paid by the state, county or person usually charged with costs in like cases in courts of justices of the peace or in the superior court, as the case may be, and in no event by the city.

Salary of chief of police.

Fees for executions.

(3) To the city clerk, for his services to the city as such clerk, per month payable monthly by the city, eighty-three dollars and thirty-three cents.

Salary of city clerk.

(4) To the street commissioner, for his services as such under the provisions of this act, per month, payable monthly, sixty-six dollars and sixty-six cents.

Salary of street commissioner.

(5) To the tax collector, for his services as such under the provisions of this act, a single commission equal to two and not exceeding two and a half per centum of the taxes by him collected and paid to the treasurer, to be computed from the treasurer's receipts for such payment.

Fees of tax collector.

(6) To the treasurer, for his services as such under the provisions of this act, a single commission not exceeding one half of one per centum on the amount actually received and paid out by him.

Commission of treasurer.

(7) To the commissioner of the sinking fund, for his services as such under the provisions of this act, per month, payable monthly, twenty dollars.

Commissioner of sinking fund.

(8) To the auditor, for his services as such under the provisions of this act, a sum not exceeding two hundred dollars per annum, payable monthly by the city at the rate of sixteen dollars and sixty-six cents per month: *Provided*, that the three last-named offices may be consolidated under a competent treasurer under a good and sufficient bond conditioned for the faithful performance of all the duties of such offices: *And provided further*, that the last two offices may be consolidated under either officer, with a good and sufficient bond, and such auditor and commissioner may be appointed from the bank officers of the city if practicable.

Salary of auditor.

Proviso.

Certain offices may be consolidated.

(9) To any officer prescribed or authorized by any of the provisions of this act such salary, fees or commissions as to the board of aldermen may seem just and proper, not exceeding that prescribed for like or similar service in this section.

Salaries of certain other officers authorized under this act.

SEC. 83. That from and after the passage and ratification of this act the same shall be and remain the charter of the City of Raleigh; and all laws or parts of laws heretofore enacted in relation thereto and not heretofore repealed which are inconsistent with this act are hereby repealed.

Certain conflicting laws repealed.

Ratified the 28th day of February, A. D. 1899.

CHAPTER 154.

An act to incorporate the town of "Goldpoint" in Martin county.

The General Assembly of North Carolina do enact:

Section 1. That the town of Goldpoint, in the county of Martin, be and is hereby incorporated under the style and name of the town of "Goldpoint," and as such shall be governed by and subject to the provisions of chapter sixty-two of The Code of North Carolina.

Incorporated.

Corporate name.

Sec. 2. That the corporate limits of said town shall be as follows: "Beginning at clay hole, near the residence of H. S. Williams, on county road leading from Robersonville to Goldpoint and running westward about three hundred (300) yards to a lightwood stake in John E. Roberson's field; thence northerly so as to strike county road at the colored church, and along said road whole distance about eight hundred (800) yards to a stake on said county road; thence eastward across B. H. Roberson's fields a straight line to a stake in the field known as Daniel place; thence southward a straight line to about six hundred (600) yards to a stake; thence westward about three hundred (300) yards to the beginning."

Corporate limits

Sec. 3. That the officers of said town shall consist of a mayor, constable and three commissioners, and the following-named persons shall fill said offices until the first Monday in May, eighteen hundred and ninety-nine (1899) or until their successors are elected and qualified as directed by law: G. A. Crofton, mayor; J. A. Bryan, constable, and J. H. Roberson, R. T. Taylor and B. H. Roberson, commissioners.

Town officers.

Temporary officers.

Sec. 4. That the said officers shall be governed in their powers and duties by chapter sixty-two of The Code of North Carolina.

Powers of officers.

Sec. 5. This act shall be in force from and after its ratification.

Ratified the 28th day of February, A. D. 1899.

CHAPTER 155.

An act to amend and consolidate the charter of the town of Red Springs, Robeson county.

The General Assembly of North Carolina do enact:

Section 1. That the inhabitants of the town of Red Springs shall continue as heretofore a body corporate under the name and style of "The Town of Red Springs," and under such name is hereby invested with all the privileges, immunities and franchises, property and all other rights heretofore belonging or appertaining to the town of Red Springs, and in and by that name may sue and be sued, plead and be impleaded. acquire and hold property, real and personal, for the use of the town as its board of commissioners may deem necessary and expedient. Incorporated. Body corporate. Corporate name. Corporate powers.

Sec. 2. That A. B. Pearsall shall be mayor and R. W. Livermore, John T. McNeill, W. F. Williams, Lucius McRae, B. W. Townsend and Dr. B. F. McMillan shall be commissioners, and that C. S. O'Neil shall be constable and D. R. McIver shall be town clerk and treasurer; the same are hereby declared the officers of said town with the powers and duties of the officers of the town of Red Springs until their successors are duly elected and qualified as hereinafter provided. Temporary officers.

Sec. 3. That the corporate limits of said town shall be and are hereby declared to be included within and up to the following boundaries, to-wit: Beginning at a point one-half of a mile due north of the center of Main street where it intersects the Cape Fear and Yadkin Valley Railroad and runs thence due east one-half of a mile; thence due south one mile; thence due west one mile; thence due north one mile; thence due east one-half mile to the beginning. Corporate limits.

Sec. 4. That the officers of said town shall consist of a mayor and six commissioners, to be elected by the qualified voters of said town on the first Monday in May annually. Officers of town.

Sec. 5. That said election of mayor and commissioners shall be held at some place within the corporate limits of said town, to be selected by the mayor and commissioners, and no person shall be entitled to vote at said election or at any election held in said town for municipal purposes, unless he shall be an elector of the state of North Carolina and shall have resided ninety days next preceding the day of election within the said corporation. Election of officers, when held.

Sec. 6. That it shall be the duty of the commissioners of said town on the first Monday in March in each year to appoint a registrar and three judges of election who shall be qualified voters of said town, and who shall within ten days thereafter be notified of their appointment by the constable of said town. The regis- Appointment of registrar and judges.

Notice of election.

trar so appointed shall immediately make publication at the door of the mayor's office and three other public places in said town of his appointment as such. He shall be furnished with a registration book by the commissioners of said town, and it shall be his duty to revise the existing registration book of said town in such a manner that said book shall show an accurate list of electors previously registered and still residing in said town without requiring such electors to be registered anew. He shall also, between the hours of sunrise and sunset each day (Sundays excepted) for thirty days preceding each election, keep open said books for the registration of any electors residing in said town entitled to register whose names have never before been registered in said town, or do not appear on the revised list, but the commissioners of said town may, if they think proper, upon giving thirty days notice at four public places in said town require an entirely new registration of voters before any election held therein.

Registration.

Registrars and judges of election.

Sec. 7. That the registrar and judges of election, before entering upon the discharge of their duties, shall take the oath prescribed by article six, section four of the constitution of North Carolina before some justice of the peace of Robeson county.

Challenge day.

Sec. 8. That it shall be the duty of the registrar and judges of election to attend at the polling place in said town with the registration books on the Monday preceding the election from the hour of nine o'clock a. m. until the hour of five o'clock p. m., when and where the said book shall be open to the inspection of the electors of the said town, and any of the electors shall be allowed to object to the name of any person appearing in said book. In case of any such objection the registrar shall enter upon his book opposite the name of the person so objected to the word "challenged," and shall appoint a time and place on or before the election day, when he, together with said judges of election, shall hear and decide said objection, giving due notice to the voter so objected to: Provided, that nothing contained in this section shall be construed to prohibit the right of any elector to challenge or object to the name of any person registering or offering to register at any other time than that above specified. If any person challenged or objected to shall be found not qualified as provided for in this charter, his name shall be erased from the registration book and he shall not be allowed to vote at any election held in said town for municipal purposes.

Proviso.

Election, how held.

Sec. 9. That the said judges of election, together with the registrar, who shall take with him the registration book, shall assemble at the polling place on the day of the election held in said town and shall open the polls at seven o'clock a. m. They shall superintend said election and shall keep the polls open until sunset, when the polls shall be closed and the votes for mayor and commissioners counted out by them. They shall keep poll books and write in them the name of every person voting at said election, and at the close thereof shall certify said poll lists and deposit them with the clerk and treasurer of said town, and said poll lists shall in any trial for illegal or fraudulent voting be received as evidence. If for any cause any of the judges of election shall fail to attend, the registrar shall appoint some discreet person or persons to fill the vacancy, who shall be sworn by him before acting.

Voters shall vote by ballot.

Sec. 10. That the voters shall vote by ballot, having the names of the mayor and commissioners on one ballot, either in writing or printed on white paper and without any device, and the person having the highest number of votes shall be declared elected by the judges of election, who shall certify said fact to the town clerk and treasurer, and in case of a tie the judges of election shall determine by ballot who is elected.

Persons eligible to office.

Sec. 11. That no person shall be eligible to any office in said town unless he shall be a qualified voter therein.

Notification of mayor and commissioners of their election.

Sec. 12. That immediately after each election it shall be the duty of the town clerk and treasurer to notify in writing the mayor and commissioners elect of their election.

When officers elect shall qualify.

Sec. 13. That the mayor and commissioners elect shall within three days after having been notified by the town clerk and treasurer, before some justice of the peace in said county, take the oath prescribed for public officers, and an oath that they will faithfully and impartially discharge the duties imposed upon them by law.

Persons refusing to qualify shall be fined.

Sec. 14. That any person elected mayor or commissioner of said town under the provisions of this charter, refusing to qualify and act as such for one month after such election, shall forfeit and pay the sum of two hundred dollars, one-half to the use of the person suing for the same and the other half to said town, to be applied by the commissioners of said town to the use and benefit thereof; the said sum shall be recovered in an ordinary civil action before a justice of the peace of said county in the name of the state of North Carolina.

Election of town clerk and treasurer.

Sec. 15. That said commissioners shall at the first meeting after their election select some one as town clerk and treasurer, who shall hold office for one year or until his successor shall be elected and qualified. He shall act as secretary to the board of commissioners, and as treasurer of said town, and before entering upon the discharge of the duties of his office shall give good and sufficient bond with sureties, to be approved by the commissioners of said town in the sum of two thousand dollars, payable to the state of North Carolina and conditioned upon his faithfully ac-

Bonds.

counting for and paying over all moneys that may come into his hands as treasurer of said town and for the faithful discharge of his duties as secretary of said board of commissioners. The commissioners of said town may require of the town clerk and treasurer a monthly statement and exhibit of receipts and disbursements, and if he shall fail for thirty days after having been required to make such exhibit to render the same, it shall be and is hereby declared a breach of his official bond, and the commissioners are authorized and empowered to declare the office vacant and to appoint his successor. All suits entered on the official bond of any of the officers of said town shall be in the name of the state of North Carolina, to the use of the board of commissioners of the town of Red Springs against the said official and his sureties.

Monthly statement of clerk and treasurer.

Election of constable.

Sec. 16. That said commissioners shall at the first meeting after their election select some one to act as constable of said town, who shall hold his office for one year or until his successor is elected and qualified. He shall, before entering upon the discharge of the duties of his office, enter into bond in the sum of two thousand dollars with good and sufficient sureties, to be approved by the board of commissioners, payable to the state of North Carolina and conditioned upon his faithfully executing and returning to the proper authority all process that may come into his hands as constable aforesaid, upon his faithfully accounting for and paying over to the proper authority all moneys that may come into his hands from any source as constable aforesaid, upon his faithfully collecting and paying over all taxes levied by the commissioners of said town and in all other respects executing to the best of his ability and honestly and faithfully all the duties imposed upon him by this charter or by the board of commissioners of said town. And the said board of commissioners may also elect and provide for the pay of such number of policemen and watchmen for said town as in their judgment may be necessary to efficiently carry out and enforce the ordinances and regulations thereof and the criminal laws of the state in said town. The said policemen and watchmen when elected shall be qualified in the manner provided for the constable, and shall, in the enforcement of the general laws of the state and the ordinances and regulations of said town, have all the powers conferred on the town constable by the provisions of this act and the general laws of the state and such as may hereafter be provided. The said policemen and watchmen may be required to give bond for the faithful discharge of their duties in such sums as the commissioners may fix, and may be removed by them at any time for neglect of duty, drunkenness or other cause.

Bond of constable.

Election of policemen and watchmen.

How qualified.

Sec. 17. That the mayor of said town of Red Springs is hereby constituted a special court, with all the jurisdiction and powers in criminal offenses occurring within the limits of said town which are or hereafter may be given to justices of the peace; he shall preserve and keep the peace, and may cause upon proper proceedings, persons charged or convicted of crimes in other counties or states who may be found within the town limits, and bound or imprisoned, to appear at the proper tribunal to answer for their offenses. He shall also have jurisdiction to issue process, to hear and determine all misdemeanors consisting of a violation of the ordinances and regulations of said town, to enforce penalties by issuing executions upon any adjudged violation thereof, to execute the laws, rules and regulations and ordinances made by the commissioners of said town in pursuance of any of the provisions of this charter or the general laws of the state. **Jurisdiction of mayor.**

Sec. 18. That the mayor may issue his warrants upon his own information of any violation of any town ordinance without a written affidavit, and may issue the same to any constable of the town or to such other officer as may be clothed with the powers of the constable, or to such other officer as the justice of the peace may issue his precepts. **Mayor may issue warrants upon certain information.**

Sec. 19. That the mayor shall preside at all meetings of the town commissioners and vote in no case except in an equal vote between said commissioners; then he shall give the casting vote. He shall keep a faithful minute of all precepts issued by him and of all judicial proceedings. Judgments rendered by him shall have all the force, virtue and validity rendered by a justice of the peace, and may be executed and enforced against the parties in the courts of Robeson county and elsewhere, and by the same means and manner as if the same had been rendered by a justice of the peace of Robeson county. **When mayor may vote at meeting of commissioners.**

Sec. 20. That every violation of a town ordinance shall be a misdemeanor. and shall be punished by a fine of not more than fifty dollars [or] imprisonment not more than thirty days. **Violation of town ordinances a misdemeanor.**

Sec. 21. That the mayor shall have power to imprison for fines imposed by him under the provisions of this act and in such cases the prisoners shall only be discharged as now or as may hereafter be provided by law. **Mayor may imprison for fines.**

Sec. 22. That all fines collected by him under the provisions of the foregoing act for violation of town ordinances shall go to the use of the said town. **Fines, how applied.**

Sec. 23 That the mayor shall be entitled by law to the same fees as a justice of the peace in like cases, and an additional salary to be allowed by the commissioners if they see fit. **Fees of mayor.**

Sec. 24 That the commissioners shall form one board and a majority of them shall be competent to perform all the duties prescribed for commissioners unless otherwise provided. Within **Majority of commissioners may be competent to perform duties.**

First meeting. five days after their election they shall convene for the transaction of business, and shall fix their stated days for meeting during the year, which shall be as often as once a month during the same. Special meetings of the commissioners shall also be held on the call of the mayor or a majority of the commissioners, and of every such meeting when called by the mayor, the commissioners not joining in the call, to be notified verbally or in writing.

Powers and duties of commissioners. Sec. 25. That the commissioners shall have power to make and provide for the execution of such ordinances, by-laws, rules and regulations for the good government of the town as they may deem necessary, and shall have power and it shall be their duty to provide for and secure the peace, good order and tranquillity of the town against disturbance by quarrels, loud, profane and obscene language, riots, affrays, trespasses or other breaches of the peace, or irregularities of whatever nature tending to disturb the peace of the citizens. Streets. They shall provide for the repairing of the streets, sidewalks and alleys and cause the same to be kept clean and in good order, take all proper means to prevent and extinguish fires. make regulations for the observance of the Sabbath, suppress and remove nuisances, prohibit the indecent exposure of the person and prohibit and suppress the sauntering around, advertising or practising their vocation by lewd women, by imposing such fines and imprisonments in all cases within the jurisdiction of a justice of the peace as they shall deem adequate.

To what territory police power applies. Sec. 26. That any ordinance passed by said commissioners by virtue of the police powers vested in them by this charter or the general laws of the state shall apply to the territory within one-fourth of a mile of the corporate limits as above set out, unless in the ordinances it is otherwise provided: Provided, however, that this clause shall not be construed to permit the passage of any ordinances to apply to the territory beyond the corporate limits which shall levy any tax on the polls or property of the inhabitants beyond the same or to the restriction of the kind or class of buildings erected outside of said corporate limits.

Nuisances. Sec. 27. That the commissioners may require the abatement and removal of all nuisances and shall have power to pull down Dangerous buildings. any old house. barn or other building in said town when the same may be considered dangerous from fire or other causes to the safety of the person or property of adjacent residents: Proviso. Provided, however, that before such removal the owner of such property shall be notified in writing by the clerk of such board of the action, and allow one month for the repairing or removal of such building. That all damage may be agreed upon by the mayor and the party whose property is removed under this section. and in case they can not agree each shall select a disinterested person, and if they can not agree they may select a third person, and the decision of two of these shall be final, except an appeal is filed within ten days. Damages.

Sec. 28. That the commissioners may build or establish a guard house in which to secure or confine offenders against town ordinances, and for feeding such persons the town constable or other officer shall be allowed such compensation as is allowed the keeper of the common jail in Robeson county: Provided, in the above case that no prisoner or offender shall be confined in said guard house more than twenty-four hours without first having his case heard and determined before the mayor. Guard house. Proviso. Limit of confinement of prisoners.

Sec. 29. That the commissioners shall have power to lay out or open any new street or streets within said town limits deemed necessary by them, and they shall have the power at any time to widen, enlarge, change, extend, narrow or discontinue any street or streets within said corporate limits whenever they may so determine, by making a reasonable compensation to the owners of property damaged thereby. In cases where owners of land can not agree with the commissioners regarding the value of land or property and the damages, the mayor of the town shall issue his warrant to the town constable commanding him to summon three disinterested freeholders of said town who, together with two freeholders as above, to be selected by party claiming damages, shall determine the value of said property and assess the damages, after which they shall return a report of their proceedings, findings and so forth, into the office of the mayor, there to be filed. Before proceeding to view said premises and assess said damages the parties so summoned shall take oath before the mayor or a justice of the peace to make a fair, just and impartial discharge of the duties of appraiser and assessor and report the same. If the party damaged or claiming damages refused to select two appraisers as provided above the report of the three summoned in behalf of the town shall be final: Provided, that if either a majority of the commissioners or the opposite party be dissatisfied with the report of the freeholders, then they may appeal to the superior court of Robeson county, and in that case the report of the valuation and the proceedings therein shall be sent in by said appraisers to said court, there to be determined. Streets and sidewalks. May condemn land. Disagreement as to price. Arbitrators. Assessors shall take oath. Either may appeal.

Sec. 30. That the board of commissioners of said town shall have power annually to levy and cause to be collected taxes for necessary town purposes on all real property, all moneys, credits, investments in bonds, stocks, joint stock companies, all personal property and all other subjects of taxation now taxed or which may hereafter be taxed by the general assembly of North Carolina for state and county purposes, and on the taxable polls within said town: Provided, however, that the taxes levied by Levy of taxes. Subjects of taxation. Proviso.

Maximum tax rate.

them shall not exceed sixty-six and two-third cents on the one hundred dollars valuation of all real and personal property within said town and two dollars on each taxable poll, to meet all the liabilities of the town in the way of indebtedness, bonded or otherwise, which now exists or which may hereafter be created, and the valuation of all property within said town as taxed by said commissioners shall be the same as that at which it was assessed for taxation on the first day of June in that year for state and county purposes: Provided, that the board of commissioners of said town at a regular meeting after ten days' notice to any person liable to taxation in said town may raise the valuation of such property in said town as they shall deem unreasonably low, and they may also, in order to discover and have properly listed all solvent credits, stocks, bond, etc., subject to taxation in said town, summon any person whom they may have reason to believe is the owner of any property of such nature which is unlisted, or which being listed is not properly valued, to appear before the said board of commissioners at a regular meeting and to answer under oath such questions as may tend to discover the existence of any property of the character above named. And in the event any person so summoned shall fail or refuse to appear and answer such questions as are proper under the provisions of this section, the said board of commissioners may proceed to investigate the matter by other evidence, and may summon and examine any witnesses necessary for a just decision of the question at issue, and may require, by proper order, the production of any books, records or other papers or evidences of the existence of such property that they may deem proper or necessary. And if a majority of said board of commissioners shall decide that any person is the owner of any property of the character above set out that is not listed or not properly valued they shall order the same to be entered on the tax list or the value increased by the town clerk and treasurer, and the said property so listed shall be subject to the payment of all taxes levied by the said town and collected as other taxes therein.

Proviso.

After notice commissioners may raise valuation of property.

Unlisted property.

Persons summoned and failing to appear.

Taxes, when due.

Sec. 31. That all taxes levied by the commissioners of said town, except license or privilege taxes, shall be due and payable on the first day of October in each year to the constable or tax collector of said town, and after that time may be collected by him by distraining any personal property of the taxpayer to be found within said town.

Notice to persons by tax lister.

Sec. 32. That on the first Monday in July of each and every year the town clerk and treasurer of said town shall, by advertisement at the mayor's office door and four other public places in said town, notify all persons within said town liable to taxation to come forward and make returns of their tax lists to him within thirty days from that date. All persons owning property in said town and liable to taxation shall make returns of all their taxable property to said clerk under oath, and he is hereby authorized and empowered to administer to them (such taxpayers) an oath that he will well and truly return all property owned by him within said town and liable to taxation under the provisions of this charter; said list so returned shall state the age of the taxpayer and all property, real and personal, liable to taxation owned by him, with an accurate description of all real estate owned by him on June the first of that year when he was required by law to return the same to the list taker of Red Springs township to be assessed for taxation for state and county purposes.

Return of taxable property.

Sec. 33. That all persons owning any property within said town liable for taxation for town purposes shall return the same to the town clerk and treasurer as provided in section thirty-two of this charter, and all property therein liable to such taxation owned by minors, lunatics or persons non compos mentis shall be returned as herein provided by their guardian or guardians if they shall have any such.

Property liable for taxation.

Sec. 34. That all the property liable to taxation for town purposes in said town and held by guardians, executors, administrators or trustees shall be returned by them in that capacity, and the individual property of all such guardians, executors, administrators or trustees shall first be distrained or attached by the constable or tax collector of said town for the satisfaction of the taxes due on all property so returned by them, and the constable or tax collector of said town is hereby authorized, at any time after the taxes may be due the town on said property as aforesaid, to distrain any personal property of such guardians, executors, administrators or trustees to be found in said town.

Return of property by guardians and others.

Sec. 35. That the town clerk and treasurer shall make out a full and complete list of all taxable property in said town so returned to him and of the taxable polls in said town, and if any person or persons in said town liable to taxation shall fail to make return to the town clerk as herein provided for for thirty days after the first Monday in July of each year, the town clerk shall make return of the taxable property of such person or persons, and his age, if he is liable to poll tax, and such person or persons so failing to make return of their property and poll shall be liable to double taxation on their property and poll, to be collected as other property and poll taxes. The town clerk of the said town shall complete the tax list and place it or a certified copy thereof in the hands of the constable or tax collector of said town on the third Monday in August in each year. Such tax list or certified copy thereof, certified by the town clerk, when placed in the

List of taxable property shall be made out by clerk and treasurer.

Failure to return tax.

hands of the town constable or tax collector of said town shall have the force and effect of an execution.

Lien for taxes.

Sec. 36. That the lien of the town taxes shall attach to all real property subject to taxation on and after the third Monday in August in each year and shall continue until such taxes, together with any penalty that shall accrue thereon, shall be paid. All personal property of taxpayers liable to taxation within the town shall be liable to be seized and sold after ten days' notice at the mayor's office and four other public places in said town in satisfaction of taxes by the town constable or tax collector of said town after said taxes shall have become due and payable.

Personal property liable.

Taxes due and unpaid, how collected.

Sec. 37. That whenever the taxes due said town shall be due and unpaid the constable or tax collector of said town shall immediately proceed to collect them as follows: First, if the party charged or his agent have personal property in said town equal in value to the taxes charged against him the constable or tax collector shall seize and sell the same under the same rules as sheriffs are required to sell personal property under execution, and his fees for such levy or sale shall be fifty cents; second, if the party charged has not personal property to be found in said town of sufficient value to satisfy his taxes, the constable or tax collector of said town shall levy upon any lands of the delinquent to be found within the town. The levy shall contain an accurate description of the lands with the name of the owner or owners, the amount of taxes due by the delinquent, and a list thereof shall be by the constable or tax collector of said town returned to the town clerk and treasurer, who shall enter the same in a book kept for that purpose, charging therefor the sum of twenty-five cents for each levy; third, the constable or tax collector shall notify the delinquent of such levy, and of the day and place of sale by service of a notice, stating these particulars, on him personally, if he be a resident of said town. If the delinquent does not reside in said town, and his residence is known or can by reasonable diligence be ascertained, the notice shall be mailed postpaid to such delinquent. If the residence of the delinquent can not with reasonable diligence be ascertained the constable or tax collector shall post a notice substantially as above described at the door of the mayor's office and four other public places in said town at least thirty days before the sale of the land, and this last mentioned notice shall be posted as in all cases of sales of land for taxes in said town; fourth, the sale shall be made at the mayor's office in said town and shall be on one of the days prescribed for sale of real estate under execution and shall be conducted in all respects as are sales under execution. If the delinquent resides out of said town and his address be known to the town constable or tax collector he shall mail to him within one

Fees of tax collector.

Description with levy.

Delinquent shall be notified.

Non-resident delinquents.

month after such sale notice of the sale and date thereof, of the name and address of the purchaser, of the sum bid and of the amount of the taxes and costs to be paid by such delinquent as a condition of its redemption.

Sec. 38. That the whole tract or lot of land belonging to a delinquent person or company shall be set up for sale at the same time and shall be struck off to him who will pay the amount of taxes with all the expenses for the smallest part of the land. At all such sales the mayor may become a bidder and purchase the whole lot or tract of land for the taxes due and expenses, for the use of the town in case no one will offer to pay the taxes and costs for a less penalty. Sale of property for unpaid taxes.

Sec. 39. That the delinquent may retain possession of the property for twelve months after sale, and within that time redeem it by paying the purchaser the amount paid by him and twenty-five per centum in addition thereto. At the time of said payment to the purchaser he shall give to the delinquent a receipt therefor. If he shall refuse or can not be found in said town the delinquent may pay the same to the town clerk and treasurer, and he shall give him a receipt therefor, and such payment shall be equivalent to payment to the purchaser. After such payment to the purchaser or town clerk all rights under the purchaser shall cease. Property may be redeemed within a year.

Sec. 40. That at the time of such purchase of real estate for taxes the town constable or tax collector, on receipt of the amount bid for such real estate, shall give the purchaser a receipt stating the amount bid, by whom and for what purpose, and describing the land sold, stating further the owner of said lands and the amount of taxes due thereon. Purchaser shall have receipt.

Sec. 41. That if delinquent, his agent or attorney shall fail to redeem as provided in section thirty-nine hereof for twelve months, at the expiration of that time the purchaser may present his receipt referred to in section forty hereof, and the town constable or tax collector of said town shall execute a deed in fee to the purchaser, and if the purchaser is dead, to his heirs-at-law or assigns for the lands for which said purchaser agreed to pay the amount called for in the receipt, and for said service the constable or tax collector shall be allowed one dollar to be paid by the purchaser. The deed from the constable or tax collector to the purchaser shall be registered in the register's office of Robeson county within six months from the time of the execution and delivery thereof, and when so registered shall convey to the grantee all the estate in the lands for which the said purchaser bid, which the delinquent, his agent or attorney had at the time of sale for taxes. Failure to redeem property sold for taxes.

Sec. 42. That all real estate bid in by the mayor of said town

Real estate bid in by the mayor for taxes.

for the use of the town at sales made by the constable or tax collector for taxes may be redeemed as hereinbefore provided by the payment on the part of the delinquent, his agent or attorney of the amount bid and twenty-five per centum additional to the town clerk and treasurer within twelve months from date of such sale.

Levy of privilege taxes.

Sec. 43. That the commissioners of said town shall have the power to annually levy and cause to be collected for the necessary expenses of the town such privilege taxes as shall seem to them fair [and] equitable on the professions, callings, trades, occupations and all other business carried on in said town; that is to say, on every lawyer, merchant, physician, dentist, druggist, artisan, mechanic, daguerrean artist or other taker of pictures; on all officers or agents of incorporated companies; on all clerks or employees of other persons or corporations; on every drummer, editor, printer, butcher, tinner, carpenter, shoemaker, wheelwright, carriage, buggy or wagon maker, jeweller, confection[er], grocer, harness maker, saddler, blacksmith; on every billiard or bagatelle table, public or private bowling nine or ten pin alley; on all lectures for reward; on all riding or pleasure vehicles; on all gold, silver or metal watches; on all pianos; on all pistols; on every livery, feed or sale stable; on every person hiring any number of horses; on every cotton gin; on every turpentine or other distillery; on every hotel, boarding house, restaurant or eating saloon; on all drays, carts, wagons, carriages, buggies, road carts, bicycles; on all horses, cattle, sheep, hogs, goats or dogs owned or kept in said town or allowed to run at large therein; on every stallion, jack, bull or boar kept or exhibited in said town; on all itinerant traders and peddlers; on all banks, railroads, telephone and telegraph companies; on all saw and planing mills, brick, lath or shingle mills; on all sash, door and blind, furniture or cotton factories, and on all incorporated companies of whatever nature or kind; on all and every person or persons, company or companies who may exhibit, sing, play, act or perform, or on anything for which they charge or receive any gratuity, fee or pay or award [reward] whatsoever within the limits of said town, and in every opera house or public hall to which an admission fee is charged, and the commissioners of said town shall prescribe when the license tax herein provided for shall be due and payable.

Privilege taxes.

Manufacture or sale of spirituous liquor within five miles of corporate limits prohibited.

Sec. 44. That it shall be unlawful for any person or company to manufacture any spirituous or malt liquor or to sell or in any manner, directly or indirectly, to receive any compensation for any spirituous or malt liquors, wine or cider or any other intoxicating liquor within the corporate limits of said town of Red Springs or within five miles from the corporate limits thereof, as set out in section three hereof; and any person violating the provisions of this section shall be guilty of a misdemeanor and shall be punished upon a conviction thereof by a fine not exceeding one hundred dollars or by imprisonment not exceeding twelve months

Penalty.

Sec. 45. That the board of commissioners of said town shall have power to provide for the establishment, organization and equipment, government and pay of such number of fire companies as they may deem necessary and proper for the protection of the said town against damage by fire, and in case of a fire occurring in said town, the mayor, or in his absence, a majority of the commissioners of said town who may be present, may order the blowing up, pulling down or destroying of any house or building deemed necessary to stop the progress of the fire.

Fire companies.

Sec. 46. That the said commissioners shall also have power to establish fire limits within said town, within which it shall not be lawful for any person to erect or build any wooden house or structure or make any wooden addition to any building or repair or cover the outside surface of any building with any material other than metal or slate; they may prohibit the removal of any wooden building from without to within such fire limits as they shall establish, and shall have power to enforce obedience to their regulations under this section by punishing such persons as violate the same by a fine of not more than fifty dollars or imprisonment of not more than thirty days, and shall further have the power to cause the removal of any structure or building erected contrary to the laws by them enacted under the power vested in them by this section.

Empowered to establish fire limits.

Sec. 47. That the town of Red Springs is hereby authorized and empowered to create a debt for public improvements, such as grading and paving streets and sidewalks, sewerage and drainage, waterworks, fire engines, lighting the streets and buildings, purchasing land for a cemetery, and the erection of necessary buildings thereon, and other improvements of a public character, to an amount not exceeding ten thousand dollars, and may issue bonds to that amount or any less amount for any one, or more or all of said purposes in the name of "The Town of Red Springs," in such denomination and form and payable at such place and time not exceeding thirty years, and bearing interest at no greater rate than six per centum per annum, payable annually or semi-annually, as the board of commissioners may determine.

May create a debt for public improvements.

Maximum amount.

Rate of interest.

Sec. 48. That the bonds for the aforesaid purposes or any one of them shall not be issued until approved by a majority of the qualified voters of said town, after thirty days' notice at the door of the mayor's office and four other public places in said town at an election to be held under the same rules and regulations as are provided by this charter for elections in the said town; such

Bonds shall be issued on approval of qualified voters.

Manner of holding election.

notice shall set forth the object for which bonds are to be issued, the amount of the same, the rate of interest, the time when they mature, and the rate of tax to be levied to pay the principal and interest on said bonds. The qualified voters approving the issue of such bonds and the levy and collection of the taxes to pay the same shall deposit in a ballot box a written or printed ballot with the word "Approved" thereon; and those disapproving the same shall deposit a like ballot with the word "Disapproved" thereon If at such election a majority of the qualified voters shall vote "Approved," then the mayor and board of commissioners of the said town shall issue the bonds provided for in such notice and shall levy and cause to be collected the taxes therein named and authorized by this act. At such election, upon the proper notice being given as above set out, the question of issuing bonds for more than one purpose, within the meaning of this act, may be voted on in separate boxes, under the same rules and regulations as above set out; but in such a case the ballots shall contain the purpose of the bonds with the word "Approved" or "Disapproved" following, as the voter may desire: Provided, that no election shall be ordered unless a petition requesting the same, signed by a majority of the qualified voters of said town be presented to the mayor and commissioners thereof, setting forth the matter above required in the notice of election.

Form of ballot.

Bonds for various purposes, how voted upon.

Bonds issued under signature of mayor.

Sec. 49. That said bonds shall be issued under the signature of the mayor of said town and attested by the town clerk and treasurer, under the official seal of said town, and the mayor shall, under the direction of the board of commissioners, dispose of said bonds at a sum not less than par value.

Commissioners empowered to levy special tax and create sinking fund.

Sec. 50. That for the purposes of paying the interest on said bonds as it falls due and for providing a sinking fund for the redemption of said bonds when due, or for purchasing and canceiling the same before due, it shall be the duty of the board of commissioners of said town at the time fixed for the levy of other taxes in the same, to levy and cause to be collected with the other taxes each year, so long as any of the said bonds are unpaid, a sufficient special tax upon all the subjects of taxation set out in section thirty of this act, which taxes so collected shall at all times be kept separate and distinct and used only for the purposes above set out: Provided, that so much of the tax levied and collected each year as may not be required to pay the interest on said bonds and which can not be applied to the purchase or discharge of said bonds shall be invested so as to secure the payment at maturity of the principal of said bonds; and to insure the due investment of the above-described amounts from time to time it shall be the duty of the treasurer of said town, under such regulations as the board of commissioners thereof shall from time to

Proviso.

Treasurer shall make investment of sinking fund.

time prescribe, to make investments of such amounts, and to do and perform all such other services in connection with said bonds as said commissioners may prescribe: Provided further, that the board of commissioners of said town may require an official bond of the clerk and treasurer not exceeding five thousand dollars for the faithful discharge of all his official duties pertaining to his said office.

Sec. 51. That the bonds authorized to be issued by this act and their coupons shall not be subject to taxation by said town until after they become due or tender of payment shall have been made by the town through its treasurer, and the coupons shall be received in payment of town taxes for any fiscal year in which they become due or thereafter; and if the holders of any said bonds or coupons shall fail to present the same for payment at the time or times and place therein named, he shall not be entitled to any interest thereon for the time they have been outstanding after maturity. Bonds and coupons not subject to taxation.

Sec. 52. That the clerk and treasurer shall keep a record in which shall be written the name of every purchaser of a bond and the number and amount thereof; and he, the said town clerk and treasurer of said town, shall keep an accurate account of the coupons and bonds which shall be paid and cancelled, so that the true state of the bonded indebtedness of the town shall be readily seen and ascertained at any time by any taxpayer of said town. Record shall be kept of purchasers of bonds.

Sec. 53. That all laws and clauses of laws in conflict with this act are hereby repealed in so far as this act is concerned. Conflicting laws repealed.

Sec. 54. That this act shall be in full force and effect from and after its ratification.

Ratified the 28th day of February, A. D. 1899.

CHAPTER 156.

An act to incorporate the North Carolina Mutual and Provident Association.

The General Assembly of North Carolina do enact:

Section 1. That John Merrick, Dr. A. M. Moore, J. E. Shepard, W. G. Pearson and D. T. Watson, of Durham; T. O. Fuller, of Warrenton, and E. A. Johnson and N. C. Bruce, of Raleigh, and their associates, successors and assigns, be and they are hereby created a body politic and corporate under the name and style of the "North Carolina Mutual and Provident Association," whose motto shall be "Merciful to All," and as such shall be ca- Corporators. Body corporate Corporate name. Motto.

pable of suing and being sued, shall have and use a corporate seal, shall exist for sixty (60) years and shall have all the powers and privileges belonging to corporations under the laws of North Carolina.

Duration of existence.

Object of corporation.

Sec. 2. That the object of the said corporation shall be the relief of the widows and orphans, of the sick and of those injured by accident, and the burial of the dead; and to this end the corporation may issue certificates to its members agreeing to pay at their death, or in the event of their injury by accident, sums of money to the beneficiaries named therein; may provide for the payment of sick benefits and for the further care of the sick and for the burial of the dead, and may adopt such by-laws, rules and regulations, fixing the assessments, dues and premiums to be paid to it by its members, the manner of electing its directors, the members necessary to make a quorum of the members of the corporation and of the directors, and generally for the government of the corporation as are not contrary to law.

Principal lodge.

Sec. 3. That the principal lodge or office of said corporation shall be in Durham, North Carolina, but the board of directors may establish lodges or branch offices anywhere in this or other states; and the said corporation, its lodges and property shall be exempt from all taxation and from the rules governing insurance companies.

Property of such lodges exempt from taxation.

Sec. 4. That the said association or corporation shall have the right to take by gift, purchase or otherwise property both real and personal not exceeding one hundred thousand dollars, and to hold and dispose of same at pleasure.

Individual liability.

Sec. 5. That none of the members of the corporation shall be individually liable for its debts, contracts or torts, except to the extent of the assessments, dues and premiums agreed to be paid by them.

Certain per cent shall be turned over to Colored Orphan Asylum at Oxford.

Sec. 6. That a certain per centum of the proceeds, to be fixed by the board of directors, shall be turned over to the Colored Orphan Asylum at Oxford, North Carolina.

Sec. 7. This act shall be in force from and after its ratification.

Ratified the 28th day of February, A. D. 1899.

CHAPTER 157.

An act to allow the city of High Point to issue bonds.

The General Assembly of North Carolina do enact:

Aldermen of High Point empowered to issue bonds.

Section 1. That the board of aldermen of the city of High Point is hereby authorized and empowered to issue bonds in the name of the city of High Point, in such denominations and forms as it may determine, to an amount not exceeding fifty thousand dollars, payable at such times and places as the board of aldermen may prescribe: Provided, that the time of payment of such bonds shall not be less than thirty years and more than sixty years from their date.

Sec. 2. That the said bonds shall bear interest at no greater rate than five per centum per annum, and the interest shall be made payable annually or semi-annually, as the board of aldermen may prescribe, and said bonds shall in no case be sold, hypothacted or otherwise disposed of for less than their par value. Rate of interest of bonds.

Sec. 3. The said bonds shall be signed by the mayor, attested by the city secretary and treasurer, and sealed with the corporate seal of the city, and shall have interest coupons attached thereto; which said bonds and their coupons shall be exempt from city taxation until after they become due and the coupons shall be receivable in payment of city taxes. That for the purpose of paying said bonds at maturity, and the said coupons as they become due, it shall be the duty of the board of aldermen, and they are hereby empowered so to do, to levy and collect each year a sufficient special tax upon all subjects of taxation which are now or may hereafter be embraced in the subjects of taxation under the charter of said city, and in the manner and at the same time as other taxes are collected under said charter: Provided, that the total rate of taxes, both general and special, shall never exceed one dollar and fifty cents on each hundred dollar valuation of property: Provided further, that the taxes collected under this act for the payment of said bonds and interest coupons as aforesaid shall be used for no other purpose, and it shall be the duty of the city treasurer, as said coupons are paid off and taken up, to cancel the same, and report not less than twice a year to the board of aldermen, the number and amount of coupons so cancelled. Bonds, how certified. Aldermen empowered to levy special tax for redemption of bonds as they become due. Proviso. Maximum tax rate. Proviso. Taxes collected under this act shall be used only for certain purposes.

Sec. 4. That the board of aldermen shall not issue said bonds, nor any of them, nor collect said tax until they shall have been authorized and empowered so to do by a majority of the qualified voters of said city, at an election or elections to be held at such times and places as the said board shall appoint, of which notice shall be given for twenty days in some newspaper published in said city; and at the said election or elections, those favoring the issue of said bonds, or of any of them as specified in the call of such election or elections, and the levy and collection of the tax for the payment of said bonds and coupons, shall vote "Issue," and those opposed to it shall vote "No Issue": Provided, that the said board may, in its discretion, order a new registration of voters. Bonds shall be issued only after election. Form of ballot.

Sec. 5. That said board may call an election under this act at any time it may see fit, after giving the proper notice and When election may be called.

observing the general election laws of the state; and the rejection by the voters of any proposition submitted to them under this act, shall not prevent a submission of the same or other propositions to the said voters at any other time that the board of aldermen may appoint, and that the said board may continue to call elections under this act until the whole amount of fifty thousand dollars shall have been issued.

Succeeding elections may be held.

Purpose of issuance of bonds.

Sec. 6. That said bonds may be issued for the purpose of building or buying, conducting and operating an electric light plant and electric power plant, gas plant, or both, and to furnish lights to the streets of said city, and lights for private use to its citizens, if the board of aldermen see fit, and to charge for said lights and power furnished for private use, and to erect, build, buy and operate waterworks, and to supply private citizens water, and charge for same, and to maintain and operate waterworks and to furnish for the use of the city; to build, construct, enlarge and maintain the sewer system; to build a city hall and market house, and other necessary buildings, and to rent stalls or other parts of public buildings, and to grade, curb, macadamize, pave, and improve the streets of the city: Provided, however, that the said board of city aldermen shall, in the resolution calling the election and the notice of the people of said election, state the maximum amount of bonds to be issued under said election, and the purpose or purposes for which the said bonds are to be issued, specifying the maximum amount to be issued for each purpose, and the bonds shall be issued for no other purpose than that specified as aforesaid, provided that the purchaser of said bonds shall not be required to see to the application of the purchase money.

Electric lights.

Waterworks.

Sewerage.

Street improvements.

Aldermen shall have entire supervision of works thus constructed.

Sec. 7. That the said board of aldermen shall have entire supervision and control of any and all of the parts or works, now established, or hereafter established under this act, and is hereby authorized to elect all such agents, servants and employees as it may deem proper, and pay the same from any of the revenues of the city not otherwise appropriated, and do all other proper things to carry into effect the true intention of this act.

Conflicting laws repealed.

Sec. 8. All laws or parts of laws in conflict herewith are hereby repealed.

Sec. 9. This act shall be in force from and after its ratification.

Ratified the 28th day of February, A. D. 1899.

CHAPTER 158.

An act to amend and supplement the articles of incorporation granted Robert L. Steele, Thomas C. Leak, Henry C. Wall, Walter L. Steele, Alfred M. Scales and William Entwistle, under the corporate name of "The Roberdell Manufacturing Company," by the clerk of the superior court of Richmond county, North Carolina, on or about the eleventh day of May, Anno Domini eighteen hundred and eighty-two.

The General Assembly of North Carolina do enact:

Section 1. That H. C. Wall, T. C. Leak, W. I. Everett, R. L. Steele, G. S. Steele, William Entwistle, James P. Leak, and their associates, successors and assigns, who are and will be the associates, successors and assigns of the original incorporators of "The Roberdell Manufacturing Company," shall be and are hereby declared a body corporate and politic, under the name and style of "The Roberdell Manufacturing Company," for the purpose of using and erecting mills and machinery for the manufacturing of yarn and fabrics of cotton, woolen and other textile fabrics, and manufacturing the same into clothing of any kind they may deem expedient, near the town of Rockingham, Richmond county, North Carolina; and shall have all the corporate power now possessed by said "The Roberdell Manufacturing Company," and by said corporate name may sue and be sued, plead and be impleaded, defend and be defended unto, answer and be answered in any of the courts of this state; may have and use a common seal, alterable and renewable at their pleasure; may establish such by-laws, rules and regulations for the government of said corporation as they may deem proper, not inconsistent with the law of the land; may purchase and hold real estate for the use of said corporation, so the same shall not exceed five hundred (500) acres in quantity; may acquire and hold personal property and effects to whatever extent may be necessary, profitable and convenient for the purposes of their organization; and may do and corry on a general mercantile business in their corporate capacity; may gin cotton, grind grain and generally shall have authority to do all acts and things for the proper and convenient carrying on of the business for which they were established, including a mercantile business, and which other corporate bodies of like character have under the general law, not inconsistent with or contrary to the constitution and laws of this state or of the United States.

Corporators. Body corporate. Corporate name. Principal office. Corporate name. Corporate powers.

Sec. 2. That the capital stock of said corporation may be as much as two hundred thousand dollars, but shall not exceed that amount, and shall be divided into shares of one hundred

Capital stock.

Corporate liabilities. dollars each, with only corporate liabilities until the first day of January, 1940; stockholders in said corporation shall not be personally liable for the debts or contracts of said corporation.

Election of directors. Sec. 3. That the stockholders in said corporation shall elect at the end of the term of the present board of directors, not less than five nor more than seven in number for a board of directors, who shall manage the affairs of the corporation for one year from the date of their election, and until their successors shall be chosen, and said board of directors, as early as practicable, shall elect one of their number president, and appoint such other officers, agents and employees as in their judgment the said corporation may require, and shall have power to do all other acts and things for the ordering and management of the affairs of said corporation, incident to the position and ancillary to the purpose for which the corporation is created, subject always to the law of the land.

Election of officers.

Compensation of officers. Sec. 4. That compensation to the president and directors shall be fixed by the stockholders, and to the other officers and employees by the board of directors; and the said board of directors shall have authority to take bond of any officer or officers having in charge the finances of the corporation, and bring action upon a breach thereof.

Annual meetings, when and where held. Sec. 5. That an annual meeting of the stockholders shall be held at such time and place as the stockholders may direct, and the board of directors shall have power to call a meeting of the stockholders at such times and places as they may deem to the interest of the corporation; and one-fifth in interest of the stockholders in said corporation may call a meeting of the stockholders when they see proper to; and at each and any meeting of the stockholders of said corporation each stockholder shall be entitled to one vote for each share of stock held by him in said corporation.

Empowered to build dams, etc. Sec. 6. That said corporation shall have authority to construct dams, buildings, walls, and all other works necessary for the purpose for which they are established, and may purchase, make and use all machinery, tools, implements and fixtures necessary and convenient for such ends, and may use any motive power which may be deemed conducive to the interest of said corporation.

Corporate powers. Sec. 7. That said corporation shall have power to borrow money for the purposes of their business to an amount not exceeding one hundred thousand lollars, at such rate of interest as may be agreed upon, not exceeding that allowed by law per annum, and to issue under their corporate seal obligations to pay the same, which said obligations shall be assignable by endorsement.

Sec. 8. That the board of directors shall have authority to keep open their books of subscription until the whole of the capital stock shall be subscribed, and may prescribe the terms upon which new stockholders may be admitted, so they respect the legal rights of old stockholders. Books may be kept open for subscriptions.

Sec. 9. That this act shall take effect and be in force from and after its ratification, and remain in force until the first day of January, Anno Domini 1940.

Sec. 10. All laws and clauses of laws and all acts of the clerk of the superior court for Richmond county, North Carolina, in conflict with this act are hereby repealed. Conflicting laws repealed.

Ratified the 28th day of February, A. D. 1899.

CHAPTER 159.

An act to authorize the City of Raleigh to issue bonds for public improvements and to levy a special tax.

The General Assembly of North Carolina do enact:

Section 1. That for the purpose of paving, macadamizing and otherwise improving such of the public streets of the city of Raleigh, as the board of aldermen of said city may determine to improve, and for making such other public improvements as the said board of aldermen may determine to make, the City of Raleigh is hereby authorized and empowered to issue its bonds to an amount not exceeding one hundred thousand dollars, of such denominations and in such proportions as the board of aldermen may deem advisable, bearing interest from the date thereof at a rate not exceeding five per centum per annum, with interest coupons attached, payable half yearly, at such times and at such place or places as may be deemed advisable by said board of aldermen, said bonds to be of such form and tenor and transferable in such way, and the principal thereof payable or redeemable at such time or times not exceeding thirty years from the date thereof, and at such place or places as the board of aldermen may determine. Aldermen of Raleigh empowered to issue bonds for certain improvements. Amount of bonds. Bonds, when redeemable.

Sec. 2 That the board of aldermen shall set apart for the special purpose of paving, macadamizing and otherwise improving the streets of the City of Raleigh, the whole of the proceeds arising from the sale of the bonds authorized by this act: Provided, that not more than fifty thousand dollars may be expended in any one year. Aldermen shall set aside certain proceeds. Proviso.

Sec. 3. That none of the bonds authorized by this act shall be disposed of either by sale, exchange, hypothecation or otherwise for a less price than their par value, nor shall said bonds or Bonds, at what price to be sold.

their proceeds be used for any other purpose than those declared in said sections one and two respectively; and any officer of the said City of Raleigh violating or aiding or abetting any person in the violation of this section shall be guilty of a misdemeanor, and upon conviction thereof, shall be fined not less than five hundred dollars and imprisoned not less than six months, and shall moreover be liable to the said city in a sum double the amount lost to the city by such violation.

Purpose for which used.

Bonds and coupons not subject to taxation.

Sec. 4. That the bonds authorized to be issued by this act and their coupons shall not be subject to taxation by the said city until after they become due and tender of payment shall have been made by the city, and the coupons shall be receivable in payment of city taxes, or other city dues for any fiscal year in which such coupons become due, or thereafter; and if the holder of any of said bonds or coupons shall fail to present the same for payment at the time or times, and at the place or places therein named, he shall not be entitled to any interest thereon for the time they have been outstanding after maturity.

Interest shall not be paid after certain time.

Aldermen empowered to levy special tax.

Sec. 5. That for the purpose of providing for the payment of the interest accruing on and the principal at maturity of the bonds issued under authority of this act, the board of alderden of said city shall annually, and at the time of levying other city taxes, levy and lay a particular tax on all persons and subjects of taxation on which the said board of aldermen now are or may hereafter be authorized to lay and levy taxes for any purpose whatsoever, said particular tax to be not less than six nor more than eight cents on the one hundred dollars assessed valuation on property, and not less than eighteen nor more than twenty-four cents on each taxable poll. The taxes provided for in this section shall be collected in the manner and at the times other city taxes are collected, and shall be accounted for and kept separate from other city taxes, and shall be applied exclusively to the purposes for which they are collected. So much of said taxes as may be required to pay the interest on the bonds issued by authority of this act, as it falls due, and cannot be applied to the purchase or discharge of the bonds for which said taxes are levied and collected, shall be invested so as to secure the payment at maturity of the principal of the said bonds; and to insure the due investment of the amount collected from year to year in excess of that required to pay the said interest, the board of aldermen shall cause the said excess to be turned over to the commissioner of the sinking fund of the City of Raleigh, whose duty it shall be, under such general rules and regulations as said board of aldermen shall from time to time prescribe, to make investments of so much of the taxes collected and turned over to him as aforesaid, as shall be appli-

Special tax rate.

How collected.

For what purpose applied.

Commissioner of sinking fund.

cable as aforesaid to the payment of the principal of said bonds issued under this act, and to do or perform all such other services in connection with said bonds as said board of aldermen may prescribe, and such commissioner shall give bond and receive such compensation for his said services as said board of aldermen may determine. Bond of sinking fund commissioner. Compensation.

Sec. 6. That the provisions of sections one and five of this act shall be submitted to a vote of the qualified voters of the city of Raleigh, at an election to be held in said city on a day to be designated by the board of aldermen at any time after ten days from and after the ratification of this act, and after a public notice of the registration of such electors as is herein provided, designating the times and places at which such registration shall be had, and of the time when and places where the said election shall be held, which notice shall contain a copy of sections one and five, or a synopsis of the same, given for thirty days prior to said new registration, and published in two or more newspapers published in the City of Raleigh. And for the purpose of holding and conducting said election the city of Raleigh is hereby divided into four wards, each of which shall constitute a single voting precinct, the boundaries of which shall be as follows: The area included between the centres of Hillsboro street and Halifax street, and the extensions thereof to the centre of Union square, on the south and east respectively, and the exterior boundaries of said city on the north and west, shall constitute the first ward, or voting precinct. The area included between the centres of Halifax street and New Bern avenue, and the extensions thereof to the centre of Union Square, on the west and south respectively, and the exterior boundaries of said city on the north and east, shall constitute the second ward or voting precinct. The area included between the centres of New Bern avenue and Fayetteville street and the extensions thereof to the centre of Union square, on the north and west respectively, and the exterior boundaries of said city on the east and south, shall constitute the third ward, or voting precinct; and the area included between Fayetteville street and Hillsboro street, and the extensions thereof, to the centre of Union square, on the east and north respectively, and the exterior boundaries of said city on the south and west, shall constitute the fourth ward or voting precinct: Provided, that the wards or voting precincts herein constituted are for the sole purpose of holding and conducting the election herein provided and none other. The clerk of said city shall select and appoint three registrars in and for each of the wards or voting precincts aforesaid, and shall furnish them with proper registration books, and the said registrars shall, at the times and places designated by the board

Election on question of bonds shall be ordered. Registration. Division of wards. Boundaries of first ward. Boundaries of second ward. Boundaries of third ward. Boundaries of fourth ward. Proviso. Purpose for which wards are created. Appointment of registrars.

Registration books, when opened.

Election, how held.

Form of ballot.

When aldermen may issue bonds.

Proviso.

Successive elections may be ordered.

Conflicting laws repealed.

of aldermen, open said registration books and take a new and distinct registration of the qualified voters therein, as provided in elections for the aldermen of the City of Raleigh. Said election shall be held and returns thereof made, except as above provided, under the same rules and regulations as exist in the case of elections for aldermen of the city. Those qualified voters approving the issue of the bonds provided for in section one, and the levy and collection of the particular taxes provided for in section five of this act shall deposit in a ballot box a slip containing the printed or written word "Approved," and those disapproving the same shall deposit a like slip with the printed or written word "Disapproved." If a majority of such voters shall vote "Approved," it shall be deemed and held that a majority of the qualified voters of the City of Raleigh are in favor of giving the board of aldermen authority to issue the bonds authorized by section one of this act, and to levy the particular taxes authorized in section five of this act, and the board of aldermen shall have such authority. But if a majority of the qualified voters shall vote "Disapproved," then the board of aldermen shall not have such authority: Provided, that if at any election held under this act a majority of the qualified voters shall fail to vote in favor of issuing said bonds, it shall not prevent the board of aldermen of said city from ordering another election under this act at any time after the lapse of six months from the date of such former election; and if at such other election a majority of the qualified voters shall vote "Approved," it shall have the same force and effect as if no election had been previously held.

Sec. 7. That all laws and clauses of laws in conflict with the provisions of this act are hereby repealed.

Sec. 8. That this act shall be in force from and after its ratification.

Ratified the 28th day of February, A. D. 1899.

CHAPTER 160.

An act to incorporate the Cape Fear Power Company.

The General Assembly of North Carolina do enact:

Corporators.

Body corporate.

Corporate name.

Section 1. That R. Percy Gray, W. M. Morgan, S. T. Morgan and J. S. Manning, and their associates and successors be and they are hereby declared a body politic and corporate under the name and style of the "Cape Fear Power Company," and by that name shall have sixty years succession, and sue and be sued, plead and be impleaded, make and use a corporate seal and alter the same at pleasure, contract and be contracted with; and shall have and enjoy all the rights and privileges necessary for the purposes of this act.

Capital stock may be increased.

Sec. 2. That the capital stock of the said company shall be fifty thousand dollars, and may be increased from time to time, with the consent of a majority of the stockholders, to any additional amount by the issue and sale of shares of common and preferred stock, or both, upon such terms and conditions and under such regulations as the board of directors, with the approval of a majority of the stockholders of said company shall prescribe, but the par value of each share of stock shall be one hundred dollars; and the directors with the like approval of the stockholders may receive cash, labor, material, bonds, stocks, contracts, real or personal property, in payment of subscriptions to the capital stock, and may make such subscriptions payable in such manner or amounts and at such times as may be agreed upon with the subscribers, and whenever one hundred shares shall have been subscribed and the sum of one thousand dollars paid in cash, the subscribers, under the direction of a majority of the corporators hereinbefore named, who themselves shall be subscribers, may organize the said company by electing a board of directors and providing for the election or appointment of such other officers as may be necessary for the control and management of the business and affairs of said company, and thereupon they shall have and exercise all the powers and functions of a corporation under this charter and the laws of this state. Every subscriber to or holder of the stock of said company shall be liable for the debts of the said company to an amount equal to the amount unpaid on the stock subscribed for and held by him and no more.

Par value of stock.

When company may be organized.

Individual liability.

May borrow money.

Sec. 3. It shall be lawful for the said corporation, upon such terms as the stockholders or board of directors by their authority may determine, to borrow money, to issue its notes, obligations, bonds and debentures from time to time as they may elect, and to secure the same by mortgage or mortgages on its property and franchises in whole or in part as they may deem necessary or expedient; and it shall be lawful for the said corporation to acquire by original subscription, contract or otherwise, and to hold, manage, pledge, mortgage, sell, convey and dispose of or otherwise deal with, in like manner as individuals may do, shares of the capital stock, notes, bonds and other obligations of other companies organized under the laws of any of the United States.

Corporate powers.

Corporate powers.

Sec. 4. That the said company is authorized and empowered to supply to the public, including both individuals and corporations, whether private or municipal, within the counties of Guilford, Rowan, Davidson, Cabarrus, Mecklenburg and elsewhere in the state of North Carolina, power in the forms of electric current, hydraulic, pneumatic and steam pressure, or any of the said forms and in any or all other forms for use in driving machinery, and for light, heat and all other uses to which the power so supplied can be applicable, and to fix, charge, collect and receive payment therefor; and for the purpose of enabling the company to supply power as aforesaid the company is authorized and empowered to buy or otherwise acquire, generate, develop, store, use, transmit and distribute power of all kinds, and to locate, acquire, construct, equip, maintain and operate from an initial point on the Deep river and Cape Fear river, or any stream not navigable within the state of North Carolina where the company may establish a plant, either directly to consumers or users or to a distributing point in the city of Raleigh, and from the same or any other initial point in the said state of North Carolina either directly to consumers or users or to a distributing point in the city of Salisbury, and from the same or any other initial point in the said state of North Carolina either directly to consumers or users or to a distributing point in the town of Concord, and from the same or any other initial point in the said state of North Carolina either directly to consumers or users, or to a distributing point in the city of Charlotte, and from the same or any other initial point in the said state of North Carolina either directly to consumers or users, or to any other distributing point in North Carolina which the said company may establish by the most practicable routes, to be determined by the board of directors of the company, lines for the transmission of power by wires or poles or underground, and by cables, pipes, tubes, conduits and all other convenient appliances for power transmission with such connecting lines between the lines above mentioned, and also such branch lines within the said territory and elsewhere as the board of directors of the company may locate or authorize to be located for receiving, transmitting and distributing power; and the company may acquire, own, hold, sell or otherwise dispose of water power and water privileges in the state of North Carolina, and may locate, acquire, construct, equip, maintain and operate all necessary plants for generating and developing by water, steam or any other means, and for storing, using, transmitting, distributing, selling and developing power, including dams, gates, bridges, sluices, tunnels, stations and other buildings, boilers, engines, machinery, switches, lamps, motors and all other works, structures and appliances in the state of North Carolina: Provided, that the amount of land which the company may at any time hold within the state of North Carolina for any one water power and appurtenant works, as well as the land flowed or submerged with the water accumulated by a dam shall not exceed five thousand (5,000) acres ex-

Corporate power.

Proviso.

Maximum of land permitted to be held.

clusive of right-of-way: And provided further, that lines and appurtenances hereinbefore authorized for distributing power and light are to be constructed when on public streets or highways of any county, city or town under such reasonable regulations as the authorities respectively thereof shall, upon application from the company, prescribe.

May sell electrical power.

Sec. 5. That the said company shall have power, in addition to the powers hereinbefore enumerated, to carry on and conduct the business of generating, making, transmitting, furnishing and selling electricity for the purposes of lighting, heat and power and transmission of power, and to furnish and sell and contract for the furnishing and sale to persons, corporations, towns and cities of electricity for illuminating purposes or as motive power for running and propelling engines, cars, machinery and apparatus, and also for all other uses and purposes for which electricity is now or may be hereafter used, and to construct, maintain and operate a plant or plants for manufacturing, generating and transmitting electricity; to deal in, generate, furnish, supply and sell electricity, gas and all other kinds of power, forces, fluids, currents, matter and materials used or to be used for the purpose of illumination, heat and power; to carry on any and all business in anywise appertaining to or connected with the manufacturing and generating, distributing and furnishing of electricity for light, heat and power purposes, including the transaction of any and all business in which electricity is now or hereafter may be utilized, and all matters incidental or necessary to the distribution of electric light, heat and power; to manufacture and repair, sell and deal in any and all necessary appliances and machinery used in or which may be required or deemed advisable for or in connection with the utilization of electricity or in anywise appertaining thereto or connected therewith; to purchase, acquire, own, use, lease, let and furnish any and all kinds of electric machinery, apparatus and appliances; to purchase, acquire, own, hold, improve, let, lease, operate and maintain water rights and privileges and water powers; to supply water to persons, corporations, factories, towns and cities, for domestic purposes, and for use as power and for manufacturing purposes, and to charge, receive and collect such charges and rates therefor as may be deemed advisable or expedient; to construct, acquire, build and operate, maintain and lease in the state of North Carolina canals, ditches and flumes and pipe lines for the conducting of water; to maintain and operate railroads, street railways, motor lines and tramways, carry freight and passengers or freight or passengers thereon, and to charge, collect and receive tolls or fares for the same; to construct, build, purchase, buy, own, hold, lease, maintain and operate telegraph and telephone lines

Corporate powers.

Corporate powers.

wherever it may be deemed expedient, and to charge, receive and collect such charges and rates for the use of its telegraph and telephone lines and for the transmission of messages thereon as may be deemed reasonable; to construct, acquire, own, hold, lease, maintain and operate lines of wires, underground conduits, subways and other convenient conduits or appliances for the transmission of electricity and other energies, fluids, forces and currents as may be deemed advisable or expedient; to lease any part or all of its railroads, street railroads, motor lines and tramways to any other company or companies incorporated for the purpose of maintaining and operating a railroad, street railroad, motor line or tramway, and to lease or purchase, maintain and operate any part or all of any other railroad constructed by any other company upon such terms and conditions as may be agreed upon between said companies respectively; to apply to the proper authorities of any incorporated city or town or of the county in the state of North Carolina in which the railways, street railways, motor lines, tramways, telegraph lines, telephone lines, electric light and power lines, plants, underground conduits, subways, wires, poles and appliances of this corporation may extend or be designed or intended now or hereafter to extend, for a grant of any rights, powers, privileges and franchises for the maintenance or operation thereof; to accept, receive, own, hold, lease, all and singular, the same; to acquire by contract, purchase, lease or otherwise, and to accept, own and hold any rights, privileges or franchises heretofore granted to any person, firm, company or corporation, or which may be hereafter so granted by the proper authorities of any such incorporated city or town, or of any county in the state of North Carolina, to purchase, acquire, lease, rent, own, hold and improve real property in such quantities as may be deemed expedient; to build dwelling houses, and to build and operate stores, mills, schools, factories, warehouses and any and all other buildings or structures desirable or convenient; to sell and dispose of the same on such terms as may be desirable or convenient; to lay out and plot any real property belonging to or acquired by the corporation into lots, blocks, squares, factory sites and other convenient forms, and to lay out, plat and dedicate to public use streets, avenues, alleys and parks; to purchase, possess, own, hold, rent, lease and improve all and any property, real, personal and mixed, necessary, desirable or convenient for the use of the corporation or the transaction of its business or any part thereof; and to do and perform all and other matters and things necessary, proper or convenient for the accomplishment of the objects above specified.

May lease property.

Corporate powers.

May enter enter upon certain lands for particular purposes.

Sec. 6. It shall be lawful for the president and directors, their agents, superintendents, engineers or others in their employ to enter at all times upon all lands or water for the purpose of exploring or surveying the works of said company and locating the same, doing no unnecessary damage to private property; and when the location of said works shall have been determined upon and a survey of the same deposited in the office of the secretary of state then it shall be lawful for the said company, by the officers, agents, engineers, superintendents, contractors and others in its employ, to enter upon, take possession of, have, hold, use and excavate any such lands, and to erect all the structures necessary and suitable for the completion or repairing of said works, subject to such compensation as is hereafter provided: Provided always, that payment or tender of payment of all demands for the occupancy of all lands upon which the said works may be laid out be made before the said company shall enter upon or break ground upon the premises, except for surveying or locating said works, unless the consent of the owners be first had and obtained: And provided further, that such locating of its works and filing of its surveys in the office of the secretary of state shall not preclude said company from making from time to time other location of works and filing surveys of the same as its business of development requires.

May enter upon possession of necessary real estate.

Proviso.

May tender payment for lands.

Proviso.

Sec. 7. When any land or right-of-way may be required by said company for the purpose of constructing and operating its works, and for want of agreement as to the value thereof or for any other cause the same can not be purchased from the owner, the same may be taken at a valuation of five commissioners or a majority of them, to be appointed in term time on petition by the judge of the superior court of the county where some part of the land is situated: Provided, nevertheless, that if any person or persons on whose land the works may be located, or if the said company shall be dissatisfied with the valuation of the commissioners, then in that case the party so dissatisfied may file exceptions to the valuation in the pending proceedings, subject to the rules and regulations prescribed by law or the course and practice of the court. The proceedings of the said commissioners, with a full description of the land, shall be returned under the hands and seals of a majority of them to the court from which the commission issued, there after confirmation by the judge to remain a matter of record, and also to be registered in the office of the register of deeds of each county wherein the land condemned lies, and the land so valued shall vest in the said company as soon as the valuation shall have been paid or tendered: Provided, that upon application for the appointment of commissioners under this section it shall be made to appear to the satisfaction of the court that at least ten days' notice had been previously given of the application to the owner or owners

When disagreement as to value of real estate, arbitrators may be appointed.

Proviso.

Either party may appeal.

Proviso.

of the land so proposed to be condemned, or if the owner or owners be under disability, then to the guardian, if any, of such owner or owners, as well as to such owner or owners, or if the owner or owners who are not under disability, or the guardian of such owners as are under disability can not be found within the county, or the owner or owners is or are not known then that such notice of such application had been published once a week for at least four weeks in some newspaper printed in the county in which the application is made: And provided further, that the valuation provided for in this section shall be made on oath to the commissioners aforesaid, which oath may be administered by any clerk of the court, justice of the peace or other person authorized by law to administer oaths: Provided further, that the right of condemnation herein granted shall not authorize said company to remove or invade the burial ground of any individual without his or her consent.

Failure to comply with certain conditions.

Proviso.

Valuation shall be made on oath.

Proviso.

May not invade burial ground.

Extent of right to condemn land.

Sec. 8. The right of the said company to condemn land in the manner aforesaid shall extend to the condemning of strips of land not exceeding twenty-five feet in width, with necessary additional width in deep cuts and fillings required by the company for its roadways, power, transmission lines and all other lands necessary for the construction and operation of its own works, as well as the necessary water, including in the land and water thus described water powers, water privileges and land overflowed or submerged with water accumulated by the company's dams.

Works may be operated before completion of entire plant.

Sec. 9. A part of the works of said company may be constructed without completing its entire works, and the said works may be operated and electric current transmitted and delivered and charges collected therefor, notwithstanding the entire works of the company have not been completed.

Representation of stockholders in meeting.

Sec. 10. Every stockholder in the company shall at all meetings or elections be entitled to one vote for every share of stock registered in his name. The stockholders of the said company may enact such by-laws, rules and regulations for the management of the affairs of the company as they may deem proper or expedient. Meetings of the stockholders and directors may be held at Lockville, in Chatham county, where the principal office of the company shall be, or elsewhere in the state of North Carolina, at such times and places as the stockholders may in the by-laws or otherwise prescribe.

Principal office.

Directors, how elected.

Sec. 11. The board of directors shall be elected from the stockholders of said company and shall consist of such number as the stockholders shall prescribe from time to time by the by-laws, and shall be elected at the stockholders' annual meeting, to be held on such days as the by-laws of the company may direct, and shall continue in office for the term of one year from and after

Term of office

the date of their election and until their successors are elected and qualified; and they shall choose one of their number president; and in case of death, resignation or incapacity of any member of the board of directors during his term of office, the said board shall choose his successor for the unexpired term. Election of president.

Sec. 12. That a copy of any by law or regulation of the said company under its corporate seal, attested by the secretary and by the president, shall be received as prima facie evidence for and against the said company in any judicial proceeding. Copy of by-laws prima facie evidence.

Sec. 13. This act shall be in force from and after its ratification.

Ratified the 28th day of February, A. D. 1899.

CHAPTER 161.

An act to incorporate The Bank of Alamance.

The General Assembly of North Carolina do enact:

Section 1. That E. S. Parker, J. L. Scott, Jr., McBride Holt, J. B. Thompson, B. S. Robertson, Charles A. Scott, and their associates and successors and assigns, be and they are hereby created a body politic and corporate under the name and style of "The Bank of Alamance," and by such name may acquire, hold and convey real and personal property, sue and be sued, plead and be impleaded in any of the courts of the state and have a continuous succession for thirty years and a common seal for the purposes indicated in this act. Corporators. Body corporate. Corporate name. Corporate powers.

Sec. 2. That the capital stock of said corporation shall not be less than four thousand dollars, which may be increased from time to time to a sum not exceeding fifty thousand dollars in shares of fifty dollars each. Said corporation may commence business when four thousand dollars shall have been paid in. Capital stock. Shares. When commence business.

Sec. 3. That the affairs of the corporation shall be governed by a board of not more than nine nor less than five directors, who shall be elected annually by the stockholders. The directors so elected shall choose from their own number a president and a vice-president, who shall serve for one year and until their successors shall have been elected. A majority of the board shall have power to fill vacancies in its body until the next succeeding annual meeting, to make rules, regulations and by-laws for the government of said corporation and for the conduct of its business, also to appoint its officers and fix their salaries. Affairs of corporation, how governed. Officers.

Sec. 4. That the office or banking house of the corporation shall be located in the town of Graham, North Carolina. Banking house at Graham.

Corporate rights and powers.

Sec. 5. That the corporation shall have all the powers, rights and privileges and immunities granted to any bank or banking institution by the laws of North Carolina and shall have the power to receive and pay out the lawful currency of the country, to deal in mercantile paper, exchange, gold and silver coins, stocks, bonds, notes and other securities; to buy and sell real and personal property, to lend money on personal security or to make loan secured by real or personal property; to receive deposits; and for the use and loan of money may charge a rate of interest per annum as high as may be allowed by the laws of the state, and may take and receive said interest at the time of making said loan free from all other control or liability whatsoever. When married women or minors shall deposit money or other property in the bank to their own credit or in their own name, they may withdraw the same on their own individual check and be bound thereby. Deeds of real estate shall be made by the president and vice-president under the seal of the corporation. When the bank shall cause to be sold any of the property of any of its debtors on which it has a lien to secure a debt, or when such property shall be sold for its benefit, the bank may bid for and purchase any and all such property and its title thereto, when so acquired, shall be valid and binding in all respects: Provided, that nothing in this act contained shall operate or be so construed as to delay or impair the mortgagor's equity of redemption.

Deeds of real estate under sale of corporation.

Sale of property of debtors.

Proviso.

Mortgagor's equity shall not be impaired.

Transferal of stock.

Sec. 6. That the stock held by any one shall be transferred only on the books of said corporation, either in person or by attorney.

Corporate powers and privileges.

Sec. 7. This corporation in [is] invested with the powers and privileges incident to savings banks; may receive deposits in very small sums, the limit to be fixed by its board of directors, and may pay interest thereon by way of dividends out of the net earnings or as fixed according as may be agreed on between the bank and its depositors; and the board of directors are hereby fully authorized to make all needful by-laws and regulations for conducting and carrying into effect the savings bank feature of this corporation.

Sec. 8. That this act shall be in force from and after its ratification.

Ratified the 28th day of February, A. D. 1899.

CHAPTER 162.

An act to amend chapter three hundred and twenty (320) of the private acts of eighteen hundred and ninety-three, to change the corporate limits of the town of Huntersville, in Mecklenburg county.

The General Assembly of North Carolina do enact:

Section 1. That chapter three hundred and twenty (320) of the private laws of eighteen hundred and ninety-three (1893) be and the same is hereby amended by striking out all after the word "following" in line five (5), section one (1) of said chapter, down to and including the word "corner" in line ten thereof, and substituting the following: "The corporate limits of the town of Huntersville shall be as follows: Beginning one-half mile due north of the Atlantic, Tennessee and Ohio Railroad crossing, near R. H. W. Barker's storehouse, and running thence one-half mile due west; thence one mile due south; thence three fourths of a mile due east; thence one mile due north; thence one-fourth mile due west to the beginning corner, making said town one mile from its north to its south limits, and three-fourths of a mile from its west to its east limits." Chapter 320, private laws of 1893, relating to corporate limits of Huntersville, Mecklenburg county, amended.

Sec. 2. That all laws in conflict with this act are hereby repealed. Conflicting laws repealed.

Sec. 3. That this act shall be in force from and after its ratification.

Ratified the 28th day of February, A. D. 1899.

CHAPTER 163.

An act to incorporate the town of Gibson, in Richmond county, North Carolina.

The General Assembly of North Carolina do enact:

Section 1. That the town of Gibson, in the county of Richmond, state of North Carolina, be and the same is hereby incorporated under the name and style of the town of Gibson, and said town shall have all the powers and be subject to all restrictions of chapter sixty-two of The Code for the government of incorporated towns, and all acts of the general assembly of North Carolina amending the same not inconsistent with this act. Town of Gibson, Richmond county, incorporated.

Sec. 2. That the officers of the said town shall consist of a mayor, five commissioners, a constable, a clerk and treasurer and as many policemen as may be necessary in the opinion of the said Town officers.

town for preserving peace and good order therein. That the mayor and five commissioners shall be elected by the qualified voters of said town as hereinafter provided. That the other officers of said incorporation shall be elected by the commissioners. That until the first election under this act shall be held and the officers found to be elected by the same shall have qualified, W. W. Goodwin shall be mayor and T. G. Gibson, W. E. Caldwell, P. R. Mason, C. L. Gibson and Joshua Gibson shall be commissioners of said incorporation, and that the said commissioners shall elect the clerk and treasurer, constable, and policemen herein provided for, whose terms of office shall expire with the term of the said commissioners.

How elected.

Temporary officers.

Corporate limits.

SEC. 3. That the corporate limits of said town shall be and include all the territory embraced within the following boundaries, to-wit: Beginning at center of stage road and at the point where said road crosses the state line, said beginning being on a ditch bridge, and running as said state line north forty-five west twenty-four chains to a stake in said line; thence north sixty-three east to intersection of road leading from Conclave to Rockingham; thence south forty-five east to said stage road; thence continuing south forty-five east thirty chains to a corner; thence south sixty-three west to the state line; thence as said state line to the beginning.

First election of officers.

Annual election thereafter.

Qualifications of electors.

SEC. 4. That there shall be held on the first Monday in May, Anno Domini eighteen hundred and ninety-nine, and on the first Monday in May in every year thereafter, an election in said town for a mayor and five commissioners thereof; that all duly qualified electors of the county of Richmond or such county as said town of Gibson may then be within, who shall have resided ninety days in said town next preceding the day of election shall be qualified voters of the said town: Provided, they shall be registered as herein prescribed. That the commissioners shall appoint a registrar and three judges of election, who shall hold the election herein required. The registrar shall register in a book to be provided for that purpose by the commissioners all qualified electors who shall take the oath prescribed for electors in said county, and also an oath that they have been residents of the said town for ninety days preceding the election; that the registration book shall be kept open for the registration of voters on the four Saturdays preceding the Saturday before the election in each year between the hours of nine o'clock a. m. and four o'clock p. m., at which time and no other all electors shall be registered who shall present themselves and comply with the provisions of this act: that on the second Saturday preceding the election any voter of said town may challenge any person registered, and the constable shall serve a notice on the person

Appointment of registrars and judges.

Registration of qualified electors.

challenged to appear before the registrar and judges of election on the succeeding Saturday, when and where the challenge shall be heard and decided; that no challenge shall be heard at any other time; that the registrar and judges of election shall attend at the polling place with the registration book on the day of election; that the polls shall be opened at seven o'clock a. m. and shall be closed at sunset; that the vote shall be by ballot, one ballot to contain the person voted for for mayor and the names of the five persons who shall be voted for for commissioners, which ballots may be on paper of any color, and may be with or without device. That before entering on the discharge of any of their duties the registrar and judges of election shall take such oath and in such manner as is required by the laws of North Carolina for registrars and judges of state and county elections before some justice of the peace for said county; that at the close of said election the said registrar and judges of election shall count the votes for mayor and commissioners, and the person receiving the highest number of votes for the office of mayor shall be duly declared elected thereto; and the five persons receiving the highest number of votes for the office of commissioner shall be duly declared elected thereto, and said registrar and judges shall post at some public places in said town the names of the persons voted for for each office and the number of votes received by each; and the clerk and treasurer of said incorporation shall forthwith notify the persons so declared elected of the fact of their election; and that the registration and poll books of the said town shall be deposited with the clerk of superior court of Richmond county or such county as Gibson may at that time be located in, immediately after the said election, to be safely kept by him until needed for the purpose of the next election.

Constable shall serve notice on persons challenged.

Polls, when opened.

Registrar and judges of election shall take oath.

Clerk and treasurer shall notify persons elected.

Sec. 5. That no person shall be eligible to any office in said town unless he be a duly qualified voter therein. That the term of office of mayor and commissioners shall begin on the Tuesday following the election in each year, and before entering on the discharge of his duties of the said office they shall each take the oath prescribed by law for public officers before some justice of the peace for said county.

Eligibility to office.

Term of office.

Sec. 6. That the mayor shall preside at all the meetings of the commissioners and shall have power to call special meetings of the commissioners when he shall deem the same proper. That the commissioners shall elect one of their number mayor pro tempore, who shall fill the office of mayor during the absence or disability of the mayor. That the mayor shall see that the ordinances of the town are enforced, and shall have the criminal jurisdiction of a justice of the peace within the limits of the said town.

Mayor shall preside at the meeting of commissioners.

Mayor shall have criminal jurisdiction.

Powers of commissioners.

Sec. 7. That in addition to the powers conferred upon the commissioners by said chapter sixty-two of The Code of North Carolina and the acts of the legislature amending the same they shall have the power to open, change, enlarge or discontinue streets in said town, and may condemn land for this purpose upon making just compensation to the owner thereof. That in case the said commissioners shall decide to condemn any land for this purpose they shall appoint three disinterested freeholders in said town, who shall view the land proposed to be condemned, and after giving the owner thereof five days' notice to appear before them, and contest the matter if he so elect, they shall, if they deem the land necessary for said purposes, assess the damage whatever sum they think just, which sum shall be paid by the said town, and the owner or owners of the said land shall have the right to appeal to the superior court of said county from the assessment of said appraisers, notice of appeal to be given within ten days.

May condemn land.

Board of assessors

May appeal.

Empowered to levy taxes.

Sec. 8. That the commissioners shall have the power to levy taxes upon the real and personal property and polls in said town, the property tax not to exceed thirty cents on the one hundred dollars valuation and the poll tax not to exceed ninety cents on each poll taxable under the laws of the state, and the valuation of all property shall be the same as that at which it is assessed for taxation by the state and county for their purposes. That the taxes shall be listed with the clerk and treasurer of said town during the first twenty days in June in each year, and all persons failing to list their taxables shall be liable to a double tax: Provided, the clerk and treasurer may take a list of the taxes for each person failing to list from the returns for taxation for state and county purposes for the current year, which shall be as binding upon the taxpayer as if their taxables had been duly listed. All property and polls in said town on the first day of June in each year shall be listed, the town clerk and treasurer shall make out and complete the tax list and place copy thereof in the hands of the constable on the first Monday in September in each year, which shall have all the force and effect of an execution. That said tax list shall be a lien on all real property in said town, and all personal property shall be liable to be seized and sold on ten days' notice for taxes; and real estate may be sold for taxes by constable in the same manner as sales are made under execution.

Limitation to tax rate.

Taxes, how listed.

Proviso

Tax list shall be be placed in hands of constable.

Tax list a lien on all real property.

Commissioners empowered to pass ordinances.

Sec. 9. That the commissioners shall have the power to pass ordinances to be enforced by suitable fines for the preservation of the peace and regulation of the good order of said town; they shall also have the power to levy and cause to be collected such reasonable privilege taxes as they may deem proper on the professions, callings, occupations, teachers and businesses carried on in said town.

Sec. 10. That the clerk and treasurer and the constable shall each give a bond in the sum of five hundred dollars with sufficient surety, payable to the state of North Carolina, conditional for the faithful performance of the duties of their respective offices and for the proper accounting for and paying over to those entitled to the same of all sums of money which may come into their hands by reason of or under color of their respective offices; that all policemen shall give bond if required by the commissioners in the sum to be fixed by them, conditional for the faithful performance of their duties; that the term of office of the clerk and treasurer shall be the same as that of the commissioners electing him: Provided, that the commissioners may remove any person holding this office for cause; the constable and policemen shall hold office during the pleasure of the commissioners.

Treasurer, clerk and constable shall give bond.

Policemen shall give bond.

Proviso.

Commissioners may remove officers.

Sec. 11. That the board of commissioners of said incorporation shall not grant license for the sale of spirituous liquor in said town, nor shall the board of county commissioners in the county in which Gibson is now located, or in which it may hereafter be located, grant any license to sell spirituous liquors within said town.

License for sale of spirituous liquors shall not be granted.

Sec. 12. That all ordinances passed by the said commissioners shall not take effect until the same have been posted for five days at four public places in said town.

Ordinances shall be publicly advertised five days before effective.

Sec. 13. That this act shall be in force from and after its ratification.

Ratified the 28th day of February, A. D. 1899.

CHAPTER 164.

An act to refund certain bonded indebtedness of the city of Wilmington.

Whereas, the city of Wilmington owes among others certain coupon bonds bearing interest at the rate of five per centum per annum, payable semi-annually and maturing January first, nineteen hundred and twelve (1912), to the amount of one hundred and fifty thousand dollars; and certain coupon bonds bearing interest at the rate of six per centum per annum, payable semi-annually and maturing the first day of January, nineteen hundred and eighteen (1918), to the [amount] of one hundred thousand dollars; and certain coupon bonds bearing interest at the rate of five per centum per annum, payable semi-annually, and maturing first day of January, nineteen hundred and nineteen

Preamble.

(1919), to the amount of one hundred and fifty thousand dollars; and

Whereas, there is a provision contained in the said bonds which mature on the said first day of January, nineteen hundred and twelve (1912), to the effect that they may be called in and paid at any time after the expiration of ten years from their date of issue, and the said city of Wilmington, through its proper officers, is desirous of so calling in the said bonds; and

Whereas, the said city of Wilmington is desirous of refunding the aforesaid bonds which mature in the years nineteen hundred and eighteen (1918) and nineteen hundred and nineteen and (1919), or such part thereof as they may lawfully effect by exchange or otherwise; now, therefore,

The General Assembly of North Carolina do enact:

To pay certain bonds of city of Wilmington. Aldermen empowered to issue bonds

Section 1. That for the purpose of paying said bonds of the city of Wilmington which mature January first nineteen hundred and twelve (1912), the board of aldermen of the city of Wilmington by and with the sanction and approval of the board of audit and finance of said city, are authorized and empowered to issue coupon bonds bearing interest, payable semi-annually, at a rate not to exceed four per centum per annum, to an amount not to exceed one hundred and fifty thousand dollars and in denominations not less than one hundred dollars nor more than one thousand dollars, said bonds to be payable thirty years from the first day of July, eighteen hundred and ninety-nine (1899).

Interest payable semi-annually.

Issue not to exceed $150,000.

For the purpose of refunding debts. When bonds mature.

Sec. 2. That for the purpose of refunding as much of the said bonded indebtedness maturing the first day of January, nineteen hundred and eighteen (1918) [and] on January first, nineteen hundred and nineteen (1919) as may be effected with the holders thereof, the said board of aldermen by and with the sanction and approval of the said board of audit and finance are hereby authorized and empowered to issue from time to time coupon bonds bearing interest payable semi-annually at a rate not exceeding four per centum per annum to an amount not exceeding two hundred and fifty thousand dollars, and in denominations of not less than one hundred dollars and not more than one thousand dollars, said bonds to be payable thirty years after the first day of July, eighteen hundred and ninety-nine (1899), all of the said bonds to be issued under the provisions of this act shall be payable at the office of the city clerk and treasurer or elsewhere, as the said board of aldermen and the said board of audit and finance may see fit, and shall not be valid unless signed by the mayor of said city and by the chairman of the said board of audit and finance and countersigned by the said clerk and treasurer of said city.

Maximum amount to be issued.

Shall not be valid unless signed by certain persons.

Sec. 3. That said bonds shall not be sold or exchanged at a less sum and rate than their par value; they shall not be subject to taxation by the said city for any purpose whatever and the coupons from and after maturity shall be receivable in payment of any and all taxes or other indebtedness due the said city.

Shall not be sold at less than par.

Sec. 4. That the said bonds at the option of the holder or holders thereof shall be registered by the clerk and treasurer of said city, and after such registration shall be transferable only by endorsement.

Bonds to be registered.

Sec. 5. All executors, administrators, guardians, trustees and all other persons acting in a fiduciary capacity, including those who now hold or may hereafter hold any of the bonds of said city maturing during the years nineteen hundred and twelve, nineteen hundred and eighteen and nineteen hundred and nineteen are hereby fully authorized and empowered to exchange them at any time for the bonds issued under this act or to invest their funds in the same.

Executors, etc., authorized and empowered to invest funds in their hands in said bonds.

Sec. 6. Any officer or employee of the said city who shall apply the proceeds of any bond or bonds issued under this act or exchange any such in any other manner or for any other purpose than is provided for in this act, or shall issue or have issued any more of said bonds than are necessary for the specific purposes of this act shall be deemed guilty of a misdemeanor, and upon conviction shall be fined not less than two hundred dollars or imprisoned not less than two months, or both, at the discretion of the court.

Officers applying proceeds of bonds for purposes other than herein specified, guilty of a misdemeanor.

Sec. 7. That the corporate authorities of said city shall annually levy a tax upon the property of the citizens of said city and upon the polls, and upon such property of non-residents which may be situate in said city and subject to taxation, to provide for the payment of the interest that may accrue upon said bonds, and in like manner provide for the payment of the principal of said bonds at maturity by creating a sinking fund for that purpose.

Annual tax levy to provide for payment of interest on bonds, etc.

Sec. 8. That whenever any of the bonds referred to in sections one and two of this act shall be paid or exchanged they shall be burned by the chairman of the board of audit and finance in the presence of the board.

Bonds when paid, shall be burned.

Sec. 9. That all laws and clauses of laws inconsistent with the provisions of this act are hereby repealed.

Conflicting laws repealed.

Sec. 10. That this act shall be in force from and after its ratification.

Ratified the 28th day of February, A. D. 1899.

CHAPTER 165.

An act to authorize the town of Highlands, in Macon county, to issue bonds and levy special tax.

The General Assembly of North Carolina do enact:

Purpose for which bonds may be issued.

Section 1. That for the purposes of building a hall, library, reading and lecture rooms in the town of Highlands, Macon county, the commissioners of said town are hereby authorized and empowered to issue bonds of the town to an amount not exceeding three thousand dollars, of such denominations as the board of aldermen or town commissioners may deem advisable, bearing interest from date thereof not to exceed the rate of six per centum per annum, with interest coupons attached, payable yearly at such times and at such places as may be deemed advisable by said board of commissioners, said bonds to be of such form and tenor and transferable in such way, and the principal thereof payable or redeemable at such time or times, not exceeding ten years from the date thereof, and at such place or places as said board may determine. Said bonds shall be signed by the mayor and commissioners of said town.

Maximum amount of bonds.

Interest.

Principal, when payable.

Bonds, how signed.

Special tax may be levied to pay interest and principal when due.

Sec. 2. That for the purpose of providing for the payment of the interest accruing on and the principal at maturity of such bonds as may be issued under this act, the board of commissioners of said town of Highlands are authorized annually and at the time of levying other town taxes, to levy and lay a special tax on all property within the corporate limits of said town, subject to taxation, and on all taxable polls of not exceeding thirty cents on the one hundred dollars worth of property, and not exceeding ninety cents on the poll, said tax to be strictly applied for the purposes herein mentioned. So much of all taxes levied and collected in the corporate limits of said town under this act as may not be required to pay the interest on said bonds as the same falls due, and can not or may not be applied to the purchase or discharge of the bonds for which said taxes are levied and collected, shall be invested so as to secure the payment at maturity of the principal of said bonds; and to insure the due investment of the amounts collected from year to year in excess of that required to pay the said interest, the board of town commissioners shall cause the said excess to be turned over to the treasurer of said town for a sinking fund. It shall be the duty of the treasurer, under such general rules and regulations as said board of town commissioners may from time to time prescribe, to make investment of so much of the taxes collected and turned over to him as aforesaid, as shall be applicable as aforesaid to the payment

Limitation to special tax.

Surplus from special tax, how applied.

Excess shall be turned over to treasurer of town for sinking fund of the principal of said bonds issued under this act, and to do or perform all such other services in connection with said bonds as said board may prescribe. Such treasurer shall give such bond as said board may prescribe, and such bond shall be liable for all moneys coming into the hands of said treasurer.

Sec. 3. That the provisions of this act shall be submitted to a vote of the qualified voters of the town of Highlands on the first Monday in May, eighteen hundred and ninety-nine, under the rules and regulations prescribed for members of the board of commissioners of said town. The town commissioners shall cause a notice of said election and of the purpose of the same to be posted at four public places in said town for thirty days before said election. All qualified voters wishing to vote in favor of the issuing of said bonds and the levying of the tax herein provided for, shall vote a written or printed ticket with the word "Approved," and those wishing to vote against the issuing of the bonds and levying the tax shall vote a ticket with the word written or printed "Disapproved." If a majority of such voters shall vote "Approved," it shall be deemed and held that a majority of the qualified voters of the town of Highlands are in favor of issuing the bonds and levying the tax, and in such case this act shall be and remain in full force and effect. But if a majority shall vote "Disapproved," this act shall be null and void.

Provisions of this act shall be submitted to voters for ratification.

Notice of election.

Form of ballot.

Sec. 4. This act shall be in force from its ratification.

Ratified the 28th day of February, A. D. 1899.

CHAPTER 166.

An act to incorporate "The Presbyterian Female College."

Whereas, on the thirtieth day of May, eighteen hundred and ninety-six, a corporation was formed under the general laws of North Carolina, authorizing the formation of corporations before the clerk, by filing articles of incorporation before the clerk of the superior court of Mecklenburg county, under the name and style of The Presbyterian Female College, the business of which corporation being to carry on and conduct a female school and college for the education and instruction of white females, in the city of Charlotte, or near thereto, in the county of Mecklenburg, which school or college was immediately thereafter inaugurated in the city of Charlotte, and which has since that time been, and still is, conducted by the said corporation.

Preamble.

And whereas, it is the object and desire of the said corporation to enlarge its field of work and to carry on and conduct

Preamble continued.

female education, not only in the city of Charlotte, but also in the city of Statesville, county of Iredell, and at such other place or places in western North Carolina as the board of trustees hereinafter enumerated, or their successors in office, may determine; therefore,

The General Assembly of North Carolina do enact:

Corporators.

Section 1. That J. B. Shearer, A. T. Graham, J. H. Hill, J. Rumple, J. M. Rose, Jr., W. G. F. Harper, P. B. Fetzer, J. R. Howerton, J. W. Stagg, A. G. Brenizer, W. S. Alexander, John R. Irwin, Frank Robinson and A. C. Miller, and their successors in office, be and they are hereby created a body politic and corporate by the name and style of The Presbyterian Female College, and by that name shall have perpetual succession and a common seal, may sue and be sued, and may purchase, take, receive and hold any real or personal property whatever, and may sell, transfer, lease, mortgage and convey any such property. That the corporators in this section named shall constitute the board of trustees of the said Presbyterian Female College, and shall hold their office for a term of two years, or until their successors are elected, as hereinbefore provided for.

Corporate name.

Perpetual succession.

Trustees.

Constitution and by-laws.

Sec. 2. That the trustees of The Presbyterian Female College are authorized to make a constitution and by-laws for the government of such schools or collges as they may control, generally to do and perform any and all acts necessary for this [their] proper conduct and management. They shall have the right to elect a president for each school or college, and such professors, tutors and officers as they may deem proper. They shall elect one of their number president of the board of trustees, and may appoint a treasurer, secretary and such other officers and servants as may be deemed expedient, and said trustees may prescribe the mode of election of said officers, with terms thereof, and may make by-laws for regulating the duties of said trustees and of all officers appointed by them. That six trustees shall constitute a quorum for the transaction of business.

President may appoint treasurer and other officers.

Number of trustees.

How elected.

Sec. 3. That the trustees of The Presbyterian Female College shall not exceed twenty-five nor be less than ten in number, and shall be elected, one-half each by the Presbyteries of Mecklenburg and Concord respectively. That at the first meeting of the said Presbyteries after the acceptance of this charter, the number of trustees shall be fixed by the said presbyteries, subject to change within the above limits. That, in the event other presbyteries in the state of North Carolina should be admitted to participate in the management of the said The Presbyterian Female College, they shall have the right so to do and may elect such number of trustees as may be agreed upon by Mecklenburg and Concord Presbyteries, and when such trustees are elected they shall have the right to participate in the management of the affairs of the said corporation. That the said trustees so elected by the said presbyteries shall hold their office for such term or terms as the respective presbyteries may fix, or until their sucessors in office are appointed. Term of office.

Sec. 4. That the president and professors of any school or college conducted by The Presbyterian Female College, shall be the faculty thereof, and, with the advice and consent of the trustees, shall have the power to confer such degrees and marks of literary distinction as are usually conferred in colleges and universities in the United States. Power to confer degrees.

Sec. 5. That the real property of the said corporation shall not exceed five hundred thousand dollars ($500,000), and that the personal property thereof shall not exceed in value the sum of five hundred thousand dollars ($500,000), and that all the real and personal property of the said corporation shall be exempt from taxation. Maximum amount of property that can be held.

Sec. 6. That the trustees of The Presbyterian Female College be and they are hereby authorized to change the name of said college and the title name of the body politic hereby created, and in case of such change of name, the new body politic and corporate shall succeed to all the rights, powers, property, privileges and advantages conferred by this act upon The Presbyterian Female College. Trustees authorized to change name of college.

Sec. 7. That The Presbyterian Female College, the body politic created by this act, shall succeed to all the rights, powers, property, whether real or personal, privileges, advantages and franchises vested in The Presbyterian Female College, the corporation created under the general laws of this state, formed by filing articles before the clerk of the superior court of Mecklenburg county, as in the preamble of this act, hereinbefore set forth, in as full and as ample a manner as if such rights, powers, property, real and personal, privileges, advantages and franchises had been originally vested in the corporation authorized under this act. Corporate powers.

Sec. 8. That the agreement heretofore entered into by and between the presbyteries of Mecklenburg and Concord, in regard to their co-operation and the management of the schools or colleges provided for in this act, shall be and the same is hereby declared to be a part of the fundamental law governing the conduct of the said corporation, and the same shall be incorporated in the by-laws governing it; but nothing herein shall be so construed as to prevent the said Presbyteries from making any change in the said plan of co-operation. Agreement heretofore entered into between presbyteries.

Sec. 9. That the said corporation is hereby authorized to carry

Location of institutions.

on and conduct female education, not only in the city of Charlotte, but also in the city of Statesville, county of Iredell, and at such other place or places in Western North Carolina as its board of trustees or their successors in office may determine, and to this end, they are hereby authorized and empowered to establish such schools or colleges as they may deem best for the interests of the corporation, and, generally, to do and perform any and all acts necessary to be done in the prosecution of the business contemplated by this act of incorporation.

Sec. 10. That this act shall be in force from and after its ratification.

Ratified the 28th day of February, A. D. 1899.

CHAPTER 167.

An act to amend the acts of the general assembly incorporating the town of Southern Pines.

The General Assembly of North Carolina do enact:

Section 1, chapter 159, laws of 1887, amended.

Section 1. That section one of chapter one hundred and fifty-nine, act of eighteen hundred and eighty-seven, be amended by adding after the word "towns," in the fourth line, "except as hereinafter provided."

Corporate limits altered.

Sec. 2. That section two of said chapter, as amended in eighteen hundred and ninety-one and eighteen hundred and ninety-five, be amended by striking out all of said section after the word "beginning," in second line of said section, and adding: "Beginning at a point at the intersection of the old Morganton road and the Raleigh and Augusta Air Line Railroad, thence running as the said old Morganton road north sixty-five degrees twenty-nine minutes thirty seconds west (one thousand and seven feet) to a point on the west side of Bennett street; thence north forty-seven degrees fifty-seven minutes east (forty-one and six-tenths feet) to the corner of the said Bennett street and the avenue leading to the Southern Pines Cemetery; thence running with the line of said avenue north sixty-two degrees twenty-five minutes west (one thousand four hundred and thirty-one and eight-tenths feet); thence south eleven degrees four minutes thirty seconds west (three hundred and ninety-three and three-tenths feet) to the southeast corner of Southern Pines Cemetery; thence along the southerly side of said cemetery south eighty-nine degrees nine minutes twenty seconds west (two hundred and thirty-one and six-tenths feet) to the southwest corner of said cemetery; thence north fifty-nine degrees forty-one minutes forty seconds west (one thousand one hundred and forty and four-tenths feet) to the southwest corner of Morris' vineyard, the same, being the southeast corner of Tarbell's vineyard; thence north sixteen degrees fifty-six minutes twenty seconds west (three thousand five hundred and three and four-tenths feet) along the easterly line of the Rogers tract; thence north fifteen degrees twenty-eight minutes fifty seconds east (eight hundred and fifty-nine feet); thence south eighty-seven degrees thirty-four minutes east (one thousand one hundred and fifty feet); thence north fifty-one degrees seventeen minutes forty seconds east (two thousand four hundred and ninety-five and five-tenths feet) to a point on the easterly side of the Pee Dee road; thence as the Pee Dee south three degrees six minutes fifty seconds west (five hundred and fifty-six and eight-tenths feet); thence south nine degrees fifty-one minutes thirty seconds east (three hundred and seventy-three and eight-tenths feet); thence south fifteen degrees thirty-three minutes ten seconds (two hundred and fifty-three and eight-tenths feet); thence south one degree thirty-eight minutes twenty seconds west (eight hundred feet); thence south six degrees twenty-four minutes thirty seconds west (eight hundred and eighty-three and two-tenths feet) to the intersection of the Pee Dee road and the easterly side of Illinois avenue; thence as the easterly side of Illinois avenue south thirty-six degrees forty-nine minutes fifty seconds east (one thousand two hundred and twenty-three and two-tenths feet) to the intersection of the said easterly side of Illinois avenue and northerly side of Hale street; thence as the northerly side of Hale street north fifty-five degrees ten minutes ten seconds east (one thousand nine hundred and fifty and seven-tenths feet) to the centre of McDeed's creek; thence as the centre of McDeed's creek (as shown on a plan entitled "Map showing boundaries of the town of Southern Pines, Moore county, N. C.", made by H. O. Parker, civil engineer of said Southern Pines), to the intersection of said McDeed's creek and the Yadkin road; thence with the Yadkin road the following courses to the Manly line south sixty-one degrees forty-nine minutes twenty seconds east (two hundred and forty-five feet); thence south sixty-nine degrees seventeen minutes twenty seconds east (six hundred and twenty-one and eight-tenths feet); thence south forty-four degrees three minutes twenty seconds east (three hundred and seventy-eight and two-tenths feet); thence south seventy-seven degrees forty-eight minutes twenty seconds east (six hundred and seventy-four and eight tenths feet); thence south sixty-one degrees fifty-eight minutes forty seconds east (three hundred and seventy-eight and five-tenths feet) to the Manly line; thence as the Manly line south (two thousand nine hundred and fifty-eight and four-tenths feet) to the

Corporate limits.

southwest corner of Manly; thence south thirty-four degrees eight minutes twenty seconds east (two thousand six hundred and thirty-three and one-tenth feet) to the line of an old hedge row; thence as the line of the said old hedge row south fifty-five degrees fifty-one minutes forty seconds west (six thousand one hundred and fifty-one feet) to the old Morganton road; thence as the said old Morganton road north seventy-eight degrees twenty minutes thirty seconds west (nine hundred and thirty-four and one-tenth feet); thence north seventy degrees fifty-five minutes twenty seconds west (seven hundred and forty-three and seven-tenths feet; thence south seventy-three degrees four minutes ten seconds west (one hundred and thirty-two and three-tenths feet); thence north seventy-three degrees thirty-eight minutes ten seconds west (four hundred and sixteen and four-tenths feet); thence north sixty-five degrees twenty-nine minutes thirty seconds west (six hundred and seventy-six and seven-tenths feet) to the point of beginning.

Sections 3, 4 and 5 stricken out.

Sec. 3. That sections three, four and five of said act be stricken out, and add the following section, viz.:

Officers of town

Sec. 4. That the officers of said town shall consist of a mayor and five commissioners, to be elected by the qualified voters of said town annually on the first Tuesday after the first Monday in May.

Election, when held.

Sec. 5. Said election of said mayor and five commissioners shall be held at a place to be designated by the town commissioners in said town, and no person shall be entitled to vote at said election or at any election in said town for municipal purposes unless he shall be an elector of the state of North Carolina and shall have resided ninety days next preceding the day of election within the said corporation.

Appointment of registrar and judges.

Sec. 6. It shall be the duty of said commissioners of said town, on the second Monday in March in each year to appoint a registrar and three judges of election, who shall be qualified voters of said town, and who shall, within ten days after, be notified of their appointment by the clerk of said town. The registrar so appointed shall immediately make publication at the post-office and three other public places in said town, of his appointment as such. He shall be furnished with a registration book for said town by the commissioners of said town, and it shall be his duty to revise the existing registration book in said town in such a manner that the said book shall show an accurate list of electors previously registered and still residing in said town without requiring such electors to register anew. He shall also between the hours of sunrise and sunset on each day (Sundays excepted), for thirty days preceding such election, keep open said book for the registration of any elector residing in said town entitled to register whose name has never before been reg-

When registration books shall be kept open.

istered in said town, or does not appear on the revised list; but the commissioners of said town may, if they think proper, upon giving thirty days' notice at four public places in said town, require an entirely new registration of voters before any election held therein.

Sec. 7. The registrars and judges of election, before entering upon the discharge of their duties, shall take the oath prescribed by article six, section four of the constitution of North Carolina, before the mayor or some justice of the peace for Moore county.

Registrars and judges must take oath.

Sec. 8. It shall be the duty of the registrar and judges of election to attend at the polling place in said town with the registration book on the second Monday preceding the election from the hour of nine a. m. until the hour of five o'clock p. m., when and where the said book shall be open to the inspection of the electors of said town, and any of the electors shall be allowed to object to the name of any person appearing on the book. In case of any such objection, the registrar shall enter upon his book, opposite the name of the person so objected to, the word "challenged," and shall appoint a time and place on or before the election day when he, together with the said judges of election shall hear and decide said objection, giving due notice to the person objected to: Provided, that nothing contained in this section shall be construed to prohibit the right of any elector to challenge or object to the name of any person registering, or offering to register, at any other time than that specified. If any person challenged or objected to shall be found not duly qualified as provided for in this charter, his name shall be erased from the registration book, and he shall not be allowed to vote at any election held in said town for municipal purposes.

Book shall be open to inspection of public.

Challenges.

Proviso.

Challenges.

Sec. 9. The said judges of election, together with the registrar, who shall take with him the registration book, shall assemble at the polling place on the day of election in the said town and shall open the book at seven o'clock a. m. They shall superintend said election and keep the polls open until sunset, when the polls shall be closed and the votes for the mayor and commissioners shall be counted out by them. They shall keep the poll books, and write in them the name of every person voting at said election, and at the close thereof shall certify said poll lists and deposit them with the clerk of said town; and said poll books shall in any trial for illegal or fraudulent voting be used for evidence. If for any cause any of the judges of election shall fail to attend, the registrar shall appoint some discreet person or persons to fill the vacancy, who shall be sworn by him before acting.

Hours when polls shall be opened.

Vacancies on election board.

Sec. 10. That the voters shall vote by ballot, having the names of the mayor and the commissioners on one ballot, either in writing or printed on white paper and without any device, and

Judges shall certify result to clerk.

the person having the highest number of votes shall be declared elected by the judges of election, who shall certify said fact to the town clerk; and in case of a tie, the judges of election shall determine by ballot who is elected.

rsons eligible office.

Sec. 11. That no person shall be eligible to any office in said town unless he shall be a qualified voter therein.

tification of yor and com ssioners of ction.

Sec. 12. That immediately after each election, it shall be the duty of the clerk to notify in writing, the mayor and commissioners-elect of their election.

cers shall take h within five ys after elec- n.

Sec. 13. That the mayor and commissioners-elect shall, within five days after the election, before the mayor or some justice of the peace in said county, take the oath prescribed for public officers, and an oath that they will faithfully and impartially discharge the duties imposed on them by law.

orum.

Sec. 14. That a majority of said commissioners shall constitute a quorum for the transaction of business.

yor shall pre- e at meetings commis- ners.

Sec. 14. That a majority of said commissioners shall constiings of the commissioners; he shall also have the power to call meetings when he may deem it necessary, by notifying all the commissioners in writing, and shall vote only in the case of a tie. In the absence or sickness of the mayor, the commissioners of said town shall select one of their own members to act as mayor pro tempore, who shall, while acting as such, have all the power and authority conferred by this charter on the mayor of said town.

cancies occur- g, how filled

Sec. 16. That if for any cause there shall be any vacancy in the office of mayor or commissioners of said town, the board of commissioners thereof shall be and are empowered hereby to fill said vacancy or vacancies by selecting any qualified voter of said town; and their appointee or appointees shall hold office until the next regular election herein provided for.

we of com- ssioners to ss ordinances.

Sec. 17. That the said commissioners shall have power to pass all by-laws, rules and regulations for the good government of the town not inconsistent with the laws of this state and the United States.

mmissioners all elect treas- er. rm of office.

Sec. 18. That said commissioners shall at their first meeting after their election, select some one as treasurer, who shall hold office for one year, or until his successor shall be elected and qualified. He shall act as treasurer of said town, and before entering upon the discharge of the duties of his office shall give good and sufficient bonds with sureties to be approved by the board of commissioners of said town in a sum of three thousand dollars ($3,000), payable to the state of North Carolina and conditioned upon his faithfully accounting for and paying over all moneys that may come into his hands as treasurer of said town, and for the faithful discharge of his duties. All suits

nd required.

ount of bond.

entered on the official bond of any of the officers of the said town shall be in the name of the state of North Carolina to the use of the board of commissioners of the town of Southern Pines, against the said official and his sureties. Suits on official bond.

Sec. 19. The said commissioners shall at their first meeting after their election, select some one to act as constable of said town, who shall hold his office for one year, or until his successor shall be elected and qualified. He shall, before entering upon the discharge of the duties of his office, enter into bond in the sum of two hundred dollars, with good and sufficient sureties, to be approved by the board of commissioners. The constable of said town shall collect the license and privilege taxes, shall execute all processes placed in his hands by the mayor, shall have authority to preserve the peace of said town, and within the corporate limits thereof, shall have the same authority in criminal matters and be entitled to the same fee as the sheriff has in the county. Commissioners shall elect constable. Bond required. Duties of constable.

Sec. 20. That the commissioners shall or or before the first day of June following their election, select some one to act as tax collector of the said town, who shall hold his office for one year, or until his successor is elected and qualified. He shall, before entering upon the discharge of the duties of his office, enter into a bond in a sum of three thousand dollars ($3,000), with good and sufficient sureties to be approved by the board of commissioners, payable to the state of North Carolina, and conditioned upon his faithfully accounting for and paying over to the proper authority all moneys that may come into his hands from any source as said collector, and upon his faithfully collecting and paying in all taxes levied by the commissioners of said town and in all other respects executing to the best of his ability, and honestly and faithfully all the duties imposed upon him by the charter or by the board of commissioners of said town; and the collector shall receive such compensation as the board of commissioners may allow, and shall have, within the corporate limits of the town, the same authority as the sheriff of Moore county in the collection of taxes levied by the authorities thereof, except as hereinafter provided by this charter. Election of tax collector. Bond required.

Sec. 21. That chapter two hundred and seventy-four, private laws of eighteen hundred and ninety-one, section eight, be amended by adding after the word "number," in the sixth line, "or qualified voter of said town." Chapter 274, private laws of 1891, section 8, amended.

Sec. 22. That section thirteen of said chapter be amended by striking out the words "and alleys," at the end of the sixth line of said section. Section 13 amended.

Sec. 23. That section fourteen of said chapter be amended by Section 14 amended.

striking out all of said section after the word "residents," in line five thereof.

ction 17 ended. Sec. 24. That section seventeen of said chapter be amended by inserting in the seventh line of said section, between the words "hours" and "without" in said section, "Sundays and legal holidays excepted."

ction 18 ended. Sec. 25. That section eighteen of said chapter be amended by inserting after the word "parks," at the end of line five, "and establish a system of sewerage and waterworks, as hereinafter provided."

ction 21 ended. Sec. 26. That section twenty-one of said chapter be amended by striking out the word "October," in the fifth line of said section, and inserting in lieu thereof the word "January," and by adding after the word "same," in the sixth line thereof, "and ten per centum additional," and after the fifth word in the seventh line strike out "state" and insert "county."

apter 194, vate laws of 7, amended. Sec. 27. That chapter one hundred and ninety-four of private laws of eighteen hundred and ninety-seven be amended by striking out the word "marshal" wherever it may occur in said chapter, and inserting in lieu thereof the word "constable."

tion 26 ended. Sec. 28. That section twenty-six of said chapter be amended by striking out the word "shall" in the fifth line thereof and inserting in lieu thereof the word "may."

tion 28 ended. Sec. 29. That section twenty-eight of said chapter be amended by adding, after the word "mayor" in the ninth line thereof, "or confined in the guard-house."

tion 31 ended. Sec. 30. That section thirty-one of said chapter be amended by striking out subsection three thereof.

tion 35 ended. Sec. 31. That section thirty-five of said chapter be amended by striking out after the word "sum," in the fourth line thereof, the words "double the amount of regular and special taxes for the current year," and inserting "($3,000) three thousand dollars."

tion 36 ended. Sec. 32. That section thirty-six of said chapter be amended by striking out the word "forty" in the third line thereof, and inserting in lieu thereof the word "twenty," and by striking out the word "thirty," in the fourth line thereof, and inserting the word "ten"; by striking out the word "five," in the sixth line thereof, and inserting in the place thereof "six," and between the words "payable" and "annually," in the said line, insert the word "semi," and by inserting after the word "April," in line seven thereof, the words "and October."

tion 37 ended. Sec. 33. That section thirty-seven of said chapter be amended by striking out the words "the denomination of one hundred dollars each," in lines one and two of said section, and inserting in lieu thereof the words "such denomination or denominations as the board of commissioners of said town may determine," and by striking out all of said section after the word "shall," in the seventh line, and inserting "have the names of mayor and clerk lithographed thereon, as above provided for their signatures to the bonds in the said section."

Sec. 34. That section thirty-nine of said chapter be amended by adding after the words "waterworks," in the fourth line thereof, "and parks." Section 39 amended.

Sec. 35. That section forty-two of said chapter be amended by striking out the words "sixty cents," in the ninth line thereof, and insert in the place thereof the words "one dollar," and by adding after the word "town," in the eleventh line thereof, the words "and three dollars on each poll." Section 42 amended.

Sec. 36. That section forty-four of said chapter be amended by striking out the word "forty," in the eighth line thereof, and insert in lieu thereof the word "twenty," and that said section be further amended by striking out all after the word "thereto," in the nineteenth line thereof down to and including the word "elections," in the twenty-second line of same. Section 44 amended.

Sec. 37. That section forty-six be amended by adding thereto "that for the purpose of constructing and maintaining a system of waterworks and a system of sewerage, either or both, in said town, the commissioners of said town shall have authority to condemn land outside the limits of said town in the same manner and for the same purposes as herein provided for condemning land inside of said town." Section 46 amended.

Sec. 38. That section fifty-seven of said chapter be amended by adding thereto "or may appoint one health officer, who shall have all the authority and power conferred on the board of health in said section." Section 57 amended.

Sec. 39. That subsection five, under section thirty-one of said chapter, be amended by striking out all after the word "exceeding," in the second line thereof and adding "twenty-five dollars." Subsection 5, section 31, amended.

Sec. 40. That for the purpose of keeping the streets of said town in repair, in addition to the power and provisions contained in the chapter, all able-bodied male persons between the ages of eighteen and forty-five years in said town may be compelled to work on the public streets of said town not to exceed six days in any one year, under such rules and regulations as may be established by the ordinances of the town: Provided, that any person who shall furnish one able-bodied hand as substitute, or who shall pay sixty-five cents for each day so ordered, shall be held to have complied with this section. Persons between 18 and 45 may be compelled to work on streets.

Sec. 41. That any person liable to work on the streets of said town who shall fail to attend and work as herein provided for when summoned so to do, unless he has furnished a substitute or paid sixty-five cents as aforesaid, shall be guilty of mis- Failure to work on streets or provide substitute a misdemeanor.

demeanor and fined two dollars or imprisoned not more than five days.

mmissioners ll appoint rk.

Sec. 42. The said commissioners shall at their first meeting appoint a clerk, who shall hold office for one year, or until his successor is appointed and qualified. It shall be his duty to

ties of clerk.

attend all meetings of the board, to keep a full and accurate record of the same, in a book provided by said board of commissioners for such purpose, and to sign all town orders and bonds as hereinafter provided. Said clerk, and any other appointed

pointed of-rs may be oved.

officers of said town, may be removed at any time for incompetency, misbehavior, neglect of duty, or other good cause by said board of commissioners, which alone shall be the judge of such incompetency, misbehavior, neglect of duty or other cause of removal, and shall appoint others in their stead, to fill out their said terms respectively, upon such removal.

flicting laws ealed.

Sec. 43. That all laws and clauses of laws in conflict with this act are hereby repealed.

Sec. 44. That this act shall be in force from and after its ratification.

Ratified the 28th day of February, A. D. 1899.

CHAPTER 168.

An act to amend the charter of the town of Statesville.

The General Assembly of North Carolina do enact:

apter 40, pri-e laws of 1885, ended.

Section 1. That an act of the general assembly, entitled "An act to amend the charter of the town of Statesville," being chapter forty of the private laws of North Carolina of the year eighteen hundred and eighty-five, be amended as follows: Strike out section forty-one of the said act and insert the following in lieu thereof:

ermen em-ered to make ain improve its on streets.

Sec. 2. (1) That the board of aldermen shall have power to grade macadamize and pave the sidewalks of the said city, to lay out and open new streets or extend or widen those already opened, and to make such improvements thereon as the public conveniences may require.

ermen may chase neces-y land.

(2) That when in the opinion of the board of aldermen any land or right-of-way shall be required for the purpose of opening new streets or of extending or widening those already open, or for other objects allowed by this charter or by this act now made a part of the charter, the city may purchase the same from the owner or owners thereof and pay such compensation therefor as may be agreed upon; or at the option of the city, the same may be taken

.t a valuation to be made by four freeholders, residents of the ity, to be appointed in the following manner, to-wit: Two to be elected by the property owner and two to be appointed by the mayor or board of aldermen. In the event that these four can iot agree, they shall select one additional freeholder, resident in he city. The award of the commission or freeholders, or any hree of them, shall be final when reduced to writing and filed vith the city clerk.

Assessment of land by arbitrators.

(3) If any one of the said commissioners should own, control or e interested in the land upon or over which any street is pro- osed to be condemned, widened, extended, improved or used or public purposes as provided in this act, the mayor and board f aldermen may appoint another freeholder of said city not so nterested, who shall qualify and act in his stead in the particu- ar case in which such interest or disqualification exists; and pon a written challenge, made by any land owner whose prop- rty is to be taken, to any commissioner appointed by the town n the ground of interest, if such interest is found to exist, then ne mayor and board of aldermen shall select another commis- oner. But when any substitute is appointed on account of the emoval of any commissioner on the ground of interest, the town hall have the right to provide a substitute for such commission- rs as it may have selected who are interested, and the land wner shall have the right to select his substitute for any com- issioner thus disqualified.

When commissioner appointed is interested in land assessed.

(4) That the mayor may fill all vacancies caused by failure to ualify, resignation or otherwise of such commissioners as are ppointed by the town, and the land owner shall fill all vacan- es caused for like reasons of any commissioner appointed by im: Provided, such land owner fills such vacancy within five ays, otherwise the mayor and board of aldermen may fill such acancy, and the four commissioners shall fill any vacancy of the fth man for failure to qualify, resignation or otherwise: Pro- ded, if any appointee shall refuse to qualify or serve, unless ex- ised or relieved by the mayor and board of aldermen, he shall e subjected to a penalty of fifty dollars, to be recovered as other enalties before the mayor or a justice of the peace.

Mayor may fill vacancies caused by failure, to qualify.

Proviso.

(5) When it is proposed to condemn any land or property for he purposes herein specified it shall be done by an order or reso- tion of the board of aldermen at a regular or special meeting the board, stating generally, or as near as may be, the nature the improvements for which the land is required, whether anted in fee simple or an easement therein, and directing the id commissioners of valuation and assessment to proceed to sess the damages to the property to be taken, on a day to be imed in the order or resolutions or at such time as the commis

Condemnation of land.

days' notice ired.

sioners may appoint. Not less than five days' notice of the time of meeting of the said commissioners shall be issued by the mayor or the commissioners and served by one of the police of the said city by reading the same to the land owner to be notified, or by leaving a copy of the notice with him or with his agent or with some adult at his residence.

missioners l meet at ap- ted time and ss damages.

(6) The said commissioners shall, at the appointed time, meet upon the lands to be condemned and view the same and assess the damages to be paid to the owner or party entitled thereto. In making such valuation and assessment the commissioners shall take into consideration the loss or damage that may accrue to the owner by reason of the land or right-of-way being surrendered, and also any benefit or advantage such owner will receive from the opening, extending or widening of the street or the use of the property for any improvements made thereon, and shall ascertain the amount of loss or damage in excess of the said benefit or advantage, if any, or the value or amount of such benefit or advantage in exeess of loss or damage, if any, and they shall report the result in writing to the board of aldermen. The board may refuse to take the property upon the assessment of damages made by the commissioners, in which case the report may be set aside, and the title to the land shall remain in the owner until further proceedings are had to condemn the same in accordance with the provisions of this act: Provided, if the board refuse to take the property upon the assessment of damages, the town shall pay all the costs of the commissioners in making the assessment.

ort may be ide.

n shall pay s when re- is set aside.

missioners run surveys ands to ndemned.

(7) That in order to ascertain what improvements should be made to the streets and sidewalks, or in or upon any lands for any of the public improvements provided for in this act, and how much land or property will be required to be taken for streets, sidewalks, waterworks, sewerage, gas, electric lights or any other public improvements. the board of aldermen may cause such surveys as they may deem necessary to be made upon the lands to be taken or condemned.

n amount ssed is not owner of within ve months.

(8) That if the amount assessed upon any land is not paid by the owner thereof within twelve months after the assessment is made, and notice thereof is served upon him, or demand made for the payment of the amount assessed, the same may be recovered and the said lien enforced by a civil action, to be brought in the superior court of Iredell county, for the sale of the property which is thus subject to the lien and for such other relief as may be appropriate to the case. If any person whose land or rights are affected by the proceedings under this section, or the aldermen of said city are dissatisfied with the award of the commissioners, then in that case either party may appeal to the next

term of the superior court of Iredell county: Provided, however, that such appeal shall not hinder or delay the aldermen in opening or widening such street or using the property for constructing or erecting any public improvements for the benefit of the city as in any of the sections herein provided.

Either party may appeal.

Sec. 3. That where any notice required to be given by the charter of said city or any amendment thereof, and the person to be notified is a non-resident of Iredell county, the notice may be served by the sheriff or other lawful officer of any county in which the said person may be, and if the said person is a non resident of the state the notice may be served by publication thereof once a week for four weeks in a newspaper published in the city of Statesville, and the affidavit of the publisher, proprietor or foreman of said paper that said notice was so published shall be prima facie proof of such publication, and the time of notice shall be counted from the last day on which the notice was inserted in said newspaper.

Notice on non-residents, how served.

Sec. 4. The value of any benefit or advantage to any lot or land arising from the opening, extending, widening or improving any street and making any of the other improvements in any of the sections herein provided for and accruing to said lot or land in common with other lots or lands similarly situated may be assessed by the said commissioners against the lots so benefited, and shall be a lien thereon, and the payment therefor may be enforced as provided in this act. The amount of said assessment shall be stated separately in the report of the commissioners, and such common benefit derived by any lot or land shall not be considered in assessing damages to be paid to any land owner or in ascertaining the excess of any benefit over loss or damage under this act. And when any land for any public improvements shall be condemned for the use of the city, according to the provisions of the foregoing or subsequent sections, and the same has been accepted by the aldermen, the report of the commissioners, when the same has been made final and spread upon the records of the town by the city clerk, containing a description of the property condemned to the uses of the city, shall thereupon vest the title to the same in fee simple where such title is contemplated by the assessment or the title to the easement and use thereof where such title is contemplated, as the case may be: Provided, that any special improvement made upon the streets already established and for which assessments are made against the land owner shall be limited to the sidewalks, unless otherwise agreed between the land owner and the town, and when such improvement is made the town shall pay one-half the costs therefor and the land owner the other half of the costs, unless otherwise agreed.

Value of benefit to land or lot arising from opening streets to be assessed against it.

Amount of such assessment shall be kept separately in report.

Record of land so condemned and purchased shall be made.

Proviso.

Special improvements on streets.

ction 20 of said amended. Sec. 5. That section twenty of the said act to amend the charter of the town of Statesville is hereby amended so as to add to the said section after the last word, "necessary," the following: "The board of aldermen of the said city are authorized and empowered to construct and maintain for the said city a system of waterworks and sewerage for the purpose of supplying the inhabitants thereof a public system of water supply and a public system of drainage and sewerage, and they are further authorized to furnish and supply the inhabitants of the said city a system of gas and electric lights, one or both, and to this end they are hereby fully authorized and empowered to enter upon and hold for the purposes of this act and for the purposes of any other public improvements necessary for the health and well being of the said city, hitherto or hereafter established, so much of the water of any stream or springs within ten miles of the city of Statesville and such land over or through which it is proposed to construct ditches, reservoirs, necessary buildings hydrants, fixtures, lay pipes, manholes or other necessary appliances, or to construct roads for the purpose of surveying, running or laying out the lines thereof; they are authorized to take title in fee or title for the easement, to the town for any land for any of the purposes aforesaid upon such price as may be agreed upon between the owner and the board of aldermen; but if it shall be found that the owner or owners of any such stream or land can not agree upon a price to be paid by the city for the right-of-way or use thereof for the purpose of erecting and establishing reservoirs, conduits, mains, supply pipes or any other appliances necessary for the construction of the improvements aforesaid or any of them, then the said springs and streams and lands may be condemned to the uses of the city agreeably to the provisions of the foregoing sections for the condemnation of lands for street improvements. And for the purpose of successfully operating any of the said improvements aforesaid the aldermen of the city are fully authorized to extend the lines of any of the said systems of improvements in any direction thought most advisable. and to this end the board of aldermen, for the purposes of this act shall have the same powers with regard to streams and lands beyond the corporate limits of the town as they have with regard to those within the corporate limits of the town: Provided, however, that in case of discontinuance of the use of the land (where the city only acquires an easement therein) either for the purposes mentioned in this act or in the charter or upon reverter to the owners, the city shall have the right to remove any property or improvements erected under its authority upon the land: Provided, that the land owner over whose lands the town seeks an easement or right-of-way, or seeks to obtain title therefor, and which

Sidenotes: lermen thorized to nstruct and intain system waterworks. — werage. — s and electric hts — ermen empowered to take d on which er flows. — streams, may be demned if e can not be ed upon. — iso. — n use of land continued may remove erty thereon.

is situated outside of the corporate limits of the town, shall have the option to select his two commissioners from amongst any of the freeholders of the county of Iredell.

Power of aldermen to make ordinances, etc.

Sec. 6. That the board of aldermen shall have power to make and provide ordinances, by-laws, rules and regulations in order to protect any of the said systems of improvements referred to in this act, and to this end the jurisdiction of the said city shall be extended beyond the corporate limits of the town and extend over any lands, streams or property condemned and used for public improvements as aforesaid or connected with them in such way as to be necessary for their enjoyment, and the police of the city shall have power to execute the process of the mayor anywhere in Iredell county to enforce the said rules and regulations.

Police empowered to execute processes of mayor anywhere in Iredell county.

Section 14 of said charter amended. Proviso. Jurisdiction of mayor in such cases.

Sec. 7. That section fourteen of the amended charter aforesaid is amended so as to insert after the word "city," the last word in the said section, the following: "Provided, that the mayor of the city of Statesville shall have jurisdiction over and power to try any misdemeanors, the trial of which are conferred upon mayors of towns, which shall or may occur upon any of the property under the control of, belonging to, used by or connected with the city of Statesville for any of its public works, and also all such offenses as may be committed within one and one-half miles from the corporate limits of the city of Statesville, and any police officer of the city is hereby authorized to execute any precept of the mayor within the boundary of Iredell county.

Sections 3 to 12 amended.

Sec. 8. That sections three to twelve inclusive of the said amended charter shall be amended so as to add after the last word of section twelve the following: That the mayor and board of aldermen of the city of Statesville are hereby empowered to provide for holding any election for officers or other election for any purpose for the said city, to be conducted according to the provisions made in the said amended charter in the sections aforesaid or to be conducted by and under any general election law which may be enacted during the session of the present general assembly or according to the laws provided by any future general assembly: Provided, however, that no one shall be a qualified elector unless he has the qualifications mentioned in section eight of the said amended charter.

Mayor and aldermen shall provide for holding elections.

Section 20 amended.

Sec. 9. It is further enacted that section twenty of the said amended charter be further amended by adding thereto the following:

Preamble.

Whereas, the town of Statesville subscribed twenty-five thousand dollars to the capital stock of the Atlantic, Tennessee and Ohio Railroad Company in the year eighteen hundred and sixty-one, and issued bonds therefor running twenty years; and

Whereas, in eighteen hundred and eighty-five the town issued twelve thousand dollars of eight per centum bonds running twenty years for the purpose of refunding the unpaid portion of the said debt and for other purposes; and

Whereas, a balance on this issue of eighteen hundred and eighty-five of about ten thousand dollars remains unpaid; now, therefore,

In order to secure the validity of the said bonds and to obtain further time for the payment thereof, and to prevent oppressive taxation, it is provided:

dermen empowered to issue pon bonds.

(1) That the board of aldermen of the city of Statesville are hereby authorized and empowered to issue coupon bonds bearing interest, payable annually, at a rate not exceeding six per centum per annum or such less rate as may be agreed on, to the amount of ten thousand dollars, in denominations not less than one hundred dollars nor more than one thousand dollars, to be made payable twenty years after the date of their execution, with a provision therein inserted that the said bonds may be paid or redeemed within a time not less than ten years after the date of their execution, at the option of the city. This period may, however, be lengthened or shortened by the board or the provisions omitted from the bonds, as the board may decide. The said bonds and coupons shall be signed by the mayor of the city and countersigned by the clerk, and shall be made payable at such place or places as the board may determine.

:erest. ount of bonds. en bonds ture. ds, how ied.

d bonds may xchanged.

(2) That the said bonds may be exchanged for the bonds now outstanding, issued for the purposes aforesaid, or if this can not be done they may be sold and the proceeds applied to the payment of the said outstanding bonds, or part sold and part exchanged, as the case may require or as it may be agreed upon; but none of said bonds shall be sold or exchanged at a less sum or rate than their par value.

ardians, etc., horized to hange same.

(3) That all executors, administrators, guardians, trustees and other persons acting in a fiduciary capacity who now hold or may hereafter hold or become possessed of any of the bonds of the said city above referred to, are hereby fully authorized and empowered to exchange the same for bonds issued under the provisions of this act.

d bonds shall estroyed as 1.

(4) That it shall be the duty of the mayor, a member of the board of aldermen, to be appointed by the board, and the clerk and treasurer, to destroy the said eight per centum bonds as they are paid or exchanged for as aforesaid, and the clerk and treasurer shall make a record of the bonds so destroyed and of all the bonds issued under this act.

may be ed on property and polls.

(5) That the board of aldermen of the said city shall levy a tax upon the property and polls upon the citizens of the city, maintaining the constitutional equation between property and polls,

to provide for the payment of interest as it may accrue upon said bonds issued under this act, and in like manner provide for the payment of the principal of said bonds as they mature and become payable; and to insure the validity of the said bonds the board of aldermen are authorized to obtain the sanction of the voters of the city of Statesville for the refunding of the bonds aforesaid at any election they may order or provide for, agreeably to the sections of the constitution in this behalf ordained.

Sanction of voters shall be obtained for refunding said bonds.

(6) And the mayor and board of aldermen of the city of Statesville are hereby generally authorized and empowered at any time to rebond the indebtedness, all or any part thereof, of the city of Statesville whenever in their discretion they can do so, so as to issue coupon bonds bearing a lower rate of interest than those which are now existing against the city, and to this end they may provide for the issuing of bonds, at such rate of interest and running for such length of time as will inure to the best interest of the city: Provided, however, in doing so they obtain the requisite authority from the voters of the city of Statesville upon their said action, agreeably to the provisions of the constitution in this behalf ordained.

Aldermen authorized to rebond indebtedness.

Sec. 10. That all laws or parts of laws in conflict with this act, whether in the charter or amended charter of the town or in teh general laws of the state, are hereby repealed, and that this act takes effect from and after its ratification.

Conflicting laws repealed.

Ratified the 28th day of February, A. D. 1899.

CHAPTER 169.

An act to incorporate "The L E. Davis Milling Company."

The General Assembly of North Carolina do enact:

Section 1. That L. E. Davis, J. D. Davis, James W. Davis, John L. Davis, and their associates and successors, be and are hereby declared to be a body politic and corporate under the name and style of "The L. E. Davis Milling Company," and shall so continue for a period of thirty years, with capacity to sue and be sued, to maintain and defend actions under its corporate name, to take, hold, buy, sell and convey real and personal property, and to conduct, transact and carry on in its full scope and import a general milling business, with all the powers, rights, privileges and immunities hereby especially granted to enlarge, build and operate roller mills, corn mill and saw mill, and to erect dams for the purpose of operating the same and may place machinery for converting lumber into all kinds of building material.

Corporators.

Corporate name.

Duration of charter.

Corporate powers.

Where located. Sec. 2. That "The L. E. Davis Milling Company" shall be located near Goshen, in Wilkes county, North Carolina.

Capital stock. Sec. 3. That the capital stock of said milling company shall not be less than five thousand dollars divided into shares of one hundred dollars each, and by a two-thirds vote of the stockholders may from time to time be increased to an amount not exceeding thirty thousand dollars.

Books may be opened for subscription. Sec. 4. That the corporators named herein or a majority of them are hereby empowered to open books of subscription to the capital stock of "The L. E. Davis Milling Company" at such time and place and for such period as they shall determine, and the stockholders may organize at any time after five thousand dollars of stock has been subscribed and elect a president, a vice-president, a secretary and treasurer and not less than three directors, one of whom shall be the president of the company. Election of officers.

Seal. Sec. 5. That the president and directors of said company may adopt and use a common seal, and may alter the same at pleasure; may establish by-laws for the government of the company and may fix the compensation for the several officers, subject to the approval of the stockholders or a majority of them. By laws and regulations.

Individual liability of stockholders. Sec. 6. That owners of stock in this company shall not be individually liable for any contract, indebtedness or liability of this company.

Fees for services. Sec. 7. That said milling company is entitled to charge such tolls for grinding grain as are allowed by law, and for sawing lumber and furnishing material such price as may be agreed on between the company and their customers.

Sec. 8. That this act shall be in force from and after its ratification.

Ratified the 28th day of February, A. D. 1899.

CHAPTER 170.

An act to incorporate The J. C. and A. L. Cooper Farming and Distilling Company.

The General Assembly of North Carolina do enact:

Corporators. Section 1. That J. C. Cooper and A. T. Cooper, their associates, successors and assigns, be and they are hereby created a body corporate and politic by the name, style and title of "The J. C. and A. L. Cooper Farming and Distilling Company," and by that name and title shall be known, to exist for the term of sixty years, and may exercise and enjoy all the privileges, franchises and immunities incident to corporations; may sue and be sued, Corporate name. Duration of charter. Corporate powers and privileges.

plead and be impleaded, complain and defend in all courts of law and equity of record and otherwise; may purchase, secure by gift or otherwise, hold and enjoy property, real, personal and mixed, of what kind and quality soever; may construct, build, erect such buildings, structures, works and improvements thereon as may be deemed proper, and may use, manage and maintain the same; may sell convey, mortgage, transfer, grant, lease, sub-lease and dispose of any portion or the whole of their property at such prices and on such terms as may be deemed proper; also to make and have a common seal and the same to alter and renew at pleasure, and adopt such by-laws as may be necessary for the government of said company.

Sec. 2 That the said corporation is hereby authorized and empowered to conduct, transact and carry on in all its branches the manufacture and sale of ales, wines and liquors, either or all, of all descriptions whatsoever: to manufacture and sell ice in any quantity; to import, raise and sell cattle, horses, mules, hogs and sheep of any or all breeds, and to conduct a general farming business; and the said corporation may buy and sell and deal in goods, wares and merchandise of every description and kind at its own will and pleasure. **Nature of operations.**

Sec 3. The capital stock of said company shall be one thousand dollars ($1,000), with liberty to increase the same from time to time to any sum not to exceed three hundred thousand dollars, to be divided into shares of one hundred dollars ($100) each. **Capital stock.**

Sec. 4. That the corporators and stockholders of said corporation and their successors and assigns shall not be individually or personally liable or responsible for the debts, liabilities, contracts or engagements of the corporation. **Individual liability of stockholders.**

Sec. 5. That the principal place of business of said corporation shall be at their place of business near Brevard, Transylvania county, North Carolina, with power and authority to establish such other places of business as said corporation may desire, if not otherwise prohibited by law. **Principal place of business.**

Sec. 6. That all property and estate owned by said corporation shall be liable for taxes according to assessed value, and the taxes thereon shall be given in and paid by the corporation and not by the several stockholders or parties owning stock therein. **Liability of property for taxes.**

Sec. 7. The affairs of said corporation shall be managed by a president and two directors, to be elected annually and to hold office until their successors are elected and qualified, and said directors shall have power to fill any vacancy that may occur. **Affairs of corporation, by whom managed.**

Sec. 8. The officers of said corporation shall be a president and secretary and treasurer (and the same person may be secretary and treasurer), and the said officers shall be elected annually at **Officers.**

a meeting of the stockholders by the stockholders of the corporation, and in all elections by the stockholders of said corporation each share of stock shall be entitled to one vote.

Sec. 9. This act shall be in force from and after its ratification.

Ratified the 28th day of February, A. D. 1899.

CHAPTER 171.

An act to amend the charter of the city of Goldsboro, and to revise and consolidate all laws in relation to said city.

The General Assembly of North Carolina do enact:

Section 1. That the inhabitants of the city of Goldsboro shall
dy politic. be and continue as they heretofore have been a body politic and corporate, and henceforth the corporation shall bear the name
rporate name. and style of the "City of Goldsboro," and under such name and style is hereby invested with all property and rights of property
rporate powers. which now belong to the corporation under any other corporate name or names heretofore used, and by this name may acquire and hold, for the purpose of its government and welfare and improvement, all such estate as may be desired bequeathed or conveyed to it, not exceeding in value three hundred thousand dollars, and shall have in [a] right to contract and be contracted with, to sue and be sued, to plead and be impleaded, to purchase and to hold and convey real or personal property.

rporate limits. Sec. 2. That the corporate limits of the city of Goldsboro shall be as follows, viz: Beginning at a point in the center of the main track of the Wilmington and Weldon Railroad, five hundred and fifty (550) yards south of the southern boundary line of Elm street in said city and running thence south seventy-two degrees east one thousand three hundred and sixty-five (1,365) yards to a stake; thence north eighteen degrees east to Ash street, extending eastward: thence along said Ash street to Marsh branch or big ditch; thence up said branch to the center of the Atlantic and North Carolina Railroad track; thence north eighteen degrees east one hundred and forty-five (145) yards to a stake on or near said branch; thence north seventy-two degrees west to the center of the Wilmington and Weldon Railroad track; thence south eighteen degrees west along said track one hundred and seventy-five (175) yards; thence north seventy-two degrees west to a point intersected by the northern extension of the west boundary line of George street; thence north seventy-two degrees west two hundred and thirty (230) yards from said intersecting point to a stake; thence south eighteen degrees west to the southern boundary line of the old county road leading from Goldsboro to the old site of the town of Waynesboro; thence along the south line of said county road to the southeast intersection of Elm street and the new county road leading from Goldsboro to the covered bridge across Neuse river; then from said intersection along the eastern line of said new county road two hundred and seventy-five (275) yards to a stake; thence south seventy-two degrees east to the center of the main track of the Wilmington and Weldon Railroad; thence south eighteen degrees west along said track to the beginning. In locating the above boundaries the courses shall be as they were in the year eighteen hundred and forty-eight, disregarding any variation of the compass since that time.

Division of wards.

Sec. 3. That said city be and the same is hereby divided into four (4) wards, denominated the first, second third and fourth wards, and bounded and described as follows:

First ward.

The first ward: Beginning at a point in the centre of East Centre and West Centre streets, where the centre of Chestnut street intersects the same, and runs thence northwardly with the centre of said East Centre and West Centre streets to the northern boundary line of said city; then with said boundary line westerly to the northwestern corner in said boundary line; then with said boundary line southerly to a point opposite to the centre of said Chestnut street; then easterly to and with the centre of said street to the beginning.

Second ward.

The second ward: Beginning at the beginning point of the first ward and runs thence northwardly with the line of the first ward to the northern boundary line of said city; then with said boundary line easterly to the northeastern corner in said boundary line; then with said boundary line in its various courses to a point opposite to the centre of said Chestnut street on the east; then westerly to and with the centre of said street to the beginning.

Third ward.

The third ward: Beginning at the centre of the intersection of William street and Chestnut street and runs thence southerly with the center of William street and an extension thereof to the southern boundary line of the corporate limits of said city; thence with said boundary line westerly to the southwestern corner in said boundary line; then with said boundary line northerly to a point opposite to the centre of said Chestnut street extended; then easterly to and with the centre of said street to the beginning.

Fourth ward.

The fourth ward: Beginning at the beginning point of the third ward and runs thence southerly with the centre of William street and the line of the third ward to the southern boundary line of the corporate limits of said city; then with said boundary line to the southeastern corner in said boundary line; then with said boundary line northerly in its various courses to a point opposite to the centre of Chestnut street extended on the east; then westerly to and with the centre of said street to the beginning.

ection of town icers.

Sec. 4. That there shall on the first Monday in May, eighteen hundred and ninety-nine, and biennially thereafter, be elected a mayor and nine (9) aldermen for said city, who shall hold their offices until their successors are qualified; the first, third and fourth wards shall have two (2) aldermen each, and the second ward shall have three (3) aldermen. Such aldermen shall be residents of the ward for which they are chosen and they and the mayor shall be elected by all the qualified voters of said city.

pointment of istrars.

Sec. 5. That the board of aldermen of said city shall appoint, at or before their meeting in March, eighteen hundred and ninety-nine, (1899) and bienniaily thereafter, a registrar of voters for each ward in said city; said registrar shall give ten days' notice at the court-house door in said city of a registration of voters in and for said city, specifying time and place. In case of vacancy in the position of registrar from any cause, the mayor of said city shall fill the vacancy.

cancies among istrars.

gistration oks, when ened.

Sec. 6. Said registrar shall be furnished by said board of aldermen with registration books at the expense of the city, and it shall be the duty of said registrar to open his books at the time and place designated at said city at least ten days before the day of election herein provided for, and to register therein the names of all persons applying for registration and entitled to register and vote. It shall be the duty of the registrar to keep the names of the white voters separate and apart from those of colored voters. The registration books shall be closed on Saturday preceding the election at seven o'clock p. m., and no registration shall be valid unless it specifies as near as may be the age, occupation, place of birth and place of residence in the ward in which he offers to register, as well as the township or county from whence the elector has removed, in the event of removal, and the full name by which he is known.

quirements of ctors.

pointment of lges of election.

Sec. 7. That said board of aldermen at or before their meeting in April, eighteen hundred and ninety-nine, and biennially thereafter, shall appoint two judges or inspectors of election for each ward in said city, who with the registrar shall open the polls and superintend the same on the day of election herein specified, and the polls shall be opened and the election held at such place or places in such wards as said board of aldermen may fix and establish at such meeting aforesaid. In case of failure or refusal of any judge or inspector of election to serve, the registrar of the precinct or ward shall have power to appoint some competent person to fill the vacancy.

ilure of judge serve.

Sec. 8. That said board of aldermen shall provide for each ward two ballot boxes, one in which shall be deposited all voters [votes] for mayor, and the other in which shall be deposited all voters [votes] for aldermen. Each of said boxes shall have an opening through the lid of sufficient size to admit a single folded ballot and no more. The judges of election, before the voting begins, shall carefully examine the ballot boxes and see that there is nothing in them.

Ballot boxes provided for each ward.

Sec. 9. That it shall be the duty of the registrars and judges of election to attend at the polling place of their ward or precinct with the registration books on the Saturday preceding the election from the hour of nine o'clock a. m. till the hour of five o'clock p. m., when and where the said books shall be open to the inspection of the electors of said ward or precinct, and any of said electors shall be allowed to object to the name of any person appearing on said books. In case of any such objection the registrar shall enter upon his books, opposite the name of the person so objected to, the word "challenged," and shall appoint a time and place on or before the election day when he, together with said judges of election, shall hear and decide said objection, giving due notice to the person so objected to: Provided, nothing in this section shall prohibit any elector from challenging or objecting to the name of any person registered or offering to register at any time other than that above specified. If any person challenged or objected to shall be found not duly qualified, the registrar shall erase his name from the books.

Days for registration of voters.

Sec. 10. The ballots shall be written or printed on white paper without device. The mayor shall be voted for on one ballot, and the aldermen shall be voted for on one ballot.

Ballots written or printed without device.

Sec. 11. When the election shall be finished the registrars and judges of election, in the presence of such of the electors as may choose to attend, shall open the boxes and count the ballots, reading aloud the names of the persons who shall appear on each ticket; and if there shall be two or more tickets rolled up together, or any ticket shall contain the names of more persons than such elector has a right to vote for, or shall have a device upon it, in either of these cases such tickets shall not be numbered in taking the ballots, but shall be void and the said counting of votes shall be continued without adjournment until completed and the result thereof declared.

Result determined.

Sec. 12. The judges of election in each ward or precinct shall appoint one of their number or the registrar to attend the meeting of the board of city canvassers as a member thereof, and shall deliver to the member who shall have been so appointed the original return or statement of the result of the election in such ward or precinct, and the members of the several wards or

Delivery of original return.

precincts boards of election who shall have been so appointed shall attend the meeting of the board of city canvassers for such election at the mayor's office at ten o'clock a. m. on the day succeeding the election. Such board of city canvassers shall organize by electing one of their number chairman and one of their number secretary, and a majority of said board so appointed shall consitute a quorum of said board of city canvassers, and said board shall open and inspect such election returns and forthwith declare the result of said election.

eclaration of sult.

rsons qualified vote.

Sec. 13. All electors who shall have resided in the state twelve months and in the city of Goldsboro ninety days, and in the ward for which they offer to register thirty days next preceding the election, shall be entitled to register.

ections held der this act, w held.

Sec. 14. That all elections held by virtue of this act shall be held under the supervision of the sheriff of Wayne county, who shall attend the polls, and by himself and his deputies preserve order.

rm of office of ayor and alder- en.

Sec. 15. That the mayor and aldermen shall hold their offices respectively until the next succeeding election and until their respective successors are qualified.

th of mayor fore entering on duties of ce.

Sec. 16. That the mayor, immediately after his election and before entering upon the duties of his office, shall take, before a justice of the peace, the following oath: "I, A. B., do solemnly swear that I will diligently endeavor to perform faithfully and truthfully, according to my best skill and ability, all the duties of the office of mayor of the city of Goldsboro while I continue therein; and I will cause to be executed, as far as in my power lies, all the laws, ordinances and regulations enacted for the government of the city; and in the discharge of my duties I will strive to do equal justice in all cases whatsoever."

hen aldermen all qualify.

Sec. 17. That on Thursday succeeding the day of election the aldermen elected thereat shall qualify by taking the oath of office before the mayor or a justice of the peace as prescribed for commissioners of incorporated towns and when organized shall succeed to and have all the rights, powers and duties prescribed by law.

cancies occur- g in office of ayor or alder- en.

Sec. 18. That if any person chosen mayor shall refuse to be qualified, or there is any vacancy in the office after election and qualification, the aldermen shall choose some qualified person mayor for the term or the unexpired portion of the term, as the case may be; and on like occasion and in like manner the aldermen shall choose other aldermen to supply the place of such as shall refuse to act, and all vacancies which may occur, and such persons only shall be chosen as are hereinbefore declared to be eligible.

case of failure elect munici- l officers, how ection is or- red.

Sec. 19. That in case of failure to elect municipal officers as herein provided, the electors residing within said city of Goldsboro may, after ten days' notice, signed by any three of said electors and posted up at three public places within the corporate limits of said city, proceed to hold an election for municipal officers in the way and manner provided for in this act.

Sec. 20. That the mayor of said city is hereby constituted an inferior court, and as such shall within the corporate limits of the city of Goldsboro have all the powers, jurisdiction and authority of a justice of the peace in criminal cases to issue process, and also to hear and determine all causes of action which may arise upon the ordinances and regulations of the city to enforce penalties by issuing executions upon any adjudged violation thereof and to execute the by-laws, rules and regulations made by the board of aldermen. The mayor shall further be a special court within the corporate limits of the city to arrest and try all persons who are charged with a misdemeanor for violating any ordinance of the city, and if the accused be found guilty, he shall be fined, at the discretion of the court or mayor, not exceeding the amount specified in the ordinance or ordinances so violated, or, at the discretion of the mayor or court trying the same, such offender may be imprisoned not more than thirty days in the city lock-up or in the common jail of the county. And in all cases where a defendant may be adjudged to be imprisoned by the said special court, it shall be competent for said court to adjudge also that the said defendant work during the period of his confinement in the public streets or other public works of said city.

Jurisdiction and power of mayor.

Mayor a special court.

Defendant may be required to work on public streets.

Sec. 21. That the mayor may issue his precepts to the chief of police or any policeman of the city and to such other officers to whom a justice of the peace may direct his precepts, and such officers may execute such process anywhere in the county of Wayne; and the mayor shall keep a faithful minute of the precepts issued by him and all of his judicial proceedings.

Mayor shall keep a record of precepts issued.

Sec. 22. That any violation of a city ordinance shall be a misdemeanor and shall be punished by a fine of not more than fifty dollars or imprisonment of not more than thirty days. And no preliminary affidavit shall be necessary to give the mayor final jurisdiction over the offenses against the city ordinances.

Violation of city ordinances a misdemeanor.

Sec. 23. That all fines and costs collected under the provisions of this act for violation of the ordinances of said city shall go to the use of said city.

Fines, how applied.

Sec. 24. That the mayor shall receive an annual salary, to be fixed by the board of aldermen, and to be paid in monthly installments, and when present he shall preside at all meetings of the board of aldermen, and when there is an equal division upon any question or in the election of officers by the board, he shall determine the matter by his vote. He shall vote in no other case, and if he shall be absent the board may appoint one of their

Salary of mayor.

number pro tempore to exercise his duties at the board; and in the event of his absence or sickness the board of aldermen may appoint one of their own number pro tempore to exercise his duties.

dermen shall nvene within e days after ction.

Sec. 25. That the aldermen shall form one board and a majority of them shall be competeht to perform all the duties prescribed by the aldermen, unless otherwise provided. Within five days after their election they shall convene for the transaction of business, and shall then fix stated days of meeting for the year, which shall be as often at least as once in every calendar month. Special meetings of the aldermen may also be held on the call of the mayor or a majority of the aldermen; and of every such meeting when called by the mayor, all the aldermen, and when called by a majority of the aldermen, such as shall not join in the call shall be notified in writing.

rfeit of alder- n for failure to end meeting.

Sec. 26. That if any alderman shall fail to attend a general meeting of the board of aldermen or any special meeting of which he shall have notice as prescribed in this charter, unless prevented by such cause as shall be satisfactory to the board, he shall forfeit and pay for the use of the city the sum of four dollars.

wers conferred aldermen.

Sec. 27. That among the powers hereby conferred on the board of aldermen, they shall provide water, provide for repairing and cleaning the streets, regulate the market, take all proper means to prevent and extinguish fires, make regulations to cause the due observance of Sunday, appoint the police force and regulate, suppress and remove nuisances, preserve the health of the city from contagious or infectious diseases, appoint constables to execute such precepts as the mayor and other persons may lawfully issue to them, to preserve the peace and order and execute the ordinances of the city, and shall appoint and provide for the pay and prescribe duties of all such other officers as may be deemed necessary.

ection of clerk, asurer, etc., aldermen.

Sec. 28. That the aldermen, at their first meeting after their election or as soon thereafter as possible, shall appoint a clerk, a treasurer, a collector of taxes, a chief of police, and one or more assistants, who shall respectively hold their offices during the official term of the aldermen, subject, however, to removal at any time and others appointed in their stead for misbehavior or neglect in office. The board of aldermen shall fix the compensation of each of said officers, and no officer shall be allowed to receive fees. Before acting each of said officers shall be sworn to the faithful discharge of his duties and shall execute a bond payable to the city of Goldsboro in such sum as the aldermen shall determine.

Sec. 29. That the clerk shall keep regular and fair minutes of the proceedings of the board, and preserve all books, papers and articles committed to his care during his continuance in office and deliver them to his successor, and generally shall perform such other duties as may be prescribed by the board of aldermen.

Clerk shall keep minutes, etc.

Sec. 30. That every person shall be allowed to inspect the journals and papers of the board in the presence of the clerk.

Duties of treasurer.

Sec. 31. That the treasurer shall call on all persons who may have in their hands moneys or securities belonging to the city which ought to be paid or delivered into the treasury and receive the same, and shall safely keep the same for the use of the city; shall disburse the funds according to such orders as may be duly drawn on him in the manner hereinafter specified: he shall keep in a book provided for that purpose a fair and correct account of all moneys received and disbursed by him, and shall submit said account to the board of aldermen whenever required to do so. On the expiration of his term of office he shall deliver to his successor all the moneys, securities and other property entrusted to him for safe keeping or otherwise, and during his continuance therein he shall faithfully perform all duties lawfully imposed upon him as city treasurer.

Orders drawn on treasurer, how signed.

Sec. 32. That all orders drawn on the treasurer shall be signed by the mayor and countersigned by the clerk, and shall state the purpose for which the money is applied, and the treasurer shall specify said purposes in his accounts, and also the sources whence are derived the moneys received by him.

Duties of tax collector.

Sec. 33 The tax collector shall proceed forthwith to collect the taxes laid upon such subjects of taxation as the board of aldermen may direct within five days after the list shall have been placed in his hands and shall complete the same on or before the first day of April next ensuing, and shall pay the moneys and coupons on the bonds of the city as they are collected to the treasurer, taking his receipts for the same, and for this purpose he is hereby divested with all the powers which are now or may hereafter be vested in a sheriff or collector of state taxes; he shall rent out the market stalls and vegetable stands and shall prosecute all persons who retail without having paid the tax imposed, or who sell without a license. Also, at every monthly meeting of the board of aldermen he shall produce an abstract showing the sums received by him upon each subject of taxation and the amounts still due thereon; he shall further specify in said abstract the amount of cash received and the amount of certificates or other vouchers received for payment of taxes, which abstract shall be placed in the hands of the committee on finance to be filed with their chairman, and all books and documents belonging to or used in the office of the collector shall be and are hereby declared to be the property and records of the city, and shall be

Monthly report of tax collector to aldermen

at all times subject to the inspection and examination of the mayor and board of aldermen. The collector shall receive for his compensation such fees and commissions as may be allowed by the board of aldermen, and he shall on or before the fifteenth day of April in each year settle his accounts in full for the entire amount of taxes levied by the board, under the supervision of the committee of finance; and if the collector shall have been unable to collect any part of said taxes by reason of the insolvency of any of the persons owing the same or other good reasons, he shall on oath deliver a list of all such insolvents, delinquents and all other tax returns uncollected to the committee on finance, to be laid before the board of aldermen; and if approved, he shall be credited with the amount thereof or so much as may be approved; he and his sureties on his bond shall be answerable for the remainder, and for all other taxes or levies not collected and paid over by him, which he is or may be required by law to collect, and his bond shall be put in suit by the chairman of the finance committee and the city attorney.

nual statement by aldern of receipts disbursents.

Sec. 34. That the board of aldermen shall cause to be made out annually a fair transcript of their receipts and disbursements on account of the city for the general inspection of the citizens, and cause the same to be posted up at the court-house door in said city ten days before the first day in May in each year.

ty of police.

Sec. 35. That it shall be the duty of the police to see that the laws, ordinances and orders of the board of aldermen are enforced, and to report all breaches thereof to the mayor; to preserve the peace of the city by suppressing disturbances and apprehending all offenders, and for that purpose they shall have all the power and authority vested in sheriffs and county constables; they shall execute all precepts lawfully directed to them by the mayor or other judicial officers, and in the execution thereof shall have the same powers which the sheriff and constables of the county have, and they shall have the same fees on all processes and precepts executed or returned by them which may be allowed to the sheriff of the county on like process and precepts, but such fees shall be paid to the treasurer for the use of the city.

ach of official d of city cers.

Sec. 36. That for any breach of his official bond by the treasurer, clerk, tax collector or any other city officer who may be required to give an official bond, he shall be liable in an action on the same in the name of the city at the suit of the city or any person aggrieved by such breach, and the same may be put in suit without assignment from time to time until the whole penalty be recovered.

ermen emered to imve streets.

Sec. 37. That the board of aldermen shall have power to lay out and open new streets within the corporate limits of the city whenever by them deemed necessary, and have power at any time to widen, enlarge, change or extend or discontinue any street or streets or any part thereof within the corporate limits of the city; and shall have full power and authority to condemn, appropiate or use any land or lands necessary for any of the purposes named in this section, upon making a reasonable compensation to the owner or owners thereof. But in case the owner of the land and the aldermen can not agree as to the damages, then the matter shall be referred to the arbitrators, each party choosing one, who shall be a freeholder and a citizen of the city; and in case the owner of the land shall refuse to chose such arbitrator, then the sheriff of the county shall in his stead select one for him; and in case the two chosen as aforesaid can not agree, they shall select an umpire, whose duty it shall be to examine the land condemned and ascertain the damages sustained and the benefits accruing to the owner in consequence of the change; and the award of the arbitrators or umpire shall be conclusive of the rights of the parties and shall vest in the aldermen the right to use the land for the purposes specified; and all damages agreed upon by the aldermen or awarded by the arbitrators or umpires shall be paid as other city liabilities, by taxation: Provided, that either party may appeal to the superior court as now provided by law.

Arbitrators shall assess value of land in dispute.

Sec. 38. That the board of aldermen shall have authority to put to and keep at work upon the streets and public grounds of the city any person or persons who may fail to pay any fine, penalty or forfeiture which may have been imposed on such person or persons by the mayor of the city; and the said aldermen shall have authority by the ordinances and by-laws of the city to confine, control and manage such person or persons until the said fines, penalties or forfeitures, together with the cost thereof, shall be fully paid and satisfied, under such rates for labor and board as the aldermen may establish.

Persons failing to pay fine may be worked on streets.

Sec 39. That in order to raise a fund for the expenses incident to the proper government of the city, the aldermen may annually levy and collect the following taxes, viz: Upon all real estate and personal property within the corporate limits of the city; upon all money on hand: solvent credits; upon all polls and other subjects of taxation taxed by the general assembly for public purposes.

Aldermen may levy and collect certain annual taxes.

Sec. 40. That the annual tax on property enumerated in preceding section shall not exceed fifty cents on the one hundred dollars valuation thereof, nor shall the poll tax annually exceed one dollar and fifty cents.

Limitation to tax.

Sec. 41. That in addition to the subjects of taxation for state purposes, the aldermen shall have power to levy and collect a

Aldermen empowered to levy and collect special taxes.

special or license tax not to exceed one hundred dollars on the following subjects, to-wit: All itinerant merchants, peddlers or auctioneers who shall sell or offer to sell privately or at public outcry within the city limits, whether by ascending or descending bids; all drummers or commercial travellers; each express company; each telegraph office and each railroad company having a depot within the city limits; each photograph artist and person taking likeness of the human face by whatsoever art; each broker, bank or banker's office; each dealer in cotton futures; each dealer in patent rights; each sewing machine agent; all commission merchants and commercial brokers; each distiller of fruit or grain; each livery stable; every resident or non-resident huckster or trader or agent of such who buys produce on the streets for sale in other markets; each gift enterprise and lottery; each dray; each omnibus; each hotel; each barber shop; each lightning rod agent; each fire or life insurance agent; on each auctioneer; on every agency for the sale of steam engines, boilers and machinery not manufactured in this city; every dealer in buggies, wagons or other vehicles not manufactured in this city; each and every surgeon, dentist, practicing physician, optician, practicing lawyer, civil engineer, real estate agent or broker, aurist, occulist and chiropodist; on every dealer in horses or mules sold, bartered or exchanged: every cattle, horse or mule drover or dealer: and every agency for the sale of snuff, tobacco or other articles of merchandise not manufactured in this city, and all other subjects taxed by the state.

xes shall be a on property.

Sec. 42. That all taxes levied by the board of aldermen shall be a lien upon the personal property of the taxpayers from date of levy thereon and upon the real property from the first day of June of the year in which the said tax is levied. That after the first day of January of each year the tax collector is authorized to levy upon and sell upon a notice of ten (10) days the personal property of any delinquent taxpayer: and to sell the real estate of any delinquent taxpayer after a notice of thirty (30) days: Provided, said tax collector may at any time levy upon and sell said personal property upon filing an affidavit that he has reason to believe that such taxpayer is about to leave the city of Goldsboro, and that there is danger of the loss of the taxes due by him, and obtaining an order from the mayor directing him forthwith to levy upon and sell the personal property of such taxpayers; the notice provided for in this section shall be posted at the court-house door and published in some newspaper published in the city of Goldsboro; that whenever any property, real or personal, is sold for non-payment of taxes as herein provided, the city of Goldsboro may become the purchaser: Provided, there is no bidder for the property so sold for the amount of the taxes and costs due upon the same; that the tax collector shall keep a record of all sales made by him, and upon the sale of any real property as herein authorized shall deliver to the purchaser a certificate stating the name of delinquent taxpayer, the amount of taxes and costs, and describing the real estate so sold, and if within twelve (12) months the owner of said real estate shall not redeem the same by paying to the purchaser the amount of said taxes and costs, with ten per centum added thereto, the tax collector shall execute and deliver to the purchaser a deed for the said real estate, which deed shall conform as near as may be to the deeds executed by sheriffs upon sales of real estate for taxes, and shall have the same force and effect; there shall be the same fees and costs charged as upon sales by sheriffs for taxes.

Aldermen may declare certain animals nuisances.

Sec. 43. That the board of aldermen shall have power to declare all horses, mules, cattle, swine, sheep, goats and dogs running at large within the limits of the city a nuisance, and the aldermen may at their option impose a fine upon the owner or owners of said animals so running at large, or may treat the same as a nuisance and abate or prohibit by law.

Certain special taxes aldermen may levy.

Sec. 44. That in addition to the subjects of taxation enumerated in section forty-one (41) the aldermen may levy a tax on the following subjects, the amount of which tax, when fixed, shall be collected by the tax collector instantly; and if the same be not paid on demand, the same may be recovered by levying on the articles upon which the tax is imposed, or any other property of the owner may be forthwith distrained and sold to satisfy the same, namely:

Bowling alleys, etc.

I. Upon every bowling alley, billiard table, pool table, bagatelle table, shooting gallery, skating rink, or any other game allowed by law, and every victualling house or restaurant, established. used or kept in the city, a tax not exceeding fifty dollars a year.

Liquor saloons.

II. Upon every permission by the board of aldermen to retail spirituous liquors a tax not exceeding five hundred ($500) dollars.

Circuses, etc.

III. Upon every company of circus riders who shall exhibit within the city a tax not exceeding thirty ($30) dollars for each separate exhibition, the tax to be paid before the exhibition, and if not, to be double.

Theatricals.

IV. Upon every company of stage or theatrical performers, every sleight-of-hand performer, rope or wire dancer or performer; every exhibitor of natural or artificial curiosities; every single person or company of singers, dancers, Ethiopian minstrels, or performers on musical instruments who shall sing, dance, perform or play on musical instruments for reward, five dollars ($5) for each exhibition.

ows and exitions. V. Upon each show or exhibition of any other kind, and upon each concert or lecture for reward, a tax of five dollars for each exhibition.

pair of streets d sidewalks. Sec. 45. That the board of aldermen shall cause to be kept clean and in good repair the streets, sidewalks and alleys; they may establish the width and ascertain the location of those already provided and lay out and open others, and may reduce or increase the width of all of them: they may also establish and regulate the public grounds and protect the shade trees of the city.

res. Sec. 46. That the board of aldermen shall have power to establish ordinances to prevent and extinguish fires; to provide for the establishment, organization, equipment and government of fire companies; provide said companies with fire engines, fire hose and necessary appurtenances, and that in all cases of fire a majority of such board of aldermen as shall be present may, if they deem it necessary to stop the progress of the fire, cause any dwelling house or other building to be blown up or pulled down, for which they shall not be responsible to any one for damages.

elling houses other buildings y be pulled vn in case of .

y require tement and oval of nuisces. Sec. 47. That the aldermen may require and compel the abatement and removal of all nuisances within the city at the expense of the person causing the same, or the owner or tenant of the grounds whereon the same may be; and may regulate, if allowed to be established, any slaughter house or place, or the exercise within the city of any offensive or unhealthy trade, business or employment.

iving of horses, Sec. 48. That they may prohibit by penalties the riding or driving of horses or other animals in a careless or dangerous manner, or at a greater speed than seven (7) miles per hour within the city limits, and also the firing of guns, pistols, gunpowder, crackers or other explosive, combustible or dangerous materials in the streets, public grounds or elsewhere within the city.

ay regulate rkets. Sec. 49. That the aldermen may establish and regulate the markets and prescribe at what time and place within the city marketable articles shall be sold.

blic buildings. Sec. 50. That they may establish all public buildings necessary and proper for the city, and prevent the erection or establishment of wooden buildings in any part of the city where they may increase the danger of fire.

meteries. Sec. 51. That they may provide graveyards in or near the corporate limits, and regulate the same; may appoint and pay a keeper and compel the keeping and returning bills of mortality; and they may prohibit interments within the city.

ntagious seases. Sec. 52. That the board of aldermen may take such measures as they deem effectual to prevent the entrance into the city or the spreading therein of any contagious or infectious disease;

may stop, detain and examine for that purpose every person coming from places believed to be infected with such disease; and may establish and regulate hospitals within the city or within three miles (3) thereof; may cause any person in the city suspected to be infected with such disease and whose stay may endanger its health, to be removed to the hospital; may remove from the city or destroy any furniture or other articles which shall be suspected of being tainted or infected with contagious or infectious disease or of which there shall be reasonable cause to apprehend that they may pass into such a state as to generate and propagate disease; may abate by any reasonable means all nuisances which may be injurious to the public health.

Persons attempting to prevent removal of others to hospital.

Sec. 53. That if any person shall attempt by force or by threats of violence to prevent the removal to the hospital of any person ordered to be conveyed thither, the person so offending shall forfeit and pay to the city one hundred ($100) dollars, and moreover be deemed guilty of a misdemeanor.

Speed of railroad trains.

Sec. 54. That the board of aldermen may govern and regulate the speed of railroad trains while running within the corporate limits of the city, and prohibit the ringing of bells, blowing of steam whistles either during the day or night within the city limits.

Commissioners of Wayne county shall not grant license to sell liquor in Goldsboro without consent of aldermen.

Sec. 55. That it shall not be lawful for the commissioners of Wayne county to grant any license to retail spirituous liquors within the limits of the city or within one mile thereof without permission first obtained from the board of aldermen of the city in being at the time of the application to the county commissioners; and if any license shall be granted without permission in writing attested by the clerk of the board of aldermen and exhibited to the county commissioners and filed with the clerk of the board of county commissioners, the same shall be utterly void, and the person obtaining such license shall be liable to indictment as in other cases of retailing without a license, and shall, moreover, forfeit and pay to the city the sum of twenty ($20) dollars.

Penalties recoverable in name of city.

Sec. 56. That all penalties imposed by law, relating to the city of Goldsboro or by this act, by any ordinance of the city, unless otherwise provided, shall be recoverable in the name of the city of Goldsboro before the mayor or any tribunal having jurisdiction thereof.

Limitation to penalty.

Sec. 57. That the board of aldermen shall not have power to impose for any offense a larger penalty than fifty ($50) dollars, unless the same be expressly authorized, and from any judgment of the mayor by this act or for other cause of action herein allowed, the party dissatisfied may appeal in like manner and under the same rules and regulations as are prescribed for appeals from a judgment of a justice of the peace.

laries of city oers. Sec. 58. That the board of aldermen shall have power to fix the salary of the mayor, treasurer, clerk, tax collector and any other officer of the city, or increase or diminish the same from time to time as they may elect.

rporate rights d privileges. Sec. 59. That the city of Goldsboro is hereby vested with all the powers, rights, privileges and immunities enumerated in chapter sixty-two (62) of The Code, not inconsistent with any of the provisions of this act.

ty may estab- h waterworks, . Sec. 60. That the city of Goldsboro may establish a system of sewerage, may pave its streets and sidewalks, may establish a system of waterworks, or may purchase the system now in operation in said city; may establish a gas, electric or other plant for furnishing lights; may build and own a city hall and market house, and may own and operate any or all of these improvements, and may make other public improvements; and may apportion the cost of the same equally among the inhabitants; and for the purpose of providing such improvements may, as and when the board of aldermen may determine, issue its bonds from time to time to an amount not exceeding in the aggregate the sum of two hundred thousand ($200,000) dollars, of such denominations and in such proportions as the board of aldermen may deem advisable, bearing interest from the date thereof at a rate not exceeding six per centum per annum, with interest coupons attached, payable half yearly at such times and at such place or places as may be deemed advisable by said board, said bonds to be of such form and tenor and transferable in such way, and the principal thereof payable or redeemable at such time or times, not exceeding fifty (50) years from the date thereof and at such place or places, as the board of aldermen may determine; said bonds may be issued for any of said purposes or for two or more or for all.

dermen may ue bonds. mitation to ue.

en bonds ma- e.

nds shall not disposed of for than par ue. Sec. 61. That none of the bonds provided for in the above section shall be disposed of, either by sale, exchange, hypothecation or otherwise, for a less price than their par value, nor shall said bonds or their proceeds be used for any other purposes than those declared in said section.

nds shall not subject to tax- on until after . Sec. 62. That the bonds authorized to be issued by section sixty (60) hereof and their coupons shall not be subject to taxation by the said city until after they become due and tender of payment shall have been made by the city, and the coupons shall be receivable in payment of the taxes or other city dues for any fiscal year in which said coupons become due or thereafter; and if the holder of any of said bonds or coupons shall fail to present the same for payment at the time, times and at the place or places therein named, he shall not be entitled to any interest thereon for the time they have been outstanding after maturity.

Sec 63. That for the purpose of providing for the payment of the interest accruing on and the principal at maturity of the bonds herein authorized, the board of aldermen of said city shall annually and at the time of levying other city taxes levy and lay a particular tax on all persons and subjects of taxation on which the said board of aldermen now are or may hereafter be authorized to lay and levy taxes for any purposes whatever, said particular tax not to be less than five nor more than twenty cents on the one hundred dollars assessed valuation on property and not less than fifteen nor more than sixty cents on each poll for each fifty thousand ($50,000) dollars of bonds so issued. The taxes provided for in this section shall be collected in the manner and at the times other city taxes are collected, and shall be accounted for and kept separate from other city taxes, and shall be applied exclusively to the purposes for which they are levied and collected. So much of said taxes as may not be required to pay the interest on the bonds issued as it falls due, and can not be applied to the purchase or discharge of the said bonds, shall be invested so as to secure the payment at the maturity of the principal of the said bonds; and to insure the due investment of the amounts collected from year to year in excess of that required to pay the said interest, the board of aldermen shall appoint some suitable person to be styled "commissioner of the sinking fund of the city of Goldsboro," who shall hold his office for six years, and whose duty it shall be, under such rules and regulations as said board of aldermen shall from time to time prescribe, to make investments of so much of the taxes collected as aforesaid as shall be applicable as aforesaid to the payment of the principal of said bonds, and to do and perform all such other services in connection with said bonds as said board of aldermen may prescribe, and such commissioner shall give bond and receive such compensation for his services as said board of aldermen may determine.

Annual special tax levy may be made to pay interest and principal.

Limitation to special tax levy.

Said funds may be invested until bonds are due.

Sec. 64. That before any of the bonds herein provided for shall be issued, the question of issuing the same shall first be submitted to the qualified voters of said city, after thirty days' notice in some newspaper published in said city, at an election to be held under the same rules and regulations as are now prescribed by law for election of mayor and aldermen for said city. Such notice shall set forth the object for which such bonds are to be issued, the amount of the same, the rate of interest, the time when they mature and the rate of tax to be levied and collected to pay the same. Those qualified voters approving the issue of such bonds and levying and collecting of the taxes to pay the same shall deposit in a separate ballot box a written or printed

Question of issuing bonds shall be submitted to voters.

ballot with the word "Approved" thereon; and those disapproving the same shall deposit a like ballot with the word "Disapproved" thereon. If at such election a majority of such voters shall vote "Approved," then the said board of aldermen shall issue the bonds provided for in such notice and shall levy and order the collection of the taxes therein named and authorized by this act. At such election, upon the proper notice being given as herein provided for, the issuing of bonds for more than one purpose within the meaning of this act may be voted on in separate ballot boxes under the same rules and regulations as are named above; but in such case the ballots shall contain the purpose of the bonds with the words "Approved" or "Disapproved," as the elector desires, following. Said elections may be held from time to time as the board of aldermen may determine, and if at any such election a majority of the qualified voters vote "Disapproved," the same or a different proposition may be submitted to the qualified voters at another election under the provisions of this act.

rm of ballot. dermen thorized to ld certain gift city.

Sec. 65. That the city of Goldsboro is hereby authorized and empowered to accept and hold the gift of Henry Weil and Solomon Weil to said city of the tract of land known as "Herman Park," and may add to the same by gift or purchase for a public park; and the said city shall have and exercise its police powers over the same and a like power over the cemeteries owned by said city, whether the same be in its corporate limits or not, and may enact and enforce ordinances for the proper government of the same.

werage system y be extended 'ond corporate its for outlet.

Sec. 66. That if it shall be necessary in obtaining proper outlets for a system of sewerage to extend the same beyond the corporate limits of said city, then in such case the board of aldermen of said city shall have power to so extend it, and both within and without the said corporate limits to condemn land for the purposes of right-of-way or other requirements of said system; the proceedings for such condemnation to be the same as those prescribed in chapter forty-nine (49), volume one (1) of The Code.

ners of land utting on eets, etc., may assessed.

Sec. 67. That the city of Goldsboro shall have power in its discretion to assess owners of land abutting on streets paved by said city with an amount not to exceed one-third of the actual cost of such paving in front of such abutting land; and if said city shall construct a partial system of sewerage, it shall have like power of assessing not exceeding one-third of the actual cost of such sewer in front of such abutting land, but the cost of common outlets shall not be so assessed; and the cost thereof as herein provided for may be assessed upon such abutting property and added to the taxes on the same, and collected in the same manner that other taxes or assessments are collected.

Sec. 68. That all persons and corporations doing business in the city of Goldsboro, "affected with a public use," shall furnish and supply said city and the inhabitants thereof, upon proper demand therefor at reasonable and uniform rates. Persons and corporations in Goldsboro affected with a public use.

Sec. 69. That all laws or clauses or parts of laws in conflict with this act are hereby repealed. Conflicting laws repealed.

Sec. 70. That this act shall take effect and be in force from and after its ratification.

Ratified the 28th day of February, A. D. 1899.

CHAPTER 172.

An act to authorize the board of aldermen of the town of Lincolnton to issue bonds to construct waterworks, sewerage, and electric light plant.

The General Assembly of North Carolina do enact:

Section 1. That the mayor and board of aldermen of the town of Lincolnton, in the county of Lincoln, for the purpose of constructing, erecting, operating and maintaining and supplying said town with complete system of waterworks, with all the necessary appurtenances thereto belonging, and for the purpose of constructing, maintaining and operating an electric plant for lighting said town by electricity, with the necessary appurtenances thereto belonging, are authorized and empowered to issue bonds, bearing interest at the rate of six per centum per annum, to the amount of twenty-five thousand dollars of the denomination of one hundred dollars to each and every one of which shall be attached and the coupons representing the interest on said bonds, which said coupons shall be due and payable on the first day of January of each year until the maturity of said bonds. The bonds so issued by said commissioners shall run for a period of thirty years and shall be numbered consecutively from one to two hundred and fifty, and the coupons shall bear the number corresponding to the bonds to which they are attached, and shall declare the amount of interest which they represent, and when the interest is due and where payable, and shall be received in payment of all municipal taxes levied by said town. The said bonds shall be exempt from municipal taxation. For purpose of supplying town with waterworks and electric lights, commissioners of Lincolnton empowered to issue bonds. Interest on bonds. When coupons payable. Maturity of bonds. Shall be received in payment for municipal taxes.

Sec. 2. That said bonds shall be issued under the signature of the mayor of Lincolnton and attested by the signature of the clerk and treasurer of the board of aldermen of said town, and the mayor and clerk of said board of aldermen shall, under the direction of the board of aldermen of said town, dispose of said bonds as the necessity for the prosecution of the work shall require at a sum not less than their par value, and it shall be the duty of the clerk of the said board of commissioners to make and keep a record of the bonds sold, the number of the bond purchased, the name of the purchaser and the price received for the same.

rk shall keep ord of bonds d, etc.

nmissioners ll levy a cial tax to ate a sinking d.

Sec. 3. That for the purpose of paying the interest on said bonds as it falls due and to provide a sinking fund for the redemption of said bonds, it shall be the duty of the board of aldermen of said town to levy and to be caused to be collected annually a tax upon all the real and personal property of said town not exceeding fifty cents on the hundred dollars worth of property and one dollar and fifty cents on the poll, which said tax shall be levied and collected as other taxes for said town. It shall further be the duty of said board of aldermen to provide for the collection of rents, water charges and other revenues for the use of the water provided by said waterworks, and to provide for the collection of rents, charges and other revenues for the use of electric light provided by said electric light plant, and all revenues derived from such source, either from the waterworks or electric plant, shall be kept and held solely for the purpose of maintaining said system of waterworks and electric light system, and surplus after paying the expenses of maintaining said system shall be used as a part of the sinking fund for the redemption of said bonds until they shall have been fully redeemed.

ximum cial tax

mmissioners all collect ts.

mmissioners powered to rchase annuy one twentyh of bonds ued.

Sec. 4. That in order that there may not be an accumulation of money arising either from taxation or from the rents of waterworks and electric light systems after paying the annual interest accrued on said bonds, the board of aldermen of said town are authorized and empowered to purchase annually one twenty-fifth of the bonds issued at a sum not exceeding their par value, and in case no one shall offer to sell one twenty-fifth of said bonds, then the said board of aldermen are authorized to designate such bonds not exceeding one twenty-fifth of the whole number issued as they may desire to purchase, and after the designation of such bonds and a notice thereof given through a newspaper published in Lincoln county, if the holder or holders of the bonds shall refuse to surrender the same and receive their par value, with accrued interest at the time of said notice, then the holder shall not receive any interest subsequently accruing: Provided, the said bonds shall be affected with the conditions of this act only when the conditions are expressed on the face of the bonds.

y designate nds desired

holder refuses surrender same all not receive erest.

cord of purasers of said ds shall be t

Sec. 5. That the commissioners of said town shall provide a record, which shall be kept by the clerk, in which shall be entered the name of every purchaser of a bond and the number of the bond purchased and the price paid therefor and the price paid in redemption of the same, and the bonds when redeemed and recorded shall be destroyed by fire in the presence of the board of aldermen by some one of their number or by the mayor under their direction.

Sec. 6. That the said board of aldermen shall not issue said bonds or any part thereof until they shall have first caused to be held in said town an election in which there shall be submitted to the qualified voters of said town the question of a ratification of this act or its rejection, which they are authorized to do at such time as shall be deemed best for securing the voice of the people upon the question; and said election shall be held in the same manner as election for town officers. Those in favor of issuing said bonds shall vote a written or printed ticket with the words "For improvement." and those who are opposed thereto shall vote a ticket written or printed with the words "Against improvement" thereon. The result of said election shall be ascertained by the judges of election and by them certified to the board of aldermen of the town of Lincolnton within twenty-four hours after said election, and said returns shall be immediately recorded on the minutes of said board of aldermen. And if at said election a majority of the qualified voters shall vote "For improvement," then the board of aldermen of said town may issue said bonds; but if a majority of such qualified voters of said town shall vote "Against improvement," then the said board of aldermen shall not issue said bonds.

Election shall be held before bonds are issued.

Election held in same manner as for town officers.

Form of ballot.

Sec. 7. That the proceeds arising from the sale of said bonds shall be paid to the town treasurer, who shall hold the same subject to the order of the board of aldermen of said town, in carrying into effect the purposes of this act; and the said treasurer shall be liable on his official bond for said proceeds, and said board of aldermen may increase said bond from time to time as in their discretion may be necessary to provide for the safe keeping of the same.

Proceeds arising from sale of said bonds, to whom paid.

Treasurer shall be liable on official bond.

Sec. 8. That this act shall be in force from and after its ratification.

Ratified the 4th day of March, A. D. 1899.

CHAPTER 173.

An act to incorporate the town of Town Creek, Wilson county, North Carolina.

The General Assembly of North Carolina do enact:

Section 1. That the town of Town Creek, in the county of Wilson, be and the same is hereby incorporated under the name and style of "Town Creek," and as such shall be subject to and gov-

Town of Town Creek, Wilson county, incorporated.

erned by all the provisions of chapter sixty two of The Code of North Carolina not inconsistent with this act.

rporate limits. Sec. 2. That the corporate limits of said town shall be as follows: Beginning at the line of the land of Z. V. Braswell on the road leading from Tarboro to Wilson, then running south eight hundred and fifty yards to R. A. Whitehead's line; thence west four hundred yards to J. D. Daws' line; thence north two thousand one hundred yards to William Whitehead's line; thence east to J. M. Stevenson's line; thence south to the beginning.

mporary cers. Sec. 3. The officers of said corporation shall consist of a mayor, three commissioners and a constable, and until their successors are elected and qualified the said officers shall be Z. V. Braswell, F. E. Edwards, R. A. Whiethead and Dempsey Weaver, commissioners, the constable to be elected by the commissioners. Such officers shall have all the rights, powers and duties conferred on like officers by chapter sixty-two of The Code of North Carolina.

Sec. 4. This act shall be in force from and after its ratification.

Ratified the 4th day of March, A. D. 1899.

CHAPTER 174.

An act to amend and consolidate the charter of the town of Kenansville, in Duplin county.

The General Assembly of North Carolina do enact:

corporated. Section 1. That the town of Kenansville, in Duplin county, be and the same is hereby incorporated under the name and style

rporate name. wn officers of "The Town of Kenansville," and that A. P. Farrior, John A. Gavin, Sr., L. M. Cooper, J. D. Southerland and J. J. Bowden, the present commissioners of said town and their successors, are hereby declared a body corporate and politic with succession during the corporate existence of said town, and shall be styled the commissioners of the town of Kenansville. That J. O. Carr, the present mayor of said town, and the commissioners aforesaid shall continue in office and perform their duties as such until their successors shall be elected and qualified.

rporate limits. Sec 2. That the corporate limits of said town shall be as follows: Beginning at the bridge over the Grove swamp, near the James Sprunt Institute, and runs south along the Wilmington road by Mrs. H. R. Kornegay's residence to the Magnolia road; thence in an easterly direction to a point where two roads cross between the Presbyterian church and Farrior's spring; thence along the road leading to the Stanford residence to the clearing at the edge of the Cooper lot; thence around the Cooper and Millard lots, including the same, to a point in the road or street leading to Cooper's mill; thence a direct line to the Rutledge graveyard, thence down a branch in a northwesterly direction to the Grove swamp; thence up said swamp to the beginning.

Sec. 3. That the officers of said town shall consist of a mayor, five commissioners and a town constable, who shall also be tax collector, and said mayor and commissioners shall be elected annually on Tuesday after the first Monday in May by the qualified voters of said town, and shall immediately assume the duties of said office, after having first taken an oath for the faithful discharge of their duties. **Officers, when elected.**

Sec. 4. That the said town constable and tax collector shall be elected by the board of town commissioners at their first meeting after their election or as soon thereafter as is convenient, and his term of office shall expire with that of said board unless sooner removed for cause, which they are hereby empowered to do; that he shall be required to enter into bond satisfactory to the board of commissioners for the faithful discharge of his duties, and shall be required to make a monthly settlement of all taxes, fines and other moneys collected in his official capacity. **Constable and tax collector to be elected by commissioners. Term of office.** **Monthly settlements.**

Sec. 5. That said constable and tax collector shall be authorized and empowered to serve all processes issued by said mayor and collect the taxes levied by said commissioners, and his fees for such services shall be the same as are allowed sheriff, unless otherwise provided by the town commissioners; and in enforcing the collection of said taxes he shall have power and authority to levy on any personal and real property, and after due advertisement according to law, sell the same and apply the proceeds to the satisfaction of said taxes, and in serving said processes he shall be subject to and have the advantage of all laws applicable to sheriffs in similar cases **Constable and tax collector shall serve processes issued by mayor.** **Collection of taxes.**

Sec. 6. That it shall be the duty of the constable to see that the laws, ordinances and orders of the mayor and commissioners are enforced, preserve the peace of the town, suppress disturbances, and for that purpose he shall have all power and authoity vested in sheriffs and other peace officers; and he may arrest, with or without a warrant, all persons committing offenses within the jurisdiction of the mayor and bring them before the said mayor for a hearing. **Duty of constable.** **May arrest with or without warrants.**

Sec. 7. That the mayor shall preside at all meetings of the town commissioners, but shall not be entitled to a vote except in case of a tie. He shall keep a faithful minute of all precepts issued by him and of all judicial proceedings; judgments rendered by him shall have the force, virtue and validity as if rendered by a justice of the peace, and for his services he shall receive the same **Mayor shall preside at meetings of commissioners** fees as a justice of the peace, and such other salary as the commisisoners may allow.

acancies occurring among comissioners how lled.

Sec. 8. That any vacancy that may occur in the office of town commissioners shall be filled by the remaining members of the board; and any vacancy in the mayor's office shall be filled by said board of commissioners. In the absence of the mayor the said board may elect one of their members to preside at their meetings, and either the mayor or a majority of the board are hereby authorized to call special meetings whenever it may be deemed best.

mmissioners powered to en streets.

Sec. 9. That said commissioners shall have the right to open new streets in said town when and where they shall deem necessary. They shall have the right to widen, straighten, make narrower or discontinue any of the streets in said town. When in the exercise of said power it shall become necessary to take the lands of any individual, firm or corporation, they shall pay full compensation to such individual, firm or corporation: and if the said commissioners and the individual, firm or corporation who own the lands can not agree, then the said commissioners shall proceed in the manner prescribed by law for county commissioners in opening public roads, to have the damage done the individual, firm or corporation assessed, and this amount they shall pay said individual, firm or corporation [and] by this proceeding and payment shall acquire the right to open and maintain a street on said land.

ndemnation of nd

amage shall be sessed.

wer of comissioners to ake by-laws d ordinances.

Sec. 10. The commissioners of said town shall have the power to make such by-laws and adopt such ordinances for the government of said town as a majority of them may deem necessary to promote the interest and insure the good order of said town, for the improvement of the streets and the preservation of the health in the same, and to make all such other public regulations as the interests, comfort, convenience and general welfare of the citizens of said town may require.

rsons violating wn ordinances ilty of misdeeanor.

Sec. 11. That any person violating an ordinance of said town shall be guilty of a misdemeanor, and in all cases where an offender has been convicted before the mayor of said town, for the violation of any ordinance thereof, and a fine has been imposed on such offender for such violation, the mayor of said town at the time of entering the judgment against such offender or thereafter, may order that on the failure to pay such fine to the constable of said town for the space of one day, such offender shall be by the constable put to work on the streets of said town for a time to be fixed by the mayor not exceeding thirty days.

iolators of law ay be worked streets.

nnual levy and llection of xes.

Sec. 12. That the board of commissioners of said town shall have the power annually to levy and cause to be collected taxes for necessary town purposes on all real property, all moneys, credits, stocks, bonds and other personal property, and on the taxable polls within the limits of said town: Provided, however, that the taxes levied by them shall not exceed forty cents on the one hundred dollars valuation on real property and one dollar and twenty cents on each taxable poll, and the valuation of all property within said town as taxed by said town commissioners shall be the same at which it is assessed for taxation for state and county purposes.

Proviso.

Limitation to tax levy.

Sec. 13. That it shall be the duty of the town clerk and treasurer to make out from the county tax lists a tax list for the town of Kenansville, and from this list shall be made out tax books for said town to be placed in hands of constable and tax collector for collection.

Tax list made out by clerk and treasurer

Sec. 14. That the commissioners of said town shall have the power to annually levy and cause to be collected for the necessary expense of said town such privilege taxes as shall seem to them fair and equitable on the professions, callings, trades, occupations and all other business carried on in said town, and may control the markets and designate the places thereof.

Privilege taxes.

Sec. 15. That the commissioners may pass such regulations for the registration of votes and holding elections as they may think wise and just, always recognizing the qualifications for suffrage prescribed by the laws of North Carolina: Provided, however, that it shall always be the duty of the commissioners to give at least ten days' notice of said registration and thirty days' notice of said election by posting such notice at three public places in said town.

Regulations for the registration of voters.

Proviso.

Notice shall be given of registration and election.

Sec. 16. That no malt or spirituous liqurs shall be sold in said town nor shall the county commissioners have any right to grant license to any person or persons to sell the same while this act may be in force.

Sale of malt or spirituous liquors forbidden.

Sec. 17. That all acts and parts of acts not brought forward in this charter, and all laws and clauses of laws not consistent with or in any way conflicting with this act be and the same are hereby repealed.

Conflicting acts repealed.

Sec. 18. That this act shall be in full force and effect from and after its ratification.

Ratified the 4th day of March, A. D. 1899.

CHAPTER 175.

An act to authorize the commissioners of the town of Shelby to issue bonds.

The General Assembly of North Carolina do enact:

mmissioners Shelby authorized to order ction. Section 1. That the commissioners of the town of Shelby are hereby authorized, empowered and directed at any time after the ratification of this act, whenever they shall be requested so to do by the petition of one-third of the qualified voters of the town of Shelby, to cause at [an] election to be held in said town at such time as said commissioners may appoint, and to submit to the qualified voters of said town the question of issuing bonds to the ount of bonds. amount of not more than thirty thousand dollars for the purposes and under the provisions hereinafter named in this act, y levy special to create king fund. and levying and collecting annually a special tax to provide for the payment of the interest thereon and to provide a sinking fund for the payment of the principal of said bonds when they shall become due or for the payment of such part of said bonds ction shall advertised. as may be called in for payment as provided in this act. The said election shall be advertised by the commissioners for said town for thirty days prior to the day of election in some newspaper published in said town, and shall be held under the same ection, how d. rules and regulations prescribed for the election of mayor and commissioners of said town in the charter of said town and the amendments thereto. Those who are in favor of issuing said bonds and levying and collecting said taxes shall vote a written rm of ballot. or printed ticket with the words "For bonds" thereon, and those who are opposed shall vote a written or printed ticket with the words "Against bonds" thereon. The result of said election shall be ascertained by the officers of election and certified and returned by them to the commissioners for the town of Shelby, who shall verify and also certify such result and cause the same to be recorded in their minutes.

nomination of nds. Sec. 2. If a majority of the qualified voters of said town shall vote for bonds then the commissioners of said town shall issue coupon bonds not to exceed in amount the sum of thirty thousand dollars and in denominations of not less than one hundred dollars and not more than five hundred dollars, bearing interest from the date of the bonds at a rate not exceeding five per te of interest. centum per annum, payable annually on the first day of January of each year. One-half of the total amount of said bonds that may hen bonds are yable. be issued shall be made payable at the expiration of thirty years from the date thereof, and the other half at the expiration of forty years. The bonds and the coupons shall be numbered and the bonds shall be signed by the mayor of the town of Shelby and countersigned by the treasurer of said town, and a record shall be kept of all bonds, showing their number, amount and to whom sold. The coupons shall be received in payment of all taxes, fines and debts due said town. The board of commissioners of said town shall dispose of said bonds for not less than their par value and as the necessity for the prosecution of the improvements for which said bonds were voted shall require.

Record of sale of bonds shall be kept.

Sec. 3. The purpose for which the aforesaid bonds shall be issued shall be for the construction of waterworks and the supplying of said town with water and for providing an adequate protection for said town against fire and the establishment of an electric light system or other lighting system for said town, for all or either of said purposes; and when the election shall be ordered as hereinbefore provided, the order of election and the advertisement thereof shall specify the purposes for which said bonds are to be issued; and if a majority of the qualified voters of said town shall vote for bonds at said election, then the proceeds arising from the sale of said bonds shall be applied exclusively to the purposes specified in said order of election.

Purpose for which bonds issued.

Advertisement shall specify purpose of bonds.

Sec. 4. In order to pay the interest on said bonds the commissioners for said town are hereby authorized and it shall be their duty to annually compute and levy at the time of levying other taxes of said town a sufficient special tax upon all polls and all property, real and personal, and other subjects of taxation mentioned in the charter of the town of Shelby and acts amendatory thereof which shall be returned or listed for general taxation in said town, always observing the constitutional equation between the tax on property and the tax on polls, not exceeding thirty cents on the one hundred dollars valuation of property and ninety cents on each poll, with which to regularly and promptly pay the interest on said bonds. Said taxes shall be collected in the same manner and at the same time the other taxes of said town are collected, and shall be paid over by the town tax collector to the treasurer of said town, which officers shall give justified bonds in amounts amply sufficient to cover said taxes, the former officer for collecting and paying over and the latter for the safe keeping and proper disbursement of said funds.

Commissioners levy special annual tax to pay interest on bonds, etc.

Limitation to special tax.

Special tax, how collected

Sec. 5. For the purpose of creating a sinking fund for the redemption of said bonds issued under this act it shall be the duty of the commissioners of the town of Shelby at and after the expiration of twenty years from the date of said bonds to annually levy and collect a special tax in addition to that mentioned in section four of this act, and the tax provided for in this section shall equal in amount one-twentieth of the amount of bonds issued under this act, and shall be used in redeeming the afore-

Special tax may be levied to create sinking fund.

Amount of special tax for said purpose.

said bonds as hereinafter provided, and when all of said bonds shall have been redeemed said commissioners shall cease to levy said taxes. The tax provided for by this section shall be levied and collected in the same manner and with same safeguards as to officer's bond as provided in preceding section.

Taxes so collected shall be kept separate from other taxes.

Sec. 6. That the taxes levied and collected for the purposes specified in sections four and five of this act shall be kept separate and distinct from any and all other taxes and shall be used only for the purposes for which they were levied and collected; Provided, that if the taxes levied and collected for the payment of interest or for the redemption of said bonds shall in any year exceed the sum required for that purpose; the amount in excess shall be applied to the credit of the interest fund or redemption fund as the case may be for the next succeeding year, and said commissioners at the time of levying taxes for the payment of interest or for the redemption fund for said next succeeding year shall take into consideration said excess and compute and levy said taxes accordingly.

Commissioners authorized to purchase annually one-twentieth of bonds.

Sec. 7. That in order that there may not be an accumulation of money arising from taxation provided by this act, after paying the annual interest accrued on said bonds, the commissioners at and after the expiration of twenty years from the date of said bonds, are authorized and empowered to purchase annually one-twentieth of the bonds issued at a sum not exceeding their par value; and in case no one will offer to sell one-twentieth of said bonds, then the said commissioners are authorized to designate such bonds, not exceeding one-twentieth of the whole number issued, as they may desire to purchase; and after the designation of such bonds and a notice thereof given through a newspaper published in Cleveland county, if the holder or holders of said designated bonds shall refuse to surrender the same and receive their par value, with accrued interest at the time of said notice, then the holder shall not receive any interest subsequently accruing: Provided, the said bonds shall be affected by the conditions of this act only when the conditions are expressed on the face of the bonds.

When no one will sell such bonds.

Proviso.

Sec. 8. That this act shall be in force from and after its ratification.

Ratified the 4th day of March, A. D. 1899.

CHAPTER 176.

An act to authorize the town of Pilot Mountain, in Surry county, to issue bonds for public improvements and to levy a special tax, and for other purposes.

The General Assembly of North Carolina do enact:

Section 1. That for the purpose of improving the streets of the town of Pilot Mountain or providing a system of electric, gas or other artificial lighting, or for the purpose of establishing a system of waterworks for the town of Pilot Mountain, or for any one or all of said purposes at such time and in such manner as the board of commissioners may determine, the town of Pilot Mountain is hereby authorized and empowered to issue its bonds immediately or from time to time to any amount not exceeding in the aggregate the sum of twenty thousand dollars, of such denomination as the board of commissioners may fix, bearing interest from their respective dates at a rate not exceeding six per centum per annum, with coupons attached, payable semi-annually at such times and places as the board may appoint, said bonds to be payable to bearer and the principal thereof to be payable at the time and place stipulated therein not exceeding thirty years from the date thereof.

Town authorized to issue bonds.

Limitation to tax issue.

Bonds, when payable.

Sec. 2. That none of said bonds shall be sold or in any manner disposed of for less than their face value, nor shall said bonds or the proceeds arising therefrom be used for any other purposes than those set out in section one of this act.

Bonds shall not be disposed of for less than par value.

Sec. 3. That said bonds and their coupons are hereby exempt from taxation by said town of Pilot Mountain and the board of commissioners of said town are authorized and empowered to provide for receiving said coupons in payment of any taxes or other dues payable to said town at any time they may deem advisable.

Bonds and coupons exempt from taxation.

Sec. 4. That for the purpose of providing for the payment of the interest accruing on said bonds and for the purpose of creating a sinking fund for the payment of the principal at maturity, the said town of Pilot Mountain shall each year when it levies other town taxes levy and impose a special tax on all property, persons, privileges and other subjects of taxation liable for taxes for any other purposes, said special tax not to exceed sixteen and two-thirds cents on the one hundred dollars assessed valuation of property nor fifty cents on each poll, and not to be less than one-third of said amounts, the lawful equation between the two to be preserved. Said special tax shall be collected at the same time and in the same manner that other town taxes are collected and shall be kept separate and distinct from the general taxes

Special tax may be levied to pay interest and principal.

Limitation to special tax.

Shall be used exclusively for certain purposes.

and shall be used and applied exclusively for the purpose or purposes for which they are authorized under this act to be levied and collected. Said town of Pilot Mountain, through its board of commissioners, shall set apart and safely invest upon interest any amount of said taxes not required to pay interest on said bond until the principal of any or all of said bonds shall become payable, and shall apply said surplus constituting such sinking fund in payment of the principal of said bonds at maturity or in discharge of them before maturity on such just terms as they may deem advisable to make with the holders thereof.

Before bonds are issued question shall be submitted to voters.

Notice shall be given of election.

Sec. 5. That before any of the bonds provided for by this act shall be issued or sold the question of issuing the same shall first be submitted to the qualified voters of said town after thirty days' notice in some newspaper published in said town, or if none be published therein, then in some newspaper published in Surry county at any election held on the first Monday in May, eighteen hundred and ninety-nine, or on the same date any year thereafter, or at such other time as the board of commissioners may determine, said election to be held under the same laws, rules and regulations as are now prescribed by the law for election of commissioners of said town, as contained in chapter two hundred and eighty-seven, private laws of eighteen hundred and ninety-one, entitled "An act to amend the charter of the town of Pilot Mountain, in Surry county." Such notice shall set forth the object for which said bonds are to be issued, the amount of the same, the rate of interest, the date of their maturity, and the rate of taxation to be levied and collected for the payment of the same. All qualified voters favoring the issuing of bonds and the levy and collection of taxes aforesaid shall deposit in a separate ballot box a written or printed ticket or ballot with the words "For bonds" thereon, and those opposing the same shall deposit a written or printed ticket or ballot with the words "Against bonds" thereon. If at such election a majority of such voters shall vote "For bonds," then the said board of commissioners shall issue the bonds provided for in such notice and shall levy and order the collection of the taxes named in said notice and authorized by this act

Franchises may be granted to individuals to establish such works.

Sec. 6. That nothing contained in this act shall render it unlawful or operate against the power and right of the board of commissioners of said town to grant to any person or corporation the franchise and privilege of establishing, operating and conducting any system of waterworks for said town or any system of lighting for said town, and it shall be lawful for the commissioners of said town, in addition to granting such franchise, to take an interest with other persons in the establishment of such public works or stock in any corporation organized for that purpose, and pay for the same with the said bonds or the proceeds arising from the sale thereof.

Sec. 7. That all laws and parts of laws in conflict with this act are hereby repealed. Conflicting laws repealed.

Sec. 8. That this act shall be in force from and after its ratification.

Ratified the 4th day of March, A. D. 1899.

CHAPTER 177.

An act to incorporate the town of Leechville.

The General Assembly of North Carolina do enact:

Section 1. That the inhabitants of the present village of Leechville, in Beaufort county, and those living within the limits hereinafter prescribed, are hereby incorporated as a town under the name and style of "The Town of Leechville," with all the rights, powers, privileges and immunities and subject to all the provisions of chapter sixty-two of The Code of North Carolina and the amendments thereto. Incorporated. Corporate name.

Sec. 2. That the corporate limits of said town shall be as follows, to-wit: Beginning at the mouth of Campbell's Gut, which makes into the Pungo river, and thence running up Pungo river to a point called Slade's wharf; thence a westwardly course to a point, being the intersection of the Bay Lane road with the Washington and Leechville public road; thence southwardly down the Bay Lane road one-fourth of a mile, and thence a straight line to the beginning. Corporate limits.

Sec. 3. The officers of said town shall consist of a mayor and three commissioners, a town marshal, a treasurer and a town clerk. The duties of the town marshal shall be the same as prescribed for the office of constable under chapter sixty-two of The Code of North Carolina. The following-named persons shall fill the offices of mayor and commissioners until the first Monday in May, eighteen hundred and ninety-nine, and until their successors are duly elected and qualified: Mayor, D. C. Betts; commissioners, W. H. Wilkinson, S. C. Bishop and F. T. Baynor; marshal, W. G. Waters; treasurer, W. J. Harris; town clerk, N. W. Sadler. Town officers. Temporary officers.

Sec. 4. That there shall be an election held for mayor and said commissioners of said town on the first Monday in May, eighteen hundred and ninety-nine, and each succeeding year thereto, under the regulations and provisions contained in chapter sixty-two of The Code of North Carolina, and the qualifications of Election for town officers.

voters within the limits of said town shall be such as are prescribed by law.

rporate powers mayor and n. Sec 5. The mayor of said town and the said commissioners shall have all the rights and privileges conferred upon incorporated towns by chapter sixty-two of The Code of North Carolina; shall have power to elect all necessary officers herein provided and agents, and to fix their compensation and also to fix the compensation of the mayor of said town; shall have power to pass and enforce all necessary by-laws and ordinances for the government of said town not inconsistent with the laws of this state or the United States; shall have power to levy a tax on all objects of taxation as provided by law not to exceed sixteen and two-thirds cents on the hundred dollars worth of property and fifty cents on the poll, and to impose fines for the violation of the town ordinances and collect the same for the use of the town: to require bonds from their officers and agents for the faithful performance of their duties.

itation to rate.

nds may be uired.

en officers ointed shall alify. Sec. 6. That it shall be the duty of the officers appointed in this act to qualify before some justice of the peace of Beaufort county within thirty days from its ratification and to take the oath of office prescribed for such officers, and to enter upon the discharge of their duties.

all vote at all ctions. Sec. 7. That in all national, state, county and township elections hereafter held the citizens of the town of Leechville shall vote within the precinct and at the place provided under the general laws, regardless of the incorporation of said town under this act.

Sec. 8. That this act shall be enforced from and after its ratification.

Ratified the 4th day of March, A. D. 1899.

CHAPTER 178.

An act to amend the charter of the town of Blowing Rock, North Carolina.

The General Assembly of North Carolina do enact:

ermen empered to enact nances rding sanita-. Section 1. That the charter of the town of Blowing Rock, North Carolina, be and the same is hereby amended so as to confer upon the board of aldermen of said town the right to adopt ordinances and make rules with respect to the sanitary condition of said town, such ordinances made for the purpose aforesaid to apply to all territory within two miles of the incorporate limits of the town, and to be enforcible under the same penalties and forfeitures as if in the corporate limits aforesaid: Provided, that no ordinance regarding the sanitary condition of the said town of Blowing Rock, enacted by the said board of aldermen of said town regarding property situated without the corporate limits of said town, shall be enforced or enforcible until the same shall be approved by the state board of health. Proviso.

Sec. 2. That for the purpose set forth in section one the said board of aldermen are empowered to make and adopt ordinances with respect to the sewerage of all hotels, livery stables, boarding houses or other buildings within the limits set forth in section one of this act. Ordinances regarding sewerage.

Sec. 3. That this act shall be in full force and effect from and after its ratification.

Ratified the 4th day of March, A. D. 1899.

CHAPTER 179.

An act to incorporate "The Wilmington Underwriters Insurance Company."

The General Assembly of North Carolina do enact:

Section 1. That P. L. Bridgers, J. W. Norwood and N. B. Rankin, and all other persons who may hereafter be associated with them in the name and style of "The Wilmington Underwriters Insurance Company," are hereby constituted a body politic and corporate, to have succession for ninety-nine years, and by that name to sue and be sued, appear, prosecute and defend in any court or place whatsoever, and may have and use a common seal, and may hereafter change and renew the same at will, and may purchase and hold such real and personal property as may be deemed necessary to effect the objects of this association, and may sell and convey the same and [at] pleasure, and may make, establish and put in execution such by-laws, ordinances and resolutions, not being contrary to the laws of this state and of the United States, as may be necessary or convenient for the regulation, government and management of their affairs, and do and execute all such acts and things as may be necessary to carry into effect the provisions of this act. Corporators. Corporate name. Corporate powers.

Sec. 2. That the affairs of this company shall be governed and managed by a board of directors, consisting of the president and not less than three nor more than thirteen members or stockholders, as may be regulated by the by-laws of the company; and the president, who shall be ex officio a member of the board of directors, and a majority of the directors, shall constitute a quo- Affairs of company governed by directors.

ection of president and directors. rum for the transaction of business. The president and directors shall be elected at the regular annual meeting of the stockholders and shall hold office for one year and until their successors are elected. The board of directors shall elect all such other officers as may be prescribed by the by-laws of the company, and shall have power to fill all vacancies occurring [in] the office of president, director or any other office by death, resignation or otherwise until the next regular election.

pital stock. Sec. 3. That the capital of the said corporation shall be twenty-five thousand dollars, with full power and authority to increase

ay be increased. the same from time to time, as may be deemed expedient by the stockholders, to the maximum of two hundred thousand dollars; said stock shall be divided into shares of one hundred dollars each, and shall be payable by each subscriber in the manner and form prescribed by the board of directors of said corporation.

rectors may vest stock. Sec. 4. That the board of directors shall have full power to invest the capital paid in and all moneys coming into the possession of the company in real or personal estate, bonds, mortgages, gold, silver, stocks or securities of any description, and have power to sell and convey the same or change the character of the investments from time to time as the interest of the company may require.

ay issue policies insurance. Sec. 5. That this company may issue policies of insurance, duly signed by its president and secretary, against loss or damage by fire, lightning, wind or tornado, or any other insurance whatsoever that the board of directors may deem proper, including life, fire, marine and accidental insurance, and this company is hereby vested with all the power that any insurance company has or may have to transact business in this state, and they may charge such premiums as may be agreed upon by this company and the parties insured.

powered to present foreign mpanies. Sec. 6. That said company shall have power to represent as agent any life, fire, marine or accident insurance company organized outside of the state of North Carolina.

dividual bility. Sec. 7. That the stockholders of said corporation shall not be personally liable for any debt of said company nor for any loss, damage or responsibility incurred by said company.

oks may be ened for subription. Sec. 8. That the above-named persons or a majority of them are hereby authorized to open books of subscription to the capital stock of said company in the city of Wilmington and elsewhere in their discretion, and as soon as the capital stock shall have been subscribed for to the amount [of] twenty-five thousand dollars and fifty per centum thereof has been paid in to them in cash, to call a meeting of said subscribers, who shall proceed to organize said company and elect from their number a president and directors to serve until the first annual meeting of the stockholders and the election of their successors; and the said company, upon its organization as aforesaid, is hereby authorized to commence business.

Sec. 9. That nothing herein contained shall be so construed as to prevent this company from receiving any of the benefits of or from complying with any general insurance law now in force or that may hereafter be enacted. **This act shall not conflict with general insurance laws.**

Sec. 10. That this act shall be in force from and after its ratification.

Ratified the 4th day of March, A. D. 1899.

CHAPTER 180.

An act to amend the charter of the town of Kinston, in the county of Lenoir, North Carolina.

The General Assembly of North Carolina do enact:

Section 1. That the general laws of the state in regard to towns and cities so far as the town of Kinston, in the county of Lenoir, is concerned, inconsistent with this act and all special laws and charters in relation to said town are hereby repealed; and the said town of Kinston shall in the future be governed by the provisions of this act and the general laws of the state in relation to towns and cities not inconsistent herewith which are now in force or which may hereafter be enacted, together with such by laws, ordinances, rules and regulations as the board of aldermen of said town of Kinston may at their election from time to time make, pass or enact: Provided, however, that such repeal shall not in any manner invalidate the election of the present mayor and aldermen and other officers acting in said town, or any of the acts, by-laws, ordinances, rules or regulations of said mayor and aldermen which they had authority to pass by the laws heretofore in force for the government of the said town. **General laws governing cities and town inconsistent with this act repealed.**

Sec. 2. Corporate limits of said town shall be as follows: Begin at about a corner of a ditch in A. Mitchell's field and run east parallel with old line forty-seven (47) chains twenty (20) links to Coast Line Railroad; thence south five degrees six minutes, thirty seconds west to Lower Hill road thirty-one (31) chains; thence east fifteen (15) degrees north nine (9) chains twenty-seven (27) links to a ditch; thence east eleven (11) degrees thirty (30) minutes south five (5) chains twenty-seven (27) links to a post; thence east six (6) degrees thirty (30) minutes south eight (8) chains fifty-four (54) links to Orion street; thence with Orion street south two (2) degrees west forty-two (42) chains seventy- **Corporate limits.**

five (75) links to Shine street; thence west five (5) degrees thirty (30) minutes north eleven chains to Atlantic and North Carolina Railroad; thence south thirty-seven (37) degrees thirty (30) minutes west with the railroad five (5) chains to a post; thence west sixteen (16) degrees thirty (30) minutes south to a fence in Stubb's field forty and a half (40½) chains; thence west twenty (20) degrees north to north end of a bridge, eleven (11) chains forty-five (45) links; thence north thirty-eight (38) degrees west to a fence in J. G. Cox's field eighteen (18) chains twenty-three (23) links; thence north one (1) degree thirty (30) minutes east eleven (11) chains fourteen (14) links to the river bank; thence with the river to a stob on the river bank twenty-five (25) chains five (5) links; thence north four (4) degrees east forty five (45) chains seventy (70) links to corner of ditch in A. Mitchell's field, the beginning.

rporate limits.

ision of rds.

Sec. 3. That the said town of Kinston shall be divided into three wards, denominated first, second and third wards.

st ward.

First Ward—On the western side of the town the first ward shall begin at or near the corner of a ditch in A. Mitchell's field seven (7) chains and twenty (20) links north of the LaGrange road and run south four (4) degrees west to the river; thence with the river to a point just west of Harvey's mill; thence south one (1) degree thirty (30) minutes west to a point in J. G. Cox's field; thence southeast to northern corner of a bridge over a ditch in Stubb's field; thence east to an extension of McIlvane; thence north on McIlvane street to Bright street; thence west to Queen street; thence north to northern boundary of town; thence west to the beginning.

ond ward.

Second ward—Begin at northeast corner of first ward on Queen street; thence south with eastern boundary of first ward to Bright street; thence east to McIlvane street; thence south to southern boundary of town; thence east to a point on a ditch in Stubb's field; thence eastwardly sixteen (16) degrees thirty (30) minutes north to Atlantic and North Carolina Railroad; thence with the railroad northwest to Shine street; thence east on Shine street to Orion street; thence north with Orion street to Bright; thence west with Bright to East street; thence north with East to King street; thence west with King to Independence; thence north with Independence to Caswell; thence east to Atlantic and North Carolina Railroad; thence with railroad northwest to Independence; thence north with Independence to northern boundary of town; thence west on northern boundary to the beginning.

rd ward.

Third ward—Begin at northeast corner of second ward; thence south on Independence to Atlantic and North Carolina Railroad; thence southeast with railroad to Caswell; thence west with Caswell to Independence; thence south with Independence to King;

thence east on King street to East street; thence with East street south to Bright; thence with Bright street east to Orion street; thence north to a post; thence from post west across a ditch to post; thence with ditch to Tower Hill road southwest to Coast Line Railroad; thence with the railroad north to the northern boundary; thence west to the beginning.

Sec. 4. That the inhabitants of the said town of Kinston shall be and continue as they heretofore have been a body politic and corporate, and shall bear the name and style of the "Town of Kinston," and under such name and style is hereby invested with all property and rights of property which now belong or which may hereafter belong to the said corporation; and by this name and style may acquire and hold for the purpose of its government, welfare and improvement, all such estates or property or interests in estates or property, whether real or personal, as may be devised, bequeathed or conveyed to it, not exceeding in value one hundred thousand ($100,000) dollars, and in this name and style shall have the right through the board of aldermen of said town to contract and be contracted with, to sue and be sued, to plead and be impleaded, to purchase, hold and convey real or personal property, whether the said property be situated within the corporate limits of said town or not: Provided, however, that the board of aldermen of said town of Kinston shall not contract any debt on the part of the said town, pledge its faith or loan its credit unless by a vote of the majority of the votes cast in said town.

Body politic. **Corporate power.** **May hold property not exceeding certain amount.** **Proviso.**

Sec. 5. There shall annually on the first Monday in May of each year be elected six aldermen for said town of Kinston, and a mayor, who shall hold their offices until their successors are elected and qualified. The first ward shall elect two (2) aldermen; the second ward shall elect two (2) aldermen; the third ward shall elect two (2) aldermen; such aldermen shall be qualified electors and residents of the wards for which they are chosen, and shall be elected by the qualified voters of such wards. In voting for aldermen as herein provided the ballots shall be written or partly written and partly printed and shall be without device. Both the number of the ward and the name of the aldermen voted for shall distinctly appear on each ballot, otherwise the said ballot shall be void and of no effect. The ballots shall be deposited by one of the judges or inspectors of election into the box assigned by the judges or inspectors of election for the ward in which the voter resides. The ballots or votes of each ward shall be deposited in separate boxes or apartment of boxes. The ballot boxes shall be furnished by the board of aldermen of said town and shall be provided with a lock and key and an opening through the lid of sufficient size to admit of a single folded

Annual elections. **Term of office** **Aldermen.** **Ballots shall be without device.**

ballot and no more, and during the voting shall be kept locked. The judges or inspectors of election before the voting begins shall carefully examine the boxes and see that there is nothing in them.

nouncement result of ction.

Sec. 6. When the election shall be finished the registrar and judges or inspectors of election, in the presence of such of the electors of said town as may choose to attend, shall open the boxes and count the ballots, reading aloud the number of the ward and the name of the person that shall appear on the ballot; and if there shall be two or more ballots rolled up together, or any ballot shall contain the names of more persons than such elector has a right to vote for or shall have a device upon it, or in any other respect illegal, in either of these cases such ballot shall not be numbered in taking the ballots, but shall be void; and said counting of votes shall be continued without adjournment until completed. The person or persons in each ward having the greatest number of legal votes cast for him or them shall be deemed elected from that ward. It shall thereupon immediately be the duty of the judges or inspectors of election, through one of their number, to declare the result at the court-house door in said town, and the persons thus declared to be elected, upon their qualifying, shall be aldermen of said town until their successors are elected and qualified.

unting of tes shall be ntinued with- t adjournment.

pointment of istrar.

Sec. 7. The board of town aldermen shall appoint at or before their meeting in March, eighteen hundred and ninety-nine (1899) and annually thereafter a registrar of voters for said town, and said registrar shall give ten days' notice at the court-house door in said town of a registration of voters in and for said town, specifying the place in said town and the time for registration of voters. In case of a vacancy in the office of registrar from any cause the mayor of said town shall fill the vacancy or appoint some suitable person to act until the inability of the registrar be removed. The registrar or person acting in his stead, in case of inability, shall take an oath before acting as such before some officer of the county of Lenoir having authority to administer an oath, faithfully, truly and honestly to perform the duties of the office of registrar according to law.

all give notice registration.

cancy occur- g.

gistrar shall e oath.

th shall be ministered to applicants for istration.

Sec. 8. That said registrar shall be furnished by the aldermen with registration books at the expense of said town, and it shall be the duty of the said registrar to open his books at the time and place designated by him in his notice of registration at least ten days before the day of election herein provided for, and to register therein the names of all persons applying for registration and entitled to register and vote. It shall be the duty of the registrar and he is hereby authorized to administer an oath to all applicants for registration touching their qualification to register and vote, and no persons shall be qualified to vote unless he states his name in full, his birthplace and the time of his birth, and his residence for three previous years; and upon his failure to thus qualify himself he shall not be a qualified voter. It shall be the duty of the registrar to keep the names of the white voters separate and apart form those of the colored voters, and he shall designate on the registration books, opposite the name of each person registering, the ward in which he resides and his place of residence in such ward, and if any applicant for registration shall not declare his place of residence in his ward and qualify himself as set out in this section, his failure so to do shall be prima facie evidence that he is not entitled to register in such ward. And the registrar shall be the judge of the qualification herein set out.

Names of white and colored voters shall be kept separate and apart.

Sec. 9. That the board of commissioners of Lenoir county at or before their meeting in April, eighteen hundred and ninety-nine (1899), and annually thereafter, shall appoint four judges or inspectors of election for said town who, after being duly sworn by some officer of the county of Lenoir having authority to administer an oath to conduct the said election fairly, honestly, impartially and according to law; the registrar shall open the polls and superintend the same on the day of election herein specified, and the polls shall be opened at the court-house in said town from seven o'clock in the morning till sunset. The registrar and judges or inspectors of the election whose appointments are herein provided for shall at all times have authority to administer oaths and shall have all the powers of such officers appointed under the general election law. Should any of the judges or inspectors of election so appointed neglect or fail for any cause to attend at the time and places in the discharge of their duties as provided by this act the registrar and judges or inspectors of election present shall forthwith fill the vacancy.

Commissioners of Lenoir county shall appoint judges of election.

Polls, when opened and closed.

Failure of judges to serve.

Sec. 10. That the registrar and judges or inspectors of election shall meet at the court-house in said town on Friday preceding each election herein provided for with the registration books, and shall continue in session from nine o'clock a. m. till two o'clock p. m. During said session the said registration books shall be open to the inspection of the electors of the town, and any of the said electors shall be allowed to object to the names of any person appearing on said books. In case of any such objection the registrar shall enter upon his books, opposite the name of the person or persons objected to, the word "challenged"; and if the said person so challenged or objected to shall at any time upon investigation be found not duly qualified as an elector, the registrar shall erase his name from the book: Provided, however, that nothing in this section shall prohibit any elector from chal-

Books shall be opened to inspection.

Challenges.

lenging or objecting to the name of any registered or offering to register at any time other than that above specified.

rsons entitled vote.

Sec. 11. All electors who shall have resided in the state twelve months, in the town of Kinston ninety days and in the ward in which they offer to register thirty days next preceding the election shall be entitled to register and vote: Provided, that they are otherwise qualified as hereinafter set out: Provided further, that this act shall not apply to those voters who have acquired citizenship by the proposed extension of the town limits, but they shall be allowed to vote in the election of May, eighteen hundred and ninety-nine: Provided, they have been resident in the said proposed limits for ninety days: And provided further, that they have the qualification herein set out by this act.

oviso.

ections, how ld.

Sec. 12. That all elections held by virtue of this act shall be held under the supervision of the sheriff of Lenoir county, who shall attend the polls and by himself and his deputies preserve order.

rm of office of y officers.

Sec. 13. That the mayor and aldermen of said town shall hold their offices respectively until the next succeeding election and until their respective successors are qualified, and the mayor shall preside at all meetings of the aldermen and have the rights prescribed by law for such officers.

yor shall e oath.

Sec. 14. That the mayor, immediately after his election and before entering upon the duties of his office, shall take before a justice of the peace the following oath: "I, A. B., do solemnly swear that I will diligently endeavor to perform faithfully and truthfully, according to my best skill and ability, all the duties of the office of mayor of the town of Kinston while I continue therein; and I will cause to be executed as far as in my power lies all the laws, ordinances and regulations enacted for the government of the town, and in the discharge of my duties I will strive to do equal justice in all cases whatsoever."

dermen shall e oath.

Sec. 15. That on Thursday succeeding the day of election the aldermen elected thereat shall qualify by taking the oath of office before a justice of the peace of Lenoir county as prescribed for commissioners of incorporated towns, according to section three thousand seven hundred and ninety-nine (3,799), chapter sixty-two (62, volume two (2) of The Code of North Carolina; and when organized, shall succeed to and have all the rights, powers and duties prescribed by law.

cancies in ces of mayor d aldermen.

Sec. 16. That if any person elected mayor shall refuse to be qualified, or there is any vacancy in the office after election and qualification, the aldermen shall choose some qualified person mayor for the term or the unexpired portion of the term, as the case may be, and on like occasions and in like manner the aldermen shall choose other aldermen to supply the place of such as shall refuse to act, and all vacancies which may occur, and such persons only shall be chosen as are hereinbefore declared to be eligible.

Failure to elect.

Sec. 17. That in case of failure to elect aldermen for said town on said first Monday in May, the election [electors] of said town may, after ten days' notice, signed by any three of said electors and posted up at three public places within the corporate limits of said town, proceed to hold an election for aldermen of said town in the way and manner provided for in chapter sixty-two (62), volume two (2) of The Code of North Carolina.

Jurisdiction of mayor.

Sec. 18. That the court of the mayor of said town of Kinston is hereby constituted an inferior court, and as such shall in all criminal cases committed within the corporate limits of the town of Kinston have all the powers, jurisdiction and authority of a justice of the peace, and also to hear and determine all causes of action which may arise upon the ordinances and regulations of the town; to enforce penalties by issuing executions upon any adjudged violation thereof and to execute the by-laws, ordinances, rules and regulations made or passed by the board of aldermen of the town. The mayor's court shall further be a special court within the corporate limits of the town, to arrest and try all persons who may be charged with a misdemeanor for violating any by-law, ordinances, rule or regulation of the town; and if the accused be found guilty he shall be fined, at the discretion of the court or mayor, not exceeding the amount specified in the by-law, ordinance, rule or regulation so violated, or at the discretion of the mayor or court trying the same such offender may be imprisoned not more than thirty (30) days in the town lockup or in the common jail of the county of Lenoir. And that in all cases where a defendant may be adjudged to be imprisoned by the said court or mayor, it shall be competent for the said court or mayor to adjudge also that the said defendant work during the period of his confinement on the public streets or other public works of said town, or the mayor shall have the power and authority to hire the defendant on conviction to the county commissioners of Lenoir county to work on the public roads of the said county.

Mayor's court a special court.

Violators of ordinances may be imprisoned.

Defendant may be hired to county commissioners.

Violation of ordinances a misdemeanor.

Sec. 19. That any person violating any of the by-laws, ordinances, rules or regulations of the town of Kinston shall not only be subject to the penalty thereto attached, but also, in addition thereto, be guilty of [a] misdemeanor, and shall be fined not exceeding fifty (50 dollars or imprisoned in the common jail of the county or town lockup not exceeding thirty (30) days.

Precepts issued by mayor.

Sec. 20. That the mayor may issue his precepts to the chief of police or any policeman of the town, and to such other officers to whom a justice of the peace may direct his precepts, and no preliminary affidavit shall be necessary to give the mayor final jurisdiction over offenses against the by-laws, ordinances, rules and regulations of the said town.

ayor shall keep inute of precepts issued.

Sec. 21. That the mayor shall keep a faithful minute of the precepts issued by him and all of his judicial proceedings. The judgment rendered by him shall have all the force, virtue and validity of judgments rendered by a single justice of the peace, and may be executed and enforced against the parties in the courts of Lenoir and elsewhere in the same manner and by the same means as if the same had been rendered by a justice of the peace for the county of Lenoir.

nes, how applied.

Sec. 22. That all fines collected under the provisions of this act for violations of the by-laws, ordinances, rules and regulations of the said town shall go to the use of said town.

ayor shall pree at meetings aldermen.

Sec. 23. That the mayor when present shall preside at all the meetings of the board of aldermen, and when there is an equal division upon any question or in the election of officers by the board he shall determine the matter by his vote. He shall vote in no other case; and if he shall be absent at any meeting the board may appoint one of their number pro tempore to exercise his duties at the board; and in the event of absence or sickness the board of aldermen may appoint one of their own number pro tempore to exercise his duties.

ajority of alderen competent transact business.

Sec. 24. That the aldermen shall form one board, and a majority of them shall be competent to perform all the duties prescribed for the aldermen, unless otherwise provided. Within five days after their election they shall convene for the transaction of business, and shall then fix stated days of meeting for the year, which shall be as often at least as once in every calendar month. The special meetings of the aldermen may also be held on the call of the mayor or majority of the aldermen; and of every such meeting when called by the mayor, all the aldermen, and when called by a majority of the aldermen, such as shall not join in the call shall be notified in writing.

ilure of alderen to attend neral meeting

Sec. 25. That if any alderman shall fail to attend a general meeting of the board of aldermen or any special meeting of which he shall have notice as prescribed in this charter, unless prevented by such cause as shall be satisfactory to the board he shall forfeit and pay for the use of the town the sum of four (4) dollars.

wers of aldern.

Sec. 26. That among the powers hereby conferred upon the board of aldermen of said town, they may contract debts or borrow money, pledge the faith of the town, loan its credit, levy and collect by its proper officers taxes for necessary expenses only by the consent of a majority of the votes cast at an election therefore [therefor], after thirty days' public notice. It shall be the duty of the said board to appoint the day to take the vote herein provided for and to give the said public notice, which shall contain the day appointed for the voting and the object thereof. It shall be the duty of the board of commissioners of Lenoir county, upon application to them by the board of aldermen of the town at their monthly meeting prior to the day appointed for said voting to appoint a registrar of voters for said town and four (4) judges or inspectors of election, who shall in all respects prepare for and conduct the said voting as is provided for at the annual elections. Before they shall enter upon the duties of their offices by virtue of said appointment they shall take the oath provided for in this act for registrar and judges or inspectors of elections at the annual elections and shall have the same powers and authority. On the day appointed for said voting the polls shall be open at the court-house in Kinston from seven o'clock in the morning until sunset under the superintendence of the registrar, judges or inspectors of election, and the sheriff of the county, who, with his deputies, shall attend and preserve the peace, and at which time the voters to the proposition or propositions of the board of aldermen shall vote "Approved" or "Not approved." Should a majority of the votes cast at said voting approve of the said proposition or propositions, the acts and doings of the mayor and aldermen of said town in relation thereto shall be binding on the said town. The expenses incurred under this section shall be borne by the town.

Appointment of registrar and judges.

Propositions, how voted on.

Expense of election.

Sec. 27. That the board of aldermen of said town shall provide water for the town, provide for repairing and cleaning the streets, regulate the market, take all proper means to prevent and extinguish fires, make regulations to cause the due observance of Sundays, appoint and regulate the town police force, suppress and remove nuisances, preserve the health of the town from contagious or infectious diseases, appoint constables or policemen to execute such precepts as the mayor and other persons may lawfully issue to them to preserve the peace and order and execute the ordinances, by-laws, rules and regulations of the town, and shall appoint and provide for the pay and prescribe the duties of all such other officers as may be deemed necessary.

Aldermen shall provide water, etc.

Sec. 28. That the board of aldermen may, in their election at any of their meetings, appoint a town clerk, a treasurer, a collector of taxes, a chief of police and one or more assistant policemen, a town constable and such other officers as they may deem necessary, who shall respectively hold their offices during the official term of the mayor and aldermen, subject, however, to removal at any time and others appointed in their stead for misbehavior or neglect in office. Before acting each of said officers shall be sworn to the faithful discharge of his duty and shall ex-

Appointment of town clerk, treasurer and tax collector.

Shall execute bond.

ecute a bond, payable to the town of Kinston, in such sum as the board of aldermen shall determine.

lary qf clerk.

Sec. 29 That if the board of aldermen shall deem it necessary to appoint a town clerk he shall have a reasonable salary, to be fixed by the said board of aldermen, and it shall be his duty to keep regular and fair minutes of the proceedings of the board, and to preserve all books, papers and articles committed to his care during his continuance in office and deliver them to his successor, and generally to perform such other duties as may be prescribed by the board of aldermen.

urnal shall be en to inspec- n.

Sec. 30. That every person shall be allowed to inspect the journals and papers of the board in the presence of the clerk or other officers having their legal custody.

lary of treas- er.

Sec. 31. That the treasurer shall have a salary of one hundred ($100) dollars a year, and it shall be his duty to call on all persons who may have in their hands moneys or securities belonging to the town which ought to be paid or delivered into the treasury, and to safely keep the same for the use of the town; to disburse the funds according to such orders as may be duly drawn on him in the manner hereinafter specified; he shall keep in a book provided for that purpose a fair and correct account of all moneys received and disbursed by him and shall submit said account to the board of aldermen whenever required to do so. On the expiration of his term of office he shall deliver to his successor all the moneys, securities and other property entrusted to him for safe keeping or otherwise, and during his continuance therein he shall faithfully perform all duties lawfully imposed upon him as town treasurer.

all keep ord.

ders on treas- er, how signed.

Sec. 32. That all orders drawn on the treasurer shall be signed by the mayor and shall state the purposes for which the money is applied; and the treasurer shall specify said purposes in his accounts and also the sources whence are derived the moneys received by him.

x list shall ve force of gment.

Sec. 33. That all tax lists when made out, completed and delivered into the hands of the tax collector, shall have the same force and effect in the hands of said collector as a judgment and execution against the property of the person or persons charged in such list, and enforceable in the same manner by said collector in which the sheriffs of the counties enforce and collect state and county tax. The collector shall proceed forthwith to collect the taxes laid upon such subjects of taxation as the board of aldermen may direct within five days after the list shall have been placed in his hands, and shall complete the same on or before the first day of April next ensuing, and shall pay the money, certificates, vouchers and so forth, as they are collected, to the treasurer, taking his receipt for the same, and for this purpose he is

hen collection taxes shall be pleted.

hereby invested with all the powers which are now or may hereafter be invested in a sheriff or collector of state taxes; he shall rent out the market stalls and vegetable stands, prosecute all persons who retail without having paid the tax imposed or sell without a license; also at every monthly meeting of the board of aldermen he shall produce an abstract showing the sums received by him upon each subject of taxation and the amounts still due thereon; he shall further specify in said abstract the amount of cash received and the amount of certificates or other vouchers received in payment of taxes, which abstract shall be placed in the hands of the committee on finance, to be filed with their chairman, and all books and documents belonging to or used in the office of the collector shall be and are hereby declared to be the property and records of the town and shall be at all times subject to inspection and examination of the mayor and board of aldermen. The collector shall receive for his compensation such fees and commissions as may be allowed by the board of aldermen, and he shall on or before the fifteenth day of April in each year settle his account in full for the entire amount of taxes levied by the board under the supervision of the committee of finance; and if the collector shall have been unable to collect any part of said taxes by reason of the insolvency of any of the persons owing the same, or other good reasons, he shall on oath deliver a list of all such insolvents, delinquents and all other tax returns uncollected to the committee on finance, to be laid before the board of aldermen, and if approved he shall be credited with the amount thereof or so much as may be approved; he and his sureties on his bond shall be answerable for the remainder and for all other taxes or levies not collected and paid over by him which he is or may be required by law to collect, and his bond shall be put in suit by the chairman of the finance committee and town attorney.

Tax collector shall make monthly report.

Compensation of collector.

Insolvents and delinquents.

Sec. 34. That in all cases when a defendant shall be adjudged to work on the public streets or other public works of the town of Kinston by virtue of the provision of this act, the mayor so adjudging may adopt all necessary methods and means to compel the defendant to do the work so adjudged.

Persons adjudged to work on roads.

Sec. 35. That the retiring board of aldermen of the town of Kinston shall annually on or before the first day of July in each year cause to be posted at the court-house door and three other public places in said town, or in lieu thereof in some newspaper in the said town, an itemized statement of the receipts and expenditures of money by said town during the preceding year; said statement shall be verified and shall contain the names of all persons who have been paid by said town; the amount claimed by each person and the amount allowed by the mayor

Commissioners shall make annual statement.

and board of aldermen, and the amounts and sources whence received of all the funds of the said town and the amount of the indebtedness of the said town.

ties of police.

Sec. 36. That it shall be the duty of the police to see that the laws, rules and regulations of the board of aldermen are enforced, and to report all breaches thereof to the mayor; to preserve the peace of the town by suppressing disturbances and apprehending all offenders, and for that purpose they shall have all the power and authority vested in sheriffs and county constables; they shall execute all precepts lawfully directed to them by the mayor and other judicial officers, and in the execution thereof shall have the same powers which the sheriff and constables of the county have, and they shall have the same fees of all processes and precepts executed or returned by them which may be allowed to the sheriff of the county in like process and precepts, and also such other compensation as the board of aldermen may allow.

wers of police.

mpensation of ice.

each of official d.

Sec. 37. That for any breach of his official bond by the treasurer, clerk, tax collector or any other town officer who may be required to give an official bond he shall be liable in an action on the same in the name of the town, at the suit of the town or any person aggrieved by such breach and the same may be put in suit without assignment from time to time until the whole penalty be recovered.

ening and ing out eets.

Sec. 38. That the board of aldermen shall have power to lay out and open new streets within the corporate limits of the town whenever by them deemed necessary, and have power at any time to widen, enlarge, change or extend or discontinue any street or streets or any part thereof within the corporate limits of the town, and shall have full power and authority to condemn, appropriate or use any land or lands necessary for any of the purposes named in this section upon making a reasonable compensation to the owner or owners thereof. But in case the owners of the land and the aldermen can not agree as to the damages, then the matter shall be referred to arbitrators, each party choosing one, who shall be a freeholder and a citizen of the town; and in case the owner of the land shall refuse to choose such arbitrator, then the sheriff of the county shall in his stead select one for him; and in case the two chosen as aforesaid can not agree, they shall select an umpire, whose duty it shall be to examine the land condemned and ascertain the damages sustained and the benefits accruing to the owner in consequence of the change; and the award of the arbitrator or umpire shall be conclusive of the rights of the parties and shall vest in the aldermen the right to use the land for the purposes specified; and all damages agreed upon by the aldermen or awarded by the arbitrators

agreement as damages for d condemned.

bitrators.

or umpire shall be paid as other town liabilities, by taxation: Provided that either party may appeal to the superior court as now provided by law.

Sec. 39. That the board of aldermen of said town shall have power from time to time and for all times hereafter to make such by-laws, rules, regulations, orders and ordinances as to them shall seem just and reasonable for the good government of the town, and to affix penalties thereto for violations thereof; to make by-laws, rules and regulations for the proper government of their corporate meetings, with the penalties attached; to erect necessary market houses; to erect and construct public pumps and wells; to appoint inspectors of wood and weighers and inspectors of cotton, tar, pitch and turpentine and other products of the country, and to provide how such weighers and inspectors shall be paid; to appoint town watch or patrols; to erect proper and necessary guard-houses, mayor's office; to imprison any violator of any of the by-laws, rules, orders, regulations or ordinances of the town in the common jail of the county or the town lock-up; to do all other acts and things as in their judgment may be necessary for the advantage, improvement and good government of said town of Kinston; and the said by-laws, rules, orders, regulations and ordinances from time to time, alter, change, annul or discontinue as to them or a majority of them shall appear just and reasonable.

Power of aldermen to make by-laws, etc.

Market houses.

May amend or change ordinances.

Sec. 40. That all bar-rooms or places where spirituous, fermented or malt liquors, wines or cider are retailed in any quantity in or within two (2) miles of the town of Kinston, in the county of Lenoir, shall not be opened for the purpose of giving away or otherwise disposing of any of the said liquors, wines or cider between the hours of twelve o'clock Saturday night and twelve o'clock on Lord's or Sunday nights, under a penalty of a fine not exceeding fifty ($50) dollars or imprisonment not exceeding thirty (30) days for each and every offense, to be enforced by warrant issuing from the mayor of said town: Provided, this section shall not apply to said liquors, wines or cider sold or given away upon a physician's certificate in the case of sickness.

Saloons shall not be opened on Sunday.

Penalty.

Sec. 41. That the board of aldermen shall have authority to put to and keep at work upon the streets or public grounds of the town any person or persons who may fail to pay any fine, penalty or forfeiture which may have been imposed on such person or persons by the mayor of the town, and the said aldermen shall have authority, by the ordinances and by-laws of the town, to confine, control and manage such person or persons until the said fine, penalties or forfeitures, together with cost thereof, shall be fully paid and satisfied under such rates for labor and board as the aldermen may establish.

Persons failing to pay fines may be worked on public roads.

er drains, lation of.

Sec. 42. That the board of aldermen shall at any and all times and under all circumstances exercise the management and control of the water drains, public streets, sidewalks and alleys of the said town. They may exercise the management and control of the same through one or more street aldermen appointed by them. Any person or persons hindering or interfering with them or the street aldermen in the exercise of these rights shall be guilty of a misdemeanor and shall be fined not exceeding fifty ($50) dollars or imprisoned not exceeding thirty (30) days. They shall cause to be kept clean and in good repair the streets, sidewalks, alleys and water drains. They may establish the width and ascertain the location of those already provided, and lay out and open others, and may reduce the width of any or all of them; they may also establish and regulate public grounds and protect the shade trees of the town.

ons interfer- with drains ty of a mis- eanor.

nances to ent fires.

Sec. 43. That the board of aldermen shall have power to establish ordinances to prevent and extinguish fires; to provide for the establishment, organization, equipment and government of fire companies, provide said companies with fire engine, fire hose and necessary appurtenances; and that in all cases of fire a majority of such board of aldermen as shall be present may, if they deem it necessary, stop the progress of the fire, cause any dwelling house or other buildings to be blown up or pulled down, for which they shall not be responsible to any one for damages.

tement and oval of ances.

Sec. 44. That the aldermen may require and compel the abatement and removal of all nuisances within the town or within one mile thereof at the expense of the person causing the same, or the owner or tenant of the grounds whereon the same may be; and may regulate, if allowed to be established, any slaughter house or place, or the exercise within the town or within a mile thereof of any offensive or unhealthy trade, business or employment.

riding or ing.

Sec. 45. That they may prohibit by penalties the riding or driving of horses or other animals in a careless or dangerous manner or at a greater speed than six miles per hour within the town limits, and also the firing of guns, pistols, gunpowder, crackers or other explosive, combustible or dangerous materials in the streets, public grounds or elsewhere in the town.

blishment of ket houses.

Sec. 46. That the aldermen may establish and regulate the markets, prescribe at what time and place within the town marketable articles shall be sold.

ic buildings.

Sec. 47. That they may establish all public buildings necessary and proper for the town and prevent the erection or establishment of wooden buildings in any part of the town where they may increase the danger of fire.

eteries.

Sec. 48. That they may provide graveyards in or near the corporate limits and regulate the same; may appoint and pay a keeper and compel the keeping and returning bills of mortality and they may prohibit interments within the town.

May take measures to prevent entrance of contagious diseases.

Sec. 49. That the board of aldermen may take such measures as they deem effectual to prevent the entrance into the town or the spreading therein of any contagious or infectious disease; may stop, detain and examine for that purpose every person coming from places believed to be infected with such disease; may establish and regulate hospitals within the town or within three miles thereof; may cause any person in the town suspected to be infected with such disease and whose stay may endanger its health to be removed to the hospital; may remove from the town or destroy any furniture or other articles which shall be suspected of being tainted or infected with contagious or infectious diseases or of which there shall be reasonable cause to apprehend that they may pass into such a state as to generate and propagate disease; may abate by any reasonable means all nuisances which may be injurious to the public health.

May destroy furniture, etc., with disease germs.

Sec. 50. That if any person shall attempt by force or by threats of violence to prevent the removal to the hospital of any persons ordered to be conveyed thither, the person so offending shall forfeit and pay to the town one hundred $100) [dollars] and moreover be deemed guilty of a misdemeanor.

May regulate speed of trains.

Sec. 51. That the board of aldermen may govern and regulate the speed of railroad trains while running within the corporate limits of the town, and prohibit the ringing of bells, blowing of steam whistles, either during the day or night, within the town limits. They may also prohibit railroad trains or cars from standing across the public streets under penalties to be prescribed by them.

Commissioners of Lenoir county shall not grant liquor license without consent of town commissioners.

Sec. 52. That it shall not be lawful for the commissioners of Lenoir county to grant any license to retail spirituous liquors within the limits of the town or within one mile thereof without permission first obtained from the board of aldermen for the town in being at the time of the application to the county commissioners, and if any license shall be granted without permission in writing attested by the mayor and exhibited to the county commissioners and filed with the clerk of the board of county commissioners, the same shall be utterly void, and the person obtaining such license shall be liable to indictment as in other cases of retailing without a license, and shall moreover forfeit and pay to the town the sum of twenty dollars.

Fines recoverable in name of town.

Sec. 53. That all penalties imposed by law relating to the town of Kinston or by this act or by any of the by-laws, ordinances, orders, rules and regulations of the said town, unless otherwise expressly provided, shall be recoverable in the name of the town of Kinston before the mayor of said town or any tribunal having jurisdiction thereof.

ximum nalty. Sec. 54. That the board of aldermen shall not have power to impose for any offense a larger penalty than fifty ($50) dollars, unless the same be expressly authorized; and from any judgment of the mayor by this act or for other cause of action herein allowed, the party dissatisfied may appeal in like manner under the same rule and regulations as are prescribed for appeals from a judgment of a justice of the peace.

lary of mayor d aldermen. Sec. 55. That the salary of the mayor shall be four hundred ($400) dollars; that the salary of the aldermen shall be fifty ($50) dollars; that the pay or salary of all other officers of the said town shall be fixed by the aldermen of the said town, and may be increased or diminished from time to time at the election of the aldermen. That the mayor besides his salary shall be entitled to the same fees as justices of the peace on all process or precepts issued by him. The police or constable shall be entitled to the same fees for executing process as the sheriffs or constables of the counties.

ditional wers and hts. Sec. 56. That the town of Kinston, through the board of aldermen, is hereby vested with all the powers, rights, privileges and immunities enumerated in chapter sixty-two (62), volume two and elsewhere in The Code of North Carolina not inconsistent with this act.

vy and collecn of taxes. Sec. 57. That in order to raise a fund for the expenses incident to the proper government of the said town the board of aldermen of said town shall have the power to levy and collect taxes on the following persons and subjects of taxation, situated and being within the corporate limits of said town, payable in the existing national currency, and shall be assessed and collected under the rules and regulations prescribed by law, viz:

ll tax. I. On each taxable poll or male residing within the corporate limits of said town between the ages of twenty-one and fifty years, except such poor and infirm persons whom the board of aldermen of said town in their judgment may exempt there may be annually levied and collected a tax not exceeding two dollars and twenty-five cents ($2.25), the collection of which may be enforced in the same manner by the tax collector of said town as is provided by the general law of the state for the collection of the poll taxes for state and county.

rsons empted.

valorem tax. II. On all real and personal property, money on hand, solvent credits, investments in bonds, stocks, joint stock companies or otherwise, being owned within the corporate limits of said town, there may be levied and collected annually an ad valorem tax not to exceed twenty-five (25) cents on every one hundred ($100) dollars valuation thereof.

ximum

III. On the net income and profits other [than] from that derived from property taxed from any source whatever during the year preceding the first day of June in each year, there may be annually levied and collected a tax not to exceed one sixth of one per centum. The income tax shall include interest on the securities of the United States, of this state or other states or governments. In estimating the net income of the income taxpayer, a deduction of one thousand ($1,000) [dollars] shall be made in his favor. The income taxpayer shall return to the mayor of the town the net amount of his income during the first ten days of June in each year, which return shall be filed in the office of the treasurer of the town. Any income taxpayer failing to return his income tax as herein provided shall be guilty of a misdemeanor, and on conviction fined not more than fifty ($50) dollars or imprisoned not more than thirty (30) days. Tax on net incomes, etc.

Sec. 58 That in addition to the person and subjects of taxation enumerated in section fifty-seven (57) of this act the board of aldermen in said town shall have power to levy and collect as herein specified a special license or privilege tax on the following persons and subjects of taxation, viz: On all itinerant or resident merchants, peddlers or auctioneers who shall sell privately or at public outcry within the town limits, whether by ascending or descending bids. each express company, each telegraph office, each railroad company having a depot within the limits of the town, and photograph artist and persons taking likenesses of the human face by whatsoever art; each broker, each bank or banker's office, each cotton buyer, each dealer in patent rights, each sewing machine agent, all commission merchants and commercial brokers, each distiller of fruit or grain, each livery stable, every resident or non-resident huckster, each trader or agent of such who buys produce on the street for sale in other markets, each gift enterprise or lottery, each dray, each omnibus, each hotel, each barber shop, each lightning rod agent, each fire or life insurance agent, each auctioneer; on every agency for the sale of steam engines, boilers and machinery not manufactured in the town; every dealer in buggies, wagons or other vehicles not manufactured in the town; each and every surgeon, dentist, practicing physician, optician, practicing lawyer, civil engineer, real estate agent or broker, aurist, oculist and chiropodist; on every dealer in horses and mules, colts, bartered or exchanged; every cattle, horse or mule drover or dealer; every agent for the sale of snuff, tobacco or other articles of merchandise not manufactured in the town, an annual tax not to exceed fifty ($50) dollars, to be levied monthly, quarterly or yearly, and collected monthly, quarterly or yearly at the option of the board of aldermen of said town as designated in their ordinances. Levy and collection of special taxes. Auctioneers, etc. Express, telegraph and railroad companies. Photographers. Brokers. Commission merchants. Distillers. Liveries. Lotteries. Drays. Barber shops. Insurance agents. Dealers in buggies. Dentists, etc. Dealers in horses, etc. How and when levied.

x on dogs.

Sec. 59. That the board of aldermen of said town shall have power to impose annually a tax per capita on all dogs, pups or bitches not to exceed one ($1) dollar, running at large or kept within the corporate limits of the said town, and may require all dogs, pups or bitches kept within the corporate limits to wear such tax badge as they may designate. No proud bitch shall be allowed to run at large in the town under any circumstances, and when found running at large shall be killed. Any person residing within the said town having therein any dog, pup or bitch and shall not return them for taxation as required by the board of aldermen, or shall fail to pay the tax according to law, after fifteen days' public notice of the imposition thereof, shall be guilty of a misdemeanor and on conviction thereof before the mayor shall be fined not exceeding twenty ($20) dollars or imprisoned not exceeding thirty (30) days, and the dog, pup or bitch may be treated as a nuisance and destroyed

ilure to pay a misdeanor.

rses, cattle, , may be lared a nuice.

Sec. 60. That the board of aldermen of the said town shall have power to declare all horses, mules, cattle, swine, fowls, sheep and goats running at large within the limits of the town a nuisance, and may at their option impose a fine upon the owner or owners of said animals so running at large or may treat the same as nuisances and abate or prohibit by law.

cial taxes.

Sec. 61. That in addition to the persons and subjects of taxation enumerated in sections fifty eight, fifty-nine and sixty of this act the board of aldermen may levy a tax on the following subjects, the amount of which tax when fixed shall be collected by the tax collector instantly, and if the same be not paid on demand the same may be recovered by suit on the articles upon which the tax is imposed, or any other property of the owner or owners may be forthwith distrained and sold by the tax collector to satisfy the same, namely:

wling alleys,

I. Upon every bowling alley, billiard table, pooi table, bagatelle table, shooting gallery, skating rink or any other game allowed by law, and every victualling house or restaurant establishment used or kept in the town a tax not exceeding fifty ($50) dollars a year.

aliers of ors.

II. Upon every permission by the board of aldermen to retail spirituous, vinous or malt liquors a tax not exceeding one hundred and twenty ($120) dollars: Provided, that every permission granted to each dealer in spirituous, vinous and malt liquors under this subsection shall expire at the expiration of twelve months from its date, and the said dealer or dealers must then obtain another permission from the said board of aldermen upon the payment again of the tax imposed upon the granting of such permission. Any dealer or dealers who shall retail said liquors without obtaining said permission or renewing the same as is provided in this subsection shall be considered and construed to be retailing without license and punished according to the law in such cases made and provided.

III. Upon every company of circus riders who shall exhibit within the town a tax not exceeding fifty ($50) dollars for each separate exhibition, the tax to be paid before the exhibition, and if not, to be double. Circuses.

IV. Upon every company of stage or theatrical performers, every sleight-of-hand performer, rope or wire dancer or performer; every exhibitor of natural or artificial curiosities; every singer, person or company of singers, dancers, Ethiopian minstrels or performers on musical instruments who shall sing, dance, perform or play on musical instruments for reward, five dollars for each exhibition. Theatrical performances.

V. Upon each show or exhibition of any other kind and upon each concert or lecture for reward, five dollars for each lecture or exhibition. Other shows and exhibitions.

Sec. 62. That besides the persons and subjects of taxation expressly enumerated in this act, the board of aldermen of the said town shall have power to levy and collect taxes on all persons and subjects of taxation which it is in the power of the general assembly to tax for state and county purposes under the constitution of the state. Other subjects of taxation.

Sec. 63. That the assessment of the real estate within the corporate limits of the said town made from time to time by the board of assessors for Kinston township shall be taken by the board of aldermen as the valuation thereof for the purposes of taxation under this act. Should the assessment made by the said board of assessors include property partly within and partly without the limits of said town in the aggregate, then and in that case the board of aldermen of said town may apportion according to the said assessment and fix the valuation of the part within the said limits. Assessment of real estate.

Sec. 64. That the board of aldermen of said town shall annually on the first Monday in April appoint some competent person, resident of said town, to list all the real estate in said town at the valuation assessed on the same, all the personal property in said town, all polls subject to taxation, residents within said town, and all other persons and subjects of taxation which shall be required by the board of aldermen to be listed by the said list-taker. The said board of aldermen shall allow such list-taker a compensation for his services not exceeding two ($2) dollars per day for the time actually employed, to be paid by the town. Appointment of tax-lister.

Sec. 65. That the said list-taker shall advertise in five public places within the town, or in lieu thereof [in] some newspaper published in said town, immediately after his appointment, noti- Tax lister shall advertise dates of listing.

fying all taxpayers to return to said list-taker all the real estate, personal property, polls and other subjects of taxation within the corporate limits required by the board of aldermen to be then listed which each taxpayer shall own or have under his control on the first day of June, requiring said return to be made to the said list-taker within twenty days after the second Monday in June, under the pains and penalties imposed by law. That the said list-taker shall attend at the court-house in Kinston for at least ten days for the purpose of taking the list of taxes.

rsons subject tax shall ke out list.

Sec. 66. Every person required to list property, polls and other subjects of taxation as provided by the preceding section shall make out and deliver to the said list-taker a statement, verified by his oath, of all real and personal property, money on hand, solvent credits, investment in bonds, stocks, joint stock companies, poll and other subjects of taxation required to be listed in his possession or under his control on the first day of June either as owner or holder thereof, or as parent, husband, guardian, trustee, executor, administrator, receiver, accounting officer, partner, agent, factor or otherwise.

hen list shall given in.

Sec 67. The list shall be given in by the person charged or his agent within twenty days after the second Monday in June as herein prescribed: Provided, that agents for the purpose of listing property shall be appointed only by females, non-residents and persons physically unable to attend and file their list at the time prescribed in law for listing property.

rified statement shall be en list-taker.

Sec. 68. At the time and place appointed by the list-taker the taxpayer shall attend and file with the list-taker on a blank to be prepared and furnished by the board of aldermen, a verified statement of all the property of every kind and description owned by the taxpayer or under his control subject to taxation, and such other subjects required to be listed for taxation. The taxpayer shall also swear to the true value of all property and choses in action except land, which oath shall be in the following form: "I, ______, do solemnly swear (or affirm) that the list furnished by me contains a true and accurate list of all property which by law I am required to list for taxation, and that the value affixed thereon by me is a true valuation of the same, according to my best knowledge, information and belief. So help me, God." Any person making a false return of any of his subjects of taxation shall be guilty of perjury. Property held in trust or as agent, guardian, executor or administrator or in a right of a feme covert shall be returned on separate lists.

th of taxyer.

rsons making se returns.

st-taker shall turn list to ayor.

Sec. 69. The list-taker shall on or before the second Monday in July in each year return the tax list to the mayor of the town. He shall also return a list of the property in town not given in for taxation, with a description and valuation thereof made by himself and the names of the occupant and supposed owner, and a list of the taxable polls of the town not given in for taxation. The returns so made shall be open to the inspector [inspection] of all persons interested.

Sec. 70. That the board of aldermen of said town shall insert in the tax list the description and valuation of all property not given in and the names of the persons supposed to be liable for a poll tax who failed to give themselves in, and shall charge all such persons double the tax which they would otherwise be chargeable, unless satisfactory excuse therefor be rendered to the said board of aldermen on or before the first Monday in October, and all persons who are liable for a poll tax and shall willfully fail to give themselves in, and all persons who own property or have it under their control and willfully fail to list it within the time allowed, before the list-takers or the board of aldermen, shall be deemed guilty of a misdemeanor, and on conviction thereof before a mayor or a justice of the peace shall be fined not more than fifty ($50) dollars or imprisoned not more than thirty (30) days.

Aldermen shall insert in tax list property not returned.

Persons failing to list property guilty of a misdemeanor.

Sec. 71. That the board of aldermen of said town shall cause to be made out two copies of the tax list as revised and settled by them. The said list shall show in different columns the sum due by each taxpayer to the town; one of said copies shall remain in the office of the mayor of the town, the other shall be delivered to the tax collector on or before the first Monday in September in each year, and he shall receipt for the same. The mayor shall endorse on the copy given to the tax collector an order to collect the taxes therein mentioned, and such order shall have the force and effect of a judgment and execution against the property of the person charged in such list. Said order shall be in the following or in some similar form:

Two lists of returns shall be made.

State of North Carolina,
Town of Kinston.

To the tax collector of said town:

You are hereby commanded to collect the taxes herein mentioned according to the provisions and requirements of the existing law.

Order to tax collector from mayor.

In witness whereof, I hereunto set my hand and seal, ---- day of ------, 18--.

----------- [Seal.]
Mayor of Kinston.

Sec. 72. The lien of the said town taxes levied for all purposes in each year shall attach to all real property subject to such taxes on the first day of June annually, and shall continue until such taxes with any penalty which shall accrue thereon shall be

Lien of town taxes.

paid; all personal property subject to taxation shall be liable to be seized and sold for taxes, and the personal property of any deceased person shall be liable in the hands of any executor or administrator for any tax due on the same by any testator or intestate.

en taxes are
e.

Sec. 73. All taxes unless in this act otherwise provided or unless otherwise by the board of aldermen in their ordinance shall be due on the first Monday in September in each year. When paid the tax collector shall note on the tax list against the name of the party the date of the payment and the amount paid; he shall also give a receipt to the party, stating the amount paid and the date of the payment. Any tax collector who shall fail to pay over to the treasurer of the town such taxes as he may collect shall be guilty of a misdemeanor, and shall be fined or imprisoned at the discretion of the court.

en taxes are
e and collecti-

Sec. 74. The tax collector shall attend at the court-house in Kinston during the month of October in each year for the purpose of receiving taxes, of which fifteen days' notice shall be given by advertisement at three or more public places in said town: Provided, that nothing in this section shall be construed to prevent the tax collector from levying and selling after the first day of November, but he shall not sell before that day.

Sec. 75. Whenever the taxes shall be due and unpaid the tax collector shall immediately proceed to collect the same.

ners of dray
hire may be
uired to
cute bond.

Sec. 76. That the board of aldermen of said town shall have power to require of the owners of drays for public hire within the limits of the town to execute a bond with approved security, payable to the town of Kinston in such sum as they shall determine, for the safe delivery of goods or other things delivered for carriage, and for any damage that may occur to the said goods or other things during the transportation thereof. They may also require the said drays to be numbered or badged. The said bond may be put in suit by any person agreed [aggrieved] by a breach thereof, without assignment, from time to time until the whole penalty be recovered: Provided, the aldermen do not fix the penalty of said bond at more than one hundred ($100) dollars.

flicting laws
ealed.

Sec. 77. That all laws and clauses of laws coming in conflict with this act shall be and the same are hereby repealed.

Sec. 78. This act shall be in force from and after its ratification.

Ratified the 4th day of March, A. D. 1899.

CHAPTER 181.

An act to amend public laws of eighteen hundred and ninety-one, chapter five hundred and ninety-one, in regard to the Buncombe Turnpike Company, and to amend the charter of the town of Victoria.

The General Assembly of North Carolina do enact:

Section 1. That sections three and four of chapter five hundred and ninety-one of the public laws of eighteen hundred and ninety-one be and the same are hereby repealed. **Sections 3 and 4, chapter 591, public laws of 1891, amended.**

Sec. 2. That the town of Victoria shall not be required to keep up, maintain or contribute to the maintenance of any road or street which does not lie within its corporate limits, nor shall any other incorporated town be required to keep up, maintain or contribute to the maintenance of any road or street lying within the corporate limits of the town of Victoria. **Town not required to contribute to maintenance of road.**

Sec. 3. All laws and clauses of laws in conflict with this act are hereby repealed, and this act shall be in force from and after its ratification. **Conflicting laws repealed.**

Ratified the 4th day of March, A. D. 1899.

CHAPTER 182.

An act to amend chapter one hundred and ninety-nine of the laws of eighteen hundred and forty-six and eighteen hundred and forty-seven, entitled "An act for the incorporation of the town of Washington," ratified the eighteenth day of January, eighteen hundred and forty-seven.

The General Assembly of North Carolina do enact:

Section 1. That section thirty-four, chapter one hundred and ninety-nine of the laws of eighteen hundred and forty-six, eighteen hundred and forty-seven, being an act entitled "An act for the incorporation of the town of Washington," ratified the eighteenth day of January, eighteen hundred and forty-seven, be and the same is hereby repealed and the following is substituted in the place thereof, to-wit: **Section 34, chapter 199, laws of 1846-'47, amended.**

That the commissioners for the county of Beaufort shall grant a license to sell spirituous, vinous or malt liquors by the drink or small measure or otherwise within the said town to no person, firm or corporation who shall not have first obtained from the town clerk a certificate of the assent of the board of commissioners for the town of Washington to his obtaining said license, which certificate shall be prima facie evidence of good moral character in the applicant. **Commissioners shall grant license to sell spirituous liquors.**

uance of cer- cates.

That before the said clerk shall issue said certificate the person, firm or corporation desiring the same shall first obtain a license from the board of commissioners of the town to engage in the sale of spirituous, vinous or malt liquors, for which license such person, firm or corporation shall pay a tax of not less than three hundred dollars per annum and not more than five hundred dollars, said tax to be paid in semi-annual installments on the first day of January and July of each and every year. The license tax may by the consent of the board of commissioners of the town be paid monthly in advance.

cense tax.

venue from id tax, how plied.

That one-half of the revenue thus derived from this license shall be used and applied for the purposes of improving and maintaining the streets of the town and one-half to be appropriated towards the maintenance of the public graded schools of the town and to no other purposes, and shall be kept separate from all other funds of the town by the several town officers. Any surplus may be disposed of as the board of commissioners direct.

Sec. 2. That this act shall be in force from and after its ratification.

Ratified the 4th day of March, A. D. 1899.

CHAPTER 183.

An act to amend an act of this general assembly, entitled "An act to amend chapter two hundred and thirteen, private laws of eighteen hundred and ninety-seven," ratified the thirteenth day of February, eighteen hundred and ninety-nine.

The General Assembly of North Carolina do enact:

rst section of to amend apter 213, private laws of 1897, ealed.

Section 1. That the first section of an act of this general assembly, entitled "An act to amend chapter two hundred and thirteen, private laws of eighteen hundred and ninety-seven," ratified the thirteenth day of February, eighteen hundred and ninety-nine, be and the same hereby is repealed.

ditional mbers local ard of managers.

Sec. 2. That the second section of chapter two hundred and thirteen of the private laws of eighteen hundred and ninety-seven be and the same hereby is amended by inserting in the fifth line thereof, between the word "Bryson" and the word "shall," the following names: "J. D. Coward, L. J. Smith, Felix E. Alley, J. Robert Long, R. L. Watson, C. C. Cowan and E. D. Davis."

rm of office.

Sec. 3. That the members of the local board of managers of the normal department of the Cullowhee High School, mentioned in the second section of this act, to-wit: J. D. Coward, L. J. Smith,

Felix E. Alley, J. Robert Long. R. L. Watson, C. C. Cowan and E. D. Davis, shall hold their offices for six (6) years from and after the ratification of this act, and shall possess the same power as the other members of said local board of managers.

Sec. 4. That section two (2) of said chapter two hundred and thirteen, private laws of eighteen hundred and ninety-seven, be and the same hereby is amended by repealing and striking out all that part thereof after the word "department" in the ninth (9th) line thereof. Section 2 amended.

Sec. 5. That all laws and clauses of laws in conflict with this act be and the same are hereby repealed. Conflicting laws repealed.

Sec. 6. That this act shall be in force from and after its ratification.

Ratified the 4th day of March, A. D. 1899.

CHAPTER 184.

An act to incorporate the town of Oriental, in Pamlico county.

The General Assembly of North Carolina do enact:

Section 1. That the town of Oriental. in the county of Pamlico, be and the same is hereby incorporated under the name and style of "The Town of Oriental," and it shall be subject to all the provisions contained in chapter sixty-two of The Code of North Carolina, and shall have the benefit of and be subject to all the provisions of law in reference to incorporated towns not inconsistent with this act. Incorporated. Corporate name. Corporate powers.

Sec. 2. That the corporate limits of said town shall be as follows: Beginning at the mouth of Smith's creek on the north and west side of Neuse river and runs up and with the north side of the channel of Smith's creek to Camp creek; thence up Camp creek to its head and continuously up the branch of Camp creek to a point opposite the back line of what is known as the Lupton property, the same conveyed by E. W. Lupton to the Oriental Lumber Company; thence to and with the back line of said Lupton lands to the west line of R. P. Midgette; thence about a south course with the line of said R. P. Midgette to E. Paris' line; thence about an east course with said Paris' and Midgette's line and the Methodist Episcopal church's south line to Jonathan Perkins' lands; thence with said Perkins' and R. P. Midgette's line to a cross wire fence of said R. P. Midgette; thence with said fence to the gate of said R. P. Midgette; thence from said gate with the wire fence of R. P. Midgette to the first channel of Neuse river; thence with the edge of said channel to channel of Smith's Corporate limits.

creek, the beginning; that to the depth of ten (10) feet of water in said Neuse river shall be the edge of said channel of Neuse river.

wn officers.

Sec. 3. That the officers of the town shall be a mayor, three commissioners. a constable, who shall be elected by the commissioners, and such other officers as the commissioners may deem necessary and proper, as provided by said chapter sixty-two of The Code: Provided, that no person shall be a mayor, commissioner or other officer of said town unless he be a qualified voter therein.

porary cers.

Sec. 4. That until the election hereafter provided for, the mayor of said town shall be Dr. W. H. Peterson; the commissioners shall be L. B. Midgette, P. J. Delamar and B. F. Picklis.

nual election fficers.

Sec. 5. That there shall be held on the first Monday in May, eighteen hundred and ninety-nine, and on the first Monday in May every year thereafter, an election for mayor and commissioners for said town at some convenient place therein, to be selected by the commissioners, which election shall be held by a registrar and two poll holders under regulations in other respects prescribed by the state election laws, which from time to time may be enacted—at which election all duly qualified voters of the state of North Carolina under the state election laws existing at the time of such elections, residing in the corporate limits of said town, shall be permitted to vote.

wers and vileges of missioners.

Sec. 6. That the said commissioners shall have power to pass all by-laws, ordinances, rules and regulations for the good government of the town not inconsistent with the laws of this state or the United States, and to levy and collect a tax upon all subjects of state and general taxation, polls, real and personal property when deemed proper by said commissioners, not to exceed an amount equal to the tax levied by the commissioners of Pamlico county for state and general purposes, and to impose fines for the violation of town ordinances and to collect the same; also to levy and collect all such license and privilege taxes as are mentioned in chapter sixty-two of The Code. All taxes and fines collected shall be used by the town for town purposes.

vy and col- tion of taxes.

yor shall side at meet- of commis- ners.

Sec. 7. The mayor, when present, shall preside at all meetings of the board of commissioners, and shall vote only when there is a tie; and at their first meeting after oranization the commissioners shall appoint one of their number as chairman pro tempore, who shall in the absence of the mayor preside at the meetings and perform all the duties of mayor.

pointment of airman.

hen mayor d commis- ners shall vene.

Sec. 8. That within five days after the election the commissioners and mayor shall convene for the transaction of business, and then shall fix monthly meetings for the board: and called meetings of said board may be held on the call of the mayor and a majority of the commissioners may adopt by-laws enforcing the attendance of the members of the board.

Sec. 9. That all orders drawn on the treasurer by the clerk on the order of the commissioners shall be signed by the mayor and countersigned by the clerk, and the treasurer shall file all such orders as his vouchers. and at the expiration of the term of the office of treasurer he shall deliver to his successors all moneys, securities or other property intrusted to him for safe keeping or otherwise. Orders on clerk, how signed.

Sec. 10. That the commissioners of said town shall have power to collect all taxes by levy and sale of property, as in case of the levy and sale of property in the collection of taxes by the sheriff for state and general purposes. Power to collect taxes.

Sec. 11. That the said commissioners shall have the right to purchase and hold, in the name of the town of Oriental, sufficient lands for the erection of necessary buildings for town purposes, town hall. town prison and such other buildings as they may deem necessary and may erect the same. Empowered to purchase and hold lands.

Sec. 12. That the mayor shall have power to cause all persons failing to pay fines, or who shall be imprisoned for violation of any town ordinance, to work it out on the streets, and in case of working out any fines the commissioners shall adopt the price. Persons failing to pay fines may be worked on streets.

Sec. 13. That as soon as practical after the ratification of this act the mayor and commissioners herein named shall take the oath of office and convene for the transaction of business. When mayor and commissioners shall take oath.

Sec. 14. That the town of Oriental is hereby vested with all the powers, rights, privileges and immunities enumerated in chapter sixty-two (62) of The Code, volume two, and elsewhere in The Code as amended by subsequent acts of the general assembly not inconsistent with any provisions of this act. Powers with which town is vested.

Sec 15. That this act shall be in force from and after its ratification.

Ratified the 4th day of March, A. D. 1899.

CHAPTER 185.

An act to incorporate The Industrial Benevolent Association of North Carolina.

The General Assembly of North Carolina do enact:

Section 1. That J. L. Meynberg, D M. Hardy, George E. Hood, B. R. King and A. J. Brown, and their successors, be and they are hereby created a body politic, to be known by the name, style and title of The Industrial Benevolent Association of North Carolina, and subordinate branches working under the juris- Corporators. Body politic. Corporate name.

diction of said association, and by such name and title shall exist for a term of sixty years, and be capable of suing and being sued, pleading and being impleaded, and of purchasing, leasing, holding and receiving in its corporate name property, real and personal and mixed, and of making such rules and regulations as the association may enact, not in conflict with the laws of the state and the United States.

uration of arter rporate pow-s.

urpose of corporation.

Sec. 2. To insure the life of persons of good bodily health who are acceptable, to collect assessments levied upon its members by the association, and upon satisfactory proof of the death of a member who has complied with all the rules and regulations. levy such assessments as the association may order, and pay the amount thus collected to the beneficiary named in the certificate held by such deceased member or may charge members and industrial policy holders such premium in advance as the association sees fit under its rules and regulations.

rporate seal.

Sec. 3. That the said association shall have a corporate seal for making and doing its legal acts and proceedings, which it may alter from time to time as it may direct.

dividual bility.

Sec. 4. That private property of members of the said association shall be exempt from the corporate debts of the said association or members thereof.

ection of cers.

Sec. 5. That the association shall provide for the election of such officers as the association may deem necessary to transact the business of the corporation, to fix the compensation for their services, who shall hold office until their successors are duly elected and qualified. That the said officers shall hold office under such rules and regulations as the by-laws of the association shall provide.

rm of office.

rectors shall be tified before eration in -laws can made.

Sec. 6. That no by-law of the association shall be made or altered except by first giving each director thirty days' notice in writing or by advertising two months in a state daily paper, and by two-thirds vote of its whole number of directors, which shall not be less than three nor more than fifteen members of the association.

ch member all have one te.

Sec. 7. That each member of the association shall have one vote in the election of its directors.

ay issue indusal policies.

Sec. 8. That this association may issue industrial policies of insurance not exceeding five hundred dollars on each life or person, under such rules and regulations as a majority of the board of directors see fit to adopt. But the holders of industrial policies shall have no vote in the management of the association unless they be certificate members of the association.

Sec. 9. That this act shall be in force from and after its ratification.

Ratified the 6th day of March, A. D. 1899.

CHAPTER 186.

An act to amend, revise and consolidate the charter of the City of Salisbury.

The General Assembly of North Carolina do enact:

SECTION 1. That the inhabitants of the City of Salisbury be and continue as they have heretofore been a body politic and corporate, and henceforth the said corporation shall bear the name and style of "City of Salisbury," and under that name is hereby invested with all the property and rights of property which now belong to the present corporation of the City of Salisbury, or any other corporate name or names heretofore used; and by the corporate name of "City of Salisbury," may purchase and hold for purposes of its government, welfare and improvement, all such property and estate, real and personal, within or without said city, as may be deemed necessary or convenient therefor, or as may be conveyed, devised or bequeathed to it, and the same may, by its board of aldermen, from time to time sell, dispose of and re-invest, as shall be deemed advisable by the proper authorities of said corporation.

Body politic.

Corporate name.

Corporate powers and rights.

SEC. 2. The corporate limits of the City of Salisbury shall be as follows: Begin at the centre of the site of the old court-house and run four lines: One north of west along and upon the extension of Inniss street, three thousand six hundred and fifty-five feet; another south of east along and upon the extension of Inniss street, two thousand seven hundred and twenty feet; another south of west along and upon the extension of Main street, three thousand one hundred and sixty-five feet; another north of east along and upon the extension of Main street, three thousand six hundred and fifty-five feet. And the corporate limits of said town shall be compressed within a parallelogram included within four lines running at right angles to said lines at the termination thereof, and extending each way until they intersect each other respectively. All that territory lying west from the intersection of Main and Inniss streets, and between said Main and Inniss streets, shall be known as the west ward; all that territory lying north from the intersection of Main and Inniss streets and between said streets shall be known as the north ward; all that territory lying east from the intersection of Main and Inniss streets and between said streets, shall be known as the east ward, and all that territory lying south from the intersection of Main and Inniss streets and between said streets, shall be known as the south ward.

Corporate limits.

Corporate limits.

Division of wards.

SEC. 3. The government of the said city shall be composed of

Government of city.

a mayor and eight aldermen, who, with the city marshal, who shall also be tax collector, shall be elected biennially on the first Monday in May by the qualified voters of said city as herein provided, and said aldermen shall be *bona fide* residents of the four wards of said town as follows: Two in each ward.

ities of mayor.

SEC. 4. The mayor shall preside at the meetings of the board of aldermen, but shall have no vote except in case of a tie. At the first meeting succeeding their election, the board of aldermen shall elect a presiding officer, to be styled the mayor *pro tempore*, who, in the absence of the mayor, or in case of his sickness or death, or when the mayor shall authorize him, shall exercise all the authority conferred by law upon the mayor. All vacancies in the offices of mayor and mayor *pro tempore* and aldermen shall be filled by the board of aldermen, and said appointees shall hold their offices until the next regular biennial election, except the mayor *pro tempore*, who shall hold his office for one year.

ection of esiding officer.

ities of mayor o tem.

rm of office.

ection of reg- rar and judges election.

SEC. 5. The board of aldermen of the City of Salisbury, on or before the first Monday in April preceding each biennial election, shall elect one registrar and two judges of election for each of the four wards of said city to conduct the election which shall be held under the rules, regulations and penalties of the general election law, except as modified by this act. The said board shall make publication of the persons so selected at the court-house door immediately after such appointment, and shall cause a notice to be served upon such appointees. If any such registrar or judge of election shall die or fail to perform his duties, the sheriff of said county shall appoint another in his place. Each ward of said town shall be an election precinct. Special elections shall be held under the rules and regulations for the regular biennial elections.

ections, how ld.

ilure of regis- r or judges serve.

dermen shall 'nish registra- n books.

SEC. 6. Each registrar shall be furnished by the board of aldermen of said city with all necessary registration books; and it shall be the duty of the registrar to arrange the registration books of his ward before each election in such manner that said books shall show an accurate list of the electors entitled to vote in such ward at said election. And he shall erase from the books the names of all persons not entitled to vote in said ward at said election. The registrars shall keep open their books for the registration of electors on Wednesday, Thursday and Friday preceding the election. There shall be a new registration of voters for the election to be held on the first Monday in May in the year eighteen hundred and ninety-nine.

hen registra- n book shall opened.

rsons shall vote ly in ward in ich they are ual residents.

SEC. 7. No person shall be entitled to vote in any other ward than the one in which he is an actual and *bona fide* resident, nor unless he shall have continuously resided in said ward for ninety days preceding the election. And no registration shall be valid unless it specifies the number of the ward and the owner and number of the lot on which the person proposing to vote shall reside.

SEC. 8. The mayor of said city shall furnish to each registrar a plat or chart of his ward, with each lot of said ward plainly numbered thereon. As far as possible the old historical numbers shall be retained. Each block or square shall contain four lots, which shall be numbered, whether the streets adjoining them have actually been numbered or not. If the mayor shall fail to deliver to any registrar the said plat or chart for ten days after the appointment of said registrar, it shall be the duty of the registrar to prepare the said plat or chart. Any mayor or registrar violating this section shall be guilty of a misdemeanor.

Mayor shall furnish chart to registrar.

Failure of mayor to deliver chart a misdemeanor.

SEC. 9. Each class of officers shall be voted for in separate boxes. The mayor and city marshal and tax collectors shall be voted for in one box on one ballot; the aldermen for the north ward shall be voted for in one box on one ballot; the aldermen of the east ward shall be voted for in one box on one ballot; the aldermen of the south ward shall be voted for in one box on one ballot; the aldermen of the west ward shall be voted for in one box on one ballot.

Each class of officers shall be voted for in separate boxes.

SEC. 10. The board of aldermen of said city, or upon their failure, the several registrars, shall provide for each ward ballot boxes for each class of officers to be voted for, in which boxes the electors may deposit their ballots for such officers respectively.

Ballot boxes shall be provided by aldermen.

SEC. 11. Each elector in person shall deposit his ballot for each class of officers in the proper ballot box; and no person shall dictate to him at the polls how or for whom he shall vote, or interfere in any way with his voting. If among the number of officers voted for there shall be any two or more having an equal number of votes, and either would be duly elected but for the equal vote, the registrars shall determine who shall be chosen.

Electors shall deposit ballot in person.

When tie vote occurs, registrars shall decide.

SEC. 12. On the next day after the election, at ten o'clock in the forenoon, the registrars of the several wards shall meet at the court-house and canvass and judicially determine the returns, and shall give a certificate to each candidate whom they shall ascertain to be duly elected.

When returns announced.

SEC. 13. The mayor and aldermen shall be installed in their respective offices at twelve o'clock, meridian, on the third Monday in May next after their election.

Installation of mayor and aldermen.

SEC. 14. The aldermen of said city shall establish as many voting places therein as they shall, from time to time, deem necessary: *Provided*, that there shall be at least one such voting place in every ward thereof.

Voting places.

th of mayor.

Sec. 15. Before entering upon the duties of this office, the mayor shall take and subscribe before some person authorized by law to administer oaths, the following oath: "I...., do solemnly swear that I will perform to my best skill, judgment and ability all and every the duties of the office of mayor of the City of Salisbury while I continue in said office, and will cause to be executed, as far as my power lies, all laws, ordinances and regulations made for the government of said city, and in the discharge of my duties I will do justice in all cases. So help me, God." Said oath shall be by him immediately filed in his office.

th of aldermen

Sec. 16. Each alderman, before entering upon the duties of his office, shall take, before the mayor, an oath that he will truly and impartially perform the duties of an alderman of the City of Salisbury according to his best skill, judgment and ability.

cancies in ce of mayor

Sec. 17. If the person elected mayor of said city shall neglect or refuse to qualify at the time provided therefor, or if after he shall have qualified there shall occur any vacancy in the office of mayor of said city, or if the mayor shall become a non-resident of said city, or for three consecutive months shall absent himself therefrom, the aldermen of said city shall, at their next regular meeting, declare said office of mayor vacant, and shall, at their next regular meeting thereafter, choose by ballot some competent person as mayor of said city for the term, or the

cancies in ce of alder- n.

unxpired portion of the term, as the case may be. In like manner all vacancies in the office of aldermen shall be filled by the remaining aldermen.

usal to alify a misde- anor.

Sec. 18. That any person elected mayor or alderman who shall neglect or refuse to qualify and act as such, shall be guilty of a misdemeanor, and upon conviction thereof shall be fined fifty dollars or imprisoned thirty days.

isdiction of yor.

Sec. 19. The mayor of the City of Salisbury is hereby constituted a special court, with all the jurisdiction and powers in criminal offenses, occurring within the limits of said city, which are now or may hereafter be given to justices of the peace, and shall also have exclusive original jurisdiction to hear and determine all misdemeanors consisting of a violation of an ordinance or ordinances of said city, except where legally the mayor and mayor *pro tempore* are incompetent to try the same, in which case the cause shall be, upon application of the defendant, removed for trial to such other court in the county of

isdiction of yor.

Rowan as would, but for this section, have jurisdiction of the same; and such legal incompetency shall be construed to mean only such incompetency as would disable a judge of a superior court to try under similar circumstances a cause pending in such last-mentioned court. The proceedings of said mayor's court shall be the same as are now, or may hereafter be, prescribed for courts of justices of the peace, except as otherwise herein provided; and in all cases there shall be a right of appeal on the part of a defendant adjudged guilty, to the next court of Rowan county having superior general criminal jurisdiction. In all such cases of appeal the mayor, or mayor *pro tempore*, shall require bond from the defendant with such surety as is, in his judgment, sufficient to insure the defendant's appearance at the next succeeding term of the appellate court, and on defendant's failure to furnish such bond the mayor, or mayor *pro tempore*, shall commit such defendant to the common jail of Rowan county. Said mayor's court shall also have jurisdiction to try all actions for the recovery of any penalty imposed by law or this act, or by any ordinance of said city, for any act done within said city of which a justice's court would have jurisdiction. Such penalty shall be sued for and recovered in the name of said City of Salisbury, in the mayor's court or in the superior court of Rowan county having jurisdiction under the general law and this charter, and if incurred by a minor, shall be recovered from and in an action against his parent or guardian, or if he be an apprentice, against his master. From any judgment of the mayor's court for such penalty imposed or allowed to be imposed by this act, or for the violation of any ordinance of said city, either party may appeal to the next term of the superior court of Rowan county, in like manner and under the same rules and regulations as are prescribed for appeals from judgments of justices of the peace; and in case the mayor or mayor *pro tempore*, respectively, as the case may be, shall be disabled by reason of relationship, or otherwise incompetent to hear and dtermine such action, the same may be instituted and prosecuted in any court within said county,which would, but for this section, have jurisdiction thereof, under the same rules and regulations as if instituted and tried in said mayor's court, where applicable. In all cases where judgment may be entered up against any person or persons for fines and penalties, according to the laws and ordinances of said city as for criminal offenses, and the person or persons against whom the same is so adjudged refuse, fail or are unable to pay such judgment, it shall be lawful for the mayor or mayor *pro tempore*, of said city, to order and require such person or persons to work the streets or other public works of said city, under the supervision of the marshal or street overseer thereof, and under such rules and regulations as may be, from time to time, prescribed by the board of aldermen thereof, until at a fair rate of wages, to be prescribed by said board of aldermen, such person or persons shall have worked out the full amount of such judgment and costs of prosecution; or such mayor or mayor *pro tempore*, if he deem best, shall have power

Penalties may be sued for in name of Salisbury.

Penalties against minors recoverable from guardian or parent.

Either party may appeal.

When mayor or mayor pro tempore are incompetent to hear actions.

'sons failing to fines may be rked on eets.

to provide, under such rules and regulations as to him may seem best, for the employment of such person or persons on the public streets, public highways or other public works, or at other labor for individuals or corporations until, at such fair rate of wages, so prescribed by said board of aldermen, such person or persons shall have worked out the full amount of such judgment and costs of prosecution.

nalties and ts shall be paid treasurer.

SEC. 20. All penalties and costs, except the mayor's costs, and fees of witnesses collected for any misdemeanor declared by this act, or for any violation of any ordinance of said city, whether in the court in which the prosecution originated or in the court to which it was carried by appeal, shall belong to said city, and immediately upon collection shall be paid to the treasurer of said city, and all judgments rendered in any court for such penalties shall belong to and be controlled by said city and collected in the same manner in which, by law, such judgments would, but for this section, be collected and enforced. All penalties hereinbefore provided to be recovered in the name of said City of Salisbury, shall belong and, upon collection, be paid to said city, and all judgments for the same shall belong to and be controlled by said city and be collected in the same manner as other judgments for money are collected, and may be docketed in the superior courts of this state in the same manner as is by law provided for the docketing of judgments, and when so docketed shall be and constitute liens in the same manner and to the same extent as other judgments so docketed.

dgments for alties may be keted.

yor may issue cepts to riff of Rowan nty.

SEC. 21. The mayor or mayor *pro tempore* of said city may issue his precepts to the sheriff of said county of Rowan or to any constable or marshal, or to any officer to whom a justice of the peace may direct his precepts.

ord of pre- ts shall be pt.

SEC. 22. The mayor and mayor *pro tempore* respectively of said city shall keep a faithful minute of the precepts issued by him, and of all his judicial proceedings. Precepts issued by said mayor or mayor *pro tempore* shall be executed by the officer or officers to whom they are directed, or any of them, anywhere in the county of Rowan.

yor's office.

SEC. 23. The mayor of said city shall keep his office in some convenient part of said city, designated by the board of aldermen thereof. He shall keep the seal of the corporation and perform such duties as are by this act prescribed and as shall be from time to time by law or by the ordinances of said city prescribed. The salary of the mayor of said city shall be five hundred dollars per annum, payable in monthly installments on the warrant of the clerk of the board of aldermen, drawn

ary of mayor.

on the treasurer of said city and countersigned by the chairman of the finance committee of said board of aldermen.

SEC. 24. The mayor of said city shall preside, when present, at all meetings of the board of aldermen thereof, and in all cases of a tie vote of the aldermen present, upon any question, or in the election of any officer by said board of aldermen, he shall have the right to vote, but shall not be allowed to vote in any other case. Mayor shall provide at meetings of aldermen.

SEC. 25. The aldermen of said city shall form one body, to be known as the board of aldermen, and a majority of them shall constitute a quorum and be competent to perform all the duties prescribed for the board of aldermen, unless otherwise provided. Corporate title of aldermen.

SEC. 26. The board of aldermen shall convene at the mayor's office on the third Monday in May of each year, for the transaction of business, and at such meeting shall designate stated days for its meeting, until the third Monday in May thereafter next ensuing, and such meetings shall be provided for and held at least once a month. Special meetings of the board of aldermen may be held at any other time than that designated for a regular meeting on call of the mayor or of a majority of the aldermen, and of every such meeting, when called by the mayor, all the aldermen then in said city shall be notified, and when called by a majority of the aldermen, such aldermen as are in the city and do not join in the call shall be notified. Time at which aldermen shall meet. Special meetings.

SEC. 27. The board of aldermen, when convened, shall have power to make such ordinances, rules and regulations for the proper government of the said city as they deem necessary, and provide for the proper execution thereof as they may think best. Power of aldermen to make ordinances.

SEC. 28. Among the powers hereby conferred upon the board of aldermen are the following: To provide a sufficient supply of pure water for said city. To provide for the repairing and cleansing the streets and sidewalks of said city, in the manner and to the extent such board may deem best. To establish and regulate a market or markets in said city, and erect or lease and use a suitable market house or market houses therefor. To provide proper and effectual means and regulations to prevent and extinguish fires in said city. To make suitable regulations for the due observance of Sunday in said city, and to provide for the enforcement of the same. To appoint and regulate city watchers. To prevent, suppress and remove nuisances in said city. To regulate the manner in which dogs may be kept in said city. To make proper provisions and take all necessary measures to preserve said city from contagious diseases or infectious diseases and to declare and enforce quarantine and quarantine regulations therein. To appoint all policemen and other officers therefor which they may deem proper, to execute such Powers of aldermen. Water supply. Repairing streets. Market house. Fees. Observance of Sunday. City watchers. Nuisances. Dogs. Contagious diseases. Appointment of policemen.

precepts as the mayor may lawfully issue to them, and to preserve the peace and good order of said city. To establish and maintain one or more public cemeteries of such size as they may deem necessary within or without the corporate limits of said city, and provide for the care and maintenance of the same and the proper regulation, control and prosecution thereof. To make provision and take all proper measures to preserve the peace and order of said city, and to execute all the laws and ordinances thereof. To enact and pass such laws, ordinances and regulations as said board may deem necessary to preserve the health of said city, and to provide for the due enforcement of the same. To determine, when necessary, the boundaries of the streets, lots and alleys of said city, and to establish new streets, lanes and alleys therein, and to make and keep for public inspection, and cause to be made and kept, accurate records of said streets, lots, lanes and alleys and their boundaries. To make provision for licensing and regulating auctioneers and auctions in said city, and provide for the enforcement of the same. To restrain and prohibit and punish gambling in said city. To provide for licensing, regulating or restraining theatrical and other public amusements within said city, and all bills, posters and advertisements thereof, and to enforce all such provisions. To establish and regulate all necessary inspections within said city, whether of buildings or otherwise. To license, regulate and restrain bar-rooms and other places where spirituous liquors are sold within said city. To lay and provide for the collection of all taxes authorized by law to be laid, levied or collected by said city, and enforce the collection of the same. To impose, collect and appropriate fines, penalties and forfeitures for the breach of the ordinances and regulations of said city. To pass all laws, ordinances and regulations necessary or proper to carry into effect the intent and meaning of this act: *Provided*, they are not incompatible with the constitution or laws of this state. To appoint and provide for the pay and prescribe the duties of all such other officers of said city as may, by said board of aldermen, be deemed necessary. To prescribe and regulate and to issue license for omnibuses, hacks, drays and other vehicles used therein for the transportation, for hire, of persons or things. To prescribe and regulate rates and charges of telephone, electric light and waterworks companies, which are operating under a franchise heretofore or which may hereafter be granted by the said town or city.

meteries.

blic peace and ler.

alth of city.

undaries of eets.

ctioneers.

mbling.

eatrical usements.

spections.

r-rooms.

llection of es.

nes and penies.

oviso dinances shall compatible th laws of the te.

cers.

ecial license.

tes and arges, of ephone and ctric light and terworks arges

pointment of rk and treaser.

SEC. 29. That the board of aldermen at its first meeting in May in every year, shall appoint a clerk and a treasurer, which officers shall hold their offices, respectively, for the term of one year from and after appointment, and until their successors, respectively, shall be appointed and qualify, subject, however, to be removed at any time for incompetency, misbehavior, neglect of duty, or other good cause, by said board of aldermen, which alone shall be the judge of such incompetency, misbehavior, neglect of duty, or other cause of removal, and shall appoint others in their stead to fill out their terms, respectively, upon such removal. Before entering upon the duties of their offices, respectively, every one of said officers shall be sworn by the mayor of said city, or other person authorized to administer oaths, to the faithful discharge of their respective duties, and may be required to execute a bond payable to said City of Salisbury in such sum as shall be prescribed by said board of aldermen, with good and sufficient surety or sureties approved by said board of aldermen, for the faithful discharge of their said duties, respectively; and such bond shall be duly probated in the manner by law allowed, and recorded in the office of the clerk of the board of aldermen in a book prepared and kept by such clerk for that purpose. The originals of such bonds shall be deposited with the mayor of said city, as soon as they have been so registered; and a copy from said registry of any such bond, duly certified by said clerk of the board of aldermen under his hand and seal of said city, shall at all times be received as evidence in any court in an action for the enforcement of the penalty thereof or in any other action, or for any other purpose whatsoever. Said board of aldermen shall also, at their first meeting in May in every year, appoint one or more policemen, and all such other officers for said city as to said board of aldermen may seem meet, and such policemen and other officers shall hold their respective offices for such times, not to exceed one year from and after their appointment, and shall receive such compensation, respectively, as shall be prescribed by said board of aldermen, subject, however, to be removed at any time by said board of aldermen at its pleasure, and the said board of aldermen may, from time to time, increase or decrease the number of such policemen and other officers, and appoint other persons to fill any vacancies therein, which, in the opinion of said board of aldermen should be filled; any such appointees to hold their offices upon the same terms and subject to the same powers of said board of aldermen as the persons in whose stead they were so appointed held their offices, respectively. The duties of such policemen or other officers shall be from time to time prescribed and designated by said board of aldermen.

Said officers shall take oath.

Shall execute bond.

Originals of bonds shall be deposited with mayor.

Appointment of policemen.

Compensation of policemen.

Duties of policemen.

SEC. 30. It shall be the duty of the clerk of the board of aldermen to attend the meetings of the board of aldermen, both regular and special, to keep regular and fair minutes of all proceedings of said board of aldermen, to preserve, in an office to be designated by said board of aldermen and where the public may,

Clerk of board shall attend meetings.

at all reasonable hours, inspect the same, all books, papers, and other articles committed to his care by said board of aldermen during his continuance in office, and subject to the control of said board of aldermen, and deliver the same to his successor, and regularly to perform all such other duties as may be, by said board of aldermen, from time to time, prescribed, and he shall receive such compensation as such board of aldermen shall prescribe.

ties of treasr.

Sec. 31. It shall be the duty of the treasurer of said city to receive and safely keep all moneys which shall be paid into his hands as such treasurer for the use of said city, to disburse the funds of said city according to such orders as shall be drawn on him by proper authority, to demand of all persons such moneys or securities as they or any of them may have in their hands belonging to said city which ought to be paid or delivered into the treasury thereof, and to perform all such other duties as may, from time to time, be required of him by law or by said board of aldermen.

asurer shall p record of ipts and dissements.

He shall keep, in a book provided for that purpose, a fair and correct account of all moneys received and disbursed by him and of all securities and other property entrusted to him for safe keeping or otherwise, and at the expiration of his term of office, or the sooner termination thereof, shall deliver to his successor all such moneys, securities and other property belonging to said city then in his hands.

pensation of surer.

He shall receive such compensation as said board of aldermen shall, from time to time, prescribe. All orders drawn on him shall be signed by the mayor of said city, and shall state the purpose for which the money therein called for is applied, and the treasurer shall in his accounts specify such purposes. He shall also state in his accounts the sources respectively from which all moneys received by him are derived, and shall, when required to do so, submit to the mayor or board of aldermen his vouchers for any and all disbursements made by him, and his said accounts in full:

viso.

Provided, that the board of aldermen may provide for the appointment of an auditor and adopt any system for the drawing of orders upon the treasurer and for the paying out of the money of the city as in their judgment will best protect the interests of the city.

ermen may vide for apıtment of an itor.

ɔointment of yor pro tem.

Sec. 32. Said board of aldermen shall, at their first meeting in May in every year, appoint one of their own number to be mayor *pro tempore* of said city, and in case of any vacancy in that office, shall fill the same with some member of their own body.

ies of mayor tem.

It shall be the duty of such mayor *pro tempore* at all times with [within] his term of office, when the mayor of said city shall for any reason be unable to discharge his duties as such mayor, to act as mayor and perform all the duties pertaining to such office during the time when the mayor is so unable to discharge the same. And for that purpose such mayor *pro tempore* shall, during such times, have and exercise all the powers and rights which pertain to said mayor, as well in holding said mayor's court and presiding at the meeting of the said board of aldermen as in all other respects. Such mayor *pro tempore* shall hold his office for the term of one year from and after his appointment, or until the next annual election of mayor *pro tempore* as hereinbefore provided, and until his successor shall be duly appointed and qualified.

Term of office of mayor pro tem.

Salary of aldermen.

Sec. 33. The salary of each alderman of said city shall be twenty-five dollars a year, to be paid when and as said board of aldermen, from time to time shall direct: *Provided*, that two dollars shall be deducted from the salary of each alderman for each regular meeting he shall fail to attend.

Duties of city marshal and tax collector.

Sec. 34. The duties of the city marshal and tax collector shall be those hereinafter provided and such as shall, from time to time, be prescribed by law and said board of aldermen, and he shall receive as compensation for his services in collecting taxes not exceeding five per centum of all taxes collected by him, to be retained by him from such collections when and as often as he shall make a settlement thereof with said board of aldermen.

City marshal subject to be removed.

Sec. 35. The city marshal shall be subject to be removed from office at any time for incompetency, misbehavior, neglect of duty, insubordination or other good cause shown by the board of aldermen, which alone shall be the judges of such incompetency, misbehavior, neglect of duty, insubordination or other cause of removal.

Appointment of public inspector.

Sec. 36. Said board of aldermen may appoint at their first meeting in May in every year, a public inspector, whose duty it shall be to carefully inspect and examine all articles of food offered for sale within said city, and whose salary shall be fixed, from time to time, by said board of aldermen, which shall also fill any vacancy occurring in said office, and such officer shall be subject to be removed at any time by said board of aldermen for cause satisfactory to it. Should such inspector find an article of food offered for sale within said city to be unclean, impure, tainted, diseased, stale, or otherwise unfit for human food, whether such article be vegetable, animal or manufactured, he shall at once notify the person offering it for sale to cease so offering the same, and to refrain from selling it in said city, and to immediately remove said article without said city, and in case he is not immediately obeyed, it shall be his duty to seize all such articles and cause them to be immediately destroyed. Any policeman of said city, when called on by said public inspector to assist him in effecting such seizure and destruction, shall promptly render such assistance and arrest

Duties of public inspector.

Impure food may be condemned.

Policemen may be called in to assist in condemnation of such food.

any person who shall resist him or said public inspector in making such seizure and destruction, or either, and take such persons before the mayor to be dealt with according to law. Said public inspector shall also inspect and examine any cistern, well, spring or other source of water supply within said city, which he shall [have] reason to believe to be impure and unfit for human use, and if upon such inspection or examination he shall not be fully satisfied that the water therein or therefrom is thoroughly pure and wholesome, he shall notify the owner thereof, or the person having charge of the same, to stop the use thereof by himself and others until a thorough analysis thereof has been made, and he shall at once cause an analysis thereof to be made by the state chemist, or other competent person, and if the report of said analysis does not remove from his mind all doubt in regard to the purity of such water, he shall cause the place from which the same was procured, if a cistern, to be thoroughly emptied and cleansed, and if a well or spring, to be filled or by some other means rendered incapable to be used. All expenses incurred in making said inspection and analysis, except for his own services, he shall report to the mayor of said city, and the amount of such expense shall be by said mayor charged to the owner of such cistern, well, spring or other source of water supply, and shall be collected by the city marshal in the same way as taxes are collected.

id inspector all also ex ine wells, terns, etc.

pure water.

cers, etc., aid city shall speculate claims inst city.

Sec. 37. It shall be unlawful for any officer or officers, appointee or appointees, employee or employees, of said city to speculate in or purchase at a discount any claim, paper, or evidence of indebtedness, whether allowed or not allowed or disallowed, of said city, or of the county of Rowan. The provisions of this section shall apply to any person and every person employed in any capacity by said city, and shall hold good throughout the entire period of such employment and for six months after the termination thereof, and any violation of this section shall cause the forfeiture of every such claim, paper and evidence of indebtedness which shall have been so speculated in or purchased at a discount and the payment thereof by said city and by said county.

whom plied.

ces shall be le on official d for breach luty.

Sec. 38. For any breach of his official bond by any officer of said city who is or may be required to give such bond, such officer shall be liable to an action on the same, in the name of said city, by said city, or any person aggrieved by such breach, and each bond may, without assignment, be from time to time put in suit until the whole penalty thereof be recovered.

Sec. 39. No mayor, alderman or other officer, appointee or employee of said city shall become a contractor for work to be done by said city, or subcontractor therefor, or employed or interested therein, directly or indirectly, and any person herein offending shall, by the very act, forfeit his office or employment, and shall be guilty of a misdemeanor, and said board of aldermen may declare any such contract null and void.

No city officer shall become a contractor for city work.

SEC. 40. It shall be unlawful for any person to resist or obstruct an officer of said city in the discharge of his duties as such, by force, threats or otherwise, and any person so offending shall be guilty of a misdemeanor, and shall be fined not less than ten dollars nor more than fifty dollars, or imprisoned not exceeding thirty days.

SEC. 41. No person who is not a duly qualified elector of [said] city shall be eligible to hold office therein, and any duly qualified elector thereof shall be competent to be elected to and hold any office of said city.

Persons eligible to office.

SEC. 42. In order to raise funds for the current expenses of said city, and thereafter for the improvement of the same, and the payment of the interest on its bonded debt, and the creation of a fund to meet the principal of that debt when due, the board of aldermen of said city may at their first meeting in June of every year, lay and provide for the collection of the following taxes:

Aldermen empowered to lay and levy annual tax.

(1) On all real and personal property within the limits of said city, and all other subjects taxable by the general assembly of this state, as specified and valued under the provisions of law, an *ad valorem* tax not exceeding ninety cents on every hundred dollars of such valuation as of the first day of June of every year.

Ad valorem tax.

(2) On all persons residing in said city on the first day of June in every year, subject to poll tax under the laws of this state, a poll tax not exceeding two dollars and seventy cents each.

Poll tax

(3) On every omnibus carrying persons for hire, a license tax not exceeding twenty dollars per annum; and on every hack, carriage, wagon, express wagon, dray or other vehicle transporting persons, freight, baggage or other articles for hire, a license tax not exceeding ten dollars per annum; and on fixing the license tax on the above enumerated vehicles, said board of aldermen shall discriminate between one-horse, two-horse and four-horse vehicles, and between the different kinds of vehicles, as to them shall seem just. Said board of aldermen shall at their first meeting in June in every year, fix the amount of license tax on every kind of such vehicles; and every person intending to use any such vehicle in said city shall, before using the same, pay to the tax collector of said city the amount of the license tax so fixed on such

Omnibuses, etc.

vehicle, and obtain from said tax collector a license stating the kind of such vehicle and the amount of such payment. Any person who shall use any such vehicle without having procured the license therefor as in this section mentioned shall be guilty of a misdemeanor, and on conviction shall be fined not more than fifty dollars or be imprisoned not more than thirty days.

cense shall be tained from x collector.

press, telegaph, telephone, s, waterworks mpanies, etc

cense tax on oss receip's

(4) On every express company, telegraph company, telephone company, gas company, waterworks company, electric light company, power company,street railroad company doing business or having an office in said city, a license tax not exceeding in amount one per centum of the gross receipts by it on its said business in said city, received during the preceding year up to and including the thirty-first of May next before the date of fixing such license tax; and the manager or agent in charge of the business of any such company in said city on the first day of June in every year shall, on that day, or if that day be Sunday or a legal holiday, on the next day thereafter, make to the clerk of the board of aldermen of said city, who shall have power in such case to administer oaths, a written return under oath signed by him of the amount of such gross receipts. Any such manager or agent who shall fail or refuse to make such return on the day whereon the same should be made, as hereinbefore provided, shall be guilty of a misdemeanor and on conviction fined not more than fifty dollars or imprisoned not more than thirty days. Every such company whose manager or agent, as aforesaid, shall fail or refuse to make such return at the time hereinbefore provided therefor, or which shall fail to pay the license tax upon its said business within the time prescribed by the board of aldermen for such payment, shall be guilty of a misdemeanor, and upon conviction shall be fined one thousand dollars. The amount of such license tax, upon the failure of such manager or agent to make such return as hereinbefore provided shall be fixed by said board of aldermen at its next meeting after the day on which such return should be made, as hereinbefore provided, or at some other meeting thereafter in the same month, by determining the amount of such gross receipts as nearly as they can ascertain the same, and of such amount so determined, which, for such purpose shall be taken and deemed to be the amount of such gross receipts, taking one per centum thereof as such license tax.

nager refusing make such urns guilty of isdemeanor.

mpanies failto pay such

nalty.

ctioneers.

(5) Said board of aldermen shall have power to license in said city auctioneers, to prescribe their duties and fix their compensation or rate of charges. Every such auctioneer, before acting as such, shall pay to the tax collector of said city a license

tax, to be prescribed by said board of aldermen, not exceeding fifty dollars and obtain from him the certificate of such appointment and the payment of such tax; and any person who shall act as auctioneer in said city without having paid the tax as aforesaid, or without having obtained such certificate, shall be guilty of a misdemeanor, and on conviction shall be fined not more than fifty dollars, or imprisoned not more than thirty days.

Tax to be prescribed by board.

Person acting as auctioneer without license guilty of a misdemeanor

SEC. 43. The clerk of said board of aldermen shall procure from the proper officer or officers, or other person or persons to whom the tax listers of said county shall be required by law to return the lists taken by them, and as soon as such lists shall have been so returned in each year all said lists which relate to property and polls within said city, and such other papers, records and documents pertaining to matters taxable by said city, as may be or should be in his office or possession, or their offices or possession. From such lists, papers, records and documents so procured, or required to be procured, said clerk of the board of aldermen shall immediately make a full and complete list showing the name of every taxpayer in every ward of said city, and the items of property, personal and real, in every one of such wards upon which he is required to pay taxes, and the respective values of each, according to said lists, and the respective names and ages and colors of the persons resident in said wards severally, who are liable to pay a poll tax in said city, and shall charge to every one of said taxpayers his taxes upon his property in every of said wards, calculated at, the rate of taxation for such property prescribed by said board of aldermen for that year, and shall charge all persons resident within said wards, respectively, who are liable to pay poll tax in said city, with the amount of their respective poll tax as prescribed by said board of aldermen for that year, and also showing the aggregate amount of property according to such valuations, and of taxes and polls in every of said wards, and the full aggregate of the same in said city. Said clerk of the board of aldermen shall submit such list so made by him to said board of aldermen at their next meeting after he shall have so completed the same, and said list, when approved by said board of aldermen, whether as amended or not by it, shall constitute the regular tax list of said city for that year, subject to any and all amendments, corrections, modifications, additions and subtractions which said board of aldermen shall, from time to time, make therein; but said board of aldermen shall have no power to raise or lower the valuation of real estate for tax purposes as fixed in the manner prescribed by law. It shall be the duty of said board of aldermen to see that all subjects of taxation within said city are duly

Clerk of board shall receive tax lists.

Clerk shall make a list of taxpayers.

Clerk shall submit list to board of aldermen.

Aldermen may make alterations in tax list.

entered from time to time, upon said list at their proper places, and that the taxes which should be paid by or upon the same are duly enforced and collected, and to take all proper measures necessary for the due accomplishment of that result.

dermen shall eserve tax list.

Sec. 44. Said board of aldermen shall preserve said list among its records, shall, immediately after its approval of the same, cause to be made a copy of so much and such parts thereof as may be required for the use of the tax collector or in collecting the taxes of said city; said copy shall be delivered to said tax collector on or before the first Monday in September in each year, and he shall receipt for the same. Said clerk of the board of aldermen shall endorse on said copy an order to said tax collector to collect the taxes therein mentioned, and such order shall have the force and effect of a judgment and execution against the real and personal property of the persons charged in said city respectively.

hen copy shall delivered to x collector.

der from clerk tax collector all have force judgment.

hen collection taxes shall be mpleted.

Sec. 45. The tax collector of said city, upon his receipt of said copy of such parts of said tax list shall proceed immediately with the collection of the taxes in such copy mentioned, and of all such as may be from time to time added thereto by said board of aldermen, and shall complete such collection by the first day of December next after such receipt; but said board of aldermen may extend the time for the completion of such collection for such period or periods as it may deem best, not longer than the first day of March next thereafter. Said tax collector shall pay over, at least as often as once a week, to the treasurer of said city all moneys collected by him as taxes, after deducting from each collection the amount of his compensation for making it, as hereinbefore provided; and for every such payment he shall take said treasurer's receipt and exhibit it to said board of aldermen at its next meeting.

ay be extended aldermen.

eekly settle- ents shall be ade by tax llector.

xes levied, ted and col- ted as pro- ded for by neral act.

Sec. 46. All taxes of said city shall be listed, levied, assessed and collected, except as is in this charter otherwise provided, in the same manner and under the same rules and regulations, and subject to the same penalties, as are provided by law or shall hereafter be provided by law for the listing, levying, assessing and collecting state and county taxes in this state.

en for taxes all attach to real property.

Sec. 47. The lien of city taxes levied for all purposes in each year shall attach to all real property which was subject to such taxes on the first day of June annually shall constitute liens and continue until such taxes, with any penalty which shall accrue thereon shall be paid. All personal property in said city subject to taxation shall be liable to be seized and sold for taxes by said tax collector, and the personal property of any deceased person therein shall be liable in the hands of any executor or administrator for any tax due on the same by any testator or intestate;

rsonal property ble to be seized taxes.

and any property, whether real or personal, in said city, conveyed or assigned after the first day of June in any year to any trustee, or trustees, assignee or assignees for the benefit of creditors shall be liable in the hands of such trustee or trustees, assignee or assignees for all taxes levied, laid or assessed upon the same in that year, and may be sold for the payment of such taxes in the same manner as if such conveyance or assignment had not been made.

Fiscal year.

SEC. 48. The fiscal year of said city shall begin with the first day of June in every year.

Poll and ad valorem taxes, when due.

SEC. 49. The poll taxes and *ad valorem* taxes of said city shall become due on the first day of September in every year.

Taxes due and unpaid.

SEC. 50. Whenever any taxes in said city shall be due and unpaid, the tax collector thereof shall proceed to collect the same as follows:

Collector may seize personal property anywhere in Rowan county.

(1) If the person charged have personal property anywhere in the county of Rowan of a value as great as the tax charged against him or against his property, said tax collector shall seize and sell the same as the sheriff is required to sell personal property under execution.

May levy on any lands of delinquent in Rowan county.

(2) If the person charged have not personal property to be found in said county of Rowan of a value as great as the tax chargedagainst him and his property, said tax collector shall levy upon the lands of the delinquent in said county of Rowan or any part of such lands, and, after due advertisement, sell the same for the payment of said taxes. Such advertisement shall be made in some newspaper published in said county of Rowan for at least twenty days immediately preceding such sale, and by posting a notice of such sale at the court-house door in said city at least twenty days before such sale, which shall contain at least a concise description of the real estate to be sold, the name of the person who appears upon the tax list as owner thereof, the amount of taxes for which said sale is to be made and the day and place of such sale. Said tax collector may divide such real estate into as many parts as he may deem convenient, employing, if necessary, a surveyor for that purpose and in such case shall sell as much thereof as shall be required to pay such taxes and all expenses attendant thereon, together with all penalties; and if such real estate shall not be so divided, he shall sell the whole. For every piece of real estate, or part thereof so advertised, said tax collector shall also collect, in the same manner as such taxes, the sum of fifty cents to defray the expenses of such advertisement. All such sales shall be made at the court-house door of said county of Rowan, at public auction to the highest bidder for cash, upon any day of the month or week except Sunday or a legal holiday, and if no person will

Advertisement shall be made.

Sales shall be made at court-house door.

bid enough to pay such taxes, penalties and expenses, in case such real estate is sold without such division, said tax collector shall bid on the behalf of said city the amount of said taxes, penalties and expenses, and if no higher bid shall be made, the same shall be struck off to said city, and if no person will bid amount or amounts in case said land is sold in parcels sufficient in the aggregate to pay such taxes, penalties and expenses, such real estate shall be then immediately sold as a whole, and if no person will bid enough for the whole to pay said taxes, penalties and expenses, said tax collector shall bid for the whole on behalf of said city the amount of said taxes, penalties and expenses, and if no higher bid shall be made, the same shall be struck off to said city; and in all cases where real estate shall be struck off to said city as herein provided, it shall belong to said city in fee-simple, unless redeemed in the manner prescribed by law or this charter. Said tax collector shall immediately thereafter return to the board of aldermen of said city, by filing the same with the clerk of said board, a statement of his proceedings, showing the purchaser or purchasers of such real estate, and the amounts for which each piece or part thereof was sold, which shall be entered by the clerk of said board upon the minute book of said board of aldermen, and if there shall be a surplus after paying said taxes, penalties and expenses, the same shall be paid to the treasurer of said city, subject to the demand of the person entitled to the same.

x collector y bid in property in behalf town.

all belong to y in fee-simple.

llector shall with aldern statement proceedings.

ners of said l estate may eem same hin a year.

Sec. 51. The owner of any real estate or interest therein sold as aforesaid, his heirs, executors, administrators or assigns, may redeem the same within one year after the sale, upon the same terms and conditions and subject to the same provisos and in the same manner as are prescribed by law for the redemption of real estate sold for state and county taxes, except that all the duties, functions and powers provided in such law to be discharged and exercised by the sheriff or tax collector shall be discharged and exercised by the tax collector of said city.

x collector ll execute to rchaser certifie of sale.

Sec. 52. On any such sale of real estate said tax collector shall execute to the purchaser a certificate similar to that required or allowed by law to be executed upon the sale of real estate for state and county taxes, which may be assigned or transferred by the purchaser, whether an individual or said city, as such last-mentioned certificates are allowed by law to be assigned or transferred, and if the real estate sold as aforesaid shall not be redeemed as hereinbefore provided, said tax collector or his successor in office, under the direction of said board of aldermen at any time within one year after the expiration of one year from the date of sale, on request of the holder of such certificate and production of the same, shall execute to the purchaser, his heirs or assigns, a deed in fee-simple for the conveyance of the real estate described in such certificate, and if such certificate shall have been lost, said board of aldermen, on being fully satisfied thereof by due proof, shall direct said tax collector to execute such conveyance, and said tax collector shall so execute the same. Any such deed shall be similar in form to the deed directed by law to be executed to a purchaser of real estate sold for state and county taxes who is entitled to a conveyance of the same, and shall be subject to the same rules, provisions, presumption and conclusions as such last-mentioned deed, and effective to the same extent as such last-mentioned deed: *Provided*, that nothing in this section shall be so construed as to interpret any act or statute, or any part of act or statute of this state directing any conveyance to be executed for real estate sold for the state or county taxes, to mean that the fact stated in such conveyance to be conclusive of the facts stated in said deed or conveyance, so as to preclude rebutting evidence of the facts contained in any such deed or conveyance executed in like manner by the tax collector of the said city.

After one year deed in fee simple shall be executed to purchaser.

Proviso.

Shall not conflict with statute of of this state.

SEC. 53. No such sale of real estate for taxes shall be considered invalid on account of the same having been charged in any other name than that of the rightful owner if said real estate be in other respects sufficiently described to insure its identification.

Such sales shall not be considered invalid when charged in other name.

SEC. 54. In addition to other subjects listed for taxation in said city, the board of aldermen thereof may lay, and cause to be collected, taxes on the following subjects, respectively, the amount of which, when laid, shall be collected by the tax collector of said city immediately, and if the same be not paid on demand, they may be recovered by suit or seizure and sale of the articles on which they are severally imposed or of any other property of the owner in said county of Rowan in the same manner as personal property is sold for taxes as hereinbefore provided:

Special taxes aldermen empowered to levy.

Articles on which tax is imposed may be seized and sold.

(1) On all itinerant merchants or peddlers offering to vend in said city, a privilege tax not exceeding fifty dollars a year in addition to a tax not exceeding one per centum on the amount of their purchases, respectively, and among such itinerant merchants or peddlers shall be included also all itinerant venders of medicines or other articles.

Itinerant merchants.

(2) On every shooting gallery, billiard table, bowling alley or alley of like kind, bowling saloon, bagatelle table, pool table or place of any other game or play, with or without a name, kept for profit, or kept in a house where spirituous, vinous or malt liquor is sold, or in a house used or connected with hotel or restaurant, a privilege tax not exceeding fifty dollars.

Shooting galleries, billiard tables, etc.

tels, restau-ts, etc.

(3) On every hotel, restaurant or eating house, a privilege tax not exceeding fifty dollars. Said board of aldermen shall have the power to classify, into as many classes as to them shall, from time to time, seem best, such hotels, restaurants and eating houses according to the character of the business done by them, and to determine according to the character of such business to which class any hotel, restaurant or eating house properly belongs, and prescribe a different privilege tax for every class, in no case exceeding said sum of fifty dollars a year.

cuses

(4) On every company of circus riders, performers or exhibitors or showmen, by whatsoever name called, who shall exhibit within said city, or within one mile of the corporate limits thereof, a license tax not exceeding one hundred dollars [for] every performance or separate exhibition, and on every side-show connected therewith a license tax not exceeding twenty dollars for every performance or separate exhibition. The tax herein specified shall be paid before performance or exhibition, otherwise it shall be double.

eatrical per-mances.

(5) On every person or company exhibiting within said city or within one mile of the corporate limits thereof, any stage or theatrical plays, sleight-of-hand performance, rope walking, wire walking, or menageries, a tax not exceeding twenty-five dollars for every twelve hours allowed for exhibition. Said tax to be paid before exhibiting, otherwise to be double.

hibitions for ard.

(6) On every exhibition, for reward, of artificial curiosities, except models of useful inventions, within said city, or within one mile of the corporate limits thereof, a license tax not exceeding twenty-five dollars, said tax to be paid before exhibition, otherwise to be double.

ows, peform-ces, etc., for ard.

(7) On every show, performance or exhibition of any kind, and on every concert, for reward, and every strolling musician within said city, or within one mile of the corporate limits thereof, a license tax not exceeding ten dollars, said tax to be paid before exhibition, or to be double.

nerant elers

(8) On each and every of the following subjects and occupations said board of aldermen may, at its discretion, impose an annual privilege tax as follows: On itinerant jewelers or silversmiths, not exceeding fifty dollars; on dentists, itinerant, not exceeding ten dollars; on photographers, not exceeding twenty-five dollars; on dealers in leaf tobacco, not exceeding ten dollars; on hucksters' stands, not exceeding twenty dollars; on itinerant dealers in lightning rods, not exceeding twenty-five dollars; on itinerant venders or agents for sale of any patented article, not exceeding twenty dollars; on banks, banking business or bank agents, not exceeding one hundred dollars; on

nerant ntists. otographers. alers in leaf acco. cksters. ghtning rod alers tented articles. nks.

note-shavers, brokers, money lenders and real estate agents, not exceeding one hundred and fifty dollars; on every tobacco manufacturer of any kind, and every cigar and every cigarette manufacturer, not exceeding one hundred dollars; on every tobacco warehouse, not exceeding fifty dollars; on retail dealers in fresh meats, not exceeding thirty dollars; on boarding houses, not exceeding ten dollars; on ice-cream saloons, not exceeding ten dollars; on dealers in fertilizers and agents for the sale thereof, not exceeding one hundred dollars; on every lumber dealer or dealer in bricks or other building materials, or manufacturers thereof, or agents thereof, not exceeding thirty dollars for every yard, warehouse, office or place of business; on soda fountains, not exceeding ten dollars; on brewers, manufacturing and selling their own products by wholesale, not exceeding fifty dollars; on manufacturers of patent medicines, or medicines of any kind usually called proprietary, not exceeding one hundred dollars; on skating rinks, not exceeding twenty dollars; on dogs, not exceeding two dollars; on dealers in or agents for carriages, buggies, wagons, sewing machines, tobacco, cigars, cigarettes, bicycles, tinware, stoves, ranges, heaters, or cotton yarn not manufactured in said county of Rowan, not exceeding one hundred dollars; on every person, firm or company selling pistols, bowie knives, dirks, slung-shots, brass or metallic knuckles, or other deadly weapons of like character, in addition to all other taxes, a license tax not exceeding five hundred dollars. Said board of aldermen may, at its discretion, impose said annual privilege taxes upon said objects and occupations, respectively, or upon any of them, and may, at its discretion, in so doing, impose different taxes upon different objects or occupations as to which the limit hereinbefore prescribed is the same.

Brokers. Real estate agents. Tobacco manufacturers. Tobacco warehouses. Dealers in fresh meats. Boarding houses. Ice-cream saloons. Dealers in fertilizers. Lumber dealers. Soda fountains. Brewers. Manufacturers of patent medicines. Skating rinks. Dogs. Dealers in buggies, etc.

(9) On every person, company or firm selling spirituous, vinous or malt liquors, a license tax for every place in which such business is or is to be conducted by retail, not exceeding one thousand dollars ($1,000), to be paid annually in advance. Every person desirous of engaging in such business in said city shall apply to said board of aldermen at its first meeting in April in any year, for license to do so, and said board of aldermen may, in its discretion, direct or decline to direct the tax collector of said city to issue such license to any such applicant, or for any place in said city where such business is desired to be conducted. Upon any direction of said board of aldermen so to do, and the payment in advance to him of the license tax therefor, it shall be the duty of said tax collector to issue to the person, company or firm named in said direction a license to conduct, at the place named in such direction, the business in such direction specified for the period of one year, to com-

Retailers of liquors, etc. Persons desirous of engaging in said business shall apply for license.

hen license mmences. mence on the first day of May next after such direction by said board of aldermen. Any person, company or firm having obtained such license, who shall, within the period therein named, at any time fail, neglect or refuse to comply with any rule or regulation therefor, or within such period prescribed by such board of aldermen for the conduct, control or regulation of such business, shall forfeit thereby such license, and upon such forfeiture being declared by said board of aldermen, such person, firm or company shall no longer be entitled to engage in said business within said period or under said license, and shall not be entitled to have refunded to him, them or it, any part of the license tax for such license paid. Retail dealers in beer shall pay a license tax not exceeding fifty dollars. Any person who shall sell, or aid in selling, or offer for sale in said city any spirituous, vinous or malt liquors without having a license therefor, shall be guilty of a misdemeanor for every such act, and upon conviction thereof shall be fined not exceeding fifty dollars or imprisoned not more than thirty days.

rsons failing comply with dinances or les forfeit ense.

etail dealers beer.

rsons selling uors without ense guilty of misdemeanor.

(10) On any other business, trade, occupation, calling or profession engaged in, carried on in whole or in part, in or having an office or place of business in the corporate limits of said city, not otherwise herein taxed or authorized to be taxed, a privilege tax to be fixed by said board of aldermen. On peddlers in produce, a privilege tax not exceeding fifty dollars. On every opera house or theatrical house, not exceeding one hundred dollars. On opticians and oculists, not exceeding fifty dollars: *Provided*, that local physicians, lawyers and dentists are exempted from the provisions of this section and the provisions of any other section of the act of which this act is amendatory, that may, by expressed or implied provisions, authorize the board of aldermen to impose a special tax upon physicians, lawyers or dentists practicing their profession in said city.

n other business t herein entioned.

pticians and ulists. roviso.

(11) On livery-stable keepers, a privilege tax not exceeding twenty-five dollars. On bicycles liveries, not exceeding twenty-five dollars. On boot-blacks, not exceeding ten dollars. On dealers in fish and oysters, not exceeding fifty dollars. On dealers in second-hand clothing, not exceeding two hundred dollars. On keepers of pawn-shops, not exceeding one hundred dollars. On auction houses, not exceeding one hundred dollars. On each bicycle, not exceeding fifty cents. On dealers in fresh meats, not exceeding fifty dollars.

ivery stables. icycle liveries. oot-blacks. ealers in fish. ealers in second-nd clothing. awn shops. uction houses. icycles. ealers in fresh eats.

(12) Said board of aldermen may require and provide for the payment in advance of any license tax or privilege tax in this act authorized, and any person who in such case shall engage in any business, trade, occupation, calling or profession upon or for which in any manner any such tax is allowed to be imposed

ldermen may quire payment advance of ecial taxes.

without having paid such tax, shall be guilty of a misdemeanor, and upon conviction shall be fined not more than fifty dollars or imprisoned not more than thirty days.

Persons liable failing to pay said tax, guilty of misdemeanor.

SEC. 55. On each telephone, telegraph and electric light pole heretofore or hereafter erected in said city, said board of aldermen shall have power to levy a tax not exceeding ($1) one dollar.

Telephone, telegraph and electric light poles.

SEC. 56. Whenever, in the opinion of the board of aldermen of said city, it is advisable to obtain land or right-of-way therein for the purpose of operating a new street therein, or widening or straightening a street therein, or making culverts or waterways for carrying water out of any street therein, and said board of aldermen and the owner or owners of such land or right-of-way can not agree as to the amount of damages consequent thereupon, as well as to the special advantage which may result to the owner or owners thereof by reason of such opening, widening or straightening of the street or making of such culvert or waterway, said board of aldermen may direct the mayor of said city to issue, and he shall thereupon issue his writ under the seal of said city, commanding the chief of police thereof to summon a jury of six freeholders of said city, unconnected by consanguinity or affinity with any of the persons supposed to be affected by said proposed improvements, in which writ the proposed improvement shall be fully described and the persons who are supposed to be affected thereby shall be named. Such chief of police shall, in obedience to said writ, summon a jury of six freeholders as aforesaid, and direct them to assemble at the mayor's office in said city, at a time by such chief of police appointed, not less than twenty nor more than thirty days after the date of such writ. Such chief of police shall also serve notice of time of meeting of the jury upon all the persons who are named in such writ as supposed to be affected by such proposed improvement, at least fifteen days before the date appointed for the meeting of the jury. Such notice shall be in writing and signed by said chief of police and addressed to the person or persons upon whom service thereof is made, and shall state the time appointed for such meeting of the jury, and designate briefly the proposed improvement, and may be issued as a single notice to all persons named in said writ or as a separate notice to every one of them or to any two or more of them. Such notice shall be served upon the person or persons therein named, or his, her or their agent, by reading the same to him, her or them, and if any such person or his, her or their agent can not be found in said city, the mayor of said city shall, upon affidavit thereof made and filed before him by such chief of police, direct such notice to be served by posting a copy of

Land necessary for new streets.

Disagreement as to price.

Assessors appointed.

Chief of police shall serve notice of time of meeting of assessors.

Notice shall be served.

tice may be sted.

the same at the court-house door in said county of Rowan, for at least fifteen days immediately preceding the time appointed for the meeting of such jury, and upon such direction of the mayor, it shall be the duty of such chief of police to so post the same, and such posting shall, upon the expiration of the time in such order designated, be a sufficient service of such notice and the party shall then be duly notified of such proceedings. Such chief of police shall duly return such writ and all such notices with his return thereon in writing endorsed, together with any such order of the mayor, to said board of aldermen at its next meeting after the time appointed for the meeting of the jury aforesaid. At the time appointed for the meeting of the jury such chief of police, or in case of his inability to do so, another chief of police or deputy chief of police of said city, shall fill any vacancy which has occurred from any cause in the number of persons theretofore summoned as such jury with other competent jurors, and shall cause the jury as then constituted, to assemble at the office of the mayor of said city, when every one of them shall be sworn by such mayor or other competent person to faithfully, truly and impartially assess the damages, if any, which in his judgment will be done to the property of every person named in the writ, and will also assess any special benefit, advantage or enhanced value which will be caused to the property of any person named in the writ. Immediately after the jury shall have been so sworn they shall proceed, accompanied by such chief of police or deputy chief of police, to view the land of every person named in the writ, and shall assess the damages, if any, to every one of the premises which they have viewed, and the special benefit, advantage or enhanced value, if any, which will accrue by reason of said proposed improvement to every one of the premises which they have viewed. Said jury shall forthwith return to said board of aldermen, by filing it with the clerk thereof, a statement in writing, signed by every one of them, or a majority of them in case they can not agree, setting forth distinctly a full itemized report of their proceedings, and stating separately the amounts of damages or special benefits, or both, as the case may be, which they have assessed to every one of the premises so viewed by them. The chief of police in charge of said jury shall keep them together until they shall have agreed on all matters submitted to them as aforesaid, and have made and signed their report as aforesaid, or in case of their inability to so agree, or twenty-four hours from the time of their return from reviewing said premises, to said office of the mayor, to which they shall so return in every case immediately for deliberation, and until they have

ry shall be orn. all assess mages.

ry shall file ort with ermen.

signed a report as hereinafter specified, upon any disagreement, if such jury shall be evenly divided so that they are unable to agree on their report, or any part thereof, they shall make and sign a report stating that fact and setting forth such items as a majority of them have agreed upon, if any such there be, and the names of the persons as owners and the particular premises in regard to the damage, special benefit or enhanced value of which they are evenly divided, or in regard to which a majority of them can not agree; which report shall be filed in the same manner as the report hereinbefore provided for. On receipt of any such report showing any disagreement of the jury, said board of aldermen shall, at its next meeting after the filing of such report, direct the mayor of said city to issue, and he shall thereupon issue under the seal of said city, his order to chief of police of said city to at once summon a new jury, qualified for such duty as hereinbefore specified, and of the same number as hereinbefore directed, to be composed of different persons from those who constituted the jury so disagreeing, and such new jury shall proceed immediately, after being duly sworn, as aforesaid, to take into consideration all parts of the report of the former jury, on which that jury was not able to agree, and to view the premises in regard to which such disagreements were had, in the manner hereinbefore directed, and shall make their report in the same manner as hereinbefore provided. Such course shall continue from time to time, until all the matters in such original writ directed to be decided shall have been determined. At the first meeting of said board of aldermen after a complete report or reports upon the matter in said writ ordered to be directed shall have been filed as aforesaid, said board of aldermen shall consider and pass upon such reports. If said board of aldermen shall determine that any item of damages so assessed is excessive, it may reject such report or reports and discontinue the proposed improvement, and in case of such discontinuance, no other proceeding shall within twelve months thereafter be commenced for a similar purpose in relation to any of the premises affected thereby or any part of the same without the written consent of the owner thereof. It shall be competent for said board of aldermen, in passing upon any such report or reports, to decrease or remit any item or items of special benefit, advantage or enhanced value therein contained, if it think proper so to do. If said board of aldermen shall think proper, it shall order such report or reports, or such report or reports so modified by it as to special benefit or advantages or enhanced value, approved, and the lands condemned in said proceedings shall vest in said city, so long as they may be used respectively for the purpose

Disagreement of jury.

In case of disagreement new jury shall be summoned.

Aldermen may reject report.

Aldermen may order report modified.

Lands condemned shall vest in the city.

of said improvement, so soon as the amount of damages assessed to them respectively, decreased by the amount of special benefit, advantage and enhanced value so assessed against them respectively, shall have been paid as [or] tendered to the owner or owners of such premises respectively or deposited as hereinbefore provided. In case of an appeal on any item as hereinafter provided, such damages on the premises as to which such appeal is taken, decreased by the amount of special benefits, advantage and enhanced value assessed against the same, shall be deposited with the clerk of the superior court of said county of Rowan, to be disposed of as so assessed, or as upon such appeal adjudged, subject to be reduced by any special benefits, advantages and enhanced value against such premises, assessed as aforesaid, or on such appeal adjudged. Any special benefit, advantage or enhanced value so assessed against any premises, or on appeal adjudged against the same, unless paid or set off by damages assessed thereon, or on appeal adjudged on the same shall, upon such approval of the board of aldermen, in case no appeal is taken upon such assessments of special benefits, advantage or enhanced value or damages, or upon final judgment in case of any such appeal, become and be a lien in favor of said city on said premises on which it has been so assessed or adjudged, as of the time when the board of aldermen passed upon the report regarding the same when said approval was had or appeal taken, and shall be paid to said city in equal installments, one, two and three years respectively, after the completion of such improvement, or in case of appeal and completion of such improvement before final judgment thereon, after such final judgment, and if any such installments shall remain unpaid for thirty days after its maturity all such installments then unpaid shall become due, and the premises so assessed or charged shall be sold for the payment of the same and the expenses of such sale and costs by the tax collector of said city, under the same rules, regulations, restrictions, rights of redemption, provisions and effects as are prescribed in this charter for sale of real estate for unpaid taxes. Any owner of premises mentioned in any such report who is dissatisfied with the amount of damages assessed therein, as done to said premises, or with any amount of special benefits, advantage or enhanced value therein assessed against the same, or said board of aldermen, if dissatisfied with any item in said report, any [may] appeal, on any item with which he, she or they are so dissatisfied, from such report thereon or the action of the board of aldermen on such report, to the next term of the superior court of said county of Rowan, by serving upon the adverse party a written notice of such appeal within ten days after said

case of appeal.

ns in favor of y.

tallments due thirty days.

ner of prop y or aldermen y appeal.

board of aldermen shall have so passed upon such report. On any such appeal, the appellate court shall have power to increase, affirm or diminish the amount of the item appealed on, but not to adjudicate the necessity of the improvement, and such appeal shall in no wise hinder or delay the board of aldermen in making or carrying out the proposed improvement, but it shall be lawful for it to enter upon and use the property so condemned as and for such purpose at any time after the expiration of two days from the date when the amount of damages assessed by the jury, decreased by special benefits, advantage and enhanced value, as aforesaid, shall have been paid or tendered or in case of appeal deposited as aforesaid.

Appellate court shall have power to increase or diminish assessment.

SEC. 57. Whenever any land, real estate, water, water-course or right-of-way, whether or not within the limits of said city, shall, in the opinion of said board of aldermen, be required for the purpose of erecting, making or establishing reservoirs, dams or ponds, tanks or other receptacles of water, or for laying conduit, main or supply pipes, or for obtaining a supply of water, or the erection or construction of houses, stations or machinery to be used in so doing, for the use of said city or its inhabitants, or for any other purpose connected with the successful operation of waterworks, in or for said city, and the owner or owners of such property and said board of aldermen can not agree as to price to be paid therefor, the same may be condemned in the manner prescribed in this charter for the condemnation of land for streets, except only that when the property so condemned lies without the limits of said city, the jury shall be composed, one-half of competent jurors from within said city and the other half of competent jurors of said county of Rowan, from without said city. For the purpose of successfully establishing, constructing and operating the waterworks hereby contemplated, said board of aldermen shall have full power to extend such waterworks, or any branch or branches thereof beyond the limits of said city, in any direction or directions which to it may seem advisable, and to exercise all rights and privileges in the establishment, construction, operation, repair and control of such waterworks, and any and all branches thereof, beyond the limits of said city, as they now are or hereafter may be empowered to exercise within such limits. In case of the discontinuance of the use of any property actually condemned for any of the purposes in this, or the preceding section allowed, and its reverting to its original owners by reason thereof, said city shall have the right to move therefrom any property, structure, machinery or improvement by it or under its authority erected, put or placed thereon.

Land, water-courses, etc., not in corporate limits, required for use of town, may be condemned.

Of whom jury shall be composed when land is out of corporate limits.

In case of discontinuance of use of land, city empowered to remove structures, etc., from said land.

tablishment of eets.

SEC. 58. Said board of aldermen may establish the width and ascertain the location of the streets, alleys and sidewalks of said city already established and may reduce the width thereof, or discontinue any of them. It may also establish, acquire, improve and control parks or other pleasure grounds for the use of said city, and may pass ordinances and regulations for the proper protection, maintenance, management and control of the same. It may also protect and control the shade trees already growing or hereafter planted on the streets, public squares, public grounds, public alleys and sidewalks of or within said city, and may remove any such trees from time to time, or plant others on such streets, public squares, public grounds, public alleys and sidewalks as to it may seem meet. Said board of aldermen may also permit the erection of telegraph poles, telephone poles, electric light poles, street car poles, and other poles upon the streets, public squares, public grounds, public alleys and sidewalks of said city, or prohibit or prevent such erection of the same, and may control and regulate all such poles as shall have been or hereafter may be so erected, and the use of the same at any and all times, and may remove or cause to be removed the same, or any of them at any time or times, and in such manner and upon such notice as to it may seem proper. It shall also have power to regulate, control, license, prohibit and remove all structures and things, of whatsoever name or character erected, constructed, put or placed on, above or under the streets, public squares, public grounds, public alleys and sidewalks of said city.

y control rks.

ade trees.

y remove es.

y permit the ction of poles.

vileges, char-, etc., may be dified by ermen.

SEC. 59. All privileges and franchises and charters, whatsoever, granted by the board of aldermen of said city, and all ordinances thereof conferring any such privileges, franchises or charters, may be altered, amended, modified, repealed or revoked by said board of aldermen from time to time, anything in such privileges, franchises, charters or ordinances contained to the contrary notwithstanding.

ditions upon ich street way can be structed.

SEC. 60. Any street railroad which has or hereafter may construct its lines of road or part thereof over any of the streets of said city, shall maintain such road or part thereof, or construct the same only upon the following conditions: It shall use only such rails and other material as the board of aldermen may designate; it shall properly grade, complete and pave the street between its rails in such manner as said board of aldermen may direct; it shall keep such street between said rails in good condition and repair, and in such condition and repair as said board of aldermen may from time to time order, so long as it shall use the same; if it shall fail to comply with any provision of this section, or to keep any such street in condition and repair as aforesaid, said board of alder-

ls.

ding of ets.
ets between s.

men may cause anything to be done which said railroad has so failed to do, and the costs thereof shall be charged against such railroad and constituted a lien from the commencement of the work paramount to every other lien upon the charter and franchises of such railroad and upon all the property of whatever kind of such railroad in said county of Rowan and such property may be sold for the payment thereof in the manner herein prescribed for the sale of property for taxes, and any such failure on the part of said railroad shall operate as a forfeiture of its right to use such streets, or any of them, or any part of them as such board of aldermen may determine.

Aldermen may cause such things to be done as railway may fail to do and tax them with costs.

Property may be sold for payment of costs.

SEC. 61. Whenever any street in said city shall have been graded, guttered and curbed in whole or in part, including the sidewalks, in [it] shall be incumbent on the owner or owners of the land along said street or part thereof so improved, to pave the sidewalk on their own sides respectively, the full width across their respective fronts, with such materials and in such manner as the board of aldermen of said city shall direct. When such land corners on two or more streets without such sidewalks, the owner or owners thereof shall pave the half of the sidewalks on such streets along his fronts which the board of aldermen may direct, at his own cost, and said city shall pave the other half thereof at its cost. Whenever any street shall have been graded, guttered and curbed, the board of aldermen of said city shall, through its clerk, notify the owner or owners of the lands fronting or cornering thereon, to at once pave the sidewalks thereof as hereinbefore provided; and should [the] owner or owners fail for fifteen days after such notice to comply therewith, said board of aldermen, unless it shall extend the time thereof, shall cause said sidewalk to be so built and charge the cost thereof against such lots respectively, and cause the same to be entered by its clerk in a book to be kept by him for that purpose; and the said clerk shall place in the hands of the tax collector of said city, immediately, copies of such charges, and said tax collector shall forthwith proceed to collect the same and account therefor in the same manner as taxes of said city. The amount of such charges shall be, and constitute from the commencement of the work for which they are charged, liens on the respective lots upon which they are so charged, and if any of them is not paid on demand, so much of the lot upon which it is charged as may be sufficient to pay the same, with interest and costs, for the whole of such lot, shall be advertised and sold by the tax collector of said city for the payment of the same under the same rules and regulations, rights of redemption, excepting and in the same manner as are prescribed in this act for the sale of real estate for unpaid taxes; but said board of

Owners of property may be required to pave sidewalks.

When owners fail for fifteen days to comply with order.

Tax collector shall collect charges.

aldermen may, in its discretion, divide any such charge in such manner that the same may be paid in three equal annual installments from and after the commencement of such work, with interest thereon at six per centum per annum from the date of such commencement.

dermen may ild system of terworks, werage, etc.

SEC. 62. Said board of aldermen may from time to time, lay, build and construct in said city such system or systems of waterworks, water pipes, sewerage and sewer pipes, and extensions of the same, as to it may seem advisable, or cause the same to be so laid, built and constructed, and shall keep the same in proper condition and repair, with proper connections, and make all necessary provisions for so doing, and shall control and regulate such system and every part thereof, and may require the owner or owners of any improved lot in said city, on any public street or alley where such water and sewer pipes have been laid, or are conveniently accessible, or on any line of pipes, to connect such lot with such sewer and water pipes in the manner and at the places designated by said board of aldermen upon like notice, terms and conditions as are hereinbefore provided for paving sidewalks, and upon failure of the owner or owners to so connect the same within the time in such notice required, said board of aldermen may enter upon such lot and make such connections and charge the costs thereof against said lot in the same manner as in [is] hereinbefore provided in the case of sidewalks, and such costs so charged shall be collected and shall constitute a lien upon such lot in the same manner and to be enforced in the same manner and with like power and privileges as is hereinbefore provided in regard to sidewalks.

ners of prop y may be uired to nect with verage.

nd within or hout limits essary for erage pur- es may be demned.

SEC. 63. When any land or right-of-way within or without the limits of said city shall in the opinion of the board of aldermen thereof be required for the purpose of laying sewer pipes or making manholes, or for any other purpose connected with the successful operation of such sewer system or systems, and the owners of such property and said board of aldermen can not agree as to the damage by reason thereof, the same shall be condemned and damages assessed therefor in the manner hereinbefore prescribed for the condemnation of land for waterworks or purposes connected therewith. For the purpose of succesfully constructing and operating such sewerage system or systems said board of aldermen shall have power to extend the same and any branch or branches thereof beyond the limits of said city, in any direction or directions which it may think proper, and to exercise all rights and privileges in the establishment, construction, operation, repair and control of such sewer system or systems and any and all branches thereof, whether within or without the limits of said city, as to it shall seem proper.

w valued.

Sec. 64. Said board of aldermen may take such measures as it may deem effectual to prevent the entrance into said city, or spread therein of any and all contagious, infectious or other diseases of whatever nature, and for that purpose may establish, maintain, enact, regulate, conduct and enforce all quarantine and other rules, regulations and requirements, which in its opinion may be necessary for the preservation of the health of said city and the protection thereof from all manner of sickness or disease whatsoever, with all rights of entry upon property, and all other rights of every character necessary thereof.

Entrance of contagious diseases.

Sec. 65. The board of aldermen of the City of Salisbury, at their first regular meeting in June, in the year eighteen hundred and ninety-nine, shall elect a regular pracicing physician for the term of four years, which said regular practicing physician, together with the mayor, the chairman of the finance committee of the board of aldermen, and the chairman of the board of county commissioners of Rowan county, shall be and constitute the board of health of the City of Salisbury: *Provided*, that the board of aldermen of the city shall have power to fill any vacancy that may occur in said board of health by death, removal, resignation or other cause.

Board of health of Salisbury.

Proviso.

Aldermen empowered to fill vacancies occurring in said board.

Sec. 66. That the board of health shall have general charge and supervision of the public health of said city, shall make such sanitary investigations and institute such inquiries as in its judgment may be necessary to ascertain the condition of the general health of the inhabitants of the said city; shall investigate the causes of all the diseases dangerous to the public health, whether epidemic or otherwise; shall ascertain as far as possible, the causes of mortality, the effects of location, employments, vocations and conditions upon public health; shall make inspection of the sanitary conditions of all public buildings of said city, including school buildings, both public and private, at least twice a year, at intervals of not over six months, and oftener, if in the judgment of the said board of health it shall be necessary: *Provided*, that the said board shall make a careful inspection of the sanitary conditions of the city prison at least once in each and every month. The said board of health shall report to the said board of aldermen of said city, the result of all investigations made by it, at least once every six months, and oftener, if it shall be deemed necessary. Said report shall be accompanied with suggestions and recommendations to the proper authorities, as may seem advisable. Said board of health shall have general supervision and control of all matters of sanitation affecting the health of said city, including the healthfulness of the water supply, milk and other dairy supplies, and all other articles of food and drink, drugs and druggists' supplies; the

Duties and powers of board of health.

Shall make inspection of sanitary conditions.

Proviso.

Said board shall make annual inspection of city prison.

Report of board to aldermen.

drainage of all lots and buildings and houses of every kind and description, whether used for residence or business purposes. Said board of health shall have authority, and power is hereby expressly given it, to declare nuisances of every character whatsoever, and abate the same, so far as in its judgment may be necessary for the convenience of the public health; shall enforce the making of accurate reports and the keeping of full and complete records of all infectious and contagious diseases, whether epidemic or of other character, and of births and deaths, and permits of burial. Said board to prescribe, regulate and determine the plumbing, ventilation and drainage of all buildings, public and private, and the connection of said sewers with outside sewers; shall prepare and prescribe a system of connections and submit the same to a joint board to be composed of the board of aldermen and the board of health of said city, and upon the adoptions of said system by said joint board, each individual member having one vote, there shall be appointed by the said joint board an expert sanitary inspector, who shall examine all plumbing and connections, and see that the law governing the same shall be fully complied with; and any person refusing to comply with such law after five days' notice so to do, shall upon conviction, be fined five dollars for each day he so refuses to comply, each day to constitute a separate offense; and said board of health may cause anything to be done which the owner of said premises has so failed to do, and the expenses thereof shall constitute a lien on said premises from the time of performing such work, paramount to all other liens except taxes and assessments, and be collected in the same manner as the liens for constructing sidewalks in said city. Said expert inspector, when so ordered by the board of health, shall have authority, and power is hereby given him, to condemn, close up and prevent the occupation of and summarily eject all persons from any and all buildings or rooms therein which are not properly and sufficiently ventilated, and which are liable to be unhealthy on account of the dampness or exclusion of light, or which from any cause whatsoever are made unsuitable for habitation or dangerous to the health of the occupants thereof.

id board shall clare nuisances.

pointment of pert sanitary pector.

Sec. 67. That all employees and officers connected with the sanitary department of the city shall be elected by said board of health; the number of employees and officers, the salary of each, and all matters pertaining to said sanitary department and necessary for its successful operation shall be determined and controlled by the said board of health: *Provided*, that the annual expenditure of the said board of health for all purposes shall not exceed the total amount annually apportioned by the board of aldermen to the sanitary department of said city.

ployees and cers con ted with itary depart- nt elected by d board.

viso.

penditures ll not exceed ount appor- oed.

SEC. 68. That the said board of health shall have the authority to select the place or places to which the garbage of the city shall be removed and the manner of its disposition. It shall have authority to make contracts or procure means for the removal of said garbage. It shall also have supervision and control of all the property of said city in the sanitary department. Garbage.

SEC. 69. That the sanitary inspector, and such assistance [assistants] as shall be provided and elected by said board of health, and shall be and are hereby constituted special policemen of the City of Salisbury, with such power and authority as may be necessary to execute and enforce all laws and ordinances relating to governing the said sanitary department of said city. They shall wear such badges, indicative of their authority, as may be prescribed by said board of health. Such inspectors and assistants shall hold their offices for such term or terms as may be prescribed by said board of health, not to exceed two years from the date of their election, subject, however, to the removal at any time by said board of health. Sanitary inspectors shall be appointed by said board. Term of office.

SEC. 70. Said board of health shall have authority, and power is hereby expressly given it to require and compel the abatement and prevention of any and all sanitary nuisances in the City of Salisbury, and shall specify a reasonable time within which its orders in reference thereto shall be complied with; and in the event that the owner, agent or occupant of the premises or in connection with which any nuisance shall be committed or be about to be committed, shall refuse, fail or neglect to comply with any order of said board of health to remove, abate, prevent or discontinue the same within the time in such order required, he or she shall be guilty of a misdemeanor, and for each offense, upon conviction, shall be fined not more than fifty dollars or imprisoned not more than thirty days; and the said board of health may, at any time, proceed to remove, abate, prevent or discontinue such nuisances, and the cost of so doing shall be charged upon such premises and constitute a lien thereon paramount to all liens, except taxes or assessments of said city, from the time of so doing, and shall be collected and enforced in the same manner in all respects as liens for the expense of constructing sidewalks in said city. Abatement and prevention of nuisances.

SEC. 71. That the said board of health shall have general oversight and care of all sources of water supply to the said city, and to the individual citizens thereof, whether by public or private pipes, wells or springs; and shall, from time to time, as it may deem necessary and expedient, cause examinations of said water to be made for the purpose of ascertaining whether the same are adapted for use or in a condition likely to affect injuriously the health of those using the same, and for the purposes aforesaid, it Board of health shall have general supervision of water supply.

ay employ pert assistance

may employ such expert assistance as it may deem necessary. Said board of health shall have authority, and power is hereby expressly given it to condemn, and, as far as may be practicable, destroy all such sources of water supply to the citizens of said city, as it may deem necessary for the protection of the health of said city, or the individual citizens thereof; and any person or prsons using any water from any source condemned by the said board of health shall, on conviction, be fined five dollars for each and every offense.

SEC. 72. That the said board of health shall, from time to time, recommend to the board of aldermen of said city the passage of such ordinances as may be necessary for the proper enforcement of the provisions of this act. The clerk of the board of aldermen shall be *ex officio* clerk of the board of health, and shall perform for said board similar duties to those required of him as clerk of the board of aldermen.

ard may uire and npel abatement of isances

SEC. 73. Said board of aldermen may require and compel the abatement of all nuisances in said city, at the expense of the person causing the same, or the owner or tenant of the land whereon any such nuisance shall be, or may itself abate the same, or cause the abatement thereof; it may also prevent any such nuisance; it may also prohibit, or license and regulate the establishment, within said city, of any slaughter house, or house for the storage of any explosive, unhealthy, dangerous or noxious substances in any quantities whatever in said city, or within one hundred yards of its corporate limits, or the exercise therein of any dangerous, noxious, offensive or unhealthy trade, business or employment. If the owner, agent, tenant or occupant of any premises in said city or in connection with which any nuisance shall be committed or about to be committed, shall refuse, fail or neglect to comply with any order of said board of aldermen to remove, abate, prevent or discontinue the same within the time in such order required, he or she shall be guilty of a misdemeanor, and for each offense, upon conviction, be fined not more than fifty dollars, or imprisoned not more than thirty days; and said board of aldermen may at any time proceed to remove, abate, prevent or discontinue or cause to be discontinued such nuisance, and the costs of so doing shall be charged upon such premises and constitute a lien thereon paramount to all liens except taxes or assessments, of said city, from the time of so doing, and shall be collected and enforced in the same manner in all respects as liens for the expense of constructing sidewalks, as hereinbefore provided.

y prohibit ughter houses thin the city.

dermen empowered to prevent horses, dogs, ., running at ge.

SEC. 74. Said board of aldermen shall have power to prevent dogs, horses, cattle, hogs and other brutes from running at large in said city, either in day time or at night.

SEC. 75. Said board of aldermen shall have power to regulate, control and protect in such manner and to such extent as to it may seem proper, the streets, alleys, sidewalks, public square, parks, city hall, fire department, markets, voting places, cemeteries and other property of said city, whether real or personal, within the limits thereof or beyond such limits, and may pass and enforce all ordinances, rules and regulations therefor, from time to time, which it may deem proper.

Protection of streets, cemeteries, etc.

SEC. 76. Said board of aldermen may establish, regulate and control markets in said city, and for that purpose may acquire, purchase and hold in fee simple and lease real estate in said city, and erect, construct and maintain thereon suitable buildings for marketing purposes, and may make, pass, provide and enforce ordinances, rules and regulations as to it may seem proper for the government and management of any such market house or market houses; may prescribe at what times and places in said city marketable things may be sold, and in what manner, whether by weight or measure, may be sold in said city grain, meal, wood, coal, fuel, flour, hay, straw, shucks, and all marketable articles; may erect scales for the purpose of weighing the same, appoint a weighmaster, fix his fees and direct what shall be required to be weighed on such scales, and by whom said fees shall be paid; and may appoint a keeper or keepers of such market or markets and prescribe his or their duties, powers, authority, fees and compensation. And it shall be lawful for said board of aldermen to impose taxes on wagons and carts or other vehicles, or any person selling farm products, garden truck, fish, oysters, meat, vegetables, chickens or other things on the public streets of said city; and it may regulate, control, prohibit, prevent and punish such sales at its discretion.

Control and regulation of markets.

May erect scales.

SEC. 77. Said board of aldermen may establish fire limits in said city within which it shall be unlawful for any person or persons to erect, construct or repair any building of wood or other material inflammable or peculiarly subject to fire; and it shall be the duty of the said board of aldermen to notify the owner or owners of any partially consumed roofless building located within the fire limits to remove the same, and upon failure of said owner or owners to tear down and remove said partially destroyed or roofless building within sixty days, the mayor of said city shall have the same torn down and removed at the expense of the owner. Said expense will be a lien upon the lot from which said building was removed, and the same shall be collected by the city marshal in the same manner as is herein provided for the collection of taxes.

Establishment of fire limits.

May notify persons to remove partially consumed buildings.

SEC. 78. Said board of aldermen may establish, construct, maintain, regulate and control in said city all public buildings

May hold land in fee simple.

necessary or proper for the best interest or good government or conduct of the affairs of said city; and for that purpose may purchase, acquire and hold in fee simple, any lot or lots or other real estate whatsoever, or in its discretion may from time to time, lease such buildings, lots and real estate.

ay prohibit terment in city.

Sec. 79. Said board of aldermen may prohibit interment in said city or at any place or places therein, and may cause to be kept and returned bills of mortality and births therein, under such rules and regulations as to it may seem proper.

lls of mortality.

anagement d equipment of e companies

Sec. 80. Said board of aldermen may provide for the establishment, organization, equipment, management, regulation, government and control of all fire companies of any kind or kinds in said city, and may purchase and maintain all necessary buildings, outfits, animals, wagons, tools, implements, machinery and other articles or things of any kind or kinds for the efficient maintenance, control and operation of the same. In all cases of a fire or conflagration in said city, a majority of the members of said board of aldermen who may be present shall, if they deem it necessary in order to arrest the progress of such fire or conflagration, cause any house or structure to be blown up or pulled down or destroyed or removed, in whole or in part, under their supervision, and none of them shall be responsible to any one therefor when any such act is so caused to be done in good faith.

ay order houses stroyed to pre- nt spread of nflagration.

bts incurred said town all not be sub- ct to be levied on.

Sec. 81. All debts and liabilities of said city heretofore or hereafter contracted or incurred shall be paid and discharged alone by taxation upon subjects properly taxable by it to the extent allowed by law, and no such debt or liability shall be subject to be levied upon or collected by execution against said city or any property, real or personal, held by it, and no execution therefor shall issue against said city on any judgment obtained thereon.

ldermen shall blish annual atement of ances of city.

Sec. 82. Said board of aldermen shall cause to be made out and published in some newspaper in some city at end of every calendar year, an itemized statement of the receipts and disbursements of said city for the year immediately preceding, and the amount of money then in the hands of its treasurer. The mayor of said city shall prepare and submit to said board of aldermen, at its last meeting in April of every year, a condensed statement of all receipts and disbursements, and the general business of said city for the year immediately preceding the submission of such reports respectively.

ty shall not in y event pay sts on appeal defendant.

Sec. 83. In no case where a defendant in any criminal prosecution shall have appealed from the judgment of the mayor of said city, shall said city be adjudged in such appellate court to pay the costs of such prosecution or any part thereof, whether upon such appeal such defendant shall be convicted or acquitted, or such judgment appealed from, reversed or affirmed.

Notices provided for in this act, how served.

Sec. 84. All notices provided in this act to be given or served by said city, or any of its officers or employees, shall, unless otherwise herein provided, be served by a policeman of said city, by the delivery of a copy thereof to the person or persons directed, required or allowed to be served, if such person or persons can be found in said county of Rowan; and if any such person can not be found in said county such policeman shall make affidavit thereof before the mayor of said city, who shall thereupon direct such service to be made of such notice by posting a copy thereof at the court-house door in said city for such length of time as such notice shall be required to be given, if any, and if no such time be required, then for a single time; and such policemen shall so post such copy, and such posting shall be deemed a sufficient service of such notice in such case.

When person can not be found service may be posted.

Aldermen may borrow money not exceeding $10,000.

Sec. 85. Said board of aldermen may borrow in any fiscal year, a sum or sums of money not exceeding in the aggregate ten thousand dollars outstanding at any one time, in such amount as the same may be needed for the necessary expenses of said city at a rate of interest not exceeding six per centum, and execute therefor the note or notes of said city, sealed with the seal of said city, and to be in such form as the board of aldermen may from time to time, prescribe; but such aggregate sum shall may, from time to time, prescribe; but such aggregate sum shall not, in any such fiscal year, exceed the aggregate taxation of said city for that year on general subjects of taxation therein, and all such loans made in any fiscal year shall be paid out of the general taxes for that year, and no such loan shall be made to come due at a date later than the expiration of the fiscal year in which it is made, and no sum whatsoever shall be borrowed under the provisions of this section until all preceding loans made thereunder in any previous fiscal year or years shall have been paid in full of principal and interest.

Arrests may be made by policemen anywhere in Rowan county.

Sec. 86. Arrests may be made by any policeman of said city, anywhere in said county of Rowan, whenever the officer making such arrest has in his hands a warrant against the person arrested, issued by the mayor of said city or a justice of the peace of said county of Rowan or other competent authority, or whenever any misdemeanor or violation of any ordinance of said city has been committed in his presence, or whenever a misdemeanor or violation of any ordinance of said city has been committed and he has reasonable cause to believe that the person so arrested is guilty of such offense and may make his escape before a warrant can be obtained, or whenever a warrant has been issued against the person so arrested and is outstanding unexecuted in the hands of any policeman of said city, or in the hands of the sheriff or any deputy sheriff or constable of said Rowan county.

making rests policemen all have powers sheriff.

SEC. 87. In making arrests the policemen of said city shall have all the powers of a sheriff or constable of said county of Rowan, as well as all the powers by this act conferred upon them.

licemen may mmon standers to sist them in aking arrest.

SEC. 88. Whenever any arrest is made by an officer of said city he may summon any of the bystanders or other persons having information in regard to the matter for which such arrest is made, as witnesses to attend as such at the hearing of the charge upon which such arrest is made, and any such summons shall be effectual and binding in the same manner as if made by subpœna, for such person so summoned, duly issued and served in such cases.

urt may post ne hearing of ses.

SEC. 89. When any arrest shall have been made, as in this charter provided, the person so arrested shall be carried by the officer making such arrest or some other officer of said city, before said mayor's court for trial, and such court may, for cause satisfactory to it, postpone the hearing of any such case to such time as it may think proper. In case of any continuance in the mayor's court, such person shall, until the time set for the hearing of his cause, be imprisoned in said city prison or admitted to bail by the presiding officer of said court.

fendant may imprisoned til time set for al.

rsons sent-ced may be nfined in ison according sentence.

SEC. 90. Whenever any person shall upon conviction in said mayor's court be sentenced to imprisonment or ordered to be imprisoned until such person shall have complied with the judgment of said court, such person shall, for such period or until such time, be confined accordingly in the prison of said city, unless otherwise in this act provided.

rsons may be nfined in unty jail stead of city ison.

SEC. 91. The mayor of said city may order any person confined in the jail of Rowan county instead of the city prison, if in his judgment the same may be necessary, in like cases as he could imprison such person in the city prison; it shall in every such case be the duty of the sheriff or jailor of said county to receive any such person with mittimus as hereinbefore provided in regard to the prison of said city, into such county jail, and keep such persons, until such trial, or for such punishment, or until such persons shall have complied with the judgment of the court in the same manner as such person would otherwise but for the provisions of this section have been subject to be kept in the city prison of said city.

ilor shall ceive persons us committed.

action shall instituted ainst city til claim has st been made writing to dermen.

SEC. 92. No action shall be instituted or maintained against said city upon any claim or demand whatsoever, of any kind or character, until the claimant shall have first presented his or her claim or demand in writing to said board of aldermen, and said board of aldermen shall have declined to pay or settle the same as presented or for ten days after such presentation neglected to enter or cause to be entered upon its minutes its determination in regard thereto; the statute of limitations shall not begin to run until the expiration of the ten days from such demand or until refusal by said board to pay such claim, provided such demand shall be made in thirty days from the time the cause of action arose.

SEC. 93. No action for damages against said city of any character whatever, to either person or property, shall be instituted against said city, unless within ninety days after the happening or infliction of the injury complained of the complainant, his executors or administrators, shall have given notice to the board of aldermen of said city of such injury, in writing, stating in such notice the date and place of the happening or infliction of such injury, the manner of such infliction, the character of the injury and the amount of damages claimed therefor; but this shall not prevent any time of limitation prescribed by law from commencing to run at the date of the happening or infliction of such injury, or in any manner interfere with its running.

Notice shall be given of injury within ninety days after such injury is received.

SEC. 94. That there shall be appointed by the board of aldermen of the City of Salisbury, at their first regular meeting in May in the year one thousand eight hundred and ninety-nine, a school committee of the City of Salisbury, which shall consist of six members, who shall be citizens of said city. The said school committee shall be divided by said board of aldermen, at the time of their appointment, into three classes of two each. The term of the office of the first class shall expire at the end of two years from the date of their appointment, and the term of the office of the second class shall expire at the end of four years from their appointment, and the term of office of the third class shall expire at the end of six years from the said date. Whenever the term of office of any class shall expire as above provided, their successor shall be appointed for a term of six years by said board of aldermen, and whenever any vacancy occurs in said committee, except by the expiration of the term of office; such vacancy for the unexpired term of the member or members shall be filled by the board of aldermen. The school committee of said city shall have exclusive control of the public schools and all public school interests and all public school property, real and personal, in said city; shall prescribe all rules and regulations for the conduct of said schools; the control of said interest; of the government of said property; shall employ and fix the compensation of all such officers and teachers of the public schools therein as to it shall seem proper, and remove or change the

Appointment of school committee by aldermen.

School committee, how divided.

Term of office.

Said committee shall have exclusive control of said schools.

same in its discretion; shall prescribe the time for which such officers and teachers shall be employed from time to time, and the times and places at which such schools shall be kept open and conducted; shall designate the character of such schools respectively, and shall do all other acts necessary for the proper conduct or management, government, regulation and control of said public schools, public school interests, and public school property, and the mayor of said city shall be ex-officio chairman of said school committee: *Provided*, that no person connected with said city schools as committeeman, officer, teacher or otherwise shall accept employment in any manner from any publisher, person or book concern publishing or selling or dealing in school books, school supplies or school furniture; any person violating this provision shall be guilty of a misdemeanor, and upon conviction thereof shall be fined not less than one hundred dollars or imprisoned not less than sixty days, and such conviction shall, *ipso facto*, work a forfeiture of any office or position held by said offender in said schools in said city, and such offender shall be forever disabled from holding any office or position in any manner connected with said city schools.

oviso.

rsons connected with city hools shall not cept employ-nt as agent of ok company.

nalty.

ildren who all be admitted public schools.

SEC. 95. All children, who are *bona fide* residents of said city, between the age of six years and twenty-one years, shall be admitted into said schools as pupils therein, free of tuition charges, and said school committee shall be exclusive judges of the *bona fides* of such residents.

parate schools all be maintained for the ces.

SEC. 96. Said schools shall be separated and kept separate in such a manner that only white children shall be admitted to the white schools and other children to other schools, and the said school committee shall be the exclusive judges of whether or not any applicant for admission to any of said schools is entitled to enter or attend the same under the provisions of this section.

mmittee shall portion school ney.

SEC. 97. The school committee provided for by this act shall apportion the money raised or received for educational purposes in the City of Salisbury as shall be just to the white and other races, without discrimination in favor of or to the prejudice of either race, due regard being paid to the cost of keeping up and maintaining the different schools for the different races.

hool commit- shall make nual report to ermen.

SEC. 98. That said school committee shall make to the board of aldermen of the said city annually, at such time as is required under the general school laws of the state, a report containing an accurate census of the school population of said city, showing the work done and money expended under their direction in the City of Salisbury on account of the public schools therein. The school committee hereby created shall be a body corporate by the name and style of the school committee of the City of Salisbury, and by that name shall exercise all the powers and author-

hool commit- a body corrate.

ty conferred upon them, and perform all the duties required of hem for the purpose of carrying out the full intent and meanng of this act. The officers of the committee shall consist of a hairman, a secretary, and such other officers as they may deem ecessary. Said corporation shall have a corporate seal, which t may alter or change at pleasure. That said school committee hall not have power to transfer, sell, mortgage or convey any f the property, real or personal, now held or hereafter to be eld by the City of Salisbury for school purposes, and shall not ontract any debt in any fiscal year, as fixed by the charter of aid city, in excess of the amount of the school funds received, r to be received by the treasurer of said city for school purposes in such fiscal year. The treasurer of said city shall be the reasurer of the school committee.

Corporate powers.

Treasurer of Salisbury shall be treasurer of schools.

SEC. 99. The following acts are hereby repealed: An act for he incorporation of the town of Salisbury, ratified the twentyeventh day of January, eighteen hundred and fifty-nine; three cts to amend the charter of the town of Salisbury, ratified repectively on the sixteenth day of February, eighteen hundred nd fifty-nine; on the seventeenth day of December, eighteen hunred and fifty-two, and on the twenty-second day of February, eighteen hundred and sixty-one; also an act to extend the corporate limits of the town of Salisbury and to amend the charter of said town, ratified on the twenty-seventh day of February, eighteen hundred and seventy-seven, and chapter sixty-nine of the private laws of eighteen hundred and sixty-three; chapter thirty-four of the private laws of eighteen hundred and eightyfive, ratified on the twenty-third day of February, eighteen hundred and eighty-five; chapter sixty-nine, private laws of eighteen hundred and eighty-nine, ratified on the first day of March, eighteen hundred and eighty-nine; and chapter fifty-two, private laws of eighteen hundred and ninety-three, ratified on the eleventh day of February, eighteen hundred and ninety-three; chapter two hundred and one, private laws of eighteen hundred and ninety-seven, ratified on the eight day of March, 1897. But the repeal of said act shall not revive any other act relating to said town.

Certain acts relating to charter of Salisbury repealed.

SEC. 100. All laws and parts of laws in conflict with this act are hereby repealed.

Conflicting laws repealed.

SEC. 101. Any person violating any of the provisions of, or neglecting or refusing to attend to or execute any of the duties required of him by this act shall be guilty of a misdemeanor, and shall be fined or imprisoned as the court may direct.

Persons violating or refusing to execute provisions of this act guilty of a misdemeanor.

SEC. 102. This act shall be in force from and after its ratification.

Ratified the 6th day of March, A. D. 1899.

CHAPTER 187.

An act for the relief of A. L. Cooper, former tax collector of the town of Murphy, in Cherokee county.

The General Assembly of North Carolina do enact:

L. Cooper powered to llect arrears of xes for town of urphy for 95.

Section 1. That A. L. Cooper, former tax collector of the town of Murphy, in the county of Cherokee, may and he is hereby authorized and empowered to collect all arrears of taxes now due and which were levied for the town of Murphy for the year eighteen hundred and ninety-five, and said A. L. Cooper may appoint one deputy to assist in the collection of such arrears of taxes; and the said A. L. Cooper and his deputy, if he has one, may collect said arrears of taxes by and under the law governing the collection of taxes for the town of Murphy for the year eighteen hundred and ninety-five and any year since.

Sec. 2. That this act shall take effect from and after its ratification.

Ratified the 6th day of March, A. D. 1899.

CHAPTER 188.

An act to amend the charter of the town of Rocky Mount, North Carolina.

The General Assembly of North Carolina do enact:

ction 20, chapter 316, laws of 91, amended.

Section 1. That section twenty, chapter three hundred and sixteen, laws of eighteen hundred and ninety-one be amended by inserting after the word "sale" and before the word "all" in line four of said section the words: "If any poll tax shall not be paid within sixty days after the same shall be demandable it shall be the duty of the tax collector of said town, if he can find no property of the person liable sufficient to satisfy the same, to attach any debt or other property incapable of manual delivery, due or belonging to the person liable, or that may become due to him before the expiration of the calendar year, and the person so owing such debt or having such property in possession shall be liable for such tax."

ction 1, chapter 3 private laws 1897, amended.

Sec. 2. That section one, chapter one hundred and forty-eight, private laws of eighteen hundred and ninety-seven, be amended by striking out all after the word "ward" in line eleven down to and including the word "law" in line thirteen of said section, and by striking out the word "now" in line fourteen and inserting the word "them."

Sec. 3. That chapter forty-eight, section one, of the private laws f eighteen hundred and ninety-nine [?], be amended by striking ut all after the word "commissioners" at the end of line six down o and including the word "year" in line nine, and that it be urther amended by adding after the word "the" and before the ord "other" in line [----] the words "mayor and." Chapter 48, section 1, private laws of 1899 [?], amended.

Sec. 4. That all laws and clauses of laws in conflict with this ct are hereby repealed. Conflicting laws repealed.

Sec. 5. That this act shall be in force and effect from and after its ratification.

Ratified the 6th day of March, A. D. 1899.

CHAPTER 189.

An act to incorporate the "African Methodist Episcopal Zion Publication House" at Charlotte, North Carolina.

The General Assembly of North Carolina do enact:

Section 1. That Right Reverends J. W. Hood, T. H. Lomax, C. C. Petty, C. R. Harris, I. C. Clinton, A. Walters, G. W. Clinton, John Holliday, J. B. Small; and Reverends M. R. Franklin, R. H. Simmons, J. B. Colbert, F. M. Jacobs, J. H. White, T. J. Manson, Solomon Johnson, C. H. Smith, G. L. Blackwell, J. W. Smith, R. B. Bruce and John C. Dancy and R. J. Crockett, laymen, their associates and successors, be and the same are hereby created a body politic and incorporate under the name and style of the "African Methodist Episcopal Zion Publication House" at Charlotte, North Carolina, and under and by said corporate name and style may sue and be sued, plead and be impleaded, contract and be contracted with in all the courts of this state, in the courts of the United States and all the courts of any state in the United States. It shall continue for a period of thirty years' may have and use a common seal, which it may alter at pleasure, and may transact business in any of the states of the United States by complying with the laws of the same. All of the real and personal property acquired or belonging to said corporation shall be exempt from all taxation under the laws of this state so long as the same is used and applied to the benefit of the religious society known as the "African Methodist Episcopal Zion Church of America." Corporators. Body politic. Corporate name. Place of business. Corporate powers.

Sec. 2. That said corporation shall have power and authority to carry on in all of its branches the general publishing and printing business. It may publish one or more newspapers and periodicals by any name desired, and may publish, handle, pur- Purpose of corporation to carry on general printing business.

chase and sell all kinds of books, tracts, treatise and pamphlets: Provided, that all the money received or the profits that may accrue on the same shall belong to and be applied to the use, purpose and benefit of the religious society known as the "African Methodist Episcopal Zion Church in America." It shall have the right to acquire, hold and own such real property as may be necessary for the proper and convenient transaction of its business; but the said real property shall be purchased, held, controlled, owned and disposed of under the rules and regulations prescribed in the "book of discipline" of the "African Methodist Episcopal Zion Church of America" and in no other way.

plication of ofits.

y own real ate

vernment in king by-laws, les, etc.

Sec. 3. That the corporators herein named and their successors in office shall be governed, in making the rules, by-laws and regulations for the transaction of the business of this corporation, by the "book of discipline" of the "African Methodist Episcopal Zion Church in America": Provided, that the same shall not be inconsistent with the laws of this state, the United States or in any state in which it may transact its business.

ection of cers.

Sec. 4 That in the election of its officers, appointment of its agents and employees the said corporators and their successors in office shall be governed by the rules and regulations prescribed in the "book of discipline" of the "African Methodist Episcopal Zion Church in America," and the duties, compensation and term of office and employment shall be the same as are prescribed in said "book of discipline."

Sec. 5. This act shall be in force from and after its ratification.

Ratified the 6th day of March, A. D. 1899.

CHAPTER 190.

An act to incorporate the Kinston and Jacksonville Railroad Company.

The General Assembly of North Carolina do enact:

rpose of corporation.

Section 1. That for the purpose of constructing, maintaining and operating a railroad from Kinston, in Lenoir county, to Jacksonville, in Onslow county, by way of Tuckaho, in Jones county, and Richlands, and near Catharine Lake, in Onslow county.

rporators.

G. W. Taylor, F. W. Harget, J. W. Burton, Frank Padrick, John F. Koonce, Frank Andrews, S. B. Taylor, J. F. Boggs, O. B. Cox, Joseph E. Rhodes, Frank Thompson, Wayne Venterz, R. D. Thompson, J. L. Nicholson, J. W. Mills, L. W. Harget, M. B. Steed, H. W. Humphrey, F. D. Koonce, J. R. Franks, H. F. Brown, F. M. Dixon, F. B. Koonce, W. S. Herbert, J. C. Wooten,

A. Mitchell, D. Oettinger, J. W. Grainger, W. A. Laroque, B. W. Canady, S. H. Abbott, E. F. Cox, and their associates, successors and assigns are hereby made and constituted a body corporate under the name and style of "The Kinston and Jacksonville Railroad Company," with the said corporators, their associates, successors and assigns, under said corporate name, shall have a corporate existence and as such may exercise the powers herein granted in perpetuity as a body politic; and by that name may sue and be sued, plead and be impleaded in any court in the state of North Carolina, and may have and use a common seal, which it may change or alter at pleasure; and shall be capable of purchasing, holding, owning, possessing, leasing and conveying property, real, personal and mixed, and of acquiring the same by gift or devise or otherwise for the purposes herein contemplated; and the said company shall have and enjoy all the rights and immunities which other corporate bodies may lawfully exercise, and may make all necessary by-laws and regulations for its government not inconsistent with the constitution and laws of the United States and of the state of North Carolina.

Body corporate. Corporate name. Corporate powers.

Sec. 2. That the capital stock of said company shall be five hundred thousand dollars, which may be increased to one million dollars, and may be created by subscription on the part of individuals, municipal or other corporations in shares of the value of one hundred dollars each, which may be made in money, bonds, lands, labor or material necessary for the construction of said railroad.

Capital stock. May be increased.

Sec. 3. That books of subscription to the capital stock of said company may be opened by such persons and at such times and places and under such rules and regulations as the corporators named in section one of this act or a majority of them may direct, after giving twenty days' notice of the opening of said books in one or more newspapers of the state, and said books may be kept open for such a length of time as may be deemed expedient or until the whole of the capital stock is subscribed. That certificates shall be issued to each stockholder for the number of shares of stock subscribed, and each share shall be entitled to one vote, and said stock may be transferred in such manner and form as may be prescribed by the by-laws of the company, and the stockholders shall not be individually liable for anything beyond the amount of their subscription to said capital stock.

Books of subscription may be opened. Shares of stock entitled to one vote for each share.

Sec. 4. That when the sum of ten thousand dollars has been subscribed to the capital stock of said company and five per centum paid in thereon or secured to be paid it shall be the duty of the corporators, any five of whom may act for the purposes, to call a general meeting of the subscribers to the capital stock of said company, of which meeting due public notice shall be given

When company shall be organized.

ction of ectors. ection of president. ary and cers.

at least twenty days aforetime, specifying the date, place and object of said meeting, at which a majority of the stock subscribed shall be represented in person or by proxy duly verified, and at said meeting the stockholders shall proceed to elect from their body a board of directors, to be composed of not less than five persons, and said directors shall forthwith elect one of their number president and also elect such other officers and appoint such agents as they think necessary and proper; fix the salaries of such president, officers and agents and their terms of office, and do and perform all other acts and things necessary to the complete organization of said company and to carry into effect the objects of this charter.

ıen work of ıstruction ll begin.

Sec. 5. That after the company shall be organized as aforesaid the board of directors shall proceed to have constructed as speedily as possible a railroad on the route designated in section one of this act, and may erect a bridge and build their railroad tracks thereon over any navigable stream by putting a sufficient draw in the bridge or other structure so as not to impede navigation; and may lay down tracks and make connections with any other railroads leading into or through the town of Kinston, in Lenoir county, and Jacksonville, in Onslow county, and may begin and continue the construction of said railroad at any point or points the company may determine upon, and use any portion thereof, before the completion of the entire line, and may convey and transport persons and property thereon and charge compensation for the same.

cessary lands y be connned. ree disinterested persons ll be appointto assess value land.

Sec. 6. That whenever any lands shall be required for the construction of said railroad or for warehouses, water stations, sidings, switches, turnouts, workshops, depositories or other buildings or structures, or for other purposes, and if the president and directors can not agree with the owner of said lands as to the terms of acquiring the right and title thereto for the construction and use of said railroad, such bonds may be taken and acquired by said company in the following manner: The sheriff of the county in which such lands may be situated shall, at the request of the president of said railroad, signified by a petition in writing, summon three disinterested and competent freeholders of his county, who shall ascertain the value of such lands under oath, to be administered by the sheriff, and in appraising the same and determining the amount of compensation to be paid for said lands to the owner thereof by said railroad company the said freeholders shall take into consideration the actual value of said lands before the construction of the proposed railroad and the enhanced value of the lands caused by the construction of said railroad, and the particular loss or damage, if any, which the owner may sustain by the seizure and condemnation of said lands to the use of said railroad company, and make a written report of their proceedings under their hands and seals to said sheriff, who shall immediately deliver a copy thereof to the owner of the land, and also one to the president of the railroad company; and upon the payment or tender by the president of the road of the amount so assessed or appraised by the said freeholders; the title to the real estate so seized and appraised shall thereby vest in said corporation, and the company may enter, possess and hold said lands for the construction use and equipment of said railroad: Provided, either party may appeal to the superior court of the county within ten days after delivery of such report, upon the question of the amount so assessed, which shall be tried by a jury of the county wherein the lands are situated: And provided further, that not more than one hundred feet from the center of the railroad bed shall be liable to be so condemned: And provided further, that no part of any yard, garden, family burying ground or burying ground attached to any dwelling house or to any plantation or any cemetery or church lot or school lot shall be subject to be taken or condemned for the construction of said railroad without the consent in writing of the lawful owners or trustees thereof.

Report of proceedings returned to sheriff.

Title shall vest in corporation.

Proviso.

Either party may appeal within ten days.

Proviso.

Certain lands exempted from condemnation.

Sec. 7. That for the purpose of raising funds requisite to the construction and equipment of said railroad the president and directors of said company shall be authorized and empowered to issue coupon bonds or other evidence of debt to an amount not exceeding five hundred thousand dollars. That said bonds may be in denominations of one hundred dollars, five hundred dollars, one thousand dollars and five thousand dollars, and run for such time not exceeding thirty years from the date of issue, and bear a rate of interest not greater than six per centum per annum, and the principal and interest be payable at such times and places as the president and said board of directors may specify. That said bonds or other evidence of debt shall be signed by the president, countersigned by the secretary and attested by the common seal of the corporation, and may be sold, hypothecated or disposed of at such times as the president and the board of directors may determine.

Authorized to issue coupon bonds

Amount of bonds.

Denomination.

Date of maturity.

Bonds, how signed.

Sec. 8. That to secure the payment of these bonds and the interest thereon as the same becomes due the said Kinston and Jacksonville Railroad Company may execute and deliver mortgage deeds with or without power of sale to such trustee or trustees as may be selected and agreed on, the said mortgage deeds to be signed by the president, countersigned by the secretary and attested by the common seal of the corporation, conveying its railway franchise and property, including its road bed, superstructure, equipments, choses in action, evidences of debt and all

May execute and deliver mortgage deeds.

at least twenty days aforetime, specifying the date, place and object of said meeting, at which a majority of the stock subscribed shall be represented in person or by proxy duly verified, and at said meeting the stockholders shall proceed to elect from their body a board of directors, to be composed of not less than five persons, and said directors shall forthwith elect one of their number president and also elect such other officers and appoint such agents as they think necessary and proper; fix the salaries of such president, officers and agents and their terms of office, and do and perform all other acts and things necessary to the complete organization of said company and to carry into effect the objects of this charter.

ection of rectors.

ection of president.

lary and cers.

Sec. 5. That after the company shall be organized as aforesaid the board of directors shall proceed to have constructed as speedily as possible a railroad on the route designated in section one of this act, and may erect a bridge and build their railroad tracks thereon over any navigable stream by putting a sufficient draw in the bridge or other structure so as not to impede navigation; and may lay down tracks and make connections with any other railroads leading into or through the town of Kinston, in Lenoir county, and Jacksonville, in Onslow county, and may begin and continue the construction of said railroad at any point or points the company may determine upon, and use any portion thereof, before the completion of the entire line, and may convey and transport persons and property thereon and charge compensation for the same.

hen work of onstruction all begin.

Sec. 6. That whenever any lands shall be required for the construction of said railroad or for warehouses, water stations, sidings, switches, turnouts, workshops, depositories or other buildings or structures, or for other purposes, and if the president and directors can not agree with the owner of said lands as to the terms of acquiring the right and title thereto for the construction and use of said railroad, such bonds may be taken and acquired by said company in the following manner: The sheriff of the county in which such lands may be situated shall, at the request of the president of said railroad, signified by a petition in writing, summon three disinterested and competent freeholders of his county, who shall ascertain the value of such lands under oath, to be administered by the sheriff, and in appraising the same and determining the amount of compensation to be paid for said lands to the owner thereof by said railroad company the said freeholders shall take into consideration the actual value of said lands before the construction of the proposed railroad and the enhanced value of the lands caused by the construction of said railroad, and the particular loss or damage, if any, which the owner may sustain by the seizure and condemnation of said lands

cessary lands y be condemned.

ree disinterested persons all be appointed to assess value land.

to the use of said railroad company, and make a written report of their proceedings under their hands and seals to said sheriff, who shall immediately deliver a copy thereof to the owner of the land, and also one to the president of the railroad company; and upon the payment or tender by the president of the road of the amount so assessed or appraised by the said freeholders; the title to the real estate so seized and appraised shall thereby vest in said corporation, and the company may enter, possess and hold said lands for the construction use and equipment of said railroad: Provided, either party may appeal to the superior court of the county within ten days after delivery of such report, upon the question of the amount so assessed, which shall be tried by a jury of the county wherein the lands are situated: And provided further, that not more than one hundred feet from the center of the railroad bed shall be liable to be so condemned: And provided further, that no part of any yard, garden, family burying ground or burying ground attached to any dwelling house or to any plantation or any cemetery or church lot or school lot shall be subject to be taken or condemned for the construction of said railroad without the consent in writing of the lawful owners or trustees thereof.

Report of proceedings returned to sheriff.

Title shall vest in corporation.

Proviso.

Either party may appeal within ten days.

Proviso.

Certain lands exempted from condemnation.

Sec. 7. That for the purpose of raising funds requisite to the construction and equipment of said railroad the president and directors of said company shall be authorized and empowered to issue coupon bonds or other evidence of debt to an amount not exceeding five hundred thousand dollars. That said bonds may be in denominations of one hundred dollars, five hundred dollars, one thousand dollars and five thousand dollars, and run for such time not exceeding thirty years from the date of issue, and bear a rate of interest not greater than six per centum per annum, and the principal and interest be payable at such times and places as the president and said board of directors may specify. That said bonds or other evidence of debt shall be signed by the president, countersigned by the secretary and attested by the common seal of the corporation, and may be sold, hypothecated or disposed of at such times as the president and the board of directors may determine.

Authorized to issue coupon bonds

Amount of bonds.

Denomination.

Date of maturity.

Bonds, how signed.

Sec. 8. That to secure the payment of these bonds and the interest thereon as the same becomes due the said Kinston and Jacksonville Railroad Company may execute and deliver mortgage deeds with or without power of sale to such trustee or trustees as may be selected and agreed on, the said mortgage deeds to be signed by the president, countersigned by the secretary and attested by the common seal of the corporation, conveying its railway franchise and property, including its road bed, superstructure, equipments, choses in action, evidences of debt and all

May execute and deliver mortgage deeds.

its real and personal property of whatever description and kind; and the said mortgage deeds and all other agreements the said company may enter into which by law are required to be registered, when duly executed and proved, shall be recorded in the office of the register of deeds in the county of Lenoir, and also in the county of Jones and in the county of Onslow.

rectors of state son authorized deliver 300 n to aid in structing said d.

Sec. 9. That the route designated in section one of this act for the location of said railroad will cause its line to pass through a considerable body of state lands in which the state of North Carolina has a direct pecuniary interest, and which lands are now entrusted to the state board of education, and the construction of said railroad will contribute largely to the reclamation of said lands and add much to their value. The board of directors of the North Carolina penitentiary are authorized to contract with and deliver to the president and directors of the Kinston and Jacksonville Railroad Company as many as three hundred able-bodied convicts at four dollars per month for each convict for such a length of time as said railroad company may desire their employment to aid in the grading and further construction of said railroad: Provided, the said railroad company shall furnish, without cost or expense to the state, to said convicts while in the service of said company, food, medical aid when necessary and suitable quarters for the comfort and security of said convicts, and bear the necessary expense of guarding them, and return them to the penitentiary on the termination of the contract.

viso.

mpany shall nish food, etc., convicts.

all have a ht-of-way ty feet wide

Sec. 10. That the said Kinston and Jacksonville Railroad Company shall have a right-of-way sixty feet wide on each side of its track over the lands owned by the state or state board of education through which the line of said railroad may pass.

ght to transrt and convey ssengers.

Sec. 11. That said railroad company shall have the exclusive right to transport and convey persons and property on said railroad to be by them constructed at such rates and charges as may be fixed by the board of directors, subject to such general laws regulating the same as the general assembly from time to time may enact.

Sec. 12. That this act shall take effect and be in force from and after its ratification.

Ratified the 6th day of March, A. D. 1899.

CHAPTER 191.

An act to incorporate the Foscoe and Montezuma Telephone Company.

The General Assembly of North Carolina do enact:

Section 1. That C. W. Phipps, W. C. Goss, W. V. Callaway, J. L. Banner, J. A. Woody, J. H. Blalock, W. Aldridge, Joseph Phipps, M. F. Presnell, Vassas Brothers, Vance Brothers, M. B. Hughes, Will Aldridge, J. C. Carpenter, C. C. Banner, J. E. Harris, A. S. Ridenour, A. Graybeal, J. G. Loven, J. B. Johnson, Jordan Cook and J. C. Shull, and their associates, successors and assigns, are hereby constituted and declared a body politic and corporate under the name and style of "The Foscoe and Montezuma Telephone Company," and by that name and style may sue and be sued, plead and be impleaded in any and all courts of this state; adopt and use a common seal, and may alter the same at will, and have the privileges, franchises, rights and powers hereby specially granted, and also those conferred upon corporations by the laws of the state of North Carolina. Corporators. Body corporate. Corporate name. Corporate powers.

Sec. 2. The principal office and place of business of said corporation shall be at Montezuma, county of Mitchell, state of North Carolina. Principal office.

Sec. 3. The general business of said corporation shall be the erection and maintenance and operation of telegraph and telephone lines as provided for by the general statutes in the counties of Watauga and Mitchell and the counties adjoining thereto, and in such other parts of the state of North Carolina and adjoining states as may be found desirable, and to do all such other acts as are or may hereafter be necessary or advantageous in conducting a general telegraph or telephone business not inconsistent with the laws of North Carolina. General business.

Sec. 4. The amount of the capital stock of said corporation shall be five hundred dollars, divided into one hundred shares of par value of five dollars each, but said capital stock may be increased to two thousand dollars should the stockholders of said corporation so elect. Capital stock. Division of shares. May be increased.

Sec. 5. The principal officers of said corporation shall be a president, vice-president, general manager, secretary and treasurer and five directors, who shall be elected annually by the stockholders in regular meeting, and shall hold their offices respectively for one year and until their successors shall be chosen. They shall constitute an executive board, to be known as the board of directors, and shall manage and govern the affairs of the corporation under the direction of the stockholders. Officers of corporation. Annual election.

Sec. 6. The annual meeting of stockholders shall be held at its office at Montezuma on the first Saturday of August of each and every year for the election of officers and the transaction of such Annual meeting of stockholders.

other business as may properly come before the meeting, but the date of such annual meeting may be changed by a vote of the majority of the stockholders at a meeting, regular or called, and a meeting of the stockholders for general or special purposes other than the election of officers may be held upon the call of the president and board of directors or by a majority of them. At all regular meetings or called meetings the stockholders representing a majority of the capital stock of the corporation which is taken shall constitute a quorum for the transaction of business which may come before the meeting. Each and every stockholder shall be entitled to one vote for each share of stock owned by such stockholder.

te of such eeting may be anged.

mporary cers of corration.

Sec. 7. The following-named persons shall fill the offices provided for in section five of this act until the first Saturday in August above mentioned and until their successors are elected and qualified as provided for: C. W. Phipps shall hold the office of president; W. C. Goss, that of vice-president; J. L. Banner, that of secretary and treasurer; W. V. Callaway, that of general manager; J. A. Woody, J. H. Blalock, W. Aldridge, Joseph Phipps and M F. Presnell, that of directors.

cretary and asurer, election of.

quired to give nd.

Sec. 8. The secretary and treasurer of this corporation shall be elected by the stockholders annually and shall hold his office for the term of one year and until his successor is elected and qualified as above provided for, unless he shall sooner be removed from office by the board of directors. He shall give bond with full and sufficient surety, to be approved by the directors, for the faithful performance of the duties of his office, for the proper accounting for all moneys which may come into his hands as treasurer, and for the proper application of the same.

ay make, alter d repeal by-s.

Sec. 9. The corporation shall have the right, by a majority vote of the capital stock which is taken, to adopt, make, alter and repeal such by-laws as may be necessary for the proper government of the corporation and for the prosecution of business not in conflict with the provisions of these articles of incorporation or the laws of this state.

de of filling ancies.

Sec. 10. The stockholders may prescribe by the by-laws a mode of filling vacancies which may occur in any of its offices or directors by death or otherwise.

dividual bility.

Sec. 11. The stockholders of the said corporation shall not be individually liable for any of its debts, obligations or other liabilities.

ration of corration.

Sec. 12. That the duration of the corporation hereby created and the powers herein granted shall continue for a period of thirty years.

Sec. 13. That this act shall be in force from and after its ratification.

Ratified the 6th day of March, A. D. 1899.

CHAPTER 192.

An act for the relief of the commissioners of the town of Bakersville.

The General Assembly of North Carolina do enact:

Section 1. That John S. Wilson, John Dail and John Riddle, the present board of commissioners for the town of Bakersville, be and they are hereby authorized and empowered through their proper officers to collect the back taxes due the said town of Bakersville for the year eighteen hundred and ninety-six and for the year eighteen hundred and ninety-seven. This act to apply only to the corporation tax due the town of Bakersville.

Commissioners of Bakersville empowered to collect arrears of taxes for 1896.

Sec. 2. This act shall be in force from and after its ratification.

Ratified the 6th day of March, A. D. 1899.

CHAPTER 193.

An act to incorporate the Grand Commandery of Knights Templar of North Carolina.

The General Assembly of North Carolina do enact:

Corporators.

Section 1. That the officers of the Grand Commandery of Knights Templar of North Carolina, to-wit: Mumford D. Bailey, grand commander; Walter E. Storm, deputy grand commander; William F. Randolph, grand generalissimo; James D. Bullock, grand captain general; James D. Miller, grand prelate; DeWitt E. Allen, grand senior warden; John C. Drewry, grand junior warden; William Simpson, grand treasurer; Horace H. Munson, grand recorder; Arthur J. Wills, grand standard bearer; James K. Norfleet, grand sword bearer; Ferdinand Ulrich, grand warder; Robert H. Bradley, grand sentinel, and their successors in office, shall be and they are hereby incorporated and made a body politic or corporate under the name, style and title of the Grand Commandery of Knights Templar of North Carolina in said state of North Carolina, and by that name may have succession, a common seal, sue and be sued, plead and be impleaded in any of the courts of the state; contract, be contracted with; acquire, hold and dispose of personal property and real estate as may be required for the convenient transaction of business, and have all such powers as are necessary for corporations to transact business.

Body politic. Corporate name. Corporate powers.

Empowered to pass by-laws, regulations, etc.

Sec. 2. That said corporation, having passed all necessary by-laws and regulations necessary for the government of said Grand Commandery of Knights Templar, and the same not being inconsistent with the constitution of North Carolina and its laws or the constitution of the United States are declared valid, with right to change, amend or modify or enact new by-laws or regulations as often as in their opinion necessary, the same not being in conflict with the constitution and laws of North Carolina and the constitution of the United States.

Sec. 3. This act shall be in force from and after its ratification.

Ratified the 6th day of March, A. D. 1899.

CHAPTER 194.

An act to alter the limits of Roxobel, in Bertie county.

The General Assembly of North Carolina do enact:

porate limits xobel red.

Section 1. That the corporate limits of the town of Roxobel, in Bertie county, be and they are hereby included within the following limits, to-wit: Commencing at a point on the road leading from Roxobel to Jackson, one thousand yards from the cross-roads at Roxobel, and thence turning to the right at right-angles with said road and running one thousand yards, and thence turning to the right and at right-angles and running two thousand yards, and thence at right-angles turning to the right and running two thousand yards, and thence at right-angles turning to the right and running two thousand yards, and thence turning to the right and running to the first station on the Roxobel and Jackson road, a distance of one thousand yards from the said cross-roads at Roxobel.

porary cers.

Sec. 2. That until an election can be held in said town, under the law now regulating elections of town officers in chapter sixty-two of The Code, the following shall be the officers of said town, to-wit: W. J. Watson, mayor; J. B. Sadler, constable; Leroy Capehart, J. H. Liverman and E. B. Hardy, commissioners, who shall qualify and hold their offices until their successors are elected and qualified, and they are hereby clothed with all the powers conferred on such officers by the act of the general assembly creating said town and by chapter sixty-two of The Code.

wers conferred officers.

Sec. 3. That said officers shall have the same powers as are conferred on the officers in the act incorporating said town, and that no liquor shall be sold in said town until the petition asking for license shall be endorsed by the board of town commissioners in regular session, and that all laws in conflict with this act are repealed.

Sec. 4. This act shall be in force from and after its ratification.

Ratified the 6th day of March, A. D. 1899.

CHAPTER 195.

An act to authorize the city of Fayetteville to establish and operate a system of waterworks and sewerage, and to issue bonds therefor.

Whereas, by reason of its revenues from other sources and because under the provisions of chapter one hundred and fifty-three (153) of the private laws of eighteen hundred and ninety-three (1893), and the act amendatory thereof, passed by the general assembly of eighteen hundred and ninety-nine 1899), entitled "An act to amend chapter one hundred and fifty-three (153) of the private laws of eighteen [hundre l] and ninety-three," etc., and ratified on January twenty-sixth, eighteen hundred and ninety-nine, sufficient taxes are now levied and not otherwise appropriated to amply provide for the payment of the interest on the coupon bonds hereinafter provided for as it falls due and to create a sinking fund sufficient to fully pay off said bonds as well as to meet all the other obligations and liabilities of the said city: Preamble.

The General Assembly of North Carolina do enact:

Section 1. That the city of Fayetteville, through its board of aldermen or their legally constituted agent or agents, be and is hereby authorized and empowered to establish and maintain a system of waterworks and sewerage, either or both, for the use of the said city and its citizens and of persons living in its suburbs, and to that end may purchase, hold, establish, maintain and operate all necessary lands, works, machinery and appliances wherewith to furnish a sufficient quantity of pure and wholesome water and a proper system of sewerage, either or both. Fayetteville empowered to establish system of waterworks.

Sec. 2. For the foregoing purpose it shall be lawful for the said the city of Fayetteville to issue and sell at a price not less than par the coupon bonds of said city to an amount not exceeding sixty thousand dollars ($60,000), said bonds to be in denominations of one hundred dollars ($100) and five hundred dollars ($500), and to run for a period of thirty years from the issue of the same, and to bear interest at a rate not exceeding six per centum per annum, payable semi-annually on the first (1st) day of June and December of each year after their issue. May issue and sell bonds. Amount of issue. Date of maturity. Interest.

Sec. 3. Said coupon bonds shall be consecutively numbered and signed by the mayor and clerk of the city of Fayetteville, and it shall be the duty of the said clerk to keep an accurate account of the same. Bonds, how numbered, etc.

Sec. 4. The coupons of said bonds shall be receivable by the tax collector and treasurer of the city of Fayetteville in payment of all taxes and dues to the said city. Coupons receivable as taxes.

Sec. 5. It shall be lawful for the said the city of Fayetteville, y provide a stem of sewer-e. in addition to supplying the public demands of said city as hereinbefore provided, to provide water and sewerage, either or both, for private use at a uniform rate to be prescribed by the board of aldermen of said city, and the receipts arising from such rentals shall be kept by the treasurer of the said city and shall be applied to the payment of interest on said bonds as the coupons may fall due, and to the further purpose of creating a sinking fund of two thousand dollars ($2,000) per annum, which sinking fund it shall be the duty of the authorities of said city to lay aside annually from any funds in the treasury not otherwise appropriated, and from any surplus arising from said rentals in excess of amounts sufficient to pay the interest on said bonds. And the sinking fund above provided for may be temporarily applied to the payment of operating expenses of said waterworks plant or sewerage plant, either or both, as the case may be, and any deficiency in amount necessary for the payment of either interest, sinking fund or operating expenses of said system shall be paid from the current tax receipts of said city and shall be charged as necessary "water expense"; and to this end the twenty (20) per centum of the tax now levied for the benefit of the city of Fayetteville for water purposes under its charter may be used. Should there be any excess from private rentals over the amount necessary to pay said interest, sinking fund and operating expenses, such excess shall be used for the payment of the ordinary expenses and liabilities of said city.

y authorities all levy annual to create king fund.

cess from tals.

king fund ll not be used other purpose.

Sec. 6 It shall be unlawful for the authorities of the said the city of Fayetteville to use the sinking fund herein provided for otherwise than as above provided for, and it shall be the duty of the board of audit and finance of said city to safely invest, at not less than the legal rate of interest, annually, the sinking fund herein provided for under the advice of the city attorney, or said board of audit and finance may purchase, at a price not exceeding the face value of said bond or bonds, any of the outstanding bonds herein provided for from any person desirous of disposing of the same.

ministrators l others may est funds in d bonds.

Sec. 7. All administrators, executors, guardians and other persons acting in a fiduciary capacity are hereby authorized and empowered to invest the funds intrusted to them in said bonds.

mmittees ll be appointed select site for nt, etc.

Sec. 8. The board of aldermen of the city of Fayetteville in the event of the erection or purchase of a waterworks plant provided for in this act shall appoint three freeholders of the city of Fayetteville who, with the assistance of the city engineer, shall locate the site for said waterworks plant and who shall survey, map out and designate with proper metes and bounds an ample watershed to secure the purity of the water flowing and draining into the stream from which said water supply may be taken, and to locate and plan a suitable reservoir for said water supply.

Sec. 9. Any person who shall willfully place or deposit in the stream from which said water supply may be taken or any of its tributaries, or upon the ground drained by them or any of them within a distance from said reservoir, to be marked, designated and published by the three freeholders and engineers aforesaid, or upon the water-shed herein provided for, any dead carcass of any animal or any filthy or poisonous substance or any other substance or thing by which the water of said streams, or its tributaries shall be rendered or may become liable to the [be] rendered unwholesome, contaminated or otherwise unfit for domestic purposes, shall be guilty of a misdemeanor. **Persons placing dead carcasses, etc., in streams used, guilty of a misdemeanor.**

Sec. 10. It shall be unlawful for any person to erect, establish or maintain upon the water-shed of the stream upon which said waterworks plant may be located or any tributary thereof within the boundaries and marks and designations provided for in this act, any establishment or works the effect of which in its operation or use shall be deleterious to the water of the stream upon which said plant shall be located or its tributaries above the points and boundaries named, and any such establishment, contrivance and works is hereby declared to be a public nuisance: **Works deleteriously affecting water shall not be established along streams used.** Provided, that all such establishments, contrivances and works which are standing, established and maintained at the time of the survey provided for in this act shall be condemned as provided in this act for condemning land, and shall be removed. **Proviso.**

Sec. 11. It shall be the duty of the superintendent of health of the county of Cumberland, together with the board of health of the city of Fayetteville to exercise due surveillance over the water-shed, streams and tributaries mentioned in the preceding section, and to report to the board of aldermen of the city of Fayetteville, whose duty it shall be to abate the nuisance therein declared and forbidden in the manner provided by existing laws. **Superintendent of health of Cumberland county shall exercise control over sheds, etc.**

Sec. 12. Any person who shall willfully injure any of the property of said waterworks plant or in any manner willfully and maliciously interfere with or obstruct the operation of its works, or shall cast, throw, place or deposit any deleterious substance in any of the filters, mains, pipes, tanks, reservoirs or other receptacle of water connected with the said water plant or waterworks, shall be guilty of a misdemeanor. **Persons injuring property guilty of a misdemeanor.**

Sec. 13. The board of aldermen and the city engineer of the city of Fayetteville, and any agent or agents appointed by said board of aldermen are hereby authorized and empowered to enter upon the lands of all persons, firms and corporations within or without the limits of said city, for the purpose of making the surveys provided for in this act, laying or putting down any **Aldermen empowered to condemn lands.**

pipes, drains, machinery or appliances, or for the purpose of erecting any reservoirs or other necessary buildings or doing any other act necessary to be done towards the erection and maintenance of such system of waterworks or sewerage, either or both, and towards the maintenance and protection of the same when erected, and may, by proper proceedings as hereinafter provided for, condemn such real estate, easement or interest in real estate as may be necessary for the purpose of this act.

ceedings for h condemna- n.

Sec. 14. The proceedings for the condemnation of land or any easement or interest therein for the use of said waterworks or water plant and the sewerage provided for in this act, the appraisal of land or interest therein, the duties of commissioners of appraisal the right of either party to file exceptions, the report of the commissioners, the mode, and manner of appeal, the power and authority of the court or judge to file judgment and the manner of its entry and enforcement and the rights of the city of Fayetteville pending appeal, shall be as prescribed in chapter forty-nine (49) of The Code of North Carolina and acts amendatory thereof for condemning land for the use of railroads: Provided, that all the provisions in said chapter requiring petitions to state incorporation, the subscription and payment of stock, surveys, maps of routes or any other maps, and signatures by directors, shall not be necessary in carrying into effect this act:

viso.

ermen not uired to in- ute proceed- s.

Provided further, that it shall not be necessary for the board of aldermen of the said city or their agents or the city engineer to institute any proceeding or file any petition or to pay into court any money before entering upon or taking possession of any land for constructing and operating the said plant: Provided further, that nothing in this act shall prevent the city of Fayetteville from acquiring any right or title or interest in any land or easements in lands by gift or purchase, nor to prevent the arbitration of any differences which may arise between the said the city of Fayetteville and any person owning or interested in any land or easements or rights in lands which may be required or needed for the erection, operation and maintenance of said waterworks plant or water plant

ction shall be d to vote on ance of ds.

Sec. 15. An election shall be held at the market house in the city of Fayetteville on the first (1st) Tuesday in April, eighteen hundred and ninety-nine, for the purpose of ratifying or disapproving, by a majority of the qualified voters of said city, the issuance of the bonds herein provided for. It shall be the duty of the mayor to cause daily publication of this act in full to be made in some newspaper published in said city not less than ten days immediately preceding said election, not including Sundays.

pointment of istrar.

Sec. 16. The board of aldermen of the city of Fayetteville shall appoint a registrar of voters for the said the city of Fayetteville, who shall register such citizens of said city as are not at present registered and who would be entitled to vote at the election, and shall cause publication and notice to be given as provided by section seven (7) of chapter one hundred and fifty-three (153) of the private laws of eighteen hundred and ninety-three (1893): Provided, that if upon a vote a majority of the board of aldermen of the city of Fayetteville shall so declare at a meeting to be held twenty days before the time provided for in this act for said election, a new registration shall be had of the voters of said city as provided by law, upon the question of issuing bonds under the provisions of this act or upon any other question submitted to the voters of said city at the same time.

Duties of registrar.

Sec. 17. The duties of registrar so to be appointed, the registration and the oath of election shall be as provided by section eight (8), nine (9) and ten (10) of chapter one hundred and fifty-three (153) of the private laws of eighteen hundred and ninety-three (1893).

Appointment of judges of election.

Sec 18. The board of aldermen of said city shall appoint two judges of election to hold said election, and the duties and powers and qualifications of said judges of election shall be the same as are provided by said chapter one hundred and fifty-three (153) of the private laws of eighteen hundred and ninety-three (1893); and all matters and questions as to the election herein provided for shall be determined according to the provisions of chapter one hundred and fifty-three (153) of the private laws of eighteen hundred and ninety-three (1893), sections seven (7) to fourteeen (14) inclusive of both.

Form of ballots.

Sec. 19. The ballots to be used at the election herein provided for shall be of white paper and without device, and shall contain the word "Water" or the words "No water," and the bonds herein provided for shall be issued only in case a majority of the qualified voters of said city shall vote "Water": Provided, however, that in case an election on any other subject than the bonds provided for in this act shall be held on said first (1st) Tuesday in April, eighteen hundred and ninety-nine, in the said the city of Fayetteville, the officers appointed to hold said other election shall hold the election provided for in this act, and it shall not be necessary in such case to appoint the election officers provided for in the preceding sections of this act.

Conflicting laws repealed.

Sec. 20. All laws and parts of laws in conflict with this act are hereby repealed.

Sec. 21. This act shall be in force and effect from and after its ratification.

Ratified the 6th day of March, A. D. 1899.

CHAPTER 196.

An act relating to the Presbyterian church at Louisburg, North Carolina.

eamble. Whereas, in eighteen hundred and thirty-three there was conveyed to trustees for the benefit of the Presbyterian church in Louisburg a certain lot of land lying at the corner of Main and Middle streets in said town, said deed being for the consideration of two hundred dollars and providing that in case the said trustees should so elect they were empowered to sell one-half of the said lot of land for the benefit of said church (but the said trustees have never exercised the right of such sale); and

Whereas, the successors of said original trustees, to-wit: W. T. Hughes, A. C. Hughes, W. G. Rackley, J. A. Turner and J. J. Allen, under the direction of said church, desire to rebuild the said church edifice, but to do so it will be necessary to borrow money on the pledge of the said property; now, therefore,

The General Assembly of North Carolina do enact:

stees empow I to pledge ain property ecurity for ney. [Section 1.] That the said trustees be and they are hereby empowered to pledge the said property to secure the payment of such sum of money as shall be borrowed for the benefit of said church, with power in the mortgage to sell and convey the said property, should a sale be necessary, free and clear from all limitations and uses. The deed of mortgage from said trustees shall be signed by not less than three of said trustees and by the clerk of the said church.

[Sec. 2.] This act shall be in force from and after its ratification.

Ratified the 6th day of March A. D. 1899.

CHAPTER 197.

An act to incorporate Whitehead Academy.

The General Assembly of North Carolina do enact:

orators. Section 1. That Tyrell R. Caudill, Josh T. Fender, Henderson C. Cheek, Wiley P. Maxwell, John M. Wagoner, Thomas A. Fender, Fielden W. Cheek, Morgan U. Spicer, Isom Fender, Solomon M. Edwards. William L. Hoppers, John F. Watson, their associates and successors, are hereby constituted a body corporate by the name of the Whitehead Academy; and that they and all who shall be duly elected members of said corporation shall be and remain a body corporate by that name forever, and shall

y corporate. orate name. orate pow-

be the trustees of said academy, with power to contract and be contracted with, to sue and be sued; to acquire property by gift, grant, bequest, devise or otherwise, and hold and convey the same, whether real personal or mixed; to have and use a common seal and alter the same at pleasure; to make and alter by-laws for the government of the corporation, its officers, agents and servants.

Authorized to receive real estate, etc.

Sec. 2. The trustees of the said academy are hereby authorized to receive all the real estate, goods, chattels, choses in action and property of every description whatever which has heretofore been given, conveyed, purchased, bequeathed, devised or in any other way secured to the Whitehead Academy, with the interest and for the purpose of establishing and maintaining an institution of learning at Whitehead, North Carolina, at which place the institution shall remain permanently located; and all the said funds and estates, as well as all other property, real, personal and mixed, which may be received by them, of which the said corporation shall be seized and possessed, shall be free from taxation, and shall be appropriated for purposes connected with the institution in such a manner as shall most effectually promote virtue and piety and the gaining of useful knowledge.

Purpose of corporation.

Exempted from taxation.

Election of president and other officers.

Sec. 3. That trustees shall have power to effect a president of their body, a secretary, treasurer and such other officers as the interests of the institution may require, who shall hold their offices at the pleasure of the board; also a principal for the government of the academy, who shall be ex officio a member of the board of trustees, and such teachers and other officers of the said academy as they shall judge most for the interest thereof; and to determine the duties, salaries, responsibilities and tenures of their several offices, and to remove each or any of them when the interest of the academy shall require it; they shall have full power and authority to determine in what times and places the meetings shall be holden and the manner of notifying the trustees to convene at such meetings. And they are further empowered to purchase or erect and keep in repair such houses and other buildings as they shall judge necessary for the academy, and also to make and ordain, as occasion may require, reasonable rules, orders and by-laws not repugnant to the constitution and the laws of this state or of the United States, with reasonable penalties for the good government of said academy and for the regulation of their own body, and through the principal of the institution, to grant to such persons as may be recommended by him and his associates a suitable certificate, which shall be signed by the principal of the academy and the president and secretary of the trustees, and shall have affixed thereto the seal of the academy.

May grant certificates.

Vacancies occurring.

Term of office.

Sec 4. They shall have power to fill all vacancies which ma occur in their own board by death, resignation or expiration of the term of office or other cause, and to elect additional members thereto; but the tenure of their office and the manner of their nomination and election and the number of which the board shall consist, also the number which shall constitute a quorum for the transaction of business, shall be determined by by-laws made by the trustees.

Apportionment of public school funds.

Sec. 5. The trustees shall maintain room and equipments for the teaching of all the public school funds that may be apportioned from time to time to the public school at Whitehead, North Carolina.

To whom academy opened.

Sec. 6. The academy in all its departments shall be open to all white persons of suitable age and approved character, without distinction of sex, and no person shall be refused admission to or denied any of its privileges or honors on account of sex or the religious opinions which may be entertained; but any student may be suspended or expelled from the institution whose habits are idle or vicious or whose moral character is bad.

Sale of liquor within one mile of academy unlawful.

Sec. 7. That it shall be unlawful to sell or manufacture malt, spirituous or vinous liquors within one mile (air line) of said academy.

Violation of section 7 a misdemeanor.

Sec. 8. That any person or persons violating the provisions of section seven of this act shall be guilty of a misdemeanor, and upon conviction fined not more than fifty dollars or imprisoned not more than thirty days.

Unlawful to sell liquors, pistols, etc., to students.

Sec. 9. That it shall be unlawful for any person or persons to sell or otherwise dispose of, directly or indirectly, to any student or students of Whitehead Academy malt, vinous, spirituous or any other intoxicating liquors, pistols or cartridges or any other weapon that is generally carried concealed.

Violation of section 9 a misdemeanor.

Sec. 10. That any person or persons violating the provisions of section nine of this act shall be guilty of a misdemeanor, and upon conviction fined not more than fifty dollars or imprisoned not more than thirty days.

Conflicting laws repealed.

Sec. 11. That all laws and clauses of laws in conflict with the provisions of this act are hereby repealed.

Sec. 12. That this act shall be in force from and after its ratification.

Ratified the 6th day of March, A. D. 1899.

CHAPTER 198.

An act to incorporate the town of Forestville, Wake county, North Carolina.

The General Assembly of North Carolina do enact:

Section 1. That the town of Forestville, in Wake county, North Carolina, be and the same is hereby incorporated under the name and style of the "Town of Forestville," and shall be subject to all the provisions of law of chapter sixty-two (62) of The Code or other existing laws in reference to incorporated towns. **Incorporated. Corporate name.**

Sec. 2. That the corporate limits of said town shall be one-fourth (¼) mile east, three-eight (⅜) mile south, one-fourth (¼) mile west, and one-half (½) north of "J. R. Dunn old store place." **Corporate limits.**

Sec. 3. That the officers of said corporation shall consist of a mayor and five commissioners, and the following-named persons shall fill said offices until the first Monday in May, Anno Domini nineteen hundred (1900), viz: Mayor, S. W. Allen; commissioners, W. P. Nuckler, A. C. Dunn, J. Q. Phillips, G. S. Patterson and P. P. Loyd. **Town officers. Temporary officers.**

Sec. 4. There shall be an election held for the officers mentioned in this act on the first Monday in May, nineteen hundred, and each succeeding year thereafter, under the same laws and restrictions that county and state elections are held, and all legal voters within said corporation who have resided in the state twelve months and within the corporate limits ninety days previous to the day of election shall be entitled to vote at said election. **Annual elections.**

Sec. 5. That said commissioners shall have power to pass all by-laws and rules and regulations for the good government of the town not inconsistent with the laws of the state or United States, and shall have power to levy and collect a tax on all subjects of state taxation not to exceed one dollar on the poll and thirty-three and one-third cents on the one hundred dollars worth of property, real and personal; to impose fines and penalties and collect the same. They shall also have power to appoint a clerk, treasurer or other officers if they deem it necessary, and shall fix the pay of said offices of said town. **Power of commissioners to pass rules, regulations, etc.**

Sec. 6. That this act shall be in force from and after its ratification.

Ratified the 6th day of March, A. D. 1899.

CHAPTER 199.

An act to amend the charter of the town of Farmville.

The General Assembly of North Carolina do enact:

Section 1. That the inhabitants of the town of Farmville shall be and continue as heretofore they have been, a body politic and corporate, and henceforth the corporate limits shall have the name and style of the "Town of Farmville," and under such name and style is hereby invested with all the property rights which now belong to the corporation under any other corporate name or names, and in and by this name may sue and be sued, plead and be impleaded; acquire and hold property, real and personal, for the use of the town, as its board of commissioners may deem necessary and expedient.

ody corporate. orporate name. rporate rights.

Sec. 2. That the corporate limits of said town shall be as follows: Five hundred yards each way from where Church street crosses Main street at the old church well.

orporate limits.

Sec. 3. That hereafter the town shall be divided into two wards, denominated as the first and second wards: That portion of the town lying north of a straight line running through the town with the southwestern line of R. L. Davis' Bruner lot, S. F. Pollard's and Ione B. Hooker's lots shall constitute the first ward, and that portion of the town lying south of the said line shall constitute the second ward.

ivision of ards.

Sec. 4. There shall on the first Monday in May, eighteen hundred and ninety-nine, and on the first Monday in May annually thereafter, be elected five commissioners for said town, who shall hold their offices until their successors are qualified, four of whom shall be chosen from the first ward and one from the second ward, and such commissioners shall be residents of the ward for which they are chosen and shall be elected by the qualified voters of the said ward, and must have resided in the state twelve months and in the corporation ninety days next preceding the day of election.

nnual elections. ection of commissioners.

Sec. 5. That the board of commissioners of the town of Farmville shall select at their regular meeting in March, eighteen hundred and ninety-nine, and annually thereafter, a registration of voters for each of the two wards of the town of Farmville, both of whom shall be qualified voters, one from each ward, and shall cause publication to be made at [——] public places in the said ward and notice to be served on such person by the constable of the town, and shall give ten days' notice of a registration for voters in and for said wards, specifying the time and place and the names of the registrars.

gistration of ters.

Sec. 6. That the registrars shall be furnished by the said board of commissioners with registration books, and it shall be their duty, after being qualified, to perform the functions of their office fairly and impartially according to law; that they shall open their books for registration of any electors in said town and entitled to such registration whose names have never before been registered in said town or do not appear in the revised list, and to register therein the names of all persons applying for registration and entitled to register and vote in that ward in which such registrar has been appointed. But the board of commissioners, upon ten days' notice, may direct that there shall be an entirely new registration of voters whenever they may deem it necessary for a fair election.

Duties of registrars.

Commissioners may order new registration.

Sec. 7. That the board of commissioners in the town of Farmville shall, in the year eighteen hundred and ninety-nine, and annually thereafter, appoint two judges or inspectors of election for each ward of the town of Farmville, one from each of the two leading political parties. After they have been duly sworn by the mayor or the justice of the peace to conduct the election fairly and impartially and according to law, it shall be the duty of said registrars and the judges or inspectors of the election to open the polls in the ward in which they have been respectively appointed and superintend the same for the municipal election to be held on the first Monday in May next succeeding.

Appointment of judges of election.

Sec. 8. All electors who are qualified to vote under the constitution of North Carolina and have resided in the town of Farmville and in the ward for which they offer to register ninety days next preceding the election shall be entitled to register hereunder.

Persons entitled to vote.

Sec. 9. The polls shall be opened on the day of election from seven o'clock in the morning until sunset of the same day; the commissioners for each ward shall be voted for on one ballot.

Polls, when opened.

Sec. 10. That at the close of the election the votes shall be counted by the judges, and such persons voted for as commissioners having the largest number of votes shall be declared elected commissioners of their respective wards.

Votes counted by judges.

Sec. 11. After the ballots are counted they shall be carefully preserved and shall be, together with the poll list, which shall be signed by the judges of the election, and the registration books, delivered to the clerk of the town of Farmville for preservation. The registrars and inspectors shall also furnish to each person as commissioner in their ward a certificate of election.

Ballots shall be preserved.

Sec. 12. That on Tuesday succeeding the day of such election each commissioner elected thereat shall, before entering upon the duties of his office, take before the mayor or some justice of the peace an oath that he will truly and impartially perform the

When commissioners shall qualify.

duties of commissioner for the town of Farmville according to the best of his skill, ability and judgment.

ction of yor. Sec. 13. That the board of commissioners at their first meeting after their election shall choose some person, not one of their own number, to be mayor of said town, to hold his office until his successor shall qualify, who shall preside at the meetings of the board of commissioners and have the rights and powers and perform all duties prescribed by law for such officers. For misconduct in office the mayor may be removed from his office by a vote of three-fifths of the entire number of the board of commissioners, and upon such office becoming vacant for any cause the board of commissioners shall fill the same for the unexpired term.

rm of office.

yor may be oved.

yor shall take h. Sec. 14. That the mayor, immediately after his election and before entering on the duties of his office, shall take his oath of office before a justice of the peace.

m of office of missioners. Sec. 15. That the commissioners shall hold offices until the next ensuing election and until their respective successors are qualified.

sons elected yor and refing to qualify. Sec. 16. That if any person elected mayor shall refuse to be qualified, or if there is a vacancy in the office after election and qualification, or if the mayor be absent from the town or unable to discharge the duties of his office, the commissioners shall choose some qualified person for the term or the unexpired portion of the term or during his absence or disability, as the case may be, to act as mayor; and he shall be clothed with all the authorities and powers given under this charter to the regularly elected mayor, and the commissioners shall on like occasions and in like manner choose other commissioners to supply the place of such as shall refuse to act, and of all vacancies which may occur, and such persons only shall be chosen as are heretofore declared to be eligible: Provided, in the event of the mayor's absence or sickness or inability to act the board of commissioners may appoint one of their number pro tempore to exercise his duties.

isdiction of yor. Constied a special irt. Sec. 17. That the mayor of the town of Farmville is hereby constituted a special court, with all the jurisdictions and powers in criminal offenses occurring within the limits of the said town which are or hereafter may be given to justices of the peace. He shall preserve and keep the peace and may cause, upon proper proceedings, to be arrested persons charged or convicted of crimes in other counties or states who may be found in the town limits and bound or imprisoned to appear at the proper tribunal to answer for their offenses. He shall also have jurisdiction to issue process, and exclusive original jurisdiction to hear and determine all misdemeanors consisting of a violation of the ordinances of

y issue proses, etc.

the said town; to hear and to determine all causes of action, to recover fines and penalties for the violation of the ordinances and regulations of said town and enforce penalties by issuing executions upon any adjudged violations thereof; to execute the laws and rules made by the commissioners, and his endorsement of the name of witnesses upon a summons or warrant shall be authority for the officer to execute the same.

Proceedings in mayor's court.

Sec. 18. That all proceedings in the mayor's court shall be the same as are now or hereafter shall be prescribed for courts of justices of the peace, and in all cases there shall be a right of appeal to the superior court of Pitt county. That whenever a defendant or witness or other person shall be adjudged to be imprisoned by the said court, it shall be competent for the said court to sentence such person to imprisonment in the county jail for a term not exceeding thirty days.

To whom processes issued.

Sec. 19. That the mayor may issue his process and warrants to the constable or police of the town of Farmville, and to such other officers to whom a justice of the peace may issue his precepts and the same may be served by the constable of the town or other officer authorized to serve process anywhere in the county of Pitt.

Mayor shall keep minute of precepts issued.

Sec. 20. That the mayor shall keep a faithful minute of the precepts issued by him and all of his judicial proceedings. The judgments rendered by him shall have all the force, virtue and validity of the judgments rendered by a justice of peace, and may be executed and enforced against the parties in the county of Pitt and elsewhere in the manner and by the same means as if the same had been rendered by a justice of the peace for the county of Pitt.

Mayor shall preside at meetings of commissioners

Sec. 21. That the mayor when present shall preside at all meetings of the board of commissioners. and when there is an equal division upon any question or in the election of officers by the board, he shall determine the matter by his vote. He shall vote in no other case, and if he shall be absent the board may appoint one of their number pro tempore to exercise his duties at the board. and in the event of his absence or sickness the board of commissioners may appoint one of their own number pro tempore to exercise his duties.

When commissioners shall convene.

Sec. 22 That the commissioners shall form one board and a majority of them shall be competent to perform all the duties prescribed for the commissioners unless otherwise provided; within five days after their election they shall convene for the transaction of business and shall then fix stated days of meeting for the year, which shall be as often as once in every month. The special meetings of the board may also be held on the call of the mayor or a majority of the commissioners.

wer of commissioners to ke ordinances.

Sec. 23. That the commissioners when convened shall have power to make and provide for the execution thereof [of] such ordinances, by-laws, rules and regulations for the better government of the town as they may deem necessary: Provided, the same be allowed by the provisions of this act and be consistent with the laws of the land. They shall provide for repairing and cleansing the streets, make regulations to cause the due observance of Sunday, appoint and regulate town constables or policemen, suppress and remove nuisances; regulate, control and tax the business of the junk shops; preserve the health of the town; appoint constables to execute such precepts as the mayor and other persons may lawfully issue to them; to preserve the peace and order and execute the ordinances of the town; regulate the hours for the sale of spirituous liquors by all persons required to be licensed by the board; and during periods of great excitement may prohibit the sale of spirituous liquors by all such persons for such times as the board may deem necessary; may pass ordinances imposing penalties for violations thereof, not to exceed a fine of twenty-five dollars or imprisonment for thirty days; and the constable or policeman of the town of Farmville when appointed shall have the power to execute any process, criminal or civil in the county of Pitt, which may be directed to them by the said mayor or other lawful authority; and shall appoint and provide for the pay and prescribe the duties of all such other officers as may be deemed necessary.

isances.

stable and cemen emered to issue cesses.

ties of policen.

Sec. 24. That it shall be the duty of the policeman to see that the laws, ordinances and the orders of the board of commissioners are enforced, and to report all breaches thereof to the mayor; to preserve the peace of the town by suppressing the disturbances and apprehending offenders; for that purpose they shall have all the powers and authorities vested in sheriffs and county constables; to prevent as far as possible all injuries to the town property, streets and sidewalks, and to report to the mayor any repairs needed, and to perform such other duties as may be required of them by the board of commissioners; they shall have authority, if resisted in the execution of their official duties, to summons a sufficient number of men to aid them in enforcing the law, and if any person so summoned shall refuse to assist, the policeman is hereby directed to proceed against them as the law directs.

pointment of k, treasurer tax collector

Sec. 25. That the commissioners at their first meeting after their election shall appoint a clerk, a treasurer, a collector of taxes and a town constable or chief of police, who shall respectively hold their offices during the official term of the commissioners, subject, however, to be removed at any time and others appointed in their stead, for misbehavior or neglect in office.

Before acting each of said officers shall be sworn to the faithful discharge of his duties, and shall execute a bond, payable to the town of Farmville in such sum as the commissioners shall determine.

Sec. 26. That the citizens of the town of Farmville and others liable to be taxed under the charter shall on the days prescribed for listing state and county taxes render on oath to the clerk of the town, who is hereby constituted as commissioners of affidavits for that purpose, on a blank to be prepared and furnished by the board of commissioners, a list of their property and subjects for which they may be liable to be taxed under all the rules and penalties prescribed for listing state and county taxes and as prescribed in this charter. The list shall state the age of the party with reference to his liability to a poll tax, and shall also contain a verified statement of all real and personal property and such interests and estates therein as are taxable, and that all persons who are liable for a poll tax to the said town and shall willfully fail to give themselves in, and all persons who own property or whose duty it is to list property and who willfully fail to list it within the time allowed by law, shall be deemed guilty of a misdemeanor to the same extent as for failure to list state and county taxes, and on conviction thereof before the mayor of the town or a justice of the peace of Farmville township, shall be fined not more than ten dollars or imprisoned not more than ten days, and it shall be the duty of the tax collector of the said town to prosecute offenders against this section.

Persons liable to taxation shall return list under oath.

Persons failing to list property liable to taxation guilty of a misdemeanor.

Sec. 27. That as soon as the tax list can be completed by the clerk and turned over to the board of commissioners they shall proceed to levy the tax on such subjects of taxation as they shall determine, and shall place the tax list in the hands of the tax collector for collection, who shall proceed forthwith in the collection and shall complete the same on or before the first day of December next ensuing, and shall pay the moneys as they are collected to the treasurer of the town, and the tax collector shall receive for his compensation not more than five per centum on the amount collected, as the board of commissioners shall determine. That if any person liable to taxes on subjects directed to be listed shall fail to pay them within the time prescribed for collection, the collector shall proceed forthwith to collect the same by distress and sale, all sales to be made after public advertisement for the space of ten days in some newspaper published in the county of Pitt, if the property be personal, and twenty days if the property be realty, and the said collector shall have the right to levy upon and sell any personal property situated outside the limits of the town and within the county of Pitt belonging to the de-

When commissioners shall proceed to levy tax.

When collection shall be completed.

Compensation of collector.

Taxes may be collected by distress.

Collector may levy upon personal property.

linquent tax payer of the town in order to enforce the payment of taxes due the town by said delinquent.

xes due and paid by December.

Sec. 28. That when the tax due on any lot or other land (which is hereby declared to be a lien on the same) shall remain unpaid on the first day of December, the tax collector shall either proceed to collect the same by levy and sale of personal property belonging to the owner of said lot or shall report the fact to the commissioners, together with a particular description of the real estate, and thereupon the commissioners shall direct the same to be sold before the mayor's office door in the town of Farmville by the collector. The collector shall, before selling the same, make a full advertisement of the said real estate at the mayor's office door and two other public places in said town for twenty days, and shall also serve upon the owner thereof a written notice of the taxes due and the day of sale, but such notice need not be given to any person having or claiming any lien on said land by way of mortgage or otherwise. Whenever the owners are not in the town or for any cause can not be served with notice, then the advertisement of real estate belonging to such owners shall be made for one week in some newspaper published in the county of Pitt and the collectors shall sell a portion of said real estate or the whole.

vertisement of .e required.

llector shall urn account proceedings to mmissioners.

Sec. 29. That the collector shall return an account of his proceedings to the commissioners, specifying the portion into which the land was divided and the purchaser thereof and the prices of each, which shall be entered on the book of proceedings of the commissioners; and if there should be a surplus after paying the said taxes the same shall be paid into the town treasury, subject to the demands of the owner.

nd sold for xes may be deemed within year.

Sec. 30. That the owner of any land sold under the provisions of this charter and amendments, his heirs, executors and administrators, or any person acting for them, may redeem the same within one year after the sale by paying to the purchaser the same [sum] by him paid and twenty-five per cent. on the amount of taxes and expenses, and the treasurer shall refund to him without interest the proceeds, less double the amount of taxes.

hen not reemed town ay convey real tate in full to rchaser.

Sec. 31. That if the real estate sold as aforesaid shall not be redeemed within the time specified, the corporation shall convey the same in full to the purchaser.

ecial taxes.

Sec 32. That in addition to the subjects listed for taxation the commissioners may levy a tax on the following subjects, the amount of which tax when fixed shall be collected by the constable of the town instantly, and if the same be not paid on demand the same may be recovered by suit, or the articles upon which the tax is composed [imposed] or any other property of the owner may be forthwith distrained and sold to satisfy the same:

(1) Upon all itinerant merchants or peddlers offering to vend in the town, a license not exceeding ten dollars, except such only as sell books, charts or maps, or wares of their own manufacture, but not excepting venders of medicines by whomsoever manufactured. Itinerant merchants.

(2) Upon every permission by the board of commissioners to retail spirituous, vinous or malt liquors a tax of not less than twenty-five dollars a year. Liquor license.

(3) Upon every company of circus riders or performers by whatever name called, who shall exhibit within the town or in one mile thereof, a license tax not exceeding twenty-five dollars. Circuses.

(4) Upon every other occupation, profession or business not herein specially named, a license tax not exceeding ten dollars per year. Other occupations.

(5) Upon every horse or mule allowed to run at large a tax not exceeding five dollars. Horses, mules, etc.

(6) That they may prohibit and prevent by penalties the riding or driving of horses or other animals at a greater speed than eight miles an hour or in a reckless manner within the town, and also the firing of guns, pistols, crackers, gunpowder or other explosives, combustible or dangerous material in the streets or elsewhere within the town. Fast riding or driving may be prohibited.

Sec. 33. That it shall not be lawful for the commissioners of Pitt county to grant any license to sell spirituous, vinous or malt liquors within the limits of the town of Farmville or within one mile thereof without permission first obtained from the board of commissioners of the town of Farmville in being at the time of the application to the county commissioners, and if any license shall be granted without permission in writing, attested by the clerk of the board of town commissioners and exhibited to the county commissioners and filed with the clerk of the board of county commissioners, the same shall be utterly void, and the person obtaining such license shall be liable to indictment as in other cases of selling liquors without license, and for every offense of such selling shall moreover forfeit and pay to the town ten dollars. County commissioners shall not grant liquor license without permission of commissioners of Farmville.

Sec. 34. All bar-rooms or places for the sale of spirituous, vinous or malt liquors shall be closed from nine o'clock every night until four o'clock the next morning, and no person or persons shall, during or between these times in any licensed liquor saloon, sell or give away any spirituous, vinous or malt liquors except in case of sickness, and then only upon a certificate from a practising physician, and one or more persons except the proprietors or their attendants seen going in or out of a bar-room between the said hours above mentioned shall be prima facie evidence of the Closing of bar-rooms.

olation of this tion. nalty. guilt of the proprietor of said bar-room. Any person violating this section shall forfeit and pay to the town a fine of five dollars.

r-rooms shall closed on nday. Sec. 35. All bar-rooms for the sale of spirituous, vinous or malt liquors shall remain closed on Sundays and no person or persons shall, in any licensed liquor saloon, sell or give away any spirituous, vinous or malt liquors on Sunday, except in case of sickness and then only upon a certificate from a practising physican, and one or more persons, except the proprietors or their attendants, seen going in or out of a bar-room on Sunday shall be prima facie evidence of the guilt cf the proprietor of said barroom of the violation of this section, and such proprietor shall forfeit and pay to the town a fine of ten dollars for every offense, and any person convicted of the violation of this section shall have their license revoked and shall never be granted license to sell liquor in the town of Farmville again.

es and pen- es, how ap- ed. Sec. 36. That all the fines and penalties imposed by and collected under the judgment of the mayor of the town of Farmville sitting as a justice of the peace, shall belong to and inure to the exclusive benefit of the town of Farmville.

is charter in n of former rters. Sec. 37. That this charter shall hereafter be in lieu of former charters and shall be the charter of the town of Farmville.

Sec. 38. That this act shal' be in force from and after the ---- day of ------, eighteen hundred and ninety-nine.

Ratified the 6th day of March, A. D. 1899.

CHAPTER 200.

An act to consolidate and amend the charter of the city of Burlington.

The General Assembly of North Carolina do enact:

apter 19, pri- e laws of 1866, laws amend- ry thereof, ended. Section 1. That chapter nineteen, private laws of eighteen hundred and sixty-six, incorporating the town of Company Shops, and all acts amendatory thereof be amended to read as follows: That the inhabitants of the city of Burlington shall be and continue as heretofore they have been a body politic and corporate, and henceforth the corporation shall bear the name and style of "The City of Burlington," and under that name and style is hereby invested with all the property and rights of property which now belong to the present corporation of the city of Burlington or any other corporate name or names heretofore used, and by the corporate name of "The City of Burlington" may purchase and hold for its government all such estate, real and personal, as may be conveyed, devised or bequeathed to it, and the same may from time to time sell, dispose of and reinvest, as

dy corporate. porate name. porate pow- .

shall be deemed advisable by the board of commissioners of the said corporation of the city of Burlington, and under the name and style of "The City of Burlington" said corporation may sue and be sued, plead and be impleaded in any and all the courts of this state; contract and be contracted with, and adopt and use a common seal, which may be altered at the pleasure of the board of commissioners.

Sec. 2. That the corporate limits of the city of Burlington shall remain the same as in the original charter of the town of Company Shops. The same special enactments prohibiting the sale and manufacture of spirituous and fermented liquors shall remain in full force and effect. Corporate limits unchanged. Enactments regarding liquor.

Sec. 3. That the city of Burlington shall be divided into four wards as follows: The first ward shall contain all that part of the city west of the track of the North Carolina Railroad and north of Main street. The second ward all that part of the city east of the track of the North Carolina Railroad and north of Tarpley street. The third ward all that part of the city east of the track of the North Carolina Railroad and south of Tarply street. The fourth ward all that part of the city west of the North Carolina Railroad and south of Main street. Division of wards.

Sec. 4. The administration and government of said city shall be vested in one principal officer, to be styled the mayor, and a board of eight aldermen. Administration and government, in whom vested.

Sec. 5. The mayor shall be elected by the qualified voters of the whole city voting in their respective wards. Mayor, how elected.

Sec. 6. Each ward shall elect two aldermen and such aldermen shall be residents of the ward for which they are chosen, and shall be elected by the qualified voters of such ward for the time and in the manner hereinafter prescribed. Election of aldermen.

Sec. 7. The board of aldermen shall make regulations to cause the due observance of Sunday, to appoint and regulate a police force to execute such precepts as the mayor and other persons may lawfully issue to them; to preserve the peace and order of the city and to execute the ordinances thereof; to suppress and remove nuisances, preserve the health of the city from contagious or infectious diseases, and shall appoint and provide for the pay and prescribe the duties of all such other officers as may be deemed necessary. Powers of aldermen.

Sec 8. The election for mayor and the board of aldermen of the city of Burlington shall be held on the first Monday in May, in the year eighteen hundred and ninety-nine and upon the first Monday in May in each succeeding year thereafter. Municipal election, when held.

Sec. 9. That on the first Monday in May, eighteen hundred and ninety-nine, four aldermen, one from each ward, shall be elected for a term of two years, and four for a term of one year, Next election. Term of office of aldermen.

and at each annual election thereafter four aldermen from each ward shall be elected for a term of two years.

nual election mayor.

Sec. 10. The mayor shall be elected annually for a term of one year.

ties of mayor.

Sec. 11. That the mayor when present shall preside at all the meetings of the board of aldermen; and when there is an equal division upon any question or in the election of officers by the board he shall determine the matter by his vote. He shall vote in no other case, and if he shall be absent the board may appoint one of their number pro tempore to exercise his duty.

dermen shall first meeting stated days meeting.

Sec. 12. That the aldermen shall form one board, and a majority of them shall be competent to perform all the duties prescribed unless otherwise provided. At their first meeting they shall fix stated days of meeting for the year, which shall be as often at least as once in every month. Special meetings of the aldermen may also be held on the call of the mayor or a majority of the aldermen, and at every such meeting when called by the mayor all the aldermen shall be notified, and when called by a majority of the aldermen such as shall not join in the call shall be notified.

dinances, and forcement of me.

Sec. 13. That the board of aldermen when convened shall have power to make and provide for the execution thereof such ordinances, by-laws, rules and regulations for the better government of the city as they may deem necessary, not inconsistent with this act or with the laws of the land.

cancies occurg.

Sec. 14. In case of a vacancy in the office of mayor or aldermen the board of aldermen shall at the first meeting after the vacancy proceed to elect a successor, who shall hold his office until the next annual election.

pointment of istrar and spectors of ction.

Sec. 15. The board of aldermen, for the purpose of holding the election for said officers shall appoint a registrar and two inspectors for each ward, the two inspectors to be of different political parties. The registrar in each ward shall keep the registration book open for thirty days preceding each election at his usual place of business, and the books shall close for registration at twelve o'clock m. on the Saturday next preceding the day of election, and no one shall vote at these elections without registration: Provided, any one coming of age after the books close for registration and on or before the day of election may register and vote on the day of election. The registrar and the inspectors for each ward shall post a written notice at three public places ten days before each election of the time and place of holding said election. The registrars, before entering upon the discharge of their duties, shall be sworn by the mayor to faithfully perform their duty according to law. The inspectors shall be sworn by some justice of the peace as in election for members of the

rsons entitled vote.

tice of election all be given.

eneral assembly, and they shall conduct the election in like anner and during the same hours of the day as elections for embers of the general assembly: and at the close of the pol. they, together with the registrar, shall make out and sign a report, giving the name, office for which voted and number of votes cast for each candidate or other person voted for. This report shall then be placed in an envelope, sealed and directed to the mayor of the city of Burlington. It shall be the duty of each registrar to file this report, the registration book and a poll of the votes, which must be kept with the mayor within twenty-four hours from the closing of the polls. On Thursday night succeeding each election at the usual hour of meeting, the mayor of the city of Burlington and the board of aldermen shall meet in the mayor's office, open and count the votes as given in the different wards and declare the result of the election. The board of aldermen at such meeting shall make or cause to be made two returns or statements showing the tabulated vote for each and every person voted for for mayor and aldermen. This tabulated statement shall be spread upon the minutes of the board and a copy be posted in the mayor's hall and a copy sent to the clerk of the superior court of Alamance county, to be by him enrolled in the book of election returns.

Report of result.

When report shall be filed.

Aldermen shall count votes.

Tabulated statement shall appear on minute book.

Sec. 16 The qualifications of the electors shall be the same as that prescribed by the laws of the state of North Carolina for the election of members of the general assembly.

Qualification of electors.

Sec. 17. That among the powers hereby conferred on the board of aldermen for the purpose of the public improvement of the city, providing lights, water, sewerage, macadamizing streets and paving sidewalks, they may borrow money or create a public debt, issue bonds and levy additional taxes for the payment of the interest on the same, and to provide a sinking fund for the liquidation of the said debt or debts or bonds at maturity only after they have passed an ordinance by a three-fourths vote of the entire board at two separate regular meetings, submitting the question of creating a debt or issuing bonds to a vote of the people, and a majority of the qualified registered voters have voted in favor thereof; thirty days' notice shall be given of such election in some newspaper published in Burlington, at which election those who favor creating the debt or issuing bonds shall vote "Approved," and those who oppose it shall vote "Not approved," but the bonded indebtedness of the city shall never exceed the sum of thirty thousand dollars. The board, when it shall deem it necessary, may order a new registration of voters. This election shall be held under the same rules and regulations as those prescribed for election of mayor and aldermen.

Powers conferred on aldermen.

Question of issuing bonds.

Form of ballot.

New registration may be ordered.

Sec. 18. The board of aldermen shall have power, in the name powered to ke contracts, of the city of Burlington, to make contracts and to become the owners or part owners of electric light plant and water plants, and shall have power to contract with private individuals, firms or corporations for light or water supplies and to charge a reasonable compensation therefor.

city officer ll become tractor for work. Sec. 19. That no mayor or aldermen or other officer of the city government shall directly or indirectly become a contractor for work to be done by the city, and any person herein offending shall be guilty of a misdemeanor.

en right-of- necessary, d may be demned. Sec. 20. When any land or right-of-way shall be required for the purpose of opening or laying out new streets or widening those already open, and the land owner or owners and said aldermen can not agree upon the price which the land owner or owners will take and convey said land to the city, the same shall be taken at a valuation of three freeholders of the said city, to be chosen as follows: The aldermen shall select one, the owner or owners of the land one, within three days after notice in writing to the land owner or owners from the aldermen of their selection, and the two freeholders thus selected shall select the third man, also a freeholder, and these persons shall assess the damages, if there be any, within five days after the notice from the aldermen to the land owner or owners above mentioned; and if the owner or owners of the land fail to select a man within three days as aforesaid, then the aldermen shall select two men, and the two thus selected shall select a third man, and the three men thus selected shall assess the damages to the land within the time aforesaid. The said freeholders when so chosen shall be first duly sworn by the mayor or a justice of the peace, and shall view the premises of the land to be condemned, and in making valuation shall take into consideration any benefit or advantage such owner or owners may receive from the opening or widening of such street; and shall ascertain and report to the aldermen under their hands and seals what amount or sum shall be paid to the land owner or owners, which report, on being confirmed by the board of aldermen and spread upon the minutes of said city, shall have the force and effect of a judgment in favor of said land owner or owners against said city of Burlington: Provided, that either party may appeal to the next term of the superior court of Alamance county upon the question of damages, and notice of appeal must be served in writing within ten days from the report of the freeholders; but no appeal shall delay the opening of any street.

ction of itrators. — ltrators shall worn. — ult shall be orted to ermen. — viso. — her party y appeal.

en owners and are in- ts, lunatics, Sec. 21. That in case the owner or owners of land over which a right-of-way is desired, as stated in preceding section, are infants, lunatics or non-residents, it shall be the duty of the aldermen to file a petition before the clerk of the superior court of

Alamance county on behalf of the said city of Burlington, making defendants the parties over whose land the said right of-way is desired, and such petition shall set forth in detail the lands over which said right of-way will run and the terminal of said street, and such proceedings as to notice and time of hearing shall be governed by the laws governing other special proceedings, and upon the hearing the clerk shall appoint three disinterested persons, citizens and freeholders of the city of Burlington, as commissioners, who shall view the premises and shall ascertain and report to the clerk under their hands and seals what amount or sum shall be paid to the land owner or owners, and the order of the clerk of the superior court, together with the report of the commissioners, shall be spread upon the minutes of the city of Burlington, and shall pass the title of said land to the city of Burlington, and shall have the force and effect of a judgment in favor of said land owner or owners against said city of Burlington.

Order of clerk shall be spread on minutes.

Sec. 22. That all property the subject of taxation by the state and county shall be likewise subject to taxation by the city of Burlington, and it shall be the duty of the mayor of said city to obtain from the office of the register of deeds for Alamance county the assessed value of all property belonging to citizens of the city of Burlington, and to compute the tax upon the same and have it ready to turn over to the tax collector by the first Monday in October of each year, at which time the taxes of said city shall be due and payable.

Property subject to taxation.

Tax, when due.

Sec. 23. That every owner of a lot which shall front any street on which a sidewalk has been established shall improve it in such manner as the aldermen may direct such sidewalk, as far as [it] may extend along such lot, and on failure to do so within twenty days after written notice from the board of aldermen served by the chief police officer of the city upon the said owner, or if he be a non resident of the county of Alamance, upon his agent; or if such non-resident have no agent in said county or personal notice can not be served upon the owner or agent, then after publication of a notice by the chief of police for thirty days in some newspaper published in Alamance county, calling on the owner to make such repairs, the aldermen may cause the same to be repaired either with bricks, stone or gravel, at their discretion, and the expense shall be paid by the person in default. Said expense shall be a lien upon said lot, and if not paid within six months after completion of the repairs, such lot may be sold, or enough of the same to pay such expenses and cost; and it shall be lawful for and the duty of the mayor of said city, after advertising time and place of sale for thirty days in some newspaper published in Alamance county, to offer said lot for sale to the highest bidder

Owners of lots fronting streets may be required to improve sidewalks.

Failure of owner to make improvement as directed.

t may be sold r expenses curred by commissioners. for cash. The [owner] shall have twelve months from day of sale in which to redeem said lot by paying the amount expended in the repairs and ten per centum interest to the last and highest bidder at said sale upon the amount expended in repairs and costs of sale. In case said owner fails to redeem said lot in twelve months, upon the payment to him of the purchase-money and costs the mayor shall make a good and fee simple deed to the purchaser: Provided, no owner of any lot as above set out shall pay more than one-third of the cost of such improvement.

nflicting laws pealed. Sec. 24. That all acts and parts of acts in conflict herewith are hereby repealed.

cers governed chapter 62 of e Code. Sec. 25. That in addition to the powers herein contained, the said officers shall be governed in their powers and duties by chapter sixty-two, volume two, of The Code of North Carolina.

Sec. 26. That this act shall be in force from and after its ratification.

Ratified the 6th day of March, A. D. 1899.

CHAPTER 201.

An act to incorporate the Salisbury Savings Bank.

The General Assembly of North Carolina do enact:

rporators. Section 1. That John S. Henderson, M. S. Brown, L. H. Clement, P. B Beard, D. R. Julian, A. H. Boyden and E. H. Cuthrell, their associates, successors and assigns, are hereby constituted and declared a body politic and corporate by the name and style of "The Salisbury Savings Bank," with its principal place of business in the city of Salisbury, and by that name may sue and be sued plead and be impleaded in any court of the state, and have a continual succession for the term of thirty years, with the rights, powers and privileges of corporations and banks under the general laws of the state.

rporate name. rporate pow-

pital stock. Sec. 2. The capital stock of said corporation shall not be less than ten thousand dollars, in shares of one hundred dollars each, and such capital stock may be increased from time to time as said corporation may elect by a vote of its shareholders to a sum not exceeding one hundred thousand dollars.

y be increased.

hen company y be organd. Sec. 3. Whenever five thousand dollars shall be subscribed and one-half paid in the capital stock of said corporation, the above-named corporation or a majority of them shall call a meeting of the subscribers to said stock at such time and place and on such notice as they may deem sufficient to organize said corporation; and such stockholders shall elect such directors as are hereinafter provided by section four of this act, who shall hold their office for one year and until their successors shall be chosen; and said directors shall elect a president and such other officers as they may think proper. to serve during their continuance in office. The remaining half of said subscribed capital shall be paid within one year after bank begins business.

Sec. 4. The officers of this corporation shall consist of a president, vice-president, cashier, teller, and such other officers as may be provided in the by-laws, and a board of directors of not less than seven nor more than nine directors, who are to be elected annually by the stockholders, and are to hold office until their successors are duly chosen; the directors so elected shall appoint the officers aforesaid. It shall be lawful for one person to perform the duties of more than one office in said corporation, and at all meetings of stockholders each share shall be entitled to one vote. Officers of said corporation. Directors.

Sec. 5. It shall be the duty of the board of directors and they are hereby empowered to make rules and regulations and by-laws for the government of the said corporation and for the conduct of its business; also to fix the salaries of its officers and to fill vacancies on its board. A majority of said board shall constitute a quorum to do business. They may adopt and use a common seal and alter the same at pleasure. Directors shall make by-laws, etc. Quorum.

Sec. 6. The corporation is especially invested with the power and authority to carry on, conduct and operate a savings bank business in all its branches, and may receive deposits in very small sums, the limits to be fixed by its board of directors, and may pay interest thereon by the way of dividends out of the net earnings or at fixed rates, according as it may be agreed between the company and its depositors; and the board of directors are hereby authorized to make all needful by-laws and regulations for conducting and carrying into effect the different features of this branch of its corporation; and shall also have a right to conduct a general banking business. Purpose of corporation.

Sec. 7. Said corporation may purchase and hold all such real and personal property as may be necessary for its own business purposes and such as may be conveyed to it to secure or satisfy any debt due to it or for any other purpose; and such as may be sold under a foreclosure of any mortgage made to said corporation or sold under execution or order of any court to satisfy any debt due to it, and may sell and convey and exchange the same at pleasure, and use or reinvest the proceeds thereof as may be deemed best; and said corporation is hereby authorized and empowered to invest the capital stock or funds of said company or such money and funds as may be deposited with said company for that purpose from time to time in the stocks, bonds or other securities of the United States or of this or any other state of the United States, or of any corporation under the laws thereof or May purchase and hold real estate.

any other stock or property whatsoever, and to dispose of the same in such manner as may appear to said company most advantageous.

y receive os'ts cf ney, etc.

Sec. 8. Said corporation may receive a [on] deposit all sums of money which may be offered it for the purpose of being invested in such sums and at such times and on such terms as the board of directors may agree upon; and if money be deposited by a minor or feme covert, such money may be withdrawn by the minor or feme covert without the consent of the parent or guardian or husband of said minor or feme covert; and his or her check or receipt shall be binding upon said minor or feme covert as if he or she were of full age, and fully discharge said corpora[illegible] tion from any and all liability therefor.

powered to ept trusts from rts, etc.

Sec. 9. Said corporation shall have power to receive moneys in trust, and shall have power to accept and execute any trust that may be committed to it by any court, corporation, company, person or persons, and it shall have power to accept any grant, assignment, transfer, desire [devise] or bequest and hold any personal or real estate in trust created in accordance with the laws of this state, and then to execute the same on such terms as [may] be established and agreed upon by its board of directors; and said corporation is hereby authorized and empowered to act [illegible]s trustee or assignee, and to receive on deposit all funds in lit[illegible]gation in the various courts in this state, and pay therefor such [illegible]erest as may be agreed on, not exceeding the lawful rate. [illegible] have power and authority to receive for safe keeping o[illegible] all money, bonds, stock, diamonds and silver plate and [illegible]valuables and charge and collect a reasonable compensati[illegible] f[illegible] the same, which charges shall be a lien upon said deposit until the same be paid; and generally to do and carry on the business of a safety and deposit company; and any receiver, executor, administrator, assignee, guardian or committee of a lunatic, and any public officer is hereby authorized to deposit with the said company for safe keeping any money or bonds, stocks, securities or other valuables which have or may come into his possession or under his control by virtue of his office or appointment aforesaid.

rk of corpora- . how trans- ed.

Sec. 10. The stock of this corporation shall be transferred only on the books of the company, either in person or by power of attorney; and no stockholder shall transfer his stock except by the consent of the directors of the corporation, if he be indebted to the corporation as principal, security or otherwise, until such indebtedness is paid off and discharged; and for all such indebtedness said corporation shall have a lien superior to all other liens upon the stock of said stockholder.

Sec. 11. This act shall be in force and effect from and after its ratification.

Ratified the 6th day of March, A. D. 1899.

CHAPTER 202.

An act to incorporate the Commercial and Savings Bank of Goldsboro, North Carolina.

The General Assembly of North Carolina do enact:

Section 1. That G. A. Norwood, Jr., K. E. Bizzen, S. W. Isler, W. W. Crawford, G. C. Royall and L. D. Gully, their associates, successors and assigns, are hereby constituted and declared a body politic and corporate by the name and style of The Commercial and Savings Bank, and shall continue for a term of sixty years, if accepted by the stockholders within five years of the date of its ratification, with capacity to take, hold and convey real and personal estate with all of the powers, rights and privileges granted any bank or banking institution incident to or belonging to corporations, banks or banking institutions as set forth or referred to in the general laws of North Carolina. Corporators. Corporate name. Corporate powers.

Sec. 2. The capital stock of said corporation shall not be less than fifteen thousand dollars ($15,000), but may be increased from time to time by the stockholders as may be agreed upon to a sum not exceeding two hundred thousand dollars ($200,000), divided into shares of one hundred dollars ($100) each. Capital stock.

Sec. [illegible] The corporators named in the first section of this act, or a ma[illegible]ity of them, are hereby empowered to open books of sub[illegible] to the capital stock of said ban[illegible] at such time and place, [illegible] such period or periods as shall be determined. Books for subscription to stock may be opened.

[illegible] Whenever fifteen hundred dollars or over shall have been [illegible]scribed and paid in, the before-named corporators, or a majority of them, shall call a meeting of the subscribers to said stock at such time and place and on such notice as they deem sufficient, and such subscribers shall elect from among their number such directors and officers as they may deem proper, who shall hold office for one year and until their successors are appointed; said directors shall have authority to fill all vacancies that may occur in their own body and in any office or position of the bank until the next annual meeting of the stockholders. The corporation shall do a general banking business in all of its forms and branches, and take interest or discount in advance as may be agreed upon, not in excess of the legal rate. The corporation may receive on deposit moneys held in trust from executors, administrators, guardians and others, and may issue certificates of deposit bearing such legal rate of interest as may be agreed upon between the parties; executors, administrators, guardians and others making such deposits are hereby authorized and empowered to accept certificates: Provided, that nothing in this section shall be construed as releasing any executor, admin- When meeting of stockholders held. Corporate powers.

istrators, guardian or any other person who has the custody of any trust fund from liability under their bond or bonds.

powered to establish savings nk.

Sec. 5. The corporation shall have authority to establish a savings bank department and operate same and receive deposits of sums of money of one dollar ($1) and upwards, and pay the same with interest, as may be agreed upon with depositors.

posits by minors d femes covert.

Sec. 6. When any deposits shall be made by any person being a minor or feme covert, the said corporation may, at its discretion, pay to such minor or feme covert, and such payment shall be to all intents and purposes valid in law to fully discharge the said corporation from any and all liability on account thereof.

rporate powers d rights.

Sec. 7. This corporation shall have all the rights, powers and privileges conferred upon the Citizens Trust Company in chapter thirty-eight, private laws of North Carolina, of eighteen hundred and eighty-three, not inconsistent with this act: Provided, this act shall not authorize the establishment of branch banks, and provided nothing herein shall authorize the charging of a greater rate of interest than that prescribed by law.

Sec. 8. This act shall be in force from and after its ratification.

Ratified the 28th day of February, A. D. 1899.

CHAPTER 203.

An act to incorporate the Raleigh Banking and Trust Company.

The General Assembly of North Carolina do enact:

rporators.

Section 1. That Charles E. Johnson, Charles H. Belvin, W. A. Linehan, James A. Briggs, Charles Root, Charles M. Busbee, Thomas B. Crowder, Joseph B. Batchelor, Julius Lewis, F. O. Moring, Perrin Busbee, J. W. Harden Jr., F. H. Briggs, and their associates and successors, are hereby created a body politic and corporate under the name and style of The Raleigh Banking and Trust Company, and by such name shall have all franchises, rights and privileges incident to a corporation.

·porate name.

oks of subscription may be opened

Sec. 2. The corporators above named, or any five of them, may open books of subscription, and after four hunderd shares of fifty dollars each shall have been subscribed, upon ten days' notice issued by said corporators, or any five of them, the subscribers may meet and organize by the election of a board of not less than five directors, who shall manage the affairs of the company for one year, or until their successors are elected, and who shall elect a president and all other necessary officers, employees and agents. The company shall have authority to trans-

ction of officers.

act business whenever four hundred shares have been subscribed, and fifty per centum thereof paid.

Capital stock. May be increased.

Sec. 3. The capital stock of the said corporation shall not be less than twenty thousand dollars ($20,000), but the same may be increased from time to time to an amount not to exceed five hundred thousand dollars, to be divided into shares of the par value of fifty dollars each.

Principal office.

Sec. 4. The principal office and place of business of said corporation shall be in the city of Raleigh, state of North Carolina; and its officers shall consist of a board of at least five directors, a president, vice-president, cashier, and such other employees as the board shall from time to time deem necessary to properly conduct the business of the bank. The board of directors shall be elected annually by the stockholders; the directors so elected shall choose the officers aforesaid, and may require the cashier, and such other employees as they may think advisable, to give bond, with approved security, for the faithful performance of their respective duties. At all stockholders' meetings each share of stock shall be entitled to one vote, either in person or by proxy.

Directors and officers, when elected.

Bond may be required.

Corporate powers.

Sec. 5. The corporation hereby created shall have power to make contracts; to have and use a common seal; to sue and be sued in the courts as fully as natural persons; to buy, hold, possess and convey real, personal and mixed property; to make by-laws for the regulation and management of the business of the company; and to do all lawful acts and things and exercise all lawful powers and privileges which a corporate body may do.

Corporate rights and powers.

Sec. 6. That said corporation shall have the right to do a general banking business, to receive deposits, to make loans and discounts, to obtain and procure loans for any person, company, partnership or corporation; to invest its own money or the money of others; to lend and invest money in or upon the security of mortgage, pledge, deed or otherwise, on any lands, hereditaments, or personal property, or interest therein of any description, situate anywhere; to lend money upon, or purchase or otherwise accept bills of lading or the contents thereof, bills, notes, choses in action, or any and all negotiable or commercial papers, or any crops or produce whatever, and what is known as cash credits, or any stock, bullion, merchandise or other personal property, and the same to sell or in anywise dispose of, and to charge any rate of interest on any such loans not exceeding the rate allowed by law.

May make certain agreements.

Sec. 7. That said corporation may subscribe to, purchase, acquire or lend money upon any stock, shares, notes, bonds, debentures, or other securities of any government, state, municipality, corporation, company, partnership or person, and hold, deal in, sell or distribute the same among the stockholders; may negotiate or place in behalf of any corporation, company, partnership or person, shares, stocks, debentures, notes, mortgages or other securities, with or without guaranty or collateral obligation by said company; and may sell or subscribe any of the property, real or personal, or any interest acquired therein by it, to any other corporation for any portion of its bonds, securities, obligations or capital stock as may be agreed upon, without liability on such stock so purchased or subscribed for beyond the agreed terms of said purchase or subscription. That said corporation may also receive on deposit all sums of money which may be offered it for the purpose of being invested, in such sums and at such times and on such terms as the board of directors may agree to, as an investment or otherwise.

rporate powers.

vested with powers usually given to nking institutions.

Sec. 8. The said corporation shall be invested with all the powers and privileges usually incident to banking institutions and to savings banks, with the right to receive deposits, the limit to be fixed by its board of directors, and to pay interest thereon at fixed rates or by way of dividends out of the net earnings, according to the terms to be agreed upon between the corporation and its depositors; and the board of directors are hereby fully authorized to adopt all other rules and regulations for conducting and carrying into effect the savings bank feature of this corporation.

posits of minors d femes covert.

Sec. 9. The said corporation may receive deposits from minors and married women, and open accounts with them in their own name, whether for investment or otherwise; and when any deposit shall be made in the name of any minor or married woman the said company may deal with such minor or married woman in reference thereto as though he or she were sui juris, and payment made to such minor or married woman, on his or her receipt or acquittance, or his or her check drawn against such deposit, shall be a valid and sufficient release and discharge to such corporation for such deposit and any interest thereon, or any part thereof.

ay become surety bonds.

Sec. 10. That said corporation shall have power to become surety on the bond of any state, county, city or town official, or on the bond of any administrator, guardian, trustee, corporation or natural person, or on undertakings of all kinds in any court of justice as fully as a natural person, by the signature and justification of any of its executive officers authorized by the rules and regulations of the company to do so.

ay act as agent, tor or trustee.

Sec. 11. That said corporation shall have the right to act as agent, factor or trustee for any state, county, town, municipality, corporation, company or individual, on such terms as to agency and commission as may be agreed upon, in registration, selling and countersigning, collecting, acquiring, holding, dealing in and disposing of, on account of any state, county, town municipality, corporation, company or person, bond, certificates of stock, or any description of property, real or personal, or for guaranteeing the payment of such bonds, certificates of stock, etc., and generally for managing such business; and may charge such premiums, commissions or rate of compensation as may be agreed on, in and for any of the matters and things authorized by this charter.

Sec. 12. That the stock of said corporation shall be transferred only upon its books, either in person or by proxy, and no stockholder shall transfer his stock, except by consent of the board of directors, while he is indebted to the corporation as principal, security or otherwise; and for all such indebtedness said corporation shall have a lien superior to all other liens upon the stock of said holder.

Transferral of stock.

Lien of corporation on stock.

Sec. 13. That said corporation shall have power to receive money in trust; to become executor or administrator of any estate, and to accept and execute any other trust that may be committed to it by any court, corporation, company, person or persons; and it shall also have power to accept any grant or transfer, devise or bequest, and hold any real or personal estate, or trust created in accordance with the laws of this state, and to execute the same on such terms as may be established and agreed upon by the board of directors.

May become executor and administrator.

Sec. 14. That in all cases when application shall be made to any court of this state for the appointment of any receiver, trustee, administrator, assignee, commissioner, or guardian of any minor or of any lunatic or insane person, it shall be lawful for such court, if it shall think fit, to appoint the Raleigh Banking and Trust Company such receiver, trustee, administrator, assignee, commissioner or guardian, and the accounts of such corporation in such fiduciary capacity shall be regularly settled and adjusted as if it was a natural person, and upon such settlement or adjustment all proper, legal and customary charges, cost and expense shall be allowed to said corporation for its services, care and management in the premises, and the said corporation, as such receiver, trustee, administrator, executor, assignee, commissioner or guardian, shall be subject to all orders or decrees made by the proper tribunal under the laws of this state: Provided, that any oath required by law to be taken, in order for qualification to any of the offices or trust above mentioned, may be taken by any officer of said company, and the oath prescribed by law may be so modified as to apply to corporations instead of individuals.

Said corporation may be appointed trustee, receiver, etc.

Shall be subject to orders and decrees.

Sec. 15. The said corporation is hereby fully authorized and empowered to act as trustee or assignee for any insolvent person, firm or corporation, and to receive on deposit all funds in litigation in the various courts of this state, and pay therefor such

May act as trustee or assignee for insolvent persons.

interest as may be agreed upon, not exceeding the lawful rate. It shall have power and authority to receive for safe keeping on deposit all money, bonds, stocks, diamonds and silver plate, and other valuables, and charge and collect a reasonable compensation for the same, which said charge shall be a lien upon such deposit until paid, and generally to do and carry on the business of a safety deposit and trust company. Said corporation shall also have power to issue bills or notes to circulate as currency in such denominations as the board of directors may authorize, and under such regulations as may be hereafter authorized and provided by the laws of this state and the United States.

ditional powers d privileges con-red.

Sec. 16. That in addition to the powers above conferred, said corporation may build, erect, maintain, conduct and operate one or more warehouses or depots for the storage of goods, wares, merchandise, cotton and other products, and to charge and receive commissions, rents and compensation for the storage and keeping thereof, which charge shall constitute a first lien upon the property so stored; make rules, regulations, contracts and by-laws fixing terms and prices for storage, manner of inspection, forms of receipts, insurance of property stored, and all other matters affecting the safe and prudent conduct of such business; make advances of money or credit upon cotton or other product and merchandise stored as aforesaid, and do all such things as may be wise and profitable in and about said storage business as are not contrary to law; and the receipts issued by said company shall be and are hereby declared to be negotiable instruments and pass by endorsement and delivery, and to entitle the holder thereof to the property marked and designated therein, in like manner as the original holder would be had not such an assignment been made: Provided, that in the absence of any stipulation in the receipt or any contract between the said company and any disposition of property in said warehouses, the said company shall be held and deemed to be liable to exercise only ordinary care in the custody and protection of such property.

ceipts issued by id company nego-ble instruments.

oviso.

nen receipt con-ns no stipula-n.

wers set forth in s act not for-ted by non-use. oviso. all organize hin five years.

Sec. 17. That the powers and privileges set forth in this act shall not be deemed forfeited by non-user: Provided, the said corporation is organized within five years from the date of the ratification of this act.

Sec. 18. This act shall be in force from and after its ratification.

Ratified the 28th day of February, A. D. 1899.

CHAPTER 204.

An act to provide a light plant for the town of Tarboro.

The General Assembly of North Carolina do enact:

Section 1. That the Board of Public Works of the town of Tarboro, approved by the act of the board of commissioners of said town, is hereby authorized, in manner and form provided by "Act to provide water-works and sewerage for said town," enacted at this session of the general assembly, to submit to the qualified voters of said town, at such time as said board may direct, the question of issuing bonds of the town of Tarboro not to exceed ten thousand dollars, in like manner as provided for in said act to provide water and sewerage, for the purpose of establishing a plant and operating same to furnish light to said town and its citizens. Board of public works may submit to voters question of issuing bonds to buy and maintain light plant.

Sec. 2. That all provisions of said act to provide water-works and sewerage are extended to this act, and power hereby conferred, as if the provisions of said act applicable hereto were embodied herein. Provisions of previous act extended.

Sec. 3. This act shall be in force from and after its ratification.

Ratified the 1st day of March, A. D. 1899.

CHAPTER 205.

An act to provide water-works and sewerage for the town of Tarboro, North Carolina.

The General Assembly of North Carolina do enact:

Section 1. That the board of commissioners of the town of Tarboro is hereby authorized and directed to submit to the qualified voters of the said town, on a day to be fixed by said board, between April fifteenth and April seventeenth, eighteen hundred and ninety-nine, the question whether the said town of Tarboro shall issue bonds of said town in an amount not to exceed forty thousand dollars ($40,000) for the purpose of providing and maintaining a system of water-works and sewerage for the said town, or purchasing the system of water-works heretofore constructed by Tarboro Water Supply Company. The said election shall be held and conducted under the same rules and regulations and penalties now prescribed by law for the election of commissioners of said town. And at said election each voter shall vote a Commissioners of Tarboro authorized to submit question of bonds for water-works and sewerage to voters. Limitation to issue. Election, how conducted.

m of ballot. written or printed ballot, with the words "For water-works and sewerage," or "Against water-works and sewerage."

missioners l appoint board ublic works. Sec. 2. The board of commissioners of the town of Tarboro shall be authorized, and is directed, within ten days after the ratification of this act, to elect or appoint seven residents of the town, who shall constitute and be called The Board of Public Works of the town of Tarboro, whose term of office shall begin at their election and continue until the second Monday in May, nineteen hundred and two, and until their successors are elected; that, at the regular meeting of the board of commissioners of said town, next after the first Monday in May, nineteen hundred and two, and every two years thereafter, there shall be elected by the said board of commissioners seven resident voters of said town as members of said board of public works. The members of said board of public works shall take an oath before the mayor to faithfully discharge the duties of their office, and in case of vacancies the same shall be filled by the board of commissioners.

m of office.

mbers of said rd shall take h.

omination of ds. Sec. 3. If, at the election as required by section one of this act, a majority of the votes cast shall be cast "For water-works and sewerage," then the board of public works aforesaid are hereby authorized and empowered to have said bonds prepared in denominations to be fixed by them, and running for a period or periods of years, not exceeding forty years, and at a rate of interest not exceeding six per cent., and payable at such place or places as said board may designate, and to sell said bonds, or so many as may be necessary, after public advertisement, publicly or privately, on the best terms obtainable, not less than par. For the due execution of said bonds they shall be signed by the president of the board of public works, attested by the secretary of said board and countersigned by the mayor of the town and the treasurer, attested by the seal of the town. And the money derived from the sale of said bonds, the said board of public works shall use in providing and maintaining a system of water-works and sewerage for the use and as the property of said town, furnishing for the use of said town all water necessary for public use and to all citizens of the town who may desire water or sewerage on such conditions and at such rates as said board of public works may prescribe; and the said board is hereby fully authorized and empowered to perform any and all acts not inconsistent with this act, which are necessary to establish and maintain a system of water-works and sewerage for the town of Tarboro and the citizens thereof.

en bonds made.

w bonds shall be cuted.

ney derived m sale of bonds.

wers of board of blic works.

neys derived m sale of bonds, applied. Sec. 4. All moneys derived from the sale of said bonds and every other source pertaining to said water-works and sewerage, shall be paid to the treasurer of said board of public works, to be disbursed under the direction of said board. The treasurer elected by said board of public works shall be elected annually

ction of treasr of board.

on the second Monday in May of each year, and before entering upon the discharge of his duties shall execute a bond, payable to the town of Tarboro, to safely keep all moneys that may come to his hands, and in all things to faithfully discharge the duties of treasurer, the amount of said bond to be fixed by the board of public works, who shall fix his compensation and prescribe the oath to be taken as treasurer.

Shall execute bond.

Sec. 5. It shall be the duty of the board of commissioners of Tarboro to set apart from the taxes levied and collected for the town, one-fourth or twenty-five per cent. of the same, for the purpose of carrying out the provisions of this act—the same to be subject to be drawn from the town treasury by the board of public works on its order or orders. And the said appropriation, together with the income from said water-works and sewerage, is hereby pledged for the payment of the aforesaid bonds and the interest coupons thereto. But should the full amount not be required in any year to maintain the system of water-works and sewerage, the residue to be covered into the town treasury for general purposes of the town; the coupons of the aforesaid bonds to be taken for all town taxes.

Certain amount of taxes shall be set aside.

When full amount is not required.

Sec. 6. If, for any reason the aforesaid election shall not be held within the time herein specified, then the same may be held at a later date, to be fixed by the board of commissioners, if requested by said board of public works, under the same rules and regulations herein specified.

Election may be held at later date.

Sec. 7. That this act shall be in force from and after its ratification.

Ratified the 1st day of March, A. D. 1899.

CHAPTER 206.

An act to amend chapter seventy-seven, private laws of eighteen hundred and eighty-three.

The General Assembly of North Carolina do enact:

Section 1. That section three (3), chapter seventy-seven (77), private laws of eighteen hundred and eighty-three (1883), be amended by striking out the word "twenty" in line eight (8) of said section and inserting in lieu thereof the word "thirty," and by striking out the word "sixty" in line nine (9) of said section and inserting in lieu thereof the word ninety.

Commissioners of Mt. Pleasant, Cabarrus county, empowered to levy tax of 30 cents.

Sec. 2. That this act shall be in force from and after its ratification.

Ratified the 2d day of March, A. D. 1899.

CHAPTER 207.

An act to amend the charter of the town of Wilkesboro, North Carolina.

The General Assembly of North Carolina do enact:

apter 240, private vs 1889, amended.

Section 1. That chapter two hundred and forty of the private laws of North Carolina, eighteen hundred and eighty-nine, entitled "An act to amend the charter of the town of Wilkesboro, N. C.," be and the same is hereby amended as follows:

1. In line six, section seven, after the word "the" and before the word "first" insert the words "Tuesday after."

2. That the following clauses be added to section thirty-one: "6. For the purpose of providing a sinking fund with which to pay the bonded indebtedness of said town, the commissioners may annually levy and collect a tax on real estate and personal property situated therein, not to exceed fifty cents on every one hundred dollars value, and on all taxable polls a tax not exceeding one dollar and fifty cents on those who may be residents in the town on the first day of June of each year, or who have been so resident, within thirty days next preceding that day." "7. When said tax as provided in clause six shall be levied, it shall be collected in the manner prescribed for the collection of other taxes, and this fund shall be kept separate and apart from all other funds of said town, and it shall be the duty of the treasurer of said town to apply said funds to the liquidation of the bonded indebtedness as often as an amount sufficient to pay off one bond shall come into his hands."

mmissioners y levy and col- t special tax.

apter 199, laws 7, amended.

Sec. 2. That chapter one hundred and ninety-nine of the private laws of North Carolina, eighteen hundred and ninety-seven, be and the same is hereby amended as follows:

1. In line eleven strike out the words "in each year" and insert in lieu thereof the word "biennially."

2. In line twelve of section one, after the word "the" and before the word "first" insert the words "Tuesday after."

plications for lor license.

3. After the word "license" in line thirty of section one, add "and upon certificate of the town commissioners that license has been granted to any applicant or applicants therein named to retail spirituous, malt and vinous liquors in said town, the county commissioners of Wilkes county shall grant state and county license to the applicant or applicants named in said certificate."

flicting laws ealed.

Sec. 3. That all laws and parts of laws in conflict herewith be and are hereby repealed, and this act shall be in force from and after its ratification.

Ratified the 2d day of March, A. D. 1899.

CHAPTER 208.

An act to amend the charter of Siler City, Chatham county, chapter eighty-eight, private laws of eighteen hundred and eighty-seven.

The General Assembly of North Carolina do enact:

Section 1. That chapter eighty-eight of the private laws of eighteen hundred and eighty-seven be and the same is hereby amended by adding and annexing to the territory included in the boundaries mentioned in section two of said act the following additional territory, to-wit: Commencing at a stone in the incorporation line on the west side of the public road leading to the Siler mill, and running north eighty-five poles to a stone, thence west to the Cape Fear and Yadkin Valley Railroad, thence down the railroad to the original incorporation line, thence east to the beginning, and all of said bounded territory shall henceforth be a part of the town of Siler City, subject to all the duties and obligations and entitled to all the privileges of said town. Boundary lines extended.

Sec. 2. That the present mayor and commissioners and other officers of the town of Siler City be and the same are hereby declared to be like officers, with the powers and duties appertaining to the same, until their successors are elected and qualified as hereinafter provided. Present officers continued.

Sec. 3. That the board of commissioners shall, on the first Tuesday in April, eighteen hundred and ninety-nine, and in each succeeding year, appoint a registrar and two judges of election who shall hold the elections for the town officers on the first Monday in May, under the same regulations as those governing the election of the members of the general assembly, and report the result to the next meeting after the election to the town commissioners. Appointment of registrar and judges of election.

Sec. 4. That all citizens resident in said town over eighteen and under fifty years of age shall be liable to do six days work each year upon the streets and sidewalks. In lieu of said labor they may pay three dollars, which shall be expended in improving streets and sidewalks. Persons liable to road duty.

Sec. 5. The town commissioners shall have power, whenever they deem it necessary, or to the interest of the town, to condemn any land for the purpose of opening any new street, or for the lengthening or widening or the changing of any street, and for that purpose shall appoint a jury of not less than three nor more than five freeholders of the town, who, after being notified of their appointment and sworn by the mayor or justice of the peace, shall meet on or at the premises or land to be condemned and assess the damages that the owner may sustain by reason of such condemnation, deducting, however, from the same the estimated value of the improvements that may accrue to the prem- Commissioners may condemn land for necessary purposes. Assessors of valuation.

ises by the opening or improvement of the streets. The owner or owners of the land shall first have at least five days' notice of the time and place of meeting of the jurors; said notice to be served by the town constable, or any other person authorized by law to serve notices. The jury shall return a report of their proceedings to the board of town commissioners, who may confirm the same, and after paying or tendering to the owner the amount of damages assessed may subject the land condemned for the desired purpose: Provided, however, that if the owner of the land or the commissioners be dissatisfied with the valuation thus made, then in that case either party may appeal to the next superior court.

viso.

her party may eal.

ointment of tax ector. er to impose es.

Sec. 6. That the board of commissioners of said town shall have power annually to appoint a tax collector, and to impose and levy a tax upon all real and personal property within the corporate limits of said town, and also upon all moneys on hand, solvent credits, and upon all polls, and all other subjects of taxation taxed by the general assembly for public purposes, not to exceed twenty cents on the one hundred dollars worth of property, and sixty cents on the poll; and the tax list made out by them or under their supervision and placed in the hands of the tax collector, shall have the force and effect of a judgment and execution for the taxes so assessed and appearing in such lists respectively.

x list shall have ce and effect of gment.

wer of tax collector in collection taxes.

Sec. 7. That in the collection of taxes for the said town the tax collector shall have all the powers and authorities, and may use the same methods as is provided by law for sheriffs, both in collecting the taxes and in conveying title of property to purchaser sold for taxes: Provided, that any lands sold for taxes shall be sold on the premises.

xes may be ied on special bjects.

Sec. 8. That in addition to the subjects listed for taxation the commissioners may levy a tax on the following subjects, the amount of which tax when fixed shall be collected by the town marshal; and if the same be not paid on demand, the same may be recovered by distress and levy on the articles upon which the tax is imposed, or any other property of the owner may be levied on and sold to satisfy the same, namely, upon all itinerant merchants or peddlers vending or offering to vend in the town, a tax not more than ten dollars a year except such only as sell books, charts or maps; upon each show or exhibition of any kind, on each sleight-of-hand performance, and on every traveling musician, a tax not exceeding ten dollars; on every daguerrean or other artist taking likenesses or enlarging those already taken, or soliciting orders for the same, of the human face, by whatever process, a tax not exceeding ten dollars; on every person who, as principal or agent, shall sell, outside his regular place of business, soda water, milk shakes, lemonade, candy, ice-cream,

ecial subjects of xation.

oranges, cakes or meals, from any stand, a tax not exceeding five dollars; on every trade, calling or occupation or business, not herein named and taxed, and which are now taxable under the state law, or may hereafter be made subject to taxation by the legislature from time to time, a tax not exceeding ten dollars.

Sec. 9. That it shall be unlawful for any person or persons or corporation to buy and sell, or deal in, or retail at their place of business, or anywhere else within the corporate limits of said town, the following articles, to-wit: ale, beer lager or porter; cider, bitters, except such bitters as possess genuine medicinal properties. Unlawful to sell liquor, etc., within corporate limits.

Sec. 10. That it shall be unlawful for any person or persons to keep or be connected with any house of ill-fame within the corporate limits of the town. Any person violating section nine or ten, or any part thereof, shall be guilty of a misdemeanor, and on conviction thereof shall be fined not more than twenty-five dollars for each offence. Unlawful to keep houses of ill-fame.

Sec. 11. That the portion of section six of the charter of the town of Siler City, as to levying taxes, be and the same is hereby repealed. Section 6 repealed.

Sec. 12. The commissioners shall have power to abate all nuisances within the corporate limits of said town, at the expense of the person causing the same, or the owner or tenants, or corporation, of the ground wherever the same shall be, and any person or persons or corporation failing to abate such nuisance, after receiving ten days' notice, shall be guilty of a misdemeanor, and upon conviction thereof shall be fined not more than fifty dollars. Abatement of nuisances.

Sec. 13. The commissioners shall have power to remove at the expense of the owner of the property, or remedy, and defective flues, pipes or other places where fire is used endangering other property, upon complaint of any person, or where they, the said commissioners, see the necessity of such a change. Removal of property endangering other property.

Sec. 14. That the cemetery for the burial of white people shall be known by the name of Oak Hill Cemetery. No colored person shall be buried within the above-named cemetery. No colored person or any one else shall be buried inside the limits of the town corporation outside the cemetery. Any person or persons violating either clauses of this section shall be guilty of a misdemeanor, and upon conviction shall be fined one hundred dollars. Cemeteries.

Sec. 15. That the town commissioners may move any dead body buried within the town, outside of the cemetery, to a point which they may think more suitable. Commissioners may remove dead bodies.

Sec. 16. That the commissioners shall have power to condemn buildings subject to fire, etc., and prevent the building of any house which might prove to be a nuisance. Buildings subject to fires may be condemned.

Sec. 17. That the mayor shall have power to commit any person convicted of violation of any town ordinance to the county or

ersons may be mmitted to jail worked on reets in default of ne.

town jail until the fine and cóst imposed by him, and jail fees, are paid; and in all cases where a defendant is adjudged to be imprisoned by the said mayor, it shall be competent for him to adjudge also that the said defendant work during the period of his confinement on the public streets of the town or public roads of the county.

id territory constitutes school district.

Sec. 18. That all the territory embraced within the limits of the town of Siler City as amended by this act constitute a public school district for the white race, to be known as Siler City school district.

ines for violation ordinances, how plied.

Sec. 19. That all fines collected for the violation of any town ordinance shall go into the town treasury for the benefit of the town.

Sec. 20. That this act shall be in force from and after its ratification.

Ratified the 2d day of March, A. D. 1899.

CHAPTER 209.

An act supplement to and to amend and re-enact section one of an act entitled "An act to incorporate the North and South Carolina Railroad Company," ratified on the twenty-second day of February, eighteen hundred and ninety-nine.

The General Assembly of North Carolina do enact:

mended and re-acted.

Section 1. That section one of an act entitled "An act to incorporate the North and South Carolina Railroad Company," ratified on the twenty-second day of February, eighteen hundred and ninety-nine, be amended and re-enacted so as to read as follows:

rporators.

Section 1. That Henry S. Haines, Afred P. Thorn, Jhon S. Cunningham, James A. Lockhart, John N. Vaughan, W. B. Hatcher, Richard B. Tunstall, F. W. Tatem, W. H. Stirling, James A. Leak, W. C. Hardison, John D. Leak, J. A. Long, and John C. Drewry, and such other persons as are now or may hereafter be associated with them, are hereby created and declared to be a body politic and corporate, under the name and style of the North and South Carolina Railroad Company, and in that name may sue and be sued, plead and be impleaded, shall have power to adopt a common seal and to change the same at will, and shall be capable of taking by purchase, gift or in any other way real or personal property, and of holding, leasing, conveying or in any other manner dealing with the same; and the said corporation shall also have and enjoy all the rights, privileges and immunities which corporate bodies may lawfully exercise or enjoy, and may

ody corporate. rporate name. rporate powers.

make ordinances, by-laws and regulations, consistent with the laws of this state and of the laws of the United States for the government of all under its authority, for the management of its estates and for the due and orderly conduct of its affairs, and shall also be subject to all the general restrictions imposed by the laws of this state upon railroad companies. It may build branch roads not exceeding fifty miles in length from any points on its main line, and for this purpose shall have all the powers, privileges and rights contained in this act, which are hereby made to apply to such branch roads as well as to the main line.

Sec. 2. That this act shall be in force from and after its ratification.

Ratified the 2d day of March, A. D. 1899.

CHAPTER 210.

An act to amend the charter of the town of Cary, Wake county, North Carolina.

The General Assembly of North Carolina do enact:

Section 1. That the persons residing within the corporate limits of the town of Cary, Wake county, North Carolina, which are particularly set forth in section two of this act, shall be and continue as they have been, a body corporate under the name and style of the town of Cary, and shall have power to purchase and hold real estate for the benefit of the town, to sue and be sued, to plead and be impleaded as any other corporation, and shall also have the rights of and be subject to the general laws of the state in relation to corporations of like kind not inconsistent with this act. Body corporate. Corporate name. Corporate powers.

Sec. 2. The corporate limits of said town shall be as follows: Beginning at a stake fifteen feet north of the North Carolina Railroad in the western line of Hillsboro street, running south eighty-six and one-half degrees, and parallel with the North Carolina Railroad eleven hundred and fifty feet to a stake, thence north ten hundred and fifty feet to a stake, thence south eighty-four degrees east two hundred and fifty feet to a stake, thence south eleven hundred feet to a stake, thence west six hundred and eighty-seven feet to a stake, thence south two and one-half degrees west twenty-six hundred and seventy-five feet to a stake, thence north seventy-eight and one-half degrees west sixteen hundred and thirty feet to a stake, thence north thirteen and one-half degrees west thirty-one hundred and fifty feet to the beginning point. Corporate limits.

cers. Sec. 3. That the officers of said corporation shall consist of a mayor, five commissioners and a town marshal and such assistant marshals as the board of commissioners may deem proper to appoint. ayor and commissioners, how elected The mayor and commissioners shall be elected by the qualified voters of the town, and the marshal and his assistants by the board of commissioners, with such compensation and period of service as said commissioners may determine, but said period of service shall not extend beyond the term of office of said commissioners. arshal shall give nd. The said marshal shall, upon entering on his duties as such, enter into a bond which shall be approved by said commissioners, with good security, payable to the town of Cary, in an amount to be fixed by said commissioners, conditioned for the faithful performance of his duties as town marshal.

rsons entitled to te in said elections. Sec. 4. That such persons as are qualified voters of this state within the said corporate limits of the town of Cary as set forth in section two of this act, who have resided in said county of Wake for ninety days and in said corporate limits for thirty days preding any election held in said town, shall be entitled to vote at said election.

ıen mayor shall e oath of office. Sec. 5. That it shall be the duty of the mayor of said town to take the oath of office required by section three thousand seven hundred and ninety-eight of The Code of North Carolina, and enter upon the duties of his office within five days after his election; and the said commissioners elected for said town at any election shall meet and organize within five days next after their election, th of commissioners. and they shall take the oath of office before some person qualified to administer oaths that they will faithfully and impartially perform their duties as commissioners to the best of their knowledge and ability during their term of office.

mmissioners powered to levy cial tax. Sec. 6. That the commissioners of said town shall have power to levy a tax for the purposes of said town each year, not to exceed one dollar on the poll and thirty-three and one-third cents on the one hundred dollars valuation of real and personal property within the limits of the said town of Cary, said valuation to be the same as that placed upon said property to raise revenue for state and county purposes, and all taxes allowed by this act shall be levied according to article five, sections one and three of the constitution of the state.

powered to improve streets. Sec. 7. That the board of commissioners of the said town of Cary shall have power to grade, macadamize or pave the streets and sidewalks of said town, and to lay out streets, change and open new streets or widen those already opened, and to make such improvements thereon as the public convenience may require, and the said board shall be the judges of the improvements required. The said board may condemn any land for the public use for said town under the same rules and regulations as are hereinafter provided for the laying out of public streets in this act.

Sec. 8. That when any land or right of way is required for the purpose of opening new streets, or for other objects allowed by this act, and for want of agreement between the town authorities and the owners of said land as to compensation or otherwise, the same may be taken at a valuation to be made by three freeholders of the town to be chosen by the board of commissioners, and in making said valuation said freeholders, after being duly sworn by the mayor, shall at once proceed to condemn said lands, and take into consideration the loss or damage which may accrue to the owners in consequence of the said lands or right of way being surrendered, and also any benefit or advantage such owners may receive from the opening or widening of such streets or other improvements, and ascertain the sum which shall be paid to the owner of said property, and report the same to the board of commissioners under their hands and seals, which, on being confirmed by the board and spread upon the minutes, shall have the effect of a judgment against said town of Cary, and shall pass the title to said town of Cary of the lands so taken: Provided, that if any person over whose land the said street may pass, or improvement be created, or the commissioners, be dissatisfied with the valuation thus made, then in either case the party dissatisfied may appeal to the next term of the superior court for Wake county: Provided, however, that such appeal shall not hinder or delay the commissioners from opening or widening such streets or creating such improvements. Any freeholder who shall refuse to act after having been duly appointed by the board, and having been notified in writing by the marshal of the town, shall be fined twenty-five dollars by the mayor for each week's failure to act after being so notified.

Condemnation of land necessary for town.

Either party may appeal. Proviso.

Appeal pending shall not delay work.

Sec. 9. That all taxes levied by the commissioners of said town on property and polls shall be due and collectible the first day of October in each year. And should any taxes remain unpaid for more than three months after becoming due, the same shall thereafter bear interest at the rate of six per cent. per annum until paid, and shall also be a lien upon the lands upon which they are levied. And if any taxes are assessed against any person or property by said commissioners, and the same shall not be paid by the first day of March next after they [become] due, the town marshal may levy upon any personal property belonging to the delinquent by virtue of the tax list in his hands and sell the same, after written notice of the time and place of sale for ten days served on the delinquent by the town marshal, and also posted at the mayor's office and three other public places in the town, and from the proceeds of said sale the said town marshal shall pay the said delinquent taxes due

Taxes, when due.

Notice shall be served on delinquent.

and the costs of sale, which shall not exceed twenty-five cents, and pay balance to the delinquent tax-payer. If no tangible personal property can be found by the town marshal to satisfy the taxes of any tax payer, it shall be the duty of said marshal to attach any debt or other property due or belonging to the delinquent tax payer, or which may become due him upon the expiration of the calendar year, and the person or corporation owing said debt, or having such property in possession, shall be liable for said tax to the amount of said debt or property. Any person or corporation who on demand shall refuse to give said marshal a statement showing the names of persons employed by them and the amounts due said employees, who are liable for taxes, shall be guilty of a misdemeanor.

bts may be attached for taxes.

rsons refusing to e marshal statements of amount e employees.

Sec. 10. No real estate shall be sold for taxes by said town marshal if the same can be collected from personal property either by sale or attachment; but if the taxes due said town cannot be collected, and the same shall remain unpaid until the first day of April next after they become due, then the said town marshal shall be authorized to sell any land in said town belonging to any delinquent tax payer to satisfy the taxes due by said delinquent tax payer. Before doing so, however, the said town marshal shall advertise the time and place of such sale for thirty days in some newspaper published in Wake county, and also by posting the same at the court-house door of Wake county and the mayor's office in the town of Cary for thirty days. The place at which sale shall occur shall be at the court-house door of Wake county, and the time of sale shall be the first Monday in May after said taxes become due. When any purchaser shall bid off any land at said sale, he shall immediately pay the amount bid by him to said town marshal who shall give to said purchaser a certificate substantially the same in form as that given by a sheriff upon a sale by him of land for state and county taxes. The purchaser shall pay the said marshal a fee not exceeding fifty cents for said certificate and the same shall be signed by said marshal. The said marshal shall keep a book showing the lands sold by him for taxes, the name of the purchaser and the sum for which each tract was sold and the amount paid for such certificate. The owner of any land sold for taxes as aforesaid, or any person having an interest in the same, may redeem said land at any time before the first day of January next after said sale: Provided, said owner or interested person shall pay said purchaser twenty per cent. on the amount paid by him on account of the taxes and certificate aforesaid. Any town marshal who shall be directly or indirectly concerned personally in the purchase of any real estate sold by him for taxes shall be guilty of a misdemeanor.

hen marshal may l real estate for es.

rshal shall advertise before selling.

me of such sale.

nd sold may be deemed within rtain time.

Sec. 11. Unless the land sold for taxes as provided for in the preceding section shall be redeemed by the time limited therein, the said town marshal shall execute to the purchaser and his heirs or assigns, a deed conveying the land sold by him for taxes upon the production of the certificate calling for the same, and upon the loss of any certificate and being fully satisfied thereof by due proof, the marshal shall execute and deliver the proper conveyance. The deed made by said town marshal as herein provided shall be substantially the same in form as that executed by sheriffs before the sale by them of land sold for the non payment of state and county taxes. When land is not redeemed.

Sec. 12. That the mayor of said town of Cary shall have the same jurisdiction as a justice of the peace, in all criminal actions within the corporate limits of said town or within two miles thereof. That all fines collected by said mayor in criminal actions shall be paid into the town treasury. Jurisdiction of mayor.

Sec. 13. That the present mayor and commissioners of the town of Cary shall hold their office until the first Monday of May, eighteen hundred and ninety-nine, and until their successors are elected and qualified, and on the first Monday of May, eighteen hundred and ninety-nine, there shall be elected a mayor and five commissioners for the said town of Cary under the rules and regulations established by chapter seventy-two, volume two of The Code of North Carolina, and said commissioners shall hold their offices for two years after their election, and every two years after the said first Monday in May, eighteen hundred and ninety-nine, there shall be elected a mayor and five commissioners for the said town of Cary under the rules and regulations above mentioned. That in the absence of any officer from the town, or during the sickness of any officer the commissioners may appoint some person to fill the office during the absence or disability of said officer. In case of the resignation of any officer of the town the board of commissioners may appoint some person to fill the unexpired term. Present officers continued. Term of office. During absence or sickness of officers.

Sec. 14. That the commissioners of said town of Cary may elect a secretary and treasurer for the town, who shall be clerk of the board of commissioners, and who shall enter into bond with good security payable to the town of Cary in an amount to be fixed by said board for the faithful performance of the duties of his office. The mayor of the said town of Cary shall be the custodian of said bond. Election of secretary and treasurer. Bond required.

Sec. 15. That the commissioners of said town shall constitute a sanitary committee, and all orders made by them for the preservation of the health of the citizens of the town shall be put into effect by the marshal of the town. Any person who shall fail to comply with any order made by the board of commissioners after having been notified in writing by the said marshal shall be deemed guilty of a misdemeanor. Commissioners constituted sanitary committee.

x list subject to trol of commissioners.

Sec. 16. That the tax lists of the town when placed in the hands of the tax collector shall at all times be subject to the control of the commissioners, and shall at all times be subject to the inspection of the public.

rshal may make est for violation ordinances and te laws.

Sec. 17. That if any person shall be found violating the laws of the state, or the town ordinances in said town, or within two miles of the corporate limits thereof, the town marshal shall forthwith arrest the offender with or without warrant and carry him before the mayor to answer the charge and to be dealt with according to law.

oceedings in yor's court.

Sec. 18. That all proceedings before the mayor's court shall be the same as are now, or hereafter prescribed for courts of justice of the peace, and in all cases there shall be a right of appeal to the superior court of Wake county. That whenever a defendant or other person shall be adjudged to be imprisoned by the mayor's court, it shall be competent for said court to sentence such person to imprisonment in the jail of the county for a term not exceeding thirty days, and to adjudge also that such person work during the period of his sentence on the streets of the public works of the town of Cary or the roads of Wake county.

rsons convicted y be imprisoned.

ecial taxes.

Sec. 19. That the commissioners of the town shall have power to tax all circuses, shows, theatres, and all exhibitions for money or reward as they may deem proper not inconsistent with the laws of the state.

sdemeanor to sell uor within corrate limits.

Sec. 20. That it shall be unlawful for any person to sell any vinous, spirituous or malt liquors, cider or brandy peaches within the corporate limits of the said town of Cary or within two miles of the said corporate limits, and any person violating the provisions of this section shall be guilty of a misdemeanor and upon conviction shall be fined in the discretion of the court.

ner of property utting on street all keep sidelk in repair.

Sec. 21. That it shall be the duty of the owner of any real property abutting on any sidewalk of the town, to keep said sidewalk in good repair at his own expense, and on his failure or neglect to do so, after being notified by the town marshal in writing said marshal may hire the work done and the cost of such improvement shall become a lien on such abutting property, and such property shall be subject to sale as for taxes for said cost.

pointment of gistrar and inectors of election.

Sec. 22. That the board of town commissioners shall, not less than thirty days before any election in said town of Cary, appoint one registrar and two inspectors of election, whose duty it shall be to register the qualified voters of the said town of Cary and conduct the said election, which shall be done according to section sixty-two, volume two of The Code, and the general election laws of North Carolina.

Sec. 23. All laws and clauses of laws in conflict with this act are hereby repealed. Conflicting laws repealed.

Sec. 24. This act shall be in force from and after its ratification.

Ratified the 3d day of March, A. D. 1899.

CHAPTER 211.

An act to incorporate the town of Wallace in Duplin county.

The General Assembly of North Carolina do enact:

Section 1. That the town of Wallace, in Duplin county, be and the same is hereby incorporated under the name of the town of Wallace, and that it shall have the benefit and be subject to all the provisions of the law existing in reference to incorporated towns not inconsistent with this act. Incorporated.

Sec. 2. That the corporate limits of said town shall be as follows: Beginning at the whistle-post one-half mile north of the Wilmington and Weldon warehouse, and runs thence north seventy-three and one-half east one hundred and forty-nine poles to a stake by the Teacheys road, thence with the southwest edge of said road south fifty-five east nineteen poles to a stake, thence south sixteen and one-half east one hundred and twelve poles to a stake at the west edge of Teacheys road, thence with said road south ten west thirty-seven poles to a stake, J. L. Boney's and Dr. Graham's corner; thence their line north eighty-eight and one-half east fifteen poles to a stake, thence with the town line sixteen and one-half east one hundred and sixty-eight poles to a stake, thence south seventy-three west ninety poles to a stake, C. B. Johnson's line; thence his line south eight poles to a stake, thence south seventy-six and one-half with his line sixty-nine poles to the cattle guard, thence north sixteen and one-half west one pole to the whistle-post, thence south seventy-three and one-half west fifty poles to a stake, J. W. Boney's line; thence his line south sixty west one hundred and nineteen poles to a stake at the edge of Rockfield creek, thence up said creek to G. L. Blanton's corner, thence his line north forty-seven and one-half west six poles to a stake, thence north thirty-four east eighteen poles to a stake, thence south fifty-six west fourteen poles to a ditch, and thence up said ditch with L. B. Carr's and J. G. Southerland's line to a stake, J. G. Southerland's corner; thence G. L. Blanton's line south fifty-six east nine poles to a stake, thence north sixteen and one-half west two hundred and thirty-five poles to a stake in Westbrook's field, thence north Corporate limits.

seventy-three and one-half east one hundred and sixty poles to the beginning.

ficers of town.

Sec. 3. That the officers of said town shall consist of a mayor, five commissioners and a town constable, who shall also be tax collector, and said mayor and commissioners shall be elected annually on the first Monday in March by the qualified voters of said town, and shall immediately assume the duties of their office, and that the following shall be mayor and commissioners until the first Monday in March, nineteen hundred, and until their successors are elected and qualified: Mayor, D. E. Boney; commissioners, B. R. Graham, J. D. Mallard, G. H. Robinson, C. B. Johnson and W. H. Carter.

mporary officers.

nstable and tax llector elected by mmissioners.

Sec. 4. That said town constable and tax collector shall be elected by the board of commissioners at their first meeting after their election, or as soon thereafter as is convenient, and his term of office shall expire with that of said board unless sooner removed for cause; that he shall be required to enter into a bond to an amount satisfactory to the board of commissioners for the faithful performance of the duties of his office, and shall make a montnly settlement with said commissioners of all taxes, fines and other moneys collected in his official capacity.

nstable and tax llector shall serve ocesses, collect xes, etc.

Sec. 5. That said constable and tax collector shall be authorized and empowered to serve all processes issued by said mayor, and collect the taxes levied by said commissioners, and his fees for said services shall be the same as are allowed the sheriff of the said county of Duplin, unless otherwise provided by the town commissioners, and in enforcing the collection of said taxes he shall have power and authority to levy on any personal or real property, and after due advertisement according to law, sell the same and apply the proceeds to the satisfaction of said taxes; and in serving said processes he shall be subject to and have the advantage of all laws applicable to sheriffs in similar cases.

ay levy on personal and real property.

ties of constable.

Sec. 6. That it shall be the duty of the constable to see that the laws, ordinances and orders of the commissioners are enforced, preserve the peace of the town, suppress disturbances, and for that purpose he shall have all power and authority vested in sheriffs and other peace officers, and he may arrest with or without a warrant all persons violating an ordinance of said town and bring them before the mayor for a hearing.

ayor shall preside meetings of commissioners.

Sec. 7. That the mayor shall preside at all meetings of the town commissioners, but shall not be entitled to a vote except in case of a tie. He shall keep a faithful minute of all precepts issued by them and of all judicial proceedings; judgments rendered by him shall have all the force, virtue and validity as if rendered by a justice of the peace, and for his services the mayor shall receive the same fees as a justice of the peace, and such other salary as the commissioners may allow.

Sec. 8. Any vacancy that may occur in the office of mayor or town commissioner, from death, resignation or otherwise, shall be filled by the remaining members of said board, and in the absence of the mayor they may elect a mayor pro tem. to preside at their meetings.

Sec. 9. That every violation of a town ordinance shall be a misdemeanor and shall be punished by a fine not exceeding fifty dollars, or imprisonment not more than thirty days; and when any defendant shall fail to pay such fine and cost as may be imposed on him by the mayor, said mayor may sentence him to work on the streets of said town at such a rate per day as the commissioners may determine until said cost and fine are paid, and all fines collected under this act shall go into the public treasury for the use of the town.

Violation of town ordinances a misdemeanor.

Defendant failing to pay fine may be worked on streets.

Sec. 10. That the commissioners shall have the power, and it shall be their duty to provide for and secure the peace, good order and tranquility of the town; to pass ordinances against disturbances by quarrels, profane or obscene language, riots, affrays, trespasses or other breaches of the peace of whatever nature tending to disturb the peace of the citizens. They shall have full power to provide for the repairing of the streets and sidewalks, to make the necessary regulations for the observance of the Sabbath; to abate nuisances, and to make necessary regulations to prevent dogs or stock from running at large in the town; and may enforce the ordinances of said town by such fines and imprisonment, always in the jurisdiction of justices of the peace, as they may deem adequate.

Powers of commissioners.

Streets and sidewalks.

Sec. 11. That said commissioners may levy a tax on all polls, personal and real property taxable under the laws of the state, and in levying said tax may be guided as to valuation by the certificate of the register of deeds of Duplin county, setting forth the amount and value of property listed by each inhabitant of said town: Provided, if the commissioners shall deem it impracticable to ascertain the value in this manner they may appoint a tax lister and prescribe the duties thereof. That said commissioners shall have authority to levy a tax on all businesses, trades and professions, not inconsistent with the laws of North Carolina, and to tax all venders of medicines, goods, wares or merchandise of whatever kind at such a rate as they may think just and proper

May levy tax.

Proviso.

May appoint tax lister.

Sec. 12. That the commissioners may pass such regulations as to the registration of voters and holding elections as they may think wise and proper, always recognizing the qualifications as to voters as may be prescribed by the laws of North Carolina: Provided, however, that it shall always be the duty of the com-

Registration of voters.

Proviso.

Irty days' notice .ll be given of istrations. missioners to give at least thirty days' notice of said registration at three public places in said town.

license shall be inted for sale of uors. Sec. 13. No malt, spirituous or vinous liquors shall be sold in said town; nor shall the county commissioners have any right to grant license to any barkeeper in said town while this act may be in force.

nflicting laws pealed. Sec. 14. That all laws and clauses of laws in conflict with this act, and all legislation that may have been previously enacted concerning said town in conflict with this act be and the same are hereby repealed.

Sec. 15. That this act shall be in force from and after its ratification.

Ratified the 4th day of March, A. D. 1899.

CHAPTER 212.

An act to incorporate the town of Hildebran in Burke county.

The General Assembly of North Carolina do enact:

corporated. Section 1. That the town of Hildebran, in the county of Burke, be and the same is hereby incorporated under the name and style rporate name. of the town of Hildebran, and in that name, by its commission- rporate powers. ers, may sue and be sued, contract and be contracted with, plead and be impleaded; may acquire and hold real and personal property for the use of the town, and may convey the same, as the commissioners may think best.

rporate limits. Sec. 2. That the corporate limits of said town shall be the territory embraced in a circle the radius of which shall extend one-half mile in every direction from a point at the middle of the railroad track, at the crossing of the main or public dirt road, over said track nearest Hildebran station, as it exists at present.

.ective officers. hen elected. Sec. 3. That the elective officers of said town shall consist of a mayor and five commissioners, who shall be elected the first Monday in May, in the year eighteen hundred and ninety-nine, and annually on the first Monday of each May thereafter, by the qualified voters of said town, which said officers shall hold their respective offices for one year or until their successors are elected and shall qualify.

mporary officers. Sec. 4. That J. O. Cook is hereby constituted mayor of said town, and Aaron J. White, D. H. Page, John W. Bailey, Joseph Flowers and James Bridges are constituted commissioners, all of whom shall exercise and perform the duties of said offices as hereinafter defined until their successors are elected on the first

Monday of May in the year eighteen hundred and ninety-nine and have duly qualified.

Sec. 5. Any person who is a qualified elector of the State of North Carolina and shall have resided in the said town sixty days next preceding the day of election, shall be a qualified voter and shall be entitled to vote at any municipal election in said town.

Persons qualified to vote in town elections.

Sec. 6. That no person except a duly qualified elector of said town shall be eligible as mayor or commissioner of said town.

Eligibility for office.

Sec. 7. That the mayor and commissioners of said town shall form the board of commissioners or town council, and they may order an election for any purpose they may see fit and whenever they may deem necessary; a majority of the board shall constitute a quorum for the transaction of business.

Mayor and commissioners may order election.

Sec. 8. That the mayor shall, thirty days before the first Monday in May, or thirty days before any other election, appoint a suitable person to act as registrar within the corporation of said town, and the registration books shall be open at least twenty days. The town marshal shall notify said person of his appointment, and the said registrar shall at once post a notice, at as many as two public places in said town, of his appointment, and shall designate the place where he will keep the books open and the time after which the books shall be closed, and when and for what purpose the election shall be held.

Appointment of registrar and judges of election.

Sec. 9. In all elections the polls shall be opened at any place in the corporation that may be designated by the board of commissioners.

Place of voting.

Sec. 10. The book of registration of the voters of the town shall be furnished the poll holders, and no person shall be allowed to vote unless his name be found therein.

No person shall be allowed to vote unless name is on registration book.

Sec. 11. Any person offering to register shall be required to take an oath that he is a citizen of North Carolina, and has resided in the town of Hildebran sixty days preceding that date, or is otherwise entitled to register; and if any person shall wilfully swear falsely in said oath, he shall be guilty of perjury.

Persons registering shall take oath.

Sec. 12. That within twenty-four hours after the close of the registration for each election, the registration books shall be opened for the inspection of the citizens of the town, and it shall be lawful for any elector to challenge the right of any person to register or vote, and the judges of election shall decide the right of such person to register or vote.

Registration books open for inspection.

Sec. 13. That for the purpose of electing said officers the commissioners shall, at least twenty days before election, appoint three inspectors, who shall be qualified voters, and the inspectors, before they proceed to act, shall be sworn before the mayor or a justice of the peace to conduct the election fairly and impartially, and according to law; and in the absence of any inspector his place shall be filled by the mayor or registrar. On the

Inspectors of election.

day of election the inspectors, with the registrars, shall duly attend the polls at the time and they shall be judges of the polls, receive the votes and conduct the election in like manner, and during the same hours of the day as elections for members of the general assembly.

ndidates shall be ted for in separate xes.

Sec. 14. The candidates for mayor and commissioners shall be voted for in separate boxes on a separate ballot, printed or written.

tes, how counted.

Sec. 15. That at the close of election the votes shall be counted by inspectors, and such person or persons receiving the largest number of votes shall be duly declared elected to fill the board of commissioners, and the officers so elected shall be notified by the inspectors of their election. But if it shall be found that there is a tie between two or more persons for any office the commissioners shall, within five days after their qualification, proceed to select out of the number of persons so tied a person or persons to fill the office or offices so left vacant. And, if at any time, there may be a vacancy in the board, the commissioners may fill the vacancy from among the qualified electors of the town.

hen a tie occurs.

spector shall cer- y result.

Sec. 16. That the inspectors shall certify and subscribe one poll list and return it to the clerk of the board, who shall keep a record of the same.

yor and commis- ners shall take th.

Sec. 17. That the mayor and each commissioner after election, and before entering on the duties of their office, shall take an oath before a justice of the peace to perform the duties of mayor or commissioners for the town, truly and impartially, and according to their best skill, judgment and ability, and they shall hold their offices until the next election, and until their successors are qualified.

rsons elected re- ing to qualify.

Sec. 18. That any person elected mayor or commissioner, who shall refuse to qualify and act as such, shall forfeit and pay to the equal use of the town and of him who shall sue for the same, five dollars.

risdiction of yor.

Sec. 19. That the mayor of said town is hereby constituted an inferior court, and as such, shall, within the corporate limits of said town, have all the power, jurisdiction and authority of a justice of the peace, to keep and preserve the peace, to issue process, to hear and determine all causes of action which may arise under the ordinances and regulations of the town, to enforce penalties by issuing execution upon adjudged violation therefor, and to execute the by-laws, rules and regulations made by the board of commissioners; the mayor shall further be a special court within the corporate limits of the town to arrest any and all persons who are charged with misdemeanors for violating any ordinance of the town, and if the accused be found guilty he shall be fined at the discretion of the mayor or court, not exceeding the amount specified in the ordinance or ordinances so

ecial court.

violated, or at the discretion of the mayor or court trying the same such offender may be imprisoned not more than thirty days in the common jail of the county, or fined not exceeding fifty dollars.

If the accused be dissatisfied with the judgment of the mayor or court he may appeal to the proper court, in like manner as prescribed for appeals from judgments of a justice of the peace. Defendant may appeal.

The fee of the mayor shall be as follows: For every warrant issued by him for the recovery of any penalty, or for other cause of action, fifty cents; for every judgment rendered thereon, one dollar, to be taxed among the costs on submission or conviction of the offender; for the use of town seal for other than town purposes, fifty cents; for every certificate for other than town purposes, twenty-five cents; for all other purposes the same fees as are allowed to justices of the peace. Fees of mayor.

Sec. 20. That the mayor shall keep faithful minutes of the precepts issued by him, and of all judicial proceedings; the judgments rendered by him shall have all the force, virtue and validity of judgments rendered by a justice of the peace, and may be executed and enforced against the parties in the county of Burke and elsewhere, in the same manner and by the same means as if the same had been rendered by a justice of the peace of Burke county. Mayor shall keep record of precepts issued.

Sec. 21. That the mayor shall keep his office in some convenient part of the town. He shall perform all the duties as shall from time to time be prescribed, and, when present, shall preside at all meetings of the board of commissioners, and shall have the deciding vote in case of a tie, but he shall vote in no other case. If he shall be absent the board may appoint one of their number to exercise the duties of the mayor to act during his absence. Duties of mayor. Shall preside at meetings.

Sec. 22. That the mayor and commissioners shall, at their first regular meeting, appoint a secretary and treasurer, who may be one of their number, a marshal, and any other officers they may think necessary, who shall receive such compensation for their services as the board may determine. Mayor and commissioners shall appoint secretary and treasurer.

Sec. 23. That within five days after their election the board of commissioners shall convene for the transaction of business, and shall then fix stated days of meeting for the year. A special meeting may be called by the mayor or a majority of the commissioners whenever it seems advisable, and the board may fix a fine or penalty for the non-attendance of any member thereof, and such fine or penalty shall be recovered as other fines and penalties for breaches of the town ordinances. When commissioners shall meet.

Sec. 24. That the board when convened shall have power to make and provide for the execution of such ordinances, by-laws and regulations for the better government of the town as they Power of board to make ordinances.

viso.

deem necessary: Provided, the same be allowed by the provisions of this act, and be consistent with the laws of the state.

stable shall be collector.

Sec. 25. That by virtue of his office the town constable or marshal shall be tax collector, unless the board shall order otherwise, in which event they shall appoint some person to such office. The town tax collector shall have the same powers, and be subject to the same penalties, in collecting the town taxes as sheriffs or tax collectors have in the collection of state and county taxes.

stable em- ered to serve ers.

ests.

Sec. 26. The town constable or marshal is empowered to serve papers and make arrests within the town limits of Hildebran. It shall be his duty to preserve the peace and good order of the town, and to do so he shall have power to make arrests without warrant or other process of all disorderly persons or any person or persons violating any by-laws, ordinances or regulations of the town or attempting to escape; and, if within the hours of seven A. M. and nine P. M., take such unruly person or persons forthwith before the mayor to answer for such violations and disorderly conduct; but if such arrest be made at any other time than that above mentioned, then the person or persons so arrested shall be taken to the lock-up or jail and be safely kept until such hour on the following day at the earliest moment as the mayor may set for the hearing. Any person who may be so intoxicated as to be incapacitated, shall be locked up and safely held until they have become duly sober or in proper condition for trial. The town marshal shall do any other duties that may be prescribed by the board, who shall fix the compensation for such service.

ection of cala- ose.

Sec. 27. That the board of commissioners shall appropriate the necessary amount of funds from the town treasury to purchase or lease a site and erect thereon a building to be used as a calaboose or lock-up, in which persons who violate the ordinances or regulations of the town may be confined while awaiting trial or be imprisoned during the serving of any sentence of imprisonment which may be imposed upon them by the mayor.

le of spirituous uors unlawful.

Sec. 28. That it shall be unlawful for any person or persons to sell any spirituous, vinous or malt liquors within said town, and that the board of commissioners shall have no power to grant license to any person or persons to sell vinous or malt liquors within the corporate limits of said town. And that any person violating this section shall be guilty of a misdemeanor, and upon conviction shall be fined or imprisoned, or both, at the discretion of the court.

axes.

Sec. 29. That in order to raise a fund for the expenses incident to the government of said town, the commissioners may annually levy and collect the following taxes, viz: (1) On real and personal property, moneys, credits, investments, et cetera, which the owner is required to list for state and county taxes in the town, a tax not exceeding twenty cents on every hundred dollars worth of property and not exceeding sixty cents on each taxable poll. Maximum ad valorem and poll tax.

Sec. 30. That if any person liable for taxes on subjects determined to be liable [taxable], shall fail to pay them within the time prescribed for collection, the collector shall proceed forthwith to collect the same by distress and sale, after public advertisement in three public places for ten days if the property is personalty, and if real estate for twenty days; and when the tax due on any lot or other lands which is hereby declared a lien on the same shall remain unpaid on the first day of January, and there is no other property visible but such lot or land of the person in whose name listed, liable to distress and sale, known to the collector, he shall report the fact to the board, with a description of the real estate, and thereupon the board shall direct the same to be sold upon the premises, by the collector, after advertising as above, when the collector shall divide the said lands into as many parts as may be convenient (for which purpose he may employ a surveyor), and shall sell as many thereof as may be required to pay all the taxes and expenses attendant thereon. If the same cannot be conveniently divided, the collector shall sell the whole, and if no person will pay the whole of the taxes and expenses for the whole land, the same shall be struck off to the town, and if not redeemed as hereinafter provided shall belong to the town in fee. Persons failing to pay taxes when due. Liens.

Sec. 31. That the board may require and compel the removal of all nuisances within the town at the expense of the person causing the same, or the owner or the tenant of the grounds on which the same may be; the [board] may also prevent the establishment within the town, and may regulate the same, if allowed to be established, any slaughter-house or place, or for the exercise within the town of any offensive or unhealthy trade, business or employment. Removal of nuisances.

Sec. 32. That the board of commissioners of the town of Hildebran shall have power, whenever they deem it necessary or to the interest of the town, to lay out or open new streets, or to widen, enlarge, change, extend or discontinue any street or streets, or any part thereof, within the corporate limits of said town; and shall have full power and authority to condemn, appropriate or use any land or lands necessary for the purpose named in this section upon making reasonable compensation to the owners or owner thereof; and in case the owner or owners and the commissioners cannot agree as to the damages, then the matter shall be referred to arbitration, each party choosing one who shall be a freeholder and citizen of said town. But if the owner or owners of the land shall refuse to choose such arbitrator within two days after notice, then the board shall select one in his stead for him; Commissioners may open and repair streets. Condemnation of land.

and in case the two chosen aforesaid cannot agree, they shall select an umpire within two days after their appointment, and if they cannot agree on the third man within said time then the board may also appoint the third man. It shall be the duty of the arbitrators aforesaid to meet on the premises or land to be condemned, and assess the damages that the owner or owners may sustain by reason of such condemnation, deducting, however, from the same the estimated value of the improvement that may accrue to the premises by the opening or improvement of the street or the changing or discontinuing of the same. The owner or owners shall have at least ten days' notice of the condemnation, for the purpose of appointing his arbitrator, said notice to be served by the town marshal or any other person authorized to serve notices. In case the arbitrators, after the selection of the third man aforesaid, cannot agree as to the damages then the opinion of any two shall prevail and be returned as the award of the arbitration. The arbitrators shall return a report of their valuation to the board of commissioners, who may confirm the same, and after the confirmation of the same shall cause the same to be entered on their minute book; and the said report so confirmed shall be in all respects the same as a judgment against said town; and said confirmation shall be a complete perfect appropriation of said land or lands for said purposes: Provided, however, that the owner or owners, is dissatisfied with the report of the arbitrators, may, if the same be confirmed, appeal to the next term of the superior court of the county, where the same may be heard anew as to the amount of damages sustained; but the said appeal shall not have the effect of staying the proceedings for making the desired improvement; and all damages agreed on by the commissioners or awarded by the arbitrators shall be paid as other liabilities of the town by taxation.

ner of land shall ve notice.

oviso. peal may be en from assessnt of arbitrators.

cers entrusted h funds of town y be required to e bond.

Sec. 33. That all officers who may be intrusted with the funds of the town shall be required to give bond in such sum as the board may require.

alties recovere in name of n.

Sec. 34. That all penalties imposed relating to the town, or by this act, by any ordinance of the town, unless otherwise provided, shall be recoverable in the name of the town of Hildebran before the mayor, or any tribunal having jurisdiction thereof.

tain persons le to road duty.

Sec. 35. That every male person residing in the town of Hildebran, over eighteen and not over forty-five years of age, who is subject to road duty under the laws of the state, and not exempted by physical disability or otherwise, shall be required to work on the public streets of the town as many days in each year and under such regulations as the board of commissioners may designate, not inconsistent with the state laws: Provided, however, that every such person may be exempted from public street duty for the current municipal year upon the payment of seventy-five cents per day.

Sec. 36. That the said town of Hildebran shall have the benefit of and be subject to all the provisions of law now existing in reference to incorporated towns not inconsistent with this act, and of such laws as may hereafter be enacted for the government of towns and cities. Certain rights and restrictions.

Sec. 37. That this act shall be in force from and after its ratification.

Ratified the 4th day of March, A. D. 1899.

CHAPTER 213.

An act to amend the charter of the city of Wilmington.

The General Assembly of North Carolina do enact:

Section 1. That an act entitled "An act to amend the charter of the city of Wilmington," ratified the ninth day of March, A. D. eighteen hundred and ninety-five, and also an act entitled "An act to amend the charter of the city of Wilmington," ratified the fifth day of March, A. D. eighteen hundred and ninety-seven, be and they are hereby repealed, and all laws and clauses of laws concerning the city of Wilmington existing at the time of the ratification of the act of March ninth, eighteen hundred and ninety-five, are hereby declared to be in full force and effect, except so far as they are amended by this act. Certain acts relating to charter of Wilmington repealed.

Sec. 2. That the election of aldermen shall be held according to the charter of the city of Wilmington and the acts amendatory thereto, except that the registration books may be open for only ten days previous to the election. Election of aldermen.

Sec. 3. No member of the board of aldermen shall be eligible to the office of mayor or other city office or employment, until the expiration of the term for which such aldermen may have been elected or appointed. Aldermen shall not be eligible to office of mayor.

Sec. 4. The mayor of the city shall receive a salary in lieu of any and all other compensation, to be fixed by the board of audit and finance, of not less than twelve hundred dollars nor more than two thousand dollars per annum, which salary shall not be diminished during his term of office. Compensation of mayor.

Sec. 5. No person arrested by the city police for a violation of the laws of North Carolina or the ordinances of the city shall be brought before any other person than the mayor for trial or submission except upon the usual affidavit for removal now provided by [illegible] Certain defendants shall be fined only by mayor.

mps or vagrants y be arrested.

Sec. 6. It shall be the duty of the mayor to have all persons who are tramps or vagrants, as defined by the laws of North Carolina, brought before him and to notify such tramps or vagrants to find employment within twenty-four hours or leave the city; and upon failure or refusal to do so within said time to arrest and put them to work on the streets or other city property for a period not exceeding thirty days.

:ms of city clerk, orney and treasr.

Sec. 7. The terms of the city attorney and the city clerk and treasurer shall be for two years, beginning on the first Monday in April of each year in which the new board of aldermen are to be elected under existing laws, and shall not be removed except for cause.

ard of audit and ance.

Sec. 8. That Jesse Wilder, C. W. Yates, S. P. McNair, H. C. McQueen and W. A. Riach be and they are hereby appointed members of the board of audit and finance, whose terms shall commence upon the expiration of the term of the members of the present board, and shall continue for two years and until their successors are appointed.

tice of primaries oe filed.

Sec. 9. That whenever the executive committee of any political party of citizens in the city of Wilmington decide to take by primary election the sense of the members of the said party as to the proper person or persons to be presented on behalf of that party to the voters of the city at an election to be held in the city, under the laws of this state, for the election of aldermen in the several wards of the city, and as to the proper persons to be presented to the board of aldermen as the candidates of that party for the offices of mayor and chief of police, and for the selection of the members of the city executive committee of such party, the said committee shall file a notice of the primary, with such rules for its conduct as it may adopt, not inconsistent with this act, with the city clerk and treasurer of said city, at least ten days before the time designated for the holding of said primary. Such notice and rules shall be signed by the chairman or acting chairman and attested by the secretary of said executive committee, and by their certified oath to true and correct copies of the original adopted by a majority of said committee. Said notice shall state the places where the voters belonging to that party are requested to cast their votes for the candidates as herein stated; and there shall be only one such place designated for each ward of the city; and the day on which such primary election is to be held, not less than ten days before the city election, and the hours within which it is to be held and the names of the inspectors appointed to hold such primary election and receive the votes that may be cast thereat and make report and return thereof, and the time when such return and report shall be made to the committee directing such primary election to be held; and, also, the date at which a second primary shall be held,

at notice of primary shall design e.

as hereinafter provided, in cases where no one voted for shall have received a majority vote of those cast at the first primary. On the filing of the said notice, and, if the said committee shall have adopted rules for the conduct of said primary, upon the filing of said rules, as provided, with the city clerk and treasurer, the said officer shall immediately cause the same to be copied in a book to be kept and preserved in his office for that purpose, and the said notice and rules to be published in three issues each of at least two, or more in his discretion, of the daily newspapers published in said city, under his certificate that the same were filed in his office and the primary called pursuant thereto.

Persons entitled to take part in primary.

Sec. 10. That no person can vote or take part in the proceedings of any primary election who is not by the laws of the state a lawful elector at the time such primary election is held.

Executive committee may declare certain forms for electors.

Sec. 11. That the executive committee appointing the inspectors to hold such primary election may declare the terms and conditions on which legal electors offering to vote at such election shall be regarded and taken as proper members of the party at whose instance or in whose interest such primary election has been called or may be held, and therefore entitled to vote at such election as a member of that party, and to provide rules and regulations, not inconsistent with this act, for the conduct of such primary. And upon the filing and publication of said rules and regulations, as hereinbefore provided, any person who shall knowingly and willfully violate or attempt to violate the same shall be guilty of a misdemeanor and upon conviction shall be fined or imprisoned in the discretion of the court trying the same: Provided, that the rule or regulation so violated or attempted to be violated be not inconsistent with the provisions of this act or the law of the state. And the record of he said rules and regulation in the office of the city clerk and treasurer shall be received in any court of this state as the evidence of the primary rules and regulations adopted by said party.

Persons violating rules of committee.

Right of persons to vote in primary may be challenged.

Sec. 12. That any recognized member of the party in whose interest such election is held may challenge the right of any person offering to vote at such election and the inspectors there authorized to hold, and holding, such election shall determine on the evidence there furnished whether the person so offering is entitled to vote at such election, and shall receive or reject such votes so offered as to them the evidence for or against the right of the persons so offering to vote shall reasonably warrant.

When polls shall be opened.

Sec. 13. That the polls shall be open for such primary elections from seven A. M. to seven P. M., and all votes shall be by ballot. The report of the committee so directing such primary election by the officers holding the same, shall be in writing, with which the original ballots shall be returned and the poll list of the voters made at the time of the voting and the reasons on which any challenged vote was received or rejected. Said committee shall carefully examine the returns and reports so made and thereupon decide who are the persons that have been chosen by the majority vote cast in the primary election, and as candidates of the party for the office of aldermen at the approaching election; and such of the executive offices of the city to be voted for by the aldermen then to be elected as are mentioned in section nine. The majority vote in a ward shall determine the result in that ward as to the persons to be, the candidates of the party in that ward for aldermen and the committeemen for the ward to serve on the party's city executive committee. The majority of the aggregate vote cast in all the wards shall determine who shall be the party candidates for mayor and such other of the officials as are mentioned in section nine. The said committee shall without delay publish in at least one issue each of two daily newspapers published in said city, the tabulated statement of the result of the primary and declare who shall have been nominated and for what office, and also for what offices by reason of no person having received a majority of the vote cast there has been a failure to nominate. Thereupon, the second primary shall be held, as may be necessary because of the failure to nominate, at the time designated in the first notice, and by the same inspectors appointed to hold the first primary, no other than the first notice being necessary; and at such primary only the two persons who shall have been voted for and received the highest and next highest vote in the first primary for candidate for a particular office shall be voted for in the second primary for that office; unless, either of those shall publicly withdraw by letter addressed to the said committee, in which event the third highest shall be then substituted for the person so withdrawing, or the fourth highest; and so on, if the person voted for the first and entitled to be voted for in the second primary shall in said manner withdraw. And the vote shall be canvassed and the result declared in the same manner as herein provided for the first primary.

jority vote in d shall determ ne result.

sult of primary ll be published.

cept as herein ovided, primaries all be regulated election law.

SEC. 14. That except as herein provided all elections at primary elections under this act shall be regulated by the election law of the said city in force at the time such primary election is held as nearly as the same can be done.

rsons illegally ting, etc., guilty misdemeanor.

SEC. 15. That if any person who is not entitled to vote under this act shal. vote at any primary election held hereunder, or vote more than once, or personate another person, or in any name other than his own legal name, or in any manner disturb the orderly proceedings of any such election, or intimidate, or in any manner attempt to intimidate, or to deter from voting, or bribe, or attempt to bribe, any lawful voter, or impose, or attempt to impose on any lawful voter, a ticket or ballot other than it appears on its face to be, such person or persons shall be guilty of a misdemeanor, and on conviction shall be fined not less than ten dollars, or be sentenced to hard labor upon the streets of the city for not more than three months, one or both at the discretion of the court trying the case. Penalty.

Sec. 16. That the inspectors who may hold such primary elections under this act, and return the votes, proceedings, and actions thereof, herein provided, shall before assuming the duties make oath before some officer authorized to administer an oath, that they will honestly, faithfully and to the best of their ability, do and perform all the duties of their respective offices, and any willful violation of said oath or of any oath taken under the provisions of this act, shall be held to be perjury, and shall be punished as provided by the laws of the state for the crime of perjury. Inspectors shall take oath before entering upon duties.

The chief of police and the sheriff of New Hanover county are required that good order is preserved at such election, and may arrest and present for commitment to the nearest officer clothed with the power of justice of the peace, all persons who may be guilty of any violation of the provisions of this act. Order shall be preserved at primaries.

Sec. 17. That the inspectors holding such primary election under the provisions of this act may of their own motion, or in case of the challenge of any person offering to vote, if they deem there is any doubt of the propriety under the provisions of this act of the vote so offered, require of the person so offering to vote his oath to the fact which authorized the vote, and if the person so offering to vote declines to make the oath so demanded, his vote shall be rejected. Persons offering to vote may be required to take oath.

Sec. 18. That the costs and expenses of holding such primary election shall be borne by the city. The compensation of each of the inspectors shall be three dollars a day, and all other charges and expenses shall be reasonable. Expense of holding such primary.

Sec. 19. That there shall be three inspectors of election appointed for each election precinct at such primary election and in making the appointment of inspectors, the executive committee shall so far as possible select qualified voters from a list of names agreed upon by a majority of the candidates before the primary election, provided such agreed list is filed with the committee, on such day as may be designated by the committee. Three inspectors shall be appointed for each precinct.

Sec. 20. That the executive committee of the city when they are petitioned by one hundred qualified electors of the same political party the committee belongs to, shall call and cause to be held a primary election as provided for in this act, and should the committee refuse to call or hold such primary election as petitioned for, they shall be guilty of a misdemeanor and upon conviction be punished by imprisonment in the county jail not less than thirty days or more than ninety days. On application of 100 members, executive committee shall order primary

flicting laws ealed. Sec. 21. That all laws and parts of laws in conflict with the provisions of this act be and the same are hereby repealed.

Sec. 22. That this act shall be in force from and after its ratification.

Ratified the 4th day of March, A. D. 1899.

CHAPTER 214.

An act to incorporate the Burlington and Southern Railroad Company.

The General Assembly of North Carolina do enact:

porators. Section 1. That R. L. Holt, J. H. Holt Jr., E. C. Holt, W. I. Holt, F. L. Williamson and J. W. Williamson, their associates, successors and assigns, be and are hereby created and constituted a body politic and corporate under the name of the Burlington and Southern Railroad Company, and under that name and style they and their successors and assigns shall have succession for sixty years and shall have power to sue and be sued, plead and be impleaded, to prosecute and defend to final judgment and execution in all courts of this state; shall have a common seal and shall have power to purchase, hold and convey lands, tenements, goods and chattels necessary or expedient to the purposes and objects of this corporation; they shall have power also to make such by-laws and regulations for the government and conduct of the business of the corporation as they may deem necessary, not inconsistent with the laws and constitution of this state.

ly corporate. porate name. porate powers.

Sec. 2. That said corporation is hereby authorized and empowered to survey, lay out, construct, equip, maintain and operate by steam or other motive power a railroad with one or more tracks from some point on the North Carolina Railroad at or near the city of Burlington in Alamance county, to the town of Pittsboro in Chatham county, or to some point on the line of a railway in the counties of Guilford, Randolph or Chatham, as it may deem best.

ital stock. y be increased. Sec. 3. That the capital stock of said company shall be fifty thousand dollars with the privilege and power of increasing the same to five hundred thousand dollars, divided into shares of the par value of one hundred dollars each. The capital stock shall be raised by subscription on the part of individuals, townships, municipal or other corporations.

oks of subscrip- n may be opened. Sec. 4. That the corporators herein named may cause books of subscription to be opened at such times and places as they may appoint, and said corporations, at any time after the sum of ten thousand dollars has been subscribed to the capital stock of said company and ten per cent. thereof has been paid, shall be authorized and empowered to call together the subscribers to the capital stock for the purpose of completing the organization of the said company in accordance with the provisions of this act. When company may be organized.

Sec. 5. That at the time of such organization, and annually thereafter, such stockholders or subscribers shall select from their number not less than seven nor more than eleven directors of said company, who shall hold their offices for one year and until their successors shall be elected and qualified; and the directors chosen at such meeting and annually thereafter shall elect one of their number president of said company and also a secretary and treasurer, and such other officers as may be provided for in the by-laws of said company, who shall hold office for one year or until their successors shall be elected and qualified; the said directors shall have power to fill any vacancy in the directors or officers of said company that shall occur by reason of resignation, death or otherwise. In all meetings and elections provided for in this act by the stockholders each share of stock represented, either in person or by proxy, shall be entitled to one vote. Election of directors. Election of officers. Term of office.

Sec. 6. The said company shall issue certificates of stock to its members and the transfer of stock may be made as provided by the by-laws. Certificates of stock

Sec. 7. That the several townships of the counties through which or into which the said railroad may pass are respectively authorized and empowered to make such subscriptions to the capital stock of said company in such amounts as may be settled upon in the manner hereinafter prescribed: Provided, no subscription shall be valid until the same has been ratified by the qualified voters of the township as hereinafter provided. Townships authorized to subscribe to capital stock.

Sec. 8. That the board of commissioners of any county in which any part of said railroad may be located are authorized and required, whenever one-fifth of the voters of any township in their county shall petition them in writing, to have submitted to the voters of said township a proposition to subscribe a specific sum to the capital stock of said company, to cause an election to be held in said township at the voting place or places therein, after thirty days' notice of said election by advertisement in some newspaper of the county, if there be one, and at the courthouse door and at four or more public places in said township, and to submit to the qualified voters of such township the election of subscribing to the capital stock of said company the sum of money specified in said written petition of at least one-fifth of the voters of said township as aforesaid asking for said election; at the election, those who favor subscription shall vote a ballot upon which shall be written or printed the words "For subscription," and those who oppose shall vote a ballot upon which shall Commissioners of any county authorized to order election on petition. Form of ballot.

be written or printed the words "Against subscription"; such election when ordered shall be held under the rules and regulations prescribed by law for holding elections for members of the general assembly. The returns of any election held by any township under the provisions of this act shall be made to the board of county commissioners of the county in which said township is on the Saturday next after the day of election, and the said board shall meet at the court-house on that day and shall on that day canvass the returns; and if a majority of the qualified voters of said township shall have voted "For subscription," then the subscription so authorized may be made to the capital stock of said company for said township by the chairman of the board of county commissioners.

turns of election.

nds may be ued.

Sec. 9. That in payment of any subscription made as provided in the next preceding section the board of commissioners of the county wherein the township is shall issue bonds to an amount not exceeding the sum so authorized to be subscribed, the said bonds shall be in the sum of one hundred dollars each, and shall express upon their face by what authority and for what purpose tney are issued. They shall be coupon bonds and bear interest at a rate of no more than six per cent., payable on the first days of January and July in each year by the treasurer of the county in which said township is, and shall have coupons attached for each payment of interest provided; and both the said bonds and each coupon shall be signed by the chairman of the board of commissioners. The bonds herein provided shall run for a period o1 thirty years from and after the first day of January next after they are issued.

nomination.

erest.

ds, how signed.

mmissioners may special tax to interest and cipal.

Sec. 10. That to provide for the payment of the interest on any bonds that may be issued under the provisions of this act the board of commissioners of the county in which the township is, on account of which said bonds shall be issued, shall, in addition to other taxes, compute and levy upon the proper subjects of taxation in such township a sufficient tax each year to pay the interest on said bonds and one-thirtieth of the amount of the principal thereof, which latter shall be and constitute a sinking fund to be invested bv said board of commissioners to meet the redemption of said bonds at their maturity, which said taxes shall be collected by the sheriff of said county under the same rules and regulations and subject to the same penalties as may be provided for by law for the collection of other taxes, and shall be paid by the sheriff to the treasurer of the county, who shall pay the interest on said bonds, and the coupons taken up by him shall be evidence of such payment.

missioners of or city shall r election on ion.

Sec. 11. The board of commissioners or aldermen of any town or city in any county in which any part of said railroad may be, shall be authorized and required, when one-fifth of the voters in said town or city shall request in writing that a proposition to subscribe a specific sum to the capital stock of said company may be submitted to the voters of said town or city, to cause an election to be held therein under the same rules and regulations as are prescribed hereinbefore for elections in townships, except that the returns shall be made to the aldermen or commissioners of said town or city, who shall canvass the same; and if a majority of all the qualified voters of said town or city shall have voted for subscription, then the mayor or chief officer of said town or city. And in addition to the other tax upon the subjects of taxation in said town or city the said aldermen or commissioners thereof shall compute and levy a tax each year sufficient to pay the interest on said bonds and one-thirtieth of the principal, which latter shall constitute a sinking fund to be invested to meet the redemption of said bonds at maturity; and the taxes levied under the provisions of this section shall be collected in the same manner as other taxes are collected and subject to the same rules and to the same penalties and remedies against the collectors for failure to collect and account for the same.

Returns of election, how made.

Special tax shall be levied to pay interest and principal.

How collected.

Sec. 12. That said company shall have the right to have lands condemned for its right of way and for necessary warehouses and other buildings according to law; and shall have also full power and authority to sell or lease its road-bed, superstructure, property and franchise to any other company, corporation or persons, and also the power to contract with any other corporation or construction company, or any individual for the construction, maintenance or operation of its road, and to purchase or lease and hold the bonds or stock of any other railroad in this state or to consolidate with any connecting line of railroad.

Company may condemn lands.

Sec. 13. That said company shall be authorized to begin the construction of said road at any point on the line where it may be located, and may operate any portion of it when completed, and shall have exclusive right of transportation over the same.

May begin construction of road at any point along line.

Sec. 14. That said company shall have the right to borrow money for the construction and operation of its railroad, and to make, issue and negotiate and sell its bonds in such sums and in such amounts as may be agreed upon and as the directors may deem expedient; and said bonds shall bear a rate of interest no greater than six per cent. per annum, and both the interest and the principal shall be payable at such time and places as the board of directors may determine; and said company shall have power to secure the payment of same by mortgage or deed of trust on its property, estate, rights and franchises, on such terms and to such trustee or trustees as the board of directors may think proper, and said mortgage, deed or deed of trust, when duly registered in the county of Alamance shall convey all

Empowered to borrow money, etc.

the property and estate in said company without registration in any county.

hts, powers and ileges. Sec. 15. That in addition to the powers, rights and privileges herein granted to said company it shall have all the rights, powers and privileges given by law to like corporations.

Sec. 16. That this act shall be in force from and after its ratification.

Ratified the 4th day of March, A. D. 1899.

CHAPTER 215.

An act to amend and consolidate the charter of the town of Lumberton, Robeson county.

The General Assembly of North Carolina do enact:

Section 1. That the inhabitants of the town of Lumberton shall continue to be as heretofore a body corporate under the name and style, "The Town of Lumberton," and under such name is hereby invested with all the privileges, immunities and franchises, property and all other rights heretofore belonging or appertaining to the town of umberton, and in and by that name may sue and be sued, plead and be impleaded, acquire and hold property, real and personal, for use of the town as its board of commissioners may deem necessary and expedient.

porate name. porate powers privileges.

officers. Sec. 2. That E. K. Proctor, Jr., shall be mayor and O. C. Norment, W. I. Linkhaw, T. N. Higley and Dr. J. D. McMillan shall be commissioners, and that F. J. Floyd shall be town constable, and C. B. Skipper shall be town clerk and treasurer; the same are hereby declared the mayor, commissioners, constable and clerk and treasurer, with the powers and duties of the officers of the town of Lumberton, until their successors are elected and qualified as hereinafter provided.

porate limits. Sec. 3. That the corporate limits of said town shall be and are hereby declared to be included within and up to the following boundaries, to-wit: Beginning on the east side of Lumber river at the mouth of a small branch that divides the lands of Mrs. McE. McMillan and W. W. Prevatt, and runs up the said branch to a bridge on the Carthage road, thence parallel with Sixth street in the town of Lumberton south eighty-seven and one-half degrees east to the east edge of the Fayetteville road, thence along said road about south seventeen degrees west to the northwest corner of a lot now owned by Mrs. A. H. McLeod, thence along the line of that lot south seventy-three degrees east (October sixteenth, eighteen hundred and sixty-six) four hundred and seventy-seven feet to the northeast corner of said lot, thence south seven hundred feet to McLeod's corner on the north side of the Elizabeth road near the A. M. E. Zion church, then along the north edge of the Elizabeth road till a line running parallel with Elm or Front of the town of Lumberton (about south two and one-half degrees west) will touch the Whiteville road at the bridge over a small branch near the cemetery, thence parallel with said Elm or Front street to said bridge, thence down the said branch to the north edge of the right of way of the Carolina Central Railroad, thence south three hundred feet to a stake on the south side of said road, thence parallel with the said road about north sixty-six degrees west till the line reaches the south line of a tract of land conveyed by John Willis to Jacob Rhodes and others, dated August fourteenth, seventeen hundred and eighty-seven, and recorded in Book A, page sixty, in the office of the register of deeds of Robeson county, thence along that line eighty-seven and one-half degrees west to an iron bar driven in a stump on the east edge of Lumber river, thence up the said river to the beginning.

Officers of town, when elected.

Sec. 4. The officers of said town shall consist of a mayor and four commissioners, to be elected by the qualified voters of said town annually on the first Monday in May.

Persons entitled to vete.

Sec. 5. Said election of mayor and commissioners shall be held at the court-house in said town, and no person shall be entitled to vote at said election, or at any election held in said town for municipal purposes, unless he shall be an elector of the state of North Carolina, and shall have resided ninety days next preceding the day of election within the said corporation.

Appointment of registrar and judges of election.

Sec. 6. It shall be the duty of the commissioners of said town, on the first Monday in March in each year, to appoint a registrar and three judges of election, who shall be qualified voters of said town, and who shall, within ten days thereafter, be notified of their appointment by the constable of said town. The registrar so appointed shall immediately make publication at the door of the court-house and three other public places in said town of his appointment as such. He shall be furnished with a registration book by the commissioners of said town, and it shall be his duty to revise the existing registration book of said town in such a manner that said book shall show and accurate list of electors previously registered and still residing in said town, without requiring such electors to he registered anew. He shall also, between the hours of sunrise and sunset on each day (Sundays excepted) for thirty days preceding each election keep open said book for the registration of any electors residing in said town entitled to register, whose names have never before been registered in said town, or do not appear on the revised lists, but the commissioners of said town may, if they think proper, upon giving thirty days' notice at four public places in said town, require an entirely new registration of voters before any election held therein.

gistrar and ges shall take h.

Sec. 7. The registrar and judges of election, before entering upon the discharge of their duties, shall take the oath prescribed by article six, section four of the constitution of North Carolina before some justice of the peace of Robeson county.

ien voters shall registered.

Sec. 8. It shall be the duty of the registrar and judges of election to attend at the polling place in said town, with the registration book, on the Monday preceding the election from the hour of nine o'clock A. M. until the hour of five o'clock P. M., when and where the said book shall be open to the inspection of the electors of the said town, and any of the electors shall be allowed to object to the name of anv person appearing in said book. In case of any such objection, the registrar shall enter upon his book opposite the name of the person so objected to, the word "Challenged," and shall appoint a time and place, on or before the election day, when he, together with said judges of election, shall hear and decide said objection, giving due notice to the voter so objected to: Provided, that nothing contained in this section shall be construed to prohibit the right of any elector to challenge or object to the name of any person registering or offering to register at any other time than that above specified. If any person challenged or objected to shall be found not duly qualified as provided for in this charter, his name shall be erased from the registration book, and he shall not be allowed to vote at any election held in said town for municipal purposes.

ection to pers registered.

viso.

ctors may challge.

nner of conduct election.

Sec. 9. The said judges of election, together with the registrar, who shall take with him the registration book, shall assemble at the polling place on the day of the election held in said town and shall open the polls at seven o'clock A. M. They shall superintend said election and shall keep the polls open until sunset, when the polls shall be closed and the votes for mayor and commissioners counted out by them. They shall keep poll books and write in them the name of every person voting at said election, and at the close thereof shall certify said poll lists and deposit them with the clerk and treasurer of said town, and said poll books shall, in any trial for illegal or fraudulent voting, be received as evidence. If for any cause any of the judges of election shall fail to attend, the registrar shall appoint some discreet person or persons to fill the vacancy, who shall be sworn by him before acting.

iges of election ll certify result.

Sec. 10. The voters shall vote by ballot, having the name of the mayor and commissioners on one ballot, either in writing or printed on white paper and without any device, and the person having the highest number of votes shall be declared elected by the judges of election, who shall certify said fact to the town lerk and treasurer, and in case of a tie the judges of election hall determine by ballot who is elected.

Eligibility to office.

Sec. 11. That no person shall be eligible to any office in said own unless he shall be a qualified voter therein.

Mayor and commissioners shall be notified of election.

Sec. 12. That immediately after each election, it shall be the luty of the town clerk and treasurer to notify, in writing, the ayor and commissioners-elect of their election.

Mayor and commissioners shall take oath.

Sec. 13. That the mayor and commissioners-elect shall, within hree days after having been notified by the town clerk and treasurer, before some justice of the peace in said county, take the oath prescribed for public officers, and an oath that they will faithfully and impartially discharge the duties imposed upon them by law.

Mayor and commissioners refusing to qualify.

Sec. 14. That any person elected mayor or commissioner of said town under the provisions of this chapter refusing to qualify and act as such for one month after such election shall forfeit and pay the sum of two hundred dollars, one-half to the use of the person suing for the same and the other half to said town, to be applied by the commissioners of said town to the use and benefit thereof; the said sum shall be recovered in an ordinary civil action before a justice of the peace of said county in the name of the state of North Carolina.

Election of town clerk.

Sec. 15. That said commissioners shall, at their first meeting after their election, select some one as town clerk and treasurer who shall hold office for one year, or until his successor shall be elected and qualified. He shall act as secretary to the board of commissioners and as treasurer of said town, and before entering upon the discharge of the duties of his office shall give good and sufficient bond, with sureties, to be approved by the board of commissioners of said town, in the sum of two thousand dollars, payable to the state of North Carolina, and conditioned upon his faithfully accounting for and paying over all moneys that may come into his hands as treasurer of said town, and for the faithful discharge of his duties as secretary of said board of commissioners. The commissioners of said town may require of the town clerk and treasurer a monthly statement and exhibit of receipts and disbursements, and if he shall fail for thirty days after having been required to make such exhibit to render the same, it shall be and is hereby declared a breach of his official bond, and the commissioners are authorized and empowered to declare the office vacant and to appoint his successor. All suits entered on the official bond of any of the officers of said town shall be in the name of the state of North Carolina, to the use of the board of commissioners of the town of Lumberton against the said official and his sureties.

Monthly statement may be required of clerk.

Suits entered on official bond.

Election of constable.

Sec. 16. The said commissioners shall at the first meeting after their election select some one to act as constable of said town, who shall hold his office for one year or until his successor is elected and qualified. He shall, before entering upon the discharge of the duties of his office, enter into bond in the sum of two thousand dollars, with good and sufficient sureties, to be approved by the board of commissioners, payable to the state of North Carolina, and conditioned upon his faithfully executing and returning to the proper authority all process that may come into his hands as constable aforesaid, upon his faithfully accounting for and paying over to the proper authority all moneys that may come into his hands from any source as said constable, upon his faithfully collecting and paying over all taxes levied by the commissioners of said town, and in all other respects executing to the best of his ability and honestly and faithfully all the duties imposed upon him by this charter or by the board of commissioners of said town. And the said commissioners may also elect and provide for the pay of such number of policemen and watchmen for said town as in their judgment may be necessary to efficiently carry out and enforce the ordinances and regulations thereof, and the criminal laws of the state in said town. The said policemen and watchmen, when elected, shall be qualified in the manner provided for the constable, and shall in the enforcement of the general laws of the state and the ordinances and regulations of said town, have all the powers conferred on the town constable by the provisions of this act, and the general laws of the state, and such as may be hereafter provided. The said policemen and watchmen may be required to give bond for the faithful discharge of their duties in such sums as the commissioners may fix, and may be removed by them at any time for neglect of duty, drunkenness, or other cause.

[margin: all give bond.] [margin: ties of constable.] [margin: alification of icemen.] [margin: y be required to e bond.]

[margin: risdiction of yor.]

Sec. 17. The mayor of said town of Lumberton is hereby constituted a special court with all the jurisdiction and powers in criminal offences occurring with the limits of said town which are or hereafter may be given to justices of the peace; he shall preserve and keep the peace, and may cause, upon proper proceedings, persons charged or convicted of crimes in other counties or states, who may be found in the town limits, to be arrested and bound or imprisoned to appear at the proper tribunal to answer for their offences. He shall also have jursdiction to issue process, to hear and determine all misdemeanors consisting of a violation of the ordinances and regulations of the said town, to enforce penalties by issuing executions upon any adjudged violations thereof, to execute the laws and rules and ordinances made by the commissioners of said town.

[margin: uance of warts.]

Sec. 18. That the mayor may issue his warrants upon his own information of any violation of any town ordinance without a written affidavit, and may issue the same to any constable of the town, or to such other officer as may be clothed with the powers of the constable, or to such other officer as the justice of the peace may issue his precepts.

Sec. 19. That the mayor shall preside at all meetings of the town commissioners, and vote in no case except in an equal vote between said commissioners, then he shall give the casting vote. He shall keep a faithful minute of all precepts issued by him and of all judicial proceedings. Judgments rendered by him shall have all the force, virtue and validity as if rendered by a justice of the peace, and may be executed and enforced against the parties in the courts of Robeson county and elsewhere, and by the same means and manner as if the same had been rendered by a justice of the peace of Robeson county. Mayor shall preside at meetings of commissioners.

Sec. 20. That every violation of a town ordinance shall be a misdemeanor, and shall be punished by a fine of not more than fifty dollars or imprisonment of not more than thirty days. Violation of ordinances a misdemeanor.

Sec. 21. That the mayor shall have power to imprison for fines imposed by him under the provisions of this act, and in such cases the prisoners shall only be discharged as now or as may hereafter be provided by law. Mayor empowered to imprison in certain cases.

Sec. 22. That all fines collected under the provisions of the foregoing act for violation of town ordinances shall go to the use of the said town. Fines, how applied.

Sec. 23. That the mayor shall be entitled by law to the same fees as a justice of the peace in like cases, and an additional salary to be allowed by the commissioners if they see fit. Compensation of mayor.

Sec. 24. That the commissioners shall form one board, and a majority of them shall be competent to perform all the duties prescribed for commissioners, unless otherwise provided. Within five days after their election they shall convene for the transaction of business, and shall fix their stated days for meeting during the year, which shall be as often as once a month during the same. Special meetings of the commissioners shall also be held on the call of the mayor or a majority of the commissioners, and of every such meeting when called by the mayor the commissioners not joining in the call to be notified verbally or in writing. Duties and board of commissioners.

Sec. 25. That the commissioners shall have power to make and provide for the execution of such ordinances, by-laws, rules and regulations for the good government of the town as they may deem necessary, and shall have power, and it shall be their duty, to provide for and secure the peace, good order and tranquility of the town against disturbance by quarrels, loud, profane or obscene language, riots, affrays, trespasses or other breaches of the peace, or irregularities of whatever nature tending to disturb the peace of the citizens. They shall provide for the repairing of the streets, sidewalks and alleys, and cause the same to be kept clean and in good order, take all proper means to pre- Duties of commissioners.

vent and extinguish fires, make regulations for the observance of the Sabbath, suppress and remove nuisances, prohibit the indecent exposure of the person, and prohibit and suppress the sauntering around, advertising or practicing their vocation by lewd women, by imposing such fines and imprisonments, in all cases within the jurisdiction of a justice of the peace as they shall deem adequate.

rdinances shall ply to territory thin one-fourth ile of corporate its.

Sec. 26. That any ordinances passed by said commissioners by virtue of the police power vested in them by this charter or the general laws of the state shall apply to the territory within one-fourth of a mile of the corporate limits as above set out, unless in the ordinances it is otherwise provided: Provided, however, that this clause shall not be construed to permit the passage of any ordinance to apply to the territory beyond the corporate limits which affects stock running at large beyond the said limits, or which shall levy any tax on the polls or property of the inhabitants beyond the same, or to the restriction of the kind or class of buildings erected outside of said corporate limits.

oviso.

all not affect ock at large out-le limits.

atement of nuinces.

Sec. 27. That the commissioners may require the abatement and removal of all nuisances, and shall have power to pull down any old house, barn or other building in said town when the same may be considered dangerous from fire or other causes to the safety of the person or property of adjacent residents: Provided, however, that before such removal, the owner of such property shall be notified in writing by the clerk of such board of the action and allow one month for repairing or removing such building. That all damages may be agreed upon between the mayor and the party whose property is removed under this section, and in case they cannot agree each shall select a disinterested person, and if they cannot agree they may select a third person and the decision of two of these shall be final, except an appeal is filed within ten days.

oviso.

ner of property all be notified.

mages agreed on.

mmissioners ay build guard use.

Sec. 28. That the commissioners may build or establish a guard-house in which to secure or confine offenders against town ordinances; and for feeding such prisoners the town marshal, constable or other officer shall be allowed such compensation as is allowed the keeper of the common jail in Robeson county: Provided, in the above case that no prisoner or offender shall be confined in said guard-house more than twenty-four hours without first having his case heard and determined before the mayor.

oviso.

mmissioners powered to lay t and open streets

Sec. 29. That the commissioners shall have power to lay out or open any new street or streets within the corporate limits of said town whenever deemed necessary by them, and they shall have the power at any time to widen, enlarge, change, extend, narrow and discontinue any street or streets within said corporate limits whenever they may so determine, by making a reasonable compensation to the owners of property damaged

Disagreement as to value of land.

hereby. In cases where owners of land cannot agree with the ommissioners regarding the value of land or property and the lamages, the mayor of the town shall issue his warrant to the own constable commanding him to summon three disinterested reeholders of said town, who, together with two freeholders as bove, to be selected by party claiming damages, shall determine he value of said property, and assess the damages, after which hey shall return a report of their proceedings, findings and so orth, into the office of the mayor there to be filed.

Assessors shall take oath.

Before proeeding to view said premises and assess said damages, the paries so summoned shall take oath before the mayor or a justice f the peace to make a fair, just and impartial discharge of the uties of appraiser and assessor and report the same. If the party damaged or claiming damages refuses to select two ppraisers as provided above, the report of the three summoned n behalf of the town shall be final: Provided, that if either a ajority of the commissioners or the opposite party be dissatised with the report of the freeholders, then they may appeal to he superior court of Robeson county, and in that case the report of the valuation and the proceedings therein shall be sent in by said appraisers to said court, there to be determined.

Annual levy of tax.

Sec. 30. That the board of commissioners of said town shall have power annually to levy and cause to be collected taxes for necessary town purposes on all real property, all moneys, credits, investments in bonds, stocks, joint stock companies, all personal property, and all other subjects of taxation now taxed or which may hereafter be taxed by the general assembly of North Carolina for state and county purposes, and on the taxable polls within said town:

Proviso. Maximum tax levy.

Provided, however, that the taxes levied by them shall not exceed sixty-six and two-third cents on the one hundred dollars valuation of all property within said town, and two dollars on each taxable poll, to meet all the liabilities of the town in the way of indebtedness, bonded or otherwise, which now exists, or which may be hereafter created; and the valuation of all property within said town, as taxed by said commissioners, shall be the same as that at which it was assessed for taxation on the first day of June in that year for state and county purposes:

Proviso.

Valuation of property may be raised.

Provided, that the board of commissioners of said town may, at a regular meeting, after ten days' notice to any person liable to taxation in said town, raise the valuation of such property in said town as they shall deem unreasonably low, and they may also, in order to discover and have properly listed all solvent credits, stocks, bonds, etc., subject to taxation in said town, summon any person whom they may have reason to believe is the owner of any property of such nature which is unlisted, or which being listed is not properly valued, to appear before the said board of commissioners at a regular meeting and to answer under oath such questions as may tend to discover the existence of property of the character above named. And in the event any person so summoned shall fail or refuse to appear and answer such questions as are proper under the provisions of this section, the said board of commissioners may proceed to investigate the matter by other evidence, and may summon and examine any witnesses necessary for a joint decision of the question at issue, and may require by proper order the production of any books, records, papers or evidence of the existence of such property that they may deem proper or necessary, and if a majority of said board of commissioners shall decide that any person is the owner of any property of the character above set out that is not listed or not properly valued, they shall order the same to be entered on the tax list or the value increased by the town clerk and treasurer, and the said property so listed shall be subject to the payment of all taxes levied by the said town, and collected as other taxes therein.

es, when due.

Sec. 31. That all taxes levied by the commissioners of said town, except license or privilege taxes, shall be due and payable on the first day of October of each year to the constable or tax collector of said town, and after that time may be collected by him by distraining any personal property of the tax payer to be found within said town.

en tax returns ll be made.

Sec. 32. That on the first Monday in July of each and every year, the town clerk and treasurer of said town shall, by advertisement at the court-house door and four other public places in said town, notify all persons within said town liable to taxation to come forward and make returns of their tax lists to him within thirty days from the publication of said notice. All persons owning property in said town, and liable to taxation, shall make returns of all their taxable property to said clerk under oath, and he is hereby authorized and empowered to administer to such tax payers an oath that he will well and truly return all property owned by him within said town and liable to taxation under the provisions of this charter; said list so returned shall state the age of the tax paver, and all property real and personal liable to taxation owned by him, with an accurate description of all real property owned by him on June the first of that year, when he was required by law to return the same to the list taken of Lumberton township, to be assessed for taxation for state and county purposes.

h shall be adistered to tax er.

required to rn taxes.

Sec. 33. That all persons owning any property within said town liable for taxation for town purposes shall return the same to the town clerk, as provided in section thirty-two of this charter, and all property therein liable to such taxation owned by minors, lunatics, or persons non compos mentis, shall be returned as herein provided by their guardian or guardians, if they shall have any such.

Sec. 34. That all property liable to taxation for town purposes in said town and held by executors, administrators or trustees shall be returned by them in that capacity, and the individual property of all such guardians, executors, administrators or trustees shall first be distrained or attached by the constable or tax collector of said town for the satisfaction of the taxes due on all property so returned by them; and the constable or tax collector of said town is hereby authorized, at any time after the taxes may be due the town on said property as aforesaid, to distrain any personal property of such guardian, executors, administrators or trustees to be found in said town.

Property held by trustees, etc., to be returned by them.

Sec. 35. That the town clerk and treasurer shall make out a full and complete list of all taxable property in said town so returned to him, and of the taxable polls in said town, and if any person or persons in said town liable to taxation shall fail to make returns to the clerk as herein provided for, for thirty days after the first Monday in July in each year, the town clerk shall make return of the taxable property of such person or persons, and his age, if he is liable to poll tax, and such person or persons so failing to make returns of their property and poll shall be liable to double taxation on their property and poll, to be collected as other property and poll taxes. The town clerk of the said town shall complete the tax list and place it, or a certified copy thereof, in the hands of the constable or tax collector of said town on the third Monday in August in each year. Such tax list, or certified copy thereof, certified by the town clerk, when placed in the hands of the constable or tax collector of said town, shall have the force and effect of an execution.

Persons failing to return tax liable to double tax.

Tax list shall have force and effect of execution.

Sec. 36. That the lien of the town taxes shall attach to all real property subject to taxation on and after the third Monday in August in each year, and shall continue until such taxes, together with any penalty that shall accrue thereon, shall be paid. All personal property liable to taxation of tax payers within the town shall be liable to be seized and sold, after ten days' notice at the court-house and four other public places in said town in satisfaction of taxes by the town constable or tax collector after said taxes shall have become due and payable.

Lien of taxes shall attach to real property.

Personal property liable to be seized.

Sec. 37. That whenever the taxes due said town shall be due and unpaid, the constable or tax collector of said town shall immediately proceed to collect them as follows: First, if the party charged or his agent have personal property in said town equal in value to the taxes charged against him the constable or tax collector shall seize and sell the same under the same rules as sheriffs are required to sell personal property under execution, and his fees for such levy or sale shall be fifty cents; second, if the party charged has not personal property to be found in said

Taxes due and unpaid.

town of sufficient value to satisfy his taxes, the constable or tax collector of said town shall levy upon any lands of the delinquent to be found within the town. The levy shall contain an accurate description of the lands with the name of the owner or owners, the amount of taxes due by the delinquent, and a list thereof shall be by the constable or tax collector returned to the town clerk and treasurer, who shall enter the same in a book to be kept for that purpose, charging therefor the sum of twenty-five cents for each levy; third, the constable or tax collector shall notify the delinquent of such levy and of the day and place of sale by service of a notice, stating these particulars, on him personally if he be a resident of said town. If the delinquent does not reside in said town, but his residence is known or can by reasonable diligence be ascertained, the notice shall be mailed post-paid to such delinquent. If the residence of the delinquent cannot with reasonable diligence be ascertained, the constable or tax collector shall post a notice substantially as above described, at the court-house door and four other public places in said town at least thirty days before the sale of the land, and this last mentioned notice shall be posted as in all cases of sale of land for taxes in said town; fourth, the sale shall be made at the court-house in said town and shall be on one of the days prescribed for sale of real estate under execution, and shall be conducted in all respects as are sales under execution. If the delinquent resides out of said town and his address be known to the constable or tax collector, he shall mail to him within one month after the sale, notice of the sale and date thereof, of the name and address of the purchaser, of the sum bid and of the amount of the taxes and costs to be paid by such delinquent as a condition of its redemption.

en residence of inquent cannot ascertained.

ice of sale shall given delinquent

e of land for es.

Sec. 38. That the whole tract or lot of land belonging to a delinquent person or company shall be set up for sale at the same time, and shall be struck off to him who will pay the amount of taxes, with all the expenses, for the smallest part of the land. At all such sales the mayor may become a bidder and purchase the whole lot or tract of land for the taxes due and expenses, for the use of the town, in case no one will offer to pay the taxes and costs for a less quantity.

en property may redeemed.

Sec. 39. That the delinquent may retain possession of the property for twelve months after sale, and within that time redeem it by paying the purchaser the amount paid by him, and twenty-five per centum in addition thereto. At the time of said payment to the purchaser, he shall give to the delinquent a receipt therefor. If he shall refuse or cannot be found in said town, the delinquent may pay the same to the town clerk and treasurer, and he shall give him a receipt therefor, and such payment shall be equivalent to payment to the purchasers; after such payment to the purchaser or town clerk, all rights under the purchase shall cease.

Receipt shall be given purchaser.

Sec. 40. That at the time of such purchase of real estate for taxes, the town constable or tax collector, on receipt of the amount bid for such real estate, shall give the purchaser a receipt stating the amount bid, by whom and for what purpose, and describing the land sold, stating further the owner of said lands and the amount of taxes due.

When deed in fee may be executed to purchaser.

Sec. 41. That if the delinquent, his agent or attorney, shall fail to redeem, as provided in section thirty-nine hereof, for twelve months, at the expiration of that time the purchaser may present his receipt referred to in section forty hereof, and the town constable or tax collector of said town shall execute a deed in fee to the purchaser, and if the purchaser is dead, to his heirs at law or assigns for the lands for which said purchaser agreed to pay the amount called for in the receipt, and for said service the constable or tax collector shall be allowed one dollar, to be paid by the purchaser. The deed from the constable to the purchaser shall be registered in the register's office of Robeson county within six months from the time of the execution and delivery thereof, and when so registered shall convey to the grantee all the estate in the land for which the said purchaser bid, which the delinquent, his agent or attorney had at the time of sale for taxes.

Deed shall be registered.

Estate bid in by mayor.

Sec. 42. That all real estate bid in by the mayor of said town for the use of the town, at sales made by the constable or tax collector for taxes, may be redeemed as hereinbefore provided, by the payment on the part of the delinquent, his agent or attorney, of the amount bid and twenty-five per centum additional to the town clerk and treasurer within twelve months from date of such sale.

Levy and collection of special taxes.

Sec. 43. That the commissioners of said town shall have the power to annually levy and cause to be collected for the necessary expenses of the said town such privilege taxes as shall seem to them fair and equitable on the professions, callings, trades, occupations and all other business carried on in said town, that is to say on every lawyer, merchant, physician, dentist, druggist, artisan, mechanic, daguerrean artist, or other picture; on all officers or agents of incorporated companies; on all clerks or employees of other persons or corporations; on every drummer, editor, printer, butcher, tinner, carpenter, shoemaker, wheelwright, carriage, buggy or wagon maker, jeweler, confection grocer, harness maker, saddler, blacksmith; on every billiard or bagatelle table, public or private bowling, nine or ten pin alley; on all lectures for reward; on all riding or pleasure

Special taxes.

vehicles; on all gold, silver or metal watches; on all pianos; on all pistols; on every livery, feed or sale stable; on every person hiring any number of horses; on every cotton gin; on every turpentine or other distillery; on every boarding house, hotel, restaurant or eating saloon; on all drays, carts, wagons, carriages, buggies, bicycles; on all horses, cattle, sheep, hogs, goats or dogs owned or kept in said town or allowed to run at large therein; on every stallion, jack, bull or boar kept or exhibited in said town; on all itinerant trades and peddlers; on all banks, railroads, telephone and telegraph companies; on all saw and planing mills, brick, lath or shingle mills; on all sash, door and blind, furniture or cotton factories, and on all incorporated companies of whatever nature or kind; on all and every person or persons, company or companies who may exhibit, sing, play, act, or perform on anything for which they charge or receive any gratuity, fee or pay, or reward whatever within the limits of said town, and on every opera house or public hall to which an admission fee may be charged, and the commissioners of said town shall prescribe when the license tax herein provided for sha.. be due and payable.

e of liquor hin five miles orporate limits hibited.

Sec. 44. That it shall be unlawful for any person or company to manufacture any spirituous or malt liquors or to sell or in any manner, directly or indirectly, to receive any compensation for any spirituous or malt liquors, wines or cider or any other intoxicating liquors within the corporate limits of said town of Lumberton, or within five miles of the corporate limits thereof as set out in section three of this act; and any person violating the provisions of this section shall be guilty of a misdemeanor, and shall be punished upon conviction thereof by a fine not exceeding one hundred dollars or by imprisonment, not exceeding twelve months or both.

alty.

ipment of fire panies.

Sec. 45. That the board of commissioners of said town shall have power to provide for the establishment, organization and equipment, government and pay of such number of fire companies as they may deem necessary and proper for the protection of the said town against damage by fire; and in case of a fire occurring in said town the chief of the fire department or mayor, or in their absence a majority of the commissioners of said town who may be present, may order the blowing up or pulling down or destroying any house or building deemed necessary to stop the progress of the fire.

missioners establish fire ts.

Sec. 46. That the said commissioners shall also have power to establish fire limits within said town, within which it shall not be lawful for any person to erect or build any wooden house or structure, or make any wooden additions to any building, or repair or cover the outside surface of any building with any material other than metal or slate; that they may prohibit the removal of any wooden building from without to within such fire limits as they shall establish; and shall have power to enforce obedience to their regulations under this section by punishing such persons as violate the same by a fine of not more than fifty dollars, or imprisonment of not more than thirty days, and shall further have the power to cause the removal of any structure or building erected contrary to the laws by them enacted under the power vested in them by this section.

Sheriff required to receive prisoners in jail without mittimus.

Sec. 47. That the sheriff or jailer of the county of Robeson is hereby required without a mittimus to receive into the jail of the county as his prisoner any person taken up in the night time by the constable, police or watchmen, and to keep such person until the morning, when such person or offender shall be brought before the mayor or some justice of the peace, resident in said town, and be lawfully dealt with, and for such services the sheriff or jailer shall be entitled to such fees as he is in other like cases; or such prisoner may be confined in the town guard house.

Proceedings in mayor's court.

Sec. 48. That all proceedings in the mayor's court shall be the same as are now or may hereafter be prescribed for courts of justices of the peace, and in all cases there shall be a right of appeal to the superior court of Robeson county; that whenever a defendant or witness or other person shall be adjudged to be imprisoned by the said court, it shall be competent for the court to sentence such person or persons to imprisonment in the county jail or town guard house for a term not exceeding thirty days, and to adjudge also that such persons may be worked during the period of their confinement on the public streets or on the public works of the said town under the supervision of the town constable, policeman or other police officer.

Ordinances in relation to vagrants.

Sec. 49. That the commissioners of said town shall have authority to pass such ordinances in relation to vagrants as they may deem necessary to the good government of the town, and any person who may be in habit of sauntering about the town not engaged in any lawful occupation, or of loafing about the streets without visible means of support, shall be guilty of a misdemeanor, and on conviction thereof before the mayor shall pay a fine of not exceeding fifty dollars or be imprisoned not more than thirty days. The said mayor is hereby constituted a special court to hear and determine such offence, and upon failure of any person convicted of such offence to pay such fine as may be imposed upon him and the cost of his arrest and conviction, he shall have authority to imprison such person in the county jail or other prison, and the commissioners of Lumberton may work such person on the public streets or public works of

Jurisdiction of mayor.

the town under the supervision of the constable or other police officer during the terms of their sentence, or they may hire out such person until the fine and costs are paid.

ıning at large of s, cattle, etc.

Sec. 50. That the commissioners of said town shall have power under such ordinances as they may enact to prevent the running at large of all dogs, hogs, horses, cattle and all other brutes within the corporate limits of said town, and the manner in which same shall be kept, and they may prohibit the keeping of hogs within the corporate limits of said town.

powered to con- ıct sewerage.

Sec. 51. That the said board of commissioners shall have power to construct and maintain a permanent system of sewerage and drainage for the said town, and protect and regulate the same by adequate ordinances; and if it shall be necessary in obtaining a suitable and proper outlet for the said system to extend the same beyond the corporate limits of said town, they may condemn a right of way to and from such out let, and any damage shall be adjusted in the same manner as is provided for the opening of new streets under section twenty-nine of this act.

y acquire land construct ldings.

Sec. 52. That the commissioners of said town may acquire land and erect and establish any public buildings thereon that may be necessary for the use of the mayor, town council, hose-reel company, hook and ladder company or any other necessary town purposes; and may establish and maintain a definite and permanent system of fire alarms for the government, use and benefit of said town.

itary regula- s.

Sec. 53. That the commissioners of said town may take such steps as they may deem necessary to prevent the entrance into the town or the spreading therein any contagious or infectious disease; and may stop, detain and examine for that purpose any and every person coming from places believed to be infected with such disease; and may cause any person in the town suspected to be infected with such disease and whose stay may endanger the health of the town to be removed to such place as the mayor may direct; and may remove from said town or destroy any furniture or other article which shall be suspected of being tainted or infected with contagious or infectious diseases, or of which there shall be reasonable cause to apprehend that they may pass into such a state as to generate and propagate disease; and may abate by any reasonable means all nuisances of whatever nature or kind which may be injurious to the public health.

ıtement of nui- ces.

poration may over expenses removal of per- s from town.

Sec. 54. That in case any person shall be removed from said town under the provisions of section fifty-three of this act the corporation may recover before the mayor or any justice of the peace of such person the expense of his removal, support, nursing and medical attendance, and burial expenses also in case of death.

Sec. 55. That if any person shall attempt by force or by threat of violence to prevent the removal to such place as the mayor may direct of any person ordered to be conveyed thither, the person so offending shall forfeit and pay to the town the sum of fifty dollars and moreover be guilty of a misdemeanor.

Persons interfering with removal.

Sec. 56. That the mayor may at any time, upon charges preferred, or upon finding the constable, policeman, watchmen or other employee of the town guilty of misconduct, have power to suspend such officer from service until the board of commissioners shall convene and take action in the matter, and upon hearing the proofs in the case, the board may discharge or restore such officer, and the pay of such officer shall cease from the time of his suspension by the mayor to the time of his restoration by the commissioners; any violation of the orders of a superior shall be good cause for suspension, and the mayor shall suspend any of the above named officers who may be found drunk while on duty.

Suspension of officers by mayor.

Sec. 57. That the said board of commissioners shall have power to pass ordinances for the good government and order of the town aforesaid, and to that end they may pass an ordinance providing that in case any officer of the town has sufficient reason to believe and does believe, that there exists any house of ill-fame, or gambling house where games of chance are being carried on within the corporate limits of said town as set out in section three of this act, or within one-fourth of a mile in any direction from the same, that such officer may, with or without a warrant, enter said premises and arrest any person or persons so engaged as keeper or occupants of said houses of ill-fame or gambling houses, and require such person or persons to appear before the mayor for violation of the ordinances against such houses of ill-fame or gambling houses, and to be dealt with according to law.

Commissioners empowered to pass ordinances.

Sec. 58. That the board of commissioners of said town shall have power to pass ordinances for the protection of the persons and property of the citizens of the same, and to that end may pass an ordinance making it unlawful to discharge any gun, pistol or other firearm within the corporate limits of said town or within one-fourth of a mile from the corporate limits of said town as set out in section three of this act, and any person found guilty of violating the provisions of this section may be punished in the same manner as if the offence had been committed within the corporate limits as aforesaid.

Ordinances regarding firearms, etc.

Sec. 59. That chapter eighty-eight [of the] private laws of eighteen hundred and ninety-seven is hereby declared to be in full force and effect, and all laws in conflict with this act are hereby repealed in so far as this act is concerned: Provided,

Chapter 88, private laws 1897 effective.

however, that this section shall not have the effect to repeal or modify chapter four hundred and seventy-five, public laws of eighteen hundred and ninety-three as amended and re-enacted at this session of the general assembly.

Sec. 60. That this act shall be in force from and after its ratification.

Ratified the 4th day of March, A. D. 1899.

CHAPTER 216.

An act to incorporate the Allen Brothers and Hill Company.

The General Assembly of North Carolina do enact:

:porators. Section 1. That James M. Allen, William H. Allen, Kemp P. Hill, and F. H. Allen, together with such other persons as they may associate with them, their successors and assigns, be and dy corporate. they are hereby created a body politic and corporate under the :porate name. name and style of the "Allen Brothers and Hill Company," by ·porate powers. which name they may sue and be sued, plead and be impleaded, prosecute and defend actions and special proceedings, adopt, have and use a common seal which they may alter at their pleasure, may make by-laws, rules and regulations for the government of said corporation, not inconsistent with the laws of North Carolina, and shall have and enjoy the rights, privileges, powers and immunities usually pertaining to corporations.

ital stock. Sec. 2. That the capital stock of said corporation shall be fifteen thousand dollars, with the privilege of increasing the same not exceeding twenty-five thousand dollars, by consent of those holding a majority of the stock. Said stock is to be divided into shares of the par value of one hundred dollars each.

en company y be organized. Sec. 3. That when the sum of fifteen thousand dollars shall have been subscribed and paid in, the said corporators, or a majority of them, shall have authority to call a meeting of the stockholders for the purpose of organization, and at such meeting to elect officers of the company, which shall consist of a cers. president, a secretary and treasurer, and a board of directors to be composed of not less than three members, and such other officers as may be necessary; prescribe their duties, fix their pensation. compensation, and designate the officer whose duty it shall be to make contracts and purchases for the company, and who shall sign checks, drafts, notes and all other instruments for the corporation. A majority of the whole number of shares subscribed orum. for and paid in shall be necessary for a quorum for the transaction of any business. A majority of all the stock subscribed and paid in shall be sufficient for the election of officers, and the transaction of all business. The number of shares necessary to constitute a quorum or for the transaction of any business may be changed at any regular general meeting of the stockholders.

Sec. 4. That a regular general meeting of the stockholders shall be held once in each and every year, at a time and place to be fixed by the by-laws, at which meeting the officers and directors shall be elected, and who shall serve until their successors are elected. The president may call meetings of the stockholders for general or special purposes, and may appoint the time and place for said meeting. Regular general meetings.

Sec. 5. That the principal office and place of business of said corporation shall be in Louisburg, Franklin county, North Carolina, but the directors may establish other offices and conduct their business wherever it may be found convenient and useful for the corporation. Principal office.

Sec. 6. That said corporation shall have full power to buy and sell goods, wares and merchandise of every kind and description, fertilizers, farm supplies, horses, mules, wagons, buggies, carriages, and vehicles of every kind; shall have power to buy, sell, lease, contract for, own and hold real estate, and personal property of all kinds; to improve such real estate as it may purchase or acquire, by constructing any and all such buildings as it may deem expedient, or in any other lawful manner, for the purpose of enhancing its value, or utilizing the same; may build and equip stores and warehouses, and other business houses and residences; may borrow and lend money, and make, accept, issue and purchase promissory notes, bonds, deeds and mortgages; may mortgage and pledge its property, both real and personal, to secure loans, and may do any and all things necessary or desirable for the profitable conduct of the business, if the same be not prohibited by law. Corporate powers.

Sec. 7. That said corporation is hereby authorized to pay for such real estate and personal property as it may purchase or otherwise acquire, with and by its capital stock; and it shall be lawful for the said corporation to receive in full or part payment of subscription to the capital stock, money, lands, buildings, labor, leases, materials, stocks, bonds, or other property. Payment of capital stock.

Sec. 8. That the duration of the said corporation shall be fifteen years from the ratification of this act. Duration of corporation fifteen years.

Sec. 9. That the corporators and stockholders of said corporation, and their successors and assigns, shall not be individually or personally liable or responsible for the debts, liabilities, contracts, engagements, or torts of this corporation. Individual liability

Sec. 10. This act shall be in force from and after its ratification.

Ratified the 4th day of March, A. D. 1899.

CHAPTER 217.

An act to incorporate the Wilson Savings Bank.

The General Assembly of North Carolina do enact:

porators. Section 1. That J. F. Farmer, W. D. Hackney, John E. Woodard, E. K. Wright, M. T. Moye, S. C. Wells, B. F. Lane, W. D. P. Sharp, W. M. Farmer, S. H. Crocker, W. W. Farmer, Silas Lucas, A. B. Deans, John D. Daws and K. H. Watson, and their associates, successors and assigns, be and they are hereby created y corporate. a body politic and corporate under the name and style of "The porate name. Wilson Savings Bank," and by such name may acquire, hold and convey real and personal property, sue and be sued, plead and be impleaded in any courts of the state, and have a continual succession for sixty years, and a common seal, for the purpose indicated in the title.

ital stock. Sec. 2. That the capital stock of said corporation shall not be less than ten thousand dollars, which may be increased from time to time to a sum not exceeding one hundred thousand dollars in shares of twenty-five dollars each, payable as follows: Ten per centum of each share in cash and ten per centum per month for each month thereafter until the full sum is paid; said corporation may, however, commence the business of banking when five thousand dollars of the capital stock aforesaid has been paid in. ividual ility. The stockholders shall be liable to the extent of the par value of their stock and nothing more for any debt, contract or engagement of said corporation.

ks of sub- ption may be ned. Sec. 3. The corporators in the first section named or any three of them are hereby authorized and empowered to open books of subscription to the capital stock of said bank at such time or times, at such places and for such periods as they shall determine, until the same be wholly subscribed.

ganization. Sec. 4. Whenever the whole number of shares of the capital stock shall have been subscribed, the before-named corporators or any three of them shall call a meeting of the subscribers to said stock at such time and place and on such notice as they may ction of ectors. deem sufficient, and such stockholders shall elect nine directors, who shall hold office for one year and until their successors are viso. qualified: Provided, that no person shall be a director in said alification for ector. corporation without having subscribed and taken at least five shares of said stock.

ectors shall scribe rules, ulations, etc. Sec. 5. It shall be the duty of the board of directors to prescribe rules, regulations and by-laws for the government thereof; to choose officers, fix salaries, fill vacancies and generally do and perform such duties as the rules, regulations and by-laws of this corporation shall prescribe, when the same shall have been rati fied by a majority in numbers and value of the stockholders voting thereon in person or by proxy.

Principal office.

Sec. 6. The principal office or banking house of this corporation shall be located in the town of Wilson and state of North Carolina.

Corporate powers.

Sec. 7. That this corporation shall have the power to receive and pay out the lawful currency of the country, to deal in exchange, gold and silver coin, stocks, bonds, notes, and other securities; to loan money to, or receive deposits of money or other property or evidences of debt from, corporations, minors, apprentices, femes covert or other persons on such terms and time and manner and collection and payment as may be agreed upon between the parties, and for the use and loan of money may charge interest at the rate of six per centum per annum, and may take and receive said interest at the time of making said loan, free from all other control, contract or liability whatever; to invest in the stocks, bonds or other securities of this or any other state or of the United States, or of any corporation under the laws thereof, and to take such real and personal property conditioned in such form for the payment of the principal and interest of money loaned, advanced or expended, as may be deemed most safe, expedient and beneficial; and may purchase and hold real estate for their own use, to cost not exceeding ten thousand dollars, in addition to such real estate as may be conveyed to said corporation for security or in payment of debts due said corporation.

Corporate powers.

Sec. 8. That said corporation shall have power and authority to guarantee the payment of principal and interest of notes, bonds, bills of exchange and other securities or evidences of debt, including the obligations of such corporations and individuals as may have secured their payment by deed of trust made to the corporation for such special purpose, and to receive for any guarantee such compensation as the parties may agree upon, and may charge therefor interest at the rate of six per centum per annum, and may take and receive the interest at the time [of] making said transaction.

Sec. 9. That this act shall be in force from and after its ratification.

Ratified the 6th day of March, A. D. 1899.

CHAPTER 218.

An act to incorporate the Surety Banking Company.

The General Assembly of North Carolina do enact:

rporators. Section 1. That B. S. Jerman, J. J. Thomas, Josephus Daniels. George Allen and H. W. Jackson, their associates, successors or assigns, are hereby created and declared a body politic and corporate by the name and style of the "Surety Bonding Company," with right of sixty years succession, and with capacity to take, hold, rent, lease and convey real and personal estate; and may exercise and enjoy all the privileges, franchises, powers and immunities granted to corporations by the general laws of this state; and by which name they may sue and be sued, plead and be impleaded, complain and defend in all the courts of the land, whether of law or of equity, of record or otherwise.

rporate name.

ration of arter.

rporate powers.

pital stock. Sec. 2. The capital stock of said company shall be one hundred thousand dollars, which may be increased from time to time at the option of the stockholders of said company to any amount not exceeding five hundred thousand dollars. So soon as twenty five thousand dollars of said capital stock shall have been subscribed and ten per centum thereof paid in cash or in bonds, stock or other property taken in lieu of cash, it shall be lawful for said company to organize and commence business. The capital stock of said company shall be divided into shares of one hundred dollars each; shall be deemed personal property; shall be transferable in the manner prescribed by the by-laws of said company, and each share shall entitle its holder to one vote in all meetings of the stockholders, to be cast in person or by proxy as the by-laws may prescribe.

y be increased.

hen company y be organized. vision of ares.

ks of sub- ption may be ned. Sec. 3. That the corporators named in the first section of this act or a majority of them, are empowered to open books of subscription to the capital stock of said company at such times and places as they shall determine, and when the required amount of capital stock is subscribed and paid as provided in section two of this act, they may call a meeting of the stockholders in the city of Raleigh, and if at such meeting the stockholders who are present have a majority of the votes (if not another meeting shall be called) they may proceed to take proper measures for the collection of the stock subscribed for and to adopt such by-laws and regulations for the government of the company as they may deem proper and may elect such number of directors as they may deem necessary to serve for one year and until their successors shall be chosen or for such other term as they may prescribe.

asures for lection of ck.

ection of cers. Sec. 4. That the directors shall elect such officers for said company and shall employ such clerks and employees as may be pro-ded for by the by-laws of said company to serve during such rm as the by-laws of said company shall prescribe. The direct-s and other officers and employees of said company shall per- rm such duties and receive such compensation as may be pre-ribed or provided for in the by-laws.

Duties and compensation.

Sec. 5. That said company shall have the power to become rety for and guarantee the faithful performance of all duties id obligations of persons holding places of public or private ust or responsibility; to execute as surety all bonds or under-kings of any official or any private person; to guarantee the ithful performance of any trust, contract or agreement (other an life, fire or accident insurance policies); to act as surety a any bonds or undertakings required or permitted in all actions r proceedings in law or equity; to guarantee, endorse and se-re the payment of notes, bonds, bills of exchange, checks, rents, nnuities, certificates of stock, choses in action and other evi-ences of indebtedness and guarantee titles to property.

Company empowered to become surety on bonds.

Sec. 6. That the said company shall have the right to act as gent, factor or trustee for any state, county, city, town, town-hip or any other municipality, corporation or individual in reg-stering, selling, countersigning, collecting or otherwise dealing rith or disposing of any bonds, certificates of stock, notes or any ther description of property, real or personal; may accept and xecute trusts of any and every description which may be com-iitted or transferred to them, with the consent by any person or ersons, company or corporation, or by authority of law.

May act as agent for states, cities, towns, etc.

Sec. 7. That said company may accept the office or appoint-ent of executor, trustee, mortgagee, assignee or guardian when uch office or appointment is created and made by the last will nd testament of any person or persons or by any conveyance or ther assignment in writing of any individual, firm, company or orporation, and may be specially committed, assigned or given y such last will and testament, conveyance or instrument in vriting or such as may be generally conferred by law, which fficial appointment shall, however, be exercised, subject to the aws of North Carolina.

May accept the office of executor, trustee, etc.

Sec 8. That the said company may charge and receive for do-ng and performing all of the matters and things authorized by his act, such premiums, commissioners or other rate of compen-ation as may be agreed upon or as may be fixed by law.

Empowered to make certain charges.

Sec. 9. That no incorporator or stockholder shall be in anywise ndividually liable or responsible for any debt, obligation, con-ract, engagement or tort of said company.

Individual liability.

Sec. 10. That the principal office of said company shall be at Raleigh, North Carolina, but the company may have branch offices or agencies anywhere in the state of North Carolina or

Principal office.

Branch offices may be established.

CHAPTER 218.

An act to incorporate the Surety Banking Company.

The General Assembly of North Carolina do enact:

rators. orate name. tion of ter. rate powers.

Section 1. That B. S. Jerman, J. J. Thomas, Josephus Danie George Allen and H. W. Jackson, their associates, successors assigns, are hereby created and declared a body politic and co porate by the name and style of the "Surety Bonding Company with right of sixty years succession, and with capacity to tak hold, rent, lease and convey real and personal estate; and m exercise and enjoy all the privileges, franchises, powers and i munities granted to corporations by the general laws of th state; and by which name they may sue and be sued, plead a be impleaded, complain and defend in all the courts of the lan whether of law or of equity, of record or otherwise.

tal stock. be increased. n company be organized. sion of es.

Sec. 2. The capital stock of said company shall be one hu dred thousand dollars, which may be increased from time time at the option of the stockholders of said company to an amount not exceeding five hundred thousand dollars. So soon twenty five thousand dollars of said capital stock shall have bee subscribed and ten per centum thereof paid in cash or in bond stock or other property taken in lieu of cash, it shall be lawfu for said company to organize and commence business. The ca ital stock of said company shall be divided into shares of on hundred dollars each; shall be deemed personal property; sha be transferable in the manner prescribed by the by-laws of sai company, and each share shall entitle its holder to one vote i all meetings of the stockholders, to be cast in person or by prox as the by-laws may prescribe.

s of sub- tion may be ed. sures for ction of

Sec. 3. That the corporators named in the first section of this ac or a majority of them, are empowered to open books of subscri tion to the capital stock of said company at such times and place as they shall determine, and when the required amount of ca ital stock is subscribed and paid as provided in section two of thi act, they may call a meeting of the stockholders in the city o Raleigh, and if at such meeting the stockholders who are presen have a majority of the votes (if not another meeting shall b called) they may proceed to take proper measures for the collec tion of the stock subscribed for and to adopt such by-laws an regulations for the government of the company as they ma deem proper and may elect such number of directors as they ma deem necessary to serve for one year and until their successor shall be chosen or for such other term as they may prescribe.

tion of ers.

Sec. 4. That the directors shall elect such officers for said com pany and shall employ such clerks and employees as may be pro 'ided for by the by-laws of said company to serve during such erm as the by-laws of said company shall prescribe. The direct-ırs and other officers and employees of said company shall per-orm such duties and receive such compensation as may be pre-cribed or provided for in the by-laws.

Duties and compensation.

Sec. 5. That said company shall have the power to become surety for and guarantee the faithful performance of all duties and obligations of persons holding places of public or private trust or responsibility; to execute as surety all bonds or undertakings of any official or any private person; to guarantee the faithful performance of any trust, contract or agreement (other than life, fire or accident insurance policies); to act as surety on any bonds or undertakings required or permitted in all actions or proceedings in law or equity; to guarantee, endorse and secure the payment of notes, bonds, bills of exchange, checks, rents, annuities, certificates of stock, choses in action and other evidences of indebtedness and guarantee titles to property.

Company empowered to become surety on bonds.

Sec. 6. That the said company shall have the right to act as agent, factor or trustee for any state, county, city, town, township or any other municipality, corporation or individual in registering, selling, countersigning, collecting or otherwise dealing with or disposing of any bonds, certificates of stock, notes or any other description of property, real or personal; may accept and execute trusts of any and every description which may be committed or transferred to them, with the consent by any person or persons, company or corporation, or by authority of law.

May act as agent for states, cities, towns, etc.

Sec. 7. That said company may accept the office or appointment of executor, trustee, mortgagee, assignee or guardian when such office or appointment is created and made by the last will and testament of any person or persons or by any conveyance or other assignment in writing of any individual, firm, company or corporation, and may be specially committed, assigned or given by such last will and testament, conveyance or instrument in writing or such as may be generally conferred by law, which official appointment shall, however, be exercised, subject to the laws of North Carolina.

May accept the office of executor, trustee, etc.

Sec 8. That the said company may charge and receive for doing and performing all of the matters and things authorized by this act, such premiums, commissioners or other rate of compensation as may be agreed upon or as may be fixed by law.

Empowered to make certain charges.

Sec. 9. That no incorporator or stockholder shall be in anywise individually liable or responsible for any debt, obligation, contract, engagement or tort of said company.

Individual liability.

Sec. 10. That the principal office of said company shall be at Raleigh, North Carolina, but the company may have branch offices or agencies anywhere in the state of North Carolina or

Principal office.

Branch offices may be established.

at such other places in the United States as the stockholders of the company may designate or authorize, such branch offices and agencies to be subject to such rules and regulations as prescribed in the by-laws of said company.

ers and ileges not :ited by non-

Sec. 11. That the powers and privileges granted herein shall not be deemed forfeited by non-use: Provided, the company is organized within five years from the date of ratification of this act.

'iso. pany shall rganized hin five rs.

Sec. 12. That this act shall be in force from and after its ratification.

Ratified the 6th day of March, A. D. 1899.

CHAPTER 219.

An act to incorporate Roxboro Cotton Mills.

The General Assembly of North Carolina do enact:

porators.

Section 1. That J. A. Long, A. R. Foushee, J. S. Bradsher, F. A. Lukin, R. I. Featherstone, A. S. DeVlaming, C. T. Wilson, T. J. Stephens, J. M. Blalock, J. C. Pass, J. S. Cunningham, W. F. Reade, A. J. Hester, W. W. Kitchen, R. E. Long, B. N. Duke, J. S. Carr, G. W. Watts and W. W. Fuller, and their associates, successors and assigns be and they hereby are created a body politic and corporate under the name and style of Roxboro Cotton Mills, with capital stock of twenty-five thousand ($25,000) dollars, divided into shares of the par value of one hundred dollars each, with liberty and authority to the majority of the stockholders to increase said capital stock at any time and from time to time to any amount not exceeding in the aggregate five hundred thousand dollars ($500.000), divided into shares of the par value of one hundred dollars each, and with privilege to said company to commence business when two thousand five hundred dollars ($2,500) of its capital stock has been subscribed for and paid in; and by unanimous vote of all the stockholders the capital stock of said company, after it has been increased, may at any time or from time to time be reduced: Provided, it shall never be less than its original capital stock of twenty-five thousand dollars ($25.000).

porate name. ital stock.

y be increased.

ital stock y be reduced.

:ation of rter.

Sec. 2. That said corporation shall have succession for sixty (60) years; it may adopt a common seal, which it may break or alter at pleasure; in its corporate name it may sue and be sued, prosecute and defend actions or special proceedings in all courts of the land; it may divide its capital stock into such classes and

porate pow-

sue it upon such terms and conditions as its stockholders may esire, and after the original or any increase thereof has been sued its stockholders may, by unanimous consent, convert one lass of stock into another or modify and change the terms and onditions upon which any or all of it has been issued; it may sue the whole or any part of its capital stock in payment for roperty acquired for the company upon such terms and conditions as its board of directors may deem advisable; it may buy, ease, exchange, hold, sell and convey real and personal property t its will and pleasure; it may construct, build and erect such uildings, works and improvements upon property of its own or f others, by their permission as may be deemed proper, and may quip, operate, use and maintain the same; it may in any way it nay desire, manufacture, handle and deal in cotton, wool, jute, emp, silk or any other textile, either singly or in combinations f two or more of them; it may buy, sell and exchange goods, vares and merchandise of all kinds; it may purchase, lease, use nd maintain any works or improvements connected or intended o be connected with the works and improvements of said company; it may consolidate or unite with any other company now reated or to be hereafter created under the laws of this or any ther state, retaining its own name or that of the company united or consolidated with; by a vote of those holding a majority of its outstanding share capital it may at any time or from time to time change its name; it may borrow money and as security therefor it may issue its notes, bonds or other obligations, and if deemed advisable, secure the payment of the same by a mortgage or deed of trust upon its franchises and property or any part of it; it may acquire, hold, own and enjoy stock in the capital of any company now in existence or hereafter to be created under the laws of this state or any other state or country, and stock in its capital may be owned, held and enjoyed by any company now created or to be hereafter created; it may acquire, construct, equip and operate telephone and telegraph lines and electric light and power plants. Corporate powers. May change its name.

Sec. 3. That the principal office of said company shall be at Roxboro, in Person county, North Carolina; but it may establish and maintain branch offices, agencies, factories, depots, warehouses, stores and works anywhere in the United States or elsewhere that its directors may deem advisable. Principal office.

Sec. 4. That it may make such by-laws, rules and regulations as the stockholders may desire, not inconsistent with the constitution and laws of this state. May make by-laws, etc.

Sec. 5. That the corporators and stockholders of said company and their associates, successors and assigns shall not be individ- Individual liability.

ually or personally liable or responsible for the debts, contracts, obligations, engagements or torts of said company.

o notice of first eeting required. Sec. 6 That no notice or publication whatever of the first meeting of said corporation shall be given or required: Provided, all of the corporators named herein waive in writing such notice and fix a time and place for such meeting.

Sec. 7. That this act shall be in force from and after its ratification.

Ratified the 6th day of March, A. D. 1899.

CHAPTER 220.

An act to repeal a portion of and to re-enact section four of "An act to provide for the enlargement, increase of depth and completion of the Albemarle and Chesapeake Canal," ratified February second, eighteen hundred and fifty-seven.

The General Assembly of North Carolina do enact:

ortion of ction 4 of an it ratified February 2nd, 1857, mended. Section 1. That so much of section four of an act ratified on the second day of February, eighteen hundred and fifty-seven, entitled "An act to provide for the enlargement, increase of depth and completion of the Albemarle and Chesapeake Canal" as authorizes and directs the governor to annually appoint three directors of said company, is hereby repealed, and the said section is hereby amended and re enacted so that the same shall read as follows: Section 4. That all provisions of the charter of the said company requiring the majority of its directors to be resident citizens of North Carolina are hereby repealed.

Sec. 2. This act shall be in force from and after its ratification.

Ratified the 6th day of March, A. D. 1899.

CHAPTER 221.

An act to incorporate Slayden, Fakes and Company, of Asheville, North Carolina.

The General Assembly of North Carolina do enact:

rporators. Section 1. That W. J. Slayden, B. B. Fakes, C. S. Davis and such other persons as they may associate with them, and their successors and assigns, are hereby created and constituted a body

dy corporate. rporate name. politic incorporated under the name and style of Slayden, Fakes & Co., and under that name and style may have a corporate seal may sue and be sued, plead and be impleaded, contract and be contracted with, and enjoy all the rights, privileges, powers and immunities given to corporations under chapter sixteen of volume one of The Code of North Carolina and the acts amendatory thereof.

Sec. 2. That the capital stock of said corporation shall be one hundred thousand dollars, with the privilege of increasing the same at any time and from time to time to any sum not exceeding two hundred and fifty thousand dollars, divided into shares of the par value of one hundred dollars each. Capital stock.

Sec. 3. That said corporation is hereby authorized and empowered to conduct a general mercantile business in all its branches, both wholesale and retail; may buy and sell and deal in goods, wares and merchandise of every kind and description. Nature of business.

Sec. 4. That said corporation shall have power to lease, purchase, hold, sell and convey real estate and personal property of every kind and description, and shall have power to borrow money and issue bonds and any other evidences of indebtedness, and to execute any mortgage deed, trust or lien to secure the payment thereof. Corporate powers.

Sec. 5. That the affairs of said corporation shall be managed by the stockholders themselves or in a manner prescribed by such by-laws, rules and regulations for the conduct and management of the corporate affairs and its business as they may deem necessary or expedient and not inconsistent with the laws of the state. Affairs of corporation, how managed.

Sec. 6. That the officers of said corporation shall consist of a president, secretary and treasurer, and the last two offices may be filled by one person, to be elected as prescribed by the by-laws, rules and regulations of the corporation. Officers of corporation.

Sec. 7. That the duration of said corporation shall be thirty years.

Sec. 8. That the said corporation shall have the right to receive goods, wares and merchandise, lands or other real or personal property in payment of its capital stock, and when the amount paid in shall reach one hundred thousand dollars, stock to that amount may be issued to the stockholders. Payment of capital stock.

Sec. 9. That for the purpose of organization W. J. Slayden shall be president of said corporation and C. S. Davis secretary and B. R. Fakes treasurer, who shall hold their offices until their successors are elected by the stockholders of said corporation, or otherwise, as shall be provided by the by-laws, rules and regulations of said company. Temporary officers.

Sec. 10. That the stockholders in the said corporation shall not be personally liable for the debts and liabilities of the corporation. Individual liability.

Sec. 11. That the place of business and office of said corpora-

ce of business. tion shall be in the city of Asheville, state of North Carolina, but the said corporation shall have the right to establish branch stores in other places in said state.

Sec. 12. This act shall be in force from and after its ratification.

Ratified the 6th day of March, A. D. 1899.

CHAPTER 222.

An act to incorporate the Knights of Hyde, a mutual benefit home insurance association

amble. Whereas, certain citizens of the state of North Carolina and county of Hyde, have associated themselves together under the name and style of the "Knights of Hyde, a Mutual Benefit Home Insurance Association," with the intention and purpose of promoting charity, benevolence, morality, industry and intelligence, and of providing for the families of deceased members indemnity for their loss by death by an assessment against the living members; therefore,

The General Assembly of North Carolina do enact:

porators. Section 1. That president Dallas Wahab, secretary and treasurer S. S. Mann; and directors for Currituck township, B. D. Harris and Asa J. Smith; and directors for Swan Quarter township, W. Sanford Harris and I. H. Swindell; and directors for Lake Landing township, S. J. Beckwith and J. M. Hall; and directors for Fairfield township, R. L. Young and W. B. Nixon, their successors, associates and assigns, be and they are hereby
ly corporate. incorporated and created a body politic under the name and
porate name. style of the "Knights of Hyde, a Mutual Benefit Home Insurance Association," and by such name and title shall have and use a common seal, contract and be contracted with, sue and be
porate pow- sued, plead and be impleaded, and shall have power and right of purchasing, leasing, holding, granting receiving and conveying in its corporate name property, real, personal and mixed, and of making such laws, by-laws, rules and regulations as the said corporation may deem necessary for the proper transaction of its business, the same not to be in conflict with the laws of this state or of the United States.

ncipal office. Sec. 2. That the principal office of the said corporation shall be established in the village of Swan Quarter, North Carolina, and the business of the said corporation shall be confined to the county of Hyde.

Sec. 3. That the officers of this corporation shall hold their respective offices for a period of one year; and at the expiration of their term of office an election shall be held for the election of their successors, who shall hold office for a period of one year, and there shall be held every year thereafter an election for officers for the corporation. Term of officers of corporation. Annual election of officers

Sec. 4. That the objects of the corporation shall be to unite for mutual benefit all acceptable white persons, citizens and residents of the state of North Carolina and the county of Hyde, of every profession, business and occupation; to give all possible moral and material aid in its power to its members and those depending on its members; to promote benevolence and charity by establishing a benefit fund, out of which, on satisfactory evidence of the death of a member who has complied with all its lawful requirements, the corporation is to pay to the family of the deceased member, or as such deceased members may have recommended in his application for membership, a sum of money, which sum of money shall be such an amount as may be derived from or produced by the levy of an assessment upon each and every member in good standing with the said corporation at the time of such death. The manner of making such levy and the amount of the same to be regulated by the constitution, by-laws and regulations of the said corporation. Objects of corporation. Benefit fund.

Sec. 5. That the private property of the members of the corporation shall be exempt from the debts of the corporation. Individual liability.

Sec. 6. That said corporation shall have power to collect, hold and disburse the funds named in its objects for the benefit of its members, and said funds shall be exempt from execution, and under no circumstances shall be liable for the debts of any of its living or deceased members, except when a deceased member shall have directed in his application for membership that the benefit accruing at his death shall be paid to his estate. Corporate powers.

Sec. 7. That said corporation shall be exempt from any privilege, state, county, city or town taxes. Exempt from taxes.

Sec. 8. That this act shall be in force from and after its ratification, and shall remain in force ninety-nine (99) years.

Ratified the 6th day of March, A. D. 1899.

CHAPTER 223.

An act to amend chapter two hundred and seventy-one of the private acts of eighteen hundred and ninety-five.

The General Assembly of North Carolina do enact:

tion 11, chap-271, private s of 1895, ended.

Section 1. That section eleven of chapter two hundred and seventy-one of the private acts of the general assembly of eighteen hundred and ninety-five be amended by adding thereto the following: Provided, that the said trustees may, by and with the written consent of J. S. Wynne, Esq., and upon such terms as may be agreed upon, transfer, deliver and convey unto the trustees of the Methodist Orphanage the funds and property now in their hands or that may hereafter come to their hands or within their control, to be used and employed by the said trustees of the Methodist Orphanage in the establishment or support (so far as said property may avail for such purpose) of a hospital or sanitarium for the care of the sick children in said orphanage or the sick inmates of any of the homes or departments under the control of said trustees of the Methodist Orphanage, and after such transfer and conveyance the trustees named in this act shall cease to be responsible therefor.

rustees of cer-in funds may nvey same to ethodist phanage.

esponsibility trustees shall se after trans. r.

Sec. 2. This act shall be in force from and after its ratification.

Ratified the 6th day of March, A. D. 1899.

CHAPTER 224.

An act to amend the charter of the D. A. Tompkins Company of Charlotte, North Carolina.

The General Assembly of North Carolina do enact:

dditional cor-rate powers nferred on the A. Tompkins mpany of arlotte.

Section 1. That the D. A. Thompkins Company, a corporation organized under the laws of this state and now having its principal office at Charlotte, shall have the following enumerated powers in addition to those already conferred upon it by law and the terms of its charter, to-wit: To acquire and hold, by subscription or purchase, stock in any other industrial corporation organized under the laws of this state or of any other state; to erect and operate mills for the manufacture of yarn or cloth out of any material and to acquire and hold land for the purposes of such manufacturing; to construct and operate railroads and tramways from any railroad track to the site of such mill or mills as may be erected by it; and to acquire and hold rights-of-way for the purpose of constructing such railroads or tramways; to operate, in connection with such manufacturing establishments, stores for the sale of goods, wares and merchandise; to establish warehouses and make and collect charges for the storage of goods therein, and to advance money on property deposited in such warehouses; to construct and operate street railways under contract with the proper authorities of any city or town; to construct and operate plants for the furnishing of light for any of the cities or towns of the state under contract with the proper authorities thereof, and to have, use and hold all such property, real or personal, as may be convenient or necessary for the successful conduct of any business which it may lawfully engage in under the powers hereby conferred upon it.

Sec. 2. This act shall take effect whenever at a regular or special meeting of the stockholders of said corporation the same shall be duly accepted by the said stockholders as an amendment of the charter of the corporation. **When this act is effective.**

Ratified the 6th day of March, A. D. 1899.

CHAPTER 225.

An act to repeal chapter one hundred and eighty-four, of the private laws of eighteen hundred and ninety-seven, entitled "An act to incorporate the Iverson Lumber and Broom Company of Yancey and Mitchell counties.".

The General Assembly of North Carolina do enact:

Section 1. That chapter one hundred and eighty-four of the private laws of North Carolina of the session of eighteen hundred and ninety-seven, entitled "An act to incorporate the Iverson Lumber and Broom Company, of Yancey and Mitchell counties," be and the same is hereby repealed. **Chapter 184, private laws of 1897, repealed.**

Sec. 2. That this act shall be in force from and after its ratification.

Ratified the 6th day of March, A. D. 1899.

CHAPTER 226.

An act to extend the time for the organization of the Lumberton and Lumber River Railroad Company.

The General Assembly of North Carolina do enact:

Section 1. That the time for organizing and beginning the construction of the Lumberton and Lumber River Railroad Company, under the terms of its charter heretofore granted, and the amendments thereto, be and the same is hereby extended for two years from the ratification of this act. **Time for beginning construction of Lumberton and Lumber River Railroad extended**

Sec. 2. This act shall be in force from and after its ratification.

Ratified the 6th day of March, A. D. 1899.

CHAPTER 227.

An act to incorporate the Merchants and Manufacturers Storage and Warehouse Company.

The General Assembly of North Carolina do enact:

rporators. Section 1. That Ashley Horne, Charles W. Horne, Charles H. Belvin, Frank K. Ellington, Ed. H. Lee and Charles G. Latta, or any three of them, and their successors, associates and assigns, dy corporate. are hereby constituted a body corporate by the name of "The rporate name. Merchants and Manufacturers Storage and Warehouse Company," by which name said corporation shall have all the privileges, franchises and rights incident to a corporation.

pital stock. Sec. 2. The capital stock of said corporation shall be for such a total sum, and be divided into such number of shares and of such amount for each share, as the majority of the stockholders oviso. in general meeting may determine: Provided, that such capital stock shall be not less than seven thousand and five hundred mitation to ck. dollars ($7,500) or more than fifty thousand dollars ($50,000), and that said corporation shall have authority to organize and transact business when seven thousand five hundred dollars ($7,500) of its capital stock is subscribed for and paid up, in cash or in property, to the value of seven thousand five hundred dollars ($7,500). y issue ck. The said corporation may issue stock, both common and preferred, with such regulations as may be prescribed by a majority of the stockholders; the certificates for this stock shall be issued only when fully paid for, and shall not thereafter be liable for assessment for any purpose whatsoever; the shares of stock shall be deemed personal property and be transferable on the books of said corporation in accordance with the by-laws made in that pital stock y be increased. behalf. The capital stock may be increased from time to time to such an amount as may be deemed proper, until the limit of fifty thousand dollars ($50,000) be reached.

rporate pow-. Sec. 3. The corporation hereby created shall have power to make contracts, to have and use a common seal; to sue and be sued in any court as fully as natural persons; to buy, hold, possess and convey real, personal and mixed property; to make bylaws for the regulation and management of the business of the company; to do all lawful acts and things and exercise all lawful powers and privileges that a corporate body may do.

ture of busi ss rporate pow-. Sec. 4. That said corporation may conduct warehouses and depots for the storage of cotton and other personal property and issue certificates or receipts therefor, which certificates or receipts shall be negotiable by endorsement and delivery, entitling the holder to the property mentioned in said certificates or receipts without regard to the depositor of the property, and the said company shall exercise ordinary care in the custody and care of the property stored with it, and may charge a reasonable compensation for such services.

Sec. 5. It shall be lawful for said company to borrow such sums of money from time to time as the interest of the company may require, and to issue and dispose of its promissory notes or bonds; and said company may mortgage, pledge or hypothecate any part of its property or franchises to secure the payment of such bonds or promissory notes. May borrow money.

Sec. 6. The stockholders in general meeting shall make and establish such by-laws, rules and regulations, not inconsistent with the laws of North Carolina and the United States, as they may deem best for the management of the business of the company, and elect a board consisting of not less than three nor more than five directors, who shall hold their office for one year or until their successors are duly elected, and the said board of directors shall elect such officers and agents as they may deem necessary, and they may require any or all of such officers and agents to enter into bond, payable to the said company, in such sum as they may deem necessary, conditioned upon the faithful discharge of their duties. Shall make by-laws, etc. Directors. Term of office.

Sec. 7. That the stockholders of the company shall not be individually liable for any of its debts, torts or liabilities. Individual liability.

Sec. 8. That the principal office and place of business of said company shall be in the city of Raleigh, North Carolina, but they may establish warehouses, offices and agencies for the transaction of business at such other places as they may deem proper. Principal office.

Sec. 9. That said corporation shall exist for thirty years and enjoy all such rights and privileges, liberties and immunities, franchises and powers as pertain to other corporate bodies. Duration of charter.

Sec. 10. That all rights, powers and privileges as set forth in this act shall not be deemed forfeited by non-user: Provided, the corporation is organized within five years from the date of the ratification of this act. Rights not forfeited by non-user. Proviso.

Sec. 11. That this act shall be in force from and after its ratification.

Ratified the 6th day of March, A. D. 1899.

CHAPTER 228.

An act to incorporate the Wright Lumber Company of Star, North Carolina.

The General Assembly of North Carolina do enact:

rporators. Section 1. That Z. T. Wright, G. H. Wright and James Allen, together with their associates and successors, be and they are hereby created and constituted a body corporate under the name of "The Wright Lumber Company," and by that name shall be entitled to sue and be sued, plead and be impleaded in any court in or out of the state of North Carolina; shall have and use a common seal and alter the same at pleasure; and have all the rights and privileges and subject to all regulations and restrictions now existing and applicable to such corporations under the laws of this state.

rporate name.

rporate powers.

rporate powers. Sec. 2. That said corporation may acquire, buy, sell and hold lands and timber and all kinds of personal property in this state, and may conduct a general lumber business in all of its branches; it may maintain saw-mills, planing mills and dry-kiln; it may acquire, manufacture, hold and sell all kinds of machinery; it may manufacture, buy and sell sash, doors, blinds and everything of whatever kind that is made from lumber: it may manufacture, buy, sell and dispose of furniture of every description; it may conduct in all of its branches the business of carrying on and operating a flour and grist mills and cotton gins, and to that end may buy, sell and dispose of corn, wheat, oats, barley, rye, flour, meal, cotton and cotton seed, and the products of the same; it may conduct and carry on in all of its branches the general mercantile business.

ture of business.

powered to construct lines of tramway, etc. Sec. 3. That the said corporation is hereby authorized to make, construct, equip, maintain and operate lines of tramway, with one or more tracks, and all necessary branches, turnouts, switchings and sidings, using such motive power as may be determined upon by the board of directors from any point on the Aberdeen and Ashboro Railroad, in the counties of Montgomery and Moore, through, along, over and across any portion of the said counties of Montgomery and Moore to any point or points in said counties, and erect such depots, stables, offices, shops and other buildings, structures, fixtures and appliances as are necessary and proper for conducting the business of said tramroads and company, and to demand and receive such sum or sums of money for the carriage of passengers and freight as the directors may think proper, not to exceed five cents per mile for passengers, and not exceeding one cent per mile for each one hundred pounds

ximum rate owed to be arged.

of freight by the tram-car load, and for parcels such compensation as may be reasonable.

Sec. 4. That whenever any land may be required for the purposes of constructing, equipping, maintaining and operating the said line or lines of tramway, or for constructing, maintaining, equipping and operating all necessary branches, switches, turnouts and sidings and the erection and maintaining of the necessary stables, depots, offices, shops and other buildings, structures, fixtures and appliances, proper for conducting the business of the said tramways by said company, it shall have the power to have the same assessed and condemned for its purposes in the manner prescribed in The Code of North Carolina, chapter forty-nine (49) of volume one, section one thousand nine hundred and forty-three (1,943,) and the sections following. **May condemn land.** **Land, assessment of.**

Sec. 5. That the said company shall have the right to lease or sell its road and franchises or any part thereof to any person or corporation and may acquire the property and franchises of or an interest in any other corporation by purchase, lease, subscription to or purchase of its capital stock or otherwise. **May lease or sell road, etc.**

Sec. 6. That the capital stock of the company shall be ten thousand dollars, divided into one hundred shares of one hundred dollars each, and may from time to time be increased to any amount not exceeding forty thousand dollars, whenever a majority of the stockholders in value shall determine. **Capital stock.**

Sec. 7. That the said company shall have power to contract debts and borrow money for the legitimate purposes of the corporation, and to make and issue notes, and shall have power to issue bonds and other evidences of debt and indebtedness for any obligations incurred in the conduct of its business, and shall have power to execute a mortgage or mortgages, as deeds of trust upon or conveying its property, franchise and income to secure the payment of any indebtedness of said company as it may deem expedient. **May contract debts, etc.**

Sec. 8. That the officers of said corporation shall consist of a president, secretary and treasurer, whose duties shall be prescribed by the by-laws of said company, and to be elected at their first meeting, and that the president, secretary and treasurer shall constitute the board of directors of said corporation; and that upon the election of said officers the said company shall be deemed to be fully organized, and may obtain subscriptions, issue stocks, bonds and other evidences of indebtedness, and begin the operations of such manufacturing establishments, mills, gins and tramroads and tramways as they or it may have already erected, and may enter into contracts for the construction and may construct tramroads [and] buildings and purchase any articles connected with the business herein mentioned, and **Officers of corporation.**

do any and all other lawful things necessary to carry out the purposes of the company.

incipal office. Sec. 9. That the principal office of said company shall be kept at Star, Montgomery county, North Carolina, and it may establish branch offices at such points in this state as it may deem necessary, and this corporation shall continue for a period of thirty years, subject to the general laws regulating corporations.

rsons obstructing, removing or facing property guilty of misdemeanor. Sec. 10. That any person or persons who shall unlawfully and willfully remove, obstruct, injure, deface or destroy any part of the property of said company shall be deemed guilty of a misdemeanor, and upon conviction be fined or imprisoned in the discretion of the court.

dividual bility. Sec. 11. That the stockholders of said company shall not be individually liable for any of its debts or engagements

Sec. 12. That this act shall be in force from and after its ratification.

Ratified the 6th day of March A. D. 1899.

CHAPTER 229.

An act to incorporate the Methodist Orphanage.

The General Assembly of North Carolina do enact:

rporators. Section 1. That Rev. J. W. Jenkins, Rev. J. N. Cole, Rev. E. C. Glenn, Joseph G. Brown, J. S. Wynne, E. J. Parish, L. B. Bynum, R. T. Gray, T. N. Ivey, H. C. Wall, W. E. Stringer, W. R. Allen, F. A. Woodward, Uriah Vaughan and H. L. Smith, and their associates and successors be and they are hereby declared and dy corporate. constituted a body politic and corporate under the name and rporate name. style of the "Trustees of the Methodist Orphanage," and as such rpetual succession. shall have perpetual succession and a common seal, which they may alter at pleasure, and shall be capable in law to sue and be sued, plead and be impleaded in all courts of the state.

rporate powers. Sec. 2. That said corporation shall have power to lease, purchase, take and receive by gift or devise, and hold in fee simple or lesser estate or estates all manner of lands, tenements, rents, annuities and other hereditaments, and shall further be capable in law to take, receive and possess all moneys, stocks, bonds, books, goods and chattels which may have been or may hereafter be given to it or to any person or persons for it, by deed, devise, bequest or othewise. A misnomer of the corporation in any deed, will or other conveyance shall not have the effect to invalidate isnomer of corporation shall t invalidate struments. the conveyance if the corporation shall be therein described with sufficient certainty to identify it or if the intent of the grantor or testator to make the said corporation the beneficiary shall sufficiently appear on the face of the instrument or otherwise.

Sec. 3. That said corporation shall be capable in law to bargain, sell and convey any and all lands, tenements, hereditaments and personal property held and owned by the corporation when the grant, devise or other conveyance does not otherwise provide. **Empowered to bargain, sell, etc.**

Sec. 4. That said corporation shall have power to make and establish such by-laws, rules and regulations for the government and conduct of the orphanage, home, asylum or retreat or other institution or department established by it and under its control as to said trustees may seem proper and necessary and as are not in conflict with the constitution and laws of this state and of the United States: Provided, the said corporation shall be under the jurisdiction, control and direction of the North Carolina Conference of the Methodist Episcopal Church, South. **By-laws, rules and regulations.** **Shall be under control of North Carolina Conference of M. E. Church, South.**

Sec. 5. That of the trustees named in the first section hereof (seven) shall hold office until the first day of January, nineteen hundred and two, and eight until the first day of January, nineteen hundred and four (the holders of said terms to be decided by agreement or lot at the first meeting of the said trustees), after which dates they may be succeeded by themselves or such other persons as may be elected by the North Carolina Conference of the Methodist Episcopal Church, South, at its session held in the years nineteen hundred and one and nineteen hundred and two, for terms of office of three and five years respectively, and thereafter by the said North Carolina Conference at its regular session next preceding the expiration of the terms of office of the said trustees, for such terms of office as they may originally have been elected to. The number of trustees may be increased by the said North Carolina Conference to any number not exceeding the number of presiding elders' districts within its bounds: Provided, that in the case of increase in the number of the board of trustees by the said North Carolina Conference, the additional members shall be elected for terms of office of five years each, excepting every third added member, who shall be elected for a term of office of three years, and such additional members shall be reelected or their successors elected thereafter at its regular annual session next preceding the expiration of the terms of office of said additional trustees, for such terms of office as they may have originally been elected to. A majority of said trustees shall constitute a quorum for the transaction of business. Whenever a vacancy shall occur by death, resignation or removal of a trustee, his successor shall be elected at the annual session of the said conference next thereafter held; and upon the failure of the conference to elect such successor at such time the remaining trus- **Term of office of trustees.** **Number of trustees may be increased.** **Proviso.** **Term of office of additional trustees.**

tees shall have power to fill the vacancy, but such new trustee shall hold only for the remainder of the term of his predecessor.

ection of president and ›retary.

Sec. 6. That the said trustees shall elect one of their own number president, and out of their number a secretary and treasurer, but nothing herein contained shall be so construed as to prevent the trustees from separating the office of secretary and treasurer.

ection of superintendent.

They may also elect a superintendent for the institution and such subordinate officers and employ such teachers, curators and servants as they may deem necessary for the successful operation of the institution. They shall also fix the salary of each officer, but the superintendent, by and with the consent of the trustees,

mpensation.

may employ and fix the compensation of such servants as may be necessary.

cation of phanage.

Sec. 7. That the said trustees may establish at or near the city of Raleigh, in the county of Wake, or at any other place within the bounds of the North Carolina Methodist Episcopal Church, South, an orphanage or home for the care, control, education, maintenance and support of such orphan children, indigent or otherwise, as said trustees may desire to provide for, which children shall be received only upon compliance with such rules as the trustees may prescribe for their reception. Said trustees may make by-laws for the government of the home and for the preservation of good morals therein, and may discharge any child so received in the orphanage or home whenever in their opinion the good of the institution so requires, and any child or children when so received shall be under the care and control of the trus-

rsons removchildren from hanage witht consent of stees, guilty of sdemeanor.

tees, and any person who shall take or remove from the orphanage or home and [any] child or children without the consent of the trustees, or who shall aid [or] abet in such removal shall be guilty of a misdemeanor, and shall be punished by fine or imprisonment, or both, in the discretion of the court. Said trustees shall also have the power to require any person or persons placing any minor child in said institution, as a condition of its admission, to surrender all right as parent, guardian or custodian of such child to the person of such child, and any document or writing signed for such purpose shall be effectual to for any right or claim at law or in equity of such parent, guardian or custodian the [to] the person of such child until his or her arrival at the age at which, under the laws of this state, he or she [is] freed from the control of pa-

y place chiln in homes.

rent or guardian. The said corporation shall also have power to place any child committed to its care in a good home and under the care and tutelage of suitable persons under such general rules and regulations and contract as the trustees may from time to time establish so as they may agree upon in any particular case: and in case any child shall be ill treated in any respect, physically, morally or otherwise, the trustees shall have power to reclaim such child. For any violation [of] or any contract made between the corporation and any person who shall receive a child therefrom, it may maintain an action in any court, either in its own name or in the name of the child.

The treatment of children at homes. Violation of contract between corporation and persons receiving children.

Sec. 8. That the said corporation may also establish and maintain, under such rules and regulations and under such names or designation as it may adopt, subject to the approval of the North Carolina Conference of the Methodist Episcopal Church, South, a home or homes for the wornout or superannuated Methodist preachers and their wives and helpless children, or for the widows and helpless children of deceased Methodist preachers.

May establish home for superannuated ministers.

Sec. 9. That said corporation shall also establish and maintain, under such name or designation and under such rules and regulations as the trustees may adopt, subject to the approval of the North Carolina Conference of the Methodist Episcopal Church, South, a hospital or hospitals for the care of the sick inmates of any of the homes under its control, and may receive and keep separate from the other funds of the corporation any donation by deed, will or otherwise that may be made for the support or benefit of such hospital or hospitals.

May establish hospital for care of sick.

Sec. 10. That it shall be unlawful for any person to set up or continue any gaming table or any device whatsoever for playing at any game of chance or hazard by whatever name called, or to exhibit any circus or theatrical performance within one-fourth of a mile of any orphanage house for orphan children under the control of the said corporation without the consent of the trustees thereof: Provided, that this section shall not be effective if said orphanage shall be established within oné-fourth of a mile from the corporate limits of Raleigh, and shall not interfere with the conduct or operation of any fair held by any agricultural association within enclosed grounds.

Certain games and performances within one-fourth a mile of orphanage prohibited.

Sec. 11. That the property of said corporation used for its purposes shall not be subject to taxation.

Exempt from taxation.

Sec. 12. That the said trustees and their successors shall hold their meetings from time to time as often as may be necessary, and shall make a report to each annual session of the North Carolina Conference of the Methodist Episcopal Church, South.

Meetings of trustees.

Sec. 13. That in case for any cause said corporation should determine to abandon the purposes for which it is hereby established all property belonging to it shall be devoted to such religious, charitable, benevolent or educational purposes as may be determined upon by the North Carolina Conference of the Methodist Episcopal Church, South, subject, nevertheless, to such limitations as may be contained in any will or deed or other instrument by which any of said property may have been conveyed to said corporation.

Application of property if corporation shall abandon purposes for which established.

nflicting laws pealed

Sec. 14. All laws and clauses of laws in conflict with the provisions of this act are hereby repealed.

Sec. 15. This act shall be in force from and after its ratification.

Ratified the 6th day of March, A. D. 1899.

CHAPTER 230.

An act to incorporate the Cape Fear Terminal Railway Company.

The General Assembly of North Carolina do enact:

rporators.

Section 1. That Iredell Meares, M. G. Guthrie, W. G. Curtis, William Weeks, William A. Williams, William H. Green and such other persons as may become associated with them as stockholders, and their successors, be created a body politic and corporate under the name of "The Cape Fear Terminal Railway Company," and shall have the right to sue and be sued, to have a common seal; to purchase or acquire for the necessary purposes of the company, by gift or devise, estate, real, personal or mixed, and to hold, lease or sell the same, as the interest of said company may require, and shall make and exercise all such by-laws and regulations for its government as may be necessary or expedient for that purpose not inconsistent with the constitution of the state or of the United States; and shall have all the rights and enjoy all the privileges and immunities possessed and enjoyed by any other railroad company under the laws of North Carolina: Provided, that this section shall not be construed to exempt the property of said corporation from being taxed.

rporate name.

rporate rights d powers.

oviso.

t exempted m taxation.

thorized to struct raild.

Sec. 2. That said company is hereby authorized to construct a railroad or railroads of one or more tracks and of any guage whatever from any point in the city of Wilmington, North Carolina, or from the shores of the Cape Fear river, opposite to or near the said city of Wilmington, through the county of Brunswick to any point in the city of Southport, North Carolina, and through said county via Southport or otherwise to the state lines dividing the states of North Carolina and South Carolina, and from the shores of said Cape Fear river at any point in or near the city of Southport through any or all of the counties of Brunswick, Columbus, Robeson, Richmond, Anson or Cumberland to any point on the line of the Carolina Central or Cape Fear and Yadkin Valley Railroads; and thence on in a northern or northwestern direction through any of the counties of the state lines dividing the states of North Carolina and Virginia.

rritory versed.

pital stock.

Sec. 3. The capital stock of said company shall be one million dollars, divided into shares of one hundred dollars each, but said company may, by a concurrence of two thirds in value of all its stock, increase its capital stock from time to time to an amount deemed necessary to the interest of said company.

May be increased.

Sec. 4. Books of subscription may be opened by said corporators or by the directors at such times and places and under such rules and regulations as a majority may determine, and the said corporators or a majority of them may, at any time after the sum of ten thousand dollars has been subscribed to the capital stock of said railroad company and five per centum cash paid thereon, have power to call together the subscribers to said shares of stock for the purpose of completing the organization of said company.

Books of subscription may be opened.

Sec. 5. That the president shall, under the direction of the board of directors, issue certificates of stock to the stockholders, which shall be transferable in such manner as may be prescribed by the by-laws of the company.

President shall issue certificates of stock.

Sec. 6. Said company shall be authorized to borrow money for the construction and operation of said railroad and for the purpose of this act, and to issue coupon or regular bonds for the amount so borrowed, and to mortgage said road and the other property of said company to secure the payment of said bonds, principal and interest.

Authorized to borrow money.

Sec. 7. The said railroad company shall have the power to cross the tracks of other railroads and to connect with any railroad now or hereafter chartered, and to lay down and to use tracks through any town or city, and with the consent of the corporate authorities of said town or city, upon such terms as they may prescribe.

Empowered to cross tracks of other roads.

Sec. 8. The said railroad company shall have power to build branches to the main stems in any direction not exceeding fifty miles in length, and may build, purchase and hold, charter or connect with such ocean steamers or vessels, river steamers, vessels or boats as may be desired to run and use from or to the terminal points or on any water-course in connection with the road to be constructed by said company.

May build branches.

Sec. 9. The said company is hereby authorized and empowered to erect and construct at or near the town of Southport, in the county of Brunswick, wharves, piers, docks, basins, warehouses, elevators, cotton presses and coal shutes, suitable for the accommodation of steamships, vessels and boats and for the convenient loading, unloading, shipping, receiving and storing of all kinds of merchandise and personal property for safe keeping, and may conduct the business usually transacted by warehousemen, wharfingers and lightermen, and may charge and collect compensation for the storage, dockage, wharfage and lighterage

Empowered to erect certain structures at Southport.

and for all labor incident thereto, including the expense of weighing, insuring, keeping and delivering such merchandise or personal property at such rates and on such terms as may be agreed upon between it and its customers; and for any advances made by it on merchandise or property stored or deposited with it for shipment, and for all its charges and expenses incident thereto, the said company shall have a preferred lien on said merchandise and property, which shall be paid before the said company shall be required to deliver the same.

y hold land.

Sec. 10. That said company is hereby fully empowered to take, by purchase or otherwise, and to hold in fee simple or any other manner any number of acres of land, besides what may be necessary for the right-of way, depots, warehouses, shops and other necessary buildings, not exceeding in value at any time the sum of one million dollars ($1,000,000): Provided, that the value of the land is to be fixed by the price paid for the same, and increase in value by improvements made by said corporation or otherwise not to be considered in ascertaining the value of the lands: Provided further, that this act shall not be construed to have any effect upon the valuation of said lands for taxation.

y condemn terways.

Sec. 11. That the said corporation, for the purpose of drainage and for the purpose of navigation and transportation with any and all kinds of boats or rafts, is hereby vested with power to widen, deepen or straighten the channels or runs and to cut canals in the Green swamp and other swamps in the counties of Columbus and Brunswick, North Carolina, as may be useful or necessary in the conduct of the business of said corporation; and it is hereby vested with all the rights and privileges secured to canal companies by chapter thirty-eight of The Code of North Carolina and any amendments thereto. And in case said corporation is unable to agree with the owner for the purchase of any real estate required for the purpose of constructing any canal, it shall have the right to acquire title to the same in the same manner and by the special proceedings prescribed in chapter forty-nine of said Code and any amendments thereto.

y acquire title canals con- ucted by it.

ction may ordered by ies, towns, inties, etc., to te on subscrip- n to stock.

Sec. 12. That upon the written application of one fifth of the qualified voters asking from any county, city, town or township any contribution, donation or subscription to its capital stock, said application stating the amount of donation or subscription asked, the terms and conditions of the same, the county commissioners of such county or proper authorities of such city, town or township shall appoint a day and order an election to be held thereon in such county, township, city or town in the manner prescribed by law for holding other elections, at which said election the legally qualified voters shall be entitled to vote for or against such subscription or donation. Said election to be held

tice shall be en of election.

at the usual voting places after thirty days' notice specifying the amount of subscription, contribution or donation to be voted for, and to what company it is proposed to donate, contribute or subscribe, which notice shall be printed in some newspaper, if any there be published in said county, city, town or township, and by posting the same in three or more conspicuous places therein; such election shall be held by persons appointed in the manner that persons are appointed for holding other elections in said county, city or town, and the returns thereof shall be made and the results declared and certified as prescribed by law in such other elections, and such results so verified shall be filed with the register of deeds in such county, city or town, and shall be taken as evidence of the same in any court in the state.

Result of election shall be certified.

Sec. 13 That if the result of said election shall show that the majority of the qualified voters of said county, township, city or town favor said contract, contribution, donation or subscription to the capital stock of said railroad to the amount voted for in such election, then the said county commissioners, if said election shall have been held in a county or township thereof, or the proper authorities of said city or town, shall immediately make such subscription to the capital stock of said railroad, payable in cash or the bonds authorized to be issued under this act as may be agreed upon, shall issue the bonds of said county, township, city or town, to the amount so voted for at said election, in such forms and denominations and running for such length of time as may be determined on by said county commissioners or proper authorities of said city, town, county or township, bearing interest at a rate not greater than six per centum per annum, said interest to be payable semi-annually and evidenced by coupons on said bonds; and said designated authorities shall deliver said bonds so issued, or pay in cash, as may be agreed, to said Cape Fear Terminal Railway Company upon receiving therefor for the use and benefit of said county, township, city or town, proper certificates of stock in said company to the amount of subscription so voted as aforesaid.

Bonds shall be issued when the vote is favorable to subscription of stock.

Rate of interest of bonds.

Sec. 14. That to provide for the interest on said bonds and their redemption at maturity, the county commissioners or proper authorities of any county, city, town or township shall, in addition to other taxes, each year compute and levy on all property and polls of any such county, township, city or town a sufficient tax to pay such interest, and after ten years a tax sufficient to provide each year for the interest on said subscription bonds, and a sum equal to one-fortieth of the principal thereof for a sinking fund; the sum levied and collected for said sinking fund to be paid over to the county treasurer or other officer of said county, city or town authorized by law to perform the duties of treasurer

Proper authorities empowered to levy special tax to pay interest and principal.

or commissioner of sinking fund and by him invested in said bonds, and the amount of interest maturing on such bonds shall be collected and likewise invested; all said bonds when purchased, also all interest coupons attached shall be stamped "sinking fund" on face of same; but in case said treasurer or other officer shall be unable to invest the sinking funds herein provided for in said bonds at or below their par value, he shall invest the same in such solvent bonds or securities as may be selected and approved by the board of county commissioners aforesaid or proper authorities of any city or town.

terest coupons, w stamped.

id special tax all be set aside a distinct fund.

Sec. 15. That all taxes which shall be levied upon and collected from said railroad company by any county, city, town or township, under the general revenue acts, as from other citizens and property, upon any real or personal property belonging to said corporation and situated within said county, city, town or township, shall be set aside as a distinct fund and applied exclusively by the proper authorities thereof, if said county, city, town or township shall have subscribed to the capital stock of said company, and issue bonds in payment therefor to the liquidation and payment of the interest accruing on said bonds issued on account of such subscription so long as said bonds shall be outstanding and remaining unpaid. If the said tax so levied upon said company should be insufficient to pay the interest upon the said subscription bonds, then the difference shall be paid out of the tax to be levied and collected and provided in section twelve of this act; but if in any year the tax paid by said company should be more than the sum required to pay the said interest for that year, then the surplus may be applied to the general purposes of said county, city, town or township.

hen tax levied insufficient pay interest d principal.

y sell or lease other compa- s.

Sec. 16. That the said company, after it shall have been organized, shall have the power to connect with any railroad company that has been already organized or that may hereafter be organized, or to sell or lease any part of [or] the whole of its main line or branches thereof to any other railroad company; and if a portion or the whole of either of said lines shall be sold to any other company, then the company purchasing shall take the line so purchased, with all the franchises herein granted as appurtenant and manage of [the] said line under its own corporate name.

ght to trans- rt passengers, ight, etc.

Sec. 17. That said company shall have exclusive right to carry and transport freight and passengers over and along said road, and upon vessels and boats run in connection with the same, at such rates as said company shall prescribe, subject to such general laws regulating the same as the general assembly may from time to time establish.

y construct hout complet- road.

Sec. 18. That the said company may construct a part of the said road without building the entire line, and may charge for transportation thereon, beginning at or near Wilmington or Southport, North Carolina.

Sec. 19. That said company may build its roads by such route as it may deem most advantageous and expedient, and shall have the right to cross any navigable stream or canal on its route: Provided, a draw sufficient not to impede navigation is placed in its bridges over such streams or canals. **Road may be built by such route as company deems best.**

Sec 20. That the said company is empowered to construct and operate a telegraph or telephone line upon any part of its route. **Empowered to construct telegraph or telephone line.**

Sec. 21. That this act shall be in force from and after its ratification, and all laws and clauses of laws in conflict with this act are hereby repealed.

Ratified the 6th day of March, A. D. 1899.

CHAPTER 231.

An act to incorporate "Linden Grove Number Two (2) United Ancient Order of Druids," of the city of Wilmington, county of New Hanover.

The General Assembly of North Carolina do enact:

Section 1. That George Ziegler, Aquilla J. Marshall, Dr. Frank H. Russell, and all others who are members at present and all who in future may become members of "Linden Grove Number Two (2) of the United Ancient Order of Druids," a charitable and fraternal institution located and existing in the city of Wilmington and in the county of New Hanover, are hereby constituted and declared to be a body politic and corporate in deed and in law under the name, style and title of "Linden Grove Number Two, United Ancient Order of Druids," and by such corporate name shall have perpetual succession and shall be forever capable in law to take, hold and sell real estate in fee simple or otherwise, and to mortgage and let the same, and to take and [any] real or personal estate by purchase, gift, grant, devise or bequest or by other lawful means, and sell, transfer or dispose of the same; to borrow or lend money and to give or take any and all kinds of security or securities for the same; to have a common seal, and the same to break, alter and renew at pleasure; to sue and be sued, plead and be impleaded; to make, pass, accept, establish, adopt, change, alter and amend from time to time and to put into execution any and all such by-laws, rules and regulations necessary to maintain, conduct and carry on the affairs of the corporation, and generally to do and perform all such matters and things that may be necessary as shall not be **Corporators.** **Corporate name.** **Where located.** **Corporate powers and rights.**

inconsistent with the constitution and laws of this state or the constitution of the United States.

dividual bility. Sec. 2. That no member shall be held individually liable for any debts or liabilities of the corporation.

Sec. 3. That this act shall be in force from and after its ratification.

Ratified the 6th day of March, A. D. 1899.

CHAPTER 232.

An act to incorporate the "United Benefit Society" of the city of Wilmington, North Carolina.

The General Assembly of North Carolina do enact:

rporators. Section 1. That John McRae, B. C. Wright, John H. Webber, James G. Blain and Charles H. Stanford, and all other persons who may become members by application and acceptance, be dy corporate. and they are hereby constituted a body politic and corporate unrporate name. der the name and style of the "United Benefit Society," of Wilmington, North Carolina.

ject and purse of corporan. Sec. 2. That the object and purpose of said corporation shall be to promote the general good and welfare of its members and their families, to improve their social and literary standing; to build, erect and maintain schools and academies whenever they may deem it necessary and expedient, and to provide means to defray the funeral and burial expenses of its members.

incipal place business. Sec. 3. That the principal place of operation of said business society shall be in the city of Wilmington, but that branch societies may be organized from time to time in any part of the state under such laws, rules and regulations as may be prescribed by said corporation.

ration of arter. Sec. 4. That the length of duration of said corporation shall be thirty years.

dividends or pital stock. Sec. 5. That there shall be no capital stock and no dividends or profits paid to its members, nor shall any member be held individually liable for any debts or liabilities of said corporation.

incipal officers corporation. Sec. 6. The principal officers shall be a president, vice-president, secretary, treasurer and a board of advisors, consisting of five members, of which the president shall be ex officio chairman. The offices of secretary and treasurer may be consolidated and held by one member, and the office of vice-president may not be filled if the board of advisors shall so elect.

rporation, w governed. Sec. 7. The corporation shall be governed by the officers and advisors, who shall be elected and hold office at such times and in such manner and for such terms, and who shall have powers and authority, as shall be prescribed in by-laws regularly adopted for its government.

Sec. 8. That the corporation shall be capable in law to take, hold and sell real estate, in fee simple or otherwise, and to mortgage and let the same, and to take and hold real and personal estate by purchase, gift, grant, devise or bequest or by other lawful means, and to sell, transfer or dispose of the same; to borrow or lend money, and to give or take any and all kinds of security or securities for the same; to have a common seal, and the same to break, alter and renew at pleasure; to sue and be sued, plead and be impleaded; to prescribe and fix the amount or amounts of funeral benefits to be paid upon the death of any of its members, and to whom paid; to fix and regulate the amount of dues, fines or assessments to be paid by each member; and to make, pass, accept, establish, adopt, alter and amend from time to time and to put into execution, any and all such by-laws, rules, conditions and regulations necessary to organize, conduct, maintain and carry on the affairs of the corporation and generally to do and perform all such matters and things that may be necessary as shall not be inconsistent with the constitution and laws of this state or the constitution of the United States.

May take, hold and sell real estate.

Seal.

Sec. 9. That it shall have full power and authority to regulate and prescribe its membership and to reject any and all applications for membership, and to expel any member or members for immoral conduct, drunkenness, engaging in immoral business, non payment of dues, fines or assessments, or for any other cause which may appear just and reasonable to the board of advisors, after due consideration, under such rules and regulations as may be prescribed in its by-laws.

Regulation of membership.

Sec. 10. That this act shall be in force from and after its ratification.

Ratified the 6th day of March, A. D. 1899.

CHAPTER 233.

An act to amend the charter of Mount Airy.

The General Assembly of North Carolina do enact:

Section 1. That section four of chapter ninety of the private laws of eighteen hundred and ninety-seven be and the same is hereby repealed.

Section 4, chapter 90, private laws of 1897, repealed.

Sec. 2. That the commissioners of the town of Mount Airy shall order an election to be held on the first Monday in July, eight-

Election shall be ordered on question of sale of liquors.

een hundred and ninety-nine, in the town of Mount Airy to ascertain whether or not spirituous or malt liquors may be sold in the said town. At said election those in favor of sale shall vote a written or printed ballot with the word "License," and those opposed to sale shall vote a written or printed ballot with the words "No license." The manner of holding such election and the penalties for illegal and fraudulent voting in this election shall be the same as in the annual elections for mayor and commissioners of the town of Mount Airy. The commissioners shall give thirty days' notice of the time of holding said election in a newspaper published in the town.

rm of ballot.

anner of holding election.

mmissioners all give notice.

dges of election shall declare ult.

Sec. 3. That the judges of election shall on the day following the election declare the number of votes cast for and against the sale, and if a majority of the votes cast at such election shall have written or printed thereon the words "No license," it shall be unlawful for the commissioners of the town of Mount Airy or the commissioners of the county of Surry to grant a license to any person or persons or corporation to sell spirituous or malt liquors with [within] the corporate limits of the town of Mount Airy until another election shall be held reversing such election.

onflicting laws ealed.

Sec. 4. That all laws and clauses of laws in conflict herewith are hereby repealed.

Ratified the 6th day of March, A. D. 1899.

CHAPTER 234.

An act relating to electric lights and telephones in the town of Waynesville.

The General Assembly of North Carolina do enact:

nmissioners Waynesville horized to nt franchise five years to tain enterses.

Section 1. That the board of aldermen of the town of Waynesville are hereby authorized and empowered, if in their opinion they should deem it necessary, in order to secure for said town electric lights and telephones, or either, to grant to any person or persons, corporation or corporations, the exclusive privilege of constructing, equipping and operating a system of electric lights and telephones, or either, in said town, for five years from the first day of May, eighteen hundred and ninety-nine, under such rules and regulations as the said board of aldermen may prescribe.

Sec. 2. That this act shall be in force from and after its ratification.

Ratified the 6th day of March, A. D. 1899.

CHAPTER 235.

An act to amend, revise and consolidate the charter of the city of Durham, in the county of Durham, the state of North Carolina.

The General Assembly of North Carolina do enact:

Section 1. That the inhabitants of the city of Durham shall be, and continue as they have been, a body politic and corporate, and henceforth the corporation shall bear the name and style of "The City of Durham," and under such name and style is hereby invested with all the property and rights of property which now belong to the corporation, and by this name may acquire and hold for the purpose of its government, welfare, and improvement, all such estate as may be devised, bequeathed or conveyed to it, and the same may from time to time sell, dispose of and invest as shall be deemed advisable by the proper authorities of the corporation. Body politic. Corporate name. Corporate rights and powers.

Sec. 2. That the corporate limits of said city shall extend one half mile north, south, east and west, from the present location of the warehouse of the North Carolina Railroad in said city, making the corporate limits one mile square. Corporate limits.

Sec. 3. That no person shall be entitled to vote at any election held in the city of Durham, unless he shall be a qualified elector under the laws and constitution of the state of North Carolina and shall have resided next preceding the day of election ninety days within the corporation. Persons entitled to vote at municipal elections.

Sec. 4. That no person shall be eligible as mayor or alderman, or other officer, unless he shall be a qualified voter, as prescribed in section three of this charter. Eligibility for mayor and other officers.

Sec. 5. That for the purpose of elections, the city of Durham shall be divided into such precincts as the board of aldermen may direct: Provided, the said board of aldermen shall make the voting places and the boundaries of said precincts conform, as nearly as may be practicable, to those designated and prescribed by the general law for election of state and county officers. Election precincts. Proviso.

Sec. 6. That a registration shall be had of the voters of the city for each precinct, and that a copy of the registration shall be furnished the poll-holders, and no person shall be allowed to vote unless his name shall be found thereon. Registration.

Sec. 7. That the board of aldermen, or upon their failure to act, the mayor, shall appoint a suitable person for each precinct to act as registrar within his precinct of the corporation of said city, and the registration shall close on the second Saturday before the day of election. Appointment of registrars.

nen registrars all attend.

Sec. 8. The registrars shall attend the voting place of their respective precincts, between the hours of nine o'clock a. m. and four o'clock p. m., for four consecutive Saturdays, beginning on the fifth Saturday next preceding the day of election, and keep open said registration books for the registration of such electors residing in said precinct as may be lawfully entitled to register and vote therein, who have not before been admitted to registration in said precinct, or whose names do not appear in the list of registered voters therein. The registrars, before admitting anyone to register as a duly qualified voter, shall require the elector to take the following oath: "I, ..., do solemnly swear (or affirm) that I will support and maintain the constitution and laws of the United States and the constitution and laws of North Carolina, not inconsistent therewith; and that I have been a resident of North Carolina for twelve months, and of the city of Durham for ninety days next preceding this date; that I am a duly qualified elector, and that I have not registered for this election in any other precinct, and that I am a bona fide resident of precinct No........, in the city of Durham. So help me, God." And upon taking said oath, the registrar shall enter the name, age, residence and day of registration of said elector, upon the registration books of the precinct as a duly qualified voter therein: Provided, however, if on the day of election, or between the closing of the registration books and the day of election, any one shall become twenty-one years of age, or otherwise qualified to vote, by reason of residence, he shall be allowed to register and vote on that day.

gistrar shall ear electors.

rm of oath.

mes, how ered.

oviso.

gistration oks shall be ned to inction.

Sec. 9. That on the first Monday after the close of the registration books, at or before ten o'clock a. m., they shall be deposited in the office of the mayor of the city and be opened for the inspection of the citizens.

allenges.

Sec. 10. It shall be lawful to challenge the right of any person to vote, either on the day of election when he offers to vote, or on the day of registration when he offers to register; and if it shall appear to the judges of election, or a majority thereof, or to the registering officer, that such person is disqualified to vote under the constitution and laws of the state, he shall be excluded from registration, or, if he has been registered, from voting.

nual election mayor and ermen.

Sec. 11. That there shall, on the first Monday in May, one thousand eight hundred and ninety-nine, and on the first Monday in May biennially thereafter, be elected a mayor and seven aldermen for said city who shall hold their offices until their successors are qualified, said officers to be elected by the qualified voters of the whole city.

pointment of ction inctors.

Sec. 12. That for the purpose of electing said officers, the aldermen shall, at least twenty days before the election, appoint two inspectors for each precinct, who shall be qualified voters residing in the precinct, and the inspectors shall give ten days' notice thereof by public advertisement, and the inspectors, before they proceed to act, shall be sworn by the mayor or a justice of the peace, to conduct the election fairly and impartially, and according to law, and in case of the absence of any inspector, his place shall forthwith be supplied by the mayor.

Inspector shall be present on day of election.

Sec. 13. That on the day of election the inspectors shall give due attendance at the time and place; shall be judges of the polls; receive the votes and conduct the election in like manner, and during the same hours of the day, as election for members of the general assembly.

Mayor and aldermen shall be voted for in separate boxes.

Sec. 14. That the mayor shall be voted for in one box, on one ballot, written or printed, and the aldermen in another box, on one ballot, written or printed.

Counting of ballots.

Sec. 15. That at the close of the election the inspectors shall proceed to count the ballot and shall meet at the mayor's office at ten o'clock a., m. of the next succeeding day, to canvass the election and declare the result thereof; and such persons voted for as mayor having received the highest number of votes shall be declared duly elected mayor for the ensuing term of two years, and of those persons voted for as aldermen, the seven receiving the highest number of votes shall be declared duly elected aldermen of the city for the ensuing term of two years, and such mayor and aldermen shall be notified of their said election, by the inspectors, on the day succeeding their election.

When a tie vote occurs.

Sec. 16. That if among the persons voted for as mayor there shall be an equal number of votes between any two or more having the largest number, the aldermen elect shall proceed within five days after their qualification to select a mayor of such persons, and if among the persons voted for as aldermen there shall be a like tie, the remaining aldermen within five days after their qualification shall select of such the person or persons to be aldermen.

Inspectors shall certify two poll lists.

Sec. 17. That the inspectors for each precinct shall certify and subscribe two poll lists, and return one of them to the clerk of the board of aldermen, who shall keep it among the archives of the city and the other to the register of deeds of the county.

Oath of mayor.

Sec. 18. That the mayor, immediately after his election and before entering upon the duties of his office, shall take the following oath: "I (A. B.,) do hereby solemnly swear that I will diligently endeavor to perform faithfully and truly, according to my best skill, judgment and ability, all of the duties of the office of the mayor of the city of Durham while I continue therein, and will cause to be executed, as far as in my power lies, all the laws, ordinances and regulations made for the government of the city, and in the discharge of my duties I will do equal justice in all cases whatsoever."

ldermen shall ke cath.

Sec. 19. That each alderman before entering on the duties of the office, shall take before the mayor or some justice of the peace, an oath, that he will truly and impartially perform the duties of alderman for the city, according to the best of his skill, ability and judgment.

rm of office.

Sec. 20. That the mayor and aldermen shall hold their offices, respectively, until the next succeeding election, and until their respective successors are qualified.

ilure of mayor aldermen to alify.

Sec. 21. That if any person chosen mayor shall refuse to be qualified, or there is a vacancy in the office after election and qualification, the aldermen shall choose some qualified person mayor for the term, or for the unexpired portion of the term, as the case may be; and on like occasions and in like manner the aldermen shall choose other aldermen to supply the place of such as shall refuse to act, and fill all vacancies which may occur, and such persons only shall be chosen as are hereafter declared to be eligible.

nalty for fusal to qualify.

Sec. 22. That any person elected mayor or alderman who shall refuse to be qualified and act as such, shall forfeit and pay, for the equal use of the city and of him who sues therefor, twenty-five dollars.

illful failure aldermen to ve notice of ction.

Sec. 23. That if the aldermen shall willfully fail to give the notice of election or to hold and declare the same in the manner herein prescribed, such of them as shall be in default shall forfeit and pay, for the equal use of the city and for him who shall sue therefor, twenty-five dollars.

ty shall not rfeit any corrate rights by lure to elect cers.

Sec. 24. That the city shall not lose any of its corporate rights and privileges by failure to elect officers on the first Monday in any year, when an election ought regularly to be held.

ilure to elect day named.

n days' notice all be given d election ld.

Sec. 25. That in case of failure to elect municipal officers on any said first Monday in May of any year when an election ought regularly to be held, the electors residing within the corporate limits may, after ten days' notice, signed by seven of said electors, and posted at three places within the corporate limits and published in some newspaper printed in the city, proceed to appoint registrars and inspectors, in like manner as the board of aldermen or mayor are herein authorized to do, and such registrars and inspectors shall hold an election for municipal officers, in the way and manner herein provided for registrars and inspectors, appointed by the board of aldermen or mayor.

yor consti ted a special urt.

risdiction of ayor.

Sec. 26. That the mayor of the city of Durham, while acting as such, is hereby constituted a special court, with all the authority, jurisdiction and powers in criminal offenses occurring in the corporate limits of said city, or within one-half mile thereof, that e now or hereafter may be given by law, to justices of the peace, ıd shall also have exclusive original jurisdiction to hear and ;termine all misdemeanors consisting of a violation of the ornances of said city, and all causes of action within the jurisdicon of a justice of the peace involving penalties imposed by this ıarter, or ordinances enacted thereunder. The proceedings in ıid court shall be the same as are now or may hereafter be preribed for courts of justices of the peace, and in all cases there ıall be a right of appeal to the superior court of Durham county, ıd in all cases where the defendant shall be adjudged by the ıid mayor to be imprisoned or to pay fines or penalties according law or the ordinances of the city, and the person of persons gainst whom the same is adjudged refuses or is unable to perrm such judgment, it shall be lawful for the mayor to sentence ıe defendant or such persons to imprisonment in the jail of urham county, for a term not exceeding thirty days, and to ljudge also, that the defendant, or any such person work, during ıe period of his confinement, on the public streets or other pubc works of said city or until, at a fair rate of wages, such peron or persons shall have worked out the full amount of such nes and penalties and cost of prosecution. The said special ourt shall have power, jurisdiction and authority of a justice of he peace, to hear and determine all causes of action to recover nes and penalties for a violation of the ordinances of the city of urham.

In all cases there shall be a right to appeal.

Defendants unable to pay fine may be worked on streets.

Sec. 27. That the mayor may issue his precepts to the policeıen of the city, and to such other officers to whom a justice of the eace may direct his precepts, and such policemen or other officers re authorized to execute such precepts or process throughout he county of Durham.

Policemen shall execue precepts of mayor.

Sec. 28. That the mayor shall keep a faithful minute of the recepts issued by him and of all his judicial proceedings. The ıdgments rendered by him shall have all the force, virtue and alidity of judgments rendered by a justice of the peace, and may e executed and enforced against the parties, in the county of urham and elsewhere, in the same manner and by the same ıeans as if the same had been rendered by a justice of the peace or the county of Durham.

Mayor shall keep a minute of precepts.

Sec. 29. That the mayor shall keep his office in some convenient art of the city. He shall perform such duties as from time to ime shall be prescribed, and he shall receive such compensation nd fees as may be allowed by law or the ordinances of the orporation.

Mayor's office.

Compensation of mayor.

Sec. 30. That the mayor, when present, shall preside at all ıeetings of the board of aldermen; and when there is an equal ivision upon any question, or in the election of the officers by

Mayor shall preside at meeting of aldermen.

the board, he shall determine the matter by his vote. He shall vote in no other case. The board of aldermen shall, at their first meeting, designate one of their own members, to exercise the duties of the mayor, as prescribed in the charter, when the mayor shall be absent, on account of sickness or other causes; the said mayor pro tempore is hereby invested with all the powers and authority conferred upon the mayor by this charter, to try and determine actions.

ection of mayor ɔ tem.

jority competent to transt business.

oviso.

hen aldermen ıll convene.

Sec. 31. That the aldermen shall form one board, and a majority of them shall be competent to perform all the duties for the aldermen, unless otherwise provided; within five days after their election they shall convene for the transaction of business, and shall then fix stated days of meeting for the year, which shall be as often at least as once in every calendar month. Special meetings of the aldermen may also be held on the call of the mayor or a majority of the aldermen, and of every such meeting, when called by the mayor, all of the aldermen, and when called by a majority of the aldermen, such as shall not join in the call shall be notified in writing.

mpensation of ermen.

Sec. 32. That the board of aldermen shall have power to vote each member of the board a sum not exceeding one hundred dollars per annum as a compensation for his services; and if any member shall fail to attend any general meeting of the board of aldermen, or any special meeting of which he shall have notice, as aforesaid, unless prevented by such cause as shall be satisfactory to the board, he shall forfeit and pay for the use of the city the sum of five dollars.

wer of alderɜn to make linances, etc.

Sec. 33. The board of aldermen, when convened, shall have power to make such ordinances, rules and regulations for the proper government of the city as they may deem necessary, and provide for the proper enforcement and execution thereof, in such manner as they may think best.

wers of aldern.

ater supply.

Sec. 34. Among the powers hereby conferred upon the aldermen are the following: To provide a sufficient water supply, fix charges and rates therefor, and provide all necessary rules and regulations for the government and conduct of the business of such persons and corporations as are engaged in furnishing water for the use of the said city of Durham and the inhabitants

ghts.

thereof; to provide lights, fix charges and rates therefor, and prescribe all necessary rules and regulations for the government and conduct of the business of such persons or corporations as are engaged in furnishing lights for the use of the said city and the inhabitants thereof; to open, grade build, curb and pave new streets; to repair, widen, ascertain location of, change, keep clean, alter and vary the established streets or grades of streets, alleys and sidewalks in said city; to improve, repair, grade, curb or pave the sidewalks or pavements now established, or that may hereafter be established in the said city, or cause the same to be improved, repaired, graded, curbed or paved, and to recover from the owner or occupant of lots (fronting or adjoining the pavements in which curbing or pavement shall be made) one-half of the expense of the work, which expense shall be a lien on the said lot or lots: Provided, always, that the owner of such lot shall have twenty days' notice, in writing, of the order of the board, and if, for any reason, personal notice can not be given, the same shall be published for twenty days in the newspapers of the city of Durham. To construct or to contract for the construction of a system of sewerage for the city, and protect and regulate the same, by adequate ordinances; and if it shall be necessary, in obtaining proper outlets for such a system, to extend the same beyond the corporate limits of the city, then in such case the board of aldermen shall have power to extend it, and, both within and without the corporate limits, to condemn property for the purpose of right-of-way, or other requirements of the system, the proceedings of such condemnation to be the same as those prescribed hereinafter for condemning private property for streets, or as near as may be, in the manner prescribed in chapter forty-nine, volume one, of The Code of eighteen hundred and eighty-three. To purchase, establish and regulate public grounds, including one or more parks, have charge of, improve, adorn and maintain the same, and protect the shade trees of the city. And in order to carry out, execute and enforce the powers hereinbefore given in this section, to borrow money, pledge the faith of the city of Durham, or loan its credit and levy and collect the taxes necessary to pay off and discharge any such debt, principal and interest, with the consent of the majority of the qualified voters of the city, which consent shall be obtained at an election, held after thirty days' public notice, whereat those who shall consent shall vote, "Approved", and those who do not consent shall vote, "Disapproved"; but they shall not borrow any sum of money when the existing aggregate indebtedness of said city equals in amount one-tenth of the aggregate tax value of the property of said city, as shown by its tax books of the preceding year, or exceeds the same, nor any sum which, when added to the aggregate indebtedness of the city then already existing, would render the full amount of the indebtedness of the city larger than one-tenth of the aggregate tax value of the property of the said city, as shown by its tax books for the preceding year; and in any public notice of a proposition to borrow the money so submitted to the votes of the qualified voters of the said city, as above provided, shall be included a statement of the then existing aggregate indebtedness of said

Street improvements.

May recover from owner of lots fronting pavements curbed.

Sewerage.

May extend system outside corporate limits.

Condemnation of land.

Public grounds.

To discharge debts of city.

Consent of voters necessary.

city, other than that hereinafter provided for, and of the aggregate tax value of the property of said city, as shown by the tax books for the preceding year, and for the purposes for which such money is to be borrowed. To establish and regulate a market or markets in the said city, and erect or lease and use a suitable market house, or market houses therefor. To prevent cellars being opened or made under the sidewalks or streets of the city, the deposit of trash boxes or other rubbish or obstructions upon the sidewalks or streets. To regulate the speed of locomotives and trains, and to regulate and prevent fast driving within the city, and also the firing of firearms, fireworks and all explosives or combustibles or dangerous material in the streets, public grounds or elsewhere within or near the city. To provide for the better protection of life, limb, person and property at the crossing of the streets of said city and the railroad tracks now located, or which may be hereafter located, in the city; to require the railroad companies operating said tracks to erect gates or place flagmen to warn the public of the approach of trains and engines. To provide proper and effectual means and regulations to prevent and extinguish fires in said city, and for such purpose to direct the destruction of buildings, for which neither the city, the aldermen or other person shall be responsible in damages. To divide the city into fire districts and prescribe the kind of buildings that may be erected therein. To sell or cause to be sold publicly or privately any property, real or personal, belonging to the city, and direct the mayor, when necessary, to make proper conveyance therefor. To make suitable regulations for the observance of Sunday in said city, and to provide for the enforcement of same. To appoint and regulate city watches. To prevent, suppress and remove nuisances in said city. To regulate the manner in which dogs may be kept in said city. To make such provisions as they may deem necessary to preserve the health of said city, and to take all necessary measures to preserve said city from contagious or infectious diseases, and to declare and enforce quarantine and quarantine regulations therein, with all the rights of entry upon the property and other rights of every character necessary therefor. To establish, regulate and maintain hospitals within the city or five miles thereof. To cause any person in the city or within two miles of its corporate limits suspected to be infected with contagious or infectious diseases, whose presence may endanger its health, to be removed or confined. To remove or destroy any furniture or other articles which may be suspected of being tainted or infected with such disease, and neither the city or any officer or person directing or causing such removal or destruction shall be responsible therefor in damages. To establish

bile notices of oposition to rrow money. at is included.

arkets.

llars.

st driving.

rearms.

otection of e, limb, etc.

ilroad companies required to ect gates.

vision of city to districts.

ty watchers.

isances.

ealth.

spitals.

rsons with contagious diseases y be removed.

and maintain one or more public cemeteries of such size as they may deem necessary within or without the corporate limits of said city, and provide for the care and maintenance of the same and the proper regulation, control and protection thereof. To appoint policemen and other officers to execute such precepts as the mayor and other persons may lawfully issue to them, to preserve order and execute the ordinances of the city, and to appoint and provide for the pay of, and prescribe the duties of all such officers as may be deemed necessary. To make provisions and take all proper measures to preserve the peace and order of the city, and to execute all laws and ordinances thereof. To determine, when necessary, the boundaries of the streets, lots and alleys of the said city, and to establish new streets, lanes and alleys therein, and to make and keep for public inspection and cause to be made and kept, accurate records of said streets, lots, lanes and alleys and their boundaries. To make provisions for licensing and regulating auctioneers and auctions in said city, and provide for the enforcement of same. To provide for licensing, regulating and restraining theatrical and other public amusements within the city, and all bills, posters and advertisements, and to enforce all such provisions. To establish and regulate all necessary inspections within said city, whether of buildings or otherwise, and order and compel the removal of dangerous or defective buildings. To license, regulate and restrain bar-rooms and other places where spirituous liquors are sold within the city. To lay and provide for the collection of all taxes authorized by law to be laid, levied or collected by said city, and enforce the collection of the same. To impose, collect and appropriate fines, penalties and forfeitures for a breach of the ordinances and regulations of the city. To prescribe and regulate the charges for the carriage of person, baggage and freight by omnibus, street car, wagons, drays or other vehicles in the city, and to issue licenses for omnibuses, hacks, drays and other vehicles used therein for the transportation for hire, of persons or things. To protect the hackmen, carriage drivers, keepers of restaurants, boarding houses and hotels from being cheated, defrauded or deprived of just compensation for services rendered, or accommodation furnished, and if necessary for such purposes to make and enact ordinances prescribing fines and penalties. To pass all laws, ordinances and regulations necessary or proper to carry into effect the intent and meaning of this act: Provided, they are not incompatible with the constitution or laws of this state.

Cemeteries.

Appointment of policemen.

Boundaries of streets.

Auctioneers.

Theatricals.

Bar rooms.

Collection of taxes.

Fines and forfeitures.

Hackmen, carriage drivers, etc.

Sec. 35. That the board of aldermen shall, at their first meeting after election, appoint a clerk, a treasurer and a collector of taxes; each of said officers shall respectively hold his office during

Appointment of clerk and treasurer.

ief of fire de rtment and ice.

cers shall e oath.

the official term of the aldermen and until his successor is qualified, subject to be removed, however, and another appointed in his stead, for misbehavior or neglect of the duties of his office; and at such time and meeting the aldermen shall elect a chief of the fire department, a chief of police and one or more policemen or constables, who shall hold office during good behavior and until removed by causes satisfactory to the board of aldermen. Before acting, each of said officers shall be sworn to the faithful discharge of his duty, and shall execute a bond, with justified securities, payable to the city of Durham, in such sum as the aldermen shall determine, conditioned for the faithful performance of the duties of said office.

ary and ties of clerk.

Sec. 36. That the clerk shall have a reasonable salary, and it shall be his duty to keep regular and fair minutes of the proceedings of the board, and to preserve all books, papers and articles committed to his care, during his continuance in office, and deliver the same to his successor and to perform such other duties as may be prescribed by the aldermen.

rnal of board ll be public.

Sec. 37. That any person shall be allowed to inspect the journals and papers of the board in the presence of the clerk, under a penalty of two dollars on the clerk for every refusal, to be paid to him who shall sue for the same.

ary and ties of treas- r.

Sec. 38. That the treasurer shall have a reasonable salary, and it shall be his duty to call on all persons who may have in their hands any money or securities belonging to the city, which ought to be paid or delivered into the treasury, and to safely keep the same for the use of the city; to disburse funds according to such orders as may be duly drawn on him, in the manner hereinafter specified; he shall keep in a book, provided for that purpose, a fair and correct account of all moneys received and disbursed by him, and shall submit said account to the aldermen whenever required to do so. On the expiration of his term of office, he shall deliver to his successor all the moneys, securities and properties entrusted to him for safe keeping, or otherwise, and during his continuance therein, he shall faithfully perform all the duties lawfully imposed upon him as city treasurer.

ers drawn on asurer, how ned.

Sec. 39. That all orders drawn on the treasurer shall be signed by such persons as shall be designated by the aldermen, and state the purpose for which the money is applied, and the treasurer shall specify said purposes in his accounts, and also the sources from whence are derived the moneys received by him.

ties of police- n.

Sec. 40. That it shall be the duty of the policemen to see that the laws, ordinances and orders of the aldermen are enforced, and to report all breaches thereof to the mayor; to preserve the peace of the city by suppressing disturbances and apprehending offenders, and for that purpose they shall have all the power and authority vested in sheriffs and county constables; they shall execute all precepts lawfully directed to them, by mayor or others, and in the execution thereof shall have the same powers which the sheriffs and constables of the county have, and they shall have such fees on all processes and precepts executed or returned by them as may be allowed by the board of aldermen, not to exceed fees allowed the sheriff and constables of the county, for like services, and also such other compensation as the aldermen may allow.

Powers of mayor.

Sec. 41. That the policemen shall have the same powers, and be bound by the same rules in this respect, as the constables of the county of Durham, to apprehend all offenders against the state, within the limits of the city, and to carry them before the mayor or some justice of the peace, and for such duty they shall have such fees as may be allowed by the board of aldermen, not to exceed fees allowed to constables of the county for like duties, to be paid by the party offending, if found guilty.

Duties and powers of tax collector.

Sec. 42. That it shall be the duty of the tax collector to collect the general taxes provided for in this charter, and such special taxes as the collection of is not otherwise provided for herein. For such purpose, he is hereby vested with the same power and authority and subjected to the same fines and penalties as the sheriff or tax collector of Durham county is, or may be by law, and for his service he shall receive such compensation as the aldermen may fix, not to exceed two (2) per centum of the taxes collected. He shall, at no time retain in his hand over three hundred dollars, for a longer time than seven days, under a penalty of ten per centum per month, to the city, upon all sums so retained.

Bond of tax collector.

Before receiving the tax list from the clerk as is provided in this charter, the tax collector shall give bond, payable to the city of Durham, with justified sureties, in such amount as the aldermen may determine: Provided, it shall not be less than ten thousand dollars, nor more than double the amount of taxes for the preceding year.

Failure of tax collector to exhibit tax list a misdemeanor.

Sec. 43. All tax lists which have been or which may hereafter be placed in the hands of the tax collector, shall be at all times subject to the control of the authorities imposing the tax, or their successors in office, shall be exhibited to the authorities for inspection and correction, and if the tax collector fails, or refuses to exhibit his list for such purpose upon such demand, he shall be deemed guilty of a misdemeanor, and upon conviction shall be imprisoned not more than two years, and fined not exceeding five hundred dollars, at the discretion of the court.

Settlement between tax collector and treasurer.

Sec. 44. The board of aldermen, at or before the first meeting in March of each year, shall appoint two or more of their number to be present and assist at the accounting and settlement between the tax collector and the treasurer of the taxes for the preceding year. In such settlement he shall be charged with the sums appearing by the tax lists as due for city taxes, and all special taxes with which he is chargable, and he shall be allowed all credits authorized by the board of aldermen. The accounts when so audited shall be reported to the board of aldermen, and when approved by them shall be recorded in the minute book of said board and shall be prima facie evidence of their correctness, and impeachable only for fraud or specified error.

counts shall reported to ard.

ilure of tax lector to tle.

Sec. 45. In case the tax collector of the city of Durham shall fail, neglect or refuse to account with the city treasurer and assistant committee, as herein required, or pay what may be rightfully found due on such account, on or before the fifteenth day of March of the next succeeding year after the taxes are levied, he shall forfeit and pay to the state, for the use of the city of Durham, a penalty of five hundred dollars. It shall be the duty of the mayor upon the neglect, failure or refusal of said tax collector to account as aforesaid, to cause an action to be brought in the superior court of the county of Durham, on the bond of the said tax collector against him and his sureties, to recover the amount owing by him and the penalty aforesaid; if the tax collector shall fraudulently and corruptly fail to account, as aforesaid, he shall be guilty of a misdemeanor, and upon conviction thereof shall be sentenced to pay a fine in the discretion of the court, or be imprisoned not less than three months nor more than twelve months.

nalty.

cancy in office tax collector.

Sec. 46. If any tax collector shall die during the time appointed for collecting taxes, then his sureties may collect them, and for that purpose shall have all the power and means for collecting the same from the taxpayers as the tax collector would have had, and shall be subject to all the remedies for collection and settlement of taxes on their bonds or otherwise as might have been had against the tax collector if he had lived.

e within ich tax collector shall lect taxes.

Sec. 47. The tax collector (and in case of his death, the sureties) shall have six months and no longer from the day prescribed for his settlement for city taxes, to finish the collection of all taxes, but the extension of time for collection shall not extend his time of settlement of city taxes as aforesaid.

ach of cial bonds.

Sec. 48. That for any breach of his official bond by the city clerk, policemen, tax collector, or any other officers who may be required to give an official bond, he shall be liable in an action on the same, in the name of the city, or any person aggrieved by such breach, and the same may be put in suit without assignment, from time to time, until the whole penalty is recovered.

vy and coltion of taxes.

Sec. 49. In order to raise funds for the current expenses of the city and thereafter for the improvement of the same and the payment of the interest on its bonded debt, and the creation of a fund to meet the principal of that debt when due, the board of aldermen of the city shall, at their first meeting in June, or as soon thereafter as practicable in every year, lay and provide for the collection of the following taxes: (1) On real and personal property within the limits of said city, and all other subjects taxable by the general assembly of the state, as specified and valued under the provisions of law, an ad valorem tax not exceeding one dollar on every hundred dollars of such valuation, as of the first day of June of every year. (2) On all persons residing in said city on the first day of June in every year subject to poll-tax under the laws of the state, a poll-tax not exceeding three dollars each. (3) On every express company, telegraph company, electric light company, water company and power company, doing business and having an office in said city, a license tax not exceeding in amount one per centum of the gross receipts by it, at its office in said city, received during the preceding year up to and including the thirty-first of May next before the date of fixing such license tax. Whenever any company of the character above named shall be operated partly in this state and partly without the state, the above tax shall be upon the gross receipts (at its said office) on the business done within the state, the receipts upon interstate business being prorated in the ratio which the distance within the state bears to the entire distance of transmission or transportation. The manager or agent in charge of the business of any such company in said city on the first day of June in every year, shall, on that day, or if that day be a Sunday or a legal holiday, on the next day thereafter, make to the clerk of the board of aldermen of said city, who shall have power in such case to administer oaths, a written return under oath, signed by him, of the amount of such gross receipts. Any such manager or agent who shall fail or refuse to make such returns on the day whereon the same shall be made, as hereinbefore provided, shall be guilty of a misdemeanor, and on conviction fined not more than fifty dollars or imprisoned not more than thirty days. Every such company, whose manager or agent, as aforesaid, shall fail or refuse to make such returns at the time hereinbefore provided for, or which shall fail to pay the license tax upon its said business, within the time prescribed by the board of aldermen for such payment, shall be guilty of a misdemeanor, and upon conviction, shall be fined one thousand dollars. The amount of such license tax, upon the failure of such agent or manager to make such return as hereinbefore provided, shall be fixed by the said board of aldermen at its next meeting after the day on which such return should be made as hereinbefore provided, or at some other meeting thereafter, by determining the amount of such gross receipts, as nearly as they can ascertain the same, and of

Ad valorem tax.

Poll tax.

Express, telephone and telegraph companies.

Manager of such company shall make return of gross receipts.

Penalty for failure to make return.

such amount so determined, which, for such purpose, shall be taken and deemed to be the amount of such gross receipts, taking one per centum thereof as such license tax. (4) In addition to the other subjects listed for taxation in said city, the board of aldermen thereof may lay and cause to be collected taxes on the following subjects, as a license tax for the privilege of carrying on the business or doing the act named, respectively, the amount of which, when laid, shall be collected by the chief of police of said city immediately, and if the same be not paid on demand, they may be recovered by suit or seizure, or sale of the articles on which they are severally imposed, or of any property used in carrying on such business, or of any other property of the owner in said county of Durham, in the same manner as in [is] hereinafter provided for the sale of personal property by the tax collector for ad valorem taxes: (1) Upon every leaf tobacco dealer, a tax not exceeding twenty-five dollars a year. (2) Upon commission merchants, auctioneers or brokers, a tax not exceeding one hundred dollars a year. (3) Upon every stock or bond broker, or upon every person, firm or corporation keeping an office in said city, where margins are bought or sold, or stock market transactions engaged in, a tax not exceeding five hundred dollars a year. (4) Upon every omnibus used for the carriage of persons for hire, a tax not exceeding twenty dollars a year; and upon every hack, carriage or other vehicles used for the transportation of freight or other articles of hire, a tax not exceeding fifteen dollars a year; and a discrimination may be made between one- and two-horse vehicles in the tax: Provided, however, a distinction may be made between residents and non-residents of the city operating such vehicles or conveyances. (5) Upon every keeper of livery, livery or sales stables or stock yard, a tax not exceeding twenty-five dollars: Provided, a distinction may be made between resident and non-resident keepers of such. (6) Upon all dogs kept in the city, and which are so kept on the first day of June, a tax not exceeding three dollars a year: Provided, a discrimination may be made in the sexes of the dogs in the tax. (7) Upon every transient merchant, trader or street peddler offering to vend in the city, a tax not exceeding one hundred dollars a year, or twelve dollars a month, except only as sell books, charts or maps. (8) Upon every public billiard table, shooting gallery, bowling alley, or alley of like kind, skating rink, bagatelle table, or table, stand or place for any other game or play, with or without a name, kept for hire or kept in a place where liquor is sold, or a house used or connected with such house, or a hotel or restaurant, a tax not exceeding one hundred dollars a year nor less than fifteen dollars a year. (9) Upon every hotel, boarding house, victualing house or restaurant, established, opened or kept in the city, a tax not exceeding fifty dollars a year. (10) Upon every per-

af tobacco lers.

nmission rchants. okers.

ery stables.

rs.

nsient merchants.

liard tables.

tels and rding houses,

mission or license of the board to wholesale or retail spirituous, vinous or malt liquors, a tax not exceeding five hundred dollars a year, to be paid annually, semi-annually or quarterly, as the board shall determine: Provided, the board of aldermen may make a distinction between wholesale and retail dealers, or spirituous, vinous or malt liquors. (11) On every exhibition or a circus or menagerie within the city, or two miles thereof, one hundred dollars for each separate exhibition, and on each side show, twenty-five dollars, to be paid before the exhibition, or if not paid then, the same to be doubled. (12) Upon every dog or pony show or exhibition, within the city or a mile thereof, a license tax not exceeding twenty dollars. (13) Upon every hall, building or place hired, leased or let for theatrical plays, operas or other stage exhibition of any kind, a tax not exceeding two hundred and fifty dollars a year. (14) Upon every exhibition within the city, of stage or theatrical plays, sleight-of-hand performances, rope-dancing or walking, a tax not exceeding twenty-five dollars, to be paid before exhibiting, or the same to be doubled: Provided, this section shall not apply where such exhibition or performance is given in a hall or building or place licensed under this charter. (15) Upon each exhibition, for reward, of waxworks or curiosities of any kind, natural or artificial, a tax not exceeding ten dollars. (16) Upon each exhibition of any other kind, and on each concert, for reward, and on every strolling musician, a tax of five dollars, except when the exhibition or concert is given for charitable or benevolent purposes, or to aid in any public improvement or enterprise of the city. (17) Upon every manufacturer, dealer in, or agent for sewing machines or musical instruments, a tax not exceeding fifty dollars a year. (18) Upon every street huckster, photographer, merchandise or produce broker, a tax not exceeding twenty-five dollars a year. (19) Upon every itinerant dentist, itinerant medical practitioner, optician, portrait or miniature painter, daguerrean artist, photographer, and every other person taking likenesses of the human face, a tax of five dollars a month: Provided, license shall not be granted or issued for less period than one month. (20) Upon every itinerant person or company peddling lightning rods, stoves or ranges, a tax of fifty dollars a month on each wagon (if wagons are used); if wagons are not used, the tax shall be paid for each agent: Provided, license shall not be granted or issued for less period than one month. (21) Upon every bill-poster, a tax of not more than ten dollars per annum: Provided, the aldermen may authorize license for less time or period than one year. (22) Upon every horse drover selling horses, a tax not exceeding fifty dollars a month. (23) On banks, banking business or bank agents, a tax not exceeding one hundred dollars a year. (24) On dealers in fertilizers and agents for the

Bar-rooms.

Proviso.

Circuses.

Dog or pony shows.

Opera houses.

Sleight-of-hand performances, etc.

Proviso.

Exhibitions for reward.

Other exhibitions.

Sewing machine agents.

Hucksters.

Itinerant dentists.

Itinerant lightning-rod dealers.

Bill-posters.

Horse drovers.

Banks.

Dealers in fertilizers.

sale thereof, a tax not exceeding twenty-five dollars. (25) On every lumber dealer or dealer in bricks or other building materials, or manufacturers thereof, or agents thereof, not exceeding twenty dollars for every yard, warehouse, office or place of business. (26) On every person, firm or company selling pistols, bowie knives, dirks, slung-shots, brass or metallic knuckles, or other deadly weapons of like character, in addition to all other taxes, a license tax not exceeding fifty dollars a year. (27) On any other business, trade, occupation, calling or profession engaged in, carried on, in whole or in part, in, or having a place of business in the corporate limits of said city not otherwise herein taxed or authorized to be taxed, a privilege tax to be fixed by the board of aldermen.

alers in pistols,

her businesses.

rsons engaging business without paying tax, ilty of a misdemeanor.

Sec. 50. Every person, clerk or agent who shall practice any trade or profession, or use any franchise, or engage in any business taxed by the board of aldermen of the city of Durham, under this charter, without having paid the tax, and having obtained the license required, shall be deemed guilty of a misdemeanor, and shall be fined not exceeding fifty dollars or imprisoned not more than thirty days, for each offense, and for each day this section is violated such person, clerk or agent shall be guilty of a separate offense.

rsons liable to xation shall ake return der oath.

Sec. 51. That the citizens of the city of Durham, and others having property or polls, liable to be taxed on account of any of the foregoing subjects, shall, during the time for listing their state and county taxes, render to such persons as may be designated by the aldermen of the city, on oath a list of their property and subjects for which they may be liable to be taxed, together with the value thereof as fixed in the list returned for county taxation, and from said lists, or such list as may be revised by the board of equalization, the clerk of the board of aldermen shall, within sixty days after the expiration of the time for taking such lists, make out, in a book kept or provided for that purpose, an alphabetical list of all persons, companies and owners of property who have so made their returns in the same manner as the tax lists are made out by law for the state and county taxes, and if any person fail to render such list, he shall pay double the tax on any subject for which he is liable to be taxed.

erk shall make t alphabetical t of tax returns.

ppointment of ard of equalition.

Sec. 52. Whenever, in their opinion, it may be advisable, in order to secure uniform valuation of property subject to taxation under this charter, the board of aldermen shall appoint three or more residents of the city to constitute a board of equalization, whose duties, compensation and length of service shall be prescribed by said board of aldermen.

hen taxes all be levied.

Sec. 53. That on or before the first day of August of each year, the board of aldermen shall proceed to lay the taxes on such subjects of taxation as are allowed by law, and shall, immediately after the approval of the same, cause to be made a copy of so much and such parts of said tax list as may be required for the use of the tax collector in collecting the taxes of the city; the said copy shall be delivered to the tax collector on or before the first Monday in September, in each year, and he shall receipt for the same. The clerk of the board of aldermen shall endorse on said copy an order to the said tax collector to collect the taxes therein mentioned, and such order shall have the force and effect of a judgment and execution against the real and personal property of the persons charged in said copy respectively. The said tax collector shall proceed forthwith in the collection, and shall complete the same on or before the tenth day of March next ensuing, and shall pay the moneys as they are collected to the treasurer.

Order shall have force of judgment against real and personal property.

When collector shall complete collections

Sec. 54. That if any person liable to taxes on subjects directed to be listed shall fail to pay them within the time prescribed for collection, the collector shall proceed forthwith to collect the same by distress and sale, after public advertisement, for the space of ten days in some newspaper published in the city, or at three public places, if the property be personalty, and twenty, if the property be realty. Whenever any taxes in said city shall be due and unpaid, the tax collector therefor shall proceed to collect the same as follows: (1) If any person charged have personal property anywhere in the county of Durham, of value as great as the tax charged against him or against his property, the said tax collector shall seize and sell the same as the sheriff is required to sell personal property under execution. (2) If the person charged have not personal property to be found in said county of Durham, of value as great as the tax charged against him, or against his property, said tax collector shall levy upon the lands of the delinquent in the said county of Durham, or any part of such lands, and, after due advertisement, sell the same for the payment of said taxes. Such advertisement shall be made in some newspaper published in said county of Durham, for at least twenty days immediately preceding the sale, and posting a notice of such sale at the court-house door in the city at least twenty days before such sale, which shall contain at least a concise description of the real estate to be sold, the name of the person who appears upon the tax list as owner thereof, the amount of taxes for which said sale is to be made, and the day and place of such sale; the said tax collector shall divide the land into as many parts as may be convenient (for which purpose he is authorized to employ a surveyor), and shall sell as many thereof as may be required to pay said taxes and all expenses attendant thereon. If the same can not be conveniently divided, the collector shall

Persons liable and failing to return taxes.

sell the whole; and if no person shall pay the whole of the taxes and expenses for the whole land, the same shall be struck off to the city, and if not redeemed, as hereinafter provided, shall belong to said city in fee.

al estate sold taxes may be eemed.

Sec. 55. The owner of any real estate, or interest therein, sold as aforesaid, his heirs, executors, administrators or assigns, may redeem the same within one year after the sale, upon the same terms and conditions, and subject to the same provisos, and in the same manner, as are prescribed by the law for the redemption of real estate sold for state and county taxes, except that all the duties, functions and powers provided in such law to be discharged and exercised by the sheriff or tax collector shall be discharged and exercised by the tax collector of the city.

llector shall ecute certifie to purchaser.

Sec. 56. On any such sale of real estate, said tax collector shall execute to the purchaser a certificate similar to that required or allowed by law to be executed upon the sale of real estate for state and county taxes, which may be assigned or transferred by the purchaser, whether an individual or said city, as such last mentioned certificates are allowed by law to be assigned or transferred; and if the real estate sold as aforesaid shall not be redeemed as hereinbefore provided, said tax collector or his successor in office, under the direction of the said board of aldermen, at any time within one year after the expiration of one year, from the date of the sale, on request of the holder of such certificate and production of the same, shall execute to the purchaser, his heirs and assigns, a deed in fee simple for the conveyance of the real estate described in such certificate, and if such certificate shall have been lost, said board of aldermen, on being satisfied thereof, by due proof, shall direct the said tax collector to execute such conveyance, and said tax collector shall so execute the same. Any such deed shall be similar in form to the deed directed by law to be executed to a purchaser of real estate sold for state and county taxes, who is entitled to a conveyance of the same, and shall be subject to the same rules, provisions, presumptions and conclusions as such last mentioned deed, and effective to the same extent as the last mentioned deed.

real estate not redeemed thin a year, rchaser shall ve a deed in simple.

ch sale all not be alid because tered in other me.

Sec. 57. No such sale of real estate for taxes shall be considered invalid on account of the same having been charged in any other name than that of the original owner of said real estate, provided such real estate be in other respects sufficiently described in notice of sale to insure identification.

xes, how listed d levied.

Sec. 58. All taxes of said city shall be listed, levied, assessed and collected, except as in this charter otherwise provided, in the same manner and under the same rules and regulations, and subject to the same penalties as are provided by law, or shall hereafter be provided by law, for the listing, levying, assessing and collecting state and county taxes in this state.

Sec. 59. When any lien or charges for repairs or improvements of the sidewalks of the city, or for the inspection, removal or destruction of buildings, and for the suppression and removal of nuisances, or other lien or charges of whatever nature or kind, authorized by the city charter, shall be due and unpaid the city, the tax collector thereof shall proceed to collect the same, by the same process and in the same manner as he is authorized to collect taxes due upon the property subject to such lien or charge, as provided in section fifty-four of the charter. Liens for improvement of sidewalks.

Sec. 60. That in the absence of any contract or contracts with said city in relation to the lands used or occupied by it for the purpose of streets, sidewalks, alleys or other public works of said city, signed by the owner thereof, or his agent, it shall be presumed that the said land has been granted to said city by the owner or owners thereof, and said city shall have good right and title thereto, and shall have, hold and enjoy the same as long as the same shall be used for the purpose of the said city, and no longer. Unless the owner or owners of said land, or those claiming under them shall, at the time of the occupation of the said land, as aforesaid, apply for an assessment of said land, as provided for in the charter of said city, within two years next after said land was taken, he or they shall be forever barred from recovering said land, or having any assessment or compensation therefor: Provided, nothing herein contained shall effect [affect] the rights of feme coverts or infants until two years after the removal of their respective disabilities. In absence of contract with city in relation to lands used by it. Proviso. Certain rights not affected

Sec. 61. That when any land or right-of-way shall be required by the city of Durham for the purpose of opening up new streets or for other objects allowed by this charter, and for want of agreement as to the value thereof the same can not be purchased by owners, the same may be taken at a valuation to be made by five freeholders of the city, three of whom shall be chosen by the aldermen and two by the land owner, and in making said valuation, said freeholders, or a majority of them, after being duly sworn by the mayor or a justice of the peace for the county, or a clerk of the court of record, shall take into consideration the loss or damage which may accrue to the owner or owners in consequence of the land or right-of-way being surrendered; also any special benefit or advantage such owner may receive from the opening of such street or other improvement, and shall state the value and amount of each, and the excess of loss or damage over and above the advantages shall form the measure of valuation of said land or right of way: Provided, nevertheless, that if any person over whose land the said street may Land necessary to town may be condemned. Assessors chosen. Proviso.

pass, or improvement be erected, or the aldermen be dissatisfied with the valuation thus made, then, in that case, either party may have an appeal to the next superior court of Durham county, to be held thereafter, under the same rules, regulations and restrictions as now govern appeals from judgments of justices of the peace, and the said freeholders, or a majority of them, shall return to the court to which the appeal is taken their valuation, with proceedings thereon, and the land so valued by the freeholders shall vest in the city as soon as the valuation may be paid or lodged in the hand of the clerk of the superior court, in case of its refusal by the owner of the land, and so long as it may be used for the purposes of the same: Provided, however, that such an appeal shall not hinder nor delay the aldermen opening such streets or erecting such improvements: And provided further, that in case of the discontinuance of the use of the land and it reverts to the owner, the city shall have the right to recover any improvement by its authority erected.

ther party may peal.

oviso.

dermen shall t be delayed in ening streets,

mmissioners Durham unty shall not ant liquor ense without rmission of ermen.

Sec. 62. That it shall not be lawful for the commissioners of Durham county to grant any license to sell, by wholesale or retail, spirituous, vinous or malt liquors within the limits of the city or within one mile thereof, without permission first obtained from the board of aldermen in office at the time of the application to the county commissioners; and if any license shall be granted without such permission in writing, attested by the clerk of the board and exhibited to the court and filed with the clerk of the board of county commissioners, the same shall be utterly void, and the person obtaining such license shall be liable to indictment, as in other cases of retailing without license, and for every offense of selling, shall, moreover, forfeit and pay to the city the sum of one hundred dollars. That it shall not be lawful for any person to sell spirituous liquors within the corporation or in one mile thereof without first having obtained license and paid tax in accordance with this section.

ilure of cers to turn er books, etc., successors a isdemeanor.

Sec. 63. The mayor and aldermen, tax collector and all other officers of the city who shall, on demand, fail to turn over to their successors in office the property, books, moneys, scales or effects of the city, shall be deemed guilty of a misdemeanor, and upon conviction shall be imprisoned for not more than two years and fined not exceeding five hundred dollars, at the discretion of the court.

nes, how plied.

Sec. 64. That all fines and penalties collected for violation of this charter or the ordinances made in pursuance thereof shall go into the city treasury and belong to the city of Durham.

person shall ld more than e office.

Sec. 65. That on and after May the fifteenth, one thousand eight hundred and ninety-nine, no person shall hold more than one office in the municipal government, and a member of the school committee of the city of Durham is hereby declared to be an officer of the city, for the purposes of this section.

Sec. 66. That all laws and parts of laws in conflict with this act are hereby repealed: Provided, nothing contained in this act shall be construed as altering or changing the term of office of any persons elected on the first Monday in May, eighteen hundred and ninety-seven, and the several persons elected at that time as the officers of the town of Durham shall continue in their respective offices as officers of the city of Durham until the election and qualification of their successor, under this charter. Conflicting laws repealed.

Sec. 67. That it shall be the duty of the board of aldermen, on the first days of July, October, January and April of each year, to publish, at the court-house door of Durham county and in some newspaper published in the city of Durham, an itemized statement of the receipts and disbursements of said city, from each and every source, and said board of aldermen shall annex to said July and January quarterly statements, a statement of the total indebtedness of said city, how evidenced and when due. Annual statement of receipts and disbursements shall be made.

Sec. 68. That this act shall be in full force and effect from and after its ratification.

Ratified the 6th day of March, A. D. 1899.

CHAPTER 236.

An act to amend the charter of the city of Asheville.

The General Assembly of North Carolina do enact:

Section 1. That subsection four of section forty-two of chapter three hundred and fifty-two of the private laws of eighteen hundred and ninety-five be and the same is hereby amended by striking out the first line of said subsection and the second line down to and including the word "annum" in said second line and inserting in lieu thereof the following words: "On every omnibus carrying persons for hire, and on every street hack or carriage being on the street of said city at any place other than the passenger depot for the purpose of obtaining business, a license tax not exceeding fifteen dollars per annum." Subsection 4, section 42, chapter 352, private laws of 1895, amended.

Sec. 2. That said subsection four be and the same is hereby further amended by inserting between the word "every" and the word "hack" in the second line of said subsection four the word "other." Further amended.

Sec. 3. That this act shall be in force from and after its ratification.

Ratified the 6th day of March, A. D. 1899.

CHAPTER 237.

An act to incorporate the Yadkin Power Company.

The General Assembly of North Carolina do enact:

rporators. Section 1. That John A. Ramsay, F. E. Boardman, M. A. M. Armstrong, J. Lee Maxwell, together with all other persons and corporations who shall be associated with them and become stockholders in the corporation hereby incorporated, their successors and assigns, be and they are hereby created and constituted a body politic and corporate by and under the name and title of the Yadkin Power Company, by which name the said corporation may sue and be sued, plead and be impleaded, appear, prosecute and defend in any courts whatsoever all suits and actions; may contract and be contracted with, and shall have all privileges hereby specially granted, and such others as may be necessary for the free enjoyment of the same, and said corporation shall continue for sixty years.

dy corporate. rporate name rporate powers.

rporate rights d powers. Sec. 2. That the said corporation shall enjoy all the rights and privileges, liberties and franchises and powers conferred upon and pertaining to other corporations or corporate bodies and not forbidden by the laws of the United States and of North Carolina.

l. Sec. 3. That the corporation shall have the right to make a common seal and alter the same at pleasure.

ture of business to be conducted. Sec. 4. That the corporation is hereby authorized and empowered to conduct, transact and carry on in all its branches the manufacture of any kind of material they so choose, either woodworking, cloth or any textile industry they may see fit, either of iron, wood, leather or any material, and sell its merchandise at will or pleasure, or may create, maintain or lease any flouring mill, sawmills or any kind of mills or buildings, machine shops or private dwellings and other business premises, and may maintain them as may be necessary to carry on its business.

ay acquire ds, etc. Sec. 5. The said corporation, its successors or assigns, is hereby authorized and empowered to buy or own, lease or deal in or otherwise acquire lands, tenements, hereditaments and all manner of real and personal property, including cotton mills, factories, houses, water powers, mineral rights, roads, bridges and railroads and tramways, and other kind of personal property or real property whatsoever to such an extent as may seem proper, and as fully as citizens of the state may do, and may sell and convey or lease the same to other persons or corporations, and said corporation is authorized to pay for such real estate and personal property as it may purchase or otherwise acquire with and by its capital stock, and may issue bonds and execute mortgages to secure the payment thereof. It may also subscribe to the stock of any other corporation. May subscribe to stock of other corporations.

Sec. 6. That the said corporation shall have the right and authority to build, erect and maintain any dam or dams across the channels of the Yadkin river at or near Mott's Falls, between the counties of Rowan, Davidson, Stanly and Montgomery, in the state of North Carolina or any other place on the Yadkin river and its tributaries for the purpose of utilizing water power, and may also build, construct, maintain and operate canals, bridges, aqueducts, waterways, waste ways, wells and reservoirs as shall be needful for its mills and manufactories, water systems, power plants or other works or for any other purpose found necessary or expedient. It shall have the right to lay water mains for the purpose of supplying water to any town, village or city in the state; to construct, maintain and operate, either above or underground, suitable wires, conductors or tubes for the conducting or transmitting electricity to any city or town or village within the state for the purpose of lighting such city or towns or for other purposes, such as heating or any use that electricity may be put to, and for the purpose of constructing railways. The said corporation when unable to purchase at an agreed price may enter upon and condemn private property for right-of-way and for necessary plants and stations by paying a reasonable price therefor, and in case such price can not be agreed upon the said corporation may have the same condemned as is provided under the general law for the condemnation of private property for said road purposes. Empowered to build dams. Empowered to lay water mains. May condemn land when necessary.

Sec. 7. That said corporation shall have the right, power and authority, as soon as they deem practicable, [to] proceed to locate the works of the said company, and may change the said location from time to time if they consider it expedient to do so; also to construct and maintain and equip with rolling stock and railroads or tramways, plank roads or turnpikes; to operate vehicles, by electricity, water moters or compressed air on any or all roads, and also maintain [and] operate such telegraph or telephone poles or lines and apparatus as may be necessary, and shall likewise have the right, power, franchise, to charge such tolls, fares or fees or compensations as is reasonable for the use service or travel over such roads, turnpikes or bridges, canals, telegraph or telephone lines as it may erect, construct or operate. May locate works as soon as deemed practicable.

Sec. 8. That the capital stock of this company shall not be less than twenty-five thousand dollars ($25,000), but the said corporation shall have authority to organize and transact business whenever the sum of twenty-five thousand dollars of its capital stock shall have been subscribed and five per centum thereof paid either in money or property, which corporation is authorized to Capital stock. When company may be organized.

hold. The said corporation may issue bonds, stock, both common and preferred, with such regulation as to the issue thereof as may be prescribed by a majority of the stockholders. The stockholders, by a two-thirds vote at any election, may increase the capitalization to any amount as they may see fit, but not to exceed one million dollars. The certificates of shares shall be issued in the said corporation only when the same are paid for the par value of the stock to be one hundred dollars each, and said shares shall not be liable thereafter for any assessment for any purpose whatsoever. The said company's shares shall be deemed personal property and be transferable upon the books of the company in the method provided for in its by-laws. But no shares shall be transferred until all previous calls thereon shall have been fully paid or declared forfeited for non-payment of calls thereon.

ck may be reased.

Sec. 9. That the directors and stockholders and incorporators, their successors or assigns, shall not be individually or personally liable or responsible for the acts, debts liabilities, contracts, engagements, defaults, commission or torts of the corporation, or for any claim, payment, loss, injury, transaction, matter or thing whatsoever related to or connected with the company, and no stockholder shall be liable to pay for more than he subscribed for.

lividual bility.

Sec. 10. That the principal place of doing business of the said company shall be in Salisbury, N. C., but said corporation shall have the privilege of holding its meetings at any place as the board of directors may designate.

incipal place business.

Sec. 11. That all property of the company shall be liable for taxes under the general law of North Carolina.

perty of comy liable for es.

Sec. 12. That the affairs of the company shall be managed by a president, vice-president and a board of directors, and persons named in the first selection are constituted provisional directors of the corporation, of which majority shall constitute a quorum, and they shall hold office as such directors until the first election of directors under the provision of this act, and shall have power forthwith to open stock books and procure subscriptions of stock to said corporation as soon as shares to the amount of twenty-five thousand dollars shall be subscribed. Any one or more of the directors may call a meeting of the subscribers at Salisbury, North Carolina, for the purpose of organizing the corporation, electing directors, etc., etc., giving at least five days' notice in writing to the subscribers of the time and place and purpose of the meeting of directors. At such meeting the shareholders may choose not more than seven nor less than three persons from among the shareholders as directors of the company, three of whom shall always constitute a quorum. The directors shall annually be elected by ballot at regular meetings of the stock-

airs of com y, how man- d.

rm of office.

lled meetings.

holders and shall act under such by-laws and regulations as the corporation may from time to time adopt; and shall hold office until their successors are elected. Thereafter the regular meetings of the stockholders for the election of directors and other general purposes shall be held once in each and every year in such place and on such day and upon such notice as the by-laws may direct. All vacancies in the board of directors shall be filled by officers of the company. The capital stock of said corporation shall be divided into shares of one hundred dollars each, and at all meetings the stockholders shall be entitled to as many votes as he owns shares of the stock of the corporation to be cast in person or by proxy, and at all meetings any shares represented by proxies shall be dated for the said annual meeting or any meeting of the corporation within one year from date, and not to be held over from time to time or voted upon after being used at any previous annual meeting. The majority of the stock shall constitute a quorum. The stockholders of the corporation shall have full powers to make all by-laws, rules, regulations not provided by law for the government of the affairs of the company, for meetings, calls upon stock subscribed, and for the enforcements of such calls, by forfeitures of stock or otherwise.

Annual elections shall be held.

Vacancies arising.

Sec. 13. That the board of directors at their first meeting and annually thereafter shall elect from among their number a president and vice-president. They shall also elect a secretary and treasurer, and shall have the right to name his salary and term of office, and may require of him a satisfactory bond. The failure to elect directors shall not dissolve the corporation. That this act shall be deemed and taken as a public act, and a copy of any by-laws or regulations of the corporation under its corporate seal and purporting to be signed by the president and vice-president shall be received as a prima facie evidence for or against the corporation in any judicial proceeding.

Election of officers.

Failure to elect directors shall not dissolve the company.

Ratified the 6th day of March, A. D. 1899.

CHAPTER 238.

An act to authorize J. T. Benbow to reinter certain dead bodies.

The General Assembly of North Carolina do enact:

Section 1. That J. T. Benbow be authorized and empowered to remove certain dead bodies now buried in his field, in Yadkin county, and to properly and decently reinter the said bodies in the cemetery of the Baptist church in the town of East Bend, in said county of Yadkin.

J. T Benbow authorized to remove certain dead bodies.

Sec. 2. That this act shall be in force from and after its ratification.

Ratified the 6th day of March, A. D. 1899.

CHAPTER 239.

An act to amend the charter of the city of Asheville.

The General Assembly of North Carolina do enact:

ennial election mayor.

Section 1. That there shall be elected by the qualified voters of the city of Asheville on the first Monday in May, eighteen hundred and ninety-nine, and every two years thereafter, on the first Monday in May, a mayor for said city, who shall be a resident and qualified voter thereof, and whose duties, when elected and qualified, shall be the same as those now prescribed by law and such as may hereafter be prescribed by law for mayor of said city, and who shall hold his said office for the term of two years from and after his election and until his successor shall be duly elected and qualified.

ection of ermen.

Sec. 2. That there shall be elected by the qualified voters of the said city of Asheville on the first Monday in May, eighteen hundred and ninety-nine, and every four years thereafter on the first Monday in May, three aldermen for said city, who shall be residents and qualified voters thereof, and whose duties shall be the same as those now prescribed by law, and such as may be hereafter prescribed by law for aldermen for said city, one of whom shall be elected without regard to the ward of said city in which he may reside, and shall be known as alderman at large, and one of whom shall be at the time of his election a resident and qualified voter of ward one; and the other shall be at the time of his election a resident and qualified voter of ward three of said city; and each of said aldermen shall hold his said office for four years from and after his election and until his successor shall be duly elected and qualified.

ties of alder- n.

rm of office.

ction of alder- n at large.

Sec. 3. That there shall be elected by the qualified voters of said city on the first Monday in May of the year nineteen hundred and one, and every four years thereafter on the first Monday in May, three aldermen for said city, who shall be residents and qualified voters thereof, and whose duties shall be the same as those now prescribed by law and such as may hereafter be prescribed by law for aldermen of said city, one of whom shall be elected without regard to the ward of said city in which he may reside, and shall be known as alderman at large, and one of whom shall be at the time of his election a resident and qualified voter of ward two; and the other shall be at the time of his election a resident and qualified voter of ward four of said city, and each of said aldermen shall hold his said office for four years from and after his election and until his successor shall be duly elected and qualified.

m of office.

Sec. 4. That the aldermen of said city elected on the first Monday in May, eighteen hundred and ninety-eight, and now holding office therein, and such alderman or aldermen as have been or may hereafter be elected by the board of aldermen of said city to fill any vacancy or vacancies caused by the death or resignation or removal of any alderman or aldermen elected on the said first Monday in May, eighteen hundred and ninety-eight, shall continue to hold their said offices respectively until the first Monday in May of the year nineteen hundred and one and until their respective successors shall be duly elected and qualified.

Vacancies occurring on board of aldermen.

Sec. 5. That there shall also be elected for the city of Asheville by the qualified voters of said city, under the rules and regulations as now provided by law or such as may hereafter be provided by law for the election of a mayor for said city on the first Monday in May, eighteen hundred and ninety-nine, and every two years thereafter, on the first Monday in May, a "chief of police," a "tax collector," a "treasurer," a "city clerk" a "supeintendent of waterworks" and a "police justice," who shall be citizens and qualified voters of said city and whose respective duties shall be the same as now are prescribed by law and such as may hereafter be prescribed by law for said officers respectively, and said officers shall hold their respective offices for the term of two years from and after their election and qualification and until their respective successors are duly elected and qualified.

Election of other city officers.

Sec. 6. That in case a vacancy shall occur in any of the offices mentioned in the preceding sections of this act, by death, resignation or otherwise, the board of aldermen of said city shall elect some resident and qualified voter of said city, possessing the qualifications herein required for the office in which such vacancy may occur, to fill such vacancy, who shall hold the office to which he is appointed until the next regular election for said city, when some resident and qualified voter of said city, possessing the qualifications herein required, shall be elected to fill the unexpired term, in case such term shall not already have expired, or to fill said office.

Vacancies occurring in city offices.

Term of office of successor.

Sec. 7. That the mayor and aldermen and other officers elected in said city and now holding office therein as such, whose terms have not expired, shall hold their said respective offices until their said terms shall have respectively terminated and as hereinbefore provided.

Present officers shall hold office until term expires.

Sec. 8. That sections five, six, seven and eight of chapter three hundred and fifty-two of the private laws of eighteen hundred and ninety-five, entitled "An act to amend, revise and consolidate the charter of the city of Asheville," and section seventeen of chapter one hundred and nine, and section three of chapter

Sections 5, 6, 7 and 8, chapter 352, private laws of 1895, repealed.

one hundred and sixty-three of the laws of eighteen hundred and ninety-seven, be and the same are hereby repealed.

tions 4, 5, 6, 7, 10, 11, 12, 13 1 16, chapter private laws 1897, repealed.

Sec. 9. That sections four, five, six, seven, eight, nine, ten, eleven, twelve. thirteen and sixteen of chapter one hundred and sixty-three of the private laws of the year eighteen hundred and ninety-seven be and the same are hereby repealed.

ctions here- er held, how ducted.

Sec. 10. That the elections hereinbefore provided for shall be held under the same rules and regulations as are now prescribed or may hereafter be prescribed for the election of members of the general assembly, but the powers and duties in such rules and regulations conferred upon and directed to be exercised by the sheriff are hereby conferred upon and directed to be exercised in said elections by the chief of police of said city, and the power and duties in said rules and regulations conferred upon and directed to be exercised by any other officer or officers, body or bodies, board or boards, or his, their or its appointees or employees respectively, are hereby conferred upon and directed to be exercised by the board of aldermen of said city or its employees or appointees respectively in said elections. Every citizen residing within the corporate limits of said city who is qualified to vote for members of the general assembly, and who shall have resided in said city for ninety days and in the precinct in which he offers to vote for fifteen days preceding any such election, immediately, shall be entitled to vote at such election, upon compliance with the law regarding the registration of votes thereat. And the board of aldermen of said city are hereby authorized and empowered in its discretion to order and require a new registration of all the voters of said city whenever it may see fit, such new registration to be conducted in the same manner and under the same rules and regulations as are now prescribed or may hereafter be prescribed for the registration of voters at elections of members of the general assembly. Each elector shall vote one ballot, on which shall be placed the names and offices of the persons voted for, either written or printed. At any such election the person who shall receive the highest number of votes for any office allowed to be voted for at such election shall be declared elected to that office. At the conclusion of any election the judges thereof shall ascertain and declare the result, and the chief of police of said city shall immediately, in person or by deputy, proclaim such result at the front door of the city hall of said city, and thirty-six hours thereafter such judges shall certify to the mayor of the said city such result in writing signed by them, which writing shall be filed by the mayor in his office. If at any such election any two or more persons receive an equal number of votes for the same office and no other person shall receive as great a number of votes for such office, the judges of election shall

(Margin notes: alified voters. — llots. — dges shall ertain and lare result election.)

decide who of those receiving such equal votes is elected to such office.

Other elections in city conducted in same manner.

SEC. 11. Every other election in said city for municipal purposes shall be held and conducted in the same manner and under the same rules and regulations as are above prescribed for election for mayor and aldermen in so far as the same are applicable.

Section 15, chapter 163, private laws of 1897, amended.

SEC. 12. That section fifteen of the said chapter one hundred and sixty-three of the private laws of eighteen hundred and ninety-seven be amended by striking out all of said section after the word "follows" in the seventh line thereof and inserting in lieu thereof the following: To appoint a marshal or marshals for said city, and all policemen and other officers therefor which they may deem proper, whose elections are not otherwise provided for by law, to execute such precepts as may lawfully issue to them, and to preserve the peace and good order of said city.

Section 19, chapter 163, private laws of 1897, amended.

SEC. 13. That section nineteen of said chapter one hundred and sixty-three of the private laws of the year eighteen hundred and ninety-seven be amended by striking out the word "four" in the ninth line from the bottom of said page three hundred and thirty-nine of said private laws of eighteen hundred and ninety-seven and inserting in lieu thereof the word "two."

Section 38, said chapter, amended.

SEC. 14. That section thirty-eight of chapter one hundred and sixty-three of the "private laws of eighteen hundred and ninety-seven" be and the same is hereby amended by adding thereto the following: But said school committee shall not be required to use said school funds for the purpose of erecting new school buildings, making additions to the ones now owned by said city or furnishing said school buildings with heating apparatus or making any other permanent improvements of like kind and nature to said school property beyond the ordinary wear and tear of the same, nor for paying fire insurance on said school property, but such new buildings, additions, improvements and insurance shall be provided by the said board of aldermen out of the general funds of said city, or otherwise, as said board shall determine.

Grading and paving of streets.

SEC. 15. That the mayor and board of aldermen of the city of Asheville shall have full power and authority, and it is hereby made their duty to grade, pave, macadamize and otherwise improve for travel and drainage the streets and public squares and alleys of said city, and put down crossings, curbings and cross drains, and otherwise properly improve them, and that the said mayor and board of aldermen shall begin the said work at once and prosecute the same as vigorously as practicable under the provisions of the charter of the said city.

SEC. 16. That in order to more fully carry out the duty imposed

ner of prop-y fronting ewalks shall assessed.

by section fifteen of this act, the said mayor and board of aldermen shall assess two-thirds of the cost of the grading, paving, macadamizing, constructing cross drains, side drains and all other necessary drains and crossings or otherwise improving said roadways or streets proper on the real estate abutting on the street, public square, alley or roadway or portion thereof so improved or repaired, assessing one third of the cost of such improvements on the real estate abutting on each side of the street or part thereof so improved or repaired: Provided, that whenever any such street, public alley or roadway or the part thereof so proposed to be graded, paved, macadamized or otherwise impoved, lies as much as one thousand feet from the point where the electric light tower on Court square in said city now stands, the said mayor and board of aldermen shall not be authorized to pave, macadamize or otherwise improve the same by virtue of this act, or to levy assessments upon the property abutting on such streets or alleys or the parts thereof so paved. macadamized or improved lying outside of the said radius as in this act set forth, until and unless the persons owning land abutting on such street or alley or the portion thereof proposed to be improved which has more than one-half of the frontage abutting on such streets or alley or the portion thereof proposed to be improved, shall in writing request the said mayor and board of aldermen to make such improvement; but the nature and kind of the material used in such improvement so made shall be left to the discretion of said board of aldermen in all cases.

viso.

ualization of h assessments

Sec. 17. That to equalize the assessments on real estate for the purposes described in section sixteen of this act the said mayor and board of aldermen shall estimate the total cost of such improvement made throughout the entire length of such work and improvement, and shall then prorate the cost thereof on the real estate abutting thereon in proportion to the frontage on the street or portion of the street so improved, and charge to and assess upon the real estate upon each side of the street upon which said work is done its pro rata share of one-third of the cost of such improvement made under the provisions of this act: Provided, however, in order to avoid obstructing land owners in subdividing and selling their property by reason of the liens hereby created upon the same, such land owners may subdivide their lands in such manner as they may see fit, and shall file in the office of the city clerk a plat of such subdivisions, making the lots fronting on the streets so paved or improved of any desired frontage, but not less than one hundred feet in depth. and the assessments made and the liens created by virtue of this act for street improvements shall thereafter affect and attach to such front lots only, not less than one hundred feet depth; and where in such

viso.

ndowners may divide land.

cases any lands fronting on such improvements are so subdivided into lots each of said lots fronting on such improvements shall be and remain charged with its ratable proportion of said assessments and lien according to its frontage. Whenever the said mayor and board of aldermen shall order paving or other improvements to be made on any street or any part thereof in the said city, they shall have the same accurately surveyed and a permanent grade thereof established, and cause an accurate map to be made of the various lots and properties abutting on said street or the portion thereof so proposed to be improved, showing the exact frontage of each lot, and also the subdivisions, if any, and the said map shall be filed in the office of the city clerk, to be subject to public inspection; and when the assessments and liens herein provided for shall have been made upon the various lots and properties on the street, the said city clerk shall write upon the said map the amount assessed upon the same, and he shall keep a record book showing such assessments, liens and the date and amount of all payments made on any of said assessments and liens.

Paving and other improvements may be ordered surveyed.

Clerk shall keep a record of such liens.

Sec. 18. That the amount of the assessments for such street improvements as hereinbefore provided, being estimated on each piece of real estate as above directed, shall be a lien on such real estate, and the said mayor and board of aldermen shall cause the city engineer to make a survey and a report of the amount of the work done and the cost thereof, upon what street or portion thereof, showing the name of each abutting owner thereon, the number of front feet of each lot and the pro rata share of such cost of such street improvement to be assessed against such real estate; and upon the adoption and approval of the said report, the liens authorized by this act shall become complete and operative, and shall be paramount to all other liens on said real estate except the liens for taxes thereon, and the said report shall be transcribed upon the minutes of the said board of aldermen, and the amount of said liens and of said assessments against all property abutting on said streets as aforesaid shall become due and payable as follows, to-wit: One-fifth in thirty days after the adoption of said report and the balance in four equal annual installments, which deferred payments shall bear interest at the rate of six per centum per annum from the date of the approval of said report until paid; and upon the filing of said report the said mayor and board of aldermen shall cause ten days' notice to be given by publication in some newspaper published in the city of Asheville, stating that such report has been filed in the office of the city clerk, and that at the first regular meeting of the said board of aldermen to be held after the expiration of the said ten days' notice the said board of aldermen would consider said report,

Such assessments shall be liens on real estate.

City engineer may make survey and report work done.

When such assessments are due and payable.

and if no valid objection be made thereto the same would be adopted and approved by said board. Any owner of land affected by said liens for assessments shall have the right to be heard concerning the same before the said board of aldermen by filing objections thereto in writing, duly verified by his oath, in the office of the city clerk at least two days prior to the first meeting of the board at which said report may be approved and confirmed, but not thereafter, and any person so objecting to the confirmation or approval of said report shall state in said objections in writing what part, if any, of said assessments he admits to be lawfully chargeable to his said land and what part thereof he disputes, and said board of aldermen shall hear said objections, and shall thereafter approve or confirm said report and overrule said objections or modify or correct said report in such manner as to make the same correspond with the true intent and meaning of this act. Any person who shall have filed objections as aforesaid to the confirmation of said report shall have the right within ten days after the approval or confirmation of the same by the said board of aldermen, and not after that time, to appeal from the said decision of the said board of aldermen to the next term of the superior court of Buncombe county, North Carolina, by serving upon said city notice in writing of his intention so to do, and specifying in said notice the item or items in said report which he disputes, and by filing within said time in the office of the clerk of the superior court of Buncombe county a written undertaking in at least the sum of two hundred dollars, with sufficient sureties, to be justified before and approved by said clerk, to the effect that said appellant will pay to said city all such costs and damages as it may sustain by reason of such appeal, if the court shall finally render judgment against said appellant. In case of an appeal as aforesaid a copy of said report, in so far as it affects the property of the appellant, as the same was approved by the mayor and board of aldermen, a copy of the objections of the appellant thereto, and of said notice duly certified by the city clerk, shall constitute the record on appeal, and when filed in the office of the clerk of the superior court of said county, the same shall be docketed on the civil issue docket in the name of the person taking such appeal against the city of Asheville as "an appeal from an assessment," and the cause shall then be deemed to be at issue without any further plea on the part of said city, but said city shall have the right to file a further answer or defense thereto if it be so advised, and said cause shall stand for trial at the next term of court, beginning more than ten days after the docketing of said appeal: Provided, that if said appeal is not docketed and said bond is not filed by the appellant within ten days after the confirmation of

ner of lands :cted shall be rd.

rsons filing 'ections to such ort may ɔeal within days after its option.

all serve notice writing.

all give bond.

rtain records stituting record on appeal.

viso.

said report, all right to prosecute such appeal shall be thereby forfeited. And upon the trial of the issues arising on such appeal, if all the issues be found in favor of the appellant, the lien for said assessments shall be discharged; if, however, the issues or any of them be found in favor of the city of Asheville to any amount, and if it be thereby ascertained that the appellant is due to said city any amount by virtue of the matters therein referred to, or that said land is subject to a lien for said assessments or any part thereof, then the amount so found in favor of the city of Asheville, with interest thereon, together with costs thereon accrued, which cost shall be assessed as costs in other civil actions, shall be and continue a lien against the property upon which the original assessment was placed from the date of the approval of said report by said board of aldermen, and shall be collected by the tax collector in such manner as the other assessments herein provided for are collected. The adoption and approval of said report of the city engineer by said mayor and board of aldermen shall complete the said liens for the amount therein stated against each of the separate pieces of real estate therein described, and the same shall become due and payable as aforesaid; and in case of a failure to pay either of said assessments or any installment thereof within thirty days after its maturity, then the whole thereof shall become immediately due and payable, and an execution shall be issued by the said city clerk directed to the tax collector of said city, who shall advertise the land upon which the said assessments so in default have been made as aforesaid, in the same manner as is required by law for the sale of land for taxes under the provisions of the charter of said city, and shall sell the said land or a portion thereof at the courthouse door in Buncombe county, North Carolina, in the same manner as he is required to sell real estate in said city in case of the failure to pay the taxes due thereon, and shall give to the purchaser a receipt stating the time the land was advertised, the date of sale, the name of the purchaser, the price paid, the amount of the assessments due thereon, the costs of the sale, the name of the owner or owners of the land sold, the interest in said land so sold as aforesaid, and a description of the same; and the owner or owners of the land so sold as aforesaid shall have twelve months within which to redeem the said lands from such sale by paying to the tax collector of said city the amount for which said lands were sold, together with twenty per centum per annum additional thereto. In making such sale the said tax collector shall set up and offer for sale the whole of the real estate to be so sold, and the same or the smallest interest thereof shall be struck off to the person who will pay the amount of the assessments due theroen, with all costs and expenses for making the

When appeal is not filed within ten days shall be forfeited.

Land subject to lien if any issue is found favorable to city of Asheville.

Adoption of report complete a lien.

Clerk shall advertise land for sale.

Shall give receipt to purchaser.

Land may be redeemed within twelve months.

llection of fee pay for advertising.

sale for the smallest interest in said land. For every piece of real estate or part thereof so advertised said tax collector shall also collect in the same manner as such assessments are collected the sum of fifty cents to defray the expenses of such advertisement.

es shall be de to highest der.

All such sales shall be made to the highest bidder for cash on any day of the week or month except Sunday or legal holidays, and he shall be deemed the highest bidder who will pay such assessments and expenses of the sale for the smallest interest in said real estate, and if no person shall bid enough to pay such assessments and expenses, said tax collector shall bid on behalf of the city of Asheville the amount of such assessments and expenses; and if no higher bid shall be made, the same shall be struck off to the said city of Asheville; and in all cases where real estate shall be struck off to the said city, as hereinbefore

ere struck off city belongs to n fee simple.

provided. the same shall belong to the city in fee simple unless redeemed in the manner prescribed by law, and said tax collector shall immediately thereafter make a return to the board of aldermen of said city by filing with the clerk of said city a statement of the proceedings showing the purchaser or purchasers of said real estate, and the amount or interest in such real estate or each part thereof that was sold, which shall be entered by the

cord of sale ll be made by rk.

city clerk upon the minute books of the said board of aldermen; if the land so sold as aforesaid is not redeemed within twelve months, then the tax collector of said city shall make to the purchaser or purchasers a deed in fee simple for the said lands or the interest thereof so sold as aforesaid, and the said deed shall oper-

ed shall erate to convey e to land in simple. viso.

ate to convey to the purchaser and his heirs the title to the said land in fee simple: Provided, however, that the owner of any land subject to the liens and assessments hereinbefore mentioned shall have the privilege of paying off all of said assessments at any time before maturity, and upon such payment the said liens shall be released and discharged.

yor and aldern shall have lusive control treet work.

Sec. 19. That the said mayor and board of aldermen of said city, by their proper officers, shall have the exclusive control and management of the work of improving of said streets, and the costs thereof shall be paid out of the street improvement fund provided for in this act, and out of any other funds belonging to the said city [of] Asheville that may be available for such purpose, the said city itself being liable for the costs of all curbing and for one-third of the costs and expenses of improving the street or roadway between the curbings and the abutting land on

viso.

each side, assuming the liability hereinbefore created: Provided, however, that whatever of the cost of the street improvements which may be paid by or assessed against the property of any

essment inst street lway or raild company.

street railroad or railway company as provided for by law, shall be deducted from the proportion of the costs of such improvement for which the said city is liable as aforesaid, whether such street railway or street railroad shall run through the center or upon either side of the street so improved as aforesaid, and the amount to be paid by said street railway or street railroad company as provided for by law shall not in any event be deducted from any sum assessed against the abutting land owners under the provisions of this act.

Mayor and aldermen empowered to sell and transfer liens.

Sec. 20. That said mayor and board of aldermen are hereby authorized and empowered to assign, sell and transfer the said liens created by this act and all sums owing thereon, either absolutely or upon condition, to any person or persons in order to enable them to raise means to carry into effect the provisions hereof, and if any such liens shall be transferred as aforesaid and shall not be paid to the owner thereof when due, they shall be collected by the tax collector of said city in the same manner as other assessments hereinbefore provided for in this act, and the amount thereof when collected shall be paid by said tax collector to the owner or owners of said liens, less his compensation for collecting the same, which shall be fixed by said board of aldermen, but shall not exceed two per centum of the amount actually collected by him.

Funds derived from assessments, how applied.

Special fund.

Sec. 21. That all funds derived from assessments heretofore or hereafter levied by said mayor and board of aldermen of the city of Asheville upon private property, on account of improvements of the streets upon which such property abuts, shall, when collected and received by the city of Asheville, constitute a special fund, to be designated as "street improvement fund," and the same, with the funds derived from the taxes hereinafter authorized to be levied, shall be kept separate from all other funds of the said city, and a separate record thereof shall be kept by the city clerk, and said funds and every part thereof shall be applied by said mayor and board of aldermen exclusively to the grading, paving, macadamizing or otherwise improving the streets of said city according to the true intent and meaning of this act. And in order to supplement said street improvement fund, and to enable said mayor and board of aldermen to carry into effect the provisions of this act, the said mayor and board of aldermen are hereby authorized and empowered to levy annually and cause to be collected by the city tax collector, in addition to the taxes otherwise provided by law, and under the same rules and regulations as general poll and property taxes are provided for by law, a special street tax in said city not to exceed twenty cents on the one hundred dollars valuation of property and sixty cents on the poll, for the purpose of carrying into effect the provisions of this act, and the funds derived from such taxes shall be and constitute a part of the "street improvement fund" hereinbefore

Special street tax may be levied.

Maximum special tax.

mentioned, and shall be applied exclusively to the purposes hereinbefore set forth.

ayor and alder- en empowered enter into con- acts.

Sec. 22. That said mayor and board of aldermen are hereby authorized and empowered to make and enter into any and all contracts and agreements, and to pass, ordain and to enforce any and all orders, rules and regulations that may be necessary and proper to carry out the provisions of this act.

nflicting laws pealed.

Sec. 23. That all laws and clauses of laws in conflict with this act are hereby repealed.

Sec. 24. That this act shall be in force from and after its ratification.

Ratified the 6th day of March, A. D. 1899.

CHAPTER 240.

An act to incorporate the Trans-Appalachian Railway System.

The General Assembly of North Carolina do enact:

rporators.

Section 1. That H. L. Miller and D. W. Beach, of Washington, District of Columbia, and S. D. Dunavant, W. C. Ervin, S. T. Pearson, F. P. Tate, J. R. Ervin and W. E. Walton, of the county of Burke and state of North Carolina, and such persons as may be associated with them, their successors and assigns, be and they are created a body politic and corporate under the name and style of "The Trans-Appalachian Railway Company," which shall have perpetual succession and may sue and be sued, plead and be impleaded, contract and be contracted with, adopt and use a common seal, and change the same at pleasure, and be capable of taking and holding by purchase, gift or devise, or in any other manner, real and personal property, and of leasing, selling or conveying the same or dealing with the same in any manner. And said corporation shall have and enjoy all privileges, rights and immunities which corporate bodies may lawfully exercise, and make all necessary by-laws necessary for its government or which its directors may deem proper and expedient, not inconsistent with law.

dy corporate. rporate name. rporate pow- s.

pital stock.

Sec. 2. That the capital stock of said corporation shall be one hundred thousand dollars, divided into shares of one hundred dollars each, with power and authority to the directors of said company to increase the same at any time to an amount not exceeding twenty-five thousand dollars ($25,000) per mile for every mile of road completed or owned by said company. And subscriptions to the capital stock may be made by individuals, corporations, counties, cities, towns or townships, and said sub-

vision of ares. ay be increased.

scription may be paid in money, labor, land, materials, cross-ties, stocks, bonds or other securities or in any other way that may be agreed upon between the company and the subscribers, and the company may receive donations of any kind of property of labor.

Sec. 3. That the incorporators or any two of them, in person or by attorney, shall have the power to open books of subscriptions to the capital stock of said company at such times and places as they may deem best and keep the same open as long as they may deem expedient; that whenever the sum of ten thousand dollars has been subscribed to the capital stock of said company the incorporators may, when they deem proper, after ten days' notice by mail to the subscribers, call together the subscribers of said shares of stock at any place in or out of the state, and said subscribers shall then complete the organization of the corporation by electing a board of not less than three nor more than fifteen directors, and at such meeting and at all meetings of the stockholders of said company, each share of stock shall be entitled to one vote, which may be cast by the owner of said shares or by proxy, verified as the by-laws adopted may prescribe, and at all stockholders' meetings a majority of the stock subscribed shall constitute a quorum, and said stockholder shall adopt by-laws prescribing for the government of said corporation, and the board of directors so elected shall meet at such time and place, either in or out of the state, as may be agreed upon and elect from their number a president and elect such other officers as the by-laws may prescribe or that they may deem necessary, and may do and perform all other acts that they may deem necessary to carry into effect the object of this charter.

Books of subscription may be opened.

When company may be organized.

Quorum.

Election of officers.

Sec. 4. That said company shall have the right to construct, and it is hereby authorized and empowered to construct, operate and maintain a railroad with one or more tracks, standard guage or otherwise, by such route as may be deemed most advantageous and expedient, from any point on the Carolina Central Railroad, at or between the town of Shelby and the town of Lincolnton, through the counties of Cleveland, Lincoln, Burke, Caldwell, Mitchell, Watauga or Ashe, or any one or more of said counties to some point on the North Carolina and Tennessee line or the North Carolina and Virginia line; and it may also construct, maintain and operate such lateral branch lines as may be necessary or advantgeous to the extension completion or successful operation of said railroad; and may also construct, maintain and operate telegraph and telephone lines along the route of said road. And said railroad company may use either electricity or steam as motive power, to condemn and hold during its corporate existence all lands within fifty (50) feet of the center of the track of said

Nature of business.

Company may decide on route.

Route.

Motive power.

company on either side, and to purchase and hold such other tracts of land as may be needed by said company for railroad purposes or to increase the amount of freight shipped over its road. And said company shall have power and authority to construct dams, culverts, trestles and bridges over and across streams, valleys and depressions, and to cross at grade or over or under, to intersect, join or unite its railway with any other railroad now constructed in this state upon the lands of such other company at any point in its route, and to build all necessary turnouts, sidings, switches and other conveniences required for the successful operation of said road; and said company may acquire, by purchase or lease, or may consolidate with any other railroad now built or projected, and assume its corporate name, or may sell or lease any part of the whole of its lines to any other railroad company, and if a portion of or the whole of its lines or line shall be sold to any other company, then the company purchasing shall take the line so purchased, with all the franchise herein granted, and may manage the same under its own corporate name: Provided, such consolidated company shall be a domestic corporation under the laws of North Carolina.

powered to onstruct dams.

y unite with ier railways.

oviso. nsolidated mpanies shall domestic corration.

Sec. 5. That it shall be lawful for any officer or agent, surveyor or engineer or other employee of said company to enter upon lands for the purpose of exploring, leveling or doing anything necessary or proper to be done for laying out said railroad and locating the same; and upon the location and construction of said road, or any part thereof, if no agreement with the owners of the land through which the road shall be constructed shall have made by the company, the land on either side of the center of the track for a distance of fifty (50) feet shall be vested in said company, and the proceedings for the condemnation of said land and for the recovery by the owners for the value thereof, shall be the same as prescribed in The Code of North Carolina. And in making the valuation, the commissioners shall take into consideration the loss or damage that may accrue to the owner in consequence of the right-of-way being surrendered or other property for station house, turnouts, water tanks, depots or warehouses.

cer or agent company may plore on lands.

nd for fifty feet all be vested in mpany.

luation of demned d.

y issue bonds.

Sec. 6. That said company shall have power and is authorized to issue bonds of the company, either coupon or registered, to any amount necessary, not exceeding twenty-five thousand dollars ($25,000) per mile for every mile of road completed or owned by said company, and to secure the payment of said bonds by executing a mortgage or mortgages or deed of trust upon any or all of its property and the franchise of said company, on such terms as the directors may prescribe, and any such conveyance, when registered in the counties in which said property is situated, shall constitute a lien upon the franchise of the company and all of its property in the counties in which such mortgage is registered.

Right of company to transport passengers and freight and fix rates for same.

Sec. 7. That said company shall have the right to transport and carry passengers and freight over and along its said line and branches, and mails and express matter, and to charge such fares and tolls for the same as may be prescribed by the board of directors, not inconsistent with law, and to fix rates for the use or services of its telegraph or telephone lines, not inconsistent with law, and to do any and all things necessary or expedient for the proper management of said company as usually exercised or performed by railroad companies; and to purchase and hold stock in any other railroad or transportation company, express company, telegraph or telephone company or other corporation, or may purchase or lease the same and operate the same or contract with such company or corporation for the transportation of passengers or freight.

Counties, cities, etc., may subscribe to capital stock.

Sec. 8. That any county, city, town or township along the line of said railroad or any of its branches, or at any terminal point of said road, or any of its branches, may subscribe to the capital stock of said company in the following manner. Upon the presentation in writing, signed by at least one-fourth of the freeholders in said county, city, town or township to the board of commissioners of said county, or to the proper authorities of said city [or] town, requesting them to submit to the qualified voters of the county, township, city or town where said petitioners may reside a proposition to subscribe a definite sum, named in said petition, to the capital stock of said company.

Within thirty days after petition is filed election shall be ordered.

The board of commissioners of said county, or the proper authorities of said city or town, shall, within thirty days after the filing of said petition, order an election to be held in such county, township, city or town, and submit to the qualified voters therein the question of subscribing to the capital stock of said company the amount specified in said petition, at which election all those qualified to vote who are in favor of such subscription shall vote a ballot on which shall be written or printed the words "For subscription," and those opposed to such subscription shall vote a ballot on which shall be written or printed the words "Against subscription," and the election for this purpose shall be conducted in the same manner and subject to the same rules and regulations as are or may be provided for the election of county officers by the general election laws of the state of North Caro ina. Such election shall be held, after thirty days' notice thereof shall have been given, specifying the amount of the proposed subscription, and the returns thereof shall be made to the board of commissioners of the county or the proper authorities of such

Form of ballot.

Election, how held.

city or town; and if a majority of the qualified voters vote for subscription, then the board of commissioners of said county or the proper authorities of said city or town shall immediately make said subscription, and may pay for the same in cash, or may issue coupon bonds to the amount of said subscription in order to pay for the same, and said bonds shall, upon their face, indicate on account of what county or township or city or town they are issued. Said bonds shall be in denominations of not less than one hundred dollars nor more than one thousand dollars each, and shall run for twenty years and bear interest at five per centum per annum, payable semi-annually.

nds may be ßued in payent for stock.

Sec. 9. That in case a subscription is made to said railway company by any county, township, city or town in North Carolina as prescribed herein, it shall be the duty of the board of commissioners of said county or the proper authorities of said city or town to obtain the necessary authority, if bonds are issued, to levy a special tax, sufficient to meet the interest charges, if necessary, and to provide a sinking fund with which to pay off and discharge the principal of said bonds from the general assembly at its session held next after the making of said subscription.

oper authoris may levy ecial tax to pay terest and incipal.

Sec. 10. That the stockholders shall provide in the by-laws for their regular meetings, but directors' meetings may be held at any time or place, either in or out of this state, as the directors or a majority of them may determine, and the stockholders shall not be individually liable for the debts of the corporation. That said company shall maintain an office in the town of Morganton and shall at all times have an agent or attorney resident of said town.

gular meetgs.

incipal office.

Sec. 11. That if work is not begun and prosecuted upon said road within five (5) years from the ratification of this act, then this charter is to become void, otherwise to remain in full force and effect.

ork shall begin thin five years.

Sec. 12. That this act shall take effect from and after its ratification.

Ratified the 6th day of March, A. D. 1899.

CHAPTER 241.

An act to incorporate the North Wilkesboro and Boone Turnpike Company.

The General Assembly of North Carolina do enact:

Section 1. That for the purpose of constructing a turnpike road from North Wilkesboro, in Wilkes county, to Boone, Watauga county, North Carolina, the formation of a corporation with a capital stock not exceeding twenty thousand dollars ($20,000), to

rpose of corpotion.

pital stock.

be styled "The North Wilkesboro and Boone Turnpike Company," is hereby authorized. Corporate name.

Sec. 2. That the said company be and is hereby authorized to construct, maintain and operate a turnpike road, extending from the town of North Wilkesboro, by the most practicable route that may be selected, to Boone; and that for the purpose of raising the capital stock of said company and to acquire the means of completing said road as contemplated by this charter, it shall be lawful to open books of subscription in the town of North Wilkesboro, and in the town of Boone, or at such other places as may be deemed advisable, under the direction of any three of the following-named persons, to-wit: J. E. Finley, E. S. Blair, R. W. Gwyn, L. E. Davis, L. L. Church, W. L. Hendrix, E. F. Lavill and J. C. Horton. Company authorized to operate a turnpike.

Sec. 3. That the capital stock of said association shall be divided into shares of ten dollars each, and whenever one hundred of such shares shall be subscribed for on the books authorized to be opened for that purpose, the subscriber for the same and their future associates, and their successors and assigns, are hereby declared to be a body politic and corporate by the name and style of "The North Wilkesboro and Boone Turnpike Company," with all the rights, powers and privileges incident or belonging to corporations, as set forth or referred to in the chapter of The Code of North Carolina, entitled "Corporations," and by that name may sue and be sued, plead and be impleaded, answer and be answered unto in any court in this state; may appoint all necessary officers and agents and prescribe their duties; and may purchase, accept, hold and convey any property, real and personal, necessary for the purpose hereinbefore and hereinafter mentioned; and may contract, have and use a common seal, and do all other acts incident to and connected with said corporation, and necessary for the control and transaction of its business: Provided, that nothing shall be done in conflict with the laws of this state. Capital stock, how divided. Corporate name. Corporate rights and powers. Proviso. Shall not conflict with laws of this state.

Sec. 4. That so soon as one hundred shares of the capital stock of said corporation shall be subscribed for, it shall be lawful for any three of the persons hereinbefore named to call a general meeting of such subscribers by notifying each one in writing at least two days prior to such meeting, or by publication in some newspaper published in either county through which the road passes for two weeks, and such subscribers at such meeting shall elect from among themselves a board of directors of not less than five, and the directors to be chosen at such meeting and at the subsequent annual meetings of the stockholders as they may be fixed by the by-laws of said corporation shall elect one of their number president of said corporation at said meeting or at any sub- When company may be organized. Election of directors.

sequent meeting of the stockholders of said corporation. They may adopt all such by-laws as may be considered necessary for the good management of said corporation, and all matters not provided for by such by-laws shall be regulated and done as the board of directors shall from time to time order and direct.

option of by-s.

yments of ital stock.

Sec. 5. That the board of directors may require payments of subscriptions to the capital stock of said corporation to be made in such installments as they may think proper; and in case any subscriber shall fail to pay the amount of his subscription after fifteen days' notice given in writing, the directors may sell said share or shares of stock so subscribed for by him by public auction, or so many of them as may be sufficient to pay the amount of his subscription then remaining unpaid, and if a balance shall remain unpaid after applying the proceeds of the sale as aforesaid, the same may be recovered by the corporation from such delinquent subscriber before any court having jurisdiction of the amount so remaining unpaid.

ds may be demned.

Sec. 6. That whenever any lands may be required for said turnpike, either for a roadway or for toll houses or other appurtenances thereto, and an agreement can not be made with the owner or owners of such lands, the company or owner may in writing apply to the clerk of the superior court of Wilkes or Watauga counties (having regard to the county in which the land is situated or located) to cause the damages, if any, to be assessed by three disinterested referees, one to be chosen by the owner, one by the corporation and one by the clerk of the court; if either party or both shall fail to appoint after five days' notice of the application to the clerk, then the clerk shall appoint instead. The referees so appointed being duly notified by the clerk shall, being first duly sworn by some person authorized to administer oaths to act impartially, lay off a right-of-way not exceeding forty feet in width, as the company may elect, and also if required by the company shall lay off a suitable site or sites for a toll house or houses not exceeding one acre of land at each toll house and assess the damage, if any, to the owners of the land, taking into consideration any benefit or advantages to accrue to such owner from the making of such road and return their award in writing within ten days to said clerk, and such award of such referees or any two of them when returned shall become a judgment of the superior court of said county on which execution may issue as on other judgments of the superior court, if the amount is not paid by said company within ten days after notice of such return. If either party is dissatisfied with the award of the referees they may appeal to the superior court as in other cases of appeal. So soon, however, as an award is returned by a majority of such referees as aforesaid, whether there is an appeal or not, the com-

nages assessed eferees.

erees shall oath.

a awards become a ment.

er party may al.

pany may enter upon the lands referred to in such award and use them for making such turnpike road or erecting toll houses, as the case may be.

Sec. 7. That said company shall be authorized to demand, recover and receive from all persons using the road such compensation no greater than the following fare or toll: For four-horse or four ox team, forty (40) cents each way; two-horse or two-ox team, twenty-five (25) cents each way; two-horse buggy or hack, thirty-five (35) cents; one-horse buggy, twenty-five (25) cents; one-horse wagon, fifteen (15) cents; horse and rider, ten (10) cents; loose horses or cattle, five (5) cents each; sheep, three (3) cents each. Any person who shall use any part of said road without paying the fare and toll due and payable for such use, and demanded by any officer or agent of said company at the established toll gate, shall be guilty of a misdemeanor, and on conviction before any justice of the peace of the county of Watauga or Wilkes, according to the respective jurisdiction, shall pay a fine of not less than two dollars ($2) nor more than five dollars ($5), and upon failure to pay such fine, together with the cost of the proceeding against him, shall be imprisoned by the justice of the peace before whom the case shall have been tried not less than five (5) days nor more than twenty (20) days. All such fines as may be collected by virtue of the provisions of this section shall be paid over to the school fund of the county in which collected.

Toll fares, etc.

Persons using roads without paying fare a misdemeanor.

Sec. 8. That so soon as said turnpike shall have been completed from North Wilkesboro up the north side of Yadkin river to Lewis Fork creek, or so as to intersect or connect with the public road leading from Deep Gap to Holmes ford of the Yadkin, in case this route is chosen for said road; or when said road is completed an equal distance on any other route that may be chosen in locating same, the said company is hereby authorized to erect a toll gate across said turnpike at some convenient place as the board of directors may select, and said company shall also have power and authority to erect a gate or gates at such other place or places on said road after it is constructed as may be deemed advisable by the said board of directors, and at such place or places may demand, recover and receive the fare or toll authorized by this act and no more.

When said company is authorized to erect toll gate.

Sec. 9. That the fares or tolls received for the use of said road shall be expended in keeping the toll houses, making and constructing said turnpike and keeping the parts thus made in repair until the whole turnpike from North Wilkesboro to Boone is completed, and after said road is completed as aforesaid the said company shall be authorized to declare dividends for the benefit of the stockholders: Provided, however, that in case said company should issue and sell its bonds or mortgage its prop-

How tolls shall be received and used.

erty, road and franchises in order to acquire the means for putting through and completing said road, the net receipts from tolls and fares, after all expense of operating and keeping said road in repair is paid, shall be applied to discharging such indebtedness and liabilities.

mpany may ue bonds.

Sec. 10. That at any time after said company is organized as provided for in this act, if it should be desired in order to secure necessary means for completing said road, they shall have power when authorized by vote of a majority of the directors to issue and sell its bonds to an amount not exceeding three hundred dollars per mile, bearing interest at not more than six per centum per annum, to run for such period as may be determined by said board of directors; said bonds to be signed by the president, attested by the secretary and sealed with the corporate seal of the company; and may, if authorized by the board of directors, execute mortgages on all or any part of the road property and franchises of said company to secure the payment of such bonds or other obligations, or may sell or lease same at pleasure.

ɔw bonds shall signed.

rsons obstructg or damaging ad.

Sec. 11. Any person who shall in any manner injure or obstruct the road of said company or any bridge connected therewith, besides being liable for damages in a civil action, shall be guilty of a misdemeanor, and on conviction thereof before any court having jurisdiction shall be fined or imprisoned, or both, in the discretion of the court.

dividual bility.

Sec. 12. That the stockholders shall not be individually liable for the debts of the corporation.

Sec. 13. That this act shall be in force from and after its ratification.

Ratified the 6th day of March, A. D. 1899.

CHAPTER 242.

An act to repeal an act entitled "An act to amend the charter of the town of Burlington, Alamance county, North Carolina."

The General Assembly of North Carolina do enact:

lating to ction of conble and street mmissioner.

Section 1. That chapter one hundred and twenty-eight (128), private laws of eighteen hundred and ninety-seven (1897), be and the same is hereby repealed.

Sec. 2. That this act shall be in full force and effect from and after its ratification.

Ratified the 6th day of March, A. D. 1899.

CHAPTER 243.

An act to revise, amend and consolidate the act of incorporation of the town of Louisburg, North Carolina, and the acts amendatory thereof.

The General Assembly of North Carolina do enact:

Section 1. That W. H. Macon, George H. Cooper, James M. Allen and R. G. Hart, and their successors in office, are hereby incorporated into a body corporate and politic, by the name of the "Commissioners of the Town of Louisburg," and under such name and style may adopt a corporate seal, sue and be sued, plead and be impleaded, acquire by purchase, bequest or other conveyance, such real and personal property anywhere within Louisburg township as may be requisite and necessary for the proper government of the town; hold, invest, improve, use, govern, control and protect, and under the hand of the mayor and two commissioners attested by the corporate seal may sell or dispose of the same and have all the powers, rights and privileges necessary, belonging or usually pertaining to municipal corporations, and all property and rights of property, powers, privileges and franchises derived from or granted by any law now in force with reference to the town of Louisburg or the government of said town, or any law granting franchises or powers of any kind to the corporation styled the commissioners of the town of Louisburg, in addition to the powers conferred on incorporate towns in chapter sixty of The Code of North Carolina, not inconsistent herewith, are hereby invested in the said commissioners of the town of Louisburg, and the same shall be exercised and administered for the government and benefit of the town of Louisburg by the mayor and commissioners thereof, and they shall also be liable in their corporate capacity for all debts, claims, obligations and duties which now exist against the said corporation under whatever name or style. Corporators. Body corporate. Corporate name. Corporate powers.

Sec. 2. The corporate limits of the town shall remain as they now exist and shall be identical with the boundaries and limits fixed and determined by section twenty-five of chapter two hundred and forty-two of the laws of North Carolina passed by the general assembly at its session of eighteen hundred and fifty-four and eighteen hundred and fifty-five entitled an act to provide for the better government of the town of Louisburg in the county of Franklin. Corporate limits.

Sec. 3. That all municipal bonds already issued by the town of Louisburg or the commissioners thereof, as well as all other valid indebtedness, shall be binding upon the town of Louisburg and Municipal bonds shall be binding.

the commissioners thereof in their corporate capacity, and all bonds which may or shall be hereafter issued by the board of commissioners of the town of Salisbury under the authority of an act of the present general assembly ratified on the fourteenth day of January, eighteen hundred and ninety-nine, entitled "an act to authorise the town of Louisburg to issue bonds for public improvements and to levy a special tax and for other purposes," shall when issued become the valid indebtedness of the town of Louisburg and of the commissioners thereof in their corporate capacity, and shall be paid according to the terms thereof.

tain bonds, en issued, ll become id indebted- s.

sent officers tinued.

SEC. 4. That the present mayor of Louisburg shall hold office until his successor is elected and qualified and the present members of the board of commissioners shall hold their office until their successors are elected and qualified, and as such shall have the same power and authority now conferred upon them by law, and such additional authority as shall be conferred upon the mayor and board of commissioners by this act.

nual elections.

SEC. 5. That there shall on the first Tuesday in May, one thousand eight hundred and ninety-nine and on the first Tuesday in May annually thereafter be elected four commissioners for said town, who shall hold their offices until their successors are qualified, and at the same time there shall be elected a mayor for said town who shall hold his office for one year and until his successor shall be elected and qualified. The mayor and commissioners shall be residents and qualified voters of the said town and shall be elected by the qualified voters thereof.

ection of reg- ar of voters.

SEC. 6. The board of commissioners shall at their regular meetings in March, eighteen hundred and ninety-nine, or as soon after the ratification of this act as may be practicable and annually thereafter at their regular meeting in March, select a registrar and shall cause publication thereof to be made at the courthouse door and notice of his appointment served on said registrar, and shall give ten days' public notice of a registration of voters in and for said town, specifying time and place and the name of the registrar.

en registra- books shall opened.

SEC. 7. Said registrar shall be furnished by said board of commissioners with a registration book and it shall be the duty of said registrar to open his book at such place in the town of Louisburg as may be designated by said commissioners on the first Saturday in April next preceding the election, and to register therein the names of all persons applying for registration and entitled to register and vote in the said town, keeping the names of the white voters separate and apart from those of the colored voters and designating on the registration books opposite the names of each person registering the place of his residence in said town, and if any applicant for registration shall not disclose the place of his residence his willful failure so to do shall be *prima facie* evidence that he is not entitled to register. Any person offering to register shall be required to take an oath that he has been a *bona fide* resident of North Carolina for twelve months, of the town of Louisburg for ninety days next preceding that date, and that he has not been convicted of any crime which, by the laws of North Carolina disqualifies him for voting. In said oath he shall specify the place of his residence. If any person shall willfully swear falsely in such affidavit he shall be deemed guilty of a felony, and on consideration [conviction] thereof shall be punished as for larceny: Provided, that after the first registration shall have been made, as provided for herein, a new registration shall not be held annually unless the board of commissioners shall at their regular meeting in March determine that the same is necessary, and by due advertisement give notice of the same and the place where the book of registration shall be opened; but a revision of the registration book shall be made, beginning on Saturday next preceding each election to be held for said town in accordance with the provisions of the general law.

Persons offering to register shall take oath.

Proviso.

New registration shall not be held annually.

SEC. 8. The registration book shall be kept open for ten days exclusive of Sunday, and after the same are closed no person shall be allowed to register, but the registrar shall, upon application before said book is closed, register all persons not then qualified to vote in said town who will have become so qualified on or before the day of election. Immediately after the book is closed it shall be deposited in the office of the mayor; and under his charge, all citizens of Louisburg desiring so to do may inspect them.

When registration book shall be kept open.

SEC. 10. Whenever any person shall offer to register in said town the registrar may examine him on oath regarding his qualification to register, and may hear evidence thereof, and upon such examination it shall be unlawful for any person to interfere or suggest answers to the person being examined, and any one so offending, upon conviction before the mayor or some justice of the peace of Franklin county, he shall be fined not more than ten dollars. The board of commissioners of said town shall have the authority to provide by ordinance for the punishment of any person who interferes with the registrar or judges of election in the discharge of their duties. If the registrar shall decide that the applicant for registration is entitled to register, he shall record his name as herein prescribed, giving age and color of the applicant and the place of his residence in the town. Any person not known to the registrar to be a voter, offering to vote at an election in said town, upon challenge, may be required to prove his identity, and upon his failure [so] to do his vote shall not be received.

Persons offering to register may be examined.

Commissioners empowered to pass ordinances punishing persons interfering with registrars or judges of election.

h of person istering.

SEC. 11. Any person offering to register in said town shall take and subscribe the following oath or affirmation: "I do solemnly swear that I am or will be twenty-one years of age; that I have been or will have been an actual *bona fide* resident of North Carolina for twelve months and an actual *bona fide* resident of the town of Louisburg for ninety days on the first Tuesday of May next, and that I have not been convicted of any crime which under the laws of North Carolina disqualify me to vote. So help me, God."

pointment udges of tion.

SEC. 12. The board of commissioners of the town of Louisburg shall at their meeting in March, one thousand eight hundred and ninety-nine, and annually thereafter, appoint two judges of election for the said town to open the polls and superintend the same for the municipal election to be held on the first Tuesday in May next succeeding, and the polls shall be opened at such place in the town as the board shall designate. The registrar and judges of election shall be sworn by an officer authorized to administer oaths before entering upon the duties of their respective offices.

o shall be itled to vote

SEC. 13. All electors who have been *bona fide* residents of North Carolina for twelve months and of the town of Louisburg for ninety days next preceding the election shall be entitled to register hereunder. A resident in said town shall be construed to be permanent citizenship thereof and not a temporary resident. The polls shall be opened on the day of the election from seven o'clock in the morning until sunset the same day. No person whose name has not been duly registered shall be allowed to vote, and any one offering to vote may be challenged at the polls, and if the judges of election shall sustain the challenge his ballot shall not be received. Ballots shall be on white paper and without device. There shall be one ballot box with the words "For mayor" labelled thereon in plain and distinct roman letters, into which box shall be deposited by the judges of election all ballots cast for mayor. There shall be another ballot box with the words "For commissioners" labelled thereon in plain and distinct roman letters, into which box shall be deposited by the judges of election all ballots cast for commissioners. The commissioners shall be voted for on one ballot, and no ballot shall contain the names of more than four commissioners. All ballots found in the wrong box shall be counted, unless the judges of election shall decide that such ballot or ballots so found are not *bona fide* ballots of qualified electors.

llenges.

m of ballots.

nting of lots in wrong lot box.

l books shall kept. Names ersons voting ll be kept.

SEC. 14. The judges of election shall keep a poll book and write in it the names of every person voting at said election, and at the close thereof shall certify said poll-list and deposit it with the secretary of said town, and said poll book shall in any trial for illegal or fraudulent voting be received as evidence. If for any cause any of the judges of election shall fail to attend, the registrar shall appoint some discreet person or persons to fill the vacancy, who shall be sworn by him before acting. When the election is ended, the registrar and judges of election shall proceed immediately to count the ballots and ascertain the result thereof.

Judges and registrar shall decide result in case of tie vote.

SEC. 15. If any of the persons voted for in the town two or more shall have an equal number of votes, and either would be elected but for the equal vote, the judges of election and registrar in said town shall decide the election between such persons. As soon as the result of the election in town is determined a certificate thereof shall be made under the hands of the registrar and judges, setting forth in writing and words the number of votes each candidate received, which certificate they shall deliver to the mayor, who shall, at twelve o'clock m. on the day after the election, make proclamation thereof at the court-house door. The registrar and judges of election shall furnish to each person elected as commissioner in said town a certificate of his election.

Registrar and judges shall furnish certificates of election.

Registrar shall give casting vote when judges can not decide.

SEC. 16. Whenever under the provisions of this act any question is to be decided by the judges of election, and said judges can not decide the same by reason of a tie vote, the registrar shall give the casting vote.

Elections shall be held under supervision of chief of police.

SEC. 17. That all elections held by virtue of this act shall be held under the supervision of the chief of police of the town of Louisburg, who shall attend the polls, and by his regular force of police and such additional numbers whom the mayor may appoint as special deputies, preserve order.

When mayor and commissioners shall qualify.

SEC. 18. That on the Tuesday next succeeding the day of election the mayor and commissioners elected thereat shall qualify by taking the oath now provided by law, and shall succeed to and have all the rights, powers and duties now provided by law for such mayor and board, as well as those conferred on them by the provisions of this act.

Oath of office.

SEC. 19. That the mayor, each commissioner, and every other officer of said town, before entering upon the duties of his or their office, shall take, subscribe and file with the town clerk the following oath of office: "I........, do solemnly swear (or affirm) that I will support and defend the constitution of the United States, and the constitution and laws of North Carolina not inconsistent therewith, and I will faithfully perform the duties of the office of..........on which I am about to enter, according to my best skill and ability. So help me, God."

Subscribed and sworn before me this .... day of.......... 1899.

When mayor shall keep office.

SEC. 20. That the mayor shall have and keep his office in the town hall, or in some other convenient building provided by the board of commissioners, and keep and hold such office open, and be therein present for the transaction of his official duties, during not less than six hours per day, between the hours of eight o'clock a. m. and six o'clock p. m., Sunday alone excepted, unless elsewhere engaged upon official duty within the town, or absent therefrom with the knowledge and consent of the board of commissioners; he shall have the custody of the corporate seal; preside when present over all meetings of the board of commissioners; have a casting vote in all cases of equal division therein; a general custody, direction, supervision and control of all the public employees, work and works, improvements, grounds, buildings and property of the town, not otherwise provided for by this act or by the board of commissioners; may, after a full and fair hearing, suspend for cause, until the next meeting of the board of commissioners, any officer or employee of the town charged with dereliction of official duty or the violation of any of the provisions of this act; and shall perform such other duties as are, or may be, prescribed by this act, or the ordinances of said town.

ce hours.

ties of mayor.

mpensation of yor.

Sec. 21. That the mayor of said town shall not receive any fees in any case tried before him, whether he has final jurisdiction or only to act as a committing magistrate, but the fees now prescribed by law for the mayor shall be collected and recovered into the treasury of said town. The mayor shall receive as compensation for his services and salary as the commissioners may fix, payable out of the town treasury, in such sums and at such periods as the commissioners may prescribe.

mmissioners y grant nchises.

Sec. 22. The commissioners of said town shall have the power to grant to any street railway company or other persons the right to use the streets of said town to operate railway lines in the town under such terms as they may contract.

risdiction of yor.

Sec. 23. That the mayor of the town of Louisburg is hereby constituted a special court to be known as the mayor's court, with exclusive original jurisdiction of all offenses arising from the violation of the provisions of this act, or of the ordinances, by-laws, rules and regulations of the board of commissioners, made in pursuance hereof and with all the jurisdiction, power and authority which is now, or hereafter may be, given to the justices of the peace, for the trial and determination of such criminal causes as may arise within the corporate limits of said town, under the general laws of North Carolina, or within one mile of said corporate limits, and to that end he may issue his summons, warrant or other process, have the party brought before him, hear, determine and give judgment thereon, issue execution, impose fines, penalties and forfeitures, as the case may be, and direct the enforcement thereof subject to the limitations of this act as to the amounts of such penalties, and subject, also, to the same right of appeal as is provided for courts of justices of the peace: *Provided*, that no cause arising upon the violation of any of the provisions of this charter, or of any ordinance, rule or regulation made in pursuance hereof, shall be removed from the mayor's court to a justice of the peace for trial: *And provided further*, that in case a defendant, a witness, or other persons, shall be adjudged to be imprisoned by said mayor's court, it shall be competent for the said court to sentence such person to imprisonment in the county jail for a term not exceeding thirty days, and to adjudge, also, that such person work during the period of his or her confinement, on the public streets or works of the town, or on the public roads or works of the county of Franklin, and in case such imprisonment be for the non-payment of a fine, a penalty or costs, he shall have credit thereon at the rate of sixty-five cents per day for every day in which he shall so work upon the public streets, roads or other works of the town or county.

Proviso.

No cause shall be removed for trial.

Proviso.

Persons may be sentenced to work on public roads.

SEC. 24. That the mayor may issue process to the chief of police or to the town police, or to any other officer in the county of Franklin to whom a justice of the peace may issue similar process, and such process, when attested by the corporate seal, shall run anywhere in the state of North Carolina, and they shall execute the same: *Provided*, that neither the chief of police nor the town police shall execute any process beyond or outside of the boundaries of Louisburg township, unless the offense was committed, or cause of action arose, within the corporate limits of the town and in violation of the provisions of this act.

Processes issued by mayor.

Proviso.

Arrests shall not be made outside corporate limits when offense was committed within same

SEC. 25. That the judgment rendered by the mayor, under the provisions of this act, shall have all the force, virtue and validity of judgments rendered by a justice of the peace; may be enforced and executed against the parties in the county of Franklin, and elsewhere, in the same manner and by the same means. The fines and penalties imposed by him shall be collected by or paid over to the chief of police, who shall pay over an amount for the same, as hereinafter directed, to the use of the town of Louisburg. All fines, costs and penalties heretofore imposed by the mayor of said town, whether collected or yet to be collected, shall be and are hereby declared to be the property of said town subject to the power of the commissioners to dispose of the same as of the other public moneys of said town.

Judgments of mayor, force and effect

SEC. 26. That it shall be the duty of the mayor to keep an exact account and true record of all the fines, penalties and forfeitures by him imposed under any of the provisions of this act, or for the violation of any ordinance, by-law, rule or regulation made in pursuance hereof, in a separate book, to be furnished by the board of commissioners therefor, showing the name and residence of each offender, the nature of the offense,

Mayor shall keep record of fines, penalties, etc

the date of hearing or trial, the amount of fine or penalty imposed, and if known, when and by whom paid to the chief of police.

ilure of mayor qualify.

Sec. 27. That if any person who has been elected mayor shall fail, neglect or refuse to qualify, or if a vacancy shall occur in the office after election and qualification, other than by expiration of term, or if the mayor be absent from the town or unable to attend or discharge the duties of his office from any other cause, then and in such case the board of commissioners shall choose some qualified person to perform the duties of the absent mayor during the period of his absence, or disability, or to the end of the term, as the case may be; and the mayor so chosen shall have all the power and authority which is vested in the regular elected mayor under this act; and the board of commissioners shall in like manner fill all vacancies for the unexpired term which may occur in the town government, choosing only such persons as are eligible to original election under the provision of this act. For drunkenness, immorality or misconduct in office, the mayor or any member of the board of commissioners may be removed from his or their office by a two-thirds vote of the entire number of commissioners, and upon such offices being vacant the board of commissioners shall fill the same for the unexpired term.

cancies occur- g among cers filled by ermen.

ties of police n.

Sec. 28. That it shall be the duty of the chief of police, and of the town police force under his immdiate charge and direction, to see that the laws of the town and the ordinances of the board of commissioners, and the orders of the mayor, are executed and enforced, and all breaches thereof reported to the mayor; to preserve the peace and order of the town; to suppress disturbances, and arrest and carry before the mayor all offending against any laws, town, state or national, who may be found within the corporate limits; to execute all warrants or other processes, lawfully directed to him by the mayor or other competent authority against any person or persons charged with the commission of any crime or misdemeanor within the corporate limits of the town; and if in any violation of any of the provisions of this act, they may pursue and continually follow and arrest such offenders anywhere in the county of Franklin, and in the performance of such duties they shall have all the power and authority of and be governed by the same provisions of the law as sheriffs and constables in their respective jurisdictions.

ef of police ll attend yor's court, lect fines, etc.

Sec. 29. That it shall also be the duty of chief of police to attend upon the mayor's court; to collect such fines, penalties and forfeitures as may be imposed by him upon offenders for the violation of any of the provisions of this charter, or of the ordinances, rules and regulations of the board of commissioners made in pursuance hereof, of which he shall keep an exact record in a book to be furnished by the board of commissioners, showing the name and residence of the offender, the nature of the offense, the date of the hearing thereon before the mayor, the amount of the fine, penalty or forfeiture imposed, the date of its collection and the date of payment thereof, by the chief of police to the treasurer; and the signature of the treasurer on the last column and same line of each such entry shall be the only sufficient voucher of the chief of police for such payment in each case.

Proceedings before mayor shall not be removed to other courts.

SEC. 30. That no person shall have the right in any proceeding before the mayor to remove the same to any other court for trial, as is provided for removal of causes from one justice of the peace to another, as is provided in section nine hundred and seven of The Code, but in all cases parties shall have the right of appeal as herein provided.

Defendants may appeal.

Within ten days after election mayor and commissioners shall convene.

SEC. 31. That the mayor and commissioners shall form a board, and a majority of them shall be competent to perform all the duties prescribed for the commissioners, unless otherwise provided. Within ten days after their election they shall convene for the transaction of business, and shall fix stated days of meetings for the year, which shall be as often, at least, as once every calendar month. Special meetings of the commissioners may be held on the call of the mayor or a majority of the commissioners, and all commissioners, when the meeting is called by the mayor, and those not joining in the call when made by a majority of the board, shall be notified.

Commissioners empowered to provide for execution of ordinances.

SEC. 32. That the commissioners, when convened, shall have power to make and provide for the execution thereof of such ordinances, by-laws, rules and regulations for the better government of the town as they may deem necessary: *Provided*, the same be allowed by the provisions of this act and are consistent with the constitution and laws of the state.

Proviso.

Election of clerk and treasurer.

SEC. 33. That the commissioners, at their first meeting after their election, shall appoint a clerk and treasurer, who shall respectively hold their offices during the official term of the commissioners who appointed them, subject, however, to be removed at any time and others appointed in their stead for misbehavior or neglect in office. Before acting, the person or persons holding said office shall be sworn to the faithful discharge of his duty, and shall execute a bond, payable to the town of Louisburg, in such sum as the commissioners shall determine.

Shall make oath and execute bond.

Clerk shall be present at meetings and keep record of proceedings.

SEC. 34. That it shall be the duty of the town clerk to be present at all the meetings of the board of commissioners; to keep record, in a book to be provided therefor, regular and fair minutes of the proceedings of the board, and when thereto required, of the mayor's court; to preserve all the books, records, documents, papers and other articles committed to his use, care or custody during his term of office and deliver them in good order and condition to his successor, and generally to perform such other duties as may be prescribed by this chapter or by the board of commissioners, and he shall receive a reasonable salary to be fixed by the board of commissioners.

easurer shall ke annual tement to missioners.

SEC. 35. That the treasurer shall make out annually a fair transcript of the receipts and the disbursements on account of the town for the general inspection of the citizens, and cause the same to be posted before the door of the mayor's office at the end of the fiscal year, or printed in some newspaper published in the town of Louisburg.

easurer shall l in all moneys onging to n.

SEC. 36. That it shall be the duty of the treasurer to call on all persons who may have in their hands any money or securities belonging to the town, which ought to be paid or delivered into the treasury, and to safely keep the same for the use of the town, disburse the funds according to such orders as may be duly drawn on him in the manner hereinafter specified; he shall keep in a book provided for that purpose a fair and correct account of all moneys received and disbursed by him, and shall submit said accounts to the commissioners when required to do so. On the expiration of his term of office he shall deliver to his successor all the moneys, securities and other property entrusted to him for safe keeping or otherwise, and during his continuance therein he shall faithfully perform all duties lawfully imposed upon him as town treasurer. For his services he shall receive such compensation as may be fixed by the board of commissioners.

mpensation of asurer.

ders drawn on asurer, how ned.

SEC. 37. That all orders drawn on the treasurer shall be signed by the clerk and countersigned by the mayor, and shall state the purposes for which the money is applied, and the treasurer shall specify said purposes in his accounts, and also the sources whence are derived the moneys received by him.

pointment of lice force.

SEC. 38. The board of commissioners shall have power to appoint a police force, to consist of a chief of police and such number of policemen as the good government of the town may require, who shall hold their office for such term as may be fixed by the board. The members of the police shall give bond in such sums as the board of commissioners may prescribe for the faithful discharge of the duties imposed by law and the ordinances of the town, and to faithfully account for all moneys that may come into their hands from fines and penalties, etc. The chief of police shall have the supervision and control of the police force, and it shall be his duty to report to the mayor any dereliction of duty on the part of any member of the police force, to see that

ities of chief of lice.

the laws and ordinances of the town are enforced and do such other things as may be required of him by the board. The chief of police and each member of the force shall have all the power and authority vested in sheriffs and constables for the preservation of the peace of the town by suppressing disturbances and apprehending offenders. They shall execute all processes directed to them by the mayor or others, and in the execution thereof shall have the same powers which sheriffs and constables have. The chief and members of the police force shall take an oath before the mayor for the faithful performance of the duties required by law and ordinances. That said policemen shall have power to take bail for appearance of defendants or other persons charged with violations of town ordinances in the manner and to the extent that such power is vested in sheriffs, and in case any person or persons shall not appear the mayor may issue a *scire facias* and enter judgment final against the defaulting party and sureties. The chief of police shall have the power to rearrest upon the same warrant a defendant or party who has been convicted and turned loose upon the statement that he will pay fine and costs, upon failure to pay same, or in case of an escape.

Chief and members of police force shall take oath.

SEC. 39. The chief and other policemen shall be entitled to and shall receive the fees arising from the execution of all precepts issued by the mayor or others, which shall be the same as that of sheriffs for like service. The board of commissioners shall pass ordinances for the government and direction of the police and fix their compensations. In times of exigency the mayor may appoint temporarily additional policemen for such time as shall appear necessary, not exceeding one week, who shall take the same oath and be subject to the same control as regular policemen.

Policemen entitled to fees arising from execution of precepts.

SEC. 40. The mayor may at any time upon charges preferred, or upon finding said chief or any member of said police force guilty of misconduct, have power to suspend such members from service until the board of commissioners shall convene and take action in the matter; and upon hearing the proofs in the case, the board may discharge or restore such members, and the pay of such members so suspended shall cease from the time of suspension to the time of his restoration to service. Any violation of the regulations or orders of any superior shall be good cause for dismissal, and the mayor may suspend the chief or any member of the police force if found drunk while on duty.

Policemen may be suspended by mayor.

Cause for dismissal.

SEC. 41. The board of commissioners shall require the entire police force to wear badges and to be so uniformed as to be readily recognized by the public as peace officers. And the police shall generally have power to do whatever may be necessary to preserve the good order and peace of the town and secure the inhabit-

Police force shall be uniformed.

ants from personal violence and their property from loss or injury.

reach of official nd.

SEC. 42. That for any breach of his official bond by the clerk, treasurer, chief of police, tax collector or any other officers who may be required to give an official bond, such officer and his sureties shall be liable in an action on the same, in the name of the town, at the suit of the town, or any person aggrieved by such breach, and the same may be put in suit without assignment from time to time untl the whole penalty be recovered.

eriff of Frank- county re- ired to receive isoners with- t mittimus

SEC. 43. That the sheriff or jailer of the county of Franklin is hereby required, without a mittimus, to receive into the jail of the county as his prisoner any person taken up in the night by the police force and to keep such person safely until morning, when the offender shall be brought before the mayor or some magistrate resident in the town, and be lawfully dealt with, and for such services the jailer shall be entitled to such fees as he is in other like cases, or such prisoners may be confined in the town prison.

pointment of ighmaster d inspector.

SEC. 44. That the said board of commissioners may, as soon after election as necessary, appoint a weighmaster and inspector, whose duty it shall be to inspect all flour, provisions, forage and all other marketable produce sold in said town, and in their judgment requiring weighing or inspection, and the said officer so appointed shall give bond with approved security, payable to the town of Louisburg, in an amount to be fixed by the board, conditioned for the faithful discharge of all duties imposed by law or the ordinances of the town, and shall take an oath before the mayor before entering upon his duties; and the board of commissioners shall have power to remove him for misbehavior or neglect or malpractice in office, and appoint a successor instead; and the board of commissioners are hereby authorized and empowered to regulate the fee to be paid for such weighing and inspection, and by them to be paid, and to make all necessary ordinances for the government of the said officer, and to impose fines and penalties for their violations. They shall have power also to appoint building inspectors and also fire inspectors, who shall make their report to the board of commissioners.

mpensation.

all take oath.

y be removed.

ilding in ctors.

pointment of gineer, town orney, etc.

SEC. 45. They may also appoint a town engineer, a town attorney or attorneys, employ detectives, and to offer rewards for the capture and conviction of criminals, and to exercise like powers in the premises in order to bring offenders against the laws of the state and town ordinances, when the offense is committed in the town limits, to justice, and to use any funds belonging to the city not otherwise appropriated to carry out this purpose.

SEC. 46. That all moneys arising from taxes, fines, penalties, forfeitures, or any other sources whatsoever, shall be the property of the town, and be paid into the town treasury, where it shall remain until lawfully appropriated by a majority of the board of commissioners, in specific items, for the exclusive use and benefit of the town and the people resident therein, unless otherwise expressly provided in this act, exclusive of special taxes to pay principal and interest on bonded indebtedness.

How moneys belonging to town shall be applied.

SEC. 47. Any person who shall resist, or in any manner interfere with a police officer of the town of Louisburg, while engaged in the discharge of his official duties, by threat, force, violence or otherwise shall be guilty of a misdemeanor and upon conviction before the mayor of said town shall be subject to a fine of fifty dollars or imprisonment for thirty days.

Persons resisting or interfering with police officer.

SEC. 48. Any person imprisoned by the mayor for violation of the law or any ordinance of said town, or for the non-payment of any fine, penalty or costs, may be placed in the county jail of Franklin county for safe keeping, and during such imprisonment such persons may be worked upon the streets of said town or any other public improvement.

Persons imprisoned for fines may be worked on public roads.

SEC. 49. The commissioners of said town shall have the authority to pass such ordinances in relation to vagrants as they may deem necessary for the good government of the town, and any person who may be in the habit of sauntering about the town, not engaged in any lawful occupation, or of loafing about the streets, or who may spend his time in gambling and without visible means of support, shall be guilty of a misdemeanor, and on conviction therefor before the mayor shall pay a fine of not exceeding fifty dollars or be imprisoned not exceeding thirty days. The said mayor is constituted a special court to hear and finally determine such offenses; and upon failure of any person convicted of said offense to pay such fine and costs of his arrest and conviction, he shall have authority to imprison such person in the county jail or town prison, and the commissioners of Louisburg may work such persons on the streets or other public works of said town, or they may hire said persons to private persons until the fine and costs are paid.

Ordinances relative to vagrants.

Mayor constituted special court to determine such offenses.

SEC. 50. The said commissioners shall have power to establish fire district in said town and to prohibit within the said district under proper penalties the erection, alteration, removal from one place to another within said limits, or removal from without said limits into the same, or repairing of any wooden building or buildings, or building or buildings with other than brick or stone outside walls, or building of any character, the erection, repairing or alterations of which they shall consider to increase the danger from fire; and shall prohibit within said

Establishment of fire districts.

limits the covering or roofing or the repairing the roof [of] any building with any material which they shall consider to increase the danger of fire. The commissioners shall have power to make all such rules and regulations for the carrying into effect the provisions of the preceding section and the enforcement of the collection of the fines and penalties that may be imposed by them under the said section, and any person violating any of said rules or regulations shall be subject to a fine of fifty dollars or imprisonment in the county jail for thirty days.

ommissioners all make cessary pro sions to carry to effect preding sections.

rsons unable pay fines ay be worked roads.

SEC. 51. That in all cases where judgments may be entered up against any person or persons for fines or penalties according to the laws or ordinances of the town of Louisburg and the person or persons against whom the same is so adjudged refuses or is unable to pay such judgment, it may and shall be lawful for the mayor before whom such judgment is entered to order and require such person or persons so convicted to work on the streets or other public works until at a fair rate of wages such person or persons shall have worked out the full amount of the judgment and costs of the prosecution, and may use all necessary means to compel work by reasonable correction and punishment.

wn may convey lands and her property.

SEC. 52. That the town of Louisburg may convey lands and all other property which is transferable by deed of bargain or sale, or other property deed, sealed with the common seal, signed by the mayor and two members of the board of commissioners and tested by a witness.

licemen shall rve civil prosses.

SEC. 53. That it shall be lawful for the policeman to serve all civil process that may be directed to them for any court within their respective counties under the same regulations and penalties as are or may be prescribed by law in the case of constables.

wn commisners may conact with county mmissioners r prisoners.

SEC. 54. That it shall be lawful for the corporate authorities of said town in their discretion to contract in writing with the board of county commissioners for the employment of such prisoners as may be confined in the county jail by order of the court, on the streets or any of them for the construction and improvement of the same.

o town officer all become a ntractor for rk given out town.

SEC. 55. That no mayor or commissioners, or other officers of the town government, shall directly or indirectly become a contractor for work to be done by the town, and any person herein offending shall be guilty of a misdemeanor.

gulations rerding cellars.

SEC. 56. That no cellar shall be built under any sidewalk in the town, or entrance established on the sidewalk to any cellar, whereby the free passage of persons may be delayed, hindered or interrupted, and every offender herein shall forfeit and pay to the town twenty-five dollars for every day the same may remain.

SEC. 57. The board of commissioners shall have the power, and it shall be their duty, to prohibit all trades, occupations or acts which are a nuisance, from being carried on in said town, and the power and authority of said board of commissioners for the abatement and removal of nuisance shall extend one mile beyond the town limits. They shall have power, and it shall be their duty, to cause all ponds, sunken lots, and other places in which water stands and stagnates, to be drained and filled up and to secure from the owner or occupier the expenses, which expenses as above shall be a lien on the lot, which may be enforced as liens for taxes: *Provided*, the owner [or] occupant of said lots, after ten days' notice, shall neglect or refuse to remove or abate said nuisance. They shall have authority to cause all nuisances arising from any cause within and for one mile without the town limits to be removed or abated, and for the removing or abating any such nuisance the person creating the same shall pay the expenses as above required.

Prohibition of nuisances.

Proviso.

Owners of lots refusing to abate nuisances.

SEC. 58. That the commissioners shall have power to prevent dogs, horses, cattle and all other brutes from roaming at large in the town.

Dogs, horses, cattle, etc., running at large.

SEC. 59. That the commissioners may establish and regulate the market and prescribe at what time and place and in what manner within the corporation marketable articles shall be sold, grain, meal, flour (if not packed in barrels), fodder, hay or oats in straw; appoint a keeper of the market, prescribe his duties, and he shall have power to prevent forestalling and regrating.

Establishment and regulation of market.

SEC. 60. That the board of commissioners shall have power to regulate the manner and terms on which bodies may be interred in the public cemetery and have said cemetery kept in proper repair. They shall have power to purchase, when they deem proper, land adjoining any cemetery for its enlargement. They shall also have the power to forbid any and all interments of dead bodies within the limits of said town, or any part thereof whenever they shall deem it expedient, and to pass ordinances for the protection of the cemeteries; may appoint and pay a keeper and compel the keeping and returning a bill of mortality.

Interment of bodies.

SEC. 61. That they may provide for the establishment, organization, equipment, government and pay of such members of fire companies as they shall deem necessary and proper; that in case of a fire occuring in said town the mayor, or in his absence a majority of the fire committee who may be present, may order the blowing up or pulling down or destroying any house or other structure deemed necessary to stop the progress of the fire, and

Establishment and government of fire companies.

no person shall be liable, civilly or criminally, for acting in such case in obedience to such orders, but the town shall be liable to pay a fair price for the same.

gulations regarding overhead res.

Sec. 62. That they shall have power to make ordinances regulating the erection and maintenance of over-head electric or other wires; to prevent obstruction to streets and to prevent accidents or injuries to the citizens; to prohibit or control the firing of firearms, fire-crackers, torpedoes, and other explosive material, and to govern or prohibit the sale thereof in the town; the pace and speed at which horses may be ridden or driven through the streets; the speed at which railroad engines and trains and street cars shall run within the town limits; to prohibit said railroads from stopping their engines or cars in said streets, and to require said railroads to keep the crossings in good repair; the arrangement of all stove pipes and flues in buildings; the manner in which powder and other explosive and inflammable substances may be kept and sold; the manner in which commercial fertilizers are stored; the manner in which hogs may be kept, and to prevent them from running at large in said town, and may exclude the keeping of hogs within the town; and to cause all alleys, lots, cellars, privies, stables, styes and other places of like character to be examined by a sanitary policeman, to be appointed for that purpose. It shall be their duty, on complaint, to cause by their order the sanitary policeman to have the said places cleaned and the nuisance abated, and the said sanitary policeman or any other person appointed by the board or charged with that duty, shall have authority to enter the premises described to be in bad order and have the same cleaned, and the expense of abating such nuisance shall be recovered from the occupant or owner of said premises by action of debt in any court having competent jurisdiction. That they shall also have power to make regulations and ordinances for the due observance of Sunday.

ay prohibit sale explosives.

gulation of tilizers.

ay order, on mplaint, sanitry policemen have certain aces cleaned.

easures to prent entrance d spread contagious seases.

Sec. 63. That they may take such measures as they may deem effectual to prevent the entrance into the town or the spreading therein of any contagious or infectious diseases; may stop, detain and examine for that purpose every person coming from places believed to be infected with such disease; may establish and regulate hospitals within the town or within three miles thereof; may cause any person in the town suspected to be infected with such disease and whose stay may endanger its health to be removed to the hospital if the town have one; if not, where the mayor may direct; may remove from the town or destroy any furniture or other article which may be suspected of being tainted or infected with contagious or infectious diseases, or of which there shall be reasonable cause to apprehend that they may pass into such a state as to generate and propagate disease; may abate by any reasonable means all nuisances which may be injurious to the public health.

Corporation may recover expenses of removal of persons to hospital.

SEC. 64. That in case any person shall be removed to the hospital, or to the place directed by the mayor the corporation may recover before the mayor or any justice of the peace, of such person, the expense of his removal, support, nursing and medical attendance, burial expenses also in case of death.

Persons attempting to prevent such removal guilty of a misdemeanor.

SEC. 65. That if any person shall attempt by force or by threat of violence to prevent the removal to the hospital, or place selected by the mayor as aforesaid, of any person ordered to be conveyed thither, the person so offending shall forfeit and pay to the town one hundred dollars, and moreover be deemed guilty of a misdemeanor.

May construct system of sewerage.

SEC. 66. That the said board of commissioners shall have power to construct a system of sewerage for the town and protect and regulate the same by adequate ordinances, and for this purpose shall have power to condemn lands of private owners in the same way that lands are condemned for streets; and if it shall be necessary in obtaining a proper outlet to the said system to extend the same beyond the corporate limits, to condemn a right-of-way to and from such outlet, it shall be done as herein provided for opening new streets and other public purposes, and in addition thereto shall have power and authority to compel citizens living along the line of said sewerage or in the vicinity thereof, to connect their premises, drain or other pipes with said sewerage so as to drain all the premises along the line of said sewerage, and to provide water supplies for the town either by erecting waterworks or by contracting with other persons or corporations; and make all such other public improvements as the health of the citizens and the safety of the property may require.

Extension of sewerage.

Persons living along line of sewerage may be compelled to connect.

May acquire lands.

SEC. 67. That the board of commissioners may acquire by gift or grant lands or easements thereon, or rights-of-way over the same, or the right of use of springs, branches or water-courses for the purpose of erecting and operating waterworks, or conducting the water of the town.

Whenever land is necessary to town it may be condemned.

SEC. 68. That whenever in the opinion of the commissioners it is advisable to obtain land or the right-of-way in the town for the purpose of opening new streets, or widening or straightening streets already established, or the making of culverts or waterways for carrying water out of the streets, or for laying sewer pipes, or for any other necessary public purpose, and the commissioners and the owners of property affected by such proposed improvements can not agree as to the amount of damages consequent thereupon, as well as to special advantages which may result to the owners thereof, or to owners of property in the close vicinity of such proposed opening, widening or straightening of said street, or the building or otherwise establishing of such culvert or water-way, sewers or other public improvements, the mayor, upon order of the commissioners, shall issue his writ under the seal of his office, commanding the chief of police or other officers of the town to summon a jury of six freeholders of said town unconnected by consanguinity or affinity with any of the persons supposed to be affected by said improvement, and in said writ the proposed improvement shall be fully described and the persons mentioned who are supposed to be affected thereby. In obedience to said writ, the officer shall summon the jury of six freeholders as aforesaid and appoint a day for them to assemble at the mayor's office; the day so appointed shall not be less than ten nor more than twenty days from the date of the writ. The officer in charge shall also serve notice of the time of the meeting of the jury upon all persons who are named in the writ, as supposed to be affected by said proposed improvements, which notice shall be at least ten days before the day appointed for the meeting of the jury, and in case any such persons, their tenant or agent, can not be found within the town, then a poster at the court-house door, stating in as few words as possible the proposed improvements and the date appointed for the meeting of the jury shall be sufficient notice. On the day appointed for the meeting of the jury the officer, if he has not already summoned them, shall proceed to do so, or to fill any vacancy which may have occurred from any cause in the number which he may have previously summoned, and shall cause them to assemble at the mayor's office, where each of them shall take an oath to be administered by the mayor or other competent person that he will faithfully, truly and impartially assess the damages, if any, which may in his judgment be done to the property of each person named in the writ or to any other person whose property may in his judgment be damaged by the proposed improvement, and that he will also assess any special benefit or advantage or enhanced value which may be caused to the property of any person named in the writ, or to any other property in the immediate vicinity of the proposed improvement. Immediately after the jury shall have taken the oath as above prescribed, they shall proceed, accompanied by the officer, to view the land of each person mentioned in the writ, and the land of any other person in the immediate vicinity of the proposed improvement which they may consider to be directly affected thereby. And they shall assess the damages, if any, specifying the amount to which each and every one of the premises which they shall have viewed shall be entitled, and the jury shall at

sessors shall appointed.

en assessors all meet.

cancies among essors.

essors shall e oath.

ll view land.

the same time take into consideration any special benefit, advantage or enhanced value which in their judgment may have [been] received by reason of said proposed improvement, and shall state the amount of such special benefit, advantage or enhanced value of each and every one of the owners of said premises. The jury shall forthwith return to the mayor in writing a statement, to be signed by each of them, or if [of] a majority of them, in case they can not agree, setting forth distinctly a full report of their proceedings and stating the amount of damages or advantages which they shall have assessed to each person: *Provided*, that in case the jury shall be evenly divided and therefore unable to agree on the whole or any part of said report, they shall state that fact, setting out such parts as a majority of them have agreed on, and also the names of the persons as to the damage or disadvantage of whom they are evenly divided; and thereupon the mayor shall order the officer to summon at once a new jury of six freeholders to take into consideration that part of the report of the first jury on which they were not able to agree, and shall continue this course until an agreement is arrived at, and if necessary the mayor is authorized to extend the meeting of the jury from day to day to accomplish the object of this section. As soon as practicable after receiving the report of the jury the mayor shall call a meeting of the board of commissioners and submit the report to them, and if the commissioners shall conclude that the damages assessed by the jury are excessive they may decline to pay the same and discontinue the proposed improvement. If the jury shall find that the proposed improvement will enhance the value of real estate adjacent thereto the amount of such valuation of benefit shall vest in the town and become a lien on the premises mentioned in report of the jury, and shall be due to the town on the completion of the proposed work and payable in three equal annual instalments, and if not paid at maturity the lot so assessed, or so much thereof as may be necessary to pay said instalments and costs, shall be sold by the tax collector to pay the same under the same rules, regulations and restrictions, rights of redemption and savings as are prescribed in this charter for the sale of unpaid taxes: *Provided, nevertheless*, that if any person who is reported in the jury's report to be affected by the proposed improvement be dissatisfied with the amount of damage or of enhanced value with which he has been assessed, or if the commissioners be dissatisfied with any item in the report, then in that case either party may appeal on the item with which they are dissatisfied, to the next term of the superior court of Franklin county, by giving the adverse party or parties ten days' notice, in writing. The appellate court, in either case, shall have power to increase or diminish the

Assessors shall return to mayor a statement in writing.

Proviso.

When jury is unable to agree.

New jury shall be summoned.

Report shall be submitted to commissioners.

Real estate adjacent when enhanced in value.

Proviso.

Either party may appeal.

amount of damages or enhanced valuation which has been assessed, but shall in no wise adjudicate the necessity of the improvement, and the questions of damage or benefits shall be submitted to a jury under the direction of the judge, to be assessed by the jury under the ordinary rules of action for damages: *Provided, however,* that such appeal shall in no wise hinder or delay the commissioners in making the proposed improvements, but it shall be lawful for them or their agents to enter upon and use the property so condemned as soon as the same has been condemned by the board. That when any land, water or water-courses or right-of-way, either within or without the corporate limits of the town of Louisburg, shall, in the opinion of the commissioners, be required for the purpose of erecting or establishing reservoirs, laying conduit, main or supply pipes or sewer pipes, or obtaining a supply of water for the use of said town or the citizens thereof or for any other purposes connected with the successful operation of waterworks or sewers in said town, and the owners of such property can not agree with the commissioners as to the price thereof, the proceedings for condemnation shall be the same as is prescribed in foregoing section for condemnation of land for streets. And for the purpose of successfully operating waterworks or sewer pipes contemplated by this section, the commissioners of the town of Louisburg are fully authorized to extend the lines of waterworks or sewer pipes beyond the town limits in any direction thought most advisable, and with all the rights and privileges belonging to said commissioners within the town limits in addition to the authority herein granted: *Provided, however,* that in case of discontinuance of the use of the land either for the purposes mentioned in this or the preceding section, and on its reverting to the owners, the town shall have the right to remove any property or improvements under its authority erected thereon: *Provided, further,* that the owner or owners of land, right-of-way, water or water-courses required for the purposes mentioned shall have at least twenty days' written notice, under the seal of the mayor's office, of the time and place of meeting and of the purposes of the jury. If a resident of the town of Louisburg, said notice shall be served by its officers, if in the town; if not, for the purposes of this act it shall be sufficient if the notice be left at his known place of residence. If a non-resident and his post-office address is known, a registered letter with postage prepaid addressed to him and deposited in the post-office at Louisburg, and a return receipt for said letter shall be deemed and taken as sufficient notice. If his address is not known, publication for two weeks shall be made in some newspaper

viso.

h appeal shall hinder commissioners in king improvements.

missioners horized to end waterks beyond porate limits.

viso.

ers of water-, etc., shall e notice.

published in Louisburg of the time and place of meeting of the jury and of the purposes thereof.

Sec. 69. That the commissioners shall cause to be kept clean and in good repair the streets, sidewalks and alleys. They may establish the width and ascertain the location of those already established and lay out and open others, and may widen or reduce the width of streets now established in their discretion. They may establish parks for pleasure grounds for the citizens of the town and pass ordinances for the protection of shade trees.

Improvement of streets.

Sec. 70. That when there is no sidewalk and has never been any in existence in convenient walking order along any lot in said town, the owner may be required to pay such proportion of the expenses of making a sidewalk along such lot as three disinterested assessors, freeholders of said town, to be appointed by the commissioners, may estimate that the property is enhanced in value by such improvement: *Provided*, that the owner shall have the privilege of building said sidewalk along his lot immediately and in the manner prescribed by the commissioners, instead of paying the amount with which he has been assessed, and if the owner of such lot shall neglect or refuse to put down said sidewalk when directed to do so by the commissioners, and shall refuse or neglect to pay the amount so assessed against him to the treasurer of the town, said sidewalk shall be made by the town and the amount assessed against the owner of such lot shall be a lien on the same, and if not paid on demand, so much of said lot shall be sold as may be sufficient to pay said assessment and the costs, under the same rules and regulations, rights of redemption and savings as are prescribed in this charter for unpaid taxes. Before making such assessment, the assessors shall appoint a time and place of meeting, and shall give at least three days' notice thereof to all parties interested, stating the purposes of such meeting, and after being duly sworn by the mayor or other competent person they shall proceed to make the assessment and report the same to the mayor in writing: *Provided, however*, that either party may appeal to the superior court of Franklin county, where all questions of amount of assessment and other issues and questions of fact shall be tried by a jury under the direction of the judge, but the commissioners, notwithstanding the appeal, may proceed with the work. That the owner of a lot which shall front on a street on which a sidewalk has been established shall repair or improve said sidewalk in such manner as the commissioners may direct, as far as it extends along such lot; and upon failure to do so immediately upon notice of the commissioners to such owners, then, after advertisement at the court-house door and upon the said lot for five days, the commissioners may cause the same to be

Owner of lot may be required to pay proportion of making sidewalks.

Proviso.

Owner may build walk instead of paying amount assessed.

Proviso.

Either party may appeal.

repaired in such manner and with material as to them may seem proper, and the expenses shall be paid by the person in default, and said expenses shall be a lien upon said lot, and if not paid on demand, such lot or so much thereof as is necessary shall be sold by the collector of taxes to pay expenses and costs of sale under the same rules, regulations and restrictions, rights of redemption and savings as are prescribed in this charter for sale of land for unpaid taxes.

ayor and commissioners, after irty days' notice, may sell at ction any operty belonging to town.

Sec. 71. That the mayor and a majority of the board of commissioners of the town of Louisburg shall have power at all times to sell at public outcry, after thirty days' notice, to the highest bidder, any property, real or personal, belonging to the town, and apply the proceeds as they think best. The mayor and commissioners are fully authorized to make title to any property sold under this act: The Code, section three thousand eight hundred and twenty-six.

naltles recoverle in name of wn.

Sec. 72. That all penalties imposed by law relating to the town, or by this act, or by any ordinance of the town, unless otherwise provided, shall be recoverable in the name of the state and town of Louisburg, before the mayor and any other tribunal having jurisdiction thereof: *Provided*, any person failing to pay the taxes or fines imposed in accordance with the authority of this charter shall be required to work upon the public streets to the value of said fine or taxes if he has no property which can be distrained.

oviso.

rsons may be quired to work roads.

ayor and commissioners failing attend meetgs.

Sec. 73. The mayor or any member of the board of commissioners for said town who shall fail, neglect or refuse to attend any regular meeting of the board, or any special meeting called by a majority of the board in which he joined, or who, having had written notice, by mail or otherwise, of a special meeting of the board, called by the mayor or by a majority of the board in which he did not join, shall fail, neglect or refuse to attend such regular or special meeting, or to give to the board, on or before the next ensuing regular meeting thereof, a satisfactory excuse therefor, shall forfeit and pay to the chief of police, to the use of the town, the sum of three dollars for each offense.

wer of commissioners to ss ordinances.

Sec. 74. That the said board of commissioners shall have power to pass ordinances for the good government and order of said town, and to that end may pass an ordinance providing that in case any officer of said town has sufficient reason to believe and does believe that there exists any house of ill-fame, or gambling houses where games of chance are being carried on, or where liquors are being illegally sold, that such officers may, with or without warrant, enter said premises and arrest any person or persons so engaged as keepers or occupants of said houses of ill-fame, or gambling house, or houses where liquors are allowed to be illegally sold, and require such person or persons to appear before the mayor for violation of the ordinances against such houses of ill-fame, gambling place or tippling houses.

SEC. 75. That any person or persons violating any ordinance of the town of Louisburg shall be deemed guilty of a misdemeanor, and shall be subject to the provisions of this act.

Persons violating ordinances guilty of a misdemeanor.

SEC. 76. The tax collector, whose appointment is herein provided for, shall be vested with the same power and authority in the collection of taxes that sheriffs have and subject to the same fines and penalties for failure and neglect of duty. He shall be charged with the sums appearing by the tax-lists as due for town taxes. He shall be credited in settlement as sheriffs are credited with amounts in suit by appeal, all poll-taxes and taxes on personal property uncollectable by reason of insolvency. The board of commissioners at the meeting before the last regular meeting in each fiscal year, shall appoint one or more of their number to be present and to assist at the accounting and settlement between the tax collector and town treasurer and to audit and settle the accounts of the town clerk and treasurer. The amounts so audited shall be reported to the board of commissioners, and when approved by them shall be recorded in the minute book of said board and shall be *prima facie* evidence of their correctness and impeachable only for fraud or specified error. It shall be the duty of said board to remove any tax collector who shall fail to settle and fully pay up the taxes by law due from him, and he shall not be eligible for reelection to said office. And it shall always be lawful for the board of commissioners to designate one of the town policemen as tax collector, who shall give the same bond and perform the same duties provided for a regular tax collector. In case no policeman shall be designated as tax collector, then the board of commissioners shall, at their regular meeting in August of each year, elect a tax collector and fix his bond and compensation.

Powers of tax collector.

Settlements of tax collector.

Commissioners shall designate policeman as tax collector.

SEC. 77. That in order to raise a fund for the expenses incident to the proper government of the town, the commissioners may annually levy and collect the following taxes, namely:

Levy and collection of taxes.

(1) On all real and personal property within the corporate limits, including money on hand, solvent credits, investments in bonds, stocks and all other subjects taxed by the general assembly, *ad valorem*, a tax not exceeding one dollar on every hundred dollars value.

Ad valorem tax.

(2) On all taxable poll residents in the town on the first day of June of each year, or so resident within sixty days next preceding that day, a tax not exceeding three dollars per poll.

Poll tax.

(3) Upon every omnibus used for the carriage of persons for hire, a license not exceeding fifteen dollars per year; and upon

Omnibus, hacks, etc.

every hack, carriage or other vehicle, including express wagons, used for the carriage of persons or baggage for hire, and upon every dray used for the transportation of freight or other articles for hire, a license tax not exceeding five dollars a year; and a discrimination shall be made between one- and two-horse vehicles.

gs.

(4) Upon all male dogs kept in the town and which may be so kept on the first day of June a tax of three dollars and upon every bitch five dollars.

ine and ts.

(5) Upon all swine and goats not prohibited by the commissioners to remain in the town, when confined, a tax not exceeding one dollar a head.

croachments sidewalks by rches, etc.

(6) Upon all encroachments on the trees or sidewalks by porches, piazzas, stairways, passages or other projections or excavations suffered or allowed by the commissioners, a tax not exceeding one dollar nor less than twenty-five cents per square foot.

press, tele- one and tele- ph companies.

(7) Upon any express company and upon every telegraph or telephone company doing business in the town, a tax not exceeding one per centum of its gross receipts in the town, to be given in, upon oath, by the managing agent of such company, annually, at the time when other taxes are listed, and under the same penalty as that prescribed in the law of the state for the failure to give in.

ares and cer- cates of stock

(8) Upon all shares and certificates of stock issued by every bank, banking association or other incorporated institution located within the corporate limits, whether such institution or banking association has been organized under the laws of the state or of the United States, *ad valorem*, a tax not exceeding one dollar on every hundred dollars value: *Provided*, that the owner of such shares or certificates of shares of stock are resident of the town, and that the assessment shall be with regard to the value of the stock on the first day of June annually: *And, provided further*, that the value of the property of such bank or association otherwise taxed by said town, and its property exempt from taxation, be deducted from the aggregate amount of such bank or association's capital stock.

viso.

viso.

rsons liable to ation shall urn tax list der oath.

SEC. 78. That the citizens of Louisburg and others liable to be taxed under this charter shall, on the day prescribed for listing state and county taxes, render on oath to the clerk of the town, who is hereby constituted a commissioner of affidavits for that purpose, on a blank to be prepared and furnished by the board of commissioners, a list of their property and subjects for which they may be liable to be taxed, under all the rules and penalties prescribed in this chapter. The list shall state the age of the party, with reference to his liability to a poll tax, and shall also contain a verified statement of all the real and personal property of every kind, and such interests and estates therein as are taxable, moneys, credits, investments in bonds, stocks, joint stock companies, annuities, or otherwise not herein accepted, and all other subjects taxed by this charter and by the general assembly, in possession or under control or in charge of the person required to render said list, either as owner or holder thereof, or as parent, husband, guardian, trustee, executor, administrator, receiver, accounting officer, partner, agent, factor or otherwise. The party listing shall also swear to the true value of all property, choses in action and other subjects, except land, which oath shall be in the following form, to-wit: "I, ... do solemnly swear (or affirm) that the list furnished by me contains a true and accurate list of all property which by law I am required to list for taxation, and that the value fixed thereon by me is a true valuation of the same, according to my best knowledge and belief and information. So help me, God." Any person making a false return shall be deemed guilty of perjury. Property held in trust, or as agent, guardian, executor, or administrator, or in right of a *feme covert*, shall be returned on separate lists. Persons owning shares in incorporated companies within the town limits, taxable by this charter, are not required to deliver to the clerk a list thereof, but the president or other chief officer of such corporation shall deliver to the clerk a list of all shares of stock held therein and the value thereof, and the tax assessed on shares of stock in such corporations shall be paid by the corporation respectively.

Form of oath to which party listing shall subscribe.

Property held in trust, etc., shall be returned on separate lists.

SEC. 79. That all bridges, express, gas, manufacturing, street railroad and transportation companies, and all other companies and associations incorporated under the laws of this state situated or having its principal place of business within the corporate limits of the town, shall, in addition to the other property required by this act to be listed, make out and deliver to the clerk a sworn statement of the amount of its capital stock, setting forth particularly: first, the name and location of the company or association; second, the amount of stock authorized and the number of shares in which such capital stock is divided; third, the amount of capital stock paid up; fourth, the market value, or if no market value, then the actual value of the shares of stock; fifth, the assessed valuation of all its real and personal property, which real and personal property shall be listed and valued as other real and personal property is listed and assessed under this charter. The aggregate amount of the fifth item shall be deducted from the aggregate value of its shares of stock as provided by the fourth item, and the remainder, if any, shall be listed by the clerk, in the name of such company or corporation, as

Corporations and others shall make oath to certain facts.

capital stock thereof. In all cases of failure or refusal of any person, officer, company or association, to make such return or statement, it shall be the duty of the clerk to make such return or statement from the best information which he can obtain.

rmation to eturned by ks.

Sec. 80. That every bank (not incorporated), banker, broker, or stock jobber shall, at the time fixed by this charter for listing personal property, make out and furnish the clerk a sworn statement, showing: (1) The amount of property on hand or in transit. (2) The amount of funds in the hands of other banks, banking brokers or others, subject to draft. (3) The amount of checks or other cash items not included in either of the preceding items. (4) The amount of bills receivable, discounted or purchased, and other credits due or to become due, including amounts receivable and interest accrued but not due, and interest due and unpaid. (5) The amount of bonds and stocks of every kind, state and county warrants and other municipal securities, and shares of capital stock of joint stock or other companies or corporations, held as an investment or in any way representing assets. (6) All other property pertaining to said business, other than real estate, which real estate shall be listed and assessed as other real estate is listed and assessed under this act. (7) The amount of deposits made with them by other parties. (8) The amount of all accounts payable, other than current deposit accounts. (9) The amount of bonds and other securities exempt by law from taxation, specifying the amount and kind of each, the same being included in the preceding fifth item. The aggregate amount of the first, second and third items in said statement shall be listed as moneys. The amount of the sixth item shall be listed the same as other similar personal property is listed under this chapter. The aggregate The aggregate amount of the ninth item shall be deducted from the aggregate amount of the fourth item of said statement, and the amount of the remainder, if any, shall be listed as credits. The aggregate amount of the ninth item shall be deducted from the aggregate amount of the fifth item of such statement, and the remainder shall be listed as bonds or stocks.

cipal officers ilroad companies shall list company's erty.

Sec. 81. That all the real and personal property of any railroad, or so much thereof as shall be located within the corporate limits of the town, including road-beds, rights-of-way, main and side tracks, depot buildings and grounds, section and tool houses, machines and repair shops, general office buildings and store houses, rolling stock and personal property, necessary for the construction, maintenance and successful operation thereof, shall be listed for purposes of taxation by the principal officers or agents of such companies with the clerk, in the manner provided by law for the listing and valuation of real and personal prop-y, and shall be taxed as other real and personal property, der the rules, regulations and methods now or hereafter to be ovided by the general assembly of North Carolina for ascer. ning and listing the value thereof.

Persons and companies failing to properly return property.

Sec. 82. That if any person or company shall fail to render the clerk the list of property and other taxables required to be ndered by this charter, within the time prescribed for listing ite and county taxes, such person or company shall pay double e tax assessed on any subject for which said person is liable be taxed.

Clerk shall examine persons on oath.

Sec. 83. That the clerk shall be particular to examine each rson on oath as to whether he has other property than that ated in his return, which he may claim is not liable to taxation. ich property, except bonds of the United States and this state, d of the town of Louisburg, shall be entered and noted on the x-lists.

Clerk shall make out alphabetical list of persons liable for tax.

Sec. 84. That from the returns and lists made, as provided this charter, the clerk shall, within thirty days after the exration of the time for taking said lists, make out, in a book ept or provided for that purpose, an alphabetical list of the rsons, companies and owners of property who have so made eir returns, in the same manner as tax lists are made out by w for the state and county taxes; and the said clerk shall copy said book the assessments, on file in the register of deeds' fice of Franklin county, of all property within the town limits.

When tax shall be levied.

Sec. 85. That as soon as the tax list can be completed the board commissioners shall proceed to levy the tax on such subjects taxation as they shall determine, and shall place the tax list the hands of the tax collector for collection, who shall proed forthwith in the collection, and shall complete the me on or before the first day of December next ening, and shall pay the moneys, as they are collected, to the easurer; on the first day of December there shall be a penalty one per centum added to the amount of all taxes due, and an lditional one per centum on the first day of each month thereter until the same are paid.

When collection of taxes shall be completed.

When tax on banks is due.

Sec. 86. The taxes imposed upon the shares or certificates of ock in any bank or banking association (state or national) iall be paid by the cashier, or other principal officers of such ink or banking association, directly to the town tax collector, ithin thirty days after notice from said tax collector of the nount of tax due; and upon the failure of said cashier or princial officer to pay the tax collected as aforesaid, he shall forthith institute an action against the bank or banking association r the recovery of the same in the proper courts in said county Franklin.

capital stock thereof. In all cases of failure or refusal of any person, officer, company or association, to make such return or statement, it shall be the duty of the clerk to make such return or statement from the best information which he can obtain.

rmation to turned by s.

Sec. 80. That every bank (not incorporated), banker, broker, or stock jobber shall, at the time fixed by this charter for listing personal property, make out and furnish the clerk a sworn statement, showing: (1) The amount of property on hand or in transit. (2) The amount of funds in the hands of other banks, banking brokers or others, subject to draft. (3) The amount of checks or other cash items not included in either of the preceding items. (4) The amount of bills receivable, discounted or purchased, and other credits due or to become due, including amounts receivable and interest accrued but not due, and interest due and unpaid. (5) The amount of bonds and stocks of every kind, state and county warrants and other municipal securities, and shares of capital stock of joint stock or other companies or corporations, held as an investment or in any way representing assets. (6) All other property pertaining to said business, other than real estate, which real estate shall be listed and assessed as other real estate is listed and assessed under this act. (7) The amount of deposits made with them by other parties. (8) The amount of all accounts payable, other than current deposit accounts. (9) The amount of bonds and other securities exempt by law from taxation, specifying the amount and kind of each, the same being included in the preceding fifth item. The aggregate amount of the first, second and third items in said statement shall be listed as moneys. The amount of the sixth item shall be listed the same as other similar personal property is listed under this chapter. The aggregate The aggregate amount of the ninth item shall be deducted from the aggregate amount of the fourth item of said statement, and the amount of the remainder, if any, shall be listed as credits. The aggregate amount of the ninth item shall be deducted from the aggregate amount of the fifth item of such statement, and the remainder shall be listed as bonds or stocks.

cipal officers ilroad companies shall list company's erty.

Sec. 81. That all the real and personal property of any railroad, or so much thereof as shall be located within the corporate limits of the town, including road-beds, rights-of-way, main and side tracks, depot buildings and grounds, section and tool houses, machines and repair shops, general office buildings and store houses, rolling stock and personal property, necessary for the construction, maintenance and successful operation thereof, shall be listed for purposes of taxation by the principal officers or agents of such companies with the clerk, in the manner provided by law for the listing and valuation of real and personal property, and shall be taxed as other real and personal property, under the rules, regulations and methods now or hereafter to be provided by the general assembly of North Carolina for ascertaining and listing the value thereof.

Persons and companies failing to properly return property.

Sec. 82. That if any person or company shall fail to render to the clerk the list of property and other taxables required to be rendered by this charter, within the time prescribed for listing state and county taxes, such person or company shall pay double the tax assessed on any subject for which said person is liable to be taxed.

Clerk shall examine persons on oath.

Sec. 83. That the clerk shall be particular to examine each person on oath as to whether he has other property than that stated in his return, which he may claim is not liable to taxation. Such property, except bonds of the United States and this state, and of the town of Louisburg, shall be entered and noted on the tax-lists.

Clerk shall make out alphabetical list of persons liable for tax.

Sec. 84. That from the returns and lists made, as provided by this charter, the clerk shall, within thirty days after the expiration of the time for taking said lists, make out, in a book kept or provided for that purpose, an alphabetical list of the persons, companies and owners of property who have so made their returns, in the same manner as tax lists are made out by law for the state and county taxes; and the said clerk shall copy in said book the assessments, on file in the register of deeds' office of Franklin county, of all property within the town limits.

When tax shall be levied.

When collection of taxes shall be completed.

Sec. 85. That as soon as the tax list can be completed the board of commissioners shall proceed to levy the tax on such subjects of taxation as they shall determine, and shall place the tax list in the hands of the tax collector for collection, who shall proceed forthwith in the collection, and shall complete the same on or before the first day of December next ensuing, and shall pay the moneys, as they are collected, to the treasurer; on the first day of December there shall be a penalty of one per centum added to the amount of all taxes due, and an additional one per centum on the first day of each month thereafter until the same are paid.

When tax on banks is due.

Sec. 86. The taxes imposed upon the shares or certificates of stock in any bank or banking association (state or national) shall be paid by the cashier, or other principal officers of such bank or banking association, directly to the town tax collector, within thirty days after notice from said tax collector of the amount of tax due; and upon the failure of said cashier or principal officer to pay the tax collected as aforesaid, he shall forthwith institute an action against the bank or banking association for the recovery of the same in the proper courts in said county of Franklin.

llector empowered to collect taxes by distress and sale.

SEC. 87. That if any person liable to taxes on subjects directed to be listed, shall fail to pay them within the time prescribed for collection, the collector shall proceed forthwith to collect the same by distress and sale; all sales to be made after public advertisements, for the space of ten days, in some newspaper published in the town, if the property to be sold be personalty, and of twenty days if the property be realty. And the said collector shall have the right to levy upon and sell any personal property situated outside of the limits of the town and within the county of Franklin, belonging to a delinquent taxpayer of the town, in order to enforce the payment of taxes due the town by said delinquent.

x due on lot a n on same.

SEC. 88. The tax due on any lot or subdivision of land, is hereby declared to be a lien on the same, and if it shall remain unpaid on the first day of December next after the assessment, the tax collector shall either proceed to collect the same by a levy and sale of personal property belonging to the owner of said lot, or shall report the fact to the commissioners, together with a particular description of the real estate, and thereupon the commissioners shall direct the same to be sold at the court-house door, in the town of Louisburg, by the collector. The collector shall, before selling the same, make a full advertisement of the said real estate, at the court-house door, and at three or more public places in said town, for twenty days, and shall also serve upon the owners thereof a written or printed notice of the taxes due and the day of sale, but such notice need not be given to any person having or claiming any lien on said land by way of mortgage or otherwise. Whenever the owners are not in the town or for any cause can not be served with notice, then the advertisement of real estate belonging to such owners shall be made for one week in some newspaper published in the town of Louisburg, and the collector shall divide the said land into as many parts as may be convenient (for which purpose he is authorized to employ a surveyor), and he shall sell as many thereof as may be required to pay said taxes and all expenses attendant thereon. If the same can not be conveniently divided the collector shall sell the whole, and if no person shall pay the whole of the taxes and expenses for the whole land, the same shall be struck off to the town, and if not redeemed, as hereinafter provided, shall belong to the said town in fee: *Provided*, that such sale shall in no case affect the lien of any lawful encumbrance which can be shown to have been listed and taxes paid thereon to the town.

lector shall urn account of eedings to missioners.

SEC. 89. That the collector shall return an account of his proceedings to the commissioners, specifying the portions into which the land was divided, and the purchaser or purchasers thereof, and the price of each, which shall be entered on the book of proceedings of the commissioners, and if there shall be surplus after paying said taxes, the same shall be paid into the town treasury, subject to the demand of the owner.

Land sold may be redeemed within a year.

Sec. 90. That the owner of any land sold under the provisions of this charter, his heirs, executors and administrators, or any person acting for them, may redeem the same, within one year after the sale, by paying to the purchaser the sum by him paid, and twenty-five per centum on the amount of taxes and expenses, and the treasurer shall refund to him without interest the proceed less double the amount of taxes.

If said land is not redeemed within a year same may be conveyed to purchaser in fee.

Sec. 91. That if the real estate sold, as aforesaid, shall not be redeemed within the time specified, the corporation shall convey the same in fee to the purchaser or his assignee, by deed executed under the hand of the mayor and two commissioners, attested by the corporate seal, and the recitals in such conveyance, or in any other conveyance of land sold for taxes due the town, that the taxes were due, or of any other matter required to be true or done before the sale might be made, shall be *prima facie* evidence that the same was true and done.

Special taxes, commissioners empowered to levy.

Sec. 92. That in addition to the subjects listed for taxation the commissioners may levy a tax on the following subjects, the amount of which tax when fixed shall be collected by the collector of taxes, and if it be not paid on demand the same may be recovered by suit, or the articles upon which the tax is imposed or on any other property of the owner may be forthwith distrained and sold to satisfy the same, viz:

Itinerant merchants.

(1) Upon all itinerant merchants or peddlers vending or offering to vend in the town, a license tax not exceeding fifty dollars a year.

Circuses.

(2) Upon every company of circus riders or performers, by whatever name called, who shall exhibit within the limits of the town, or within one mile thereof, a license tax not exceeding one hundred dollars for each performance or separate exhibition, and upon every side-show connected therewith a license tax not exceeding twenty dollars, the tax to be paid before the exhibition, and if not, to be doubled.

Theatrical performances.

(3) Upon every person or company exhibiting in the town, except for religious, educational or charitable purposes, stage or theatrical plays, sleight-of-hand performances, rope-dancing, tumbling, wire-dancing, spinning-jenneys or merry-go-rounds, or menageries, a tax not exceeding twenty dollars for every twelve hours allowed for exhibitions, the tax to be paid before exhibiting or the same shall be doubled: *Provided, however*, that this section shall not apply to licensed houses who take out annual license.

Proviso.

hibitions for ard.

(4) Upon every exhibition for reward of artificial curiosities (models of useful invention excepted) in the town, a tax not to exceed twenty dollars, to be paid before exhibition or the same be doubled.

hibitions of y kind.

(5) Upon each show or exhibition of any kind, and on each concert for reward, unless for religious or benevolent purposes, in the town, and on every strolling musician, a tax not exceeding ten dollars, to be paid before exhibition or the same shall be doubled.

ctioneers.

(6) Upon every auctioneer or crier of goods at public auction, a license tax not exceeding twenty dollars per year: *Provided*, that their [this] section shall not conflict with the provisions of section twenty-two hundred and eighty-four of The Code, and shall not be construed to include tobacco warehouse auctioneers.

okers, etc.

(7) Upon every stock and bank broker, sewing machine company or agent for such company, dealer in or manufacturer's agent of musical instruments, keeper of sales stables, livery stables, or stock yards doing business in the town a license tax not exceeding twenty-five dollars.

l-posters.

(8) Upon every bill-poster, street huckster, photographer, merchandise or produce broker, ice dealer, dealer in wood and coal or either, insurance agencies and every skating-rink or shooting-gallery, waterworks, express company and oil company, a license not exceeding ten dollars a year.

graph, telene and tric light panies.

(9) That every telegraph, telephone or electric light company, itinerant dealer in lightning rods and stores, shall pay a license not exceeding twenty-five dollars per annum.

e-walkers,

(10) Each rope-walker, itinerant optician, itinerant dealer in any specific, carriage, buggy or wagon, each dancing school, every stallion or jack standing in the town, persons soliciting orders for photographs or pictures, selling jewelry or any other article having a prize given therewith, or any itinerant person taking or enlarging likenesses of a human face on order or otherwise, each dealer in patent rights, itinerant traders, shall pay a license tax not exceeding ten dollars a year.

lleries.

(11) Each distillery of fruits or grain, each distiller or compounder of spirituous liquors, each gift enterprise or lottery, every railroad company having a depot or office in town, a license tax not exceeding fifty dollars a year.

ucting ness without se. iso.

(12) Any person carrying on business in the town without having paid the license tax according to the ordinance of the town, shall be fined twenty dollars: *Provided*, that any person taking out license after the first of May shall pay a tax on such license as in the foregoing sections, proportioned according to the unexpired term of the year according to the discretion of the mayor.

(13) Upon all subjects taxed under Schedule B, chapter one

hundred and thirty-six, laws of North Carolina, session of one thousand eight hundred and eighty-three, not hereinbefore provided for, shall pay a license tax of ten dollars, and the board of commissioners shall have power to impose a license tax on any business carried on in the town of Louisburg not before enumerated herein, not to exceed ten dollars a year. Other subjects of taxation.

(14) Upon every billiard table, bowling alley or alley of like kind, bowling saloon, bagatelle table, pool table, or table, stand or place for any other game or play, with or without a name, kept for hire, or used or connected with a hotel or restaurant, or contiguous or adjacent thereto, a license not exceeding fifty dollars. Upon every hotel, restaurant or eating house, a license tax not exceeding twenty-five dollars. Billiard tables, bowling alleys, etc.

S53. 93. That all laws and clauses of laws in conflict with this act are hereby repealed. Conflicting laws repealed.

SEC. 94. That this act shall be in force from and after its ratification.

Ratified the 6th day of March, A. D. 1899.

CHAPTER 244.

An act to incorporate the High School of Swain county, under the name and style of the James L. Robinson Institute in Swain county.

The General Assembly of North Carolina do enact:

Section 1. That L. Lee More, S. B. Gibson, D. Dehart, A. V. Calhoun, John S. Woodard, R. T. Cunningham, A. H. Hayes, E. C. Monteeth, John Enloe, T. P. Sawer, W. T. Conley, E. Everett, D. K. Collins, A. M. Fry, S. B. Allison, their associates and successors, be and they are hereby created a joint stock company, a body politic and corporate, for the purpose of maintaining a school of high grade in the town of Bryson City, North Carolina, Swain county, for the intellectual and moral training of the children and young men and women of the white race, under the name and style of the James L. Robinson Institute, and in that name may sue and be sued, plead and be impleaded, contract and be contracted with, acquire, hold and convey in their corporate capacity property, real and personal, and exercise all acts in relation thereto or incident to the ownership of real and personal property and for the promotion of education. Corporators. Body corporate. Location of school. Purpose of corporation.

Sec. 2. That said trustees shall, if they deem proper, establish a school of law in said institute, and secure the services of some competent instructor to preside over the same, who shall receive School of law may be established.

as compensation for his services such sum as may be determined upon by said trustees.

rpetual succession.

Sec. 3. That the members of said corporation shall have perpetual succession, shall elect their officers, and may, if they deem it advisable, have a common seal.

cers.

Sec. 4. That the officers of said corporation shall be a president, vice-president, treasurer, secretary and five directors, three of whom shall constitute a quorum for the transaction of business, and all of whom shall be elected by the stockholders annually.

st meeting, en held.

Sec. 5. That the first meeting for the election of officers shall be held within sixty days from the ratification of this act, and these shall continue to hold their offices until their successors are elected; and the annual meeting of stockholders shall be on the first Monday in June of each year, unless otherwise ordered by the stockholders.

laws.

Sec. 6. That at the first regular meeting of the stockholders they shall have power to make such by-laws not inconsistent with the laws of the state as shall be deemed necessary to promote the object of the corporation, and from time to time to make such charges [changes] as they may deem best.

ital stock.

Sec. 7. That the capital stock of said corporation shall not be less than five thousand nor more than ten thousand dollars and shall be divided into shares of twenty-five dollars each, and to be paid at such times and in such manner as the board of directors may direct.

sion of res.

questions ded by ority of kholders.

Sec. 8. That at the meetings of stockholders all questions may be decided by a majority vote, each share being entitled to one vote, and a majority of all the stock shall be represented in person or by proxy, to constitute a legal meeting of stockholders.

dent may meetings.

Sec. 9. That the president of said corporation, with the advice and consent of the directors, shall have power to call a meeting of the stockholders whenever he may deem it proper.

n corpora- may con-

Sec. 10. That except for building purposes said corporation shall have no power to contract indebtedness exceeding three hundred dollars, nor shall it have power to execute any mortgage or to create other lien than mechanics' and laborers' liens upon its property; and the stockholders shall not be individually liable for any indebtedness of said corporation.

vidual lity.

ointment of uctors.

Sec. 11. That the said board of directors shall have power to appoint such teachers as may be necessary in and over said school, and may remove the same for misbehavior, inability or neglect of duty; they shall also have power to make all necessary rules and regulations for the government of said school, not inconsistent with the laws of this state.

held for it of school pted from ion.

Sec. 12. That land held by any of the officers of said corporation for the benefit of said school shall be and the same is hereby exempted from all kinds of public taxation.

Sec. 13. That any license to retail spirituous, vinous or malt liquors at or within three miles of said school shall be void. **Sale of liquor within three miles prohibited.**

Sec. 14. That if any person shall sell, give or carry to any student or students of said institute or school at or within three miles thereof any spirituous or intoxicating liquors, also wines, beers or cordials, by whatsoever name the same may be called, without special permission in writing from the president of said school, he shall forfeit and pay the sum of two hundred dollars, to be recovered in any court of record, one-half to the use of the informant and the other half to the use of said school, and the offender shall furthermore be guilty of a misdemeanor, and upon conviction thereof in the superior court of Swain county shall be fined at the discretion of the court. **Persons giving students liquor guilty of a misdemeanor.**

Sec. 15. All laws or clauses of laws in conflict with this act are hereby repealed. **Conflicting laws repealed.**

Sec. 16. This act shall take effect from and after its ratification.

Ratified the 6th day of March, A. D. 1899.

CHAPTER 245.

An act to amend chapter fifty-eight, laws of eighteen hundred and seventy-nine.

The General Assembly of North Carolina do enact:

Section 1. That chapter fifty-eight of private laws of eighteen hundred and seventy-nine, entitled "An act concerning Rock Spring Camp Ground," state of North Carolina, be amended as follows: **Chapter 58, private laws of 1879, amended.**

Sec. 2. That the trustees of Rock Spring Camp Ground, on the first Monday in May, eighteen hundred and ninety nine, and annually thereafter, elect a mayor and three commissioners and a marshal. **Election of officers.**

Sec. 3. That it shall be the duty of the mayor and commissioners and marshal elected to meet before some justice of the peace or other officer authorized to administer oaths and take the oath usual for such officers. **Officers shall take oath.**

Sec. 4. That the said commissioners shall have power to pass all by-laws and rules for the good government of the camp ground not inconsistent with the laws of the state and United States. **Commissioners empowered to pass by-laws.**

Sec. 4. That the mayor shall have the same power and authority to issue process and try all cases that may come before him as is given to other mayors of incorporated towns and cities, and **Power of mayor to issue processes.**

shall retain all fines collected by him for the use of the aforesaid camp ground. The election of the aforesaid officer shall be held as for other municipal officers.

Sec. 6. That this act shall be in force from and after its ratification.

Ratified the 6th day of March, A. D. 1899.

CHAPTER 246.

An act to incorporate Asheville Tobacco Company

The General Assembly of North Carolina do enact:

rporators. Section 1. That J. A. Porter, R. R. Porter and C. L. Porter, their associates, successors and assigns, are hereby created a body politic and corporate under the name of Asheville Tobacco Company, and under that name and style may have a corporate seal, sue and be sued, plead and be impleaded, contract and be contracted with, and enjoy all the rights, privileges and immunities given to corporations under chapter sixteen of The Code of North Carolina and the acts amendatory thereof.

rporate name.

rporate powers.

pital stock. Sec. 2. That the capital stock of said corporation shall be five thousand dollars, with the privilege of increasing the same at any time and from time to time to any sum not exceeding fifty thousand dollars, divided into shares of the par value of one hundred dollars each.

ay be increased.

ture of business. Sec. 3. That said corporation is hereby authorized and empowered to conduct, transact and carry on in all its branches the business of manufacturing, buying and selling tobacco, and may buy, sell and deal in goods, wares and merchandise of every kind and description at its will and pleasure, either as jobbers, wholesalers or retailers.

y lease, purchase and hold l estate. Sec. 4. That said corporation shall have the power to lease, purchase, hold, sell and convey real estate, and to borrow money and issue bonds or other evidences of indebtedness so created, and secure the payment of the same by mortgage of its property, franchises and effects or otherwise.

airs of corporation, how verned. Sec. 5. That the affairs of said corporation shall be managed by its stockholders, but they may make such by-laws, rules and regulations for the conduct and management of the corporate affairs and its business as they may deem necessary and expedient not inconsistent with the laws of the state.

ces of corporation Sec. 6. That the offices of said corporation shall consist of a president, secretary and treasurer, and the last two officers may be filled by one person to be elected as prescribed by the by-laws, rules and regulations of the corporation, but until such rules and regulations are made the said R. R. Porter shall act as president and the said J. A. Porter as secretary and treasurer, who shall hold their respective offices until their successors are elected and qualified. That on and after the ratification of this act the said corporation shall be considered organized. Temporary officers.

Sec. 7. That the duration of said corporation shall be thirty years. Duration of charter.

Sec. 8. That the said corporation shall have the right to purchase the business, good-will, machinery, fixtures and furniture of any existing firm or concern, and to pay for the same by the issuance of stock to the seller; and when the sum of five thousand dollars is paid in, whether in cash or otherwise, the said stock may be issued to the stockholders. May purchase plants from other concerns.

Sec. 9. That the said stockholders and members of said corporation shall not be personally liable for the debts and liabilities of the corporation. Individual liability.

Sec. 10. That the principal office of the said corporation shall be in Asheville, North Carolina, but the said corporation may establish branches at other places or by a majority vote of its stockholders may move to some other place. Principal office.

Sec. 11. This act shall be in force from and after its ratification.

Ratified the 6th day of March, A. D. 1899.

CHAPTER 247.

An act to incorporate The Asheville Savings Bank.

The General Assembly of North Carolina do enact:

Section 1. That G. W. Purefoy, J. H. Tucker, O. D. Revell and J. D. Murphy, and their associates, successors and assigns, be and they are hereby created a body politic and corporate under the name and style of "The Asheville Savings Bank," and by such name may acquire, hold and convey real and personal property, sue and be sued, plead and be impleaded in any of the courts of this state, and have a continued succession for ninety-nine years, and a common seal, and shall have all the powers, rights, and privileges granted to any banking institution under the laws of the state of North Carolina. Corporators. Body corporate. Corporate name. Corporate powers

Sec. 2. That the capital stock of said corporation shall not be less than ten thousand dollars, which may be increased from time to time to a sum not exceeding one million dollars, in shares of one hundred dollars each. Said corporation may commence its Capital stock. May be increased.

hen corporan may commence business. business when ten thousand dollars of the capital stock aforesaid has been paid in. The stockholders shall not be individually liable for the debts or torts of the corporation, except as provided by law.

ard of directs. SEC. 3. That five persons shall constitute a board of directors of this corporation, to be selected when said corporation shall be organized, who shall continue in office until their successors are chosen: Provided, that no person shall be a director in said corporation without having first subscribed and taken at least two shares of said stock.

option of laws. SEC. 4. It shall be the duty of the board of directors to prescribe rules and regulations and by-laws for the government thereof; to choose officers, fix salaries, fill vacancies and generally do and perform such duties as the rules, regulations and by-laws of this corporation shall prescribe, when the same shall have been duly ratified by a majority in number and value of the stockholders voting thereon in person or by proxy.

ture of business. SEC. 5. That this corporation shall have power to receive and pay out the lawful currency of the country; deal in exchange, gold and silver coin, stocks, bonds, notes and other securities; to loan money to or receive deposits of money or other property or evidences of debt from corporations, minors, apprentices, femes coverts or other persons, on such terms and time and manner of collection as may be agreed upon between the parties; and for the use and loan of money may charge legal interest, and may take and receive such interest at the time of making such loan, free from all other control, contract or liability whatever; to invest in the stocks, bonds or other securities of this or any other state of the United States, or of any corporation created under the laws thereof or any municipality of this or any other state, and to take such real and personal property, conditioned in such form for the payment of the principal and interest of money loaned, advanced or expended, as may be deemed most safe, expedient and beneficial.

(Margin: ay charge terest.)

y guarantee yment of tes, bonds, etc. SEC. 6. That said corporation shall have the power and authority to guarantee the payment of principal and interest of notes, bonds, bills of exchange and other securities and evidences of debt, including the obligations of such corporations, individuals and municipalities as may have secured their payment by deed of trust made to this corporation for such special purpose, and to receive for any guarantee such compensation as the parties may agree upon, and may charge interest therefor, and may take and receive such interest and compensation at the time of making such transaction or transactions.

(Margin: mpensation owed.)

ay receive oney in trust. SEC. 7. That said corporation shall have power to receive money in trust and accumulate the same, at legal interest, and to allow interest at the legal rate; to accept and execute trusts of every description as fully as a natural person could which may be committed to said corporation by any person or persons, corporation or corporations whatsoever, or by order or decree or authority of any court of record, upon such terms as may be agreed upon, provided or declared in regard thereto; to act as agent for the purpose of issuing, registering or countersigning certificates of stock, bonds or other evidences of debt of any state, corporation, association, municipality or public authority, on such terms as may be agreed upon; to lease and rent real estate, and collect rents from the same, upon commission, to be agreed upon between the parties; to accept and execute trusts for married women in respect to their separate property or estate, and to act as agent for them in the management, sale and disposition of their property or properties, real and personal.

Courts may appoint company guardian, administrator, etc.

Sec. 8. That in all cases where an application may be made in a court having jurisdiction to appoint a guardian of an infant, committee of an idoit, lunatic or insane person, administrator of any person dying intestate or executor of any person dying testate, trustee or receiver, such court shall have power to appoint such corporation as such guardian, committee, executor, administrator, trustee or receiver, upon the like application that any natural person might be so appointed. And it shall be lawful for any person, by deed, will or any other writing, to appoint said corporation trustee, executor, guardian, assignee or receiver; and as such executor, administrator, assignee or receiver, guardian of an infant, committee of an idiot, lunatic or insane person, said corporation may lawfully act, and as such shall be subject to all the obligations and liabilities of a natural person acting in like capacity, and subject to be removed like natural persons, and subject to all the laws of North Carolina applicable to natural persons holding such fiduciary positions.

Said corporation may be appointed trustee, etc.

Persons having custody of bonds, etc., may deposit same with corporation.

Sec. 9. That it shall be lawful for any individual, executor, administrator, guardian, committee, receiver, assignee, trustee, public officer or other person having custody of any bonds, stocks, securities, moneys, funds, credits or other valuables to deposit the same for safe keeping with said corporation: Provided, that the deposit shall not exonerate such individual from liability.

Courts making said corporation guardian, etc., may compel obedience to orders.

Sec. 10. That every court wherein said corporation shall be appointed or shall be allowed to qualify as guardian, committee, executor, administrator, trustee or receiver, or in which it may be made a depository of moneys or other valuables, shall have power to make all orders and compel obedience thereto, and require such corporation to render all accounts which such courts might lawfully make or require, as if such corporation was a natural person; and the court, if it deem necessary, may from time to time appoint suitable persons to investigate the affairs and management of said company, or the court may, if it deem necessary, examine the affairs of said company under oath or affirmation as to the security aforesaid.

thorized to est moneys eived in st, etc.

Sec. 11. That said corporation is authorized to invest moneys received in trust or deposit, loan or otherwise, and to take, have and hold estate and property, real and personal or mixed, obtained with the money aforesaid, or with funds belonging to said corporation, and to sell, grant, mortgage, convey, by way of deed of trust or otherwise, encumber, lease or dispose of the same, and to that end may execute all deeds or other instruments concerning the same; to deal in exchange, foreign or domestic, securities, mortgages, notes, bonds or other evidences of debt, certificates of indebtedness, stocks of incorporated companies, loans, bonds of the United States or of any city, county or other municipality or of any incorporated company or individual.

ds given by corporation y be approved.

Sec. 12. Whenever any bond, undertaking, recognizance, obligation or stipulation, municipal or otherwise, or the rules or the regulations of any board, body corporate, municipal or otherwise, required or permitted to be made, given, tendered or filed for the security or protection of any person or persons, corporation, municipality or other organization whatsoever, conditioned for the doing of or not doing of any act or thing whatsoever, as specified in such bond, recognizance, obligation, stipulation or undertaking specified, any and all heads of departments, public officers, said county, town or municipality, and any and all boards, courts, judges and municipalities now and hereafter required or permitted to accept or approve the sufficiency of any such bond or recognizance, obligation, stipulation or undertaking, may in the discretion of such head of department, court, judge, public officer or municipality, accept such bond, recognizance, obligation, stipulation or undertaking, and approve the same whenever the same is executed or the conditions thereof are guaranteed by such corporation.

ers and others may pt and ap- e bonds d by said pany.

Sec. 13. Whenever any such bond, recognizance, obligation, stipulation or undertaking is so required or permitted to be made, given, tendered or filed with any surety, or with two or more sureties, the execution of the same or the guaranteeing the performance of the conditions thereof shall be executed when executed or guaranteed by said corporation, and any and all heads of departments, courts justices, boards and municipalities, and any and all public officers, state, county, town or municipal, whose duty it might be or shall be hereafter to accept or approve the sufficiency of any such bonds, recognizance, obligation, stipulation or undertaking, may accept and approve the same when executed or guaranteed by said corporation; and said corporation is hereby vested with full power and authority to execute or guarantee such bonds, recognizance, stipulations, obligations or undertakings, whether given under the laws of this state or of the United States, or of any state or county.

Shall have power to endorse notes, etc.

Sec. 14. That said corporation shall have power to guarantee, endorse and secure the payment and punctual performance and collection of notes, debts, bills of exchange, contracts, bonds, accounts, claims, rents, annuities, mortgages, choses in actions, evidences of debt, certificates of property values, checks, and the title to property, real and personal, indebtedness of companies, individuals, partnerships, cities, counties, municipalities in this state, on such terms or commission as may be agreed upon or established by said company and the parties dealing therewith.

May receive deposits etc., upon storage.

Sec. 15. That said corporation may receive upon storage, deposit or otherwise, merchandise, moneys, funds, credits, specie, plate, stock, promissory notes, mortgages and deeds of trust, certificates and evidences of debts, contracts and all other personal properties whatsoever; take charge and custody of real and personal estates and securities and advance money thereupon on such terms as may be established by such corporation and agreed upon between the parties: and in all cases in which public officers of municipalities, or the officers of private corporations are authorized to deposit moneys, funds, credits, stocks, bonds or other evidences of debt, such deposits by such officers or corporations may be made with said corporation, and said corporation may be appointed and is hereby authorized to act as redemption agent of any bank or banking association created or existing under the laws of this state.

Authorized to act as redemption agent of banking institutions.

May sell at public auction securities held by them.

Sec. 16. That it shall be lawful for said corporation to sell at public auction or private sale all properties or securities of whatsoever kind mentioned or specified in any contract or agreement between the corporation and the other party or parties, after the maturity of an obligation under said contract or agreement, upon giving the party or parties in interest ten days' notice of its intention to sell such property or securities, and to reimburse itself out of the proceeds of such sale for the money due it, with interest, storage, costs and charges, and to indemnify itself for any loss it may have sustained for the non-fulfillment of such contract, or by reason of any misrepresentation, fraud or concealment.

Empowered to discount and endorse notes, bills, etc.

Sec. 17. That said corporation shall have power to discount and endorse promissory notes, bills of exchange, domestic and foreign, and shall have all the powers, privileges and immunities which any bank or banking institution incorporated by the laws of this state has.

Sec. 18. That said company or corporation shall have power to ay borrow oney, as rected by board directors. borrow money in such amounts and at such rate of interest and payable at such time and places as the board of directors may determine, and issue its notes, certificates or registered or coupon bonds under its corporate seal. It may receive money on deposit or on open account or on certificate and deposit, and pay interest thereon or not, as may be agreed upon between the parties.

ce of corpora- n. Sec. 19. That the office for the transaction of business of said corporation shall be in Asheville, in the state of North Carolina, and the said corporation shall exist for sixty years.

Sec. 20. That this act shall be in force from and after its ratification.

Ratified the 6th day of March, A. D. 1899.

CHAPTER 248.

An act to incorporate the town of Saratoga in Wilson county.

The General Assembly of North Carolina do enact:

corporated. Section 1. That the town in Wilson county now known as Saratoga, be and the same is hereby incorporated under the name and style of Saratoga, and it shall have the benefit of and shall be subject to all the provisions of law now existing in reference to incorporated towns not inconsistent with this act.

rporate limits. Sec. 2. That the corporate limits of said town shall be as follows: Beginning at the crossing of the Plank road and the Tarboro road and runs along the Plank road north forty-seven west one hundred poles to a post; thence south forty-three west eighty poles to a post; thence south forty-seven east one hundred and sixty poles to a post; thence north forty-three east one hundred and sixty poles to a post; thence north forty-seven west one hundred and sixty-four poles to a post; thence south forty-three west eighty poles to a post at the Plank road, the beginning.

rm of officers. Sec. 3. That the officers of said corporation shall be a mayor, five commissioners and a town constable, the constable to be selected by the commissioners, and the following-named persons shall fill the said offices until the next regular election for municipal corporations: John T. Moore, mayor; commissioners, Patrick Bailey, William Price, J. Lawrence Gay, Dr. C. B. Walton and R. E. Bynum. The said officers shall have all the rights, powers and duties conferred by law.

mporary cers.

mmissioners powered to ss by-laws and dinances. Sec. 4. The said commissioners shall have power to pass by-laws, rules and regulations for the good government of the town not inconsistent with the laws of the state and of the United States, and to levy and collect a tax on all subjects of state taxation, and to impose fines for violation of town ordinances and collect the same, and also levy and collect such license and privilege taxes as are provided by law.

Sec. 5. That at the next regular election for mayor and commissioners the question as to whether liquor shall be sold in said town [shall] be submitted to the qualified voters of said town. Those favoring the sale of liquor shall vote a ticket with word "License" thereon, and those opposed will vote a ticket with the words "No license." If a majority shall vote for license, no license shall be granted by the commissioners of Wilson county unless the commissioners of said town shall endorse and approve the same. At next regular election question as to whether or not liquor shall be sold in corporate limits shall be submitted.

Sec. 6. That the following words of chapter four hundred and eleven, section one, of the laws of eighteen hundred and ninety-seven, to-wit: "Wilson county, within two miles of the Freewill Baptist church at Saratoga" be and the same is hereby repealed. Portion of chapter 411, section 1, laws of 1897, repealed.

Sec. 7. That this act shall be in force from and after its ratification.

Ratified the 6th day of March, A. D. 1899.

CHAPTER 249.

An act to incorporate the Northampton Electric and Water Power Company.

The General Assembly of North Carolina do enact:

Section 1. That Nicholas D. Wilkins, of the county of Northampton; William J. White and Benjamin S. Bronson, of the county of Warren, in the state of North Carolina, and such others as are now or may hereafter be associated with them, and their successors and assigns, are hereby constituted a body politic and corporate by the name and title of "Northampton Electric and Water Power Company," and under that name and style may sue and be sued, implead and be impleaded, contract and be contracted with, adopt and use a common seal, which it may alter at pleasure; shall have perpetual succession, and shall have and enjoy all the rights and privileges, powers, immunities, liberties and franchises pertaining to corporations. Incorporated. Body corporate. Corporate name. Corporate powers.

Sec. 2. That said company shall have full power: Corporate powers.

(1) To buy, lease, exchange, own, hold, sell and convey real property, situate in the counties of Northampton, Halifax and Warren, North Carolina, especially those lands along the Roanoke river between Gaston and Robinson's ferry, in any amount or quantity, in fee simple, or for a less interest, with all rights and privileges in connection therewith: Provided, the amount

or quantity so held by the company does not exceed at any one time five thousand acres.

develop and ilize water wer.

(2) To develop and utilize the water power of the Roanoke river between Gaston and Robinson's ferry, North Carolina, and on both sides of that stream, for manufacturing purposes, and for the construction and operation of mills and factories of any kind and for any purpose, and for generating, using and applying electricity and electric power; and to that end to erect and maintain all necessary dams, waste-ways and obstructions in and across said river, and cut and construct all such canals and waste-ways from and to said river upon the lands of said company as may be required to fully develop and utilize such water power:

oviso.

Provided, that in the construction and maintenance of said dams, canals and waste-ways, and in the develop [development] and use of said water power, neither the rights or property of persons owning lands on the said river, nor the rights, franchises, privileges or property of any other corporation shall be interfered with or encroached upon in any unreasonable manner to the substantial injury of any other person or corporation.

ght of property all not be erfered with unreasonable nner.

ild and equip lls.

(3) To build and equip mills and factories of any kind and for any purpose on its said property and development, and operate, sell or lease the same, or make such other disposition of them as it may deem best.

build and rate railroad.

(4) To erect and build and operate a railroad from the site or plant where the factory or factories may be located, to some place on the Raleigh and Gaston Railroad, in the county of Halifax or Warren; and also to erect and maintain and operate lines for the use and transmission of electric power along its said railroad, and is hereby vested with all the rights, privileges and powers as are allowed to railroad companies and telegraph companies under and pursuant to chapter forty-nine of the first volume of The Code of North Carolina for the erection, construction and operation of said railroad and lines.

sell, lease and nate water wer.

(5) To sell, lease and donate the water power, electric power and sites for mills, factories and other structures that may be developed by the construction and maintenance of its aforesaid dams, waste-ways and canals.

lay out cer- n lands.

(6) To lay out its lands not needed for the construction and maintenance of its dams, waste-ways, canals and railroad, nor for the operation of the mills, factories and other plants that may be located thereon, into parks, blocks and building lots, and if it so desire, erect suitable structures and buildings thereon, and sell, lease and donate the same, whether improved or unimproved.

do any and all ings expedient developing ter power.

(7) To do any and all things expedient for acquiring, utilizing, improving, developing and disposing of its property, and to that end contract with any person or corporation to purchase and sell to it such lands, water rights and easements and electric power

it may desire or need for its aforesaid purposes, and also to develop the water power and construct and erect dams, waste-ways, canals, mills and factories it may determine upon; and also the said railroad and electric line, and make payment therefor in money or shares of its capital stock, or both.

Capital stock. Division of shares.

Sec. 3. That the capital stock of said company shall be one hundred thousand dollars, to be divided into shares of one hundred dollars each, and may be increased from time to time to an amount not exceeding one million dollars, as may be authorized by the stockholders at their general or special meetings. Shares of stock may be issued and sold or subscribed for, and payment therefor may be made in money, lands, services, work, labor and materials, contributed, employed and furnished for and in the prosecution and objects of the company, and upon such terms and at such price and rates as the company, by its president and board of directors, may determine and agree upon.

Individual liability.

Sec. 4. That the stockholders and corporators of said company, their associates, successors and assigns shall not be responsible for the debts, contracts, obligations, engagements, assurances or torts of said company beyond or further than the property which they may own as stockholders therein, or than to such amount as may be due and unpaid severally upon the shares of stock purchased or subscribed for by them respectively at the stipulated price therefor.

Temporary officers of corporation.

Sec. 5. That Nicholas D. Wilkins is hereby appointed president and William J. White is appointed secretary and treasurer, to act as such and hold their offices as such until their successors shall be elected by the stockholders in such manner as may be prescribed by the by-laws of the company; and the principal office of the company shall be in the town of Warrenton, in Warren county, until the same shall be changed by the stockholders in meeting assembled.

Authority and power of stockholders.

Sec. 6. That the stockholders shall have authority to pass such by-laws for the regulation and management of the affairs of the company, and to alter the same, as they may deem best, and to prescribe the number of directors and establish such offices and assign the duties thereto as they may deem to the best interest of the company, and to establish the principal office of the company and change the place at pleasure; and to regulate the terms of the officers, their respective salaries, and to make rules for the transfer of stock of the company, and for the times and places of the meetings of the stockholders. And the aforesaid incorporators may manage the affairs of the said corporation as directors until others are duly elected under the provisions of this charter.

Sec. 7. That this act shall be in force from and after its ratification.

Ratified the 6th day of March, A. D. 1899.

CHAPTER 250.

An act to amend the charter of Warsaw in Duplin county.

The General Assembly of North Carolina do enact:

ction 4, chapter , private laws 1885, amended. Section 1. That section four (4), chapter ninety-one (91), private laws of eighteen hundred and eighty-five (1885), be amended to read as follows:

nnual election officers. The officers of the town of Warsaw shall consist of a mayor and five commissioners, to be elected annually on the first Tuesday in June by the qualified voters of said town; also a constable, secretary and treasurer, to be chosen by the board of commissioners immediately after its organization, to hold for one year or until their successors are elected and qualified; and it shall be the duty of the mayor to give notice of the election ten days previous thereto by posters written or printed, and put up at three or more public places within the corporate limits of said town; and if the board of commissioners of Duplin county shall fail or neglect to appoint inspectors, two resident citizens shall be appointed by the mayor, who with himself shall hold said election.

esent officers ntinued. Sec. 2. That all the present officers of said town shall continue in office and perform the duties thereof until first Tuesday in June next.

Sec. 3. That this act shall be in force from and after its ratification.

Ratified the 6th day of March, A. D. 1899.

CHAPTER 251.

An act to incorporate the town of Alexis in Gaston county.

The General Assembly of North Carolina do enact:

corporated. Section 1. That the town of Alexis, in the county of Gaston, be and the same is hereby incorporated by the name and style

rporate name. of Alexis, and shall be subject to all provisions of law contained in chapter sixty-two, volume two, of The Code, now in force in relation to the incorporated towns.

rporate limits. Sec. 2. That the incorporate limits of said town shall be one-half mile in every direction from the place where the Rozzell Ferry dirt road now crosses the Carolina Central Railroad.

wn officers. Sec. 3. That the officers of said town shall consist of a mayor, three commissioners and a constable.

Sec. 4. That there shall be an election held for the election of a mayor, three commissioners and a constable for said town on the first Monday in May, eighteen hundred and ninety-nine, and on said day in every year thereafter by the qualified voters within the limits of said corporation. Annual election of officers.

Sec. 5. That until their successors are elected and qualified under the provisions of this act the following-named persons shall fill said offices: S. A. Straup, mayor; and C. F. Abernethy, J. L. Hoover, Q. Y. Straup, commissioners; and F. L. Howard, constable. Temporary officers.

Sec. 6. That the manufacture and sale of intoxicating drinks of any kind shall be forever prohibited within the corporate limits of said town. Manufacture and sale of liquors prohibited.

Sec. 7. That this act shall be in force from and after its ratification.

Ratified the 6th day of March, A. D. 1899.

CHAPTER 252.

An act to incorporate the Winston-Salem Gas and Lighting Company.

The General Assembly of North Carolina do enact:

Section 1. That R. J. Reynolds, W. R. Reynolds, E. B. Jones, E. H. Wilson, J. O. Magruder and such other persons, companies or corporations as may hereafter be associated with them, their successors and assigns, are hereby created a body politic and corporate by the name of the Winston-Salem Gas and Lighting Company, for the term of sixty years, to enjoy all rights and privileges usually conferred upon corporations. Corporators. Body corporate. Corporate name.

Sec. 2. That the capital stock of said company shall be one hundred thousand dollars represented by one thousand shares of the par value of one hundred dollars, with privilege of increasing the same from time to time as a majority of the stockholders may deem necessary to a sum not exceeding two hundred thousand dollars. Capital stock. May be increased.

Sec. 3. That as such corporation they may sue and be sued, plead and be impleaded, prosecute and defend actions and special proceedings; have a common seal, which they may change at will; make all such by-laws, rules and regulations for the government of the corporation as they may see fit, not in conflict with the laws of the state or United States; they may elect such officers as they may see fit, provide their compensation, duties and terms of service, and may do any and all other acts necessary in the conduct of said business not prohibited by law. Corporate powers.

thorized to erate light,

Sec. 4. That said company is hereby authorized and empowered to manufacture, produce, lease and sell light, heat and power made from or by the use of gas, electricity, coal, oil, steam, water or any other product or material or combination, or a combination of any other product or material for any or all of said purposes; and said company shall have the power to maintain and operate such plant or plants and appliances as may be necessary to manufacture and distribute for sale or use light, heat and power from the sources above named, and to do any and all things that may be necessary for the proper conduct of said business.

rporate pow-

That said company shall also have the right and the power to lease, purchase, hold, sell and convey patents relating to or in any way identified with said business, and they shall also have the power to lease, purchase, hold, sell and convey such real and personal estate as the company may deem necessary for the proper prosecution of its business; and to borrow money and issue bonds or other evidences of indebtedness so created, and to secure the payment of the same by mortgage upon its property or effects [or] otherwise, or may also receive subscriptions to its capital stock in cash, real or personal property of any kind, at such rates or upon such terms as the corporation may deem best.

y acquire ht-of-way.

Sec. 5. That said corporation may acquire right-of-way to lay, plant and bury its pipes and mains through, over or under the streets, thoroughfares, public squares, rights-of-way granted to other corporations, private property of the citizens of the cities of Winston-Salem, by a consent of the respective town governments or their lawful authorized agents. And after such consent shall have been obtained from the respective cities said company shall have the right to maintain the same along said streets, thoroughfares, public squares, and private property if necessary, by condemnation proceedings conducted in all respects and with like rights and powers and in like manner as provided for acquisition for rights-of-way of telegraph companies in chapter forty-nine, volume one, of The Code.

ncipal office.

Sec. 6. That the principal office of said company shall be in the city of Winston, North Carolina.

ividual oility.

Sec. 7. That the corporators, stockholders and their successors and assigns shall not be individually or personally liable or responsible for the debts, contracts, obligation or torts of the corporations or its agents.

Sec. 8. This act shall be in force from and after its ratification.

Ratified the 6th day of March, A. D. 1899.

CHAPTER 253.

An act to incorporate the Great Council of North Carolina, Improved Order of Red Men.

The General Assembly of North Carolina do enact:

Section 1. That J. B. Hathaway, J. R Davis, J. R. Sanders, T. T. Anthony, W. Ben Goodwin and T. T. Whitcomb and their successors and associates in office, with such other persons as under the rules or usages of the order are now or hereafter may be associated with them as members, be and they are hereby created a body politic and corporate under the name and style of the Great Council of North Carolina, Improved Order of Red Men, and by such name and style may sue and be sued, plead and be impleaded and shall exist for thirty years and have a common seal. Corporators. Body corporate. Corporate name.

Sec. 2. The said corporation, for the purposes of its organization which are hereby declared to be social and benevolent in their character, may purchase, hold, alien or encumber estate, real and personal, at any point or points in the state: Provided, that such real estate shall not at any time exceed in value the sum of one hundred thousand dollars ($100,000) altogether. May hold property, etc.

Sec. 3. It shall have power from time to time to establish or change its places of session as well as the location of its principal offices, at or to such place or places in the state as it may deem expedient or proper. May change location of offices

Sec. 4. It shall have power, in furthering the purposes of its organization, to establish subordinate councils of tribes at different points in the state, and for their and its own better control and government may from time to time declare and promulgate such constitutions, by-laws and rules, being not inconsistent with the general law, as to it may seem expedient and proper. May establish subordinate councils.

Sec. 5. This act shall be in force from and after its ratification.

Ratified the 6th day of March, A. D. 1899.

CHAPTER 254.

An act to incorporate the town of Jerome in Johnston county.

The General Assembly of North Carolina do enact:

Section 1. That the town of Jerome, in the county of Johnston, be and the same is hereby incorporated into a body politic under the name and style of the town of Jerome, and under this name shall have all the rights, powers and privileges conferred Incorporated. Corporate name.

upon towns and cities by chapter sixty-two (62) of the Code, volume two.

rporate limits.

Sec 2 That the corporate limits of the town of Jerome shall be as follows:

The Atlantic Coast Line depot shall be the center of said town and the corporate limits shall extend therefrom one-fourth (¼) of a mile north, east, south and west.

mporary cers.

Sec. 3. That J. C. Beland, W. E. Smith, Troy Batten and J. R. Creech are hereby constituted and appointed the board of commissioners for said town, and A. B. Peacock is hereby constituted and appointed mayor of said town, and upon taking the oath of office required by law they shall have full power to execute the ordinances of said town, and shall hold their offices until the first Monday in May, eighteen hundred and ninety-nine, and until their successors are duly elected and qualified, and at the time and in the manner prescribed by law their successors shall be elected, but the board of commissioners shall then be reduced to three (3) in number.

›wers of cers.

mmissioners powered to x saloons, etc.

Sec. 4. That the board of commissioners of said town are hereby authorized to impose a license tax upon all persons in the corporate limits selling or retailing wines or liquors, not exceeding fifty (50) dollars per annum. and to levy and collect a tax upon real and personal estate not to exceed twenty (20) cents on the one hundred dollars and a poll tax not to exceed sixty cents on the poll.

They are also authorized to levy and collect taxes upon all the subjects enumerated in said chapter sixty-nine, volume two, of The Code.

Sec. 5. This act shall be in force from and after its ratification.

Ratified the 6th day of March, A. D. 1899.

CHAPTER 255.

An act to authorize the New Columbus Bridge Company of Columbus, Ohio, to remove a steel bridge erected by it across the Tar river in Yancey county, or to establish the same as a toll bridge.

The General Assembly of North Carolina do enact:

ew Columbus ›idge Company powered to ove certain ›idge.

Section 1. That the New Columbus Bridge Company of Columbus, Ohio, be and said company is hereby allowed and empowered to remove the bridge lately constructed by said company across Tar river, between Yancey and Mitchell counties, in North Carolina, when the said company shall choose to do so.

Sec. 2. That if said comapny shall choose to allow said bridge to remain at the point where it is now situated the said company shall be allowed to charge the following rates as toll for the passage over said bridge, to-wit: For each person on foot, not more than three cents; for each person on horseback, not more than ten cents; for each one-horse wagon or buggy, not more than fifteen cents; for each two horse wagon or carriage or wagon or carriage drawn by more than one horse, not more than twenty cents; for each head of loose cattle, sheep, horses or hogs, not more than one cent each.

Rates said company shall charge if bridge is allowed to stand.

Sec. 3. That any person who shall pass or attempt to pass, or shall drive or cause to be driven, over said bridge any stock or wagon mentioned in this act, without first paying the toll for the same, shall be guilty of a misdemeanor, and upon conviction thereof shall be fined not more than fifty dollars or imprisoned not more than thirty days, and shall be subject to indictment for said offense in either of said counties of Yancey or Mitchell.

Persons riding, driving, etc., over bridge without paying toll, guilty of a misdemeanor.

Sec. 4. That this act shall be in force from and after its ratification.

Ratified the 6th day of March, A. D. 1899.

CHAPTER 256.

An act to amend the charter of the town of Winterville, Pitt county.

The General Assembly of North Carolina do enact:

Section 1. That section two of chapter ninety-five of the private laws of eighteen hundred and ninety-seven be amended by striking out all of said section after the word "follows," in line two of said section, and inserting the following words: "Beginning at a point on the main road five hundred yards west of the railroad and runs north twenty and one-half east six hundred yards; thence east one thousand yards; thence south twenty and one-half west one thousand two hundred yards; thence west one thousand yards; then [thence] north twenty and one-half east six hundred yards to the beginning."

Section 2, chapter 95, private laws of 1897, amended.

Sec. 2. That section eight of said chapter be amended by striking out the word "twenty" in line seven of said section and inserting the word "fifty" in its place, and by striking out the words "sixty cents" in line eight and inserting the words "one dollar and fifty cents" in their place.

Section 8 amended.

Sec. 3. That this act shall be in force from and after its ratification.

Ratified the 6th day of March, A. D. 1899.

CHAPTER 257.

An act to incorporate the Pungo and Mattamuskeet Railroad Company.

The General Assembly of North Carolina do enact:

rporators. Section 1. J. M. Rhodes, P. Mulherin, Asa J. Smith and G. Brinn and their assigns, be and they are hereby constituted and created a body politic and corporate by the name of the "Pungo and Mattamuskeet Railroad Company," and shall continue such corporation for a period of ninety-nine years. That such company shall have power and authority to make by-laws and regulations for its government and management; to elect and appoint all necessary officers and prescribe their powers and duties, and to have and use a common seal which it may alter at pleasure; to acquire by purchase, lease or otherwise, and to hold, own, possess, mortgage, lease and sell such real, personal and mixed property as may be necessary or convenient to carry out the purposes of this charter, and to have and exercise all and every other power, privilege, franchise and rights necessary to similar corporations and not inconsistent with the laws of this state or the provisions of this act.

rporate name. ration of nchise. rporate pow- s.

powered to struct and intain a rail- ad. Sec. 2. That the said railroad company is hereby authorized and empowered to construct, maintain and operate a railroad with one or more tracks and of such gauge as may be determined, from the village of Makleyville, in the county of Hyde, and thence running eastwardly, touching at or near Sladesville, Brickhouse forks, Swan Quarter, Swindell, Juniper bay, Douglass bay, Englehard, and Fairfield, with the privilege of building and operating branch roads not exceeding twenty (20) miles in length. That in constructing and operating said branch roads, the said company shall have all the rights and privileges granted to the main line.

pital stock. Sec. 3. That the capital stock of said company shall be $3,000.00 (three thousand dollars), and the same may be increased from time to time as a majority of the capital stockholders may determine, not exceeding two hundred thousand dollars (200,000.00). That the stock of said company shall be divided into shares of fifty dollars ($50.00) each, for which certificates shall be issued, and each share shall be entitled to one vote, and the stockholders shall not be individually liable beyond the amount of their subscriptions to the capital stock. That the said corporators, or a majority of them, acting in person or by proxy, shall cause a book or books of subscription to be opened by a commissioner or commissioners to be appointed by them, at such times and places and under such rules and regulations as they or a majority of them may prescribe. That said corporators or a majority of them, acting in person or by proxy,

y be increased. itation to pital stock dividual bility.

after the sum of three thousand dollars ($3,000.00) has been subscribed, shall call a meeting of the stockholders who shall have subscribed to the capital stock for the purpose of completing the organization of the company, of which personal notice of ten (10) days shall be given to each subscriber. That at such meeting the stockholders shall elect a board of directors, consisting of five members, who shall immediately elect one of their number president of the company. The directors shall elect all of the officers of the company. The stockholders, by a majority vote at any meeting, may increase the directors to any number not exceeding eleven.

When company may be organized.

Election of directors.

Sec. 4. That subscriptions to the capital stock of said company may be made in money, land, labor or materials necessary for the construction and equipment of said road in lands, stocks or other valuable credits, in such manner and on such terms as may be agreed upon by the said company.

Subscriptions to stock.

Sec. 5. That said company is hereby authorized and empowered to merge and consolidate its capital stock, property, franchise, rights and privileges with those of any other railroad company or companies now existing or hereafter created under the laws of this state, whenever a majority of the stockholders of this company shall so desire: Provided, that the railroad company with whom this company may be consolidated shall have a continuous traffic arrangement and connection either by rail or by steamboats and barges crossing any intervening body of water, and the said consolidation may be effected by its directors in such manner and on such terms and conditions and under such name and style as a majority of its stockholders may determine.

May consolidate with other companies.

Sec. 6. That it shall be lawful for any railroad or transportation company created by the laws of this state or any other state, from time to time, to subscribe or to purchase or to hold the stock and bonds, or either, in this company, or to guarantee or endorse such bonds or stock, or either of them; and it shall or may be lawful for any railroad or transportation company created by the laws of this or any other state to purchase, use or lease the road, property and franchise of this company for such time and upon such terms as may be agreed upon by this company and such company or companies as shall be parties to the contract. That it shall be lawful for this company to subscribe to or purchase and to hold the stock or bonds, or both, of any other railroad or transportation company chartered by this or any other state, or to guarantee the stock or bonds of any such company, or to purchase, lease or operate the road or line, property or franchise of any such railroad or transportation company.

Other corporations may subscribe to stock.

Sec. 7. That meetings of stockholders shall be held annually,

nual meetings tockholders. at such time and place as may be determined by them in this state, and at all annual meetings the president and directors shall render to the stockholders an account of the affairs of the company. Special meetings of stockholders may be called by the president, or by a majority of the directors, by giving ten days' notice thereof by mailing such notice to each stockholder to his last post-office address. Similar notice shall be given of the annual meeting of stockholders.

nual report.

cial meetings.

ction of cers.

Sec. 8. The board of directors of this company shall elect a president and all other officers which they may deem necessary in the construction and operation of the railroad and affairs of this company. The directors shall be elected annually by the stock holders. The term of office of both directors and officers shall be one year, but they shall serve until their successors are elected and qualified. In case of a vacancy in any office or in the board of directors, by death or resignation or otherwise, the said board of directors may fill the same for the unexpired time.

m of office.

bscriptions to ital stock.

Sec. 9. That the directors are authorized to permit subscriptions to the capital stock to be paid in installments until the whole of their subscription shall be paid. If any stockholder shall fail to pay the sum required of him by the directors within one month after the same shall have been required, it shall be lawful for the said president and directors to sell at public auction and convey to the purchaser the share or shares of such stockholder so failing, giving thirty (30) days' previous notice of the time and place of sale in one or more newspapers published in this state, and after retaining the sum due and costs of sale out of the proceeds, to pay the surplus, if any, to the delinquent owner or his legal representative; and, if the sale shall not produce the balance due on the subscription and costs of sale, the said company may recover the said balance from the original subscriber or his assignee, or the personal representative of either of them, by civil action, in any court having jurisdiction.

paid for res of stock y be sold at tion.

thorized to struct one or re lines.

Sec. 10. That said company is hereby authorized at its option to construct and operate one or more lines of railroad and from any other points to its lines of railroad, and to establish a schedule of charges for the use of same and to collect the same; and said company may connect such lines of telegraph or telephone with the lines of any other company in this state, and may lease, rent or sell this right, and any telegraph or telephone lines constructed by the company.

thorized to rrow money.

Sec. 11. That the said company is hereby authorized to borrow money to such extent and in such manner as may be authorized by its stockholders, and to pay thereon a rate of interest not exceeding six per centum, as may be necessary in the construction and operation of said railroad, and to issue therefor such bonds, either coupon or registered, or other evidences of debt, in such a manner and of such form as may be determined by the directors, and to secure such loans, both as to principal and interest, by such mortgages or deeds of trust on the whole of the property and franchises of the company or any part thereof, as may be deemed advisable. May issue bonds.

Sec. 12. That this company shall have power and authority to appropriate and occupy such land as may be necessary for the construction of said railroad and its branches, of the width of one hunderd feet (100 ft.); that is to say, a right-of-way of fifty (50) feet from each side of the center of said track; and such additional land as may be necessary for station houses, depots, warehouses and other purposes necessary for the construction and operation of said railroad and its branches, and the power of condemnation of same shall be such as is provided under the general laws of North Carolina. Occupation of land. Right-of-way.

Sec. 13. That the townships of Currituck, Swan Quarter and Lake Landing, in the county of Hyde, may subscribe to the capital stock or invest the first mortgage bonds of this railroad company, to be secured by the joint bonds of each of said townships, bearing not exceeding six per centum interest, subject to the approval of the qualified voters of said townships. Townships may subscribe to stock.

Sec. 14. That the board of commissioners of Hyde county are authorized, and it shall be their duty, whenever one-fourth of the aggregate of all the qualified voters in said townships shall petition the same, to cause an election to be held in each of said three townships at the legal voting places therein, after at least thirty days' notice of said election, posted at three public places in each township, and to submit to the qualified voters of each of said townships the question of subscribing to the capital stock of the said Pungo and Mattamuskeet Railroad Company,or of loan to said railroad company to be secured by the first mortgage bonds of said company, a sum of money not less than thirty thousand dollars ($30,000.00) and not more than forty thousand dollars ($40,000.00); at such election, those in favor of said subscription to the capital stock or first mortgage bonds shall deposit a ballot on which shall be written or printed the words, "For subscription," and those opposed shall deposit a ballot on which is written or printed the words, "Against subscription," such election to be held in all respects as required by the general law for the election of members of the general assembly, except as are herein otherwise provided. The reports of said election shall be made to the county commissioners on Tuesday next after the day on which the said election is held, who shall on that day declare the result of said election and enter the same on their minutes; and if a majority of all the qualified voters in the three several townships shall vote for subscription, then Commissioners shall order an election. Maximum amount. Form of ballot.

the subscription or loan so authorized shall be made by the said board of county commissioners. That for the purposes of this act, the voters of said three townships shall be considered jointly or in the aggregate and the liability created under the provisions of this act shall be deemed and held to be a joint and not a several liability. The amounts of the bonds to be issued by the said townships, that is to say, as to whether the amount shall be more than thirty thousand dollars ($30,000.00) and not exceeding forty thousand dollars ($40,000.00) or any intermediate sum shall be determined by the said board of county commissioners. The question whether the bonds of said township shall be subscribed to the capital stock of said railroad company or shall be subscribed as a loan to the said company to be secured by its mortgage bonds, shall be determined by said railroad company through its board of directors, which determination shall be made after the election herein provided, and when notice of said action of the said railroad company shall be filled [filed] with the clerk of the board of commissioners of Hyde county the said commissioners shall proceed to issue said bonds as authorized for the purpose indicated by the said railroad company. If the said railroad company shall determine that said bonds shall be a subscription to the capital stock of said railroad company, then each of the said townships shall be entitled to be represented in all general meetings of the stockholders, and for this purpose, the board of county commissioners shall appoint some suitable person from each township to represent jointly the shares of stock of said townships at the meetings of said company. This appointment shall be evidenced by the certificate of the clerk of the county commissioners, and shall be given for one year and until their successor or successors are appointed; but if the said railroad company shall determine that the bonds aforesaid shall be in the nature of a loan secured by mortgage, as aforesaid, then the said board of county commissioners, through their chairman, shall proceed to issue the said bonds upon the execution of the mortgage by said railroad company as aforesaid.

int liability.

ount of ads deter ned by county mmissioners.

wnships en- ied to vote in eral meetings.

wnship resentatives.

Sec. 15. For the payment of any subscription made either to the capital stock or as a loan to the said company as provided in the preceding section, the board of county commissioners of Hyde county shall issue bonds to the amount authorized to be subscribed or loaned, payable to bearer, and the said bonds shall express on their face by what authority and for what purpose they are issued; such bonds shall be coupon bonds of the denomination of not more than one thousand dollars ($1,000.00) or less than one hundred dollars ($100.00), and shall bear interest at a rate not exceeding six per centum, the interest payable

nat bonds shall press on face.

nomination of nds.

on the first day of March of each successive year by the treasurer of said company, at some bank in the town of Washington, N. C., to be designated by said treasurer. The said bonds shall be due and payable as follows: one thousand dollars in amount ten years after the first day of March succeeding the year in which said bonds are issued and one thousand dollars on the first day of March in each successive year thereafter: Provided, that the board of commissioners of Hyde county, by giving ninety (90) days' notice thereof preceding the first day of March in any year and making publication of the same in some newspaper published in the state may pay off at the same time as the next installment of interest such bonds and of such an amount as may be named in said publication, payable at the same bank at which the installment of interest is paid. The interest upon said bonds so called in shall thereupon cease and determine after the said first day of March.

Maturity of bonds.

Sec. 16. That to provide for the payment of interest on said bonds, the board of county commissioners shall, in addition to other taxes each year, compute and levy upon the proper subjects of taxation in the townships of Currituck, Swan Quarter and Lake Landing a sufficient tax to pay the interest on said bonds issued as aforesaid, and in order to pay the said bonds as they mature and such other bonds as they may anticipate the payment of, the said commissioners shall, at the expiration of ten years from the date of their issue, annually compute and levy an additional tax of one thousand dollars ($1,000.00) or more, in their discretion, until all their bonds are paid, which taxes shall be collected by the sheriff of Hyde county under the same rules and regulations as are provided for collecting other taxes, and he and his sureties shall be liable to the same penalties and subject to the same remedies as are now prescribed by law for the faithful collecting and paying over all taxes to the state and county. The said taxes when collected shall be paid over to the county treasurer, as other taxes are paid, and the said treasurer and his sureties shall be liable to the same penalties and subject to the same remedies as are now prescribed by law for accounting for and paying out the state and county taxes. The said treasurer shall first pay the interest on said bonds and the coupons be retained as vouchers and evidences of payment, and the balance of money shall be retained in his hands for the purpose of creating a sinking fund for the payment of the principal of the remaining bonds in the order in which they are payable, and the management and control of said sinking fund shall be vested in the said board of county commissioners, provided it shall not be expended for any other purposes.

Special tax may be levied and collected to create a sinking fund.

Additional tax levy.

How collected.

To whom paid.

Bonds, how signed.

Sec. 17. Said bonds shall be signed by the chairman of board of county commissioners and the clerk of the said board, and the coupons shall be signed by the chairman alone.

wnship bonds all not be alidated.

Sec. 18. That nothing herein shall be taken or construed in any wise to invalidate the said bonds of the several townships in case the said taxes should for any reason fail to be applied to the payment of the said interest or any part thereof.

upons receiv-le for taxes.

Sec. 18. The coupons of said bonds shall [be] receivable for taxes under this act and it shall be the duty of the sheriff to receive them when tendered if they are due and payable.

ew registration ay be ordered.

Sec. 20. That it shall be lawful for the county commissioners at their discretion to order a new registration or said election under the provisions of law.

rpose of bonds ued.

Sec. 21. That the bonds of the several townships issued under this act shall only be issued for the purpose of constructing a railroad from Makleyville along the route hereinbefore provided, at least as far as Juniper bay.

hen bonds all be issued.

Sec. 22. That if the result of the said election shall be favorable for the issuing of said bonds, then said bonds shall be issued as hereinbefore provided within sixty days after the result of said election as declared by said board of county commissioners. When issued, the bonds, together with all coupons, shall be deposited with some bank or trust company agreed upon by the county commissioners and the said railroad company, to be held in trust by said bank or trust company until satisfactory evidence is produced of the completion of said road from Makleyville, along the route hereinbefore provided, at least as far as Juniper bay, whereupon their bonds and coupons shall be delivered to the president of said railroad company or to such person as may be designated by said railroad company, and upon such delivery the said railroad company shall issue its certificates of stock or its own bonds secured by first mortgages, dependent upon whether the said township bonds are issued in subscribing to the said capital stock, or as a loan to said railroad company, as hereinbefore provided. That when the said bonds are issued they, with the coupons attached, shall be numbered and a record kept by the clerk of the board of commissioners of Hyde county, showing the numbers, amounts and dates of maturity of the same respectively.

nds, how posited.

mpany shall sue certificates stock for nds.

wnships mak-g subscriptions all be considered as acting intly.

Sec. 23. That for the purpose of this act, the townships which shall make said subscriptions or loan shall be deemed and considered as acting jointly and not severally, both in the matter of the election and in their liability for the bonds issued hereunder, and each of said townships are hereby created bodies politic and corporate, with power to carry out the provisions of this act, and the county commissioners of Hyde county are declared to be for all purposes corporate agents of the said townships.

Sec. 24. That this company shall have the right to dispose of, negotiate or sell these bonds secured by mortgage on the whole or any part of its franchise and property upon such terms as the president and directors shall deem most advantageous to the company. Company may dispose of bonds.

Sec. 25. That any officer failing and refusing to perform his duties under this act shall be guilty of a misdemeanor. Officers failing to perform duty guilty of a misdemeanor.

Sec. 26. --at the railroad authorized by this act shall be commenced within four years from the date of the ratification of this act.

Sec. 27. That this act shall be in force from and after its ratification. When road shall be commenced.

Ratified the 6th day of March, A. D. 1899.

CHAPTER 258.

An act to incorporate "The Carolina Banking, Loan and Trust Company."

The General Assembly of North Carolina do enact:

Section 1. That J. S. Carr, Wm. A. Guthrie, Leo. D. Heartt, Wm. M. Morgan, G. W. Watts, R. W. Winston, J. S. Manning, F. L. Fuller, T. B. Fuller, W. H. Branson, Melville Jeffries, T. H. Martin, T. M. Gorman, J. H. Sharpe, D. A. McCauley, D. C. Parks, V. Ballard, their present and future associates and successors are hereby constituted and declared to be a body politic and corporate by the name and style of "The Carolina Banking, Loan and Trust Company," and as such shall have succession for the term of sixty years, and by that name may sue and be sued, appear, prosecute and defend in any court or place whatsoever, and may make contracts, buy, hold, possess and convey real estate and personal property and have and use a common seal, and may break and renew the same at will and may make, establish and put in execution such by-laws, rules and regulations not contrary to the laws of North Carolina or of the United States as may be necessary for the regulation and management of its affairs, and do all such acts and things as may be necessary to carry into effect the provisions of this act, and shall have all the powers, rights and privileges granted to any bank or banking institution under the general law of the state of North Carolina. Corporators. Body corporate. Corporate name. Corporate powers

Sec. 2. The corporate powers of the company shall be vested in a board of directors, to be elected by the stockholders annually, who shall hold their office for one year and until their successors have been appointed. Said board of directors shall consist Corporate powers vested in a board of directors.

ber of direct- of as many stockholders as the by-laws provide, but not less than five. A majority of the board shall constitute a quorum to do business. The said board shall have each and every power necessary to carry out the business of this company and to enable it to exercise all the powers and franchises of the corporation. It may appoint an executive committee from their number, consisting of not less than three, having like power when the board is not in session, and shall have power to make all by-laws and prescribe such regulations for the transaction of its business as it shall deem necessary, not inconsistent with the laws of this state and of the United States, and may amend, alter, suspend or add to the same at pleasure, subject to a like restriction.

cutive committee may be ointed.

ital stock. be increased.

Sec. 3. The capital stock of said corporation shall not be less than twenty-five thousand dollars nor more than one million of dollars, to be divided into shares of fifty dollars each; and when not less than the minimum amount of stock has been subscribed and ten thousand dollars paid in in cash, the stockholders may elect a president, vice-president, a secretary and treasurer, and such other officers as it may deem expedient, and not less than five directors, which officers shall serve for one year, and thereafter until their successors are elected. Election of officers of the company shall be by ballot, unless the same be dispensed with, and a plurality of votes shall elect. At meetings of stockholders each stockholder shall be entitled to one vote, in person or by proxy, for each share of the capital stock of the company held by him and transferred to him on the books of the company not less than thirty days immediately preceding such election.

tion of ers.

resentation ockholders.

tal stock be invested onds, etc.

Sec. 4. The capital stock of said company may be invested in bonds, notes or other evidences of debt secured by deed of trust or mortgage upon real or personal property or otherwise, safely secured, or in securities or bonds of the United States or the bonds of the state of North Carolina, or the bonds of any incorporated city or town or county in this state, as in the discretion of the board of directors shall seem best. If any subscriber shall fail to pay his stock or any part thereof as the same is required of him, the entire residue of his stock shall be deemed to be due and may be recovered in the name of the corporation, either by motion to the court of the county where the delinquent may reside upon giving him ten days' notice of the motion, or by ordinary civil action, or the entire stock of such delinquent may be sold by order of the board of directors for cash at the office of said company, after advertisement of such sale for ten days in some newspaper published in the town of Durham, N. C.; and if at such sale the price should not be sufficient to discharge the amount unpaid with all costs of such sale, the subscriber shall be liable for the deficiency in a civil action.

criber failing y stock.

re stock of quent may ld.

Sec. 5. The said company shall have power to receive money in trust and accumulate the same at legal rate of interest, and to allow interest not exceeding the legal rate; to accept and execute trusts of every description as fully as a natural person could which may be committed to said company by any person or persons whatsoever, or by any corporation, or by order or decree, or authority of any court of record, upon such terms as may be agreed upon, provided or declared in regard thereto; to act as agent for the purpose of issuing, registering of countersigning certificates of stock, bonds or other evidences of debt of any state, corporation, association, municipality or public authority, on such terms as may be agreed upon; to lease and rent real estate and collect rents from the same; to accept from and execute trusts for married women in respect of their separate property or estate, and to act as agent for them in the management, sale and disposition of their properties.

May receive money in trust.

Corporate powers.

Sec. 6. That in all cases where an application may be made to any court having jurisdiction to appoint a curator, guardian of an infant, committee of an idiot or insane person, administrator of any person dying testate or intestate, trustee or receiver, such court shall have power to appoint said company as such curator, guardian, committee, administrator, trustee or receiver upon the like application that any person might be so appointed; and it shall be lawful for any person by deed, will or any other writing to appoint said company a trustee, executor, guardian, assignee or receiver; and as such executor, guardian of an infant, committee of an idiot or insane person, administrator, trustee, executor, assignee or receiver, said company may lawfully act, and as such shall be subject to all like capacities, and subject to be removed like natural persons.

Court may appoint said company guardian, etc.

Said company may be appointed trustee, executor, etc.

Sec. 7. That it shall be lawful for any individual, executor, administrator, guardian, committee, receiver, assignee, trustee, public officers or other person having the custody of any bonds, stocks, securities, moneys, or other valuables, to deposit the same for safe keeping with said company: Provided, that the deposit shall not exonerate such individual from liability.

Persons having bonds, etc., may deposit them with said company.

Sec. 8. That every court wherein said company shall be appointed or shall be allowed to qualify as guardian, committee, executor, administrator, trustee or receiver, or in which it is made the depository of moneys or other valuables, shall have power to make all orders and compel obedience thereto and require said company to render all accounts which such court might lawfully make or require if such company was a natural person; and the court if it deem necessary, may from time to time appoint suitable persons to investigate the affairs and management of said company, or the court may, if it deem necessary, examine the officers

Courts may compel obedience to orders from said company.

cers of com- ıy may be mined under h.

of said company, under oath or affirmation as to the security aforesaid.

npany author- d to invest ney received trust.

Sec. 9. That said company is authorized to invest moneys received in trust or deposit, loan or otherwise, and to take, have and hold estates, real, personal or mixed, obtained with the money aforesaid, or with funds belonging to said company, and to sell, grant, mortgage or otherwise encumber, lease or dispose of the same, and to that end may execute all deeds or other instruments concerning the same; to deal in exchange, foreign or domestic, securities, mortgages, bonds, certificates of indebtedness, stocks of incorporated companies, notes, loans, bonds of the United States or of any city, county or of any incorporated company or individual.

rsons apply- deposits of pany to per- al use guilty embezzlement.

Sec. 10. That any officer or employee of said company who shall apply any of the deposits of any kind of said company to his own or to the use of any person or person [persons] not entitled thereto shall be deemed guilty of embezzlement, and upon conviction shall be punished by imprisonment in the penitentiary for a term of not less than one nor more than five years, and shall be responsible in any suit at law for injury, loss, expense or damages incurred by reason of its prosecution or in consequence of said act, either to the company or to any party aggrieved, damaged or injured thereby.

fficiency of ds given by pany may be proved by thority.

Sec. 11. Whenever any bond, recognizance, obligation, stipulation or undertaking is by law, or rules and regulations, municipal or otherwise, or the rules or regulations of any board, body corporate, municipal or otherwise, required or permitted to be made, given, tendered or filed for the security or protection of any person or persons, corporation, municipality or other organization whatsoever, conditioned for the doing of or not doing of any act [in] such bond, recognizance, obligation, stipulation or undertaking specified, any and all heads of departments, public officers, state, county, town or municipal, and any and all boards, courts, judges and municipalities, now and hereafter required or permitted to accept or approve the sufficiency of any such bond, recognizance, obligation, stipulation, or undertaking, may, in the discretion of head of department, court, judge, public officer or municipality, or officers or boards of a private corporation, accept such bond, recognizance, obligation, stipulation or undertaking and approve the same whenever the same is executed or the conditions thereof are guaranteed by said compnay.

hen bonds y be accepted certain cer as suf- ient.

Sec. 12. Whenever any such bond, recognizance, obligation, stipulation or undertaking is so required or permitted to be made, given, tendered or filed with one surety or with two or more sureties, the execution of the same, or the guaranteeing the performance of the conditions thereof, shall be sufficient when executed or guaranteed by said company, and any and all heads of departments, courts, judges, boards and municipalities and any and all public officers, state, county, town or municipal, or officers of a private corporation, whose duty it may be, or shall hereafter be, to accept or approve the sufficiency of any such bond, recognizance, obligation, stipulation or undertaking, may accept and approve the same when executed or guaranteed by said company; and said company is hereby vested with full power and authority to execute or guarantee such bonds, recognizances, stipulations, obligations or undertakings, whether given under the laws of this state or of the United States, or of any state. That said company shall have power to guarantee, endorse and secure the payment and punctual performance and collection of notes, debts, bills of exchange, contracts, bonds, accounts, claims, annuities, mortgages, choses in action, evidence of debt, certificates of property values, checks, and the title to property, real and personal indebtedness of companies, partnerships, cities, counties, municipalities, et cetera, in this state, on such terms or commissions as may be agreed upon or established by said company and the parties dealing therewith.

Empowered to guarantee and endorse notes, etc.

Sec. 14. That said company may receive upon storage, deposit or otherwise, merchandise, moneys, specie, plate, stocks, promissory notes, certificates and evidences of debts, contracts and all other personal properties whatsoever; take charge and custody of real and personal estates and securities and advance money thereupon on such terms as may be established by said company; and in all cases in which public officers, municipal or private corporations are authorized to deposit moneys, stocks, bonds or evidences of debt, such deposits by such officers or corporations may be made with said company, and said company may be appointed and is hereby authorized to act as redemption agent for any bank or banking association created or existing under the laws of this state.

May receive upon storage deposits, etc.

Authorized to act as redemption agent for banking institutions.

Sec. 15. That it shall be lawful for the said company to sell at public auction all property or securities of what kind soever mentioned, or specified in any contract or agreement between the company and the other party or parties after the maturity of an obligation under said contract or agreement upon giving ten days' notice by advertisement of the time and place of sale in some newspaper published in the county where said company is carrying on its business, and to reimburse itself out of the proceeds of such sale for the money due it, with interest, storage, costs and charges and to indemnify itself for any loss it may have sustained by the non-fulfilment of such contract, or by reason of any misrepresentation, fraud or concealment.

May sell at auction securities held by them.

Sec. 16. That said company is authorized to make, execute

strumeuts of rporation, how gned.

and issue in the transaction of its business all papers, receipts, certificates, vouchers, bonds and contracts which shall bear the impress or stamp of the seal of the company, and shall be signed by the president or vice-president and countersigned by the secretary or cashier.

dividual ability of stockolders.

Sec. 17. The stockholders of said company shall be individually liable, equally and ratably, and not one for another, for all contracts, debts, bonds, recognizances, obligations, stipulations and undertakings of said company to the extent of the amount of their stock therein at the par value thereof, in addition to the amount invested in such stock.

rincipal office.

Sec. 18. The officer for the transaction of the business of the company shall be in Durham, Durham county, in the state of North Carolina, and the said company shall exist for sixty years.

hen company ay issue notes pass as money.

Sec. 19. Whenever by any general banking law of the state, state banks shall be allowed to issue notes to pass as currency or money, this company shall have power to issue such notes in the same proportion and upon the same terms and conditions as provided for other state banks in said general law.

Sec. 20. That this act shall be in force from and after its ratification.

Ratified the 6th day of March, A. D. 1899.

CHAPTER 259.

An act to incorporate the Bank of East Carolina.

The General Assembly of North Carolina do enact:

rporators.

Section 1. That George Green, N. M. Jurney and Thomas G. Hyman, and their present and future associates, successors and assigns, be and they are hereby constituted, created and declared to be a body politic and corporate under the name and style of "The Bank of East Carolina," and shall so continue for the period of thirty years, with capacity to sue and be sued, maintain and defend actions and special proceedings in its corporate name; to take, hold, buy, sell, lease and exchange and convey real and personal estate, and to conduct, transact and carry on in its full scope and import a general banking business, with all the powers, rights, privileges and immunities hereby specially granted, and in addition those contained in chapter four (4), volume two (2) of The Code, entitled "Banks," and all such laws as may in the future be passed relative to banks.

dy corporate.

rporate name.

iration of arter.

rporate powers.

Sec. 2. That the capital stock of said bank shall be twenty-five thousand dollars in shares of one hundred dollars each, with liberty to the stockholders or a majority of them to increase said capital stock from time to time to one hundred and twenty-five thousand dollars.

Sec. 3. That the office and place of business of said banking company shall be in the city of New Bern, state of North Carolina, and its officers shall consist of a president, vice-president, cashier and teller, and board of not less than three (3) nor more than nine (9) directors, who are to be elected annually by the stockholders—the directors so selected to choose the officers aforesaid, and shall require the president, the cashier and the teller each to give bond with approved security for the faithful performance of their respective duties.

Place of business.

Officers.

Annual election of directors.

Bond of officers.

Sec. 4. That it shall be the duty of the board of directors, and they are hereby fully empowered to make rules, regulations and by-laws for the government of said corporation and for the conduct of its business; also to fix the salaries of its officers and to fill vacancies on the board of directors; said board of directors shall be chosen by a majority of the corporators named herein at the first meeting to be called by them, which said board of directors shall hold office for one year and until their successors are duly elected, a majority of said board to constitute a quorum for the transaction of business.

Rules of corporation.

Board of directors, how chosen.

Sec. 5. That the said company shall have the right to do a general banking business, to receive deposits, to make loans and discounts; to obtain and procure loans for any person, company, partnership or corporation; to invest its own money or the money of others; to lend and invest money in or upon the security of mortgage, pledge, deed or otherwise on any lands, hereditaments or personal property or interest therein of any description, situated anywhere; to lend money upon or purchase or otherwise acquire bills of lading or the contents thereof, bills, notes, choses in action, or any and all negotiable or commercial papers, or any crop or produce whatever; or any stock, bullion, merchandise or other personal property, and the same to sell or in anywise dispose of, and to charge any rate of interest on all such loans not exceeding the rate allowed by law.

Nature of business.

Corporate powers.

Sec. 6. That said company may subscribe to, purchase, acquire or lend money upon any stock, share, note, debenture or other securities of any government, state, municipality, corporation, company, partnership or person, and hold, deal in, sell or distribute the same among the stockholders; may negotiate or place in behalf of any corporation, company, partnership or person, shares, stocks, debentures, notes, mortgages or other securities, without guaranty or collateral obligation by this company; and

Corporate powers.

may sell or subscribe any of the property, real or personal, or any interest acquired therein by it to any corporation for any of its bonds, securities, obligation or capital stock as may be agreed upon without liability on such stock so purchased or subscribed for beyond the agreed terms of said purchase or subscription.

bility on ɔk.

y receive ms of money deposit.

Sec. 7. Be it further enacted: that said corporation may receive on deposit all sums of money which may be offered it for the purpose of being invested in such sums and at such times and on such terms as the board of directors may agree upon; and when married women, minors or apprentices deposit money or other things of value in said bank, either generally or specially to their own credit, they or any of them may draw the same out on their check or order and be bound thereby, and such minor, married woman or apprentice shall be bound by said individual check or order, and the said check or order shall be a valid and sufficient release to said corporation against said minors, married women or apprentices, and all persons whatever.

y act as agent, ., for state, nties or nicipalities.

Sec. 8. That said company shall have the right to act as agent, factor or trustee for any state, county, town, municipality, corporation, company or individual on such terms as to agency and commission as may be agreed on in registering, selling and countersigning, collecting, acquiring, holding, dealing and disposing of on account of any state, county, town, municipality, corporation, company or person, bonds, certificates of stock or any description of property, real or personal, or for guaranteeing the payment of such bonds, certificates of stock, etc., and generally for managing such business, and may charge such premiums, commissions or rates of compensation as may be agreed on in and for any of the matters and things authorized by this charter.

arges allowed.

wer to receive execute sts.

Sec. 9. That said corporation shall have power to receive money in trust, and shall have power to accept and execute any trust that may be committed to it by any court, corporation, company, person or persons; and it shall have power to accept any grant, assignment, transfer, devise or bequest, and to hold any real or personal estate or trust created in accordance with the laws of this state, and then to execute the same on such terms as may be established and agreed upon by its board of directors; and said corporation is hereby fully authorized and empowered to act as trustee or assignee and to receive on deposit all funds in litigation in the various courts of this state, and pay therefor such interest as may be agreed upon not exceeding the lawful rate. It shall have power and authority to receive for safe keeping on deposit all money, bonds, stocks, diamonds, and silver plate and other valuables and charge and collect a reasonable compensation for the same, which said charge shall be a lien on

y act as trus- or assignee

y receive posits, etc , on e keeping.

such deposits until paid, and generally to do and carry on the business of a safety deposit and trust company.

Sec. 10. That said company is hereby given the right to insure or guarantee the payment of any dividends, bonds, notes, undertakings, mortgages or other securities or evidences of indebtedness of any person, partnership or corporation for any price and in any consideration agreed on. May insure or guarantee payment of bonds, etc.

Sec. 11. That this company is specially invested with the powers and privileges usually incident to savings banks; may receive deposits in very small sums, the limit to be fixed by the board of directors, and may pay interest thereon by way of dividends out of the net earnings or by fixed rates according as may be agreed between the company and its depositors; and the board of directors are hereby fully authorized to make all needful by-laws and regulations for conducting and carrying into effect the savings bank features of this corporation. Additional corporate powers.

Sec. 12. That when this bank shall sell the property of its debtors on which it has a lien to secure a debt, or when such property shall be sold for its benefit, it may bid for, buy and hold any and all such property free from lien or incumbrances, and its title thereto shall be absolute and unconditional, and shall be in all respects valid and binding against all persons. When property of debtors is sold.

Sec. 13. That the board of directors shall by the by-laws fix the time of the annual meeting of the stockholders of this corporation and how the said meeting shall be called, and also provide for special meetings, and at all general or special meetings the stockholders may be represented in person or by proxy, and each share of stock shall be entitled to one vote. Annual meetings. Special meetings.

Sec. 14. That the stockholders of this corporation shall not be individually liable for any of the debts, contracts or liabilities of the corporation except as is prescribed by law. Individual liability.

Sec. 15. That the stock held by any one shall be transferred only on the books of said corporation, either in person or by power of attorney. Stock, how transferred.

Sec. 16. That this act shall be in force from and after its ratification.

Ratified the 6th day of March, A. D. 1899.

CHAPTER 260.

An act to incorporate the town of Manly, Moore county, North Carolina.

The General Assembly of North Carolina do enact:

Section 1. That the town of Manly, in the county of Moore, be and the same is hereby incorporated under the name and style of "Manly," and that S. J. Ellington, M. G. Hatcher, W. K. Incorporated. Corporate name.

mmissioners.

Wood, Alexander Cameron and A. B. Gunter, of said town, and their successors in office shall be and are hereby declared a body corporate and politic, with succession during the corporate existence of said town, and shall be styled the "Commissioners of the town of Manly," and as such shall have power to sue and be sued, plead and be impleaded, and have and use a common seal. That D. D. F. Cameron shall be mayor of said town, and with the commissioners aforesaid shall continue in office as such and perform all the duties pertaining to their offices of mayor and commissioners of said town until their successors shall be elected and qualified as hereinafter provided.

rporate title.

yor.

rm of office.

rporate limits.

rporate limits.

Sec. 2. That the corporate limits of said town shall be and hereby [are] declared included within and up to the following boundaries, to-wit: Beginning at a point one-half mile north fifty-three and one-half degrees west from a point in the center of the Seaboard Air Line Railroad track, opposite the center of the Manly passenger depot (the said beginning being one-half mile away from the said point near the depot, at a right-angle from the railroad), running thence north thirty-six degrees thirty minutes east parallel with said railroad two thousand six hundred and forty feet (or one-half mile); thence (turning a right-angle) south fifty-three degrees thirty minutes east two thousand six hundred and forty feet to the center of said railroad track, one-half mile northeasterly from the center of Manly depot; thence continuing south fifty-three degrees thirty minutes east two thousand six hundred and forty feet; thence south thirty-six degrees thirty minutes west parallel with the railroad five thousand two hundred and eighty feet, or one mile, to a stake; thence south fifty-seven west two thousand feet to a corner of Southern Pines' new incorporate boundary; thence with it north thirty-four degrees eight minutes twenty seconds west two thousand six hundred and thirty-three and one-tenth feet; thence north two thousand nine hundred and fifty-eight and four-tenths feet to the Yadkin road; thence continuing north about five hundred and thirty feet to an intersection of the reverse of the first line; thence as it north thirty-six degrees thirty minutes east nine hundred and twenty five feet to the beginning. Description of boundaries given by magnetic bearings, bearing date of this charter.

wn officers.

Sec. 3. The officers of said town shall consist of a mayor and five commissioners, to be elected by the qualified voters of said town annually on the first Monday in May.

ction of town cers, where d.

Sec. 4. Said election of said mayor and commissioners shall be held at the mayor's office in said town, and no person shall be entitled to vote at said election or at any election in said town for municipal purposes unless he shall be an elector of the state of North Carolina and shall have resided ninety days next preceding the day of election within said corporation. Qualifications for voting.

Sec. 5. It shall be the duty of the commissioners of said [town] on the second Monday in March in each year to appoint a registrar and three judges of election, who shall be qualified voters of said town and who shall within ten days thereafter be notified of their appointment by the constable of said town. The registrar so appointed shall immediately make publication, at the door of the mayor's office and three other public places in said town, of his appointment as such; he shall be furnished with a registration book by the commissioners of said town, and it shall be his duty to revise the existing registration book of said town in such a way that it shall show an accurate list of electors previously registered and still residing in said town, without requiring such electors to register anew. He shall also, between the hours of sunrise and sundown (Sundays excepted) on each day for thirty days preceding each election, keep open said book for the registration of any electors residing in said town entitled to register whose names have never before been registered, and any of the electors shall be allowed to object to the name of any person appearing in said book. In case of any such objection the registrar shall enter upon his book, opposite the name of the person so objected to, the word "challenged," and shall appoint a time and place on or before the election day when he, together with said judges of election, shall hear and decide said objection, giving due notice to the voter so objected to: Provided, that nothing contained in this section shall be construed to prohibit the right of any elector to challenge or object to the name of any person registering or offering to register at any time other than that specified. If any person challenged or objected to shall be found not duly qualified as provided for in this charter, his name shall be erased from the registration book, and he shall not be allowed to vote at any election in said town and his name shall not appear on the revised list; but the commissioners of said town may, if they think proper, upon giving thirty days' notice at four public places in said town, require an entirely new registration of voters before any election held therein.

Appointment of registrar and judges. Duties of registrar. When registration book shall be kept open. Challenges. Proviso. Certain challenges not prevented. Commissioners may give notice.

Sec. 6. The registrar and judges of election, before entering upon the discharge of their duties, shall take the oath prescribed by article six, section four, of the constitution of North Carolina, before some justice of the peace of Moore county. Registrar and judges shall take oath.

Sec. 7. It shall be the duty of the registrar and judges of election to attend at the polling places in said town with the registration book on Monday preceding the election from the hours of nine o'clock a. m. until the hour of five o'clock p. m., when Registration book open to inspection.

and where the said book shall be open to the inspection of the electors of said town held in said town for municipal purposes.

urs between ich polls shall kept open.

Sec. 8. The said judges of election, together with the registrar, who shall take with him the registration book, shall assemble at the polling place on the day of the election held in said town, and shall open the polls at seven o'clock a. m. They shall superintend said election and keep the polls open until sunset, when the polls shall be closed and the voters [votes] for mayor and commissioners shall be counted out by them. They shall keep poll books and write in them the name of every person voting at said election, and at the close thereof shall certify said poll lists and deposit them with the clerk and treasurer of said town, and said poll books shall in any trial for illegal or fraudulent voting be received as evidence. If for any cause any of the judges of election shall fail to attend, the registrar shall appoint some discreet person or persons to fill the vacancy, who shall be sworn by him before acting.

unting of llots.

ilure of judges attend.

llots, how t.

Sec. 9. The voters shall vote by ballot, having the name of the mayor and commissioners on one ballot, either in writing or printed on white paper, and without any device, and the person having the highest number of votes shall be declared elected by the judges of election, who shall certify said fact to the town clerk and treasurer; and in case of a tie the judges of election shall determine by ballot who is elected.

igibility to ce.

Sec. 10. That no person shall be eligible to any office in said town unless he shall be a qualified voter therein.

tification of cers elected.

Sec. 11 That immediately after each election it shall be the duty of the town clerk and treasurer to notify in writing the mayor and commissioners elect of their election.

hen mayor d commis- ners shall alify.

Sec. 12. That the mayor and commissioners elect shall, within three days after having been notified by the town clerk and treasurer, before some justice of the peace of said county, take the oath prescribed for public officers, and on [an] oath that they will faithfully and impartially discharge the duties imposed on them by law.

fficers refusing qualify.

Sec. 13. That any person elected mayor or commissioner of said town, under the provisions of this charter, refusing to qualify and act as such for one month after such election, shall forfeit and pay the sum of fifty dollars, one half to the use of the person suing for same and the other half to said town, to be applied by the commissioners of said town to the use and benefit thereof. Said sum shall be recovered in any ordinary civil action before a justice of the peace of said county in the name of the state of North Carolina.

uorum.

Sec. 14. That a majority of said commissioners shall constitute a quorum for the transaction of business.

Sec. 15. That the mayor, when present shall preside at all meetings of the commissioners; he shall also have power to call meetings when he may deem it necessary, and may vote only in case of a tie. In the absence or sickness of the mayor, the commissioners of said town shall elect one of their own number to act as mayor pro tempore, who shall while acting as such have all the power and authority conferred by this charter on the mayor of said town.

Mayor shall preside at meetings of aldermen.

Sec. 16. If for any cause there should be a vacancy in the office of mayor or commissioner of said town the board of commissioners shall be and are hereby empowered to fill said vacancy or vacancies, and their appointee or appointees shall hold office until the next regular election herein provided for.

Vacancies occurring.

Sec. 17. That said commissioners shall at the first meeting after their election select some one as town clerk and treasurer, who shall hold office for one year or until his successor shall be elected and qualified. He shall act as secretary to the board of commissioners and as treasurer of said town, and before entering upon the duties of his office shall give good and sufficient bond, with sureties to be approved by the board of commissioners of said town in the sum of five hundred dollars or any other sum the said commissioners may think sufficient, payable to the state of North Carolina, and conditioned upon his faithfully accounting for and paying over all moneys that may come into his hands as treasurer of said town, and for the faithful discharge of his duties as secretary of said board of commissioners. The commissioners of said town may require of said clerk and treasurer a monthly statement and exhibit of receipts and disbursements; and if he fail, if for thirty days after having been required to make such exhibits, to render the same, it shall be and is hereby declared a breach of his official bond, and the commissioners are authorized and empowered to declare the office vacant and to appoint his successor. All suits entered on the official bond of any of the officers of said town shall be in the name of the state of North Carolina to the use of the board of commissioners of the town of Manly against the said official and his sureties.

Election of town clerk.

Treasurer.

Shall give bond.

Monthly statements.

Failure to render statement.

Suits shall be in name of the state.

Sec. 18. The said commissioners shall at the first meeting after their election select some one to act as constable of said town, who shall hold his office for one year or until his successor is elected and qualified. He shall before entering upon the discharge of the duties enter into bond in the sum of five hundred dollars, or such sum as the commissioners of said town may deem proper, with good and sufficient sureties, to be approved by the board of commissioners, payable to the state of North Carolina and conditioned upon his faithfully executing and returning to proper authorities all process that may come into his hands as

Election of constable.

Bond shall be required.

constable, upon his accounting for and paying over to the proper authorities all moneys that may come into his hands from any source as said constable: upon his faithfully collecting and paying over all taxes levied by the commissioners of said town, and in all other respects executing to the best of his ability honestly and faithfully all the duties of his office imposed upon him by this charter or by the board of commissioners of said town.

mmissioners powered to ke by-laws, inances, etc.

Sec. 19. The commissioners of said town shall have the power to make such by-laws and adopt such regulations or ordinances for the government of said town as a majority of them may deem necessary to promote the interests and insure the good order and government of said town, for the improvement of the streets, and the preservation of health in the same, and to make all such other police regulations as the interest, comfort and convenience of the citizens of the said town may require.

atement of isances.

Sec. 20. The commissioners of said town may pass laws for abating and preventing nuisances of any kind therein.

olation of inances a sdemeanor.

Sec. 21. Any person or persons violating any ordinance of said town shall be deemed guilty of a misdemeanor, and shall be punished upon conviction thereof before the mayor of said town by a fine not exceeding fifty dollars or by imprisonment not exceeding thirty days.

enders failing pay fine may rk on roads.

Sec. 22. In all cases where an offender has been convicted before the mayor of said town for the violation of any of the ordinances thereof, and a fine has been imposed on such offender for said violation the mayor of said town at the time of entering judgment against such offender thereof may order that on failure to pay such fine to the constable of said town for the space of one day such offender so convicted shall be by the constable of Manly put to work on the streets of said town for a time to be fixed by the mayor, not exceeding ten days, when he shall be discharged.

risdiction of yor.

Sec. 23. The mayor of said town shall have the power to hear and determine all charges or indictments against any person or persons for the violation of the ordinances of said town, and in addition thereto shall have all the power, jurisdiction and authority of a justice of the peace over all crimes and criminal offenses committed within the corporate limits of said town.

nstable shall ecute processes.

thority of stable.

Sec. 24. The constable of said town shall execute all process placed in his hands by the mayor, shall have authority to preserve the peace of said town, and within the corporate limits thereof shall have the same authority in criminal matters and be entitled to the same fees as a sheriff has in the county; and in the collection of the taxes of the said town, levied by the authorities thereof, shall have the same power and authority as are given to sheriffs by law, except as hereinafter provided for by this charter.

Sec. 25. It shall not be lawful for the mayor or any commissioner of said town, town clerk or constable or any other official officer of said town to demand or receive either directly or indirectly any consideration for work or labor done or material furnished to said town by said officials: Provided, however, that the commissioners of said town may determine the compensation or salary of the mayor, town clerk and treasurer and town constable.

Town officers shall not receive consideration for certain services for town.

Proviso.

Compensation of officers.

Sec. 26. The commissioners of said town shall have power to open and lay out any new street or streets within the corporate limits of said town whenever a majority of them may think necessary, and shall have power at any time to widen, enlarge, make narrower, change or discontinue any street or streets or any part thereof within the corporate limits of said town, and shall have power to condemn and appropriate any land necessary for the purposes of this section, on making compensation as hereinafter provided to the owner or owners of such lands. It shall be the duty of the commissioners of said town to tender through their clerk and treasurer the amount they may think the owner of any land may be entitled to as damages for the opening out, changing or discontinuing any street or streets across his lands, and if such amount shall not be accepted in full satisfaction therefor the mayor of said town shall have the power to issue an order directed to the town constable commanding him to summon as jurors six citizens of said town, freeholders, connected neither by consanguinity nor affinity with the mayor or commissioners of said town or the person or persons over whose land said street proposed to be changed or discontinued runs, or over whose lands said proposed new street will run; said order shall direct the town constable to summons said jurors to meet on the land over which the proposed street is to be laid out or changed or discontinued on a day not exceeding ten days from the day of summoning them, and the owner or owners of said land shall be notified by the constable of said town of the summoning of said Jurors and the time and place of their meeting for five days before the day when the said jurors will meet to open and lay out any new street or alter, change or discontinue any street already laid out; said jurors attended by the constable, after being sworn by the mayor to do strict and impartial justice between the parties, shall proceed to lay open lay out, change, narrow or widen such street or streets as the case may be, and shall assess the damages sustained by the owner or owners of such land, and in assessing the damages they shall consider the improvements to said land or lands caused by the opening or laying out, chang-

Improvement of streets.

Condemnation of lands.

Assessors of value of property.

Owners of land condemned shall be notified.

Considerations in estimating value of lands.

ing, making narrower or wider of said street or streets, and such estimated improvement shall be deducted from the damages assessed by them; and the said jurors shall under their hands and seals make a return of their proceedings to the mayor of said town, and the board of commissioners of said town shall make compensation to such owner or owners of said land for the amount of damages so assessed on the return of the report of said jurors to the mayor of said town, and the payment or tender of payment to the owner or owners of said land by the town clerk and treasurer under the order and direction of said commissioners of the amount of damages so assessed. Said new street or streets so laid out, altered or changed, made narrower or wider shall be in all respects one of the streets of said town, and under the control of the board of commissioners of said town.

port of jurors.

ewalks, conıction and air of.

Sec. 27. The said commissioners shall have the power to construct and repair sidewalks on any of the streets of the said town.

wn market.

Sec. 28. The commissioners of said town may establish a market and regulate the same and prescribe at what place in the corporation shall be sold marketable things and in what manner, whether by weight or measure.

evention of ntagious eases.

Sec. 29. The commissioners of said town may take such measures as they may deem requisite or pass such ordinances or regulations as they may think necessary to prevent the entrance into or spreading within the limits of said town of any contagious or infectious disease or diseases, and may take any action necessary in their opinion to preserve the public health of said town.

cense to retail uors shall not granted by inty commisners without nsent of town missioners.

Sec. 30. That it shall not be lawful for the board of commissioners of Moore county to grant any license to retail spirituous or malt liquors within the corporate limits of said town without permission first obtained from the board of commissioners of said town, in being at the time of application to the said county commissioners; and if any license to retail spirituous or malt liquors within said town shall be granted by said county commissioners without such permission in writing, attested by the clerk or secretary of [the] board of commissioners of said town and exhibit[ed] to the board of county commissioners and filed with their clerk and entered on the minutes of their proceedings, the same shall be utterly void.

nual levy of

Sec. 31. The board of commissioners of said town shall have power annually to levy and cause to be collected taxes for necessary town purposes on all real property, all moneys, credits, investments in bonds, stocks, joint companies and all other personal property and on the taxable polls within the limits of said town: Provided, however, that the taxes levied by them shall not exceed forty cents on the hundred dollars valuation on all real and personal property and one dollar and twenty cents on

bjects of taxan.

oviso.

nitation to issue.

each taxable poll, and the valuation of all property within said town as taxed by said town commissioners shall be the same as that at which it is assessed for taxation for state and county purposes.

Sec 32. That all taxes levied by said town commissioners shall be due and payable on the first day of October in each year to the constable of said town, and after that time may be collected by him by distraining any personal property of the taxpayer to be found within said town. Taxes, when due.

Sec. 33. On the first Monday in June in each year the town clerk and treasurer of said town shall by advertising at the door of the mayor's office and at four other public places in town, notify all persons in said town liable to taxation to come forward and make returns of their tax list to him within thirty days from publication of said notice. All persons within said town and liable to taxation shall make returns of all their taxable property to said town clerk under oath, and he is hereby authorized and empowered to administer to such taxpayers an oath that he will well and truly return all property owned by him within said town and liable to taxation under the provisions of this charter; said list so returned shall state the age of the taxpayer and all property, real or personal, liable to taxation owned by him, with an accurate description of all real property owned by him, when he is required by law to return the same to the list taker of the township in which Manly is situated, to be assessed for taxation for state and county purposes. Notice shall be given of time of listing taxes. Tax lists returned under oath.

Sec. 34. All persons owning any property within said town liable to taxation for town purposes shall return the same to the town clerk as provided in section thirty-three (33) of this charter and all property therein liable to such taxation owned by minors, lunatics or persons non compos mentis, shall be returned as herein provided by their guardian or guardians, if they shall have any such. Persons who shall return tax lists.

Sec. 35. All property liable to taxation for town purposes in said town and held by executors, administrators or trustees shall be returned by them in that capacity, and the individual property of all such guardians, executors, administrators or trustees shall first be distrained or attached by the constable for the satisfaction of the taxes due on all property so returned by them, and the constable of said town is hereby authorized at any time after the taxes may be due the town on said property as aforesaid to distrain any personal property of said guardians, executors, administrators or trustees to be found in said town. Property may be distrained, or attached for taxes.

Sec. 36. The town clerk and treasurer of said town shall make out a full and complete list of all taxable property in said [town] List of taxable property shall be made out.

so returned to him, and of taxable polls in said town, and if any person or persons in said town liable to taxation shall fail to make return to the clerk as herein provided for for thirty (30) days after the second Monday in July in each year, the town clerk shall make return of the taxable property of such person or persons and his age, if he is liable to poll tax; and such person or persons so failing to make return of their property and poll shall be liable to double property and poll tax, to be collected as other property and poll taxes. The town clerk of the said town shall complete the tax list and place it or a certified copy thereof in the hands of the constable of said town on the third Monday in August each year. Such tax list or a copy thereof certified by the clerk when placed in the hands of the town constable shall have the force and effect of an execution.

x list in hands constable shall ve force of ecution.

en of taxes on al property.

Sec. 37. The lien of the town taxes shall attach to all real property subject to taxation on and after the third (3d) Monday in August of each year. and shall continue until such taxes, together with any penalty that shall accrue thereon shall be paid. All personal property liable to taxation of taxpayers within the town shall be liable to be seized and sold after ten (10) days' notice at the mayor's office and four (4) other public places in said town in satisfaction of taxes by the town constable after said taxes shall have become due and payable.

rsonal property ble.

xes due and paid.

Sec. 38. When the taxes due of said town shall be unpaid, the constable of said town shall immediately proceed to collect them as follows: First, if the party charged or his agents have personal property in said town equal in value to the taxes charged against him, the constable shall seize and sell the same under the same rules as sheriffs are required to sell personal property under execution, and his fees for such levy or sale shall be fifty (50) cents; second, if the party charged has not personal property to be found in said town of sufficient value to satisfy his taxes, the constable of said town shall levy upon any lands of the delinquent to be found within the town. The levy shall contain an accurate description of the lands with the name of the owner or owners, the amount of the taxes due by delinquent, and a list thereof shall by the constable [be] returned to the town clerk and treasurer, who shall enter the same in a book to be kept for that purpose, charging therefor the sum of twenty-five (25) cents for every levy; third, the constable shall notify the delinquent of such levy and of the day and place of sale by service of a notice, stating these particulars, on him personally if he be a resident of said town; if the delinquent does not reside in said town but his residence is known, or by reasonable diligence [can] be ascertained, the notice shall be mailed post-paid to such delinquent; if the residence of the delinquent can not with reasonable dili-

le of property · taxes.

hat levy shall ntain.

cord of sale.

n-resident linquents.

gence be ascertained, the constable shall post a notice substantially as above described at the mayor's office and four (4) other public places in said town at least thirty (30) days before the sale of the land, and the last-mentioned notice shall be posted as in all cases of sales of land for taxes in said town; fourth, the sale shall be made at the mayor's office in said town, and shall be on one of the days prescribed for the sale of real estate under execution, and shall be conducted in all respects as are sales under execution. If the delinquent resides outside of said town and his address be known to the constable, the constable shall within one month after the sale mail to him a notice of the sale and the date thereof, of the name and address of the purchaser, of the sum paid, and of the amount of the tax and costs to be paid by such delinquent as a condition of its redemption.

Where sale shall be made.

Constable shall notify delinquent of sale.

Sec. 39. The whole tract belonging to a delinquent person or company shall be set up for sale at the same time and shall be struck off to him who will pay the amount of the taxes with all the expenses for the smallest part of the land; at all such sales the mayor may become a bidder and purchase the whole lot or tract of land for the taxes due and expenses for the use of the town, in case no one will offer to pay the taxes and cost for a less quantity.

Said land, how put up and sold.

Mayor may bid in property for town.

Sec. 40. The delinquent may retain possession of the property for twelve (12) months after the sale, and within that time redeem it by paying the purchaser the amount paid by him and twenty-five (25) per centum in addition thereto; at the time of said payment to the purchaser he shall give to the delinquent or [a] receipt therefor. If he shall refuse or can not be found in said town, the delinquent may pay the same to the town clerk and treasurer, and he shall give him a receipt therefor, and such payment shall be equivalent to payment to the purchaser. After such payment to the purchaser or town clerk all rights under the purchase shall cease.

Land may be redeemed within twelve months.

Sec. 41. At the time of such purchase of real estate for taxes the town on the receipt of the amount bid for such real estate shall give the purchaser a receipt, stating the amount bid, by whom and for what purpose, and describing the land sold, stating further the owner of said land and the amount of taxes due.

Town shall give purchaser a receipt.

Sec. 42. If the delinquent, his agent or attorney shall fail to redeem as provided in section forty (40) hereof for twelve (12) months, at the expiration of that time the purchaser may present his receipt referred to in section forty-one (41) thereof, and the town constable of said town shall execute a deed in fee to the purchaser, and if the purchaser is dead, to his heirs-at-law or assigns for the land for which said purchaser agreed to pay the amount called for in the receipt, and for said service the consta-

Failure to redeem property within a year, purchaser entitled to deed in fee simple.

e of constable ble shall be allowed one dollar ($1), to be paid by the purchaser. The deed from the constable to the purchaser shall be registered in the register's office of Moore county within six (6) months from the time of its execution and delivery, and when so registered shall convey to the grantee all the estate in the land for which the said purchaser bid which the delinquent, his agent or attorney had at the time of sale for taxes.

al estate bid in mayor.

Sec. 43. All real estate bid in by the mayor of said town for the use of said town at sales made by the constable for taxes may be redeemed as hereinbefore provided by the payment on the part of the delinquent, his agent or attorney, of the amount bid and twenty-five (25) per centum additional to the town clerk and treasurer within twelve (12) months.

nual levy of es.

vilege taxes.

Sec. 44. The commissioners of said town shall have power to annually levy and cause to be collected for the necessary expenses of said town such privilege taxes as shall seem to them fair and equitable on the profession, callings, trades, occupations and all other business carried on in said town; that is to say, on every merchant, lawyer, physician, dentist, druggist, artisan, mechanic, daguerrean artist or other pictures; on all officers or agents of incorporated companies; on all clerks or employees of other persons or corporations; on every drummer, unless the state license under which he acts shall have been issued to such drummer by the treasurer of the state in the name of such drummer, and not in the name of the person, firm or corporation for whom he is acting or doing business; on all editors, printers, butchers, tinners, carpenters, shoemakers, wheelwrights, carriage, buggy or wagon makers, jewelers, liquor dealers, confection grocers, bartenders, harness makers, saddlers, blacksmiths; on billiard or bagatelle able, public or private boarding, nine or ten-pin alley; on all lectures for reward; on all riding or pleasure vehicles; on all gold, silver or metal watches; on all pianos and organs; on all pistols, dirks, bowie knives or sword canes; on every livery stable, cotton gin or turpentine or other distillery; on every hotel or boarding house, restaurant or eating saloon; on all drays, carts, wagons, carriages, buggies; on all horses, cattle, sheep, hogs, goats or dogs owned or kept in said town; on every stallion, jackass kept or exhibited in said town; on all itinerant trades, peddlers or bankers; on all and every person, company or companies who may exhibit, sing, play, act or perform on anything for which they charge or receive any gratuity, fee or reward or award whatsoever within the limits of said town, and the commissioners of said town shall prescribe when the license tax herein provided for shall be due and payable.

bjects of ial taxation.

le of spirituous uors.

Sec. 45. The board of commissioners of said town shall have full and complete control of the sale or vending of spirituous or malt liquors, wines or cider within the limits of said corporation, and may permit the same to be sold by persons of good moral character, resident therein; shall prescribe the rules and regulations under which the same may be sold; shall prescribe the amount of the license tax therefor and when the same shall be due and payable, and shall have full power and authority to revoke and annul any license by them granted at any time, without refunding any part of the license tax. License tax.

Sec. 46. That it shall be the duty of the town clerk and treasurer to post all ordinances adopted by the board of commissioners at the mayor's office and four other public places in said town for five (5) days, and all ordinances shall go into effect from and after the expiration of five days from the time they have been posted. Ordinances shall be posted for five days.

[Sec.] 47. That all laws heretofore passed for the government or regulation of the town of Manly in conflict with this act be and the same are hereby repealed. Conflicting laws repealed.

Sec. 48. That this act shall be in force from and after its ratification.

Ratified the 6th day of March, A. D. 1899.

CHAPTER 261.

An act to enable the town of Salem to establish a workhouse.

The General Assembly of North Carolina do enact:

Section 1. That the mayor and commissioners of the town of Salem, in Forsyth county, are authorized and empowered, either alone or in conjunction with the authority of the city of Winston, to purchase and provide a farm and to establish thereon a workhouse for the detention and employment of criminal classes. Mayor and commissioners of Salem authorized to establish work house.

Sec. 2. That all persons duly convicted of crimes, violations of town ordinances and other violations of law by the mayor or other officers within the town of Salem having jurisdiction thereof, may be sentenced by such mayor or other such officer for a term in said workhouse and on said farm, and all such persons thus sentenced may be required to work during the term fixed by such sentence. Persons who may be sent to said work house

Sec. 2 [3]. That the cost of providing such farm and the establishing a workhouse thereon, as well as the maintenance thereof, may be borne by the town of Salem and the city of Winston in the proportion to be agreed upon by the authorities of the two respective towns, as either or both may provide and maintain a Costs incident thereto borne by Salem.

separate farm or workhouse for the purposes herein explained in the discretion of the authorities of the respective corporations, and in either event the provisions of this act shall be applicable.

Sec. 4. That this act shall be in force from and after its ratification.

Ratified the 6th day of March, A. D. 1899.

CHAPTER 262.

An act to amend the charter of the town of Clayton.

The General Assembly of North Carolina do enact:

Section 1. That the inhabitants of the town of Clayton shall be and continue as they heretofore have been, a body politic and corporate, and henceforth the corporation shall bear the name and style of the "Town of Clayton," and under such name and style is hereby invested with all property and rights of property which now belong to the corporation under any other corporate name or names heretofore used, and by this name may acquire and hold for the purpose of its government and welfare and improvement, all such estate as may be devised, bequeathed or conveyed to it, not exceeding in value three hundred thousand dollars and shall have right to contract and be contracted with, to sue and be sued, to plead and be impleaded, to purchase and to hold and convey real or personal property.

rporate name. rporate powers.

rporate limits.

Sec. 2. That the corporate limits of the said town of Clayton, in the county of Johnston, shall be as follows: Beginning at a stake in the old corporation line two hundred and ten feet southeast from O'Neill street, runs a line parallel with said street north forty-five degrees east eleven chains to a stake; thence north forty-five degrees west four hundred and seventy-six feet to a stake; thence east forty-five degrees west eleven chains to a stake in the old corporation line; thence north forty-five degrees west eleven chains to a stake in said line; thence nineteen and twenty-two one-hundredths chains to a post oak on the south side of Raleigh road; thence south forty-five degrees west four and forty-four one-hundredths chains to N. C. R. R.; thence with said railroad south forty-five degrees east six and ninety-six one-hundredths chains to a stake in the old corporation line; thence forty-five degrees west to a stake on the lands of J. T. Ellington; thence south forty-five degrees east eighty-two chains to a stake on the lands of Harry Durham; thence north forty-five degrees east thirty-seven chains to a stake on the lands of J. D. Dodd; thence forty-five degrees west to the beginning. That A. J. Farmer, Charles W. Horne and D. L. Barbour are hereby constituted and appointed a board of commissioners for said town, and E. L. Hinton is hereby constituted and appointed mayor of said town, upon their taking the oaths of office required by this act, and they shall have full power to execute the by-laws and ordinances of said town until their successors shall be elected at the next general election for town officers under the provisions of this act.

Commissioners appointed.

Mayor.

Powers of said appointees.

Sec. 3. There shall be annually on the first Monday in May of each year be elected three commissioners for said town, who shall hold their offices until their successors are qualified.

Annual election.

Sec. 4. The board of commissioners of Johnston county shall appoint at or before their meeting in March, one thousand eight hundred and ninety-nine and annually thereafter a registrar of voters of said town. Said registrar shall give ten days' notice at thre public places in said town of a registration of voters in and for said town, specifying time and place; in case of vacancy in the position of registrar from any cause, the chairman of the board of commissioners of Johnston county shall fill the vacancy.

Appointment of registrar.

Vacancies.

Sec. 5. Said registrar shall be furnished by said county commissioners with registration books at the expense of the town, and it shall be the duty of said registrar to open his books at the time and place designated by said county commissioners in said town, at least thirty days before the day of election herein provided for, and to register therein the names of all persons applying for registration and entitled to register and vote. It shall be the duty of the registrar to keep the names of the white voters separate and apart from those of colored voters, and he shall designate on the registration books opposite the name of each person registering the place of residence, and if such applicant for registration shall not disclose his place of residence, his willful failure to do so shall be prima facie evidence that he is not entitled to registration.

Registration furnished by county commissioners.

When registration books shall be opened.

Names of voters of different races kept separately.

Sec. 6. The board of commissioners of Johnston county, at or before their meeting in April, one thousand eight hundred and ninety-nine and annually thereafter, shall appoint two judges or inspectors of election for said town, who, with the registrar, shall open the polls and superintend the same on the day of election hereinafter specified. The judges of election, whose appointments are herein provided for shall have authority to administer oaths, and shall have all the powers of such officers under the general laws regulating elections.

Appointment of judges.

Sec. 7. All electors that shall have resided in the state twelve

Persons entitled to vote.

months, and in the town of Clayton ninety days next preceding the election shall be entitled to register.

ection of yor. Sec. 8. That the legally qualified voters of said town of Clayton shall, on the first Monday in May, one thousand eight hundred and ninety-nine and on each succeeding first Monday in May thereafter, by ballot, elect a mayor for the said town of Clayton, a majority of all the votes cast being necessary to elect said mayor. He shall preside at all meetings of the board of commissioners, and have the right and powers and perform all the duties heretofore prescribed by law for said officers.

wer of mayor.

ection of chief police. Sec. 9. That at all the elections held by virtue of this act, the chief of police of said town shall attend the polls, and by himself and by his assistants preserve order.

rm of office of yor and commissioners. Sec. 10. That the mayor and commissioners shall hold their offices respectively until the next succeeding election, and until their respective successors are qualified.

th of mayor. Sec. 11. That the mayor, immediately after his election and before entering upon the duties of office, shall take before a justice of the peace the following oath: "I, A. B., do solemnly swear that I will diligently endeavor to perform faithfully and truthfully, according to my best skill and ability, all the duties of the office of mayor of the town of Clayton while I continue therein, and I will cause to be executed, as far as in my power lies, all the laws, ordinances and regulations enacted for the government of the town of Clayton, and in the discharge of my duties I will strive to do equal justice in all cases whatsoever."

hen commissioners shall alify. Sec. 12. That on Thursday succeeding the day of election the commissioners elected thereat shall qualify, by taking the oath of office, before the mayor or a justice of the peace, as prescribed for commissioners of incorporated towns according to section fifteen, chapter three (one hundred and eleven) Battle's Revisal, and when organized, shall succeed to and have all the rights, powers and duties prescribed by law.

hen mayor uses to qualify. Sec. 13. That if any person chosen mayor shall refuse to be qualified, or there is any vacancy in the office after election and qualification, the commissioners shall choose some qualified person mayor for the term or unexpired portion of the term, as the case may be, and all like occasions, and in like manner the commissioners shall choose other commissioners to supply the places of such as shall refuse to act, and all vacancies which may occur, and such persons only shall be chosen as are hereinbefore declared to be eligible.

cancies on ard of commissioners.

case of failure lect municipal cers. Sec. 14. That in any case of failure to elect municipal officers on any said first Monday in May, the electors residing within the said town of Clayton may, after ten days' notice, signed by any three of said electors and posted up at three public places within the corporate limits of said town, proceed to hold an election of municipal officers in the way and manner provided for in Battle's Revisal, chapter one hundred and eleven.

Jurisdiction of mayor.

Sec. 15. That the mayor of said town is hereby instituted an inferior court, and as such shall, within the corporate limits of the town of Clayton, have all the power, jurisdiction and authority of justices of the peace in criminal cases, to issue process, and also to hear and determine all causes of action which may arise upon the ordinances and regulations of the town; to enforce penalties by issuing executions upon any adjudged violation thereof, and to execute the by-laws, rules and regulations made by the board of commissioners. The mayor shall further be a special court within the corporate limits of the town to arrest and try all persons who are charged with a misdemeanor for violating the ordinances of the town, and if the accused be found guilty, he shall be fined at the discretion of the court or mayor, not exceeding the amount specified in the ordinance or ordinances so violated; or at the discretion of the mayor or court trying the same such offender may be imprisoned not more than thirty days in the town lockup or common jail of the county, and that in all cases where a defendant may be adjudged to be imprisoned by said special court it shall be competent for said court to adjudge also that the said defendant work during the period of his confinement in the public streets or other public works of said town.

Mayor constituted a special court.

Persons failing to pay fines may be worked on public roads.

To whom mayor may issue precepts.

Sec. 16. That the mayor may issue his precept to the chief of police or any policeman of the town, and to such officers to whom a justice of the peace may direct his precepts.

Force of judgments rendered by mayor.

Sec. 17. That the mayor shall keep a faithful minute of the precepts issued by him and all of his judicial proceedings. The judgments rendered by him shall have all the force, virtue and validity of judgments rendered by a single justice of the peace, and may be executed and enforced against the parties in the courts of Johnston and elsewhere in the same manner and by the same means as if the same had been rendered by a justice of the peace for the county of Johnston.

Violation of town ordinances a misdemeanor.

Sec. 18. That any violation of a town ordinance shall be a misdemeanor, and shall be punished by a fine of not more than fifty dollars or imprisonment of not more than thirty days, and no preliminary affidavits shall be necessary to give the mayor final jurisdiction over the offenses against the town ordinances.

Fines, how applied.

Sec. 19. That all fines collected under the provisions of this act for violation of the ordinances of said town shall go to the use of the said town.

When mayor shall vote.

Sec. 20. That the mayor when present shall preside at all meetings of the board of commissioners, and when there is any equal division upon any question or/in the election of officers by the board, he shall determine the matter by his vote. He shall vote in no other case, and if he shall be absent they may appoint one of their number chairman pro tempore to exercise his duties at the board, and in event of his absence or sickness, the board of commissioners may appoint one of their own number pro tempore to exercise his duties. (Battle's Revisal, chapter three (one hundred and eleven) section eight.

hen commissioners shall onvene for nsaction of siness.

Sec. 21. That the commissioners shall form one board and a majority of them shall be competent to perform all the duties prescribed for the commisioners, unless otherwise provided. Within five days after the election they shall convene for the transaction of business and shall then fix stated days of the meetings for the year, which shall be as often at least as once in every calendar month. The special meetings of the commissioners may also be held on the call of the mayor or a majority of the commissioners, and of every [and] each meeting when called by the mayor, all the commissioners, and when called by a majority of the commissioners such as shall not join in the call shall be notified in writing.

ilure of commissioners to end meeting.

Sec. 22. That if any commissioner shall fail to attend a general meeting of the board of commissioners, or any special meeting of which he shall have notice, as prescribed in this chapter, unless prevented by such cause as shall be satisfactory to the board, he shall forfeit and pay for the use of the town the sum of two dollars.

wers conferred commission-.

Sec. 23. That among the powers hereby conferred on the board of commissioners, they may borrow money only by the consent of a majority of the qualified registered voters, which consent shall be obtained by a vote of the citizens of the corporation after thirty days' public notice, at which time those who consent to the same shall vote, "Approved," and those who do not consent shall vote, "Not approved." They shall provide water, provide for repairing and cleansing the streets, regulate the market, take all proper means to prevent and extinguish fires, make regulations to cause the due observance of Sunday, appoint and regulate the town police force, supress and remove nuisances, preserve the health of the town from contagious or infectious diseases, appoint constables to execute precepts, as the mayor and other persons may lawfully issue to them, to preserve the peace and order, and execute the ordinances of the town, and shall appoint and provide for the pay and prescribe the duties of all such other officers as may be deemed necessary.

provement of eets.

ntagious eases, etc.

pointment of wn officers.

Sec. 24. That the commissioners, at their first meeting after their election, or as soon thereafter as possible, shall appoint a clerk, a treasurer, a collector of taxes, a chief of police, and, if necessary, one or more assistants, who shall respectively hold their offices during the official term of the commissioners, subject, however, to removal at any time, and others appointed in their stead, for misbehavior or neglect in office. Before acting, each of said officers shall be sworn to the faithful discharge of his duties, and shall execute a bond payable to the town of Clayton, in such sum as the commissioners shall determine.

Term of office.

Said officers shall be sworn.

Sec. 25. That the clerk shall have a reasonable salary and it shall be his duty to keep regular and fair minutes of the proceedings of the board, and to preserve all books, papers and articles committed to his care during his continuance in office, and deliver them to his successor and generally to perform such other duties as may be prescribed by the board of commissioners.

Compensation of officers.

Sec. 26. That every person shall be allowed to inspect the journals and papers of the board in the presence of the clerk.

Inspection of journals of town.

Sec. 27. That the treasurer shall have a reasonable salary, and it shall be his duty to call on all persons who may have in their hands moneys or securities belonging to the town which ought to be paid or delivered into the treasury and to safely keep the same for the use of the town; to disburse the funds according to such orders as may be duly drawn on him in the manner hereinafter specified; he shall keep in a book provided for that purpose a fair and correct account of all moneys received and disbursed by him, and shall submit said account to the board of commissioners whenever required to do so. On the expiration of his term of office he shall deliver to his successor all the moneys, securities and other property entrusted to him for safe keeping or otherwise, and during his continuance therein he shall faithfully perform all duties lawfully imposed upon him as town treasurer.

Compensation of treasurer.

Duties of treasurer.

Sec. 28. That all orders drawn on the treasurer shall be signed by the mayor and countersigned by the clerk, and shall state the purpose for which the money is applied, and the treasurer shall specify said purpose in his accounts, and also the sources whence are derived the moneys received by him.

Orders drawn on treasurer, how signed.

Sec. 29. The tax collector shall proceed forthwith to collect the taxes laid upon such subjects of taxation as the board of commissioners may direct within five days after the list shall have been placed in his hands, and shall complete the same on or before the first day of April next ensuing, and shall pay the moneys, certificates, vouchers and so forth, as they are collected, to the treasurer, taking his receipt for the same; and for this purpose he is hereby invested with all the powers which are now or may hereafter be invested in a sheriff or collector of state taxes; he shall rent out the market stalls and vegetable stands, prosecute all persons who retail without having paid the tax imposed or sell without a license; also at every monthly

Collection of taxes.

When collection of taxes shall be completed.

Powers of tax collector.

meeting of the board of commissioners he shall produce an abstract showing the sums received by him upon each subject of taxation, and the amount still due thereon; he shall further specify in said abstract the amount of cash received and the amount of certificates or other vouchers received in payment of taxes, which abstract shall be placed in the hands of the town commissioners, to be filed with their chairman, and all books and documents belonging to or used in the office of collector shall be, and are hereby, declared to be the property and records of the town, and shall be at all times subject to the inspection and examination of the mayor and board of commissioners. The collector shall receive for his compensation such fees and commissions as may be allowed by the board of commissioners, and he shall, on or before the fifteenth day of April in each year, settle his accounts in full for the entire amount of taxes levied by the board under the supervision of the town commissioners, and if the collector shall have been unable to collect any part of said taxes by reason of the insolvency of any persons owing the same, or other good reasons, he shall, on oath, deliver a list of all such insolvents, delinquents and all other tax returns uncollected to the mayor, to be laid before the board of commissioners, and if approved, he shall be credited with the amount thereof, or so much as may be approved; he and his sureties on his bond shall be answerable for the remainder and for all other taxes or levies not collected and paid over by him, which he is or may be required by law to collect, and his bond shall be put in suit by the mayor and the attorney.

mpensatson of llector.

st of insolvents.

all be credited th approved solvents.

nual transcript of receipts d disbursements shall made by commissioners.

Sec. 30. That the board of commissioners shall cause to be made out annually a fair transcript of their receipts and disbursements of [on] account of the town, for the general inspection of the citizens, and cause the same to be posted up at the mayor's office in said town ten days before the day of the annual election of commissioners.

ties cf police.

Sec. 31. That it shall be the duty of the police to see that the laws, ordinances and orders of the board of commissioners are enforced and to report all breaches thereof to the mayor; to preserve the peace of the town by suppressing disturbances and apprehending all offenders, and for that purpose they shall have all the power and authority vested in sheriffs and county constables; they shall execute all precepts lawfully directed to them by the mayor or other judicial officers, and in the execution thereof shall have the same powers which the sheriff and constables of the county have, and they shall have the same fees on all processes and precepts executed or returned by them which may be allowed to the sheriff of the county on like process and

es of police.

precepts, and also such other compensation as the board of commissioners may allow.

Sec. 32. That for any breach of his official bond by the treasurer, clerk, tax collector, or any other town officer who may be required to give an official bond, he shall be liable in an action on the same in the name of the town or at the suit of the town, or any person aggrieved by such breach, and the same may be put in suit without assignment from time to time until the whole penalty be recovered.

B each of official b nd by town officers.

Sec. 33. That the board of commissioners shall have power to lay out and open any streets within the corporate limits of the town, and shall have full power and authority to condemn, appropriate or use any lands necessary for any of the purposes named in this section, upon making a reasonable compensation to the owner or owners thereof; but in case the owner of the land and the commissioners can not agree as to the damages, the matter shall be referred to arbitrators, each party choosing one, who shall be a freeholder and a citizen of the town; and in case the owner of the land shall refuse to choose such arbitrator, then the sheriff of the county shall in his stead select one for him, and in case the two chosen as aforesaid can not agree they shall select an umpire, whose duty it shall be to examine the lands condemned and ascertain the damages sustained and the benefits accruing to the owner in consequence of the change; and the award of the arbitrators or umpire shall be conclusive of the rights of the parties and shall vest in the commissioners the right to use the land for the purposes specified, and all damages agreed upon by the commissioners or awarded by the arbitrators or umpire shall be paid as other town liabilities, by taxation: Provided, that either party may appeal to the superior court as now provided by law.

Improvement of streets.

Condemnation of land.

Selection of assessors.

Proviso Either party may appeal.

Sec. 34. That the board of commissioners shall have authority to put and keep at work upon the streets or public grounds of the town any person or persons who may fail to pay any fines, penalties or forfeitures which may have been imposed on such person or persons by the mayor of the town, and the said commissioners shall have authority by the ordinances and by-laws of the town to confine, control and manage such person or persons until the said fines, penalties or forfeitures, together with the cost thereof, shall be fully paid and satisfied, under such rates for labor and board as the commissioners may establish.

Persons failing to pay fines may be worked on roads.

Sec. 35. That in order to raise a fund for the expenses incident to the proper government of the town, the commissioners may annually levy and collect the following taxes, viz: On all real and personal property within the corporate limits of the town; upon all money on hand, solvent credits; upon all polls

Annual levy of tax.

Subjects of taxation.

and other subjects of taxation taxed by the general assembly for public purposes.

itation to valorem tax.

Sec. 36. That the annual tax on property enumerated in preceding section shall not exceed fifty cents on one hundred dollars valuation thereof, nor shall the poll tax annually exceed one dollar and fifty cents.

y and collec- n of special es

Sec. 37. That in addition to the subjects of taxation for state purposes, the commissioners shall have power to levy and collect a special or license tax not to exceed fifty dollars on the following subjects, to-wit: all itinerant merchants, peddlers or auctioneers who shall sell or offer to sell, privately or at public outcry, within the town limits, whether by ascending or descending bids; each express company, each telegraph office and each railroad company having a depot within the town limits; each photograph artist and person taking likenesses of the human face by whatsoever art; each broker, bank or banker's office; each dealer in cotton futures; each dealer in patent rights; each sewing machine agent; all commission merchants and commercial brokers; each distiller of fruit or grain; each livery stable; every resident or non-resident huckster or trader or agent of such who buys produce on the street for sale in other markets; each gift enterprise and lottery; each dray; each omnibus; each hotel; each barber shop; each lightning-rod agent; each fire or life insurance agent; on each auctioneer; on every agency for the sale of steam engines, boilers and machinery not manufactured in this town; every dealer in buggies, wagons or other vehicles not manufactured in this town; each and every surgeon, dentist, practicing physician, optician, practicing lawyer, civil engineer, real estate agent or broker, oculist and chiropodist.

ctioneers, etc

press, tele- ph and rail d companes otographers.

kers and ks.

ing ma- nes, etc.

ery stables

cksters.

t enterprises

ber shops

htning-rod nts.

ctioneers.

rgeons, den- s, etc.

al estate nts

rses, etc., run- g at large y be declared isances.

Sec. 38. That the board of commissioners shall have power to declare all horses, mules, cattle, swine, sheep, goats and dogs running at large within the limits of the town a nuisance, and the commissioners may at their option impose a fine upon the owner or owners of the said animals so running at large, or may treat the same as a nuisance and abate or prohibit by law.

ditional cial taxes.

Sec. 39. That in addition to the subject of taxation enumerated in section thirty-eight, the commissioners may levy a tax on the following subjects, the amounts of which tax, when fixed, shall be collected by the tax collector instantly, and if the same be not paid on demand, the same may be recovered by suit upon the articles upon which the tax is imposed, or any other property of the owner may be forthwith distrained and sold to satisfy the same, namely:

wling alleys. liard tables.

1. Upon every bowling alley, billiard table, pool table, bagatelle table, shooting gallery, skating rink, or any other game allowed by law, and on every victualing house or restaurant, estab-

lished, used or kept in the town, a tax not exceeding fifty dollars a year.

II. Upon every permission by the board of commissioners to retail spirituous liquors, a tax not exceeding one hundred dollars. Liquor license

III. Upon every company of circus riders who shall exhibit within the town, a tax not exceeding thirty dollars for each separate exhibition, the tax being paid before the exhibition; if not, to be doubled. Circuses.

IV. Upon every company of stage of theatrical performers, every sleight-of-hand performer, rope or wire dancer or performer, every exhibitor of natural or artificial curiosities, every single person or company of singers, dancers, Ethiopian minstrels or performers on musical instruments, who shall sing, dance, perform or play on musical instruments for reward, five dollars for each exhibition. Theatrical performances.

V. Each show or exhibition of any other kind, and upon every concert or lecture for reward, a fine of five dollars for each exhibition. Exhibitions of other kind.

Sec. 40. That the board of commissioners shall cause to be kept clean and in good repair the streets, sidewalks and alleys; they may establish the width and ascertain the location of those already provided, and lay out and open others; may reduce the width of all of these; they may also establish and regulate the public grounds and protect the shade trees of the town. Repair of streets.

Sec. 41. That the board of commissioners shall have power to establish ordinances to prevent and extinguish fires, to provide for the establishments or organization, equipment and government of fire companies, provide said companies with fire engines, fire hose and necessary appurtenances. Prevention of fires.

Sec. 42. That the commissioners may require and compel the abatement and removal of all nuisances within the town at the expense of the person causing the same, or the owner or tenants of the grounds, whoever the same may be, and may regulate the same, if allowed to be established, any slaughter house or place or the exercise within the town of any offensive or unhealthy trade, business or employment. Abatement of nuisances.

Sec. 43. That they prohibit by penalties the riding or driving of horses or other animals in a careless or dangerous manner, or at a greater speed than ten miles per hour, within the town limits, and also the firing of guns, pistols, gunpowder, crackers or other explosive, combustible or dangerous materials in the streets, public grounds or elsewhere within the town. Fast riding and driving.

Sec. 44. That the commissioners may establish and regulate the markets, [and] prescribe at what time and place [in] the town marketable articles shall be sold. Regulation of markets.

ublic buildings. Sec. 45. That they may establish all public buildings necessary and proper for the town and prevent the erection or establishment of wooden buildings in any part of the town where they may increase the danger of fire.

ppointment of lice force. Sec. 46. That the board of commissioners are hereby authorized and empowered to appoint and employ the police force for said town, of persons residing either in or out of the corporate limits of saia town.

emeteries. Sec. 47. That they may provide graveyards in or near the corporate limits, and regulate the same; may appoint and pay a keeper, and compel the keeping and returning bills of mortality, and they may prohibit interments within the town.

revention of ntagious disses Sec. 48. That the board of commissioners may take such measures as they may deem effectual to prevent the entrance into the town of the spreading therein of any contagious or infectious disease; may stop, detain and examine for the purpose every person coming from places believed to be infected with such diseases; may establish and regulate hospitals within the town or within three miles thereof; may cause any person in the town suspected to be infected with such disease, and whose stay may endanger its health, to be removed to the hospital; may remove from the town or destroy any furniture or other articles which shall be suspected of being tainted or infected with contagious or infectious diseases or of which there shall be reasonable cause to apprehend that they may pass into such a state as to generate and propagate diseases; may abate by any reasonable means all nuisances which may be injurious to the public health.

ay remove seased persons

rsons attempting to prevent moval of hers guilty of a isdemeanor. Sec. 49. That if any person shall attempt by force or threats of violence to prevent the removal to the hospital of any person ordered to be conveyed thither, the person so offending shall forfeit and pay to the town one hundred dollars, and moreover be deemed guilty of a misdemeanor.

egulation of eed of trains. Sec. 50. That the board of commissioners may govern and regulate the speed of railroad trains while running within the corporate limits of the town, and prohibit the ringing of bells, the town limits.

mmissioners of hnston county all not grant uor license thout permission of town mmissioners. Sec. 51. That it shall be unlawful for the commissioners of Johnston county to grant any license to retail spirituous liquors within the limits of the town or within one mile thereof, without permission first obtained from the board of commissioners for the town it [in] being at the time of the application to the county commissioners; and if any license shall be granted without permission in writing, attested by the clerk of the board of commissioners, and exhibited to the county commissioners, and filed with the clerk of the board of county commissioners, the same shall be utterly void, and the person obtaining such license shall be liable to indictment, as in other cases of retailing without a license, and shall, moreover, forfeit and pay to the town the sum of twenty dollars. Such license void.

Sec. 52. That all penalties impressed [imposed] by law relating to the town of Clayton, or by this act, by any ordinance of the town, unless otherwise provided, shall be recoverable in the name of the town of Clayton before the mayor or any tribunal having jurisdiction thereof. Penalties recoverable in name of town.

Sec. 53. That the board of commissioners shall not have power to impose for any such offense a larger penalty than fifty dollars, unless the same be expressly authorized, and from any judgment of the mayor by this act, or for other cause of action herein allowed, the party dissatisfied may appeal in like manner and under the same rules and regulations as are prescribed for the appeals from a judgment of a justice of the peace. Maximum penalty.

Sec. 54. That the board of commissioners shall have power to fix the salary of the mayor, treasurer, clerk, tax collector and any other officer of the town, or increase or diminish the same from time to time as they may elect. Salary of mayor and other officers.

Sec. 55. That the town of Clayton is hereby vested with all the powers, rights, privileges and immunities enumerated in chapter one hundred and eleven and elsewhere in "Battle's Revisal," not inconsistent with any of the provisions of this act. Corporate powers.

Sec. 56. That all laws and clauses of laws coming in conflict wit. this act be, and the same are hereby, repealed. Conflicting laws repealed.

Sec. 57. That this act shall be in force from and after its ratification.

Ratified the 6th day of March, A. D. 1899.

CHAPTER 263.

An act for the relief of members of the Tarboro fire company.

The General Assembly of North Carolina do enact:

Section 1. That all active firemen of the city of Tarboro, North Carolina, belonging to regular organized fire companies having fire apparatus and being recognized and under control of chief of fire department as part of the fire department of the city of Tarboro, in the county of Edgecombe, and who attend not less than fifty per centum of the alarms of fire in the said city during each fiscal year beginning April first, eighteen hundred and ninety-nine, shall be credited and allowed the amount of their annual city poll tax. Certain firemen of Tarboro allowed annual poll tax.

retary shall ep record of tendance of remen.

Sec. 2. That the secretary of each company shall keep a correct account of the yearly attendance of each active member of his company at fires and alarms, and the list of such members as have attended at not less than fifty per centum of alarms of fires, sworn to by the secretary of such company before a justice of the peace of Edgecombe county and endorsed by the clerk of the fire department, and when presented to the treasurer of the city of Tarboro shall be sufficient evidence to entitle such active firemen to the above credit or allowance of city poll tax as stated in section one.

Sec. 3. This act shall be in force from and after its ratification.

Ratified the 6th day of March, A. D. 1899.

CHAPTER 264.

An act to re-enact and amend the charter of the Polk County Railroad Company, being chapter one hundred and thirty-four, laws of eighteen hundred and eighty-seven.

The General Assembly of North Carolina do enact:

ction 1, chapter , laws of 1887, ended.

Section 1. That section one, chapter one hundred and thirty-four, laws of eighteen hundred and eighty-seven, be and the same is hereby amended by inserting before the words, "and their associates" in line twelve the following: "That for the purpose of constructing a railroad through Polk county, North Carolina, from any town or station on the Carolina Central Railway via Columbus and Mills Springs to the state line between Tennessee and North Carolina, as may be most practicable, J. G. B. Livingston, Robert Hamilton, N. H. Hill, George Collins, John W. McFarland, Grayson Arledge, J. R. Foster, J. A. Thome, A. C. Boone, Lynch Whiteside, J. C. Powell, L. F. Thorne, H. E. Gray, J. P. Arledge."

tion 3, said t, amended.

Sec. 2. That section three of said act be and is hereby amended by striking out after the word "of" in line one to the word "to" in line two, and insert "N. H. Hill, H. E. Gray, J. P. Arledge," and by striking out the word "the" in line six; also in lines ten and eleven strike out the words "to Columbus or Mills Springs," and in line twelve for "fifty" insert "ten."

ction 14 ended.

Sec 3. That section fourteen of said act be and is hereby amended by inserting after the word "annually" in line five, "at the court house in Polk county"; and in same line strike out "twenty" and insert "thirty."

Sec. 4. That said act be further amended by adding after section sixteen the following sections, to be called seventeen, eighteen, nineteen, twenty, twenty-one: Additional sections.

Sec. 17. Said company shall be authorized to begin the construction of said road at any point on the projected line, and may operate any portion of it when completed, and shall have the exclusive right of transportation over the same. Authorized to begin construction of road at any point along projected line.

Sec. 18. That said company shall have power and are hereby authorized to build branch roads and to construct and operate telegraph and telephone lines along its main line and branches. May build branch roads.

Sec. 19. That for the purpose of aiding in raising the capital stock of said railroad company, it shall and may be lawful for any county, township, city or town which is interested in its construction to subscribe to the capital stock of said company such sum or sums, in bonds or money, as a majority of their qualified electors may authorize, under the same rules and regulations as are by this chapter provided for Polk county. County, townships or towns may subscribe to capital stock.

Sec. 20. That said act is hereby ratified and confirmed in all respects and is continued in full force as heretofore, except only as herein specially amended. Said act continued in full force as amended.

Sec. [21.] This act shall be in force from and after its ratification.

Ratified the 6th day of March, A. D. 1899.

CHAPTER 265.

An act to be entitled an act to incorporate Rich Square Academy, Northampton county.

The General Assembly of North Carolina do enact:

Section 1. That J. A. Mancey, G. G. Maggett, W. M. Brewer, W. H. Roberts, Alfred Moore, W. L. Lassiter, E. D. Bishop, E. E. Roberts, Charles Bullocks, Solomon Harrell, John Manley, and their associates and successors, are hereby incorporated a body politic for educational purposes under the name and style of "Trustees of Rich Square Academy," in the county of Northampton, state of North Carolina, and as such may have all the powers of the like institutions and may sue and be sued, plead and be impleaded; said corporation shall have corporate existence for a period of sixty years. Corporators. Body corporate. Corporate name.

Sec. 2. That said corporation may purchase and hold such property, real and personal, as they may deem necessary for the purposes of the above-named, and may convey the same at pleasure. May purchase and hold property.

-laws and rules government.

Sec. 3. That said trustees shall have power to make all needful and necessary by-laws for their own government, and by a vote of two-thirds of said trustees at a regular meeting may increase the number of said trustees not to exceed thirty in all, and by a majority vote appoint the additional trustees, and when so appointed they shall have the same power and be subject to the same duties as if named in this act.

culty of acad- y, how ected.

Sec. 4. That the faculty of said Rich Square Academy, by the advice and with the consent of said trustees, shall have power to grant certificates of merit and diplomas upon the published courses of the instructions of students completing the same, but not to confer degrees or titles.

Sec. 5. That this act shall be in force from and after its ratification.

Ratified the 6th day of March, A. D. 1899.

CHAPTER 266.

An act to authorize the city of Salisbury to issue bonds to secure and supply to said city electric light plant, sewerage, waterworks, and for other purposes.

The General Assembly of North Carolina do enact:

dermen thorized to ue bonds. ximum ount.

Section 1. That the board of aldermen of the city of Salisbury is hereby authorized and empowered to issue, to an amount not exceeding one hundred thousand dollars ($100,000), bonds in the name of said city, in such denomination and form as the said board of aldermen [may] determine, with which to establish, construct, purchase or otherwise secure and maintain a system of electric lights; also purchase or construct, erect, equip and operate a system of waterworks and a system of sewerage for the use of said city and its inhabitants.

rpose of said ue.

turity of ds.

Sec. 2. That said bonds shall be made payable at such place and time as may be determined upon by said board of aldermen, but the time of payment of principal of said bonds shall be fixed at not less than twenty years nor more than thirty years.

rest.

Sec. 3. That said bonds shall bear interest at not more than five (5) per centum per annum, and the interest shall be made payable semi-annually, and said bonds shall in no case be sold, hypothecated or otherwise disposed of for less than their par value, and the money arising from the sale thereof shall be used to purchase or erect an electric light plant and appurtenances, and for the purchase or construction, erection, equipment and operation of a system of waterworks, and the purchase, erection,

ceeds from ds, how ap- ed.

equipment and operation of a system of sewerage, including such real estate and other property and machinery as may be necessary in establishing and operating the same.

Bonds shall not be issued until question is submitted to people.

Sec. 4. That said bonds shall not be issued until authorized by a majority of the qualified voters of said city at a public election to be held at such time and place as the board of aldermen shall appoint, at which election those favoring the issue of said bonds shall vote "For issue of bonds," and those opposing it shall vote "Against issue of bonds"; and it shall be the duty of said board of aldermen to give notice of the time, place and purpose of such election for thirty days in some newspaper published in the city of Salisbury; that said election shall be held in like manner and under the same rules and regulations, as far as the same are pertinent and applicable, as other elections are held in said city.

Form of ballot.

Bonds, how signed.

Sec. 5. If the powers hereby conferred and hereinbefore provided shall be exercised, and a majority of the qualified voters of said city shall vote to issue said bonds, then the said board of aldermen shall issue said bonds, and they shall be signed by the mayor, attested by the treasurer of the city and sealed with the corporate seal of the city; and said bonds and their coupons shall be exempt from city taxation until after they shall become due and the coupons thereon shall be receivable in payment of city taxes.

Exempt from municipal taxation.

Annual special tax may be levied to create sinking fund.

Sec. 6. That for the purpose of a sinking fund and of paying said coupons as the same shall become due, it shall be the duty of said board of aldermen, and they are hereby empowered so to do, to levy and collect a sufficient special tax each and every year upon all subjects of taxation which may be now or hereafter embraced in the subject of taxation under the charter of said city, which taxes so collected shall be used for no other purpose, and shall be kept separate from all taxes; and it shall be the duty of the said city treasurer as the said coupons are paid off and taken up to cancel the same, and he shall report not less than twice a year to the board of aldermen the manner and amount of coupons so cancelled: Provided, that no levy of taxes shall be made as to make the rate of all taxes, general and special, more than one dollar and fifty cents on the hundred dollars.

Treasurer shall make annual report.

Empowered to establish and maintain electric light plant.

Sec. 7. That the said city of Salisbury shall have power and authority to establish, construct or purchase, and at all times maintain in the said city an electric light and power plant, including all machinery and appliances necessary and appurtenant to the same, and to purchase or construct, erect, equip and operate a system of waterworks; also purchase, erect, equip and operate a system of sewerage, and all rights and privileges required to accomplish and maintain the same, and to secure the full benefit thereof to the said city and its customers within or near said city, and the said city shall have full power and right to purchase and hold such real estate and personal property as shall be necessary to enable it to build, erect and maintain such electric light and power plant in the said city, and to use the streets of said city for planting its poles and other purposes; and to purchase or construct, erect, equip and operate a system of waterworks; also purchase, erect, equip and operate a system of sewerage; and may enter by its officers, agents and servants upon the lands of other persons and corporations for the above purposes, and contract for and purchase the same; and if unable to agree for the purchase of said lands with the owners of the same, then the said city shall have the right by its board of aldermen to condemn the same in the manner now provided in the charter of said city for the condemnation of land for streets and other public purposes.

powered to rchase and ld real estate.

aterworks. werage.

dermen may er succeeding ctions.

Sec. 8. If a majority of the qualified voters of the city shall not vote in favor of the issue of bonds herein provided for at the first election, the board of aldermen [may] at any time thereafter, not oftener than once in each twelve months, as they may deem fit, and of their own motion, again submit the same question to a vote of the qualified voters of the city on the same notice and terms as is required for said first election; and if a majority of the qualified voters shall be in favor of the issue of said bonds, then this act and all of its provisions shall be and remain in full force and effect, and the said board of aldermen shall take the steps provided in this act for carrying out the provisions of said act.

Sec. 9. That this act shall take effect and be in force from and after its ratification.

Ratified the 6th day of March, A. D. 1899.

CHAPTER 267.

An act to allow S. H. Fine to run a ferry across French Broad river for the benefit of his customers.

The General Assembly of North Carolina do enact:

H. Fine au- rized to run y at certain int.

Section 1. That S. H. Fine, of Madison county, and his successors in business, be and they are hereby allowed to run a ferry across the French Broad river at or near the mouth of Big Pine creek, in said county, for the benefit of foot passengers only.

Sec. 2. That this act shall be in force from and after its ratification.

Ratified the 6th day of March, A. D. 1899.

CHAPTER 268.

An act to amend the charter of the town of Kings Mountain.

The General Assembly of North Carolina do enact:

Section 1. That chapter two hundred and fifty-four, laws of eighteen hundred and ninety-one, and section two of chapter seventy-three, private laws of eighteen hundred and seventy-three and eighteen hundred and seventy-four, be and the same are hereby repealed, and the following be substituted therefor, viz.: "That the corporate limits of said town of Kings Mountain shall extend from the center of the crossing of King and Piedmont streets in said town three-fourths (¾) of a mile in every direction, making said corporate limits a circle with a radius three-fourths of a mile in length." Corporate limits of Kings Mountain extended.

Sec. 2. That all laws and clauses of laws in conflict with this act are hereby repealed. Conflicting laws repealed.

Sec. 3. That this act shall be in force from and after its ratification.

Ratified the 8th day of March, A. D. 1899.

CHAPTER 269.

An act to authorize the town of Fremont to subscribe to the stock of the Great Eastern Railway and other purposes.

The General Assembly of North Carolina do enact:

Section 1. That the town of Fremont, in the county of Wayne, is hereby authorized to subscribe an amount not exceeding ten thousand dollars to the capital stock of the Great Eastern Railway Company, on condition that said company shall run its roadway to or through said town of Fremont. Town of Fremont authorized to subscribe to capital stock.

Sec. 2. That the proposition to subscribe said amount to the capital stock of said railway company, and to levy a tax for the payment of same, shall be submitted to the qualified electors of said town of Fremont at an election to be held at any time subsequent to the ratification of this act, after twenty (20) days' notice, specifying the amount of subscription to be voted for. Proposition to subscribe shall be submitted to voters.

Sec. 3. That at said election those favoring said subscription shall vote a ballot on which shall be written or printed the words, "For subscription," and those opposing said subscription shall vote a ballot upon which shall be written or printed the words "Against subscription." Form of ballot.

anouncement of sult.

Sec. 4. That the day succeeding the election the board of town commissioners of said town shall compare the votes as returned by the poll holders and judges of election and declare the result.

yment of capital ock.

Sec. 5. That if the result of said election shall show that the majority of the qualified voters of said town have voted in favor of said subscription to the capital stock of said railway company, then the commissioners of said town shall make said subscription to the capital stock of said railway company, payable in such terms as may be agreed upon between the commissioners of said town and the authorities of said railway company.

mmissioners ay issue bonds to y stock.

Sec. 6. That in order to pay said subscription the commissioners of said town may issue bonds of said town in such denominations as to them may seem best, running not exceeding thirty (30) years, bearing interest not exceeding six per cent. per annum, payable annually, with coupons attached, and sell the same at not less than their par value.

ecial tax may be vied to provide nking fund.

Sec. 7. That to provide for the payment of interest on said bonds and their redemption at maturity, the commissioners of said town are authorized each year to compute and levy on all property and polls of said town a sufficient tax to pay such interest and to provide a sinking fund for the payment of said bonds at maturity.

pointment of istees to sell nds.

Sec. 8. That for the purpose of carrying out the provisions of this act, and for paying the interest and investing the sinking fund, the commissioners of said town are hereby authorized to appoint not exceeding three (3) trustees, who shall have the supervision and control of selling said bonds and paying said subscription and investing the sinking fund and paying the interest on said bonds, and paying off said bonds at maturity, which trustees shall give bonds in such sums as to the commissioners of said town shall seem proper for the faithful performance of their duties.

Sec. 9. That this act shall be in force from and after its ratification.

Ratified the 8th day of March, A. D. 1899.

CHAPTER 270.

An act to amend the charter of the Cape Fear and Northern Railway Company.

The General Assembly of North Carolina do enact:

t incorporating pe Fear and d Northern Rail- y Company ended.

Section 1. That the act incorporating the Cape Fear and Northern Railway Company, ratified the 9th day of March, A. D. eighteen hundred and ninety-one, and all other acts amendatory thereof, be amended as follows, a majority of the stockholders in general meeting concurring, to-wit: The said The Cape Fear and Northern Railway Company may extend its line of railway, with one or more tracks, from any point on the Cape Fear river between Northington's ferry and Fayetteville, to the town of Fayetteville, or the city of Wilmington, or the town of Southport, or either or all of said lines.

May extend road.

Sec. 2. That the said company may extend and maintain its railway from and between the places mentioned in the first section of this act, with the privilege of constructing branch roads not to exceed twenty-five miles in length, and connecting with such other places or railways in and out of this state as may be deemed advisable by said company, either from the present constructed line of railway or lines that may hereafter be constructed.

When construction of road may be commenced.

Sec. 3. That said company may commence the construction of the extension of its railway at any point or points on its line or lines or divisions, and use any portion or portions or divisions of its said railway that may be constructed before its final completion, and charge for transportation and passage thereon.

Capital stock may be increased.

Sec. 4. That the capital stock of the said The Cape Fear and Northern Railway Company may be increased to an amount not o exceed two million dollars, in shares of one hundred dollars ach, and the said company may at any time increase its capital o such an amount as may be found necessary to carry out the ntention and purpose of this act.

Company may receive subscriptions to stock.

Sec. 5. That to provide the means, in whole or in part, for the xtension of the said The Cape Fear and Northern Railway Company, and for the construction of branches or lateral roads, the aid company may receive subscriptions in money, labor or proprty, as said company may agree, and may at its discretion issue nd execute a mortgage deed to secure the payment thereof on ts entire extended line, with the franchises and rights connected herewith, and may sell or negotiate such bonds at such rates as he board of directors shall deem for the best interest of the company, and the proceeds arising from the sale of such bonds shall e applied to the construction and equipment of the line, ranch or division so bonded.

May negotiate bonds.

May consolidate or unite with other companies.

Sec. 6. That said railway company shall have the privilege, pon the concurring vote as aforesaid, to consolidate or unite vith any other railroad, or to purchase or lease any other raiload within or without the state, under any general railroad law, erms or rules as may be agreed upon, not inconsistent with the aws of this state.

Counties, cities, towns, etc., may subscribe to stock.

Sec. 7. That any corporation, county, city, town or township nterested therein may subscribe to stock for said purpose, or otherwise contribute to such work in such manner and in such amount as shall be determined by the proper authorities of such corporation, county, city, town or township, and agreed upon with the said The Cape Fear and Northern Railway Company, and said subscription or contribution shall be made according to the general laws of the state of North Carolina.

idemnation of d.

Sec. 8. In the construction of the extended line or proposed branches the said company shall be entitled to the same rights, powers and privileges with respect to the acquisition of such land, and the condemnation thereof, as may be necessary therefor, as are conferred upon the said The Cape Fear and Northern Railway Company by its charter or any other amendments thereto.

pany not exempted from taxa-

Sec. 9. That nothing in this act shall be construed to exempt the property of said company from taxation for state and county purposes.

ll exercise such ers within two rs.

Sec. 10. That said company shall elect to exercise the powers and receive the benefits of this act within two years from its ratification, and not thereafter.

Sec. 11. That this act shall be in force from and after its ratification.

Ratified the 8th day of March, A. D. 1899.

CHAPTER 271.

An act to amend an act entitled "An act to amend the charter of the city of Charlotte," ratified March the first, eighteen hundred and eighty-one, being chapter forty of the private laws of eighteen hundred and eighty-one.

The General Assembly of North Carolina do enact:

pter 40; private s 1881, amended.

Section 1. That chapter forty of the private laws of eighteen hundred and eighty-one, entitled "An act to amend the charter of the city of Charlotte," be and the same is hereby amended by adding thereto the following:

rd of water missioners ointed.

Sec. 2. That E. T. Cansler and R. J. Brevard, W. C. Dowd and R. H. Jordan be and they are hereby constituted a board of water commissioners for the city of Charlotte, of which board the mayor of the city of Charlotte shall be ex officio chairman. That at all meetings of the said board the mayor shall preside, but shall vote only in case of a tie.

m of office.

Sec. 3. That the two commissioners first named above shall hold office until the first Monday in June, nineteen hundred, or until their successors shall be appointed, and that the two commissioners last named shall hold their office until the first Monday in June, eighteen hundred and ninety-nine, or until their successors are appointed.

Sec. 4. That the board of aldermen of the city of Charlotte at their regular meeting in June, eighteen hundred and ninety-nine, shall elect two commissioners to succeed the two last named above, and at their regular meeting in June, nineteen hundred, said board of aldermen shall elect two commissioners to succeed the two first above-mentioned, and said commissioners so elected shall hold office for two years from the date of their election, and until their successors are appointed. That thereafter said board of aldermen shall, at their regular meetings in June of any year that the term of office of any commissioners shall expire under this act, elect their successors, and said persons so elected shall hold office for two years from the date of their election, and until their successors are appointed.

Election of successors.

Regular election of water commissioners.

Sec. 5. That the commissioners appointed by this act, and their successors in office, shall take an oath to faithfully discharge the duties of the said office, to be administered by the mayor of the city of Charlotte. That on or before the first day of April, eighteen hundred and ninety-nine, the commissioners herein appointed shall assemble and organize, and the mayor of the city of Charlotte shall be ex officio chairman of the board; and when so organized they shall be known as the board of water commissioners of the city of Charlotte, and shall be a corporation under the corporate name of the board of water commissioners of the city of Charlotte, and as such corporation they shall have power to sue and be sued, to hold real estate and to enjoy the usual privileges of a corporation.

Commissioners shall take oath.

When commissioners shall organize.

Sec. 6. That a majority of said board shall constitute a quorum for the transaction of business, and all contracts and engagements, acts and doings of said board within the scope of their duty or authority shall be obligatory upon, and be in law considered as if done by the board of aldermen of the city of Charlotte; and said board shall, for and in the name of the board of aldermen of the city of Charlotte, take and hold the land, real estate, rights, franchises and property of every kind now owned by said board of aldermen for the city of Charlotte or that may hereafter be purchased, for the purpose of operating and maintaining a system of water-works for the said city; and they shall have power to acquire such additional property and make such additional improvements thereof as may be necessary to supply the city of Charlotte with a sufficient supply of good and wholesome water.

Quorum.

May hold real estate, rights, etc., in name of aldermen.

ay condemn land necessary purposes.

Sec. 7. That in case it becomes necessary to purchase additional lands or water rights necessary to the operation of said system of water-works, and there should be a disagreement between the owner of any such lands or water rights, [and the board] as to the price to be paid therefor, or as damages done thereto, it shall be lawful for either party to apply to the clerk of the superior court of Mecklenburg county, who shall thereupon appoint three disinterested persons to examine said property and assess the value thereof or the damage done to the same, who, after taking an oath before said clerk to administer the same impartially, shall proceed to assess the same and make return of their actions and doings to the said clerk of the superior court, who shall enter the same upon the minutes of the court and enter judgment according to the said report: Provided, that in case either party is dissatisfied with said award, he or they may appeal to the superior court of said county at term time, and have said case tried as is provided for cases of appeal from the clerk to the court in term time: Provided, also, that either party desiring to appeal from the judgment of the clerk shall give the opposite party notice within ten days after the rendition of the said judgment. That this act shall not be construed to allow said board to take said land until the damages awarded are paid.

(Margin notes: essessment of d. — oviso. ther party may peal. — oviso. otice of appeal. — nd shall not be ken until dam- es paid.)

npowered to e certain property.

Sec. 8. That the said board of water commissioners and all persons acting under their authority, shall have the right to use the ground or soil of any road, railroad, highway, lane or alley for the purpose of enlarging or improving the plant or system of water-works owned by the city of Charlotte, upon condition that they shall not permanently injure any such property; that the same shall be restored to its original condition or damages done thereto shall be repaired by the said board.

hall regulate distribution of water.

Sec. 9. That said board shall regulate the distribution and use of water for all places and for all purposes where the same may be required, and from time to time shall fix a price for the use thereof and the time of payment; and they shall erect such a number of public hydrants and in such places as they shall see fit, and shall direct in what manner and for what purposes the same shall be used; and they shall erect such a number of public places for urinating, and also have public water-closets, all of which shall be established or erected in the city of Charlotte; all of which they may change at their discretion: Provided, however, that all hydrants or appliances required and furnished for the purpose of extinguishing fires shall be erected at the expense of the board of aldermen of the city of Charlotte, and shall be placed as they direct and shall be under their exclusive control and direction.

(Margin notes: roviso. ydrants, etc., ected at expense town.)

Sec. 10. That the said board shall have full power and authority to require the payment in advance for the use or rent of the water furnished by them in or upon any building, place or premises; and in case prompt payment shall not be made, they may shut off the water from such building, place or premises after five days' notice, and shall not be compelled again to supply said premises, building or place with water until the arrears, with interest thereon, shall be fully paid.

May require payment in advance of water rentals.

Sec. 11. That the said board shall make no contract for the price of using the water for a longer time than three years.

No contract longer than three years shall be made.

Sec. 12. That if any person or persons shall maliciously or wilfully divert the water, or any portion thereof, from the said water-works, or shall corrupt or render the same impure, or shall destroy or injure any canal, aqueduct, pipe or other property used or acquired for procuring or distributing the water, said person shall be guilty of a misdemeanor, and upon conviction shall be fined not exceeding five hundred dollars or shall be imprisoned not exceeding one year, at the discretion of the court.

Persons diverting or rendering water impure guilty of misdemeanor.

Sec. 13. That all land and property of every kind held by the said board of water commissioners for the purposes aforesaid shall be exempted from taxes and assessments.

Said land exempt from taxation.

Sec. 14. And said board shall have power to make rules and regulations with respect to the introduction of water into or upon any premises, and from time to time to regulate the use thereof in such manner as shall seem to them necessary and proper; and the members of said board, and all engineers, superintendents or inspectors in their service are hereby authorized and empowered to enter, after demand made and refusal, at all reasonable hours any dwellings or other place where such water is taken and used where unnecessary waste thereof is known or suspected,, and examine and enquire into the cause thereof; and if any person refuses to permit such examination, or opposes or obstructs such officer in the performance of such duty, he, she or they, so offending, shall forfeit and pay the sum of ten dollars, to be recovered before any justice of the peace in an action by the said board, and the supply of water may also be cut off until the required examination is made and the required alterations and repairs are made.

Regulations with respect to water on premises.

Sec. 15. That the said board of water commissioners shall collect, or cause to be collected, all rents, forfeitures or emoluments arising from the operation of said system of water-works of the city of Charlotte. They shall cause accurate accounts to be kept of all receipts and expenditures of money coming into their hands, and shall, at least once in each year, make a detailed report thereof to the board of aldermen of the city of Charlotte. They shall pay, or cause to be paid, such moneys as shall come

Collection of rents, etc.

whom revenue d.

into their hands to the treasurer of the board of water commissioners, which money shall be disbursed by the treasurer of the board only upon the warrant of said board of water commissioners.

rk and treasr of commisners.

Sec. 16. That the city clerk and treasurer of the city of Charlotte shall be ex officio clerk and treasurer of said board of water commissioners, and for his services as such he shall receive such compensation as shall be fixed by the said board.

t of operation, w paid.

Sec. 17. That the said board of water commissioners shall, out of any money received by them, pay, first, the costs and expenses of operating the plant or system of water-works under their control, including costs of such improvements as they may deem necessary for the efficient working of the same, and the net balance, if any, they shall pay over to the treasurer of the city of Charlotte.

;erest on bonds.

Sec. 18. That the board of aldermen, out of such net balance, if any, shall pay, first, the interest upon such of the bonds of the city of Charlotte as were sold for the purpose of raising money to purchase said system of water-works, and the balance remaining after the payment of such interest shall be invested by the treasurer of the city of Charlotte, under the direction of the board of aldermen, and shall remain and be known as a sinking fund to meet the payment of said bonds at their maturity.

mpensation of ter commissions.

Sec. 19. That the members of said board of water commissioners shall receive such compensation as shall be fixed by the board of aldermen and shall not exceed the sum of one hundred dollars each per annum. That the amount of said compensation shall be fixed at the time of their entrance into office and shall not be changed during their said terms.

nflicting laws pealed.

Sec. 20. That all laws and parts of laws in conflict with this act are hereby repealed.

Sec. 21. That this act shall be in force from and after its ratification.

Ratified the 8th day of March, A. D. 1899.

CHAPTER 272.

An act to amend chapter sixty-four, private laws of eighteen hundred and eighty-nine.

The General Assembly of North Carolina do enact:

Section 1. That section six of chapter sixty-four of the private acts of eighteen hundred and eighty-nine be amended by inserting after the word town in the second line of said section the following words "by prescription or otherwise." Sale of liquor in Ellenboro, Rutherford county, by prescription or otherwise, unlawful.

Sec. 2. That this act shall be in force from and after its ratification.

Ratified the 8th day of March, A. D. 1899.

CHAPTER 273.

An act to amend chapter three hundred and eleven of the private laws of North Carolina, eighteen hundred and ninety-three.

The General Assembly of North Carolina do enact:

Section 1. That chapter three hundred and eleven of the private laws of North Carolina, eighteen hundred and ninety-three, be and the same is hereby amended as follows: Private acts, 1893, chapter 311, amended.

1. Strike out that part of section five after the word "telegraphs" in line thirty-two of said section.

2. Whenever the word "twenty-five thousand dollars" or the figures "($25,000)" appear in said act, strike out the same and insert in lieu thereof the words "ten thousand dollars" or the figures "($10,000)."

3. Strike out the word "five" in line one of section seventeen and insert in lieu thereof the word "ten."

Sec. 2. That this act shall be in force from and after its ratification.

Ratified the 8th day of March, A. D. 1899.

CHAPTER 274.

An act to amend chapter one hundred and thirty-six, private acts of eighteen hundred and ninety-five.

The General Assembly of North Carolina do enact:

Section 1. That chapter one hundred and thirty-six, private acts of eighteen hundred and ninety-five, be amended by adding thereto a section as follows, to be numbered section three, to-wit: In addition to the powers and privileges conferred upon the said The Raleigh Electric Company as to the successor to the Raleigh Street Railway Company, it shall have all the rights, powers and privileges usually belonging or pertaining to gas light companies Additional powers granted to Raleigh Electric Company.

incorporated under the laws of this state, and to that end may have the power to erect its plant and lay its mains and branch pipes in the city of Raleigh and vicinity: Provided, that before using the streets of the city of Raleigh for such purpose it shall obtain the consent of the board of aldermen of the city of Raleigh.

ɔviso.

y purchase ıer property and nchises.

Sec. 2. That said company may purchase and own the capital stock, property and franchises, either or all, of any other company.

ivate acts, 1895, mbered section ır.

Sec. 3. That section three of said chapter one hundred and thirty-six, private acts of eighteen hundred and ninety-five, shall be numbered section four.

nflicting laws ealed.

Sec. 4. That all laws and clauses of laws in conflict with the provisions of this act be and the same are hereby repealed.

Sec. 5. That this act shall be in force from and after its ratification.

Ratified the 8th day of March, A. D. 1899.

CHAPTER 275.

An act to charter the town of Wakefield, Wake county, North Carolina.

The General Assembly of North Carolina do enact:

wn of Wakefield, ke county, in- ·porated.

Section 1. That the persons residing within the corporate limits of the town of Wakefield, Wake county, North Carolina, which are particularly set forth in section two of this act shall be and are hereby incorporated by the name and style of the Town of Wakefield, and shall be subject to all the provisions contained in chapter sixty-two, volume two of The Code of North Carolina not inconsistent with this act.

nits and boun- ries of said town.

Sec. 2. That the corporate limits of the said town shall be as follows: Beginning at a point four hundred feet north of Taylor street on a line with the west side of Foster street, thence south with said line to a point in a line with south side of Johnston street, thence east with said line to a point on a line with west side of Perry street, thence north with said line to a point four hundred feet north of Taylor street, thence west on a parallel line with Taylor street to the beginning.

cers, when cted.

Sec. 3. That the officers of said town shall consist of a mayor, five commissioners and a town marshal. That the said mayor and commissioners shall be elected by the qualified voters of said town, and the said marshal shall be elected by said commissioners.

Sec. 4. That until the election hereinafter provided for shall be held, the mayor and commissioners shall consist of the following persons: Mayor, S. P. Green; commissioners, J. A. Kemp, T. L. Honeycutt, M. C. Chamblee, G. M. Bell and C. E. Pippin, who shall hold their respective offices until their successors are elected and duly qualified. Officers pro tem.

Sec. 5. That there shall be held on the first Monday in May, in the year eighteen hundred and ninety-nine, an election for mayor and five commissioners, and every year thereafter, in some convenient place in said town, notice of which shall be given for thirty days in three public places in said town. Annual election.

Sec. 6. That any qualified voters of this state shall be eligible for mayor and commissioners. Eligibility of officers.

Sec. 7. That all persons entitled to vote in the county of Wake for members of the general assembly, and who have been bona fide residents of said town for ninety days next preceding the election, and shall be otherwise entitled to vote, may vote at said election. Qualifications of electors.

Sec. 8. That the mayor of said town of Wakefield shall have the same jurisdiction as a justice of the peace in all criminal actions arising within the corporate limits of said town or within two and one-half miles thereof. Jurisdiction of mayor.

Sec. 9. That in addition to the powers conferred on the commissioners of incorporated towns enumerated in chapter sixty-two, volume two of The Code of North Carolina, the said commissioners shall have power to lay out and open any new street or streets within the corporate limits of said town, whenever they deem necessary, and of the necessity thereof the commissioners shall be the sole judges, within said corporation; and they shall have power at any time to widen, enlarge, change, extend or discontinue any street or streets, or any part thereof, within the corporate limits of said town; and shall have full power and authority to condemn, appropriate or use any land or lands necessary for any of the purposes named in this section, upon making a reasonable compensation to the owner thereof; but in case the owner or owners of the land sought to be condemned or appropriated for public use by the commissioners and the commissioners cannot agree as to the compensation, then the matter shall be referred to arbitration, the commissioners to choose one and the owners of the land another freeholder and a qualified elector of said town, and in case the owner of said land sought to be condemned shall refuse to choose such an arbitrator then the mayor shall choose in his stead such an arbitrator for him, and in case the two chosen as aforesaid cannot agree, then they shall elect an umpire, like qualified as themselves, whose duty it shall be to examine the land sought to be condemned and ascer- Powers of commissioners. Commissioners may lay out, etc., streets, and condemn land.

tain the damage that will be sustained by and the benefits accruing to the owner in consequence of the taking and using and appropriating said land, and award to the owner, if any, that [which] shall be paid by the town for the use of the land so taken, and the award of the arbitrator, or any two of them, shall be conclusive of the right to the use of said land, and shall vest in the commissioners the right to use said land for the purposes for which it was condemned, and the damages, as agreed upon between the owners of the land and the commissioners, or awarded by the arbitrator, shall be paid as other town liabilities: Provided, that either party may appeal to the superior court of Wake county.

mmissioners y prohibit stock m running at ge.

Sec. 10. That the said commissioners may prohibit the running at large of horses, cattle, hogs, sheep, jacks, jennets, goats and other live stock in the corporate limits of said town, and are hereby empowered to make such rules and regulations as they may deem best for the impounding and sale of the animals mentioned in this section, as well as other stock not mentioned, found running at large in the corporate limits of said town contrary to the ordinances of said town.

ohibition of in- icating liquors.

Sec. 11. That it shall be unlawful for any person or persons to manufacture, sell or give away, or dispose of in any way, directly or indirectly, any spirituous liquors or intoxicating drinks of any kind, for reward or hope of reward, within the corporate limits of said town or within two and one-half miles thereof, and if any person shall violate the provisions of this act he shall be guilty of a misdemeanor.

wers of taxation.

Sec. 12. That said commissioners shall have power to levy and collect taxes on all subjects of taxation in said corporate limits, not exceeding ten cents on every one hundred dollars worth of property and thirty cents on each poll, maintaining the constitutional equation between property and poll.

plication of xes, fines, for- tures, etc.

Sec. 13. That said commissioners shall have power to apply the taxes collected under this act, together with fines, forfeitures and penalties for violation of the town ordinances, to the improvement of the public streets in said town as they may find necessary.

ho required to rk streets.

Sec. 14. That all parties subject to road duty be required to work the streets in said town and not on public roads outside the corporate limits of said town.

Sec. 15. This act shall be in force and take effect from and after its ratification.

Ratified the 8th day of March, A. D. 1899.

CHAPTER 276.

An act to incorporate the town of Virgilina, in the county of Granville, North Carolina.

The General Assembly of North Carolina do enact:

Section 1. That the town of Virgilina, in the county of Granville, be and the same is hereby incorporated by the name and style of the Town of Virgilina, and it shall have the benefit of and be subject to all the provisions of law now existing in reference to incorporated towns not inconsistent with this act. Town of Virgilina, Granville county, incorporated.

Sec. 2. That the corporate limits and boundaries of said town shall be as follows: Beginning in centre of Florence avenue where it intersects the Virginina and North Carolina state line, thence west with said line one-half (½) mile to a stone, thence south one-half (½) mile to a stone, thence east one mile (1) to a stone, thence north one-half mile (½) to a stone in state line, thence west one-half mile to the beginning. Limits and boundaries.

Sec. 3. That the officers of said incorporation shall consist of a mayor, three commissioners and a constable, and the following named persons shall fill said offices until the first Monday in May, nineteen hundred, viz.: Mayor, Rufus Amis; commissioners, Wm. M. Pannebaker, Wm. D. Amis, Joseph C. Baldeirie; constable, Benjamin R. Puryear. Officers.

Sec. 4. That there shall be an election held for officers mentioned in this act, on the first Monday in May, A. D. nineteen hundred, and each succeeding year thereafter, with the same restrictions and regulations under which county and state elections are held; and all citizens who are qualified under the laws of the state shall be entitled to vote at said elections. Election to be held on first Monday in May, 1900.

Sec. 5. That the said commissioners shall have power to pass all by-laws, rules and regulations for the good government of the town, not inconsistent with the laws of the state and United States, and levy and collect a tax on all subjects of state taxation not to exceed one-half (½) of the state tax; and to impose fines for the violation of the town ordinances and collect the same. Powers of commissioners.

Sec. 6. That the manufacture and sale of intoxicating liquors of any name, distilled, fermented or malt, are forever prohibited within the corporate limits. Manufacture and sale of liquors forbidden.

Sec. 7. That the constable of said incorporation shall have authority to pursue, to a distance of five (5) miles from the corporate limits, and arrest without warrant any person who has committed a crime within said corporate limits and is fleeing to escape the lawful punishment of such crime. When constable may arrest without warrant.

Sec. 8. That this act shall be in force from and after its ratification.

Ratified the 8th day of March, A. D. 1899.

CHAPTER 277.

An act to amend section three of chapter twelve, private laws of eighteen hundred and eighty-nine.

The General Assembly of North Carolina do enact:

Reduction of number of directors in Merchants and Planters Bank of Milton.

Section 1. That in line six of section three, chapter twelve of the private laws of eighteen hundred and eighty-nine, strike out the word "ten" and insert in lieu thereof the word "five."

Sec. 2. That this act shall be in force from and after its ratification.

Ratified the 8th day of March, A. D. 1899.

CHAPTER 278.

An act to allow the North Carolina Investment Company further time to organize.

The General Assembly of North Carolina do enact:

North Carolina Investment Company to have further time to organize.

Section 1. That chapter one hundred and fifty-four of the private acts of eighteen hundred and ninety-three be continued in full force and effect until March first, nineteen hundred and five, so as to allow said company further time to organize and begin operation.

Sec. 2. That this act shall be in force from and after its ratification.

Ratified the 8th day of March, A. D. 1899.

CHAPTER 279.

An act to amend the charter of the town of Lillington, in Harnett county.

The General Assembly of North Carolina do enact:

Charter of Lillington, Harnett county, amended.

Section 1. That the charter of the town of Lillington in Harnett county be amended as follows:

"That the corporate limits of said town be extended according to metes and bounds to be prescribed by the present board of commissioners of said town, acting with the mayor at their meeting to be held on the first Monday in April, eighteen hundred and ninety-nine.

Sec. 2. That the ordinances fixing the new boundaries of said town be immediately published in three public places, within the territory covered by said metes and bounds, whereupon said new territory shall comprise a part of the said town. Ordinances fixing new boundaries to be published.

Sec. 3. That the secretary of state shall certify a copy of this act to the mayor of said town immediately upon its ratification. Secretary of State to certify act to mayor.

Sec. 4. That this act shall be in force from and after its ratification.

Ratified the 8th day of March, A. D. 1899.

CHAPTER 280.

An act to repeal chapter sixty-six, private laws of North Carolina of eighteen hundred and ninety-seven.

The General Assembly of North Carolina do enact:

Section 1. That chapter sixty-six of the private laws of eighteen hundred and ninety-seven of North Carolina be and the same is hereby repealed. Relating to construction of fence around Pollocksville, Jones county.

Sec. 2. That this act shall be in force from and after its ratification.

Ratified the 8th day of March, A. D. 1899.

CHAPTER 281.

An act to incorporate the State Council Junior Order United American Mechanics.

The General Assembly of North Carolina do enact:

Section 1. That the State Councilor, State Vice-Councilor, State Council Secretary, and members who at present are or in the future may be of the State Council Junior Order United American Mechanics of North Carolina are hereby constituted and declared to be a body corporate under the name and title of "State Council Junior Order United American Mechanics," and by such name shall have perpetual succession, and have a common seal, may sue and be sued, plead and be impleaded, acquire, hold and transfer property and pass all such necessary by-laws and regulations as shall not be inconsistent with the constitution and laws of this state or the constitution of the United States. State Council Junior Order American Mechanics incorporated.

Sec. 2. This act shall be in force from and after its ratification.

Ratified the 8th day of March, A. D. 1899.

CHAPTER 282.

An act to incorporate the State Line Lodge, number three hundred and seventy-five (375), Ancient, Free and Accepted Masons, in the town of Grover, North Carolina.

The General Assembly of North Carolina do enact:

te Line Lodge, . 375, A. F. and M., in Grover, veland county, orporated

Section 1. That the Master, Warden and members who at present or in the future may be of State Line Lodge number three hundred and seventy-five of Ancient Free and Accepted Masons located in the town of Grover, in the county of Cleveland, are hereby constituted and declared to be a body corporate under the name and style of "State Line Lodge number three hundred and seventy-five (375) Ancient Free and Accepted Masons," and by such name shall have perpetual succession and may have a common seal, may sue and be sued, plead and be impleaded, acquire, hold and transfer property and pass all such necessary by-laws and regulations as shall not be inconsistent with the constitution and laws of this state and the constitution of the United States.

Sec. 2. That this act shall be in force from and after its ratification.

Ratified the 8th day of March, A. D. 1899.

CHAPTER 283.

An act to amend, revise and consolidate the charter of the town of Chapel Hill.

The General Assembly of North Carolina do enact:

arter of the town Chapel Hill ended.

Section 1. That the inhabitants of the town of Chapel Hill shall be and continue as they have been a body politic and corporate, and henceforth the corporation shall bear the name and style of the town of Chapel Hill, and under such name and style shall have the right to sue and be sued, contract and be contracted with, and is hereby invested with all the property and rights of property which now belong to the corporation, and by this name may acquire and hold for the purpose of its government, welfare and improvement, all such estate as may be devised, bequeathed or conveyed to it, not exceeding in value two hundred thousand dollars, and the same may from time to time sell, dispose of and invest as shall be deemed advisable by the proper authorities of the corporation.

Sec. 2. That the corporation boundaries of the town of Chapel Hill shall be as follows: Beginning at a stone post six hundred yards northwest of the intersection of the center line of Franklin street and the west boundary of Merrit street, in a line at right angles to the main part of Franklin street; thence two thousand six hundred and twenty-two (2622) yards east northeast parallel to the course of the main part of Franklin street to marked stone and pointers; thence southeast at right angles to the course of the main part of Franklin street fifteen hundred and forty-nine (1549) yards to marked stone and pointers; thence two thousand six hundred and twenty-two (2622) yards west southwest parallel to the course of the main part of Franklin street to marked stone and pointers; thence northwest fifteen hundred and forty-nine (1549) yards at right angles to the course of the main part of Franklin street to the beginning, containing eight hundred and forty-one (841) acres, more or less, all courses to be laid down on a copy of the map of Chapel Hill made in eighteen hundred and fifty-nine, and on any subsequent map of Chapel Hill that may be made by order of the board of aldermen. Change of boundaries.

Sec. 3. That the present mayor of Chapel Hill shall hold office until his successor is elected and qualified, and the present members of the board of commissioners shall be and constitute the board of aldermen of the town of Chapel Hill until the expiration of their term of office, and as such shall have the same power and authority now conferred upon them by law and such additional authority as may be conferred upon the board of aldermen of the town of Chapel Hill by this act. Officers, term of office and authority

Sec. 4. That no person shall be entitled to vote for mayor or aldermen, unless he shall be an elector of the state of North Carolina, and shall have resided next preceding the day of election ninety days within the corporation. Suffrage.

Sec. 5. That no person shall be eligible as mayor or alderman or other officer, unless he shall be a qualified voter as prescribed in the next preceding section of this charter. Eligibility to office.

Sec. 6. That a registration shall be had of the voters of the town, and that a copy of the registration shall be furnished the poll-holders, and no person shall be allowed to vote unless his name shall be found thereon; the board of aldermen may order a new registration or revision of the book, by giving thirty days' notice of each new registration or revision before the opening of the registration book. Registration and elections.

Sec. 7. That the registration shall be closed ten days before the election, and after the closing of the same no person shall be allowed to register; however, the registrar is authorized and empowered before said book shall be closed to register therein all persons, who not then being of the age of twenty-one years, but Registration to be closed ten days before election; proviso.

otherwise qualified to register, may arrive at the age of twenty-one years on or before the day of election.

ayor to appoint gistrar, and registration books to kept open fifteen ays.

Sec. 8. That the mayor shall, thirty days before the first Tuesday in May in each year, appoint a suitable person to act as registrar within the corporation of said town, and the registration books shall be open fifteen days; the chief of police shall notify said person of his appointment, and said registrar shall at once post a notice at the postoffice door of his appointment, and shall designate the place where he will keep the registration books, and the time after which the books will be closed, and when and for what purpose the election will be held.

ooks to be deposed in mayor's ce and opened r inspection.

Sec. 9. That within twenty-four hours after the close of the registration for each election, the registration books shall be deposited in the office of the mayor of the town, and be opened for the inspection of the citizens.

oters may be allenged.

Sec. 10. It shall be lawful to challenge the right of any person to vote, either on the day of election, when he offers to vote, or on the day of registration, when he offers to register; and, if it shall appear to the judges of election, or a majority thereof, or to the registering officer, that such person is disqualified, he shall be excluded from registration, or, if he has been registered, from voting.

lections to be eld annually.

Sec. 11. That there shall on the first Thursday in May, one thousand eight hundred and ninety-nine, and on the first Tuesday in May annually thereafter, be elected a mayor and five aldermen for said town, who shall hold their office until their successors are qualified; the mayor and aldermen to be elected by the qualified voters of the whole town.

ayor and alderen elected by opular vote.

spectors to be pointed by mayor aldermen.

Sec. 12. That for the purpose of electing said officers, the aldermen, and in cases of failure by the aldermen, the mayor shall at least twenty days before the election appoint two inspectors, who shall be qualified voters, and the inspectors shall give ten days' notice thereof by public advertisement, and the inspectors before they proceed to act shall be sworn by the mayor or a justice of the peace to conduct the election fairly and impartially and according to law, and in case of the absence of any inspector his place shall forthwith be supplied by the mayor, and in his absence or failure to act by the other member of the election board.

egistrar and inectors shall tend and conduct ection.

Sec. 13. That on the day of election the registrar and the inspectors shall give due attendance at the time and place; shall be judges of the polls; receive the votes and conduct the election in like manner and during the same hours of the day as election for members of the general assembly.

rm of ballot.

Sec. 14. That the candidates for mayor shall be voted for on one ballot without device, written or printed on white paper, and the candidates for aldermen in another box, on one ballot, without device, written or printed, on white paper.

Sec 15. That at the close of the election the registrar and inspectors shall proceed to count the ballot and declare the result thereof; and such person voted for as mayor having received the highest number of votes shall be declared duly elected mayor for the ensuing term of one year; and of those persons voted for as aldermen the five receiving the highest number of votes shall be declared duly elected aldermen of the town for the ensuing term of one year; and such mayor and aldermen shall be notified of their said election by the inspectors on the day succeeding their election.

Registrar and inspectors to count the ballots and declare the result.

Sec. 16. That if among the persons voted for as mayor there shall be an equal number of votes between any two or more having the largest number the aldermen-elect shall proceed within five days after their qualification to select a mayor of such persons; and if among the persons voted for as aldermen there shall be a like tie the remaining aldermen within five days after their qualification shall select of such the person or persons to be aldermen.

In case of tie for mayor or aldermen, who declared elected.

Sec. 17. That the inspectors shall certify and subscribe one poll-list and, together with the registration book, deliver them to the mayor, who shall keep them among the archives of the town. As soon as the result of the election is determined a certificate thereof shall be made under the hands of the registrar and judges, setting forth in writing and words the number of votes each candidate received, which certificate they shall deliver to the mayor on the day following the election to be recorded in the town journal.

Inspectors to certify and subscribe poll list and deliver same and registration book to mayor.
Certificate of result to be delivered to mayor and recorded.

Sec. 18. That the mayor immediately after his election and before entering on the duties of his office shall take before a justice of the peace the following oath: "I, (A. B.) do solemnly swear that I will diligently endeavor to perform faithfully and truly, according to my best skill, judgment and ability all the duties of the office of mayor of the town of Chapel Hill while I continue therein, and will cause to be executed as far as in my power lies, all the laws, ordinances and regulations made for the government of the town; and in the discharge of my duties I will do equal justice in all cases whatsoever."

Mayor to take oath before entering upon duties of his office.

Sec. 19. That each alderman, before entering on the duties of the office, shall take before the mayor or some justice of the peace, an oath that he will truly and impartially perform the duties of aldermen for the town, according to the best of his skill, ability and judgment.

Aldermen to take oath before entering upon duties of office.

Sec. 20. That the mayor and aldermen shall hold their offices respectively until the next succeeding election and until their respective successors are qualified.

Term of office.

How vacancies in office to be filled.

Sec. 21. That if any person chosen mayor shall refuse to be qualified, or there is a vacancy in the office after election and qualification, the aldermen shall choose some qualified person mayor for the term, or the unexpired portion of the term, as the case may be; and on like occasions, and in like manner, the aldermen shall choose other aldermen to supply the place of such as shall refuse to act, and fill all vacancies which may occur; and such persons only shall be chosen as [are] and hereafter declared to be eligible.

Penalty for refusal to qualify when elected.

Sec. 22. That any person elected mayor or alderman, who shall refuse to be qualified, and act as such, shall forfeit and pay for the equal use of the town, and of him who sues therefor, twenty-five dollars.

Penalty for aldermen failing to give notice of election, or to hold and declare same.

Sec. 23. That if the aldermen shall fail to give the notice of election, or to hold and declare the same in the manner prescribed, such of them as shall be in default shall forfeit and pay for the equal use of the town, and for him who will sue therefor, twenty-five dollars.

Corporate rights not to be affected by failure to elect officers.

Sec. 24. That this town shall not lose any of its corporate rights and privileges by failure to elect officers on any first Tuesday in May of any year when an election ought regularly to be held.

Failure to hold election on first Tuesday in May, election to be held in way provided in chapter 62, of Code.

Sec. 25. That in case of failure to elect municipal officers on any said first Tuesday in May of any year when an election ought regularly to be held, the electors residing within the corporate limits may, after ten days' notice, signed by any thirty-five of said electors, and posted up at three places within the corporate limits, proceed to hold an election for municipal officers, in the way and manner provided for in chapter sixty-two of The Code entitled "Towns and cities."

Mayor's jurisdiction.

Sec. 26. That the mayor of the town of Chapel Hill, while acting as such is hereby constituted a special court, with all the authority, jurisdiction and powers in criminal offences occurring within the corporate limits of said town, and within one-half mile thereof, that are now, or hereafter may be given by law to justices of the peace; and shall also have exclusive original jurisdiction to hear and determine all misdemeanors consisting of a violation of the ordinances of said town. The proceedings in said court shall be the same as are now, or hereafter shall be prescribed for courts of justices of the peace; and in all cases there shall be a right of appeal to the superior court of Orange county, and in all cases where a defendant shall be adjudged to be imprisoned by the said mayor, it shall be competent for said court to sentence the defendant to imprisonment in county jail for a term not exceeding thirty days, and to adjudge also that the defendant work during the period of his confinement on the public streets or other public works of said town of Chapel Hill

Defendants may be imprisoned in county jail and also worked on streets, public roads or public works of Chapel Hill.

or on the public roads. The said special court shall have the power, jurisdiction and authority of a justice of the peace to hear and determine all causes of action, to recover fines and penalties for a violation of the ordinances of the town of Chapel Hill.

Jurisdiction of mayor to recover fines and penalties.

Sec. 27. That the mayor may issue his precepts to constables of the town, and to such other officers to whom a justice of the peace may direct his precepts.

Precepts to issue to constable.

Sec. 28. That the mayor shall keep a faithful minute of the precepts issued by him and all his judicial proceedings. The judgment rendered by him shall have all the force, virtue and validity of judgments rendered by a single justice of the peace, and may be executed and enforced against the parties in the county of Orange and elsewhere in the same manner and by the same means as if the same had been rendered by a justice of the peace for the county of Orange.

Minutes of precepts and judicial proceedings to be kept.

Force and effect of mayor's judgment.

Sec. 29. That the mayor shall keep his office in some convenient part of the town. He shall perform such duties as shall from time to time be prescribed. That the mayor shall receive as compensation for his services such salary as the aldermen may fix, payable out of the town treasury in such sums and at such periods as the aldermen may prescribe, and for his services in the performance of magisterial duties in the mayor's court, under the provisions of this act, he shall be entitled to such fees and allowances as justices of the peace and clerks of the superior court are entitled to receive for the performance of like duty, to be taxed on the paper as part of the costs in each case, and paid by the state, county or person usually charged with the costs in like cases in courts of justices of the peace or the superior court, as the case may be, and in no event by the town.

Office of mayor to be kept in town.

Duties, compensation and salary.

Sec. 30. That the mayor when present shall preside at all meetings of the board of aldermen; and when there is an equal division upon any question, or in the election of officers by the board, he shall determine the matter by his vote. He shall vote in no other case. That in the absence of the mayor from the court or in case of his inability to perform the duties of his office on account of sickness or any other cause, it shall be the duty of the board of aldermen to designate one of their own number to hold pro tempore the mayor's court of said town and to perform the duties of the office, and the said mayor pro tempore is hereby invested with all the powers and authority conferred upon the mayor by the charter of said town to try and determine all actions arising within the jurisdiction of said mayor.

Mayor shall preside at meetings of board of aldermen, and vote only in case of tie.

Who to preside and be mayor pro tem. when mayor absent

Sec. 31. That the aldermen shall form one board, and a majority of them shall be competent to perform all the duties prescribed for the aldermen, unless otherwise provided; within five days after their election they shall convene for the transaction of

Duties of aldermen.

Aldermen to meet once every calendar month, and upon call of mayor or majority of aldermen.

business, and shall then fix stated days of meeting for the year, which shall be as often at least as once in every calendar month. The special meetings of the aldermen may also be held on the call of the mayor, or a majority of the aldermen; and of every such meeting when called by the mayor, all of the aldermen, and when called by a majority of the aldermen, such as shall not join in the call, shall be notified in writing.

Failure of aldermen to attend meetings, shall forfeit $5.

Sec. 32. That if any member shall fail to attend a general meeting of the board of aldermen or any special meeting of which he shall have notice as aforesaid, unless prevented by such cause as shall be satisfactory to the board, he shall forfeit and pay for the use of the town the sum of five dollars.

Aldermen shall have power to make and provide for executing ordinances, by-laws, etc.
Proviso.

Sec. 33. That the aldermen when convened shall have power to make and provide for the execution thereof such ordinances, by-laws, rules and regulations for the better government of the town as they may deem necessary: Provided, the same be allowed by the provisions of this act and be consistent with the laws of the land.

Aldermen may provide water, lights, regulate the market, remove nuisances, preserve public health.

Sec. 34. That among the powers hereby conferred on the board of aldermen, they may provide water and lights, shall provide for repairing and cleaning the streets, regulate the market, take all proper means to prevent and extinguish fires, make regulations to cause the due observance of the Sabbath, appoint and regulate town watches, suppress and remove nuisances, preserve the health of the town (from contagious or infectious diseases), appoint a chief of police and additional policemen to execute such precepts as the mayor and other persons may lawfully issue to them to preserve the peace and order and execute the ordinances of the town, and shall appoint and provide for the pay and prescribe the duties of all such other officers as may be deemed necessary from time to time.

Clerk, treasurer, chief of police and collector of taxes appointed by aldermen.

Sec. 35. That the board of aldermen shall, at their first meeting after election, or as soon thereafter as possible, appoint a clerk, a treasurer, a chief of police and a collector of taxes, who shall respectively hold their offices during the official term of the aldermen, and until their successors are qualified, subject to be removed at any time, however, and others appointed in their stead, for misconduct or neglect of the duties of their said offices. The board of aldermen shall have power to provide, by suitable ordinances, for the establishment, organization, equipment and government of a fire and police department, and a board of health; and at any regular meeting the board may elect a chief of the fire department, a chief of police, and one or more policemen, who shall hold office during good behavior and until removed for causes satisfactory to the board of aldermen, or until the time appointed for the next regular election of the clerk and treasurer. Before acting each of said officers shall

Fire and police departments to be established.

sworn to the faithful discharge of his duty, and shall execute ond with justified sureties residing within the limits of the n of Chapel Hill, payable to the town of Chapel Hill in such as the aldermen shall determine, conditioned for the faith- performance of the duties of said office: Provided, that the ıds of clerk and treasurer, and of the chief of police and tax lector shall not be less than one thousand dollars respectively.

Said officers shall take oath and give justified bond.

Proviso.

ec. 36. That the board may combine the offices of clerk and asurer, and of chief of police and tax collector, and invoke the ties upon one or more persons, the offices nevertheless to re- in the same.

Certain offices may be combined.

'ec. 37. That the clerk shall have a reasonable salary, and it all be his duty to keep regular and fair minutes of the pro- edings of the board, and to preserve all books, papers and ticles committed to his care during his continuance in office, d deliver to his successor, and generally to perform such other ties as may be prescribed by the aldermen.

Clerk shall have reasonable salary, keep minutes of proceedings of board, etc.

Sec. 38. That every person shall be allowed to inspect the urnals and papers of the board, in the presence of the clerk, paying twenty-five cents for each inspection under a penalty two dollars on the clerk for every refusal, to be paid to him o will sue for the same.

Any person may inspect journals and papers of board

Sec. 39. That the treasurer shall have a reasonable salary, and shall be his duty to call on all persons who may have in their ınds any money or securities belonging to the town, which ıght to be paid or delivered into the treasury, and to safely eep the same for the use of the town; to disburse the funds. ccording to such orders as may be duly drawn on him in the ıanner hereinafter specified; he shall keep in a book provided ɔr that purpose a fair and correct account of all moneys ːceived and disbursed by him, and shall submit said account to ıe aldermen whenever required to do so. On the expiration of ıs term of office, he shall deliver to his successor all the moneys, ːcurities and properties entrusted to him for safe keeping or ːherwise, and during his continuance therein, he shall faithfully ɜrform all duties lawfully imposed upon him as town treasurer.

Salary and duties of treasurer.

Sec. 40. That the treasurer shall prepare annually an itemized ɩatement of the receipts and disbursements on account of the ɔwn for the general inspection of the citizens and cause the ıme to be posted at the post office door within ten days after ıe first Tuesday in May of each year; and for the failure to ɔmply with the requirements of this section, the treasurer shall ɔrfeit and pay for the use of the town fifty dollars, to be recov- ered before any justice of the peace on the relation of any citi- ɜn of the town.

Treasurer shall publish annually itemized statement of receipts and disbursements.
Penalty for failure.

Sec. 41. That all orders drawn on the treasurer shall be signed y the mayor and such other persons as may be designated by

Duties of treasurer concerning payments from treasury.

the aldermen, and also the purpose for which the money is applied, and the treasurer shall specify said purposes in his accounts and also the sources whence are derived the moneys received by him.

Duties of chief of police.

Sec. 42. That it shall be the duty of the chief of police to see that the laws, ordinances and orders of the aldermen are enforced, and to report all breaches thereof to the mayor; to preserve the peace of the town by suppressing disturbances and apprehending offenders, and for that purpose he shall have all the powers and authority vested in sheriffs and township constables; he shall execute all precepts lawfully directed to him by the mayor or others, and in the execution thereof shall have the same powers which the sheriff and constables in the county have, and he shall have such fees on all process and precepts executed or returned by him as may be allowed by the board of aldermen, not to exceed the fees allowed the sheriff and constables in the county for like services, and also such other compensation as the aldermen may allow. The chief of police and assistant policemen shall have the power to rearrest, upon the same warrant, a defendant or party who has been convicted and released on the statement that he will pay fine and costs, upon failure to pay same, or in case of an escape.

Fees of chief of police.

Defendant may be arrested for failure to pay fine and costs

Chief of police and assistants may arrest for violation of State laws.

Sec. 43. That the chief of police and assistant policemen shall have the same powers and be bound by the same rules in this respect as constables in the county of Orange, to apprehend all offenders against the state within the limits of the town, and to carry them before the mayor or some justice of the peace; and for such duty he shall have such fees as may be allowed by the board of aldermen, not to exceed the fees allowed to constables in the county for like duties, to be paid by the party offending, if found guilty.

Persons arrested to be confined in town prison; allowed bail.

Sec. 44. The town officers, policemen, or watchmen arresting any person for violating any ordinance of said town, may confine the same in the town prison until such person can be brought before the mayor or other court, having jurisdiction, for trial; but said person may give bail, in the same manner as bail is given to sheriffs for his or their appearance before the mayor or other court.

Additional policemen may be appointed in case of exigency.

Sec. 45. In times of exigency, the mayor may appoint, temporarily, additional policemen for such time as may appear necessary, not exceeding one week, who shall take the same oath, and be subject to the same control and entitled to the same fees as the regular policemen.

Chief of police or assistants may be suspended by mayor.

Sec. 46. That the mayor may at any time upon charges preferred or upon finding the said chief of police or any members of said police force guilty of misconduct have power to suspend such members from service until the board of aldermen shall convene and take action in the matter; and upon hearing the proofs in the case the board may discharge or restore such members and the pay of such members so suspended shall cease from the time of suspension to the time of his restoration to service. Any violation of the regulations or orders of any superior shall be good cause for dismissal, and the mayor may suspend the chief or any member of the policing force if found drunk while on duty.

Violations of orders of any superior, good cause for dismissal.

Drunkenness of chief of police or member of force.

Sec. 47. That the board of aldermen shall require the chief of police and other policemen to wear badges and may require them to be so uniformed as to be readily recognized by the public as peace officers. And the police shall generally have power to do whatever may be necessary to preserve the good order and peace of the town and secure the inhabitants from personal violence, and their property from loss or injury.

Chief of police and members of force to wear badges and be uniformed.

Sec. 48. That the aldermen may provide a patrol or watch for the town and prescribe the duties and powers of the several officers, members and classes thereof, and shall pay such patrol or watch, or may class the inhabitants into such patrol or watch.

Patrol or watch may be provided.

Sec. 49. That for any breach of his official bond by the town clerk, chief of police, tax collector, or any other officers who may be required to give an official bond, he shall be liable in an action on the same, in the name of the town, at the suit of the town, or any person aggrieved by such breach, and the same may be put in suit without assignment from time to time until the whole penalty be recovered.

Breach of official bond.

Sec. 50. That in order to raise a fund for the expenses incident to the proper government of the town, the aldermen may annually levy and collect the following taxes, namely: Schedule A—I. An ad valorem tax of not exceeding fifty cents on every one hundred dollars value of real property in the town of Chapel Hill, and on all money, credits, investments in lands, stock in joint stock companies or otherwise, required to be listed by the state laws of North Carolina. (II.) On each taxable poll who may be a resident in the town of Chapel Hill on the first day of June of each year, or who may have been so residing within thirty days next preceding that day as a bona fide citizen, except such as the board of aldermen may exempt, and so record, a tax not exceeding one dollar and fifty cents.

Taxation.

Schedule A. Ad-valorem tax of not exceeding 50 cents on every $100 value of real property, etc.

On each taxable poll a tax not exceeding $1.50.

Schedule B—I. The tax in this schedule as set forth in the divisions named below, shall be imposed as a license tax for the privilege of carrying on the business or doing the act named, the amount of which tax, when fixed, shall be collected by the tax collector, and if it be not paid on demand, it may be recovered by suit, or the article upon which the tax is imposed, or any other property owned, may be forthwith distrained and sold to satisfy the same; and nothing in this schedule contained shall

Schedule B. Privilege tax; remedy for collecting.

be construed as to relieve any person from the payment of the ad valorem taxes required in the preceding schedule: 1. Upon merchandise a tax not exceeding ten dollars a year. 2. Upon leaf tobacco dealers a tax not exceeding five dollars a year. 3. Upon commission merchants, auctioneer broker a tax not exceeding ten dollars a year. 4. Upon every omnibus for the carriage of persons for hire a tax not exceeding fifteen dollars a year; and upon every hack, carriage or other vehicle used for the transportation of freight or other articles for hire a tax not exceeding ten dollars a year; and a discrimination may be made between one and two-horse vehicles in the tax. 5. Upon all dogs kept in the town, and which are so kept on the first day of June, a tax not exceeding three dollars a year: Provided, a discrimination may be made in the sexes of dogs in the tax: Provided further, that any person owning a dog listed under the ordinance passed hereunder, who fails to pay the tax levied for the year preceding by the first day of January of each year, shall be subject to a fine of five dollars, and an additional fine of five dollars for each ten [days] said tax remains unpaid. 6. Upon every transient merchant trader or street peddler offering to vend in the city, a tax not exceeding one hundred dollars a year, or twelve dollars a month, except only such as sell books, charts or maps. 7. Upon every public billiard table, bowling alley, or alley of like kind, skating rink, bagatelle table or table, stand or place for any other game or play, with or without a name, kept for hire, or used or connected with a hotel or restaurant, or otherwise, a tax not exceeding one hundred dollars a year, nor less than fifty dollars a year. 8. Upon every hotel, victualing house or restaurant established, opened or kept in the town, a tax not exceeding fifty dollars a year. 9. On every exhibition of a circus or menagerie within the town, or a mile thereof, one hundred dollars for each separate exhibition; and on each side-show twenty-five dollars to be paid before the exhibition, or if not paid then, the same to be doubled. 10. Upon each exhibition within the town or a mile thereof, of stage or theatrical plays, sleight-of-hand performance, rope dancing or walking, a tax not exceeding twenty-five dollars, to be paid before exhibiting, or the same to be doubled. 11. Upon each exhibition for reward of wax-works or curiosities of any kind, natural or artificial, a tax not exceeding ten dollars. 12. Upon each exhibition of any other kind, on each concert for reward, and on every strolling musician, a tax of five dollars except when the exhibition or concert is given for charitable or benevolent or educational purposes, or to aid any public improvement of the town. 13. Upon every goat or hog running at large in the town, a tax of two dollars, and every such goat or hog may be seized and impounded, and if the owner, on being notified, will not pay the tax, the animal shall be sold

Merchandise, leaf tobacco dealers, commission merchants, auctioneer or broker.
Omnibus for hire.
Hacks, carriages or other vehicles used for transportation of freight, etc.
Dogs.
Provisos.
When subject to increased tax.
Transient merchants, traders or street peddlers.
Public billiard tables, bowling alleys, etc.
Hotel, restaurant, etc.
Circuses, menageries and side-shows
Theatres, sleight-of-hand performers, and rope-dancing or walking.
Wax-works, or curiosities.
Any other kind of exhibition.
Strolling musician.
Goats and hogs.

therefor at such place as the aldermen may designate, after giving three days' notice. 14. Upon every auctioneer or crier of goods at public auction allowed to be taxed by this charter, a tax not exceeding twenty-five dollars: Provided, that this section shall not conflict with the provisions of section two thousand two hundred and eighty-four of The Code of North Carolina. 15. Upon every stock and bond broker, sewing-machine company, dealer in or manufacturer's agent of musical instruments, keeper of a livery or livery and sale stables or stock yards, a tax not exceeding thirty-five dollars. 16. Upon every street huckster, photographer, merchandise or produce broker, or shooting-gallery, a tax not exceeding twenty-five dollars a year. 17. Upon every itinerant dentist, itinerant medical practitioner, optician, portrait or miniature painter, daguerrean artist, photographer, and every person taking or enlarging likenesses of the human face, a tax of five dollars a month. 18. Upon every itinerant person or company peddling lightning ro ds stoves or ranges, a tax of fifty dollars a year on each wagon (if wagons are used), if wagons are not used the tax shall be on each agent. 19. Upon every bill-poster, a tax of not more than ten dollars per annum. 20. Upon every horse drover selling horses at public auction, a tax not exceeding fifty dollars a month.

Auctioneers. Proviso. Stock or bond broker, sewing-machines, musical instruments, livery or horse and sale stables, etc. Street huckster, photographer, merchandise or produce broker and shooting-gallery. Itinerant medical practitioner, optician, portrait painter or other artist. Peddlers of lightning-rods, stoves or ranges. Horse drovers.

Sec. 51. Provided, nevertheless, that no property or subjects of taxation, which are specially exempt from taxation by the laws o. the state, shall be taxed by the town.

Proviso.

Sec. 52. That any person carrying on business in the town without having paid the license tax according to the ordinances of the town, shall be fined twenty dollars, in addition to the payment of the tax: Provided, that any person taking out license after the first of January shall pay tax on each license in the foregoing sections except that provided for in division four (4) of schedule B, section fifty of this charter, proportioned according to the unexpired term of the year according to the discretion of the mayor. Upon all subjects taxed under schedule B, chapter one hundred and sixty-eight, laws of North Carolina, session of eighteen hundred and ninety-seven, not herein provided for, shall pay a license tax of ten dollars; and the board of aldermen shall have power to impose a license tax on any business carried on in the town of Chapel Hill, not before enumerated herein, not to exceed ten dollars a year.

Penalty for violation of this act. Proviso. Subjects taxed under Schedule B, chapter 168, Laws of 1897, not herein provided for, license tax of $10. Other subjects may be taxed.

Sec. 53. That the citizens of the town of Chapel Hill, and others liable to be taxed on account of any of the foregoing subjects, shall, during the time for listing their state and county taxes, render to such persons as may be designated by the aldermen of the town, on oath, a list of their property and subjects for which they may be liable to be taxed; and any person who shall fail to render such list within the time allowed by law, before the first

Listing of taxes under oath. Violation of this section, misdemeanor.

day of July shall be deemed guilty of a misdemeanor to the same extent as for a failure to list state and county taxes, and on conviction thereof before the mayor of said town or any justice of the peace, shall be fined not more than twenty dollars or imprisoned not more than ten days; and it shall be the duty of the tax collector of said town to prosecute offenders against this section: Provided, that in the discretion of the aldermen the tax list may be made directly from the tax abstracts filed each year with the county lister, except as to land not situated within the corporate limits of the town of Chapel Hill, and that the board shall have authority to revise, correct or amend the assessments taken from said abstracts.

ty of tax collector to prosecute.

oviso.

xes to be laid on before first day August.

x list to be placed hands of collector on or before st day of September.

Sec. 54. That on or before the first day of August of each year, the board of aldermen shall proceed to lay the taxes on such subjects of taxation as are allowed by law, and shall, on or before the first day of September of each year, place the tax list in the hands of the collector for collection, who shall proceed forthwith in the collection, and shall complete the same on or before the first day of January next ensuing, and shall pay the moneys, as they are collected, to the treasurer, and the collector for his compensation shall receive such pay as the aldermen may allow.

mpensation of llector.

xes may be colcted by distress; vertisement.

Sec. 55. That if any person liable to taxes on subjects directed to be listed shall fail to pay them within the time prescribed for collection, the collector shall proceed forthwith to collect the same by distress and sale, after public advertisement for the space of ten days in some newspaper published in the town, or at three public places, if the property be personalty, and of twenty days if the property be realty.

oceedings to sell nd for tax due on me.

Sec. 56. That when the tax due on any lot or other land (which is hereby declared to be a lien on the same), shall remain unpaid on the first day of January, and there is no other visible estate, but such lot or lands of the person in whose name it is listed, liable to distress and sale, known to the collector, he shall report the fact to the aldermen, together with a particular description of the real estate, and thereupon the aldermen shall direct the same to be sold upon the premises by the collector, after advertising for twenty days in some newspaper published in the town, or in three public places, when the collector shall divide the land into as many parts as be convenient (for which purpose he is authorized to employ a surveyor), and shall sell as many thereof as may be required to pay said taxes and all expenses attendant thereon. If the same cannot be conveniently divided, the collector shall sell the whole; and if no person shall pay the whole of the taxes and expenses for the whole land, the same shall be struck off to the town, and if not redeemed as hereinafter provided, shall belong to said town in fee.

ınd may be sold parcels.

hen land may be rfeited to the wn.

Sec. 57. That the collector shall return an account of his proceeding to the aldermen, specifying the portions into which the land has been divided and the purchasers thereof, and the prices of each, which shall be entered on the book of proceedings of the aldermen, and if there shall be a surplus after paying said taxes and expenses of the sale, the same shall be paid into the town treasury, subject to the demand of the owner.

Account of collector's proceedings to be returned to aldermen.

Surplus, if any, after paying taxes, paid into town treasury.

Sec. 58. That the owners of any land sold under the provisions of this charter, his heirs, executors and administrators, or any other person acting for them, may redeem the same within one year after the sale, by paying to the purchaser the sum paid by him, and twenty-five per cent. on the amount of taxes and expenses, and the treasurer shall refund to him, without interest, the proceeds, less double the amount of taxes.

Land may be redeemed within one year.

Sec. 59. That if the real estate sold as aforesaid shall not be redeemed within the time specified, the corporation shall convey the same in fee to the purchaser or his assigns, and the recital of such conveyance, or in any other conveyance of land sold for taxes due the town, that the taxes were due, or of any other matter required to be true or done, before the sale might be made, shall be prima facie evidence that the same was true and due.

When town may convey such land in fee.

Sec. 60. That the real estate of infants or persons non compos mentis shall not be sold for taxes, and when the same shall be owned by such in common with other persons free of such disability, the sale shall be made according to section three thousand six hundred and ninety-one of The Code.

Real estate of infants or persons non compos mentis.

Sec. 61. That all the moneys arising from taxes, donations, or other sources, shall be paid to the treasurer, and no appropriation thereof shall be made but by the board constituted of a majority of the aldermen.

What done with moneys arising from taxes.

Sec. 62. That when any land or right of way shall be required by said town of Chapel Hill for the purpose of operating new streets, alleys or sidewalks or altering existing streets, alleys or sidewalks or for other objects allowed by this charter, and for want of agreement as to the value thereof the same cannot be purchased from the owner or owners, the same may be taken at a valuation to be made by five freeholders of the town, three of whom shall be chosen by the aldermen, and two by the land owner; and in making said valuation, said freeholders, or a majority of them, after being duly sworn by the mayor or a justice of the peace for the county, or a clerk of a court of record, shall take into consideration the loss or damage which may accrue to the owner or owners in consequence of the land or right of way being surrendered, also any special benefit or advantage such owner may receive from the opening or altering of such street, alley or sidewalk or other improvement, and state the value and amount of each, and the excess, if any, of loss or damage over

Condemnation of land for streets, alleys, etc., proceedings.

Damages accruing to or benefits derived by owner of land to be considered.

and above the advantages shall form the measure of valuation of said land or right of way; and if said advantages be considered equal to or greater than the damages inflicted, the jury shall so declare: Provided, nevertheless, that if any person over whose land the said street, alley or sidewalk may pass, or improvement be erected, or tne aldermen be dissatisfied with the valuation thus made, then in that case either party may have an appeal to the next superior court of Orange county to be held thereafter, under the same rules, regulations and restrictions as now govern appeals from judgments of justices of the peace, and the said freeholders, or a majority of them, shall return to the court to which the appeal is taken, their valuation with the proceedings thereon, ana the land so valued by the freeholders shall vest in the town so long as it may be used for the purposes of the same as soon as the valuation may be paid or lodged in the hands of the clerk of the superor court in case of its refusal by the owner of the land: Provided, however, that such an appeal shall not hinder or delay the aldermen opening such streets, alleys or sidewalks or erecting such improvements: And provided further, that in case of discontinuance of the use of the land and it reverts to the owner, the town shall have the right to recover any improvements under its authority erected.

ssatisfied party y appeal to superior court.

oceedings of eholders to be urned to court.

peal not to hin- aldermen opening streets, etc. en town may over improvents.

iat declared olic streets.

Sec. 63. That all public roads lying within the corporate limits of said town, and all streets, as now constituted, constructed and used, are hereby declared, made and construed public streets of said town.

thority of aldern over streets, eys, etc.

Sec. 64. That the aldermen shall have the exclusive power to open, close, alter or change the streets, alleys and ways of said town, and also their grade, and the power to have made a map or plot showing the present lay of the streets in said town, and such other streets, alleys and ways, etc., as they in their judgment shall deem expedient and best for the future development of said town, which map or plot when so made, shall be the scheme, grade and rule of said streets and alley in said town, and no person shall be allowed to open, lay out or establish any street, alley or way otherwise than in accordance with said map or plot; Provided, said commissioners may cause to be made sucn alterations in said map or plot as in the future may seem expedient and best. Any person violating the provisions of this section shall be guilty of a misdemeanor and fined twenty-five dollars.

lation of this tion, misdeanor.

ther authority r streets, public unds, etc.

Sec. 65. That tne aldermen shall cause to be kept clean and in good repair the streets, sidewalks and alleys. They may establish the width and ascertain the location of those already provided and lay out and open others. They may also establish and regulate the public grounds and shall care for and protect the shade trees of the town.

Sec. 66. That if any owner or lesse of land in the town of Chapel Hill, on being notified to repair his sidewalks, shall fail or neglect to repair as ordered, he shall be deemed guilty of a misdemeanor, and fined not more than five dollars for each day's neglect to make such repairs, a notice of ten days by any officer of the town being sufficient in any event.

Owner or lessee of land required to repair sidewalks; penalty.

Sec. 67. That where there are no sidewalks in convenient walking order, along any lot in said town, the owner may be required to pay such portion of the expense of making the sidewalk along said lot as three assessors, unconnected with the owner, and disinterested, to be appointed by the aldermen, may estimate that the said property is benefited by the improvement; such expense to be a lien on the property, enforcible as liens for repairing sidewalks under existing laws: Provided, that there shall be right of appeal by either party to the superior court.

Who to pay expense of making sidewalks.

Cost of improvement to be lien on property.

Proviso.

Sec. 68. That before making such appointment, the assessors shall appoint a day when they shall hear parties interested on the subject, giving at least three days' notice of the time and place of their sitting. From their decision the town or lot owners may appeal to the superior court of Orange county, but the aldermen may, notwithstanding an appeal under this or any other act, proceed with the work of opening and grading the new sidewalk.

Parties interested to be notified by assessors.

Either party may appeal.

Sec. 69. All persons owning or occupying buildings with eaves, porches or porticos projecting or extending over the sidewalks or streets in the town, shall be required to place proper drains and gutters, so as to prevent water from falling on sidewalks or streets, and shall be required to place under-ground drains for carrying off water from said gutters, and no person shall be allowed to place any awning or shed over the streets or sidewalks so as to allow water to drip on sidewalks. Persons offending against this section shall be fined fifty dollars for every day said buildings are permitted to remain without gutters, and awnings or sheds are permitted to drip water on sidewalks after being notified by police to alter the same.

Sidewalks and streets protected from rain by drains and gutters.

Penalty for violation of this section.

Sec. 70. That the aldermen may require and compel the abatement and removal of all nuisances within the town, and at the expense of the person causing the same, or the owner or tenant of the ground whereon the same may be, and may also prevent the establishment within the town, and may regulate the same, if allowed to be established, any slaughter-house or place or the exercise within the town of any offensive or unhealthy trade, business or employment.

Removal of nuisances to be at expense of person causing same.

Slaughter-houses and offensive or unhealthy trades, etc.

Sec. 71. That the aldermen shall have the power to prevent dogs, horses, cattle, and all other brutes from running at large in the town.

Certain animals not to run at large.

Sec. 72. That they may prohibit and prevent by penalties, the

ast driving, discharging fire-arms, plosion of gunwder, etc.

riding or driving of horses or other animals at a speed greater than six miles per hour within the town; and also the firing of guns, pistols, crackers, gunpowder or other explosive, combustible or dangerous material in the streets, public grounds or elsewhere within the town, and govern the sale thereof.

rganization of fire partment. hen necessary to op fire, houses ay be blown up, c.

Sec. 73. That they may provide for the establishment, or organization, equipment and government of fire companies; and in all cases of fire, a majority of such of the aldermen or the mayor and two of the aldermen, as shall be present, may, if they deem it necessary to stop the progress of the fire, cause any house to be blown up or pulled down; for which they shall not be responsible to any one in damages.

stablishment of re limits.

Sec. 74. That they may establish in the said town fire limits, with such boundaries as they may determine, within which they may prescribe by general rules or special permits, the kind of buildings which may be erected, so as to provide against accidents by fire, and may prohibit the erection of wooden buildings within the same. They may also provide for the inspection of all buildings now erected or hereafter to be erected and condemn such as are unsafe or dangerous to life or limb by reason either of their defective construction or dilapidation, and they may notify the owner or owners to remove or repair such as are condemned within thirty days, and if the owner or owners shall refuse to remove or repair the same, or shall neglect to do so, for the space of thirty days, the aldermen shall have the power to remove the same, which expense shall be a lien on the lot, and the owner or owners shall be liable for all such loss as may be incurred by the aldermen, and the aldermen shall not be liable for damages.

ispection and condemnation of ildings; owners be notified.

xpense of removal of buildings be lien on lot.

ldermen may control and regulate iblic cemeteries.

Sec. 75. That the board of aldermen shall have power to regulate the manner and terms on which bodies may be interred in the public cemetery, and have said cemetery kept in proper repair; they shall have power to purchase where they may deem proper, land adjoining any cemetery for its enlargement or for the establishment of one or more additional cemeteries within one mile of the town; they shall also have power to forbid any and all interments of dead bodies within the limits of said town or any part thereof wherever they shall deem it expedient, and to pass ordinances for the protection of the cemeteries; and may appoint and pay a keeper and compel the keeping and returning a bill of mortality.

uarantine against ertain disease, stablish hospitals, c.

Sec. 76. That they may take such measures as they deem effectual to prevent the entrance into the town, or the spreading therein of any contagious or infectious disease, may stop, detain and examine for that purpose every person coming from places believed to be infected with such disease; may establish and regulate hospitals within the town or three miles thereof; may ause any person in town, suspected to the infected with such isease, and whose stay may endanger its health, to be removed o the hospital; may remove from the town or destroy any furniure or other articles which shall be suspected of being tainted r infected with contagious or .nfectious disease, or of which here shall be reasonable cause to apprehend that they may pass nto such a state as to generate and propagate diseases, may .bate by reasonable means all nuisances which may be injurious :o the public health.

Protection to public health.

Sec. 77. That in case any person shall be moved to the hos-)ital or to the place directed by the mayor, the corporation may ·ecover before the mayor or any justice of the peace of such)erson the expense of his removal, support, nursing and medical ttendance, and burial expenses also, in case of death.

Expense of removal, medical attendance, etc., of sick person.

Sec. 78. That if any person shall attempt by force or by threat of violence to prevent the removal to the hospital or place selected by the mayor as aforesaid of any person ordered to be conveyed thither, the person so offending shall forfeit and pay to the town one hundred dollars and moreover to be deemed guilty of a misdemeanor.

Violation of this section misdemeanor.

Sec. 79. That for the violation of any by-law or rule made by the said aldermen, they may prescribe penalties not exceeding fifty dollars for each offense, to be recovered before the mayor, intendant or magistrate of police without any stay of process, mesne or final, and when judgment shall be given for any such penalty, the party convicted may, unless the penalty and costs be paid, be immediately committed to jail for the space of thirty days, or until payment thereof shall be made or else the mayor or intendant or magistrate of police may issue execution therefor: Provided, that any party dissatisfied with such judgment shall be allowed an appeal to the next superior court for the county, upon entering into recognizance with sufficient surety for his appearance at said court, and also for the penalty and costs.

Authority of aldermen to prescribe penalties, etc.

Proviso.

Sec. 80. That all penalties imposed by law relating to the town by this act, or by any ordinance of the town, unless otherwise provided, shall be recovered in the name of the town of Chapel Hill, before the mayor or any tribunal having jurisdiction thereof.

Suit to be in name of town.

Sec. 81. That the aldermen shall not have power to impose for any offense a larger penalty than fifty dollars, unless the case be expressly authorized, and from any judgment of the mayor for any penalty which is imposed or allowed to be imposed by this act, or for any other cause of action herein allowed, the party dissatisfied may appeal in like manner and under the same rules and regulations as are prescribed for appeal from the judgment of a justice of the peace.

When penalty limited to $50.

Dissatisfied party may appeal.

nvicted person fusing or unable pay costs may worked on :eets, etc.

Sec. 82. That in all cases where judgment may be entered against any person or persons for fines or penalties according to the laws and ordinances of any incorporated town, and the person or persons against whom the same is adjudged, refuses or is unable to pay such judgment, it may and shall be lawful for the mayor, before whom such judgment is entered, to order and require such person or persons so convicted to work on the streets or other public works of the town or on the public roads of the county, until at fair rates of wages such as prevail in the community, such person or persons shall have worked out the full amount of judgment and costs of prosecution.

ıthority to sell operty belonging town.

Sec. 83. That the mayor and a majority of the aldermen shall have the power at all times to sell at public outcry, after thirty days' notice, to the highest bidder, any property real or personal belonging to the town and apply the means as they may think best. The mayor is authorized to make title to any property sold under this section.

iminal jurisdic- n of mayor.

Sec. 84. That the mayor shall have and it shall be his duty to exercise all the jurisdiction, powers and duties given to justices of the peace in chapter thirty-three of Battle's Revisal, entitled "Criminal Proceedings," (The Code, chapter twenty-six), subject to the restrictions and limitations contained in the chapter: Provided, that the mayor shall not take jurisdiction of any offense committed within less than one-half mile beyond the limits of the town.

oviso.

moval of case m mayor, when t allowed.

Sec. 85. That no person shall have the right in any proceeding before the mayor to remove the same before any other inferior court for trial, as is provided for the removal of causes from one justice of the peace to another in section nine hundred and seven of The Code; but in all cases the parties shall have the right of appeal.

nalty for viola- n of city or- ıances.

Sec. 86. That any person or persons violating any ordinance of the town whether penalties be specifically prescribed or not shall be deemed guilty of a misdemeanor, and shall be fined not exceeding fifty dollars, or imprisoned not exceeding thirty days.

bts of town, how scharged.

Sec. 87. That debts contracted by the town in pursuance of authority vested in it, shall not be levied out of any of the property belonging to the town and used by it in the discharge and execution of its corporate duties and trusts, nor out of the property or estate of any individual who may be subject to pay said debts according to the course of the law in other cases.

glect of certain ties by town cers, how pun- ıed.

Sec. 88. That the mayor and aldermen, tax collector and all other officers of the town who shall, on demand, fail to turn over to their successors in office the property, books, moneys, scales or effects of the town shall be deemed guilty of a misdemeanor, and upon conviction before the superior court of Orange county, shall be imprisoned for not more than two years and fined not exceeding five hundred dollars at the discretion of the court.

Tax-lists, regulations concerning.

Sec. 89. All tax lists which have been or may hereafter be placed in the hands of the tax collector, shall be at all times subject to the control of the authorities imposing the tax, or their successors in office, shall be surrendered to the authorities for such inspection and correction, and if the tax collector fails or refuses to surrender his list upon such demand, he shall be found guilty of a misdemeanor, and upon conviction shall be subject to the penalties imposed by the preceding section.

Duties of tax collector.

Sec. 90. That the tax collector, whose election is herein provided for, shall be vested with the same power and authority in the collection of taxes that sheriffs have, and subject to the fines and penalties for failure or for failures or neglect of duty by this act imposed. He shall be charged with the sums appearing by the tax lists as due for town taxes. He shall be credited in settlement as sheriffs are credited, with amounts in suit by appeal, all poll taxes and taxes on personal property certified by the clerk of the board of aldermen of the town, by order of the board of aldermen, to be insolvent and uncollectable, an itemized list of said amounts to be spread upon the minutes of the town. He shall at no time retain in his hands over one hundred dollars for a longer time than seven days, under a penalty of ten per cent. per month to the town upon all sums so unlawfully retained. The board of aldermen, at the meeting in January of each year, shall appoint two or more of their number to be present and assist at the accounting and settlement between the tax collector and the treasurer of the taxes for the preceding year. The accounts so audited shall be reported to the board of aldermen, and when approved by them shall be recorded in the minute book of said board, and shall be prima facie evidence of their correctness, and impeachable only for fraud or specified error. In case the tax collector of the town of Chapel Hill shall fail, neglect or refuse to account with the town treasurer and assistant committee, as herein required, or to pay what may be rightfully found due on such accounts on or before the fifteenth of February of the next succeeding year after the taxes are levied, he shall forfeit and pay to the state for the use of the town of Chapel Hill a penalty of five hundred dollars. It shall be the duty of the mayor, upon the neglect, failure or refusal of said tax collector to account as aforesaid, to cause an action to be brought in the superior court of the county of Orange on the bond of said tax collector against him and his sureties to recover the amount owing by him and the penalty aforesaid; if the tax collector shall fraudulently and corruptly fail to account as aforesaid, he shall be deemed guilty of a misdemeanor, and upon conviction thereof shall be sentenced to pay a fine, in the discre-

Tax collector to account with treasurer annually, in presence of aldermen.

Penalty for failure to account annually.

Action may be brought against tax collector and sureties.

Fraud and corruption of tax collector, penalty.

tion of the court, or be imprisoned not less than three months nor more than twelve months. If any tax collector shall die during the time appointed for collecting taxes, then his sureties may collect them, and for that purpose shall have all the power and means for collecting the same from the tax payers as the tax collector would have had, and shall be subject to all the remedies for collection and settlement of taxes on their bonds, or otherwise, as might have been had against the tax collector if he had levied. The tax collector (and in case of his death the sureties) shall have six months and no longer from the day prescribed for his settlement of town taxes, February the fifteenth as aforesaid, to finish the collection of all taxes, but the extension of time for collection shall not extend his time of settlement of town taxes as aforesaid. Said tax collector before receiving the tax list from the town clerk shall give a bond as prescribed in section thirty-five of this chapter, in such amount as the aldermen may determine, the amount of said bond not to be less than one thousand dollars nor more than double the amount of taxes for the preceding year. For his services/said tax collector shall receive such compensation as the aldermen may fix, not to exceed ten per centum of the taxes collected.

ath of tax collector, sureties y collect.

ne for collection taxes may be tended.

nd of tax collector.

mpensation for llecting taxes.

Sec. 91. That every owner of a lot, which shall front any street on which a sidewalk has been established, shall improve, curb or repair, or pave in such manner as the aldermen may direct, such sidewalk as far as it may extend along such lot, the expense of the same to be divided equally between the town and the owner of such lot, and on failure of said owner to do so within twenty days after notice by the chief of police to said owner or lessee, or if he be a non-resident of the county of Orange, to his agent, or if such non-resident have no agent in said county, or if personal notice cannot be served upon such owner, lessee or agent, then after publication of said notice by the chief of police for thirty days in some newspaper published in the town of Chapel Hill, calling on such owner to make such repairs, the aldermen may cause the same to be repaired either with brick, stone, asphalt, cement or gravel, at their discretion, and the expense shall be divided equally between such owner and the town, said repairs to be done under direction of the street committee. Said one-half of the expense of such repairs shall be a lien upon the lot and bear interest from the date of the completion of the said repairs, and if the same is not paid within six months, such lot may be sold to pay said expenses and costs, under the same rules, regulations, restrictions, rights of redemption and savings as are prescribed in said charter for the sale of land for unpaid taxes.

idewalks, expense of improvement.

wn may repair idewalks, when; pense.

en for improvements.

Sec. 92. That all fines and penalties collected for violation of this charter or the ordinances made in pursuance thereof shall go into the town treasury and belong to the town of Chapel Hill.

ppropriation of ies and penalties.

Sec. 93. That the board of aldermen of said town may, at their first regular meeting in May, or at any time during the year, elect a town attorney, prescribe his duties, fix his term of office and rate of compensation. They may employ detectives and offer rewards for the capture and conviction of criminals, and exercise like powers in the premises in order to bring offenders against the laws of the state and town ordinances, when the offence is committed in the town limits, to justice and to use any funds belonging to the town not otherwise appropriated to carry out this purpose.

Election of town attorney; compensation. Detective may be employed.

Sec. 94. That in the absence of any contract or contracts with said town in relation to the land used or occupied by it for the purpose of streets, sidewalks, alleys or other public works, signed by the owner thereof or his agent, it shall be presumed that said land has been granted to said town by the owner or owners thereof; and said town shall have good right and title thereto, and shall have, hold and enjoy the same as long as the same shall be used for the purposes of said town and no longer, unless the owner or owners of said land, at the time of the occupation of said land as aforesaid, or those claiming under them, shall apply for an assessment of said land as provided for in the charter of said town, within two years next after said land was taken; and in case the owner or owners, or those claiming under them, shall not apply within two years next after said land was taken, he or they shall be forever barred from recovering said land or having any assessment or compensation thereof: Provided, nothing herein contained shall affect rights of feme coverts, or infants, until two years after the removal of their respective disabilities: Provided, this act shall not be construed as repealing or modifying section one hundred and fifty of The Code.

Streets, sidewalks, etc., when grant of land to town covered by same shall be presumed.

Rights of married women and infants protected.

Proviso.

Sec. 95. That all laws in conflict with this act are hereby repealed.

Conflicting acts repealed.

Sec. 96. That this act shall be in force from and after its ratification.

Ratified the 8th day of March, A. D. 1899.

CHAPTER 284.

An act to exempt Harrison Aldridge of Mitchell county from certain license tax on account of physical infirmity.

The General Assembly of North Carolina do enact:

Section 1. That Harrison Aldridge, of Mitchell county, be and he is hereby permitted to hold musical and magical entertain-

Harrison Aldridge exempted from payment of certain license tax.

ments without paying a license tax either to the state or county or any town in the state.

Sec. 2. That this act shall be in force from and after its ratification.

Ratified the 8th day of March, A. D. 1899.

CHAPTER 285.

An act to incorporate Caldwell Institute, Orange county, North Carolina.

The General Assembly of North Carolina do enact:

ldwell Institute, ange county, corporated.

Section 1. That R. N. Hall, Jr., D. S. Miller, Dr. A. C. Jordan, Rev. J. H. McCracken, W. D. Villiner, W. J. Miller, J. D. Nichols, T. H. Wilson, T. J. Hall, J. T. Wilson, Weldon Hall, C. E. Wilson, J. T. Wilkerson, J. C. Rountree, T. J. Riley, R. N. Hall, Sr., J. R. Wilson, W. D. Woods, D. S. Allison, W. R. McKee and Thomas T. Candler, be and they are hereby declared to be a body politic and corporate, to be known and distinguished by the name of the board of trustees of Caldwell Institute, and by that name they shall have perpetual succession and by that name may sue and be sued, plead and be impleaded.

wer of trustees fill vacancies on ard.

Sec. 2. Said board of trustees shall have the power to fill all vacancies occurring in said board caused by death, resignation or otherwise by a vote of a majority of the remaining members of said board, and the said board of trustees of Caldwell Institute shall have power in law to receive and possess all moneys, goods, chattels and real estate or other property that may be given them, and shall hold the same subject to the will of the donor in special trust that they or the profits thereof shall be applied to and for the use and benefit of said Caldwell Institute.

ustees may hold operty to use of id Caldwell Institute.

Sec. 3. Said board of trustees shall have power to employ a principal for said Caldwell Institute and such other assistants as they may deem necessary, whose duty it shall be to carry on a school for primary and high-school education upon such terms as said board may direct; and said board of trustees of Caldwell Institute may, in conjunction with the principal of said school, prescribe what course of study shall be taught therein, and make such by-laws and regulations as they may deem necessary for the good government of said school, shall have the power to issue certificates of proficiency to those students who shall pass successfully the examination upon the different courses therein taught, which certificates shall be signed by the principal of said school and by the president of the board of trustees and countersigned by the secretary of said board.

incipal and assistants may be ployed; course study, etc.

ustees may ake by-laws and gulations.

Sec. 4. Said board of trustees shall have power to adopt a corporate seal. Corporate seal may be adopted.

Sec. 5. This act shall be in force from and after its ratification.

Ratified the 8th day of March, A. D. 1899.

CHAPTER 286.

An act to amend the charter of the city of Asheville.

The General Assembly of North Carolina do enact:

Section 1. That section three of chapter one hundred and sixty-three, private laws of eighteen hundred and ninety-seven, be and the same is hereby amended by striking out of said section the following words in lines fifteen and sixteen, to-wit: "and shall thereafter be ineligible to hold office for the next succeeding term." Charter of city of Asheville amended.

Sec. 2. That this act shall be in force from and after its ratification.

Ratified the 8th day of March, A. D. 1899.

CHAPTER 287.

An act to amend chapter three hundred and twenty-one, private laws of eighteen hundred and ninety-five.

The General Assembly of North Carolina do enact:

Section 1. That throughout said chapter, the words "Miller Gap" and the word "Cranberry" each be displaced as often as it occurs by the word "Pinola." Private Laws 1895, chapter 32, amended.

Sec. 2. That in sections seven and eight, the words "where it intersects the Morganton turnpike road" be stricken out. Sections 7 and 8 also amended.

Sec. 3. That the company may, at any time, construct a branch road from their main line, at John W. Wiseman's, to the head of Bushy creek, at George Weld's, and to this end shall have all the powers and privileges pertaining to the main line. Said company may construct branch road, beginning at Jas. W. Wiseman's.

Sec. 4. That persons going to and from Linville Falls, over the branch line, and not passing through any gate on the main line, shall pay half the fare or toll that would be due and payable on the main line, and for this purpose a special toll-gate may be established. When only half toll payable.

resent terminus ay be extended.

Sec. 5. That the company may, a. such times and in such sections as they may deem fit, extend their road from its present terminus at W. J. English's towards Marion, under all the powers and privileges of its charter: Provided, however, that said sections as often as completed shall be turned over to the county of McDowell, and kept up as other public roads.

ain line shall ·oss channel at inville Falls.

Sec. 6. That the main line shall cross the channel at the top of Linville Falls by a bridge.

xemption from ll.

Sec. 7. That if a ford shall be made above said bridge, for temporary use, or to afford a choice of ways, persons crossing said ford shall not be exempt from the regular fare or toll.

Sec. 8. That this act shall be in force from and after its ratification.

Ratified the 8th day of March, A. D. 1899.

CHAPTER 288.

An act to amend chapter two hundred and twenty-one, private laws of eighteen hundred and ninety-one.

The General Assembly of North Carolina do enact:

nlawful to pay for rvices rendered id turnpike company in any other ing than money.

Section 1. That chapter two hundred and twenty-one (221), private laws of eighteen hundred and ninety-one, entitled "An act to incorporate the Valley Crucis, Shawneehaw and Elk Park Turnpike Company," be and the same is hereby amended by adding thereto the following: That it shall be unlawful for any person or any officer of said corporation to pay for any labor or any other service in constructing or repairing said turnpike road in any other thing than money. Any person violating the provisions of this section shall be guilty of a misdemeanor and shall be fined or imprisoned, or both, at the discretion of the court.

ow quorum constituted.

Sec. 2. That at all meetings of said company, after the passage of this act, the following rules and regulations shall be observed: That in order to constitute a quorum for the purpose of voting, a majority of the voting stock or shares must be present either in person or by proxy in writing and signed by the owners of the stock or shares; that the voting of said shares shall be regulated as follows, to-wit: One share shall entitle the owner thereof to one vote; three shares shall entitle the owner thereof to two votes; five shares shall entitle the owner thereof to three votes; ten shares shall entitle the owner thereof to four votes; each additional ten shares shall entitle the owner thereof to four votes; and the fractional part over ten shares shall entitle the owner thereof to the fractional part of four votes.

egulation of ting of shares.

Sec. 3. That it shall be unlawful for said corporation to pay and for any officer or member of the same to receive any greater sum for any one year than the following salaries or fees, to-wit: President, not exceeding fifty dollars; directors, not exceeding twenty-five dollars each; secretary, not exceeding twenty-five dollars; treasurer, not exceeding five per cent. on gross receipts; and the superintendent not exceeding one dollar and fifty cents per day for the actual time while employed: Provided, that he shall not receive pay for more than fifty days in one year: Provided further, that when any person is president and also a director in said company he shall receive only one salary: Provided further, that this section shall not have the effect to interfere with any salaries or fees of the officers in said company for the year eighteen hundred and ninety-nine. Any person violating the provisions of this section shall be guilty of a misdemeanor, and shall be fined or imprisoned, or both, at the discretion of the court. Salaries of officers. Proviso. Proviso. Proviso. Violation of this section misdemeanor.

Sec. 4. That this act shall be in force from and after its ratification.

Ratified the 8th day of March, A. D. 1899.

CHAPTER 289.

An act to incorporate the town of Hexlena, in Bertie county.

The General Assembly of North Carolina do enact:

Section 1. That the town of Hexlena, in Bertie county, be and the same is hereby incorporated under the name and style of Hexlena, and as such shall be subject to and governed by all the provisions of chapter sixty-two of Code of North Carolina not inconsistent with this act. Incorporated. Corporate name.

Sec. 2. That the corporate limits of the said town shall be as follows: Commencing at a point on the Powellsville road, a distance of seventy-five yards from the Hexlena cross-roads at Taylor's store, and thence across Harris' field to a point on the Windsor road, a distance of one hundred and twenty-five yards from said cross-roads, and thence at right angles with said road across T. T. Early's field a distance of two hundred and fifty yards; and thence at right angles turning to the right and running to the Conaritsa road to a point two hundred and fifty yards from said cross-roads, and thence towards the road to Williford schoolhouse, and striking said road a distance of one hundred and twenty-five yards from said cross-roads, and thence at right Corporate limits.

angles and across John Harris' field a distance of seventy-five yards, and thence at right angles and towards the Powellsville road where it strikes the point of beginning, a distance of seventy-five yards from said cross-roads.

Town officers. Sec. 3. That the officers of the said town shall consist of a mayor, three commissioners and a constable; and until their successors are elected and qualified the following shall be officers of said town: T. T. Early, mayor, and John Harris, L. J. Taylor and Charles Minton commissioners, who shall have all the powers and authority and rights conferred on like officers by The Code, chapter sixty-two: Provided, that no liquor shall be sold in said town until the petition asking for license shall be endorsed by the board of town commissioners in regular session, and that all laws in conflict with this act are repealed.

Temporary officers.

Proviso.

Petition for liquor license must be endorsed by commissioners.

Election of constable. Sec. 4. The commissioners named herein shall elect a town constable who shall hold his office until his successor is elected and qualified according to law.

Sec. 5. This act shall be in force from and after its ratification.

Ratified the 4th day of March, A. D. 1899.

CHAPTER 290.

An act to incorporate the Ozark Mills.

The General Assembly of North Carolina do enact:

Corporators. Section 1. That Geo. A. Gray, John F. Love, P. Kankin, together with all other persons who shall be associated with them and become stockholders in the corporation hereby incorporated, their successors and assigns, be and they are hereby created and constituted a body politic and corporate by and under the name and style of Ozark Mills, by which name the said corporation may sue and be sued, plead and be impleaded, appear, prosecute and defend in any court of law or equity whatsoever, and in all suits or actions, contract and be contracted with, and shall have the privileges and rights hereby specially granted, and such as may be necessary to the full exercise and enjoyment of the same.

Body corporate.

Corporate name.

Duration of charter. Sec. 2. Said corporation shall have sixty years succession and enjoy all the rights and privileges, liberties and immunities, franchises and powers conferred upon and pertaining to other similar corporations, and not forbidden by the laws of the United States and of North Carolina, as well as those rights and privileges, liberties and immunities, franchises and powers hereby specially granted.

Sec. 3. The place of business of said corporation shall be at Gastonia, in Gaston county, North Carolina. Place of business.

Sec. 4. That said corporation shall have the right to and may make and use a common seal, and alter the same at pleasure. Seal.

Sec. 5. That said corporation is hereby authorized and empowered to conduct, transact and carry on, in all its branches, the manufacture of cotton, wool, silk and any and all other fibrous and similar or kindred material into yarn, rope, cloth, or other merchantable product or products, the dyeing, bleaching, printing and finishing of such material and products, and carrying on any and all processes that may be thought to add efficiency, value or other desirable quality thereto; to gin cotton and to manufacture cotton seed, either alone or in connection with other material, into all such products as may be obtainable therefrom; the buying, selling and exchanging of all kinds of machinery, goods, wares and merchandise, including the purchasing and holding of suitable land, the purchase, construction and erection of all necessary and suitable machinery, houses and all sorts of structures and bulidings that may be convenient or useful in the prosecution of their main purpose of manufacturing as aforesaid; also the making and repairing of all kinds of machinery and supplies, such as may be used in their said business. Empowered to manufacture certain goods and wares.

Sec. 6. The principal officers of said corporation shall be the president, the vice-president, and the secretary and treasurer, who shall be stockholders, and these shall be and constitute the board of directors of said corporation. The persons named in the first section of this act, towit: George A. Gray, John F. Love and P. Kankin are hereby constituted, respectively, provisional president, vice-president, and secretary and treasurer, and as such the board of directors of said corporation, and they shall hold their respective offices until their successors are elected. Principal officers. Board of directors. Term of office.

Sec. 7. Said corporation shall be governed by the above-named officers who shall be elected annually by the stockholders' meeting, and at such meeting each stockholder can be represented in person or by proxy and shall be entitled to cast one vote for each share of stock held by him, and the by-laws shall be adopted or amended by a two-thirds vote of the capital stock of the company which is taken. Annual election of officers.

Sec. 8. The annual meeting of said corporation shall be held in Gastonia, North Carolina, on the second Tuesday in April of each year, at which time the officers shall be elected, but the time of the annual meeting may be changed by vote of stockholders as in the adoption of by-laws for the corporation. Other meetings of the stockholders may be held for special or general purposes upon the call of the president and one other director. Annual meeting, when held.

Sec. 9. The stockholders of this corporation shall not be personally or individually liable for its debts, acts, liabilities, con- Individual liability of stockholders.

tracts, engagements, defaults, omissions or torts, or for any claim, payment, loss, injury, transaction, matter or thing whatsoever relating to or connected with the company.

Capital stock. Sec. 10. The amount of the capital stock of said corporation shall be one hundred and twenty-five thousand ($125,000) dollars, divided into one thousand two hundred and fifty shares of the par value of one hundred dollars each, with the privilege of increasing the same to two thousand shares of same amount by a majority vote of the stock at any regular meeting of the stockholders. May be increased.

When certificates of stock may be issued. Sec. 11. That no certificate of stock shall be issued unless the par value thereof be fully paid, and when any certificate of stock shall have been issued no assessment shall thereafter be made thereon.

May borrow money Sec. 12. The board of directors may by resolution authorize money to be borrowed by the corporation for the purpose of aiding the conduct of its business, and prescribe how much may be borrowed and how the same shall be secured.

Sec. 13. This act shall be in force from and after its ratification.

Ratified the 6th day of March, A. D. 1899.

CHAPTER 291.

An act to amend chapter one hundred and ten, of the private laws of eighteen hundred and eighty-nine, entitled "An act to incorporate the town of Brevard.

The General Assembly of North Carolina do enact:

Section 17, chapter 110, private laws 1889, amended. Section 1. That section seventeen of chapter one hundred and ten of the private laws of eighteen hundred and eighty-nine, be and the same is hereby amended as follows, to-wit: Add at the end of said section the following words: That for the purpose of constructing, improving and repairing the streets and sidewalks in said town, the board of aldermen shall have the power to levy in addition to the taxes above mentioned, a special tax to be known as a street tax, said tax shall not exceed twenty-five cents on the one hundred dollars of property, both real and personal, and seventy-five cents on the poll. The word "property" shall be construed to mean everything taxable by the town for general purposes. Special tax for street purposes may be levied.

Section 26, chapter 110, repealed. Sec. 2. That section twenty-six of said chapter one hundred and ten is hereby repealed and the following is substituted therefor to be known as section twenty-six of said chapter: That the board of aldermen of the said town shall have full power and authority to construct, repair and otherwise improve the sidewalks upon such streets in said town as they may designate by an ordinance passed by the said board, and the said streets and the lots abutting thereon when so designated by said ordinances shall become a taxing district, and the word "lot" where it occurs in this act shall be taken to mean the whole of the frontage abutting the sidewalk constructed or improved, and shall extend back from the street the distance of one hundred and thirty-two feet.

Improvement of streets and sidewalks.

Sec. 3. In order to more effectually carry out the authority delegated and the duty imposed by the preceding sections, the board of aldermen of said town shall have authority to assess and proportion the cost of the sidewalk constructed, repaired or improved between the town and the lots abutting thereon, and they may assess two-thirds thereof on the lots abutting and one-third upon the town. The amount of the assessments against the abutting lots so improved as herein divided, being estimated and ascertained by the board of aldermen in the manner prescribed by their ordinance, shall be a lien on such lots and shall be entered upon the minutes of the said board, and if the same is not paid within thirty days after notice to the owner or his agent, the clerk of the board of aldermen shall issue execution against the said lot or lots directed to the marshal of the said town, who shall advertise the said lots, under such rules and regulations as are now and may hereafter be provided by the ordinance of the said town for the sale of real estate for taxes, and shall sell the same, and convey as other lands sold for taxes.

May assess proportion of cost for repairing sidewalk to owner of property adjoining.

When assessment is unpaid, clerk may issue execution.

Sec. 4. That any person whose land has been so assessed as provided above, who is dissatisfied with the said assessment, or who desires to contest the matter or right of assessment, shall file his petition before the mayor of the said town within thirty days after notice to him of the assessment, setting forth his grounds of objection, and the mayor shall hear the same and render his judgment thereon, from which either the petitioner or the board of aldermen may appeal to the superior court in the same way and manner as appeals are allowed from justice of the peace, and the trial in the superior court shall be de novo.

Person dissatisfied with assessment may file petition with mayor.

Either party may appeal.

Sec. 5. This act shall be in force from and after its ratification.

Ratified the 6th day of March, A. D. 1899.

CHAPTER 292.

An act to amend chapter twenty-five, laws of eighteen hundred and ninety-three.

The General Assembly of North Carolina do enact:

Section 1. That laws of eighteen hundred and ninety-three, chapter twenty-five, section two (2), be amended as follows:

Relating to incorporation of town of Waxhaw, in Union county.

After the word "thence" in line seven and the following lines, eight, nine, ten, eleven, twelve and thirteen, to the word "chain" in said line thirteen be stricken out and the following words inserted in lieu thereof: South eighty-seven east twenty-one and sixty-five one-hundredths chain to a black jack, south sixty-two and one-third west thirty-two links from A. E. Gordon's chimney corner, thence north eighty-three and one-half east seventy chains crossing the Providence road to a hub by A. R. O.; thence north eighty-seven degrees fifty minutes two thousand two hundred and eighty-three chains to a hub in J. E. Stephenson and Company's line fifty feet north from center of G. C. and N. Railway, thence with his line eighty-eight and one-fourth east nine chains to a hub in said line, thence north one and three-fourths east two hundred feet to a hub in main street, thence north eighty-eight and one-fourth west about ten chains and eighty-five links to a rock.

Cultivated land and wood land exempt from taxation.

Sec. 2. That all cultivated land and wood land not laid off in lots lying within the incorporate limits of the town of Waxhorne, shall be exempted from taxation for town purposes.

Sec. 3. That this act shall be in force from and after its ratification.

Ratified the 8th day of March, A. D. 1899.

CHAPTER 293.

An act to authorize William Howard to practice pharmacy without license.

The General Assembly of North Carolina do enact:

Section 1. That William Howard, of Edgecombe county, be and hereby authorized to register and practice pharmacy without the examination and license prescribed by the general law.

Sec. 2 That this act shall be in force from its ratification.

Ratified the 8th day of March, A. D. 1899.

CHAPTER 294.

An act to change the name of the town of Hub, in Columbus county, to Boardman.

The General Assembly of North Carolina do enact:

Name of town of Hub, in Columbus county, changed to Boardman.

Section 1. That chapter one hundred and one, private laws of eighteen hundred and ninety-one, and chapter three hundred and forty-five, public laws of eighteen hundred and ninety-seven, be mended by striking out the word "Hub" wherever the same appears in said chapters and inserting therefor the word "Boardan."

Sec. 2. That all laws in conflict with this act are hereby repealed as far as they are inconsistent with this act. Conflicting laws repealed.

Sec. 3. That this act shall be in force from and after its ratification.

Ratified the 8th day of March, A. D. 1899.

CHAPTER 295.

An act to allow Dr. J. G. Hord to run a drug store without securing pharmaceutical license.

The General Assembly of North Carolina do enact:

Section 1. That Dr. J. G. Hord, of the town of Kings Mountain, be and he is hereby authorized and allowed to run and operate a drug store in the town of Kings Mountain, North Carolina, without securing pharmaceutical license. Dr. J. G. Hord authorized to run drug store without license.

Sec. 2. That all laws and clauses of laws, in so far as they conflict with this act, are hereby repealed. Conflicting laws repealed.

Sec. 3. That this act shall be in force from and after its ratification.

Ratified the 6th day of March, A. D. 1899.

CHAPTER 296.

An act to amend chapter seventy-five of the private laws of North Carolina, ratified on the first day of March, Anno Domini, eighteen hundred and ninety-seven.

The General Assembly of North Carolina do enact:

Section 1. That section one of chapter seventy-five of the private laws of North Carolina, ratified on the first day of March, Anno Domini eighteen hundred and ninety-seven, be amended by striking out the word "Greensboro" and inserting the word 'Raleigh." Principal office of Southern Mining, Smelting and Manufacturing Company changed.

Sec. 2. That this act shall be in force from and after its ratification.

Ratified the 6th day of March, A. D. 1899.

CHAPTER 297.

An act to amend the charter of the town of Wilson.

The General Assembly of North Carolina do enact:

Charter amended.

Section 1. That chapter three hundred and eighty-seven, private laws of eighteen hundred and ninety-three, be amended as follows: That section four be struck out and insert in lieu thereof the words: "There shall, on the first Monday in May, eighteen hundred and ninety-nine, and annually thereafter, be elected by the qualified voters of said town a mayor, chief of police and five commissioners for said town, who shall hold their office until their successors are elected. One of the said commissioners shall be chosen by the voters of each ward in said town. The mayor and the chief of police shall be voted for in each ward and the person receiving the highest number of votes shall be declared elected. The commissioners shall reside in the ward for which they are elected, and shall receive no compensation for their services."

Annual election of officers.

When judges of election shall meet.

Sec. 2. That section ten be amended by adding at the end thereof the words: "And the judges of election shall meet at two o'clock p. m. on the day next after the election at the mayor's office and canvass the vote cast for mayor and chief of police, and certify the same to the clerk of the town, and the persons receiving the highest number of votes for the offices of mayor and chief of police shall be declared elected and the said clerk shall notify the persons thereof."

Commissioners empowered to establish fire limits.

Sec. 3. That section thirteen be amended by striking out in line two the word "mayor," and in line three the word "constable," and by adding thereof [thereto] the following: "The board of commissioners shall have power to establish fire limits within said town, within which it shall not be lawful for any person to erect or build any wooden house, make any wooden additions to any building or cover any building with any other material than metal or slate. They may prohibit wooden buildings from being removed from one place to another within the same, under such penalties as the board of commissioners may establish."

License tax on corporations buying and selling stocks, etc.

Sec. 4. That section thirty-three be amended by adding thereto the following: (10) That any persons or corporation engaged in the business of buying or selling stocks, provisions, cotton or grain for future delivery, or any agent of such person or corporation having an office in the town of Wilson shall before opening such office, soliciting business or accepting orders pay an annual license tax of one thousand dollars.

Sec. 5. That this act shall be in force from and after its ratification.

Ratified the 6th day of March, A. D. 1899.

CHAPTER 298.

An act to authorize the town of Franklin, in Macon county, to issue bonds and levy special tax.

The General Assembly of North Carolina do enact:

Section 1. That for the purposes of improving the streets of the town of Franklin, in Macon county, and for such other improvements as may be deemed necessary by the mayor and board of commissioners of said town, Macon county, the commissioners of said town are hereby authorized and empowered to issue bonds of the [said town] to an amount not exceeding five thousand dollars, of such denominations as the board of aldermen or town commissioners may deem advisable, bearing interest from date thereof, not to exceed the rate [of] six per centum per annum, with interest coupons attached, payable yearly, at such times and at such places as may be deemed advisable by said board of commissioners, said bonds to be of such form and tenor and transferable in such way, and the principal thereof payable or redeemable at such time or times, not exceeding ten years from the date thereof, and at such places, as said board may determine. Said bonds shall be signed by the mayor and commissioners of said town.

Commissioners authorized to issue bonds.

Interest.

Bonds, how signed.

Sec. 2. That for the purpose of providing for the payment of the interest accruing on and the principal at maturity of such bonds as may be issued under this act, the board of commissioners of said town of Franklin are authorized annually and at the time of levying other town taxes to levy and lay a special tax on all property within the corporate limits of said town subject to taxation, and on all taxable polls not exceeding thirty cents on the one hundred dollars worth of property, and not exceeding ninety cents on the poll, said tax to be strictly applied for the purposes herein mentioned. So much of all the taxes levied and collected in the corporate limits of said town under this act as may not be required to pay the interest on said bonds as the same falls due, and can not or may not be applied to the purchase or discharge of the bonds for which said taxes are levied and collected, shall be invested so as to secure the payment at maturity of the principal of said bonds; and to insure the due investment of the amounts collected from year to year in excess of that required to pay the said interest, the board of town commissioners shall cause the said excess to be turned over to the treasurer of said town for a sinking fund. It shall be the duty of the treasurer, under such general rules and regulations as said board of town commissioners may from time to time prescribe, to make investments of so much of the taxes collected and turned

Annual tax may be levied to provide sinking fund.

Tax shall be applied for no other purpose.

Excess shall be turned over to sinking fund.

over to him as aforesaid as shall be applicable as aforesaid to the payment of the principal of said bonds issued under this act; and to do or perform all such other services in connection with said bonds as said board may prescribe. Said treasurer shall give such bond as said board may prescribe, and such bond shall be liable for all moneys coming into the hands of said treasurer.

Bond of treasurer.

Question of bonds shall be submitted to voters.

Sec. 3. That the provisions of this act shall be submitted to a vote by the qualified voters of the town of Franklin on the first Monday in May, eighteen hundred and ninety-nine, under the rules and regulations prescribed for members of the board of commissioners of said town. The town commissioners shall cause a notice of said election and of the purpose of the same to be posted at four public places in said town for thirty days before said election. All qualified voters wishing to vote in favor of the issuing of said bonds and the levying of the tax herein provided for shall vote a written or printed ticket with the words "Approved," and those wishing to vote against the issuing of the bonds and levying the tax shall vote a ticket with the word written or printed, "Disapproved." If a majority of such voters shall vote "Approved," it shall be deemed and held that a majority of the qualified voters of the town of Franklin are in favor of issuing the bonds and levying the tax, and in such case this act shall be and remain in full force and effect. But if a majority shall vote "Disapproved," this act shall be null and void.

Form of ballots.

Sec. 4. This act shall be in force from and after its ratification.

Ratified the 6th day of March, A. D. 1899.

CHAPTER 299.

An act to incorporate the Davidson Mineral Railway Company.

The General Assembly of North Carolina do enact:

Corporators.

Section 1. That Wyndham Henry Wynne, Edward Hopkins and S. E. Williams and J. M. Primm. and their associates, successors and assigns, be and they are hereby created and constituted a body politic and corporate to be styled the Davidson Mineral Railway Company, and by that name to remain in succession, with full power to sue and be sued, plead and be impleaded; to acquire by gift, purchase or otherwise hold, enjoy and convey property, real, personal and mixed, and of whatever kind or class that may be necessary for the conduct and maintenance of said corporation.

Body corporate.

Corporate name.

Corporate powers.

Seal.

Sec. 2. That it shall have and is hereby authorized and empowered to keep and use a common seal; to make, alter and maintain all such by-laws as may be deemed necessary and expedient for the organization, management and control of the business to be done by said corporation, not inconsistent with the constitution and laws of the United States of America and the state of North Carolina. By-laws.

Sec. 3. That said corporation shall have power and authority to lay, cut, construct, equip, maintain and operate a railway in the county of Davidson from Lexington or Linwood, in the county of Davidson, on the Southern Railroad, to the Narrows or the Great Falls of the Yadkin river, in Montgomery county, by way of Silver Hill, Davidson county. Empowered to construct and operate railroad.

Sec. 4. That the guage or width between the rails of said road may be either broad or narrow in the common acceptation of the term, as the corporation shall deem best, not to be less than three feet wide. Gauge of road.

Sec. 5. That said proposed railway may be built and maintained for the purpose of carrying either passengers or freight, or both, with proper appliances and accommodation for the same. Purpose of construction.

Sec 6. That the power to be used by said corporation for hauling or propelling trains and cars may be either steam, electricity or other mechanical motive force or power. Power used.

Sec. 7. That in the prosecution of the business herein authorized, the said corporation shall have the right and is hereby authorized and empowered to condemn all such lands as they can not acquire by gift or purchase as may be needed for its use and enjoyment in establishing, laying out and conducting its business for right-of-way for necessary warehouses or depots or other buildings, in the same manner and form and to the same extent and under the same rules as are now provided by law in chapter forty-nine volume one, of The Code of the state and laws amendatory thereof. Empowered to condemn lands.

Sec 8. That said corporation in laying out, locating and constructing its right-of-way and road-bed thereon, may follow and use any public road or other public highway on its route without charge, let or hindrance from anyone: Provided, they or it shall leave and restore ample room and passageway or roadway for the passage, use and benefit of vehicles and other public travel along said roads or highways. May follow and use public roads.

Sec. 9 That the capital stock of said corporation shall be sixty thousand dollars, to be divided into shares of one hundred dollars each, with the privilege to increase the said capital stock to one hundred thousand dollars, if it shall be found necessary or expedient. Capital stock.

Sec. 10. That within twelve months after the passage of this act on a call signed by any three of the corporators, they and their associates may meet in Lexington, North Carolina, and ac- First meeting.

Election of officers.

cept the charter organized, and elect such officers and for such length of time as they may deem necessary for the control and management of said corporation and till their successors are elected and qualified as by the by-laws required, to-wit: President, treasurer, secretary, and etc.

Duration of charter.

Sec. 11. That said corporation shall have sixty years in which to transact its business and wind up its affairs.

May borrow money, etc.

Sec. 12. That said corporation may borrow money and pond, hypothecate or mortgage it road-bed, rolling stock or other and all its property of whatever kind for the payment of the same, not to exceed the amount of its cash subscription.

Conflicting laws repealed.

Sec. 13. That all laws and clauses of laws in conflict [or] inconsistent with this act are hereby repealed.

Sec. 14. That this act shall be in force from and after its ratification.

Ratified the 6th day of March, A. D. 1899.

CHAPTER 300.

An act to authorize the commissioners of the town of Rocky Mount to issue bonds to construct waterworks in said town.

The General Assembly of North Carolina do enact:

Commissioners of Rocky Mount authorized to issue bonds.

Section 1. That the commissioners of the town of Rocky Mount, for the purpose of constructing waterworks and supplying said town with water, are authorized and empowered to issue bonds, bearing interest at a rate not exceeding six per centum per annum, to an amount not exceeding forty thousand dollars of the denomination of one hundred dollars, to each and every one of which shall be attached the coupons representing the interest on said bonds, which said coupons shall be due and payable on the second day [of] January of each year until the maturity of said bonds. The bonds so issued by said commissioners shall run for a period of twenty years, and shall be numbered consecutively from one to four hundred, and shall declare the amount of interest which they represent, and when the interest is due, and when it is payable, and shall be receivable in payment of all municipal taxes levied by said town. The said bonds shall be exempt from municipal taxation.

Limitation to issue.

Maturity of bonds.

Interest may be received in payment for taxes.

Bonds, how signed.

Sec. 2. That said bonds shall be signed by the mayor of Rocky Mount and attested by the signature of the clerk of the board of town commissioners, with the corporate seal of said town also attached. The board of commissioners of said town shall dispose of said bonds as the necessity for the prosecution of said work

Disposition of bonds.

shall in their discretion require at a sum not less than their par value, and it shall be the duty of the said commissioners to cause a record to be made and kept of the bonds sold, the number, name of the purchaser, and the price received for the same.

Special annual tax may be levied to pay interest.

Sec. 3. That for the purpose of paying interest on said bonds as it falls due, it shall be the duty of the board of commissioners of said town to levy and cause to be collected annually as other taxes are collected a tax not exceeding twenty (20) cents on the hundred dollars worth of real and personal property in said town and not exceeding sixty cents on all taxable polls in said town, and also before the time when the principal of said bonds become due to levy and collect a further special tax to pay the same or to provide for the payment thereof, and in said levy the equation between property and poll shall be preserved according to the constitution of North Carolina. It shall be the duty of said commissioners to provide for the collection of rents, water charges, and other revenues for the use of the water provided by said waterworks, and all revenues derived from such source shall be held and kept solely for the purpose of maintaining and extending said system of waterworks, and the surplus, after paying the expenses of maintenance and extension of said system, shall be used as a part of the sinking fund for the redemption of said bonds until they have been fully redeemed.

Maximum tax.

Revenue derived how applied.

Bonds shall not be issued until question submitted to voters.

Sec. 4. That the board of commissioners shall not issue said bonds or any part thereof until the question of "Waterworks" or "No waterworks" shall be submitted to the qualified voters of said town as hereinafter provided, and unless when so submitted two-thirds of the qualified voters voting at said election shall vote "For waterworks," and unless a majority of the freeholders of said town voting at said election shall vote "For waterworks"; that is if two-thirds of the voters of said town voting at said election shall vote "For waterworks," and among said two thirds there shall be a majority of the freeholders of said town voting at said election, then and in that case the waterworks shall have been deemed to have been carried, and the bonds issued, otherwise not.

When question shall be submitted.

Sec. 5. That the question of "Waterworks" or "No waterworks" shall be submitted to the qualified voters of said town at the next annual election for town offices of said town, and at the voting place in each ward there shall be a separate box in which this vote on waterworks shall be polled, and at said election those in favor of waterworks shall vote a written or printed ticket with "Waterworks" thereon and those opposed to waterworks shall vote a written or printed ticket with "No waterworks" thereon, and at the said election the registrars and poll holders shall vote the number of freeholders in their respective wards

Form of ballot.

and the number of said freeholders who vote for and against "Waterworks," and shall certify the same, showing fully the number of votes cast for waterworks, those cast against waterworks and the number of freeholders who voted "Waterworks," and the number of freeholders who voted "No waterworks." These certificates shall be sealed and delivered to the clerk of the board of commissioners of said town, who shall present the same to the board of commissioners at their next meeting after said election, whether said meeting be a general or a special meeting and the result of the election in the several wards shall be ascertained by the said board and entered upon the record book of said town and the result posted at the door of the mayor's office of said town and at the post-office door for ten days; and if the votes so certified be in favor of waterworks, and if no exception be filed thereto within ten days, said record shall thereafter import verity, and shall be conclusive evidence of the correctness of said returns, and the same shall therefore be received in all the courts of this state and the United States as conclusive evidence of the correctness of the vote polled at said election.

Result of election ascertained.

Commissioners may order succeeding elections for purpose of voting on bonds.

Sec. 6. If at the election held at the regular election in May, eighteen hundred and ninety-nine, waterworks shall fail to carry, the commissioners of said town shall have the power from time to time and at such time as they shall appoint, as in their judgment it shall be best for the good of said town, to submit the question again to the voters of said town. If they decide to submit it at a regular election, then the registrars and poll holders shall conduct the election and report the result fully as provided in section five of this act. If they shall decide to submit it at a time other than a regular election, then the commissioners shall appoint the proper election officers and keep the registrars' books open for thirty days, and at said election they shall revise the book and register those whose names do not appear, and are fully entitled to registration, before the election; but no new registration shall be required of those already registered, and in all other respects the election shall be conducted and the report made as directed in section five of this act. The result in either event shall be declared and recorded as in section five required and with like effect: *Provided* that elections under this act shall not be held oftener than once in twelve months.

Registration of voters.

Sec. 7. That this act shall be in force and effect from and after its ratification.

Ratified the 6th day of March, A. D. 1899.

CHAPTER 301.

An act to amend the charter of the Atherton Mills, a corporation organized under the laws of this state, and having its business in the county of Mecklenburg.

The General Assembly [*of North Carolina*] *do enact:*

Section 1. That the charter of the Atherton Mills be so amended as to confer upon such corporation, in addition to those powers which it now has, the following: To subscribe for, hold and own stock in any manufacturing corporation of the like kind with itself; to build, own and operate mills for the manufacturing of yarns, cloths or other articles at such place or places as it may select, and in connection with its manufacturing enterprises, to conduct stores for the purchase and sale of goods, wares, merchandise and agricultural products, and to have, hold and operate warehouses for the storage of personal property, and to charge fees for such storage, and make advancments of money upon property hypothecated in its warehouses, and generally to do such acts as may be convenient or necessary for the carrying out the purpose of its organization, to-wit: The manufacture and sale of yarns, cloth and other articles. **Additional powers conferred.** **May hold stock in other corporations.**

Sec. 2. This act shall take effect wherever [whenever] at a regular or special meeting of the stockholders of said corporation the same shall be duly accepted by the said stockholders as an amendment of the charter of the corporation. **When this act is effective.**

Ratified the 6th day of March, A. D. 1899.

CHAPTER 302.

An act to incorporate the Cross-Roads Church Academy.

The General Assembly of North Carolina do enact:

Section 1. That the present names of the institution or academy known as the "Cross-Roads Church Academy," shall hereafter be known by the same name and that D. I. Reavis I. J. Cranfield Y. T. Rutledge, C. B. Reavis and F. M. Danner, Charles M. Bagley, N. S C. May, Melvin Hendrix, their successors in office be and they are hereby created and constituted a body politic and corporate by the name and style of trustees of the Cross-Roads Church Academy an institution of learning, situated at Cross-Roads Church in Yadkin county, North Carolina, and as such and by said name of such institution as afore- **Corporate name.** **Corporators.** **Trustees.**

Corporate powers. said, may make contracts, sue and be sued, plead and be impleaded, have perpetual succession, use a common seal, purchase, use, hold and enjoy all real and personal property as may be necessary to advance the interest of said institution of learning, and make such by-laws and regulations and rules as they, the said trustees and their successors, may deem best, not inconsistent with the laws of the United States or the state of North Carolina.

Object of the institution. Sec. 2. That the object of this institution shall be to foster and promote education, and to enable said institution to successfully carry out and accomplish its undertaking the trustees herein named are and shall be authorized to appoint such officers and teachers as may be necessary to serve the purpose and carry into effect the objects of said institution of learning.

Term of office of trustees. Sec. 3. That the trustees appointed by this act shall hold their offices for a term of two years from and after the ratification of this act and until their successors are elected and qualified, and from [and] after the first two years next ensuing after the adoption of this act, the trustees shall be elected by the stockholders of said institution: Provided, that the first election for the election of trustees under this act shall be on the first Tuesday in April nineteen hundred and two, and every two years thereafter, and the trustees elected at each and every election shall hold their offices two years and until their successors are elected and qualified.

Trustees, how elected. Proviso. When elected.

Division of stock. Sec 4. That the stock owned by this institution of learning or that may hereafter come into its hands for the purpose herein stated shall be divided into shares of five dollars each, and at each bi-annual election or at other elections held as prescribed for by the by-laws of said institution, each shareholder or stockholder sha'l be entitled to one vote for each share of stock owned and held by him, and at such election the stockholders may vote by written or printed proxy signed by them.

Organization of trustees. Sec. 5 That the trustees appointed by this act and their successors in office are hereby invested with power, on and after the ratification of this act, to meet and organize and to begin business, shall take charge of and have charge of and hold all property whatsoever now belonging to said institution of learning and all that may hereafter belong to the same, in trust for the use of and support of the said institution of learning, and they shall give notice in writing to all persons who now own stock in the said Cross Roads Church Academy to present a sworn statement of the amount of their stock to them, the said trustees, within four months after receiving such notice, and all who fail to present such certificate within the time prescribed shall forfeit their stock, which shall go to the institution. Upon receipt of the sworn statement of stock from the stockholders by the trus-

Notice shall be given to stockholders.

tees, they shall cause the same to be recorded by the secretary in the record of the institution kept for that purpose.

Sec. 6. That the property of this institution shall be exempt from taxation. Exempted from taxation.

Sec. 7. That a majority of the members present, either at a meeting of the trustees or at a meeting of the stockholders, shall constitute a quorum for the transaction of business. Quorum.

Sec. 8. That this act shall be in effect from and after its ratification.

Ratified the 6th day of March, A. D. 1899.

CHAPTER 303.

An act to amend the charter of the town of Dunn, Harnett county.

The General Assembly of North Carolina do enact:

Section 1. That section seven, chapter one hundred and ninety-one of the private laws of eighteen hundred and eighty nine, be abolished and the following substituted therefor: All elections held in said town shall be conducted under the same rules and regulations as apply to elections for members of the general assembly in the several voting precincts of the county. Section 7, chapter 191, laws of 1889, repealed. Substitute.

Sec. 2. That section twelve of said chapter be amended by adding after "meat" in line twenty eight the following: "Barber shops, fresh-fish dealers"; and add to said section the following: "Said board of town commissioners may have power to regulate the sale of fresh meats and fresh fish by restricting their sale to certain localities in said town." Section 12, of said chapter amended.

Sec 3 That said chapter be further amended as follows: "That said board shall levy a license tax of five hundred dollars upon retailers of spirituous liquors, to be paid annually or semi-annually, as said board may elect." Said chapter further amended. Tax on barrooms.

Sec. 4. That the following section: "That the board of town commissioners shall have power by suitable ordinances to establish fire limits in said town within which no wooden buildings may be erected without a permit therefor from said board, and the said board may condemn any buildings or other property within said district, and upon notice to owner require the removal of the same; upon failure or refusal of the owner to remove the same, the same may be appraised as other property is condemned for public or corporate use, and upon the payment to the owner of the appraised value the said board may cause the said condemned property to be removed." Amended.

Sections 2 and 4, chapter 164, private laws of 1897, repealed.

Sec. 5. That sections two and four, chapter one hundred and sixty-four of the private laws of eighteen hundred and ninety-seven, are hereby repealed.

Sec. 6. That this act shall be in effect from and after its ratification.

Ratified the 6th day of March, A. D. 1899.

CHAPTER 304.

An act to change the name of White-Rickle Furniture Company.

The General Assembly of North Carolina do enact:

Name of White-Rickle Furniture Company changed.

Section 1. That the name of White-Rickle Furniture Company, a corporation under the general law of the state, with principal places of business at Mebane, in the county of Alamance, be changed to White Furniture Company, and by that name said corporation to have all the rights, privileges and powers and be subject to all the liabilities of White Rickle Furniture Company.

Sec. 2. That this act shall be in force from and after its ratification.

Ratified the 6th day of March, A. D. 1899.

CHAPTER 305.

An act to incorporate the town of Wrightsville Beach, in the county of New Hanover.

The General Assembly of North Carolina do enact:

Incorporated.

Section 1. That the inhabitants and residents of Wrightsville Beach, in the county of New Hanover, be incorporated into a town to be known by the name of Wrightsville Beach.

Corporate limits.

Sec. 2. That the corporate limits of said town shall include all that land known as Wrightsville Beach and bounded by the Atlantic ocean, Moore's inlet, Wrightsville banks, channel and Mascoboro inlet.

Town officers.

Sec. 3. That the officers of said corporation shall consist of a mayor and two aldermen, and the following-named persons shall fill said offices for the first four years and until their successors are duly appointed and qualified as hereinafter provided; that is to say, Samuel H. Northrop, mayor; and William R. Kenan and Ernest Williams, aldermen.

Temporary officers.

Sec. 4. That the said mayor and aldermen shall elect a clerk and treasurer and such other subordinate officers as they in their discretion shall deem necessary and proper for the better government of the said town. The mayor shall preside at all meetings of the aldermen and shall be entitled to vote.

Election of clerk and treasurer.

Sec. 5 That the term of office of the said mayor and aldermen appointed under this act shall begin the first day of April of this year, and before that time they shall meet and take the oath of office prescribed by law before some officer authorized to administer such oaths in the county of New Hanover, and after taking such oath they shall enter upon the discharge of the duties of their office.

Term of office.

Oath of officer.

Sec 6. That in the second week of March, nineteen hundred and three, and in the second week in March every four years thereafter, the governor of the state of North Carolina shall appoint a mayor and two aldermen for the said town, but he shall have power to appoint only such persons to fill said office as shall be recommended to him by a majority of the male owners of real estate and males whose wives shall own real estate within the limits of said town and who shall be of age.

Governor shall appoint mayor and aldermen.

Sec. 7. The said mayor and aldermen shall have all the powers and authority given to aldermen and commissioners of towns and cities in this state as provided and set forth in chapter sixty-two of The Code; and shall have power to enact all such lawful ordinances as they may deem proper and necessary for the better government of said town.

Power of mayor and aldermen.

Sec. 8. That the clerk of said mayor and aldermen shall keep upon his minutes the names of all the property owners in the said town, and shall, five days prior to the first day of March, nineteen hundred and three, and five days prior to the first of March every four years thereafter, give notice to every male property holder and male whose wife shall be a property holder in the said town who shall be of age to deposit with him on the first Monday in said March, or within three days thereafter, a ballot containing the names of the persons whom he desires to recommend to the governor as mayor and aldermen of the said town for the ensuing four years. That at the expiration of the third day after the said first Monday in March, the said clerk in the presence of the mayor and aldermen of the said town, shall canvass the said ballots and announce the result thereof, and thereupon the said mayor and aldermen under their hands and the official seal of the said town shall certify to the governor the persons receiving the largest number of votes for the said offices of mayor and aldermen for the ensuing four years, and thereupon during the second week of said month the governor shall appoint the said persons so certified to him as their term of office, beginning on the first day of April and continuing for four years there-

Duties of clerk.

Names of officers recommended to governor.

after, and until their successors are duly appointed and qualified according to the provisions of this act.

Meetings of aldermen.

Sec. 9. That the mayor and aldermen of said town may hold meetings of their board at any time when they deem it necessary or convenient in the city of Wilmington, and that the ballot for persons to be recommended to the governor for mayor and aldermen as hereinbefore provided may also be taken and had in the said city of Wilmington.

Vacancies occurring in offices.

Sec. 10. Any vacancies that may occur in he office of mayor or aldermen of the said town, whether occasioned by death, resignation or otherwise, shall be filled by the remaining members, whether aldermen or mayor and aldermen.

Sec 11. This act shall be in force from and after its ratification.

Ratified the 6th day of March, A. D. 1899.

CHAPTER 306.

An act to incorporate Plummer Seminary, in Ashe county.

The General Assembly of North Carolina do enact:

Corporators.

Section 1. That S. C. Plummer, E V. Spamper, C. L. P. Plummer and Robert E. Lee Plummer, be and they are hereby declared to be a body politic and corporate, to be known and designated by the name of Plummer Seminary, and by that name shall have perpetual succession and a common seal; and said corporators and their successors shall be empowered and allowed to take, receive, possess, hold and demand all moneys, goods, chattle, bonds and tenements that shall be given them for the use of the said seminary.

Corporate name.

Power of trustees.

Sec. 2. That the said incorporators or trustees of said seminary shall have the control of the same and all its property and effects, and power to appoint officers and teachers for same.

May confer certificates.

Sec. 3. That the proper officers of said seminary shall have and are hereby given power to confer certificates on such as are usually conferred by such institutions.

Sec. 4. This act shall take effect from and after its ratification.

Ratified the 6th day of March, A. D. 1899.

CHAPTER 307.

An act to amend the charter of the town of Sanford.

The General Assembly of North Carolina do enact:

Section 1. That the inhabitants of the town of Sanford shall be and continue as they have been a body politic and corporate, and henceforth the corporation shall bear the name and style of "The Town of Sanford," and under such style and name is hereby invested with all the property and rights of property which now belong to the corporation or are posessed by it under any corporate name or names heretofore used; and by this name may acquire and hold, for the purpose of its government, welfare and improvement, all such estate as may be devised, bequeathed or conveyed to it, not exceeding in value two hundred thousand dollars; and may from time to time, as it shall be demed advisable by the proper authorities of the corporation, invest, sell or dispose of the same; and under this name shall have power to contract and be contracted with, to sue and be sued, to plead and be impleaded, to purchase and convey real estate and personal property, and shall have all powers, rights and privileges necessary or belonging to or usually appertaining to municipal corporations. Body corporate. Corporate name. Corporate powers.

Sec. 2. That the corporate limits of said town shall be as follows: The boundary line of the northern limit shall be at its nearest point to the grade crossing of the Raleigh and Augusta Air Line Railroad and the Cape Fear and Yadkin Valley Railroad one-half mile north therefrom, and shall run from this point east and west each way one-half mile; thence, at the east terminus of the east half mile aforesaid, running south one mile; thence west one mile; thence north one mile to the western terminus of the western half-mile aforesaid. Corporate limits.

Sec. 3. That the town of Sanford shall be divided into five wards, denominated first, second, third, fourth and fifth wards. The said wards shall be bounded as follows: First ward, beginning at the intersection of the Buffalo church road with the west boundary line of the town west of Dry creek; running with the center of said road to the center of Carthage street; thence with the center of Carthage street to its intersection with the south terminus of Hawkins avenue, near McPherson and Weatherspoon's store; thence with the center of Hawkins avenue to the north boundary line of the town; thence with the north and west boundary lines of the town to the beginning. Second ward, beginning in the center of Hawkins avenue, on the north boundary line; running thence with the center of said Hawkins avenue to the center of Carthage street, near McPherson and Weatherspoon's store; thence with the center of Carthage street Division of wards. Second ward.

and Charlotte avenue to the east boundary line of the town; thence with the east and north boundary lines to the beginning.

Third ward.

Third ward, beginning at the west boundary line, at the beginning point of first ward, running with the center of Buffalo church road to the center of Carthage street; thence with the center of Carthage street to Charlotte avenue; thence with the center of Charlotte avenue to the east boundary line of the town; thence south with the east boundary line to the center of McIver street; thence with the center of McIver street to the center of Chatham street, near J. D. McIver's store; thence with the center of Chatham street to the point in said street near a big oak at the corner of S. W. Brewer's residence in a direction from said oak at right angles to the street; thence in a direct line to a stone at the south corner of the Moffit Bros. foundry building; thence to the southwest corner of Steele street Methodist church lot; thence parallel with Steele street to G. A. Davis' lot; thence with his line to the west end of said lot; thence south fifty-six west to the west boundary line of the town. Fourth ward, beginning in the center of McIver street on the east boundary line of the town; running thence with the center of McIver street to the center of Chatham street, near J. D. McIver's store; thence with the center of Chatham street to a point in said street near a big oak near S. W. Brewer's residence, a corner of ward No. three (3); thence a direct line to the northeast corner of Primus Holmes' lot, near Park avenue; thence with his line east to the east corner; thence with his line to the south corner; thence directly south to W. T. Buchanan's line, near Little Buffalo creek; thence with his line to Chatham street; thence with the center of Chatham street to a point in the center of said street opposite the southwest corner of J. S. McIver's residence lot; thence crossing the C. F. and Y. V. R. R. (Cape Fear and Yadkin Valley Railroad) or Atlantic and Yadkin R. R. a direct line to the south corner of John A. Womack's residence lot; thence a direct line to the south corner of John L. Brown's residence lot; thence with his line east to the C. F. and Y. V. R. R. (Cape Fear and Yadkin Valley Railroad); thence with said C. F. and Y. V. R. R. (Cape Fear and Yadkin Valley Railroad) to the south boundary line, near Norton Alcott's; thence with the south and east boundary line of the town to the beginning. Fifth ward, all that portion of the town of Sanford not included in the first, second, third and fourth wards.

Annual election of officers.

Sec. 4. There shall, on the first Monday in May, one thousand eight hundred and ninety-nine, and on the first Monday in May annually thereafter, be elected nine aldermen for said town, who shall hold their offices until their successors are qualified, two of whom shall be chosen for each ward, except fifth ward, from which only one alderman shall be chosen. Such aldermen shall be residents of the wards for which they are chosen and shall be elected by the qualified voters of such ward, and must have resided in the state twelve months and in the corporation ninety days next preceding the day of election.

Appointment of registrar and judges of election.

Sec. 5. The board of aldermen of said town shall select, at their regular meeting in March, one thousand eight hundred and ninety-nine, and annually thereafter, a registrar of voters and two inspectors or judges of elections for each of the five wards of said town, all of whom shall be qualified voters and residents of the wards for which they are chosen, who shall be notified of their appointment within two days thereafter by the town constable, and who shall give ten days' public notice at least one public place in each ward, of a registration of voters in and for said wards, specifying time and place and the name of registrars; and shall advertise the election in at least one public place in each ward for at least ten days preceding the day of election.

Election shall be advertised.

Failure of aldermen to make such appointments.

Sec. 6. Should the aldermen of said town fail to appoint said registrars and judges of election, the sheriff of Moore county shall summon three freeholders of the town, who with him shall make such appointment; and the aldermen so failing to appoint shall each forfeit and pay to the equal use of the town of Sanford and of any person who shall sue therefor the sum of twenty dollars, recoverable before the mayor of said town, or any justice of the peace of Moore county.

Registrar shall be furnished with registration book.

Sec. 7. The registrar of each of said wards shall be furnished by the aldermen of the town with a registration book, and it shall be his duty to perform the duties of his office fairly, impartially and acording to law; to revise the existing registration book of his ward in such manner that said book shall show an accurate list of electors previously registered in said ward and still residing therein without requiring said electors to be registered anew; and such registrar shall also, between the hours of seven o'clock a. m. and nine o'clock p. m., for four successive Saturdays immediately next preceding the day of election, keep open the books for the registration of any electors residing in his said ward and entitled to register, whose names have never before been registered in said ward or do not appear on said revised lists, and shall register in said book all names of persons not so registered who may apply for registration, keeping the names of white voters separate and apart from the names of colored voters. Any person offering to register may be required to take and subscribe an oath that he has resided in the state of North Carolina twelve months and in the town of Sanford ninety days next preceding the day of election, and that he is an actual and bona fide resident of the ward in which he offers

Hours for registration.

Persons offering to register shall be required to take oath.

for registration, or is otherwise entitled to register, and that he is twenty-one years old; and if any person shall wilfully swear falsely in taking such oath he shall be deemed guilty of a misdemeanor, and on conviction shall pay a fine not exceeding one hundred dollars and be imprisoned not exceeding sixty days in the county jail. But the board of alder- an entirely new registration of voters whenever they may deem men, upon thirty days' notice, may direct that there shall be it necessary for a fair election. This new registration may, if the board so determine, be conducted by one of the registrars hereinbefore provided for, to be designated by the board, who shall keep all the registration books of the town at a place to be designated by said board.

Board of aldermen may order new registration.

When registration books shall be closed.

Sec. 8. The registration books shall be closed at nine o'clock p. m. on the Saturday next preceding the day of election; and after the same are closed no person shall be allowed to register, but the registrar shall, on application before said books are closed, on one of the days herein named for the registration of voters, register all persons not then qualified to vote in his ward who will become so qualified on or before the day of election.

Persons entitled to vote

Sec. 9. Any person who is a qualified elector of the state of North Carolina, and shall have resided for ninety days next preceding the day of election within the corporate limits of said town, and shall be an actual and bona fide resident of the ward in which he applies for registration, shall be a qualified elector and shall be entitled to register and vote in any municipal election therein; and no person who is not thus a qualified elector of said town shall be eligible as mayor or aldermen thereof.

Registrar and judges shall be sworn.

Sec. 10. After having been duly sworn by the mayor or justice of the peace to conduct the election fairly, impartially and according to law, the said registrar and inspectors or judges of election shall, at the appointed time, open the polls at such places in the wards respectively as the aldermen shall designate; they shall receive and deposit ballots in boxes provided for them, administer oaths when necessary, decide all questions of voting, and superintend and conduct the election for municipal officers in like manner and during the same hours of the day as the election of members of the general assembly, and with reference to the canvass of votes and challenges and in all other respects except as herein otherwise directed they shall have the powers and duties belonging to registrars and judges of elections as established by the laws of North Carolina with reference to general elections.

Duties and powers of judges and registrars.

Persons challenged.

Sec. 11. No person whose name has not been duly registered shall be allowed to vote, and any one offering to vote may be challenged at the polls, and if the judges of election shall sustain the challenge, such person's ballot shall not be received. Ballots shall be on white paper and without device. The aldermen for each ward shall be voted for on one ballot.

Counting of votes. Sec. 12. At the close of the election the votes shall be counted by the judges and such persons voted for as aldermen receiving the highest number of votes shall be declared elected aldermen, and if of the persons voted for as aldermen there shall be any two or more having an equal number of votes, the judges shall decide by ballot the election between such persons; and the person or persons so chosen shall be declared elected: *Proviso.* Provided, that when any question or matter is to be decided by vote of the judges of election, the registrar shall not cast his vote except *When registrar may vote.* in case of tie, in which case he shall cast the deciding vote.

Vacancies occurring among registrars and judges. Sec. 13. The aldermen shall have authority to fill any vacancy occurring in the office of inspector of election or registrar by death, permanent disability or otherwise up to the day of election, and if on that day any vacancy should be or occur, or if any inspector or registrar shall be absent at the time for the opening of the polls on said day, it shall be the duty of the mayor to fill said vacancy forthwith, and the person or persons so appointed shall have all the power vested in the regular appointed inspector or registrar, and shall be subject to the same requirements and penalties: Provided, that any inspector of elections or any registrar who shall willfully absent himself from the poll-ing place when his attendance thereat is required by law, or shall otherwise willfully delay or obstruct the business of said election, shall be guilty of a misdemeanor and shall be fined not exceeding fifty dollars or imprisoned not exceeding thirty days.

Judges shall certify to result of election. Sec. 14. At the close of the election and of the counting of the votes the judges shall immediately make out, subscribe and certify two statements of said election and return one to the register of deeds of Moore county and return the other to the clerk of the town, and the said register of deeds and the said clerk shall duly record the same in their respective offices, and the registration and poll lists shall be duly subscribed by said judges of election and returned to the clerk of the town.

Town officers shall take oath. Sec. 15. The aldermen so elected, and the mayor, after his election, and all other officers of the town required to take an oath, shall, before entering upon their duties, take and subscribe before the proper officer the respective oaths specified by chapter sixty-two, volume two of The Code, entitled "Towns and Cities."

Election of mayor by aldermen. Sec. 16. That the board of aldermen, at their first meeting after their election, shall choose some person not one of their own number to be mayor of said town, to hold his office until his successor shall qualify, who shall preside at the meetings of the board of aldermen and have the rights and powers and perform all the duties prescribed by law for such officers. For misconduct in office the mayor may be removed from his office by a vote of a majority of said aldermen, and upon such office becoming vacant for any cause the board of aldermen shall fill the same for the unexpired time.

Mayor may be removed.

Mayor or commissioners refusing to qualify.

Sec. 17. That any person elected as mayor or commissioner who shall refuse to qualify and act as such shall forfeit and pay to the equal use of the town and of him who shall sue therefor the sum of twenty-five dollars.

Jurisdiction of mayor.

Sec. 18. That the mayor of the town of Sanford is hereby constituted a special court, with all the jurisdiction and powers in criminal offenses occurring within the limits of said town which are or may hereafter be given to justices of the peace; he shall preserve and keep the peace, and may cause, upon proper proceedings, to be arrested persons charged with or convicted of crimes in other counties or states, who may be found in the town limits, and bind or imprison them to appear at the proper tribunal to answer for their offenses. He shall also have jurisdiction to issue process, to hear and determine all misdemeanors consisting of a violation of the ordinances and regulations of the town or the provisions of this act, where the same is not exclusively within the jurisdiction of the superior court, to enforce penalties by issuing execution upon any adjudged violation thereof; to execute the laws and rules made by the commissioners; and his endorsement of the names of witnesses upon a summons or warrant shall be authority for the officers to execute the same; (and he may issue process without complaint when he is satisfied that there has been a violation of the law): Provided, that he shall not have jurisdiction of laws of any nature or amount other than such whereof a justice of the peace may take cognizance, unless specially allowed by this act.

Proceedings in mayor's court.

Right of appeal.

Mayor shall keep record of precepts issued.

Sec. 19. That all proceedings in the mayor's court shall be the same as are now or may hereafter be prescribed for courts of justices of the peace, and in all cases there shall be a right of appeal to the superior court of Moore county, and causes may be removed from before the said court in the same manner as prescribed in The Code for removal from the courts of justices of the peace. The mayor shall keep a faithful record of the precepts issued by him, and of all his official proceedings. The judgments rendered by him shall have all the force, virtue and validity of judgments rendered by justices of the peace, and may be executed and enforced against all parties in Moore county and elsewhere in the same manner and by the same means as if the same had been rendered by a justice of the peace of the county of Moore.

Sec. 20. That all fines and penalties imposed and collected by the mayor, sitting as justice of the peace, and all fines and penalties imposed in consequence of a violation of the town ordinances or the provisions of this act, except as herein expressly otherwise provided shall inure to the exclusive benefit of the town of Sanford.

Fines and penalties, how applied.

Sec. 21. That when a defendant or witness or any other person shall be adjudged to be imprisoned by said court, it shall be competent for the said court to sentence such person to imprisonment in the county jail of Moore county or the calaboose or guardhouse of the town for a term not exceeding thirty days, and to adjudge that such person work during the term of his confinement on the public streets or other public works of the town; and in all cases where judgments may be entered up against any person for fines or penalties according to the laws and ordinances of said town and the person against whom the case is so adjudged refuses, or is unable, to pay such judgment, it shall be lawful for the mayor before whom such judgment is entered to order and require such person so convicted to work on the streets or other public works of the town, until, [at] such rates of wages as are now or shall be fixed by the aldermen, such person shall have worked out the full amount of such judgment and costs of the prosecution.

Persons adjudged imprisoned may be sent to Moore county jail.

Persons may work out sentence on public roads.

Sec. 22. That any person who shall violate any ordinance of the town of Sanford shall be guilty of a misdemeanor and on conviction thereof shall be fined not exceeding fifty dollars or imprisoned not exceeding thirty days.

Persons violating ordinances, guilty of a misdemeanor.

Sec. 23. That the mayor shall keep his office in some convenient part of the town, designated by the aldermen. He shall keep the seal of the corporation, and perform such duties as from time to time shall be prescribed, and he shall receive for his services the same compensation as a justice of the peace receives for like services, and may receive a salary in addition thereto as mayor or in lieu thereof, not to exceed one hundred dollars per annum, to be allowed by the board of aldermen. He shall preside at all meetings of the board of aldermen, except as otherwise herein provided, and when there is an equal division upon any question, or in the election of officers by the board, he shall determine the matter by his vote, and he shall vote in no other case.

Mayor's office.

Salary of mayor.

Sec. 24. That the aldermen shall form one board and a majority of them shall be competent to perform all the duties prescribed for the aldermen unless otherwise provided. Within five days after their election they shall convene for the transaction of business, and fix days of meetings for the year, which shall be as often as once in every month. Special meetings of the aldermen may be held on the call of the mayor or a majority

When aldermen shall convene for transactions of business.

of the aldermen, and all the aldermen, when the call is made by the mayor, and those not joining in calls, when made by a majority of the board, shall be notified.

Aldermen shall provide for enforcement of ordinances.

Sec. 25. That the aldermen when convened shall have power to make and provide for the execution thereof, such ordinances, by-laws, rules and regulations for the better government of the town as they may deem necessary: Provided, the same be consistent with the provisions of this act and the laws of the state.

Improvement of streets.

Sec. 26. The aldermen of said town shall have power to open and lay out any new street or streets within the town limits, and to widen, enlarge, make narrower, change, extend or discontinue any street or streets, or any part thereof, and to construct and repair sidewalks or any of the streets of the town; they may prevent dogs, horses, cattle, swine, and all other brutes from running at large within the town, and may prevent hogs from being kept within the town; may prohibit the riding or running of horses or other animals at a speed greater than six miles per hour within the town, and may prohibit the running of trains, engines or cars within the town at a greater speed than six miles per hour, and may require any persons or companies or corporations operating a railroad in said town to establish gates or station watchmen or flagmen at any of the public crossings of said roads, and may prohibit the firing of guns, pistols, crackers, gunpowder of other explosive, or combustibles or dangerous material on the streets or within the town; may establish and regulate the markets and employ a weighmaster and keeper of the market and fix their fees; may provide graveyards in or near the town, and regulate and maintain the same, employ a keeper, compel the keeping and returning of bills of mortality, and prohibit interments in the town; may provide for the protection against fires by the esablishment and equipment of fire companies or otherwise; may take such measures as they deem necessary to prevent the entrance into or spread within the town of infectious or contagious diseases; may abate nuisances at the cost of the person on whose premises the same may be located, and by any reasonable means may prevent encroachment on the streets by awnings, signs, porticoes or other obstructions; may fix ordinances for the due observance of Sunday, and in general have power to make such by-laws and adopt such regulations or ordinances for the government of said town as a majority of them may deem necessary to promote the interests and insure the good order and government of said town, and make all such other police regulations and ordinances as the interests, comfort and convenience of the citizens of said town may require.

May prohibit fast riding or driving, etc.

Markets.

Cemeteries.

Protection against fires.

Prevention of contagious diseases.

Abate nuisances.

Encroachment on streets.

Observance of Sunday.

Sec. 27. The said aldermen shall have power to establish, maintain and operate a plant or system of waterworks for furnishing in said town a water supply, and a plant for furnishing lights, and may establish rules and regulations for the government, maintenance and operation thereof; and for the operation, care and superintendence thereof may appoint a superintendent or superintendents, commissioners, committees, or such officers as in their opinion may be expedient, fixing their compensation, and in the discretion of the board of aldermen, requiring of them suitable bonds for the proper conduct of their offices.

Empowered to establish and maintain waterworks plant, electric light plant, etc.

Sec. 28. That the aldermen, at their first meeting after their election, shall appoint a clerk, a treasurer, a constable and a collector of taxes (the constable and tax collector may be the same person), who shall hold their offices during the official term of the aldermen who appointed them, subject to removal for misbehavior or neglect in office. The aldermen shall likewise have power to appoint a street commissioner and regulate his compensation, and may employ an attorney or attorneys for the town and fix their compensation. Before acting, the clerk shall be sworn to the faithful discharge [of] his duty, and the treasurer, the constable and the collector of taxes shall take and subscribe the oaths and execute bonds in such sum as the commissioners shall fix, which are prescribed in chapter sixty-two, volume two, of The Code, entitled "Towns and Cities."

Appointment of clerk, treasurer and other city officers.

Appointment of street commissioner.

Sec. 29. That the clerk may have a reasonable salary, fixed by the board of aldermen, and it shall be his duty to keep regular and accurate minutes of the proceedings of the board, and to preserve all books, papers and articles committed to his care during his continuance in office, and deliver them to his successor, and generally to perform such other duties as may be prescribed by the aldermen and this charter.

Salary of clerk.

Duties of clerk

Sec. 30. That the treasurer shall make out annually a fair transcript of the receipts and disbursements on account of the town and post the same for the inspection of citizens at the end of every fiscal year; and for failure so to do shall forfeit and pay to him who shall sue therefor one hundred dollars.

Salary of treasurer.

Duties of treasurer.

Sec. 31. That it shall be the duty of the treasurer to receive and hold for the use of the town all moneys or securities belonging thereto; to disburse the funds only upon order drawn upon him in the manner herein specified; he shall keep in a book provided for that purpose an accurate account of all moneys received and disbursed by him, and shall submit said account to the aldermen whenever required so to do; and shall make monthly reports to the aldermen as required by chapter sixty-two, volume two, of The Code. On the expiration of his office he shall deliver to his successor all the

Duties of treasurer.

Monthly report.

books, moneys, securities and other property entrusted to him for safe keeping or otherwise.

Orders on treasurer, how signed. Sec. 32. All orders on the treasurer shall be signed by the mayor and countersigned by the clerk, and shall state the purpose for which the money is applied, and the treasurer shall specify said purpose on his accounts, and also the sources whence are derived the moneys received by him.

Power and authority of tax collector. Sec. 33. The tax collector shall have the same power and authority in the collection of taxes as sheriffs have, and shall be subject to the same fines and penalties for neglect of duty. He shall be charged with the sum appearing by the tax list as due for town taxes. He shall be credited in settlement as sheriffs are credited, with all accounts in suit by appeals, all poll taxes and personal property taxes declared by the board insolvent and uncollectable. He shall not retain in his hands over fifty ($50.00) dollars for a longer time than five days, under a penalty of ten per centum per month to the town on all sums so retained.

Annual settlement between tax collector and treasurer. Sec. 34. The board of aldermen shall, at the meeting before the last regular meeting in each year, appoint one or more of their number to be present and assist at the accounting and settlement between the tax collector and town treasurer, and to audit and settle the accounts of the town clerk and treasurer. The accounts so audited shall be reported to the board of aldermen and when approved by them shall be recorded in the minute book of said board. It shall be the duty of said board to remove any tax collector who shall fail to settle and fully pay up the taxes by law due him, and he shall not be eligible to reelection to said office.

Annual levy of tax. Sec. 35. That in order to raise a fund for the expenses incident to a proper government of the town and improvement thereof, the aldermen may annually levy the following tax:

On real and personal property, etc. (1) On all real and personal property within the corporate limits, including money on hand, solvent credits, investments in bonds, stocks and all other subjects taxed by the general assembly, ad valorem, a tax not exceeding fifty cents on the hundred dollars worth of property.

On polls (2) On all taxable polls, a tax not exceeding one dollar and fifty cents on those who may be resident in the town on the first day of June of every year, or may have been so resident within sixty days next preceding said day.

Goods, wares and merchandise. (3) On every one hundred dollars value of goods, wares and merchandise purchased for resale by any merchant trading within the town within one year next preceding the first day of June of the year in which the same is listed, a tax not exceeding ten cents.

Dogs. (4) On all dogs kept in the town and which may be so kept on the first day of June, a tax not exceeding five dollars: Provided, however, that a discrimination within this limit may be made on the different species and sexes of dogs. Proviso.

(5) On all swine and goats not prohibited by the aldermen to remain in the town, when confined, a tax not exceeding five dollars a head. Swine and goats.

(6) On every express company, on every telegraph or telephone company doing business in the town, a tax not exceeding one per centum of its gross receipts in the town, to be given in on oath by the managing agent of such company annually at the same time when other taxes are listed, and under the same penalty as that prescribed by the law of the state. Express, telegraph and telephone companies.

(7) Upon every auctioneer or crier of goods at public auction a license tax not exceeding fifty dollars a year: Provided, that this section shall not conflict with the provisions of section twenty-two hundred and eighty-four of The Code. Auctioneers.

(8) Upon every stock and bond broker, junk dealer and pawnbroker, sewing machine company or agent of such company, dealer in or manufacturer's agent of musical instruments, keeper of sale stable or stock yards, doing business in the town, a license tax not exceeding twenty-five dollars a year. Brokers.

(9) Upon every lawyer, physician, cotton broker, bill poster, street huckster, photographer, merchandise or produce broker, ice dealer, dealer in wood and coal or either, insurance company or insurance agency for every company represented, and every skating rink and shooting gallery, a license tax not exceeding ten dollars a year. Lawyers, physicians, bill posters, etc.

(10) Upon every other occupation, profession or business not herein specially named, a license tax not exceeding twenty-five dollars a year. Other occupations.

Sec. 36. The aldermen, at the last regular meeting in April, shall appoint a list taker, whose duty it shall be to take the list of property, polls and subjects of taxation within the town. Immediately after his appointment he shall make advertisement thereof at three public places in the town, notifying all persons required by law to give in their polls or property for taxation to list the same before him during the month of June; and he shall attend for two days at a place specified in said notice, in said town, to list said property, polls and subjects of taxation. In so far as may be consistent with this act, his powers and duties shall be the same as are conferred by law on the township list taker, and his compensation shall be such as the board of aldermen may allow. It shall be his duty to obtain from the township list taker, provided the list of the latter has not been returned, and if it has been returned, then from the register of deeds for Moore county, who shall furnish the same on demand, a list of the property, with valuation thereon, as returned or to Appointment of list-taker. When taxes shall be listed. Powers and duties of tax-lister.

be returned for taxation included within the corporate limits of the town of Sanford, or subject to be taxed by this charter; and in making out his list he shall place upon all real property within the town the same valuation as is placed thereon in said township tax list for taxation for state and county purposes, and he shall return his list to the clerk of the town on or before the first Monday of July of every year.

Valuation on real property.

All persons liable to tax shall render list.

Sec. 37. All persons liable to taxation by this charter shall, during the month of June in every year, render to the list taker herein mentioned, on a blank to be furnished by the aldermen, a list of their property and subjects for which they may be liable to be taxed under all the rules and penalties prescribed for listing state and county taxes, and as prescribed in this charter. The said list or return shall be in manner and form and contents the same, as near as may be, as is required in listing state and county taxes and the verification thereof and in regard thereto the same; and any person making a false return shall be guilty of perjury. The person listing shall swear to a true value of all property, choses in action and other subjects listed except land; and property held in trust shall be returned on a separate list.

Persons or companies failing to return tax shall pay double tax.

Sec. 38. If any person or company shall fail to render to the list taker a list of property or other taxables, or if any person liable to poll-tax shall fail to give himself in within the time prescribed by this charter, such person or company shall pay double the tax assessed on any subject for which said person or company is liable to be taxed; and any person who shall list any property in the name of any person or company other than the real owner, or who shall fail to disclose the real state of the title thereto, if interrogated concerning the same, shall be guilty of a misdemeanor and shall be fined not exceeding fifty dollars or imprisoned not exceeding thirty days.

Persons liable to poll tax and failing to return same.

Sec. 39. That all persons who are liable for a poll-tax to the said town and who shall willfully fail to give themselves in, and all persons who own property subject to taxation in said town, or whose duty it is to list property, and who shall willfully fail to list the same within the time required by law, shall be guilty of a misdemeanor, and on conviction thereof shall be fined not exceeding twenty-five dollars or imprisoned not exceeding ten days.

Board of aldermen shall examine list.

Sec. 40. That the board of aldermen shall meet on the second Monday night of July of every year to examine and revise the tax list. They shall constitute a board of equalization, with full power upon notice to the party concerned, and for cause, to increase or diminish the valuation upon any property, real or personal, subject to taxation by this charter, to secure a fair distribution of the taxes; and to that end they may subpœna and examine witnesses, administer oaths and have all the power that county commissioners have with respect to the revision of the tax list: Provided, that they shall endeavor to make the list of taxables within the town conform to the list for the state and county taxation: And provided, that the increase or diminution of the valuation of any real property shall not exceed fifteen per centum of the valuation fixed therefor by the township assessors, unless it be in consequenece of some improvement added thereto or subtracted therefrom since such assessment. The board shall have power to assess the value of such portion of any property as may be included within the town limits in cases where the boundaries of the town shall cross said property, and there is in consequence thereof no assessment of the value of the same by the town assessors. The board shall have power to adjourn from time to time to complete said revision.

Proviso.

Board shall have power to assess value of property.

Sec. 41. That as soon as the tax list has been revised the board of aldermen shall proceed to levy the tax on such subjects of taxation as they shall determine, and shall place the tax list in the hands of the tax collector for collection, who shall proceed forthwith in the collection and shall complete the same on or before the first day of November next ensuing, and shall pay the moneys as they are collected to the treasurer, and the tax collector shall receive for his compensation not more than five per centum on the amount collected, as the board of commissioners shall determine. On the first day of November there shall be a penalty of one per centum added to the amount of taxes due, and an additional penalty of one per centum on the first day of every month until the same are paid.

When tax list is revised aldermen shall levy tax.

When collection of taxes shall be completed.

Penalty for unpaid taxes due.

Sec. 42. That if any person liable to taxes on subjects directed to be listed shall fail to pay them within the time specified for collection, the collector shall forthwith proceed to collect the same by distress and sale, all sales to be made after public advertisement, for the space of ten days, at five public places within the town, if the property sold be personalty, and thirty days if the property be realty; and the said collector shall have the right to levy upon and sell any personal property situated outside the limits of the town and within the county of Moore, belonging to a delinquent taxpayer, to enforce the payment of the taxes due the town by said delinquent.

Collection of taxes by distress and sale.

Personal property may be attached.

Sec. 43. That when the tax due on any lot or other land (which is hereby declared to be a lien on the same) shall remain unpaid on the first day of November, the tax collector shall either proceed to collect the same by a levy and sale of personal property belonging to the owner of said lot, or shall report the same to the aldermen with a particular description of the real

Taxes due and unpaid November 1st, how collected.

Sale of real estate for taxes.

estate, and thereupon the aldermen shall direct the same to be sold at some public place in the town designated by them; the collector shall, before selling the same, make advertisement at five or more public places in said town, and shall also serve upon the owners thereof a written or printed notice of the taxes due and the day of sale; but no notice need be given any person having or claiming any lien on said land by mortgage or otherwise. Should the owner not be in the town, or if for any cause the owner can not be served with notice, then the advertisement of said real estate shall be for four weeks in some newspaper published in the county of Moore; and the collector shall divide the said land into as many parts as may be convenient, (for which purpose he is authorized to employ a surveyor), and shall sell as many thereof as may be required to pay said taxes and all expenses attendant thereon. If the same can not be conveniently divided, the collector shall sell the whole, and if no person will pay the whole of the taxes and expenses for the whole of the land, the same shall be struck off to the town; and if not redeemed, as hereinafter provided, shall belong to the town in fee.

Notice shall be served on owner of property.

May be struck off to town.

Collector shall return an account of proceedings.

Sec. 44. That the collector shall return an account of his proceedings, specifying the portions into which the land was divided and the purchaser or purchasers thereof, and the prices of each; and if there be a surplus after paying the said taxes and expenses, the same shall be paid to the town treasurer, subject to the demands of the owners.

Land sold for taxes may be redeemed within a year.

Sec. 45. That the owner of any land sold under the provisions of this charter and amendments, his heirs, executors and administrators, or any person acting for them may redeem the same within one year after the sale by paying the purchaser the sum paid by him and twenty-five per centum on the amount of taxes and expenses; and the treasurer shall refund to him, without interest, the proceeds, less double the amount of taxes.

When not redeemed within time specified purchaser may recover deed in fee simple.

Sec. 46. That if the real estate sold as aforesaid be not redeemed within the time specified, the corporation shall convey the same in fee simple to the purchaser and his assigns; and the recitals in such conveyance, or in any conveyances of lands sold for taxes due the town, that the taxes were due, or of any other matter required to be true or done before the sale might be made, shall be prima facie evidence that the same was true and done.

Certain real estate exempted from such provisions.

Sec. 47. That the real estate of infants or persons non compos mentis shall not be sold for taxes, and when the same shall be owned by such in common with other persons free from such inability, the same shall be made according to section ninety-two, chapter ninety-nine, of The Code.

Sec. 48. That in addition to the subjects to for taxation before named, the aldermen may levy a tax on the following subjects, the amount of which tax, when fixed, shall be collected by the town constable immediately, and if the same be not paid on demand, it may be recovered by suit or the articles on which the tax is imposed, or any other property of the owner may be forthwith distrained and sold to satisfy the same: Special taxes aldermen empowered to levy and collect.

(1) Upon all itinerant merchants or peddlers offering to vend in the town, a license tax not exceeding fifty dollars a year or part thereof, except only such as sell books, charts or maps, or wares of their own manufacture, but not excepting venders of medicines, by whomsoever manufactured; not more than one person shall peddle under a single license. Itinerant merchants.

(2) Upon every company of circus riders, or performers by whatsoever name called, who shall exhibit within the town, a license tax not exceeding fifty dollars for each exhibition; and upon any side-show connected therewith, a license tax not exceeding ten dollars, the tax to be paid before exhibition; and if not, to be doubled. Circuses.

(3) Upon every person or company exhibiting within the town stage or theatrical plays, sleight-of-hand performances, rope-dancing, tumbling, wire-dancing or menagerie, a tax not exceeding twenty dollars, to be paid before exhibition, or the same shall be doubled. Theatrical exhibitions.

(4) Upon every exhibition for reward of artificial curiosities (models of useful inventions excepted), a tax not exceeding twenty dollars, to be paid before exhibition, or the same shall be doubled. Exhibitions for reward

(5) Upon each show or exhibition of any other kind, and on each concert for reward, in the town, and on every strolling musician, a tax not exceeding ten dollars, to be paid before exhibition or the same shall be doubled. Other shows.

(6) Upon any dog which may be brought into the town after the first day of June, to be kept therein, a tax not exceeding five dollars, for permission to keep said dog in the town, which permission shall not extend beyond the last day of May next ensuing. Dogs.

Sec. 49. That when any land or right-of-way shall be required by the town of Sanford for the purpose of opening new streets or for any other purpose allowed by its charter, and for want of agrement as to value the same can not be purshased from the owner or owners, the same may be taken at a valuation to be made by five freeholders of the town, to be named by the aldermen; and the said freeholders, after having been duly sworn by a justice of the peace of the county, shall assess the losses or damages which may accrue to the owner or owners in conse- Land may be condemned. Appointment of freeholders to assess value.

quence of the land or right-of-way having been surrendered, and upon payment to the owner or owners of such sum or lodgment thereof with the clerk of the superior court of Moore county, in case he shall refuse to accept it, the land so valued by the freeholders shall vest in the town so long as it may be used for the purposes of the same: Provided, that if either the owners of said land or the commissioners of the town shall be dissatisfied with such valuation, the party dissatisfied may appeal to the next term of the superior court of Moore county, to which the said freeholders shall return their valuation, with their proceedings therein; and the town shall acquire an immediate right to the use of said lands notwithstanding said appeal.

Proviso.

Either party may appeal.

Appointment of policemen.

Sec. 50. That the board of aldermen may appoint as many policemen as they deem necessary for the better control and government of the town, at such rates of pay and for such times and for such length of time as they think proper. The said policemen shall be under the control of the town constable as chief of police. The town constable, and each member of the police force shall have all the authority vested in sheriffs for the preservation of the peace of the town, and apprehending offenders. They shall execute all process directed to them by the mayor or other proper authority, and in the execution thereof shall have the same power that sheriffs or constables have. The town constable and policemen shall receive for their services such fees as sheriffs receive for like services, or in addition thereto, or in lieu thereof, such compensation as the board of aldermen may allow.

Authority of police

Compensation of constable and police.

To whom mayor may issue precepts.

Sec. 51. That the mayor may issue his precepts, processes and warrants to the town constable and to such other officers to whom a justice of the peace may issue his precepts, and the same may be served by the town constable or other officer authorized to serve process, anywhere in the county of Moore.

Persons may be detained in guardhouse.

Sec. 52. That the constable or policemen of said town may arrest any offender against the laws or ordinances thereof, without process, and if between the hours of seven o'clock p. m. and sunrise, may confine the offender in the guardhouse for safe keeping until he may be brought before the mayor and a warrant obtained for his detention and trial; and when any person arrested by the constable or policemen of said town shall be intoxicated, it shall be lawful to confine him in the guardhouse for safe keeping until he becomes sufficiently sober to be brought before the mayor for trial.

Power of aldermen to fill vacancies.

Sec. 53. That the aldermen have power at any time to fill vacancies in office of which the incumbent was appointed by said board.

Persons liable to work on roads.

Sec. 54. That all persons residing within the corporate limits who would, if they resided outside the town, be liable to work on the public roads, shall be liable to work on the streets of the town, and shall not be liable to work on roads outside the town; and any person who shall fail to attend and work on the day appointed, being liable to work on said streets, after having been summoned so to do by the street overseer or commissioner in like manner as is by law provided for summoning hands to work on the public roads, shall be guilty of a misdemeanor, and fined not exceeding five dollars or imprisoned not exceeding ten days: Provided, that if any person so summoned shall, previous to the day appointed for working said streets pay one dollar to said street commissioner, to be used in repairs of said streets, such person shall be relieved from working the streets for that day.

Persons failing to work on streets guilty of a misdemeanor.

Sec. 55. That the streets may be worked by funds raised by taxation or general funds of the town or by assessment of labor or by both.

Streets may be worked by funds raised by taxation.

Sec. 56. That any person who shall wantonly, willfully or maliciously deface, injure or destroy any of the property of the town, or shall wantonly or willfully break the pound or place where animals are confined by authority of the laws and regulations of the town, or let out any animal confined therein, such person shall be guilty of a misdemeanor, and on conviction fined not exceeding fifty dollars or imprisoned not exceeding thirty days.

Persons injuring property of town guilty of a misdemeanor.

Sec. 57. The aldermen, by proper ordinance to that effect, may cause to be seized and impounded any animal prohibited by law or the ordinances of said town from running at large in said town, and if the owner, on being notified, will not pay the cost of taking up and keeping said animal, at rates to be fixed by the aldermen, or if said owner can not be found, the animal shall be sold therefor at such place as the aldermen may designate, after three days' notice at three public places in the town.

Aldermen may cause animals to be seized and impounded.

Sec. 58. It shall be unlawful for any person or company operating any railroad in the town of Sanford to keep any public crossing in said town closed or obstructed by engine, tender, cars or in any other manner, longer than five minutes at a time, when the said crossing shall be opened and kept open for a reasonable length of time for the passage of those desiring to cross; and any person or company offending against this section shall forfeit and pay to the use of the town fifty dollars, recoverable before the mayor or any justice of the peace of Moore county; and any person or persons in charge of said train or cars and willfully violating this section, or aiding or assisting in violation thereof, shall be guilty of a misdemeanor, and fined not exceeding fifty dollars or imprisoned not exceeding thirty days: Provided, that nothing in this section shall be so construed as

Unlawful for railroads to keep public crossings closed or obstructed.

Penalty.

to prevent the necessary repairs of said crossings and roads by by said person or companies.

Question of issuing bonds shall be submitted to voters.

Sec. 59. That the aldermen of the town of Sanford are hereby authorized and empowered, and it shall be their duty, to cause an election to be held at the various polling places in said town, at such time as said aldermen may appoint, within twelve months from the ratification of this act, and to submit to the qualified voters of said town the question of issuing bonds to the amount of ten thousand dallars, for the purposes and under the provisions hereinafter named in this act, and levying and collecting annually a special tax to provide for the payment of the interest thereon and to provide for the payment of the principal of said bonds when they shall become due. The said election shall be advertised by the aldermen of the said town for thirty days prior to said election, in some newspaper published in said town, and if no newspaper be published in said town, then at least in one public place in each ward therein, and held under the same rules and regulations prescribed for the election of aldermen in the charter of said town, and amendments thereto. Those who are in favor of issuing said bonds and levying and collecting said tax shall vote a written or printed ticket with the words, "For bonds" thereon; those who are opposed shall vote a written or printed ticket with the words, "Against bonds" thereon. The result of said election shall be ascertained by the judges of election of the different wards and certified and returned by them to the aldermen of the town of Sanford in two days from the day of election, who shall verify and also certify such result and cause the same to be recorded in their minutes, and shall also make return of said result, under the signature of the mayor and clerk of said town, to the register of deeds of Moore county, who shall duly record the same.

Annual levy of special tax.

Election, how held.

Form of ballot.

Result of election shall be certified.

Proceeds from bonds, how used.

Sec. 60. That the proceeds arising from the sale of said bonds shall be applied to the following purposes: for furnishing the town of Sanford with water and lights, or either.

Amount of bonds.

Denomination of bonds.

Maturity.

Sec. 61. That if a majority of the qualified voters shall vote for bonds, then the aldermen of said town shall issue coupon bonds to the sum of ten thousand dollars, and in denominations of not less than one hundred and not more than one thousand dollars, maturing not less than twenty and not more than thirty years from date of issue. The said bonds shall bear interest from date at a rate not exceeding six per centum per annum, payable semi-annually at the office of the treasurer of said town on the first day of January and the first day of July of every year: Provided, that said bonds shall be issued and sold for the purposes named and provided for in section sixty-two of this act, and each of said bonds shall bear upon its face a reference to this act and statement that it is issued thereunder. The bonds and the coupons shall be numbered and the bonds shall be signed by the mayor of said town and countersigned by the clerk of the board of aldermen, and a record shall be kept of all bonds, showing the number, amount and to whom sold. The coupons shall be received in payment of all taxes, fines and debts due said town. Said bonds shall be sold for not less than par value.

Bonds, how signed.

Sec. 62. In order to pay the interest on said bonds, the aldermen of said town are hereby authorized, and it shall be their duty, to annually compute and levy, at the time of levying other taxes of said town, a sufficient special tax upon all polls and property, real and personal, and other subjects of taxation mentioned in the charter of said town, always observing the constitutional equation between the tax on property and the tax on polls, not exceeding thirty cents on one hundred dollars valuation of property, and ninety cents on each poll, with which to regularly and promptly pay the interest on said bonds. Said taxes shall be collected in the same manner and at the same time as [all] the other taxes of said town are collected, and shall be paid over by the town tax collector to the treasurer of said town, which officers shall give justified bonds in amounts amply sufficient to cover said taxes,—the former officer for collecting and paying over, and the latter for the safe keeping and proper disbursement of said funds.

Annual special tax may be levied to pay interest and principal.

To whom said tax paid.

Sec. 63. The taxes levied and collected for the purposes specified in section sixty-two of this act shall be kept separate and distinct from any and all other taxes, and shall be used only for the purposes for which they were levied and collected, and any mayor or aldermen who shall appropriate by vote or otherwise to any purpose, directly or indirectly, other than that for which they were levied any of said special taxes, or any part thereof, or shall in any other way violate the provisions of this act, shall be guilty of a misdemeanor: Provided, that if the taxes levied and collected for the payment of interest shall in any year exceed the sum required for that purpose, the amount in excess shall be applied to the credit of the interest fund for next succeeding year; and the said aldermen, at the time of levying the taxes for payment of interest for said next succeeding year, shall take into consideration said excess and compute and levy taxes accordingly.

Said taxes shall be kept separate.

Proviso.

Surplus of said taxes.

Sec. 64. For the purpose of paying the principal of the bonds issued under this act, it shall be the duty of said aldermen, at the time of levying other taxes, beginning at least ten years before the maturity of the respective bonds issued under authority

Special tax may be levied to pay principal.

of this act; to annually levy and collect a special tax in addition to that mentioned in section sixty-two of this act for the payment of said bonds as they mature, and the tax provided for in this section shall equal in amount one-tenth of the amount of said bond or bonds falling due next after the tenth annual levy and collection of taxes from and including said first levy and collection for said purpose, in such manner that at the maturity of each and every of said bonds a sufficient amount shall have been levied and collected for the payment thereof.

Aldermen authorized to invest money thus arising.

Sec. 65. That it shall be the duty of said aldermen to annually invest any and all money arising from the special tax collected under section sixty-four of this act in the purchase of any of said bonds at a price deemed advantageous to said town by said aldermen; but in case said bonds can not be purchased as herein provided the said aldermen may lend said sinking fund, or any part thereof, in such sums as they may deem proper, and for such lengths of time as they deem best: Provided, that said loans shall mature in such manner that such part of said loaned fund as shall be needed to pay off said bonds as they fall due shall become due at least six months before the maturity of said bonds. The said aldermen may take as security for the repayment of said loans and for the payment of the interest thereon, mortgages and deeds in trust in the name of the mayor, or sufficient real estate, or bonds issued under this act may be taken as collateral security for such loan. The notes or other evidences of debt given for any loan under this section shall be executed to and in the name of the aldermen of the town of Sanford, and shall bear interest, payable annually, at a rate not less than six per centum per annum; and in case the aldermen of said town shall not be able to invest any or all said money annually, as directed above, they may, and it shall be their duty, to cause such part as they may be unable to invest to be deposited with some bank, trust company or safe deposit company of undoubted solvency, at the best obtainable rate of interest; and any and all interest arising from the said investments shall be reinvested in the manner above provided.

Proviso.

When bonds shall mature.

Security taken by aldermen.

Interest on such loans.

Net profits arising from operation of electric light plant, etc.

Sec. 66. That the net profits arising from the operation of the water and light plants, by the town, for any year, shall be applied to the payment of said bonds or interest thereon; and the said net profits in the treasury at the time of levying tax for the payment of interest and principal of said bonds, or either, shall be taken into consideration in computing said taxes and levying the same.

Aldermen empowered to contract for water and lights.

Sec. 67. That the aldermen of said town shall have power to contract for a water supply and for furnishing the town with lights; they shall have power to make permanent and exclusive contracts with any individual, corporation or company to build waterworks and furnish said town with water, and grant exclusive privileges and permission to use the streets of the town for said purpose. They may have work done on the country roads leading into the town, and appropriate money from the town treasury not otherwise appropriated, to pay for such work and improvement. They shall have power to exempt from taxation such manufacturing establishments in the town of Sanford as they may think proper and for the best interests of the community.

May have work done on roads.

Sec. 68. That the signatures of the mayor and five of the aldermen of said town shall be sufficient in executing any deed for the conveyance of property by the town, after the same shall be ordered by a majority of the board.

Deeds for conveyance of property.

Sec. 69. That the town of Sanford shall have all the powers, rights, privileges and immunities conferred or hereafter to be conferred on towns and cities of [by] chapter sixty-two, volume two, of the Code, and amendments thereto, and by such acts as may hereafter be passed by the general assembly with reference to towns and cities, when the same are not inconsistent with this charter or within its provisions; and no powers, rights, privileges or immunities belonging to the town of Sanford by any other act or acts shall be hereby lost or abridged; and wherever in any respect this act may be silent or of no effect as to any procedure of the time and manner of doing any act, or the enforcement of any right, the general laws of North Carolina governing in that respect shall be applicable to the town of Sanford.

Corporate powers, rights, etc.

Sec. 70. That in order to facilitate the carrying into effect immediately the provisions of this act, T. L. Bass is hereby appointed mayor, and the following are hereby appointed aldermen of the town of Sanford, with all the powers and authority conveyed and conferred upon said officers by this charter, to hold their offices until their successors are elected and qualify: For the first ward, A. P. McPherson and G. H. Makepeace; for the second ward, J. B. King and W. J. Edwards; for the third ward, R. R. Riley and E. C. Moffitt; for the fourth ward, J. K. Perry and I. H. Lutterlow; for the fifth ward, John G. Phillips.

Temporary town officers appointed.

Sec. 71. That all laws inconsistent herewith or coming within the provisions of this act are hereby repealed, in so far as they affect the town of Sanford.

Conflicting laws repealed.

Sec. 72. That this act shall be in force from and after its ratification.

Ratified the 6th day of March, A. D. 1899.

CHAPTER 308.

An act to incorporate the Pungo and Mattamuskeet Railroad Company.

The General Assembly of North Carolina do enact:

Corporators. Sec. 1. That J. M. Rhodes, P. Mulherin, A. J. Smith and G. Brinn and their associates and assigns, be and they are hereby constituted and created a body politic and corporate by the name of the "Pungo and Mattamuskeet Railroad Company," and shall continue such corporation for a period of ninety-nine years. That such company shall have power and authority to make by-laws and regulations for its government and management; to elect and appoint all necessary officers and prescribe their powers and duties, and to have and use a common seal which it may alter at pleasure; to acquire by purchase, lease or otherwise, and to hold, own, possess, mortgage, lease and sell such real, personal and mixed property as may be necessary or convenient to carry out the purposes of this charter, and to have and exercise all and every other power, privilege, franchise and rights necessary to similar corporations and not inconsistent with the laws of this state or the provisions of this act.

Corporate name.

Duration of franchise.

Corporate powers.

Empowered to construct and maintain a railroad. Sec. 2. That the said railroad company is hereby authorized and empowered to construct, maintain and operate a railroad with one or more tracks and of such guage as may be determined, from the village of Makleyville, in the county of Hyde, and thence running eastwardly, touching at or near Sladesville, Brickhouse forks, Swan Quarter, Swindell, Juniper bay, Douglass bay, Englehard, and Fairfield, with the privilege of building and operating branch roads not exceeding twenty (20) miles each in length. That in constructing and operating said branch roads, the said company shall have all the rights and privileges granted to the main line.

Capital stock. Sec. 3. That the capital stock of said company shall be $3,000.00 (three thousand dollars), and the same may be increased from time to time as a majority of the stockholders may determine, not exceeding two hundred thousand dollars ($200,000.00). That the stock of said company shall be divided into shares of fifty dollars ($50.00) each, for which certificates shall be issued, and each share shall be entitled to one vote, and the stockholders shall not be individually liable beyond the amount of their subscriptions to the capital stock. That the said corporation, or a majority of them, acting in person or by proxy, shall cause a book or books of subscription to be opened by a commissioner or commissioners to be appointed by them, at such times and places and under such rules and regulations as they or a majority of them may prescribe. That said corporators or a majority of them, acting in person or by proxy,

May be increased.

Limitation to capital stock

Individual liability.

after the sum of three thousand dollars ($3,000.00) has been subscribed, shall call a meeting of the stockholders who shall have subscribed to the capital stock for the purpose of completing the organization of the company, of which personal notice of ten (10) days shall be given to each subscriber. That at such meeting the stockholders shall elect a board of directors, consisting of five members, who shall immediately elect one of their number president of the company. The directors shall elect all of the officers of the company. The stockholders, by a majority vote at any meeting, may increase the directors to any number not exceeding eleven.

When company may be organized.

Election of directors.

Sec. 4. That subscriptions to the capital stock of said company may be made in money, land, labor or materials necessary for the construction and equipment of said road in lands, stocks or other valuable credits, in such manner and on such terms as may be agreed upon by the said company.

Subscriptions to stock.

Sec. 5. That said company is hereby authorized and empowered to merge and consolidate its capital stock, property, franchise, rights and privileges with those of any other railroad company or companies now existing or hereafter created under the laws of this state, whenever a majority of the stockholders of this company shall so desire: Provided, that the railroad company with whom this company may be consolidated shall have a continuous traffic arrangement and connection either by rail or by steamboats and barges crossing any intervening body of water, and the said consolidation may be effected by its directors in such manner and on such terms and conditions and under such name and style as a majority of its stockholders may determine: Provided further, that any company consolidated under this act, or acquiring any rights thereunder, shall be domestic corporations and subject to the laws and jurisdiction of North Carolina.

May consolidate with other companies.

Sec. 6. That it shall be lawful for any railroad or transportation company created by the laws of this state or any other state, from time to time, to subscribe to or purchase or to hold the stock and bonds, or either, in this company, or to guarantee or endorse such bonds or stock, or either of them; and it shall or may be lawful for any railroad or transportation company created by the laws of this or any other state to purchase, use or lease the road, property and franchise of this company for such time and upon such terms as may be agreed upon by this company and such company or companies as shall be parties to the contract. That it shall be lawful for this company to subscribe to or purchase and to hold the stock or bonds, or both, of any other railroad or transportation company chartered by this or any other state, or to guarantee the stock or bonds of any such company, or to purchase, lease or operate the road or line, property or franchise of any such railroad or transportation company.

Other corporations may subscribe to stock.

Annual meetings of stockholders.

Sec. 7. That meetings of stockholders shall be held annually, at such time and place as may be determined by them in this state, and at all annual meetings the president and directors shall render to the stockholders an account of the affairs of the company. Special meetings of the stockholders may be called by the president, or by a majority of the directors, by giving ten days' notice thereof by mailing such notice to each stockholder to his last post-office address. Similar notice shall be given of the annual meeting of stockholders.

Annual report.

Special meetings.

Election of officers.

Sec. 8. The board of directors of this company shall elect a president and all other officers which they may deem necessary in the construction and operation of the railroad and affairs of this company. The directors shall be elected annually by the stockholders. The term of office of both directors and officers shall be one year, but they shall serve until their successors are elected and qualified. In case of a vacancy in any office or in the board of directors, by death or resignation or otherwise, the said board of directors may fill the same for the unexpired time.

Term of office.

Subscriptions to capital stock.

Sec. 9. That the directors are authorized to permit subscriptions to the capital stock to be paid in installments until the whole of their subscription shall be paid. If any stockholder shall fail to pay the sum required of him by the directors within one month after the same shall have been required, it shall be lawful for the said president and directors to sell at public auction and convey to the purchaser the share or shares of such stockholder so failing, giving thirty (30) days' previous notice of the time and place of sale in one or more newspapers published in this state, and after retaining the sum due and costs of sale out of the proceeds, to pay the surplus, if any, to the delinquent owner or his legal representative; and if the sale shall not produce the balance due on the subscription and costs of sale, the said company may recover the said balance from the original subscriber or his assignee, or the personal representative of either of them, by civil action, in any court having jurisdiction.

Unpaid for shares of stock may be sold at auction.

Authorized to construct one or more lines.

Sec. 10. That said company is hereby authorized at its option to construct and operate one or more lines of telegraph or telephone along its line or lines of railroad and from other points to its lines of railroad, and to establish a schedule of charges for the use of the same, subject to the regulations of the railroad commissioners, and to collect the same; and said company may connect such lines of telegraph or telephone with the lines of any other company in this state, and may lease, rent or sell this right, and any telegraph or telephone lines constructed by the company.

Authorized to borrow money.

Sec. 11. That the said company is hereby authorized to borrow money to such extent and in such manner as may be authorized by its stockholders, and to pay thereon a rate of interest not exceeding six per cent., as may be necessary in the construction and operation of said railroad, and to issue therefor such bonds, either coupon or registered, or other evidences of debt, in such a manner and of such form as may be determined by the directors, and to secure such loans, both as to principal and interest, by such mortgages or deeds of trust on the whole of the property and franchises of the company, or any part thereof, as may be deemed advisable. May issue bonds.

Sec. 12. That the company shall have power and authority to appropriate and occupy such land as may be necessary for the construction of said railroad and its branches, of the width of one hunderd feet (100 ft.); that is to say, a right-of-way of fifty (50) feet from each side of the center of said track; and such additional land as may be necessary for station houses, depots, warehouses and other purposes necessary for the construction and operation of said railroad and its branches, and the power of condemnation of same shall be such as is provided under the general laws of North Carolina. Occupation of land. Right-of-way.

Sec. 13. That the townships of Currituck, Swan Quarter and Lake Landing, in the county of Hyde, may subscribe to the capital stock or invest in the first mortgage bonds of this railroad company, to be secured by the joint bonds of each of said townships, bearing not exceeding six per cent. interest, subject to the approval of the qualified voters of said townships. Townships may subscribe to stock.

Sec. 14. That the board of commissioners of Hyde county are authorized, and it shall be their duty, whenever one-fourth of the aggregate of all the qualified voters in said townships shall petition the same, to cause an election to be held in each of said three townships at the legal voting places therein, after at least thirty days' notice of said election, posted at three public places in each township, and to submit to the qualified voters of each of said townships the question of subscribing to the capital stock of the said Pungo and Mattamuskeet Railroad Company, or of loan to said railroad company to be secured by the first mortgage bonds of said company, a sum of money not less than thirty thousand dollars ($30,000.00) and not more than forty thousand dollars ($40,000.00); at such election, those in favor of said subscription to the capital stock or first mortgage bonds shall deposit a ballot on which shall be written or printed the words, "For subscription," and those opposed shall deposit a ballot on which is written or printed the words, "Against subscription," such election to be held in all respects as required by the general law for the election of members of the general assembly, except as are herein otherwise provided. The reports of said election shall be made to the county commissioners on Tuesday next after the day on which the said election is held, who shall Commissioners shall order an election. Maximum amount. Form of ballot.

on that day declare the result of said election and enter the same on their minutes; and if a majority of all the qualified voters in the three several townships shall vote for subscription, then the subscription or loan so authorized shall be made by the said board of county commissioners. That for the purposes of this act, the voters of said three townships shall be considered jointly or in the aggregate and the liability created under the provisions of this act shall be deemed and held to be a joint and not a several liability. The amounts of the bonds to be issued by the said townships, that is to say, as to whether the amount shall be more than thirty thousand dollars ($30,000.00) and not exceeding forty thousand dollars ($40,000.00) or any intermediate sum shall be determined by the said board of county commissioners. The question whether the bonds of said township shall be subscribed to the capital stock of said railroad company or shall be subscribed as a loan to the said company to be secured by its mortgage bonds, shall be determined by said railroad company through its board of directors, which determination shall be made after the election herein provided, and when notice of said action of the said railroad company shall be filed with the clerk of the board of commissioners of Hyde county the said commissioners shall proceed to issue said bonds as authorized for the purpose indicated by the said railroad company. If the said railroad company shall determine that said bonds shall be a subscription to the capital stock of said railroad company, then each of the said townships shall be entitled to be represented in all general meetings of the stockholders, and for this purpose the board of county commissioners shall appoint some suitable person from each township to represent jointly the shares of stock of said townships at the meetings of said company. This appointment shall be evidenced by the certificate of the clerk of the county commissioners, and shall be given for one year and until their successor or successors are appointed; but if the said railroad company shall determine that the bonds aforesaid shall be in the nature of a loan secured by mortgage, as aforesaid, then the said board of county commissioners, through their chairman, shall proceed to issue the said bonds upon the execution of the mortgage by said railroad company as aforesaid.

Joint liability.

Amount of bonds determined by county commissioners.

Townships entitled to vote in general meetings.

Township representatives.

What bonds shall express on face.

Sec. 15. For the payment of any subscription made either to the capital stock or as a loan to the said company as provided in the preceding section, the board of county commissioners of Hyde county shall issue bonds to the amount authorized to be subscribed or loaned, payable to bearer, and the said bonds shall express on their face by what authority and for what purpose they are issued; such bonds shall be coupon bonds of the denomination of not more than one thousand dollars ($1,000.00) or less

Denomination of bonds.

than one hundred dollars ($100.00), and shall bear interest at a rate not exceeding six per cent., the interest payable on the first day of March of each successive year by the treasurer of said company, at some bank in the town of Washington, N. C., to be designated by said treasurer. The said bonds shall be due and payable as follows: one thousand dollars in amount ten years after the first day of March succeeding the year in which said bonds are issued and one thousand dollars on the first day of March in each successive year thereafter: Provided, that the board of commissioners of Hyde county, by giving ninety (90) days' notice thereof preceding the first day of March in any year and making publication of the same in some newspaper published in the state may pay off at the same time as the next installment of interest such bonds and of such an amount as may be named in said publication, payable at the same bank at which the installment of interest is paid. The interest upon said bonds so called in shall thereupon cease and determine after the said first day of March.

Maturity of bonds.

Sec. 16. That to provide for the payment of interest on said bonds, the board of county commissioners shall, in addition to other taxes each year, compute and levy upon the proper subjects of taxation in the townships of Currituck, Swan Quarter and Lake Landing a sufficient tax to pay the interest on said bonds issued as aforesaid, and in order to pay the said bonds as they mature and such other bonds as they may anticipate the payment of, the said commissioners shall, at the expiration of ten years from the date of their issue, annually compute and levy an additional tax of one thousand dollars ($1,000.00) or more, in their discretion, until all their bonds are paid, which taxes shall be collected by the sheriff of Hyde county under the same rules and regulations as are provided for collecting other taxes, and he and his sureties shall be liable to the same penalties and subject to the same remedies as are now prescribed by law for the faithful collecting and paying over all taxes to the state and county. The said taxes when collected shall be paid over to the county treasurer, as other taxes are paid, and the said treasurer and his sureties shall be liable to the same penalties and subject to the same remedies as are now prescribed by law for accounting for and paying out the state and county taxes. The said treasurer shall first pay the interest on said bonds and the coupons be retained as vouchers and evidences of payment, and the balance of money shall be retained in his hands for the purpose of creating a sinking fund for the payment of the principal of the remaining bonds in the order in which they are payable, and the management and control of said sinking fund shall be vested in the said board of county commissioners, provided it shall not be expended for any other purposes.

Special tax may be levied and collected to create a sinking fund.

Additional tax levy.

How collected.

To whom paid.

Bonds, how signed.

Sec. 17. Said bonds shall be signed by the chairman of board of county commissioners and the clerk of the said board, and the coupons shall be signed by the chairman alone.

Township bonds shall not be invalidated.

Sec. 18. The coupons of said bonds shall be receivable for any wise to invalidate the said bonds of the several townships in case the said taxes should for any reason fail to be applied to the payment of the said interest or any part thereof.

Coupons receivable for taxes.

Sec. 18. The coupons of said bonds shall be receivable for taxes under this act and it shall be the duty of the sheriff to receive them when tendered if they are due and payable.

New registration may be ordered.

Sec. 20. That it shall be lawful for the county commissioners at their discretion to order a new registration or said election under the provisions of law.

Purpose of bonds issued.

Sec. 21. That the bonds of the several townships issued under this act shall only be issued for the purpose of constructing a railroad from Makleyville along the route hereinbefore provided, at least as far as Juniper bay.

When bonds shall be issued.

Sec. 22. That if the result of the said election shall be favorable for the issuing of said bonds, then said bonds shall be issued as hereinbefore provided within sixty days after the result of said election as declared by said board of county commissioners. When issued, the bonds, together with all coupons, shall be deposited with some bank or trust company agreed upon by the county commissioners and the said railroad company, to be held in trust by said bank or trust company until satisfactory evidence is produced of the completion of said road from Makleyville, along the route hereinbefore provided, at least as far as Juniper bay, whereupon their bonds and coupons shall be delivered to the president of said railroad company or to such person as may be designated by said railroad company, and upon such delivery the said railroad company shall issue its certificates of stock or its own bonds secured by first mortgages, dependent upon whether the said township bonds are issued in subscribing to the said capital stock, or as a loan to said railroad company, as hereinbefore provided. That when the said bonds are issued they, with the coupons attached, shall be numbered and a record kept by the clerk of the board of commissioners of Hyde county, showing the numbers, amounts and dates of maturity of the same respectively.

Bonds, how deposited.

Company shall issue certificates of stock for bonds.

Townships making subscriptions shall be considered as acting jointly.

Sec. 23. That for the purpose of this act, the townships which shall make said subscriptions or loan shall be deemed and considered as acting jointly and not severally, both in the matter of the election and in their liability for the bonds issued hereunder, and each of said townships are hereby created bodies politic and corporate, with power to carry out the provisions of this act, and the county commissioners of Hyde county are declared to be for all purposes corporate agents of the said townships.

Sec. 24. That this company shall have the right to dispose of, negotiate or sell these bonds secured by mortgage on the whole or any part of its franchise and property upon such terms as the president and directors shall deem most advantageous to the company. Company may dispose of bonds.

Sec. 25. That any officer failing and refusing to perform his duties under this act shall be guilty of a misdemeanor. Officers failing to perform duty guilty of a misdemeanor.

Sec. 26. That the railroad authorized by this act shall be commenced within four years from the date of the ratification of this act.

Sec. 27. That this act shall be in force from and after its ratification. When road shall be commenced.

Ratified the 6th day of March, A. D. 1899.

CHAPTER 309.

An act to renew and amend the charter of the town of Gatesville.

The General Assembly of North Carolina do enact:

Section 1. That the act of incorporation, chapter two hundred and three, laws of eighteen hundred and seventy-seven, be and the same is hereby declared to be in full force and effect, except as the same may be modified by this act. Chapter 203, laws of 1877, in full force except as herein modified.

Sec. 2. That the corporate limits be and the same are hereby extended on the west by a line running parallel with the present western boundary line and three hundred (300) yards therefrom. Corporate limits.

Sec. 3. That until the next regular election for cities and towns, on the first Monday of May, eighteen hundred and ninety-nine, the following persons shall constitute the officers of the town of Gatesville, to-wit: T. W. Coster, Jr., mayor; Lycurgus Hofler, R. M. Reddick and L. L. Smith, commissioners; and Toney Felton, constable. Temporary officers.

Sec. 4. That it shall be unlawful for any person to retail spirituous, vinous or malt liquors within the corporate limits of the town or within one mile thereof; and the officers of the said town, together with the usual powers conferred by chapter sixty-two of The Code, shall have full power to prevent the sale within the corporate limits of all kinds of intoxicants, etc., including ale, beer, wine and cider. Sale of liquors prohibited.

Sec. 5. That this act shall be in full force and effect from and after its ratification.

Ratified the 6th day of March, A. D. 1899.

CHAPTER 310.

An act entitled an act to incorporate the Peoples Savings Bank at Asheville, North Carolina.

The General Assembly of North Carolina do enact:

Corporators. Section 1. That Erwin Sluder, E. R. Lucas and J. W. Norwood, their associates, successors and assigns, are hereby constituted Body corporate. and declared a body politic and corporate by the name and style Corporate name of the Peoples Savings Bank, with its principal place of business Place of business. in the city of Asheville, and by that name may sue and be sued, plead and be impleaded in any court of the state, and have a continual succession for the term of ninety years, with all the rights, powers and privileges of corporations and banks under the general laws of the state.

Capital stock. Sec. 2. The capital stock of said corporation shall not be less than twenty-five thousand dollars, in shares of fifty dollars each, and such capital stock may be increased from time to time as said corporation may elect, to a sum not exceeding five hundred thousand dollars.

Books of subscription may be opened. Sec. 3. The corporators named in the first section, or a majority of them, are hereby empowered to open books of subscription to the capital stock of said corporation at such time or times, at such places and for such periods as they shall determine, and the stockholders at any general meeting called after the organization of said corporation may at their discretion from time to time reopen books of subscription to said capital stock until the same as herein limited be wholly taken.

When company may be organized. Sec. 4. Whenever twenty-five thousand dollars shall be subscribed and paid into the capital stock of said corporation, the above-named corporation or a majority of them shall call a meeting of the subscribers to said stock at such time and place and on such notice as they may deem sufficient to organize said corporation; and said stockholders shall elect such directors as they may think proper, who shall hold office for one year, until their successors shall be chosen, and said directors shall elect a president to serve during their continuance in office; and said corporation, at the time of its organization, or at any general meeting held thereafter, may, by a majority of the votes cast, change the name of the corporation to the "Asheville Savings and Trust Company."

Seal. Sec. 5. The president and directors of said corporation may adopt and use a common seal, and alter the same at pleasure; Appointment of officers. may make and appoint all necessary officers and agents and fix their compensation; shall exercise and have all such powers and authority as may be necessary for governing the affairs of said corporation, and shall prescribe the rules for the conduct of said corporation consistent with the by-laws established by the stockholders; they may regulate the terms and rates on which discounts and loans may be made and deposits received, and when dividends of the profits and the amount thereof shall be made and declared; and fill all vacancies occurring in their own body and among the officers and agents of said corporation. They may call meetings of the stockholders whenever they think proper, and at all meetings the stockholders may be represented by proxy, and each share shall be entitled to one vote.

Corporate powers.

Vacancies occurring.

Sec. 6. The said corporation may receive and pay out the lawful currency of the country, deal in exchange, gold and silver coin, uncurrent paper, and public and other securities; may loan money to and receive deposits of money or other property or evidences of debt from corporations, minors, feme coverts or other persons, on such terms and time and manner of collection and payment as may be agreed upon, and for the use and loan of money may charge so high a rate of interest as is or may be allowed by the laws of the state of North Carolina and may take and receive said interest at the time of making said loan; may invest in the stock, bonds or other securities of the United States, of this or any other state in the Union [or] of any corporation under the laws thereof, and take such real or personal property as security for all loans and upon such terms as may be agreed upon.

Corporate powers.

Rate of interest.

May invest in other securities.

Sec. 7. The said corporation may purchase and hold all such real and personal property as may be necessary for its own business purpose, and such as may be conveyed to it, to secure or satisfy any debt due to it or for any other purpose, and such as may be sold under a foreclosure of any mortgage made to said corporation, or sold under an execution or order of any court to satisfy any debt due it, and may sell and convey or exchange the same at pleasure, and use or reinvest the proceeds thereof as may be deemed best.

May purchase and hold real estate.

Sec. 8. That when any deposit shall be made by any person being a minor or feme covert, the said corporation may at its discretion pay to such minor or feme covert such sums as may be due to him or her, and the receipt or acquittance of such minor or feme covert shall be to all interests and purposes valid in law to fully discharge the said corporation from any or all liabilities on account thereof.

Deposits by minors and feme coverts.

Sec. 9. That the said company be and is hereby authorized and empowered to receive and keep on deposit all such valuables, gold, silver or paper money, bullion, precious metals, jewels, plate, certificates of stocks, bonds or other evidences of indebtedness, instruments of title or other valuable papers of any kind, or any other article or thing whatsoever which may be left on deposit for safe keeping with said company, and shall be entitled

Authorized to receive and keep moneys on deposit.

Charges for compensation.

to charge such commissions or compensation therefor as may be agreed upon, and for the complete preservation and safe keeping thereof, may construct, erect or purchase such fire and burglar-proof buildings, vaults, safes or other means which may be or become necessary, and generally to transact and perform all business relating to such deposit and safe keeping or preservation of all such articles or valuables as may be deposited with said company; and also to invest the capital stock or funds of said company or such money or funds as may be deposited with said company for that purpose from time to time in the stocks, bonds or other securities of the United States or of this or any other state of the United States or any corporation under the laws thereof, or in any other stock or property whatsoever, and to dispose of the same in such manner as may appear to said company most advantageous.

May accept and exercise trusts of any description.

Sec. 10. That the said company be and is hereby authorized and empowered to accept and exercise any trust of any and every other description which may with its consent be committed or transferred to it by any person or persons whomsoever, by any bodies corporate or public, or by any court of the state of North Carolina or of the United States, or of any one of the states of the United States, and to accept the appointment and office of executor, administrator or trustee or assignee of any kind or nature, whenever such office or appointment is made or conferred by any person or persons or by any court of competent jurisdiction of this state or of any one of the United States, and in all such cases where application shall be made to any court for the appointment of any receiver, trustee, administrator, assignee, guardian of any minor or committee of a lunatic, it shall and may be lawful for such court to appoint the said company, with its assent, such receiver, trustee, administrator, assignee, guardian or committee, and where any person shall appoint the said company the executor of his or her will, or any court shall appoint the said company a receiver, trustee, administrator, assignee, guardian or committee, or shall order the deposit of any money with said company (the capital stock as paid in shall be taken and considered as the security required by law for the faithful performance of the said duties as such executor, administrator, trustee, assignee, guardian or committee, and shall be absolutely liable for any default; and in addition thereto) the court may require the said company to give such other and additional security as it may judge to be expedient, and the court may, if deemed necessary, examine the officers of the company under oath or affirmation as to the sufficiency of its capital stock on such security. The accounts of said company as such receiver, trustee, executor, administrator, assignee, guardian or committee

Guardians of minors, etc.

Courts may appoint said company receiver, etc,

Liable for default.

Accounts shall be regularly settled.

shall be regularly adjusted and settled before such court or officer as shall have jurisdiction thereof, which said court or officer shall, upon such adjustment and settlement being made, allow to said company all proper and legal and customary costs, charges, expenses and commissions for its care and management of the trusts and estates aforesaid, and shall charge the said company with interest not exceeding six per centum per annum, wherever the said company shall be liable for or chargeable with interest as such receiver, trustee, executor, administrator, assignee, guardian or committee, or upon money deposited therewith as aforesaid. The said company as such receiver, trustee, executor, administrator, assignee, guardian or committee shall be subject to all lawful orders and decrees made by the proper tribunal under the laws of this state.

Subject to certain orders and decrees.

Sec. 11. Any receiver, executor, administrator, assignee, guardian or committee of a lunatic, and any public officer, is hereby authorized to deposit with the said company for safe keeping any money or bonds, stocks, securities or other valuables which have or may come into his possession or under his control by virtue of his said office or appointment aforesaid: Provided, that the stockholders of this bank shall be held individually responsible equally and ratably and not one for another for all contracts, debts and agreements of this association to the extent of the amounts of their stock therein at the par value thereof in addition to the amount invested in such share.

Receivers, executors, etc., ordered to deposit moneys with said corporation.

Proviso.

Individual liability.

Sec. 12. All laws and clauses of laws in conflict with this act are hereby repealed.

Conflicting laws repealed.

Sec. 13. That this act shall be in force from and after its ratification.

Ratified the 6th day of March, A. D. 1899.

CHAPTER 311.

An act to amend the charter of the town of Hobgood, in Halifax county.

The General Assembly of North Carolina do enact:

Section 1. That section two, chapter one hundred and sixty of the laws of eighteen hundred and ninety-one, be amended so as to embrace the following boundaries: Beginning at the center of the junction of the Norfolk and Carolina and Scotland Neck Branch Railroad; thence along the Scotland Neck Branch Railroad nearly east two hundred and seventy yards; thence nearly south and parallel to and with the Norfolk and Carolina Rail-

Section 2, chapter 160, laws of 1891, amended.

Corporate limits extended.

road two hundred and fifty yards to a stake; thence at right angle two hundred and fifty yards to the Norfolk and Carolina Railroad; thence along the Norfolk and Carolina Railroad four hundred and fifty yards; thence at right angles with said line nearly west three hundred and twenty-five yards to a stake; thence nearly north and parallel to and with the Norfolk and Carolina Railroad nine hundred and seventy yards to a stake; thence nearly east and at right angle to and with said line three hundred and twenty-five yards to the beginning.

Ratified the 6th day of March, A. D. 1899.

CHAPTER 312.

An act to authorize the city of Asheville to issue bonds to refund its debt.

The General Assembly of North Carolina do enact:

Mayor and aldermen authorized to order election.

Section 1. That the mayor and board of aldermen of the city of Asheville at any time within two years after the ratification of this act at any election held for that purpose as hereinafter provided, be and they are hereby authorized and empowered to issue coupon bonds in the name of the city of Asheville in such denomination and form as the said mayor and board of aldermen may determine to an amount not exceeding eight hundred thousand dollars ($800,000), and for the purposes hereinafter specified, which bonds are to bear interest from their date at a rate not exceeding four per centum per annum, payable semi-annually, and be payable at such time or times and place or places as the said mayor and board of aldermen shall determine: Provided, that the time of payment of said bonds shall not be fixed at less than twenty nor more than fifty years from their date; that the said bonds shall be signed by the mayor of said city, attested by the city clerk, and under the corporate seal of said city, and the interest upon said bonds shall be evidenced by interest coupons thereto attached in the usual form; and said bonds when issued and the interest accumulating thereon shall be fully binding upon said city and its property.

Purpose of election.

Amount of bonds.

Proviso.

Maturity of bonds.

Interest on bonds.

Aldermen authorized to arrange for surrender of outstanding bonds.

Sec. 2. That said mayor and board of aldermen are hereby authorized and directed to arrange with the owners and holders of the outstanding bonds of said city as soon as practicable, to surrender the bonds or any portion thereof held by them upon the receipt by them of the par value of such bonds with the interest due thereon in money, or to exchange or surrender the said bonds held by them, or any portion thereof, for like amounts of the bonds authorized by this act, and upon perfecting such arrangement or agreement with said bondholders or any of them, said mayor and board of aldermen are directed to carry the same into effect by exchanging said bonds or any portion thereof for a like amount of said outstanding bonds or by selling the bonds authorized by this act or any portion thereof at a price not less than their par value and apply such amount of the proceeds of the sale of such bonds as may be necessary exclusively and only to the purpose of paying off and taking up the outstanding bonds of said city, and the amount of said bonds necessary to pay off the said outstanding bonds of said city shall be used for no other purpose than that above specified, and the balance of said bonds over and above what may be necessary to be used to pay off or take up said outstanding bonds at par may be by the said mayor and board of aldermen sold from time to time at a price not less than their par value for the purpose of funding or paying off any other indebtedness of the said city of Asheville and for no other purpose; but the purchaser or purchasers of said bonds or any of them shall not be bound to see to the application of the purchase-money paid therefor; that whenever any of the present bonds of said city shall be exchanged for the bonds hereby authorized to be issued or paid off by any of the proceeds of the sale of said bonds, the said bonds so exchanged or paid off shall not again be issued or sold, but shall thereafter be null and void, and shall be cancelled and destroyed by said mayor and board of aldermen.

Proceeds from said bonds applied only for purpose specified.

Sec. 3. That the mayor and board of aldermen of the city of Asheville, upon the issuing of said bonds, shall be authorized and empowered to levy and collect a tax annually upon all subjects of taxation which are now or may hereafter be embraced in the subjects of taxation under the charter of said city sufficient to meet the interest on said bonds, and pay the principal thereof when they shall become due and payable, and said taxes shall be collected in like manner as the other taxes of said city and paid into the hands of the treasurer thereof for the purposes aforesaid.

Mayor and aldermen empowered to levy special tax.

To meet interest and principal.

Sec. 4. That said bonds shall not be issued nor said taxes levied until authorized by vote of a majority of the qualified voters of the said city at a public election to be held in the same manner as elections are or may hereafter be held in said city for the election of mayor and aldermen thereof, and at such election those who favor the issuing of said bonds and levying the taxes herein provided for shall vote ballots with the word "Approved" written or printed thereon, and those opposed to issuing said bonds shall vote ballots with the words "Not approved" written or printed thereon; and if at any such election a majority of the qualified voters of said city shall vote ballots with the word

Bonds shall be authorized by a majority of voters.

Form of ballot.

"Approved" written or printed thereon, then the said mayor and board of aldermen shall issue said bonds and levy a tax sufficient to meet interest and principal thereof when due, as hereinbefore specified.

Election, when held.

The first election under this act shall be held at the next general election for mayor and aldermen of said city; and if at such election a majority of the qualified voters of said city shall not vote in favor of issuing said bonds, then the mayor and board of aldermen of said city shall at any time, and as often thereafter as they deem best, upon the petition of one-fourth of the qualified voters of the said city, order an election to be held under the rules and regulations prescribed by law for the election of mayor and aldermen of said city, and after thirty days' public notice thereof and at each of such elections the ballots shall be as hereinbefore directed; and if at any such election the majority of the qualified voters of said city shall cast ballots in favor of the issuing of said bonds as aforesaid, then the said bonds shall be issued by said mayor and board of aldermen, to be applied to the purposes and upon the terms and conditions hereinbefore stated in this act.

Succeeding elections may be held.

Sec. 5. That this act shall be in force from and after its ratification.

Ratified the 6th day of March, A. D. 1899.

CHAPTER 313.

An act to authorize the commissioners of the town of Davidson, in the county of Mecklenburg, to issue bonds to improve the streets and sidewalks of said town, and to construct waterworks.

The General Assembly of North Carolina do enact:

Commissioners of Davidson authorized to issue coupon bonds for waterworks, etc.

Section 1. That for the purpose of macadamizing and otherwise improving the public streets and sidewalks of the town of Davidson, and if practicable for the further purpose of constructing waterworks in said town, the board of commissioners of said town are hereby authorized to issue coupon bonds for such purposes: Provided, that the whole bonded indebtedness of said town so issued for the purpose of this act shall not exceed six thousand dollars.

Proviso.

Limitation to bond issue.

Denomination of bonds

Sec. 2. That said bonds shall be in such form and in such denominations, and shall be payable at such times, and shall bear such rate of interest, not exceeding six per centum per annum, payable semi-annually, as the said board may determine: Provided, that no debt shall be created and no bonds issued under this act unless the board shall have first passed an ordinance by a majority of the whole board taken and recorded at a regular meeting of the said board, submitting the question of creating the debt and issuing the bonds to a vote of the people of the said town, and a majority of the qualified voters at said election have voted in favor thereof.

Question shall be submitted to voters.

Sec. 3. That notice of such election shall be given by said commissioners in some newspaper published in the county of Mecklenburg at least once a week for four successive weeks next preceding the day of election, in which notice shall be stated the time and place fixed for such election. At such election those who favor creating the debt and issuing bonds shall vote on a written or printed ballot "Approved," and those who oppose it shall vote on a like ballot "Not approved."

Notice of election shall be given.

Form of ballot.

Sec. 4. That such election shall be held as other elections for officers of the said town are held, and it shall be the duty of the judges of such elections to make returns, showing the result of the said election to the board of commissioners of the said town.

Election, how held.

Sec. 5. That for the purpose of providing for the payment of the interest on the said bonds, as well as for the payment of the principal thereof at maturity, the commissioners of the said town shall annually, at the time of levying the other town taxes, levy a special tax on all subjects of taxation, which said commissioners now or hereafter may be allowed to levy taxes upon for any purposes whatsoever, sufficient to pay the interest on said bonds, as well as to create a sinking fund for the payment of the principal thereof at maturity.

Annual special tax may be levied to pay interest and principal.

Sec. 6. That at the election held under this act, should a majority of the voters vote not to create the indebtedness herein provided for, the said commissioners may again submit the proposition to the voters of the town of Davidson at any succeeding election; and should a majority of the said voters at such election vote in favor of creating the said debt and issuing the said bonds, the commissioners of the said town may issue the said bonds in as full and ample a manner as if the same had been authorized by a majority vote had at the first election under this act.

Succeeding elections may be held.

Sec. 7. That this act shall be in force from and after its ratification.

Ratified the 6th day of March, A. D. 1899.

CHAPTER 314.

An act to amend the charter of the town of North Wilkesboro, chapter one hundred and ninety-eight, private laws of eighteen hundred and ninety-one.

The General Assembly of North Carolina do enact:

tion 3, chapter private laws 891, amended.

Section 1. That section three of said act shall be amended as follows, viz: After the word "treasurer" in the last line thereof add the words "town constable."

tion 4, chapter laws of 1891, ended.

Sec. 2. That section four of said act [be] and the same is hereby repealed and the following put in the place thereof, viz: That there shall be an election for mayor and five commissioners on the first Tuesday in May, in the year eighteen hundred and ninety nine, and every year thereafter, under the same restrictions and regulations that state and county elections are held, with this proviso: That at their first meeting in March each year the town commissioners shall appoint one registrar and two judges of election, who are to hold said election; and the result shall be declared by the mayor of said town.

nual election town officers

·tion 10 ended.

Sec. 3. That section ten of said act shall be amended as follows: That in line five of said section the word "ten" shall be substituted in place of the word "twenty."

tion 16 ended.

Sec. 4. That section sixteen of said act shall be amended by striking out the words "not exceeding" in line five thereof and inserting between the word "dollar" and the word "and" in line six the following, viz: "To be paid quarterly in advance to the town treasurer without compensation to the tax collector"; and by adding at the end of said section the following words: "Upon every express company doing business in said town a tax of twenty-five dollars per annum, and upon every telegraph company a tax of ten dollars per annum."

x on express d telegraph mpanies.

ction 17 ended.

Sec. 5. That section seventeen of said act be amended as follows: "That all license taxes shall be applied toward keeping in repair the streets of said town instead of being applied to the support of the schools."

Sec. 6. That this act shall be in force from and after its ratification.

Ratified the 6th day of March, A. D. 1899.

CHAPTER 315.

An act to change the name of "Falls Manufacturing Company."

The General Assembly of North Carolina do enact:

Section 1. That section one of chapter one hundred and ninety-six of the laws of eighteen hundred and ninety-one be and the same is hereby amended by striking out the words "Falls Manufacturing Company" in line six of said section and inserting in place thereof the words "Neuse River Milling Company." **Section 1, chapter 196, laws of 1891, amended.**

Sec. 2. That the incorporators and subscribers to the capital stock of said Falls Manufacturing Company are hereby granted two years from the date of the ratification of this act to reorganize and begin work, under the provisions of this act. **Time in which to begin work.**

Sec. 3. That this act shall be in force from and after its ratification.

Ratified the 6th day of March, A. D. 1899.

CHAPTER 316.

An act to incorporate "The Merchants and Farmers Bank of Dunn."

The General Assembly of North Carolina do enact:

Section 1. That W. A. Erwin, F. L. Fuller, E. F. Young, M. T. Young, V. L. Stephens, D. H. McLean and their associates and successors be and they are hereby constituted and declared to be a body politic and corporate under the name and style of "The Merchants and Farmers Bank of Dunn," shall not continue for a period of sixty years, and under such name may acquire, hold and convey real and personal estate, may sue and be sued, plead and be impleaded in any of the courts of this state or elsewhere; may make by-laws and regulations for its own government and the due and orderly conducting of its affairs and the management of its property: Provided, the same be not inconsistent with the laws of this state or of the United States; and may conduct, transact and carry on in its full scope and import a general banking business, with all the rights, powers and privileges and immunities hereby specially granted, and those contained in chapter four, volume two, of The Code of North Carolina, entitled "Banks," as well as in the constitution and laws of this state as now existing. **Corporators. Body corporate. Corporate name. Duration of charter. Corporate powers.**

Sec. 2. That the capital stock of said corporation shall be not less than ten thousand dollars, in shares of one hundred dollars each, and said capital stock may be increased at any time or **Capital stock may be increased.**

from time to time as said corporation may elect, to any sum not exceeding five hundred thousand dollars.

Books of subscription may be opened.

SEC. 3. That the incorporators in the first section named or a majority of them are hereby authorized and empowered to open or cause to be opened books of subscription to the capital stock of said corporation at such time or times, at such place or places, and for such periods as they may deem proper; and the stockholders at any general meeting called after the due organization of said corporation may, in their discretion from time to time, re-open books of subscription to the capital stock of said corporation until the same as herein limited shall be taken.

When company may be organized.

SEC. 4. That when ten thousand dollars shall be subscribed to the capital stock of said corporation and fifty per centum of that amount shall be paid to two commissioners, who shall be appointed by the above-named incorporators or a majority of them, shall call a meeting of the subscribers to said capital stock at such time and place and upon such notice as they may deem sufficient; and said stockholders shall elect such directors as they may see proper to elect, not exceeding five, who shall hold office for one year and until their successors shall be elected and qualified; and said directors shall elect at their first meeting and annually thereafter, one of their number president of the bank, and fix his compensation and prescribe his duties, and he shall be ex-officio chairman of the board of directors; whereupon said bank may commence the transaction of its business.

Election of directors.

Election of president.

Seal.

SEC. 5. That the president and directors of said bank may adopt and use a common seal and alter the same at pleasure; may appoint all necessary officers, fix their compensation and take security for the faithful discharge of their duties; prescribe the manner of paying for stock and the transfer thereof; may do [a] general banking business on such terms and rates of discount and interest as may [be] agreed on, not inconsistent with the laws of this state or of the United States. The bank shall have a lien on stock for debts due it by the stockholders in preference to the claims of all other creditors of equal dignity.

Compensation of officers.

Corporate powers.

SEC. 6. That said bank may pay out and receive the lawful currency of the country, deal in exchange, gold and silver coin, bullion, current paper and public and other securities; may purchase and hold such personal and real estate and property as may be conveyed to secure debts to the bank, or may be sold under execution to satisfy any debt due the bank, and may sell and convey the same at pleasure; may purchase and hold real estate for the transaction of business, and at pleasure sell or exchange the same; may discount notes and other evidences of debt, and may lend money on such terms as may be agreed on not inconsistent with the laws of this state or of the United States. It may

May purchase and hold real estate.

receive on deposit money on terms such as may be agreed on by the officers and depositors, and issue certificates of said deposits, which certificates may be assignable and transferable under such regulations as may be prescribed by the president and directors; all such certificates signed by the proper officers of the bank shall be as binding as if under the seal of said bank.

Empowered to make loans upon mortgage of real estate.

Sec. 7. That said bank shall have power to make loans upon mortgage of real estates and personal property, or upon liens upon crops planted or unplanted, [with] power of sale inserted upon default in payment; to advance or loan any farmer, planter, manufacturer or other person or persons any sum or sums of money, and to secure the payment of the same by taking in writing a lien upon the prospective products of any manufacturing operations or upon any article then existing or thereafter to be made, purchased, manufactured or acquired, and lien so taken shall be good and effectual in law, provided the same shall be duly recorded under the existing laws of registration; and said bank shall have power to receive in storage or warehouse any cotton, spirits of turpentine, wheat, corn or any other produce, or any manufactured articles whatsoever, as a pledge or pledges for the repayment of money loaned upon the faith of the same, and said liens, pledges or mortgages being duly recorded as in the case of mortgages and deeds of trust made under the general law, and any sales made thereunder according to the terms therein recited shall be good and valid in law: Provided, that nothing contained in this act shall be construed to authorize the taking or receiving a greater rate of interest than the legal rate.

Failure of subscriber to pay stock.

Sec. 8. That if any subscriber shall fail to pay for his stock or any part thereof as the same may be required of him, the entire residue of his stock shall be deemed due, and may be recovered in the name of the bank either by motion in the superior court of the county wherein the delinquent resides, upon giving him ten days' notice of the motion, or by civil action in said court, or the entire stock may be sold by order of the board of directors for cash at the banking house in Dunn, North Carolina, after advertising said sale for thirty days in a newspaper published in Harnett county or in North Carolina; and if at such sale the price should not be sufficient to discharge the amount unpaid, with all costs attending the sale, the subscribers shall be liable for the deficiency in the [a] civil action.

Stock may be sold.

Subscribers liable for deficiency.

Assignment of stock not paid for, liability.

Sec. 9 That if a subscriber shall assign his stock before paying for the same in full, he and his assignees, and all subsequent assignees thereof, shall be liable for its payment, and may be sued jointly or severally by motion as aforesaid or by civil action. And in every case of a delinquency in a subscriber or other person, the subsciption shall be deemed a promissory note, payable to the bank, as well in respect to the remedy for recovering the same as in the distribution of the assets of any deceased subscriber.

Individual liability.

Sec. 10. That the stockholders of said bank shall be liable individually, equally and ratably, and not for one another, for all contracts, debts and agreements of said bank to the extent of the amount of their stock therein at the par value thereof in addition to the amount invested in such stock.

Deposits by minors and feme coverts.

Sec. 11. That when married women or minors deposit money or other property in said bank to their own credit, they may withdraw the same on their own order or check and be bound thereby, and such individual check or order of such minor or married women shall be valid and sufficient release and receipt to said bank against themselves and all other persons.

Powers of president and directors.

Sec. 12. That the president and directors shall be capable of exercising all such powers and authority as may be necessary for the better government of the affairs of said bank; shall have power to prescribe rules for the conduct of said bank, the same being consistent with the by-laws, rules and regulations established by the stockholders; may regulate the terms and rates on which discounts and loans may be made and deposits received by said bank, and shall direct when dividends of profit shall be declared. They may call a meeting of the stockholders whenever they may think proper, and any number of stockholders owning and holding one-fifth of the stock may call a special meeting by serving a personal notice, and twenty days' notice in some newspaper circulated in said county, on a majority of the other stockholders. At all meetings stockholders may be represented by proxy, each share being entitled to one vote.

Special meetings

Authorized to organize a savings bank.

Sec. 13. That said bank is authorized to organize in connection with its general banking business a department for savings, and to do a savings-bank business for the convenience of small depositors, and to make such regulations in regard thereto not inconsistent with the laws of this state or of the United States as will enable said bank to receive small deposits in savings department, not less than fifty cents in any single case, and to give certificates or other evidences of deposit, and to pay such interest as may be agreed on, not exceeding the legal rate, and to regulate the time of payment and notice of demand. But the said limit of deposit shall apply only to the savings department and not to the general business of the bank.

Charter not forfeited by non-use.

Sec. 14. The powers and privileges granted herein shall not be deemed forfeited by non use: Provided, the corporation is organized within five years from date of ratification of this act.

Sec. 15. That said corporation shall have power to negotiate loans on mortgages of real or personal estate at a rate of interest not exceeding the legal rate, and to charge and receive from the lender or borrower, or either of them, a reasonable commission therefor.

Empowered to negotiate loans, etc.

Sec. 16. That the stockholders shall be authorized to change the name of said bank and the name and title of the corporation hereby created, and in case of such change of name, the new body politic and corporate shall succeed to all the rights, powers, property, privileges and liabilities conferred by this act upon the corporation hereby created.

Name of bank may be changed.

Sec. 17. That said bank may receive and pay out all lawful currency of its own issue under all rights, powers and authority and under such instructions as may be imposed by the laws of this state and of the United States as to circulation by state banks; may deal in exchange, gold and silver coin, current and uncurrent paper, public, municipal and other securities; and for the purpose of aiding planters, farmers, manufacturers and others, said bank shall and may have power to loan any sum or sums of money and to secure the payment of the same by taking in writing lien or liens upon the crops to be raised, either then planted or to be planted in the future, or upon any article or articles then in existence, and shall have power to make loans upon mortgages and deeds in trust of real and personal property, with power of sale inserted upon default of payment said bank shall also have power to receive in storage or warehouse any cotton, tobacco, wheat, corn, peanuts, potatoes, oats or any other article of produce, trade or manufacture as a pledge or pledges for the payment of money or moneys loaned upon the faith of the same so due or advanced thereon, and upon failure to pay at the time agreed upon said property may be sold after the same advertisement as required for sale of personal property under chattel mortgage. Said bank may discount notes or other evidence of debt, buy or sell or otherwise deal in all commercial paper of every kind; may loan money to and receive deposits of the same from any and all persons, including corporations, minors, feme coverts, upon such terms and the manner and time of collection and payment as may be agreed upon, and may charge such rate of interest as allowed by the laws of the state, and may take and receive such interest at the time of making such loan or at such time as may be agreed upon. Said bank may invest in stocks, bonds or other securities of this state, the United States or any corporation, public or private, of this or any other state in the Union, and may issue its own bonds in such denominations, payable at such time and manner as it may see fit.

Corporate powers.

Nature of business.

Property may be sold in default of payments.

Sec. 18. That whenever any deposit shall be made by any minor or feme covert to said corporation, it may at its discretion pay

Deposits by minors and feme coverts.

such minor or feme covert such sum or sums as may be required by them from such deposits; and any check, draft, order, receipt or acquittance of such minor or feme covert shall be to all intents and purposes valid in law to discharge the said corporation from any and all liability on account thereof.

Corporation authorized to receive deposits.

Sec. 19. That said corporation is hereby authorized to receive on deposit all valuables, gold, silver, precious metals, jewels, certificates of stock, bonds, evidence of debt, instruments of title, and all other things of value which may be left on deposit with said corporation for safe keeping, and shall be entitled to charge such commission or compensation as may be agreed upon, and that said bank is authorized and empowered to accept and exercise any trust of any and every other description which may by its consent be committed or transferred to it by any person or persons whomsoever, by any bodies, politic or corporate, public or private, and to accept the office of executor, administrator, collector, guardian or assignee whenever such appointment is made or conferred by any person or persons or court of the state or United States, and shall be clothed with the same power and shall be under the same restrictions as private individuals in the same capacity.

Location of bank.

Sec. 20. That said bank shall be located [at] Dunn, North Carolina.

Sec. 21. That this act shall be in force and effect from and after its ratification.

Ratified the 6th day of March, A. D. 1899.

CHAPTER 317.

An act to amend chapter eighty-five of private laws of eighteen hundred and ninety-one.

The General Assembly of North Carolina do enact:

Section 1, chapter 85, private laws 1891, amended.

Section 1. That section one of chapter eighty-five of the private laws of eighteen hundred and ninety-one be amended by striking out in lines five and six of said section the words, "The Enterprise Land and Improvement Company of Cumberland county, North Carolina," and inserting in lieu thereof the words "Atlantic and Western Railroad Company."

Section 2 amended.

Sec. 2. That section two of said chapter be amended by striking out in line three of said section the word "one" and inserting in lieu thereof the word "five."

Empowered to cross certain railroads.

Sec. 3. That section six of said chapter be amended by adding to said section the words "and the said Atlantic and Western

Railroad Company shall have the right to cross the Raleigh and Augusta Air Line Railroad with its track sixteen feet above the track of said Raleigh and Augusta Air Line Railroad, so as to reach the mills of said Atlantic and Western Railroad Company."

Sec. 4. That this act shall be in force from and after its ratification.

Ratified the 6th day of March, A. D. 1899.

CHAPTER 318.

An act to incorporate the Excelsior Electric Light, Waterworks and Power Company.

The General Assembly of North Carolina do enact:

Section 1. That B. L. Davis, R. J. Cobb, C. T. Munford and J. L. Little, of the county of Pitt, and their associates, successors and assigns, are hereby created a body politic and corporate under the name and style of the "Excelsior Electric Light, Waterworks and Power Company," and by such name and title shall have perpetual succession, with all the rights, powers and privileges granted to corporations by chapter sixteen of The Code, entitled "Corporations." **Corporators.** **Corporate name.**

Sec. 2. That the capital stock of said corporation shall be ten thousand dollars, divided into shares of twenty-five dollars each; and said corporation shall have power to increase its capital stock from time to time to a sum not exceeding one hundred thousand dollars when so authorized by a majority vote of the stockholders. **Capital stock.** **May be increased.**

Sec. 3. That said corporation shall have power and authority to establish, construct and at all times maintain in or near the town of Greenville a system of waterworks and an electric light and power plant for the purpose of supplying the said town, its inhabitants and others with water and electric lights and motive power for all public and private uses and purposes for which they may be desired, and to charge, demand and collect such reasonable rates for the use of water, electric lights and of said motive power. And to this end said corporation shall have power and authority to borrow money, to make, negotiate and dispose of its promissory notes, bills and bonds, with or without coupon interest notes attached, to mortgage any or all of its property and franchise to secure the payment thereof. **Nature of business and operations.** **Rate of charges, etc.**

Sec. 4. That said corporation shall at all times have power and authority to lay, build, construct, maintain and repair, tap and remove all necessary pipes, mains, conductors, stand-pipes, hy- **Empowered to construct mains, pipes, etc.**

drants, fixtures and appurtenances in, upon, through and over any and all roads, streets, avenues, lanes, alleys and bridges within the said town and its vicinity; and also to dig any and all kind of wells, artesian or otherwise, that may be desirable for getting said water supply or establishing said electric light and motive power plants: Provided, however, it shall at its own expense and cost repair, replace and restore all streets, roads, avenues, etc., so used by it, and leave in as good condition as they were before such use. And said corporation, its officers, agents and servants may enter upon the land of any person or corporation for the above purposes, and may contract for and purchase the same: and in case any agreement can not be made between the corporation and the owner of the land or the person entitled to the beneficial interest therein, this corporation may have the same condemned to its use in the manner now provided for the condemnation of land for town purposes by the charter of said town of Greenville, and upon the same terms; and in case said land lies without the town of Greenville, then said land shall be condemned for the use of said corporation in the manner now provided by law for the condemnation of land for railroad or other public uses: Provided always, that said corporation shall pay all damages that may occur or be incurred by reason of the condemnation of land. And it shall at all times have the right to enter upon said lands for the purpose of repairing, improving or replacing said pipes, wells, electric light and motive power, fixtures, appliances, wires, lamps, poles, etc., and also the right to enter at all proper hours into the stores, hotels, dwellings or other premises where said waterworks and electric light and motive power, fixtures, pipes, wires, lamps, etc., are located for the purpose of repairing, removing or replacing the same.

Proviso. Shall repair streets, etc. Land may be condemned. Proviso. May enter upon lands for certain purposes.

Persons injuring property belonging to said company guilty of a misdemeanor.

Sec. 5. Any person who shall willfully, wantonly or maliciously tap, remove, injure, deface or destroy any main, pipe, fire plug, wire, pole, hydrant, standpipe, tank, well, reservoir, aqueduct, pump, fixtures, machinery, structure or building of any kind belonging to said corporation and used by them for the purposes aforesaid, or who shall open, use or tamper with any fire plug or hydrant, electric wire, pole, lamp or apparatus belonging or appertaining to the works of said corporation, shall be guilty of a misdemeanor, and upon conviction shall be fined not exceeding fifty dollars or imprisoned not more than thirty days; and such person or persons shall also forfeit and pay to said corporation, to be sued for and recovered in an action of debt, the damages so sustained.

Penalty.

May contract for supplying water

Sec. 6. That the said corporation is hereby authorized and empowered to contract with any and all persons, private and corporate, to supply the same with water for drinking, fire and other purposes, and to furnish them with electric lights of any and all description, and with motive power produced by electricity, and to make such contracts with said parties as shall be mutually agreeable that are not in conflict with the laws of this state.

Sec. 7. That said corporation shall have the power to engage in the manufacture of ice, furniture and such other articles of merchandise as its board of directors may deem advisable, and to purchase, construct, own and hold such warehouses, factories, buildings, machinery and other property as may be necessary, and may engage in such other business enterprises not forbidden by the laws of this state as its board of directors may determine. **Empowered to engage in certain manufacturing industries.**

Sec. 8. That said corporation may purchase, hold and convey real estate. **May hold real estate.**

Sec. 9. That this act shall be in force from and after its ratification.

Ratified the 6th day of March, A. D. 1899.

CHAPTER 319.

An act to amend the charter of the town of Nashville, Nash county.

The General Assembly of North Carolina do enact:

Section 1. That the inhabitants of the town of Nashville, in the county of Nash, shall continue as heretofore, a body corporate under the name and style of "The Town of Nashville," and shall be subject to and have the benefits of all the provisions of chapter sixty-two, volume two, of The Code of North Carolina, except as hereinafter provided, and of such amendments as have been or may be hereafter from time to time made to the same. **Body corporate. Corporate name.**

Sec. 2. That the corporate limits of said town shall embrace the following described territory, viz: Beginning at a stake on the old Raleigh road; thence south seventy degrees east one hundred and sixty poles to a red-oak on the Nashville and Wilson road; thence north twenty east two hundred and sixty-six poles to a pine in B. H. Sarsby's old field; thence north sixty degrees north one hundred and twenty-four poles to a stake in J. C. Harper' and T. T. Boss' line; thence south eighty-seven degrees west one hundred and two poles to a sweetgum on Stony creek at the mouth of a small drain; thence up the various courses of said creek to a turkey-oak; thence south forty degrees west fifty poles to a stake on Stony creek; thence up the various courses of said creek to a red-oak; thence south twelve degrees west one hundred and forty poles to a stake; thence south eighty-five degrees east ninety-eight poles to the beginning. **Corporate limits.**

Annual levy of tax.

Sec. 3. That the commissioners of said town may, not oftener than annually, lay a tax on all persons, apothecaries and druggists excepted, retailing or selling liquors or wines of the measure of a quart or less, of not less than fifty dollars and not exceeding two hundred and fifty dollars.

Conflicting laws repealed.

Sec. 4. That all laws and clauses of laws inconsistent with the provisions of this act are hereby repealed.

Sec. 5. That this act be in force from and after its ratification.

Ratified the 6th day of March, A. D. 1899.

CHAPTER 320.

An act to amend chapter one hundred and twenty-five, private laws eighteen hundred and ninety-three.

The General Assembly of North Carolina do enact:

Name of town of Hilma, Edgecombe county, changed.

[Section 1.] That chapter one hundred and twenty-five, private laws of eighteen hundred and ninety-three, be amended by substituting for the word "Hilma" wherever it occurs in said act the word "Farrar."

[Sec. 2.] That this act be in force from and after its ratification.

Ratified the 6th day of March, A. D. 1899.

CHAPTER 321.

An act to incorporate the United Mining, Developing and Construction Company.

The General Assembly of North Carolina do enact:

Corporators.

Body corporate.

Corporate name.

Corporate powers.

Section 1. That Walter George Newman, Robert J. Hornor, Joseph J. Newman, Strother M. Newman, Byron P. Stratton and Edward N. Newman, together with all other persons and corporations as become stockholders in the company hereby incorporated, are hereby constituted a body corporate and politic by and under the name of the United Mining, Developing and Construction Company, by which name the said corporation may sue and be sued, plead and be impleaded in any court of law and equity, and shall have power to make such by-laws and regulations not inconsistent with the laws of this state as may be deemed necessary for the government of said company, and which shall be binding on them and requisite to carry on business. It shall have perpetual succession, shall have and use a common seal, that may be changed or altered at will, and shall enjoy all the rights and privileges, liberties, immunities and franchises usually pertaining to a mining, metallurgical, milling, developing, construction, trading and manufacturing corporation.

Sec. 2. This company shall be organized by any one of the resident corporators giving ten days' notice in writing to the other corporators to meet in the town of Salisbury, North Carolina, in person or by proxy, within two years from the passage of this act, and a majority of the corporators shall constitute a quorum for the transaction of business, and the company may be organized when one hundred thousand dollars have been subscribed and ten per centum thereon paid in. How organized. Notice shall be given.

Sec. 3. The capital stock of said company shall be divided into shares of twenty-five dollars ($25) each, and shall be for such a total sum as the directors or stockholders in general meeting may determine: Provided, that such capital stock shall not exceed the sum of two hundred and fifty million dollars ($250,000,000), and the shares shall be personal property and are transferable as the by-laws may determine; said shares shall be non-assessable and the stockholders shall not be individually or in their private property liable for the debts of the corporation. And it shall be lawful to accept real estate, stocks and bonds of other corporations, other securities, labor and articles of value in payment of subscriptions to the capital stock of this said company. And also, that this said company may subscribe to, pay for, hold and own stock and other securities of other corporations. Capital stock. Proviso. Limitation to capital stock. Individual liability.

Sec. 4. Each stockholder, until the amount of his stock has been paid up, shall be individually liable to the creditors of the company to an amount equal to that not paid up thereon, but shall not be liable to an action therefor by any creditor before an execution against the company has been returned unsatisfied in whole or in part; and the amount due on such execution shall, subject to the provisions of the next section, be the amount recoverable with cost against such stockholders. Any stockholder may plead, by way of defense, in whole or in part, any set-off which he could set up against the company, except a claim for unpaid dividends or a salary or allowance as a president or director. Individual liability of stockholders for unpaid stock.

Sec. 5. The stockholders of the company shall not as such be held responsible for any act, default or liability whatsoever of the company, or for any engagement, claim, payment, loss, injury, transaction, matter or thing whatsoever relating to or connected with the company beyond the unpaid amount of their respective shares in the capital stock thereof. Individual liability of stockholders.

Sec. 6. The said company shall have power to purchase and

May acquire lands.

hold in fee simple, under lease or otherwise acquire lands in Rowan, Cabarrus, Stanly, Montgomery, Davidson and other counties in this state, in other states of the United States and in foreign countries, or minerals or surface rights therein or thereon, with power to sell, mortgage, lease or otherwise dispose of the same; to develop, mine, purchase, prepare, transport to any market and sell iron, ore, coal, limestone, fireclay, aluminum, nickel, zinc, manganese, baryta, gold, silver, copper, lead or any other ores or minerals, fertilizers, timber or any other product that may be found or produced upon, in or from their lands; to erect manufactories, mills, furnaces, machinery and fixtures, and manufacture and refine iron and steel, nickel, zinc, aluminum, manganese, baryta, gold, silver, copper, lead, limestone, fireclay, fertilizers, acids, chemicals or any other minerals or metals or by-products from them; lumber in all of its various branches, cotton and its products, and other fabrics, machinery and other articles, and sell and dispose of the same; that the said company may, besides having the power and privilege to construct their own works, enter into contract to construct and erect any kind of works for others, and generally to do all other acts and things which the successful prosecution of their business may require.

Corporate powers.

Empowered to use certain powers in operation of works.

Sec. 7. The said company may use steam, electricity, gas, water or any other power by which their works or manufactories can be run or operated; and may generate electrical power, transmit it and sell or otherwise dispose of any power thus generated, and for this purpose may dam rivers not navigable in the counties aforenamed, or in any territory owned or controlled by the said company.

Authorized to lay out town sites.

Sec. 8. The said company may lay out town sites and divide the same into streets and lots, and erect buildings thereon, and may sell or otherwise dispose of the same; they may also build and operate hotels in connection with the same or in connection with such mineral and medicinal springs as may be found or developed on their property; to conduct health resorts, and to promote and encourage immigration.

Empowered to construct roads, etc.

Sec. 9. That the said company shall have the right, power and authority to lay out, build and construct roads, whether rail, tram, plank or turnpike for the transportation of iron, coal, coke, ores of iron, limestone, fireclay, aluminum, nickel, zinc, manganese, baryta, gold, silver, copper, lead or any other ores or minerals, timber and other materials and persons to, from or between their lands, mines, furnaces, mills and manufactories, and also to construct such canals or drains as may be needful or required for the supply of water to said furnaces, mills or manufactories, the drainage of their mines or the transportation of coal, ores or other articles and persons as aforesaid; to bridge and dam streams of water wherever necessary, and to connect such roads or canals with the railroads, canal or slack water navigation of any company now incorporated or which may hereafter be incorporated by the laws of the state at any point the said company may select for such connection; and such roads, canals and drains shall be open to the use of the public upon the payment of such reasonable tolls and compensation and subject to such rules and regulations as said company may by their by-laws establish, not inconsistent with the laws of this state.

Damming of streams.

Such canals, etc., open to use of public.

Sec. 10. That when any land or right-of-way may be required by said company for constructing said roads, canals or drains, and for want of agreement as to the value thereof, or for any other cause, the same can not be purchased of the owners, the same may be taken and the value thereof ascertained as follows, viz: On application by the company to any justice of the peace for the county where the said land or right-of-way may be situated, it shall be his duty to issue his warrant to the sheriff of said county to summon a jury of at least five freeholders to meet on the land on the day named in such warrant, not less than five nor more than twenty days thereafter, and the sheriff on receipt of said warrant shall summon the jury and notify the owner of the land of the time and place at which he has summoned the jury to meet, and when met, if three or more appear, shall administer an oath or affirmation to them that they will impartially value the land or right-of-way in question. The proceedings of said jurors, accompanied by a description of the land or right-of-way, shall be returned under their hands and seals, or a majority of them, by the sheriff to the clerk of the superior court, there to remain as a matter of record, and on the payment of the said valuation the lands or right-of-way so valued shall vest in said company so long as the same shall be used for the purposes of said road, canal or drain: Provided, that the location of said roads, canals or drains shall not interfere with any graveyards, house, house lot or garden, without the consent of the owner thereof, and that no more land than thirty feet in width on either side from the center of said road, canal or drain shall be condemned for the purpose aforesaid: And provided further, that if any person or persons over whose lands said road, canal or drain may pass, or said company shall be dissatisfied with the valuation of said jurors, either party may have an appeal to the superior court of the county in which the land lies, but such appeal shall not delay or interrupt the use or enjoyment of said right-of-way by said company: Provided, that when the company shall appeal from the decision of the jurors aforesaid, the company shall be liable for all cost and execute their bond, with

Land may be condemned.

Appointment of assessors.

Owner of land shall be notified.

Proceedings of jurors shall be returned to clerk of court.

Proviso.

Location of works, etc., shall not interfere with certain property.

Proviso.

Either party may appeal from valuation of jury.

Proviso.

Company shall be liable for costs.

sufficient surety, payable to the owners of the land in double the amount adjudged by said jury.

Authorized to issue bonds

Sec 11. The company is hereby authorized to issue bonds under the seal of the company, signed by the president or other presiding officer and countersigned by its secretary or treasurer, and such bonds may be made payable at such times and in such manner and at such places in the United States or Great Britain, and bearing such rates of interest as the directors may think proper, and the directors shall have power to issue, sell or pledge all or any of such bonds at the best price and upon the best terms and conditions which at the time they are able to obtain for the purpose of raising money for the payment of the price of any lands or the erection of any works or otherwise for the purposes of the said company; and such bonds shall, without registration or formal conveyance, be taken and considered to be the first preferential claim and charge upon the property of the company, real and personal, then existing and at any time thereafter acquired, and each holder of the said bonds shall be held and be deemed to be a mortgagee or incumbrancer upon all the said properties pro rata with the other bondholders. The company may secure the said bonds by mortgage deed upon the whole of their real and personal property acquired and to be acquired, and by the said deed the company may grant to the holders of such bonds, or to the trustee or trustees named in the deed, every and all the powers and remedies granted by this act in respect to the said bonds, and all other powers and remedies not inconsistent with this act, and may restrict the bondholders in the exercise of any power or remedy, and all such powers, rights and remedies as are so contained in such mortgage deed shall be valid, binding and available to the bondholders as may be therein provided.

Said bonds, first claim.

Bonds may be secured.

Powers, rights, etc., in mortgage deed valid.

Provisional directors.

Quorum.

Sec. 12. The persons named in the first section of this act are hereby constituted provisional directors of the company, of whom three shall be a quorum, and shall hold office as such until the first election of directors under this act, and shall have power forthwith to open stock books and procure subscription of stock in the said company.

Persons eligible as directors.

Sec. 13. No person shall be a director of the company unless he is the holder of at least twenty shares in the stock of the company.

Sec. 14. At such general meeting the stockholders may choose not more than seven or less than three persons to be directors of the company, of whom three shall be a quorum.

Annual meeting of stockholders.

Sec. 15. Thereafter the annual general meeting of the stockholders of the company for the election of directors and other general purposes shall be held at such place and on such day and upon such notice as may be provided by by-law by the company.

Sec. 16. (1) At all general meetings of the company every stockholder shall be entitled to as many votes as he owns shares in the company, and may vote by proxy. Representation of stockholders at meetings.

(2) Election of directors shall be by ballot. Election of directors.

(3) Vacancies occurring in the board of directors may be filled for the unexpired remainder of the term by the board from among the qualified stockholders of the company. Vacancies occurring.

(4) The directors shall from time to time elect from among themselves a president and a vice-president of the company, and shall also name all other officers thereof. Election of officers.

Sec. 17. If at any time an election of directors is not made or does not take effect at the proper time, the company shall not be held to be thereby dissolved, but such election may take place at any general meeting of the company duly called for that purpose, and the retiring directors shall continue in office until their successors are appointed. Failure to elect directors shall not dissolve company.

Sec. 18. One-fourth part in value of the stockholders of the company shall at all times have the right to call a special meeting thereof for the transaction of any business specified in such written requisition and notice as they may issue to that effect. Special meetings.

Sec. 19. The directors of the company shall have full power to make all by-laws not contrary to law or to this act for the regulation of the affairs and management of the company, for making calls upon stock subscribed, for the establishment of a head office and of branch offices, and of changing from time to time the location of such offices; they shall have full power to manage the affairs of the company, and may make or cause to be made for the company any description of contract which the company may by law enter into. By-laws.

Sec. 20. No share shall be transferable until all previous calls thereon have been fully paid in or until declared forfeited for non-payment of calls thereon. Transfer of shares.

Sec. 21. The directors may refuse to allow the entry into any such book of any transfer of stock whereon any call has been made which has not been paid in. Directors may refuse entry of stock not paid for.

Sec. 22. No transfer of stock, unless made by sale under execution, shall be valid for any purpose whatever save only as exhibiting the rights of the parties thereto toward each other and as rendering the transferee liable ad interim, jointly and severally, with the transferer to the company and their creditors, until the entry thereof has been duly made in such book or books. Transfers of stock, when valid.

Sec. 23. The company shall not be bound to see to the execution of any trust, whether expressed, implied or constructive, in respect of any share; and the receipt of the stockholder in whose Execution of trusts in respect to shares.

name the same stands in the books of the company shall be a valid and binding discharge to the company for any dividends or money payable in respect of such share, whether or not notice of such trust has been given to the company, and the company shall not be bound to see to the application of the money paid up on such receipt.

Liability to persons holding stock as executors, etc.

Sec. 24. No person holding stock in the company as an executor, administrator, tutor, curator, guardian or trustee, shall be personally subject to liability as a stockholder: but the estates and funds in the hands of such person shall be liable in like manner and to the same extent as the testator or intestate, or the minor, ward or interdicted person, or the person interested in such trust funds would be, if living and competent to act and holding such stock in his own name; and no person holding such stock as collateral security shall be personally subject to such liability; but the person pledging such stock shall be considered as holding the same, and shall be liable, as a stockholder accordingly.

Executors, administrators, etc., may represent stock in meeting.

Sec. 25. Every executor, administrator, tutor, curator, guardian or trustee shall represent the stock in his hands at all meetings of the company, and may vote accordingly as a stockholder; and every person who pledges his stock may, nevertheless, represent the same at all such meetings and may vote accordingly as a stockholder.

Directors may demand of stockholders money subscribed.

Sec. 26. The directors of the company may call in and demand from the stockholders thereof respectively all sums of money by them subscribed at such times and places and in such payments or installments as the by-laws of the company require or allow, and interest shall accrue and fall due at the legal rate for the time being upon the amount of any unpaid call from the day appointed for payment of such call.

Company may enforce payment by action in court.

Sec. 27. The company may enforce payment of all calls and interest thereon by action in any court of competent jurisdiction, and in such action it shall not be necessary to set forth the special matter, but it shall be sufficient to declare that the defendant is a holder of one share or more, stating the number of shares and is indebted in the sum of money to which the calls in arrear amount, in respect of one call or more upon one share or more, stating the number of calls and the amount of each whereby an action has accrued to the company under this act; and a certificate under the seal and purporting to be signed by any officer of the company to the effect that the defendant is a stockholder, that such call or calls has or have been made, and that so much is due by him and unpaid thereon, shall be received in all courts of law and equity as prima facie evidence to that effect.

Sec. 28. If, after such demand or notice as by the by-laws of the company is prescribed, any call made upon any share or shares is not paid within such time as by such by laws may be limited in that behalf, the directors in their discretion, by vote to that effect, reciting the facts and duly recorded in their minutes, may summarily forfeit any shares whereon such payment is not made, and the same shall thereupon become the property of the company, and may be disposed of as by the by-laws or otherwise the company may ordain.

Holder may forfeit shares on which payment is not made.

Sec. 29. The directors of the company shall not declare or pay any dividend when the company is insolvent, or any dividend the payment of which renders the company insolvent or diminishes the capital stock thereof, but if any director, present when such dividend is declared, forthwith, or if any director then absent, within twenty-four hours after he has become aware thereof and able to do so, enters on the minutes of the board of directors his protest against the same, and within eight days thereafter causes such protest to be published in at least one newspaper published at or as near as may be possible to the office or chief place of business of the company, such director may thereby and not otherwise exonerate himself from liability.

Dividends, when payable.

Protest of directors.

Sec. 30. Every contract, agreement, engagement or bargain made, and every bill of exchange drawn, accepted or endorsed, and every promissory note and check made, drawn or endorsed on behalf of the company by any agent, officer or servant of the company in general accordance with his powers as such, under the by-laws of the company, shall be binding upon the company, and in no case shall it be necessary to have the seal of the company affixed to any such contract, agreement, engagement, bargain, bill of exchange, promissory note or check, or to prove that the same was made, drawn, accepted or endorsed, as the case may be, in pursuance of any by-law or special vote or order, nor shall the party so acting as agent, officer or servant of the company be thereby subjected individually to any liability whatsoever to any third party therefor.

Contracts made on behalf of company.

Parties acting as agents not individually liable.

Sec. 31 A copy of any by-law of the company, under its seal and purporting to be signed by any officer of the company, shall be received as prima facie evidence of such by-law in all courts of law or equity in North Carolina

Copy of by-law prima facie evidence of such by-law.

Sec. 32. This charter shall take effect and be in force from and after its ratification, and remain in force for the term of ninety-nine years.

Charter, when effective.

Ratified the 6th day of March, A. D. 1899.

CHAPTER 322.

An act to re-enact and amend the charter of the Polk County Railroad Company, being chapter one hundred and thirty-four, laws of eighteen hundred and eighty-seven.

The General Assembly of North Carolina do enact:

Section 1, chapter 134, laws of 1887, amended.

Section 1 That section one, chapter one hundred and thirty-four, laws eighteen hundred and eighty-seven, be and the same is hereby amended by inserting before the words "and their associates" in line twelve the following: That for the purpose of constructing a railroad through Polk county, North Carolina, from any town or station on the Carolina Central Railway via Columbus and Mill Spring to the state line between Tennessee and North Carolina as may [be] most practicable, J. G. B. Livingston, Robert Hamilton, N. H. Hill, George Collins, John W. McFarland, Grayson Arledge, J. R. Foster, J. A. Thorne, A. C. Boone, Lynch Whiteside, J. C. Powell, T. F. Thorne, H. E. Gray and J. P. Arledge.

Section 3 amended.

Sec. 2. That section three of said act be and the same is hereby amended by striking out after the word "of" in line one to the word "to" in line two and insert "N. H. Hill, H. E. Gray, J. P. Arledge" and by striking out the word "the" in line six; also in lines ten and eleven strike out the words, "to Columbus or Mill Spring," and in line twelve for "fifty" insert "ten."

Section 14 amended.

Sec. 3. That section fourteen of said act be and is hereby amended by inserting after the word "annually" in line five, "at the court-house in Polk county," and in same line strike out "twenty" and insert "thirty."

Additional sections.

Sec. 4. That said act be further amended by adding after section sixteen the following sections, to be called sections seventeen, eighteen, nineteen, twenty, twenty-one:

Where construction of road may begin.

Sec. 17. Said company shall be authorized to begin the construction of said road at any point on the projected line, and may operate any portion of it when completed, and shall have the exclusive right of transportation over the same.

May build branch roads.

Sec. 18. That said company shall have power and are hereby authorized to build branch roads and to construct and operate telegraph and telephone lines along its main line and branches.

Counties, townships and towns may subscribe to capital stock.

Sec. 19. That for the purpose of aiding in raising the capital stock of said railroad company it shall and may be lawful for any county, township, city or town which is interested in its construction to subscribe to the capital stock of said company such sum or sums in bonds or money as a majority of their qualified electors may authorize, under the same rules and regulations as are by this chapter provided for Polk county.

Sec. 20. That said act is hereby ratified and confirmed in all respects and is continued in full force as heretofore except only as herein specially amended. **Said act continued in full force, except as amended.**

Sec. 21. That this act shall be in force from and after its ratification.

Ratified the 6th day of March, A. D. 1899.

CHAPTER 323.

An act to incorporate the town of Granite Falls in Caldwell county.

The General Assembly of North Carolina do enact:

Section 1. That the town of Granite Falls, in the county of Caldwell, be and the same is hereby incorporated under the name and style of the town of Granite Falls, and [in] that name may sue and be sued, plead and be impleaded, contract and be contracted with, acquire and hold property, real and personal, for the use of the town as its board of commissioners may deem necessary or expedient. **Incorporated. Corporate name. Corporate powers.**

Sec. 2. That the corporate limits of said town shall be one mile long, three-quarters of a mile wide: Beginning at a point in the Carolina and Northwestern Railroad, three-eighths miles south of depot, and running with said road one mile—three-eighths mile wide on each side of said railroad. **Corporate limits.**

Sec 3. That the officers of said town shall consist of a mayor and three commissioners, who shall be styled a board of commissioners, Granite Falls, and the said mayor and commissioners shall be elected by the qualified voters of said town on the first Monday in May, eighteen hundred and ninety-nine, and annually thereafter, under the same rules and regulations as are prescribed by the law for the holding of such elections in the incorporate town of Lenoir, in said county of Caldwell; a constable and secretary and treasurer to be chosen by the board of commissioners immediately after its organization, to hold one year or until their successors are elected and installed into office. **Town officers. Term of office of treasurer, secretary and constable.**

Sec. 4. That the board of commissioners of said town shall have authority to assess and collect annually taxes for municipal purposes on all persons and property within the corporate limits, which are taxed for state and county purposes, under such rules and regulations as they may adopt: Provided, that the basis between persons and property shall be the same as established by the constitution of the state, and the taxes so assessed and col- **Annual levy of taxes.**

lected shall not exceed twenty cents on the hundred dollars of property and sixty cents on the poll.

Commissioners may pass ordinances.

SEC. 5. That the board of commissioners of the town may pass all ordinances they may deem necessary for the good government, quiet, peace, health and safety of the town, not inconsistent with the constitution and laws of the state and of the United States.

Sale of liquor prohibited.

SEC. 6. That it shall be unlawful for any person or persons to manufacture, sell, give away, or directly or indirectly dispose of any spirituous, vinous or malt liquors or any other drinks of whatever name or nature containing any per centum of alcohol, within the corporate limits of said town of Granite Falls.

Violation of ordinances a misdemeanor.

SEC. 7. That the willful and unlawful violation of any ordinance of the town shall be a misdemeanor, but the punishment thereof shall not exceed a fine of fifty dollars or imprisonment for more than thirty days.

Jurisdiction of mayor.

SEC. 8. That the mayor of said town, within the limits thereof, shall have and exercise true jurisdiction and power which are now or may hereafter be conferred by the laws governing cities and towns; and constable or marshal of said town shall, within the corporate limits thereof, have and exercise all the authority, rights and powers which are now or may hereafter be conferred by the laws on constables, including the right and authority to arrest any person without warrant who commits a breach of the peace or violates a town ordinance.

Constable and marshal, authority of.

Collection of taxes by constable.

SEC. 9. That the town constable shall collect and pay over to the secretary and treasurer all taxes imposed by the board of commissioners, all fines and costs, when execution is issued to him for that purpose, and return the same in due time to the secretary and treasurer. He shall see that the ordinances of the town are enforced, and report all breaches thereof to the mayor. He shall preserve the peace of the town by suppressing all disturbances in his presence and apprehending offenders and taking them before the mayor; or if they are intoxicated or in any way not in a condition to be brought before the mayor, he may confine them until they are in a condition to be brought before the mayor. He shall execute all process directed to him by the mayor within the limit of the said town and make due return thereof, and in the execution of his duties he may call to his aid such assistance as he may deem necessary. And whenever the board of commissioners may deem it necessary, they may appoint as many additional constables as they see proper. He shall have the same fees for his services as are allowed the sheriff for similar services, and such additional compensation as the board of commissioners may allow.

Duties of constable.

Constable shall execute processes.

Fees of constable.

SEC. 10. That the secretary and treasurer, before entering upon the duties of his office, shall enter into a bond conditional upon the faithful performance of his duties in the sum of five hundred dollars, payable to the state of North Carolina, with surety to be approved by the board of commissioners. And the town constable shall enter into a like bond before entering upon his duties. And the board of commissioners shall institute suit in the name of the town of Granite Falls upon the relation of the state of North Carolina for any violation of said bonds.

Secretary and treasurer shall execute bond.

Sec. 11. That the mayor shall have power to commit any offender who is sentenced to imprisonment for misdemeanor or violation of the town ordinances, or for contempt of the mayor's court, or upon failure to pay fine and cost, to the town prison or the common jail of the county, and the sheriff or jailor shall receive such persons as are committed by the mayor, and shall charge the same fees as in cases of other prisoners, or the mayor shall have power under such rules and regulations as the board of commissioners may adopt, to require any person who fail to pay fines and costs to work on the streets of the town till the fines and costs are paid.

Persons adjudged guilty of violation of town ordinance may be committed to jail.

Sec 12. That all fines and penalties imposed for the violation of the town ordinances shall be paid over to the secretary and treasurer and shall be expended for the improvement of the streets of the town or for the necessary expenses of the town.

Fines and penalties, how applied.

Sec. 13. That the mayor, immediately after the election and before entering upon the duties of his office, shall before a justice of the peace take the oath prescribed for public officers and an oath that he will faithfully and impartially discharge the duties of his office according to law.

Oath of mayor.

Sec 14. That each commissioner, before entering upon the duties of his office shall take before the mayor or some justice of the peace the oath prescribed for public officers, and an oath that he will truly and impartially perform his duties of commissioner for the town according to the best of his skill, ability and judgment.

Commissioners shall take oath.

Sec. 15. That the mayor and commissioner shall hold their offices respectively till the next ensuing election and until their respective successors shall be qualified. The mayor when present shall preside at the meetings of said board of commissioners, but shall not be entitled to a vote upon any question except in case of a tie; in the absence of the mayor the board may appoint one of their number mayor pro tempore. The said board shall have power also to fill all vacancies which may occur.

Term of office of mayor and commissioners.

Vacancies occurring.

Sec. 16 Any person qualified to serve and elected mayor or commissioner, either by the electors at their annual election or by the commissioners, to fill a vacancy or otherwise, who shall not take the oath of office within five days after his election, or

Officers failing to qualify shall pay penalty.

who having qualified shall fail to serve during the term for which he may be elected (inability from sickness, removal from the town or resignation accepted), shall forfeit and pay fifty dollars, to be recovered before any justice of the peace of Caldwell county in the name and for the benefit of the town of Granite Falls.

Empowered to open streets.

Sec. 17. That the commissioners shall have power from time to time to open out any new streets and alleys within the limits of said town by paying the owners through whose lands the said streets and alleys may run the damages, if any there be: Provided, that if the said commissioners and the owner of said land can not agree as [to] the price of the same, it shall be left to three disinterested persons, to be selected as follows: The commissioners shall select one, and the owner of the land one, and the two thus selected shall elect a third man, and the persons thus selected shall assess the damages; and if the owners of the land will not select a man, then the commissioners shall select two men, and the two thus selected shall select a third, and the three thus selected shall assess the damages to the land: Provided that either party being dissatisfied with the decision of the persons thus selected, by giving bond for payment of cost, may appeal to the superior court.

Proviso.

Term of office.

Sec. 18. That the mayor and commissioners and constable named in this charter shall hold said offices, with all the powers, privileges, rights and responsibilities which this charter confers until their successors are elected and qualified.

Additional powers.

Sec. 19. That in addition to the rights, franchises and immunities conferred by the foregoing sections the town of Granite Falls shall have and be subject to all the provisions contained in The Code of North Carolina, chapter sixty-two, not inconsistent with this act.

Appointment of registrar and judges.

Sec. 20. That the board of commissioners of Caldwell county shall at their regular meeting on the first Monday in April, eighteen hundred and ninety-nine, appoint a registrar and two judges of election from the qualified voters in the boundary set forth in section two of this act, who shall hold the first election for mayor and commissioner provided for in section three of this act. The said registrar and judges of election shall be notified of this appointment by the sheriff of Caldwell county, and they shall hold said election as prescribed in section three of this act. At the said election for mayor and commissioners of said town, to be held on the first Monday in May, eighteen hundred and ninety-nine, there shall also be submitted to the qualified voters of said town the question of incorporating said town as provided for in this act. At such election those favoring such incorporation will vote "For charter," and those opposed to such incorporation will

Question of incorporation to be submitted to voters.

Form of ballot.

vote "Against charter." If a majrity of the qualified voters in said town shall vote "For charter," then this act shall be in full force and effect, and the mayor and commissioner elected at such election shall [qualify] soon as prescribed in this act; but if a majority of said qualified voters shall fail to vote "For charter," then this act shall be of no effect. The said judge of election shall declare the result of said election and file a report thereof with the board of county commissioners of Caldwell county.

Sec. 21. That this act shall be in force from and after its ratification.

Ratified the 6th day of March A. D. 1899.

CHAPTER 324.

An act to amend the charter of Mount Airy.

The General Assembly of North Carolina do enact:

Section 1 That after the word "time" in line twenty-seven of section one of chapter three hundred and four of the private acts of the legislature [of] eighteen hundred and ninety-one, the following be inserted: "That every owner of a lot or person having as great interest therein as three years lease, which front on a street on which a sidewalk has been established, shall improve in such manner as the commissioners of the town shall direct such sidewalk as far as it may extend along such lot; and on a failure to do so within ten days after notice by the chief of police to said owner, or if he be a non resident of the county of Surry, his agent; or if such non-resident have no agent in such county, and personal notice can not be served upon him or his agent, then after publication of the notice for thirty days by the chief of police in some newspaper printed in the town of Mount Airy, the commissioners may cause same to be repaired with either brick, stone, gravel or other material, at their discretion, and the cost thereof may be assessed upon the property of such delinquent and added to the taxes against him or her, and collected in the same manner as other taxes are collected.

Owners of property adjoining sidewalks shall contribute to improvement of such.

Commissioners may require repairs.

Sec 2. That section two of chapter ninety of the private laws of the session of the general assembly of eighteen hundred and ninety-seven be and the same is hereby repealed.

Section 2, chapter 90, private laws of 1897, repealed.

Sec. 3. That all laws and clauses of laws in conflict with this act are hereby repealed.

Conflicting laws repealed.

Sec. 4. That this act shall be in force from and after its ratification.

Ratified the 6th day of March, A. D. 1899.

CHAPTER 325.

An act authorizing Concord to issue bonds if a majority of the registered voters vote in favor of bonds.

The General Assembly of North Carolina do enact:

Commissioners of Concord empowered to order election.

Section 1. That the commissioners for the town of Concord are hereby authorized and empowered to cause an election to be held at the various polling places in said town at such times as said commissioners may appoint, within twelve months from the ratification of this act, and to submit to the qualified voters of said town the question of issuing bonds to the amount of twelve thousand dollars for the purpose and under the provision hereinafter named in this act, and levying and collecting annually a special tax to provide for the payment of the interest thereon and to provide a sinking fund for the payment of the principal of said bonds when they shall become due. The said election shall be advertised by the said commissioners for thirty days immediately preceding the day of election in some newspaper published in said town, and held by inspectors and judges under the same rules and regulations provided for the election of state and county officers. Those who are in favor of issuing said bonds and levying and collecting said taxes shall vote a written or printed ticket with the words "For bonds" thereon, and those who are opposed shall vote a written or printed ticket with words "Against bonds" thereon. The result of the election shall be ascertained by the inspectors and judges of election of the respective wards and certified and returned by them to the commissioners for the town of Concord within two days from the day of election, who shall verify and also certify such result and cause the same to be recorded in their minutes.

Question to be submitted.

Amount of bonds.

Special annual tax may be levied.

Election shall be advertised.

Form of ballots.

Bonds, for what purpose used.

Sec. 2. Said bonds shall be used for the following purpose only, viz: It shall be the duty of the commissioners for the town of Concord to call in and pay all the outstanding floating indebtedness of said town at the date of the issue of said bonds. That if a majority of the qualified registered voters of said town shall vote "For bonds," and said bonds shall be sold, then it shall be unlawful for the commissioners for the town of Concord to issue any script or other evidence of indebtedness on the credit of the town for the payment of any expense or indebtedness that the town may incur in the government or improvement of the same, and should the town authorities issue such script or other evidence of indebtedness, then it shall be void and of no value.

Limitation to bond issue.

Sec. 3. If a majority of the qualified voters of said town shall vote "For bonds," then the commissioners for said town shall issue coupon bonds not to exceed in amount the sum of twelve thousand dollars, and in denomination of not less than one hundred dollars and not more than one thousand dollars, bearing interest from the date of their issue at a rate not exceeding five per centum (5 per centum) per annum, payable semi-annually, either at the Concord National Bank or the Cabarrus Savings Bank of Concord, North Carolina at the option of the holders of such bonds, on the first day of January and July of each year until said bonds are paid. The said bonds shall be made payable at the expiration of thirty years from the date thereof: Provided, that said bonds shall be issued and sold for the purpose named and only when and as needed for said purpose, and each bond shall bear upon its face the specific purpose for which it is issued. The bonds and coupons shall be numbered and shall be signed by the mayor and countersigned by the clerk of the board of commissioners and sealed with the corporate seal of the town of Concord. A record shall be kept of all bonds, showing the number, amount and to whom sold The coupons shall be received in payment of all taxes, fines and debts due said town. Said bonds shall be sold for not less than par value.

Rate of interest.

Maturity of bonds. Proviso.

Bonds, how signed.

Sec. 4. In order to pay the interest on said bonds the commissioners for said town are hereby authorized, and it shall be their duty to annually compute and levy, at the time of levying other taxes for said town, a sufficient special tax upon all poles [polls] and all property, real and personal, and other subjects of taxation mentioned in the charter of the town of Concord and acts amendatory thereto, which shall be returned or listed for general taxation in said town, always observing the constitutional equation between the tax on property and the tax on polls, not exceeding seven (7) cents on the one hundred ($100) dollars valuation of property and twenty-one (21) cents on each poll, with which to regularly and promptly pay the interest on said bonds, said taxes to be collected in the same manner and at the same time the other taxes of said town are collected, and shall be paid over by the town tax collector to the treasurer of said town, which officers shall give justified bonds in amounts amply sufficient to cover said taxes, the former for collecting and paying over and the latter for the safe keeping and proper disbursement of said funds.

Annual levy of special tax to pay interest and principal.

Maximum special tax.

Sec. 5. That the taxes levied and collected for the purpose specified in section four (4) of this act shall be kept separate and distinct from any and all other taxes, and shall be used only for the purposes for which they were levied and collected, and any mayor or commissioner who shall appropriate by vote or other wise to any purpose, directly or indirectly, other than that for which they were levied, any of said special taxes, or any part thereof, or shall in any other way violate the provisions of this

Said special taxes shall be kept separate.

Appropriation of taxes to any purpose other than specified, a misdemeanor.

act, shall be guilty of a misdemeanor: Provided, that if the taxes levied and collected for the payment of interest shall in any year exceed the sum required for that purpose, the amount in excess shall be applied to the credit of the interest fund for the next succeeding year, and said commissioners at the time of levying taxes for payment of interest for said next succeeding year shall take into consideration said excess and compute and levy said tax accordingly.

After twenty years special tax may be levied to create sinking fund to pay principal of bonds.

Sec. 6. For the purpose of creating a sinking fund with which to pay the principal of the bonds issued under this act, it shall be the duty of said commissioners, at and after the expiration of twenty (20) years from the date of said bonds, to annually levy and collect a special tax in addition to that mentioned in section four (4) of this act, and the tax provided for in this section shall equal in amount one-tenth ($\frac{1}{10}$th) of the amount of bonds issued under this act; and whenever the amount of taxes collected under this section, together with the interest accumulated from the investment thereof as provided in section seven of this act, shall be sufficient to pay off the principal of all outstanding bonds, then said commissioners shall cease to levy taxes for said sinking fund.

Commissioners may invest money arising from special tax.

Sec. 7. That it shall be the duty of said commissioners to annually invest any and all moneys arising from the special tax collected under section six (6) of this act in the purchase of any of said bonds at a price deemed advantageous to said town by said commissioners; but in case said bonds can not be purchased as herein provided, the said commissioners may lend said sinking fund or any part thereof in such sums as they may deem proper for a length of time not exceeding beyond six (6) months prior to the date of maturity of said bonds, taking as security for the payment thereof, and for the payment of the interest thereon, mortgages or deeds in trust in the name of the mayor of said town on sufficient real estate; or bonds issued under this act may be taken as collateral security for such loan. The notes or other evidences of debt given for any loan under this section shall be executed to and in the name of "the commissioners for the town of Concord," and shall bear interest, payable annually, at a rate not less than six per centum per annum; and in case the commissioners for said town shall not be able to lend any or all of said money annually as directed above, they may and it shall be their duty to cause such part as they are unable to invest to be deposited with some national or state bank, trust company or safe deposit company of undoubted solvency at the best obtainable rate of interest, and any and all interest arising from the investment as above directed shall be re-invested in the manner as above provided. But any mayor or commissioner of said town who

Money may be deposited.

shall be personally interested, directly or indirectly, in any loan, shall be guilty of a misdemeanor.

Sec. 8. That this act shall take effect from and after its ratification.

Ratified the 6th day of March, A. D. 1899.

CHAPTER 326.

An act to extend the corporate limits of the town of Trenton, Jones county, North Carolina.

The General Assembly of North Carolina do enact:

Section 1. That the corporate limits of the town of Trenton, Jones county, North Carolina be and the same are hereby extended as follows: By extending the line from its present terminus on Front street to a point in the dividing line between F. Castet and J. A. Smith; then in a southern direction parallel with Upper street to a point opposite Third street; then in an eastern direction to Third street; then with Upper street extended to the mill pond; then down and with the various courses of the mill pond and race to a point opposite Lower street; thence in a northern direction to Lower street. **Corporate limits extended.**

Sec. 2. That this act shall be in force from and after its ratification.

Ratified the 6th day of March, A. D. 1899.

CHAPTER 327.

An act supplemental to an act entitled "An act to incorporate the Black Diamond Company," which was ratified February twenty-first, eighteen hundred and ninety-nine.

The General Assembly of North Carolina do enact:

Section 1. That the act entitled "An act to incorporate the "Black Diamond Company," which was ratified February the twenty-first, Anno Domini eighteen hundred and ninety nine, be amended by striking out the word "Judge" where it appears before "S. Fowler" and inserting in lieu thereof the word "Judson," so that it will read "Judson S. Fowler" wherever it occurs in said act. **Act incorporating Black Diamond Company amended.**

Sec. 2. That this act shall be in force from and after its ratification.

Ratified the 6th day of March, A. D. 1899.

CHAPTER 328.

An act to incorporate Neuse River Institute.

The General Assembly of North Carolina do enact:

Corporators.

Section 1. That William R. Mason, Milan Brown, Richard P. Ivey, J. H. Arrington, Claven Faison, Phillip Garris, S. G. Newsome, Seldon Jeffry, Moses W. Williams, Cary Alston and David Watkins, their associates and successors, be and they are hereby incorporated for the purpose of educating the colored youths and training them the skill of labor, by the name and style of "The Neuse River Baptist Institute," in the town of Sheldon, in Halifax county, by which name they shall exist for sixty years and have a common seal; shall sue and be sued, implead and be impleaded, and purchase, take and hold lands, goods and chattels: Provided, that the amount or value of property to be held by said institute shall not exceed twenty-five thousand dollars.

Purpose of corporation. Corporate name. Duration of charter. Amount of property to be held.

Power of corporators to make by-laws, etc.

Sec. 2. The members of the institute above incorporated (and five of whom shall constitute a quorum) shall have power to make by-laws, rules and regulations not contrary to the laws of this state and of the United States, as they may deem proper for the good of the Institute; and shall have the power of appointing a president of the Institute and such teachers and other officers as to them shall appear necessary and proper, whom they may remove for misbehavior, inability or neglect of duty, and the faculty of the institute (that is to say), the president and teachers, by and with the consent of the trustees, shall have the power "to grant certificates of merit or proficiency upon the published courses of instruction to students completing the same."

May grant certificates.

Exempt from taxation.

Sec. 3. The lands and other property belonging to the Institute aforesaid shall be exempt from all kinds of public taxation.

Board of trustees.

Sec. 5 [4]. The persons named in first section of this act shall constitute the first board of trustees.

Sec. 5. This act shall be in force from its ratification.

Ratified the 6th day of March, A. D. 1899.

CHAPTER 329.

An act to incorporate the Citizens Savings Bank.

The General Assembly of North Carolina do enact:

Corporators.

Section 1. That Julian S. Carr, William A. Guthrie, W. J. Christian, W. H. Proctor, C. L. Lindsay, W. T. Carrington, Y. E. Smith, H. H. Markham, H. A. Foushee, A. E. Lewith, W. H. Rogers, V. Ballard, A. D. Markham, W. M. Yearby, J. R. Proctor, E. T. Rollins, M. E. M'Cown, C. E. King, C. A. Jordan, W. T.

O'Brien, J. E. Owens, and their associates, successors and assigns, be and they are hereby created a body politic and corporate under the name and style of "The Citizens Savings Bank," and by such name may acquire, hold and convey real and personal property, sue and be sued, plead and be impleaded in any of the courts of the state, and have a continual succession for sixty (60) years and a common seal for the purposes indicated in the title. Corporate name. Corporate powers.

Sec 2. That the said corporation shall enjoy all the rights, privileges, liberties, immunities, franchises and powers conferred upon and pertaining to other corporate bodies chartered for like purposes and not forbidden by the laws of the United States and of North Carolina. Corporate rights and privileges.

Sec. 3. That the capital stock of said corporation shall not be less than twenty-five thousand dollars, which may be increased from time to time by the consent of the majority of the stockholders to a sum not exceeding one million dollars, in shares of twenty-five ($25) dollars each, payable as follows: Ten per centum of each share in cash, and ten per centum per month for each month thereafter until the full sum is paid; said corporation may, however, commence the business of banking when five thousand dollars of the capital stock aforesaid has been paid in. The stockholders of the corporation shall be individually liable, equally and ratably, and not one for another, for all contracts, debts and agreements of the corporation to the extent of the amount of their stock therein at the par value thereof in addition to the amount invested in such stock. The stockholders of the corporation shall have full power to make all necessary by-laws, rules and regulations not forbidden by law for the government of affairs of the corporation, for meeting calls upon stock subscribed and for the enforcement of such calls by forfeiture of stock or otherwise; and at all meetings of the stockholders every stockholder shall be entitled to as many votes as he owns shares in the corporation, to be cast in person or by proxy; and at all meetings a majority of the stock subscribed, represented in person or by proxy, shall constitute a quorum. Capital stock. May be increased. Division of shares. Individual liability of stockholders.

Sec. 4. That the nine persons first named in section one of this act shall be and remain directors of this corporation until their successors are chosen: Provided, that no person shall be a director in said corporation without having first subscribed and taken at least ten shares of said stock. Directors of corporation.

Sec. 5. It shall be the duty of the board of directors, subject to the provisions of the by-laws, to prescribe rules and regulations for conducting the business of the corporation, to choose officers and prescribe their duties, fix salaries, fill vacancies, and generally do and perform such duties as the rules, regulations and by- Rules, regulations and by-laws.

laws of this corporation shall prescribe, when the by-laws shall have been duly ratified by a majority of the stockholders voting thereon in person or by proxy.

Principal office.

Sec. 6. The principal office or banking house of this corporation shall be located in the city of Durham and state of North Carolina.

Corporate powers.

Sec. 7. This corporation shall have power to receive and pay out the lawful currency of the country; deal in exchange, gold and silver coin, stocks, bonds, notes and other securities; to loan money or receive deposits of money or other property, or evidences of debt from corporation, minors or other property, or evidences of debt from corporations, minors, apprentices, femes covert or other persons, on such terms and at such rate of interest, time and manner of collection and payment as may be fixed by the board of directors and agreed upon between the parties, and for the use and loan of money may charge so high a rate of interest as may be allowed by law, and may take and receive said interest at the time of making said loan; to invest in the stocks, notes and bonds of individuals, bonds of counties, cities and towns, bonds of this state or of the United States, or of any corporation under the laws thereof, and to take such real estate and personal property conditioned in such form for the payment of the principal and interest of money loaned, advanced or expended as may be deemed most safe, expedient and beneficial. If money be deposited with said corporation by a minor or a feme covert, either as an investment or otherwise, such money may be withdrawn by such minor or feme covert without the consent of the parent or guardian of such minor or the husband of the feme covert, and his check or receipt therefor shall be as binding upon such minor or feme covert as though he or she were of full age or not married.

May take real estate as security.

Empowered to guarantee principal and interest of bonds, notes, etc.

Sec. 8. That said corporation shall have power and ample authority to guarantee the payment of the principal and interest of notes, bonds, bills of exchange and other securities or evidences of debt, including the obligations of such corporation and individuals as may have secured their payment by a deed of trust made to this corporation for such special purpose, and to receive for any guarantee such compensation as the parties may agree upon, and may charge therefor so high a rate of interest as may be allowed by law, and may take and receive the interest at the time of making said transaction.

May act as agents, trustees, etc.

Sec. 9. That said company shall have the right to act as agents, factor or trustee for any state, county, town, municipal corporation, company or individual on such terms as to the agency and commissions as may be agreed upon, in registering, selling and countersigning, collecting, acquiring, holding, dealing in and disposing of on account of any state, county, town, municipal corporation, company or person, bonds, certificates of stock of any description or property, real or personal, or for guaranteeing the payment of any such bond, certificates of stock, etc., and generally for managing such business as is usually charged by other [corporations] for similar services, and as may be agreed on, and for any of the matters and things authorized by this section.

Sec. 10. That said corporation shall have power to receive moneys in trust, and shall have power to accept and execute any trust that may be committed to it by the court, corporation, company, person or persons, and it shall have power to accept any grant, assignment, transfer, devise or bequest, and hold any personal or real estate in trust created in accordance with the laws of this state, and then to execute the same on such terms as may be established and agreed upon by the board of directors, and said corporation is hereby fully authorized and empowered to act as trustee or assignee, and to receive on deposit all funds in litigation in the various courts in this state, and pay therefor such interest as may be agreed upon, not exceeding the lawful rate. It shall have power and authority to receive for safe keeping on deposit all money, bonds, stocks, diamonds and silver plate and other valuables, and charge and collect a reasonable compensation for the same, which said charge shall be a lien upon said deposit until paid, and generally to do and carry on the business of a safety and deposit company. **May receive moneys in trust, execute trusts, etc.** **May act as assignee, etc.**

Sec. 11. That the stock of this corporation held by any one shall be transferred only on the books of the company, either in person or by power of attorney. **Transferral of stock.**

Sec. 13. That this act shall be in force from and after its ratification.

Ratified the 6th day of March, A. D. 1899.

CHAPTER 330.

An act to incorporate the town of Mint Hill, in Mecklenburg county.

The General Assembly of North Carolina do enact:

Section 1. That the town of Mint Hill, in the county of Mecklenburg, be and the same is hereby incorporated by the name and style of "The Town of Mint Hill," and shall be subject to all the provisions of chapter sixty-two and all amendments thereto of volume two of The Code. **Incorporated.** **Corporate name.**

Corporate limits.

Sec. 2. That the corporate limits of said town shall be as follows: Beginning at at [an] elm tree standing in the yard of one Walter McEwen, where the Matthews public road crosses the old Lawyers public road, and running thence north fifty-one degrees east to a white-oak on north side of Matthews road on H. M. Lipe's land; thence north fourteen and one half degrees east to stake twenty-four yards on north side of Charlotte road at top of rise between H. M. Lipe's and J. C. Dennis; thence south seventy five degrees east crossing Concord road at D. A. Henderson and H. M. Lipe's corner, running north of tenant house on D. A. Henderson's land to two white oaks on W. C. Miller's land; thence south twenty-two degrees east crossing Charlotte road to a stump on south side of said road; thence south thirty degrees west crossing a branch and Church road leading by E. U. Alexander's farm to a persimmon tree south of his house; thence south eighty-seven degrees west crossing branch and Church road leading by J. M. Wilson's farm to a stake on Church road leading by D. W. Miller's farm; thence south eighty-five degrees west crossing a branch to a stake on T. J. Flow's farm on east side of Lawyers road, near tenant house; thence north thirty-five and one-half degrees west to the beginning.

Town officers.

Sec. 3. That the officers of said corporation shall consist of a mayor, three commissioners and one constable, and the following-named persons shall fill said offices until the first Monday in May, nineteen hundred, and until their successors are elected and qualified, viz: E. U. Alexander, mayor; W. B. Estridge, D. A. Henderson and Walter McEwen, commissioners; and J. A. Crowell as constable who shall hold their offices until their successors are elected and qualified under the provisions of this act.

Temporary officers.

Annual election for town officers.

Sec. 4. That there shall be an election for the officers mentioned in this act held in said town on the first Monday in May, nineteen hundred, and annually thereafter as required by the general laws regulating elections in cities and towns in North Carolina.

Officers shall take oath.

Sec. 5. That it shall be the duty of the persons appointed to offices under the provisions of this act to meet and take the oath prescribed by law for such officers before some justice of the peace of said county, or other person qualified to administer an oath, within thirty days from the passage of this act, and enter upon the discharge of their respective duties, and the constable, before entering upon the duties of his office, shall be required to execute a bond in the sum of two hundred dollars, to be approved by the commissioners of said town.

Sec. 6. That this act shall be in force from and after its ratification.

Ratified the 6th day of March, A. D. 1899.

CHAPTER 331.

An act to amend chapter forty-two, private laws of North Carolina of eighteen hundred and ninety-one, to amend the charter of the town of Maxton.

The General Assembly of North Carolina do enact:

Section 1. That chapter forty-two (42), private laws of North Carolina of eighteen hundred and ninety-one (1891) be and the same is hereby amended as follows: Chapter 42, private laws of 1891, amended.

Sec. 2. That section eleven of said chapter be and the same is hereby amended by adding thereto the following paragraphs: Section 11 amended.

(17) Upon every express company, telegraph company and telephone company having an office or exchange in said town, a tax not exceeding twenty-five dollars ($25) per year: Provided, that such tax shall be collected by the tax collector when determined; and if the same be not paid on demand, the same may be recovered by suit brought by the tax collector for the use of the town, or any property of the company liable for such tax may be forthwith distrained and sold to satisfy the same after ten days advertisement at three public places within the limits of the town: Provided further, that discrimination may be made between foreign telegraph and telephone companies operating through extra municipal lines, and domestic companies operating local or infra-municipal lines, upon every of which letter [latter] there shall be a tax not exceeding ten dollars per year. Additional special tax commissioners may levy. Proviso. Discrimination may be made.

(18) Upon every carriage shop, a tax not exceeding ten dollars per year. Carriage shops.

(19) Upon every blacksmith shop, a tax not exceeding five dollars per year. Blacksmiths.

(20) Upon every barber shop, a tax not exceeding five dollars per year. Barber shops.

(21) Upon every jeweler's, silversmith's goldsmith's or other shop for making or repairing jewelry, silverware, watches, clocks, etc., a tax not exceeding five dollars per year. Jewelers.

(22) Upon every shoe shop, a tax not exceeding three dollars per year. Shoe shops.

(23) Upon every shop of whatever description other than those above specified for making, altering or repairing any wood, iron, tin, brick or stone material, a tax not exceeding five dollars per year. Other shops.

(24) Upon every undertaker's establishment, a tax not exceeding five dollars per year. Undertakers.

(25) Upon every meat market or stall, a tax not exceeding fifty dollars per year. Meat markets.

(26) Upon every livery or sale stable or stock yard, where Livery stables.

horses or mules, or both, or vehicles, harness, saddles, bridles, whips, blankets, etc., or any of them, are kept for hire or trade, or both, a tax not exceeding twenty-five dollars per year: Provided, that any person who shall hire a horse, mule or vehicle for the carriage of a person or persons, or shall engage in the sale of the aforesaid articles, or any of them, shall be liable under this section and taxed accordingly.

Proviso.

Authorized to create a debt for public improvements.

Sec 3. That the town of Maxton is hereby authorized and empowered to create a debt for public improvements, such as grading and paving streets and sidewalks, sewerage and drainage, waterworks, fire engines, lighting the streets and buildings, purchasing land for a cemetery, and the erection of necessary buildings and improvements thereon, and other public improvements, to an amount not exceeding twenty thousand dollars, and may issue bonds to that amount or any less amount for any one or more or all of said purposes in the name of the "Town of Maxton," in such denomination and form and payable at such place and time, not exceeding thirty years, and bearing interest at no greater rate than six per centum per annum, payable annually or semi-annually, as the board of commissioners may determine.

Issue of bonds shall be approved by voters.

Sec. 4. That the bonds for any of the aforesaid purposes shall not be issued until approved by a majority of the qualified voters of said town, after thirty days' notice on the public square of the town of Maxton at an election to be held under the same rules and regulations as are now provided by the charter for elections in said town; such notice shall set forth the object for which bonds are to be issued, the amount of the same, the rate of interest, the time when they mature, and the rate of tax [to] be levied to pay the principal and interest on the bonds. The qualified voters approving the issue of such bonds and the levy and collection of the taxes to pay the same shall deposit in a ballot box a written or printed ballot with the word "Approved" thereon, and those disapproving the same shall deposit a like ballot with the word "Disapproved" thereon. If at such election a majority of such voters shall vote "Approved," then the mayor and board of commissioners of the said town shall issue the bonds provided for in such notice, and shall levy and cause to be collected the taxes therein named and authorized by this act. At such election, upon the proper notice being given as above set out, the question of issuing bonds for more than one purpose within the meaning of this act may be voted on in separate boxes under the same rules and regulations as above set out; but in such a case the ballots shall contain the purpose of the bonds with the word "Approved" or "Disapproved" following, as the voters may desire: Provided, that no election shall be ordered unless a petition requesting the same, signed by a majority

Form of ballot.

Levy and collection of taxes.

Bonds for two or more purposes.

Form of ballot.

Proviso.

of the qualified voters of said town, be presented to the mayor and commissioners thereof, setting forth the matter above required in the notice of election.

Election ordered only on petition.

Sec. 5. That said bonds shall be issued under the signature of the mayor of said town, and attested by the town clerk and treasurer under the official seal of said town, and the mayor shall, under the direction of the board of commissioners, dispose of said bonds at a sum not less than par value.

Bonds, how signed.

Sec. 6. That for the purpose of paying the interest on said bonds as it falls due, and for providing a sinking fund for the redemption of said bonds when due, or for purchasing and cancelling the same before due, it shall be the duty of the board of commissioners of said town at the time fixed for the levy of other taxes in the same to levy and cause to be collected with the other taxes each year so long as any of the said bonds are unpaid, a sufficient special tax upon all the subjects of taxation set out in section thirty-two of chapter eighty-nine, private laws of eighteen hundred and eighty-three, which taxes as collected shall at all times be kept separate and distinct and used only for the purpose above set out: Provided, that so much of the tax levied each year as may not be required to pay the interest on said bonds, and which can not be applied to the purchase or discharge of the said bonds, shall be invested so as to secure the payment at maturity of the principal of said bonds; and to increase the due investment of the above-described amounts from time to time it shall be the duty of the treasurer of said town, under such regulations as the board of commissioners thereof shall from time to time prescribe, to make investment of said amounts, and to do and perform all such other services in connection with said bonds as said commissioners may prescribe: Provided further, that the board of commissioners of said town may require an official bond of the clerk and treasurer not exceeding ten thousand dollars for the faithful discharge of all the duties pertaining to his office: Provided further, that the rate of taxation in said town (not including license and privilege taxes), shall not at any time exceed the rate of sixty-six and two-third cents on every hundred dollars valuation, and a poll tax not exceeding two dollars, with which to pay both the ordinary expenses of said town and the special taxes herein provided for.

Special annual tax may be levied to pay interest and principal on bonds.

Proviso.

Money arising may be invested.

Proviso.

Commissioners may require bond of clerk and treasurer.

Proviso.

Limitation to tax rate.

Sec. 7. That the bonds authorized to be issued by this act and their coupons shall not be subject to taxation by said town until after they become due or tender of payment shall have been made by the town through the treasurer, and the coupons shall be received in payment of town taxes for any fiscal year in which they become due or thereafter; and if the holders of any of said bonds or coupons shall fail to present the same for payment at

Bonds and coupons exempted from taxation.

Failure of holders of bonds to present same on demand.

the time or times and place therein named, he shall not be entitled to any interest thereon for the time they have been outstanding after maturity.

Clerk and treasurer shall keep record.

Sec. 8. That the clerk and treasurer of said town shall keep a record, in which shall be written the name of every purchaser of a bond and the number and amount thereof; and he shall keep an accurate account of the coupons and bonds which shall be paid and cancelled, so that the true state of the bonded indebtedness of the town shall be readily seen and ascertained at any time by any taxpayer of said town.

Regulating cemeteries.

Sec. 9. That in the event the said town should purchase lands for a cemetery, either within or without the corporate limits thereof, the commissioners thereof shall have power to pass all such rules and regulations as they may deem necessary for the proper government thereof; and it shall be a misdemeanor, punishable as in the charter of said town provided, to violate the provisions of any ordinance relating thereto.

Sale of liquor prohibited.

Sec. 10. That the sale or manufacture of spirituous, vinous and malt liquors, wines or cider, brandy peaches, bitters or other intoxicating liquors is forever prohibited within the corporate limits of the town of Maxton or within two miles thereof.

Conflicting laws repealed.

Sec. 11. That all sections, paragraphs or clauses of laws in conflict with the foregoing paragraphs are hereby repealed.

Sec. 12. That this act shall be in force from and after its ratification.

Ratified the 6th day of March, A. D. 1899.

CHAPTER 332.

An act to incorporate the Home Circle Mutual Aid Association.

The General Assembly of North Carolina do enact:

Corporators.

Section 1. That George W. Newell, John H. Uzzell, John Oliver Newell and John A. Coppedge, and their associates, successors and assigns, be and are hereby created a body corporate and politic, to be known as "The Home Circle Mutual Aid Association," and as such shall have perpetual succession and be capable of suing and being sued, pleading and being impleaded in any of the courts of this state, and shall have and use a common seal.

Body corporate.

Corporate name.

Purpose of corporation.

Sec. 2. The purposes for which this company is formed are to provide the means and facilities to enable men and women to become mutually insured, upon such terms and under such conditions as may be fixed by the by-laws of this corporation.

Sec. 3. That the said corporation may make by-laws fixing the number of its officers and defining their powers and duties; and may also make rules and regulations governing the company for the conduct of its business. By-laws and regulations.

Sec. 4. This company shall have the power to create and organize local home circles, one or more in each county, or one in two or more counties, as the need may be, in the several counties of this state, and such local circles shall be governed by and in accordance with such rules and regulations as may be made by this company. May create local home circles.

Sec. 5. That the principal office of this company shall be located in the town of Louisburg and state of North Carolina; but it may have branch offices in such other cities and towns of this state as it may see fit. Principal office.

Sec. 6. The capital stock of this company shall be not less than five thousand dollars nor more than twenty-five thousand dollars, to be divided into shares of the par value of one hundred dollars; and whenever five thousand dollars of the capital stock has been subscribed and ten per centum of the same paid in, the company may organize and begin operation. Capital stock.

Sec. 7. This act shall be in force from and after its ratification.

Ratified the 6th day of March, A. D. 1899.

CHAPTER 333.

An act to amend chapter seventy-four of the private laws of North Carolina, ratified on the first day of March, Anno Domini eighteen hundred and ninety-seven.

The General Assembly of North Carolina do enact:

Section 1. That section one of chapter seventy-four of the private laws of North Carolina, ratified on the first day of March, Anno Domini eighteen hundred and ninety-seven, be amended by striking out the word "Salisbury" and inserting the word "Winston." Principal office of Yadkin Mining, Smelting and Manufacturing Company changed from Salisbury to Winston.

Sec. 2. That this act shall be in force from and after its ratification.

Ratified the 6th day of March, A. D. 1899.

CHAPTER 334.

An act to authorize the commissioners of the town of Rockingham, Richmond county, North Carolina, to issue bonds to construct waterworks.

The General Assembly of North Carolina do enact:

Commissioners of Rockingham authorized to issue bonds

Section 1. That the commissioners of the town of Rockingham, Richmond county, North Carolina for the purpose of constructing waterworks and supplying the town with water, are hereby authorized and empowered to issue bonds, bearing interest at the rate of six (6) per centum per annum from date of their issue to the amount of fifteen thousand dollars, in denominations not less than one hundred dollars and not more than one thousand dollars, to each and every one of which shall be attached the coupons representing the interest on said bonds, which said coupons shall be due and payable on the first day of January of every year until the maturity of said bonds; the bonds issued to run for a period of thirty (30) years and shall be numbered consecutively, and the coupons shall bear the number corresponding to the bond to which they are attached, and shall declare the amount of interest which they represent, and when the interest is due, and where it is payable and shall be receivable in payment of municipal taxes levied by said town.

Amount of bonds.

Coupons, when due.

Maturity of bonds.

Coupons receivable for municipal taxes.

Bonds, how signed.

Sec. 2. That the said bonds shall be issued under the signature of the mayor of said town and attested by the signature of the clerk and treasurer of said town, and the mayor and clerk and treasurer shall, under direction and with authority of the board of the town commissioners, dispose of said bonds as the necessity for the prosecution of the work may require, at a price not less than their par value, and it shall be the duty of the clerk and treasurer of said town to make and keep a record of the bonds sold, the number of bond purchased, the name of the purchaser and the price received for same.

Record shall be kept of bonds.

Commissioners authorized to levy special tax to pay interest on bonds.

Sec. 3 In order to pay the interest on said bonds the commissioners of said town are hereby authorized and it shall be their duty to annually compute and levy, at the time of levying other taxes for said town, a sufficient special tax upon all poll and all real and personal property which shall be returned or listed for general taxation in said town, always observing the constitutional equation between the tax on property and tax on poll not to exceed twenty-five cents on the one hundred dollars valuation of property and seventy-five cents on each poll, with which to regularly and promptly pay the interest on said bonds, said taxes to be collected in the same manner and at the same time the other taxes of said town are collected, and shall be paid over by the town tax collector to the treasurer of said town, which officer shall give justified bonds in amounts amply sufficient to cover said taxes, the former for collecting and paying over and the latter for the safe keeping and proper disbursement of said funds. It shall further be the duty of said commissioners to provide for the collection of rents, water charges and other revenues for the use of the water provided by said waterworks, and all revenues derived from such sources shall be held and kept solely for the purpose of maintaining said system of waterworks, and the surplus, after paying the expenses of maintenance of said system, shall be used as a part of the sinking fund hereinafter provided for for the redemption of said bonds until they have been fully redeemed.

Tax collector and treasurer, bonds of.

Surplus used as a part of sinking fund.

Sec. 4 That the taxes levied and collected for the purpose specified in section three of this act shall be kept separate and distinct from any and all other taxes, and shall be used only for the purpose for which they were levied and collected, and any mayor or commissioner who shall appropriate, by vote or otherwise, to any purpose, directly or indirectly, other than that for which they were levied, any of said special taxes or any part thereof, or shall in any way violate the provisions of this act, shall be guilty of a misdemeanor: Provided, that if the said taxes levied and collected for the payment of interest shall in any year exceed the sum required for that purpose, the amount in excess shall be applied to the credit of the interest fund for the next succeeding year, and the said commissioners at the time of levying taxes for payment of interest for said next succeeding year, shall take into consideration said excess and shall compute and levy said tax accordingly.

Said taxes shall be kept separate.

Violation of provisions of this act a misdemeanor.

Proviso.

Sec. 5. For the purpose of creating a sinking fund with which to pay the principal of the bonds issued under this act, it shall be the duties of said commissioners, at and after the expiration of twenty (20) years from date of said bonds, to annually levy and collect a special tax in addition to that mentioned in section three of this act, and the tax provided for in this section shall equal in amount one-tenth [$\frac{1}{10}$th] of the amount of bonds issued under this act after deducting the amount of the sinking fund received from the profits derived from running said waterworks as hereinbefore provided for; and whenever the amount of taxes collected under this section, together with the interest accumulated from the investment thereof as hereinafter provided for in section six of this act, and the accrued profits from running said waterworks, shall be sufficient to pay off the principal of all outstanding bonds, then said commissioners shall cease to levy said taxes for the sinking fund.

Sinking fund to to pay off principal.

When commissioners shall cease to levy special tax.

Sec. 6. That it shall be the duty of said commissioners to annually invest any and all moneys arising from the special tax col-

Commissioners may invest moneys so arising.

lected under section five of this act and from the profits of running said waterworks in the purchase of any of said bonds at a price deemed advantageous to said town by said commissioners; but in case said bonds can not be purchased as herein provided, the said commissioners may lend said sinking fund or any part thereof in such sums as they may deem proper for a length of time not exceeding beyond six (6) months prior to the date of maturity of said bonds, taking as security for the payment thereof, and for the payment of interest thereon, mortgages or deeds in trust in name of the mayor of said town, on sufficient real estate, or bonds issued under this act may be taken as collateral security for such loans. The notes or other evidence of debt given for any loan under this section shall be executed to and in the name of "the commissioners of the town of Rockingham" and shall bear interest, payable annually, at a rate not less than six (6) per centum per annum; and in case the commissioners for said town shall not be able to lend any or all of said money annually as directed above, they may and it shall be their duty to cause such part as they are unable to invest to be deposited with some bank of undoubted solvency at the best obtainable rate of interest, and any and all interest arising from the investment above directed shall be re-invested in the manner as above provided. But any mayor or commissioner of said town, who shall be personally interested, directly or indirectly, in any such loans shall be guilty of a misdemeanor.

May purchase bonds.

Evidences of debt, in what name executed.

Funds may be deposited with some bank.

Question of issuing bonds shall first be submitted to voters.

Sec. 7. That the said board of commissioners shall not issue said bonds or any part thereof until they shall have first caused to be held in said town an election in which there shall be submitted to the qualified voters of said town the question of ratification of this act or its rejection, of issuing the bonds herein provided for or not issuing them, of levying the taxes provided for in sections three (3) and five (5) of this act or not levying said taxes, which they are authorized to do at such time as they deem best for securing the voice of the people on the question within twelve months from the ratification of this act. The said election shall be advertised by the said commissioners for thirty (30) days immediately preceding the day of election in some newspaper published in said town, and held by the same officers of election and under the same rules and regulations as are or may be provided for the election of the officers of the said town. Those who are in favor of ratifying this act, issuing said bonds and levying and collecting said taxes provided for in sections three (3) and five (5) of this act shall vote a written or printed ticket with the words "For ratification, bonds and taxes" thereon, and those who are opposed to the ratification of this act, the issuing of said bonds and levying and collecting the said taxes shall vote a writ-

Election shall be advertised.

Form of ballot.

ten or printed ticket with the words "Rejection, against bonds and taxes." The result of the election shall be ascertained by the officers thereof and certified and returned by them to the commissioners for the town of Rockingham within two days from the day of the election, who shall officially find what such finding is and cause the same to be recorded in their minutes. Result of election.

Sec. 8. That this act shall be in force from and after its ratification.

Ratified the 6th day of March, A. D. 1899.

CHAPTER 335.

An act to incorporate the North Carolina Bar Association.

Whereas certain members of the bar of North Carolina have associated themselves together under the name of the North Carolina Bar Association, with the object of cultivating the science of jurisprudence, of promoting reform in the law, of facilitating the administration of justice, of elevating the standard of integrity, honor and courtesy in [the] legal profession, of encouraging a thorough and liberal legal education and of cherishing a spirit of brotherhood among the members thereof; therefore, Preamble.

The General Assembly of North Carolina do enact:

Section 1. That Platt D. Walker, president; W. D. Pruden, John L. Bridgers, T. M. Argo, W. A. Guthrie, Geo. Rountree, J. A. Lockhart, Zeb. V. Walser, R. N. Hackett, E. J. Justice, O. F. Mason, J. C. Martin, vice-presidents, J. Crawford Biggs, secretary and treasurer; and Chas. L. Abernathy, W. R. Allen, M. N. Amis, Frank Armfield, A. B. Andrews, Jr., C. B. Aycock, Jos. B. Batchelor, F. M. Beasley, B. C. Beckwith, I. W. Bickett, J. L. C. Bird, J. R. Blair, R. B. Boone, V. H. Boyden, J. H. Bridgers, Henry R. Bryan, V. S. Bryant, C. M. Busbee, F. H. Busbee, Perrin Busbee, W. H. Carroll, Walter Clark, Heriot Clarkson, Cyrus A. Cook, C. M. Cook, R. M. Cooper, W. B. Council, F. A. Daniels, T. P. Devereaux, Claudius Dockery, W. C. Douglass, Kope Elias, A. J. Field, J. W. Ferguson, W. C. Fields, H. A. Foushee, F. L. Fuller, Solomon Gallut, S. M. Gattis, Donnell Gilliam, H. A. Gilliam, R. B. Glenn, H. B. Goodwin, R. L. Gray, R. T. Gray, J. S. Grogan, O. H. Guion, F. D. Hackett, W. C. Hammer, A. J. Harris, Hugh W. Harris, J. C. L. Harris, L. T. Hartsell, R. H. Hayes, Sherwood Haywood, A. A. Hicks, I. I. Hicks, Thos. N. Hill, F. P. Hobgood, Jr., S. T. Honeycutt, Maxey Corporators. Corporators.

L. John, E. B. Jones, F. P. Jones, J. N. Kenney, R. R. King, George M. Lindsey, H. A. London, J. C. MacRae, S. H. MacRae, R. S. McCoin, J. D. McCaul, Clement Manly, John Manning, J. S. Manning, E. S. Martin, W. C. Maxwell, Stephen McIntyre, D. H. McLean, A. W. McLean, W. G. Means, Walter E. Moore, Isaac A. Murchison, Walter Murphy, J. A. Narrow, Frank Nash, Walter H. Neal, O. S. Newlin, B. B. Nicholson, Brevard Nixon, Edmund V. Norvell, W. H. Pope, E. S. Parker, E. S. Parker, Jr., J. L. Patterson, P. M. Pearsall, W. J. Peele, C. G. Peebles, R. B. Peebles, E. K. Procktor, Jr., J. H. Pou, J. N. Pruden, H. McD. Robinson, B. S. Royster, Wiley Rush, St. Leon Scull, H. E. Shaw, H. M. Shaw, W. B. Shaw, F. M. Shannonhouse, J. E. Shepherd, S. B. Shepherd, L. M. Swink, F. M. Simmons, R. N. Simms, Thomas G. Skinner, L. L. Smith, W. B. Snow, F. S. Spruill, C. M. Stedman, Henry Stevens, W. A. Stewart, R. C. Strong, H. W. Stubbs, Ed. Chambers Smith, Chas. W. Tillett, C. F. Toms, C. D. Turner, Z. I. Walser, H. S. Ward, A. D. Ward, G. W. Ward, Chas. Whedbee, Francis D. Winston, Robt. W. Winston, L. L. Witherspoon, Chas. F. Warren, W. W. Zackery, and such other persons as are now associated with them in the unincorporated association called the North Carolina Bar Association, or as many as may be hereafter associated with them under this charter, their successors and associates, be, and they are hereby, incorporated and created a body of politic, under the name of the "North Carolina Bar Association," for the purposes hereinbefore set forth, which shall have perpetual succession and shall have the right to sue and be sued, to contract and be contracted with, shall have power to adopt a common seal, and to change the same, and shall be capable of acquiring by purchase, gift, devise, bequest or otherwise, and of holding, leasing and conveying any and all such real or personal property as may be necessary for obtaining the objects or carrying into effect the purposes of this corporation.

Body politic.

Corporate name.

Corporate powers.

Empowered to make and adopt a constitution, etc.

Sec. 2. Said corporation shall have power to make and adopt a constitution and by-laws not inconsistent with the laws of the state of North Carolina, rules and regulations for the admission government, suspension and expulsion of its members for the collection of fees and dues, the number and election of its officers, and to define their duties, and for the safe keeping of its property and the management of its affairs, and to alter, modify and change such constitution, by-laws, rules and regulations.

Interest of members shall cease on termination of membership.

Sec. 3. All interest of any member of said corporation in its property shall determine and vest in the corporation upon his ceasing to be a member thereof, by death, resignation, expulsion or otherwise.

Sec. 4. The several officers of the said association at the time of the passage of this act shall continue to hold their respective offices, with the powers, duties and emoluments provided by the constitution and by-laws of said association until their successors shall be elected and installed, and in case of any vacancy in any of said offices it shall be filled in the manner prescribed by the constitution and by-laws heretofore adopted by said association, or as the same may in conformity therewith be altered and amended by this corporation, and the present constitution and by-laws of said association shall be the constitution and by-laws of said corporation until the same shall be altered or amended by said corporation. All property, rights and interest of said association now held by any or either of the officers thereof, or any person or persons, for its use or benefit, shall by virtue of this act vest in and become the property of the corporation hereby created, subject to the payment of the debts of the said association.

Officers of corporation.

Election of succeeding officers.

Sec. 5. Such corporation in its corporate name shall have power to take, institute and prosecute any action or other proceeding in the courts of this state or elsewhere, for the purpose of punishing [and] debarring unworthy members of the profession or persons assuming its functions which may now be taken and prosecuted by any natural person.

Corporate powers.

Sec. 6. This act shall be in force from and after its raification.

Ratified the 6th day of March, A. D. 1899.

CHAPTER 336.

An act to incorporate the North Carolina Trust Company.

The General Assembly of North Carolina do enact:

Section 1. That Walter George Newman, Robert J. Horner, Joseph J. Newman, Kerr Craige, Strother M. Newman, Byron P. Stratton and Edward N. Newman, together with all other persons and corporations as become stockholders in the company hereby incorporated, are hereby constituted a body corporate and politic, by and under the name of the North Carolina Trust Company, by which name the said corporation may sue and be sued, plead and be impleaded in any court of law and equity, and shall have power to make such by-laws and regulations not inconsistent with the laws of this state as may be deemed necessary for the government of the said company, and which shall be binding on them and requisite to carry on business. It shall have perpetual succession; shall have and use a common seal,

Corporators.

Body corporate.

Corporate name.

Corporate powers.

that may be changed or altered at will, and shall enjoy all the rights, privileges, liberties, immunities and franchises usually pertaining to a banking, savings bank, safe deposit, trust, guarantee, fiscal, fiduciary, surety, agency and trading corporation.

How and when organized.

Sec. 2. This company shall be organized by any one of the resident corporations [corporators] giving ten days' notice, in writing, to the other corporators to meet in the town of Salisbury, North Carolina, in person or by proxy, within two years from the passage of this act, and a majority of the corporators shall constitute a quorum for the transaction of business, and the company may be organized when one hundred thousand dollars have been subscribed and ten per centum thereon paid in.

Provisional directors.

Sec. 3. The persons named in the first section of this act are hereby constituted provisional directors of the company, of whom three shall be a quorum, and shall hold office as such until the first general election of directors under this act. At such general meeting the stockholders may choose not more than seven or less than three persons to be directors of the company, of whom three shall be a quorum. Thereafter, the annual general meeting of the stockholders of the company for the election of directors and other general purposes shall be held at such place and on such day and upon such notice as may be provided by by-law by the company. Vacancies occurring in the board of directors may be filled for the unexpired remainder of the term by the board from among the qualified stockholders of the company. If at any time an election of directors is not made or does not take effect at the proper time, the company shall not be held to be thereby dissolved, but such election may take place at any general meeting of the company duly called for the purpose, and the retiring directors shall continue in office until their successors are appointed and qualified.

Annual election of directors.

Failure to elect directors shall not disolve corporation.

Election of president and other officers.

Sec. 4. The directors shall from time to time elect from among themselves a president and a vice-president of the company, and shall also name all other officers thereof.

Directors shall make by-laws, etc.

Sec. 5. The directors of the company shall have full power to make all by-laws not contrary to law or this act for the regulation of the affairs and management of the company, for making calls upon stock subscribed, for the establishment of a head office and of branch offices, and of changing from time to time the location of such offices; they shall have full power to manage the affairs of the company, and may make or cause to be made for the company any description of contract which the company may by law enter into.

Stock books may be opened.

Sec. 6. That the incorporators and directors named in the first section of this act shall have power forthwith to open stock books and procure subscriptions of stock in the said company;

that the capital stock of said company shall be divided into shares of one hundred dollars ($100.00) each, and shall be for such a total sum as the directors or stockholders in general meeting may determine, and that the said amount of stock may be increased or decreased from time to time by the stockholders or directors to suit the needs of the company: Provided, that such capital stock shall not exceed the sum of one million dollars ($1,000,000), and the shares shall be personal property and are transferable as the by-laws may determine and shares shall be non-assessable, and the stockholders shall not be, individually nor in their private property, liable for the debts of the corporation. And it shall be lawful to accept real estate, money, stocks, and bonds of other corporations, or other securities, labor and articles of value, in payment of subscription to the capital stock of this company. And also, that this said company may subscribe to, pay for, hold and own stock and other securities of other corporations.

Division of shares.

Limitation to capital stock.

Individual liability of stockholders.

Sec. 7. That this company shall have the right to do a general banking business, to receive on deposit and pay out, by check or otherwise, the common currency of the country; deal in exchange, gold, silver and other coin, bullion, uncurrent paper and public or other securities, including any and all forms of indebtedness; to make loans and discounts; to buy and sell exchange, and to lend its own or its depositors' funds; to obtain loans for any person, firm or corporation, and to do all things necessary towards mediating between borrower and lender, either with or without guarantee, and to charge for such service such commission as may be agreed upon between the borrower and the said company; to lend and borrow money on its own account, and to give or receive such security as may be lawful and expedient, and generally to do and to perform any other act or thing authorized by law to be done and performed by a bank of depositing and lending, according to The Code of this state, or that any other bank chartered by this state may do; and said company is hereby made a legal depository for any state, county, township, city, town or municipal funds, corporations, companies, persons, trust funds by other trustees and person in positions of trust, whatsoever.

Empowered to do a general banking business.

Sec. 8. That this said company is hereby authorized and empowered, at any time hereafter, by a resolution of the board of directors and a full compliance with the laws of this state relative thereto, in force at the time of the adoption of such resolution, to organize, in connection with its general business, a department for savings, and do a savings bank business for the convenience of small depositors, and to make such regulations in regard thereto as will enable said company to receive small

Empowered to establish savings bank.

deposits in the savings department, and to give certificates or other evidence of deposits, paying such interest thereon as may be agreed upon, consistent with the laws of the state, as to the rate, and to regulate the time of payment and notice of demand.

May acquire real estate.

Sec. 9. That said company shall have power to buy, take, acquire, hold and own all kinds of real, mixed and personal estates and properties, in the name and right of said company; and as owner thereof, or in trust for said company or for others, and convey and encumber the same, or any part thereof, as natural persons can or are authorized to do under the laws of this state, and to and with the same effect; and it shall be competent for the said company to convey and encumber real estate or any interest therein by a deed executed in the name of said company, by its president or chief officer, with the corporate seal affixed thereto, as well as the modes now exercised by other corporations; and the same may be admitted to probate and registration on the acknowledgment of the said president or other chief officer signing the same, or proof by any subscribing witness thereto, as in case of natural persons, before the proper officers.

May receive money in trust.

Sec. 10. The said company shall have power to receive money in trust and accumulate the same at such legal rate of interest as may be obtained or agreed on, or to allow interest not exceeding the legal rate; to accept and execute trusts of every description as fully as natural persons could, which may be committed to said company by any person or persons whatsoever, or by any corporation, or by order, decree, or authority of any court of record, upon such terms as may be agred upon, provided or declared thereto; to act as agents for the purpose of issuing, registering or countersigning certificates of stocks, bonds or other evidences of debt of any state corporation, association, municipality or public authority, on such terms as may be agreed upon; to lease and rent real estate and collect rents from the same; to accept from and execute trusts for married women in respect of their separate property or estate, whether real, personal or mixed, and to act as agent for them in the management, sale and disposition of their properties: Provided, however, that said corporation shall not be required to receive or hold any property or moneys, or to execute any trust contrary to its own desire. All money or property held in trust shall constitute a special deposit, and the accounts thereof shall be kept separate, and such funds and the investments or loans of them shall be specially appropriated to the security and payment of such deposits, and not be subject to any other liabilities of the company, and for the purpose of securing the observance of this proviso, said company shall have a trust department in which all business pertaining to such trust

Lease and rent real estate.

Proviso.

Moneys held in trust shall constitute special deposit.

property shall be kept separate and distinct from its general business.

Courts may appoint said company guardian, administrator, etc.

Sec. 11. That in all cases where an application may be made to any court or other public authority having jurisdiction to appoint a curator, guardian, collector, committee of an idiot or insane person, administrator of any person dying testate or intestate, trustee, commissioners, receiver, fiduciary or agent of any character, such court shall have power to appoint such company upon the like application, terms and conditions that any natural person might be so appointed; and it shall be lawful for any person, by deed, will or other writing to appoint said company a trustee, executor, guardian, committee of an idiot or insane person, assignee, fiduciary or agent of any character, and as such it shall be subject to all the obligations and liabilities and vested with all the authority and powers of natural persons acting in like capacity.

Executors, guardians and others may deposit funds with said company for investment.

Sec. 12. That it shall be lawful for any individual, executor, administrator, collector, guardian, committee, commissioner, receiver, assignee, trustee, public officer, fiduciary or other persons having the custody of any bonds, stocks, securities, money or other valuables, [to] deposit the same for investment or safe keeping with said company: Provided, nothing in this act shall be construed as releasing from liability on his bond or other sureties thereon such executor, administrator, collector, guardian, committee, commissioners, receiver, assignee, trustee, public officer or fiduciary, when any bonds, stocks, sucurities, moneys or other valuables so deposited shall be lost, destroyed or misapplied while on deposit with said company, or the same shall depreciate in value during such time on account of the performance or non-performance of some act of said company.

Subject to orders and decrees of courts.

Sec. 13. That every court wherein said company shall be appointed, or shall be allowed to qualify as guardian, committee, executor, administrator, trustee or receiver, or in which it is made the depository of moneys or other valuables, shall have power to make all orders and compel obedience thereto, and require said company to render all accounts which said courts might lawfully make or require if such company were a natural person.

Authorized to invest moneys received in trust.

Sec. 14. That said company is authorized to invest moneys received in trust on deposit, loan or otherwise, and to take, have and hold estates, real, personal and mixed, obtained with the moneys aforesaid or with funds belonging to said company, and to sell, grant, mortgage or otherwise incumber, lease or dispose of the same, and to that end may execute all deeds or other instruments concerning the same, as hereinbefore provided; to subscribe for and take stock in any other incorporated companies;

to borrow and lend money and give or take notes therefor, as the case may be; discount, buy and sell notes, bonds, drafts and other securities or evidences of debt; to lend money at such rates of interest as may be agreed upon, subject to the general laws of the state as to the rate, with privilege to charge and retain same in advance, and secure the repayment thereof by mortgages or deeds in trust, made directly to said company, or to others in trust for it, on all kinds of property; to act as agents for others in borrowing and lending money, charging such compensation therefor, by way of commission, as may be agreed upon by said company and the party for whom it is acting; to deal in exchange, foreign or domestic securities, mortgages, lands, certificates of indebtedness, stock of incorporated companies, notes, loans, bonds of the United States, or of any state thereof, of foreign countries, or of any city, county, or any incorporated company or individual.

May guarantee, indorse and secure notes.

Sec. 15. That said company shall have power to guarantee, endorse and secure the payment and punctual performance and collection of notes, debts, bills of exchange, contracts, bonds, accounts, claims, rents, annuities, mortgages, choses in action, evidences of debt, certificates of property of value, checks and the title to property, indebtedness of companies, partnerships, cities, counties, municipalities, et cetera, in this state and others, on such terms or commissions as may be agreed upon or established by said company and the parties dealing therewith.

May receive merchandise, etc., on storage.

Sec. 16. That said company may receive upon storage, or otherwise, merchandise, specie, plate, stocks, promissory notes, certificates and evidences of debt, contracts, and all other personal properties whatsoever; take charge and custody of real and personal estates and securities, and advance money thereupon on such terms as may be established or approved by said company; that in all cases in which public officers of municipal or private corporations are authorized to deposit money, stocks, bonds or evidences of debt, such deposit by such officers or corporations may be made with said company: Provided, that nothing in this act shall change the rule of law now in force as to the liability of public officers.

May sell at public auction property held as security; default in payment.

Sec. 17. That as to all property held by said company as security, it shall be lawful for the said company to sell at public auction, or private sale, in its discretion, all property of what kind soever mentioned or specified in any contract or agrement between the company and other parties, real estate excepted, after ten days shall have elapsed from the time of maturity of an obligation under said contract or agreement, or immediately upon the discovery of any fraud, misrepresentation, or concealment, in regard to the ownership, or otherwise, which might jeopardize the rights of the company, or its security, after ten days' advertisement of the time and place of sale by bills posted at the court-house door in Salisbury, North Carolina, and three other public places in Rowan county, or by an advertisement in a newspaper published at Salisbury, North Carolina; and to reimburse itself out of the proceeds of such sales for the money due it, with interest, storage, cost and other charges of all kinds, and to indemnify itself for any loss it may have sustained by the non-fulfillment of such contract, or by reason of said misrepresentations, fraud or concealment.

Shall advertise sale of such property.

Sec. 18. That the said company is authorized to make, execute and issue, in the transaction of its business, all papers, receipts, certificates, vouchers, obligations and contracts, and the same shall be binding if signed for and in behalf of the company by the president or other chief officer thereof, except for sale or transfer of real estate, which is hereinbefore provided for, unless otherwise provided for in the by-laws.

Orders signed by chief officer of company binding.

Sec. 19. That when married women, minors or apprentices lend money to or deposit same, or other things of value, with said company, in the course of the business herein provided for, or in the course of doing a banking business herein provided for, either generally or specifically, in their own or to their own name or credit, they, or any of them, may collect or draw the same, in their own name, or on their own check or order, and they and all other persons [shall] be bound thereby; and such collection, settlement, draft, checks or order shall be a valid and sufficient release and discharge to said company.

Deposits by minors and feme coverts.

Sec. 20. Whenever any bond, recognizance, obligation, stipulation or undertaking is by law, municipal or otherwise, or the rules or regulations of any board, body corporate, municipal or otherwise, required or permitted to be made, given, tendered or filed for the security or protection of any person, persons, corporation, municipality or other organization whatsoever, conditioned for the doing of or not doing of any such bond, recognizance, obligation, stipulation or undertaking specified, any and all heads of departments, public officers, state, county, town or municipal, and any and all boards, courts, judges and municipalities now and hereafter required or permitted to accept or approve the sufficiency of any such bond, recognizance, obligation, stipulation or undertaking, may, in the discretion of such head of department, court, judge, public officer or municipality, accept such bond, recognizance, obligation, stipulation or undertaking and approve the same whenever the same is executed or the conditions thereof are guaranteed by said company, and the provisions of this section shall also apply as between individuals, where bond is required to be given.

May enter on lands, etc.

Bonds executed by said company may be approved.

Sec. 21. Whenever any such bond, recognizance, obligation,

Execution of bonds. stipulation or undertaking is required or permitted to be made, given, tendered or filed with one surety or with two or more sureties, the execution of the same, or the guaranteeing the performance of the conditions thereof, shall be sufficient when executed or guaranteed by said company, and any and all heads of departments, courts, judges, boards and municipalities, and all public officers, state, county, town or municipal, all corporations and private individuals whose duty it may be or shall hereafter be to accept or approve the sufficiency of any such bond, recognizance, obligation, stipulation or undertaking, may accept and approve the same when executed or guaranteed by said company; and said company is hereby vested with full power and authority to execute or guarantee such bonds, recognizances, stipulations, obligations or undertaking, whether given under the law of this state or of the United States, or of any state or county.

May conduct an insurance department. Sec. 22. That this company may also conduct an insurance department and act as the agent of any insurance company, whether life, fire, accident or other kinds of insurable risks, for the protection of itself and its patrons, the same as a natural person or firm may do, charging the legal rates and commissions for the same.

May construct safes, etc. Sec. 23. That the said company may construct, erect, purchase or lease such fire- and burglar-proof buildings, vaults, iron and composition safes or other buildings or means which may be or become necessary, and generally to transact and perform all the business relating to such deposit and safe keeping or preservation of all such articles or valuables as may be deposited with the said company; may act as the fiscal or transfer agent of or trustee for any state, county, municipality, body politic or corporation, or for any person or persons, and in such capacity may receive and disburse money, and negotiate, sell, transfer, register and countersign certificates of stock, bonds or other evidences of indebtedness.

May act as fiscal agent, etc., for counties, towns, etc.

Capital stock of said company taken as security in its undertakings. Sec. 35. Whenever the said company shall be appointed to any place of trust enumerated in any of the foregoing sections, or whenever deposits of money or valuables of any kind shall be made with said company, the capital stock and its property and effects shall be taken and considered as security required by law for the faithful performance of its duties, and shall be absolutely liable therefor, and no other security shall be required from it, on the execution of the bond required, where one is now required of any natural person acting in such capacity.

Officers or agents of company applying funds otherwise than as provided guilty of embezzlements. Sec. 26. That any officer or employee of said company who shall apply any of the deposits of any kind of said company to his own use or to the use of any person or persons not entitled thereto, shall be deemed guilty of embezzlement, and upon conviction shall be punished by imprisonment in the penitentiary for a term of not less than one nor more than five years, and shall be responsible in any suit at law for injury, loss, expense or damages incurred by reason of its prosecution or in consequence of said act, either to the company or to any party aggrieved, damaged or injured thereby.

Sec. 27. That whenever any business is transacted or service rendered by such company, where fees, interest, discount, commissions or other charges are not specifically stated or agreed upon, the said company is empowered to charge and collect such fees, interest, discounts, commissions or other charges as may be established by the directors or allowed by the laws of the state. **When compensation is not agreed upon charges by company.**

Sec. 28. That said company shall exist and be in force and effect, with all the powers hereinbefore conferred, for the term of ninety-nine years (99) from and after the ratification of this act. **Duration of charter.**

Ratified the 6th day of March, A. D. 1899.

CHAPTER 337.

An act to amend the charter of The Bank of Carthage.

The General Assembly of North Carolina do enact:

Section 1. That section one of chapter one hundred and eighty-six of the private laws of North Carolina, passed at the session of eighteen hundred and eighty-nine, be, and the same is hereby amended as follows: After the word "that" and before the words "James D. McIver" in the first line insert "W. W. Mills, W. A. Mills, William Hayes." **Section 1, chapter 186, private laws of 1889, amended.**

Sec. 2. In line one of section three after the word "or" strike out the words "a majority" and substituting the words "any three or more." **Section 3 amended.**

Sec. 3. That section four be and the same is hereby amended as follows: In line four after the word "or" and before the word "of" strike out the words "a majority" and substitute the words "any three or more," and in line five after the word "or" strike out the words "a majority" and substitute the words "any three or more." **Section 4 amended.**

Sec. 4. That section thirteen be, and the same is hereby amended as follows: In lines six and seven strike out the words "twenty-five cents" and substitute the words "ten cents." **Section 13 amended**

Sec. 5. That the time for the organization of the Bank of Carthage, under said charter, be, and the same is hereby extended six months from the ratification of this act. **Time for organization extended.**

Sec. 6. That that [this] act shall be in force and effect from and after its ratification.

Ratified the 6th day of March, 1899.

CHAPTER 338.

An act to validate, ratify and confirm the charter granted by the secretary of state to the Linville River Railaoad Company, and to validate the transfer of the corporate rights, franchises, privileges and property of said company to the Linville Railway Company, and to charter the same.

Preamble. Wnereas, on the thirtieth day of July, eighteen hundred and ninety-six, the secretary of state granted letters of incorporation to the Linville River Railroad Company, and the said company was organized under said charter and began the construction of a railroad in Mitchell county, North Carolina, and failed, and the properties, franchises, etc., of the said company were sold at a judicial sale, and Isaac T. Mann became the purchaser of the same, and is now the sole owner of the same,

Preamble continued. And whereas, the said Isaac T. Mann has associated with himself certain parties, and wishes to complete the said road and to extend the same, and desires for the purpose of the organization to become incorporated under the name of the Linville Railroad Company; now, therefore,

The General Assembly of North Carolina do enact:

Charter of Linville River Railroad Company confirmed. Section 1. That the charter of the Linville River Railroad Company, granted by the secretary of state of North Carolina and recorded in the Book of Railroad Companies in his office, pages two hundred and twenty-seven and two hundred and twenty-nine, bearing date of thirtieth day of July, eighteen hundred and ninety-six, be, and the same is hereby ratified, approved and confirmed.

Corporators. Sec. 2. That Isaac T. Mann, now owner as purchaser under a judicial sale of the property, franchises, rights-of-way, land and all other rights and properties of the said Linville River Railroad Company, Edwin T. Mann, James P. Taylor, and such other persons as they may associate with them, be, and they are hereby constituted and made a body politic and corporate, under the name and style of the Linville Railway Company; and such corporation shall have all the rights and powers of the Linville River Railroad Company, and shall succeed to all of its properties, franchises, rights and privileges, and in addition thereto the said corporation shall have all the rights and privileges conferred upon other railroad corporations in chapter forty-nine of The Code of North Carolina and the acts amendatory thereof. The duration of this corporation shall be sixty years from July thirtieth, eighteen hundred and ninety-six.

Body corporate. Corporate name. Corporate rights and privileges.

May consolidate with other roads. Sec. 3. The said corporation shall have the power to consolidate with or lease or sell to any other railroad company, and it shall have the right to change its name by a vote of a majority of the board of directors.

Sec. 4. After completing the line of road from Cranberry to Pineola the said corporation shall have the right to extend the same to the town of Boone, in Watauga county, or to the town of Lenoir, or some other point in Caldwell county, or to either or both of them; and it may extend further to some point on the Western North Carolina division of the Southern Railway, at or near the town of Morganton. Road may be extended.

Sec. 5. The corporation by a vote of a majority of its stock may from time to time increase its capital stock to a sum not exceeding one million dollars; and it may issue bonds, not exceeding in amount ten thousand dollars for each completed mile of road, and to secure the same by mortgage or mortgages of all or any part of its line of railway. Capital stock may be increased.

Sec. 6. This act shall be in force from and after its ratification.

Ratified the 6th day of March, A. D. 1899.

CHAPTER 339.

An act to incorporate the town of Shallotte in the county of Brunswick.

The General Assembly of North Carolina do enact:

Section 1. That the town of Shallotte, in the county of Brunswick, be, and the same is hereby incorporated by the name and style of the town of Shallotte, and is hereby invested with all the powers, rights, privileges and immunities enumerated in chapter sixty-two of volume two of The Code of North Carolin. entitled, "Cities and Towns," and subject to the restrictions and liabilities specified in the same not inconsistent with this act. Incorporated. Corporate name.

Sec. 2. That the corporate limits of said town shall be as follows: Beginning at the mouth of Charles branch; then about north so as to intersect with the line of James Holmes on the east; then with his line the same course to intersect with A. S. White's line; then with his line bearing an eastward course so as to include J. B. Gray and J. M. Stanley; then westward a direct course to Mulberry swamp; then with said swamp to Shallotte river; then with said river to beginning. Corporate limits

Sec. 3. That the officers of said incorporation shall consist of a mayor five commissioners, marshal and treasurer, and the following persons shall fill said offices until the first Monday in May, eighteen hundred and ninety-nine, and until their successors in office have been elected and qualifid, viz: For mayor, Affairs of town, by whom managed.

Temporary officers.

George Leonard; for commissioners, James Holmes, Charles Hemmingway, W. A. Frink, R. V. Leonard and F. P. White; for marshal, McD. Turner; for treasurer, John W. Moore. Said officers, before entering upon the discharge of their duties, shall go before some justice of the peace of said county and take the oath of office prescribed by law for such offices.

Annual elections.

Sec. 4. There shall be an election for officers mentioned in this act on the first Monday in May, eighteen hundred and ninety-nine, and annually thereafter, under the same restrictions that state and county elections are held, and all qualified electors who have resided within the incorporate limits of said town for the period of sixty days next preceding the election shall be entitled to vote at said election.

Qualified voters.

Commissioners shall pass by-laws, etc.

Sec. 5. That the commissioners of said town shall have power to pass all by-laws, rules and regulations necessary for the good government of said town, not inconsistent with the laws of this state, and shall also have power to abate all nuisances and may impose such fines and penalties as may be necessary to abate them, and they shall have power to levy and collect a tax not exceeding fifty cents on the poll and not to exceed sixteen and two-thirds cents on the hundred dollars valuation of all property, real, personal and mixed, and shall also have power to tax all other subjects of taxation, not to exceed one-half of the state taxes.

Fines and penalties.

Tax levy.

Election of secretary.

Sec. 6. That it shall be the duty of the commissioners when organized to appoint one of their number as secretary, whose duty it shall be to keep a record of all proceedings of said commissioners, and said commissioners may require the treasurer and marshal each to enter into a bond approved by the commissioners, payable to the state of North Carolina, to the use of the town of Shallotte, conditioned for the faithful performance of their duties, approved by the commissioners.

Marshal empowered to make arrests.

Sec. 7. That when it shall be necessary for the preservation of the public peace, good order and common decency, or the protection of life, liberty, person or property of individuals, the town marshal shall have the authority, and it shall be the duty of such marshal, to arrest the body of offending parties who have violated the law in the presence of such marshal, without warrant, and take such person or persons before the mayor of said town as early as practicable, to be dealt with as the law directs, and for every resistance of such authority by such offenders or others, the party so resisting shall be punished as the ordinances of said town shall provide, and if necessary the marshal shall have power to call to his aid any bystander to assist in making any legal arrest, and any one so summoned or called, who refuses or

Marshal may call by-standers to his aid.

fails to arrest, shall, upon conviction before the mayor, be punished as the ordinances of said town shall prescribe.

Sec. 8. That the commissioners shall have the power to apply the taxes collected under this act, together with all fines and forfeitures, to the public streets of said town as they may find necessary. Application of taxes and fines.

Sec. 9. That any person violating any ordinance of said town shall be deemed guilty of a misdemeanor, but the punishment thereof upon conviction shall not exceed a fine of fifty dollars or imprisonment for thirty days. Persons violating ordinances guilty of a misdemeanor.

Sec. 10. That it shall be unlawful for any person or persons to manufacture or sell any spirituous liquors, or to sell any wine, cider, malt liquors or any other intoxicating drink within the limits of said town or within one and one-half miles of the outer limits of said town; and any person violating any of the provisions of this section shall be deemed guilty of a misdemeanor and upon conviction shall be punished by a fine not exceeding fifty dollars or imprisoned for not more than thirty days, in the discretion of the court. Sale of liquors within one and a half miles of limits a misdemeanor.

Sec. 11. That this act shall be in force from and after its ratification.

Ratified the 6th day of March, A. D. 1899.

CHAPTER 340.

An act to incorporate the town of Pinebluff.

The General Assembly of North Carolina do enact:

Section 1. That the town of Pinebluff, in the county of Moore, be and is hereby incorporated under the name and style of Pinebluff, and shall be subject to all the provisions of chapter sixty-two of The Code in reference to incorporated towns, and not inconsistent with the provisions of this act. Incorporated. Corporate name.

Sec. 2. The corporate limits of said town shall be as follows: The eastern limit shall be the line of the Raleigh & Augusta Air Line R. R.; the western limit shall be a line running north and south along the western line of the farm of E. Vander Meersch and others; the northern limit shall be the Juniper branch and a line or lines continuing in the same direction as the Juniper branch until an intersection is formed with the above defined east and west lines; the southern limit shall be the Forked creek and a line or lines continuing in the same direction as the Forked creek until an intersection is formed with the above defined east and west lines. Corporate limits.

Town officers.

Sec. 3. That the officers of said town shall consist of a mayor and five aldermen or commissioners. The mayor when present shall preside at the meeting of said board of aldermen or commissioners, but shall not be entitled to vote, except in case of a tie. In the absence of the mayor the board may elect one of their number as mayor pro tem; but the mayor shall not be entitled to vote except in case of a tie. The following named persons shall fill said offices until the first Monday in May, one thousand eight hundred and ninety-nine, and until their successors are elected and qualified, to-wit: J. C. S. Twitchell, mayor; L. S. Packard, E. Vanuer Meersch, Joseph White, G. R. Parker and R. A. Campbell, commissioners. Said officers, before entering upon the discharge of their duties, shall take and subscribe to an oath to support the constitution of the United States and constitution and laws of the state of North Carolina, and shall have power to appoint a marshal, secretary and treasurer, who shall hold their respective offices for one year and until their successors are appointed and qualified.

Temporary officers.

Shall take oath.

Provisions for annual election.

Sec. 4. That it shall be the duty of the commissioners of said town to provide for an election on the first Monday in May, one thousand eight hundred and ninety-nine, and annually thereafter, according to the laws of the state; and the officers elected shall hold their offices until thir successors are elected and qualified.

Persons entitled to vote.

Sec. 5. All qualified electors of the state who have been residents of the town for ninety days prior to any election in said town shall be entitled to vote.

Commissioners empowered to pass ordinances.

Sec. 6. That the commissioners of said town shall have power to pass all by-laws, rules and regulations necessary for the good government of said town, not inconsistent with the laws of this state; and shall also have power to abate all nuisances, and may impose such fines and penalties as may be necessary to abate them; and they shall have power to lay and collect taxes on all subjects of state taxation, not to exceed the state tax, for the necessary expenses of the town, for the support of a public free school, according to the general law of the state, and for such other purposes as are necessary for the public welfare.

Levy of taxes.

Persons violating ordinances guilty of a misdemeanor.

Sec. 7. That any persons violating any ordinance of said town shall be deemed guilty of a misdemeanor; but the punishment thereof, upon conviction, shall not exceed a fine of fifty dollars or imprisonment more than thirty days.

Sec. 8. That this act shall be in force from and after its ratification.

Ratified the 6th day of March, A. D. 1899.

CHAPTER 341.

An act to incorporate the town of Richfield in Stanly county.

The General Assembly of North Carolina do enact:

Section 1. That the village of Richfield, in the county of Stanly, be and the same is hereby incorporated by the name and style of the town of Richfield, and it shall be subject to all the provisions of law now existing in reference to incorporated towns. Incorporated. Corporate name.

Sec. 2. That the corporate limits and boundaries of said town shall be as follows, viz: The crossing of Main and Church [streets], two hundred and fifty feet from the Yadkin Railroad, shall be considered the center of said town: Beginning at the center and running five hundred and thirty-three and one-third yards each way along Main and Church streets, the outside lines being one thousand and sixty-six and two-third yards each, forming a perfect square, in accordance with the survey and plot of said town. Corporate limits.

Sec. 3. That the officers of said town shall consist of a mayor, three commissioners and marshal, and the following-named named persons shall fill said offices until the first Monday in May, eighteen hundred and ninety-nine, or until the time prescribed by law for the election of such officers, viz: For mayor, Cicero Ritchie; for commissioners, Charles F. Floyd, George G. Ritchie and W. C. Morgan: and for marshal, M. M. Ritchie. Officers. Temporary officers.

Sec. 4. There shall be an election held for officers mentioned in this act on the first Monday in May, eighteen hundred and ninety nine, and each succeeding year thereafter under the same restrictions and regulations that county and state elections are held; and all citizens within said corporation who shall have resided in the county and state the length of time required by the general law of the state for all voters, and thirty days in the corporate limits of the town, shall be allowed to vote. Annual election of town officers.

Sec. 5. That said commissioners shall have the power to pass all by-laws, rules, ordinances and regulations for the good government of the town, not inconsistent with the laws of the state or of the United States, and to levy and collect a tax on all subjects of state taxation, not to exceed sixteen and two-third cents on each one hundred dollars worth of property, and a corresponding amount of poll property, and to impose fines for the violation of town ordinances, and to collect the same, which shall go into the hands of the town treasurer, whom the mayor and commissioners may elect, for the benefit of the town. Powers of commissioners to pass by-laws, etc. Maximum tax rate.

Sec. 6. That this charter shall be subject to all conditions and privileges heretofore granted any church or school house within the corporate limits of said town in regard to the sale of spirituous or intoxicating liquors. Charter subject to certain conditions, etc.

Sec. 7. That this act shall be in force from and after its ratification.

Ratified the 6th day of March, A. D. 1899.

CHAPTER 342.

An act to incorporate "The Carolina Power Company."

The General Assembly of North Carolina do enact:

Corporators. Section 1. That Everett Waddy and Pescal Davie, of Richmond, Virginia; J. M. Mullen, of Petersburg, Virginia; W. S. Parker and W. A. Hunt, of Henderson, North Carolina, or such of them as may accept the provisions of this act, their associates and successors, be, and they are hereby incorporated and made a body politic and incorporate by the name and style of the "Carolina Power Company," and under that name and style may sue and be sued, implead and be impleaded, contract and be contracted with, adopt and use a common seal, which it may alter and renew at its pleasure; shall have perpetual succession and shall have and enjoy all the powers, immunities, liberties and franchises pertaining to corporate bodies and necessary for the purposes of this act.

Body politic.

Corporate name.

Corporate powers. Sec. 2. The said company is authorized and empowered:

May hold land (1) To acquire by purchase, lease or other operation of law, in fee simple or for a less interest, and to such extent and in such quantity as its purposes may require, the lands in the state of North Carolina along the banks of Roanoke river, and the water rights and privileges connected therewith and pertaining to said river, suitable for the utilization of the water power of said river, whether such power upon the lands and rights that may be so acquired has been fully or partially developed or wholly undeveloped, together with all rights, easements, powers and franchises, canals, dams and other structures, mills, factories, machinery, appliances, and other buildings and improvements appurtenant thereto, or located and erected thereon: Provided, that the land acquired for the purposes of their [this] sub-section shall at no time exceed five thousand acres.

May develope and utilize water power. (2) To fully develop and utilize the water power upon the property and rights so acquired by it, for navigation or manufacturing purposes, for the construction and operation of mills and factories of any kind and for any purpose, and for supplying both individuals and corporations within the state with power in form of electric current and hydraulic, pneumatic and steam pressure, or any of the said powers, and in any and all other forms for use in driving machinery and forlight, heat, and all other uses to which the power so supplied can be made applicable; and to fix, charge, collect and receive rates and tolls therefor, and to that end maintain and enlarge such dams, canals, and other structures as may be upon its property when acquired, and erect and maintain such other dams, water-ways and obstructions in and across siad Roanoke river, and cut and construct such canals and waste vays and other structures from said river, upon the lands of aid company as may be required to generate, develop, store, use, ransmit and distribute power of all kinds: Provided, that in he construction and maintenance of said dams, canals and wastevays and in the development and use of said water power, neither the rights nor property of persons owning lands on the Roanoke river, nor the rights, franchises, privileges or property of any other corporation shall be interfered with or encroached upon in any unreasonable manner, to the substantial injury of any ther person or corporation.

(3) To purchase in fee simple or otherwise other lands contiguous to the aforesaid proposed acquisitions, and to lay out the same into streets, parks, blocks and building lots; and if it so desire, erect suitable structures and buildings thereon, and sell, lease and donate the same, whether improved or unimproved: Provided, that the land acquired for the purposes of this subsection shall at no time exceed ten thousand acres. **To purchase certain bonds.**

(4) To sell, lease, donate and supply its water power for any of the purposes heretofore set out, and to build and equip mills and factories upon its property, and operate, sell or lease the same, or make such other disposition of them as it may deem best. **To sell and lease water power.**

(5) To do any and all things expedient for acquiring, utilizing, improving, developing and disposing of the property and rights needed for its aforesaid purposes, and to that end the said company may consolidate and merge its stock, property and franchises with and into those of any other company or companies incorporated under the laws of this state organized for any of the purposes for which this company is chartered, upon such terms and under such name as may be agreed upon between the companies uniting or connecting, merging or consolidating, or may acquire the said property and franchises of such other company or companies by lease or purchase, and for that purpose power is hereby given to it, and to such other company or companies, to make and carry out such contracts as will facilitate and consummate such connections, merges or consolidation, lease or purchase: Provided, that every such contract of consolidation and merges, lease or purchase, shall be recorded as and where deeds of realty are permitted and required to be recorded, and a copy thereof filed in the office of the secretary of state. **Any and all things requisite to said purpose.** **May consolidate with other companies.**

Sec. 3. The capital stock of said company shall not be less than one hundred thousand dollars, to be divided into shares of one hundred dollars each, with the right to increase the same from time to time to an additional amount, not exceeding two million dollars, by the issue and sale of shares of preferred or **Capital stock.** **Capital stock may be increased.**

common stock, or both, upon such terms and conditions and under such regulations as the board of directors, with the approval of the majority in interest of the stockholders of said company shall prescribe. Shares of stock may be paid for in cash, real or personal property, services, work, labor and materials, and bonds, stocks and property of other corporate bodies, required, employed and furnished for and in the prosecution of the objects of the company, upon such terms and at such price and rate as the board of directors may determine and agree upon.

Stock subscribed, how paid.

May borrow money.

Sec. 4. It shall be lawful for said company to borrow money and issue and sell its bonds from time to time for such sums and on such terms as its board of directors may deem expedient and proper for any of the purposes of the company, and may secure the payment of said bonds by mortgages or deeds of trust upon all or any portion of its property, real, personal or mixed, its contracts and privileges and its chartered rights and franchises, including its franchise to be a corporation, and it may, as the business of the company shall require, sell, lease, convey and encumber the same, and it shall be lawful for said company to subscribe to and hold the stock and bonds of manufacturing or other corporations, and any manufacturing or other corporations may subscribe to, guarantee and hold the stock and bonds of the said company.

May hold stock and bonds of other companies.

Individual liability.

Sec. 5. No stockholder in the said company shall be held liable or made responsible for its debts and liabilities in a larger or further sum than the amount of any unpaid subscription upon his stock.

Name may be changed.

Sec. 6. That said company may change its name whenever the holders of two-thirds of the stock of the company shall so determine at any general meeting or special meeting called for that purpose, certificate of which change to be filed in the secretary of state's office, with the signatures of the president and secretary and the seal of the company thereto affixed.

Principal office.

Sec. 7. That the principal office of said company may be at such point in Halifax or Northampton county as the by-laws may designate; but the directors may establish branch offices elsewhere, either within or beyond the limits of this state.

Conflicting laws repealed.

Sec. 8. That all sections or parts of sections of chapter sixteen (16) and forty-nine (49) of The Code of North Carolina, or of the statutes amendatory thereof, or other laws in conflict or inconsistent with this act, are hereby declared inoperative, so far as they affect the privileges, rights and powers hereby conferred.

Sec. 9. That this act shall be in force from and after the date of its ratification.

Ratified the 6th day of March, A. D. 1899.

CHAPTER 343.

An act to amend chapter fourteen of the public laws of eighteen hundred and ninety-six and eighteen hundred and ninety-seven, relating to the charter of the town of Cameron.

The General Assembly of North Carolina do enact:

Section 1. That section five of chapter fourteen of the public laws of eighteen hundred and seventy-six and eighteen hundred and seventy-seven be amended by inserting after the word "state" and before the word "tax" in line six of said section the words "and county." **Section 5, chapter 14, public laws of 1876-'77, amended.**

Sec. 2. This act shall be in force from its ratification.

Ratified the 6th day of March, A. D. 1899.

CHAPTER 344.

An act to incorporate the Salisbury and Fayetteville Coast Line Railway Company.

The General Assembly of North Carolina do enact:

Section 1. That A. C. Mauney, George Battleson and F. H. Mauney, and such other persons as may be connected and associated with them as stockholders, and their successors, be, and they are hereby created a body politic and corporate, under the name of Salisbury and Fayetteville Coast Line Railway Company, and by and in that name shall have the right to sue and be sued, plead and be impleaded in any court of law or equity; to have a common seal; shall have the right to make and pass all such by-laws and regulations for its government as may be necessary or expedient for that purpose; have the right to purchase, hold and acquire for the necessary purposes of the company, by gift, devise, or in any other manner, any estate, real, personal or mixed, and to hold, lease, mortgage or sell the same as the interest of the said company may require; and shall have all the rights and powers for the condemnation of a right-of-way over the lands of others necessary for the location and construction of said road and for the erection and location of depots, station houses, warehouses and other necessary establishments, or for altering, or extending the same; and shall have all the rights and privileges possessed and enjoyed by other railroad companies under the laws of North Carolina, and such as are specially conferred by chapter forty-nine (49) of The Code, volume first, and all amendments thereto. **Corporators. Body corporate. Corporate name. Corporate powers. May condemn land.**

May build and erect railroad.

Route of road.

Sec. 2. That the said company shall have power to build and construct a railroad, with one or more tracks, from the town of Salisbury, Rowan county, North Carolina, at some point in the valley near the gas house in said town; thence down said ravine to Town creek; thence down said creek to the Yadkin river, and down said river to a point below Swift Island opposite Little's Mills; thence to Fayetteville, Faison, Pink Hill, through Jones county to Cedar Point in said county, through any of the said counties along the proposed line of road, and shall have the right to build one or more branch lines to any point in said state.

Capital stock.

May be increased.

Sec. 3. The capital stock of said company shall be not less than five hundred thousand dollars ($500,000), divided into shares of five dollars ($5.00) each; but may be increased from time to time as the demands of said company shall require to an amount not exceeding two million dollars ($2,000,000).

Books of subscription may be opened.

Directors of company.

Sec. 4. That the persons named in section one, or either of them, shall have power to open books of subscription to the capital stock, and when the same shall be paid and subscribed in money or property to an amount not less than fifty thousand dollars ($50,000) may call a meeting of the stockholders, and organize the company. Until the election of directors, the persons named in section one shall be the directors of the company. All vacancies shall be filled by the board of directors. The principal office of the company and the place of holding the meetings shall be determined by the stockholders.

Empowered to mortgage property and franchises.

Counties, townships and towns may subscribe to stock.

Denomination of bonds.

Sec. 5. And said railway company shall have power to mortgage its property and franchises and to issue bonds on such terms and conditions and for such uses and purposes of said corporation as said company may deem necessary. That in addition to the provisions contained in the previous sections for subscriptions, it shall be lawful for any county, township, city or town, interested in the construction of said railway to subscribe to its capital stock such sum as the majority of their voters may authorize the county commissioners or the proper authorities of such city or town to subscribe, which subscription shall be made in bonds payable in such installments and at such rate per centum and at such times as the county commissioners or the proper authorities of such city or town may determine, said bonds to be of the denomination of one hundred dollars ($100) each, and shall be received by said company at par.

Commissioners shall order election on "bonds" or "no bonds"

Sec. 6. That for the purpose of determining the amount of said subscription it shall be the duty of the county commissioners of the counties through which said road may pass, or either of them, upon the written application of two hundred voters in any of said counties, or if [of] fifty voters in any township in any of said counties, specifying the amount to be subscribed therein, to submit to the qualified voters of such county or township the question of "Subscription" or "No subscription" to the capital stock of said railway company, and they shall have power to order an election specifying the time, place and purpose of said election, and shall appoint judges of election at each election precinct in said county or township, who shall hold and conduct said election, at which election the ballot shall have written or printed thereon the word "Subscription" or "No subscription," the said county commissioners having first fixed the amount proposed to be subscribed and the terms and conditions of said subscription, in accordance with the petition submitted to them, and giving notice of election in a newspaper published in the county in which the same is to be held for thirty days previous to said election; and the proper corporate authorities of any city or town in any of the said counties through which said road passes, upon a like petition of fifty voters in such city or town, shall in like manner, and after like notice submit the question of "Subscription or "No subscription" to the capital stock of said company, to the qualified electors in said city or town, and declare the result as hereafter directed in the cases of county or township elections.

Question submitted.

Ballots, form of.

Notice shall be given of election.

Sec. 7. It shall be the duty of the judges of election to make returns and to meet at their respective court-houses and count the votes and declare the result, as in other elections, which result shall be certified in writing to the chairman of the board of county commissioners or to the city or town council, as the case may be.

Duty of judges to make returns.

Sec. 8. If a majority of the ballots cast at such election shall be for subscription, then the chairman of the board of county commissioners, in the case of county or township elections, and the proper authorities in the case of city or town elections, should a majority of the ballots cast therein be for subscription, shall be authorized and required to subscribe to the capital stock of said company in behalf of said county, township, city or town, the sum which may have been fixed and named in the resolutions of said boards and notice of election and published as aforesaid, which subscription shall be made in bonds bearing interest as aforesaid. And that for the payment of the interest on said bonds, and to provide a sinking fund to pay or retire the principal thereof, according to the terms and conditions of said subscription, the said county commissioners and the said proper authorities of said city or town, as the case may be, are hereby authorized and empowered to levy and assess annually upon the taxable property of such county, township, city or town a tax of such per centum as may be necessary to pay the interest on said bonds and to pay or retire the principal thereof as aforesaid, which shall be known and styled in the tax-book as "rail-

If majority of ballots cast be for subscription, commissioners authorized to subscribe to stock.

Subscription made in bonds.

Special annual tax may be levied to provide sinking fund.

road tax" and shall be collected and paid out to the holders of the said coupons or bonds, under the same regulations as are now provided by law for the collection of taxes and the disbursement of the public funds in the said county, township, city or town respectively, so subscribing.

How collected and paid out

May cross tracks of other roads.

Sec. 9. That the said company shall have the power to cross the tracks of other railroads and connect with any railroad now or hereafter chartered and to lay down and use tracks through any town or city along the proposed line, by and with the consent of the corporate authorities of said town or city upon such terms as they may prescribe.

May construct part of road without completing all.

Sec. 10. That the said company can construct a part of said road without building the entire line, and may charge for transportation thereon both freight and passengers, at such rate as said company shall prescribe, subject to such general laws regulating the same as the general assembly [may] from time to time establish.

Sec. 11. That this act shall be in force from and after its ratification.

Ratified the 6th day of March, A. D. 1899.

CHAPTER 345

An act to incorporate the Piedmont Savings Bank.

Corporators.

The General Assembly of North Carolina do enact:

Section 1. That T. J. Brown, F. B. Efird, D. H. Browder, O. B. Eaton and L. W. Seabott, and their associates, successors and assignees be, and they are hereby created a body politic and corporate under the name and style of the Piedmont Savings Bank, and by such name may acquire, hold and convey real and personal property, sue and be sued, plead and be impleaded, in any courts of the state, and have a continual succession for (30) thirty years and a common seal for the purpose indicated in the title.

Body corporate.

Corporate name.

Corporate powers.

Sec. 2. That this corporation shall have the power to receive and pay out the lawful currency of the country, deal in exchange, gold and silver coin, stocks, bonds, notes and other securities; to loan money to or receive deposits from corporations, minors, apprentices, femes coverts, and his or her check or receipt therefor shall be as binding upon such minor or femes covert as though he or she were of full age, or a feme sole, or other persons, on such terms and time, and manner of collection and payment as may be agreed upon between the parties; and for the use and loan of money may charge the legal rate of interest, and may take and receive said interest at the time of making said loan free from all other con-

Rate of interest.

trol, contract or liability whatever; invest in stocks and bonds or other securities of this or any other state of the United States, or any corporation under the laws thereof, and to take such real and personal property conditioned in such forms for the payment of the principal and interest of money loaned, advanced or expended, as may be deemed most safe, expedient and beneficial.

Empowered to do a general banking business.

Sec. 3. That said corporation shall have power to do a general banking business; to received [receive] deposits, make loans and discounts; to lend and invest money in or upon the security of mortgages, pledges, deeds or otherwise, or lands, hereditaments, or personal property or interest therein of any description situated anywhere; to lend money upon, or purchase, or otherwise acquire bills of lading or the contents thereof, bills, notes, choses in action, or any and all negotiable or commercial papers, or any crops or produce whatever, or any stock, bullion, merchandise or other personal property, and the same to sell or anywise dispose of, and to charge any rate of interest on all such loans not exceeding the rate allowed by law.

Capital stock.

May be increased.

How payable.

Sec. 4. That the capital stock of such corporation shall not be less than ($5,000.00) five thousand dollars, which may be increased from time to time to a sum not to exceed ($200,000.00) two hundred thousand dollars, in shares of ($20.00) twenty dollars each, payable as follows: Ten per centum of each share in cash, and ten per centum per month for each month thereafter, until the full sum is paid. Said corporation may, however, commence the business of banking when ($2,000) two thousand dollars of the capital stock aforesaid has been paid in. The stockholders shall not be indivdiually liable for the debts or obligations of the corporation, and stockholders shall be non-assessable.

Individual liability.

Directors of company.

Sec. 5. That the persons first named in section one in this act shall be and remain directors of this corporation until their successors are chosen, provided that no person shall be a director in said corporation without having first subscribed and taken at least (5) five shares of said stock.

Rules prescribed by directors.

Sec. 6. It shall be the duty of the board of directors to prescribe rules, regulations and by-laws for the government thereof, to choose officers, fix salaries, fill vacancies and generally to do and perform such duties as the rules and regulations and by-laws of this corporation shall prescribe, when the same shall have been duly ratified by a majority in number and value of the stockholders voting therein in person or by proxy. The principal office of [or] banking house of this corporation shall be located in the city of Winston, county of Forsyth, and state of North Carolina, U. S. A.

Principal office.

Stock non-forfeitable.

Sec. 7. Stock in this corporation shall be non-forfeitable, but in the event of any stockholder being (3) three months in arrears at any time for installments, the cashier or treasurer may cause

Stockholders in arrears.

to be personally served upon him, a notice showing said stockholder's arrearages upon such stock, with cost for notice and with interest on the past due installments, requiring him to pay his arrearages within thirty days from notice, or his said stock will be sold by the board of directors at auction, at any regular monthly meeting of the board; from such sale all expenses, dues and interest accrued therefrom will first be paid and the balance, if any, to the holder of said stock, but in event of a deficiency after said sale, the subscriber shall be still liable for such deficiency up to the par value of his stock, and no stockholder shall be liable for more than the par value of his stock.

Stockholders liable only for par value of stock.

May buy and sell real estate.

Sec. 8. That said corporation shall have the right to buy and sell real estate at pleasure, either conditionally, by way of mortgage or otherwise.

Sec. 9. That this act shall be in force from and after its ratification.

Ratified the 6th day of March, A. D. 1899.

CHAPTER 346.

An act to enlarge the corporate limits of Colerain, in Bertie county, North Carolina.

The General Assembly of North Carolina do enact:

Corporate limits of Colerain enlarged.

Section 1. That the corporate limits of the town of Colerain, in Bertie county, are and shall be as follows: Commencing at a red oak, B. J. Mizell's and Nellie Toy's corner in J. H. Simon's line, thence north seventy-six degrees east sixty-nine and one-half poles to a fork of ditch, the northwest corner of Dr. W. B. Watford's lot; thence along said ditch said Watford's line east seventeen poles to the northeast corner of Dr. W. B. Watford's lot; thence south sixty-two east one hundred and twelve poles to an old well near the pathway in J. O. Saunder's field; thence south eleven degrees west thirty-seven poles to the river road; thence same course down "New barn road" thirty-one poles to an old gate post on the opposite side of the road; thence north eighty seven and one-half degrees west one hundred and sixteen poles to the Windsor road; thence the same course seventy-three poles to a water-oak in Britton's line; thence north eleven degrees east sixty-seven poles to Powellsville road; thence same course thirty poles to the red-oak, the commencing station, containing one hundred and fifteen and one-half acres by actual survey.

Sec. 2. That all the powers and authority given the officers of Colerain over the original territory named in the act incorporating said town are given said officers over the new limits as named in this act. Power of officers over said territory.

Sec. 3. That this act shall be in force from and after its ratification.

Ratified the 6th day of March, A. D. 1899.

CHAPTER 347.

An act to authorize town of Edenton to assist in building bridge.

The General Assembly of North Carolina do enact:

Section 1. That the board of councilmen of town of Edenton, North Carolina, are hereby authorized to contribute such sum as they may see fit, not exceeding five hundred dollars, to be used in building a bridge across Pembroke creek: Provided, such money shall not be contributed until after the commissioners of Chowan county shall have decided to erect such bridge and shall have procured, free of expense to said county, all rights-of-way to connect by a public road the town of Edenton with the main Cowpen Neck road. Commissioners of Edenton authorized to contribute a limited sum to building certain bridges. Proviso. When money shall be contributed.

Sec. 2. That this act shall be in force from and after its ratification.

Ratified the 6th day of March, A. D. 1899.

CHAPTER 348.

An act to incorporate "The Cape Fear Sewer Company."

The General Assembly of North Carolina do enact:

Section 1. That Nathaniel Jacobi, William J. Reaves, Edward P. Bailey, Henry A. Burr and L. Warren Davis, their associates, successors and assigns, be and the same are hereby created a body politic and corporate under the name of "The Cape Fear Sewer Company," and by that name shall have succession and a common seal; have power to sue and be sued, plead and be impleaded; may acquire, hold and convey real and personal estate; may contract and be contracted with, adopt by-laws and alter the same at pleasure, and shall have all the rights and privileges conferred upon corporations by chapter sixteen of The Code, entitled "Corporations." Corporators. Corporate name. Corporate powers.

Empowered to establish system of sewerage.

Sec. 2. That said corporation shall have power to establish a system of sewerage in, under and through the streets and public lanes, roads and alleys of the city of Wilmington, and lay all such necessary pipes, conduits and mains as may be deemed requisite to carry out the provisions hereof, under such rules and regulations as may be prescribed by the board of aldermen of said city, and shall have authority to charge for the use of said sewers such reasonable sums as the board of directors may from time to time adopt, and enforce the collection of such charges by severing the connection of said defaulting user with the main sewer; or in lieu thereof, if said company may decide best, shall have and enforce a lien on the lot and premises of said user having the connection with the said sewer for the said sewer charges.

May enforce lien on lot of user for non-payment of rents.

Persons injuring property guilty of a misdemeanor.

Sec. 3. That any person who shall willfully or wantonly cut, break enter, injure, damage or destroy any sewer pipe, main, trap, valve, hydrant or any of the appliances connected therewith, laid in or under any of the streets or alleys of the city of Wilmington or the vicinity thereof, without the consent of the said company or its officers or agents, shall be guilty of a misdemeanor, and fined or imprisoned, in the discretion of the court.

Capital stock.

Sec. 4. That the capital stock of said company shall be twelve hundred dollars, but the same may be increased from time to time to a sum not exceeding one hundred thousand dollars, divided into shares of the par value of fifty dollars each; but the said company may begin business when the sum of six hundred dollars each shall have been subscribed for and the same actually paid in in cash money or its equivalent in property.

Division of shares.

Duration of charter.

Sec. 5. That said corporation shall have an existence for a term of sixty years.

Affairs of company governed by directors.

Sec. 6. That the affairs of the company shall be governed by a board of five (5) directors elected by the stockholders at an annual meeting, who shall hold office for such term as the bylaws may prescribe, and said board shall hold over always until their successors are duly elected, but the stockholders at any annual meeting may increase the number of directors from time to time as they may think best.

Sec. 7. That this act shall be in force from and after its ratification.

Ratified the 6th day of March, A. D. 1899.

CHAPTER 349.

An act to incorporate the Carolina Mutual Life Insurance Company of North Carolina.

The General Assembly of North Carolina do enact:

Section 1. That Josephus Daniels, R. H. Battle, Joseph G. Brown, Fred Philips, J. J. Thomas, H. W. Jackson, C. H. Belvin, Charles E. Johnson, W. C. Stronach, Ashley Horne, E. B. Borden, John S. Cunningham, J. S. Carr, their associates, successors and assigns, are hereby made a corporation by the name of the Carolina Mutual Life Insurance Company. **Corporators.** **Corporate name.**

Sec. 2. The company shall be located and the principal office for the transaction of its business shall be in the city of Raleigh, state of North Carolina. **Principal office.**

Sec. 3. The kind of business to be undertaken by the corporation is insurance upon the lives of individuals, and every insurance appertaining thereto or connected therewith, and to grant, purchase or dispose of annuities and pure endowments, and for the insurance of the health of individuals or against accidents to them; and shall or may have perpetual succession for sixty years, and shall be capable in law of contracting and being contracted with, of suing and being sued, pleading and being impleaded, either in law or equity, in all the courts of record in this state or elsewhere. They and their successors may have a common seal, and may change the same at pleasure; and may, from time to time, make and establish such by-laws, ordinances and regulations, the same not being inconsistent with the laws of the state and United States, as may appear to them necessary or expedient for the management of said corporation, and may from time to time alter, amend or repeal the same or any of them. **Nature and kind of business.** **Seal.** **By laws and regu ations.**

Sec. 4. The insurance business of the company shall be conducted on the principal [principle] of giving to policy holders an interest in the profits of the company, as hereinafter provided in this section, unless it shall be otherwise agreed between the company and the insured. The directors shall declare such dividends as they deem proper, and such dividends shall be apportioned between the stockholders and said policy holders, who are entitled by contract, to share in such dividends. **Interest of policy-holders in profits.**

Sec. 5. Said company may reinsure any and all risks taken under its charter in such manner as the board of directors may prescribe. **May reinsure risks.**

Sec. 6. The corporate powers of this company shall be exercised by a board of directors, and such officers and agents as said board may appoint and empower, and said board of directors shall have the power to remove at pleasure any officers or agents ap- **Corporate powers, by whom exercised.**

pointed by said board. The number of directors shall not be less than five nor more than twenty-five persons, and each director shall hold at least five shares of stock in the company.

First board of directors elected by stockholders.

Sec. 7. The first board of directors shall be elected by the stockholders after said stock has been subscribed for and before the said corporation shall begin to transact any business of insurance, at an election to be held at such time and place as may be determined by a majority of the corporators named in section one of these articles of incorporation, due notice of which shall be given by mail or otherwise to each stockholder. Said board of directors shall hold their office for one year or until their successors are elected and qualified.

Sec. 8. There shall be an annual election of said board of directors at the principal office of the company.

Representation of stockholders in voting for directors.

Sec. 9. In the election of directors every stockholder in the company shall be entitled to one vote for every share of stock held by him, and such vote may be given in person or by proxy.

Election of officers.

Sec. 10. The board of directors shall immediately after their organization and annually after each election elect from their number a president and a vice-president, who shall hold office one year and until the election of their successors.

Capital stock.

Sec. 11. The amount of the capital stock of said corporation shall be one hundred thousand dollars, and the said stock shall be divided into one thousand shares of one hundred dollars each, with the privilege of increasing it to one million dollars.

Policies expressed to be for benefit of married women.

Sec. 12. Any policy issued by the Carolina Mutual Life Insurance Company on the life of any person, expressed to be for the benefit of any married woman, whether the same be effected originally by herself or her husband or by any other person, or whether the premiums thereafter be paid by herself or her husband or any other person as aforesaid, shall inure for her sole special use and benefit, and that [of] her husband's children, if any, as may be expressed in said policy, and shall be held by her free from the control or claim of her husband or his creditors or of the person effecting the same and his creditors.

May lend money.

Sec. 13. The company shall have power to lend money to policy holders on such terms as the directors of said company may prescribe, not inconsistent with the laws of this state.

Individual liability.

Sec. 14. The individual stockholders of this company shall not be personally liable for any loss or damage beyond the amount of stock subscribed respectively by them, and any undivided profits accruing from said stock.

May hold real estate.

Sec. 15. That it shall be lawful for said corporation to purchase, hold and convey real estate as follows:

Such as directors may deem necessary.

(1) Such as the board of directors may deem necessary in the transaction of the business of the company.

(2) Such real estate as shall have been mortgaged to it by way of security for loans personally contracted or for money due. Mortgaged.

(3) Such real estate as shall have been purchased upon judgment, decree or mortgage obtained or made for such debts. Purchased upon judgment.

(4) Such real estate as shall have been conveyed to said company in satisfaction of debts previously contracted in the course of its dealings. Conveyed in satisfaction of a debt.

Sec. 16. That this act shall be in force from and after its ratification.

Ratified the 6th day of March, A. D. 1899.

CHAPTER 350.

An act in aid of the public schools of the city of Asheville.

The General Assembly of North Carolina do enact:

Section 1. That section thirty-seven of chapter one hundred and sixty-three of the private laws of eighteen hundred and ninety-seven, entitled "An act to amend chapter three hundred and fifty-two, private laws of eighteen hundred and ninety-five," entitled "An act to amend, revise and consolidate the charter of the city of Asheville," be and the same is hereby amended by striking out in the seventh line of said section thirty-seven after the word "exceed" and before the word "cents" the word "twenty" and inserting instead thereof the word "thirty"; and by striking out in the eighth line of said section after the word "and" and before the word "cents" the word "sixty" and inserting in lieu thereof the word "ninety." Section 37, chapter 163, private laws of 1897, amended.

Sec. 2. That before this act shall go into effect the same shall be submitted to the qualified voters of the city of Asheville for the approval of the majority thereof, and the mayor and board of aldermen of said city are hereby directed to submit the same to the qualified voters of said city at the next election to be held therein for the election of mayor and aldermen, and under the same rules and regulations as are now or may hereafter be prescribed for said election; and at such election those who favor the school tax authorized by this act shall cast ballots having the words "For schools" written or printed thereon, and those opposed to said school tax shall cast ballots having the words "Against schools" written or printed thereon; and if at such election a majority of the qualified voters of said city shall cast ballots having the words "For schools" written or printed thereon, then the said board of aldermen shall levy and collect the Act shall be submitted to qualified voters of Asheville. When voted upon. Form of ballot.

said taxes as aforesaid for the purposes specified in this act and the acts of which the same is amendatory, and thereupon this act shall go into immediate effect.

Conflicting laws repealed.

Sec. 3. That all laws and parts of laws in conflict herewith are hereby repealed.

Sec. 4. That this act shall be in force from and after its ratification.

Ratified the 6th day of March, A. D. 1899.

CHAPTER 351.

An act to incorporate the town of Cedar Falls, North Carolina.

The General Assembly of North Carolina do enact:

Body corporate.

Corporate name.

Corporate powers.

Section 1. That the town of Cedar Falls, in the county of Randolph be, and the same is hereby incorporated into a body politic and corporate, under the name and style of the Town of Cedar Falls, and under this name may acquire and hold for the purpose of its government, welfare and improvement, by purchase, gift, devise or otherwise, any real estate or personal property, in the same manner and to the same extent that private persons may or can, and shall have the right to contract or be contracted with, sue and be sued, plead and be impleaded, and hold and convey real or personal property.

Corporate limits.

Sec. 2. That the corporate limits of said town shall embrace the territory within the following boundaries, beginning at a stake on south bank of Deep river, the Cedar Falls Manufacturing Company's corner; thence north and northeast on the outside lines to the hickory corner; thence northwest to J. M. Pound's northeast corner; thence west on his line to his and J. M. Campbell's corner; thence on J. M. Campbell's outside line to Cedar Falls Manufacturing Company's line; thence on the line to the corner on south bank of Deep river; thence west to J. M. Jummy's northwest corner; thence south on the lines of J. H. Allred and A. H. Ridding to A. H. Ridding's southwest corner; thence east to P. M. and J. F. S. Julisu's line; thence north on their line to Cedar Falls Manufacturing Company's line; thence east out the line to beginning.

Town officers.

Sec. 3. That the officers of said town shall consist of a mayor, five commissioners, a constable, treasurer and clerk; that the mayor and five commissioners shall be elected on the first Monday in May, in the year eighteen hundred and ninety-nine, and annually thereafter, who shall hold their offices until the [their] ccessors are qualified, and all other officers created by this act all be appointed by the town commissioners for a term not tending beyond the term of office for which said commisiners are elected.

Temporary officers.

Sec. 4. That Geo. L. Leonard, W. C. Richardson, A. H. Ridding, T. Williams and J. M. Campbell are hereby constituted and pointed a board of commissioners, and O. R. Cox is hereby pointed mayor, who, upon their taking the oath of office, shall ive full power to exercise and perform such duties as are reinafter prescribed by the provisions of this act, until their ccessors shall be duly elected and qualified.

Officers shall take oath of office.

Sec. 5. That all the officers herein provided for, before enterg upon their duties as such officers, shall take an oath before me justice of the peace of said county, or other officer authored to administer oaths, to faithfully and impartially discharge e duties of their offices; and the treasurer and constable or ief of police, before entering upon their duties, shall also file a nd with the board of commissioners, payable to the town of edar Falls, in such sum as the commissioners may determine: rovided, the same shall not be less than four hundred dollars, nditioned upon the faithful performance of the duties of their fice.

Proviso.

Appointment of registrar and judges of election.

Sec. 6. That the board of commissioners of said town, each ear at least forty days prior to the first Monday in May, shall ppoint a registrar, who shall give ten days' notice at three pubc places in said town, of the registration of voters of said wn, specifying time and place, and shall be furnished with gistration books at the expense of the town; and it shall be e duty of the registrar to open the books at the time and place entioned, which shall be at least twenty days before the elecon, and to register therein all persons applying for registraon, who are ascertained to be entitled to registration under e general election laws of the state, and at the time of the ppointment of said registrar the board of commissioners shall ppoint two judges of election, who with the registrars shall open e polls and superintend and conduct the same on the day of ection, which shall be held at the mayor's office in said town, nd shall be conducted in accordance with the general laws f the state regulating the election of the members of the general ssembly not inconsistent with this act; and returns of id election shall be made as provided in section thirty-seven undred and eighty-eight (3788), chapter sixty-two (62) of he Code.

Persons entitled to register.

Election, how conducted.

When mayor and commissioners shall qualify.

Sec. 7. That on Thursday succeeding the day of election the ayor and commissioners shall qualify by taking the oath as rescribed by law, and when organized shall have all the duties,

said taxes as aforesaid for the purposes specified in this act and the acts of which the same is amendatory, and thereupon this act shall go into immediate effect.

Conflicting laws repealed.

Sec. 3. That all laws and parts of laws in conflict herewith are hereby repealed.

Sec. 4. That this act shall be in force from and after its ratification.

Ratified the 6th day of March, A. D. 1899.

CHAPTER 351.

An act to incorporate the town of Cedar Falls, North Carolina.

The General Assembly of North Carolina do enact:

Body corporate.

Corporate name.

Corporate powers.

Section 1. That the town of Cedar Falls, in the county of Randolph be, and the same is hereby incorporated into a body politic and corporate, under the name and style of the Town of Cedar Falls, and under this name may acquire and hold for the purpose of its government, welfare and improvement, by purchase, gift, devise or otherwise, any real estate or personal property, in the same manner and to the same extent that private persons may or can, and shall have the right to contract or be contracted with, sue and be sued, plead and be impleaded, and hold and convey real or personal property.

Corporate limits.

Sec. 2. That the corporate limits of said town shall embrace the territory within the following boundaries, beginning at a stake on south bank of Deep river, the Cedar Falls Manufacturing Company's corner; thence north and northeast on the outside lines to the hickory corner; thence northwest to J. M. Pound's northeast corner; thence west on his line to his and J. M. Campbell's corner; thence on J. M. Campbell's outside line to Cedar Falls Manufacturing Company's line; thence on the line to the corner on south bank of Deep river; thence west to J. M. Jummy's northwest corner; thence south on the lines of J. H. Allred and A. H. Ridding to A. H. Ridding's southwest corner; thence east to P. M. and J. F. S. Julisu's line; thence north on their line to Cedar Falls Manufacturing Company's line; thence east out the line to beginning.

Town officers.

Sec. 3. That the officers of said town shall consist of a mayor, five commissioners, a constable, treasurer and clerk; that the mayor and five commissioners shall be elected on the first Monday in May, in the year eighteen hundred and ninety-nine, and annually thereafter, who shall hold their offices until the [their] successors are qualified, and all other officers created by this act shall be appointed by the town commissioners for a term not extending beyond the term of office for which said commissioners are elected.

Sec. 4. That Geo. L. Leonard, W. C. Richardson, A. H. Ridding, J. T. Williams and J. M. Campbell are hereby constituted and appointed a board of commissioners, and O. R. Cox is hereby appointed mayor, who, upon their taking the oath of office, shall have full power to exercise and perform such duties as are hereinafter prescribed by the provisions of this act, until their successors shall be duly elected and qualified. Temporary officers.

Sec. 5. That all the officers herein provided for, before entering upon their duties as such officers, shall take an oath before some justice of the peace of said county, or other officer authorized to administer oaths, to faithfully and impartially discharge the duties of their offices; and the treasurer and constable or chief of police, before entering upon their duties, shall also file a bond with the board of commissioners, payable to the town of Cedar Falls, in such sum as the commissioners may determine: Provided, the same shall not be less than four hundred dollars, conditioned upon the faithful performance of the duties of their office. Officers shall take oath of office. Proviso.

Sec. 6. That the board of commissioners of said town, each year at least forty days prior to the first Monday in May, shall appoint a registrar, who shall give ten days' notice at three public places in said town, of the registration of voters of said town, specifying time and place, and shall be furnished with registration books at the expense of the town; and it shall be the duty of the registrar to open the books at the time and place mentioned, which shall be at least twenty days before the election, and to register therein all persons applying for registration, who are ascertained to be entitled to registration under the general election laws of the state, and at the time of the appointment of said registrar the board of commissioners shall appoint two judges of election, who with the registrars shall open the polls and superintend and conduct the same on the day of election, which shall be held at the mayor's office in said town, and shall be conducted in accordance with the general laws of the state regulating the election of the members of the general assembly not inconsistent with this act; and returns of said election shall be made as provided in section thirty-seven hundred and eighty-eight (3788), chapter sixty-two (62) of The Code. Appointment of registrar and judges of election. Persons entitled to register. Election, how conducted.

Sec. 7. That on Thursday succeeding the day of election the mayor and commissioners shall qualify by taking the oath as prescribed by law, and when organized shall have all the duties, When mayor and commissioners shall qualify.

rights, powers and privileges prescribed in chapter sixty-two (62) of The Code not inconsistent with the provisions of this act.

Powers of commissioners.

Sec. 8. That among the powers conferred upon said board of commissioners, they may provide for and have opened streets through said town, provide for the working, repairing and cleaning said streets, regulate the markets, take all proper means to prevent and extinguish fires, regulate the town police force, suppress and remove all nuisances, pass ordinances for the regulation of the peace and order of the town, and for carrying out of the provisions of this act, and may appoint such officers as the board of commissioners may fix and prescribe the pay of all officers, either elected or appointed.

Mayor constituted an inferior court.

Jurisdiction of mayor.

Sec. 9. That the mayor of the town is hereby constituted an inferior court, with like powers of a justice of the peace in all criminal cases, according to the general law regulating towns and cities, contained in volume two (2) chapter sixty-two (62) of The Code, and the general laws and the laws amendatory thereto regulating the duties of justices of the peace in criminal cases, and to execute the by-laws, rules, ordinances and regulations made by the board of commissioners.

Mayor shall preside over meetings of commissioners.

Sec. 10. That the mayor when present shall preside at all meetings of the board of commissioners, and shall vote only when there is a tie; and at the first meeting after organization the commissioners shall appoint one of their number a chairman pro tempore, who shall in the absence of the mayor preside at tne meetings and perform all the duties of mayor.

Quorum.
When commissioners shall convene for business.

Sec. 11. That a majority of the commissioners shall constitute a quorum for the transaction of all business; within five days after election they shall convene for the transaction of business and then shall fix monthly meetings for the board and call meetings of said board or [on] call of the mayor, and a majority of the commissioners may adopt by-laws enforcing the attendance of the members of the board.

Orders drawn on treasurer, how signed.

Sec. 12. That all orders drawn on the treasurer by the clerk or the order of the commissioners, shall be signed by the mayor and countersigned by the clerk, and the treasurer shall file all such orders as his vouchers, and at the expiration of the term of the office of treasurer he shall deliver to his successors all moneys, securities or other property entrusted to him for safe keeping or otherwise.

Levying and collection of taxes.

Sec. 13. That the commissioners of said town may provide for the listing, levying and collection of a tax upon the property and polls in said town in accordance with the general laws regulating towns and cities.

Improvement of streets, etc.

Sec. 14. That the board of commissioners of said town shall ave power to lay out and open any streets within the corporate mits of said town whenever they may deem it necessary, and have ower at any time to widen, enlarge, charge, [change] extend or disntinue any street or streets, or any part thereof, within the corrate limits of said town, and shall have full power and authory to condemn, appropriate or use any land or lands necessary r any of the purposes named in this section, upon making a asonable compensation to the owner or owners thereof; but case the owner of the land and the commissioners can not ree as to the damages, the matter shall be referred to arbitrars, each party choosing one, who shall be a freeholder in and citizen of said town; and in case the owner of the land shall fuse to choose said arbitrator, then the sheriff of the county all, in his stead, select one for him, and in case the two chosen aforesaid can not agree, they shall select a third man, whose duty shall be to examine the lands condemned and ascertain the mages sustained and the benefits accruing to the owner in nsequence of the change, and the award shall be conclusive the rights of the parties and shall vest in the commissioners e right to use the lands for the purpose specified, and all damges agreed upon or awarded shall be paid as the other town lialities, by taxation: Provided, that either party may appeal as ovided by law.

Land may be condemned.

Damages decided by arbitrators.

Award shall be conclusive.

Either party may appeal.

Commissioners empowered to levy tax.

Sec. 15. That the board of commissioners shall have full power d authority to levy and collect a tax upon the real and pernal property and polls of said town, for the purpose of raising e money to pay [any] and all such sums as may be required to paid under the preceding sections and all other sections of is act.

Sale of liquor prohibited.

Sec. 16. That no intoxicating liquors shall be manufactured or ld within the corporate limits or within one and one-half miles the corporate limits of said town.

Commissioners empowered to levy license and privilege taxes.

Sec. 17. That the commissioners of said town may levy and llect license or privilege tax on such things as the state and unty may levy a license tax upon, and upon all itinerant merants, peddlers and auctioneers who shall sell or offer for sale ithin the limits of said town.

Vested with general municipal powers.

Sec. 18. That the town of Cedar Falls is hereby vested with l the powers, rights, privileges and immunities enumerated in apter sixty-two (62) of The Code, volume two (2) and elsehere in The Code as amended by subsequent acts of the general sembly not inconsistent with any of the provisions of this act.

Sec. 19. That this act shall be in force from and after its tification.

Ratified the 6th day of March, A. D. 1899.

rights, powers and privileges prescribed in chapter sixty-two (62) of The Code not inconsistent with the provisions of this act.

ers of commissioners.

Sec. 8. That among the powers conferred upon said board of commissioners, they may provide for and have opened streets through said town, provide for the working, repairing and cleaning said streets, regulate the markets, take all proper means to prevent and extinguish fires, regulate the town police force, suppress and remove all nuisances, pass ordinances for the regulation of the peace and order of the town, and for carrying out of the provisions of this act, and may appoint such officers as the board of commissioners may fix and prescribe the pay of all officers, either elected or appointed.

or constituted an inferior t.

sdiction of or.

Sec. 9. That the mayor of the town is hereby constituted an inferior court, with like powers of a justice of the peace in all criminal cases, according to the general law regulating towns and cities, contained in volume two (2) chapter sixty-two (62) of The Code, and the general laws and the laws amendatory thereto regulating the duties of justices of the peace in criminal cases, and to execute the by-laws, rules, ordinances and regulations made by the board of commissioners.

or shall preover meetof commisers.

Sec. 10. That the mayor when present shall preside at all meetings of the board of commissioners, and shall vote only when there is a tie; and at the first meeting after organization the commissioners shall appoint one of their number a chairman pro tempore, who shall in the absence of the mayor preside at tne meetings and perform all the duties of mayor.

rum n commisers shall con for business.

Sec. 11. That a majority of the commissioners shall constitute a quorum for the transaction of all business; within five days after election they shall convene for the transaction of business and then shall fix monthly meetings for the board and call meetings of said board or [on] call of the mayor, and a majority of the commissioners may adopt by-laws enforcing the attendance of the members of the board.

ers drawn on surer, how ed

Sec. 12. That all orders drawn on the treasurer by the clerk or the order of the commissioners, shall be signed by the mayor and countersigned by the clerk, and the treasurer shall file all such orders as his vouchers, and at the expiration of the term of the office of treasurer he shall deliver to his successors all moneys, securities or other property entrusted to him for safekeeping or otherwise.

ing and ction of s.

Sec. 13. That the commissioners of said town may provide for the listing, levying and collection of a tax upon the property and polls in said town in accordance with the general laws regulating towns and cities.

Sec. 14. That the board of commissioners of said town shall have power to lay out and open any streets within the corporate limits of said town whenever they may deem it necessary, and have power at any time to widen, enlarge, charge, [change] extend or discontinue any street or streets, or any part thereof, within the corporate limits of said town, and shall have full power and authority to condemn, appropriate or use any land or lands necessary for any of the purposes named in this section, upon making a reasonable compensation to the owner or owners thereof; but in case the owner of the land and the commissioners can not agree as to the damages, the matter shall be referred to arbitrators, each party choosing one, who shall be a freeholder in and a citizen of said town; and in case the owner of the land shall refuse to choose said arbitrator, then the sheriff of the county shall, in his stead, select one for him, and in case the two chosen as aforesaid can not agree, they shall select a third man, whose duty it shall be to examine the lands condemned and ascertain the damages sustained and the benefits accruing to the owner in consequence of the change, and the award shall be conclusive of the rights of the parties and shall vest in the commissioners the right to use the lands for the purpose specified, and all damages agreed upon or awarded shall be paid as the other town liabilities, by taxation: Provided, that either party may appeal as provided by law.

Improvement of streets, etc.

Land may be condemned.

Damages decided by arbitrators.

Award shall be conclusive.

Either party may appeal.

Sec. 15. That the board of commissioners shall have full power and authority to levy and collect a tax upon the real and personal property and polls of said town, for the purpose of raising the money to pay [any] and all such sums as may be required to be paid under the preceding sections and all other sections of this act.

Commissioners empowered to levy tax.

Sec. 16. That no intoxicating liquors shall be manufactured or sold within the corporate limits or within one and one-half miles of the corporate limits of said town.

Sale of liquor prohibited.

Sec. 17. That the commissioners of said town may levy and collect license or privilege tax on such things as the state and county may levy a license tax upon, and upon all itinerant merchants, peddlers and auctioneers who shall sell or offer for sale within the limits of said town.

Commissioners empowered to levy license and privilege taxes.

Sec. 18. That the town of Cedar Falls is hereby vested with all the powers, rights, privileges and immunities enumerated in chapter sixty-two (62) of The Code, volume two (2) and elsewhere in The Code as amended by subsequent acts of the general assembly not inconsistent with any of the provisions of this act.

Vested with general municipal powers.

Sec. 19. That this act shall be in force from and after its ratification.

Ratified the 6th day of March, A. D. 1899.

CHAPTER 352.

An act to amend and consolidate the charter of the town of Monroe.

The General Assembly of North Carolina do enact:

dy corporate. Section 1. That the inhabitants of the town of Monroe, living within the limits hereinafter described, shall be and continue as they have heretofore been a body politic and corporate, and rporate name. hereafter the corporation shall bear the name of "The City of rporate pow- Monroe," and under such name and style is hereby invested with title to all property and rights of property, real and personal, which now belong to the town of Monroe under any other name or names heretofore used, and by this name may acquire and hold for the purposes of its government, welfare and improvement, all such estates as may be devised, bequeathed or conveyed to it; and it may sell, dispose of and invest the same as shall be deemed advisable by the proper authorities of the corporation. al. It may also adopt a common seal, sue and be sued, plead and be impleaded, contract and be contracted with, and generally do any and all acts necessary for the welfare of its inhabitants and the preservation of the property of its citizens.

rporate limits. Sec. 2. That the corporate limits of said city shall be and remain as they are now established by former acts of the general assembly of North Carolina.

vernment of y vested in yor. That the government of said city and the administration of its municipal affairs shall be vested in a chief magistrate, to be styled the mayor, and five aldermen, who shall be elected by the qualified voters of said city on the first Monday in May, eighteen hundred and ninety-nine, and biennially thereafter, and at least ection of alder- n. one alderman shall be elected from each ward as hereinafter located. The said board of aldermen shall have the power and it shall be their duty to elect a chief of police, a tax collector and ection of town cers. a secretary and treasurer, and such additional policemen as shall be deemed necessary for the proper protection of the citizens and property of said city. One person may be both chief of police and tax collector, and one person may be both secretary and treasurer of said city, the latter of whom may be chosen from the board of aldermen or from the citizens of the city.

vision of rds. Sec. 3. The said city shall be divided into four wards by a straight line running along the eastern side of Lafayette street to the corporate limits at either end, and a straight line running along the northern side of Winsor street to the corporate limits of the city, and that portion of said city lying in the northeast corner of the division so made shall be the first ward, that portion in the northwest corner of the division shall be the second ırd, that portion lying in the southwestern corner shall be the ird ward, and that portion lying in the southeast corner shall the fourth ward.

Appointment of registrar.

Sec. 4. That it shall be the duty of the board of aldermen at eir meeting in March preceding the election to appoint a regrar of voters, whose duty it shall be to register all persons qualed to vote in the said election, and for that purpose he shall lvertise at the court-house door or in a newspaper published in e town the place where the said books are opened for the regration of voters, and the time in which voters may register, ıd at such time and place, beginning on the sixth Saturday efore the election and on each succeeding Saturday until the cond Saturday before the election, he shall register all persons ho have been residents of the city for six months and are qualed voters in the election of members of the general assembly of orth Carolina. The registrar is authorized to register any pern, otherwise qualified, who will attain his majority between the ose of the registration book on the second Saturday before the ection and the day of the election. And the said board of dermen shall appoint two judges of election, who with the regtrar shall constitute the election board, and shall under their ands and seals certify the result of said election in duplicate opies, one of which shall be delivered to the mayor and the ther to the register of deeds of Union county, which said reırns of election shall be registered in the office of the register of eeds and the other in the office of the clerk of the city. The egistrar and judges of election shall be sworn to the faithful discharge of their duties before holding any election or registering ny voters. On the Saturday preceding the election the books f registration shall be opened for the inspection of the citizens f said town, who may challenge the right of any person to vote whose name appears on the said registration book, and if the egistrar and judges of election or a majority of them decide that e is not a qualified voter, his name shall be erased from said ook and he shall not be allowed to vote in said election.

Persons qualified to vote.

Appointment of judges of election.

Registrar and judges shall be sworn.

Registration book shall be revised.

Sec. 5. That the registration book provided for in the precedıg section at any subsequent election shall be revised by strikıg therefrom all names of persons who have ceased to be qualied voters of said city, and by registering the names of all perons who are qualified voters and make application for registraion: Provided, that the board of aldermen shall order a new registration of voters when in their discretion they may deem it necssary to secure a correct registration of voters in any election to e held for said city.

Establishment of voting places.

Sec. 6. That the board of aldermen, if they deem it advisable, ıay establish voting places in each ward, and when so estab-

CHAPTER 352.

An act to amend and consolidate the charter of the town of Monroe.

The General Assembly of North Carolina do enact:

dy corporate. Section 1. That the inhabitants of the town of Monroe, livi within the limits hereinafter described, shall be and continue they have heretofore been a body politic and corporate, a porate name. hereafter the corporation shall bear the name of "The City porate pow- Monroe," and under such name and style is hereby invested wi title to all property and rights of property, real and person which now belong to the town of Monroe under any other nan or names heretofore used, and by this name may acquire a hold for the purposes of its government, welfare and improv ment, all such estates as may be devised, bequeathed or convey to it; and it may sell, dispose of and invest the same as shall deemed advisable by the proper authorities of the corporatio It may also adopt a common seal, sue and be sued, plead and impleaded, contract and be contracted with, and generally any and all acts necessary for the welfare of its inhabitants a the preservation of the property of its citizens.

porate limits. Sec. 2. That the corporate limits of said city shall be and r main as they are now established by former acts of the gener assembly of North Carolina.

vernment of y vested in yor. That the government of said city and the administration of i municipal affairs shall be vested in a chief magistrate, to styled the mayor, and five aldermen, who shall be elected by t qualified voters of said city on the first Monday in May, eightee hundred and ninety-nine, and biennially thereafter, and at lea ction of alder- n. one alderman shall be elected from each ward as hereinaft located. The said board of aldermen shall have the power a it shall be their duty to elect a chief of police, a tax collector a ction of town cers. a secretary and treasurer, and such additional policemen as sha be deemed necessary for the proper protection of the citizens an property of said city. One person may be both chief of poli and tax collector, and one person may be both secretary a treasurer of said city, the latter of whom may be chosen from t board of aldermen or from the citizens of the city.

ision of rds. Sec. 3. The said city shall be divided into four wards by straight line running along the eastern side of Lafayette stre to the corporate limits at either end, and a straight line runni along the northern side of Winsor street to the corporate limi of the city, and that portion of said city lying in the northea corner of the division so made shall be the first ward, that po tion in the northwest corner of the division shall be the secon ward, that portion lying in the southwestern corner shall be the third ward, and that portion lying in the southeast corner shall be the fourth ward.

Appointment of registrar.

Sec. 4. That it shall be the duty of the board of aldermen at their meeting in March preceding the election to appoint a registrar of voters, whose duty it shall be to register all persons qualified to vote in the said election, and for that purpose he shall advertise at the court-house door or in a newspaper published in the town the place where the said books are opened for the registration of voters, and the time in which voters may register, and at such time and place, beginning on the sixth Saturday before the election and on each succeeding Saturday until the second Saturday before the election, he shall register all persons who have been residents of the city for six months and are qualified voters in the election of members of the general assemply of North Carolina. The registrar is authorized to register any person, otherwise qualified, who will attain his majority between the close of the registration book on the second Saturday before the election and the day of the election. And the said board of aldermen shall appoint two judges of election, who with the registrar shall constitute the election board, and shall under their hands and seals certify the result of said election in duplicate copies, one of which shall be delivered to the mayor and the other to the register of deeds of Union county, which said returns of election shall be registered in the office of the register of deeds and the other in the office of the clerk of the city. The registrar and judges of election shall be sworn to the faithful discharge of their duties before holding any election or registering any voters. On the Saturday preceding the election the books of registration shall be opened for the inspection of the citizens of said town, who may challenge the right of any person to vote whose name appears on the said registration book, and if the registrar and judges of election or a majority of them decide that he is not a qualified voter, his name shall be erased from said book and he shall not be allowed to vote in said election.

Persons qualified to vote.

Appointment of judges of election.

Registrar and judges shall be sworn.

Registration book shall be revised.

Sec. 5. That the registration book provided for in the preceding section at any subsequent election shall be revised by striking therefrom all names of persons who have ceased to be qualified voters of said city, and by registering the names of all persons who are qualified voters and make application for registration: Provided, that the board of aldermen shall order a new registration of voters when in their discretion they may deem it necessary to secure a correct registration of voters in any election to be held for said city.

Establishment of voting places.

Sec. 6. That the board of aldermen, if they deem it advisable, may establish voting places in each ward, and when so established it shall be their duty to appoint a registrar for each ward, and judges of election for each ward in the same manner as is provided in section four of this act, whose duty shall be as hereinbefore provided; and when the certificates of election are deposited with the mayor or register of deeds of the county, it shall be their respective duties to ascertain and declare the aggregate number of votes cast for each candidate for office, and the mayor shall issue to each person elected a certificate of election.

Town officers shall take oath.

Sec. 7. That before any of the officers elected shall enter upon the discharge of his duties he shall take an oath faithfully and impartially to discharge the duties of his office to the best of his judgment and ability, and the mayor shall further take and subscribe the oath provided for justices of the peace.

Mayor, how elected.

Sec. 8. The mayor shall be elected by the qualified voters of the city, and shall hold his office for two years and until his successor is elected and qualified. The board of aldermen shall fix the salary of the mayor, to be paid out of the city treasury, [and] all fees which shall be due to the mayor for services rendered by him in trying offenders in his capacity as mayor shall be paid into the city treasury. In case a vacancy shall occur in the office of mayor, the board of aldermen shall elect a qualified person to fill such vacancy during the unexpired term.

Salary of mayor.

Jurisdiction of mayor.

Sec. 9. The mayor of said city shall be a special court, with all the jurisdiction conferred on justices of the peace in criminal cases, and he shall have jurisdiction of all violations of the city ordinances.

Defendants convicted and unable to pay fine may be sentenced to road duty.

Sec. 10. That in all cases, when a defendant shall be convicted before the mayor of said city of any misdemeanor, and shall be sentenced to pay a fine and costs, and such defendant shall refuse to pay the fine or costs or be unable to do so, it shall be lawful for the mayor to order and require such defendant to work on the streets of said city or the public roads of Union county until at a fair rate of wages such person shall have worked out the full amount of the fine and costs of the prosecution. And any person so required by the mayor to work on the streets or public roads of Union county who shall willfully refuse so to do or shall attempt to escape while engaged in said work, shall be guilty of a misdemeanor, and upon conviction thereof shall be fined not exceeding fifty dollars or imprisoned not exceeding thirty days.

To whom mayor shall direct his precepts.

Sec. 11. That the mayor shall direct his precepts or warrants to the chief of police or to any other officer to whom a justice of the peace may issue his precepts.

Mayor shall preside at meetings of aldermen.

Sec. 12. The mayor shall preside at all meetings of the board of aldermen, and in case of an equal division of the votes of the aldermen on any subject to be decided by them, shall cast the deciding vote, but otherwise shall have no vote in passing on any matter before them. In the absence of the mayor, it shall be the duty of the board of aldermen to select one of their number to preside over their meetings.

Sec. 13. At their first meeting after their election the board of aldermen shall fix regular times for their meetings, which must be at least once in every month. Special meetings of the board of aldermen may be called by the mayor or by a majority of the aldermen, of which every person not joining in the call shall receive notice, which shall be served by the chief of police or a policeman.

Provisions for the execution of ordinances.

Sec. 14. The board of aldermen shall have power to make, and provide for the execution thereof, such ordinances, by-laws, rules and regulations for the good government of the city, the health and security of its citizens, the protection of their property and lives as they may deem proper and necessary for such purposes, consistent with the laws of the land.

Improvement of streets, etc.

Sec. 15. That the board of aldermen shall have power to macadamize, repair and cleanse the streets, regulate the markets, take all proper measures to prevent and extinguish fires, establish and regulate a system of waterworks for the city, make reasonable charges for the use thereof by the citizens of the city or other consumers thereof, make and enforce all such rules and regulations for the government of the police force as shall be necessary to preserve the peace and order of the city by proper ordinances; prevent, suppress and remove nuisances, preserve the health of the people from contagious or infectious diseases, and when necessary establish a quarantine against such diseases; establish a fire limit in said city, within which it shall be unlawful to build, erect, repair or move any building built of wood or other dangerous material; to appoint and provide for the pay and prescribe the duties of any and all officers necessary to execute their ordinances and perform the duties herein required.

Fire limits.

Election of officers by aldermen.

Sec. 16. That at their first meeting or as soon thereafter as practicable, they shall elect a chief of police and tax collector, a city clerk and treasurer and city attorney, who shall respectively hold their offices during the term of the board electing them, and until their successors are elected and qualified: Provided, that any or all of such officers may be removed for misbehavior or neglect in office and others elected in their stead. Said officers shall take an oath of office for the faithful performance of their duties, which shall be administered by the mayor, and they shall also execute a bond for the faithful performance of duty and accounting for such moneys as shall come into their hands, except that no bond or oath shall be required of the city attorney.

Shall execute bonds.

lished it shall be their duty to appoint a registrar for each wa[rd] and judges of election for each ward in the same manner a[s] provided in section four of this act, whose duty shall be as he[re]inbefore provided; and when the certificates of election are [de]posited with the mayor or register of deeds of the county, it sh[all] be their respective duties to ascertain and declare the aggreg[ate] number of votes cast for each candidate for office, and the ma[yor] shall issue to each person elected a certificate of election.

[Whe]n officers [shal]l take oath.

Sec. 7. That before any of the officers elected shall enter up[on] the discharge of his duties he shall take an oath faithfully a[nd] impartially to discharge the duties of his office to the best of [his] judgment and ability, and the mayor shall further take and su[b]scribe the oath provided for justices of the peace.

[May]or, how [elect]ed.

Sec. 8. The mayor shall be elected by the qualified voters [of] the city, and shall hold his office for two years and until his su[c]cessor is elected and qualified. The board of aldermen shall [fix]

[Sala]ry of mayor.

the salary of the mayor, to be paid out of the city treasury, [an[d] all fees which shall be due to the mayor for services rendered [by] him in trying offenders in his capacity as mayor shall be pa[id] into the city treasury. In case a vacancy shall occur in the offi[ce] of mayor, the board of aldermen shall elect a qualified person [to] fill such vacancy during the unexpired term.

[Juri]sdiction of [may]or.

Sec. 9. The mayor of said city shall be a special court, with a[ll] the jurisdiction conferred on justices of the peace in crimin[al] cases, and he shall have jurisdiction of all violations of the cit[y] ordinances.

[Defe]ndants con[vict]ed and un[able] to pay fine [may] be sentenced [to ro]ad duty.

Sec. 10. That in all cases, when a defendant shall be convicte[d] before the mayor of said city of any misdemeanor, and shall b[e] sentenced to pay a fine and costs, and such defendant shall re[fuse] to pay the fine or costs or be unable to do so, it shall be law[ful] for the mayor to order and require such defendant to wor[k] on the streets of said city or the public roads of Union count[y] until at a fair rate of wages such person shall have worked o[ut] the full amount of the fine and costs of the prosecution. An[d] any person so required by the mayor to work on the streets o[r] public roads of Union county who shall willfully refuse so to d[o] or shall attempt to escape while engaged in said work, shall b[e] guilty of a misdemeanor, and upon conviction thereof shall b[e] fined not exceeding fifty dollars or imprisoned not exceedin[g] thirty days.

[To w]hom mayor [shal]l direct his [prec]epts.

Sec. 11. That the mayor shall direct his precepts or warrant[s] to the chief of police or to any other officer to whom a justice o[f] the peace may issue his precepts.

[May]or shall pre[side] at meetings [of a]ldermen.

Sec. 12. The mayor shall preside at all meetings of the boar[d] of aldermen, and in case of an equal division of the votes of th[e] aldermen on any subject to be decided by them, shall cast th[e] leciding vote, but otherwise shall have no vote in passing on any natter before them. In the absence of the mayor, it shall be the luty of the board of aldermen to select one of their number to preside over their meetings.

Sec. 13. At their first meeting after their election the board of aldermen shall fix regular times for their meetings, which must be at least once in every month. Special meetings of the board of aldermen may be called by the mayor or by a majority of the aldermen, of which every person not joining in the call shall receive notice, which shall be served by the chief of police or a policeman.

Sec. 14. The board of aldermen shall have power to make, and provide for the execution thereof, such ordinances, by-laws, rules and regulations for the good government of the city, the health and security of its citizens, the protection of their property and lives as they may deem proper and necessary for such purposes, consistent with the laws of the land. **Provisions for the execution of ordinances.**

Sec. 15. That the board of aldermen shall have power to macadamize, repair and cleanse the streets, regulate the markets, take all proper measures to prevent and extinguish fires, establish and regulate a system of waterworks for the city, make reasonable charges for the use thereof by the citizens of the city or other consumers thereof, make and enforce all such rules and regulations for the government of the police force as shall be necessary to preserve the peace and order of the city by proper ordinances; prevent, suppress and remove nuisances, preserve the health of the people from contagious or infectious diseases, and when necessary establish a quarantine against such diseases; establish a fire limit in said city, within which it shall be unlawful to build, erect, repair or move any building built of wood or other dangerous material; to appoint and provide for the pay and prescribe the duties of any and all officers necessary to execute their ordinances and perform the duties herein required. **Improvement of streets, etc.** **Fire limits.**

Sec. 16. That at their first meeting or as soon thereafter as practicable, they shall elect a chief of police and tax collector, a city clerk and treasurer and city attorney, who shall respectively hold their offices during the term of the board electing them, and until their successors are elected and qualified: Provided, that any or all of such officers may be removed for misbehavior or neglect in office and others elected in their stead. Said officers shall take an oath of office for the faithful performance of their duties, which shall be administered by the mayor, and they shall also execute a bond for the faithful performance of duty and accounting for such moneys as shall come into their hands, except that no bond or oath shall be required of the city attorney. **Election of officers by aldermen.** **Shall execute bonds.**

Salary of clerk and treasurer.

Duties of clerk and treasurer.

Sec. 19. The clerk and treasurer shall be paid a reasonable salary, to be fixed by the board of aldermen; he shall keep correctly the regular minutes of the proceedings of the board, preserve all books, papers and other things placed in his charge during his continuance in office and deliver them to his successor. He shall also keep all moneys received by him belonging to the city of Monroe and disburse the same on orders made by the board and signed by the mayor, of which he shall keep a correct and accurate account in a book provided for that purpose by the city, which account shall show the sources from which the moneys are derived, to whom paid and for what purposes; the orders for money shall be produced at any settlement made with the board of aldermen as vouchers for such payments, and he shall at all times submit his accounts for inspection, when required by the board of aldermen. He shall make quarterly settlements of his accounts and file them with the board of aldermen at their next regular meeting after the end of a quarter. He shall pay all moneys in his hands at the end of his term of office and deliver all books, papers and other things received by him as clerk and treasurer to his successor, and shall in all respects faithfully discharge the duties imposed on him by this act or the ordinances of the city.

Shall turn over moneys and books to successor.

Duties of tax collector.

Sec. 20. The tax collector shall have the same power and authority to collect the taxes due the city as is conferred upon sheriffs for the collection of the state and county taxes, and he shall be liable to the same penalties for non-performance of his duties. The amount of the tax lists shall be charged against him and he shall be credited with all sums paid to the treasurer of the city and with such insolvents as shall be allowed him by the "finance committee" of the city, who shall audit the books of the treasurer and tax collector quarterly, and make report of their finding of the financial condition of each officer to the board of aldermen, who shall cause the same to be recorded in the minutes of the board if approved by them. The tax collector shall pay over to the treasurer weekly all moneys collected by him, taking the treasurer's receipt for the same; and in the event of his failure to pay over said moneys as herein provided and required, he shall pay ten per centum monthly on such sum as he shall fail to deliver to the treasurer, and it shall be the duty of the board of aldermen to remove him from office and appoint another in his stead and institute legal proceedings on the bond of such tax collector for the recovery of such sum as may be due the city. If any person owing a poll tax shall willfully fail to pay the same for three months after it shall become due it shall be the duty of the tax collector to report such delinquent to the mayor, who shall cite said delinquent to appear and show cause

Weekly settlements of tax collector.

Persons willfully failing to pay poll tax guilty of a misdemeanor.

why said tax is not paid; and if the delinquent has not paid the said tax and willfully refuses to pay the same, he shall be guilty of a misdemeanor, and on conviction he shall pay a fine not exceeding fifty dollars or be imprisoned not exceeding thirty days: Provided, the fine shall be at least double the poll tax assessed against such delinquent, not exceeding fifty dollars. The tax collector shall not report the non-payment of any poll tax to the mayor until after he has made diligent efforts to find personal or real estate sufficient to pay said tax and exhausted his legal remedies to enforce the payment of the same by levy and sale of such property if found.

When tax collector shall report.

Sec. 21. That the board of aldermen shall elect a chief of police and such other policemen as shall be necessary for the preservation of the peace, the enforcement of the ordinances of the city and the safety of the persons and property of the residents of said city, who shall hold their offices during the term of the board electing them and until their successors are qualified. The chief of police shall give a bond in such sum as the board of aldermen shall require for the faithful performance of the duties required of him by law and the city ordinances, faithfully to account for all moneys collected by him or which may come into his hands from fines, penalties, special taxes or in any way received by him in his official capacity. The chief of police shall have oversight and supervision of the police force, and shall see that all failure on their part to discharge their duties shall be reported to the mayor. The chief of police shall attend the courts of the mayor each day and report any and all violations of law or ordinances of the city which have come to his knowledge; he shall collect all fines, penalties and costs imposed by the mayor and pay the same to the treasurer, taking his receipt therefor, after reporting the collection of such sums to the mayor, who shall cause an entry thereof to be made on a city criminal docket, to be kept for the city by the mayor: Provided, that any money due to any person in said bill of costs other than an officer of the city shall be paid to the mayor to be paid to the parties entitled to the same. He shall also see that the laws and ordinances of the city are enforced, and shall do such other things as shall be required of him by law and the ordinances of said city. The chief of police and policemen shall have all the power and authority vested in sheriffs and constables for the preservation of the peace by preventing or suppressing disturbances and arresting offenders, and shall have power to serve any precept in any criminal case anywhere in the county of Union as sheriff now has. The chief of police and every policeman shall take an oath before the mayor for the faithful performance of his duties as required by law. The said chief of police and each policeman shall be paid a sal-

Election of policemen.

Bond of chief of police.

Chief of police shall attend courts.

Duties of chief of police.

Policemen shall take oath.

ary, to be fixed by the board of aldermen. and all fees to which they may be or become entitled under the laws of the land shall be collected as a part of the costs and paid into the city treasury. It shall be the duty of the mayor to tax as costs against offenders the same fees for services rendered by the chief of police or a policeman as the sheriff would be entitled to receive for similar services. When the necessities of the town require it the mayor shall appoint extra policemen to serve for such time as he shall direct, not exceeding one week. and such extra policemen shall take the oath of a regular policeman, as hereinbefore required. The chief of police and any policeman shall be subject to removal from office by the board of aldermen for neglect of duty, improper conduct or intoxication. The mayor, upon charges being preferred or upon finding the chief or any policeman guilty of mis conduct shall have power to suspend such member of the force from service until the board of aldermen shall investigate and take official action in the matter, and upon hearing the proofs, the board may discharge or restore such member, and his pay shall cease during the time of suspension.

Fees of policemen.

Policemen may be suspended.

Improvement of streets.

Sec. 22. That the board of aldermen shall have power to lay out, open and name any street or streets within the corporate limits of said city whenever by them deemed necessary, and shall have power to widen, enlarge, change, extend or discontinue any street or streets or any part thereof within the corporate limits, and shall have full power and authority for the purposes herein expressed to condemn, appropriate or use any land or lands within said city upon making reasonable compensation to the owner or owners thereof; and in case the owner or owners of any land which shall be condemned, appropriated or used under the provisions of this act, and the board of aldermen shall fail to agree upon the compensation for such land, the matter shall be settled by arbitrators, who shall be freeholders and residents of said town, and shall be chosen by the parties, one by the aldermen and the other by the owner of said land; and in case the owner of such land shall fail or refuse, upon notice given, to choose such arbitrator, then the mayor of said city shall select one in his stead; and in case the two chosen as aforesaid can not agree, they shall select an umpire, whose duty it shall be to examine the land condemned and ascertain the damages sustained and the benefit accruing to the owner in consequence of the change, and the award of the arbitrators and umpire or any two of them shall be conclusive of the rights of the parties, and shall vest in the city of Monroe the right to use the land for the purpose herein specified; and all damages agreed upon by the parties or awarded by the arbitrators in case of disagreement, shall be paid by taxation or as other liabilities of the corporation:

Condemnation of land.

Arbitrators.

Selection of umpire.

Damages agreed upon, how paid.

Provided, that either party may appeal to the superior court as now provided by law. Either party may appeal.

Sec 23. The board of aldermen are hereby authorized and fully empowered to levy annually on all real and personal property in said city which is subject to taxation therein by the laws of the land, and on every poll, a tax not to exceed seventy-five cents on the one hundred dollars worth of property, and two dollars and twenty-five cents on each poll, which said taxes shall be used by the board of aldermen for the general purposes of said city in its government, and the payment of such expenses as are necessary or incident to the purposes of its creation. The limit of taxation herein imposed shall not in any way interfere with or repeal the right to levy special taxes necessary to pay any bonds issued by said city under any special act of the general assembly heretofore enacted or which shall be hereafter enacted for its benefit. Aldermen empowered to levy annual special tax.

Sec. 24 The city tax collector shall have all the power and authority for the collection of the taxes levied on property and polls as is or may be conferred on the sheriff of Union county, and all sales of property made by such tax collector shall be made under the same rules, regulations and provisions of law as govern the sheriff of Union county in sales for taxes, and the right to redeem any property after a sale for city taxes shall be as allowed for the redemption of property sold for county and state taxes. Power of tax collector to collect taxes. Property sold for taxes may be redeemed.

Sec. 25. The board of aldermen shall have the right to levy and cause to be collected the following additional taxes, viz: Additional taxes.

(1) On every omnibus carrying persons for hire, a license tax not exceeding twenty dollars per annum; on every hack, carriage, wagon, express wagon, dray or other vehicle carrying or transporting persons, freight, baggage, merchandise or other articles for hire, a license tax not exceeding ten dollars per annum; and in fixing the amount of license tax on the above enumerated vehicles, the aldermen shall discriminate between one-horse, two horse and four horse vehicles and the different kind of vehicles, as shall seem just to them. The taxes herein enumerated shall be fixed by the aldermen at their meetings in June of each year and the amount of license tax so fixed on every vehicle shall be paid in advance by any person intending to engage in such business, and a license shall be issued by the clerk of the board of aldermen upon the exhibiting and filing with such clerk a receipt from the tax collector for the taxes so levied. Any person desiring to use the vehicles herein enumerated may pay the tax for a shorter term than twelve months, not less than three months, by the payment of the proportionate part of said tax for the desired time. Any person who shall use any of the vehicles herein enumerated without having first obtained the license from the city treasurer shall be guilty of a misdemeanor, Omnibuses, etc.

and on conviction shall pay a fine of not more than fifty dollars or be imprisoned not more than thirty days.

Saddle horses. (2) On every saddle horse kept for hire in said city a license tax not exceeding five dollars per annum, said license to be obtained in the same manner as for vehicles as above enumerated and subject to the same fine or imprisonment for failure to so obtain the license.

Delivery wagons. (3) On every delivery wagon or other vehicle delivering goods, wares or merchandise, except those used exclusively by resident citizens in delivering merchandise from their own stores, a license tax not exceeding one hundred dollars per annum.

Express, telephone and telegraph companies, etc. (4) On every express company, telegraph company, gas company, electric light company, power company, street railroad company doing business or having an office in said city, a license tax not exceeding in amount one-fourth of one per centum of its gross receipts on its business in said city received during the preceding year up to and including the thirty-first day of May next before the date of fixing such license tax; and the manager or agent in charge of the business of any such company in said city on the first day of June in every year shall on that day, or if that day be Sunday or a legal holiday, on the next day thereafter, make to the clerk of the board of aldermen, who shall in such case have power to administer oaths, a written return under oath signed by him of the amount of such gross receipts. The failure or refusal of any manager or agent to make such returns on the day fixed for that purpose shall make such manager or agent guilty of a misdemeanor, and on conviction he shall be fined not more than fifty dollars or imprisoned not more than thirty days. The amount of such tax, on the failure or refusal of such manager or agent to make the returns as herein required, shall be determined by the board of aldermen at their next meeting after the day on which said return should have been made or at some other meeting thereafter before the first of August of each year, and they shall fix the amount of such gross receipts as nearly as they can do so, and they shall levy one-fourth of one per centum thereof as the amount of the license tax.

Failure to pay said taxes.

Itinerant merchants, peddlers, etc. (5) On all itinerant merchants, peddlers or persons vending from any stand on the streets, offering to vend in said city, a privilege tax not exceeding twenty-five dollars a year, in addition to a tax not exceeding one per centum on the amount of their purchases respectively; and among such itinerant merchants or peddlers shall be included all itinerant venders of medicines or other articles.

Shooting galleries, billiard tables, etc. (6) On every shooting gallery, billiard table, bagatelle table, pool table or place of any other game or play, bowling alley or alley of like kind, with or without a name, kept for profit or kept n a house where spirituous, vinous or malt liquor is sold, or in a house used or connected with such a house, or used or connected with a hotel or restaurant, a privilege tax not exceeding one hundred dollars.

Hotels, restaurants, etc.

(7) On every hotel, restaurant or eating-house a privilege tax not exceeding fifty dollars. The board of aldermen shall have the power to classify into as many classes as to them from time to time shall seem just, such hotels, restaurants and eating-houses according to the character and amount of business done by them and the class to which each may belong and prescribe a different tax for every class, not to exceed in any case the sum of fifty dollars.

Circuses.

(8) On every circus, company of circus riders, performers or exhibitors or showmen, by whatever name called, who shall exhibit within said city or within one-half mile thereof, a license tax not exceeding one hundred dollars for every performance or separate exhibition, and on every side-show connected therewith a license tax not exceeding twenty-five dollars for each performance or exhibition. If the tax herein levied is not paid before performance, it shall be double the amount levied for such license.

Theatrical or other performances.

(9) On every person or company exhibiting within said city or one-half mile thereof, any stage or theatrical plays, sleight-of-hand performance, rope-walking, wire-walking, a license tax not exceeding twenty-five dollars for every twelve hours allowed for such exhibition. The tax, if not paid in advance, shall be double.

Opera houses.

(10) On every opera house a tax not exceeding one hundred dollars per annum: Provided, if a license is levied on opera houses, no license tax, as allowed in the preceding subsection nine, shall be required of the exhibitors therein.

Flying jennies.

(11) On every flying jenny, merry-go-round or mechanical contrivance for amusement within said city or one-half mile thereof, run for profit, a tax of five dollars for each and every day it is run. If the tax is not paid in advance it shall be double.

Exhibition of curiosities.

(12) On every exhibition of artificial or natural curiosities for reward a tax not exceeding twenty-five dollars.

Shows, etc., not enumerated.

(13) On every show, exhibition or performance of any kind, not othewise enumerated herein, and on every concert for reward, unless given by a religious, charitable or educational company, and on every strolling musician within said city, a license not exceeding ten dollars.

Dentists. Photographers. Special taxes.

(14) The board of aldermen may also levy, at their discretion, an annual privilege tax as follows: On dentists, local or itinerant, not exceeding ten dollars; on photographers, not exceeding twenty-five dollars; on hucksters' stands, not exceeding twenty-five dollars; on itinerant dealers in lightning rods, not exceeding

twenty-five dollars; on venders or agents of patent articles, not exceeding twenty-five dollars; on banks, banking business or bank agents, not exceeding one hundred dollars; on note-shavers, money-lenders, brokers and real estate agents, not exceeding twenty-five dollars, on retail dealers in fresh meats, not exceeding twenty-five dollars, on dealers in fish and oysters, not exceeding ten dollars; on boarding houses, not exceeding ten dollars; on ice cream saloons, a tax not exceeding ten dollars; on dealers in fertilizers, not exceeding twenty-five dollars; on skating-rinks, not exceeding ten dollars; on dogs, not exceeding five dollars; on dealers in carriages, buggies, wagons, sewing machines, tobacco, cigars, cigarettes, bicycles, cotton yarn not manufactured in Union county, not exceeding twenty-five dollars; on every person, company, firm or corporation selling pistols, bowie-knives, dirks, sling-shots, brass or metallic knuckles or other deadly weapons of like character, in addition to all other taxes, a license tax not exceeding one hundred dollars.

Special taxes.

Special taxes.

Itinerant physicians, etc.

(15) On every itinerant physician, surgeon, dentist, chiropodist, optician, oculist, a tax not exceeding twenty-five dollars.

Bar-rooms.

(16) On every person, company or firm selling spirituous, vinous or malt liquors, a license tax for every place in which such business is or is to be conducted, whether by wholesale or retail, one thousand dollars, to be paid semi-annually in advance on the first days in January and July of each year, one-half at each payment. Every person desirous of engaging in such business in said city shall apply to said board of aldermen at its first meeting in June or December in any year for license to do so, and the said board of aldermen may in its discretion direct or decline to direct the tax collector to issue such license to any such applicant or for any place in said city where license is sought to be obtained for the conduct of said business. Upon the direction of the board of aldermen so to do, and the payment of the license tax therefor, it shall be the duty of the tax collector to issue to the person, company or firm named in said direction a license to conduct the business specified in said direction at the place therein named for the period of six months, to commence on the first day of January or July next after the date of such direction to the tax collector. Any license issued by the county commissioners of Union county for the sale of liquors in the city of Monroe, without a license first issued by the board of aldermen's direction to the tax collector, shall be void. Any person, company or firm having such license who shall within the period therein named at any time fail, neglect or refuse to comply with any rule or regulation theretofore or within such period prescribed by such board of aldermen for the conduct, control or regulation of such business, shall thereby forfeit such license, and upon such

Persons desiring to sell liquor shall apply to aldermen for license.

County commissioners shall not issue license without permission of town commissioners.

forfeiture being declared by the board of aldermen, such person, company or firm shall no longer be entitled to engage in said business within said period or under said license, nor shall such person, company or firm be entitled to have refunded to him, them, or it any part of the license tax paid for such license. Any person who shall sell or aid in selling or offer to sell in said city any spirituous, vinous or malt liquors without having a license therefor, or after his license shall have been declared forfeited by the board of aldermen, shall be guilty of a misdemeanor, and on conviction thereof shall be fined not more than fifty dollars or be imprisoned not more than thirty days.

Regulations governing sale of liquor.

(17) They shall levy the taxes specified in subsection sixteen for the sale of liquors upon the granting of an order for license, and no license issued by the county commissioners shall be valid unless the tax specified above shall have been paid by the applicant for license: Provided, that this charter shall not have the effect to repeal the act prohibiting the sale of liquors in Union county by a dispensary, being chapter four hundred and forty-nine of the acts of eighteen hundred and ninety-seven.

No license valid unless tax has been paid.

Proviso.

Does not repeal dispensary act.

Sec. 26. The board of aldermen shall provide for the establishment, organization, equipment, government and pay of such fire companies as they shall deem necessary and proper for the protection of the property of said town and of its citizens; and in case of a fire occurring in said city, the mayor or a majority of the aldermen present at a fire may order the blowing up, pulling down or destroying of any house or houses deemed necessary to stop the progress of the fire; and no person shall be held civilly or criminally liable for any damages resulting from his acting in obedience to such orders. They shall also establish fire limits within said city, within which it shall be unlawful for any person, company, firm or corporation to erect, build or repair any wooden house, make any wooden additions to any building or cover any building with any material other than slate or metal. They may prohibit wooden buildings from being removed into said fire limits or from being removed from one place to another within said fire limits under such penalties as the board of aldermen shall establish, which penalties may be sued for and recovered from the owner in any action in any court having jurisdiction.

Organization and pay of fire companies.

Fire limit.

Sec. 27. That the board of aldermen shall have the right and power to make ordinances to prohibit or control the firing of firearms, fire crackers, torpedoes, roman candles, sky-rockets and other explosive materials and to govern the sale thereof in the city; to limit the speed at which horses may be ridden or driven through the streets or bicycles ridden and the speed at which engines and trains of railroads shall run within the city limits;

Ordinances regulating use of fire-arms.

prohibit said railroads from stopping their engines or cars on said streets and to require the railroad companies to keep the crossings of the streets over their railroads in good repair; to control the arrangement of stove pipes and flues in buildings and the manner in which powder, dynamite and other explosives and inflammable substances may be kept, stored and sold; the manner and place of storing commercial fertilizers in said city; the manner in which dogs and hogs may be kept; to cause all alleys, street lots, cellars, privies, stables and other places of like character to be examined by a sanitary policeman, to be appointed for that purpose, and to cause by their order the sanitary policeman to have said places cleansed and the nuisances abated, and any sanitary policeman or any other person appointed by said board and charged with that duty shall have authority to enter upon the premises found to be in bad order and inspect and have the same cleansed, and the expense of cleansing said places and removing said nuisances shall be recovered from the occupant or owner of said premises by action in any court having jurisdiction.

Abatement of nuisances.

Trades and occupations becoming a nuisance prohibited.

Sec. 28. The board of aldermen shall have power and it shall be their duty to prohibit all trades or occupations which are a nuisance from being carried on in said city within one mile thereof, and to abate any such nuisances and cause their removal. They shall have power and it shall be their duty to cause all ponds, sunken lots and other places in which water stands and stagnates to be drained and filled up and to recover from the owner or occupant of such lot, the expenses for such removal, draining or filling up, which expenses shall be a lien on the lot: Provided, the owner or occupant of said lots, after ten days' notice shall neglect or refuse to remove or abate such nuisance.

Expenses of cleaning lot a lien on same.

Establishment and control of public pleasure grounds.

Sec. 29. That the board of aldermen may establish, acquire, improve and control parks or other pleasure grounds for the use of inhabitants of said city, and may pass ordinances and regulations for the proper protection, maintenance, management, government and control of the same. It may also protect and control the shade trees already growing or hereafter planted on the streets, public squares, public grounds, alleys, sidewalks of or within the city, and may remove any such trees from time to time or plant others on such alleys, grounds, streets, sidewalks and other places as may seem to them meet. Said board may also grant permission to erect telegraph poles, telephone poles, electric light poles, street car poles or other poles upon the streets, sidewalks, alleys, public grounds or squares, or prohibit or prevent such erection of the same, and may control and regulate all such poles as have been or may be erected, and the use of the same and the manner of their use, and may remove or cause to e removed the same or any of them at any time or times, and n such manner and upon such notice as may seem just and roper. It shall also have the right to control, regulate, license, rohibit or remove any and all structures or things erected, contructed, put or placed on, above or under the streets, public quares, public grounds, alleys or sidewalks of the city.

Control and regulation of structures erected in said town.

Sec. 30. That the board of aldermen may establish, acquire and naintain one [or] more public cemeteries of such size as they may eem necessary within or without the corporate limits of said ity, and provide for the care and maintenance of the same and he proper regulation, control and protection thereof. They may lso divide such cemeteries into lots of proper and convenient izes, and may fix the prices of such lots at a reasonable sum, and nay sell the same and make title to the purchaser. They may lso annually appoint some suitable person as sexton of the cemtery, whose duty it shall be to have charge over the cemetery nd to see that all entrances thereto, the walls and fences around t and the walks and avenues therein are kept in proper condiion and repair. If the person appointed sexton shall be found o be negligent, or in any way unsuitable for his position, the ldermen may remove him and appoint another in his stead.

Cemeteries.

Appointment of sexton.

Sexton may be removed for cause.

Sec. 31. It shall be unlawful for any person to behave in a rude r boisterous manner or be guilty of any indecent conduct of any ind in any cemetery in the said city of Monroe, or to injure, leface or disturb in any manner any wall, fence, grave, gravetone, monument, tomb or vault, or trees or shrubbery, and [the] exton shall promptly report any violation of this act to the chief f police.

Indecent conduct unlawful.

Sec. 32. That the board of aldermen shall have the right to grant, control, rescind any franchises, privileges or permits to any company, firm or corporation to erect, on, over, along or under the streets and alleys of said city any work, piping, elecric wires, telephone wires, street car lines or other structure, in which the public have an interest as a matter of convenience or therwise.

Empowered to grant and rescind franchises.

Sec. 33. That all privileges, powers and benefits conferred upon he aldermen of other cities in the state under the general laws or the government of cities and towns are hereby conferred upon the aldermen of the city of Monroe.

Additional privileges and powers.

Sec. 34. That in addition to the other powers conferred on the board of aldermen, they shall have power and authority to borow money with the consent of a majority of the qualified voters f said city, which consent shall be obtained at an election held fter thirty days' public notice published in a newspaper in the ity of Monroe, at which those who consent to the proposition ubmitted to them shall vote "Approved," and those who do not

May borrow money.

Approval of indebtedness by voters.

Form of ballot.

consent shall vote "Disapproved," which said indebtedness when approved by a majority of the qualified voters shall be evidenced by the bonds of the city, signed by its mayor and attested by the seal of the city and the signature of its secretary or clerk, but no bonds or other indebtedness of the city shall be issued or created in excess of one-tenth of the valuation of the property of the city as shown by its tax list of the preceding year, nor shall any sum of money be borrowed in excess of an amount which, added to the previous indebtedness of the city then owing, shall exceed one-tenth of the taxable property of the city as so shown, it being the intention of this restriction to prevent the entire indebtedness of said city at any one time from exceeding the one-tenth of the aggregate tax value of property of said city as shown by the tax books of the preceding year; and in any proposition published in said newspaper submitted to the qualified voters of said city as above provided shall be included the statement of the then existing indebtedness of said city, and of the aggregate tax value of the property of said city, together with the amount of the indebtedness proposed to be created by said election. That before any proposition to create any indebtedness shall be submitted to the qualified voters of said city, a resolution to that effect shall be passed by a three-fourths majority of the board of aldermen at two separate meetings of said board. All propositions to borrow money submitted to the qualified voters of said city shall provide for the payment of interest on the amount so proposed to be borrowed, and shall fix a limit of taxation on the one hundred dollars of property and on the polls of said city, and such tax shall observe the constitutional equation of taxation between the poll and property, making the tax on a poll equal to the tax on three hundred dollars worth of property. The said election shall be held under the provisions of this charter providing for the election of officers, but may be held at such time as the board of aldermen shall designate, either at their regular election in May or at any other time.

Resolution passed by three-fourths majority of aldermen before vote can be taken.

Sec. 35. That this act shall be in force from and after its ratification.

Ratified the 6th day of March, A. D. 1899.

CHAPTER 353.

An act to amend the charter of the city of Southport.

The General Assembly of North Carolina do enact:

Section 1. That an act entitled an act to amend the charter of the city of Southport, ratified at this session of the general assembly, be and the same is hereby amended as follows, to-wit: Act amending charter of Southport amended.

Sec. 2. That the second ward shall constitute and embrace that part of said city east of the center line of Flower street, including West street to the center line of Rhett street, thence to the center line of Moore street, thence with the center line of Moore street, eastern line of the city limits. Territory included in Second Ward.

Sec. 3. This act shall be in force from and after its ratification.

Ratified the 7th day of March, A. D. 1899.

CHAPTER 354.

An act to incorporate the Raleigh Real Estate, Trust and Insurance Company.

The General Assembly of North Carolina do enact:

Section 1. That Frank K. Ellington, John Drewry, Sherwood Higgs, Joseph G. Brown, and such other persons as may become associated with them by subscribing to or purchasing the capital stock of the company, and their successors, are hereby constituted and declared to be a body politic and corporate under the name and style of The Raleigh Real Estate, Trust and Insurance Company, for a period of sixty years, and by that name may sue and be sued, plead and be impleaded, contract and be contracted with, may adopt and have a common seal which may be altered at pleasure, and may adopt such by-laws, rules and regulations for the management and government of its business and officers as may be deemed proper. Corporators. Body corporate. Corporate name. Duration of charter. Corporate powers.

Sec. 2. The capital stock of said company shall be ten thousand dollars ($10,000), divided into shares of one hundred dollars each, but it may be increased from time to time, by and with the consent of a majority in value of the stockholders, to an amount not exceeding one hundred thousand dollars ($100,000); but said company may commence business whenever five thousand dollars ($5,000) of the capital stock shall have been bona fide subscribed for and forty per cent. thereof shall have been paid in cash. Capital stock. May be increased.

Books of subscription may be opened

Sec. 3 The corporators named in the first section of this act, or a majority of them, may open books of subscription to the capital stock of said company at such time and place, and for such period, as they may determine upon, and whenever five thousand dollars ($5,000) of the capital stock shall have been bona fide subscribed for, the said corporators, or a majority of them, may call a meeting of the subscribers or stockholders to be held in the city of Raleigh at such place and time as may be designated in the call, which may be in writing or by advertisement in some newspaper of general circulation published in Raleigh, North Carolina; and if at such meeting a majority of the stock is represented and forty per cent. of the amount subscribed shall be paid in in cash, said incorporators may organize said company by the election of such directors as they may deem proper, not exceeding seven in number, who shall manage the affairs of the company and shall hold office for one year, or until their successors shall be elected; said directors, when elected, as well as their successors, shall elect one of their own number president, and shall elect and appoint such other officers as may be provided for by the by-laws.

When meeting may be called.

Organization of company.

Officers.

Corporate powers.

Sec. 4. Said corporators shall have power to receive, purchase, buy and hold land, real estate, and property, real, personal or mixed, to issue bonds therefor and to improve, sell and dispose of the same, in such parts, parcels, way and manner as they may deem best, and to this intent and purpose may enter into agreements, contracts and conveyances, and may lease, mortgage or otherwise dispose of and convey the same, and may receive for such sales, or lease or mortgages, such moneys, securities and things as they may choose, with power to issue or endorse bonds, or borrow money, and to prescribe the form of such conveyances, agreements, contracts, leases, mortgages or other instruments of writing and determine how and by whom the same shall be executed, with further power to make loans and advances of money or other things, on such terms and on such security, real or personal, as may be agreed upon, and to engage in any mining, building or manufacturing enterprises. It may also act as agent in the collection of rents, notes, accounts, and such other evidences of indebtedness on commission, may discount, buy and sell notes, drafts, bonds and other securities or evidences of debt; may act as broker or agent in the purchase and sale of stocks and bonds, and negotiate loans and receive commissions therefor; may lend money on mortgages of real and personal property, or both, or upon crops planted and unplanted, may own, maintain or lease warehouses and carry on the business of warehousemen and forwarders, and receive on storage or deposit all kinds of produce, merchandise or other personal property and make advances on the same, and collect and receive interest

Nature of business.

May make loans, etc.

Empowered to act as warehousemen.

and commissions and compensation for storage and all labor and expenses incident thereto.

Execution of trusts

Sec. 5. That the said company be and it is hereby authorized to accept and execute trusts of any and every description which may be committed or transferred to it with its consent by any person or persons whomsoever, bodies corporate or public, or by any court in the state of North Carolina, or in any one of the states of the United States, and to accept the office and appointment of executor, administrator or guardian whenever such office or appointment is conferred or made by any person or persons, or by any court of this state or of the United States, or of any other state within the United States; and in all cases where application shall be made to any court of this state for the appointment of any receiver, trustee, administrator, executor, assignee, guardian of any minor, or committee of a lunatic, it shall and may be lawful for such court, if it shall think fit to appoint the Raleigh Real Estate, Trust and Insurance Company with its assent such receiver, trustee, administrator, assignee, guardian, or committee, and the accounts of the said company as such receiver, trustee, administrator, assignee, guardian or committee shall be regularly settled and adjusted before such tribunal; and upon such settlement and adjustment all proper legal and customary charges, costs and expenses shall be allowed to said company for its care and management of the trusts and estates as aforesaid, and the said company as such receiver, trustee, administrator, executor, assignee, guardian or committee shall be subject to all orders or decrees made by the proper tribunal by which such appointment may have been made: Provided, that said corporation shall not be eligible to an appointment by any court as executor, administrator, guardian or committee of a lunatic unless the capital stock of said corporation, with its surplus added, shall be equal to twice the value of the estate to be entrusted by said appointment to said company.

Empowered to act as executor, administrator, etc.

Compensation to be allowed company for execution of trust.

May act as agent for municipal corporation, etc.

Sec. 6. That said corporation may act as agent, factor or trustee for any state, county, township, city, town or other municipal corporation, or for any person or corporation, on such terms as to compensation as may be agreed upon, in negotiating loans, registering, selling, countersigning, collecting, holding, acquiring, dealing in and disposing of any bonds, certificates of stock, notes or any description or property, real or personal.

May become surety on bonds.

Sec. 7. That said corporation may become surety for the faithful discharge by any public officer, or by any individual, of the duties incident to his office or employment, as well as for the payment of any costs of any suit or action by any person or corporation required to give security therefor, and on any bond or undertaking required or permitted in any suit or other proceedings in any of the courts of this state, or of the United States, or under the laws of this state.

May organize savings bank.

Sec. 8. That said corporation may organize and conduct a savings bank for the convenience of its stockholders and depositors, may make such regulations in regard thereto, not inconsistent with the laws of this state, as will enable it to receive deposits and give therefor certificates or other evidence of deposit, and it may pay such interest on deposits as may be agreed upon, not exceeding the legal rate, and may regulate the time of payment and notice of demand.

Authorized to do general banking business.

Sec. 9. Said corporation may do a general banking business, and exercise all the rights, powers and privileges conferred by the laws of this state on bankers and corporations, especially those set forth in chapter four, volume two of The Code of North Carolina: Provided, that before the said corporation shall exercise the power conferred in this section, there shall be at least twenty thousand dollars ($20,000) of its stock paid in: Provided further, that the stockholders of said corporation shall be held individually responsible, equally and ratably, and not one for another, for all contracts, debts, and engagements made and incurred by it as a banking institution, to the extent of their stock therein, at the par value thereof, in addition to the amount invested in such shares.

Proviso. Certain stock shall be paid before business begins.

May issue policies of insurance.

Sec. 10. That said corporation may issue policies of insurance, duly signed by its president and secretary, against loss or damage by fire, lightning, wind or tornado, or any other insurance whatever that the directors may deem proper, including life, accident and liability insurance, any or all, and said corporation is hereby vested with all the power that any insurance company has or may have to transact business in this state, and may charge such premiums as may be agreed upon by said company and the parties insured.

Individual liability

Sec. 11. That no corporator or stockholder of said corporation shall be in anywise individually liable for any debts, obligations, contracts or torts of said corporation, but any officer of said corporation who may be guilty of fraud shall be liable, as provided in section six hundred and eighty-six, chapter sixteen of The Code.

Representation of stockholders in meetings.

Sec. 12. Each stockholder shall be entitled in all meetings of the stockholders to cast one vote for each share of stock held by him.

Sec. 13. That this act shall be in force from and after its ratification.

Ratified the 7th day of March, A. D. 1899.

CHAPTER 355.

An act to extend the charter of the "Seamen's Friend Society" at Wilmington.

The General Assembly of North Carolina do enact:

Section 1. That the charter granted to Gilbert Potter, Charles D. Ellis, Armond J. DeRossett, Oscar G. Parsley, John McRae, P. K. Dickinson and Joseph H. Flanner, incorporating them and their successors under the name and style of the Seamen's Friend Society, is hereby extended for the term of sixty years from the time fixed for the expiration of the original charter, said corporation being for the purpose of improving the social, moral and religious condition of the seamen at Wilmington. Charter extended sixty years. Purpose of corporation.

Sec. 2. That the successors of the incorporators above mentioned constitute the corporation as aforesaid, and are vested with all the rights, powers, privileges, franchises, property and assets of every description, real, personal and mixed, which may belong or appertain to the corporation hereinbefore mentioned. Successors of incorporators, rights and powers of.

Sec. 3. That this act shall be in force from and after its ratification.

Ratified the 7th day of March, A. D. 1899.

CHAPTER 356.

An act to extend the corporate limits and to amend the charter of the town of Ayden.

The General Assembly of North Carolina do enact:

Section 1. That the corporate limits of the town of Ayden be and the same are hereby enlarged and extended so that the said town shall be included and embraced in the following boundaries, to-wit: Beginning on the east side of the right of way of the Scotland Neck and Kinston branch of the Wilmington and Weldon Railroad at J. J. Harrington's corner and running from thence with said Harrington's line north fifty-seven degrees east forty-seven poles and three links; thence north eighty-one and one-half degrees east thirty-two poles and thirteen links to the southeast corner of the cemetery; thence with the line of said cemetery north nine and one-half degrees west ten poles and thirteen links to the northeast corner of said cemetery; thence north twenty-one and three-fourths degrees east fifty-four poles to Third street; thence down said street south eighty-four and one-fourth degrees east seventy-eight poles; thence north ten Corporate limits of Ayden extended.

and one-half degrees west fourteen poles; thence north thirty-six degrees west twelve and two-thirds poles to Second street; thence north five and one-half degrees east fifty-two poles; thence north eighty-three and one-half degrees west two hundred and forty poles; thence south twenty and one-half degrees west seventy-six poles; thence south eighty-three degrees east twenty-four poles to J. Griffin's line; thence south twelve and one-fourth degrees east thirty-eight poles to Henry Venter's corner; thence south thirty-nine degrees west one hundred and one-half poles to Lee street; thence north fifty-seven degrees east thirty-four poles to the beginning.

Town officers.

Sec. 2. That the officers of said town shall consist of a mayor and five commissioners, to be elected on the first Monday in May, eighteen hundred and ninety-nine, and annually thereafter in the manner prescribed by law for municipal elections. That said board of commissioners shall have the power and authority to appoint such policemen and other officers as they may deem necessary for the government of said town and to fix and determine their salaries.

Appointment of policemen.

Violators of ordinances worked on streets.

Sec. 3 That any person who shall be convicted of violating any ordinance of said town, who shall refuse or fail to pay the costs and fine imposed upon him, may be required to work upon the streets at such sum per day as may be fixed by the board of commissioners until such costs and fine are paid.

Appointment of tax collector.

Sec. 4. That in collecting the taxes of said town, the officer or person who may be appointed for that purpose shall be vested with the same power and authority as sheriffs and tax collectors are in the collection of state and county taxes.

Conflicting laws repealed.

Sec. 5. That all laws and clauses of laws in conflict with this act be and the same are hereby repealed.

Sec. 6. That this act shall be in force from and after its ratification.

Ratified the 7th day of March, A. D. 1899.

CHAPTER 357.

An act to re-enact and to amend chapter ninety-three of the laws of eighteen hundred and eighty-nine, and to extend the time for organization of the said corporation authorized thereby.

The General Assembly of North Carolina do enact:

Chapter 93, laws of 1889, re-enacted.

Section 1. That chapter ninety-three of the laws of eighteen hundred and eighty-nine, which authorized the incorporation of the Bank of Madison, be and is hereby re-enacted.

Sec. 2. That three years from the date hereof be allowed to the incorporators for the purpose of organization. Extension of time for organization.

Sec. 3. That section seven of the said chapter be and is hereby repealed. Section 7 repealed.

Sec. 4. That section three of the said chapter be amended so as to read, "not less than five directors, such number of directors as the stockholders in their by-laws may determine upon." Section 3 amended.

Sec. 5. That the said bank shall have the power to act as trustees, assignee, administrator, executor, guardian, commissioner, etc., with all the rights and privileges of natural persons serving in their several capacities. Power of bank to act as trustee, etc.

Sec. 6. That the said bank is authorized to organize, in connection with its general banking business, a department for savings, and to do a savings bank business for the convenience of small depositors, and to make such regulations in regard thereto, not inconsistent with the laws of this state or of the United states, as will enable said bank to receive small deposits in the savings department, and to give certificates or other evidences of deposits and to pay such interest as may be agreed on not exceeding the legal rate; and to regulate the time of payment and notice of demand. Authorized to organize savings bank department.

Sec. 7. That this act shall be in force from and after its ratification.

Ratified the 7th day of March, A. D. 1899.

CHAPTER 358.

An act to incorporate the Raleigh Warehouse Company.

The General Assembly of North Carolina do enact:

Section 1. That A. A. Thompson, Charles E. Johnson and J. Ludlow Skinner, all of the city of Raleigh, North Carolina, and those whom they may hereafter associate with them, and their successors and assigns, be and they are hereby declared to be incorporated into a corporation by the name and style of the Raleigh Warehouse Company, and by that name shall be empowered to purchase, hold and sell real estate, and take leases of real estate in the county of Wake and elsewhere in North Carolina; to do a warehouse business for the storage, care and custody of cotton which may be deposited or stored with said corporation for shipment, safe keeping, or otherwise; to sample, grade and ship cotton on its own account, and for others; to advance and lend money on cotton, and to negotiate for such advances upon cotton stored with it for safe keeping, or for shipment; to act as Corporators. Body corporate. Corporate name. Nature of business. Corporate powers.

agent for its customers in making contracts with insurance companies for the customary insurance of cotton stored with it, or in transit; to buy and sell cotton on the corporators' own account, and also on consignment from, or as agent for others; to charge and collect reasonable compensation for its services.

Principal place of business.

Sec. 2. The principal place of business of said corporation shall be in the city of Raleigh, North Carolina.

Duration of charter.

Sec. 3. The corporate existence of said corporation shall be fifty years.

Capital stock.

Sec. 4. The amount of capital of said corporation shall be ten thousand dollars, to be divided into one hundred shares of the amount and par value of one hundred dollars each; and said corporation is authorized to commence business when the whole of said capital stock is subscribed for, and fifty per centum of the capital is paid in cash, or its equivalent, and not before; and the capital of said corporation may be increased to an amount not exceeding one hundred thousand dollars, whenever a majority of shareholders may elect so to do.

Capital may be increased.

Individual liability

Sec. 5. No shareholder in said corporation shall be individually or personally liable for any debt, contract, tort or other liability whatever of said corporation.

Receipt shall be given for cotton stored.

Sec. 6. Whenever any cotton shall be stored with said corporation, a receipt shall be given therefor to the person or persons, copartnership or corporation from whom the cotton is received, which receipt shall be signed by such officer or employee of the said corporation as shall be authorized by the by-laws of the said corporation to sign said receipts, and every such receipt shall also have the common seal of said corporation stamped thereon; every such receipt shall bear the true date of its issue, shall state the number of bales or packages of cotton delivered to said corporation by the person or persons, copartnership or corporation to whom or to which such receipt is issued, and the distinguishing letters or marks on said bales or packages, and every such receipt shall have plainly written or printed on the face thereof the following: "The above described cotton will be delivered to the person or persons, copartnership or corporation named above, or to his, her, their or its endorsees, upon the surrender of this receipt properly endorsed, and upon the payment to this corporation of all charges due this corporation upon said cotton; but under no circumstances will said cotton, or any part thereof, be delivered to the person or persons, copartnership or corporation above named or his, her, their, or its endorsees, without the actual surrender of this receipt duly endorsed, except in the case of the accidental loss or destruction of this receipt, and then only upon the surrender of the duplicate receipt, properly endorsed, which may be issued by this corporation under the provisions of section thirteen of its charter." And on the

Form of acknowledgment on face of receipt.

Surrender and endorsement of receipt.

margin of every such receipt shall be written or printed in plain, large letters the following: "This receipt negotiable by proper endorsement."

Receipts given for cotton shall be negotiable.

Sec. 7. Each and every receipt for cotton given or issued by said corporation in accordance with the requirements of this act shall be negotiable by endorsement of the person or persons, copartnership or corporation to whom and in whose name such receipts shall be issued, and his, her, their or its subsequent endorsees, in the same manner and to the full extent that bills, bonds and other notes are negotiable under section forty-one of chapter six of volume one of The Code of North Carolina. And whenever any person or persons, copartnership or corporation to whom any such receipt for cotton shall be issued by said corporation, and whose name or names appear in the body of such receipt, shall endorse and deliver such receipt to another, the person or persons, copartnership or corporation to whom or to which said receipt shall be endorsed and his, her or their, or its subsequent endorsees, shall be deemed and held in law and in equity to be the owner or owners of the cotton described in such receipt, subject only to the charges due to said corporation on said cotton, in as full and ample a manner and degree as it would be possible for the person or persons, partnership or vorporation to whom such receipt was originally issued, or any subsequent endorsee thereof, to sell, assign, transfer, and declare the title, right and possession of, in and to the cotton described in such receipt, to the endorsee or endorsees thereof by any manner or form of actual sales and delivery of said cotton known to the law.

Receipt shall be endorsed before delivery.

After delivery of receipt persons selling shall enter into other sale or conveyance.

Sec. 8. After any cotton shall have been delivered to said corporation for storage or shipment, and receipt shall have been issued therefor, as hereinbefore provided, then, except by endorsement and delivery of such receipt, as in this act provided, no sale, assignment, transfer or mortgage of the cotton described in such receipt or other act, deed or contract thereafter made or entered into with respect to such cotton by the person or persons, copartnership or corporation to whom any such receipt shall have been issued, or by any endorsee, or endorsees, thereof, shall be of any validity to have any right, title or interest in or to the cotton described in such receipt, or to create any lien, encumbrance, right or estate, legal or equitable, in or to such cotton, so long as such cotton shall remain in the custody and under the control of said corporation, and the receipt given or issued therefor shall be outstanding and unsurrendered; but the title to such cotton shall pass or be affected and controlled only by endorsement and delivery of the corporation's receipt given or issued therefor so long as such cotton shall remain stored with, or in the custody of, or under the control of said corporation.

Officers may levy upon cotton in warehouse.

Sec. 9. Any sheriff, coroner, constable, United States marshal, or other officer, having in hand for execution any writ of execution, or other final process, may levy upon said cotton in the custody of said corporation as in the case of any other personal property stored and in the custody of a bailer, but the property and title in and to such cotton at the time of such levy shall be deemed and held to be vested in the person or persons, copartnership or corporation who shall at that time be the bona fide holder and owner of the receipt issued for such cotton; and no such levy shall in any manner affect or impair the rights of any person or persons, copartnership or corporation, who, not being the defendant or defendants in such execution, or other final process, is a bona fide endorsee for value of any such receipt for cotton, or the rights of any bona fide pledge of any such receipt, or the right of said corporation as pledgee of the cotton levied on; and if at the time of any such levy the defendant or defendants, or any of them, against whom the process is issued, shall be the real and absolute owner or owners of and have in possession the receipt issued for the cotton levied upon, he or they shall immediately surrender such receipt to the officer making such levy; and if they fail to do so when thereto required by such officer, the person or persons so refusing shall be guilty of a misdemeanor, and upon conviction thereof shall be fined or imprisoned, or both, in the discretion of the court.

Certain rights not affected by levy.

Receipt shall be surrendered to officer making levy.

On delivery of cotton, corporation released from liability.

Sec. 10. Whenever said corporation shall have delivered any cotton stored with it to the person or persons, copartnership or corporation from whom it was received, and to whom and in whose name a receipt was given, or shall have delivered such cotton to the endorsee and holder of such receipt, the original receipt in either case being properly endorsed, and surrendered to the corporation, then said corporation shall be by such delivery absolutely discharged from all further liability with respect to such cotton.

Form of endorsement on face of receipt.

Sec. 11. Whenever said corporation shall lend any money on any cotton stored with it, it shall cause to be written or printed across the face of the receipt given and issued for such cotton the following: "The cotton described in this receipt is pledged with this corporation to secure .... dollars, with interest thereon from the ...... day of ...., A. D. ......, till paid, at the rate of ...... per centum per annum. Any endorsee or holder of this receipt will take said cotton subject to the lien of said pledge and must pay said amount and interest, or whatever balance may be due thereon in addition to warehouse charges, before said cotton will be delivered to him." And the blanks in such writing across the face of such receipt shall be filled up with the true amount of the money lent by said corporation, the true date from which said amount bears interest, and the true rate of interest payable on said money. When any receipt which shall be given by said corporation shall have such writing on its face, the said corporation shall have all the rights of a pledgee in and to the cotton described in such receipt as security for the amount actually lent by it, to the holder of such receipt, and specified in such writing across the face thereof, and interest on such amount: Provided, that the amount lent shall not exceed the amount specified in such writing across the face of such receipt.

Proviso. Amount lent shall not exceed the amount specified in writing.

Sec. 12. The original holders or any endorsee of any receipt for cotton, issued by said corporation under the provisions of this act may pledge such receipt by endorsing and delivering the same to any person, copartnership or corporation, to secure any contract, obligation, debt or liability of the pledgor; and the pledgee of such receipt shall have, by the virtue of the pledge or such receipt, the same being duly endorsed, all the rights, interests and powers of a pledgee in and to and over the cotton described in such receipt, which he, she, it or they would have if such cotton were actually delivered into the actual possession of such pledgee under a binding contract or pledge.

Receipt may be pledged by endorsing same.

Sec. 13. If any receipt for cotton issued by said corporation shall by accident be lost or destroyed by the holder thereof, a duplicate may be issued by the corporation to any person or persons, copartnership or corporation to whom the original receipt was issued, or to the person or persons, copartnership or corporation to whom such original has been duly endorsed and delivered, and whose property it was at the time of such loss or destruction. But no duplicate receipt shall be issued except upon full compliance with the following provisions, that is to say: The applicant for duplicate receipt shall make affidavit before some justice of the peace of this state that the original receipt was accidentally destroyed or that it is lost and cannot after diligent search be found; that said original receipt was issued to the applicant, or that it had been duly endorsed to such applicant, stating the name or names of each and every endorser upon such receipt at the time of its loss, and that no other person or persons, copartneship or corporation has or claims any interest in and to said receipt; and the affidavit when made shall be filed with said corporation. If a corporation is the applicant for a duplicate receipt the affidavit above referred to shall be made by one of its officers. Such applicant shall also file with said corporation a bond, with at least two sureties, in the penal sum of double the market price of the cotton described in the lost or destroyed receipt at the time of applying for the duplicate, such bond to be conditioned to be void if the obligors shall save harm-

When receipt is lost or destroyed.

Duplicate receipts shall be issued on compliance with certain conditions

When a corporation is applicant for duplicate receipt.

less the said corporation from any and all loss costs, expenses and damages by reason of the issue of such duplicate receipt; and such bond shall have attached to it the affidavits of the sureties made before some justice of the peace of North Carolina to the effect that they are worth a certain amount in excess of all debts, liabilities and exemptions. And unless it appear from such affidavit that the sureties in the aggregate are worth at least the penalty of the bond over and above all debts, liabilities and exemptions no duplicate receipt shall be issued. And the officers of said corporation shall have the right to examine the sureties to such bond on oath before some justice of the peace as to their property and liabilities before accepting such bond. If any surety refuse to be thus examined when requested by the president or other officers of said corporation, the bond tendered by the applicant for a duplicate receipt shall not be deemed sufficient, and no duplicate shall be issued until a proper bond shall be given, and before issuing any duplicate receipt a notice that such duplicate has been applied for and will be issued shall be published for thirty consecutive days in some newspaper published daily in the city of Raleigh, North Carolina. Such notice shall state number of the lost or destroyed receipt; the name of the person or persons, copartnership or corporation to whom and in whose name it was originally issued; the number of bales or packages of cotton for which it was issued, with the letters and marks thereon, as described in the original receipt; the name of the applicant for the duplicate receipt, and the date on which such duplicate will be issued unless opposed on or before such day. If before the day named in such notice as the day on which the duplicate will be issued, any adverse claimant notifies the corporation in writing that there is objection to the issue of such duplicate, stating the grounds of such objection, then no duplicate shall be issued until the rights of the claimants shall be settled among themselves by agreement or judicial determination.

Bonds shall have attached affidavits of sureties.

Notice shall be made that duplicate receipt has been applied for.

When claimant objects to issuance of duplicate.

Officers and agents of company giving receipt when cotton has not been delivered, guilty of crime.

Sec. 14. If any officer, agent or employee of said corporation shall issue any receipt for cotton in the name of said corporation when, in fact, the cotton described in said receipt shall not have been actually delivered to said corporation, then such officer, agent or employee shall be guilty of a crime, and upon conviction thereof shall be imprisoned in the state's prison for a term not to exceed five years, in the discretion of the court.

Unlawful delivery of cotton by agents or officers.

Sec. 15. If any officer, agent or employee of said corporation shall deliver to any person or corporation other than a duly authorized officer of the law executing lawful process, any cotton stored with said corporation, for which cotton a receipt has been issued, without the surrender to the corporation of such receipt, duly endorsed, or the surrender of the duplicate receipt, if a duplicate receipt shall have been issued under the provisions of this act, then such officer, agent or employee shall be guilty of a misdemeanor, and upon conviction thereof shall be fined or imprisoned, or both, in the discretion of the court.

Sec. 16. The storage of any cotton with said corporation shall not affect the rights of persons or corporations having an interest in or lien upon such cotton existing and in force prior to the delivery of such cotton to said corporation: Provided, such interest or lien be such as under the laws of this state would be valid and binding as against any bona fide purchaser of such cotton from the person or corporation storing the same. And said corporation shall not be held as guarantor of the title of any cotton placed in its custody and for which it shall issue a receipt. Liens on cotton not affected by such storage.

Sec. 17. If the said corporation shall so desire they may store goods, wares and merchandise other than cotton and issue receipts therefor, and such receipts shall be issued in the same way and be negotiable upon endorsement in the same manner as receipts issued for cotton. Empowered to store goods other than cotton.

Sec. 18. This act shall be in force from and after its ratification.

Ratified the 7th day of March, A. D. 1899.

CHAPTER 359.

An act to amend the charter of the town of Apex, in Wake county.

The General Assembly of North Carolina do enact:

Section 1. That chapter fifty-two, private laws of North Carolina, session eighteen hundred and seventy-two and eighteen hundred and seventy three, entitled "An act to incorporate the town of Apex, in the county of Wake," be amended by inserting after section six of said act the following: That the mayor of the town of Apex is hereby constituted a special court, to be known as "The Mayor's Court," with exclusive, original jurisdiction of all offenses arising from the violation of the provisions of this act, of the ordinances, by-laws, rules and regulations of the board of commissioners made in pursuance hereof and the charter of said town, and with all the judicial powers and authority which is now or hereafter may be given to justices of the peace for the trial and determination of such criminal and civil causes as may arise within the corporate limits of said town under the general laws of North Carolina; and to that end he may issue his summons, warrant or other process, and of criminals have the party brought before him, hear, determine and give judgment thereon, impose fines, penalties and forfeitures, as the case may Chapter 52, private laws 1872–'73 amended. Official title of mayor's court. Summons issued by mayor.

be, and direct the enforcement thereof by imprisonment in criminal action, subject to the limitations of this act as to the amount of such penalties, and subject also to the same right of appeal as provided for courts of justices of the peace: Provided, that no cause arising upon the violation of any of the provisions of this act, or of any ordinance, rule or regulation made in pursuance hereof and of the charter, shall be removed from the mayor's court to a justice of the peace for trial; and Provided further, that in case a defendant, a witness or other person shall be adjudged to be imprisoned by the said mayor's court, it shall be competent for the said court to sentence such person to imprisonment in the county jail for a term not exceeding thirty days, and to adjudge also that such person work during the period of his confinement on the public streets or works of the town or on the public roads of the county of Wake, and in case such imprisonment be for the non-payment of a fine or penalty or cost he shall have credit thereon at the rate of fifty cents a day for every day which he shall so work on the streets, roads or other works of the county.

Right of appeal. Proviso.

Persons sentenced to prison may be worked on public roads.

Sec. 2. That among the powers conferred on the board of commissioners are these: Ascertain the location, increase, reduce and establish the width and grade, regulate the repairs and keep clean the streets, sidewalks and alleys of the town, extend, lay out, open, establish the width and grade, keep clear and maintain others, and protect the shade trees of the town; appoint a police force and fix their salaries; prohibit vagrancy and street begging; regulate, control, tax, license or prevent the establishment of junk and pawnshops, their keepers or brokers, and the sale of spirituous, vinous and malt liquors; regulate the speed of railroad locomotives, tram and electric cars, the charge for the carriage of persons, baggage and freight for hire, and the license or the prevention of the same; provide for the proper observance of the Sabbath and the preservation of the peace, order and tranquility of the town. That they prohibit and prevent by penalties the running at large of dogs, hogs, cattle and other brutes, the riding and driving of horses or other animals at a greater speed than six miles an hour or any reckless manner within the town limits, and also the firing of guns, pistols, crackers, gunpowder, and other explosives, combustibles, or dangerous materials in streets or elsewhere within the town; and to provide for the execution of such ordinances, by-laws, rules and regulations by such fines and penalties, either in money or imprisonment, for their violation, as may be authorized by this act, consistent with the laws of the land and necessary for the proper government of the town: Provided, that no penalty prescribed by the commissioners for the violation of this act, or of any ordinance, by-law,

Powers conferred on commissioners. Improvement of streets.

Police force. Vagrancy.

Pawn shops.

Running at large of hogs. Fast driving.

Firing of guns, pistols, etc.

Proviso.

Maximum penalties.

ule, or regulation made by them, shall exceed fifty dollars fine, r thirty days' imprisonment.

Principal streets.

Sec. 3. That the survey and position of the streets of the town f Apex, as made and plotted by J. P. H. Adams, on the twentieth ay of June, eighteen hundred and seventy-eight, recorded in the ffice of register of deeds in Wake county in Book fifty-four, on age three hundred and twenty-seven and three hundred and wenty-eight, shall be and the same are hereby declared to be he principal streets of said town, and said town shall have abso-ute pre-eminent right of assessment over the land covered y said streets free and discharged from all claims for damages.

Commissioners empowered to lay annual tax.

Assessment and collection of taxes.

Sec. 4. That in order to raise a fund for the expenses of the overnment and improvement of the town of Apex, the commis-ioners may annually levy a tax, not to exceed twenty-five cents n every one hundred dollars worth of taxable real and personal roperty in said town, and on all taxable polls a tax not exceed-ng seventy-five cents on each poll residing in said town, and the aid commissioners shall also have power to provide the machin-ery necessary to assess, list and collect said taxes, not inconsist-ent with this act and the laws of North Carolina. The valuation f real and personal property for taxation in said town of Apex hall be the same as that assessed for the collection of state and county taxes in White Oak township, Wake county.

Tax list, how made out.

Sec. 5. The tax list of the town of Apex shall be made out under the direction of the commissioners of said town and placed in the hands of the town marshal or tax collector of the said town on or before the first day of October in each year, and the taxes of said town shall be due and payable on the fifteenth day of October of each year; and should any taxes assessed by said town not be paid by the first day of January after they become due they shall thereafter bear interest at the rate of six per centum per annum until paid.

Taxes, a lien on real estate.

Sec. 6. The taxes assessed by said town shall be a lien upon the real estate of the tax payer owing the same until paid.

Taxes remaining unpaid, when tax lister shall levy.

Sec. 7. That if the taxes assessed against any tax payer by said town for any year shall remain unpaid until the first day of March after they become due, the town marshal or tax collector of said town shall, by virtue of the tax list in his hands, levy upon any personal property belonging to said tax payer or so much thereof as may be necessary to pay said delinquent taxes, and sell the same after ten days' notice of time and place of sale posted at the mayor's office in said town of Apex and three other public places in said town; and there shall be served by said town marshal a written or printed notice to said delinquent tax payer of said time and place of sale. From the proceeds of said sale, the said town marshal or tax collector shall pay the taxes due by said delinquent to said town and cost of sale, which shall not exceed seventy-five cents, and the balance, if any, pay to said delinquent.

chment of ts and other perty by tax ector.

Sec. 8. That if no personal property of the delinquent tax payer can be found to satisfy the taxes due by said delinquent, it shall be the duty of the said town marshal or tax collector to attach any debt or other property incapable of manual delivery, due or belonging to the person liable, or that may become due him before the expiration of the calendar year, and the person or corporation owing such debt or having such property in possession shall be liable for said tax to the extent of the debt owing or property held by him, and said liability of said person or corporation shall be discharged to the delinquent by the payment of said tax and the cost of attachment to the amount of the same.

ceedings in e of attachment.

The proceedings in case of attachment as herein provided shall be the same as now allowed by law for the collection of state and county taxes.

e of real estate unpaid taxes.

Sec. 9. Should any taxes assessed by said town as provided in this act remain unpaid until the first day of April after they become due, it shall be the duty of the said town marshal or tax collector to advertise and sell for cash any real estate in said town belonging to any delinquent tax payer, the said sale to occur at the court-house door of Wake county on the first Monday of May of each year after said taxes become due, after advertising the time and place of sale for thirty days in some one or more newspapers published in Wake county, and by giving notice of said sale to the delinquent tax payer through the mails thirty days before said sale, and the said marshal or tax collector shall also post notice of sale at the mayor's office of said town of Apex this thirty days before said sale.

e and place of e shall be adver- ed.

ount bid pay- e to marshal.

When any purchaser shall bid off land at said sale he shall immediately pay the amount bid by him to said town marshal or tax collector who shall give to said purchaser a certificate substantially the same form as that given by a sheriff upon a sale by him of land sold for state and county taxes.

rchaser shall be en certificate.

The purchaser shall pay to said marshal or tax collector a fee not exceeding fifty cents for said certificate, and the same shall be signed by said marshal or tax collector. The said marshal or tax collector shall keep a book showing the lands sold by him for taxes, the name of the purchaser and the sum for which each tract was sold and the amount paid for said certificate.

rshal shall keep ecord of land es.

demption of land ld for taxes.

The owner of any land sold for taxes as aforesaid, or any person having an interest in the same, may redeem said land at any time before the first day of January next after said sale: Provided, said owner or interested person shall pay said purchaser twenty per cent. on the amount paid by him on account of the taxes and certificate aforesaid. Any town marshal or tax collector who shall be directly or indirectly concerned personally in the purchase of any real estate sold by him for taxes shall be guilty of a misdemeanor.

Sec. 10. Unless the land sold for taxes as provided in the preceding section shall be redeemed by the time limited therein, the said town marshal or tax collector shall execute to the purchaser and his heirs and assigns a deed conveying the land sold by him for taxes upon the production of the certificate calling for the same; and upon the loss of any certificate, on being fully satisfied thereof by due proof, the said marshal or tax collector shall execute and deliver the proper conveyance. The deed made by said town marshal or tax collector as herein provided shall be substantially the same in form as that executed by sheriffs upon a sale by them of land sold for the non-payment of state and county taxes. When land is not redeemed within time specified, marshal shall execute deed.

Sec. 11. That the commissioners of said town of Apex may elect a secretary and treasurer for said town, who shall be the clerk of the said board of commissioners and who shall enter into bond, with good security, payable to the town of Apex, in an amount to be fixed by said board for the faithful performance of the duties of his office, which duties shall be fixed by said commissioners. The mayor of said town of Apex shall be the custodian of said bond. Election of secretary and treasurer.

Sec. 12. That all laws and parts of laws inconsistent with this act are hereby repealed. Conflicting laws repealed.

Sec. 13. This act shall be in force from and after its ratification.

Ratified the 7th day of March, A. D. 1899.

CHAPTER 360.

An act to incorporate the Guilford Power Company.

The General Assembly of North Carolina do enact:

Section 1. That J. S. Hunter, E. P. Wharton, G. J. Taylor and W. M. Barber, and their associates and successors, be and they are hereby declared a body politic and corporate under the name and style of the Guilford Power Company, and by that name shall have sixty years succession, and sue and be sued, plead and be impleaded, make and use a corporate seal and alter the same at pleasure, contract and be contracted with, and shall have and enjoy all the rights and privileges necessary for the purposes of this act. Corporators. Body corporate.

Sec. 2. That the capital stock of the said company shall be fifty thousand dollars, and may be increased from time to time, with Capital stock may be increased.

the consent of a majority of the stockholders, to any adequate amount by the issue and sale of shares of common and preferred stock, or both, upon such terms and conditions, and under such regulations as the board of directors, with the approval of a majority of stockholders of said company, shall prescribe; but the par value of each share of stock shall be one hundred dollars;

orate powers.

and the directors, with the like approval of the stockholders, may receive cash, labor, material, bonds, stocks, contracts, real or personal property in payment of subscription to the capital stock; and may make such subscriptions payable in such manner or amounts and at such times as may be agreed upon with the subscribers;

n company be organized.

and whenever one hundred shares shall have been subscribed for and the sum of one thousand dollars paid in cash, the subscribers, under the direction of a majority of the corporators hereinbefore named, who themselves shall be subscribers, may organize the said company by electing a board of directors and providing for the election or appointment of such other officers as may be necessary for the control and management of the business and affairs of said company; and therefore they shall have and exercise all the powers and functions of a corporation under this charter and the laws of this state.

ility of stock ebts.

Every subscriber to or holder of the stock of said company shall be liable for the debts of the said company to an amount equal to the amount unpaid on the stock subscribed for and held by him and no more.

borrow money

Sec. 3. It shall be lawful for the said corporation, upon such terms as the stockholders or board of directors, by their authority may determine, to borrow money, to issue its notes, obligations, bonds and debentures from time to time as they may elect, and to secure the same by mortgage or mortgages on its property and franchises, in whole or in part, as they may deem necessary or expedient;

deal in notes, gages, etc.

and it shall be lawful for the said corporation to acquire, by original subscription, contract or otherwise, and to hold, manage, pledge, mortgage, sell, convey and dispose of or otherwise deal with in like manner as individuals may do, shares of the capital stock, notes, bonds and other obligations of other companies, organized under the laws of any of the United States.

owered to ap- lectrical and r power.

Sec. 4. That the said company is authorized and empowered to supply to the public, including both individuals and corporations, whether private or municipal, within the counties of Guilford, Rowan, Davidson, Cabarrus, Mecklenburg and elsewhere in the state of North Carolina, power in the form of electric current, hydraulic, pneumatic and steam pressure or any of the said forms, and in any or all other forms for use in driving machinery, and for light, heat and all other uses to which the power so supplied can be applicable, and to fix charges, collect and receive payment therefor; and for the purpose of enabling the company to supply power as aforesaid, the company is authorized and empowered to buy or otherwise acquire, generate, develop, store, use, transmit, and distribute power of all kinds, and to locate, acquire, construct, equip, maintain and operate from an initial point on the Yadkin River, the Mayodian, or any stream not navigable within the state of North Carolina, where the company may establish a plant, either directly to consumers or users or to a distributing point in the city of Greensboro, and from the same or any other initial point in the said state of North Carolina either directly to consumers or users or to a distributing point in the city of Salisbury, and from the same or any other initial point in the said state of North Carolina either directly to consumers or users or to a distributing point in the town of Concord, and from the same or any other initial point in the said state of North Carolina either directly to consumers or users or to a distributing point in the city of Charlotte, and from the same or any other initial point in the said state of North Carolina either directly to consumers or users or to any other distributing point in North Carolina which the said company may establish by the most practical routes to be determined by the board of directors of the company, lines for the transmission of power by wires on poles, or underground, and by cables, pipes tubes, conduits, and all other convenient appliances for power transmission, with such connecting lines between the lines above mentioned, and also such branch lines within the said territory and elsewhere as the board of directors of the company may locate or authorize to be located for receiving, transmitting and distributing power; and the company may acquire, own, hold, sell or otherwise dispose of water-power and water privileges in the state of North Carolina, and may locate, acquire, construct, equip, maintain and operate all necessary plants for generating and developing by water, steam, or any other means, and for storing, using, transmitting, distributing, selling and developing power, including dams, gates, bridges, sluices, tunnels, stations, and other buildings, boilers, engines, machinery, switches, lamps, motors, and all other works, structures and appliances in the state of North Carolina: Provided, that the amount of land which the company may at any time hold within the state of North Carolina for any one water-power, and appurtenant works, as well as the land flowed or submerged with the water accumulated by a dam shall not exceed five thousand acres exclusive of right of way; and Provided further, that lines and appurtenances hereinbefore authorized for distributing power and light are to be constructed when on public streets or highways of any county, city or town, under such reasonable regulations as the authorities respectively thereof shall, upon application from the company, prescribe.

Nature of business. Corporate powers.

Distributing points.

Corporate powers.

Proviso.

Lines, etc., to be constructed under certain regulations.

)owered to gen-
› and sell elec-
ty.

Sec. 5. That the said company shall have power, in addition to the powers hereinbefore enumerated, to carry on and conduct the business of generating, making, transmitting, furnishing, and selling electricity for the purposes of lighting, heat, and power, and to furnish and sell and contract for the furnishing and sale to persons, corporations, towns and cities of electricity for illuminating purposes, or as motive power for running and propelling engines, cars, machinery and apparatus, and also for all other uses and purposes for which electricity is now or may be hereafter used; and to construct, maintain and operate a plant or plants for manufacturing, generating and transmitting electricity; to deal in, generate, furnish, supply, and sell electricity, gas and all other kinds of power, forces, fluids, currents, matter and materials used or to be used for the purposes of illumination, heat and power; to carry on any and all business in anywise appertaining to or connected with the manufacture and generating, distributing and furnishing of electricity for light, heat, and power purposes, including the transaction of any and all business in which electricity is now or hereafter may be utilized, and all matters incidental or necessary to the distribution of electric light, heat and power; to manufacture and repair, sell and deal in any and all necessary appliances and machinery used in or which may be required or deemed advisable for or in connection with the utilization of electricity or in anywise appertaining thereto or connected therewith; to purchase, acquire, own, use, lease, let and furnish any and all kinds of electric machinery, apparatus and appliances; to purchase, acquire, own, hold, improve, let, lease, operate and maintain water rights and privileges and water powers; to supply water to persons, corporations, factories, towns and cities for domestic purposes, and for use as power, and for manufacturing purposes, and to charge, receive and collect such charges and rates therefor as may be deemed advisable or expedient, to construct, acquire, build and operate, maintain and lease in the state of North Carolina canals, ditches and flumes and pipe-lines for the conducting of water; to maintain and operate railroads, street railways, water lines and tramways, carry freight and passengers thereon, and to charge, collect and receive tolls or taxes for the same; to construct, build, purchase, buy, own, hold, lease, maintain and operate telegraph and telephone lines wherever it may be deemed expedient, and to charge, receive and collect such charges and rates for the use of its telegraph and telephone lines and for the transmission of messages thereon as may be deemed advisable or expedient; to construct, acquire, own, hold, lease, maintain, and operate lines of wires, underground conduits, subways, and other convenient conduits or appliances for the transmission of electricity and other energies, fluids, forces and currents as may be deemed ad-

)owered to con-
ct and operate
tric plants.

manufacture
deal in ma-
iery, etc., in
nection with
t.

ɔurchase and
i water rights.

lection of
rges.

y maintain and
rate railroads.

y hold and oper-
lines of wires.

visable or expedient; to lease any part or all of its railroads, street railroads, motor lines and tramways to any other company or companies incorporated for the purpose of maintaining and operating a railroad, street railroad, motor line or tramway, and to lease or operate, maintain and operate any part or all of any other railroad constructed by any other company upon such terms and conditions as may be agreed upon between said companies respectively; to apply to the proper authority of any incorporated city or town, or of the county in the state of North Carolina, in which the railways, street railways, motor lines, tramways, telegraph lines, telephone lines, electric light and power lines, plants, underground conduits, subways, wires, poles and appliances of this corporation may extend, or be designed or intended now or hereafter to extend, for a grant of any rights, powers, privileges and franchises for the maintenance or operation thereof; to accept, receive, own, hold, lease all and singular the same; to acquire by contract, purchase, lease, or otherwise, and to accept, own and hold any rights, privileges or franchises heretofore granted to any person, firm, company or corporation or which may be hereafter so granted by the proper authorities of any such incorporated city or town, or of any county in the state of North Carolina; to purchase, acquire, lease, rent, own, hold and improve real property in such quantities as may be deemed expedient; to build dwelling houses and to build and operate stores, mills, schools, factories, warehouses, and any and all other buildings or structures desirable or convenient; to sell and dispose of the same on such terms and conditions and payments, including installment, and installment plans, as may be desirable or convenient; to lay out and plot any real property belonging to or acquired by the corporation into lots, blocks, squares, factory sites, and other convenient forms; and to lay out, plot and dedicate to public use, or otherwise, streets, avenues, alleys and parks; to purchase, possess, own, hold, rent, lease and improve all and any property, real, personal, and mixed, necessary, desirable or convenient for the use of the corporation, or the transaction of its business or any part thereof; and to do and perform all and other matters and things necessary, proper or convenient for its accomplishment of the objects (and any thereof) above specified.

May lease property

Shall apply to proper authorities for rights desired.

May acquire and hold real property.

May lay out and plat real property.

Sec. 6. It shall be lawful for the president and directors, their agents, superintendents, engineers, or others in their employ, to enter at all times upon all lands or water for the purpose of exploring or surveying the works of said company and locating the same, doing no unnecessary damage to private property; and when the location of said works shall have been determined upon and a survey of the same deposited in the office of the secretary of state, then it shall be lawful for the said company by the

Officers and agents may enter upon certain property.

officers, agents, engineers, superintendents, contractors and others in its employ to enter upon, take possession of, have, hold, use and locate any such lands, an- to erect all the structures necessary and suitable for the completion or repairing of said works, subject to such compensation as is hereafter provided:

Proviso. Tender of payment shall be made before lands are entered upon.

Provided, always, that payment or tender of payment of all demands for the occupancy of all lands upon which the said works may be laid out, be made before the said company shall enter upon or break ground upon the premises, except for surveying or locating said works, unless the consent of the owners be first had

Proviso. Company shall not be precluded from making other locations.

and obtained; and Provided further, that such locating of its works and filing of its surveys in the office of the secretary of state shall not preclude said company from making from time to time other location of works and filing surveys of the same, as its business or development requires.

Condemnation of land.

Sec. 7. When any land and right of way may be required by said company for the purpose of constructing and operating its works, and for want of agreement as to the value thereof or for any other cause, the same cannot be purchased from the owner,

Appointment of arbitrators.

the same may be taken at a valuation of five commissioners or a majority of them to be appointed in term time on petition of the judge of the superior court of the county where some part of the land is situated. In making the said valuation, the said commissioners shall take into consideration the loss or damage which may occur to the owner or owners in consequence of the

Proviso. Appeal may be taken.

land being surrendered: Provided, nevertheless, that if any person or persons on whose land the works may be located or if the said company shall be dissatisfied with the valuation of the commissioners, then in that case the party so dissatisfied may file exceptions to the valuation in the pending proceedings, subject to the same rules, regulations and restrictions as in other like cases. The proceedings of the said commissioners, with a full description of the land, shall be returned under the hands and seals of a majority of them, to the county from which the commission issued thereafter [on] confirmation by the judge to remain a matter of record, and also to be registered in the office of the register of deeds of each county wherein the land condemned lies, and the land so valued shall vest in the said company as soon as the valuation shall have been paid or tendered:

Proviso. When notice is given and owners of land cannot be found.

Provided, that upon application for the appointment of commissioners under this section it shall be made to appear to the satisfaction of the court that at least ten days' notice had been previously given of the application to the owner or owners of the land so proposed to be condemned, or if the owner or owners be under disability, then to the guardian, if any, of such owner or owners, as well as to such owner or owners, or if the owner or owners who are not under disability, or the guardian of such owners as are under disability, cannot be found within the county, or the owner or owners is or are not known, then that such notice of such application had been published once a week for at least four weeks in some newspaper printed in the vicinity of the court-house of the county in which the application is made; and Provided further, that the valuation provided for in this section shall be made on oath by the commissioners aforesaid, which oath may be administered by any clerk of the court, justice of the peace, or other person authorized by law to administer oaths: Provided further, that the right of condemnation herein granted shall not authorize said company to remove or invade the burial ground of any individual without his or her consent.

Sec. 8. The right of the said company to condemn land in the manner aforesaid shall extend to the condemning of strips of land not exceeding twenty-five feet in width with necessary additional width in deep cuts and fillings required by the company for its roadways, power, transmission lines and all other lands necessary for the construction and operation of its own works, as well as the necessary water, including in the land and water thus described water powers, water privileges and land followed or submerged with water accumulated by the company's dams. Extension of right to condemn land.

Sec. 9. A part of the works of said company may be constructed without completing its entire works, and the said works may be operated and electric current transmitted and delivered, and charges collected therefor, notwithstanding the entire works of the company have not been completed. Works may be partially constructed without completing the whole.

Sec. 10. Every stockholder in the company shall at all meetings or elections be entitled to one vote for every share of stock registered in his name. The stockholders of the said company may enact such by-laws, rules and regulations for the management of the affairs of the company as they may deem proper or expedient. Meetings of the stockholders and directors may be held in the city of Greensboro, where the principal office of the company shall be, or elsewhere in the state of North Carolina, at such times and places as the stockholders may in the by-laws or otherwise prescribe, Representation of stockholders in meetings.

Sec. 11. The board of directors shall be composed of stockholders of said company, and shall consist of such members as the stockholders shall prescribe from time to time by the by-laws, and shall be elected at the stockholders' annual meeting, to be held on such days as the by-laws of the company may direct, and shall continue in office for the term of one year from and after the date of their election, and until their successors are elected and accept the duties of office; and they shall choose one of their number president, and in case of death, resignation or incapacity of any member of the board of directors during his term of Board of directors. Annual meeting. Term of office. Vacancies occurring.

office, the said board shall choose his successor for the unexpired term.

s act shall be med a public

Sec. 12. That this act shall be deemed and taken to be a public act and a copy of any by-law or regulation of the said company, under its corporate seal purporting to be signed by the president, shall be received as prima facie evidence for and against the said company in any judicial proceedings.

Sec. 13. This act shall be in force from and after its ratification.

Ratified the 7th day of March, A. D. 1899.

CHAPTER 361.

An act to allow the town of Castalia to elect its officers under its present charter.

amble.

Whereas, by chapter sixty-four of the public laws of eighteen hundred and seventy-two and eighteen hundred and seventy-three, the town of Castalia in the county of Nash was incorporated and allowed to elect from year to year the officers therein named. And whereas, there was a failure to elect said officers in the year eighteen hundred and ninety-seven and eighteen hundred and ninety-eight, and there is doubt in minds of its inhabitants whetner or not they did not lose said right to elect their officers therein named,

The General Assembly of North Carolina do enact:

powered to ct town officers.

Section 1. That the town of Castalia, in the county of Nash, shall have and is hereby given the right to elect three commissioners and a mayor and a constable, as set out and allowed in said chapter sixty-four, under the general laws of this state governing the election of officers of incorporated towns, at an election to be held on first Monday in May, eighteen hundred and ninety-nine.

Sec. 2. That this act shall be in full force from and after its ratification.

Ratified the 7th day of March, A. D. 1899.

CHAPTER 362.

An act to incorporate the Atlantic and Western Railroad Company.

The General Assembly of North Carolina do enact:

porators.

Section 1. That Julian S. Carr, of Durham county; W. J. Edwards and N. J. Adams, of Moore county; E. F. Young, of Harnett county; J. W. Perry, of Johnston county, and F. K. Borden, of Wayne county, and their associates, successors and assigns, be and they are hereby constituted and created a body politic and corporate under the name of the Atlantic and Western Railroad Company, and as such may sue and be sued, plead and be impleaded in the courts of the state, and shall have the powers herein granted. Said company shall have power and authority to make by-laws; to buy, hold, use, sell, mortgage or otherwise transfer all such real and personal estate as may be necessary to and will advance the interest of said company; to elect or appoint all necessary officers and prescribe their powers and duties; and to have and use a common seal which it may change at pleasure, and to have and exercise all and every other power, privilege, franchise and right common or necessary to similar corporations, and not inconsistent with the laws of this state or the provisions of this act.

Body corporate. Corporate name. Corporate powers.

Sec. 2. That said company be and is hereby authorized and empowered to survey, lay out, construct and equip, maintain and operate, by steam or other motive power, a railroad with one or more tracks from some point at or near Goldsboro, in the county of Wayne, westwardly, by such route or routes as the directors of said company may determine through the counties of Wayne, Johnston, Harnett, Moore and Montgomery, and thence to or in the direction of Concord, Salisbury or Charlotte, and thence westwardly to the Tennessee state line. Said company may also build and operate branch roads, trams, etc.

Empowered to construct and operate a railroad.

Sec. 3. That for the purpose of surveying, constructing, maintaining and operating said lines of railroads said company is hereby empowered: First—To cause such examination and surveys to be made as shall be necessary to the selection of the most advantageous route or routes, and for such purpose its officers and agents, servants and employees may enter upon the land or water of any person. Second—To take and hold such voluntary grants of real estate, or other property, as may be made to it to aid in the construction, maintenance and operation of its road. Third—To purchase, hold and use all such real estate and other property as may be necessary for the construction and maintenance of its roads or stations, and all other accommodations necessary to accomplish the objects of its corporation, and to lease or buy land necessary for its use. Fourth—To lay out its road, not exceeding two hundred feet in width, and to construct the same; and for the purpose of cutting any embankments, and for obtaining gravel and other materials, may take as much land as may be necessary for the proper construction, operaton and security of the roads, or to cut down any trees that may be in danger of getting on the track or obstructing the right of way. Fifth—To construct its road across, along or upon any stream of

Corporate powers. Surveys of routes. Voluntary grants of real estate. Purchase and hold real estate, etc. To lay out road. To construct road across streams, etc.

water, watercourses, streets, highways, canal, etc., which the route of the road shall intersect or touch.

To cross other roads.

Sixth—To cross, intersect or join or unite its road with any other railroad heretofore or hereafter to be constructed, at any point on its route, or upon the ground of any other railroad company, with the necessary turnouts, siding and switches or other conveniences necessary in the construction of its roads, and may run over any part of any other railway's right of way necessary or proper to reach its freight depot in any city, town or village, or to reach any other point of its right of way otherwise inaccessible, through or near which its road may run.

To convey persons or property over their road.

Seventh—To take and convey persons or property over their road by use of steam or any mechanical power, and to receive compensation therefor, and to do all things incident to railroad business.

To erect buildings, wharves, etc.

Eighth—To erect and maintain convenient buildings, warehouses, docks, stations, fixtures and machinery, whether within or without a city, town or village, for the accommodation and use of their passengers and freight business.

Regulation of schedule.

Ninth—To regulate the time and manner in which passengers and freight shall be transported, and the compensation to be paid therefor, subject to any laws of this state upon the subject. Tenth—To borrow such sum or sums of money at such rates of interest not contrary to law, and upon such terms as said company or its board of directors shall agree upon and may deem necessary or expedient, and may execute one or more trust deeds or mortgages, or both, if occasion may require, on its roads, branches, or both, in process of construction by said company, for the amount or amounts borrowed or owing by said company, as its board of directors shall deem expedient.

May make deeds and mortgages for transferring track, etc.

Said company may make deed or mortgage for transferring their railroad track or tracks, depots, grounds, rights, privileges, franchises, immunities, machine-houses, rolling stock, furniture, tools, implements, appendages and appurtenances used in connection with its road in any manner then belonging to said company or which shall thereafter belong to it, as security for any bonds, debts or sums of money as may be secured by said trust deeds or mortgages, as they shall think proper.

Capital stock may be increased.

Sec. 4. That the capital stock of said company shall be fifty thousand dollars, and the same may be increased from time to time, as a majority of the stockholders may determine, up to one million dollars.

Division of shares.

The stock of said company shall be in shares of one hundred dollars each, for which, when fully paid for, certificates shall be issued, which shall be non-assessable, and each share shall entitle the holder to one vote, and the stockholders shall not be individually liable for the debts of the corporation.

Personal liability of stockholders.

Books of subscription shall be opened by the corporators, or a majority of them, at such time or times, place or places, and under such rules and regulations as they, or a majority of them, may prescribe. Said corporators, or a majority of them, acting in person or by proxy, after the sum of five thousand dollars shall have been subscribed, shall call a meeting of the subscribers to the said capital stock for the purpose of completing the organization of the company, and at such meeting the said subscribers to the capital stock shall elect a board of directors, consisting of not less than three nor more than eleven members, who shall immediately elect one of their number president of the company.

Election of directors.

Sec. 5. That subscriptions to the capital stock of said company may be made in money, land or material, or in bonds, stocks or other valuable credits, in such manner and on such terms as may be agreed upon by the president and directors of said company, and if any subscriber shall neglect or refuse to pay any installment when it becomes due, if required by the directors, said board may declare his stock forfeited, as well as all previous payments thereof, to the benefit and use of said company; but before so declaring it forfeited said stockholder shall have served upon him a notice in writing, in person or by depositing said notice in the postoffice, [post]paid, directed to him at the postoffice nearest his usual place of abode, stating that he is required to make such payment within sixty days from the date of said notice, at such time and place as is within named; said notice shall be served or mailed sixty days prior to the day on which payment is required to be made.

Subscriptions to stock, how made.

Sec. 6. That said company is hereby authorized and empowered to survey and consolidate its capital stock, estate, real, personal and mixed, franchises, rights, privileges and property with those of any other railroad or steamboat company or companies chartered by and organized under the laws of this or any other state whenever a majority of the stockholders of the company hereby chartered shall so desire, when the two or more railroads so to be merged shall and may form a continuous line of railroad with each other or by means of intervening road or roads; and said consolidation may be effected by its directors in such manner, and on such terms and conditions, and under such name and style as a majority of the stockholders may determine or approve.

May merge capital stock, etc., with that of other companies.

Sec. 7. That it shall and may be lawful for any railroad or transportation company, created by the laws of this or any other state, from time to time to subscribe for, purchase or hold the stock and bonds, or either, of the company incorporated by this act, or to guarantee or endorse such bonds or stock or either of them; and it shall and may be lawful for any railroad or transportation company or companies to purchase, use or lease the road, property or franchises of the said company hereby incorporated, for such time and upon such terms as may be agreed upon.

Other transportation companies may subscribe to stock.

Annual meetings of stockholders.

Sec. 8. That meetings of stockholders shall be held annually at such time and place, either in this or other state, as may be determined by them, and at all such annual meetings the president and directors shall render to the stockholders an account of the affairs of the company.

Appointment of vice-president, treasurer, etc.

Sec. 9. That the president and board of directors of said company shall have the power of appointing a vice-president, treasurer and such other officers and agents as may be necessary for conducting the construction and management of its railroad. The directors shall be elected by the stockholders annually, and shall remain in office one year, and in case of vacancies occurring by death or resignation in the office of directors, the same may be filled by the directors until the next meeting of the stockholders.

President and directors empowered to make certain expenditures.

Sec. 10. The president and directors of said company, under authority from the stockholders, shall have power to make such expenditures and contract such debts as may be necessary for the construction and operation of its railroad and business. And authority is hereby given to the said company to borrow money to such extent and in such manner as may be authorized by its stockholders, and to pay thereon such rates of interest as may be deemed advisable, and to issue therefor such bonds, whether coupons or registered, or other evidences of debt, in such manner and of such form as may be determined by the president and directors, and to secure such loans, both as to principal and interest, by such mortgages or deeds of trust on the whole of the property, income, or franchise of the company, either [whole] or any part thereof.

Shall enjoy all rights conferred by Code on like corporations.

Sec. 11. That said company shall enjoy all benefits and be subject to the provisions of section one thousand nine hundred and forty-three to one thousand nine hundred and fifty-one, both inclusive, of chapter forty-nine, volume one of The Code of North Carolina, in respect to the acquisition of land by condemnation.

Counties, townships or towns may subscribe to capital stock.

Sec. 12. That it shall and may be lawful for any county, township, city or town in or through which the said railroad may be located, or which is interested in its construction, to subscribe to the capital stock of such company such sum or sums, in bonds or money, as a majority of their qualified voters may authorize the county commissioners of such county or the municipal authorities of such town to subscribe.

Representation of counties, etc., in meetings.

Sec. 13. That in all conventions of stockholders of said company, such counties, townships or towns as may subscribe to the capital stock shall be represented by one or more delegates to be appointed for such purposes by the corporate authorities of such towns, or the county commissioners of the respective counties, or townships in such counties.

Sec. 14. That it shall be lawful for said railroad company from time to time to subscribe for, purchase or hold the stock and bonds of any other company incorporated under the laws of this state, or to guarantee or endorse such bonds or stock or either of them, and to lease, use or purchase the road, property or franchises of any such company, for such time and upon such terms as may be agreed upon. May hold stock and bonds of other companies.

Sec. 15. In the event of the consolidation of said corporation with any other corporation or corporations, the said corporation so formed by said consolidation shall be a corporation of this state and amenable to the courts of this state. In event of consolidation with other company.

Sec. 16. This act shall be in force from its ratification.

Ratified the 7th day of March, A. D. 1899.

CHAPTER 363.

An act to incorporate the Granville County Railway Company.

The General Assembly of North Carolina do enact:

Section 1. That Louis De Lacroix, L. C. Edwards, J. S. Brown, C. J. Cooper, J. Graham Hunt, Sidney W. Minor, and C. M. Rogers, their associates and successors, be and they are hereby created a body politic and corporate under the name and style of the Granville County Railway Company, with all the powers and privileges conferred upon railroad companies in chapter forty-nine (49) of The Code entitled "Railroad companies," together with power to construct and operate a railroad or railroads from Oxford, or point in Oxford township, to any point or points in Granville county or adjoining counties, that its board of directors may desire; and that the railway company hereby created is hereby vested with power to extend its line or lines of railway beyond the aforesaid counties to junction points with other lines of railroads in the state. Corporators. Body corporate. Corporate name. Corporate powers. May extend its lines.

Sec. 2. That in order to carry into effect the purposes and objects of this act the said railroad company may survey one or more routes for such railroad as they deem practicable, and shall have the power and authority to appropriate and occupy as much land as may be necessary for the construction of said railway and its branches of the width of one hundred feet, and as much additional land as may be necessary for the station-houses, depots and all other purposes necessary for the construction and operation of said railway and its branches, under the same rules and terms as are prescribed for acquisition and condemnation of land by the charter of the North Carolina Railroad Company; and shall have authority to transport passengers, freight and May survey one or more routes. Transportation of passengers and freight.

merchandise over said railway, its branches or that of any railway it may lease, upon such terms and conditions as are prescribed in the charter of the North Carolina Railway Company.

Capital stock. Capital may be increased.

Sec. 3. That the capital stock of said company shall be one hundred thousand dollars, with liberty to increase the same from time to time, as the stockholders may determine, to one million dollars, the same to be divided up into shares of one hundred dollars each.

Books of subscription may be opened

Sec. 4. That the corporators named in the act, or any one or more of them, may open books of subscription to the capital stock of said company at such times and places as they may prefer, and receive subscriptions to said capital stock, and when five thousand dollars of said stock shall have been subscribed for the subscribers thereto shall elect a board of directors, to consist of not less than three, who shall serve until the next annual meeting, or until their successors are elected and qualified, and upon the subscription of said sum of five thousand dollars and the election of said directors said company shall be deemed and held fully organized for all intents and purposes, and may proceed to carry out the objects of its charter.

Election of directors.

May consolidate with or lease other lines.

Sec. 5. That the said company shall have power to consolidate with or lease or be leased by any other railroad company now created or which may hereafter be created by the laws of this state, or to enter into arrangements for use of tracks and terminals with the same, and shall have power to contract with individuals, firms and corporations for the construction or operation of said road, and also for the equipment thereof.

Management of company in whom vested.

Sec. 6. The management of said company shall be vested in the board of directors, to be elected annually at such time and place as the stockholders may designate, and they shall have the power to make such by-laws, rules and regulations for the management of said corporation and create such offices and appoint such officers as may be necessary for the transaction of its business, and as may be consistent with the constitution and laws of the United States and of this state.

Other companies may subscribe to stock.

Sec. 7. Any railroad company, whether incorporated under this or the laws of any other state, is hereby authorized to subscribe to the capital stock of said railroad company, or to lend money or endorse the bonds or their evidence of debt of the same, and may pay for their subscription to the capital stock of said Granville County Railway Company in cash or by the issue of their bonds, stock or otherwise; and said Granville County Railway Company may mortgage its road-bed, rolling stock and franchises or other property, and may issue bonds, as the directors thereof may determine, and may provide for the conversion of such bonds into the capital stock of said company.

Sec. 8. That said railroad company may buy, sell, lease, exchange, hold and convey, use, operate and work any and all lands and mines along and near the main and branch lines of said railroad. May buy and sell lands, mines, etc., along line.

Sec. 9. That this act shall be in force from and after its ratification.

Ratified the 7th day of March, A. D. 1899.

CHAPTER 364.

An act to amend chapter two hundred and seven of the private laws of eighteen hundred and ninety-five relating to the town of Swansboro.

The General Assembly of North Carolina do enact:

Section 1. That section thirty-three of chapter two hundred and seven of the private laws of eighteen hundred and ninety-five be amended by inserting in line three of said section, after the word "property" and before the word "all," the words "except farming lands." Section 33, chapter 207, private laws 1895, amended.

Sec. 2. That this act shall be in force from and after its ratification.

Ratified the 7th day of March, A. D. 1899.

CHAPTER 365.

An act supplemental to an act ratified February twenty-first, eighteen hundred and ninety-nine, entitled "An act to incorporate the Ohio River, Franklin and Tidewater Railway Company, to confer certain powers and privileges and for other purposes."

The General Assembly of North Carolina do enact:

Section 1. That an act, ratified on the twenty-first day of February, A. D. eighteen hundred and ninety-nine, entitled "An act to incorporate The Ohio River, Franklin and Tidewater Railway Company, to confer certain powers and privileges, and for other purposes," be amended as follows: In section two of said act, where it reads "To connect with the Ohio River, Anderson and Tidewater Railway Company," strike out the word "Railway," and insert "Railroad," so that it will read thus: "To connect with The Ohio River, Anderson and Tidewater Railroad Company." Amended. "Railroad" inserted for railway.

Section 6 amended. In section six (6) where it reads after the word "decide," "and certificates of stock shall be issued on the basis of one share for every twenty-five dollars as paid," strike out the word "twenty," so that it will read after the word "decide," "and certificates of stock shall be issued on the basis of one share for every five dollars so paid."

Sec. 2. That this act shall take effect from and after its ratification.

Ratified the 7th day of March, A. D. 1899.

CHAPTER 366.

An act to incorporate the town of Belhaven in the county of Beaufort.

The General Assembly of North Carolina do enact:

Incorporated. Corporate name. Section 1. That the town of Belhaven in Beaufort county be and the same is hereby incorporated by the name and style of Belle Haven, and shall have and be entitled to all the rights and privileges, and be subject to the restrictions and liabilities, as now provided by law for incorporated towns in this state.

Corporate limits. Sec. 2. That the corporate limits of said town shall be as follows: Beginning at the northwest corner of the buildings of the Norfolk and Southern Railroad depot; thence north forty-seven east across the center of the railroad five hundred feet; thence south forty-three east to Haslins street; thence north forty-seven east with said street about nine hundred feet to Pantego street; thence with Pantego street, south forty-three east to Pungo river; thence in the various courses of Pungo river and Pantego creek to the beginning.

Annual election of town officers. Sec. 3. That an election for mayor and five commissioners shall be held on the first Monday in May, nineteen hundred, and annually thereafter under the same rules and regulations prescribed by law for holding municipal elections in this state.

Officers. Sec. 4. That the officers of said corporation shall consist of a mayor and five commissioners and the following named people shall fill said offices until the first Monday in May, nineteen hundred, or until their successors are duly elected and qualified, Temporary officers. viz.: For mayor, J. M. Lupton; for commissioners, W. R. Tooley, W. J. Bullock, J. F. Bishop, A. D. Miles, G. L. Swindle.

Commissioners empowered to adopt ordinances. Sec. 5. That said commissioners shall have power to pass all by-laws, rules and regulations for the good government of the corporation, not inconsistent with the laws of this state and the United States.

Sec. 6. That the commissioners shall have power to levy a tax on all taxable property within (the) corporate limits, not to exceed twenty-five cents on a hundred dollars valuation, or seventy-five cents on the poll; also, a special street tax on all able-bodied males between eighteen and forty-five years of age, not to exceed one dollar. Commissioners empowered to levy taxes.

Sec. 7. That it shall be the duty of the commissioners to spend the tax so levied and collected in repairing the streets and sidewalks, and in keeping them in good passable order. Repair of streets and sidewalks.

Sec. 8. That the commissioners shall have power to abate all nuisances, and for this purpose may impose such fines that may be necessary to abate them. Abatement of nuisances.

Sec. 9. That the commissioners when organized shall have power to appoint a secretary and a treasurer, also a town constable. The treasurer and constable shall enter into a bond not to exceed five hundred dollars, with approved securities. Election of secretary, treasurer and constable.

Sec. 10. That the mayor, when elected and qualified, shall have the same power to all intents and purposes that any other magistrate in the county has. Power and jurisdiction of mayor.

Sec. 11. That the mayor-elect, before entering into office, shall go before some person authorized to administer an oath, and take the oath of a justice of the peace, and he shall hold an election, as provided in section three of this act, on the first Monday in May, nineteen hundred, and each successive year. Mayor shall take oath of office.

Sec. 12. That all fines and penalties shall be paid into the town treasury for benefit of the town. Fines and penalties, how applied.

Sec. 13. That the constable-elect shall go before some person authorized to administer an oath, and take the oath usually taken by constables. Oath of office by constable.

Sec. 14. That this act shall be enforced from and after its ratification.

Ratified the 7th day of March, A. D. 1899.

CHAPTER 367.

An act to incorporate Liberty Normal College.

The General Assembly of North Carolina do enact:

Section 1. That L. C. Amick, J. Rover Smith, L. H. Smith, and such persons as they may associate with them, and their successors, are hereby [created] a body politic and corporate under the name and style of Liberty Normal College, in said name to sue and be sued, plead and be impleaded, to buy, sell, lease, and hold real and personal estate for educational purposes, and to Corporators. Body politic.

have all other rights and privileges incident to such corporations.

Capital stock.

Sec. 2. That the capital stock of this corporation shall be five thousand dollars, with privilege to increase it to fifty thousand dollars, divided into shares of ten dollars each.

May open books of subscription.

Sec. 3. That the corporators herein named shall open books of subscription, and when fifty per cent. of said five thousand dollars shall have been subscribed, and fifty per cent. of that paid in, the said stockholders may organize by electing a board of directors, consisting of not less than three nor more than five members, who shall elect a president and secretary, said board of directors being elected by a vote of a majority of stock.

Sec. 4. Said board of directors shall have power, and it shall be their duty, to elect once a year a president and faculty for said college and to fix their compensation.

Object of corporation.

Sec. 5. The object of said corporation shall be to train young men and women morally, physically, and intellectually, to prescribe courses of study, and upon its completion to grant diplomas of graduation under the seal of the college signed by the president and faculty, and to have such other powers as are incident to colleges in this state.

Empowered to hold in trust, funds donated to college.

Sec. 6. This college as incorporated shall have authority to receive and hold in trust any funds or property donated by any individual or otherwise for the benefit of the college, to be used as directed by the donor, if direction be made, otherwise by the directors of said corporation, the principal place of business of which shall be at Liberty, Randolph county, North Carolina.

Enactment of by-laws, etc.

Sec. 7. That this corporation shall have power to enact such by-laws for the government of said college as it may deem best, not inconsistent with this charter and the laws of the state.

Individual liability

Sec. 8. That no stockholder shall be liable individually for the debts of the corporation.

Sec. 9. That this act shall be in force from its ratification.

Ratified the 7th day of March, A. D. 1899.

CHAPTER 368.

An act to amend chapter forty-three of the private laws of eighteen hundred and ninety-seven, relating to the charter of the People's Mutual Benevolent Association.

The General Assembly of North Carolina do enact:

Chapter 43, private laws 1897, amended

Section 1. That chapter forty-three of the private laws of eighteen hundred and ninety-seven be amended by striking out section eight of said chapter, and that section nine be section eight of said chapter.

Sec. 2. That this act shall be in force from its ratification.

Ratified the 2d day of March, A. D. 1899.

CHAPTER 369.

An act to amend, revise and consolidate the charter of the town of Lincolnton.

Section 1. That the inhabitants of the town of Lincolnton shall be and continue, as they have heretofore been, a body politic and corporate, and henceforth the said corporation shall bear the name and style of Town of Lincolnton, and under that name is hereby invested with all the property and rights of property which now belong to the present corporation of the town of Lincolnton, or the board of commissioners of the town of Lincolnton, or any other corporate name or names heretofore used, and by the corporate name of town of Lincolnton, may purchase and hold for purposes of its government all such property and estate, real and personal, within and without said town, as may be deemed necessary or convenient therefor, or as may be conveyed, devised or bequeathed to it, and the same may from time to time sell, dispose of and reinvest, as shall be deemed advisable by the proper authorities of said corporation, and in its corporate name to contract and be contracted with, sue and to be sued, and invested with all other rights and powers necessary or usually pertaining to municipal corporations. Body politic. Corporate name. Corporate powers and privileges.

Sec. 2. That the corporate limits of the said town of Lincolnton shall be hereafter defined and located as follows: Beginning at a stake on what was formerly known as Samuel P. Simpson's line, John Hoke's corner, now Child's corner, and runs thence with Hoke's now Child's line, south eighty-four degrees east sixty-six poles to a stake and pointers, Hoke's now Child's corner; thence with another of Hoke's now Child's lines south fifty-eight degrees east sixty-eight poles to a stake; thence north fifty-two degrees east thirty and one-half poles to a rock formerly James T. Alexander's corner, now S. T. Burgin's corner; thence north forty-five degrees east one hundred and ninety-one and one-half poles to a hickory stump, Ramseur's corner, now Mrs. John Setzer's corner; thence with another of Ramseur's now Setzer's lines north forty-five degrees west sixteen poles to a stake, Ramseur's now Setzer's corner; then with her line north forty-five degrees east sixty poles to a stake; then north forty-five degrees west one hundred and seventy-six poles to a small post-oak on Vardry M'Bee's line; then with his line south forty-seven degrees west two hundred and twenty-four poles to a stone, where Reinhardt's hickory corner formerly stood, now Caleb Motz's; thence with Reinhardt's now Motz's line south fifty-eight degrees west sixty poles to a post-oak, his corner; thence to the beginning. Corporate limits.

Division of wards. Sec. 3. The town of Lincolnton shall be divided into four wards by the intersection of Main and Aspen streets, to be known as follows, to-wit:

Ward One. Ward One—That part of said territory lying northeast of said intersection, to be known and is hereby designated as ward one.

Ward Two. Ward Two—That part of said territory lying southeast of said intersection, to be known and is hereby designated as ward two.

Ward Three. Ward Three—That part of said territory lying southwest of said intersection, to be known and is hereby designated as ward three.

Ward Four. Ward Four—That part of said territory lying northwest of said intersection, to be known and is hereby designated as ward four.

Corporate powers shall be exercised by mayor and aldermen. Sec. 4. The corporate powers hereby vested in the town of Lincolnton shall be exercised, controlled and managed by a board of aldermen and mayor for said town. Said aldermen of said town shall form one body to be known as the board of aldermen, a majortity of them shall constitute a quorum and be competent to perform all the duties.

Number of aldermen. How elected. Sec. 5. The board of aldermen of said town shall consist of eight aldermen, two from each ward, to be elected by the qualified voters of each ward, the voters of each ward to vote for the aldermen of said ward and no other. *Qualifications for aldermen.* Each alderman shall be a resident of the ward from which elected, and a resident of the state twelve months and of the town ninety days, and of his ward fifteen days, and shall be elected for twelve months.

Election of mayor. Sec. 6. A mayor shall be elected from the town at large, who shall have been a resident of the state twelve months, of the town ninety days, who will hold office for twelve months, or until his successor is elected.

Election of mayor and aldermen. Sec. 7. There shall be elected by the qualified voters of said town, on the first Monday in May, eighteen hundred and ninety-nine, and every first Monday in May following thereafter, a mayor and eight aldermen, of which aldermen two shall be from ward one, two from ward two, two from ward three and two from ward four, who shall be residents of their respective wards, *Term of office.* who shall hold office for the term of one year from and after his election, and until his successor is elected and qualified. The mayor shall be elected from the town at large by the qualified *Term of office of mayor.* voters of said town, who shall hold his office for one year and until his successor is elected and qualified.

Present officers continued. Sec. 8. That the aldermen or commissioners and mayor or intendant of said town, and now holding office therein as such, whose terms have not expired, shall hold their said offices until their said terms shall have respectively terminated.

Elections, how held. Sec. 9. That the elections hereinbefore provided for shall be held under the same rules and regulations as are now prescribed, or may be hereafter prescribed, for the election of members of the general assembly; but the powers and duties in such rules and regulations conferred upon and directed to be exercised by the sheriff are hereby conferred upon and directed to be exercised by the marshal of said town, and the power and duties in said rules and regulations conferred upon and directed to be exercised by any other officer or officers, body or bodies, board or boards, or his, their or its appointees or employees, respectively, are hereby conferred upon and directed to be exercised by the board of aldermen of said town, or its employees or appointees respectively, in said election. Every citizen residing within the limits of said town who is qualified to vote for members of the general assembly, and who shall have resided in said town ninety days, in the state twelve months and in the ward in which he offers to vote for fifteen days immediately preceding any such election, shall be entitled to vote at any such election, upon compliance with the law regarding the registration of voters thereat. Each elector shall vote on one ballot on which shall be placed the names and offices of the persons voted for, either printed or written. At any such election the person who shall receive the highest number of votes for any office allowed to be voted for at such election shall be declared elected to that office. At the conclusion of any election the judges thereof shall ascertain and declare its result, and the marshal of said town shall immediately, in person or by deputy, proclaim such result at the court-house door in the town of Lincolnton, and within thirty-six hours thereafter such judges shall certify to the mayor of said town such result in writing signed by them, which writing shall be filed by the mayor in his office. If at any such election any two or more persons receive an equal number of votes for the same office, and no other person shall receive as great a number of votes for such office, the registrar shall decide who of those receiving such equal votes is elected to such office.

Persons qualified to vote.

Each elector shall vote on one ballot.

Announcement of result.

When election results in a tie vote.

Sec. 10. Every other election in said town for municipal purposes shall be held and conducted in the same manner and under the same rules and regulations as are above prescribed for election for mayor and aldermen, in so far as same is applicable.

Other elections conducted in same manner.

Sec. 11. The mayor and aldermen shall be installed in their respective offices at twelve o'clock on the first Wednesday after the first Monday in May next after their election.

Installation of mayor and aldermen.

Sec. 12. The aldermen of said town shall establish as many voting places in said town as they shall from time to time deem necessary: Provided, that there shall be at least one voting place in said town.

Voting places.

Sec. 13. Before entering upon his duties of office the mayor shall take and subscribe before some person authorized by law to administer oath, the following: "I .... do solemnly swear that I will perform, according to my best skill, judgment

Mayor shall take oath of office.

Form of oath.

and ability, all and every the duties of the office of mayor of the town of Lincolnton, while I continue in said office, and will cause to be executed, as far as in my power lies, all laws, ordinances and regulations made for the government of said town, and in the discharge of my duties I will do justice to the best of my knowledge and ability in all cases. So help me God." Said oath shall be immediately filed and kept by the clerk to the board of aldermen.

Oath shall be filed.

Aldermen shall take oath of office.

Sec. 14. Each alderman, before entering upon the duties of his office, shall take before the mayor an oath that he will truly and impartially perform the duties of an alderman of the town of Lincolnton, according to his best skill, judgment and ability.

Vacancy in office of mayor.

Election of successor to mayor.

Sec. 15. If the person elected mayor of said town shall neglect or refuse to qualify at the time provided therefor, or if after he shall have qualified there shall occur a vacancy in the office of mayor of said town, either by death, resignation, or the mayor shall become a non-resident of said town, or for three consecutive months shall absent himself therefrom, or for malpractice or malfeasance in office, the aldermen at their next meeting, or at a meeting called for that purpose, shall declare said office of mayor vacant, and shall immediately, or at their next meeting thereafter, choose by ballot some competent person as mayor of said town for the term, or the unexpired portion of the term, as the case may be. In like manner all vacancies in the office of aldermen shall be filled by the remaining aldermen.

Persons elected mayor or aldermen refusing to qualify, guilty of a misdemeanor.

Sec. 16. That any person elected mayor or alderman, who shall neglect or refuse to qualify and act as such shall be guilty of a misdemeanor, and upon conviction thereof shall be fined fifty dollars or imprisoned thirty days.

Jurisdiction of mayor.

Removal of cases for trial.

Sec. 17. The mayor of the town of Lincolnton is hereby constituted a special court with all the jurisdiction and powers in criminal offences occurring within the limits of said town, which are or may hereafter be given to justices of the peace, and shall also have exclusive original jurisdiction to hear and determine all misdemeanors consisting of a violation of an ordinance or ordinances of said town, except where legally the mayor or vice-mayor are legally incompetent to try the same, in which case the cause shall be, upon application of the defendant [removed], or the court of its own motion, [may] remove the cause for trial to such other court of the county of Lincoln as would but for this section have jurisdiction of the same; and such legal incompetency shall be construed to mean only such incompetency as would disable a judge of the superior court to try under similar circumstances a cause pending in said last-named court. The proceedings of said mayor's court shall be the same as are now or may hereafter be prescribed for courts of justices of the peace, except as otherwise provided herein; and in all cases there shall be a right of appeal on the part of a defendant adjudged to be guilty to the next term of Lincoln superior court. In all such cases of appeal, the mayor or vice-mayor shall require bond from the defendant with such surety as is in his judgment sufficient to insure the defendant's appearance at the next succeeding term of the appellate court, and on defendant's failure to furnish such bond, the mayor or vice-mayor shall commit such defendant to the common jail of the county of Lincoln. Said mayor's court shall also have jurisdiction to try all actions for the recovery of any penalty imposed by law or this act, or by any ordinance of said town, for any act done within said town, and such penalty shall be sued for and recovered in the name of the town of Lincolnton, and if incurred by a minor shall be recovered from and in an action against his or her parent or guardian, or if he or she be an apprentice, against his or her master or mistress. From any judgment for such penalty imposed by this act, or for the violation of any ordinance of said town, either party may appeal to the next term of the superior court of Lincoln county, in like manner and under the same rules and regulations as are prescribed for appeals from judgment of justices of the peace; and in case the mayor or vice-mayor, respectively, as the case may be, shall be disqualified by reason of relationship, or otherwise incompetent to hear and determine such action, the same may be instituted and prosecuted in any court within said county which would but for this section have jurisdiction thereof, under the same rules and regulations as if instituted and tried in said mayor's court where applicable. In all cases where judgments may be entered against any person or persons for fines or penalties, according to the laws and ordinances of said town as for criminal offences, and the person or persons against whom the same is so adjudged refuse, fail, or be unable to pay such judgment, it shall be lawful for the mayor or vice-mayor of said town to order and require such person or persons to work on the streets or other public works of said town under the supervision of the marshal or street overseer thereof, and under such rules and regulations as may be from time to time prescribed by the board of aldermen thereof, until at a fair rate of wages, to be prescribed by said board of aldermen, such person or persons shall have worked out the full amount of such judgment and cost of prosecution; or such mayor or vice-mayor, if he deem best, shall have power to provide, under such rules and regulations as to him may seem best, for the employment of such person or persons on the public streets, public highways, or other public works, or at other labor for individuals or corporations, until at such fair rate of wages so prescribed by said board of aldermen such person or persons shall have worked out the full amount of such judgment and costs of prosecution.

Right of appeal.

Mayor shall require bond in case of appeal.

Have jurisdiction of actions for recovery of penalties.

Either party may appeal.

Persons unable to pay fines may be worked on public streets.

Penalties and fines collected for violation of ordinances, how applied.

Sec. 18. All penalties and fines collected for any misdemeanor declared by this act, or for any violation of any ordinance of said town, whether in the court in which the prosecution originated, or in the court to which it was carried by appeal, shall belong to said town, and immediately upon collection shall be paid to the treasurer of said town; and all judgments rendered in any court for such penalties and fines shall belong to and be controlled by said town and collected in the same manner in which by law such judgments would but for this section be collected and enforced. All penalties and fines hereinbefore provided to be recovered of said town of Lincolnton shall belong and upon collection be paid to said town, and all judgments for same shall belong to and be controlled by said town and be collected in the same manner as other judgments for money are collected, and may be docketed in the superior court of this state in the same manner as is by law provided for the docketing of judgments, and when so docketed shall be and constitute liens in the same manner and to the same extent as other judgments so docketed.

To whom precepts of mayor shall be issued.

Sec 19. The mayor or vice-mayor of said town may issue his precepts to the sheriff of said county of Lincoln, or to any constable or marshal, or to any officer to whom a justice of the peace may direct his precepts.

Record of precepts issued by mayor or vice-mayor.

Sec. 20. The mayor and vice-mayor, respectively, of said town shall keep a faithful minute of the precepts issued by him and of all his judicial proceedings. Precepts issued by said mayor or vice-mayor shall be executed by the officer or officers to whom they are directed, or any of them, anywhere in the county of Lincoln.

Mayor's office.

Sec. 21. The mayor of said town shall keep his office in some convenient part of said town designated by the board of aldermen.

Seal of corporation.

He shall keep the seal of the corporation and perform the duties as are by this act prescribed, and as shall from time to time by law or by the ordinances of said town be prescribed.

Mayor shall preside at meetings of commissioners.

Sec. 22. The mayor of said town shall preside when present at all meetings of the board of aldermen thereof, and in all cases of a tie-vote of the aldermen present upon any question or in the election of any officer by said board of aldermen, he shall have the right to vote, but shall not be allowed to vote in any other case.

When mayor is absent.

If he shall be absent at any such meeting the board of aldermen may appoint one of their own number to exercise pro tempore his duties at such meeting; and in the event of his extended absence the board of aldermen may appoint one of their own number to exercise pro tempore his duties, both at the meeting of the aldermen and in the mayor's court, as well as elsewhere. But nothing herein provided shall be construed to require or allow the appointment of a mayor pro tempore in case

except where the vice-mayor shall also be absent or unable to discharge the duties of mayor.

Sec. 23. The aldermen of said town shall form one body to be known as the board of aldermen, and a majority of them shall constitute a quorum and be competent to perform all the duties prescribed for the board of aldermen, unless otherwise provided. Majority of aldermen shall constitute quorum.

Sec. 24. The board of aldermen shall convene at the mayor's office on the first Friday night of each and every month for the transaction of business. Regular meeting of aldermen.

Sec. 25. Special meetings of the board of aldermen may be held at any other time than that designated for a regular meeting on call of the mayor or a majority of the aldermen, and every such meeting called by the mayor all the aldermen in the town shall be notified, and when called by the majority of the aldermen such aldermen as are in the town and do not join in the call shall be notified. Special meetings.

Sec. 26. The board of aldermen when convened shall have power to make such ordinances, rules and regulations for the proper government of the town as they deem necessary and provide for the proper execution thereof as they think best. Aldermen empowered to make ordinances, etc.

Sec. 27. Among the powers hereby conferred upon the board of aldermen are the following:

To borrow money, with the consent of a majority of the qualified voters of said town, which consent shall be obtained at an election held after thirty days' public notice, whereat those who consent shall vote "Approved," and those who do not consent shall vote "Disapproved"; but they shall not, except as hereinafter provided, borrow any sum of money when the existing aggregate indebtedness of said town equals in amount one-eighth of the aggregate tax value of the property of said town as shown by its tax books of the preceding year, or exceeds the same, nor any sum which, when added to the aggregate indebtedness of said town then already existing, would render the full amount of the indebtedness of said town than is hereinafter provided, larger than one-eighth of the aggregate tax value of the property of the said town as shown by its tax books for the preceding year; and in any public notice of a proposition to borrow money so submitted to the voters of said town as above provided, shall be included a statement of the then existing indebtedness of said town, other than that hereinafter provided for, and of the aggregate tax value of the property of said town as shown by the tax books of the preceding year. May borrow money. Question of borrowing money shall be submitted to voters. Notice of proposition to borrow money shall include statement of indebtedness to town.

To provide a sufficient supply of pure water for said town. Water supply of town.

To provide a sufficient and adequate water system and waterworks and sewerage system for said town.

To provide an electric light plant for lighting the streets, public buildings and houses of private individuals in said town. Electric light plant.

own attorney. To employ an attorney for said town and fix his compensation.

mprovement of :reets. To provide for the curbing and paving of the streets and sidewalks of said town, and the cleaning of the same, to the extent such board may deem best.

arkets. To establish and regulate a market or markets in said town, and to erect or lease and use a suitable market-house therefor.

ires. To provide proper and effectual means and regulations to prevent and extinguish fires in said town, and to provide for the

ire companies. establishment, organization, equipment and government of fire companies.

own watchers. To appoint and regulate town watches.

bservance of Sunay. To make suitable regulations for the due observance of Sunday in said town, and to provide for the enforcement of same.

batement of nuiances. To prevent, suppress and remove nuisances in said town.

ogs. To regulate the manner in which dogs may be kept in said town.

ast riding and riving. To regulate the speed at which horses may be driven or ridden through said town.

ire. To regulate the mode or manner in which fire may be carried through said town, and the arrangement of stove-pipe flues in buildings.

ogs, goats, etc. To regulate the manner in which hogs, goats and cattle may be kept in the town and run at large.

lleys, cellars, etc. To cause all alleys, lots, cellars, privies, styes, stables and other places of similar character to be examined, cleaned, removed or abated as may be prescribed by the board.

rades and occuations, nuisances. To prohibit all trades or occupations which are nuisances from being carried on in the said town.

emeteries. To establish and maintain one or more public cemeteries of such size as they may deem necessary within or without the corporate limits of said town, and provide for the care and maintenance of same, and the proper regulation, control and protection thereof.

iring of firearms, c. That they shall have power to make ordinances to prohibit or control the firing of firearms, fire-crackers, torpedoes and other explosive material, and to govern the sale thereof in the said town.

eed of railroad ains. To regulate the speed at which railroad engines and trains shall run within the town limits and across any of the streets of said town, and to prohibit said railroads from stopping their engines or cars on said streets, and to require said railroads to keep the street crossings in good repair, and to require said railroads to provide proper gates or watchmen at all crossings in said town, and to give proper alarm or signals of the approach of any and all trains at said crossings, and to require said railroads to keep in repair and erect all necessary overhead bridges in said town, when in the discretion of said board of aldermen said bridges are necessary for the travel and passing and repassing of the citizens of said town, upon any street in said town said railroad or any of them cross.

To adopt a seal for said corporation, and same to be kept by the mayor thereof. Seal.

To require of all officers, appointed or elected by the mayor and board of aldermen of said town, to give good and sufficient bonds for the faithful performance of their duties, as the same is prescribed by law, in such sum or sums as to the board of aldermen and mayor thereof may seem proper. To regulate bond of officers.

To make provisions and take all proper measures to preserve the peace and order of said town, and to execute all the laws and ordinances thereof.

To enact and pass such laws and ordinances and regulations as said board may deem necessary to preserve the health of said town, and to provide for the due enforcement of the same. Health.

To make provisions for licensing and regulating auctioneers and auctions in said town, and provide for the enforcement of the same. Auctioneers.

To provide licensing regulating or restraining theatrical and other public amusements within said town, and all bill posters and advertisements thereof, and to enforce all such provisions. Theatricals.

To establish all necessary inspection within said town, whether of buildings or otherwise. Inspection of buildings, etc.

To license, regulate and restrain bar-rooms and other places where spirituous liquors are sold within said town. Bar-rooms.

To lay and provide for the collection of all taxes authorized by law to be laid, levied or collected by said town, and enforce the collection of the same. Levy and collection of taxes.

To impose, collect and appropriate fines, penalties and forfeitures for the breach of the ordinances and regulations of said town. Levy and collection of fines.

To pass all laws, ordinances and regulations necessary or proper to carry into effect the intent and meaning of this act: Provided, they are not incompatible with the constitution or laws of this state. Proviso.

To appoint and provide for the pay and prescribe the duties of all such other officers of said town as may by said board of aldermen be deemed necessary. Appointment and pay of other officers.

To prescribe and regulate the charges for the carriage of persons, baggage and freight by omnibus, wagons, drays, carriages and other vehicles in said town, and to issue license for omnibus, hacks, carriages, drays and other vehicles used therein for the transportation, for hire, of persons or things. Regulation of rates for vehicles.

To make proper provisions and take all necessary measures to preserve said town from contagious diseases or infectious dis- Prevention of contagious diseases.

eases, and to declare and enforce quarantine and quarantine regulations therein.

To make and pass all such rules, regulations and ordinances as may be necessary for the government, control, management or operating of all electric light plants, water-works or sewerage systems, as the board of aldermen may deem necessary.

Appointment of marshal.

To appoint a marshal or marshals for said town, and all policemen and other officers thereof which may by said board be deemed proper to execute such precepts as the mayor may lawfully issue to them, and to preserve the peace and good order of said town; and whenever, in the opinion of the board of aldermen, the peace and good order of said town requires an additional or special force to assist the regular police or marshals in preserving order and peace in said town on any occasion, or upon the assembling of any large or unusual meeting in said town, deemed dangerous to the peace and good order thereof, the board of aldermen may in their wise discretion appoint special marshals or policemen who shall be citizens of said town or the county of Lincoln, which specially appointed marshals or policemen shall be invested with all the authorities and rights under the law as the regular marshals or police of said town are invested with, and clothed with all the authorities to make arrest for infraction of the law and to perform other duties as though they were regular marshals and policemen of said town.

Appointment of extra police.

Authority of specially appointed marshals.

Election of clerk or treasurer,

Sec. 28. That the board of aldermen, at its first meeting after election in May, or not later than its regular meeting in June after election shall appoint or elect a clerk or treasurer, (or may consolidate the offices of clerk and treasurer and elect one and the same person to fill both places and be known as clerk and treasurer), and a tax collector and one or more marshals, all of which officers shall hold their offices respectively for the term of one year from and after appointment, and until their successors, respectively, shall be appointed and qualify; subject, however, to be removed at any time for incompetency, misbehavior, neglect of duty, or other good cause, by said board of aldermen, which alone shall be the judge of such incompetency, misbehavior, neglect of duty or other cause of removal, and shall appoint others in their stead to fill out his or their said term or terms, respectively, upon such removal. Said tax collector may be one of said marshals, or in event only one marshal, may be said marshal. Before entering upon the duties of their offices, respectively, every one of said officers shall be sworn by the mayor of said town, or other person authorized to administer oaths, to the faithful discharge of their respective duties, and shall execute a bond, payable to the said town of Lincolnton, in such sum as shall be prescribed by said board of aldermen, with good and sufficient surety or sureties, approved by said board of aldermen,

May be removed from office.

Officers shall be sworn.

Shall execute bonds.

for the faithful discharge of their said duties, respectively; and such bond shall be duly proven by a subscribing witness before the mayor of said town and recorded in the office of said clerk of the said board of aldermen in a book to be kept for that purpose, to be marked and called "Official bonds"; the original of such bonds as soon as recorded to be deposited and kept by the clerk of the board to the aldermen, except the bond of the clerk, which shall be filed and kept by the mayor of said town. A copy from said registry of any such official bond duly certified by the clerk of the board of aldermen under his hand and seal of said town shall at all times be received as evidence in any court, in any action for the enforcement of the penalty thereof, or in any other action, or for any other purpose whatsoever.

Original of bonds shall be recovered.

Said board of aldermen, at its pleasure, may from time to time increase or decrease the number of marshals and other officers, and appoint other persons to fill any vacancies therein which, in the opinion of said board of aldermen should be filled; any such appointees to hold offices upon the same terms and subject to the same powers of said board of aldermen as the persons in whose stead they were so appointed held their offices, respectively, in said cases reserving the right to the board of aldermen to appoint to said places for a period less than a year, and to contract for said time and to pay for the term of actual service rendered in proportion to the year. The duties of such marshals or other officers shall be from time to time prescribed and designated by said board of aldermen.

Aldermen may increase bond of officers.

Duties of marshal shall be prescribed by aldermen.

Sec. 29. It shall be the duty of the clerk of the board of aldermen to attend the meetings of the board of aldermen, to attend the meetings of the board, both regular and special, to keep regular and fair minutes of all proceedings of said board of aldermen; to preserve and keep said minutes where the public may, at all reasonable hours, inspect the same, all books, papers and other articles committed to his care by said board of aldermen during his continuance in office, subject to the control of said board of aldermen, and deliver the same to his successors, and regularly to perform all such other duties as may be by said board of aldermen from time to time prescribed, and he shall receive such compensation as such board of aldermen shall prescribe.

Duties of clerk of board of aldermen.

Compensation of clerk.

Sec. 30. That it shall be the duty of the treasurer of said town to receive and safely keep all moneys which shall be paid into his hands as such treasurer for the use of said town, to disburse the funds of said town according to such orders as shall be drawn on him by the proper authority, to demand of all persons such moneys or securities as they or any of them may have in their hands belonging to said town which ought to be paid or delivered into the treasury thereof, and to perform all such other

Duties of treasurer.

duties as may from time to time be required of him by law or by said board of aldermen.

Shall keep account of moneys received and disbursed.

He shall keep in a book provided for that purpose a fair and correct account of moneys received and disbursed by him, and of all securities and other property entrusted to him for safe keeping or otherwise; and at the expiration of his term of office or the sooner determination thereof, shall deliver to his successor all such moneys, securities and other property belonging to said town then in his hands.

Compensation of treasurer.

He shall receive such compensation as said board of aldermen shall from time to time prescribe.

Order drawn on treasurer, how signed.

All orders drawn on him shall be signed by the mayor of said town and shall state the purpose for which the money therein called for is applied, and the treasurer shall in his accounts specify such purpose.

Itemized statement.

He shall also state in his accounts the sources respectively from which all moneys received by him are derived, and shall, when required to do so, submit to the mayor or board of aldermen his vouchers for any and all disbursements made by him, and his said accounts in full.

Election of vice-mayor.

Sec. 31. Said board of aldermen shall, at their first meeting in June in each and every year, appoint one of their own number to be vice-mayor of said town, and in case of any vacancy in that office shall fill the same with some other member of their own body.

Duties of vice-mayor.

It shall be the duty of such vice-mayor, at all times during his term of office when the mayor of said town shall for any reason be unable to discharge his duties as such mayor, to act as mayor and perform all the duties pertaining to such office during the time when the mayor is so unable to discharge the same.

Rights and powers of vice-mayor.

And for that purpose such vice-mayor shall, during such times, have and exercise all the powers and rights which pertain to said mayor, as well in holding said mayor's court and presiding at the meetings of the said board of aldermen, as in all other respects. Such vice-mayor shall hold his office for the term of one year from and after his appointment, or until the next annual election of vice-mayor, as hereinbefore provided, and until his successor shall be duly appointed and qualified.

Duties of marshals.

Sec. 32. It shall be the duty of each and every marshal or marshals of the said town to see that the laws, ordinances, regulations and orders of said board of aldermen are enforced, and to report all breaches thereof to the mayor of said town; to preserve the peace and order of said town by suppressing disturbances and apprehending offenders, for which purpose he shall have all the powers and authorities vested in sheriffs or county constables;

Power of marshal to execute precepts.

and execute all criminal and civil process and precepts and notices of every character lawfully directed to him by the mayor of said town or the board of aldermen thereof, or others, and in the execution thereof he shall have the same powers anywhere in the county of Lincoln as the sheriff or constable thereof have or hereafter may have. Such marshal or marshals shall have the same power to apprehend in the limits of said town or county of Lincoln all offenders against the state, as the sheriff and constables of said county have, and to carry such offenders before the mayor of said town, and in this respect he shall be bound by the same rules as the constables of said county. It shall also be the duty of said marshal or marshals to perform such other acts and exercise such other functions as shall be from time to time directed or required of him or them by said board of aldermen.

Other duties of marshals.

The duties of tax collector of said town shall be those hereinafter provided, and such as shall from time to time be prescribed by law and by said board of aldermen; and he shall receive as compensation for his services in collecting taxes five per centum of all taxes actually collected by him, to be retained by him from such collections when and as often as he shall make a settlement thereof with said board of aldermen, and for his services in discharging any other duty such compensation as shall from time to time be prescribed by the board of aldermen.

Duties of tax collector.

Compensation.

Sec. 33. For any breach of his official bond by any officer of said town who is or may be required to give such bond, such officer shall be liable to an action on the same, in the name of said town, by said town, or any person aggrieved by such breach, and each bond may without assignment be from time to time put in suit until the whole penalty thereof be recovered.

Breach of official bond by officers of said town.

Sec. 34. That it shall be unlawful for any person to resist or obstruct any officer of said town in the discharge of his official duty as such by force, threats or otherwise, and any person so offending shall be guilty of a misdemeanor, and shall be fined twenty-five dollars or imprisoned for thirty days.

Unlawful to resist or obstruct officer.

Sec. 35. No person who is not a duly qualified elector of said town shall be eligible to hold office therein, and any duly qualified elector thereof shall be competent to be elected to and to hold any office of said town.

Eligibility to office.

Sec. 36. In order to raise funds for the current expenses of said town, and thereafter for the improvement of the same, the board of aldermen of said town shall, at their first meeting in June in every year, lay and provide for the collection of the following taxes:

Annual levy of taxes.

(1) On all real and personal property within the limits of said town, and all other subjects taxable by the general assembly of this state, as specified and valued under the provisions of law, an ad valorem tax not exceeding thirty-five cents on every hundred dollars of such valuation as of the first day of June of every year.

Real and personal property tax.

Poll tax.

(2) On every person residing in said town on the first day of June of every year subject to poll tax under the laws of this state, a poll tax not exceeding one dollar and five cents each.

Omnibuses, vehicles, etc.

(3) On every omnibus carrying for hire a license tax not exceeding ten dollars per annum; and on every hack, carriage. wagon, express wagon, dray or other vehicle transporting persons, freight, baggage or other articles for hire, a license tax not exceeding five dollars per annum; and on fixing the license tax on the above enumerated vehicles, said board of aldermen shall discriminate between one-horse, two-horse and four-horse vehicles, and between the different kinds of vehicles, as to them shall seem just. Said board of aldermen shall, at their meeting in June in every year, fix the amount of license tax on every kind of such vehicles; and every person intending to use any such vehicles in said town shall, before using the same, pay to the tax collector of said town the amount of the license tax so fixed on such vehicles and obtain from said tax collector a license stating the kind of such vehicle and the amount of such payment; but any person may, upon payment to said tax collector of the amount of license tax in such case prescribed by said board of aldermen for such period, obtain from him such license for any part of the year not less than three months, to be therein designated. Any person who shall so use any such vehicle without having procured the license therefor as in this section mentioned, shall be guilty of a misdemeanor, and on conviction shall be fined twenty-five dollars or imprisoned for thirty days.

License tax shall be paid before vehicles are used.

Persons using vehicle without first paying tax guilty of a misdemeanor.

Saddle horses.

(4) On every saddle-horse kept for hire in said town, a license tax of one dollar per annum, such license to be obtained in the same manner as licenses for vehicles hereinbefore required to be licensed, and subject to the same regulations.

Horses kept for hire.

Any person who shall keep for hire any such horse for any time whatever, without having first paid such license tax and procured such license, shall be guilty of a misdemeanor, and on conviction fined twenty-five dollars or imprisoned for thirty days.

Express, telegraph, telephone, electric light and railroad companies.

(5) On every express company, telegraph company, telephone company, electric light company and railroad company doing business or having an office in said town a license tax not exceeding in amount one per centum of the gross receipts by it on its said business in said town, received during the preceding year up to and including the thirty-first day of May next before the date of fixing such license tax; and the manager or agent in charge of the business of any such company in said town on the first day of June in every year, shall on that day, or if that day be on Sunday or a legal holiday, the next day thereafter, make to the clerk of the board of aldermen of said town, who shall have power in such cases to administer oaths, a written return under oath signed by him of the amount of such gross receipts.

Written returns of gross receipts.

Any such manager or agent who shall fail or refuse to make such return on the day whereon the same should be made, as hereinbefore provided, shall be guilty of a misdemeanor, and on conviction fined twenty-five dollars or imprisoned for thirty days. Every such company whose manager or agent, as aforesaid, shall fail or refuse to make such return at the time hereinbefore provided therefor, or which shall fail to pay the license tax upon its said business within the time prescribed by the board of aldermen for such payment, shall be guilty of a misdemeanor, and upon conviction shall be fined fifty dollars. The amount of such license tax, upon the failure of such manager or agent to make such return, as is hereinbefore provided, shall be fixed by said board of aldermen at its next meeting after the day on which such return should be made as hereinbefore provided, or some other meeting thereafter in the same month, by determining the amount of such gross receipts as nearly as they can ascertain the same, and of such amount so determined, which for such purpose shall be taken and deemed to be the amount of such gross receipts, taking one per centum thereof as such license tax. Failure to make such returns a misdemeanor. Failure to pay tax a misdemeanor.

(6) On ever dog a tax not exceeding ten dollars: Provided, that a discrimination may be made within this limit on the different species and sexes of dogs. Dogs. Proviso.

Sec. 37. That the clerk shall, on the second Monday in May of each and every year make advertisement in some newspaper published in the town notifying all persons residing in the town of Lincolnton, who own or have control of taxable property in the town on the first of June to return to him on or before the last day of June a list of their taxable property in said town. Said lists shall state the number of lots or parts of lots, and other property now taxable, or that hereafter may be taxable by the laws of the state or the ordinances of the town, and the list so returned to the clerk shall be sworn to before him, and he is hereby authorized to administer the following oath: "I . . . . . do solemnly swear that the tax return made out and signed by me, contains a full and accurate list of the number of lots owned by me in said town, a full and accurate list of all personal property, and a full and accurate list of all other stocks, bonds, incomes, solvent credits and other property subject to taxation by the laws of the state and ordinances of said town, according to my best knowledge, information and belief. So help me God." Clerk shall make advertisement of date for listing taxes. Oath administered to person making tax list.

From the returns so made the clerk shall, within thirty days after the expiration of the term for taking said list, make out in a book kept for that purpose an alphabetical list of the persons and owners of property who have so made their returns in the same manner as tax lists are made out by law for collection of state taxes. The clerk shall copy in said book the assessments Clerk shall make out alphabetical list of persons liable for tax.

made by the board of township assessors of all property within the town limits, which assessments may be revised, corrected or amended by the board of aldermen.

Clerk shall make out list of taxable polls.

Sec. 38. That the clerk shall, within thirty days from the return of the tax list, make out to the best of his knowledge and belief, by comparing his books with the returns made to the board of township assessors, or to the tax listed for the county, and by enquiry from other sources, a list of taxable poll and owners of taxable property in said town who shall have failed to return a list in the manner and time aforesaid, and said persons who failed to list as required in the preceding section shall forfeit and pay a sum to be fixed by the board of aldermen, not to exceed twice the amount of his tax, which penalty may be received or recovered as other fines and penalties imposed by the board of aldermen before the mayor or any justice of the peace.

Persons failing to list, penalty.

From such list, records, papers, and documents so procured, or required to be procured, said clerk of the board of aldermen shall immediately make a full and complete list, showing the name of every tax payer in every ward of said town, and the items of property, personal and real, in every of such wards upon which he is required to pay taxes, and the respective value of each according to said lists, and the respective names and ages and colors of the persons resident within said wards, respectively, who are liable to pay a poll tax in said town, and shall charge to every of said tax payers his taxes upon his property in every of said wards, calculated at the rate of taxation for such property prescribed by said board of aldermen for that year, and shall charge all persons resident within said ward, respectively, who are liable to pay poll tax in said town with the amount of their respective poll tax as prescribed by said board of aldermen for that year, and also showing the aggregate amount of property according to such valuations, and of taxes and polls in every of said wards, and the full aggregate of the same in said town.

Clerk shall make and complete list.

Certain facts to be given in list made out by clerk.

Clerk shall submit list to aldermen.

Said clerk of the board of aldermen shall submit such list so made by him to the said board of aldermen at their next meeting after he shall have completed the same, and said list, when approved by said board of aldermen, whether as amended or not by it, shall constitute the regular tax list of said town for that year, subject to any or all amendments, corrections, modifications, additions and subtractions which said board of aldermen shall from time to time make therein.

Aldermen shall see that subjects of taxation are duly entered.

It shall be the duty of said board of aldermen to see that all subjects of taxation within said town are duly entered from time to time upon said list at their proper places, and the taxes which should be paid by or upon the same are duly enforced and collected, and to take all proper measures necessary for the due accomplishment of that result.

Sec. 39. Said board of aldermen shall preserve said list among its records; shall immediately after its approval of the same, cause to be made a copy of so much and such parts thereof as may be required for the use of the tax collector in collecting the taxes of said town; said copy shall be delivered to said tax collector on or before the first Monday in September in each year, and he shall recept for the same. Said clerk of the board of aldermen shall endorse on said copy an order to said tax collector to collect the taxes therein mentioned, and such order shall have the force and effect of a judgment and execution against the real and personal property of the person charged in said copy respectively.

Said list shall be preserved.

Copy shall be delivered to tax collector.

Order shall have force of judgment.

Sec. 40. The tax collector of said town, upon his receipt of said copy of such parts of said tax list, shall proceed immediately with the collection of the taxes in such copy mentioned, and of all such as may be from time to time added thereto by said board of aldermen, and shall complete such collection by the first day of December next after such receipt, but said board of aldermen may extend the time for the completion of such collection for such period or periods as it may deem best, not longer than the first day of March next thereafter. Said tax collector shall pay over, at least once a week to the treasurer of said town all moneys by him collected as taxes, after deducting from each collection the amount of his compensation for making it, as hereinbefore provided; and for every such payment he shall take said treasurer's receipt and exhibit to the board of aldermen at its next meeting.

Tax collector shall proceed immediately with collection of taxes.

Weekly settlement with treasurer.

Sec. 41. All taxes of said town shall be levied, assessed and collected, except as in this charter otherwise provided, in the same manner and under the same rules and regulations, and subject to the same penalties, as are provided by law, or shall hereafter be provided by law, for the listing, levying, assessing and collecting state and county taxes in this state.

How taxes levied, assessed and collected.

Sec. 42. The lien of town taxes levied for all purposes in each year shall attach to all real property on the first day of June annually, shall be paramount to all other liens and continue until such taxes, with any penalty which shall accrue thereon, shall be paid.

Lien of town taxes shall attach to all real property.

All personal property in said town subject to taxation shall be liable to be seized and sold for taxes by said tax collector, and the personal property of any deceased person there shall be liable in the hands of any executor or administrator for any tax due on the same by any testator or intestate; and any property, whether real or personal, in said town, conveyed or assigned after the first day of June in any year to any trustee or trustees, assignee or assignees for the benefit of creditors, shall be liable in the hands of such trustee or trustees, assignee or assignees,

Personal property liable to attachment for taxes.

for all the taxes levied, laid or assessed upon the same in that year, and may be sold for the payment of such taxes in the same manner as if such conveyance or assignment had not been made.

Fiscal year.

Sec. 43. The fiscal year of said town shall begin with the first day of June in every year.

Poll and ad valorem taxes, when due.

Sec. 44. The poll taxes and the ad valorem taxes of said town shall become due on the first day of September in every year.

Taxes due and unpaid.

Sec. 45. Whenever any taxes in said town shall be due and unpaid, the tax collector thereof shall proceed to collect the same as follows:

Collector shall seize real property.

(1) If the person charged have personal property anywhere in the county of Lincoln of a value as great as the taxes charged against him or against his property, said tax collector shall seize and sell the same as the sheriff is required to sell personal property under execution.

Shall levy on any lands of delinquent in Lincoln county.

(2) If the person charged have not personal property to be found in said county of Lincoln of the value as great as the tax charged against him and his property said tax collector shall levy upon the lands of the delinquent in said county of Lincoln, or any part of such land of the delinquent in said county, and after due advertisement sell the same for the payment of said taxes. Such advertisement shall be made in some newspaper published in said county of Lincoln for at least thirty days immediately preceding such sale, and by posting notice at court-house door for thirty days before said sale, which shall contain a description of the real estate to be sold, the name of the person who appears upon the tax list as the owner thereof, the amount of taxes for which said sale is made, and the day and place of said sale.

Advertisement shall be made.

Collection of advertising expenses.

For every piece of real estate or part thereof so advertised said tax collector shall also collect, in the same manner as such taxes, the sum of fifty cents to defray the expenses of such advertisement.

Sale of property for taxes, when made.

All such sales shall be made at the court-house door of said county of Lincoln, at public auction, to the highest bidder, for cash, upon any day of the week or month, except Sunday or a legal holiday; and if no person will bid enough to pay such taxes, penalties and expenses, in case such real estate is sold, said tax collector shall bid on behalf of said town the amount of said taxes, penalties and expenses, and if no higher bid is made, the same shall be struck off to said town; and in all cases where real estate is struck off to said town as herein provided it shall belong to said town in fee simple. Said tax collector shall immediately thereafter return to the board of aldermen of said town, by filing the same with the clerk of said board, a statement of his proceedings, showing the purchaser or purchasers of such real estate, and the amount for which each piece or part

When real estate is struck off to town.

thereof sold, which shall be entered by the clerk of said board upon the minute book of said board of aldermen; and if there shall be a surplus after paying said taxes, penalties and expenses, the same shall be paid to the treasurer of said town, subject to the demand of the person entitled to the same.

Surplus of sale shall be paid to treasurer.

Sec. 46. The owner of any real estate or interest therein sold as aforesaid, his heirs, executors, administrators or assigns, may redeem the same within one year after the sale upon the same terms and conditions and subject to the same provisos and in the same manner as prescribed by law for the redemption of real estate sold for state and county taxes, except that all the duties, functions and powers provided by law to be discharged and exercised by the sheriff or tax collector, shall be discharged and exercised by the tax collector of said town.

Land may be redeemed within one year.

Sec. 47. On any such sale of real estate, said tax collector shall execute to the purchaser a certificate similar to that required or allowed by law to be executed upon the sale of real estate for state and county taxes, which may be assigned or transferred by the purchaser, whether an individual of said town, as such last mentioned certificates are allowed by law to be assigned or transferred; and if the real estate sold as aforesaid shall not be redeemed as hereinbefore provided, said tax collector or his successors in office, under the direction of said board of aldermen, at any time within one year after the expiration of one year from the date of sale, on request of the holder of such certificate and production of the same, shall execute to the purchaser, his heirs or assigns, a deed in fee simple for the conveyance of the real estate described in such certificate; and if such certificate shall have been lost, said board of aldermen, on being fully satisfied thereof by due proof, shall direct said tax collector to execute such conveyance, and said tax collector shall so execute the same. Any such deed shall be similar in form to the deed directed by law to be executed to a purchaser of real estate sold for state and county taxes who is entitled to a conveyance of the same, and shall be subject to the same rules, provisions, presumptions and conclusions as such last-mentioned deed, and effective to the same extent as such last-mentioned deed: Provided, that nothing in this section shall be construed as to interpret any act or statute or any part of act or statute of this state directing any conveyance to be executed for real estate sold for state or county taxes to mean that the facts stated in such conveyance to be conclusive of the facts stated in said deed or conveyance so as to preclude rebutting evidence of the facts contained in any such deed or conveyance executed in like manner by the tax collector of said town.

Tax collector shall execute certificate to purchaser.

If real estate sold for taxes is not redeemed tax collector shall execute a deed in fee simple to purchaser.

Form of deed.

Facts stated in conveyance conclusive of facts stated in deed.

Sec. 48. No such sale of real estate for taxes shall be considered invalid on account of the same having been charged in any other

Sale shall not be invalidated on account of having been charged in toher name.

name than that of a rightful owner if said real estate be in other respects sufficiently described to insure identification.

Additional subjects of taxation. Sec. 49. In addition to the other subjects listed for taxation in said town the board of aldermen thereof may lay and cause to be collected taxes on the following subjects respectively, the amounts of which when laid shall be collected by the tax collector of said town immediately, and if the same be not paid on demand they may be recovered by suit or by seizure and sale of the articles on which they are severally imposed, or of any other property of the owner in the county of Lincoln, in the same manner as personal property is sold for taxes as hereinbefore provided:

Itinerant merchants, etc. (1) On all itinerant merchants or peddlers offering to vend in said town, a privilege tax not exceeding fifteen dollars a year in addition to a tax not exceeding one per centum on the amount of their purchases, respectively; and among such itinerant merchants or peddlers shall be included also all itinerant venders of medicines or other articles.

Shooting galleries, billiard tables, etc. (2) On every shooting gallery, billiard table, bowling alley, or alley of like kind, bowling saloon, bagatelle table, pool table, or place of any other game or play, with or without a name, kept for profit or kept in a house where spirituous, vinous or malt liquors are sold, or in a house used or connected with such house, or used or connected with a hotel or restaurant, a privilege tax not exceeding twenty-five dollars.

Hotels, restaurants and eating-houses. (3) On every hotel, restaurant or eating-house, a privilege tax not exceeding thirty dollars. Said board of aldermen shall have the power to classify into as many classes as to them shall from time to time seem best such hotels, restaurants and eating-houses according to the character of business done by them and to determine according to the character of such business to which class any hotel, restaurant or eating-house belongs, and prescribe a different privilege tax for every class, in no case exceeding thirty dollars per year.

Circuses. (4) On every company of circus riders, performers or exhibitors, or showmen, by whatsoever name called, who shall exhibit within said town, or within one mile of the corporate limits thereof, a license tax not exceeding fifty dollars for every performance or separate exhibition, and on every side-show connected therewith, a license tax not exceeding ten dollars for every performance or separate exhibition. The tax herein specified shall be paid before performance or exhibition, otherwise it shall be double.

Side-shows.

Theatrical plays. (5) On every person or company exhibiting within said town, or within one mile of the corporate limits thereof, any stage or theatrical plays, sleight-of-hand performance, rope-walking, wire-walking, or menagerie, a tax not exceeding ten dollars for every twelve hours allowed for exhibition. Said tax to be paid before exhibiting, otherwise to be double.

(6) On every exhibition for reward of artificial curiosities within said town, or within one mile of the corporate limits thereof, a license tax not exceeding five dollars. Such tax to be paid before exhibition, otherwise to be double.

Exhibitions for reward.

(7) On every show, performance or exhibition of any kind, and on every concert for reward, and on every strolling musician within said town, or within one mile of the corporate limits thereof, a license tax not exceeding five dollars. Said tax to be paid before exhibition, or be double.

Shows and performances of any kind.

(8) On each and every of the following objects and occupations said board of aldermen may, at its discretion, impose an annual privilege tax as follows: On itinerant jewelers or silver-smiths not exceeding ten dollars; on photographers, not exceeding ten dollars; on itinerant dealers in lightning rods, not exceeding ten dollars; on retailers of fresh meats, not exceeding fifteen dollars; on boarding-houses, not exceeding ten dollars; on ice-cream saloons, not exceeding ten dollars; on soda fountains, not exceeding ten dollars; on manufacturers of patent medicines, or medicines of any kind usually called proprietary, not exceeding twenty-five dollars; on skating rinks, not exceeding twenty-five dollars; on dogs, not exceeding ten dollars.

Itinerant jewelers.
Photographers.
Itinerant dealers in lightning rods.
Retailers of fresh meats.
Boarding houses.
Ice-cream saloons.
Soda fountains.
Manufacturers of patent medicines.
Skating rinks.
Dogs.

Said board of aldermen may, at its discretion, impose said annual privilege taxes upon said objects and occupations, respectively, or upon any of them, and may, at its discretion in so doing, impose different taxes upon different objects or occupations as to which the limit hereinbefore prescribed is the same.

(9) On every person or firm selling spirituous, vinous or malt liquors, a license tax for every place in which such business is or is to be conducted, whether by wholesale or retail, such tax as the board of aldermen may deem proper and fix, not exceeding fifteen hundred dollars, to be paid annually in advance, at the time of issuing said license, or the board of aldermen may direct same to be paid semi-annually, in advance, on the first days of July and January, in each and every year, and one-half of such tax at each payment.

Bar-rooms.

Every person desirous of engaging in such business in said town, shall apply to said board of aldermen at its first meeting in June, or its first meeting in December, or at any of its regular monthly meetings, in any year, for license to do so, and said board of aldermen may, in its discretion, direct or decline to direct the tax collector of said town, to issue such license to any applicant, or for any place in said town where such business is desired to be conducted: Provided, the applicant for license shall give bond in the sum of one thousand dollars, with approved security, conditioned for the keeping of an orderly and

Persons desiring to sell liquor shall secure license from aldermen.

Proviso.

Applicant for license shall give bond

lawful house, and to comply with all the requirements of the ordinances, rules and regulations passed by the board of aldermen governing the sales of spirituous, vinous and malt liquors in said town. Upon any direction of said board of aldermen so to do, and the payment in advance to him of the license tax therefor (bond having previously been given to the board, as in this section required), it shall be the duty of said tax collector to issue to the person, company or firm named in said direction, a license to conduct, at the place named in such direction, the business in such direction specified for the period of six or twelve months (as said board may direct), to commence on the first day of July, or the first day of January, as the case may be, next after such direction by said board of aldermen.

Issuance of license.

Any person, company or firm, having obtained such license, who shall within the period therein named, at any time fail, neglect or refuse to comply with any rule or regulation theretofore or within such period prescribed by such board of aldermen for the conduct, control or regulation of such business, shall forfeit thereby such license, and upon such forfeiture being declared by said board of aldermen such person, firm or company shall no longer be entitled to engage in such business within said period or under said license, and shall not be entitled to have refunded to him, them or it, any part of the license tax for such license paid. Any person who shall sell or aid in selling, or offer to sell, in said town, or within one mile thereof, any spirituous, vinous or malt liquors, without having license therefor, shall be guilty of a misdemeanor for every such act or sale, and upon conviction thereof shall be fined fifty dollars or imprisoned for thirty days.

Persons selling liquor without license guilty of a misdemeanor

Aldermen may require payment in advance of license taxes

(10) Said board of aldermen may require and provide for the payment in advance of any license tax in this act authorized, and any person who in such case shall engage in any such business, trade, occupation, calling or profession upon or for which in any manner any such tax is allowed to be imposed, without having paid such tax, shall be guilty of a misdemeanor, and upon conviction shall be fined not more than fifty dollars, or imprisoned not more than thirty days.

County commissioners shall not grant license without consent of aldermen.

Sec. 50. That it shall not be lawful for the county commissioners of the county of Lincoln to grant any license to sell spirituous, vinous or malt liquors within the limits of the town of Lincolnton, or within two miles thereof, without permission first obtained from the board of aldermen of said town of Lincolnton, and said permission in force at said time, and if any license shall be granted without permission in writing, attested by the clerk of the board of aldermen of said town, and exhibited to the board of county commissioners of said county of Lincoln, and filed with the clerk of the board of said county commissioners, the same shall be utterly void, and the person obtaining such license shall be liable to indictment as in other cases of selling without license, and for every offence of selling shall moreover forfeit and pay to the town of Lincolnton the sum of fifty dollars.

Persons so obtaining license liable to indictment.

Sec. 51. Whenever in the opinion of the board of aldermen of said town it is advisable to obtain land or right of way therein for the purpose of opening a new street therein, or widening or straightening a street therein, or making culverts or water-ways for carrying water out of any street therein, and said board of aldermen and the owner or owners of such land or right of way can not agree as to the amount of damages consequent thereupon as well as the special advantage which may result to the owner or owners thereof by reason of such opening, widening or straightening of the street, or making of such culvert or waterway, said board of aldermen may direct the mayor of said town to issue and he shall thereupon issue his writ, under his hand and seal, commanding the marshal thereof to summon a jury of six freeholders of said town unconnected by consanguinity or affinity with any of the persons supposed to be affected by said proposed improvement, in which writ the proposed improvement shall be fully described and the persons who are supposed to be affected thereby shall be named. Such marshal shall, in obedience to said writ, summon a jury of six freeholders, as aforesaid, and direct them to assemble at the mayor's office in said town at a time by such marshal appointed, not less than twenty nor more than thirty days after the date of such writ. Such marshal shall also serve notice of the time of meeting of the jury upon all the persons who are named in such writ as supposed to be affected by such proposed improvement, at least fifteen days before the date appointed for the meeting of the jury.

Condemnation of land by aldermen.

Selection of arbitrators.

Marshal shall serve notice of meeting of jury on person affected.

Such notice shall be in writing and signed by said marshal and addressed to the person or persons upon whom service thereof is made, and shall state the time appointed for such meeting of the jury and designate briefly the proposed improvement, and may be issued as a single notice to all persons named in said writ or as a separate notice to every one of them or to any two or more of them.

Notice shall be in writing and signed by marshal.

Such notice shall be served upon the person or persons therein named, or his, or their agent, by reading the same to him, her or them, and if any such person, or his, her or their agent, can not be found in said town the mayor shall, upon affidavit thereof, made before him by such marshal, direct such notice to be served by posting a copy of the same at the court-house door in said county of Lincoln for at least fifteen days immediately preceding the time appointed for the meeting of such jury, and upon such direction of the mayor it shall be the duty of such marshal

How notice shall be served.

Copy of notice may be posted.

Posting of notice sufficient service. Marshal shall return notice.

to so post the same, and such posting shall, upon the expiration of the time in such order designated, be a sufficient service of such notice, and the party shall then be held to be duly notified of such proceeding. Such marshal shall duly return such notices with his return thereon in writing endorsed, together with any such order of the mayor, to said board of aldermen at its next meeting after the time appointed for the meeting of the jury; at the time appointed for the meeting of the jury such marshal or in case of his inability to do so another marshal or deputy marshal of said town, shall fill any vacancy which has occurred from any cause in the number of persons theretofore summoned as such jury with other competent jurors, and shall cause the jury as then constituted to assemble at the office of the mayor of said town, where every one of them shall be sworn by such mayor or other competent person to faithfully, truly and impartially assess the damages if any which in their judgment will be done to the property of every person named in the writ, and will also assess any special benefit, advantage or enhanced value which will be caused to the property of any person named in the writ. Immediately after the jury shall have been sworn they shall proceed, accompanied by such marshal or deputy marshal, to view the land of every person named in the writ and shall assess the damages if any to every one of the premises which they have viewed, and the special benefit, advantage or enhanced value if any which will accrue by reason of said proposed improvements to every one of the premises which they have viewed. Said jury shall forthwith return to said board of aldermen, by filing with the clerk thereof a statement in writing signed by every one of them, or a majority of them in case they cannot agree, setting forth distinctly a full itemized report of their proceedings, and stating separately the amount of damages or special benefits, or both as the case may be, which they have assessed to every one of the premises so viewed by them. The marshal in charge of said jury shall keep them together until they shall have agreed on the matters submitted to them as aforesaid, and have made and signed their report as aforesaid, or in case of their inability to agree, or twenty-four hours from the time of their return from viewing said premises to said office of mayor, to which they shall so return in every case immediately for deliberation, and until they shall have signed a report, as hereinafter specified, upon any disagreement. If such jury be evenly divided so that they are unable to agree on their report, or any part thereof, they shall make and sign a report stating that fact and setting forth such items as a majority of them have agreed upon, if any such there be, and the names of the persons as owners and the particular premises in regard to

Assembling of jury.

Jury shall view land condemned.

Jury shall file report with aldermen.

Marshal shall keep jury together.

When jury is unable to agree.

the damages, special benefit or enhanced value of which they are evenly divided, or in regard to which a majority of them cannot agree, which report shall be filed in the same manner as the report hereinbefore provided for. On receipt of any such report, showing any disagreement of the jury, said board of aldermen shall at its next meeting after the filing of such report direct the mayor of said town to issue, and he shall thereupon issue under his hand and seal his order to a marshal of said town to at once summon a jury, qualified for such duty as hereinbefore specified and of the same number as hereinbefore directed, to be composed of different persons from those who constituted the jury disagreeing, and such new jury shall proceed immediately after being duly sworn, as aforesaid to take into consideration all parts of the report of the former jury on which that jury was not agreed and to view the premises in regard to which such disagreements were had in the manner hereinbefore directed. Such course shall be continued from time to time until all the matters in such original writ directed to be decided shall have been determined. At the first meeting of said board of aldermen after a complete report or reports upon the matters in said writs ordered to be made shall have been filed as aforesaid, said board of aldermen shall consider and pass upon such report or reports. If the board of aldermen shall determine that any item of damages so assessed is excessive it may reject such report or reports and discontinue the proposed improvement, and in case of such discontinuance no other proceeding shall within twelve months thereafter be commenced for a similar purpose in relation to any of the premises affected thereby, or any part of the same, without the written consent of the owner thereof. It shall be competent for said board of aldermen in passing upon any such report or reports to decrease or omit any item or items of special benefit, advantage or enhanced value therein contained if it think proper to do so. If said board of aldermen shall think proper it shall order such report or reports, or such report or reports so modified by it as to special benefits or advantages or enhanced value approved, and the lands condemned in said proceedings shall vest in said town so long as they may be used respectively for the purpose of said improvements, so long as the amount of damages assessed to them respectively, decreased by the amount of special benefit, advantage, and enhanced value so assessed against them respectively, shall have been paid or tendered to the owner or owners of such premises respectively, or deposited as hereinafter provided.

Second jury shall be summoned.

Second jury shall consider parts of report submitted by first.

Aldermen shall consider and pass upon report.

Aldermen may reject report.

No other proceeding shall be commenced within twelve months.

Aldermen may decrease or omit any item.

Aldermen may order report modified

In case of an appeal on an item, as hereinafter provided, such damages on the premises as to which such appeal is taken, decreased by the amount of special benefit, advantage and

When appeal is made on an item.

enhanced value assessed against the same, shall be deposited with the clerk of the superior court of Lincoln county to be disposed of as so assessed, or as upon such appeal adjudged, subject to be reduced by any special advantage and enhanced value against such premises assessed as aforesaid or on such appeal.

Special advantages accruing to premises.

Any special benefit, advantage or enhanced value, so assessed against any premises, or any appeal adjudged against the same, unless paid or set off by damages assessed thereon, or on appeal adjudged on the same, shall upon such approval of the board of aldermen, in case no appeal is taken upon such assessment of special benefits, advantage or enhanced value or damages, or upon final judgment in case of any such appeal, become and be a lien in favor of said town on said premises on which it has been so assessed or adjudged, as of the time when the board of aldermen passed upon the report regarding the same when said approval was had or appeal taken, and shall be paid to said town in equal installments, one, two and three years respectively after the completion of such improvements, or in case of appeal, and completion of such improvement before final judgment thereon, after such final judgment, and if any such installments shall remain unpaid for thirty days after maturity all such installments then unpaid shall become due, and the premises so assessed or charged shall be sold for the payment of the same and the expenses of such sale and costs by the tax collector of said town, under the same rules, regulations, restrictions, rights of redemption, provisions and effects as are prescribed in this charter for the sale of real estate for unpaid taxes. Any owner of premises mentioned in any such report who is dissatisfied with the amount of damages assessed therein as done to said premises, or with any amount of special benefits, advantages or enhanced value therein assessed against the same, or said board of aldermen, if dissatisfied with any item in said report, any [may] appeal on any item with which he, she or they are so dissatisfied, from such report thereon or the action of the board of aldermen on such report, to the next term of the superior court of said county of Lincoln, by serving upon the adverse party a written notice of such appeal within ten days after said board of aldermen shall have so passed upon such report. On any such appeal the appellate court shall have power to increase, affirm or diminish the amount of the item appealed on, but not to adjudicate the necessity of the improvement, and such appeal shall in no wise hinder or delay the board of aldermen in making or carrying out the proposed improvement, but it shall be lawful for it to enter upon and use the property so condemned as and for such purpose at any time after the expiration of five days from the date when the amount of damages assessed by the jury, decreased by special benefits, advantage and enhanced value, as

Approval by board shall become a lien in favor of said town.

Installments remaining unpaid for thirty days, become due.

Owner of premises dissatisfied with amount assessed may appeal.

Written notice shall be served on adverse party.

Town may enter on and use property condemned

aforesaid, shall have been paid or tendered, or in case of appeal deposited as aforesaid.

Sec. 52. Whenever any land, real estate, watercourse or right of way, whether or not within the limits of said town, shall in the opinion of said board of aldermen be required for the purpose of erecting, making or establishing reservoirs, dams or ponds, tanks or other receptacles of water, or for laying conduit, main or supply pipes of water, or the erection or construction of houses, stations or machinery to be used in so doing, for the use of said town or its inhabitants, or for any other purpose connected with the successful operation of water-works in or for said town, and the owner or owners of such property and said board of aldermen can not agree as to the price to be paid therefor, the same may be condemned in the manner prescribed in this charter for the condemnation of land for streets, except only that when the property so condemned lies without the limits of said town the jury shall be composed one-half of competent jurors from within said town and the other half of competent jurors of said county of Lincoln from without said town.

Land or waterways necessary to town may be condemned.

When property lies outside of corporate limits, of whom jury shall be composed.

For the purpose of successfully establishing, constructing and operating the water-works hereby contemplated said board of aldermen shall have full power to extend such water-works or any branch or branches thereof beyond the limits of said town in any direction or directions which to it may seem advisable, and to exercise all rights and privileges in the establishment, construction, operation, repair and control of such water-works and any and all branches thereof beyond the limits of said town as they now or may hereafter be empowered to exercise within such limits. In case of the discontinuance of the use of the property actually condemned for any of the purposes in this or the preceding section allowed and its reverting to the original owners by reason thereof, said town shall have the right to remove therefrom any property, structure, machinery or improvement by it or under its authority erected, put or placed thereon.

Aldermen empowered to extend water-works.

Town may remove structures, etc., from property, use of which is discontinued.

Sec. 53. Said board of aldermen may establish the width and ascertain the location of the streets, alleys and sidewalks of said town already established, and may reduce the width thereof or discontinue any of them. It may also establish, acquire, improve and control parks or other pleasure grounds for the use of said town, and may pass ordinances for the proper protection, maintenance, management and control of the same. It may also protect and control the shade trees already growing or hereafter planted on the streets, public squares, public grounds, public alleys and sidewalks of or within said town, and may remove any such trees from time to time and plant others on such streets, public squares, public grounds, sidewalks and alleys as

Width and location of streets.

Establishment of parks.

Protection of shade trees.

May permit erection of telegraph poles, etc.,

to said board may seem best. Said board may also permit the erection of telegraph poles, telephone poles, electric light poles, and other poles upon the streets, public squares, public grounds, public alleys and sidewalks of said town or prohibit or prevent such erection of the same, and may control and regulate all such poles as shall have been or hereafter may be so erected and the use of the same at any and all times, and may remove or cause to be removed the same or any of them at any time or times, and in such manner and upon such notice as to it may seem proper. It shall also have power to regulate, control, license, prohibit and remove all structures and things of whatever name or character erected, constructed, put or placed on, above or under the streets, public squares, public grounds, public alleys and sidewalks of said town.

May remove poles.

Empowered to control certain structures.

Franchises, charters, etc., may be altered.

Sec. 54. Any railroad of whatever description, name or gauge granted by the board of aldermen of said town, and all ordinances thereof conferring any such privileges, franchises or charters, may be altered, amended, modified, repealed or revoked by said board of aldermen, from time to time, anything in such privileges, franchises, charters or ordinances to the contrary notwithstanding.

Railroads running over streets shall maintain such part on certain conditions.

Sec. 55. Any railroad of whatever description, name or gauge which has or may hereafter construct its lines of road or part thereof over any of the streets of said town shall maintain such road or part thereof or construct the same only upon the following conditions: It shall use only such rails and other material as the board of aldermen may designate; it shall properly grade, complete and pave the streets between its rails in such manner as said board of aldermen may direct; it shall keep such streets between said rails in good condition and repair, and in such condition and repair as said board of aldermen may from time to time order, so long as it shall use the same; if it fail to comply with any provision of this section, or to keep any of such streets in condition and repair as aforesaid, said board of aldermen may cause anything to be done which said railroad has so failed to do, and the costs thereof shall be charged against such railroad and constitute a lien from the commencement of the work paramount to every other lien upon the charter and franchise of such railroad and upon all the property of whatever kind of such railroad in said county of Lincoln, and such property may be sold for the payment thereof in the manner herein prescribed for the sale of property for taxes; and any such failure on the part of said railroad shall operate as a forfeiture of its right to use such streets, or any of them, or any part of any of them, as such board of aldermen may determine.

Failure to maintain street by railroad.

Lien on charter.

Property may be sold for non payment of assessment.

Sec. 56. It shall be incumbent upon all persons owning land in the town of Lincolnton to care for, improve or pave the sidewalks respectively the full width across their respective fronts with such work, material and in such manner as the board of aldermen of said town shall direct. At any time said board of aldermen shall adjudge that any of the streets of said town needs work or repair, it shall through the marshal give the owner of the property adjacent to said street, or fronting said sidewalk, notice to improve or repair said sidewalk; and should said owner or owners fail for ten days to comply with said notice and make the required improvement or repairs, as the case may be, said board of aldermen, unless it extend the time thereof, shall cause said sidewalk to be repaired, rebuilt, paved or improved in such manner as said board of aldermen may direct and charge the costs thereof against such lots respectively, and cause the same to be entered in a book by the clerk thereof to be kept for that purpose; and said clerk shall place in the hands of the tax collector of said town copies of such charges, and said tax collector shall immediately proceed to collect the same and account therefor in the same manner as taxes of said town. The amount of such charges shall constitute from the commencement of the work for which they are charged liens upon the respective lots upon which they are respectively charged, and if any of them are not paid upon demand so much of the lot upon which charged as may be sufficient to pay the same, with interest and costs, for the whole of such lot, shall be advertised and so sold by the tax collector for the payment of the same, under the same rules, regulations, rights of redemption, excepting and in the same manner as are prescribed in this act for the sale of real estate for unpaid taxes.

Owner of property adjacent to streets needing repairs, shall be notified.

On failure of owner to repair sidewalks town shall make repairs.

Cost of repairs charged to owner of property.

Amount of charges shall constitute lien on property.

Sec. 57. Said board of aldermen shall from time to time buy, build and construct in said town such system or systems of water-works, water-pipes, sewerage and sewer pipes and extension of the same as to it may seem advisable, or cause the same to be so laid, built and constructed, and shall keep the same in proper condition and repair with proper connections, and make all necessary provisions for so doing, and shall control and regulate such system and every part thereof, and may require the owner or owners of any improved lot in said town on any public street or alley where such water and sewer-pipes have been laid or are conveniently accessible, or on any line of pipes to connect such lot with such sewer and water-pipes in the manner and at the places designated by said board of aldermen, upon like notice, terms and conditions as are hereinbefore provided for paving sidewalks; and upon failure of the owner or owners to so connect the same within the time in such notice required, said board of aldermen may enter upon such lot and make connections and charge the costs thereof against said lot, in the same manner as is hereinbefore provided in the case of side-

Construction of waterworks system.

Control and regulation of water system.

Owners of lots may be required to connect with sewer pipes.

When owners refuse to make such connection, town may do so and charge costs.

walks, and such costs so charged shall be collected and shall constitute a lien upon such lot in the same manner and to be enforced in the same manner and with like powers and privileges as is hereinbefore provided in regard to sidewalks.

Land necessary for sewerage purposes may be condemned.

Sec. 58. When any land or right of any within or without the limits of said town shall in the opinion of the board of aldermen thereof be required for the purpose of laying sewer pipe or making man-holes, or for any other purpose connected with the successful operation of such sewer system or systems, and the owner or owners of such property and said board of aldermen cannot agree as to the damage by reason thereof, the same shall be condemned and damages assessed therefor in the manner hereinbefore prescribed for the condemnation of land for water-works and streets or purposes connected therewith.

Sewer system may be extended from time to time

For the purpose of successfully constructing and operating such sewer system or systems, said board of aldermen shall have power to extend the same and any branch or branches thereof beyond the limits of said town in any direction or directions as it may think proper, and to exercise all rights and privileges in the establishment, construction, operation, repair and control of such sewer system or systems, and any and all branches thereof, whether within or without the limits of said town, as to it shall seem proper.

Empowered to buy and maintain an electric light plant.

Sec. 59. The mayor and board of aldermen of the town of Lincolnton are hereby authorized and empowered, in their discretion, to buy, maintain and operate an electric plant for the purpose of furnishing light to the inhabitants of said town, and they are authorized and empowered to charge therefor such prices as they shall deem fair and reasonable, and to provide for the collection of the rents, or they may have the same erected, maintained and operated by contract or grant of franchise.

Land necessary for said purpose may be condemned.

When any land or right of way within or without the limits of said town shall in the opinion of the board of aldermen of said town be required for the purpose of erecting or carrying on or having the same erected and carried on, said electric light system in said town of Lincolnton, or for any other purpose connected with the successful operation of said system, and the owner or the owners of such property and the board of aldermen cannot agree as to the damages by reason thereof, the same shall be condemned and the damages assessed therefor in the manner hereinbefore prescribed for the condemnation of land for water-works or purposes therewith connected or for purposes connected with streets.

Measures against contagious diseases.

Sec. 60. Said board of aldermen may take such measures as it may deem effectual to prevent the entrance into said town, or spread therein, of any and all contagious, infectious or other diseases of whatever nature, and for that purpose may establish, maintain, enact, regulate, conduct and enforce all quarantine and other rules, regulations and requirements, which in its opinion may be necessary for the preservation of the health of said town and the protection thereof from all manner of sickness or disease whatever, with all rights of entry upon property, and all other rights of every character necessary therefor.

Sec. 61. Said board of aldermen may establish, construct, maintain, regulate and control in said town all public buildings necessary or proper for the best interest or good government or conduct of the affairs of said town; and for that purpose may purchase, acquire and hold in fee simple any lot or lots or other real estate whatsoever, or in its discretion may from time to time lease such buildings, lots and real estate.

May control and regulate all public buildings.

Sec. 62. Said board of aldermen may prohibit interment in said town, or at any place or places therein, and may cause to be kept and returned bills of mortality and births therein, under such rules and regulations as to it may seem proper.

May prohibit interment at certain places.

Sec. 63. Said board of aldermen may require and compel the abatement of a.. nuisances in said town at the expense of the person causing the same or the owner or tenant of the land whereon any such nuisances shall be, or may itself abate the same or cause the abatement thereof; it may also prohibit, or license or regulate the establishment within said town of any slaughter house, or house for the storage of any explosive, unhealthy, dangerous or noxious substances, or the storage of any such substances in any quantities whatever in said town or within one hundred yards of its corporate limits, or the exercise therein of any dangerous, noxious, offensive or unhealthy trade, business or employment. If the owner, agent, tenant or occupant of any premises in said town on or in connection with which any nuisances shall be committed or about to be committed, shall refuse, fail or neglect to comply with any order of said board of aldermen to remove, abate, prevent or discontinue the same within the time in such order required, he or she shall be guilty of a misdemeanor, and for such offence, upon conviction, be fined fifty dollars, or imprisoned for not more than thirty days; and said board of aldermen may at any time proceed to remove, abate, prevent or discontinue such nuisance, and the costs of so doing shall be charged upon such premises and constitute a lien thereon paramount to all liens except taxes and assessments of said town from the time of so doing, and shall be collected in the same manner in all respects as liens for the expense of constructing or repairing sidewalks as hereinbefore provided.

May require abatement of nuisances.

Oners of property failing to comply with order for abatement and prevention of nuisances, guilty of misdemeanor.

Sec. 64. Said board of aldermen shall have power to prevent dogs, horses, cattle and other brutes from running at large in said town either in day time or at night.

May prevent live stock from running at large.

Sec. 65. Said board of aldermen may prevent, prohibit and punish, and provide for prohibiting, preventing and punishing,

Fast riding and driving.

the riding or driving of horses or other animals on the streets of said town at a speed greater than in the opinion of said board may be for the safety of persons passing and repassing upon said streets; may prohibit, prevent, punish, restrain, license, restrict, regulate and control the riding or use of bicycles and tricycles on the streets, sidewalks, alleys, public squares, parks or other public grounds in said town; may prevent, punish, prohibit, license, regulate and control the firing of guns, pistols, pop-crackers, gunpowder or other explosive, combustible or dangerous things or materials on the streets, alleys, sidewalks, public squares, parks, public grounds or elsewhere in said town; and may by ordinance prevent, prohibit and punish the carrying of concealed deadly weapons in said town by any person or persons when not upon his or their own premises.

ast riding on cycles and icycles.

ire crackers, etc.

rsons keeping wdy houses ilty of a misdemeanor.

Sec. 66. Any person who shall keep in said town a bawdy house, disorderly house, house of ill-fame, or house in which prostitution, lewdness, or illicit sexual connection is permitted, shall be guilty of a misdemeanor, and, upon conviction thereof, shall be fined not exceeding fifty dollars or imprisoned not more than thirty days; and each day for which said house is kept shall constitute distinct and separate offences, and the keeping of any such house may, at any time, whether or not there has been a prosecution for any such offence, be declared a nuisance by said board of aldermen, and abated in the manner hereinbefore provided for the abatement of nuisances.

wdy houses ay be declared isances.

vners or agents using houses for sorderly houses ilty of misdemeanor.

Sec. 67. Every owner of any real property in said town or any estate therein, or agent of such owner, who shall lease, use or permit the use of the same for a bawdy house, disorderly house, or house of ill-fame, or as a place where prostitution, lewdness, or illicit sexual connection is carried on or allowed, or shall continue to lease the same to any tenant who uses the same or permit the same to be used for any of said purposes or shall suffer any person or persons to use it for any such purposes, when it is within his right or power to prevent such use, shall be guilty of a misdemeanor, and upon conviction shall for every offence be fined fifty dollars or imprisoned not more than thirty days; and each day for which the same is so used shall be and constitute a distinct and separate offence.

nalty.

rsons visiting sorderly houses ilty of a misdemeanor.

Sec. 68. Every person who, not being a resident therein, shall visit any bawdy house, disorderly house, house of ill-fame, or other house in said town where prostitution, lewdness, or illicit sexual connection is carried on, for the purpose of indulging in any such illicit connection or aiding others to indulge therein, or who shall be found in any such house for such purpose, shall be guilty of a misdemeanor and upon conviction thereof shall be fined not more than fifty dollars or imprisoned not more than thirty days; and the presence of such person in such house shall

nalty.

be prima facie evidence that he or she is there for such purpose.

Sec. 69. Said board of aldermen shall have power to regulate, control and protect, in such manner and to such extent as to it may seem proper, the streets, alleys, sidewalks, public squares, parks, fire department, market, voting places, cemeteries and other property of said town, whether real or personal, within the limits of said town, and may pass and enforce ordinances, rules and regulations therefor from time to time which it may deem proper. Control of town property.

Sec. 70. Said board of aldermen may establish fire limits in said town, within which it shall be unlawful for any person or persons to erect, construct or repair any building of wood or other material inflammable or peculiarly [subject] to fire. Fire limits.

Sec. 71. Said board of aldermen may provide for the establishment, organization, equipment, management, regulation, government and control of all fire companies of any kind or kinds in said town, may purchase and maintain all necessary buildings, outfits, animals, wagons, tools, implements, machinery and other articles and things of any kind or kinds, for the efficient maintenance, control and operation of the same. In all cases of fire or conflagration in said town, a majority of the members of the board of aldermen who may be present shall, if they deem it necessary in order to arrest the progress of such fire or conflagraton, cause any house to be blown up or pulled down or destroyed or removed, in whole or in part, under their supervision, and none of them shall be responsible to any one therefor when any such act is so caused to be done in good faith. Organization of fire companies. In case of fire houses may be blown up to arrest progress of fire.

Sec. 72. No member of a fire company in said town who receives no compensation for his services as such shall be liable to pay any poll tax therein while in good faith belonging to such company, or during such period pay any street tax therein which may be by law imposed, other than assessments on property for street or sidewalk improvement. Firemen receiving no compensation exempt from poll tax.

Sec. 73. All debts and liabilities of said town heretofore or hereafter contracted or incurred shall be paid and discharged alone by taxation upon subjects properly taxable by it to the extent allowed by law, and no such debt or liability shall be subject to be levied upon or collected by execution against said town or any property, real or personal, held by it, and no execution therefor shall issue against said town on any judgment obtained thereon. Debts and liabilities of town, how paid.

Sec. 74. In no case where a defendant in any criminal prosecution shall have appealed from the judgment of the mayor, vice-mayor or mayor pro tem. of said town shall said town be adjudged in such appellate court to pay the costs of such prosecution or any part thereof, whether upon such appeal such de- Town shall not pay costs in cases of appeal.

fendant shall be convicted or acquitted or such judgment appealed irom, reversed or affirmed.

ll notices to served by a arshal.

Sec. 75. All notices provided in this act to be given or served by said town, or any of its officers or employees, shall, unless otherwise herein provided, be served by a marshal of said town, or any of its officers or employes shall, unless otherwise herein provided, be served by a marshal of said town or his duly constituted or authorized deputy, by the reading of said notice to the person or persons directed or required to be served, if such person or persons can be found in the county of LLincoln; and if such person or persons can not be found in said county such marshal or deputy shall make affidavit thereof before the mayor of said town, who shall thereupon direct such service to be made by posting a copy thereof at the court-house door in said town, for such length of time as such notice shall be required to be given, and if no such time be required, then for a single time, and such marshal or deputy marshal shall so post such copy, and such posting shall be deemed a sufficient service of such notice in such case.

ow notices shall served.

hen persons n not be found tice may be sted.

dermen may rrow money.

Sec. 76. Said board of aldermen may borrow in any fiscal year a sum or sums of money not exceeding in the aggregate fifteen hundred dollars outstanding at any one time, in such amount as the same may be needed for the necessary expenses of the town, at a rate of interest not exceeding six per centum, and execute therefor the note or notes of said town, sealed with the seal of said town, and to be in such form as the board of aldermen may from time to time prescribe; but such aggregate sum shall not, in any fiscal year, exceed the aggregate taxation of said town for that year on general subjects of taxation therein; and all such loans shall be paid out of the general taxes for that year, and no such loan shall be made to become due at a date later than the expiration of the fiscal year in which it is made, and no sum whatsoever shall be borrowed under the provisions of this section until all preceding loans made thereunder in any previous fiscal year or years shall have been paid in full of principal and interest.

ximum rate interest.

ney borrowed, w paid.

ans made in ceding years ll first be id.

es of mayor.

Sec. 77. That the mayor shall be entitled to fees in cases brought before him, and whereof he may have jurisdiction, as are prescribed by law for justices of the peace; he shall have the same fees as are allowed justices of the peace not only in cases in which he has final jurisdiction, but also in all cases in which he may act and the parties are bound or recognized to the superior court of Lincoln county or any other county in the State upon appeal or in which he acts as a committing magistrate in which he has not final jurisdiction. In addition thereto he shall also be entitled to twenty-five cents for each and every certificate, twenty-five cents for each and every official seal, except when the

es of mayor.

seal is used for the benefit of the town, in which case no charge shall be made for the seal. The fees of said mayor shall be taxed in all cases in the manner and as prescribed to be taxed by the law of the state for justices of the peace.

Fees of marshals and policemen.

Sec. 78. The marshal or marshals and policeman or policemen, as well as special marshals or policemen, shall receive the same fees as are now prescribed by law or may hereafter be prescribed for sheriffs and constables for like service, together with such other compensation as the board of aldermen may see proper to give, but said board of aldermen shall not be required to give or pay anything, and in event they do not, said fees as prescribed for sheriff and constables shall be all said marshals or policemen shall receive for performing said duty.

Compensation of clerk and treasurer.

Sec. 79. The clerk and treasurer of the board shall each receive such compensation as the board of aldermen may prescribe and allow; in the event the said two officers, clerk and treasurer, are consolidated by said board and filled by one and the same man, said board of aldermen shall fix the compensation for the entire work and shall pay what in their discretion is right and proper for the services performed.

Arrests, when and by whom to be made.

Sec. 80. Arrests may be made by any marshal or policeman of said town anywhere in the county of Lincoln, whenever the officer making the arrest has in his hands a warrant against the person arrested, issued by the mayor, vice-mayor or mayor pro tempore of said town, or a justice of the peace of said county of Lincoln or other competent authority, or whenever any misdemeanor or violation of said town has been committed in his presence, or whenever a misdemeanor or violation of any ordinance of said town has been committed and he has reasonable cause to believe that the person so arrested is guilty of such offence and may make his escape before a warrant can be obtained, or whenever a warrant has been issued against the person so arrested and is outstanding unexecuted in the hands of any marshal, deputy marshal or policeman of said town, or in the hands of the sheriff or any deputy sheriff or constable of the county of Lincoln.

Powers of marshals and policemen in making arrests.

Sec. 81. In making arrests the marshals, deputy marshals and policemen of said town shall have the same and all the powers of a sheriff or constable of said county of Lincoln as well as all the powers of this act conferred upon them.

Officer may summon bystanders to assist in making arrest.

Sec. 82. Wherever any arrest is made by an officer of said town he may summon any of the bystanders or other person having information in regard to the matter for which such arrest is made as witnesses to attend as such at the hearing of the charge upon which such arrest is made, and any such summons shall be effectual and binding in the same manner as if made by subpoena for such person so summoned duly issued and served in such causes.

Mayor's court, when held.

Sec. 83. The mayor's court of said town shall be held therein by the mayor, vice-mayor or mayor pro tempore of said town at such time and days as the presiding officer thereof shall deem best.

Trial of persons arrested may be postponed.

Sec. 84. When any arrests shall have been made, as in this charter provided, the person so arrested shall be carried by the officer making such arrest, or some other officer of the town, before the mayor's court when the same shall be convened for the trial of causes, and such court may, for cause satisfactory to it, postpone the hearing of any such case to some other time. When any such arrests shall have been made the person so arrested shall, until said court of the mayor shall convene, be confined for safe keeping in the county jail of the county of Lincoln until such time for hearing arrives, or admitted to bail until such time, in such manner and under such rules and regulations as said board of aldermen shall prescribe; and in case of any such continuance in the mayor's court such person shall, until the time set for the hearing of the cause, be imprisoned in the county jail of the county of Lincoln, or admitted to bail by the presiding officer of said court, in such manner and under such rules and regulations as said board of aldermen shall provide, and in none of the cases of confinement in this section provided for shall any mittimus be required.

Until time set for hearing persons may be imprisoned in county jail.

On failure to pay fines persons may be committed to jail.

Sec. 85. Whenever any person shall upon conviction in said mayor's court be sentenced to imprisonment or ordered to be imprisoned until such person shall have complied with the judgment of said court, such person shall, for such period or until such time, be confined accordingly in the common jail of the county of Lincoln. It shall in every case be the duty of the sheriff of the county of Lincoln, or the jailor of said county, to receive any such person with or without mittimus as hereinbefore provided into such county jail, and keep such person until such trial or for such punishment or until such person would otherwise be discharged.

Sheriff or jailor shall receive such persons without mittimus.

Section 907 of The Code shall not be considered to apply to ordinances, etc.

Sec. 86. That section nine hundred and seven of The Code shall not be construed to apply to trials for the violation of the town ordinances by the mayor thereof, but the defendant in all such cases shall have the right of appeal: Provided, this section shall in no way abridge the provisions of section seventeen, where it shall appear said mayor or vice-mayor are incompetent to try the same

Claim shall be presented before action against town is instituted.

Sec. 87. No action shall be instituted or maintained against said town or demand whatsoever of any kind or character until the claimant shall have first presented his or her claim or demand, in writing, to said board of aldermen and said board of aldermen shall have declined to pay or settle the same as presented; or for ten days after such presentation neglected to enter or cause to be entered upon its minutes its determination in regard thereto; but nothing herein contained shall be construed to prevent any statute of limitation from commencing to run at the time such claim accrued or demand arose, or in any manner interfere with its running.

Statute of limitation not debarred.

Sec. 88. No action for damages against said town of any character whatever, to either person or property, shall be instituted against said town, unless within ninety days after the happening or infliction of the injury complained of, the complainant, his executors or administrators, shall have given notice to the board of aldermen of said town of such injury, the manner of such infliction, the character of the injury and the amount of damages claimed therefor; but this shall not prevent the statute of limitation prescribed by law from commencing to run at the date of the happening or infliction of injury, or in any manner interfere with the running.

Notice of injury, etc., shall be given commissioners within ninety days in order to institute action.

Sec. 89. That the mayor shall have jurisdiction to try all cases prescribed by this charter or by the ordinances of the town, and to hear and determine same, without requiring a complaint on oath in writing from the party injured, but may exercise said jurisdiction on the complaint of any other person or where the offence committed is in the knowledge of the mayor or presiding officer.

Jurisdiction of mayor.

Sec. 90. The mayor's court shall be a special or inferior court, in the town of Lincolnton, and the mayor, vice-mayor or mayor pro tempore shall be clothed with all the powers of judges or presiding officers of inferior courts for the purpose of executing the laws and ordinances of the said town of Lincolnton, and in all cases of appeal the person appealing shall give bond and security for the payment of all charges, costs, fines and penalties which may be assessed against him in the superior court, as required by the preceding section of this charter, before said appeal is granted.

Mayor's court a special court.

Persons appealing from mayor's court shall give bond.

Sec. 91. That the violation of any such ordinance or ordinances which may be passed by the board of aldermen of the town of Lincolnton, under and by the authority granted by this charter, shall be a misdemeanor, and punishable by a fine of not exceeding fifty dollars, or imprisonment for a period of not exceeding thirty days, and as such shall be punishable by any court of the state having jurisdiction.

Violation of ordinances a misdemeanor.

Sec. 92. That chapter ———— of the laws of eighteen hundred and seventy one, charter of the town of Lincolnton, ratified the third of March, eighteen hundred and seventy-one; chapter ————, laws of eighteen hundred and seventy-five, amending the charter of the town of Lincolnton, ratified the fifth of Febru-

Certain acts relating to charter of Lincolnton repealed.

ary, eighteen hundred and seventy-five; chapter one hundred and ninety-one of the laws of eighteen hundred and seventy-six and eighteen hundred and seventy-seven; chapter sixty-seven of the public laws of eighteen hundred and seventy-four and eighteen hundred and seventy-five; chapter two hundred and thirteen of the private laws of eighteen hundred and ninety-five, and all other laws and parts of laws heretofore constituting the charter of the town of Lincolnton or the board of commissioners of the town of Lincolnton, or either of them, or any part thereof, be and the same are hereby repealed. And all laws of a public or private nature inconsistent with the provisions of this act, or any of them, are hereby repealed. And all laws of a public or general nature inconsistent with the provisions of this act, or any of them, are hereby repealed so far only as they may affect said town, and all laws and parts of laws in conflict herewith are hereby repealed. That all laws of a public or private nature incorporating any church, school house, society, or other corporation, of any kind or character, whether same be a corporation or not, and forbidding the sale of spirituous, vinous or malt liquors, within a certain radius of said corporation as incorporated, that so much of the same that will in any way conflict or in any way prevent or interrupt the sale, or the granting of license for the sale of vinous, malt or spirituous liquors by the board of aldermen of the town of Lincolnton, as in this charter herein is provided, be and the same are hereby repealed. Said board of aldermen of said town of Lincolnton be and they are hereby vested with all the authority to grant license for the sale of vinous or malt or spirituous liquors, or not, as in their discretion, in the town of Lincolnton, as in this charter hereinbefore directed and defined; all laws in conflict be and as the same is hereby repealed, or so much thereof as interfered or interrupts such sale anywhere within the corporate limits of said town. The repeals as in this section mentioned and intended to repeal shall not, unless otherwise provided, expressly or by implication, amend any ordinance or regulation of said town, nor shall such repeal, unless otherwise herein provided, expressly or by necessary implication, affect any act done or right accruing or establishing or any suit begun before the time when such appeal shall take effect. The right, estate, duty or obligation possessed by or due to said town, or to which it is entitled by its present or any other name shall not be lost or impaired by such repeal, but the same shall remain in full force and effect, and be possessed, enforced and enjoyed in the name and for the use of the town of Lincolnton; and no right, duty, obligation or liability accrued or owing [accruing] to this state or to any corporation or person shall be, unless otherwise herein provided, expressly or by implication, lost,

nflicting laws ealed.

tain acts ating to sale of nor in Lincolnton inetive.

ermen vested h authority rant liquor nse.

ions formerly ght not cted by repeal mendments,

affected or impaired by such repeal; but the same shall, unless as aforesaid otherwise provided, expressly or by implication, remain in full force and be possessed, enforced and enjoyed by said state, corporation or person against said town.

Offences committed, etc., prior to this act not affected by act.

Sec. 93. No offence committed, and penalty, fine or forfeiture incurred under or by reason of any of the acts or ordinances hereby repealed, and before the time when such repeal shall take effect, shall be affected by such repeal, except that when any punishment, penalty or fine has been mitigated by the provisions of this act, such provisions may be extended and applied to any judgment to be pronounced after such repeal. No suit or prosecution pending at the time of such repeal for any offence committed or for any penalty, fine or forfeiture incurred under any of the acts or ordinances hereby repealed shall be affected by such repeal. No laws heretofore repealed shall be revived or re-enacted by the repeal hereby of any act repealing such law. All persons who, at the time when said repeal shall take effect, holding office under and by reason of the acts hereby repealed, or any of them, shall continue their said respective offices, with all the rights and privileges thereof, according to the tenure thereof, until their respective successors shall be elected or appointed and qualified under the provisions of this act.

Pending suits not affected.

Laws repealed not revived.

Persons holding office continued in office.

Sec. 94. This act shall be in force from and after the date of its ratification.

Ratified the 7th day of March, A. D. 1899.

CHAPTER 370.

An act to amend and extend the time of organization of the Wilkes County Bank.

The General Assembly of North Carolina do enact:

Time of organization extended two years

Section 1. That the time of organizing the Wilkes County Bank is hereby extended for two years, and upon its organization within said time it shall have all rights and privileges granted in chapter one hundred and thirty-eight of the private laws of eighteen hundred and ninety-three, and those granted in chapter seventy-nine of the private laws of eighteen hundred and ninety-five, "and the stockholders therein shall be subject to all the liabilities imposed by the provisions of chapter two hundred and ninety-eight (298) of the public laws of eighteen hundred and ninety-seven (1897);" "and provided further that said bank shall not have the right to establish any branches or agencies at any point in the state and that nothing in any of said private acts shall be construed to give them power."

Liability of stockholders.

Shall not establish branches.

Ratified the 7th day of March, A. D. 1899.

CHAPTER 371.

An act to repeal chapter thirty-three of the private laws of eighteen hundred and ninety-five, and to re-enact chapter ninety-eight of the private laws of eighteen hundred and eighty-seven.

The General Assembly of North Carolina do enact:

Act repealing incorporation of Whittier, Swain county. Section 1. That chapter thirty-three of the private laws of eighteen hundred and ninety-five be and the same is hereby repealed.

Whittier re-incorporated. Sec. 2. That chapter ninety-eight of the private laws of eighteen hundred and eighty-seven be and the same is hereby re-enacted.

Election of officers, when and how held. Sec. 3. That the election of all officers as provided for in chapter ninety-eight of the private laws of eighteen hundred and eighty-seven shall be held at the time and place and in the manner therein prescribed.

Sec. 4. That this act shall be in force from and after its ratification.

Ratified the 8th day of March, A. D. 1899.

CHAPTER 372.

An act to incorporate the town of Waco in Cleveland county.

The General Assembly of North Carolina do enact:

Town of Waco incorporated. Section 1. That the town of Waco, in the county of Cleveland, be and the same is hereby incorporated by the name and style of the town of Waco, and shall be subject to all the provisions of law contained in chapter sixty-two (62) volume two of The Code, now in force in relation to incorporated towns.

Corporate limits. Sec. 2. That the incorporate limits of said town shall be one-half mile in every direction from the railroad bridge.

Temporary officers. Sec. 3. That the officers of said town shall consist of a mayor, five commissioners and a marshal, and that until their successors are elected on the first Monday in May, eighteen hundred and ninety-nine (1899) the following officers shall serve: Mayor, C Miller; commissioners, B. H. Elliott, W. A. Putnam, M. H. Hoyle and F. M. Miller; marshal, James Putnam.

Sec. 3. That this act shall be in force from and after its ratification.

Ratified the 8th day of March, A. D. 1899.

CHAPTER 373.

An act to authorize the "Carolina Manufacturing Company" further time to organize.

The General Assembly of North Carolina do enact:

Section 1. That chapter one hundred and forty-eight of the private acts of eighteen hundred and ninety-three be continued in full force and effect until March first, nineteen hundred and five, so as to allow said company further time to organize and begin operation. **Chapter 148, private acts of 1893, continued in force.**

Sec. 2. That this act shall be in force from and after its ratification.

Ratified the 8th day of March, A. D. 1899.

CHAPTER 374.

An act to charter Farmer's Institute in Randolph county.

The General Assembly of North Carolina do enact:

Section 1. That C. H. Lewis, Marvin Kearns, M. F. Lassiter, Ivy Dorsett, Clark Johnson, Ivy Johnson and Gideon Macon, of Randolph, their associates and successors, are hereby constituted and declared a body politic and corporate for educational purposes under the name and style of Farmer's Institute, an institution of learning situated at Farmer, Randolph county, and by that name may have succession for sixty years, may sue and be sued, plead and be impleaded, contract and be contracted with, to have and to hold the buildings, grounds and all the other appurtenances thereunto belonging, and such other lands and buildings as may be necessary for the conduct of an educational institution; the said trustees to have the authority to make such by-laws and regulations and rules for the government of said institution, as they and their successors may consider best. **Corporators.** **Duration of charter.**

Sec. 2. That at the next annual meeting of the trustees on the first Saturday in July, eighteen hundred and ninety-nine, certificates of stock shall be issued to those who contributed to the erection of the school building and the purchase of the land (five dollars being a share of stock), said certificates to be duly signed by the secretary and the president of the board of trustees. **Certificates of stock shall be issued.**

Sec. 3. That all vacancies in the board of trustees caused by death or otherwise shall be filled by a vote of the stockholders, according to the number of shares held, at the annual meeting each year, which shall be held on the first Saturday in July: Provided, however, that a majority of the stockholders at a regu- **Vacancies occurring on board of trustees.**

lar meeting may change the time of holding the annual meeting by giving thirty days' notice in some newspaper published in Randolph county.

Individual liability.

Sec. 4. That the liabilities of said institution shall affect the property of the institution only, and not the private credit and property of the trustees or stockholders as individuals.

Election of officers and teachers.

Sec. 5. That the said trustees and their successors shall be authorized to appoint and elect such officers and teachers as they may consider to serve the interests of the institution and the cause of education.

Sec. 6. This act shall be in force from and after its ratification.

Ratified the 8th day of March, A. D. 1899.

CHAPTER 375.

An act to incorporate the Home Mission Committee of Asheville Presbytery.

The General Assembly of North Carolina do enact:

Corporators.

Section 1. That R. F. Campbell, T. S. Morrison, W. A. Blair and J. B. Shope and their associates, successors and assigns, be and they are hereby created a body politic and corporate under the name and style of The Home Mission Committee of Asheville Presbytery, and by such name may acquire, hold and convey real and personal property, sue and be sued, plead and be impleaded in any of the courts of the state, and have a continued succession for ninety-nine years, and have a common seal.

Corporate name.

Corporate powers.

May acquire property.

Sec. 2. That said corporation may acquire property in any way recognized by the laws of North Carolina and may convey same according to law, either in fee simple or for a less estate for a term of years by mortgage or deed of trust, or any other way recognized by the laws of North Carolina.

Election of officers.

Sec. 3. That said corporation shall have power to elect such officers as said incorporators and their successors shall determine and decide to elect, with power to fix the term of office of such officers and their duties and to make all by-laws and regulations needful and necessary for the proper conduct of the affairs of such corporation.

Exempt from payment of certain fees.

Sec. 4. That this corporation under the above name shall exist for the purpose of promoting religion and education in North Carolina, and shall be exempt from the payment of the fifty dollars required to be paid by business corporations before a charter is granted by the General Assembly of this state.

Sec. 5. That this act shall be in force from and after its ratification.

Ratified the 8th day of March, A. D. 1899.

STATE OF NORTH CAROLINA,

OFFICE OF SECRETARY OF STATE,

RALEIGH. May 29th. 1899.

I, Cyrus Thompson, Secretary of State, hereby certify that the foregoing (manuscript) are true copies of the original acts on file in this office.

CYRUS THOMPSON,
Secretary of State.

INDEX TO PRIVATE LAWS.

A.

B.

C.

D.

E.

F.

I

J.

K.

L.

M.

N.

O.

R.

U.

V

W

Y

Lightning Source UK Ltd.
Milton Keynes UK
UKHW041213260219
337728UK00017B/684/P